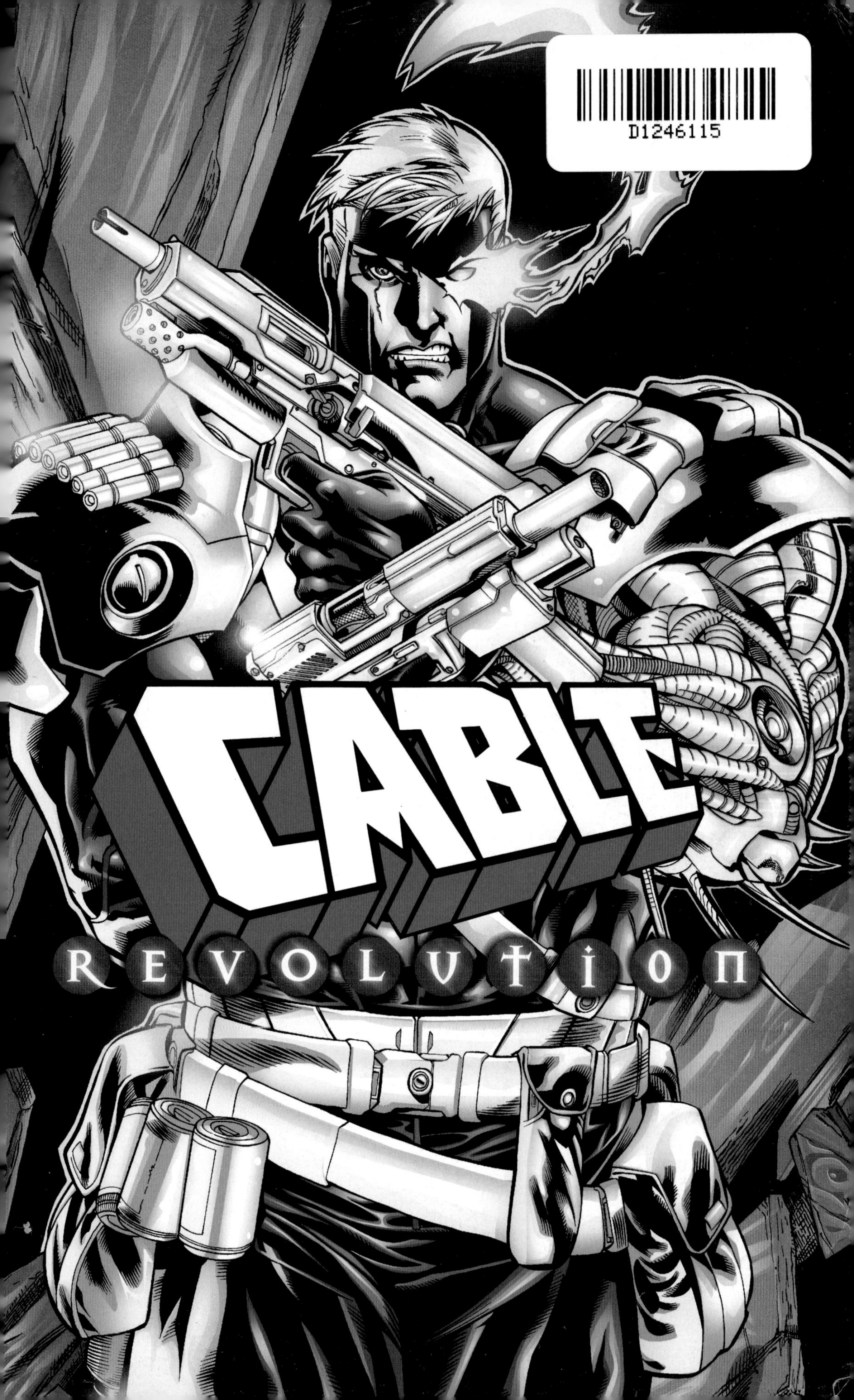
CABLE
REVOLUTION

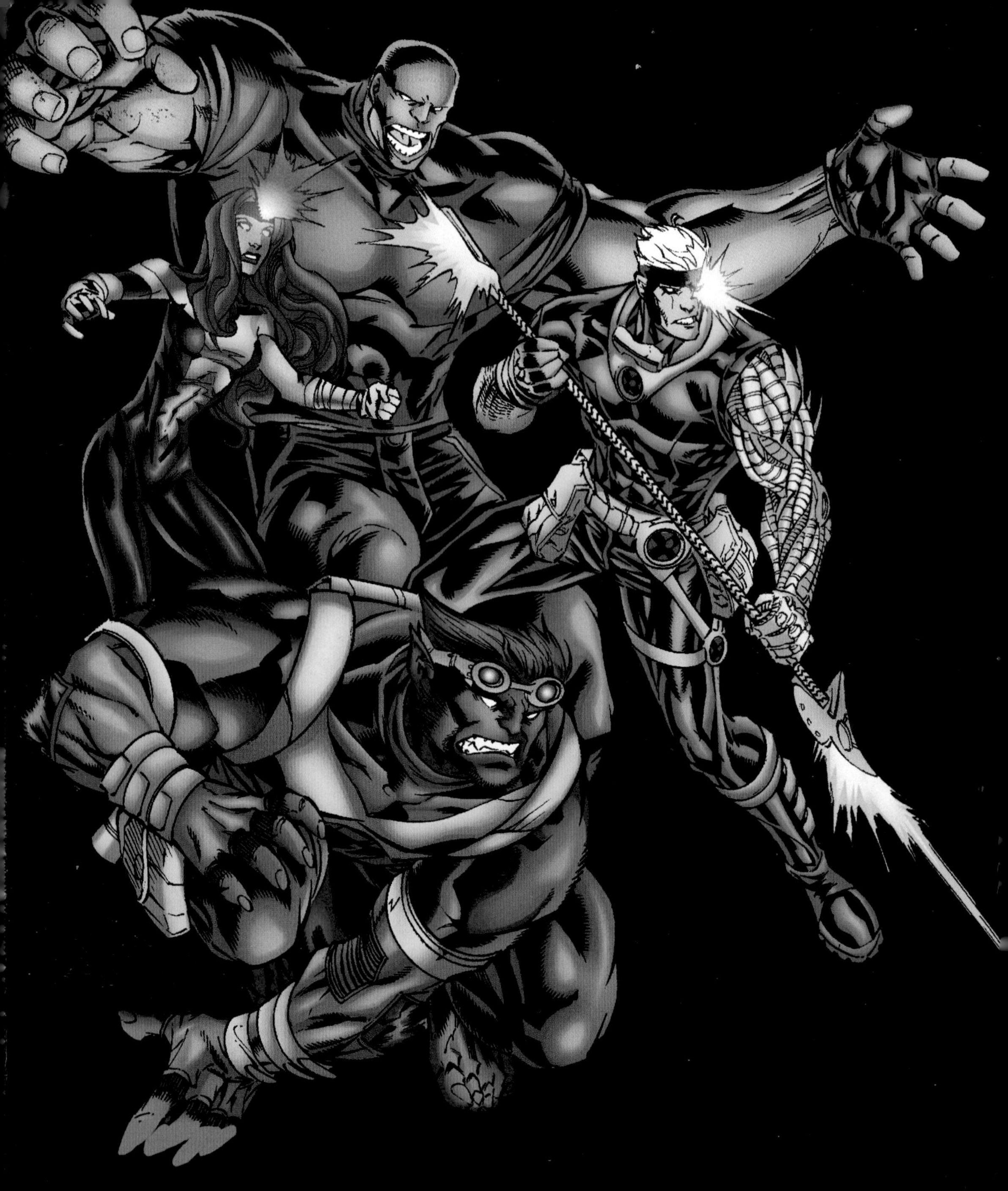

COLLECTION EDITOR: MARK D. BEAZLEY ■ ASSISTANT EDITOR: CAITLIN O'CONNELL
ASSOCIATE MANAGING EDITOR: KATERI WOODY ■ ASSOCIATE MANAGER, DIGITAL ASSETS: JOE HOCHSTEIN
SENIOR EDITOR, SPECIAL PROJECTS: JENNIFER GRÜNWALD ■ VP PRODUCTION & SPECIAL PROJECTS: JEFF YOUNGQUIST
RESEARCH & LAYOUT: JEPH YORK ■ PRODUCTION: RYAN DEVALL
BOOK DESIGNER: JAY BOWEN ■ SVP PRINT, SALES & MARKETING: DAVID GABRIEL

EDITOR IN CHIEF: C.B. CEBULSKI ■ CHIEF CREATIVE OFFICER: JOE QUESADA
PRESIDENT: DAN BUCKLEY ■ EXECUTIVE PRODUCER: ALAN FINE

CABLE
REVOLUTION

ROBERT WEINBERG
WRITER

MICHAEL RYAN, ESAD RIBIĆ & TOM DERENICK
PENCILERS

**ANDREW PEPOY, SCOTT HANNA, WALDEN WONG, NATHAN MASSENGILL,
LARY STUCKER, RICK KETCHAM, TED PERTZBORN & HARRY CANDELARIO
WITH ROBERT HUNTER & NORM RAPMUND**
INKERS

GLORIA VASQUEZ, LIQUID!, HI-FI DESIGN, ENIGMA, VLM & AVALON STUDIOS
COLORISTS

RICHARD STARKINGS & COMICRAFT'S SAIDA TEMOFONTE & CO.
LETTERERS

PETE FRANCO
ASSISTANT EDITOR

MARK POWERS
EDITOR

MICHAEL RYAN, MARK McKENNA & HABERLIN STUDIOS' DAN KEMP
FRONT COVER ARTISTS

MICHAEL RYAN
BACK COVER ARTIST

CABLE: REVOLUTION. Contains material originally published in magazine form as CABLE #79-96. First printing 2018. ISBN 978-1-302-91217-8. Published by MARVEL WORLDWIDE, INC., a subsidiary of MARVEL ENTERTAINMENT, LLC. OFFICE OF PUBLICATION: 135 West 50th Street, New York, NY 10020. Copyright © 2018 MARVEL. No similarity between any of the names, characters, persons, and/or institutions in this magazine with those of any living or dead person or institution is intended, and any such similarity which may exist is purely coincidental. Printed in the U.S.A. DAN BUCKLEY, President, Marvel Entertainment; JOHN NEE, Publisher; JOE QUESADA, Chief Creative Officer; TOM BREVOORT, SVP of Publishing; DAVID BOGART, SVP of Business Affairs & Operations, Publishing & Partnership; DAVID GABRIEL, SVP of Sales & Marketing, Publishing; JEFF YOUNGQUIST, VP of Production & Special Projects, DAN CARR, Executive Director of Publishing Technology; ALEX MORALES, Director of Publishing Operations; SUSAN CRESPI, Production Manager; STAN LEE, Chairman Emeritus. For information regarding advertising in Marvel Comics or on Marvel.com, please contact Vit DeBellis, Custom Solutions & Integrated Advertising Manager, at vdebellis@marvel.com. For Marvel subscription inquiries, please call 888-511-5480. Manufactured between 2/16/2018 and 3/20/2018 by LSC COMMUNICATIONS INC., KENDALLVILLE, IN, USA.

10 9 8 7 6 5 4 3 2 1

ALTHOUGH ROBERT WEINBERG AND MICHAEL RYAN'S CABLE RUN OFFICIALLY BEGAN WITH ISSUE #79, THEY ALSO PRODUCED THIS THREE-PAGE PROLOGUE THAT RAN AS AN INTERLUDE IN *CABLE #78*.

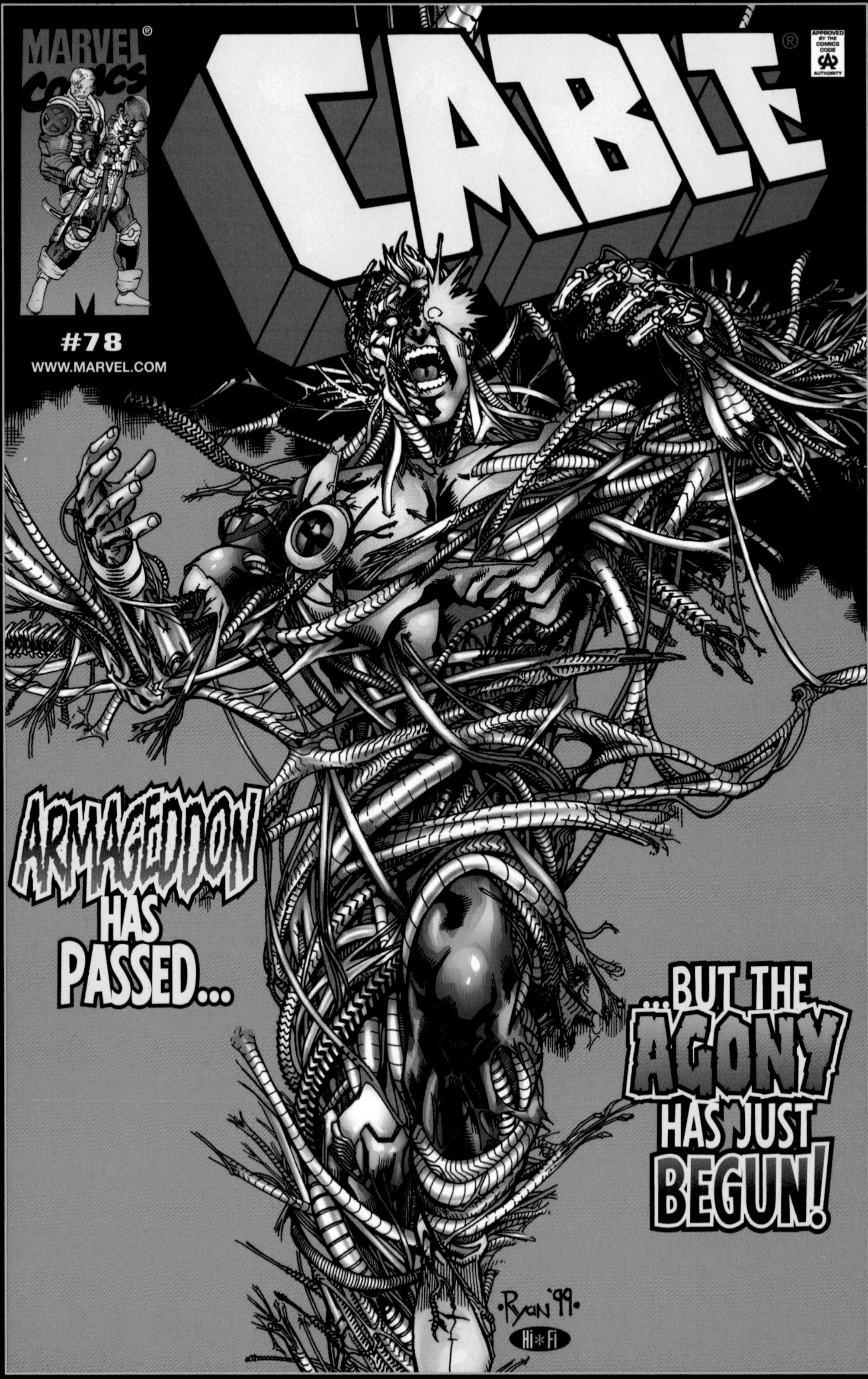
MARVEL COMICS
CABLE
#78
WWW.MARVEL.COM
APPROVED BY THE COMICS CODE AUTHORITY
ARMAGEDDON HAS PASSED...
...BUT THE AGONY HAS JUST BEGUN!
Ryan '99
Hi*Fi

INKER ANDREW PEPOY ■ COLORIST GLORIA VASQUEZ ■ LETTERER RICHARD STARKINGS & COMICRAFT

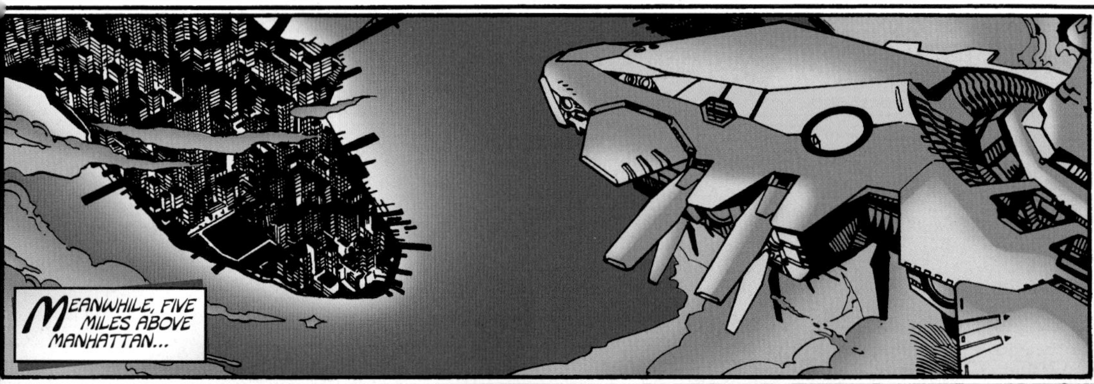
MEANWHILE, FIVE MILES ABOVE MANHATTAN...

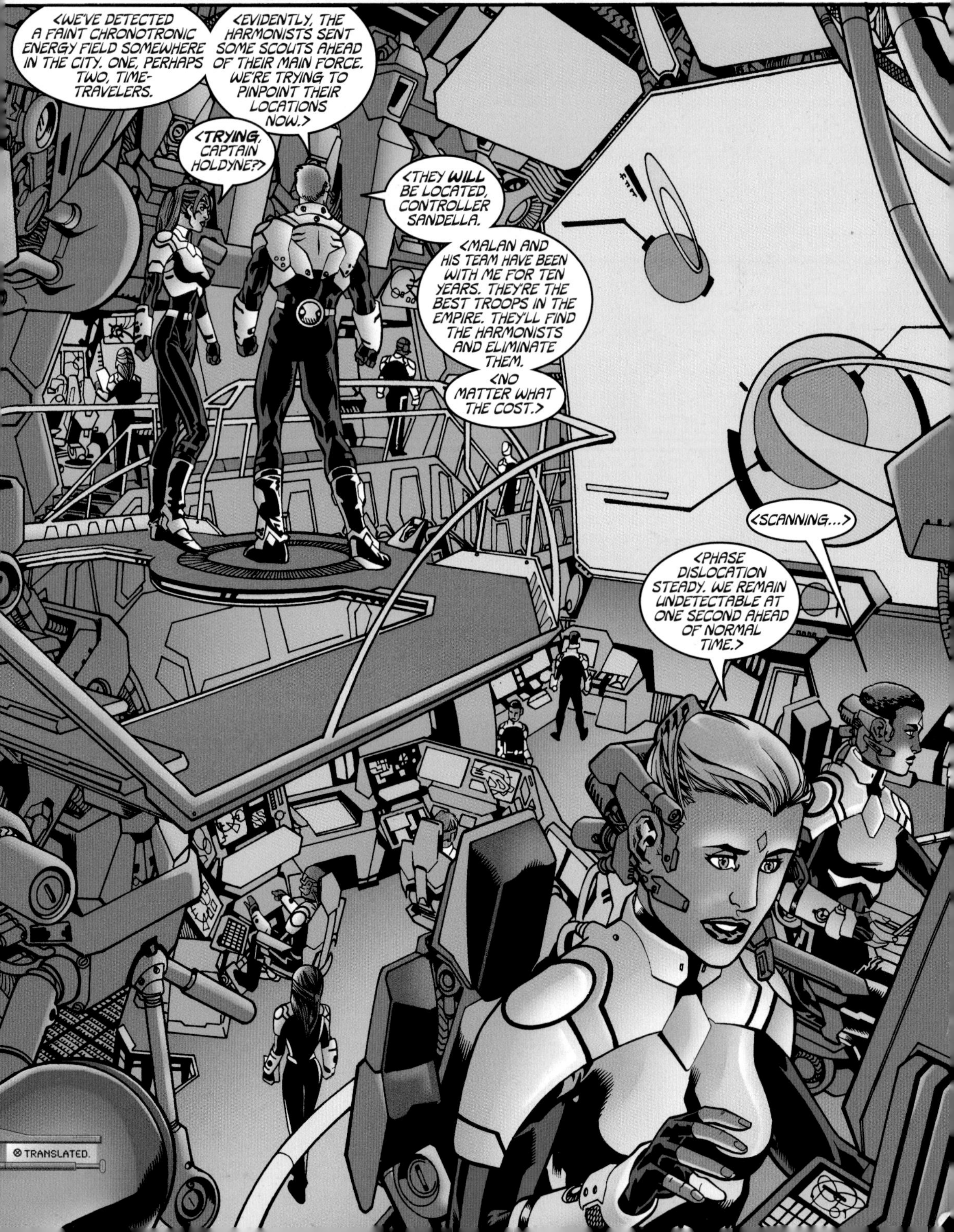
<WE'VE DETECTED A FAINT CHRONOTRONIC ENERGY FIELD SOMEWHERE IN THE CITY. ONE, PERHAPS TWO, TIME-TRAVELERS.
EVIDENTLY, THE HARMONISTS SENT SOME SCOUTS AHEAD OF THEIR MAIN FORCE. WE'RE TRYING TO PINPOINT THEIR LOCATIONS NOW.>
<TRYING, CAPTAIN HOLDYNE?>
<THEY WILL BE LOCATED, CONTROLLER SANDELLA.
<MALAN AND HIS TEAM HAVE BEEN WITH ME FOR TEN YEARS. THEY'RE THE BEST TROOPS IN THE EMPIRE. THEY'LL FIND THE HARMONISTS AND ELIMINATE THEM.
<NO MATTER WHAT THE COST.>
<SCANNING...>
<PHASE DISLOCATION STEADY. WE REMAIN UNDETECTABLE AT ONE SECOND AHEAD OF NORMAL TIME.>
⊗ TRANSLATED.

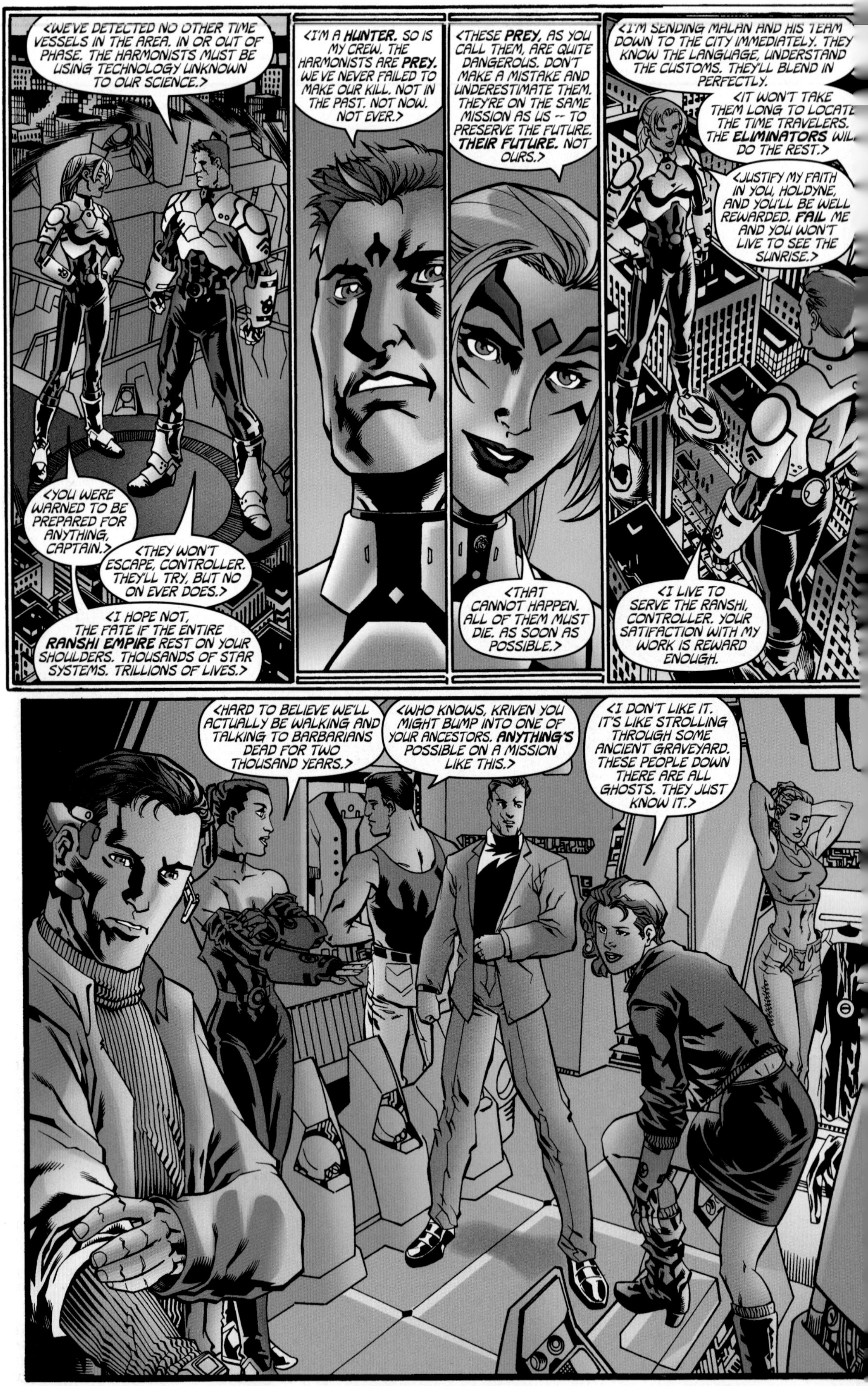
<WE'VE DETECTED NO OTHER TIME VESSELS IN THE AREA. IN OR OUT OF PHASE. THE HARMONISTS MUST BE USING TECHNOLOGY UNKNOWN TO OUR SCIENCE.>
<YOU WERE WARNED TO BE PREPARED FOR ANYTHING, CAPTAIN.>
<THEY WON'T ESCAPE, CONTROLLER. THEY'LL TRY, BUT NO ON EVER DOES.>
<I HOPE NOT, THE FATE IF THE ENTIRE **RANSHI EMPIRE** REST ON YOUR SHOULDERS. THOUSANDS OF STAR SYSTEMS. TRILLIONS OF LIVES.>
<I'M A **HUNTER.** SO IS MY CREW. THE HARMONISTS ARE **PREY.** WE'VE NEVER FAILED TO MAKE OUR KILL. NOT IN THE PAST. NOT NOW. NOT EVER.>
<THESE **PREY,** AS YOU CALL THEM, ARE QUITE DANGEROUS. DON'T MAKE A MISTAKE AND UNDERESTIMATE THEM. THEY'RE ON THE SAME MISSION AS US -- TO PRESERVE THE FUTURE. **THEIR FUTURE.** NOT OURS.>
<THAT CANNOT HAPPEN. ALL OF THEM MUST DIE. AS SOON AS POSSIBLE.>
<I'M SENDING MALAN AND HIS TEAM DOWN TO THE CITY IMMEDIATELY. THEY KNOW THE LANGUAGE, UNDERSTAND THE CUSTOMS. THEY'LL BLEND IN PERFECTLY.
<IT WON'T TAKE THEM LONG TO LOCATE THE TIME TRAVELERS. THE **ELIMINATORS** WIL DO THE REST.>
<JUSTIFY MY FAITH IN YOU, HOLDYNE, AND YOU'LL BE WELL REWARDED. **FAIL** ME AND YOU WON'T LIVE TO SEE THE SUNRISE.>
<I LIVE TO SERVE THE RANSHI, CONTROLLER. YOUR SATIFACTION WITH MY WORK IS REWARD ENOUGH.
<HARD TO BELIEVE WE'LL ACTUALLY BE WALKING AND TALKING TO BARBARIANS DEAD FOR TWO THOUSAND YEARS.>
<WHO KNOWS, KRIVEN YOU MIGHT BUMP INTO ONE OF YOUR ANCESTORS. **ANYTHING'S** POSSIBLE ON A MISSION LIKE THIS.>
<I DON'T LIKE IT. IT'S LIKE STROLLING THROUGH SOME ANCIENT GRAVEYARD. THESE PEOPLE DOWN THERE ARE ALL GHOSTS. THEY JUST KNOW IT.>

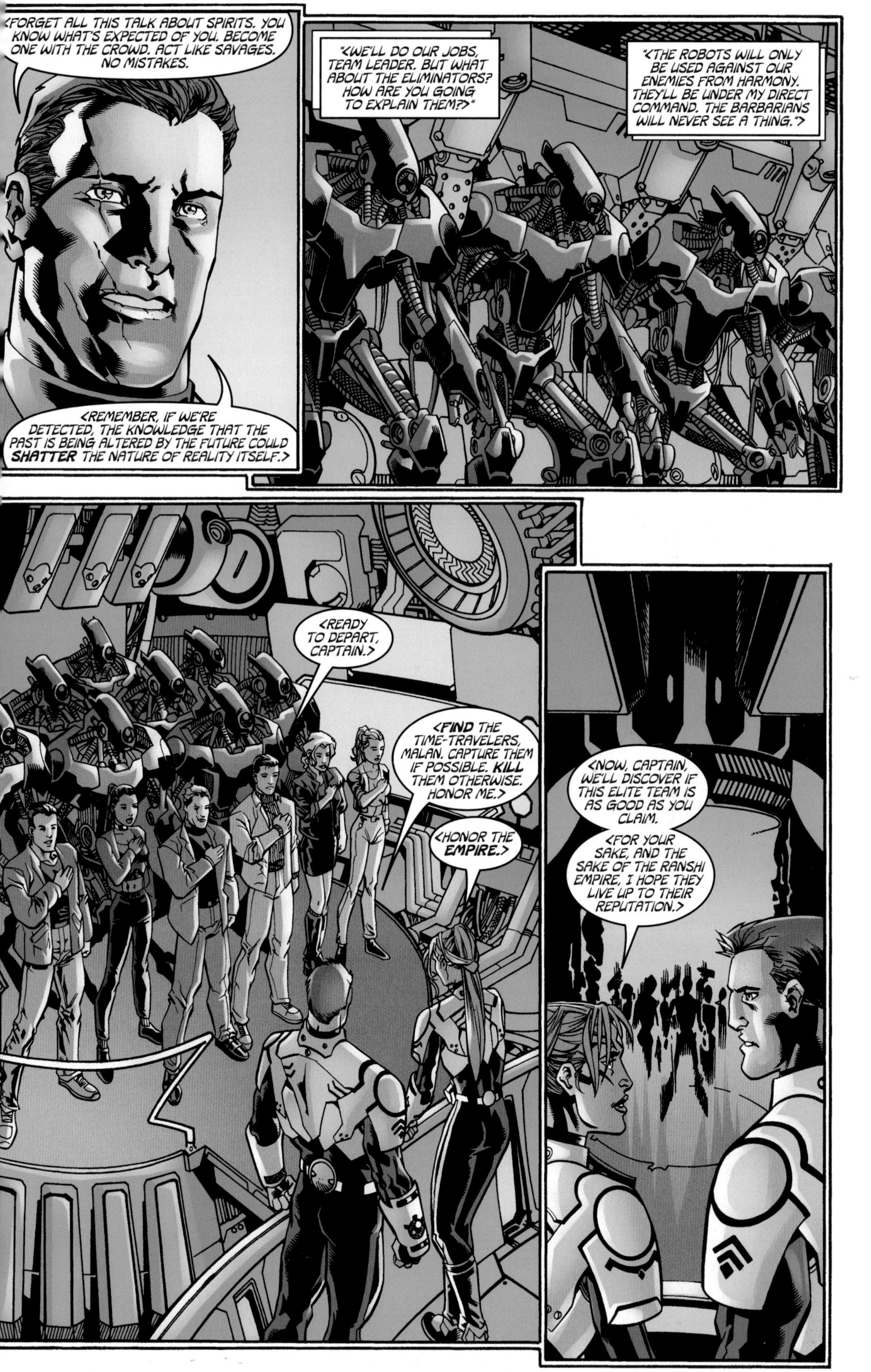
<FORGET ALL THIS TALK ABOUT SPIRITS. YOU KNOW WHAT'S EXPECTED OF YOU. BECOME ONE WITH THE CROWD. ACT LIKE SAVAGES. NO MISTAKES.
<REMEMBER, IF WE'RE DETECTED, THE KNOWLEDGE THAT THE PAST IS BEING ALTERED BY THE FUTURE COULD SHATTER THE NATURE OF REALITY ITSELF.>
"<WE'LL DO OUR JOBS, TEAM LEADER. BUT WHAT ABOUT THE ELIMINATORS? HOW ARE YOU GOING TO EXPLAIN THEM?>"
"<THE ROBOTS WILL ONLY BE USED AGAINST OUR ENEMIES FROM HARMONY. THEY'LL BE UNDER MY DIRECT COMMAND. THE BARBARIANS WILL NEVER SEE A THING.">
<READY TO DEPART, CAPTAIN.>
<FIND THE TIME-TRAVELERS, MALAN. CAPTURE THEM IF POSSIBLE. KILL THEM OTHERWISE. HONOR ME.>
<HONOR THE EMPIRE.>
<NOW, CAPTAIN, WE'LL DISCOVER IF THIS ELITE TEAM IS AS GOOD AS YOU CLAIM.
<FOR YOUR SAKE, AND THE SAKE OF THE RANSHI EMPIRE, I HOPE THEY LIVE UP TO THEIR REPUTATION.>

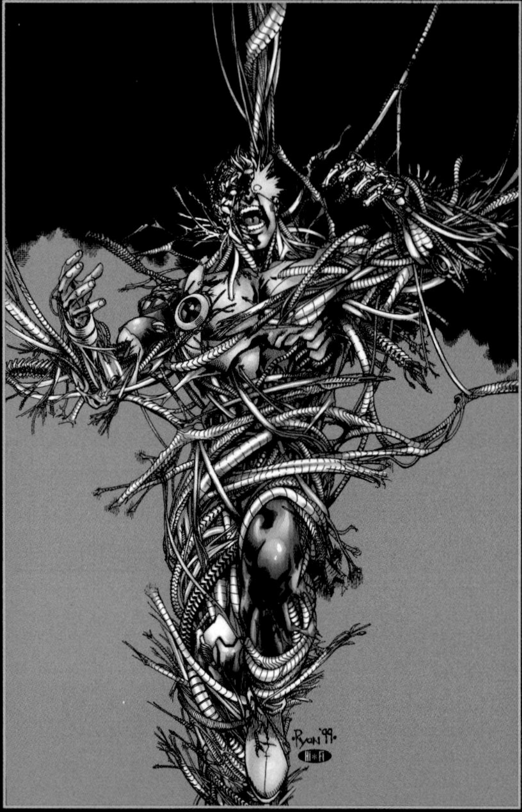
•RYAN '99•
HI-FI

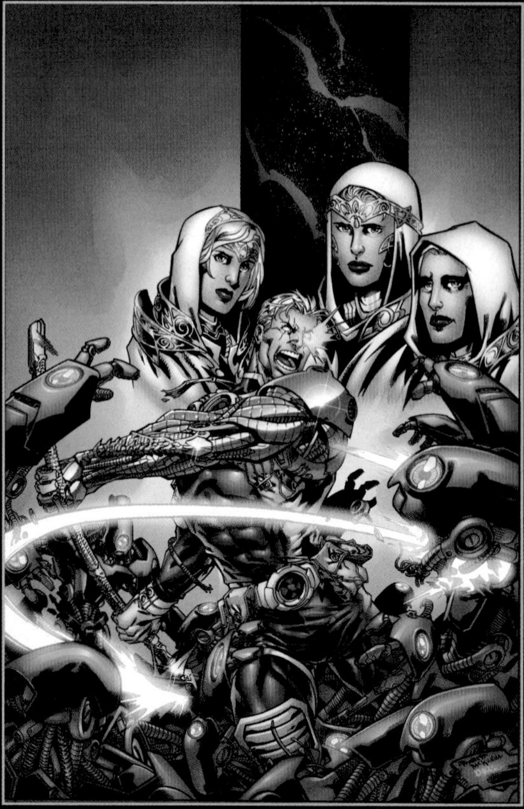

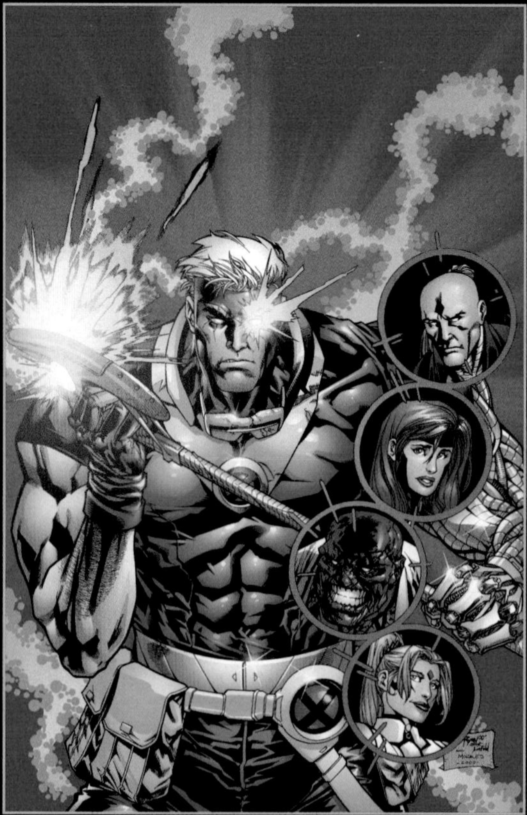

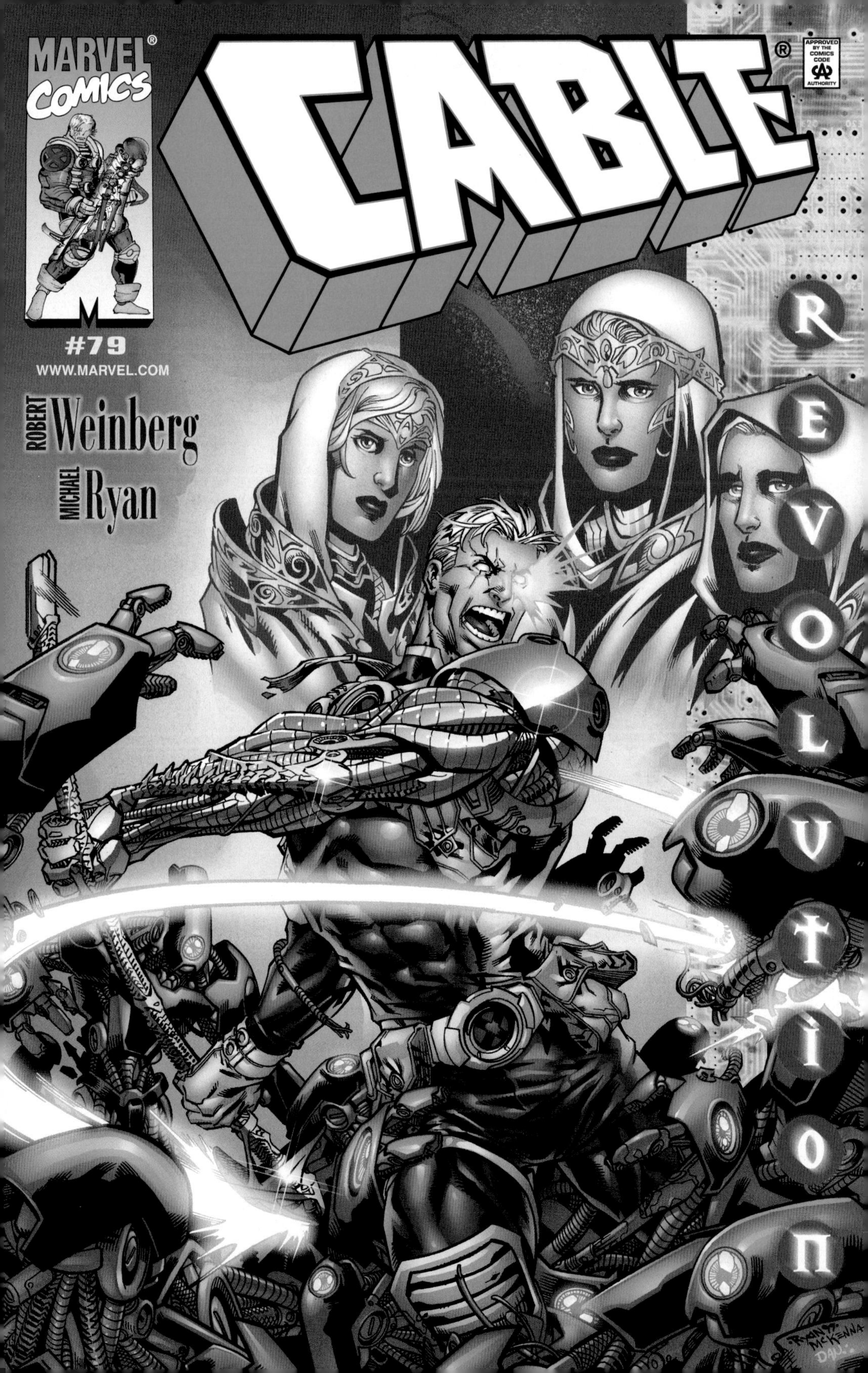
MARVEL COMICS
CABLE
APPROVED BY THE COMICS CODE AUTHORITY
#79
WWW.MARVEL.COM
ROBERT Weinberg
MICHAEL Ryan
REVOLUTION

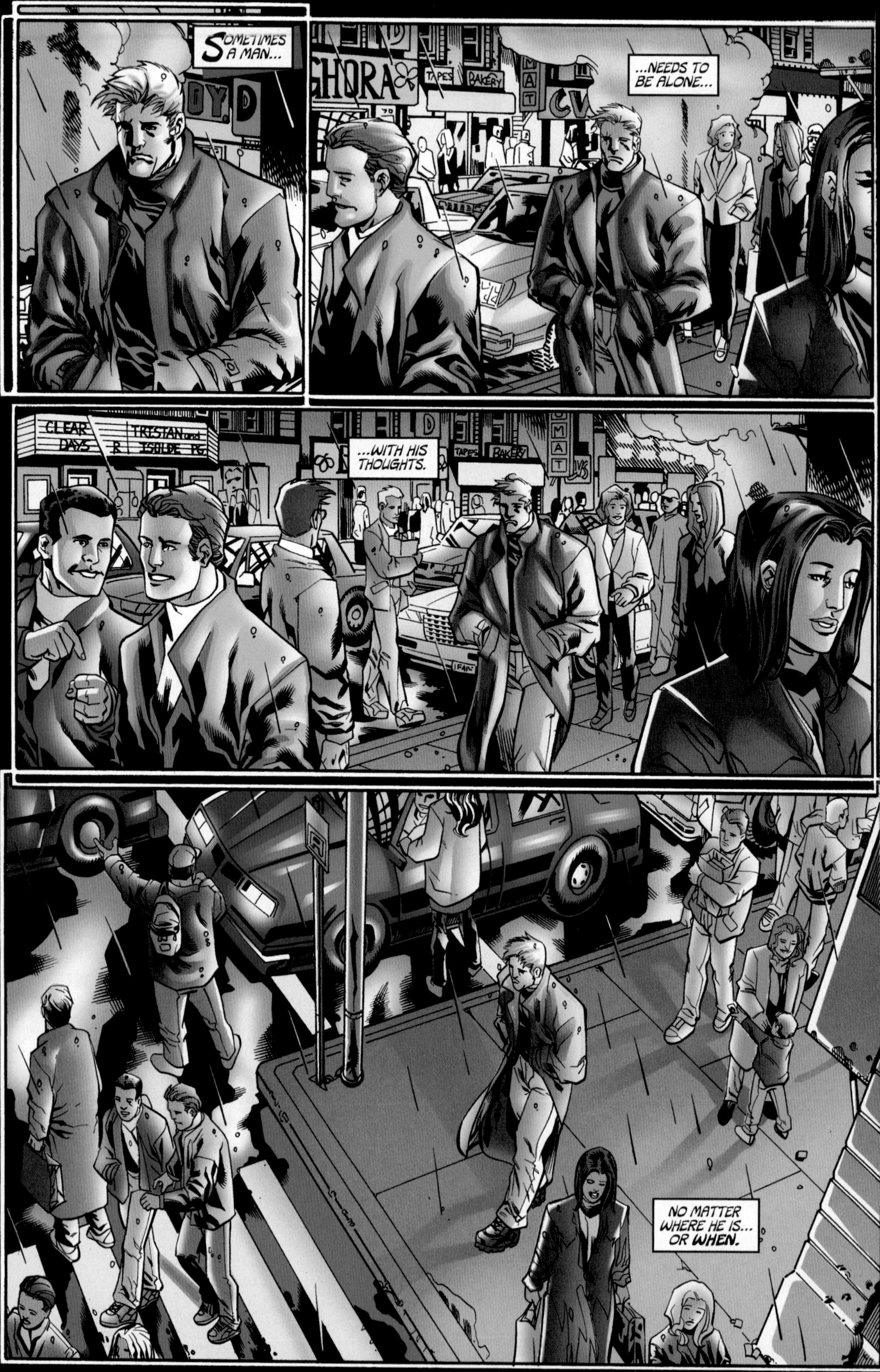
SOMETIMES A MAN...
...NEEDS TO BE ALONE...
...WITH HIS THOUGHTS.
NO MATTER WHERE HE IS... OR WHEN.

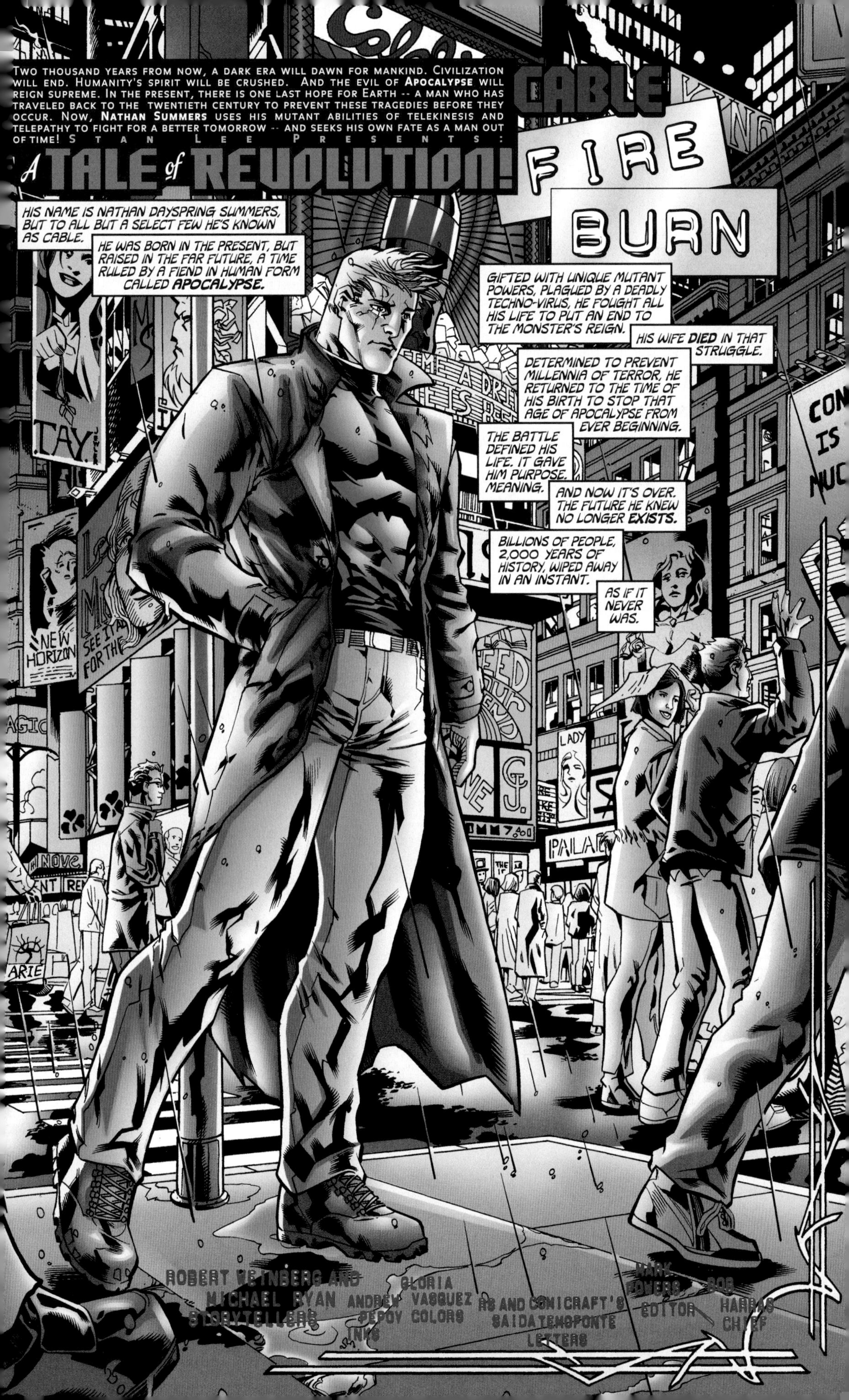
TWO THOUSAND YEARS FROM NOW, A DARK ERA WILL DAWN FOR MANKIND. CIVILIZATION WILL END. HUMANITY'S SPIRIT WILL BE CRUSHED. AND THE EVIL OF APOCALYPSE WILL REIGN SUPREME. IN THE PRESENT, THERE IS ONE LAST HOPE FOR EARTH -- A MAN WHO HAS TRAVELED BACK TO THE TWENTIETH CENTURY TO PREVENT THESE TRAGEDIES BEFORE THEY OCCUR. NOW, NATHAN SUMMERS USES HIS MUTANT ABILITIES OF TELEKINESIS AND TELEPATHY TO FIGHT FOR A BETTER TOMORROW -- AND SEEKS HIS OWN FATE AS A MAN OUT OF TIME!
CABLE
STAN LEE PRESENTS:
A TALE of REVOLUTION!
FIRE BURN
HIS NAME IS NATHAN DAYSPRING SUMMERS, BUT TO ALL BUT A SELECT FEW HE'S KNOWN AS CABLE.
HE WAS BORN IN THE PRESENT, BUT RAISED IN THE FAR FUTURE, A TIME RULED BY A FIEND IN HUMAN FORM CALLED APOCALYPSE.
GIFTED WITH UNIQUE MUTANT POWERS, PLAGUED BY A DEADLY TECHNO-VIRUS, HE FOUGHT ALL HIS LIFE TO PUT AN END TO THE MONSTER'S REIGN.
HIS WIFE DIED IN THAT STRUGGLE.
DETERMINED TO PREVENT MILLENNIA OF TERROR, HE RETURNED TO THE TIME OF HIS BIRTH TO STOP THAT AGE OF APOCALYPSE FROM EVER BEGINNING.
THE BATTLE DEFINED HIS LIFE. IT GAVE HIM PURPOSE. MEANING.
AND NOW IT'S OVER. THE FUTURE HE KNEW NO LONGER EXISTS.
BILLIONS OF PEOPLE, 2,000 YEARS OF HISTORY, WIPED AWAY IN AN INSTANT.
AS IF IT NEVER WAS.
ROBERT WEINBERG AND MICHAEL RYAN STORYTELLERS
ANDREW PEPOY INKS
GLORIA VASQUEZ COLORS
RS AND COMICRAFT'S SAIDATENOFONTE LETTERS
MARK POWERS EDITOR
BOB HARRAS CHIEF

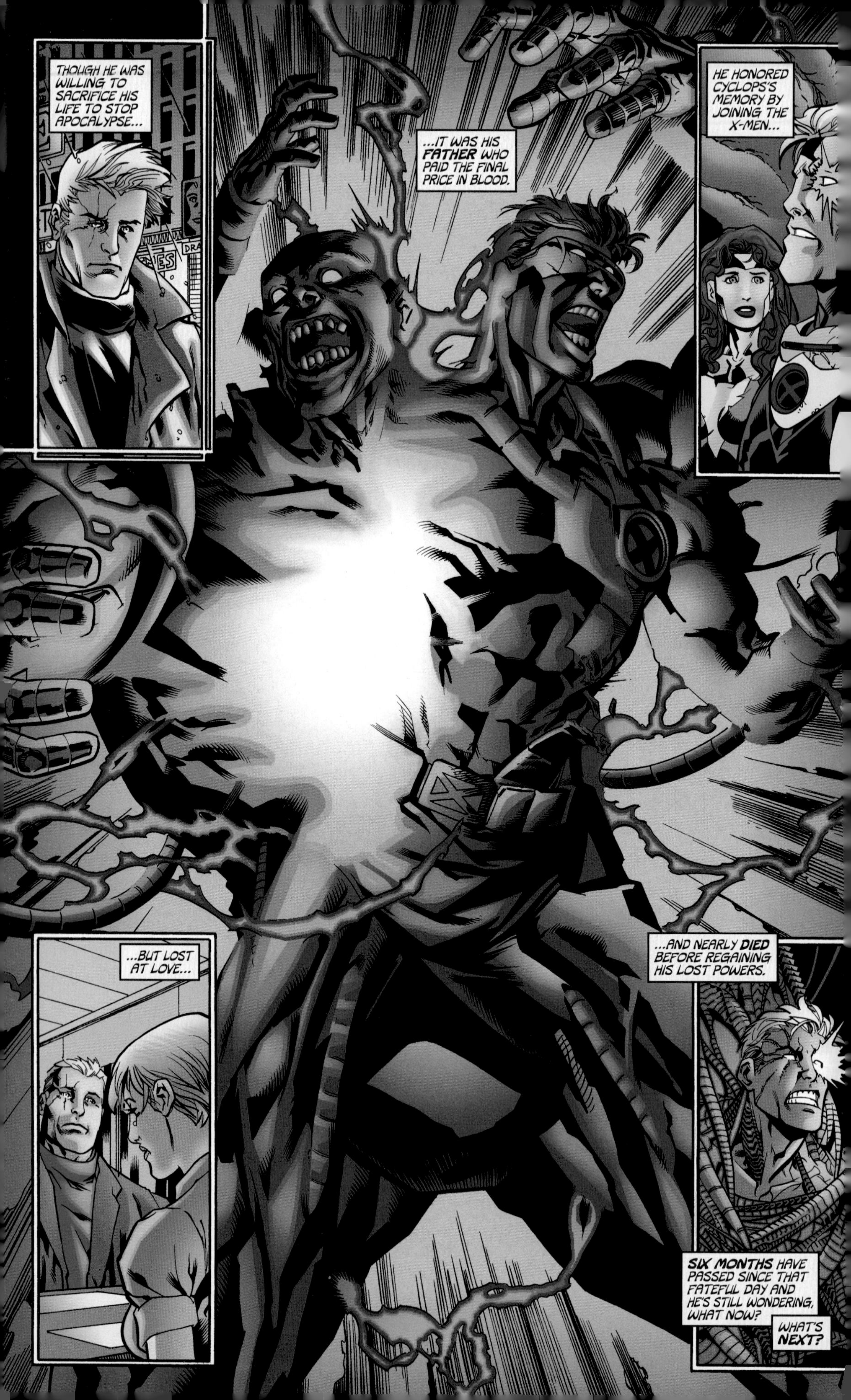

THOUGH HE WAS WILLING TO SACRIFICE HIS LIFE TO STOP APOCALYPSE...
...IT WAS HIS **FATHER** WHO PAID THE FINAL PRICE IN BLOOD.
HE HONORED CYCLOPS'S MEMORY BY JOINING THE X-MEN...
...BUT LOST AT LOVE...
...AND NEARLY **DIED** BEFORE REGAINING HIS LOST POWERS.
SIX MONTHS HAVE PASSED SINCE THAT FATEFUL DAY AND HE'S STILL WONDERING, WHAT NOW?
WHAT'S **NEXT?**

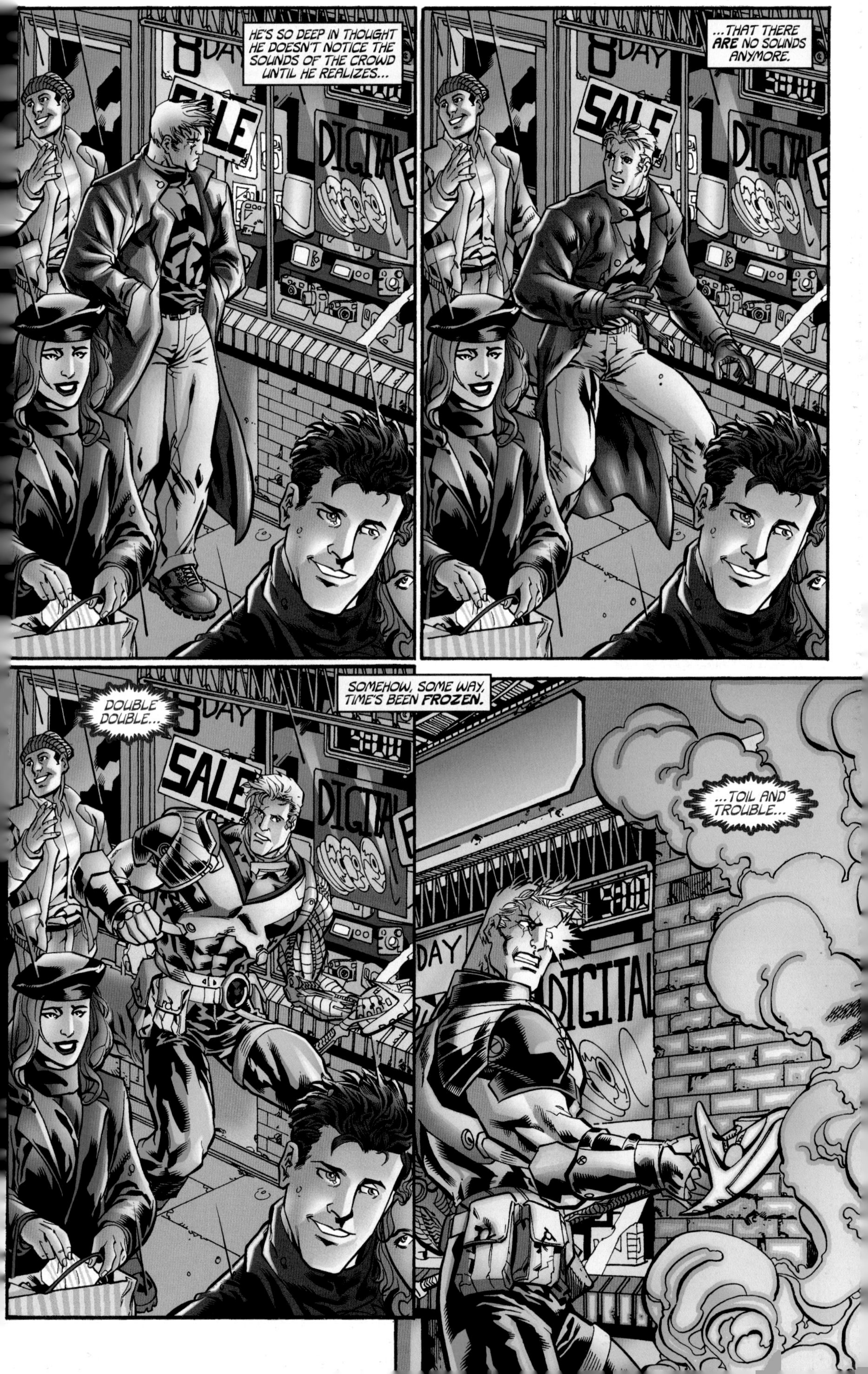
HE'S SO DEEP IN THOUGHT HE DOESN'T NOTICE THE SOUNDS OF THE CROWD UNTIL HE REALIZES...
8 DAY
SALE
DIGITAL
...THAT THERE ARE NO SOUNDS ANYMORE.
SOMEHOW, SOME WAY, TIME'S BEEN FROZEN.
DOUBLE DOUBLE...
...TOIL AND TROUBLE...

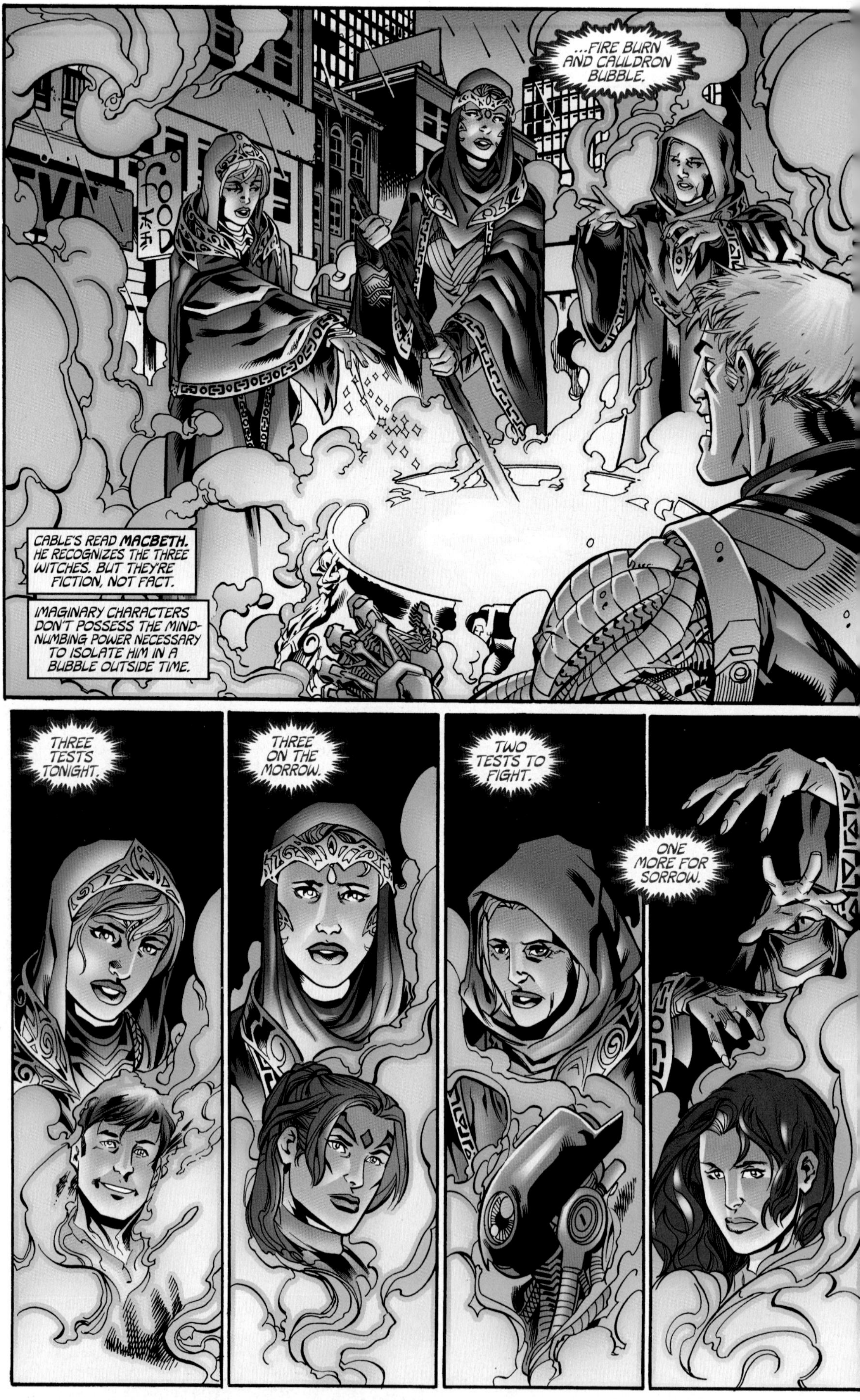

...FIRE BURN AND CAULDRON BUBBLE.
CABLE'S READ **MACBETH.** HE RECOGNIZES THE THREE WITCHES. BUT THEY'RE FICTION, NOT FACT.
IMAGINARY CHARACTERS DON'T POSSESS THE MIND-NUMBING POWER NECESSARY TO ISOLATE HIM IN A BUBBLE OUTSIDE TIME.
THREE TESTS TONIGHT.
THREE ON THE MORROW.
TWO TESTS TO FIGHT.
ONE MORE FOR SORROW.

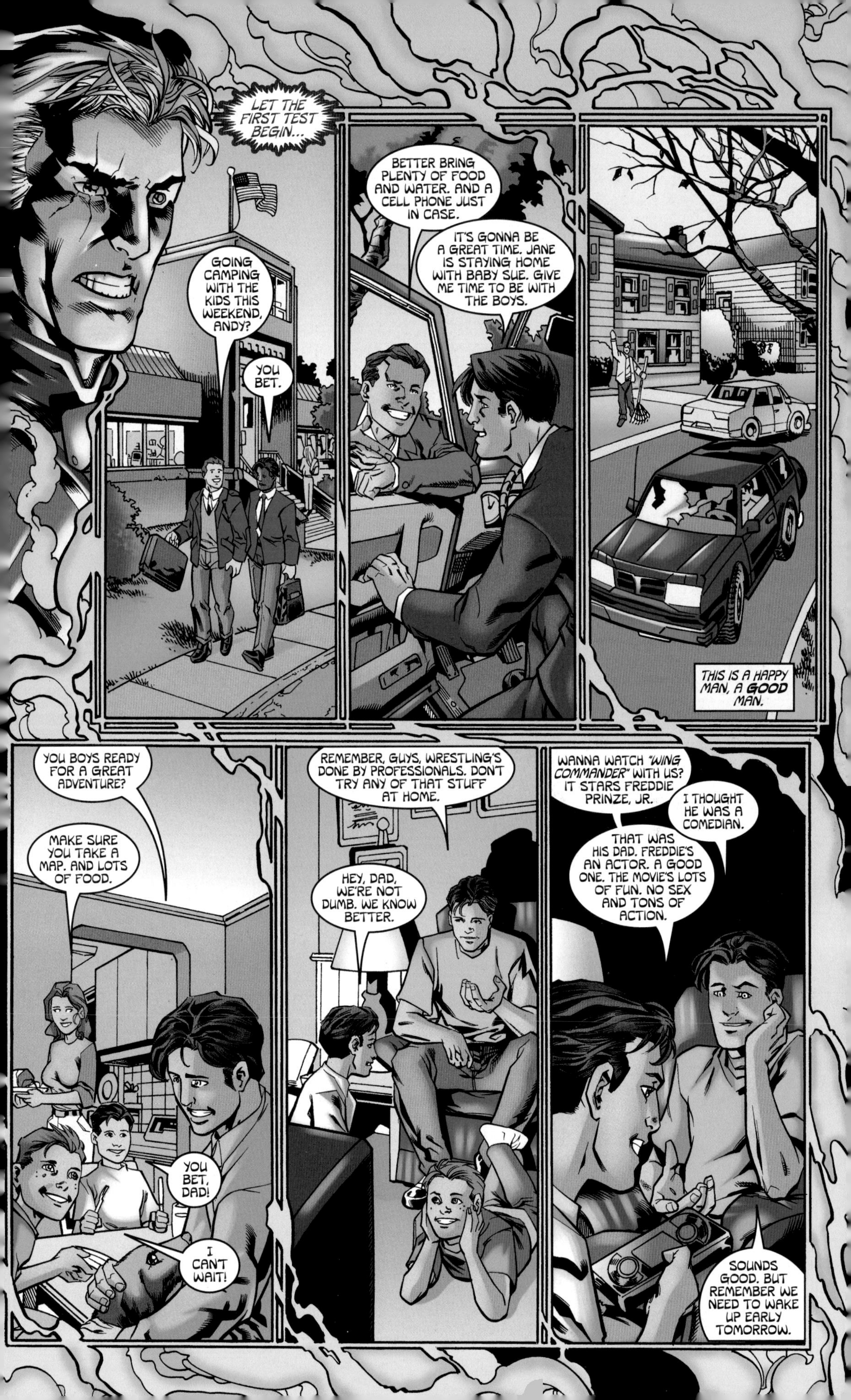
LET THE FIRST TEST BEGIN...
GOING CAMPING WITH THE KIDS THIS WEEKEND, ANDY?
YOU BET.
BETTER BRING PLENTY OF FOOD AND WATER. AND A CELL PHONE JUST IN CASE.
IT'S GONNA BE A GREAT TIME. JANE IS STAYING HOME WITH BABY SUE. GIVE ME TIME TO BE WITH THE BOYS.
THIS IS A HAPPY MAN, A **GOOD** MAN.
YOU BOYS READY FOR A GREAT ADVENTURE?
MAKE SURE YOU TAKE A MAP. AND LOTS OF FOOD.
YOU BET, DAD!
I CAN'T WAIT!
REMEMBER, GUYS, WRESTLING'S DONE BY PROFESSIONALS. DON'T TRY ANY OF THAT STUFF AT HOME.
HEY, DAD, WE'RE NOT DUMB. WE KNOW BETTER.
WANNA WATCH *"WING COMMANDER"* WITH US? IT STARS FREDDIE PRINZE, JR.
I THOUGHT HE WAS A COMEDIAN.
THAT WAS HIS DAD. FREDDIE'S AN ACTOR. A GOOD ONE. THE MOVIE'S LOTS OF FUN. NO SEX AND TONS OF ACTION.
SOUNDS GOOD. BUT REMEMBER WE NEED TO WAKE UP EARLY TOMORROW.

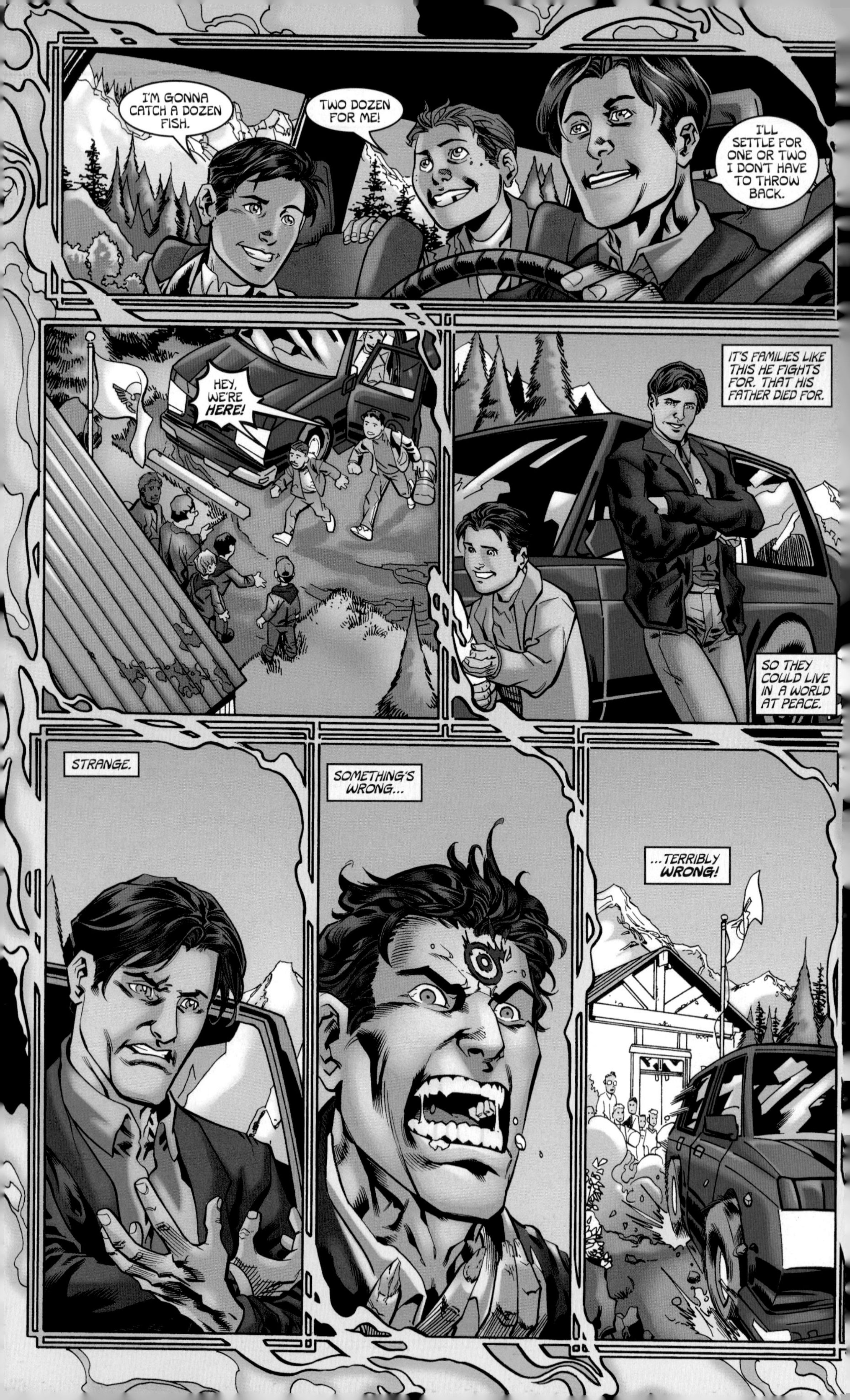
I'M GONNA CATCH A DOZEN FISH.
TWO DOZEN FOR ME!
I'LL SETTLE FOR ONE OR TWO I DON'T HAVE TO THROW BACK.
HEY, WE'RE *HERE!*
IT'S FAMILIES LIKE THIS HE FIGHTS FOR. THAT HIS FATHER DIED FOR.
SO THEY COULD LIVE IN A WORLD AT PEACE.
STRANGE.
SOMETHING'S WRONG...
...TERRIBLY *WRONG!*

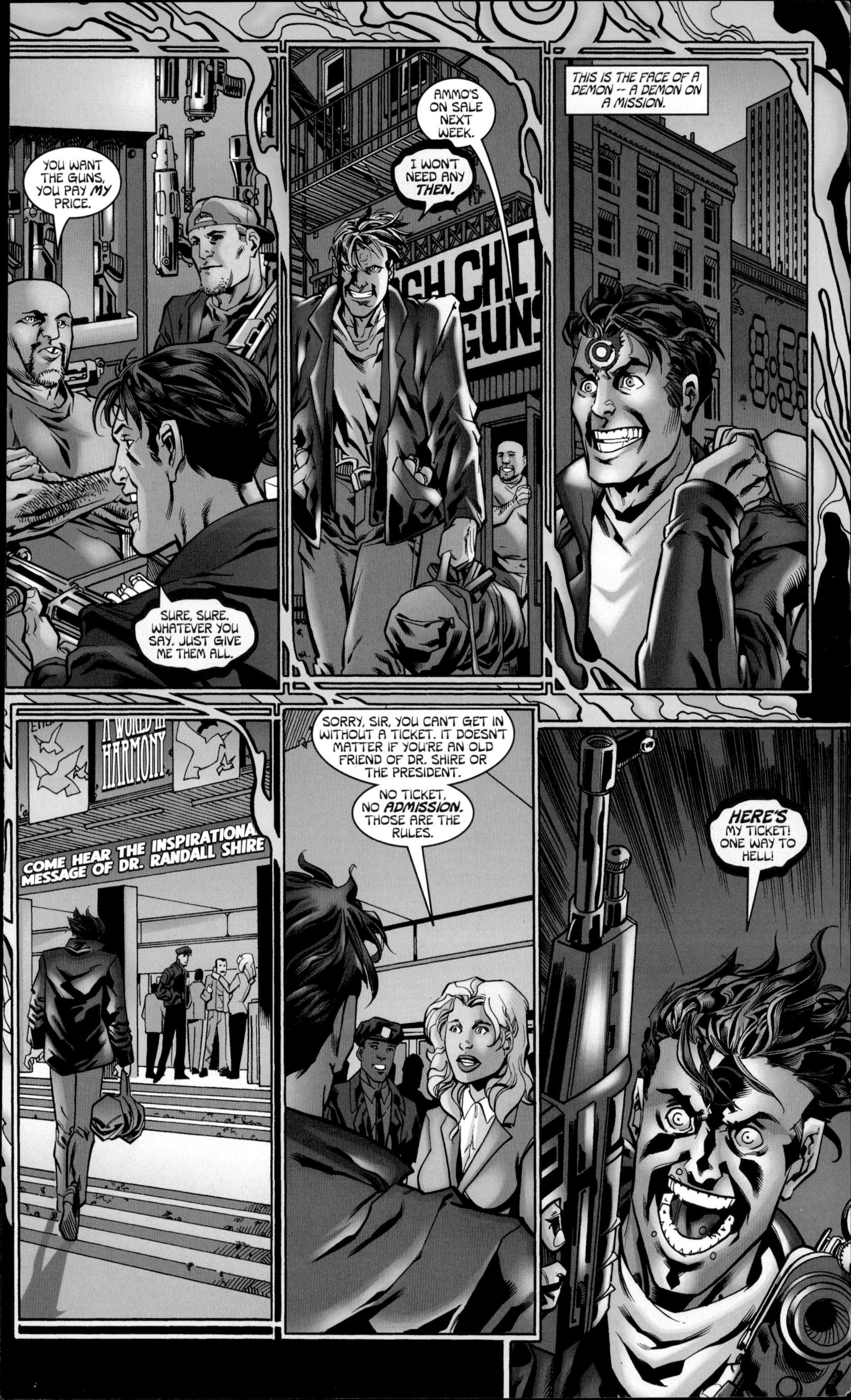
YOU WANT THE GUNS, YOU PAY MY PRICE.
SURE, SURE. WHATEVER YOU SAY. JUST GIVE ME THEM ALL.
AMMO'S ON SALE NEXT WEEK.
I WON'T NEED ANY THEN.
GUNS
THIS IS THE FACE OF A DEMON -- A DEMON ON A MISSION.
A WORLD IN HARMONY
COME HEAR THE INSPIRATIONA
MESSAGE OF DR. RANDALL SHIRE
SORRY, SIR, YOU CAN'T GET IN WITHOUT A TICKET. IT DOESN'T MATTER IF YOU'RE AN OLD FRIEND OF DR. SHIRE OR THE PRESIDENT.
NO TICKET, NO ADMISSION. THOSE ARE THE RULES.
HERE'S MY TICKET! ONE WAY TO HELL!

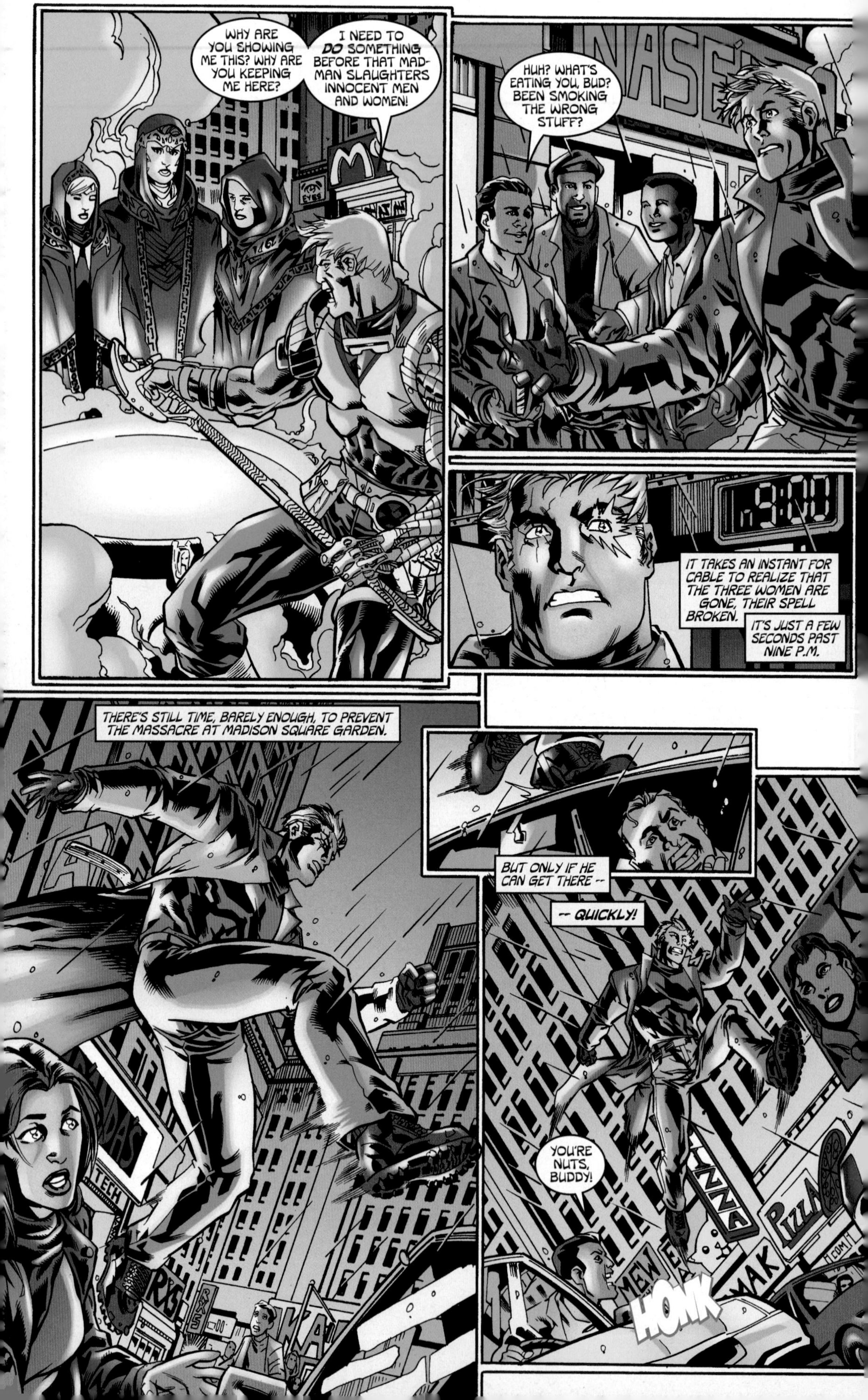
WHY ARE YOU SHOWING ME THIS? WHY ARE YOU KEEPING ME HERE?
I NEED TO DO SOMETHING BEFORE THAT MAD-MAN SLAUGHTERS INNOCENT MEN AND WOMEN!
HUH? WHAT'S EATING YOU, BUD? BEEN SMOKING THE WRONG STUFF?
IT TAKES AN INSTANT FOR CABLE TO REALIZE THAT THE THREE WOMEN ARE GONE, THEIR SPELL BROKEN.
IT'S JUST A FEW SECONDS PAST NINE P.M.
THERE'S STILL TIME, BARELY ENOUGH, TO PREVENT THE MASSACRE AT MADISON SQUARE GARDEN.
BUT ONLY IF HE CAN GET THERE --
-- QUICKLY!
YOU'RE NUTS, BUDDY!
HONK
PIZZA

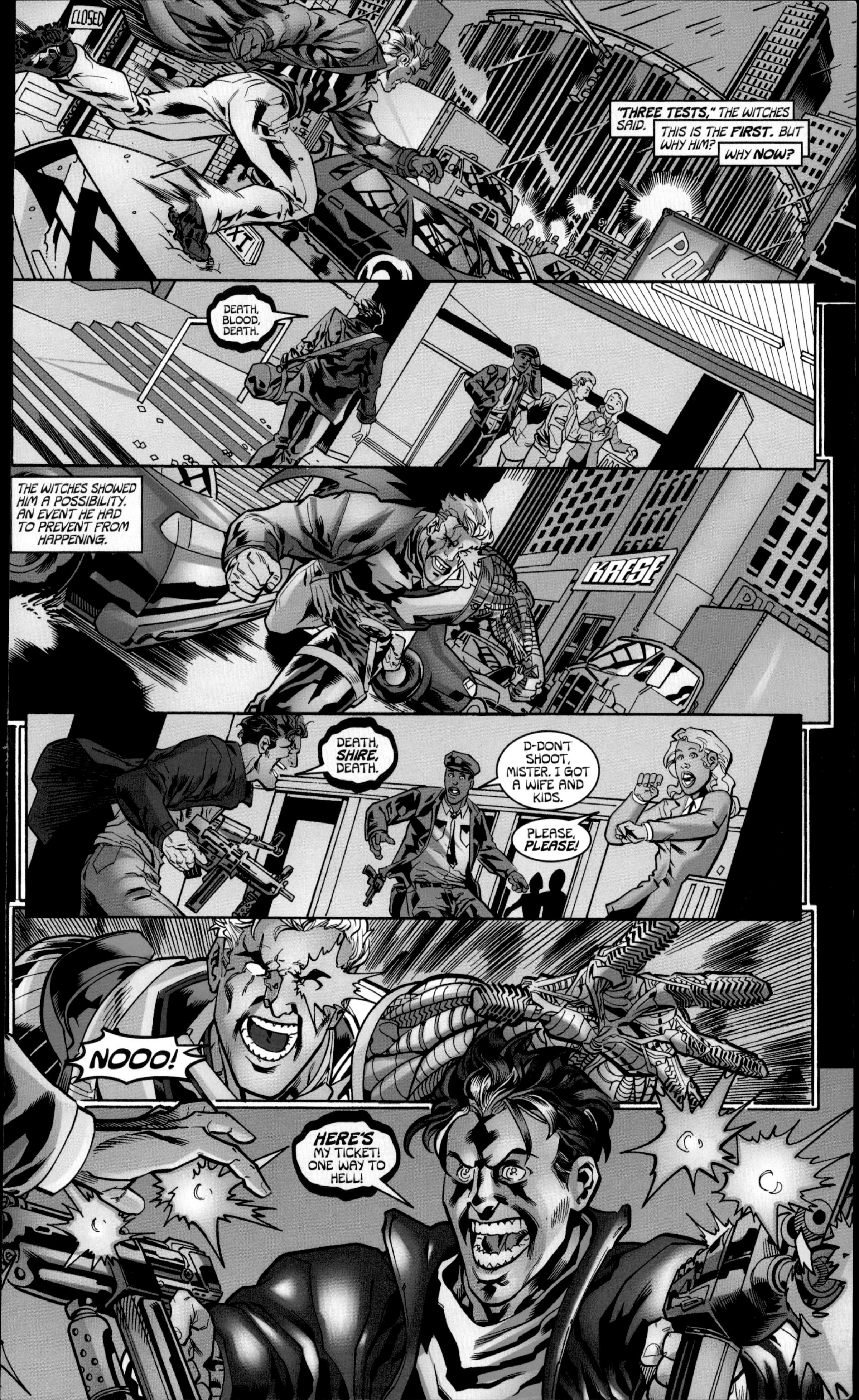
CLOSED
"THREE TESTS," THE WITCHES SAID.
THIS IS THE FIRST. BUT WHY HIM?
WHY NOW?
DEATH, BLOOD, DEATH.
THE WITCHES SHOWED HIM A POSSIBILITY. AN EVENT HE HAD TO PREVENT FROM HAPPENING.
KRESE
DEATH, SHIRE, DEATH.
D-DON'T SHOOT, MISTER. I GOT A WIFE AND KIDS.
PLEASE, PLEASE!
NOOO!
HERE'S MY TICKET! ONE WAY TO HELL!

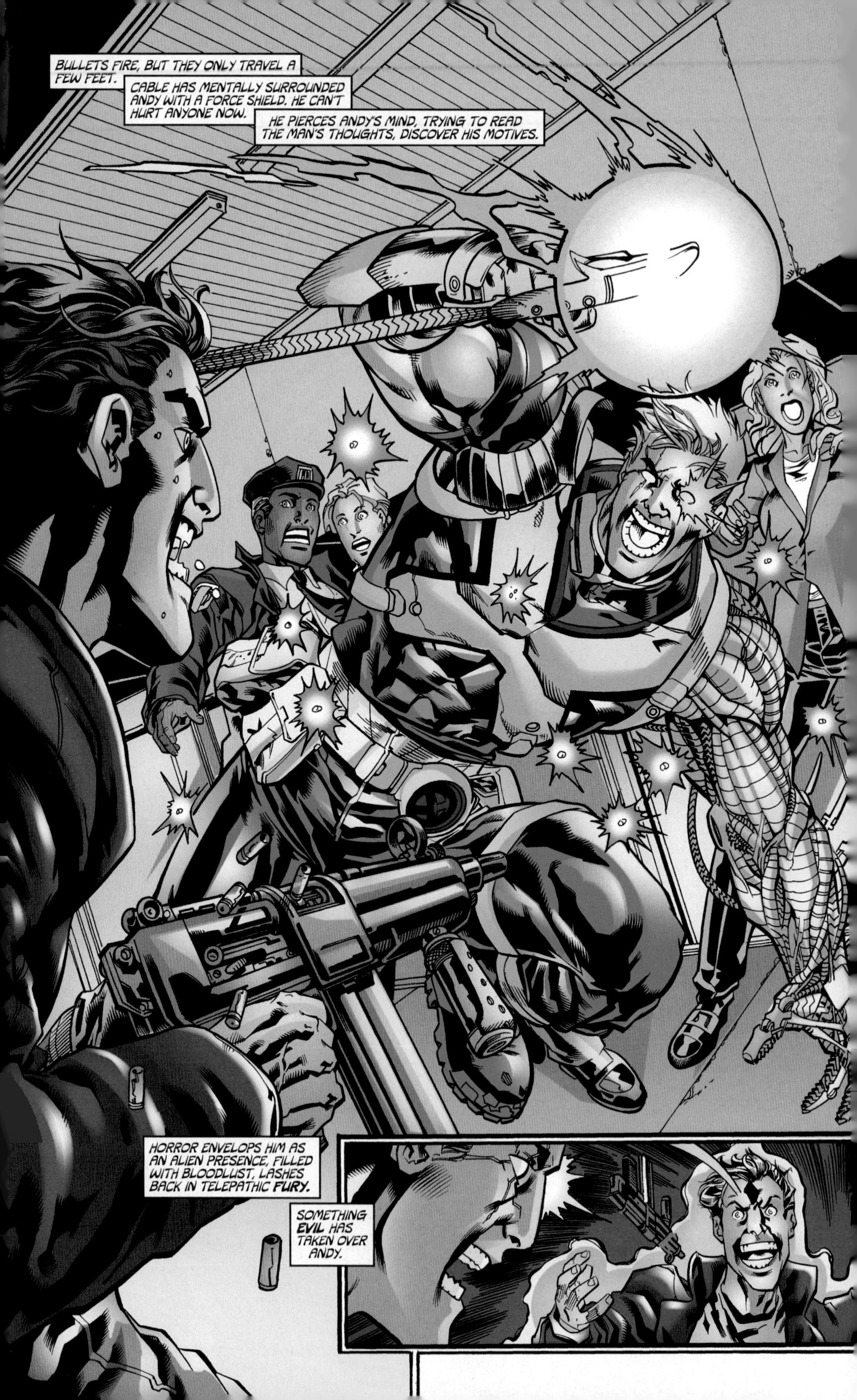

BULLETS FIRE, BUT THEY ONLY TRAVEL A FEW FEET.
CABLE HAS MENTALLY SURROUNDED ANDY WITH A FORCE SHIELD. HE CAN'T HURT ANYONE NOW.
HE PIERCES ANDY'S MIND, TRYING TO READ THE MAN'S THOUGHTS, DISCOVER HIS MOTIVES.
HORROR ENVELOPS HIM AS AN ALIEN PRESENCE, FILLED WITH BLOODLUST, LASHES BACK IN TELEPATHIC FURY.
SOMETHING EVIL HAS TAKEN OVER ANDY.

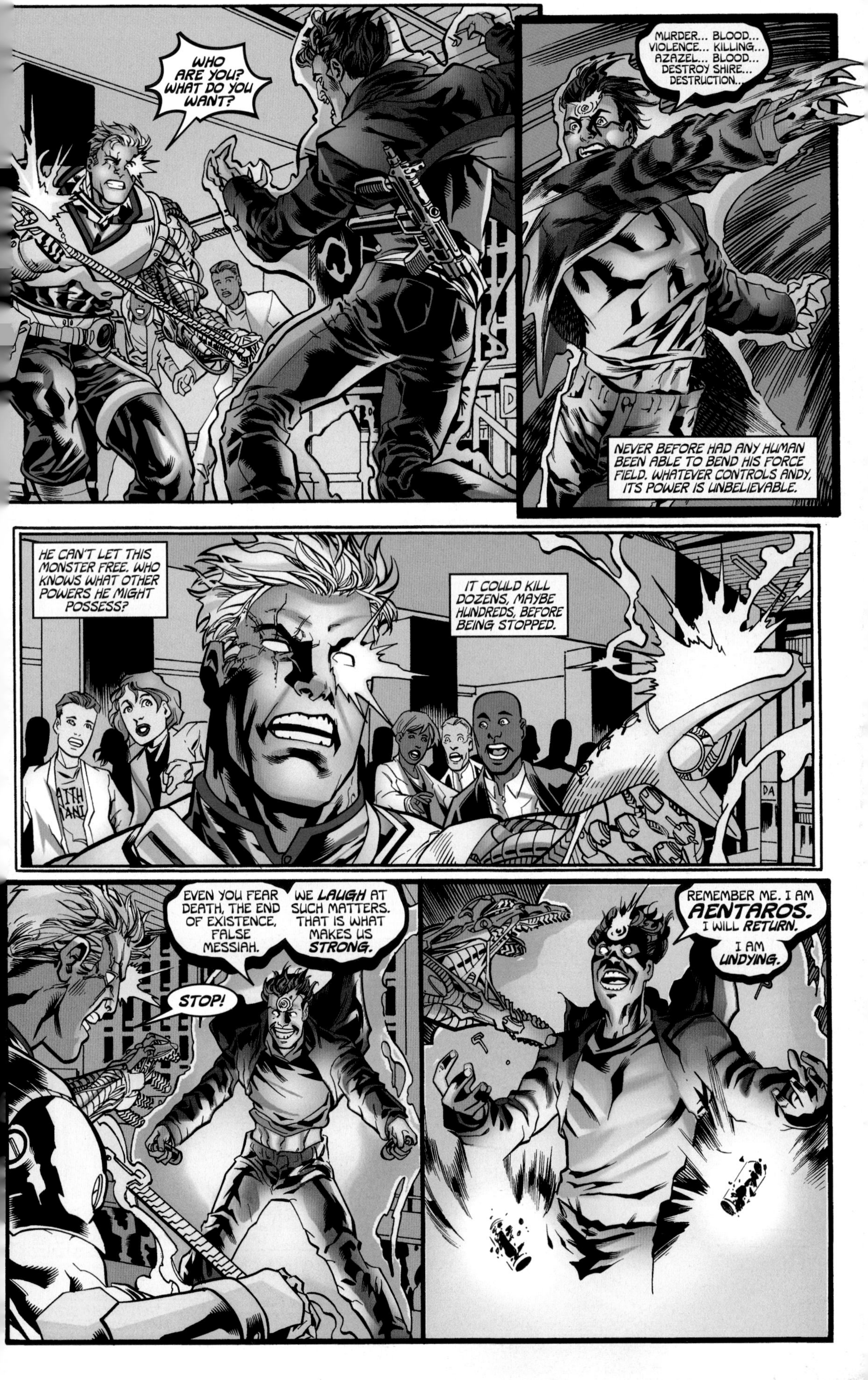
WHO ARE YOU? WHAT DO YOU WANT?
MURDER... BLOOD... VIOLENCE... KILLING... AZAZEL... BLOOD... DESTROY SHIRE... DESTRUCTION...
NEVER BEFORE HAD ANY HUMAN BEEN ABLE TO BEND HIS FORCE FIELD. WHATEVER CONTROLS ANDY, ITS POWER IS UNBELIEVABLE.
HE CAN'T LET THIS MONSTER FREE. WHO KNOWS WHAT OTHER POWERS HE MIGHT POSSESS?
IT COULD KILL DOZENS, MAYBE HUNDREDS, BEFORE BEING STOPPED.
EVEN YOU FEAR DEATH, THE END OF EXISTENCE, FALSE MESSIAH.
WE LAUGH AT SUCH MATTERS. THAT IS WHAT MAKES US STRONG.
STOP!
REMEMBER ME. I AM AENTAROS. I WILL RETURN.
I AM UNDYING.

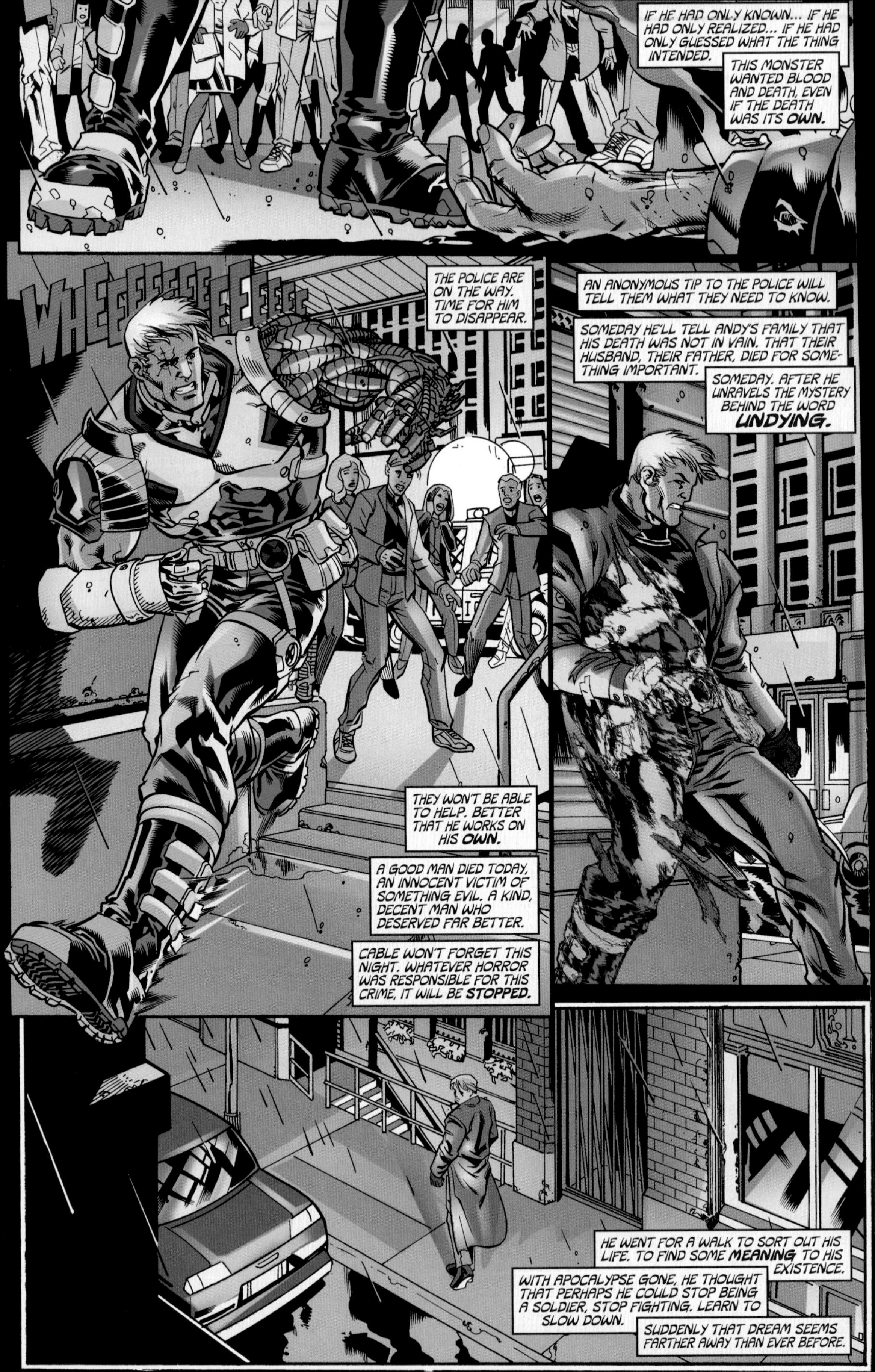

IF HE HAD ONLY KNOWN... IF HE HAD ONLY REALIZED... IF HE HAD ONLY GUESSED WHAT THE THING INTENDED.
THIS MONSTER WANTED BLOOD AND DEATH, EVEN IF THE DEATH WAS ITS OWN.
WHEEEEEEEEEEEE
THE POLICE ARE ON THE WAY. TIME FOR HIM TO DISAPPEAR.
THEY WON'T BE ABLE TO HELP. BETTER THAT HE WORKS ON HIS OWN.
A GOOD MAN DIED TODAY, AN INNOCENT VICTIM OF SOMETHING EVIL. A KIND, DECENT MAN WHO DESERVED FAR BETTER.
CABLE WON'T FORGET THIS NIGHT. WHATEVER HORROR WAS RESPONSIBLE FOR THIS CRIME, IT WILL BE STOPPED.
AN ANONYMOUS TIP TO THE POLICE WILL TELL THEM WHAT THEY NEED TO KNOW.
SOMEDAY HE'LL TELL ANDY'S FAMILY THAT HIS DEATH WAS NOT IN VAIN. THAT THEIR HUSBAND, THEIR FATHER, DIED FOR SOMETHING IMPORTANT.
SOMEDAY. AFTER HE UNRAVELS THE MYSTERY BEHIND THE WORD UNDYING.
HE WENT FOR A WALK TO SORT OUT HIS LIFE. TO FIND SOME MEANING TO HIS EXISTENCE.
WITH APOCALYPSE GONE, HE THOUGHT THAT PERHAPS HE COULD STOP BEING A SOLDIER, STOP FIGHTING. LEARN TO SLOW DOWN.
SUDDENLY THAT DREAM SEEMS FARTHER AWAY THAN EVER BEFORE.

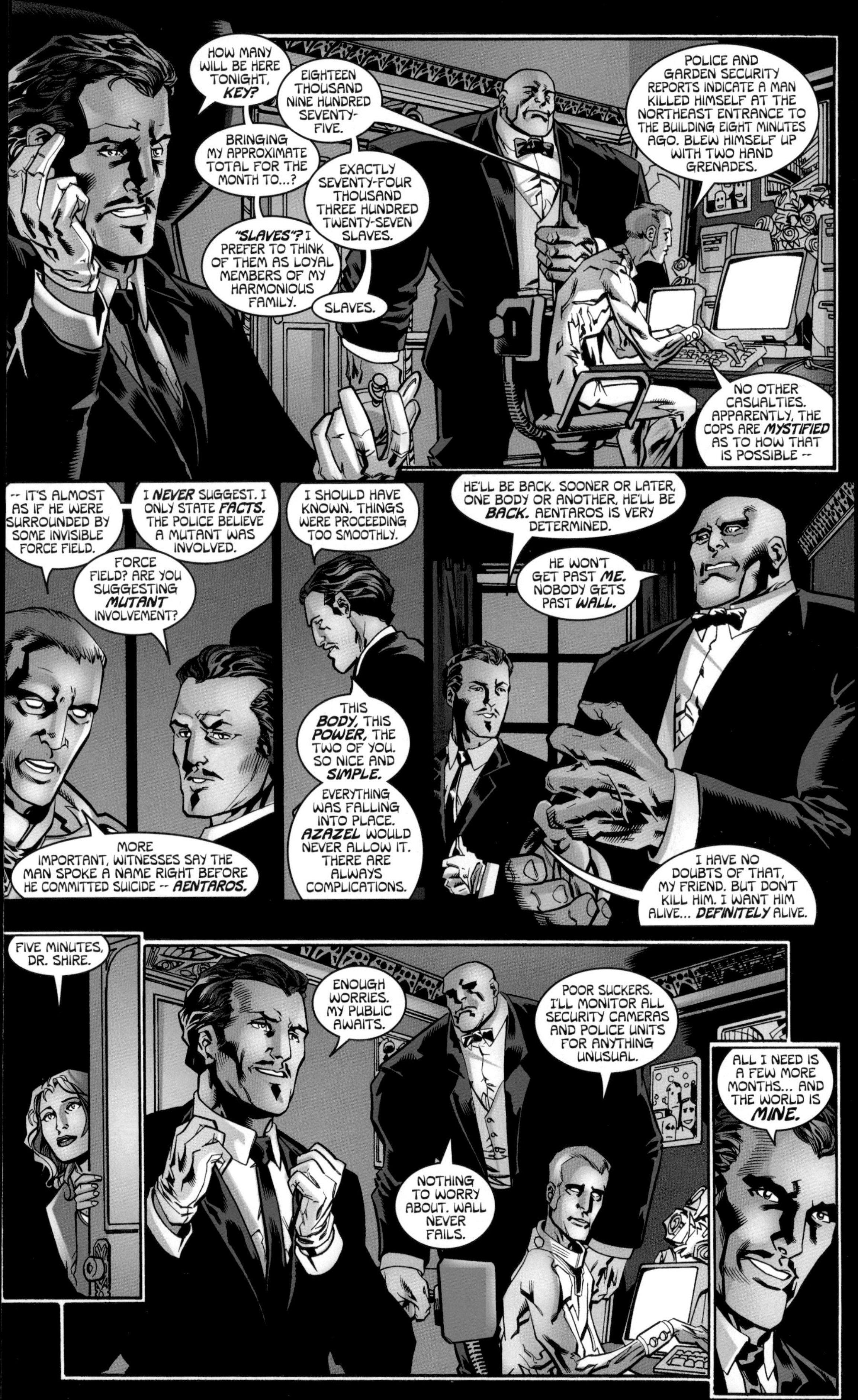
HOW MANY WILL BE HERE TONIGHT, KEY?
EIGHTEEN THOUSAND NINE HUNDRED SEVENTY-FIVE.
BRINGING MY APPROXIMATE TOTAL FOR THE MONTH TO...?
EXACTLY SEVENTY-FOUR THOUSAND THREE HUNDRED TWENTY-SEVEN SLAVES.
"SLAVES"? I PREFER TO THINK OF THEM AS LOYAL MEMBERS OF MY HARMONIOUS FAMILY.
SLAVES.
POLICE AND GARDEN SECURITY REPORTS INDICATE A MAN KILLED HIMSELF AT THE NORTHEAST ENTRANCE TO THE BUILDING EIGHT MINUTES AGO. BLEW HIMSELF UP WITH TWO HAND GRENADES.
NO OTHER CASUALTIES. APPARENTLY, THE COPS ARE MYSTIFIED AS TO HOW THAT IS POSSIBLE --
-- IT'S ALMOST AS IF HE WERE SURROUNDED BY SOME INVISIBLE FORCE FIELD.
FORCE FIELD? ARE YOU SUGGESTING MUTANT INVOLVEMENT?
I NEVER SUGGEST. I ONLY STATE FACTS. THE POLICE BELIEVE A MUTANT WAS INVOLVED.
MORE IMPORTANT, WITNESSES SAY THE MAN SPOKE A NAME RIGHT BEFORE HE COMMITTED SUICIDE -- AENTAROS.
I SHOULD HAVE KNOWN. THINGS WERE PROCEEDING TOO SMOOTHLY.
THIS BODY, THIS POWER, THE TWO OF YOU. SO NICE AND SIMPLE.
EVERYTHING WAS FALLING INTO PLACE. AZAZEL WOULD NEVER ALLOW IT. THERE ARE ALWAYS COMPLICATIONS.
HE'LL BE BACK. SOONER OR LATER, ONE BODY OR ANOTHER, HE'LL BE BACK. AENTAROS IS VERY DETERMINED.
HE WON'T GET PAST ME. NOBODY GETS PAST WALL.
I HAVE NO DOUBTS OF THAT, MY FRIEND. BUT DON'T KILL HIM. I WANT HIM ALIVE... DEFINITELY ALIVE.
FIVE MINUTES, DR. SHIRE.
ENOUGH WORRIES. MY PUBLIC AWAITS.
POOR SUCKERS. I'LL MONITOR ALL SECURITY CAMERAS AND POLICE UNITS FOR ANYTHING UNUSUAL.
NOTHING TO WORRY ABOUT. WALL NEVER FAILS.
ALL I NEED IS A FEW MORE MONTHS... AND THE WORLD IS MINE.

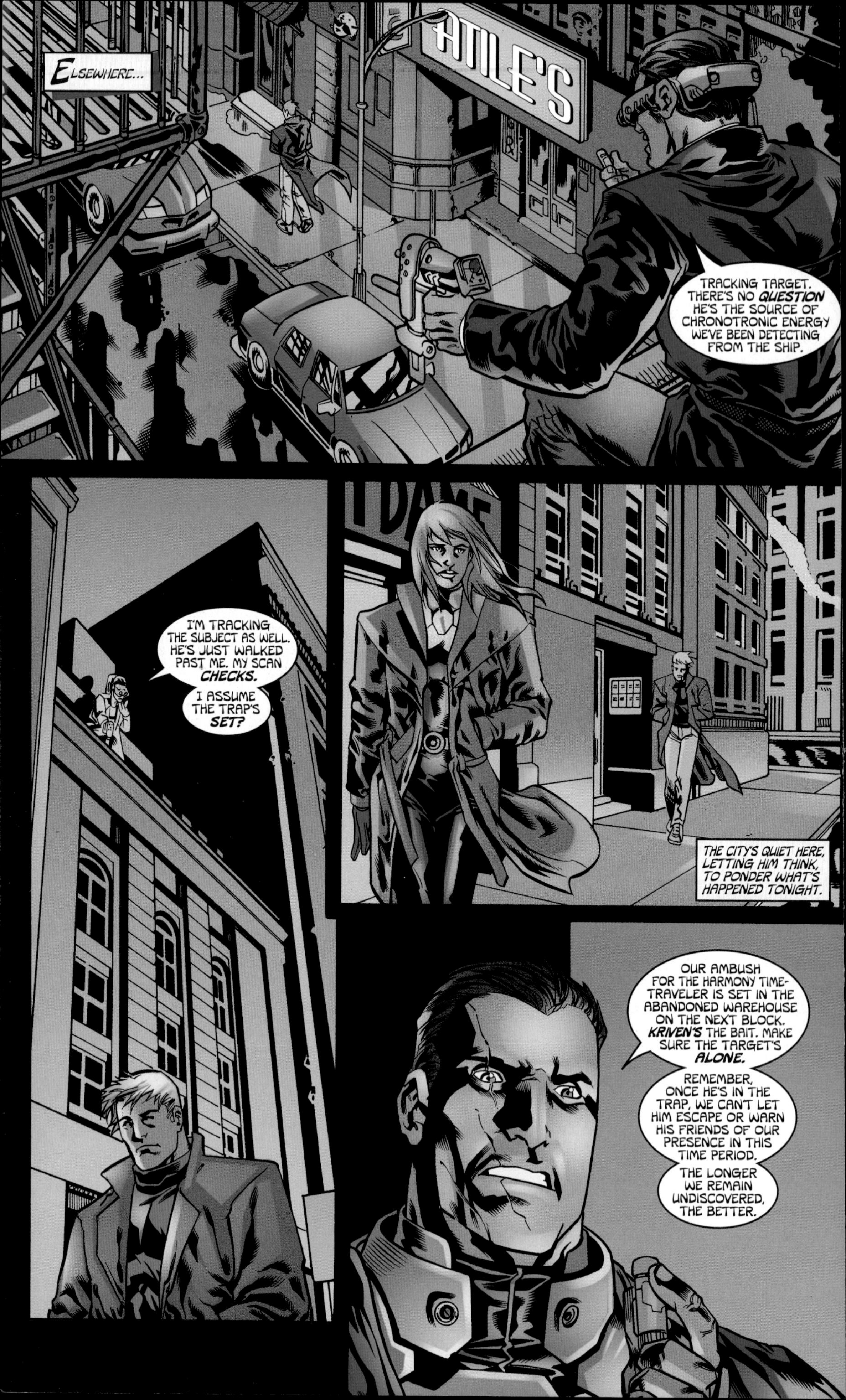
ELSEWHERE...
ATILE'S
TRACKING TARGET. THERE'S NO QUESTION HE'S THE SOURCE OF CHRONOTRONIC ENERGY WE'VE BEEN DETECTING FROM THE SHIP.
I'M TRACKING THE SUBJECT AS WELL. HE'S JUST WALKED PAST ME. MY SCAN CHECKS.
I ASSUME THE TRAP'S SET?
THE CITY'S QUIET HERE, LETTING HIM THINK, TO PONDER WHAT'S HAPPENED TONIGHT.
OUR AMBUSH FOR THE HARMONY TIME-TRAVELER IS SET IN THE ABANDONED WAREHOUSE ON THE NEXT BLOCK. KRIVEN'S THE BAIT. MAKE SURE THE TARGET'S ALONE.
REMEMBER, ONCE HE'S IN THE TRAP, WE CAN'T LET HIM ESCAPE OR WARN HIS FRIENDS OF OUR PRESENCE IN THIS TIME PERIOD.
THE LONGER WE REMAIN UNDISCOVERED, THE BETTER.

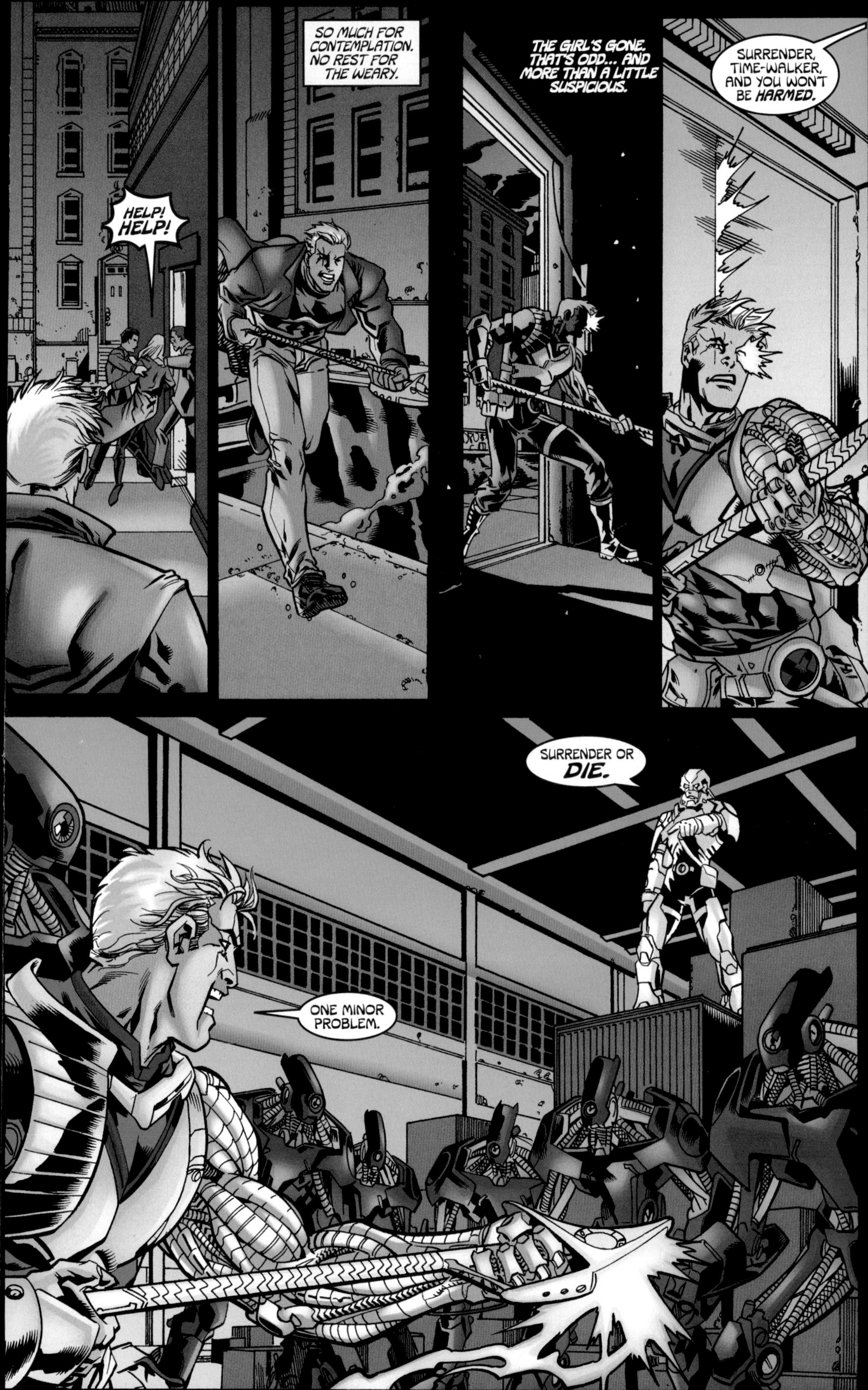
HELP! HELP!
SO MUCH FOR CONTEMPLATION. NO REST FOR THE WEARY.
THE GIRL'S GONE. THAT'S ODD... AND MORE THAN A LITTLE SUSPICIOUS.
SURRENDER, TIME-WALKER, AND YOU WON'T BE HARMED.
SURRENDER OR DIE.
ONE MINOR PROBLEM.

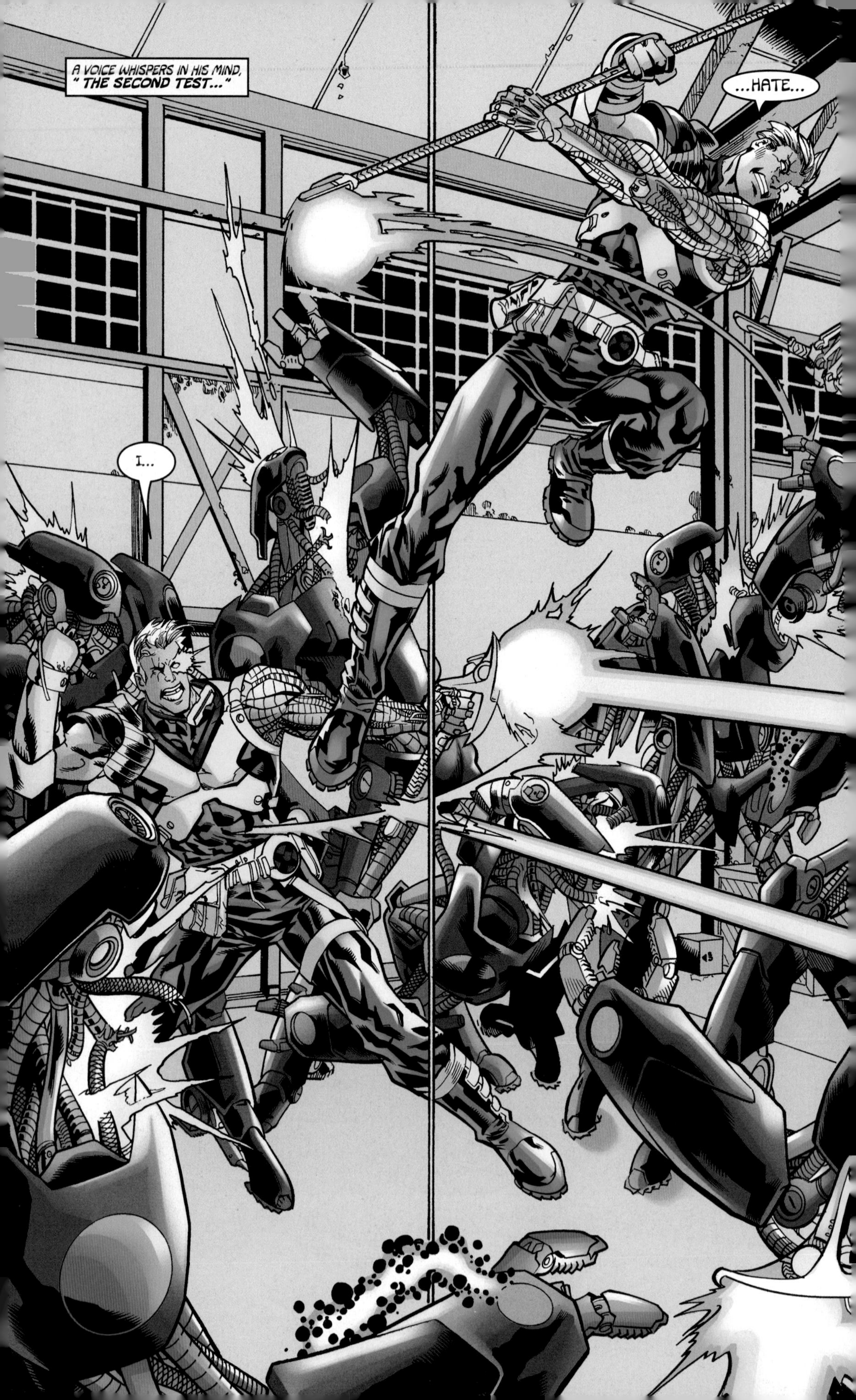
A VOICE WHISPERS IN HIS MIND, "THE SECOND TEST..."
...HATE...
I...

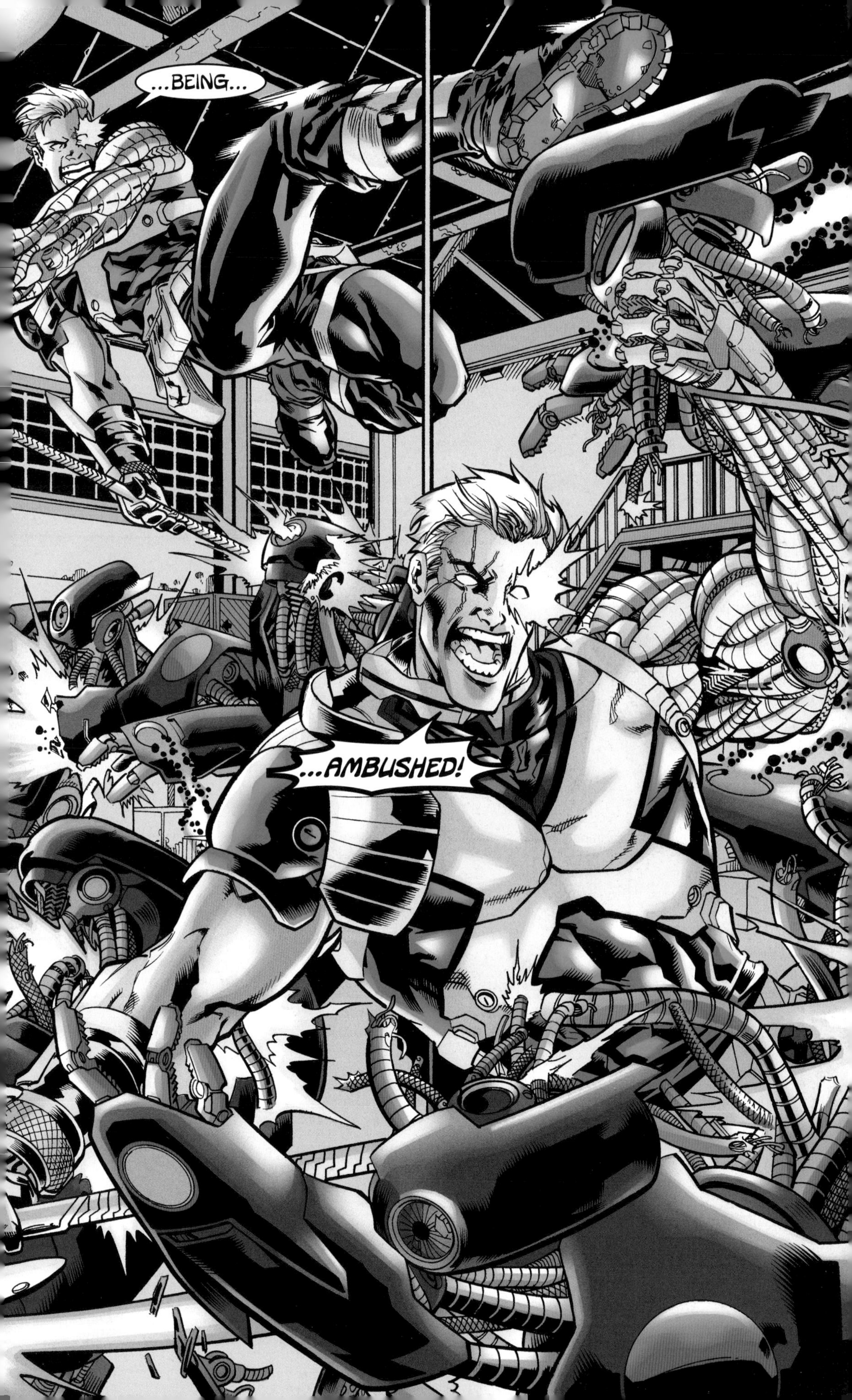
...BEING...
...AMBUSHED!

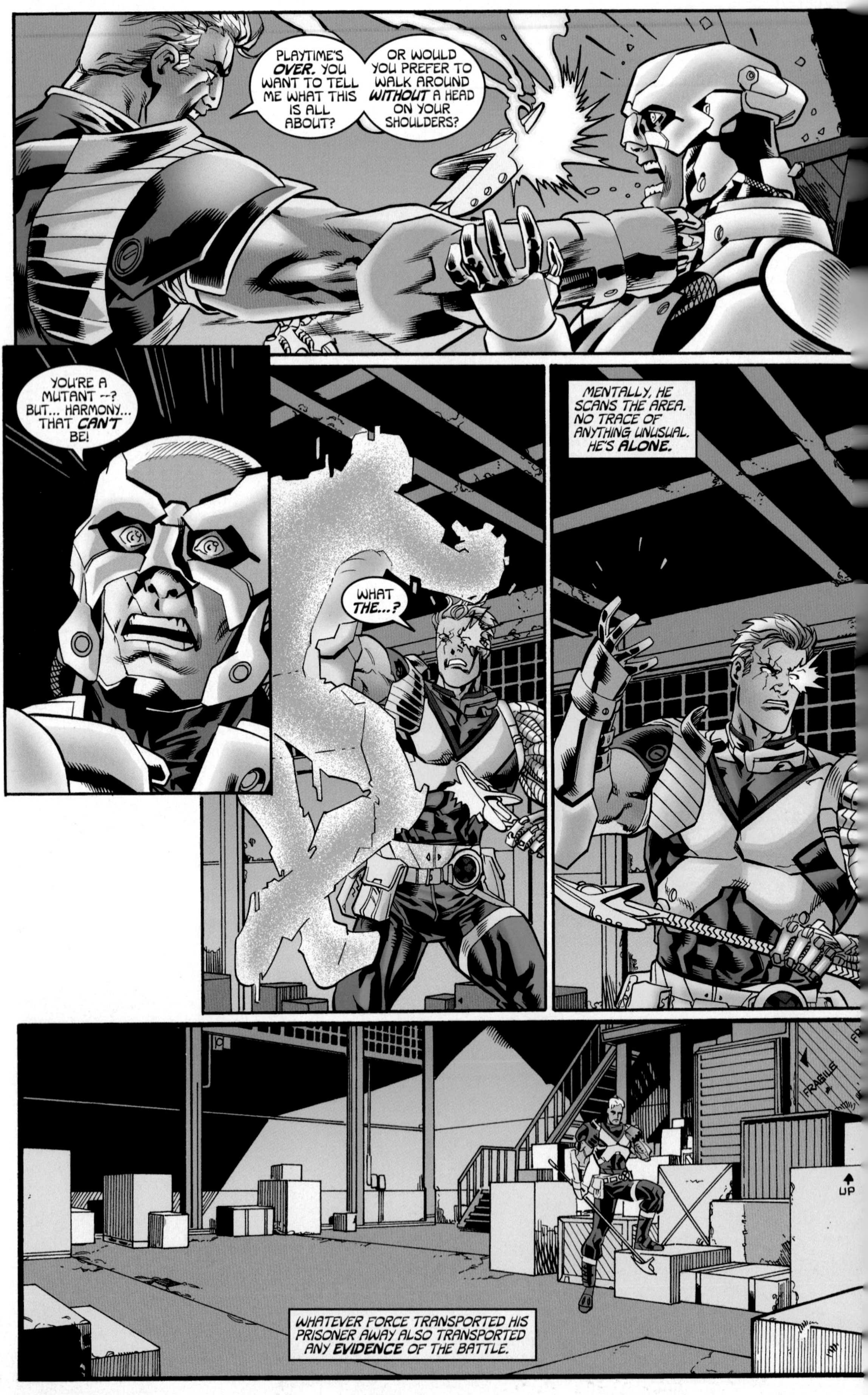
PLAYTIME'S OVER. YOU WANT TO TELL ME WHAT THIS IS ALL ABOUT?
OR WOULD YOU PREFER TO WALK AROUND WITHOUT A HEAD ON YOUR SHOULDERS?
YOU'RE A MUTANT --? BUT... HARMONY... THAT CAN'T BE!
WHAT THE...?
MENTALLY, HE SCANS THE AREA. NO TRACE OF ANYTHING UNUSUAL. HE'S ALONE.
FRAGILE
UP
WHATEVER FORCE TRANSPORTED HIS PRISONER AWAY ALSO TRANSPORTED ANY EVIDENCE OF THE BATTLE.

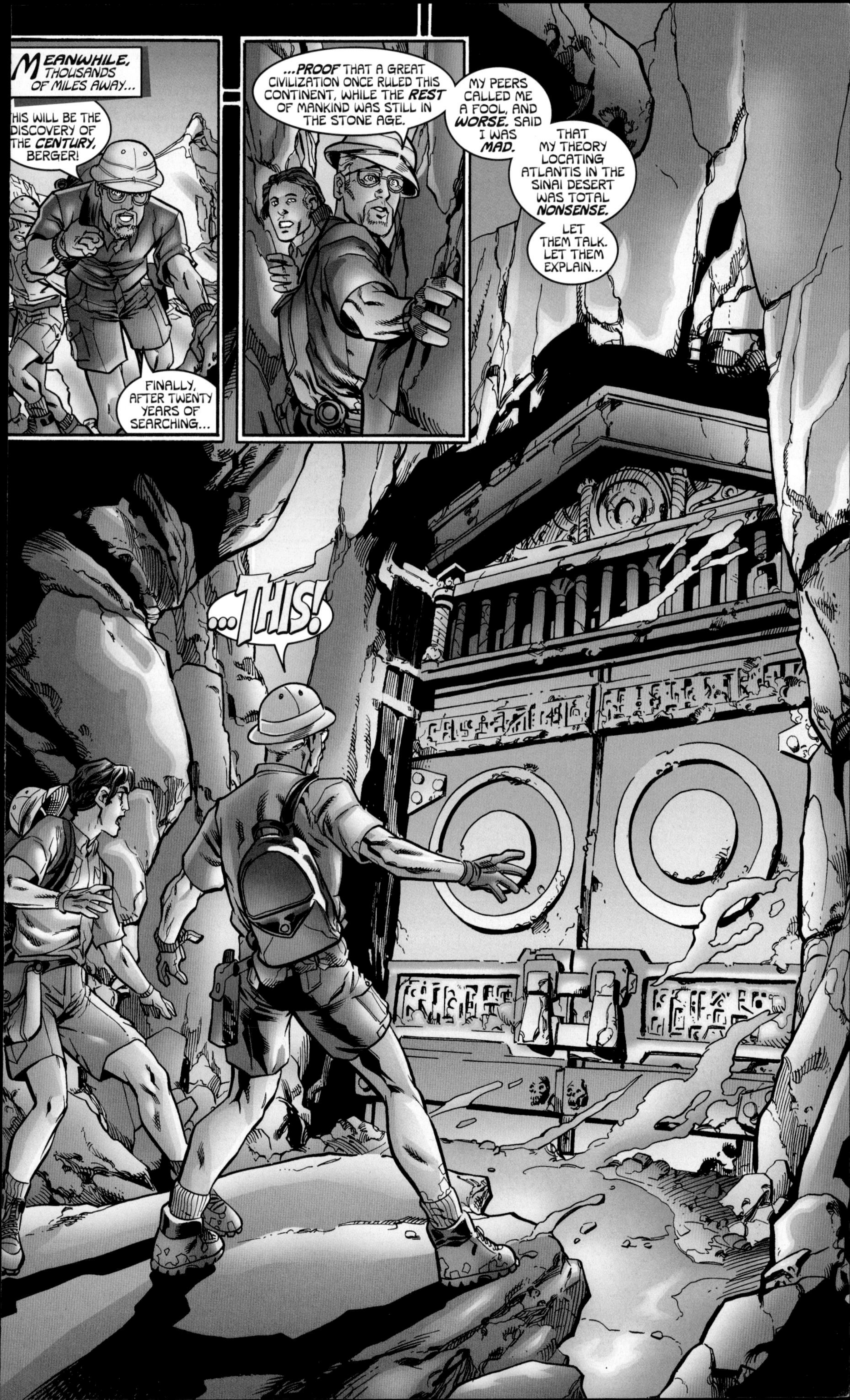
MEANWHILE, THOUSANDS OF MILES AWAY...
THIS WILL BE THE DISCOVERY OF THE CENTURY, BERGER!
FINALLY, AFTER TWENTY YEARS OF SEARCHING...
...PROOF THAT A GREAT CIVILIZATION ONCE RULED THIS CONTINENT, WHILE THE REST OF MANKIND WAS STILL IN THE STONE AGE.
MY PEERS CALLED ME A FOOL, AND WORSE. SAID I WAS MAD.
THAT MY THEORY LOCATING ATLANTIS IN THE SINAI DESERT WAS TOTAL NONSENSE.
LET THEM TALK. LET THEM EXPLAIN...
...THIS!

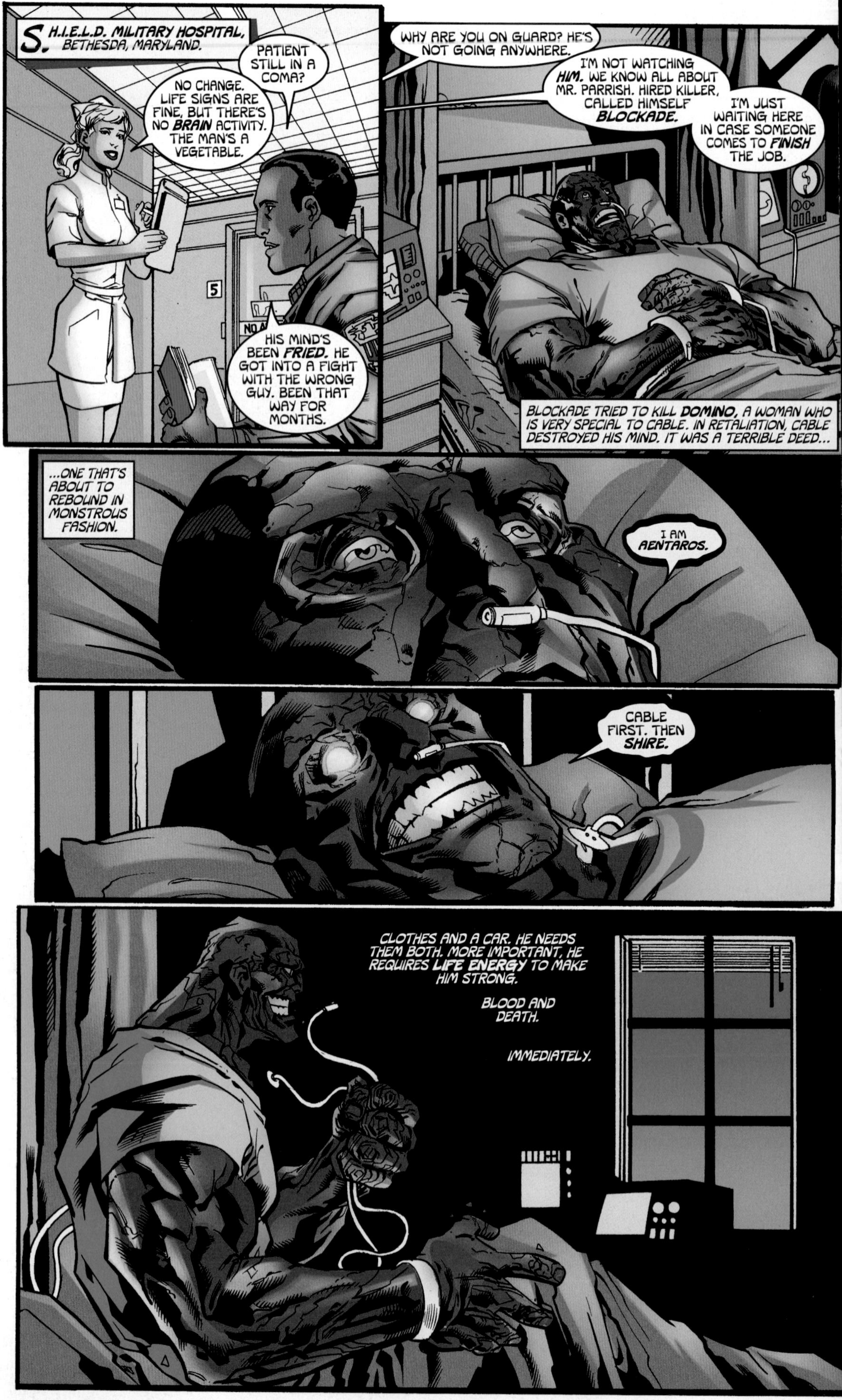
S.H.I.E.L.D. MILITARY HOSPITAL, BETHESDA, MARYLAND.
PATIENT STILL IN A COMA?
NO CHANGE. LIFE SIGNS ARE FINE, BUT THERE'S NO BRAIN ACTIVITY. THE MAN'S A VEGETABLE.
HIS MIND'S BEEN FRIED. HE GOT INTO A FIGHT WITH THE WRONG GUY. BEEN THAT WAY FOR MONTHS.
WHY ARE YOU ON GUARD? HE'S NOT GOING ANYWHERE.
I'M NOT WATCHING HIM. WE KNOW ALL ABOUT MR. PARRISH. HIRED KILLER, CALLED HIMSELF BLOCKADE.
I'M JUST WAITING HERE IN CASE SOMEONE COMES TO FINISH THE JOB.
BLOCKADE TRIED TO KILL DOMINO, A WOMAN WHO IS VERY SPECIAL TO CABLE. IN RETALIATION, CABLE DESTROYED HIS MIND. IT WAS A TERRIBLE DEED...
...ONE THAT'S ABOUT TO REBOUND IN MONSTROUS FASHION.
I AM AENTAROS.
CABLE FIRST. THEN SHIRE.
CLOTHES AND A CAR. HE NEEDS THEM BOTH. MORE IMPORTANT, HE REQUIRES LIFE ENERGY TO MAKE HIM STRONG.
BLOOD AND DEATH.
IMMEDIATELY.

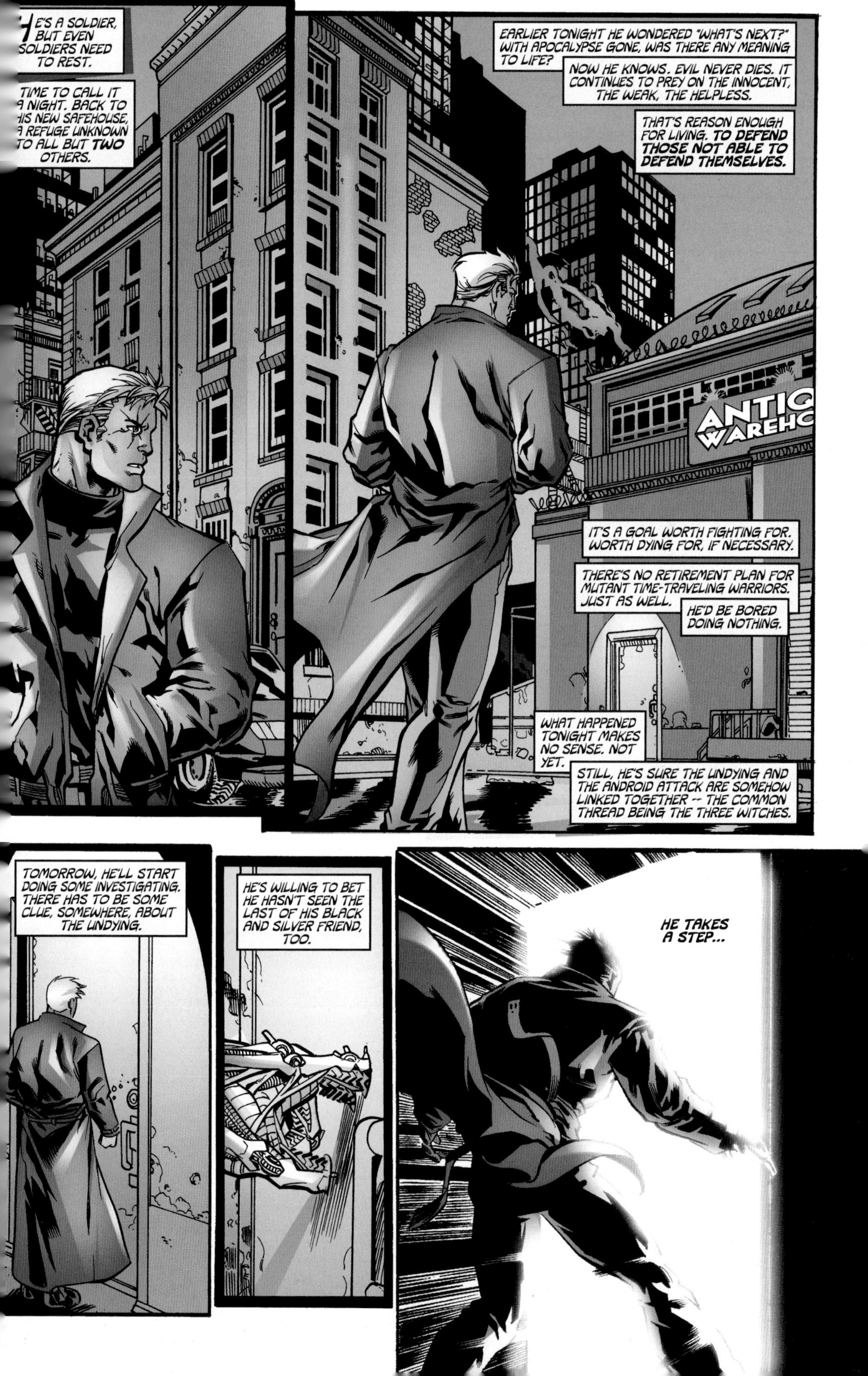
HE'S A SOLDIER, BUT EVEN SOLDIERS NEED TO REST.
TIME TO CALL IT A NIGHT. BACK TO HIS NEW SAFEHOUSE, A REFUGE UNKNOWN TO ALL BUT **TWO** OTHERS.
EARLIER TONIGHT HE WONDERED "WHAT'S NEXT?" WITH APOCALYPSE GONE, WAS THERE ANY MEANING TO LIFE?
NOW HE KNOWS. EVIL NEVER DIES. IT CONTINUES TO PREY ON THE INNOCENT, THE WEAK, THE HELPLESS.
THAT'S REASON ENOUGH FOR LIVING. **TO DEFEND THOSE NOT ABLE TO DEFEND THEMSELVES.**
ANTIQ
WAREHO
IT'S A GOAL WORTH FIGHTING FOR. WORTH DYING FOR, IF NECESSARY.
THERE'S NO RETIREMENT PLAN FOR MUTANT TIME-TRAVELING WARRIORS. JUST AS WELL.
HE'D BE BORED DOING NOTHING.
WHAT HAPPENED TONIGHT MAKES NO SENSE. NOT YET.
STILL, HE'S SURE THE UNDYING AND THE ANDROID ATTACK ARE SOMEHOW LINKED TOGETHER -- THE COMMON THREAD BEING THE THREE WITCHES.
TOMORROW, HE'LL START DOING SOME INVESTIGATING. THERE HAS TO BE SOME CLUE, SOMEWHERE, ABOUT THE UNDYING.
HE'S WILLING TO BET HE HASN'T SEEN THE LAST OF HIS BLACK AND SILVER FRIEND, TOO.
HE TAKES A STEP...

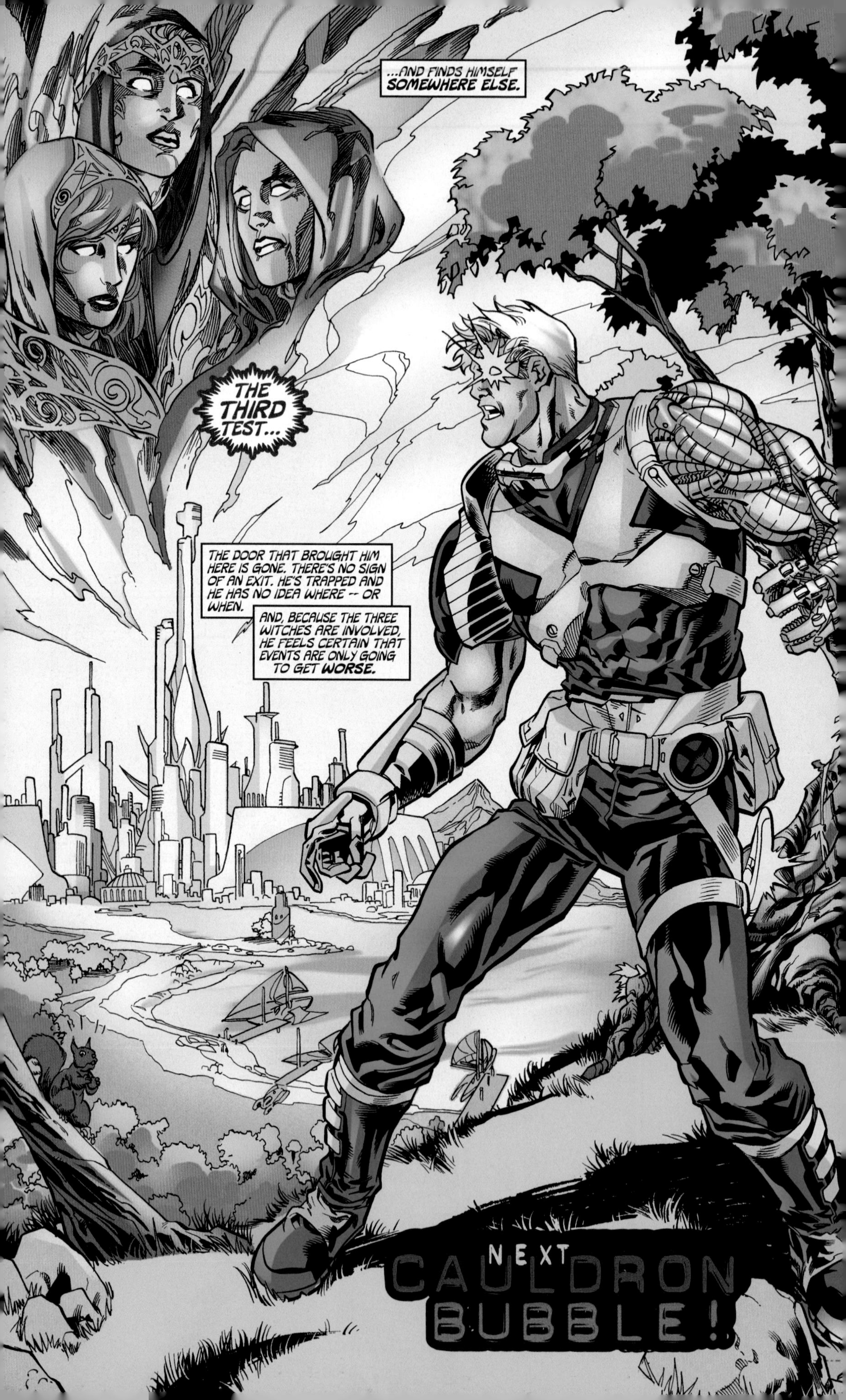
...AND FINDS HIMSELF SOMEWHERE ELSE.
THE THIRD TEST...
THE DOOR THAT BROUGHT HIM HERE IS GONE. THERE'S NO SIGN OF AN EXIT. HE'S TRAPPED AND HE HAS NO IDEA WHERE -- OR WHEN.
AND, BECAUSE THE THREE WITCHES ARE INVOLVED, HE FEELS CERTAIN THAT EVENTS ARE ONLY GOING TO GET WORSE.
NEXT
CAULDRON BUBBLE!

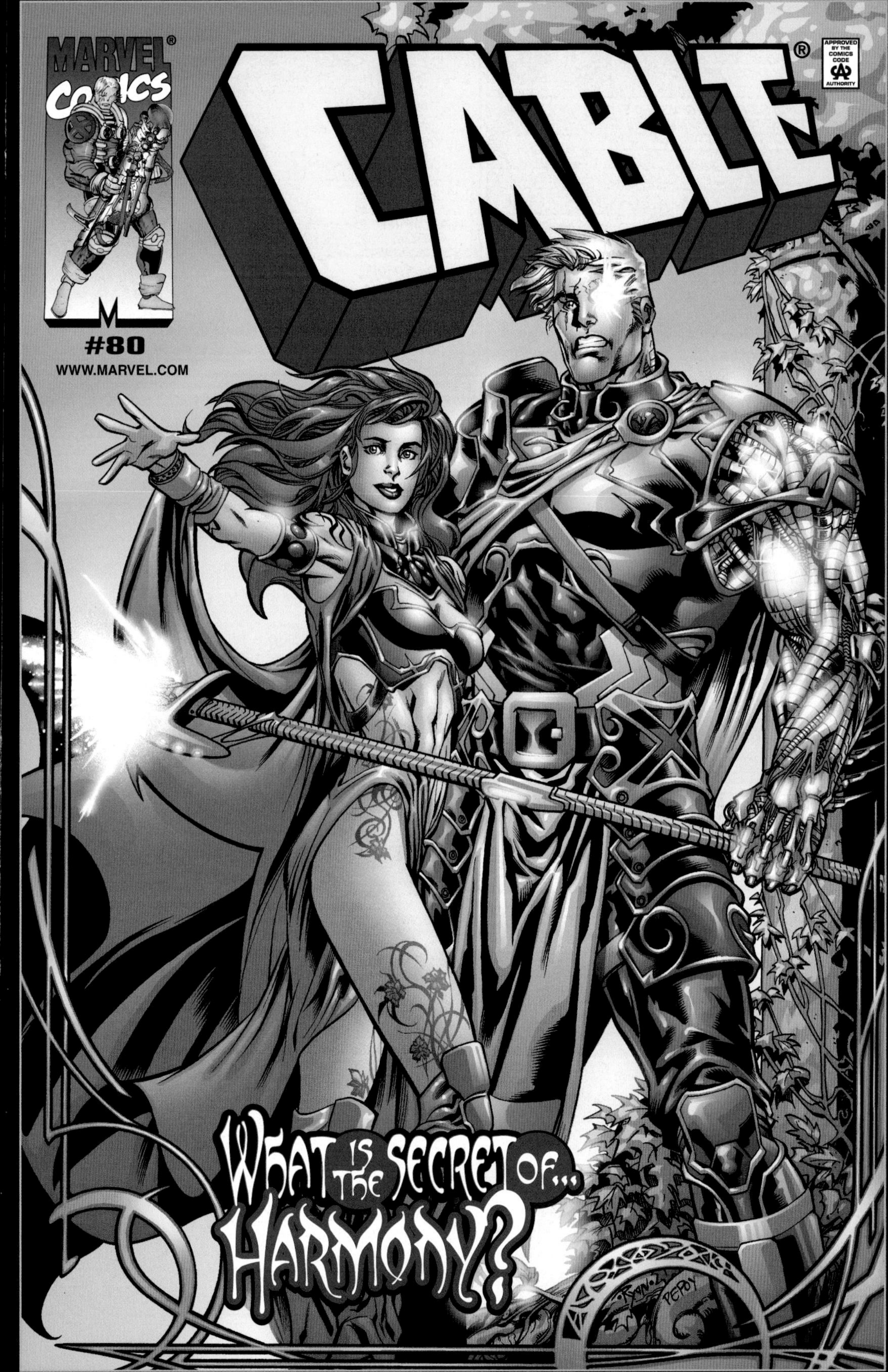
MARVEL COMICS
CABLE
APPROVED BY THE COMICS CODE AUTHORITY
#80
WWW.MARVEL.COM
WHAT IS THE SECRET OF... HARMONY?

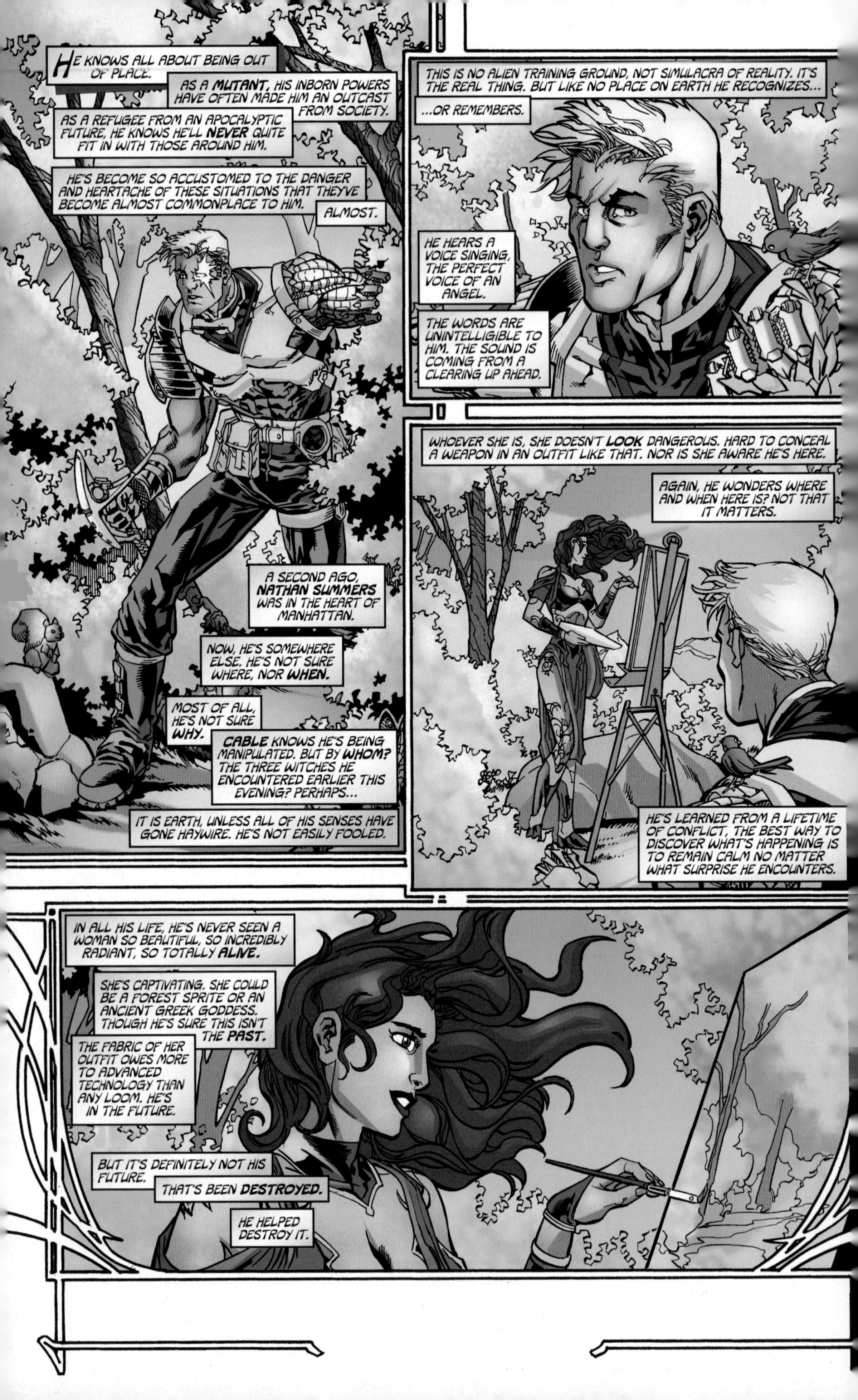
HE KNOWS ALL ABOUT BEING OUT OF PLACE.
AS A MUTANT, HIS INBORN POWERS HAVE OFTEN MADE HIM AN OUTCAST FROM SOCIETY.
AS A REFUGEE FROM AN APOCALYPTIC FUTURE, HE KNOWS HE'LL NEVER QUITE FIT IN WITH THOSE AROUND HIM.
HE'S BECOME SO ACCUSTOMED TO THE DANGER AND HEARTACHE OF THESE SITUATIONS THAT THEY'VE BECOME ALMOST COMMONPLACE TO HIM.
ALMOST.
A SECOND AGO, NATHAN SUMMERS WAS IN THE HEART OF MANHATTAN.
NOW, HE'S SOMEWHERE ELSE. HE'S NOT SURE WHERE, NOR WHEN.
MOST OF ALL, HE'S NOT SURE WHY.
CABLE KNOWS HE'S BEING MANIPULATED. BUT BY WHOM? THE THREE WITCHES HE ENCOUNTERED EARLIER THIS EVENING? PERHAPS...
IT IS EARTH, UNLESS ALL OF HIS SENSES HAVE GONE HAYWIRE. HE'S NOT EASILY FOOLED.
THIS IS NO ALIEN TRAINING GROUND, NOT SIMULACRA OF REALITY. IT'S THE REAL THING. BUT LIKE NO PLACE ON EARTH HE RECOGNIZES...
...OR REMEMBERS.
HE HEARS A VOICE SINGING, THE PERFECT VOICE OF AN ANGEL.
THE WORDS ARE UNINTELLIGIBLE TO HIM. THE SOUND IS COMING FROM A CLEARING UP AHEAD.
WHOEVER SHE IS, SHE DOESN'T LOOK DANGEROUS. HARD TO CONCEAL A WEAPON IN AN OUTFIT LIKE THAT. NOR IS SHE AWARE HE'S HERE.
AGAIN, HE WONDERS WHERE AND WHEN HERE IS? NOT THAT IT MATTERS.
HE'S LEARNED FROM A LIFETIME OF CONFLICT, THE BEST WAY TO DISCOVER WHAT'S HAPPENING IS TO REMAIN CALM NO MATTER WHAT SURPRISE HE ENCOUNTERS.
IN ALL HIS LIFE, HE'S NEVER SEEN A WOMAN SO BEAUTIFUL, SO INCREDIBLY RADIANT, SO TOTALLY ALIVE.
SHE'S CAPTIVATING. SHE COULD BE A FOREST SPRITE OR AN ANCIENT GREEK GODDESS. THOUGH HE'S SURE THIS ISN'T THE PAST.
THE FABRIC OF HER OUTFIT OWES MORE TO ADVANCED TECHNOLOGY THAN ANY LOOM. HE'S IN THE FUTURE.
BUT IT'S DEFINITELY NOT HIS FUTURE.
THAT'S BEEN DESTROYED.
HE HELPED DESTROY IT.

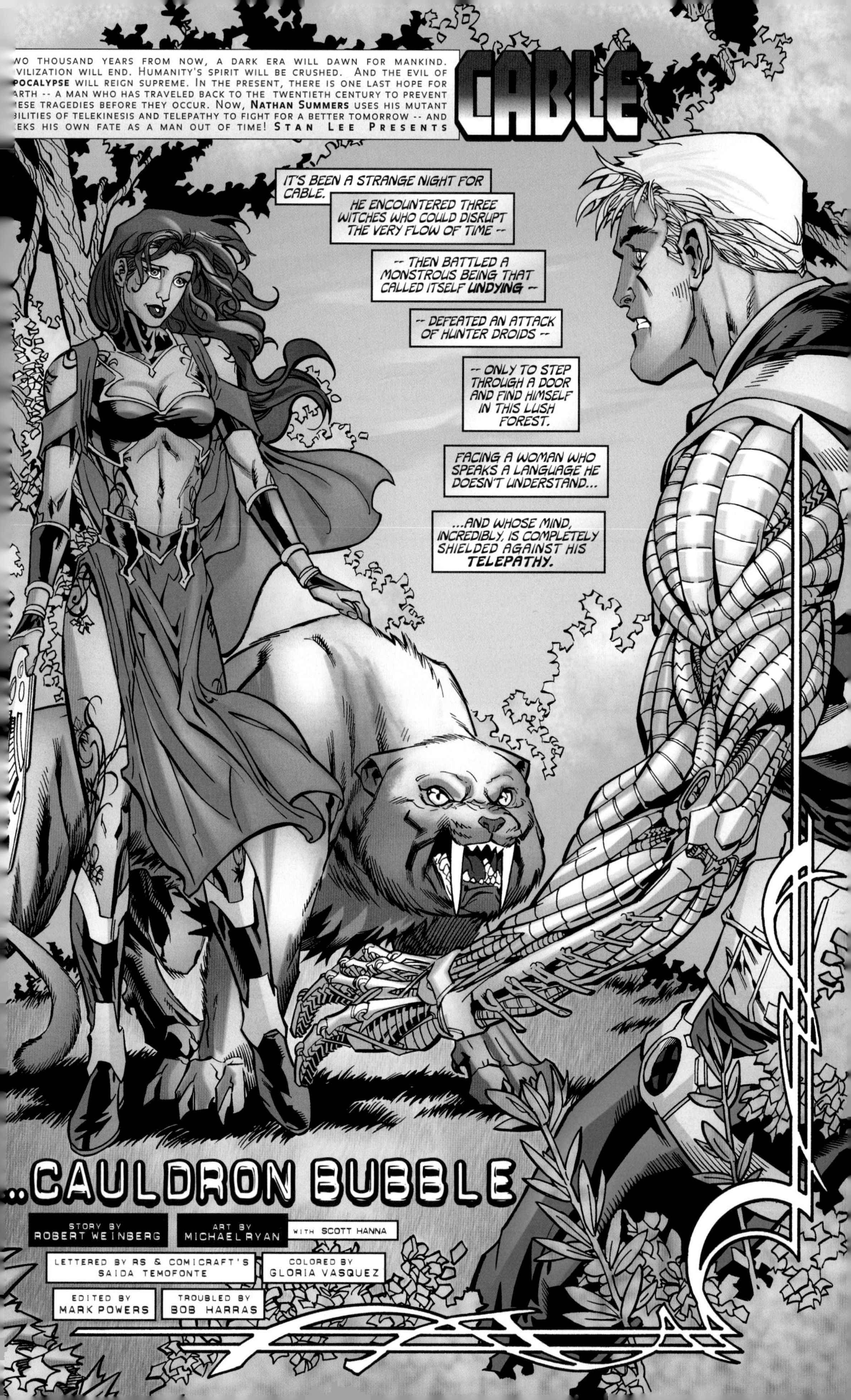
WO THOUSAND YEARS FROM NOW, A DARK ERA WILL DAWN FOR MANKIND. IVILIZATION WILL END. HUMANITY'S SPIRIT WILL BE CRUSHED. AND THE EVIL OF POCALYPSE WILL REIGN SUPREME. IN THE PRESENT, THERE IS ONE LAST HOPE FOR ARTH -- A MAN WHO HAS TRAVELED BACK TO THE TWENTIETH CENTURY TO PREVENT IESE TRAGEDIES BEFORE THEY OCCUR. NOW, NATHAN SUMMERS USES HIS MUTANT BILITIES OF TELEKINESIS AND TELEPATHY TO FIGHT FOR A BETTER TOMORROW -- AND EKS HIS OWN FATE AS A MAN OUT OF TIME! STAN LEE PRESENTS
CABLE
IT'S BEEN A STRANGE NIGHT FOR CABLE.
HE ENCOUNTERED THREE WITCHES WHO COULD DISRUPT THE VERY FLOW OF TIME --
-- THEN BATTLED A MONSTROUS BEING THAT CALLED ITSELF UNDYING --
-- DEFEATED AN ATTACK OF HUNTER DROIDS --
-- ONLY TO STEP THROUGH A DOOR AND FIND HIMSELF IN THIS LUSH FOREST.
FACING A WOMAN WHO SPEAKS A LANGUAGE HE DOESN'T UNDERSTAND...
...AND WHOSE MIND, INCREDIBLY, IS COMPLETELY SHIELDED AGAINST HIS TELEPATHY.
...CAULDRON BUBBLE
STORY BY ROBERT WEINBERG
ART BY MICHAEL RYAN
WITH SCOTT HANNA
LETTERED BY RS & COMICRAFT'S SAIDA TEMOFONTE
COLORED BY GLORIA VASQUEZ
EDITED BY MARK POWERS
TROUBLED BY BOB HARRAS

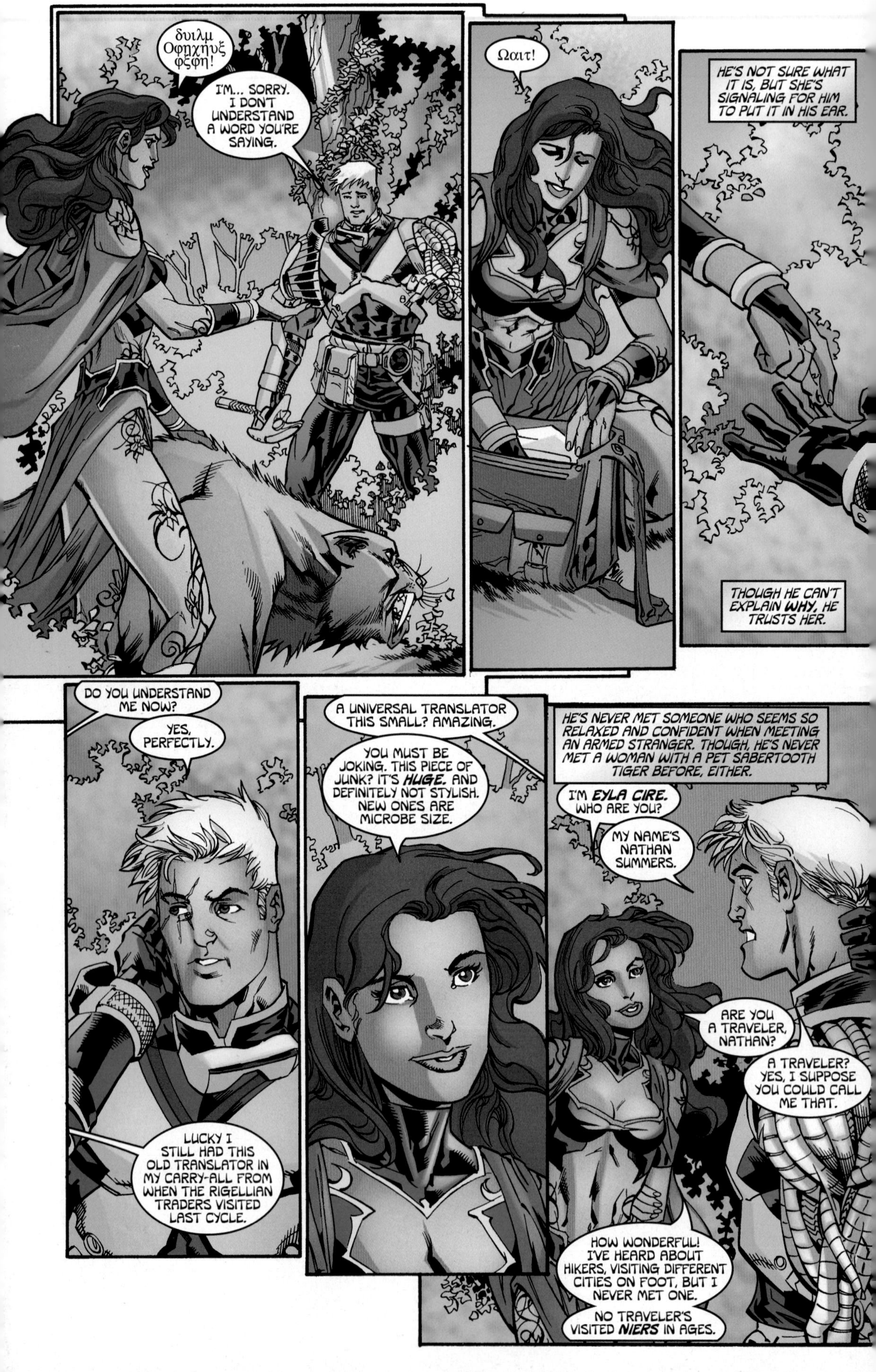
δυιλμ Οφηχηυξ φξφη!
I'M... SORRY. I DON'T UNDERSTAND A WORD YOU'RE SAYING.
Ωαιτ!
HE'S NOT SURE WHAT IT IS, BUT SHE'S SIGNALING FOR HIM TO PUT IT IN HIS EAR.
THOUGH HE CAN'T EXPLAIN WHY, HE TRUSTS HER.
DO YOU UNDERSTAND ME NOW?
YES, PERFECTLY.
LUCKY I STILL HAD THIS OLD TRANSLATOR IN MY CARRY-ALL FROM WHEN THE RIGELLIAN TRADERS VISITED LAST CYCLE.
A UNIVERSAL TRANSLATOR THIS SMALL? AMAZING.
YOU MUST BE JOKING. THIS PIECE OF JUNK? IT'S HUGE. AND DEFINITELY NOT STYLISH. NEW ONES ARE MICROBE SIZE.
HE'S NEVER MET SOMEONE WHO SEEMS SO RELAXED AND CONFIDENT WHEN MEETING AN ARMED STRANGER. THOUGH, HE'S NEVER MET A WOMAN WITH A PET SABERTOOTH TIGER BEFORE, EITHER.
I'M EYLA CIRE. WHO ARE YOU?
MY NAME'S NATHAN SUMMERS.
ARE YOU A TRAVELER, NATHAN?
A TRAVELER? YES, I SUPPOSE YOU COULD CALL ME THAT.
HOW WONDERFUL! I'VE HEARD ABOUT HIKERS, VISITING DIFFERENT CITIES ON FOOT, BUT I NEVER MET ONE.
NO TRAVELER'S VISITED NIERS IN AGES.

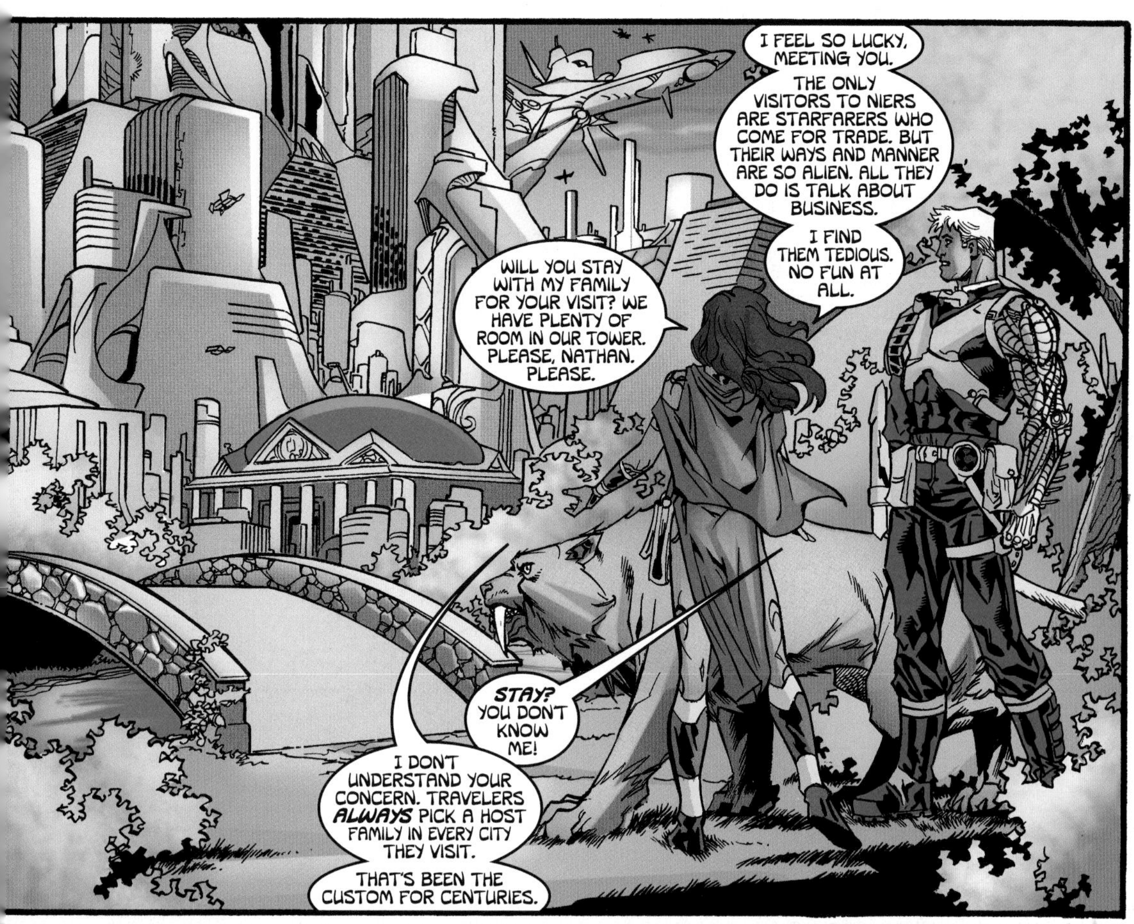
I FEEL SO LUCKY, MEETING YOU.
THE ONLY VISITORS TO NIERS ARE STARFARERS WHO COME FOR TRADE. BUT THEIR WAYS AND MANNER ARE SO ALIEN. ALL THEY DO IS TALK ABOUT BUSINESS.
I FIND THEM TEDIOUS. NO FUN AT ALL.
WILL YOU STAY WITH MY FAMILY FOR YOUR VISIT? WE HAVE PLENTY OF ROOM IN OUR TOWER. PLEASE, NATHAN. PLEASE.
STAY? YOU DON'T KNOW ME!
I DON'T UNDERSTAND YOUR CONCERN. TRAVELERS ALWAYS PICK A HOST FAMILY IN EVERY CITY THEY VISIT.
THAT'S BEEN THE CUSTOM FOR CENTURIES.

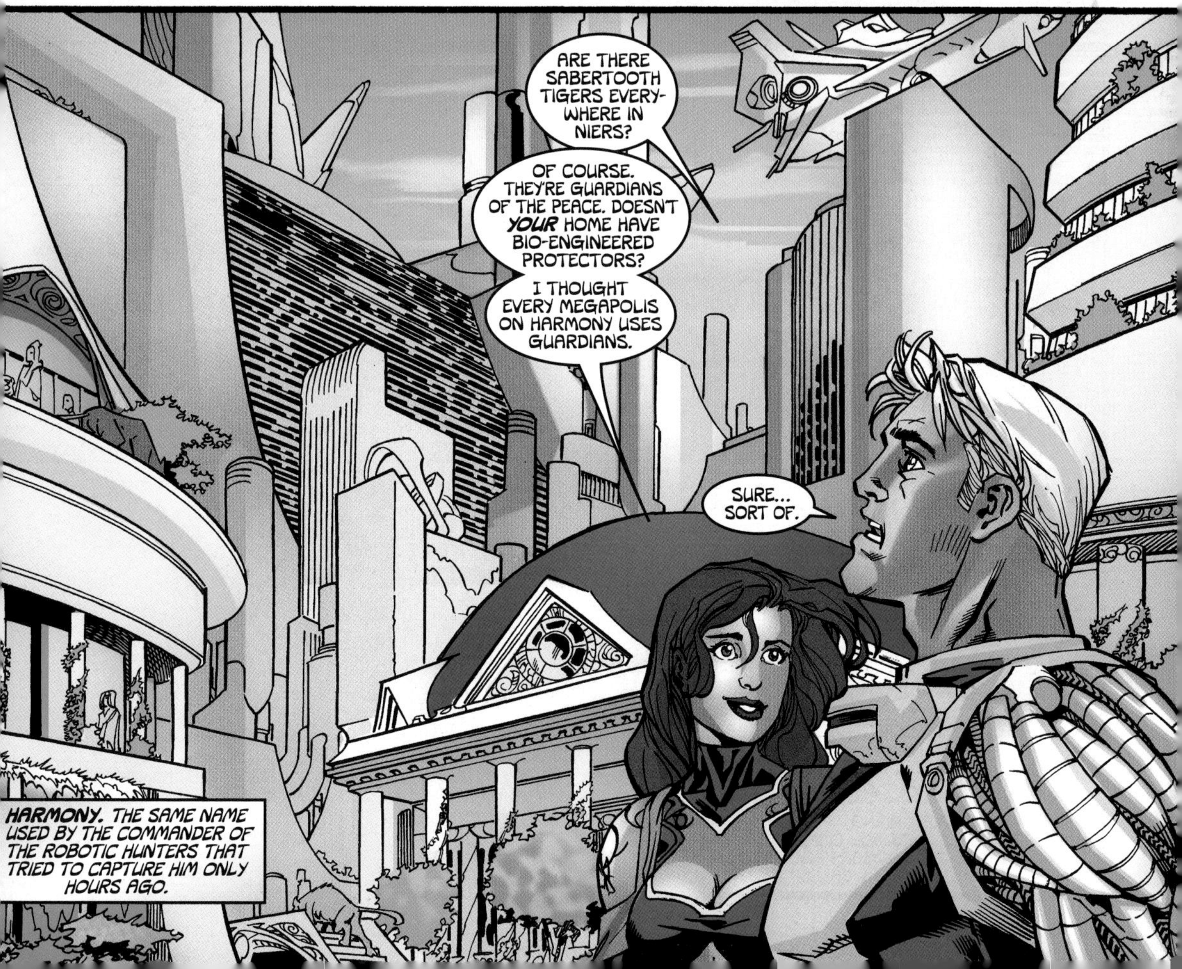
ARE THERE SABERTOOTH TIGERS EVERY-WHERE IN NIERS?
OF COURSE. THEY'RE GUARDIANS OF THE PEACE. DOESN'T YOUR HOME HAVE BIO-ENGINEERED PROTECTORS?
I THOUGHT EVERY MEGAPOLIS ON HARMONY USES GUARDIANS.
SURE... SORT OF.
HARMONY. THE SAME NAME USED BY THE COMMANDER OF THE ROBOTIC HUNTERS THAT TRIED TO CAPTURE HIM ONLY HOURS AGO.

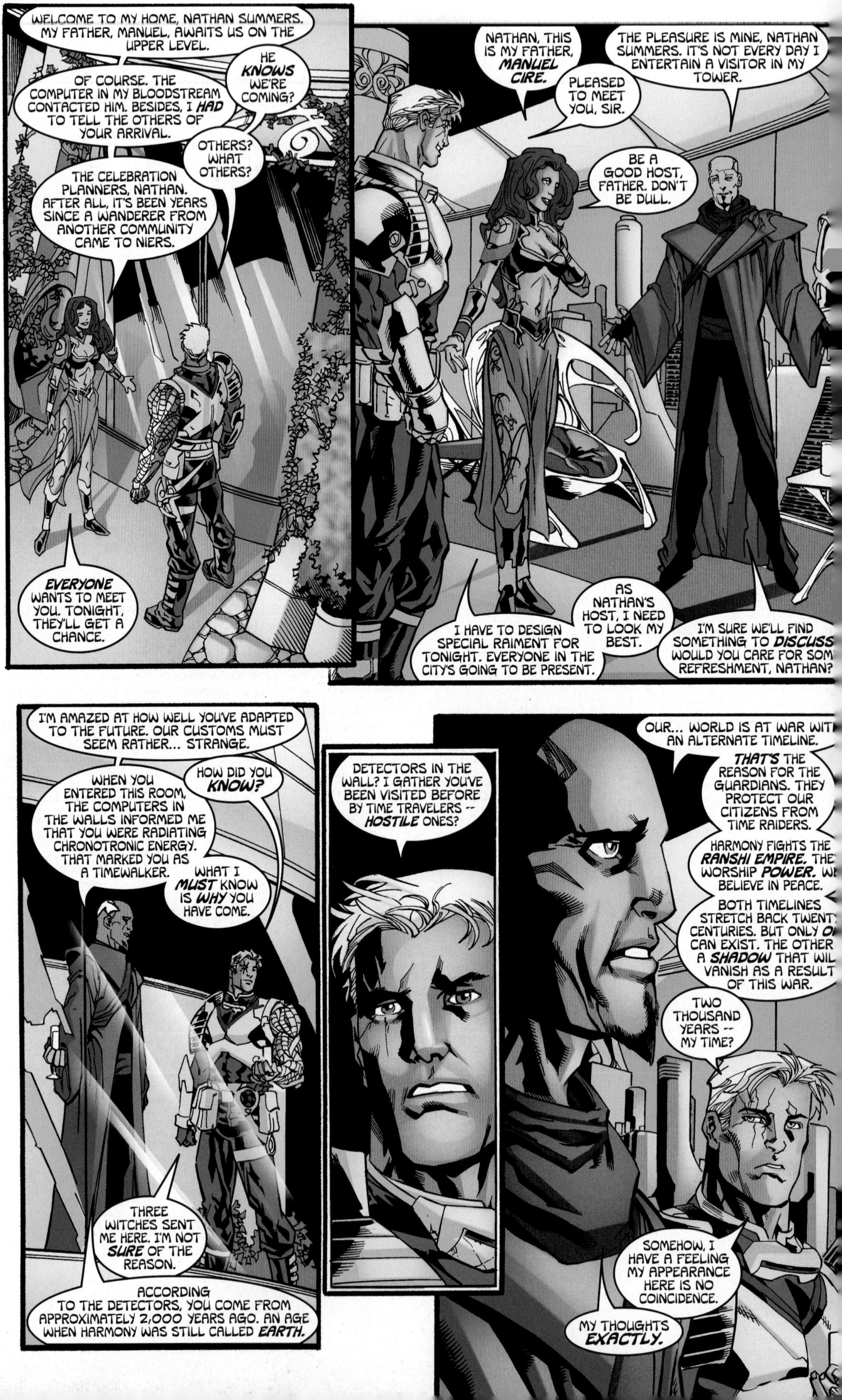
WELCOME TO MY HOME, NATHAN SUMMERS. MY FATHER, MANUEL, AWAITS US ON THE UPPER LEVEL.
HE KNOWS WE'RE COMING?
OF COURSE. THE COMPUTER IN MY BLOODSTREAM CONTACTED HIM. BESIDES, I HAD TO TELL THE OTHERS OF YOUR ARRIVAL.
OTHERS? WHAT OTHERS?
THE CELEBRATION PLANNERS, NATHAN. AFTER ALL, IT'S BEEN YEARS SINCE A WANDERER FROM ANOTHER COMMUNITY CAME TO NIERS.
EVERYONE WANTS TO MEET YOU. TONIGHT, THEY'LL GET A CHANCE.
NATHAN, THIS IS MY FATHER, MANUEL CIRE.
PLEASED TO MEET YOU, SIR.
THE PLEASURE IS MINE, NATHAN SUMMERS. IT'S NOT EVERY DAY I ENTERTAIN A VISITOR IN MY TOWER.
BE A GOOD HOST, FATHER. DON'T BE DULL.
I HAVE TO DESIGN SPECIAL RAIMENT FOR TONIGHT. EVERYONE IN THE CITY'S GOING TO BE PRESENT.
AS NATHAN'S HOST, I NEED TO LOOK MY BEST.
I'M SURE WE'LL FIND SOMETHING TO DISCUSS. WOULD YOU CARE FOR SOME REFRESHMENT, NATHAN?
I'M AMAZED AT HOW WELL YOU'VE ADAPTED TO THE FUTURE. OUR CUSTOMS MUST SEEM RATHER... STRANGE.
HOW DID YOU KNOW?
WHEN YOU ENTERED THIS ROOM, THE COMPUTERS IN THE WALLS INFORMED ME THAT YOU WERE RADIATING CHRONOTRONIC ENERGY. THAT MARKED YOU AS A TIMEWALKER.
WHAT I MUST KNOW IS WHY YOU HAVE COME.
THREE WITCHES SENT ME HERE. I'M NOT SURE OF THE REASON.
ACCORDING TO THE DETECTORS, YOU COME FROM APPROXIMATELY 2,000 YEARS AGO. AN AGE WHEN HARMONY WAS STILL CALLED EARTH.
DETECTORS IN THE WALL? I GATHER YOU'VE BEEN VISITED BEFORE BY TIME TRAVELERS -- HOSTILE ONES?
OUR... WORLD IS AT WAR WITH AN ALTERNATE TIMELINE.
THAT'S THE REASON FOR THE GUARDIANS. THEY PROTECT OUR CITIZENS FROM TIME RAIDERS.
HARMONY FIGHTS THE RANSHI EMPIRE. THEY WORSHIP POWER. WE BELIEVE IN PEACE.
BOTH TIMELINES STRETCH BACK TWENTY CENTURIES. BUT ONLY ONE CAN EXIST. THE OTHER A SHADOW THAT WILL VANISH AS A RESULT OF THIS WAR.
TWO THOUSAND YEARS -- MY TIME?
SOMEHOW, I HAVE A FEELING MY APPEARANCE HERE IS NO COINCIDENCE.
MY THOUGHTS EXACTLY.

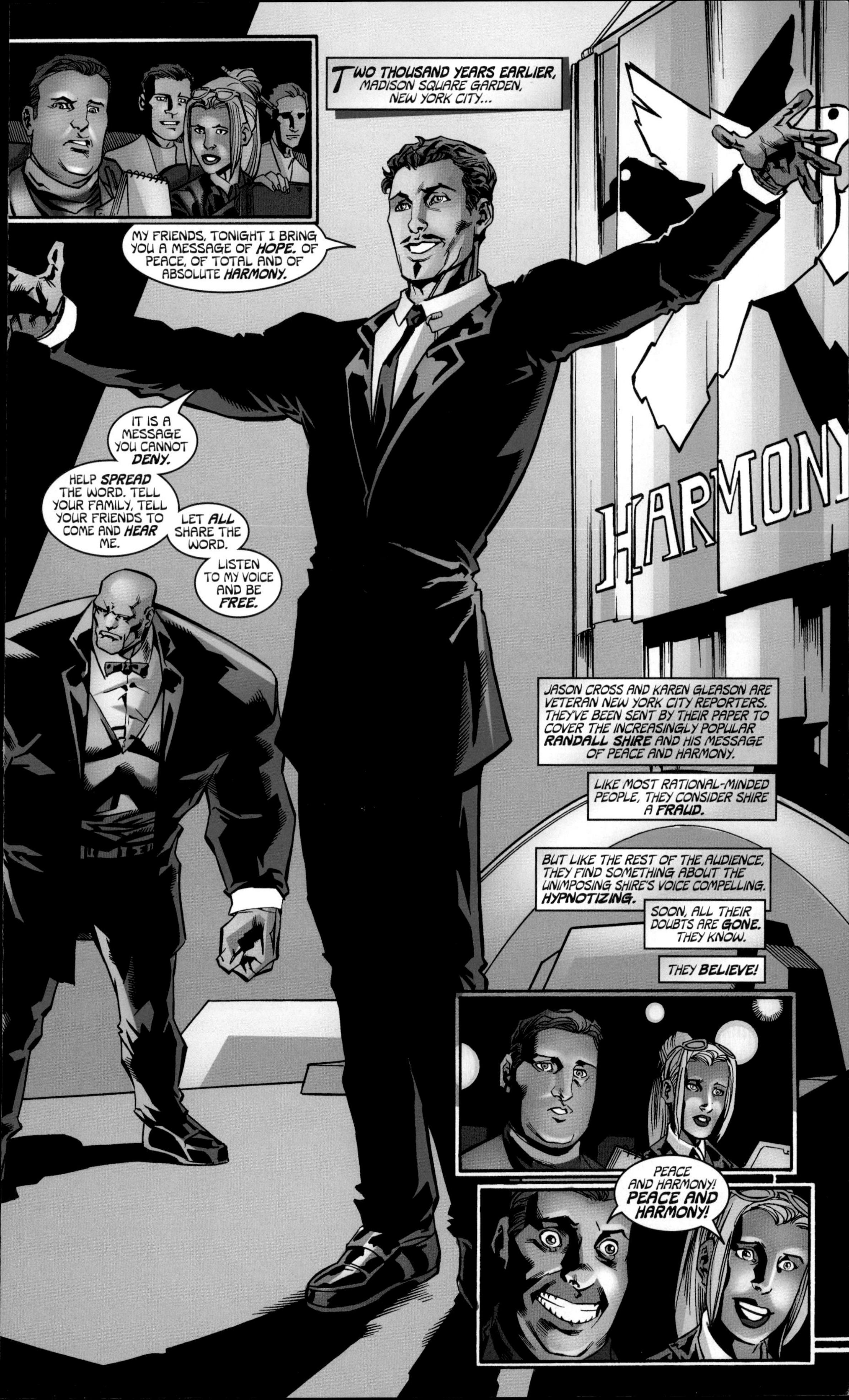
TWO THOUSAND YEARS EARLIER, MADISON SQUARE GARDEN, NEW YORK CITY...
MY FRIENDS, TONIGHT I BRING YOU A MESSAGE OF HOPE. OF PEACE, OF TOTAL AND OF ABSOLUTE HARMONY.
IT IS A MESSAGE YOU CANNOT DENY.
HELP SPREAD THE WORD. TELL YOUR FAMILY, TELL YOUR FRIENDS TO COME AND HEAR ME.
LET ALL SHARE THE WORD.
LISTEN TO MY VOICE AND BE FREE.
HARMONY
JASON CROSS AND KAREN GLEASON ARE VETERAN NEW YORK CITY REPORTERS. THEY'VE BEEN SENT BY THEIR PAPER TO COVER THE INCREASINGLY POPULAR RANDALL SHIRE AND HIS MESSAGE OF PEACE AND HARMONY.
LIKE MOST RATIONAL-MINDED PEOPLE, THEY CONSIDER SHIRE A FRAUD.
BUT LIKE THE REST OF THE AUDIENCE, THEY FIND SOMETHING ABOUT THE UNIMPOSING SHIRE'S VOICE COMPELLING. HYPNOTIZING.
SOON, ALL THEIR DOUBTS ARE GONE. THEY KNOW.
THEY BELIEVE!
PEACE AND HARMONY! PEACE AND HARMONY!

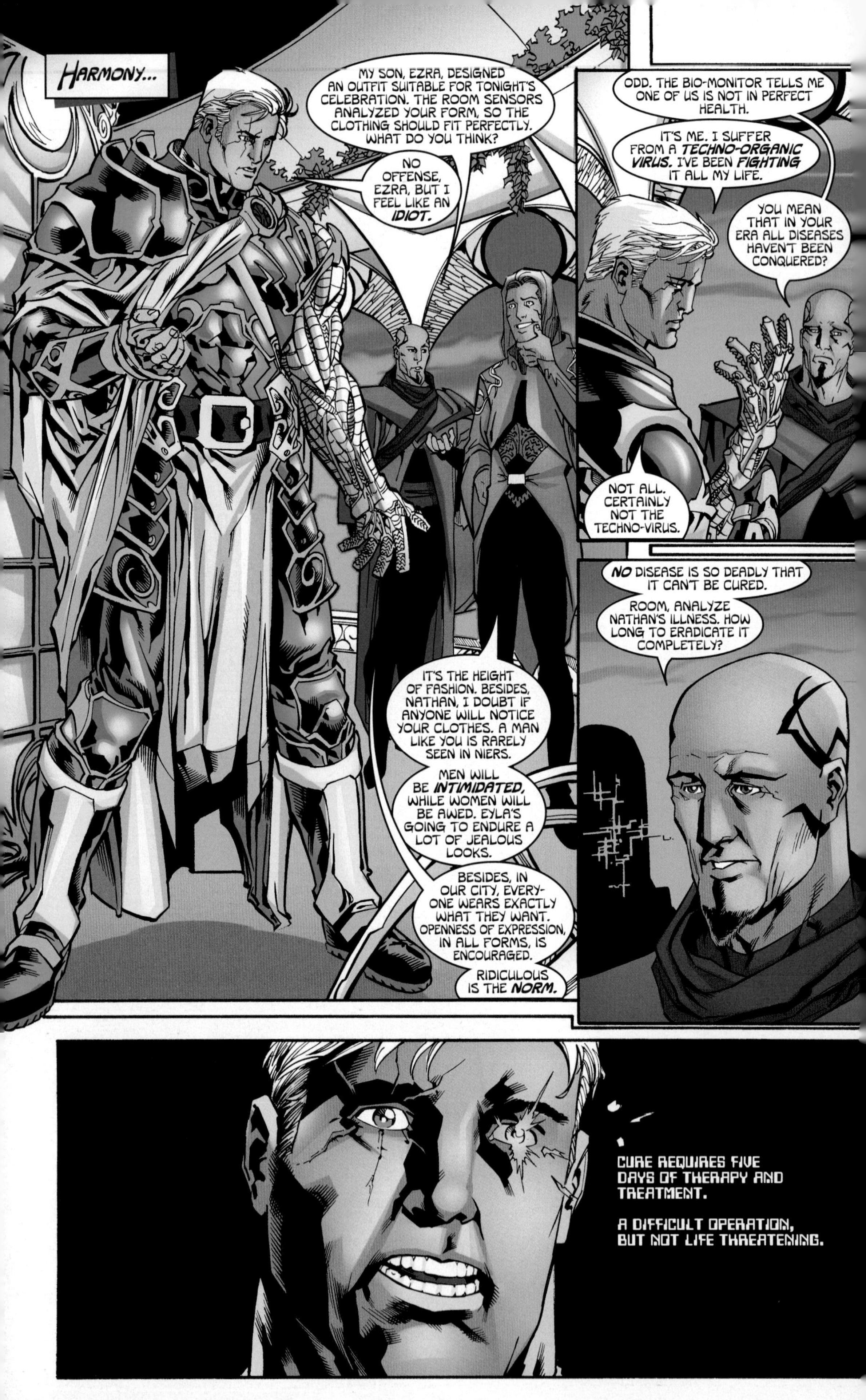
HARMONY...
MY SON, EZRA, DESIGNED AN OUTFIT SUITABLE FOR TONIGHT'S CELEBRATION. THE ROOM SENSORS ANALYZED YOUR FORM, SO THE CLOTHING SHOULD FIT PERFECTLY. WHAT DO YOU THINK?
NO OFFENSE, EZRA, BUT I FEEL LIKE AN IDIOT.
IT'S THE HEIGHT OF FASHION. BESIDES, NATHAN, I DOUBT IF ANYONE WILL NOTICE YOUR CLOTHES. A MAN LIKE YOU IS RARELY SEEN IN NIERS.
MEN WILL BE INTIMIDATED, WHILE WOMEN WILL BE AWED. EYLA'S GOING TO ENDURE A LOT OF JEALOUS LOOKS.
BESIDES, IN OUR CITY, EVERYONE WEARS EXACTLY WHAT THEY WANT. OPENNESS OF EXPRESSION, IN ALL FORMS, IS ENCOURAGED.
RIDICULOUS IS THE NORM.
ODD. THE BIO-MONITOR TELLS ME ONE OF US IS NOT IN PERFECT HEALTH.
IT'S ME. I SUFFER FROM A TECHNO-ORGANIC VIRUS. I'VE BEEN FIGHTING IT ALL MY LIFE.
YOU MEAN THAT IN YOUR ERA ALL DISEASES HAVEN'T BEEN CONQUERED?
NOT ALL. CERTAINLY NOT THE TECHNO-VIRUS.
NO DISEASE IS SO DEADLY THAT IT CAN'T BE CURED.
ROOM, ANALYZE NATHAN'S ILLNESS. HOW LONG TO ERADICATE IT COMPLETELY?
CURE REQUIRES FIVE DAYS OF THERAPY AND TREATMENT.
A DIFFICULT OPERATION, BUT NOT LIFE THREATENING.

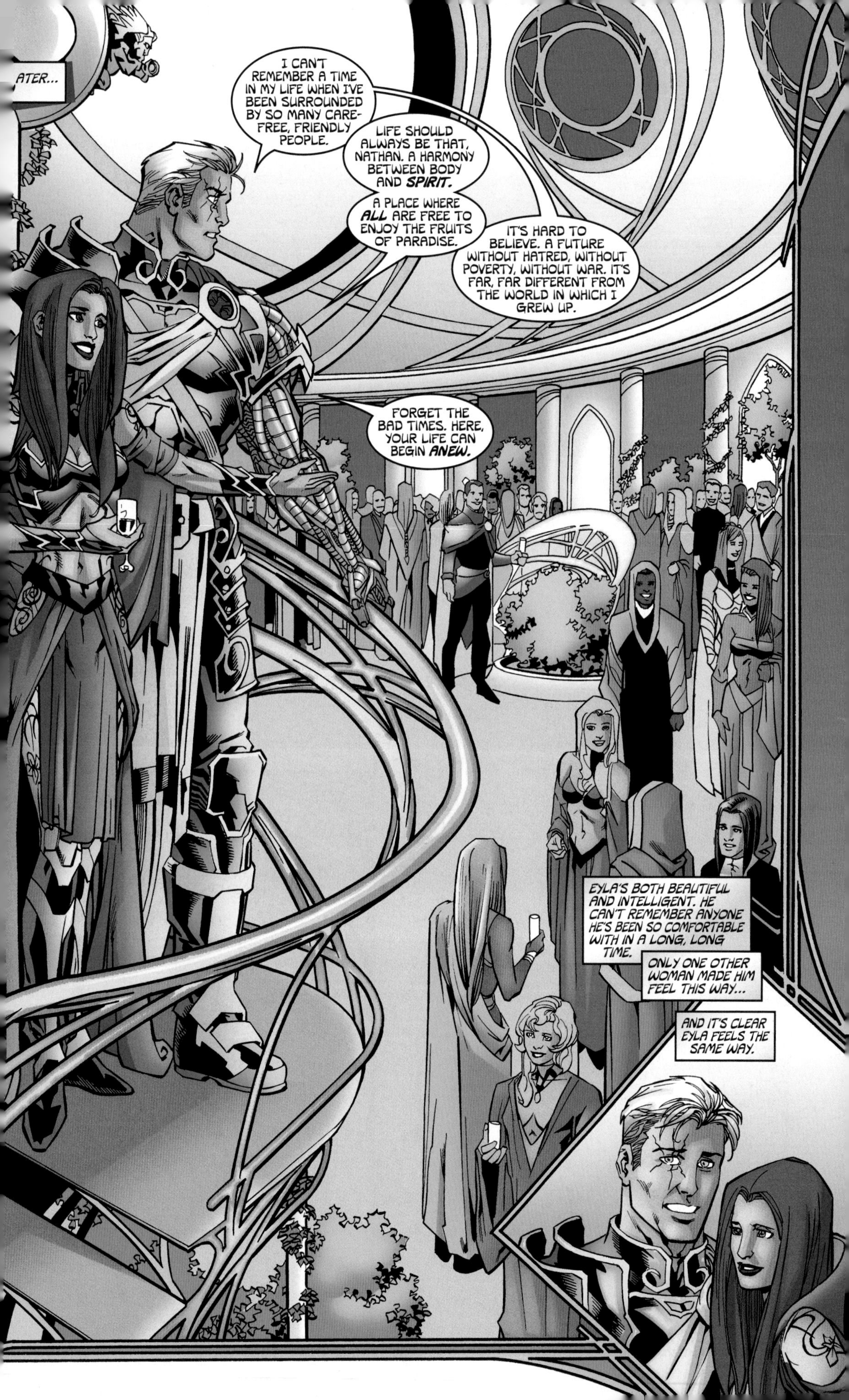

ATER...
I CAN'T REMEMBER A TIME IN MY LIFE WHEN I'VE BEEN SURROUNDED BY SO MANY CARE-FREE, FRIENDLY PEOPLE.
LIFE SHOULD ALWAYS BE THAT, NATHAN. A HARMONY BETWEEN BODY AND SPIRIT.
A PLACE WHERE ALL ARE FREE TO ENJOY THE FRUITS OF PARADISE.
IT'S HARD TO BELIEVE. A FUTURE WITHOUT HATRED, WITHOUT POVERTY, WITHOUT WAR. IT'S FAR, FAR DIFFERENT FROM THE WORLD IN WHICH I GREW UP.
FORGET THE BAD TIMES. HERE, YOUR LIFE CAN BEGIN ANEW.
EYLA'S BOTH BEAUTIFUL AND INTELLIGENT. HE CAN'T REMEMBER ANYONE HE'S BEEN SO COMFORTABLE WITH IN A LONG, LONG TIME.
ONLY ONE OTHER WOMAN MADE HIM FEEL THIS WAY...
AND IT'S CLEAR EYLA FEELS THE SAME WAY.

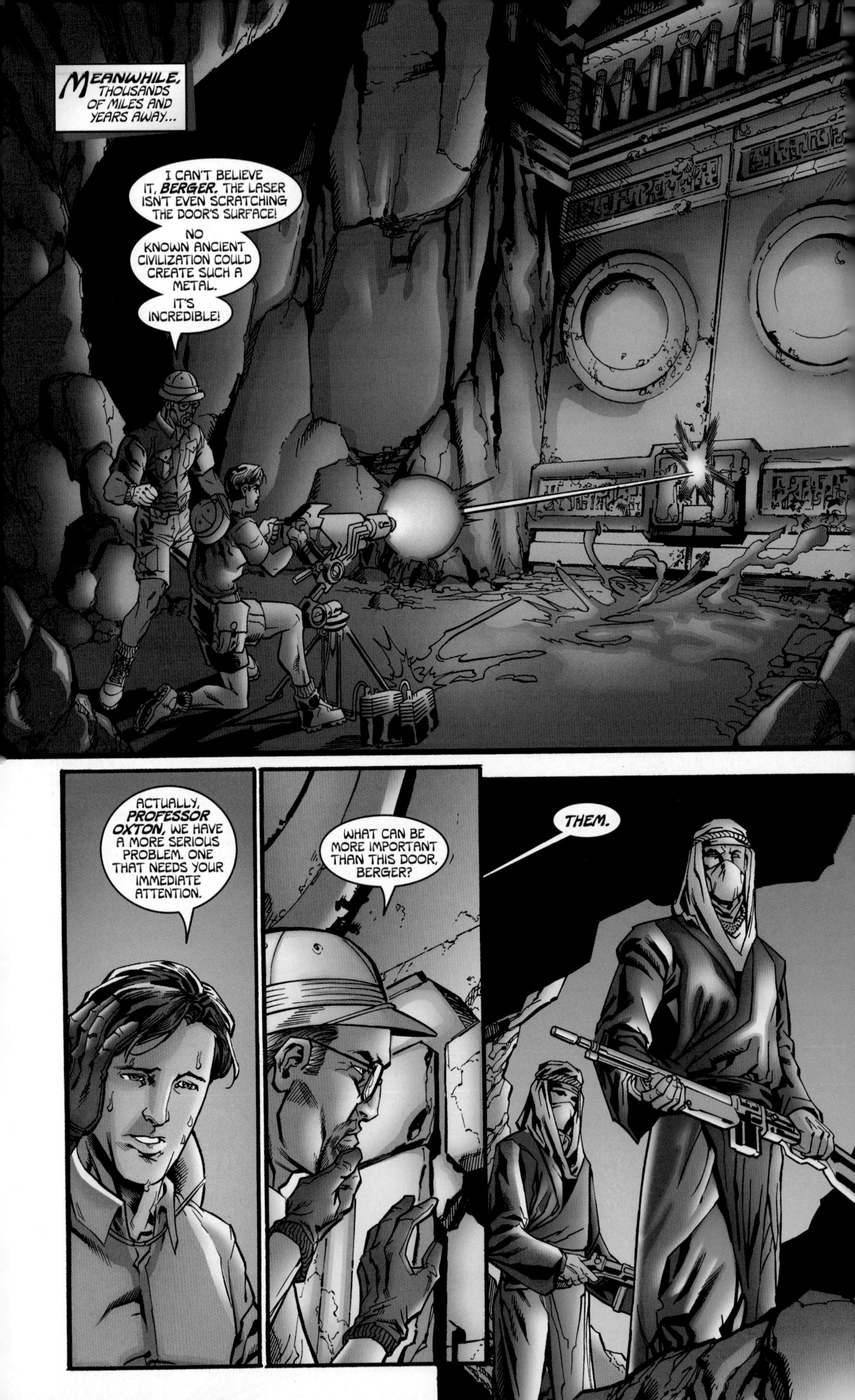
MEANWHILE, THOUSANDS OF MILES AND YEARS AWAY...
I CAN'T BELIEVE IT, BERGER. THE LASER ISN'T EVEN SCRATCHING THE DOOR'S SURFACE!
NO KNOWN ANCIENT CIVILIZATION COULD CREATE SUCH A METAL.
IT'S INCREDIBLE!
ACTUALLY, PROFESSOR OXTON, WE HAVE A MORE SERIOUS PROBLEM. ONE THAT NEEDS YOUR IMMEDIATE ATTENTION.
WHAT CAN BE MORE IMPORTANT THAN THIS DOOR, BERGER?
THEM.

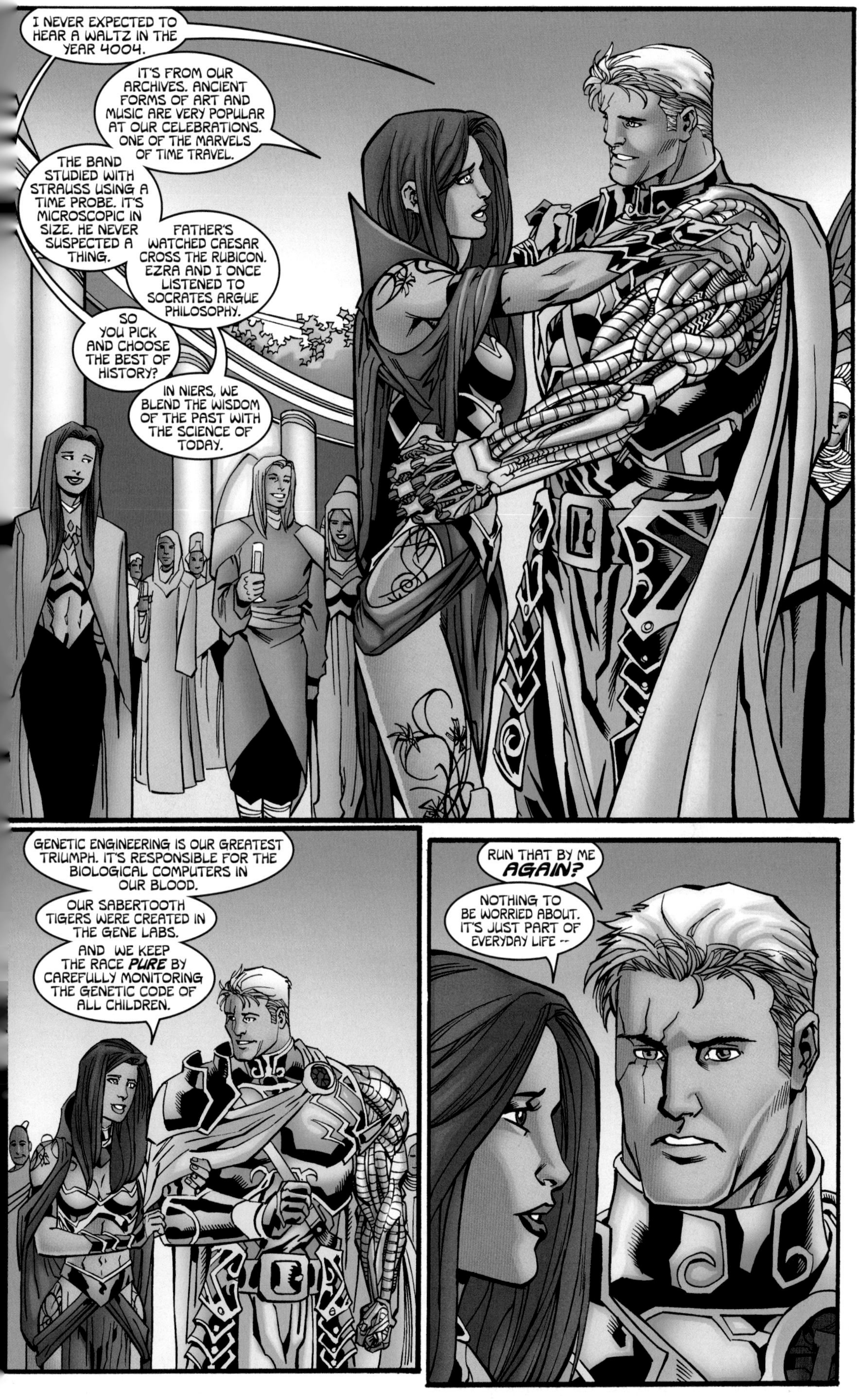
I NEVER EXPECTED TO HEAR A WALTZ IN THE YEAR 4004.
IT'S FROM OUR ARCHIVES. ANCIENT FORMS OF ART AND MUSIC ARE VERY POPULAR AT OUR CELEBRATIONS. ONE OF THE MARVELS OF TIME TRAVEL.
THE BAND STUDIED WITH STRAUSS USING A TIME PROBE. IT'S MICROSCOPIC IN SIZE. HE NEVER SUSPECTED A THING.
FATHER'S WATCHED CAESAR CROSS THE RUBICON. EZRA AND I ONCE LISTENED TO SOCRATES ARGUE PHILOSOPHY.
SO YOU PICK AND CHOOSE THE BEST OF HISTORY?
IN NIERS, WE BLEND THE WISDOM OF THE PAST WITH THE SCIENCE OF TODAY.
GENETIC ENGINEERING IS OUR GREATEST TRIUMPH. IT'S RESPONSIBLE FOR THE BIOLOGICAL COMPUTERS IN OUR BLOOD.
OUR SABERTOOTH TIGERS WERE CREATED IN THE GENE LABS.
AND WE KEEP THE RACE PURE BY CAREFULLY MONITORING THE GENETIC CODE OF ALL CHILDREN.
RUN THAT BY ME AGAIN?
NOTHING TO BE WORRIED ABOUT. IT'S JUST PART OF EVERYDAY LIFE --

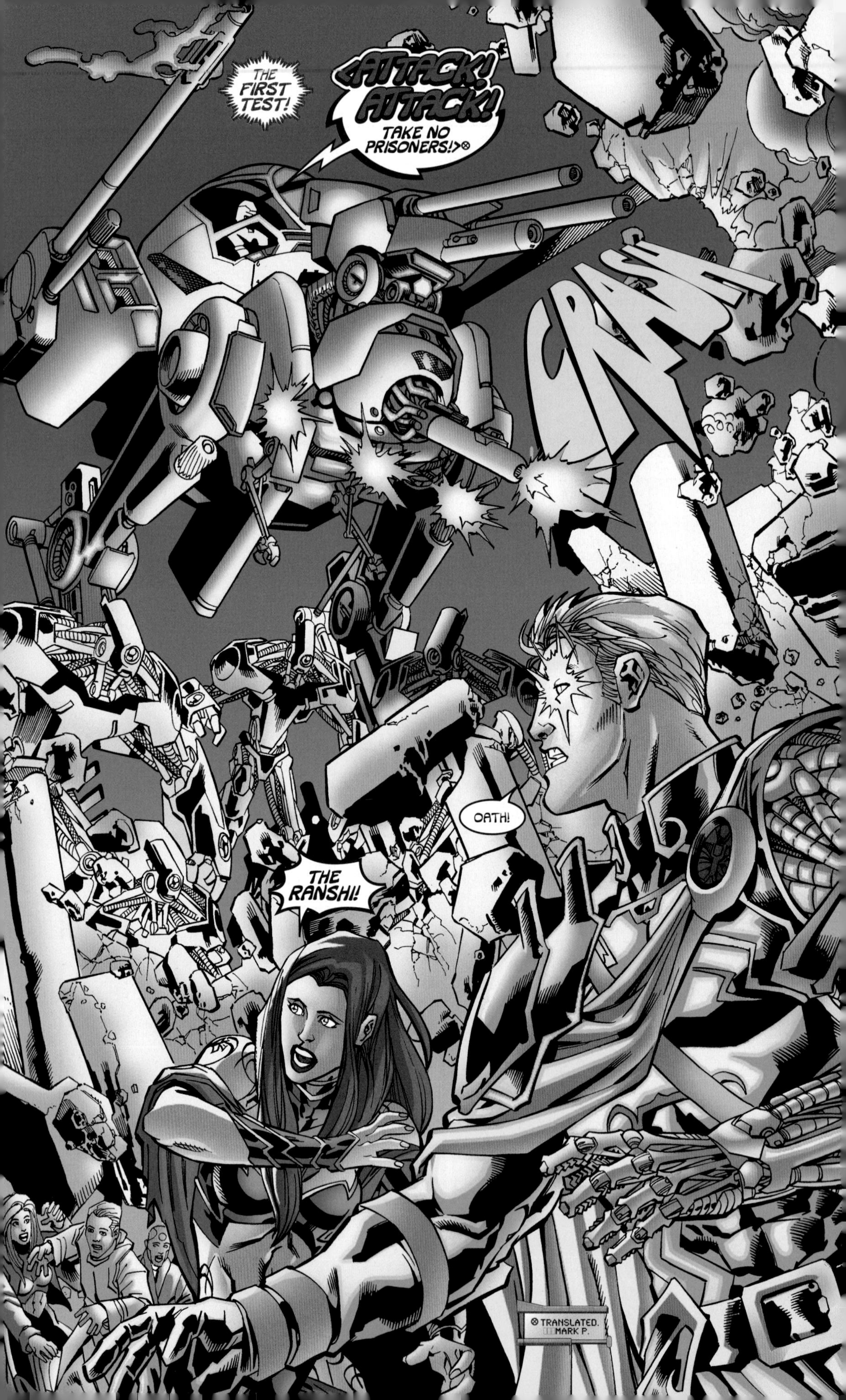
THE FIRST TEST!
<ATTACK! ATTACK! TAKE NO PRISONERS!>⊗
CRASH
OATH!
THE RANSHI!
⊗ TRANSLATED.
MARK P.

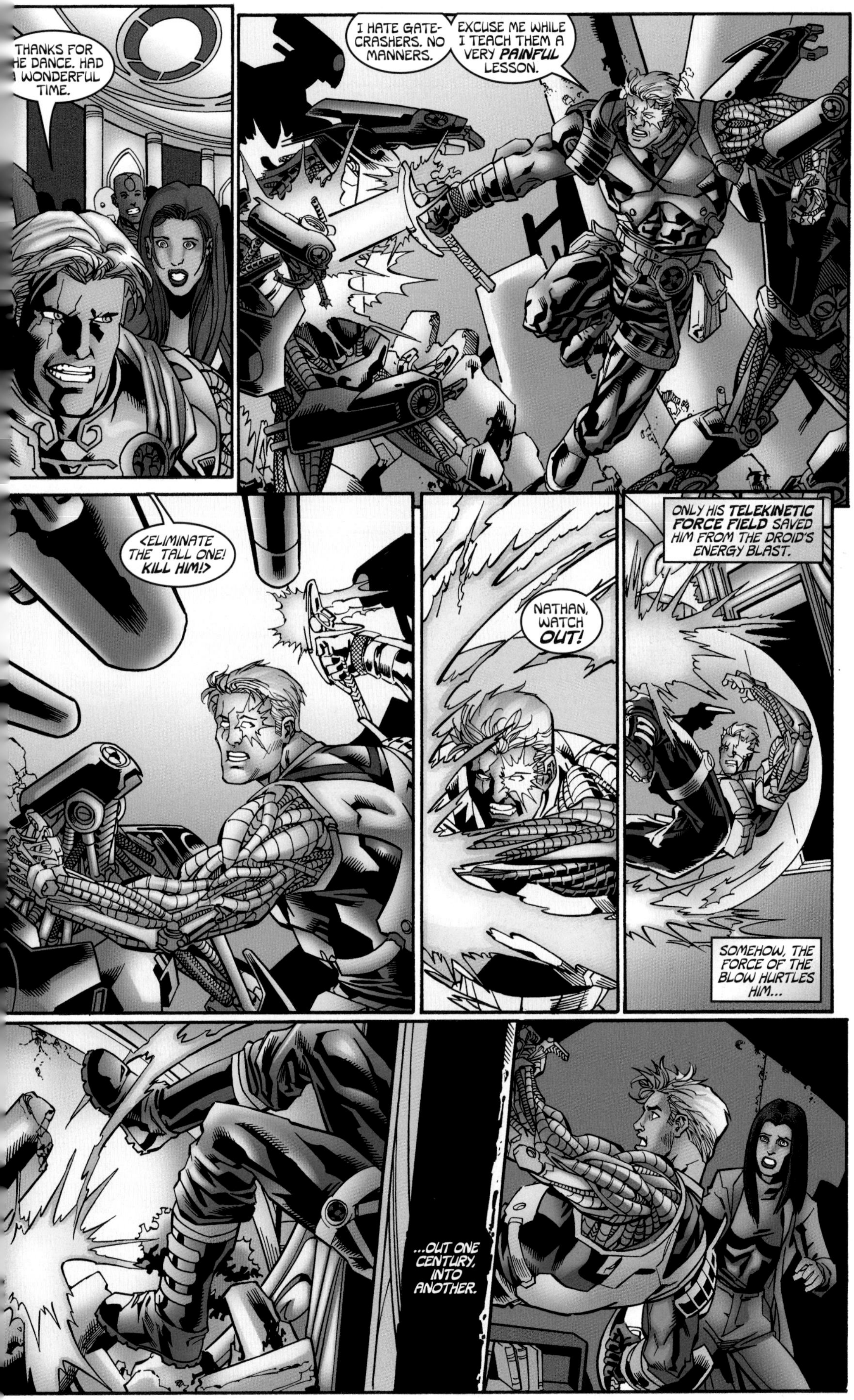
THANKS FOR THE DANCE. HAD A WONDERFUL TIME.
I HATE GATE-CRASHERS. NO MANNERS.
EXCUSE ME WHILE I TEACH THEM A VERY PAINFUL LESSON.
<ELIMINATE THE TALL ONE! KILL HIM!>
NATHAN, WATCH OUT!
ONLY HIS TELEKINETIC FORCE FIELD SAVED HIM FROM THE DROID'S ENERGY BLAST.
SOMEHOW, THE FORCE OF THE BLOW HURTLES HIM...
...OUT ONE CENTURY, INTO ANOTHER.

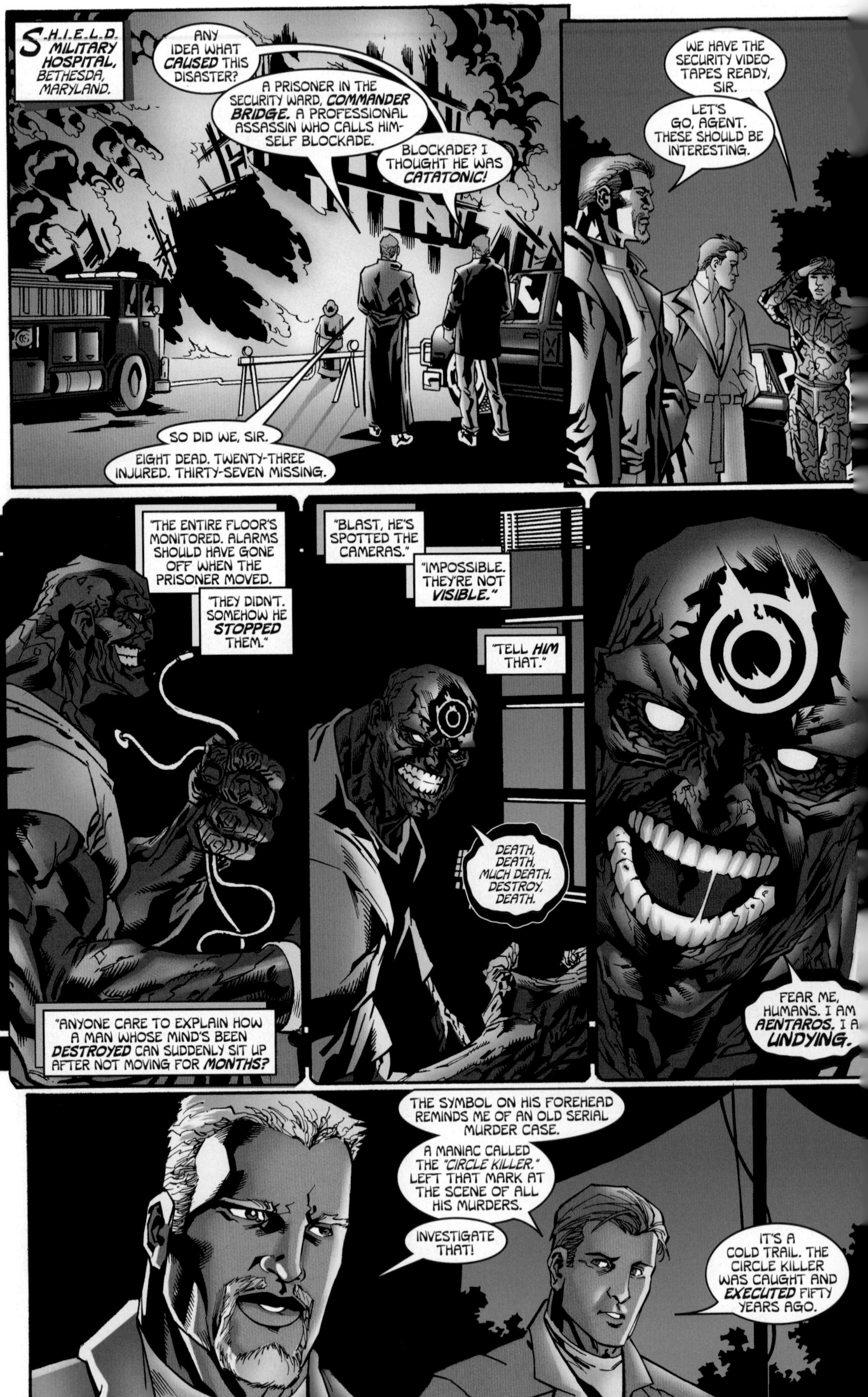
S.H.I.E.L.D. MILITARY HOSPITAL, BETHESDA, MARYLAND.
ANY IDEA WHAT CAUSED THIS DISASTER?
A PRISONER IN THE SECURITY WARD, COMMANDER BRIDGE. A PROFESSIONAL ASSASSIN WHO CALLS HIMSELF BLOCKADE.
BLOCKADE? I THOUGHT HE WAS CATATONIC!
SO DID WE, SIR.
EIGHT DEAD. TWENTY-THREE INJURED. THIRTY-SEVEN MISSING.
WE HAVE THE SECURITY VIDEOTAPES READY, SIR.
LET'S GO, AGENT. THESE SHOULD BE INTERESTING.
"THE ENTIRE FLOOR'S MONITORED. ALARMS SHOULD HAVE GONE OFF WHEN THE PRISONER MOVED.
"THEY DIDN'T. SOMEHOW HE STOPPED THEM."
"ANYONE CARE TO EXPLAIN HOW A MAN WHOSE MIND'S BEEN DESTROYED CAN SUDDENLY SIT UP AFTER NOT MOVING FOR MONTHS?
"BLAST, HE'S SPOTTED THE CAMERAS."
"IMPOSSIBLE. THEY'RE NOT VISIBLE."
"TELL HIM THAT."
DEATH, DEATH, MUCH DEATH. DESTROY, DEATH.
FEAR ME, HUMANS. I AM AENTAROS. I A UNDYING.
THE SYMBOL ON HIS FOREHEAD REMINDS ME OF AN OLD SERIAL MURDER CASE.
A MANIAC CALLED THE "CIRCLE KILLER." LEFT THAT MARK AT THE SCENE OF ALL HIS MURDERS.
INVESTIGATE THAT!
IT'S A COLD TRAIL. THE CIRCLE KILLER WAS CAUGHT AND EXECUTED FIFTY YEARS AGO.

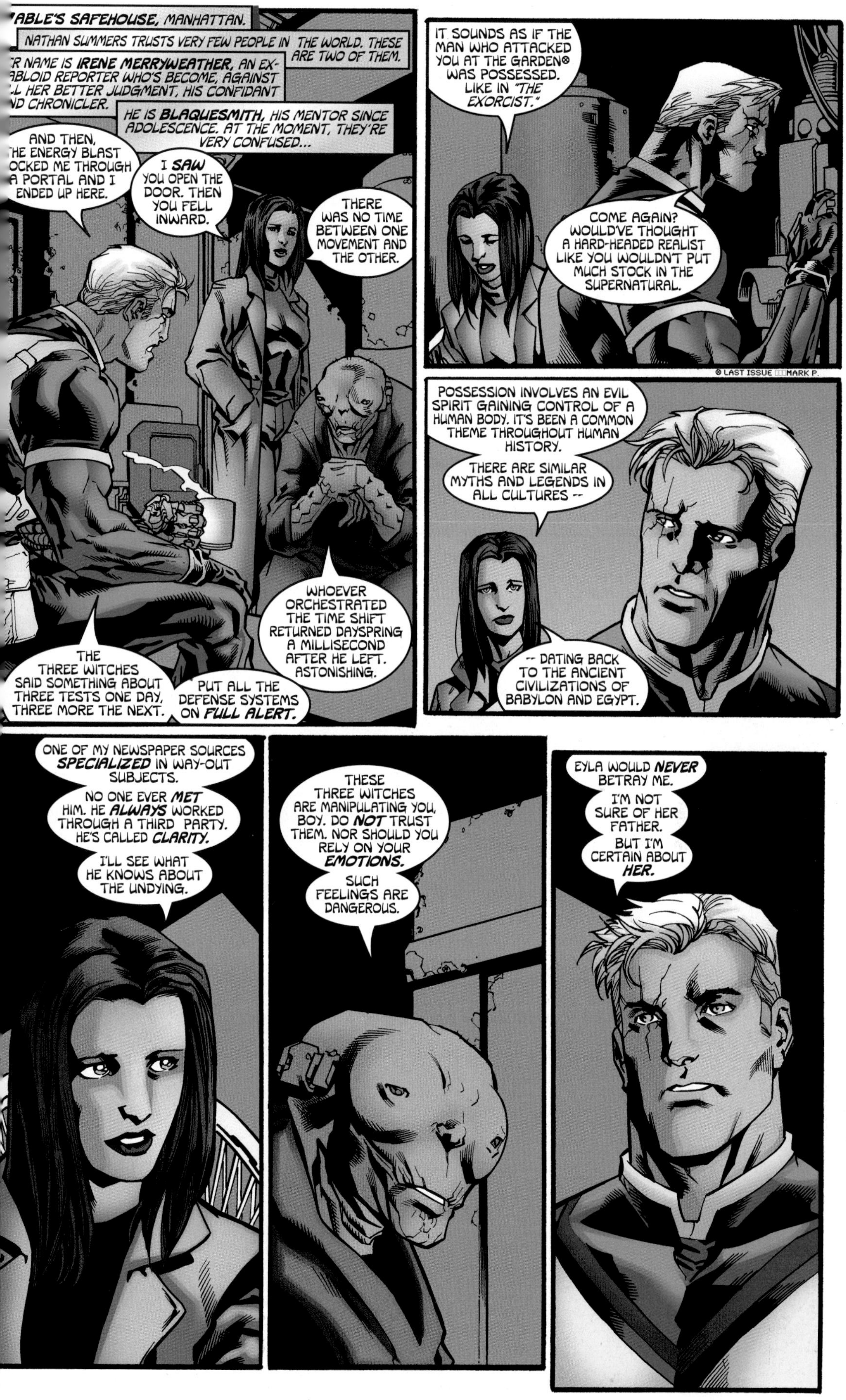

ABLE'S SAFEHOUSE, MANHATTAN.
NATHAN SUMMERS TRUSTS VERY FEW PEOPLE IN THE WORLD. THESE ARE TWO OF THEM.
ER NAME IS IRENE MERRYWEATHER, AN EX-
ABLOID REPORTER WHO'S BECOME, AGAINST
L HER BETTER JUDGMENT, HIS CONFIDANT
ND CHRONICLER.
HE IS BLAQUESMITH, HIS MENTOR SINCE ADOLESCENCE. AT THE MOMENT, THEY'RE VERY CONFUSED...
AND THEN, HE ENERGY BLAST OCKED ME THROUGH A PORTAL AND I ENDED UP HERE.
I SAW YOU OPEN THE DOOR. THEN YOU FELL INWARD.
THERE WAS NO TIME BETWEEN ONE MOVEMENT AND THE OTHER.
WHOEVER ORCHESTRATED THE TIME SHIFT RETURNED DAYSPRING A MILLISECOND AFTER HE LEFT. ASTONISHING.
THE THREE WITCHES SAID SOMETHING ABOUT THREE TESTS ONE DAY, THREE MORE THE NEXT.
PUT ALL THE DEFENSE SYSTEMS ON FULL ALERT.
IT SOUNDS AS IF THE MAN WHO ATTACKED YOU AT THE GARDEN⊗ WAS POSSESSED. LIKE IN "THE EXORCIST."
COME AGAIN? WOULD'VE THOUGHT A HARD-HEADED REALIST LIKE YOU WOULDN'T PUT MUCH STOCK IN THE SUPERNATURAL.
⊗ LAST ISSUE MARK P.
POSSESSION INVOLVES AN EVIL SPIRIT GAINING CONTROL OF A HUMAN BODY. IT'S BEEN A COMMON THEME THROUGHOUT HUMAN HISTORY.
THERE ARE SIMILAR MYTHS AND LEGENDS IN ALL CULTURES --
-- DATING BACK TO THE ANCIENT CIVILIZATIONS OF BABYLON AND EGYPT.
ONE OF MY NEWSPAPER SOURCES SPECIALIZED IN WAY-OUT SUBJECTS.
NO ONE EVER MET HIM. HE ALWAYS WORKED THROUGH A THIRD PARTY. HE'S CALLED CLARITY.
I'LL SEE WHAT HE KNOWS ABOUT THE UNDYING.
THESE THREE WITCHES ARE MANIPULATING YOU, BOY. DO NOT TRUST THEM. NOR SHOULD YOU RELY ON YOUR EMOTIONS.
SUCH FEELINGS ARE DANGEROUS.
EYLA WOULD NEVER BETRAY ME.
I'M NOT SURE OF HER FATHER.
BUT I'M CERTAIN ABOUT HER.

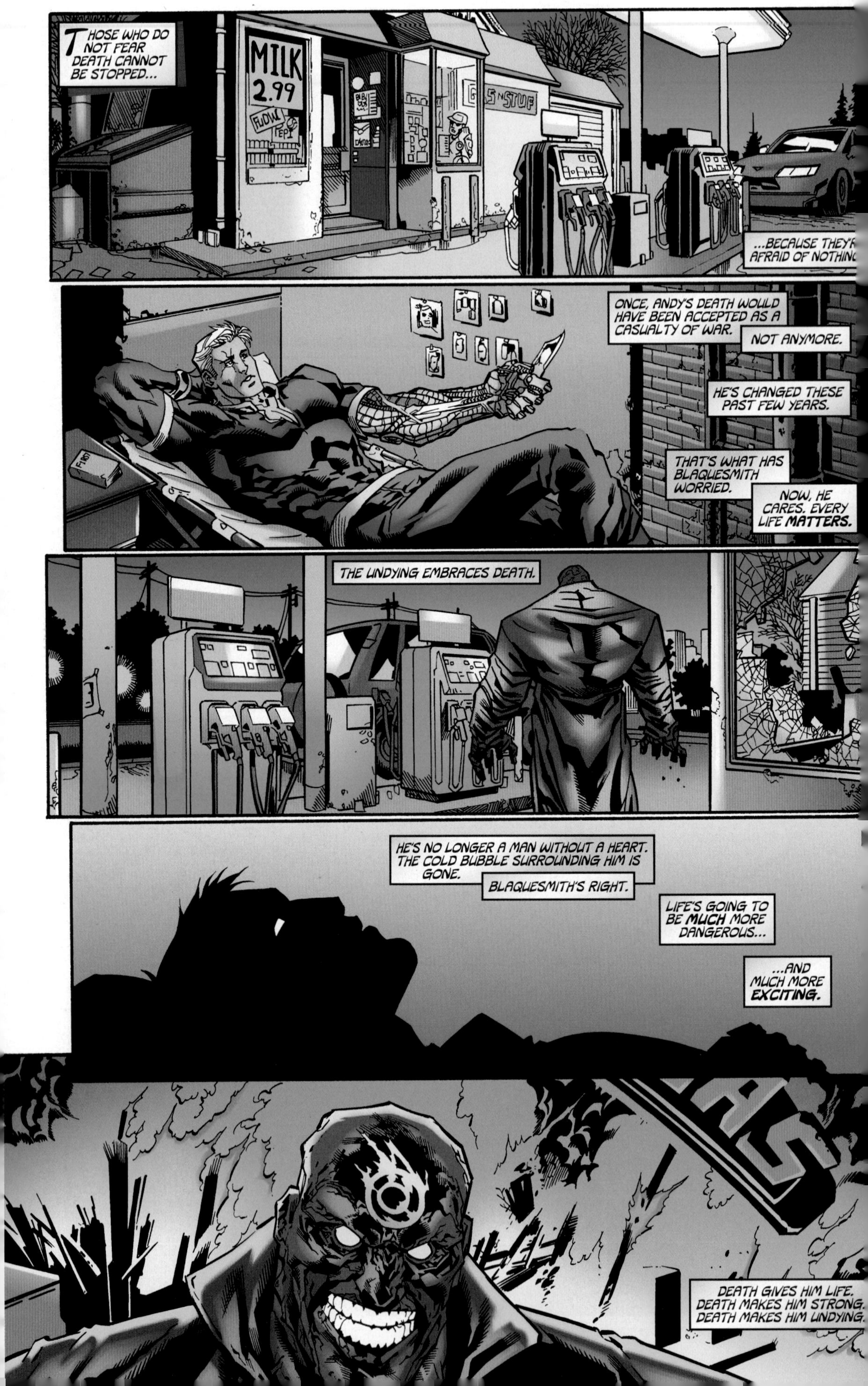

THOSE WHO DO NOT FEAR DEATH CANNOT BE STOPPED...
MILK 2.99
GAS N STUF
...BECAUSE THEY'R AFRAID OF NOTHING
ONCE, ANDY'S DEATH WOULD HAVE BEEN ACCEPTED AS A CASUALTY OF WAR.
NOT ANYMORE.
HE'S CHANGED THESE PAST FEW YEARS.
THAT'S WHAT HAS BLAQUESMITH WORRIED.
NOW, HE CARES. EVERY LIFE MATTERS.
THE UNDYING EMBRACES DEATH.
HE'S NO LONGER A MAN WITHOUT A HEART. THE COLD BUBBLE SURROUNDING HIM IS GONE.
BLAQUESMITH'S RIGHT.
LIFE'S GOING TO BE MUCH MORE DANGEROUS...
...AND MUCH MORE EXCITING.
DEATH GIVES HIM LIFE. DEATH MAKES HIM STRONG. DEATH MAKES HIM UNDYING.

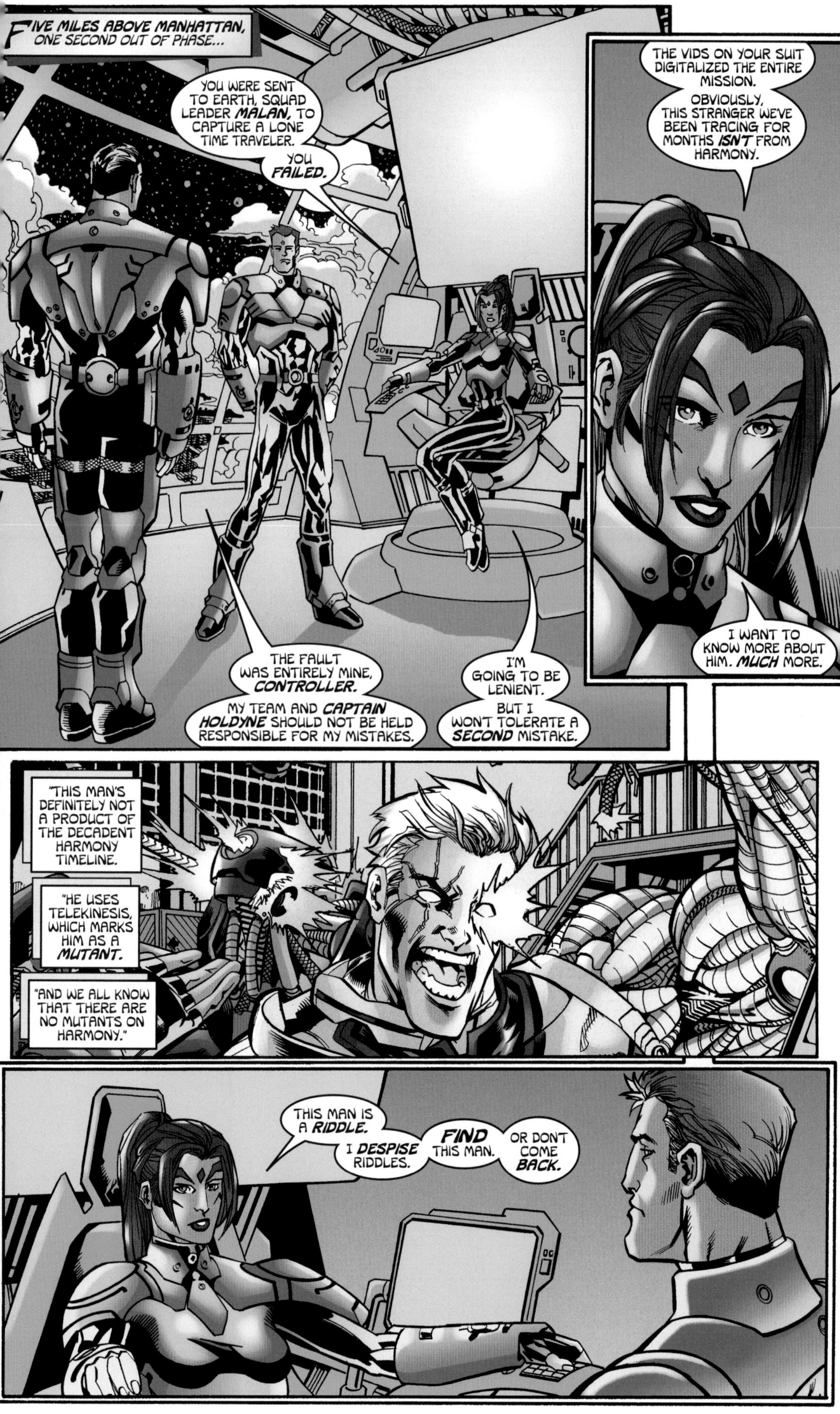
FIVE MILES ABOVE MANHATTAN, ONE SECOND OUT OF PHASE...
YOU WERE SENT TO EARTH, SQUAD LEADER MALAN, TO CAPTURE A LONE TIME TRAVELER.
YOU FAILED.
THE VIDS ON YOUR SUIT DIGITALIZED THE ENTIRE MISSION.
OBVIOUSLY, THIS STRANGER WE'VE BEEN TRACING FOR MONTHS ISN'T FROM HARMONY.
THE FAULT WAS ENTIRELY MINE, CONTROLLER.
MY TEAM AND CAPTAIN HOLDYNE SHOULD NOT BE HELD RESPONSIBLE FOR MY MISTAKES.
I'M GOING TO BE LENIENT.
BUT I WON'T TOLERATE A SECOND MISTAKE.
I WANT TO KNOW MORE ABOUT HIM. MUCH MORE.
"THIS MAN'S DEFINITELY NOT A PRODUCT OF THE DECADENT HARMONY TIMELINE.
"HE USES TELEKINESIS, WHICH MARKS HIM AS A MUTANT.
"AND WE ALL KNOW THAT THERE ARE NO MUTANTS ON HARMONY."
THIS MAN IS A RIDDLE.
I DESPISE RIDDLES.
FIND THIS MAN.
OR DON'T COME BACK.

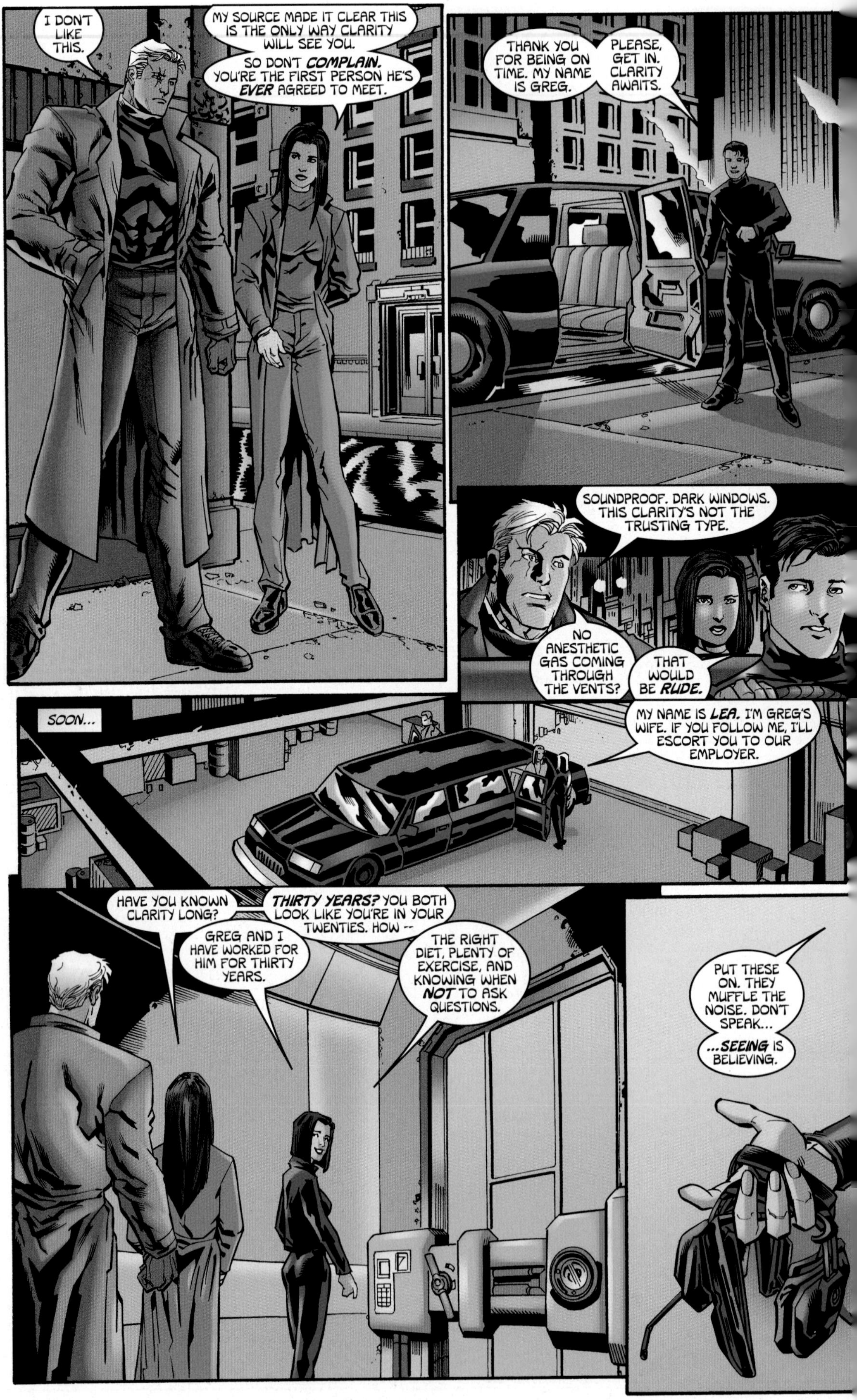
I DON'T LIKE THIS.
MY SOURCE MADE IT CLEAR THIS IS THE ONLY WAY CLARITY WILL SEE YOU.
SO DON'T COMPLAIN. YOU'RE THE FIRST PERSON HE'S EVER AGREED TO MEET.
THANK YOU FOR BEING ON TIME. MY NAME IS GREG.
PLEASE, GET IN. CLARITY AWAITS.
SOUNDPROOF. DARK WINDOWS. THIS CLARITY'S NOT THE TRUSTING TYPE.
NO ANESTHETIC GAS COMING THROUGH THE VENTS?
THAT WOULD BE RUDE.
SOON...
MY NAME IS LEA. I'M GREG'S WIFE. IF YOU FOLLOW ME, I'LL ESCORT YOU TO OUR EMPLOYER.
HAVE YOU KNOWN CLARITY LONG?
GREG AND I HAVE WORKED FOR HIM FOR THIRTY YEARS.
THIRTY YEARS? YOU BOTH LOOK LIKE YOU'RE IN YOUR TWENTIES. HOW --
THE RIGHT DIET, PLENTY OF EXERCISE, AND KNOWING WHEN NOT TO ASK QUESTIONS.
PUT THESE ON. THEY MUFFLE THE NOISE. DON'T SPEAK...
...SEEING IS BELIEVING.

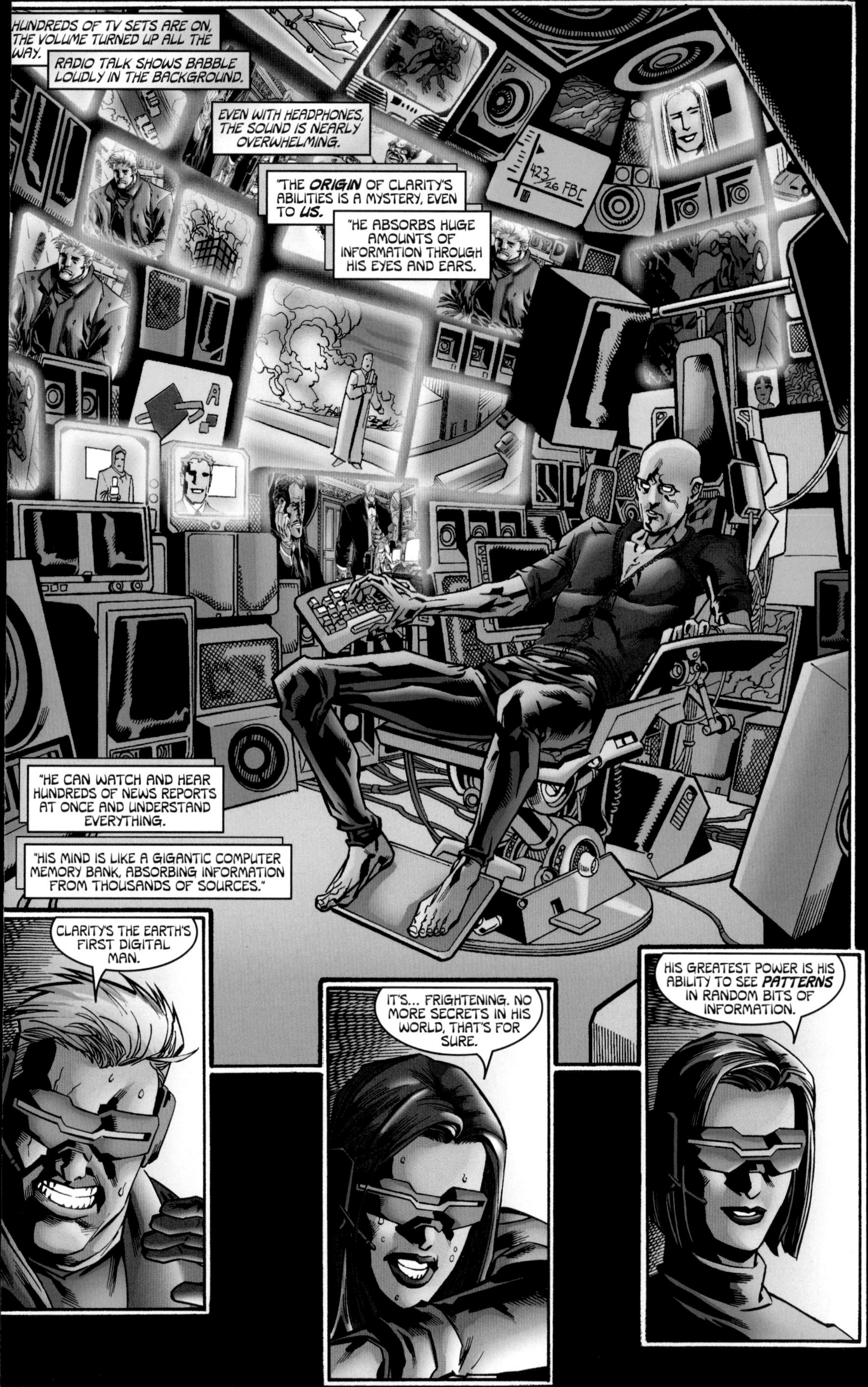

HUNDREDS OF TV SETS ARE ON, THE VOLUME TURNED UP ALL THE WAY.
RADIO TALK SHOWS BABBLE LOUDLY IN THE BACKGROUND.
EVEN WITH HEADPHONES, THE SOUND IS NEARLY OVERWHELMING.
"THE ORIGIN OF CLARITY'S ABILITIES IS A MYSTERY, EVEN TO US.
"HE ABSORBS HUGE AMOUNTS OF INFORMATION THROUGH HIS EYES AND EARS.
"HE CAN WATCH AND HEAR HUNDREDS OF NEWS REPORTS AT ONCE AND UNDERSTAND EVERYTHING.
"HIS MIND IS LIKE A GIGANTIC COMPUTER MEMORY BANK, ABSORBING INFORMATION FROM THOUSANDS OF SOURCES."
CLARITY'S THE EARTH'S FIRST DIGITAL MAN.
IT'S... FRIGHTENING. NO MORE SECRETS IN HIS WORLD, THAT'S FOR SURE.
HIS GREATEST POWER IS HIS ABILITY TO SEE PATTERNS IN RANDOM BITS OF INFORMATION.

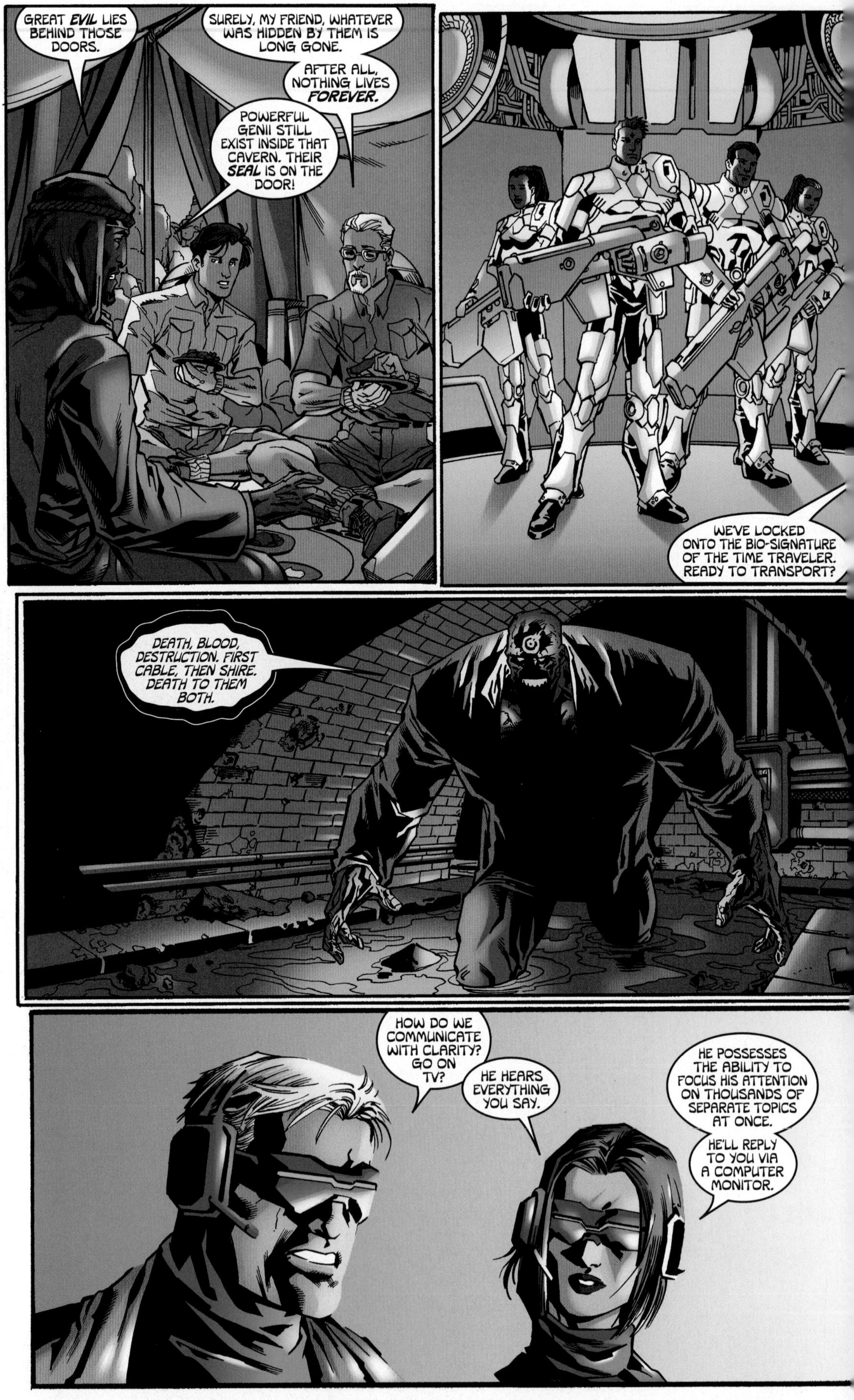
GREAT *EVIL* LIES BEHIND THOSE DOORS.
SURELY, MY FRIEND, WHATEVER WAS HIDDEN BY THEM IS LONG GONE.
AFTER ALL, NOTHING LIVES *FOREVER.*
POWERFUL GENII STILL EXIST INSIDE THAT CAVERN. THEIR *SEAL* IS ON THE DOOR!
WE'VE LOCKED ONTO THE BIO-SIGNATURE OF THE TIME TRAVELER. READY TO TRANSPORT?
DEATH, BLOOD, DESTRUCTION. FIRST CABLE, THEN SHIRE. DEATH TO THEM BOTH.
HOW DO WE COMMUNICATE WITH CLARITY? GO ON TV?
HE HEARS EVERYTHING YOU SAY.
HE POSSESSES THE ABILITY TO FOCUS HIS ATTENTION ON THOUSANDS OF SEPARATE TOPICS AT ONCE.
HE'LL REPLY TO YOU VIA A COMPUTER MONITOR.

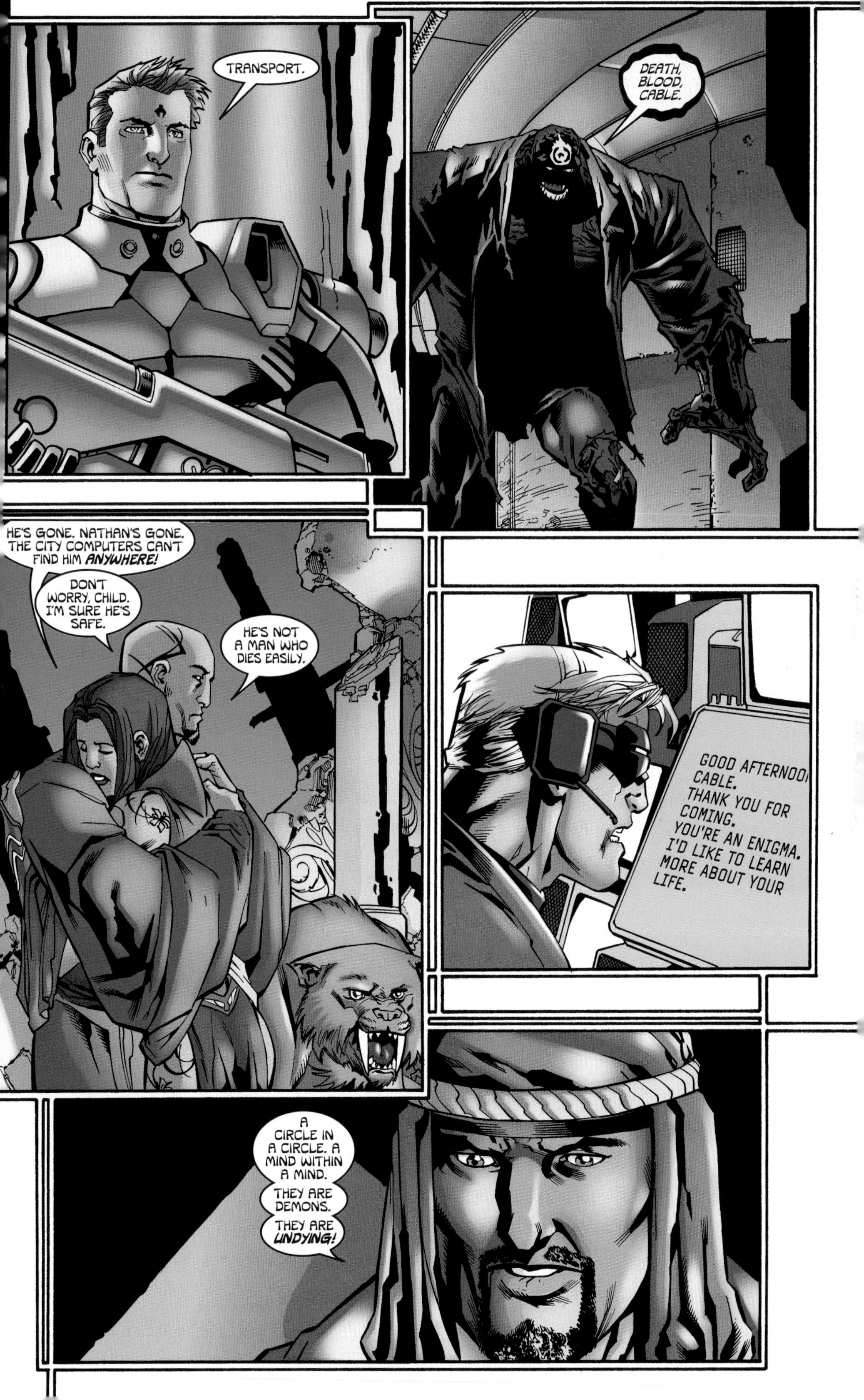
TRANSPORT.
DEATH, BLOOD, CABLE.
HE'S GONE. NATHAN'S GONE. THE CITY COMPUTERS CAN'T FIND HIM ANYWHERE!
DON'T WORRY, CHILD. I'M SURE HE'S SAFE.
HE'S NOT A MAN WHO DIES EASILY.
GOOD AFTERNOO
CABLE.
THANK YOU FOR COMING.
YOU'RE AN ENIGMA.
I'D LIKE TO LEARN MORE ABOUT YOUR LIFE.
A CIRCLE IN A CIRCLE. A MIND WITHIN A MIND.
THEY ARE DEMONS.
THEY ARE UNDYING!

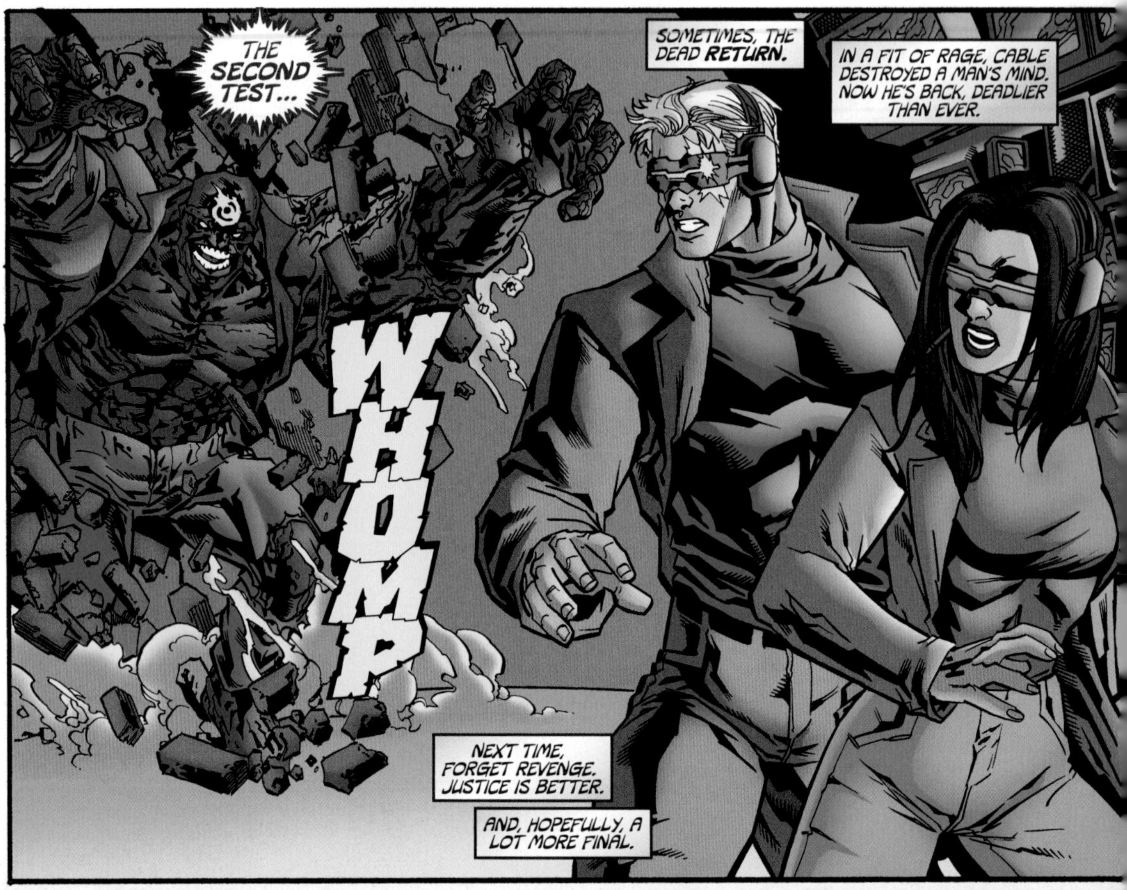
THE SECOND TEST...
SOMETIMES, THE DEAD RETURN.
IN A FIT OF RAGE, CABLE DESTROYED A MAN'S MIND. NOW HE'S BACK, DEADLIER THAN EVER.
WHOMP
NEXT TIME, FORGET REVENGE. JUSTICE IS BETTER.
AND, HOPEFULLY, A LOT MORE FINAL.

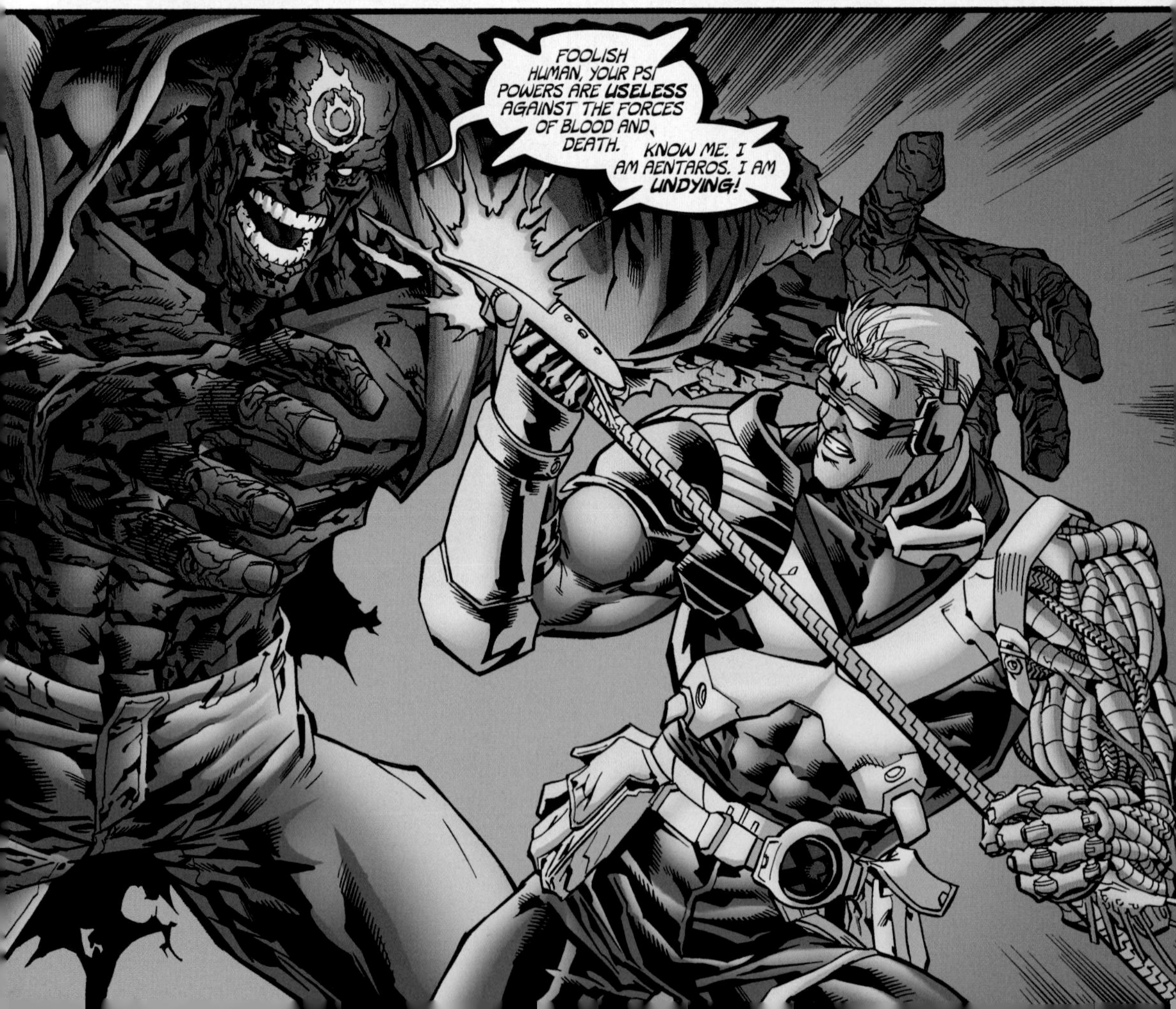
FOOLISH HUMAN, YOUR PSI POWERS ARE USELESS AGAINST THE FORCES OF BLOOD AND DEATH.
KNOW ME. I AM AENTAROS. I AM UNDYING!

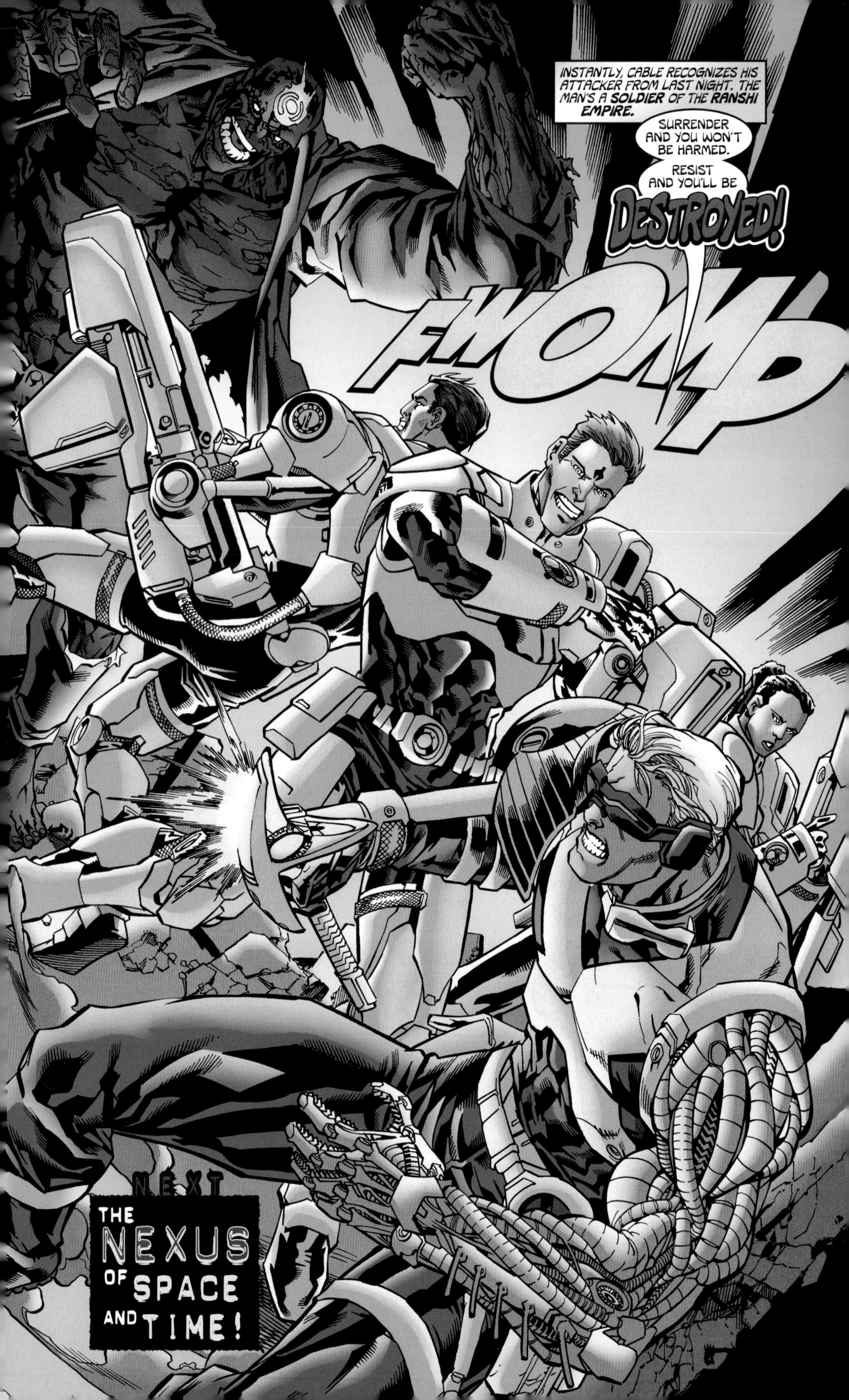
INSTANTLY, CABLE RECOGNIZES HIS ATTACKER FROM LAST NIGHT. THE MAN'S A SOLDIER OF THE RANSHI EMPIRE.
SURRENDER AND YOU WON'T BE HARMED.
RESIST AND YOU'LL BE DESTROYED!
FWOMP
NEXT
THE NEXUS OF SPACE AND TIME!

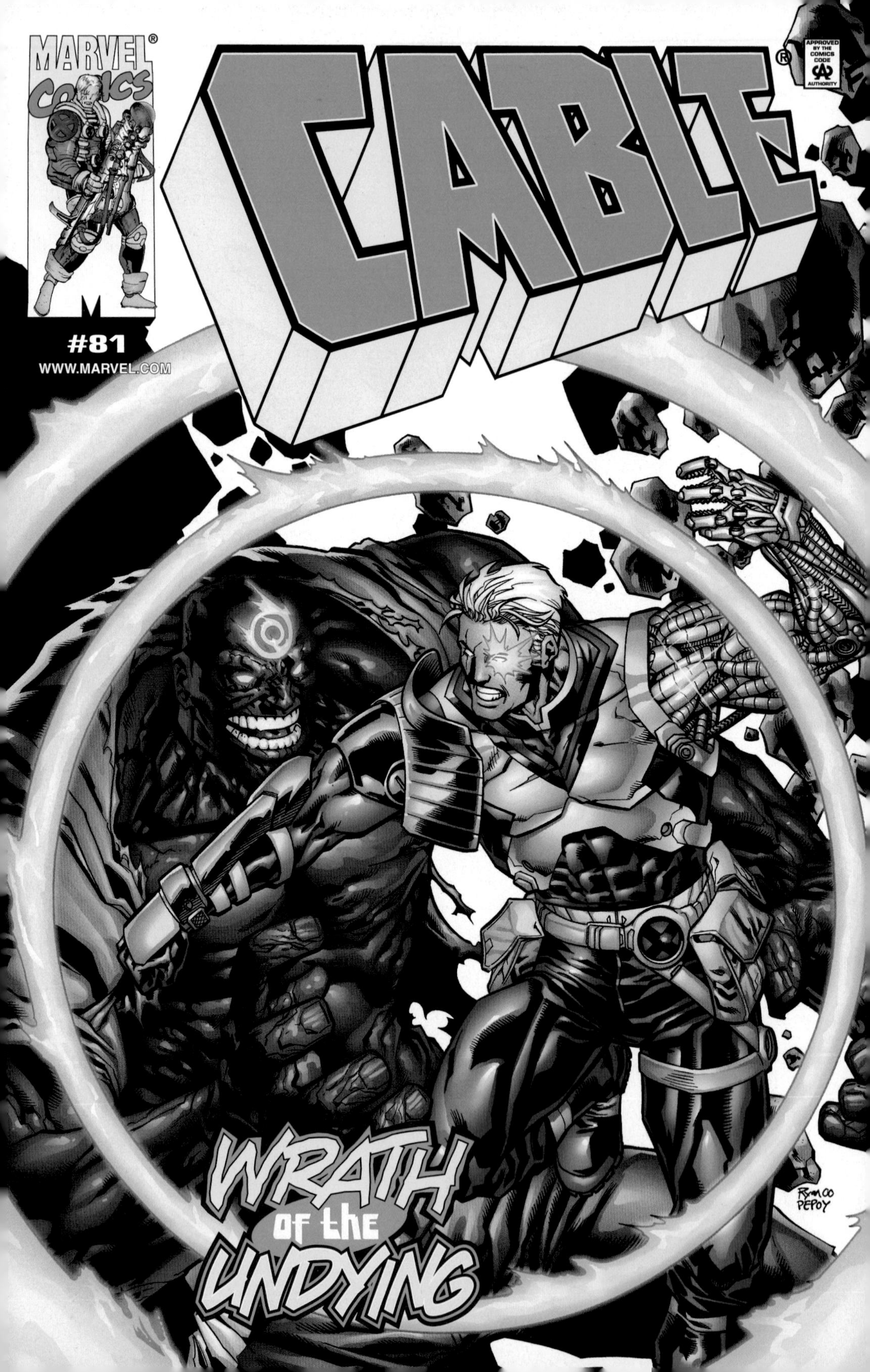

MARVEL COMICS
CABLE
#81
WWW.MARVEL.COM
APPROVED BY THE COMICS CODE AUTHORITY
WRATH of the UNDYING

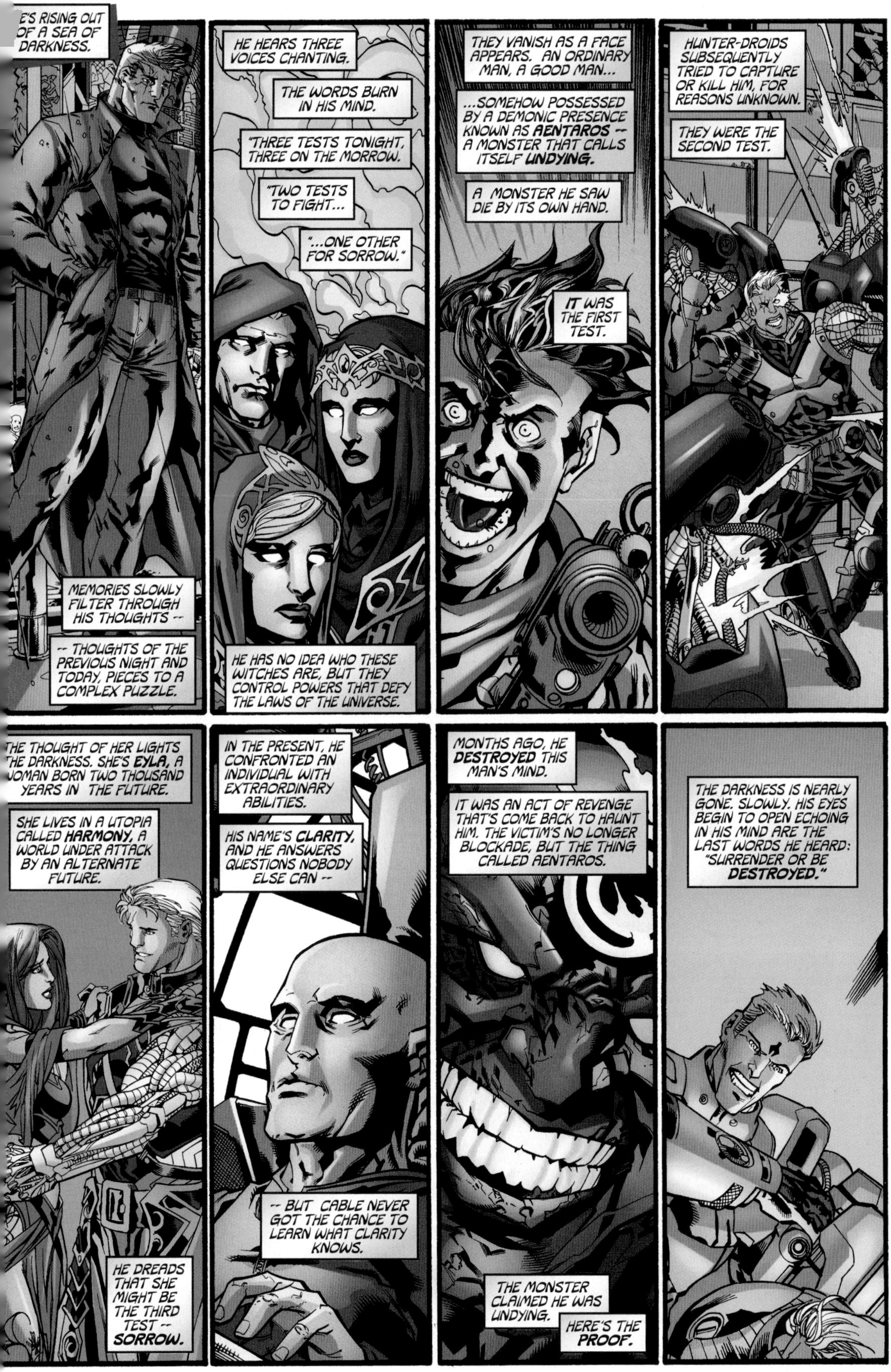

E'S RISING OUT OF A SEA OF DARKNESS.
MEMORIES SLOWLY FILTER THROUGH HIS THOUGHTS --
-- THOUGHTS OF THE PREVIOUS NIGHT AND TODAY, PIECES TO A COMPLEX PUZZLE.
HE HEARS THREE VOICES CHANTING.
THE WORDS BURN IN HIS MIND.
"THREE TESTS TONIGHT, THREE ON THE MORROW.
"TWO TESTS TO FIGHT...
"...ONE OTHER FOR SORROW."
HE HAS NO IDEA WHO THESE WITCHES ARE, BUT THEY CONTROL POWERS THAT DEFY THE LAWS OF THE UNIVERSE.
THEY VANISH AS A FACE APPEARS. AN ORDINARY MAN, A GOOD MAN...
...SOMEHOW POSSESSED BY A DEMONIC PRESENCE KNOWN AS **AENTAROS** -- A MONSTER THAT CALLS ITSELF **UNDYING.**
A MONSTER HE SAW DIE BY ITS OWN HAND.
IT WAS THE FIRST TEST.
HUNTER-DROIDS SUBSEQUENTLY TRIED TO CAPTURE OR KILL HIM, FOR REASONS UNKNOWN.
THEY WERE THE SECOND TEST.
THE THOUGHT OF HER LIGHTS THE DARKNESS. SHE'S **EYLA,** A WOMAN BORN TWO THOUSAND YEARS IN THE FUTURE.
SHE LIVES IN A UTOPIA CALLED **HARMONY,** A WORLD UNDER ATTACK BY AN ALTERNATE FUTURE.
HE DREADS THAT SHE MIGHT BE THE THIRD TEST -- **SORROW.**
IN THE PRESENT, HE CONFRONTED AN INDIVIDUAL WITH EXTRAORDINARY ABILITIES.
HIS NAME'S **CLARITY,** AND HE ANSWERS QUESTIONS NOBODY ELSE CAN --
-- BUT CABLE NEVER GOT THE CHANCE TO LEARN WHAT CLARITY KNOWS.
MONTHS AGO, HE **DESTROYED** THIS MAN'S MIND.
IT WAS AN ACT OF REVENGE THAT'S COME BACK TO HAUNT HIM. THE VICTIM'S NO LONGER BLOCKADE, BUT THE THING CALLED AENTAROS.
THE MONSTER CLAIMED HE WAS UNDYING.
HERE'S THE **PROOF.**
THE DARKNESS IS NEARLY GONE. SLOWLY, HIS EYES BEGIN TO OPEN ECHOING IN HIS MIND ARE THE LAST WORDS HE HEARD: "SURRENDER OR BE **DESTROYED.**"

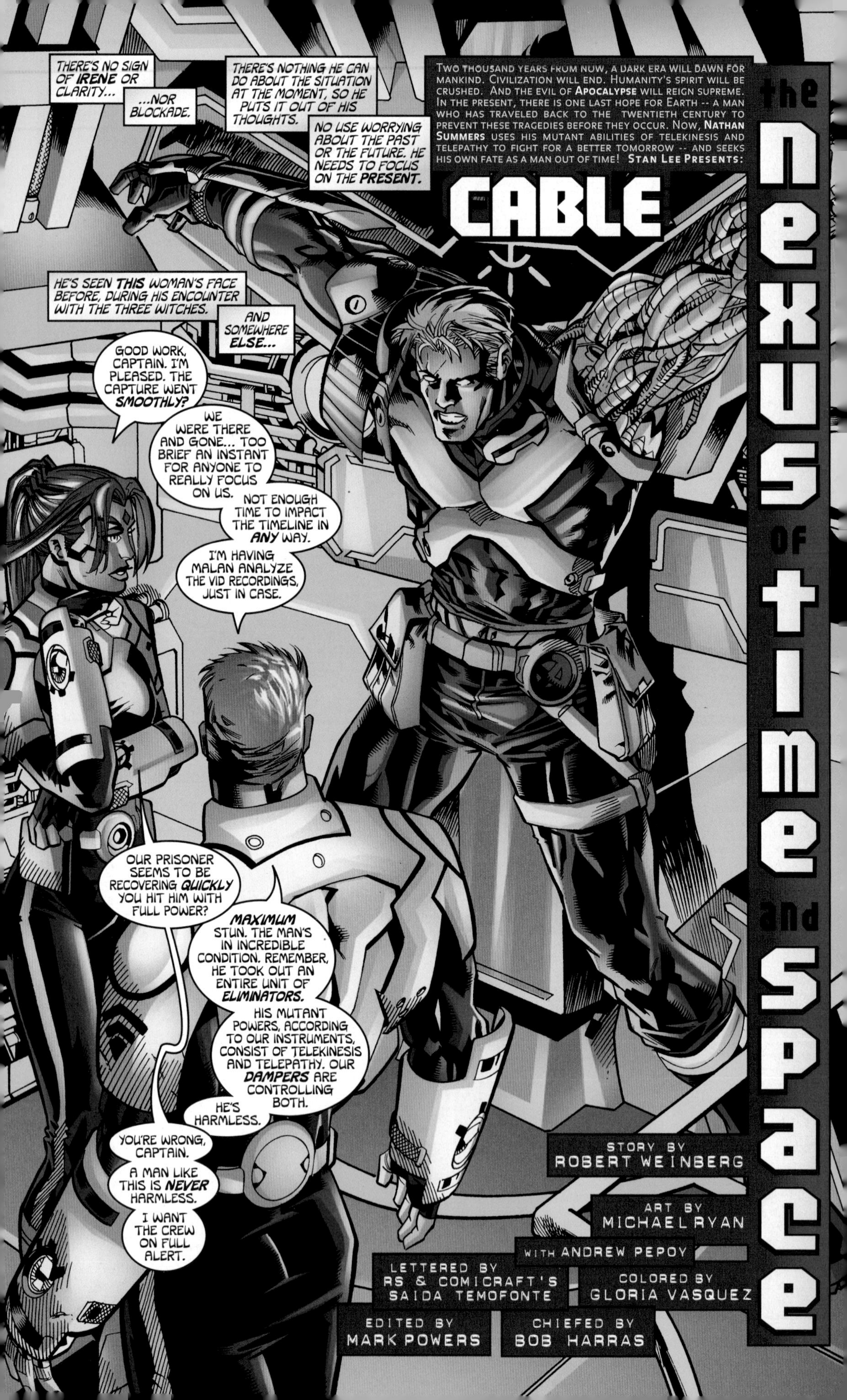

THERE'S NO SIGN OF IRENE OR CLARITY...
...NOR BLOCKADE.
THERE'S NOTHING HE CAN DO ABOUT THE SITUATION AT THE MOMENT, SO HE PUTS IT OUT OF HIS THOUGHTS.
NO USE WORRYING ABOUT THE PAST OR THE FUTURE. HE NEEDS TO FOCUS ON THE PRESENT.
TWO THOUSAND YEARS FROM NOW, A DARK ERA WILL DAWN FOR MANKIND. CIVILIZATION WILL END. HUMANITY'S SPIRIT WILL BE CRUSHED. AND THE EVIL OF APOCALYPSE WILL REIGN SUPREME. IN THE PRESENT, THERE IS ONE LAST HOPE FOR EARTH -- A MAN WHO HAS TRAVELED BACK TO THE TWENTIETH CENTURY TO PREVENT THESE TRAGEDIES BEFORE THEY OCCUR. NOW, NATHAN SUMMERS USES HIS MUTANT ABILITIES OF TELEKINESIS AND TELEPATHY TO FIGHT FOR A BETTER TOMORROW -- AND SEEKS HIS OWN FATE AS A MAN OUT OF TIME! STAN LEE PRESENTS:
CABLE
the nexus of time and space
HE'S SEEN THIS WOMAN'S FACE BEFORE, DURING HIS ENCOUNTER WITH THE THREE WITCHES.
AND SOMEWHERE ELSE...
GOOD WORK, CAPTAIN. I'M PLEASED. THE CAPTURE WENT SMOOTHLY?
WE WERE THERE AND GONE... TOO BRIEF AN INSTANT FOR ANYONE TO REALLY FOCUS ON US.
NOT ENOUGH TIME TO IMPACT THE TIMELINE IN ANY WAY.
I'M HAVING MALAN ANALYZE THE VID RECORDINGS, JUST IN CASE.
OUR PRISONER SEEMS TO BE RECOVERING QUICKLY YOU HIT HIM WITH FULL POWER?
MAXIMUM STUN. THE MAN'S IN INCREDIBLE CONDITION. REMEMBER, HE TOOK OUT AN ENTIRE UNIT OF ELIMINATORS.
HIS MUTANT POWERS, ACCORDING TO OUR INSTRUMENTS, CONSIST OF TELEKINESIS AND TELEPATHY. OUR DAMPERS ARE CONTROLLING BOTH.
HE'S HARMLESS.
YOU'RE WRONG, CAPTAIN.
A MAN LIKE THIS IS NEVER HARMLESS.
I WANT THE CREW ON FULL ALERT.
STORY BY ROBERT WEINBERG
ART BY MICHAEL RYAN
WITH ANDREW PEPOY
LETTERED BY RS & COMICRAFT'S SAIDA TEMOFONTE
COLORED BY GLORIA VASQUEZ
EDITED BY MARK POWERS
CHIEFED BY BOB HARRAS

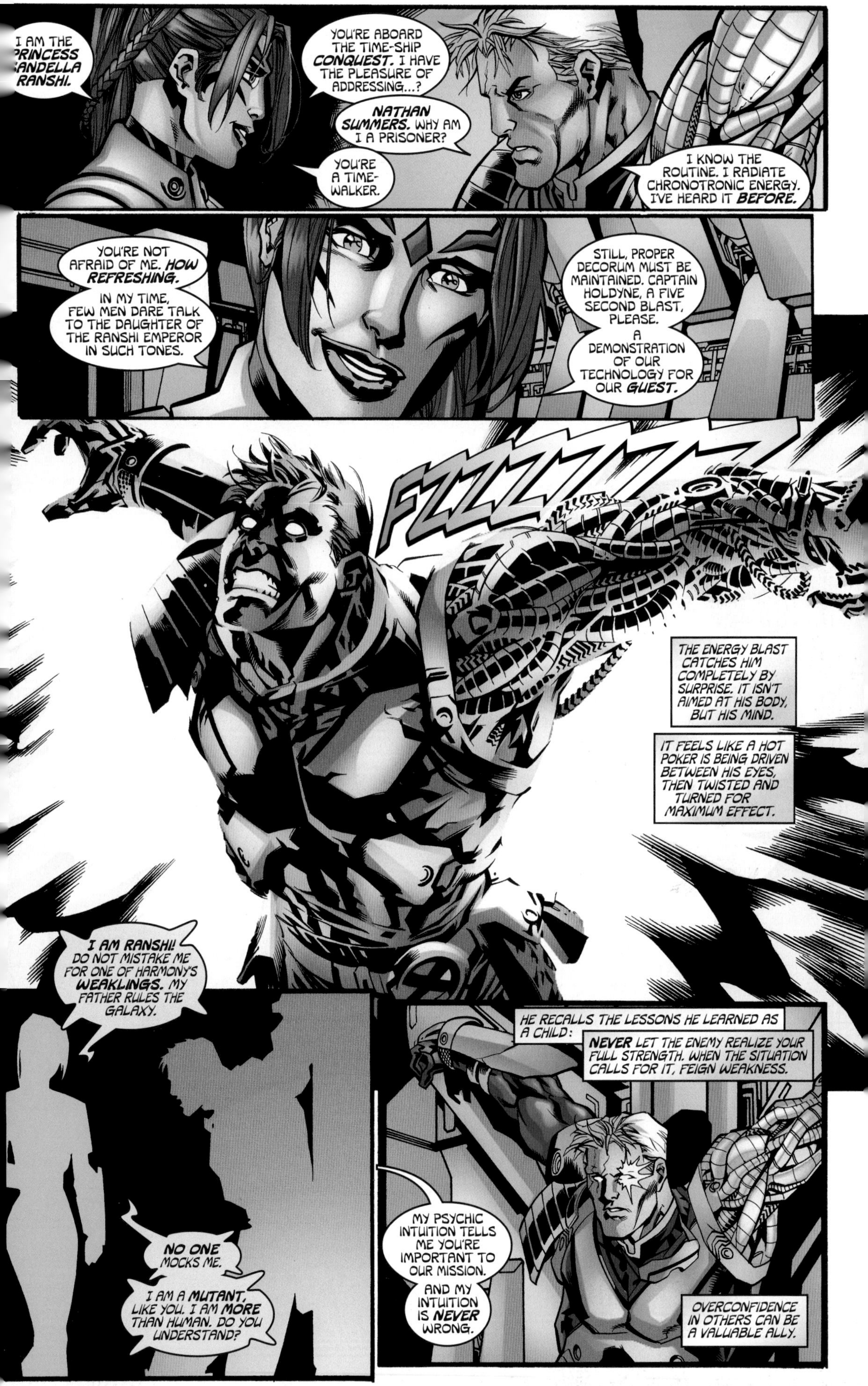
I AM THE PRINCESS SANDELLA RANSHI.
YOU'RE ABOARD THE TIME-SHIP CONQUEST. I HAVE THE PLEASURE OF ADDRESSING...?
NATHAN SUMMERS. WHY AM I A PRISONER?
YOU'RE A TIME-WALKER.
I KNOW THE ROUTINE. I RADIATE CHRONOTRONIC ENERGY. I'VE HEARD IT BEFORE.
YOU'RE NOT AFRAID OF ME. HOW REFRESHING.
IN MY TIME, FEW MEN DARE TALK TO THE DAUGHTER OF THE RANSHI EMPEROR IN SUCH TONES.
STILL, PROPER DECORUM MUST BE MAINTAINED. CAPTAIN HOLDYNE, A FIVE SECOND BLAST, PLEASE.
A DEMONSTRATION OF OUR TECHNOLOGY FOR OUR GUEST.
FZZZZT
THE ENERGY BLAST CATCHES HIM COMPLETELY BY SURPRISE. IT ISN'T AIMED AT HIS BODY, BUT HIS MIND.
IT FEELS LIKE A HOT POKER IS BEING DRIVEN BETWEEN HIS EYES, THEN TWISTED AND TURNED FOR MAXIMUM EFFECT.
I AM RANSHI! DO NOT MISTAKE ME FOR ONE OF HARMONY'S WEAKLINGS. MY FATHER RULES THE GALAXY.
NO ONE MOCKS ME.
I AM A MUTANT, LIKE YOU. I AM MORE THAN HUMAN. DO YOU UNDERSTAND?
HE RECALLS THE LESSONS HE LEARNED AS A CHILD:
NEVER LET THE ENEMY REALIZE YOUR FULL STRENGTH. WHEN THE SITUATION CALLS FOR IT, FEIGN WEAKNESS.
MY PSYCHIC INTUITION TELLS ME YOU'RE IMPORTANT TO OUR MISSION.
AND MY INTUITION IS NEVER WRONG.
OVERCONFIDENCE IN OTHERS CAN BE A VALUABLE ALLY.

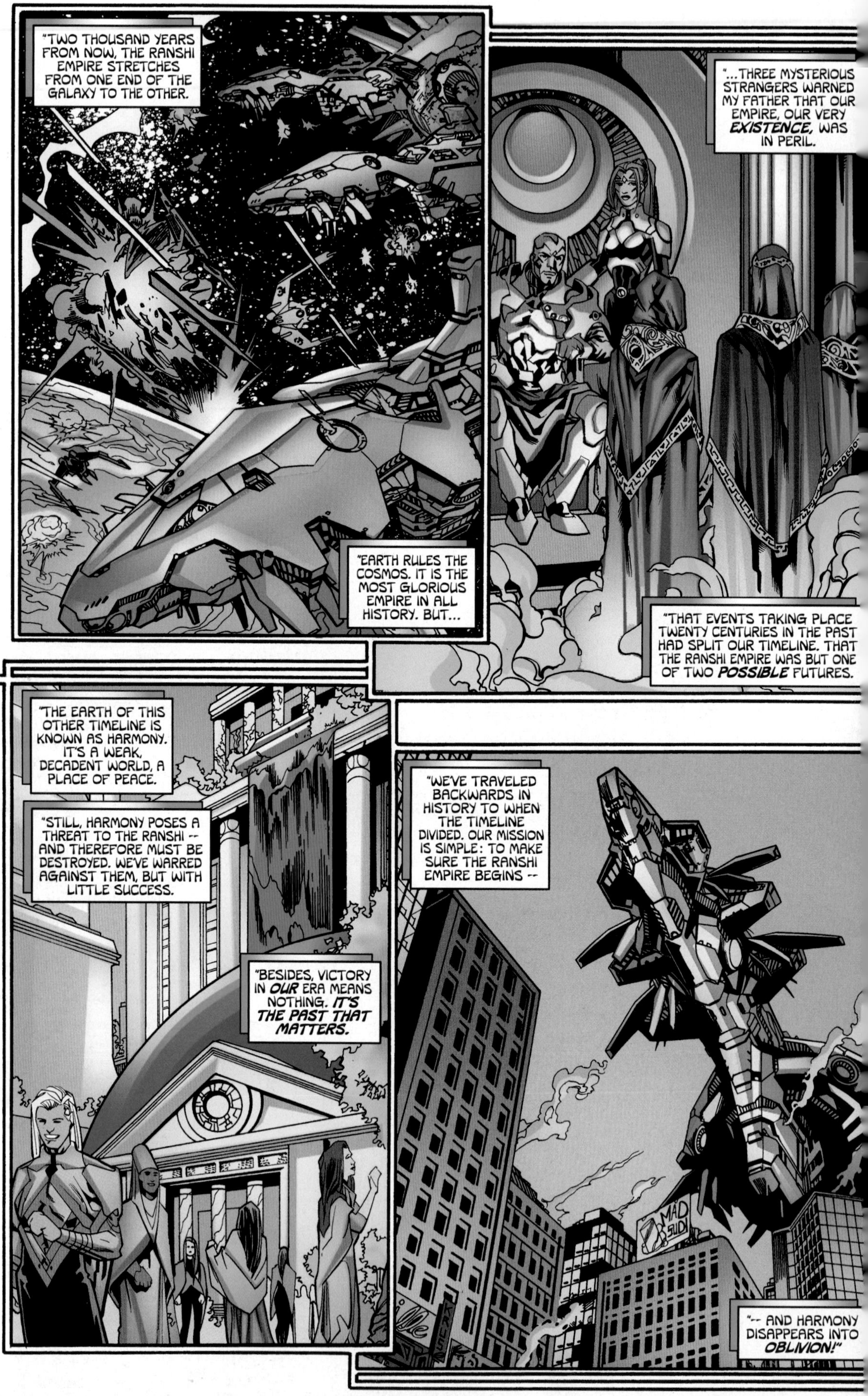
"TWO THOUSAND YEARS FROM NOW, THE RANSHI EMPIRE STRETCHES FROM ONE END OF THE GALAXY TO THE OTHER.
"EARTH RULES THE COSMOS. IT IS THE MOST GLORIOUS EMPIRE IN ALL HISTORY. BUT...
"...THREE MYSTERIOUS STRANGERS WARNED MY FATHER THAT OUR EMPIRE, OUR VERY ***EXISTENCE,*** WAS IN PERIL.
"THAT EVENTS TAKING PLACE TWENTY CENTURIES IN THE PAST HAD SPLIT OUR TIMELINE. THAT THE RANSHI EMPIRE WAS BUT ONE OF TWO ***POSSIBLE*** FUTURES.
"THE EARTH OF THIS OTHER TIMELINE IS KNOWN AS HARMONY. IT'S A WEAK, DECADENT WORLD, A PLACE OF PEACE.
"STILL, HARMONY POSES A THREAT TO THE RANSHI -- AND THEREFORE MUST BE DESTROYED. WE'VE WARRED AGAINST THEM, BUT WITH LITTLE SUCCESS.
"BESIDES, VICTORY IN ***OUR*** ERA MEANS NOTHING. ***IT'S THE PAST THAT MATTERS.***
"WE'VE TRAVELED BACKWARDS IN HISTORY TO WHEN THE TIMELINE DIVIDED. OUR MISSION IS SIMPLE: TO MAKE SURE THE RANSHI EMPIRE BEGINS --
"-- AND HARMONY DISAPPEARS INTO ***OBLIVION!"***

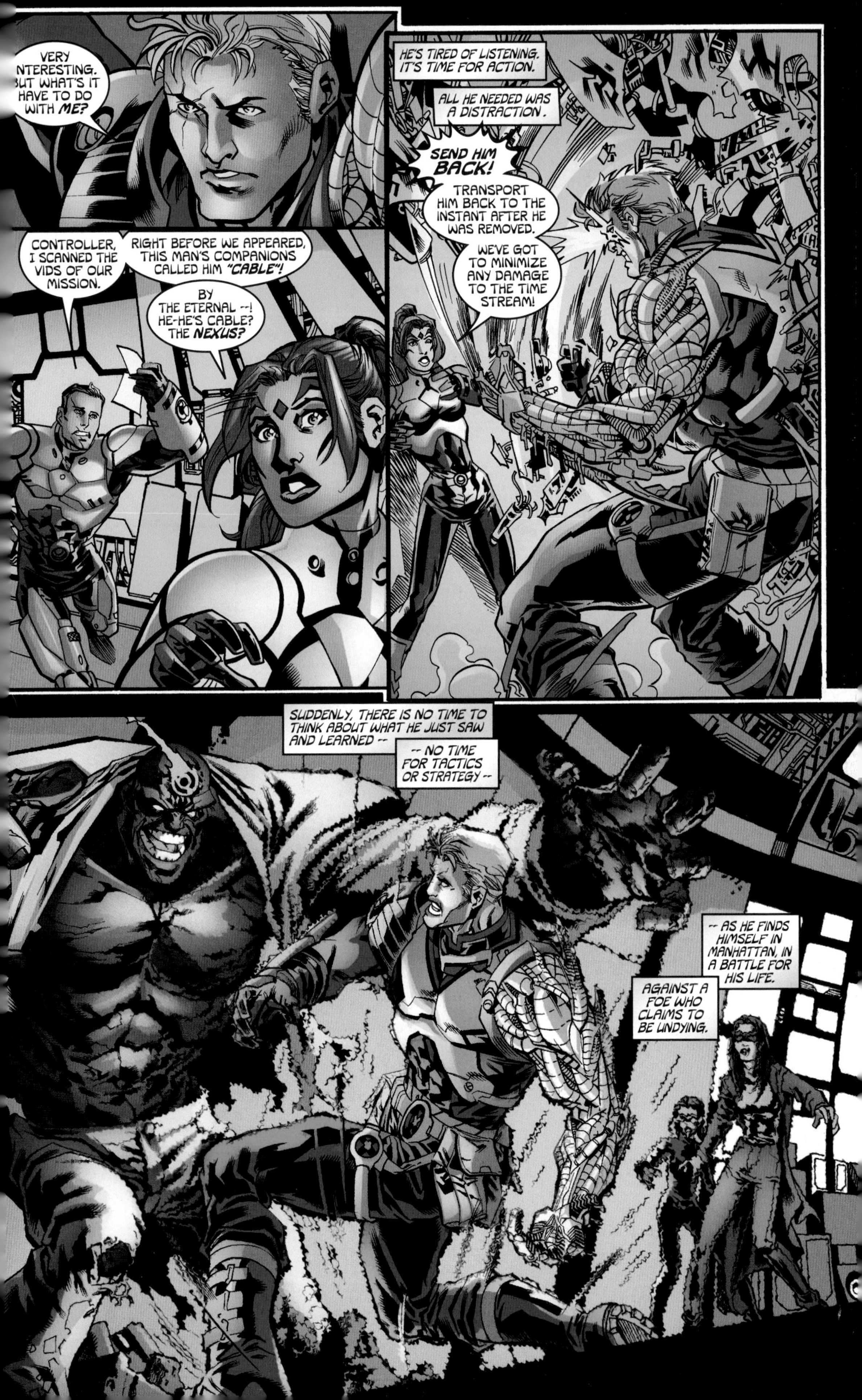
VERY INTERESTING. BUT WHAT'S IT HAVE TO DO WITH *ME?*
CONTROLLER, I SCANNED THE VIDS OF OUR MISSION.
RIGHT BEFORE WE APPEARED, THIS MAN'S COMPANIONS CALLED HIM *"CABLE"!*
BY THE ETERNAL --! HE-HE'S CABLE? THE *NEXUS?*
HE'S TIRED OF LISTENING. IT'S TIME FOR ACTION.
ALL HE NEEDED WAS A DISTRACTION.
SEND HIM BACK!
TRANSPORT HIM BACK TO THE INSTANT AFTER HE WAS REMOVED.
WE'VE GOT TO MINIMIZE ANY DAMAGE TO THE TIME STREAM!
SUDDENLY, THERE IS NO TIME TO THINK ABOUT WHAT HE JUST SAW AND LEARNED --
-- NO TIME FOR TACTICS OR STRATEGY --
-- AS HE FINDS HIMSELF IN MANHATTAN, IN A BATTLE FOR HIS LIFE.
AGAINST A FOE WHO CLAIMS TO BE UNDYING.

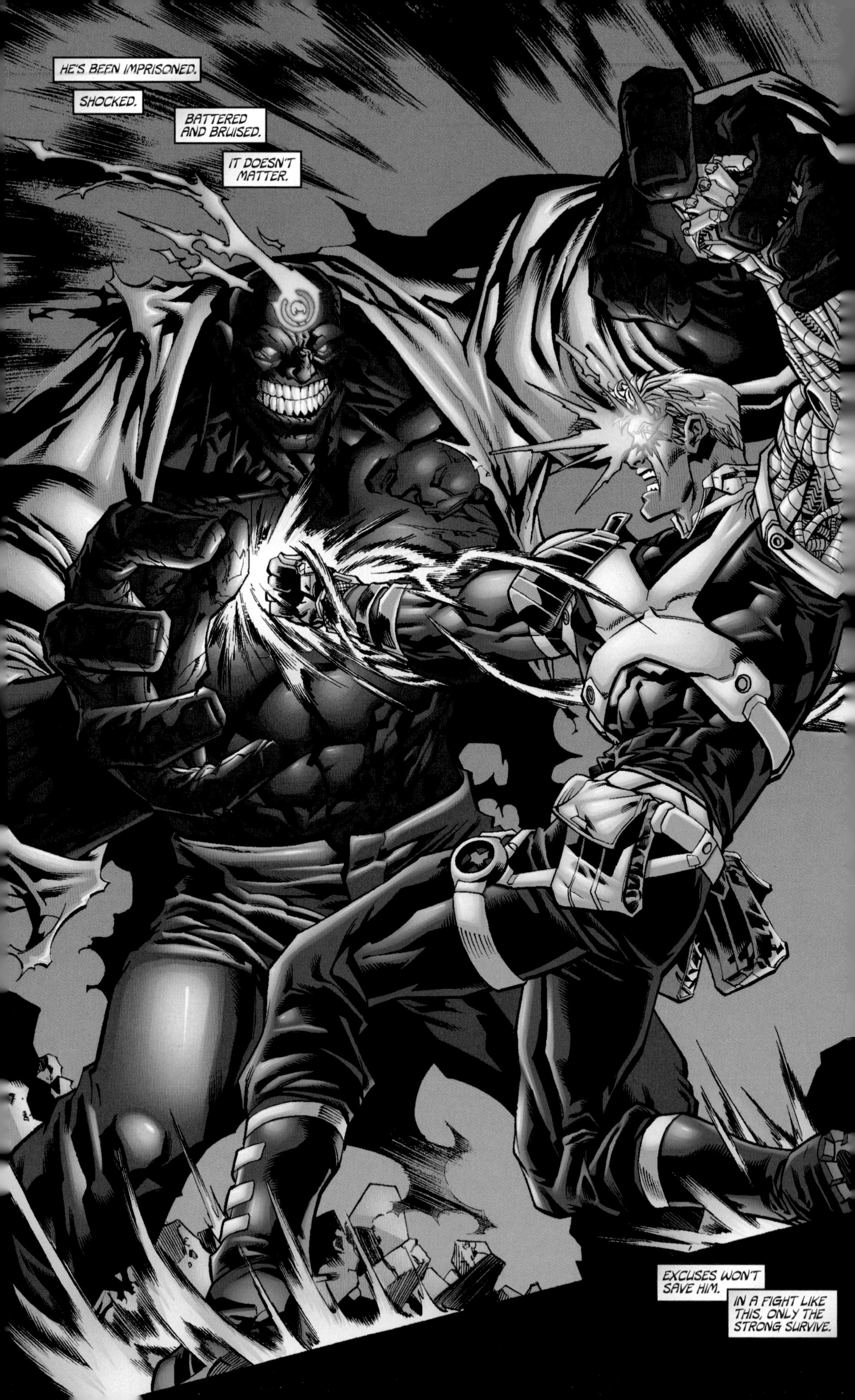
HE'S BEEN IMPRISONED.
SHOCKED.
BATTERED AND BRUISED.
IT DOESN'T MATTER.
EXCUSES WON'T SAVE HIM.
IN A FIGHT LIKE THIS, ONLY THE STRONG SURVIVE.

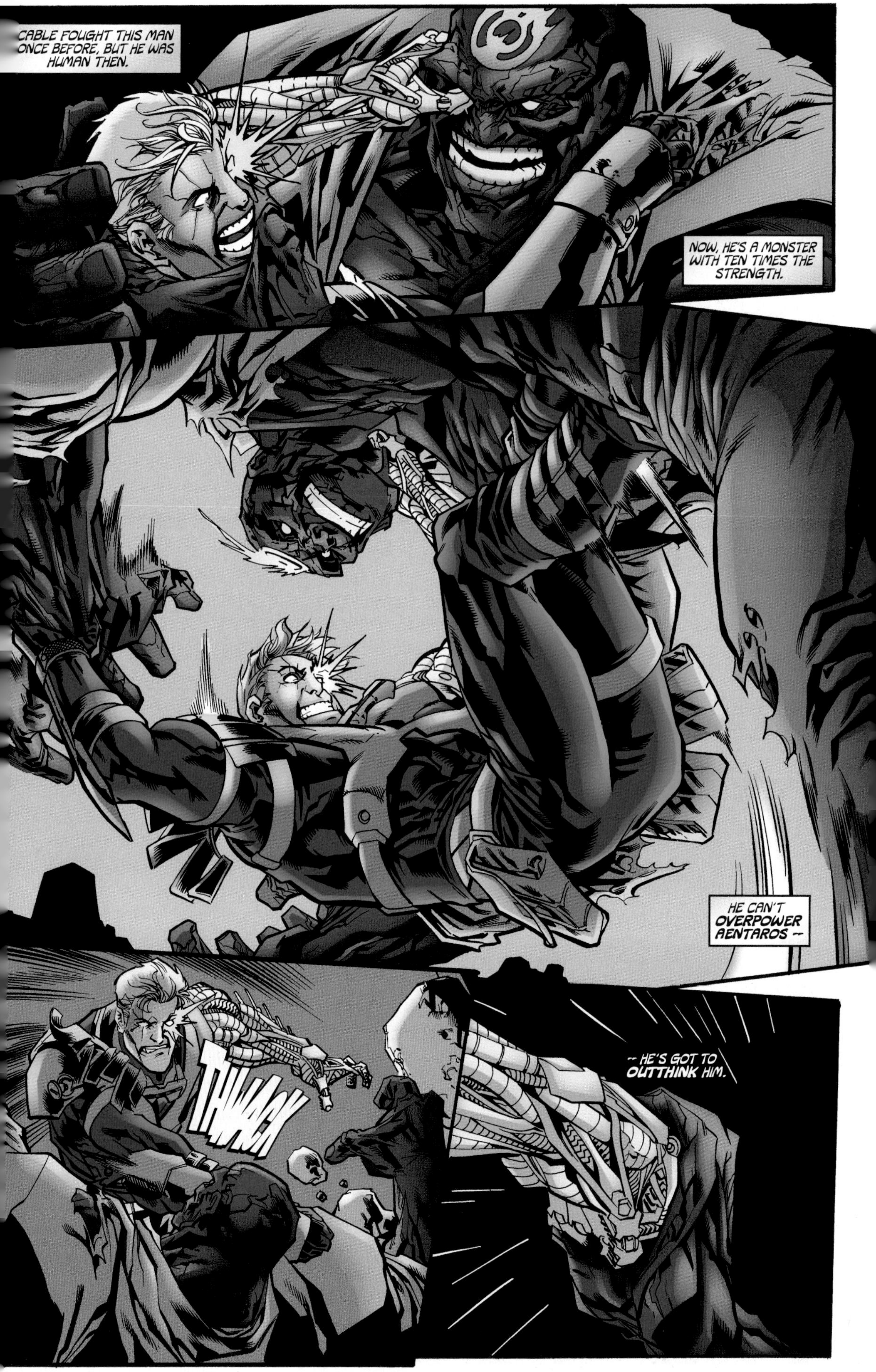
CABLE FOUGHT THIS MAN ONCE BEFORE, BUT HE WAS HUMAN THEN.
NOW, HE'S A MONSTER WITH TEN TIMES THE STRENGTH.
HE CAN'T OVERPOWER AENTAROS --
THWACK
-- HE'S GOT TO OUTTHINK HIM.

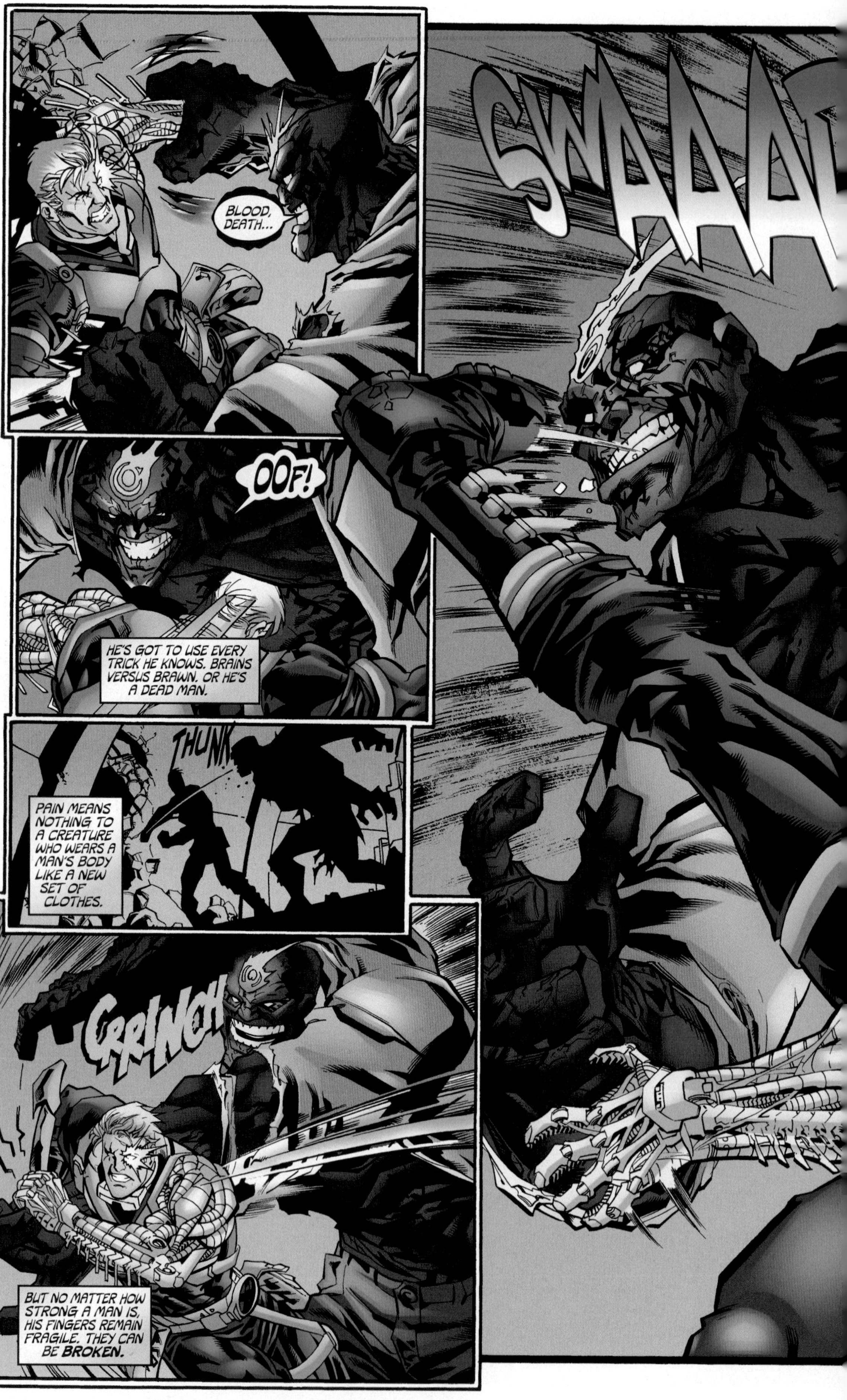
BLOOD, DEATH...
OOF!
HE'S GOT TO USE EVERY TRICK HE KNOWS. BRAINS VERSUS BRAWN. OR HE'S A DEAD MAN.
THUNK
PAIN MEANS NOTHING TO A CREATURE WHO WEARS A MAN'S BODY LIKE A NEW SET OF CLOTHES.
CRRINCH
BUT NO MATTER HOW STRONG A MAN IS, HIS FINGERS REMAIN FRAGILE. THEY CAN BE **BROKEN.**
SWAAAA

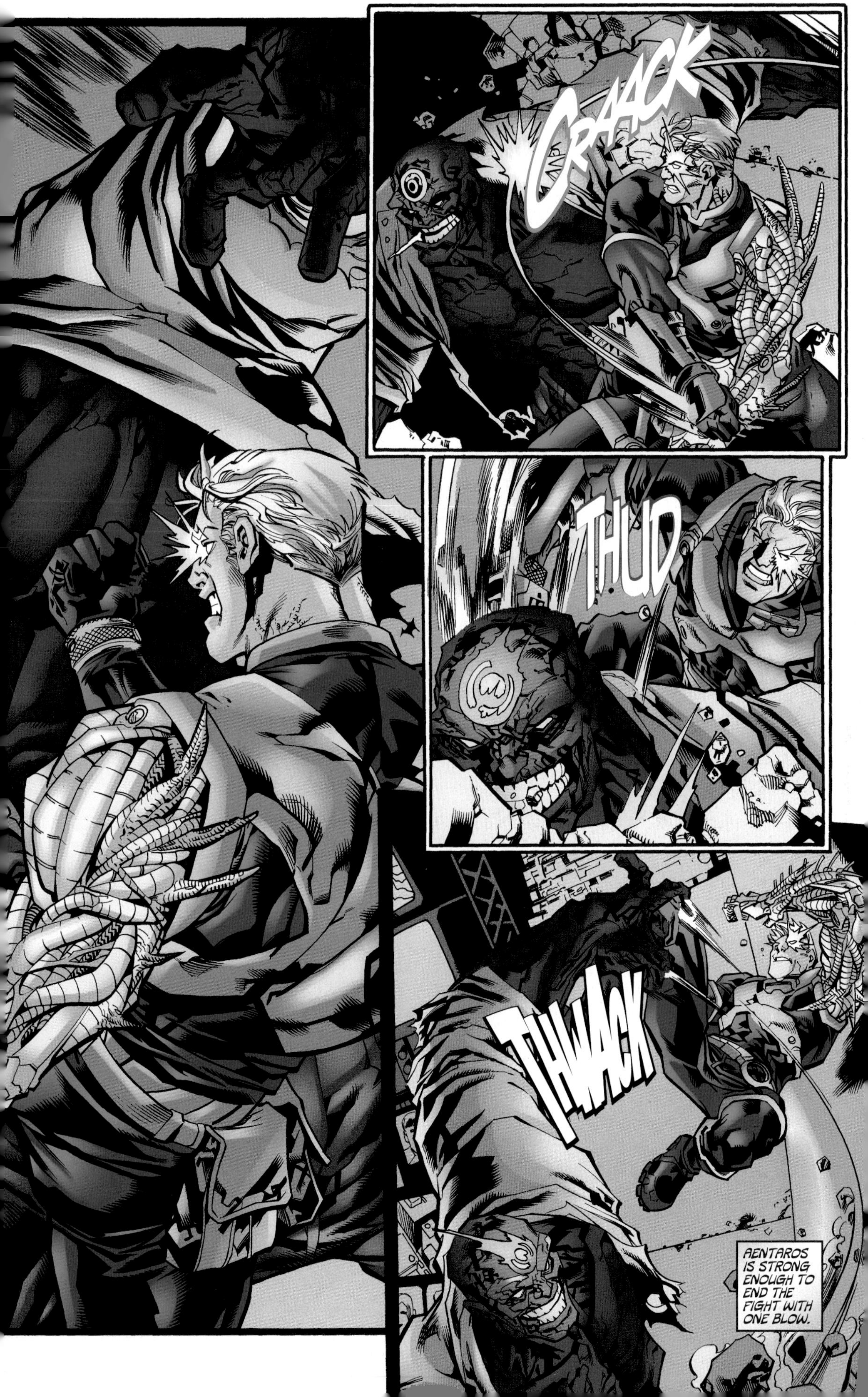
CRAACK
THUD
THWACK
AENTAROS IS STRONG ENOUGH TO END THE FIGHT WITH ONE BLOW.

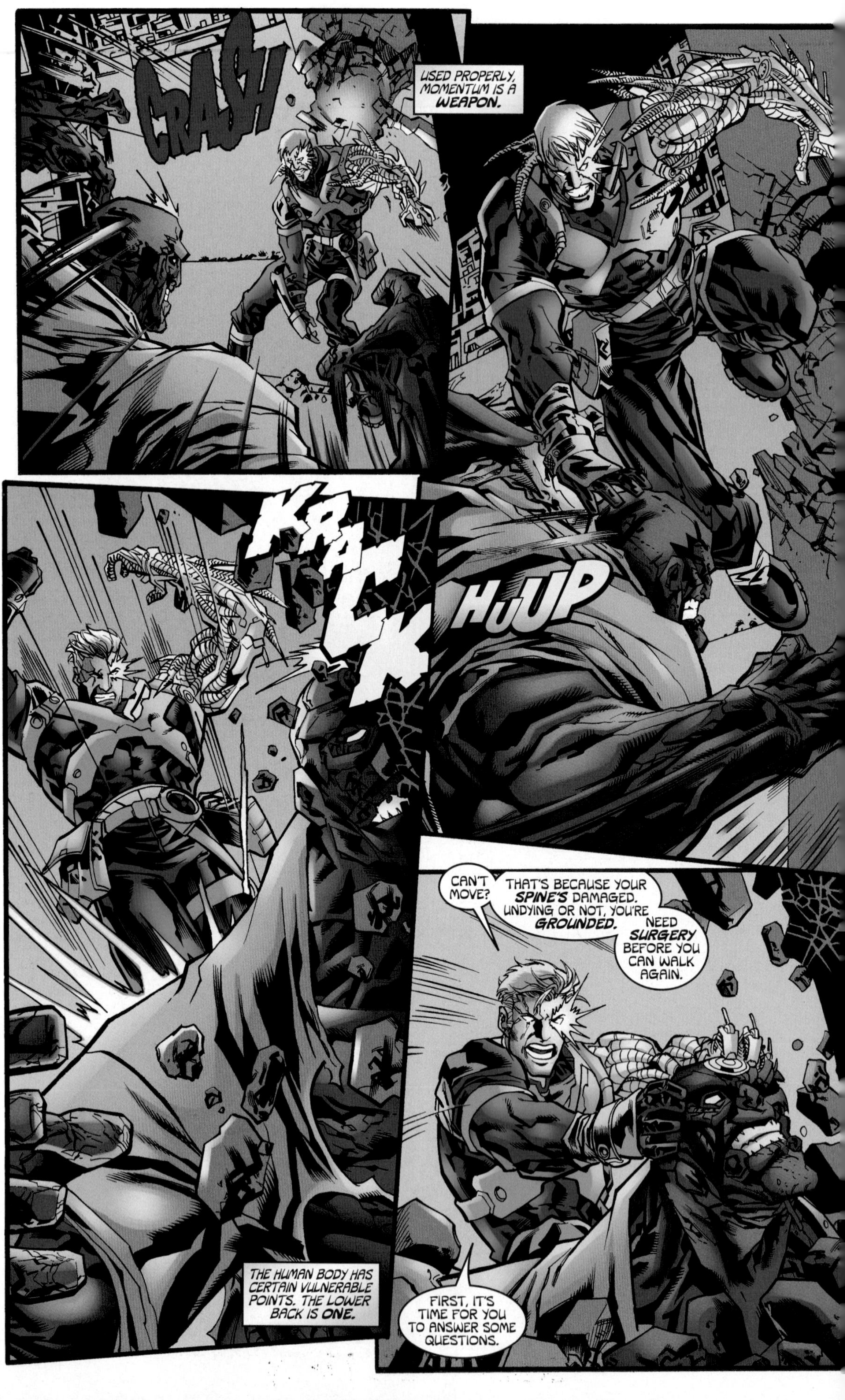
CRASH
USED PROPERLY, MOMENTUM IS A WEAPON.
KRACK
HUUP
THE HUMAN BODY HAS CERTAIN VULNERABLE POINTS. THE LOWER BACK IS ONE.
CAN'T MOVE?
THAT'S BECAUSE YOUR SPINE'S DAMAGED. UNDYING OR NOT, YOU'RE GROUNDED.
NEED SURGERY BEFORE YOU CAN WALK AGAIN.
FIRST, IT'S TIME FOR YOU TO ANSWER SOME QUESTIONS.

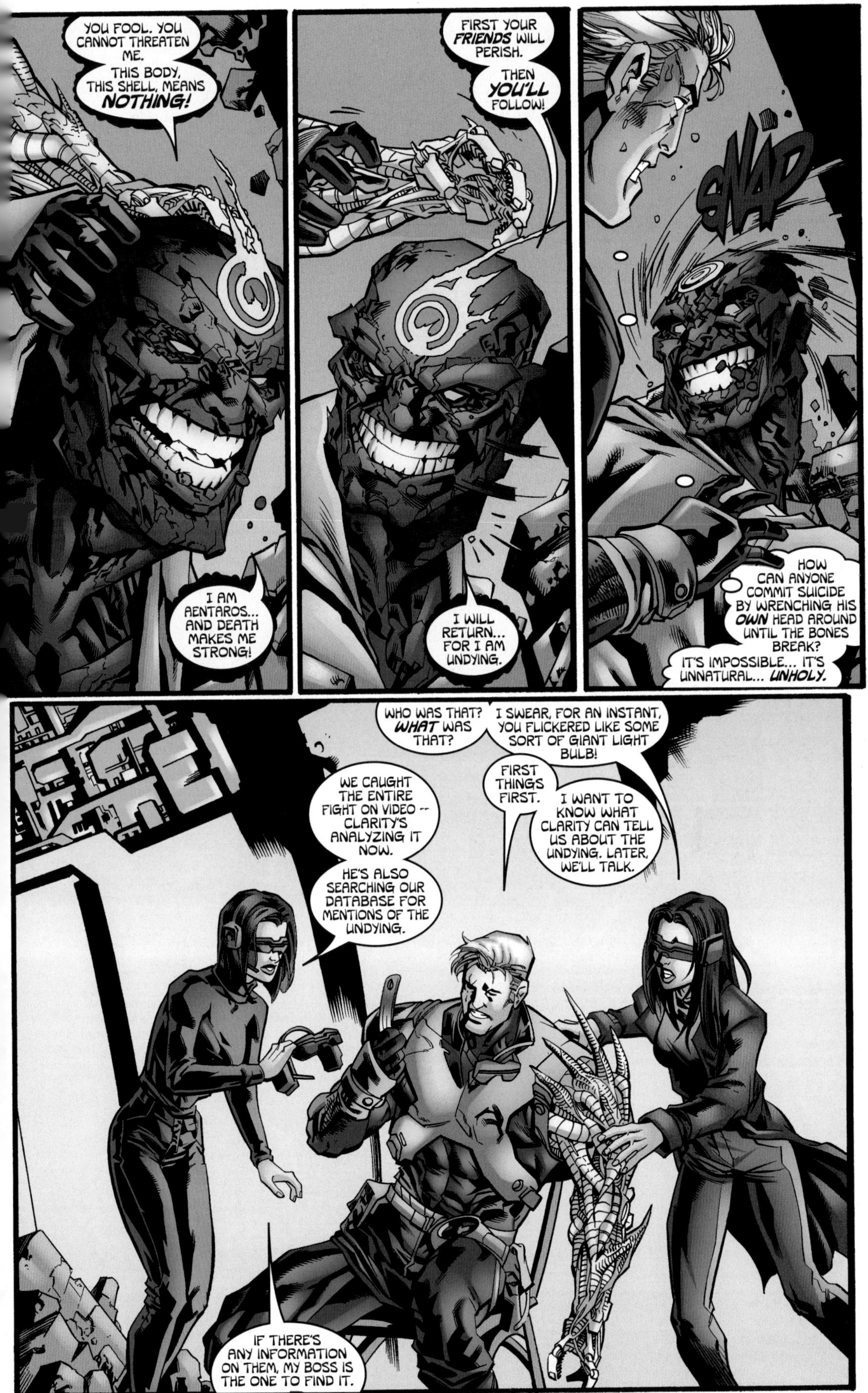
YOU FOOL. YOU CANNOT THREATEN ME.
THIS BODY, THIS SHELL, MEANS NOTHING!
I AM AENTAROS... AND DEATH MAKES ME STRONG!
FIRST YOUR FRIENDS WILL PERISH.
THEN YOU'LL FOLLOW!
I WILL RETURN... FOR I AM UNDYING.
SNAP
HOW CAN ANYONE COMMIT SUICIDE BY WRENCHING HIS OWN HEAD AROUND UNTIL THE BONES BREAK?
IT'S IMPOSSIBLE... IT'S UNNATURAL... UNHOLY.
WHO WAS THAT? WHAT WAS THAT?
I SWEAR, FOR AN INSTANT, YOU FLICKERED LIKE SOME SORT OF GIANT LIGHT BULB!
WE CAUGHT THE ENTIRE FIGHT ON VIDEO -- CLARITY'S ANALYZING IT NOW.
HE'S ALSO SEARCHING OUR DATABASE FOR MENTIONS OF THE UNDYING.
FIRST THINGS FIRST.
I WANT TO KNOW WHAT CLARITY CAN TELL US ABOUT THE UNDYING. LATER, WE'LL TALK.
IF THERE'S ANY INFORMATION ON THEM, MY BOSS IS THE ONE TO FIND IT.

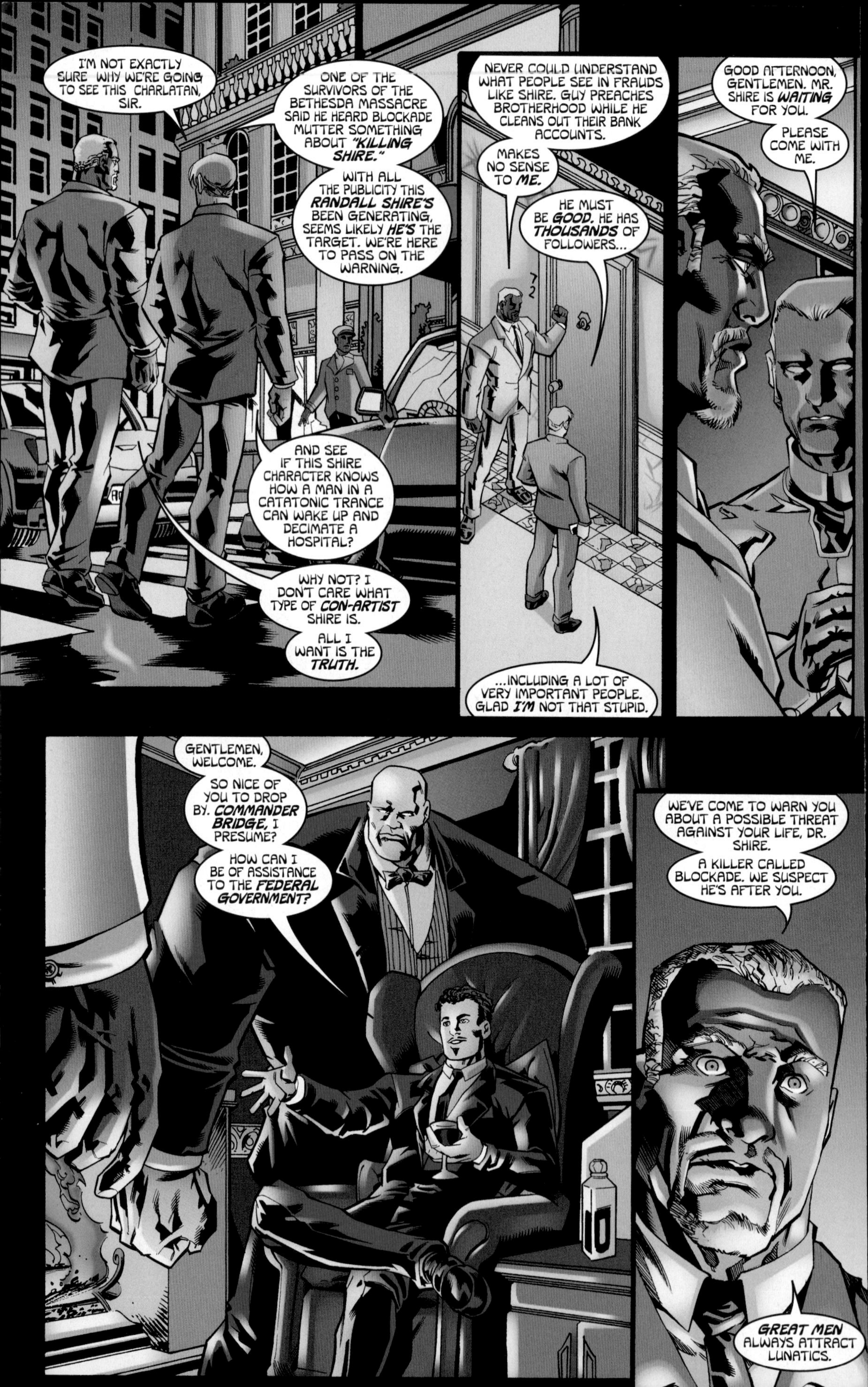
I'M NOT EXACTLY SURE WHY WE'RE GOING TO SEE THIS CHARLATAN, SIR.
ONE OF THE SURVIVORS OF THE BETHESDA MASSACRE SAID HE HEARD BLOCKADE MUTTER SOMETHING ABOUT "KILLING SHIRE."
WITH ALL THE PUBLICITY THIS RANDALL SHIRE'S BEEN GENERATING, SEEMS LIKELY HE'S THE TARGET. WE'RE HERE TO PASS ON THE WARNING.
AND SEE IF THIS SHIRE CHARACTER KNOWS HOW A MAN IN A CATATONIC TRANCE CAN WAKE UP AND DECIMATE A HOSPITAL?
WHY NOT? I DON'T CARE WHAT TYPE OF CON-ARTIST SHIRE IS.
ALL I WANT IS THE TRUTH.
NEVER COULD UNDERSTAND WHAT PEOPLE SEE IN FRAUDS LIKE SHIRE. GUY PREACHES BROTHERHOOD WHILE HE CLEANS OUT THEIR BANK ACCOUNTS.
MAKES NO SENSE TO ME.
HE MUST BE GOOD. HE HAS THOUSANDS OF FOLLOWERS...
...INCLUDING A LOT OF VERY IMPORTANT PEOPLE. GLAD I'M NOT THAT STUPID.
GOOD AFTERNOON, GENTLEMEN. MR. SHIRE IS WAITING FOR YOU.
PLEASE COME WITH ME.
GENTLEMEN, WELCOME.
SO NICE OF YOU TO DROP BY. COMMANDER BRIDGE, I PRESUME?
HOW CAN I BE OF ASSISTANCE TO THE FEDERAL GOVERNMENT?
WE'VE COME TO WARN YOU ABOUT A POSSIBLE THREAT AGAINST YOUR LIFE, DR. SHIRE.
A KILLER CALLED BLOCKADE. WE SUSPECT HE'S AFTER YOU.
GREAT MEN ALWAYS ATTRACT LUNATICS.

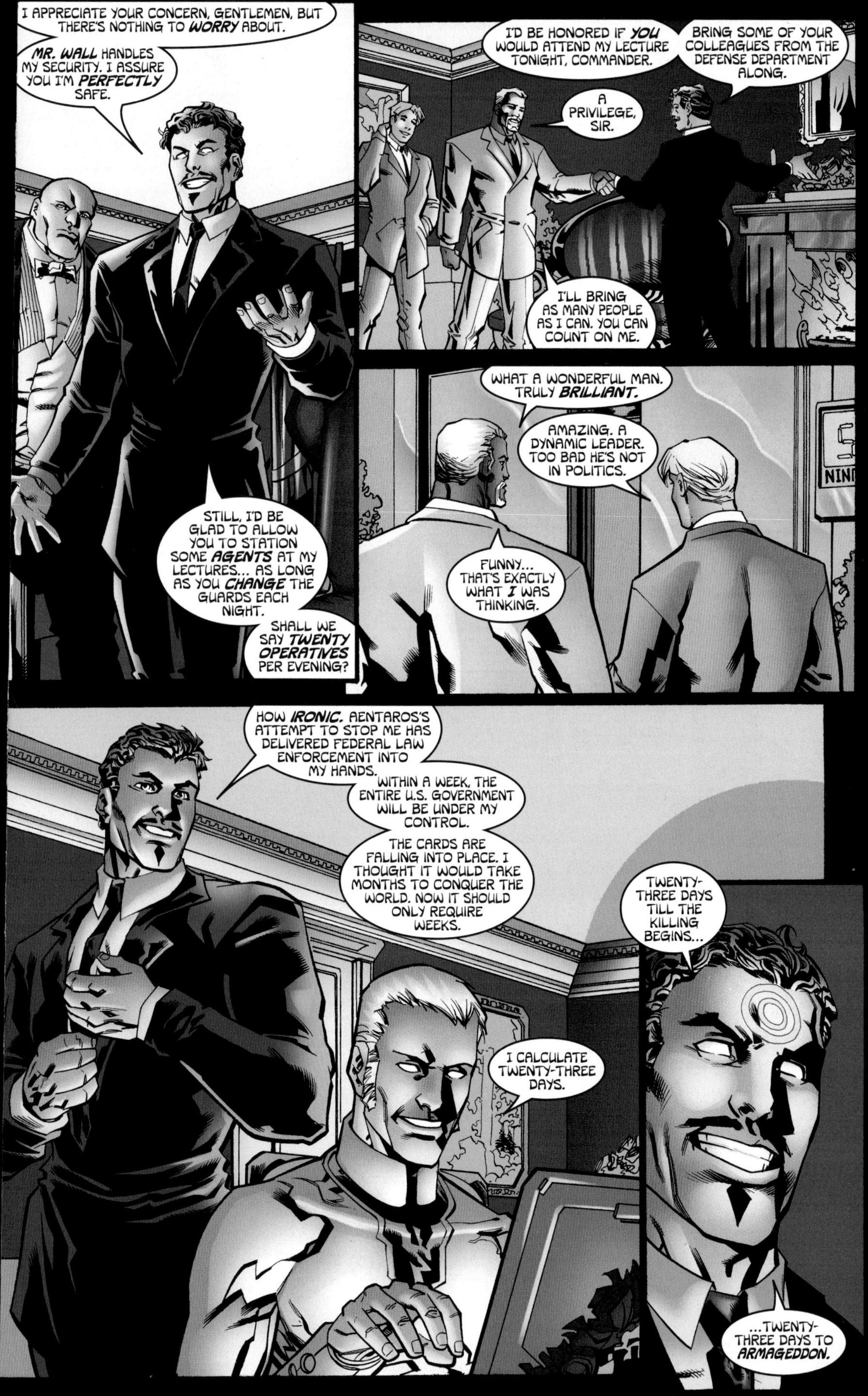
I APPRECIATE YOUR CONCERN, GENTLEMEN, BUT THERE'S NOTHING TO WORRY ABOUT.
MR. WALL HANDLES MY SECURITY. I ASSURE YOU I'M PERFECTLY SAFE.
STILL, I'D BE GLAD TO ALLOW YOU TO STATION SOME AGENTS AT MY LECTURES... AS LONG AS YOU CHANGE THE GUARDS EACH NIGHT.
SHALL WE SAY TWENTY OPERATIVES PER EVENING?
I'D BE HONORED IF YOU WOULD ATTEND MY LECTURE TONIGHT, COMMANDER.
BRING SOME OF YOUR COLLEAGUES FROM THE DEFENSE DEPARTMENT ALONG.
A PRIVILEGE, SIR.
I'LL BRING AS MANY PEOPLE AS I CAN. YOU CAN COUNT ON ME.
WHAT A WONDERFUL MAN. TRULY BRILLIANT.
AMAZING. A DYNAMIC LEADER. TOO BAD HE'S NOT IN POLITICS.
FUNNY... THAT'S EXACTLY WHAT I WAS THINKING.
HOW IRONIC. AENTAROS'S ATTEMPT TO STOP ME HAS DELIVERED FEDERAL LAW ENFORCEMENT INTO MY HANDS.
WITHIN A WEEK, THE ENTIRE U.S. GOVERNMENT WILL BE UNDER MY CONTROL.
THE CARDS ARE FALLING INTO PLACE. I THOUGHT IT WOULD TAKE MONTHS TO CONQUER THE WORLD. NOW IT SHOULD ONLY REQUIRE WEEKS.
I CALCULATE TWENTY-THREE DAYS.
TWENTY-THREE DAYS TILL THE KILLING BEGINS...
...TWENTY-THREE DAYS TO ARMAGEDDON.

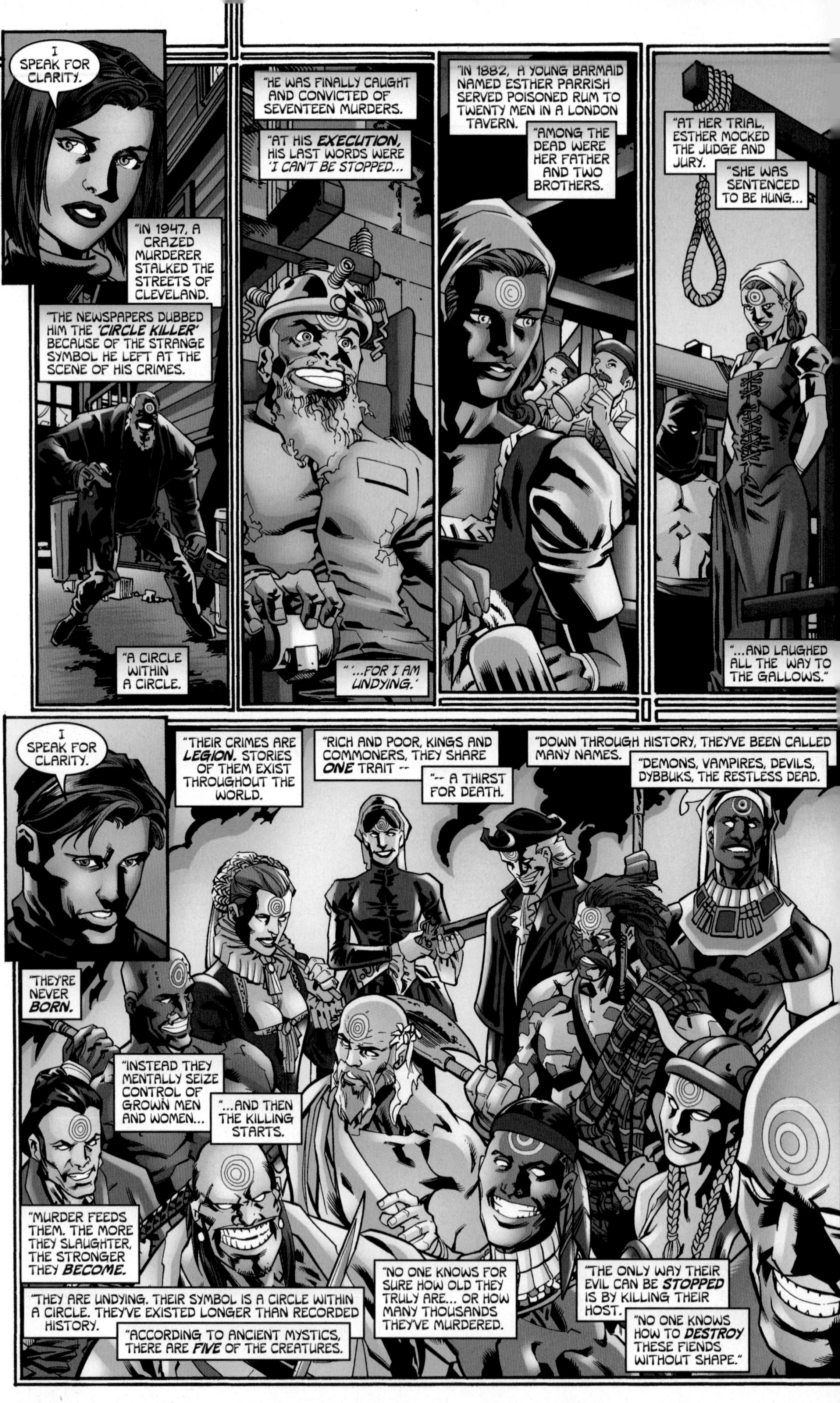

I SPEAK FOR CLARITY.
"IN 1947, A CRAZED MURDERER STALKED THE STREETS OF CLEVELAND.
"THE NEWSPAPERS DUBBED HIM THE 'CIRCLE KILLER' BECAUSE OF THE STRANGE SYMBOL HE LEFT AT THE SCENE OF HIS CRIMES.
"A CIRCLE WITHIN A CIRCLE.
"HE WAS FINALLY CAUGHT AND CONVICTED OF SEVENTEEN MURDERS.
"AT HIS EXECUTION, HIS LAST WORDS WERE 'I CAN'T BE STOPPED...
"'...FOR I AM UNDYING.'
"IN 1882, A YOUNG BARMAID NAMED ESTHER PARRISH SERVED POISONED RUM TO TWENTY MEN IN A LONDON TAVERN.
"AMONG THE DEAD WERE HER FATHER AND TWO BROTHERS.
"AT HER TRIAL, ESTHER MOCKED THE JUDGE AND JURY.
"SHE WAS SENTENCED TO BE HUNG...
"...AND LAUGHED ALL THE WAY TO THE GALLOWS."
I SPEAK FOR CLARITY.
"THEIR CRIMES ARE LEGION. STORIES OF THEM EXIST THROUGHOUT THE WORLD.
"RICH AND POOR, KINGS AND COMMONERS, THEY SHARE ONE TRAIT --
"-- A THIRST FOR DEATH.
"DOWN THROUGH HISTORY, THEY'VE BEEN CALLED MANY NAMES.
"DEMONS, VAMPIRES, DEVILS, DYBBUKS, THE RESTLESS DEAD.
"THEY'RE NEVER BORN.
"INSTEAD THEY MENTALLY SEIZE CONTROL OF GROWN MEN AND WOMEN...
"...AND THEN THE KILLING STARTS.
"MURDER FEEDS THEM. THE MORE THEY SLAUGHTER, THE STRONGER THEY BECOME.
"THEY ARE UNDYING. THEIR SYMBOL IS A CIRCLE WITHIN A CIRCLE. THEY'VE EXISTED LONGER THAN RECORDED HISTORY.
"ACCORDING TO ANCIENT MYSTICS, THERE ARE FIVE OF THE CREATURES.
"NO ONE KNOWS FOR SURE HOW OLD THEY TRULY ARE... OR HOW MANY THOUSANDS THEY'VE MURDERED.
"THE ONLY WAY THEIR EVIL CAN BE STOPPED IS BY KILLING THEIR HOST.
"NO ONE KNOWS HOW TO DESTROY THESE FIENDS WITHOUT SHAPE."

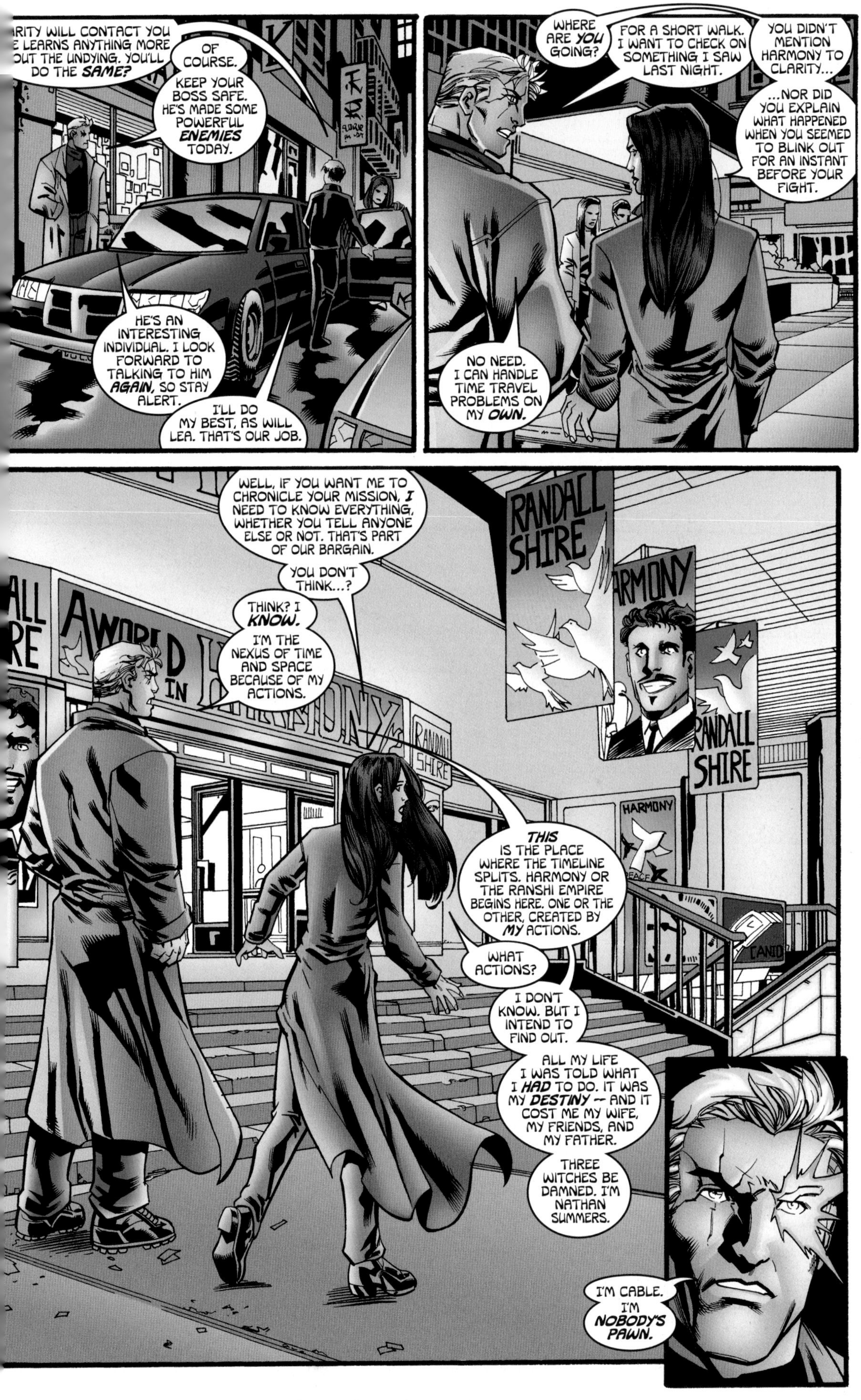

ARITY WILL CONTACT YOU
E LEARNS ANYTHING MORE
OUT THE UNDYING. YOU'LL
DO THE SAME?
OF COURSE.
KEEP YOUR BOSS SAFE. HE'S MADE SOME POWERFUL ENEMIES TODAY.
HE'S AN INTERESTING INDIVIDUAL. I LOOK FORWARD TO TALKING TO HIM AGAIN, SO STAY ALERT.
I'LL DO MY BEST, AS WILL LEA. THAT'S OUR JOB.
WHERE ARE YOU GOING?
FOR A SHORT WALK. I WANT TO CHECK ON SOMETHING I SAW LAST NIGHT.
YOU DIDN'T MENTION HARMONY TO CLARITY...
...NOR DID YOU EXPLAIN WHAT HAPPENED WHEN YOU SEEMED TO BLINK OUT FOR AN INSTANT BEFORE YOUR FIGHT.
NO NEED. I CAN HANDLE TIME TRAVEL PROBLEMS ON MY OWN.
WELL, IF YOU WANT ME TO CHRONICLE YOUR MISSION, I NEED TO KNOW EVERYTHING, WHETHER YOU TELL ANYONE ELSE OR NOT. THAT'S PART OF OUR BARGAIN.
YOU DON'T THINK...?
THINK? I KNOW.
I'M THE NEXUS OF TIME AND SPACE BECAUSE OF MY ACTIONS.
RANDALL SHIRE
HARMONY
A WORLD IN HARMONY
THIS IS THE PLACE WHERE THE TIMELINE SPLITS. HARMONY OR THE RANSHI EMPIRE BEGINS HERE. ONE OR THE OTHER, CREATED BY MY ACTIONS.
WHAT ACTIONS?
I DONT KNOW. BUT I INTEND TO FIND OUT.
ALL MY LIFE I WAS TOLD WHAT I HAD TO DO. IT WAS MY DESTINY -- AND IT COST ME MY WIFE, MY FRIENDS, AND MY FATHER.
THREE WITCHES BE DAMNED. I'M NATHAN SUMMERS.
I'M CABLE. I'M NOBODY'S PAWN.

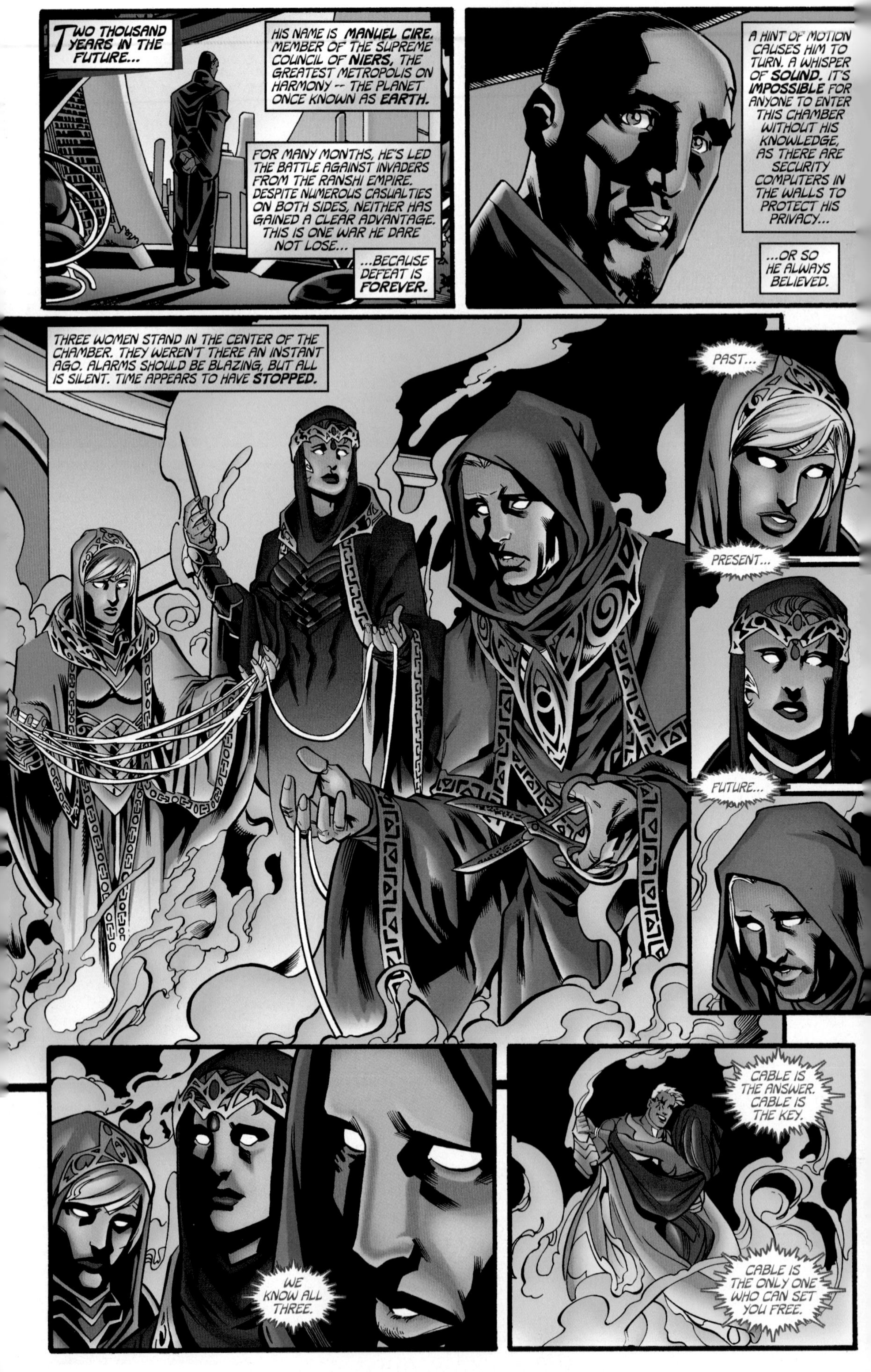
TWO THOUSAND YEARS IN THE FUTURE...
HIS NAME IS MANUEL CIRE, MEMBER OF THE SUPREME COUNCIL OF NIERS, THE GREATEST METROPOLIS ON HARMONY -- THE PLANET ONCE KNOWN AS EARTH.
FOR MANY MONTHS, HE'S LED THE BATTLE AGAINST INVADERS FROM THE RANSHI EMPIRE. DESPITE NUMEROUS CASUALTIES ON BOTH SIDES, NEITHER HAS GAINED A CLEAR ADVANTAGE. THIS IS ONE WAR HE DARE NOT LOSE...
...BECAUSE DEFEAT IS FOREVER.
A HINT OF MOTION CAUSES HIM TO TURN. A WHISPER OF SOUND. IT'S IMPOSSIBLE FOR ANYONE TO ENTER THIS CHAMBER WITHOUT HIS KNOWLEDGE, AS THERE ARE SECURITY COMPUTERS IN THE WALLS TO PROTECT HIS PRIVACY...
...OR SO HE ALWAYS BELIEVED.
THREE WOMEN STAND IN THE CENTER OF THE CHAMBER. THEY WEREN'T THERE AN INSTANT AGO. ALARMS SHOULD BE BLAZING, BUT ALL IS SILENT. TIME APPEARS TO HAVE STOPPED.
PAST...
PRESENT...
FUTURE...
WE KNOW ALL THREE.
CABLE IS THE ANSWER. CABLE IS THE KEY.
CABLE IS THE ONLY ONE WHO CAN SET YOU FREE.

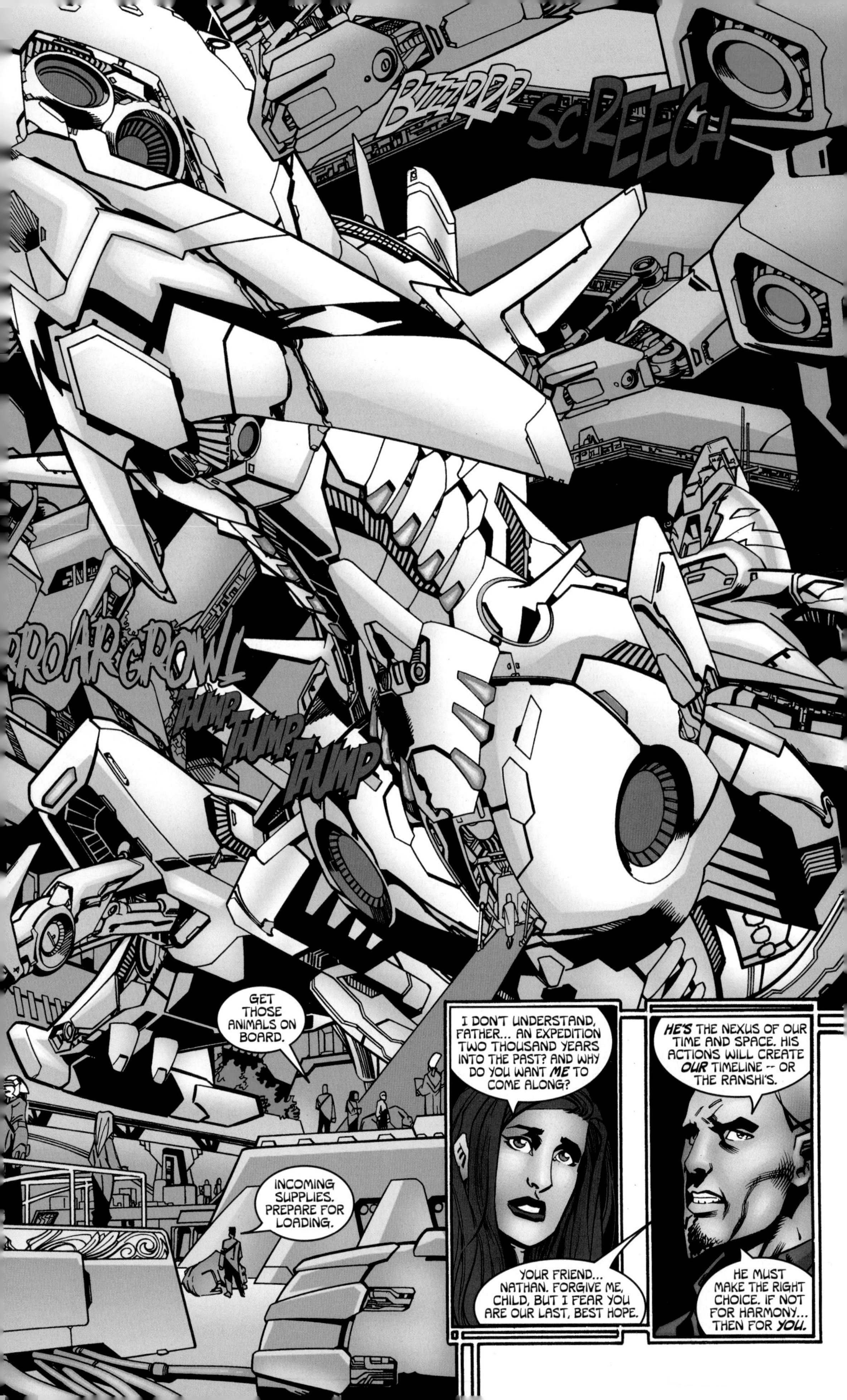
BZZZRRR
SCREECH
RROARGROWL
THUMP THUMP THUMP
GET THOSE ANIMALS ON BOARD.
INCOMING SUPPLIES. PREPARE FOR LOADING.
I DON'T UNDERSTAND, FATHER... AN EXPEDITION TWO THOUSAND YEARS INTO THE PAST? AND WHY DO YOU WANT *ME* TO COME ALONG?
YOUR FRIEND... NATHAN. FORGIVE ME, CHILD, BUT I FEAR YOU ARE OUR LAST, BEST HOPE.
HE'S THE NEXUS OF OUR TIME AND SPACE. HIS ACTIONS WILL CREATE *OUR* TIMELINE -- OR THE RANSHI'S.
HE MUST MAKE THE RIGHT CHOICE. IF NOT FOR HARMONY... THEN FOR *YOU*.

I CAN'T LET AENTAROS CONTINUE TO KILL ITS HOST EVERY TIME I DEFEAT IT.

A SECOND MAN HAS DIED, AND THE ENTITY IS OBVIOUSLY SEARCHING FOR A NEW BODY.

BLAQUESMITH, I NEED AN IMMOBILIZING TRAP --

-- A PORTABLE UNIT I CAN USE TO KEEP THE UNDYING PARALYZED FOR HOURS, NO MATTER *WHAT* ITS STRENGTH.

A DEVICE THAT CHANNELS THE CREATURE'S KINETIC ENERGY IN A LOOP, S THE HARDER IT TRIES T MOVE, THE *TIGHTER* THE BONDS HOLDING IT.

A SIMPLE TASK, BOY. WHEN ARE YOU GOING TO BRING ME A *REAL* CHALLENGE?

CLARITY WAS A HELP, BUT THERE'S MORE TO THIS SITUATION THAN JUST THE UNDYING. THE THREE WITCHES MADE THAT CLEAR.

THE UNDYING HAVE BEEN AROUND FOR THOUSANDS OF YEARS. SO EXACTLY HOW DO THEY TIE IN WITH HARMONY AND THE RANSHI?

MORE IMPORTANT, WHAT *LINKS* THE TWO TIMELINES AND THE UNDYING WITH RANDALL SHIRE?

RANDALL SHIRE BECOMES *"RANSHI"* AFTER A BUNCH OF CENTURIES.

HARMONY IS NO STRETCH. YOU WANT ME TO INVESTIGATE SHIRE?

DEFINITELY. ONE MORE THING... BE *CAREFUL.*

IT'S HARD FOR HIM TO ADMIT, BUT HE CONSIDERS IRENE *FAMILY.* AND AFTER ALL THE LOVED ONES HE'S SEEN DIE, HE WORRIES ABOUT *LOSING* HER.

HOW SWEET. YOU'RE WORRIED ABOUT ME.

I USED TO BE AN INVESTIGATIVE REPORTER, REMEMBER? I CAN TAKE CARE OF *MYSELF.*

IT'S THE FIRST TIME HE'S EVER SHOWN CONCERN FOR HER SAFETY.

IT'S NICE TO REALIZE HE CONSIDERS HER IMPORTANT.

MEANWHILE I'LL CONTACT MY OLD BUDDY, G.W. BRIDGE. TELL HIM WHERE HE CAN FIND BLOCKADE'S BODY. MAKE SOME ARRANGEMENTS FOR A DECENT BURIAL.

BLOCKADE WAS A HIRED GUN, BUT HE STILL DESERVED BETTER THAN WHAT HE GOT.

WHAT HAPPENED TO HIM IS PARTLY *MY* FAULT. BESIDES, I NEED TO MAKE PEACE WITH G.W....

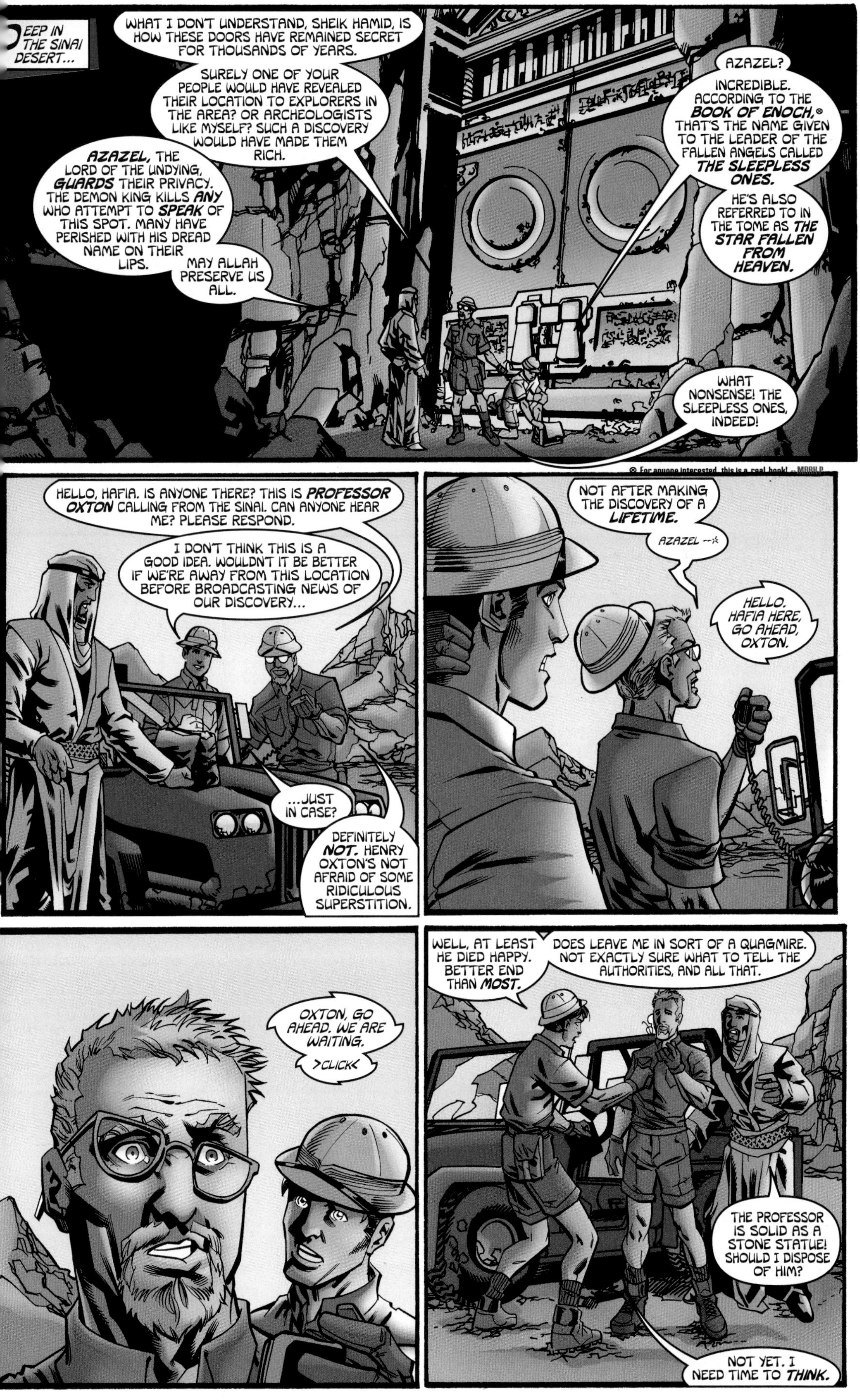
DEEP IN THE SINAI DESERT...
WHAT I DON'T UNDERSTAND, SHEIK HAMID, IS HOW THESE DOORS HAVE REMAINED SECRET FOR THOUSANDS OF YEARS.
SURELY ONE OF YOUR PEOPLE WOULD HAVE REVEALED THEIR LOCATION TO EXPLORERS IN THE AREA? OR ARCHEOLOGISTS LIKE MYSELF? SUCH A DISCOVERY WOULD HAVE MADE THEM RICH.
AZAZEL, THE LORD OF THE UNDYING, GUARDS THEIR PRIVACY. THE DEMON KING KILLS ANY WHO ATTEMPT TO SPEAK OF THIS SPOT. MANY HAVE PERISHED WITH HIS DREAD NAME ON THEIR LIPS.
MAY ALLAH PRESERVE US ALL.
AZAZEL?
INCREDIBLE. ACCORDING TO THE BOOK OF ENOCH,⊗ THAT'S THE NAME GIVEN TO THE LEADER OF THE FALLEN ANGELS CALLED THE SLEEPLESS ONES.
HE'S ALSO REFERRED TO IN THE TOME AS THE STAR FALLEN FROM HEAVEN.
WHAT NONSENSE! THE SLEEPLESS ONES, INDEED!
⊗ For anyone interested, this is a real book! -- MARK P.
HELLO, HAFIA. IS ANYONE THERE? THIS IS PROFESSOR OXTON CALLING FROM THE SINAI. CAN ANYONE HEAR ME? PLEASE RESPOND.
I DON'T THINK THIS IS A GOOD IDEA. WOULDN'T IT BE BETTER IF WE'RE AWAY FROM THIS LOCATION BEFORE BROADCASTING NEWS OF OUR DISCOVERY...
...JUST IN CASE?
DEFINITELY NOT. HENRY OXTON'S NOT AFRAID OF SOME RIDICULOUS SUPERSTITION.
NOT AFTER MAKING THE DISCOVERY OF A LIFETIME.
AZAZEL --*
HELLO. HAFIA HERE, GO AHEAD, OXTON.
OXTON, GO AHEAD. WE ARE WAITING.
>CLICK<
WELL, AT LEAST HE DIED HAPPY. BETTER END THAN MOST.
DOES LEAVE ME IN SORT OF A QUAGMIRE. NOT EXACTLY SURE WHAT TO TELL THE AUTHORITIES, AND ALL THAT.
THE PROFESSOR IS SOLID AS A STONE STATUE! SHOULD I DISPOSE OF HIM?
NOT YET. I NEED TIME TO THINK.

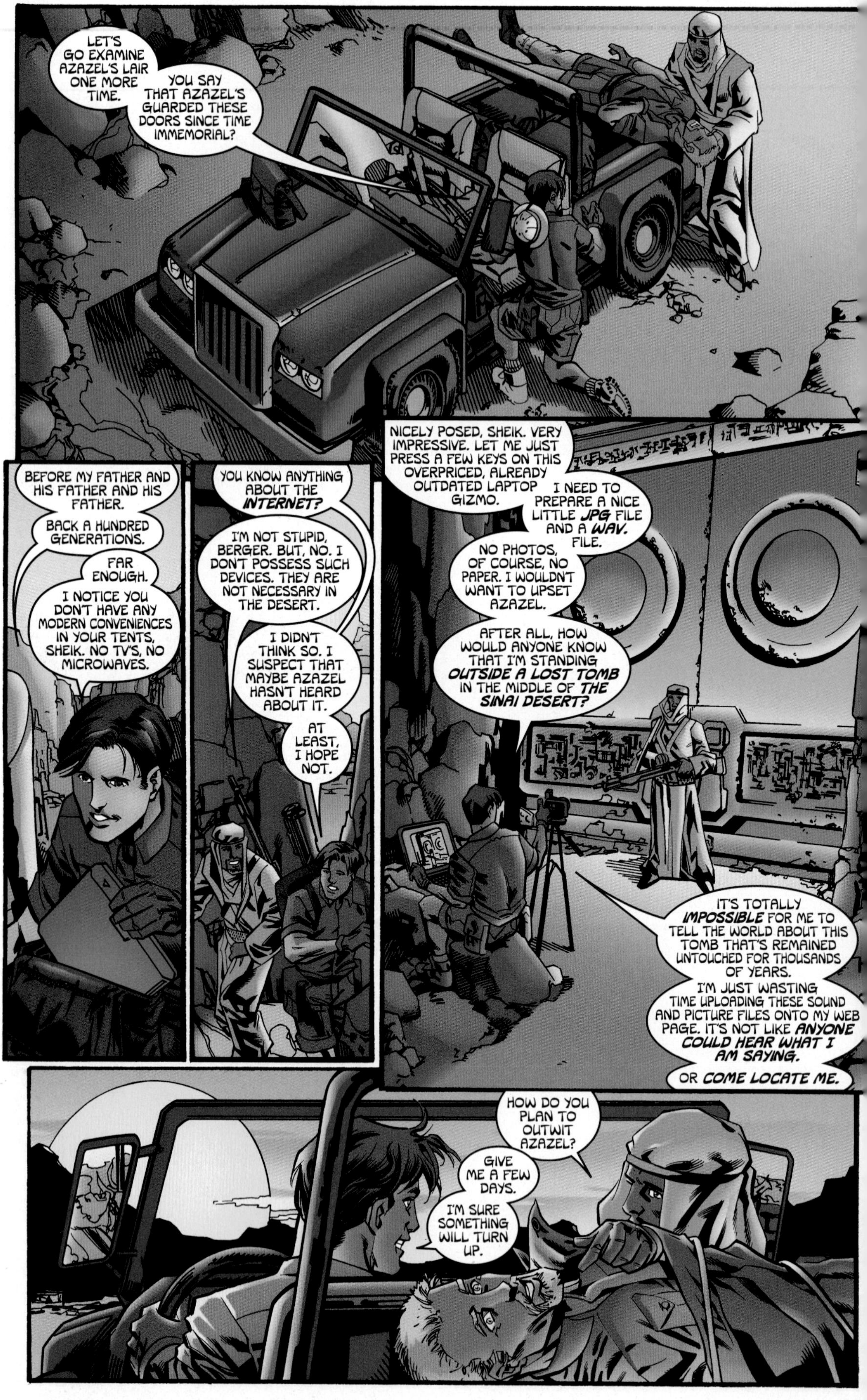
LET'S GO EXAMINE AZAZEL'S LAIR ONE MORE TIME.
YOU SAY THAT AZAZEL'S GUARDED THESE DOORS SINCE TIME IMMEMORIAL?
BEFORE MY FATHER AND HIS FATHER AND HIS FATHER.
BACK A HUNDRED GENERATIONS.
FAR ENOUGH.
I NOTICE YOU DON'T HAVE ANY MODERN CONVENIENCES IN YOUR TENTS, SHEIK. NO TV'S, NO MICROWAVES.
YOU KNOW ANYTHING ABOUT THE INTERNET?
I'M NOT STUPID, BERGER. BUT, NO. I DON'T POSSESS SUCH DEVICES. THEY ARE NOT NECESSARY IN THE DESERT.
I DIDN'T THINK SO. I SUSPECT THAT MAYBE AZAZEL HASN'T HEARD ABOUT IT.
AT LEAST, I HOPE NOT.
NICELY POSED, SHEIK. VERY IMPRESSIVE. LET ME JUST PRESS A FEW KEYS ON THIS OVERPRICED, ALREADY OUTDATED LAPTOP GIZMO.
I NEED TO PREPARE A NICE LITTLE JPG FILE AND A WAV. FILE.
NO PHOTOS, OF COURSE, NO PAPER. I WOULDN'T WANT TO UPSET AZAZEL.
AFTER ALL, HOW WOULD ANYONE KNOW THAT I'M STANDING OUTSIDE A LOST TOMB IN THE MIDDLE OF THE SINAI DESERT?
IT'S TOTALLY IMPOSSIBLE FOR ME TO TELL THE WORLD ABOUT THIS TOMB THAT'S REMAINED UNTOUCHED FOR THOUSANDS OF YEARS.
I'M JUST WASTING TIME UPLOADING THESE SOUND AND PICTURE FILES ONTO MY WEB PAGE. IT'S NOT LIKE ANYONE COULD HEAR WHAT I AM SAYING.
OR COME LOCATE ME.
HOW DO YOU PLAN TO OUTWIT AZAZEL?
GIVE ME A FEW DAYS.
I'M SURE SOMETHING WILL TURN UP.

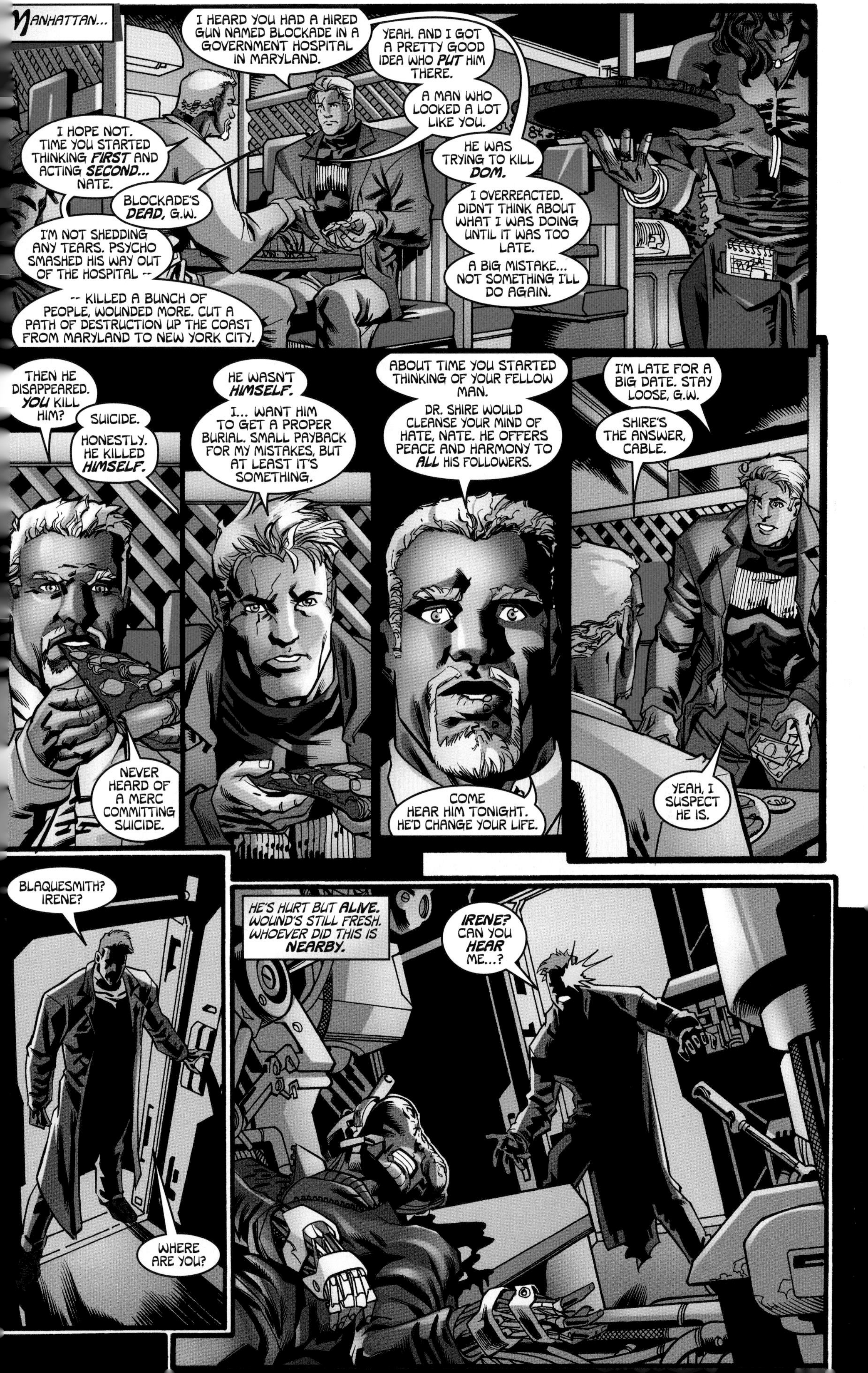
MANHATTAN...
I HEARD YOU HAD A HIRED GUN NAMED BLOCKADE IN A GOVERNMENT HOSPITAL IN MARYLAND.
YEAH. AND I GOT A PRETTY GOOD IDEA WHO PUT HIM THERE.
A MAN WHO LOOKED A LOT LIKE YOU.
HE WAS TRYING TO KILL DOM.
I HOPE NOT. TIME YOU STARTED THINKING FIRST AND ACTING SECOND... NATE.
BLOCKADE'S DEAD, G.W.
I OVERREACTED. DIDN'T THINK ABOUT WHAT I WAS DOING UNTIL IT WAS TOO LATE.
A BIG MISTAKE... NOT SOMETHING I'LL DO AGAIN.
I'M NOT SHEDDING ANY TEARS. PSYCHO SMASHED HIS WAY OUT OF THE HOSPITAL --
-- KILLED A BUNCH OF PEOPLE, WOUNDED MORE. CUT A PATH OF DESTRUCTION UP THE COAST FROM MARYLAND TO NEW YORK CITY.
THEN HE DISAPPEARED. YOU KILL HIM?
SUICIDE.
HONESTLY. HE KILLED HIMSELF.
NEVER HEARD OF A MERC COMMITTING SUICIDE.
HE WASN'T HIMSELF.
I... WANT HIM TO GET A PROPER BURIAL. SMALL PAYBACK FOR MY MISTAKES, BUT AT LEAST IT'S SOMETHING.
ABOUT TIME YOU STARTED THINKING OF YOUR FELLOW MAN.
DR. SHIRE WOULD CLEANSE YOUR MIND OF HATE, NATE. HE OFFERS PEACE AND HARMONY TO ALL HIS FOLLOWERS.
COME HEAR HIM TONIGHT. HE'D CHANGE YOUR LIFE.
I'M LATE FOR A BIG DATE. STAY LOOSE, G.W.
SHIRE'S THE ANSWER, CABLE.
YEAH, I SUSPECT HE IS.
BLAQUESMITH? IRENE?
WHERE ARE YOU?
HE'S HURT BUT ALIVE. WOUND'S STILL FRESH. WHOEVER DID THIS IS NEARBY.
IRENE? CAN YOU HEAR ME...?

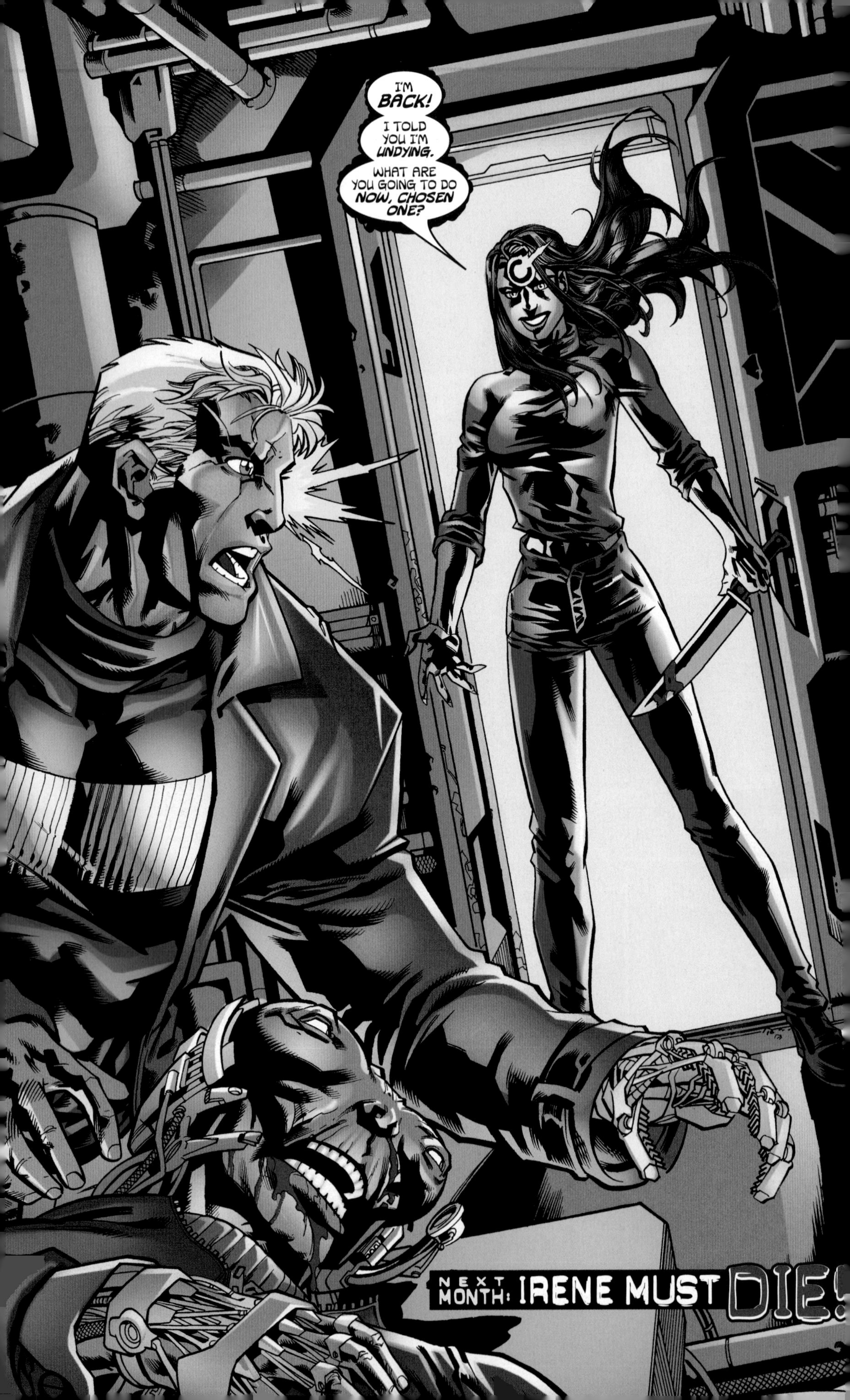
I'M BACK!
I TOLD YOU I'M UNDYING.
WHAT ARE YOU GOING TO DO NOW, CHOSEN ONE?
NEXT MONTH: IRENE MUST DIE!

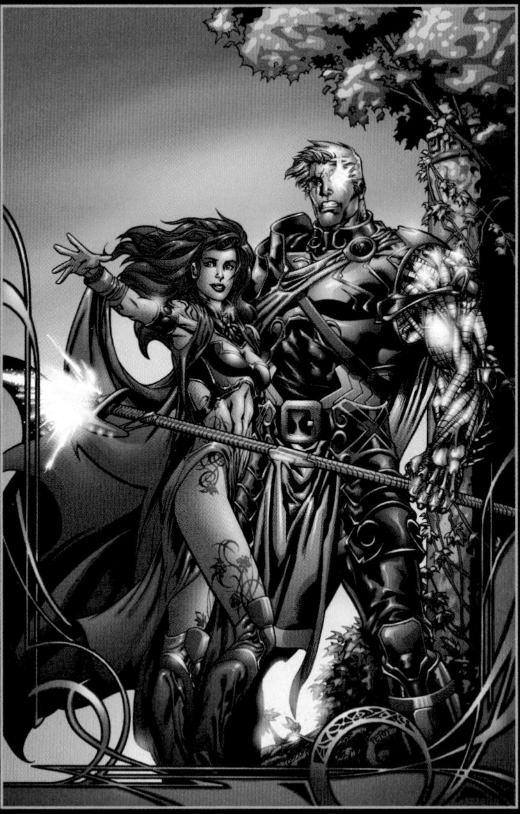
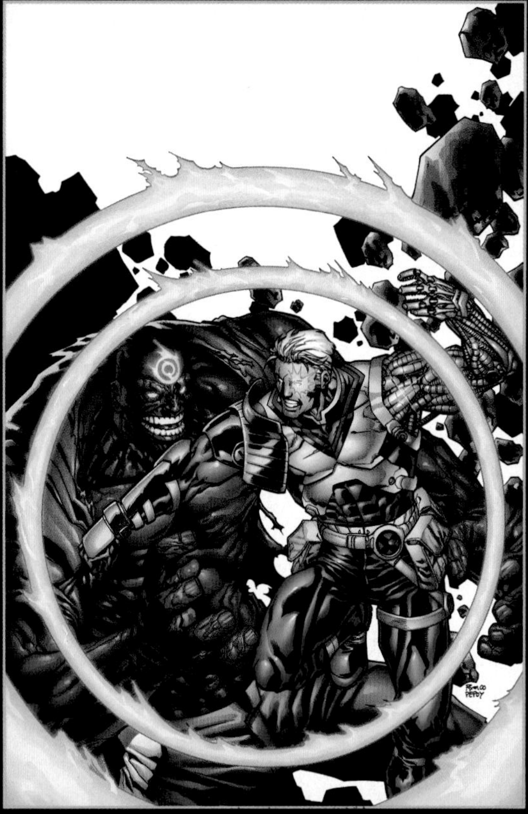
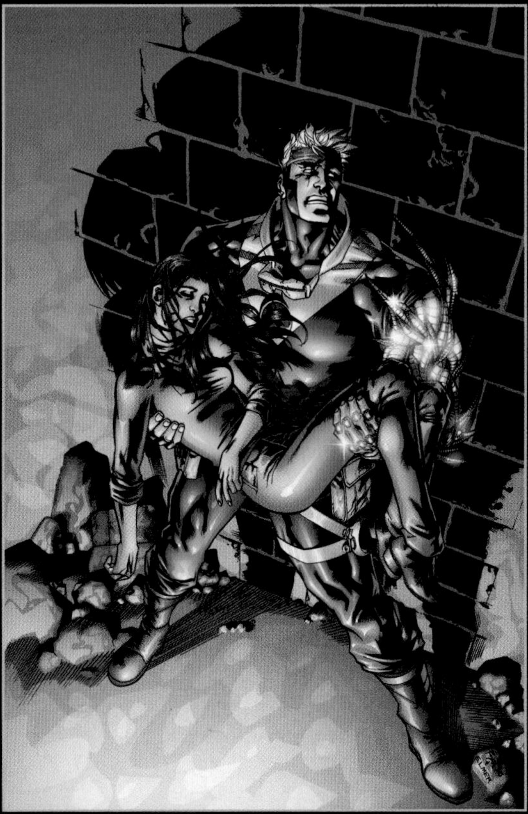

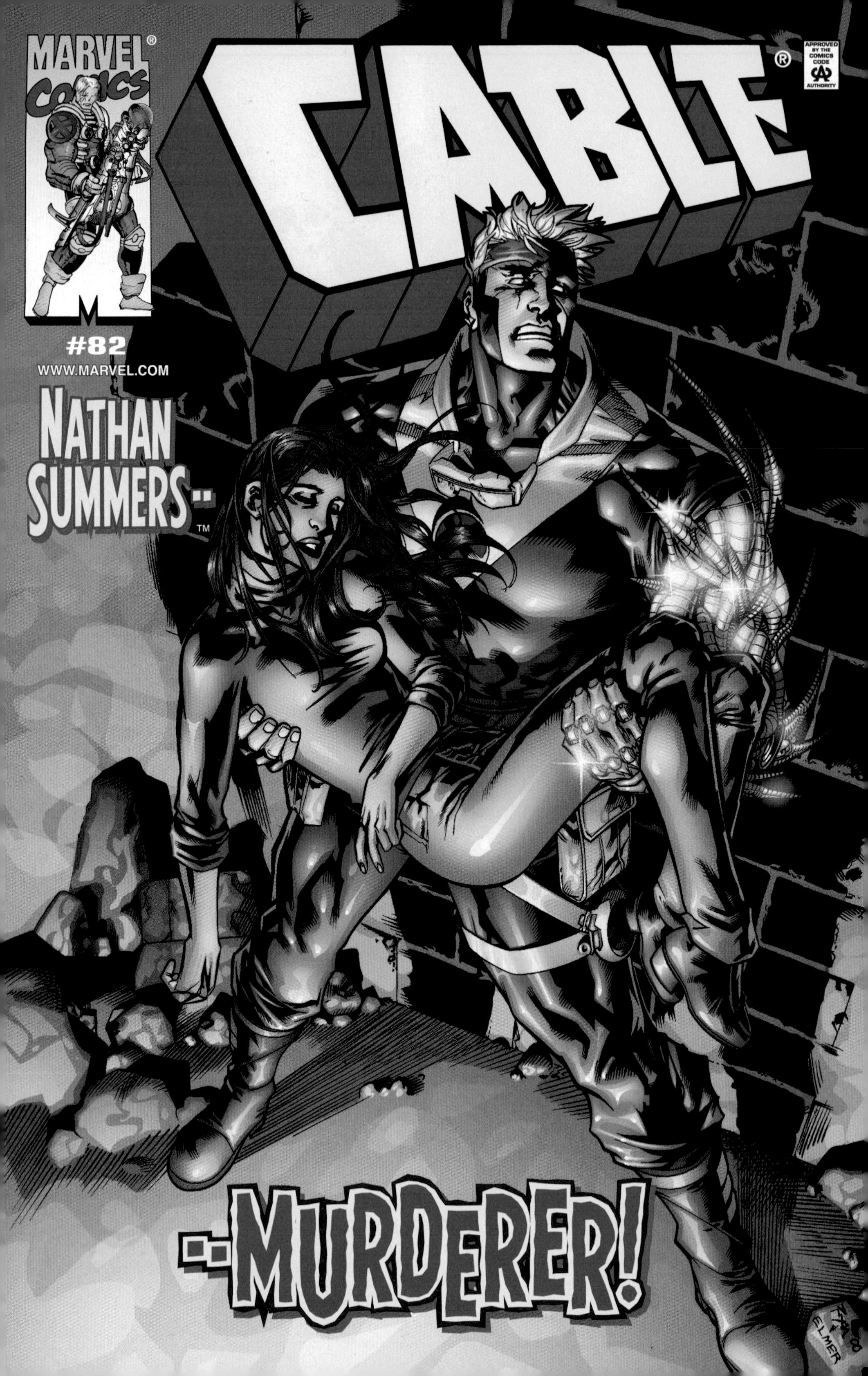
MARVEL® COMICS
CABLE®
APPROVED BY THE COMICS CODE AUTHORITY
#82
WWW.MARVEL.COM
NATHAN SUMMERS--™
--MURDERER!

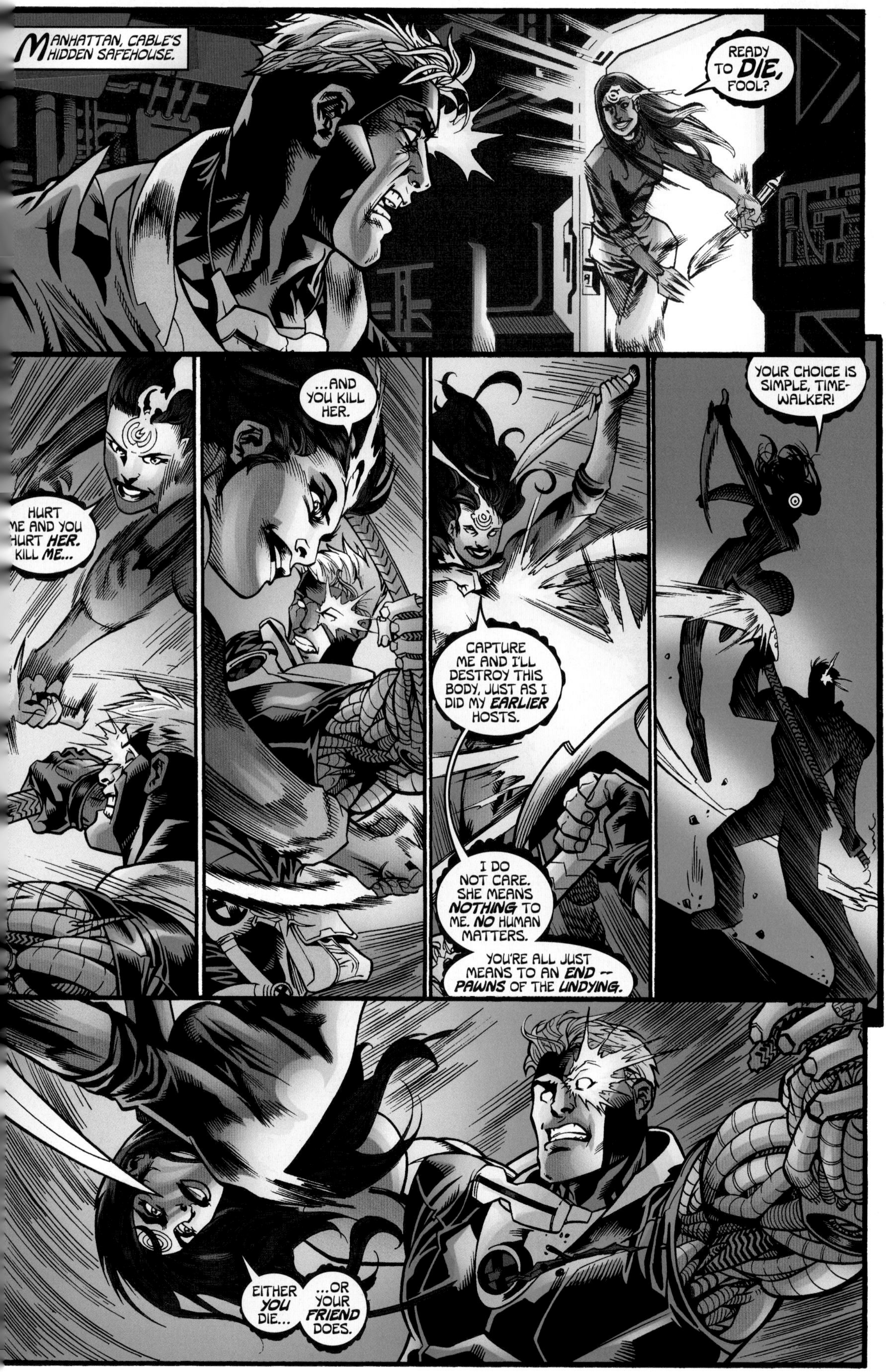
MANHATTAN, CABLE'S HIDDEN SAFEHOUSE.
READY TO DIE, FOOL?
HURT ME AND YOU HURT HER. KILL ME...
...AND YOU KILL HER.
CAPTURE ME AND I'LL DESTROY THIS BODY, JUST AS I DID MY EARLIER HOSTS.
I DO NOT CARE. SHE MEANS NOTHING TO ME. NO HUMAN MATTERS.
YOU'RE ALL JUST MEANS TO AN END -- PAWNS OF THE UNDYING.
YOUR CHOICE IS SIMPLE, TIME-WALKER!
EITHER YOU DIE...
...OR YOUR FRIEND DOES.

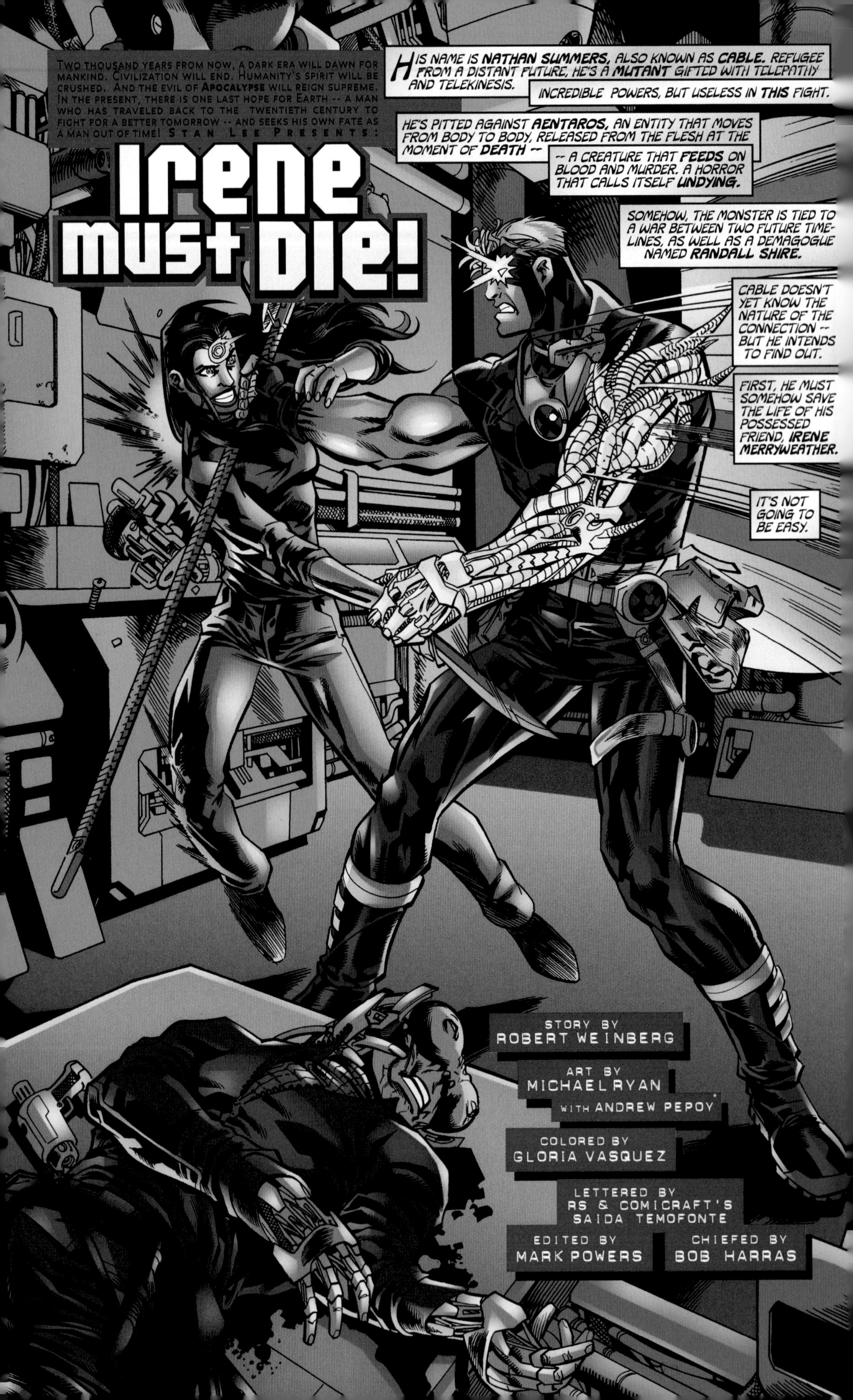
TWO THOUSAND YEARS FROM NOW, A DARK ERA WILL DAWN FOR MANKIND. CIVILIZATION WILL END. HUMANITY'S SPIRIT WILL BE CRUSHED. AND THE EVIL OF APOCALYPSE WILL REIGN SUPREME. IN THE PRESENT, THERE IS ONE LAST HOPE FOR EARTH -- A MAN WHO HAS TRAVELED BACK TO THE TWENTIETH CENTURY TO FIGHT FOR A BETTER TOMORROW -- AND SEEKS HIS OWN FATE AS A MAN OUT OF TIME! STAN LEE PRESENTS:
IRENE MUST DIE!
HIS NAME IS NATHAN SUMMERS, ALSO KNOWN AS CABLE. REFUGEE FROM A DISTANT FUTURE, HE'S A MUTANT GIFTED WITH TELEPATHY AND TELEKINESIS.
INCREDIBLE POWERS, BUT USELESS IN THIS FIGHT.
HE'S PITTED AGAINST AENTAROS, AN ENTITY THAT MOVES FROM BODY TO BODY, RELEASED FROM THE FLESH AT THE MOMENT OF DEATH --
-- A CREATURE THAT FEEDS ON BLOOD AND MURDER. A HORROR THAT CALLS ITSELF UNDYING.
SOMEHOW, THE MONSTER IS TIED TO A WAR BETWEEN TWO FUTURE TIME-LINES, AS WELL AS A DEMAGOGUE NAMED RANDALL SHIRE.
CABLE DOESN'T YET KNOW THE NATURE OF THE CONNECTION -- BUT HE INTENDS TO FIND OUT.
FIRST, HE MUST SOMEHOW SAVE THE LIFE OF HIS POSSESSED FRIEND, IRENE MERRYWEATHER.
IT'S NOT GOING TO BE EASY.
STORY BY ROBERT WEINBERG
ART BY MICHAEL RYAN WITH ANDREW PEPOY
COLORED BY GLORIA VASQUEZ
LETTERED BY RS & COMICRAFT'S SAIDA TEMOFONTE
EDITED BY MARK POWERS
CHIEFED BY BOB HARRAS

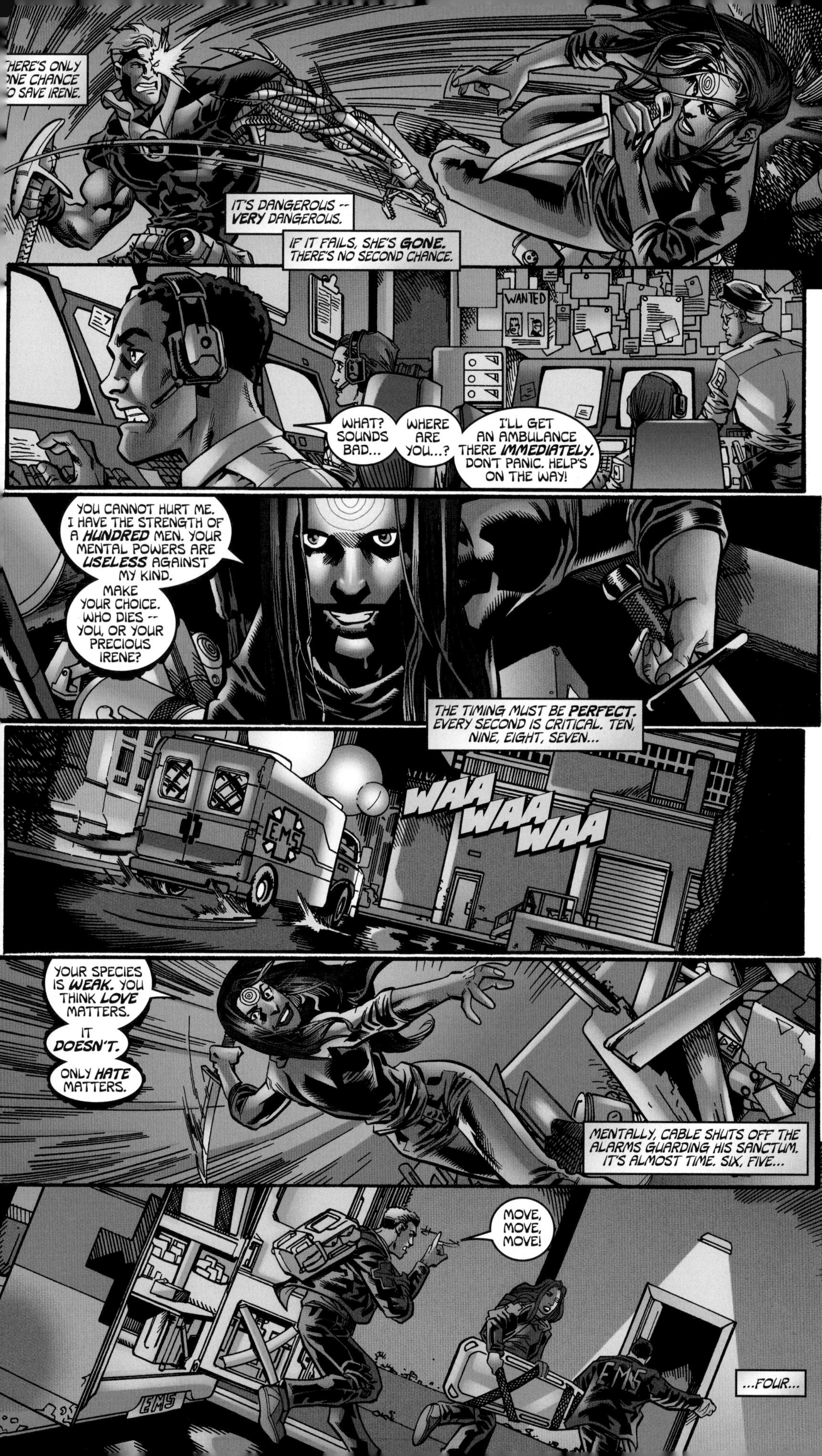
THERE'S ONLY ONE CHANCE TO SAVE IRENE.
IT'S DANGEROUS -- VERY DANGEROUS.
IF IT FAILS, SHE'S GONE. THERE'S NO SECOND CHANCE.
WANTED
WHAT? SOUNDS BAD...
WHERE ARE YOU...?
I'LL GET AN AMBULANCE THERE IMMEDIATELY. DON'T PANIC. HELP'S ON THE WAY!
YOU CANNOT HURT ME. I HAVE THE STRENGTH OF A HUNDRED MEN. YOUR MENTAL POWERS ARE USELESS AGAINST MY KIND.
MAKE YOUR CHOICE. WHO DIES -- YOU, OR YOUR PRECIOUS IRENE?
THE TIMING MUST BE PERFECT. EVERY SECOND IS CRITICAL. TEN, NINE, EIGHT, SEVEN...
WAA WAA WAA
EMS
YOUR SPECIES IS WEAK. YOU THINK LOVE MATTERS.
IT DOESN'T.
ONLY HATE MATTERS.
MENTALLY, CABLE SHUTS OFF THE ALARMS GUARDING HIS SANCTUM. IT'S ALMOST TIME. SIX, FIVE...
MOVE, MOVE, MOVE!
EMS
...FOUR...

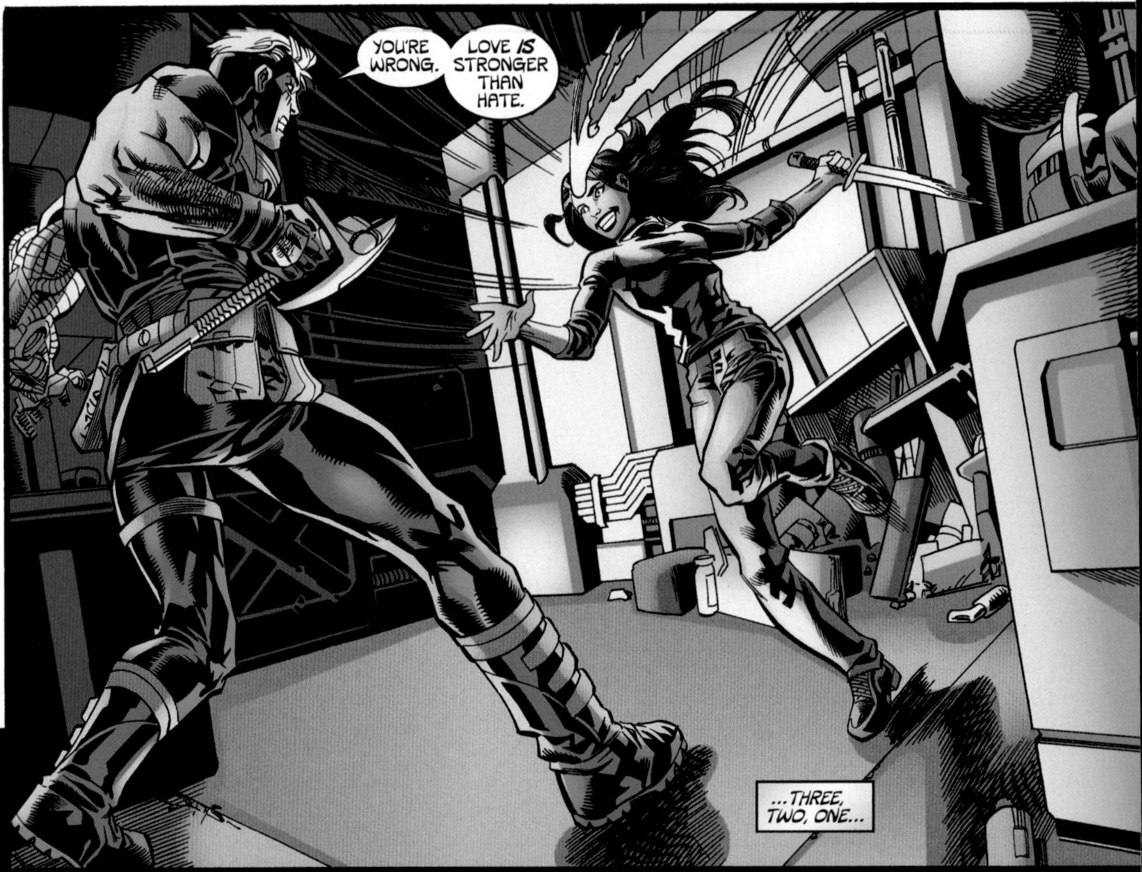
YOU'RE WRONG.
LOVE IS STRONGER THAN HATE.
...THREE, TWO, ONE...
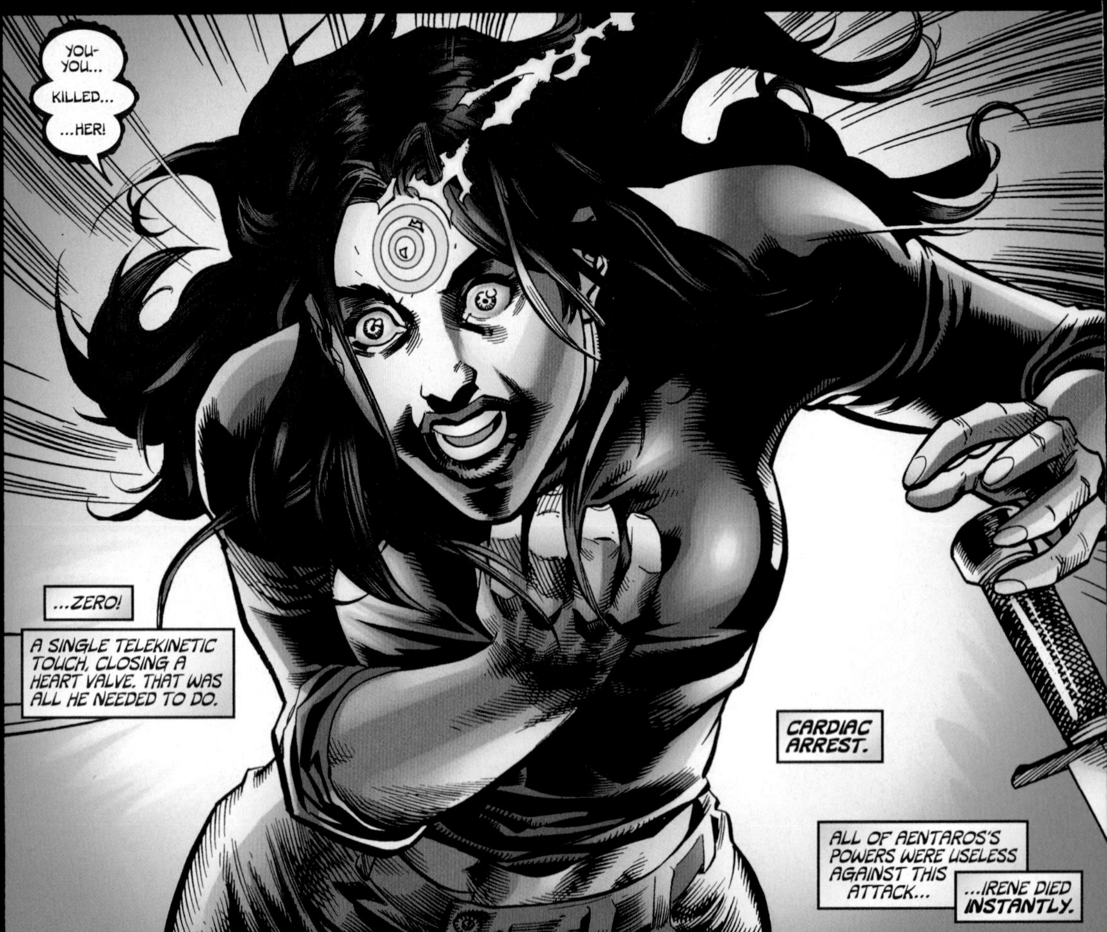
YOU- YOU...
KILLED...
...HER!
...ZERO!
A SINGLE TELEKINETIC TOUCH, CLOSING A HEART VALVE. THAT WAS ALL HE NEEDED TO DO.
CARDIAC ARREST.
ALL OF AENTAROS'S POWERS WERE USELESS AGAINST THIS ATTACK...
...IRENE DIED INSTANTLY.

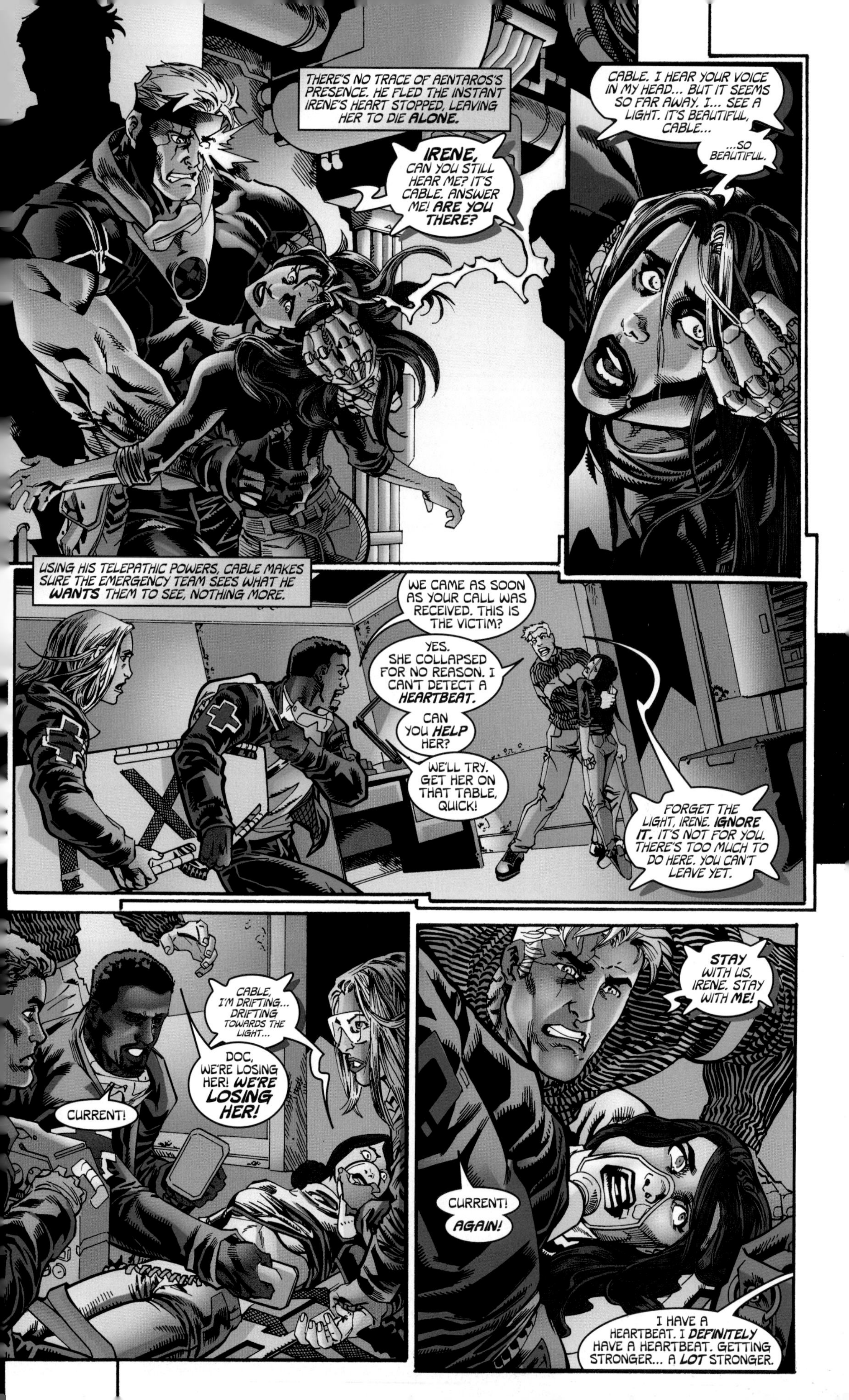
THERE'S NO TRACE OF AENTAROS'S PRESENCE. HE FLED THE INSTANT IRENE'S HEART STOPPED, LEAVING HER TO DIE ALONE.
IRENE, CAN YOU STILL HEAR ME? IT'S CABLE. ANSWER ME! ARE YOU THERE?
CABLE. I HEAR YOUR VOICE IN MY HEAD... BUT IT SEEMS SO FAR AWAY. I... SEE A LIGHT. IT'S BEAUTIFUL, CABLE...
...SO BEAUTIFUL.
USING HIS TELEPATHIC POWERS, CABLE MAKES SURE THE EMERGENCY TEAM SEES WHAT HE WANTS THEM TO SEE, NOTHING MORE.
WE CAME AS SOON AS YOUR CALL WAS RECEIVED. THIS IS THE VICTIM?
YES. SHE COLLAPSED FOR NO REASON. I CAN'T DETECT A HEARTBEAT.
CAN YOU HELP HER?
WE'LL TRY. GET HER ON THAT TABLE, QUICK!
FORGET THE LIGHT, IRENE. IGNORE IT. IT'S NOT FOR YOU. THERE'S TOO MUCH TO DO HERE. YOU CAN'T LEAVE YET.
CABLE, I'M DRIFTING... DRIFTING TOWARDS THE LIGHT...
DOC, WE'RE LOSING HER! WE'RE LOSING HER!
CURRENT!
STAY WITH US, IRENE. STAY WITH ME!
CURRENT! AGAIN!
I HAVE A HEARTBEAT. I DEFINITELY HAVE A HEARTBEAT. GETTING STRONGER... A LOT STRONGER.

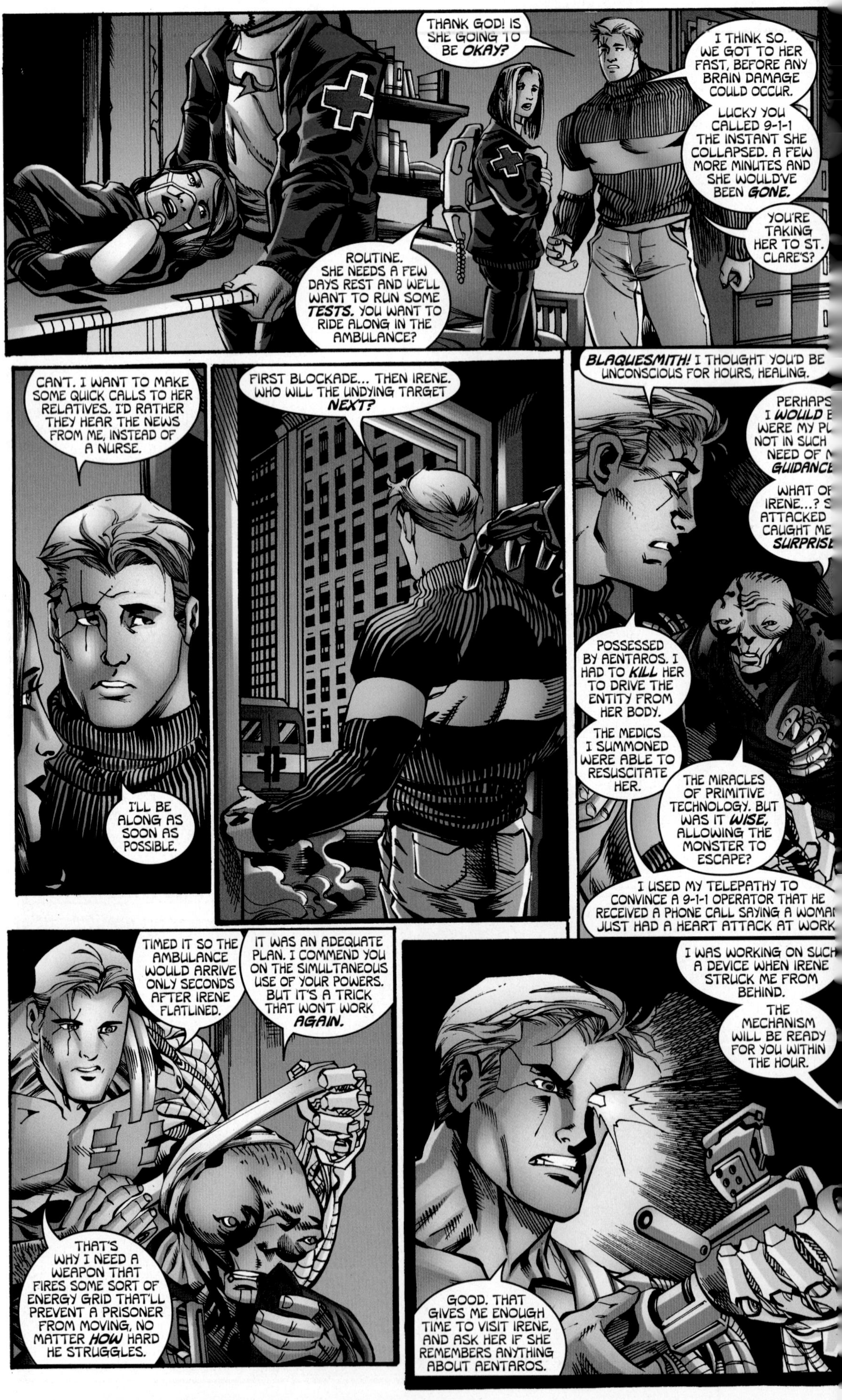
THANK GOD! IS SHE GOING TO BE *OKAY?*
I THINK SO. WE GOT TO HER FAST, BEFORE ANY BRAIN DAMAGE COULD OCCUR.
LUCKY YOU CALLED 9-1-1 THE INSTANT SHE COLLAPSED. A FEW MORE MINUTES AND SHE WOULD'VE BEEN *GONE.*
YOU'RE TAKING HER TO ST. CLARE'S?
ROUTINE. SHE NEEDS A FEW DAYS REST AND WE'LL WANT TO RUN SOME *TESTS.* YOU WANT TO RIDE ALONG IN THE AMBULANCE?
CAN'T. I WANT TO MAKE SOME QUICK CALLS TO HER RELATIVES. I'D RATHER THEY HEAR THE NEWS FROM ME, INSTEAD OF A NURSE.
I'LL BE ALONG AS SOON AS POSSIBLE.
FIRST BLOCKADE... THEN IRENE. WHO WILL THE UNDYING TARGET *NEXT?*
BLAQUESMITH! I THOUGHT YOU'D BE UNCONSCIOUS FOR HOURS, HEALING.
PERHAPS I *WOULD* B WERE MY PL NOT IN SUCH NEED OF M *GUIDANCE*
WHAT OF IRENE...? S ATTACKED CAUGHT ME *SURPRISE*
POSSESSED BY AENTAROS. I HAD TO *KILL* HER TO DRIVE THE ENTITY FROM HER BODY.
THE MEDICS I SUMMONED WERE ABLE TO RESUSCITATE HER.
THE MIRACLES OF PRIMITIVE TECHNOLOGY. BUT WAS IT *WISE,* ALLOWING THE MONSTER TO ESCAPE?
I USED MY TELEPATHY TO CONVINCE A 9-1-1 OPERATOR THAT HE RECEIVED A PHONE CALL SAYING A WOMA JUST HAD A HEART ATTACK AT WORK
TIMED IT SO THE AMBULANCE WOULD ARRIVE ONLY SECONDS AFTER IRENE FLATLINED.
IT WAS AN ADEQUATE PLAN. I COMMEND YOU ON THE SIMULTANEOUS USE OF YOUR POWERS. BUT IT'S A TRICK THAT WON'T WORK *AGAIN.*
THAT'S WHY I NEED A WEAPON THAT FIRES SOME SORT OF ENERGY GRID THAT'LL PREVENT A PRISONER FROM MOVING, NO MATTER *HOW* HARD HE STRUGGLES.
I WAS WORKING ON SUC A DEVICE WHEN IRENE STRUCK ME FROM BEHIND.
THE MECHANISM WILL BE READY FOR YOU WITHIN THE HOUR.
GOOD. THAT GIVES ME ENOUGH TIME TO VISIT IRENE, AND ASK HER IF SHE REMEMBERS ANYTHING ABOUT AENTAROS.

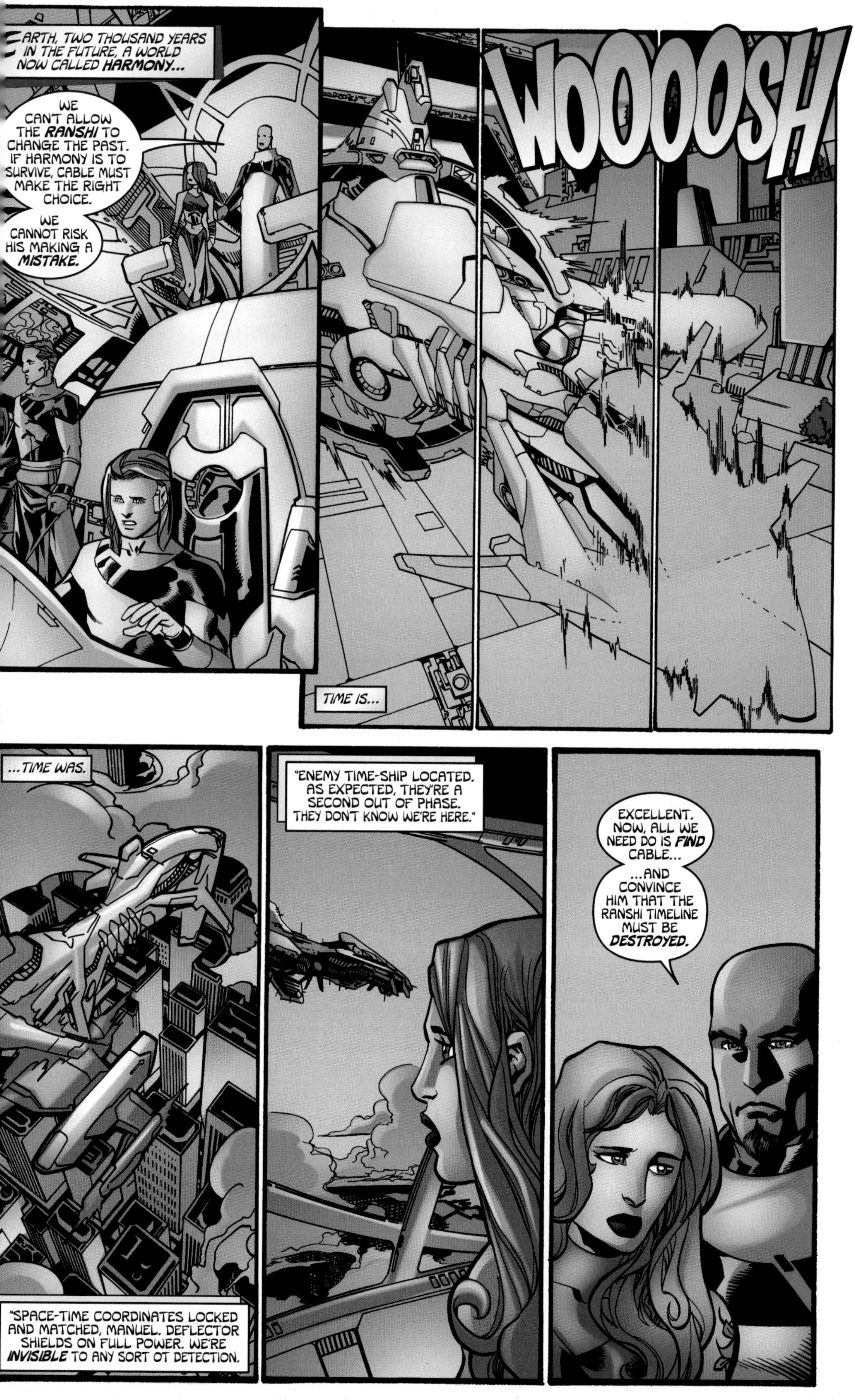
EARTH, TWO THOUSAND YEARS IN THE FUTURE, A WORLD NOW CALLED HARMONY...
WE CAN'T ALLOW THE RANSHI TO CHANGE THE PAST. IF HARMONY IS TO SURVIVE, CABLE MUST MAKE THE RIGHT CHOICE.
WE CANNOT RISK HIS MAKING A MISTAKE.
WOOOOSH
TIME IS...
...TIME WAS.
"SPACE-TIME COORDINATES LOCKED AND MATCHED, MANUEL. DEFLECTOR SHIELDS ON FULL POWER. WE'RE INVISIBLE TO ANY SORT OT DETECTION.
"ENEMY TIME-SHIP LOCATED. AS EXPECTED, THEY'RE A SECOND OUT OF PHASE. THEY DON'T KNOW WE'RE HERE."
EXCELLENT. NOW, ALL WE NEED DO IS FIND CABLE...
...AND CONVINCE HIM THAT THE RANSHI TIMELINE MUST BE DESTROYED.

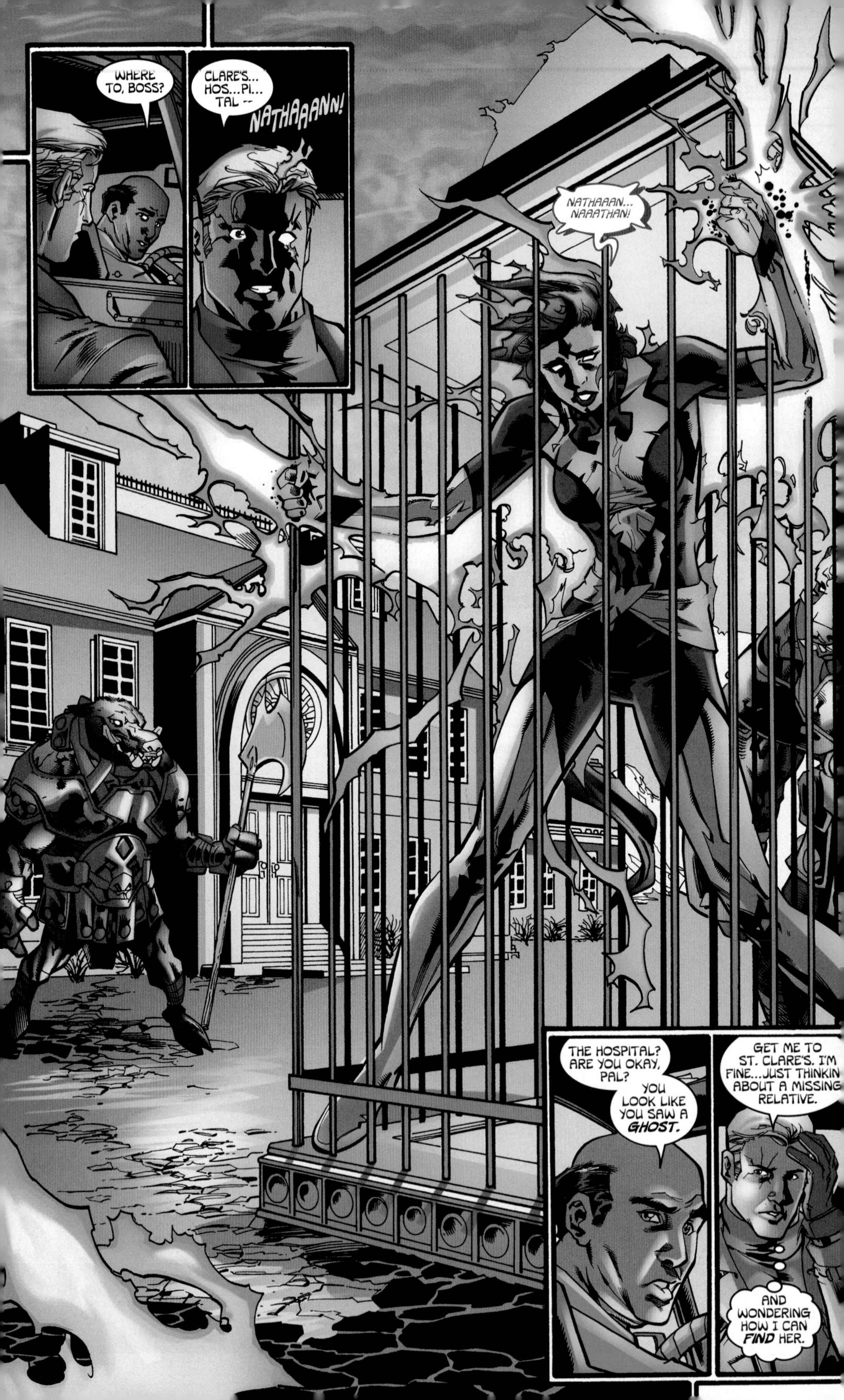
WHERE TO, BOSS?
CLARE'S... HOS...PI... TAL --
NATHAAANN!
NATHAAAN... NAAATHAN!
THE HOSPITAL? ARE YOU OKAY, PAL?
YOU LOOK LIKE YOU SAW A GHOST.
GET ME TO ST. CLARE'S. I'M FINE...JUST THINKIN' ABOUT A MISSING RELATIVE.
AND WONDERING HOW I CAN FIND HER.

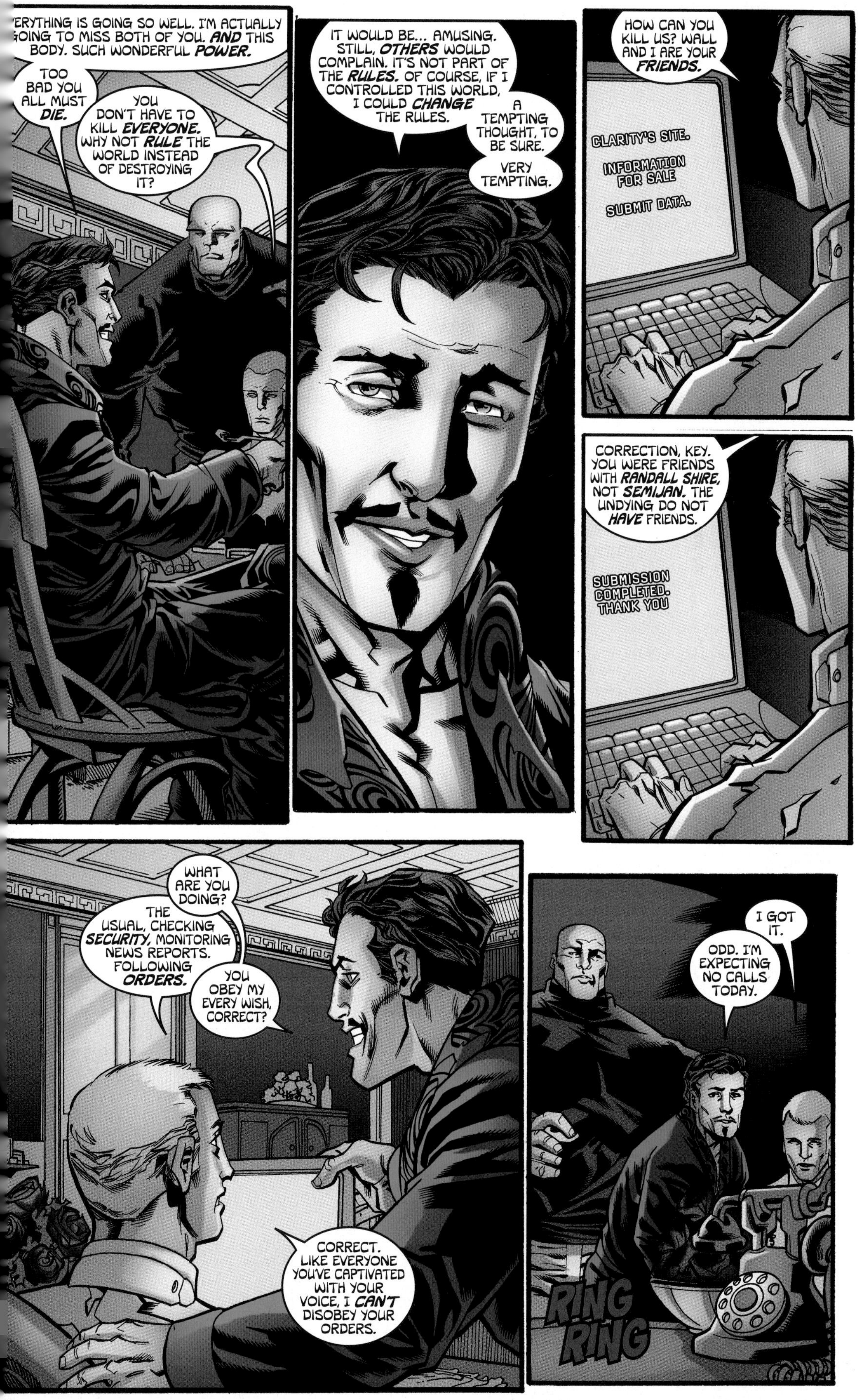

VERYTHING IS GOING SO WELL. I'M ACTUALLY GOING TO MISS BOTH OF YOU. AND THIS BODY. SUCH WONDERFUL POWER.
TOO BAD YOU ALL MUST DIE.
YOU DON'T HAVE TO KILL EVERYONE. WHY NOT RULE THE WORLD INSTEAD OF DESTROYING IT?
IT WOULD BE... AMUSING. STILL, OTHERS WOULD COMPLAIN. IT'S NOT PART OF THE RULES. OF COURSE, IF I CONTROLLED THIS WORLD, I COULD CHANGE THE RULES.
A TEMPTING THOUGHT, TO BE SURE.
VERY TEMPTING.
HOW CAN YOU KILL US? WALL AND I ARE YOUR FRIENDS.
CLARITY'S SITE.
INFORMATION FOR SALE
SUBMIT DATA.
CORRECTION, KEY. YOU WERE FRIENDS WITH RANDALL SHIRE, NOT SEMIJAN. THE UNDYING DO NOT HAVE FRIENDS.
SUBMISSION COMPLETED. THANK YOU
WHAT ARE YOU DOING?
THE USUAL, CHECKING SECURITY, MONITORING NEWS REPORTS. FOLLOWING ORDERS.
YOU OBEY MY EVERY WISH, CORRECT?
CORRECT. LIKE EVERYONE YOU'VE CAPTIVATED WITH YOUR VOICE, I CAN'T DISOBEY YOUR ORDERS.
I GOT IT.
ODD. I'M EXPECTING NO CALLS TODAY.
RING RING

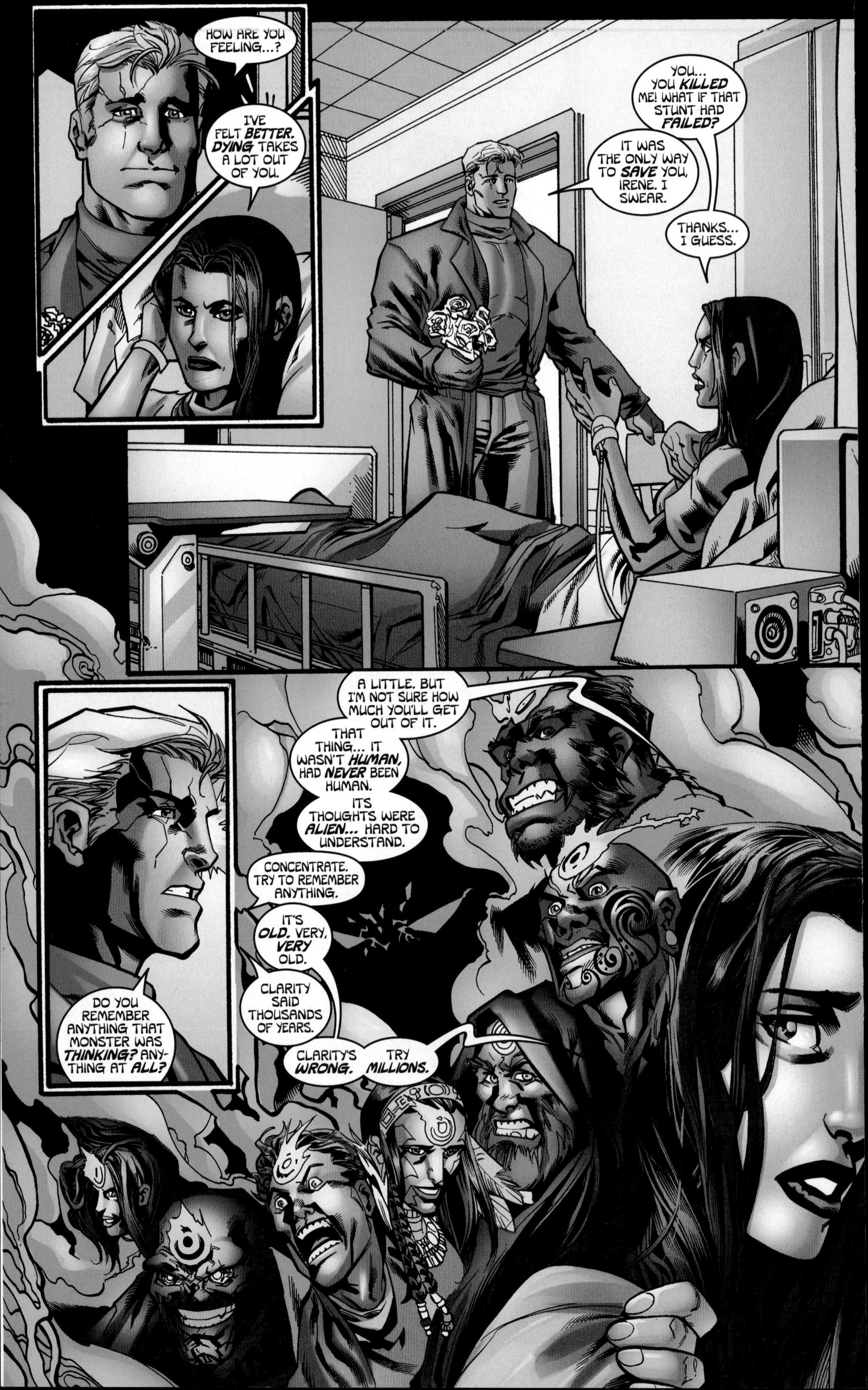
HOW ARE YOU FEELING...?
I'VE FELT BETTER. DYING TAKES A LOT OUT OF YOU.
YOU... YOU KILLED ME! WHAT IF THAT STUNT HAD FAILED?
IT WAS THE ONLY WAY TO SAVE YOU, IRENE. I SWEAR.
THANKS... I GUESS.
DO YOU REMEMBER ANYTHING THAT MONSTER WAS THINKING? ANYTHING AT ALL?
A LITTLE. BUT I'M NOT SURE HOW MUCH YOU'LL GET OUT OF IT.
THAT THING... IT WASN'T HUMAN, HAD NEVER BEEN HUMAN.
ITS THOUGHTS WERE ALIEN... HARD TO UNDERSTAND.
CONCENTRATE. TRY TO REMEMBER ANYTHING.
IT'S OLD. VERY, VERY OLD.
CLARITY SAID THOUSANDS OF YEARS.
CLARITY'S WRONG. TRY MILLIONS.

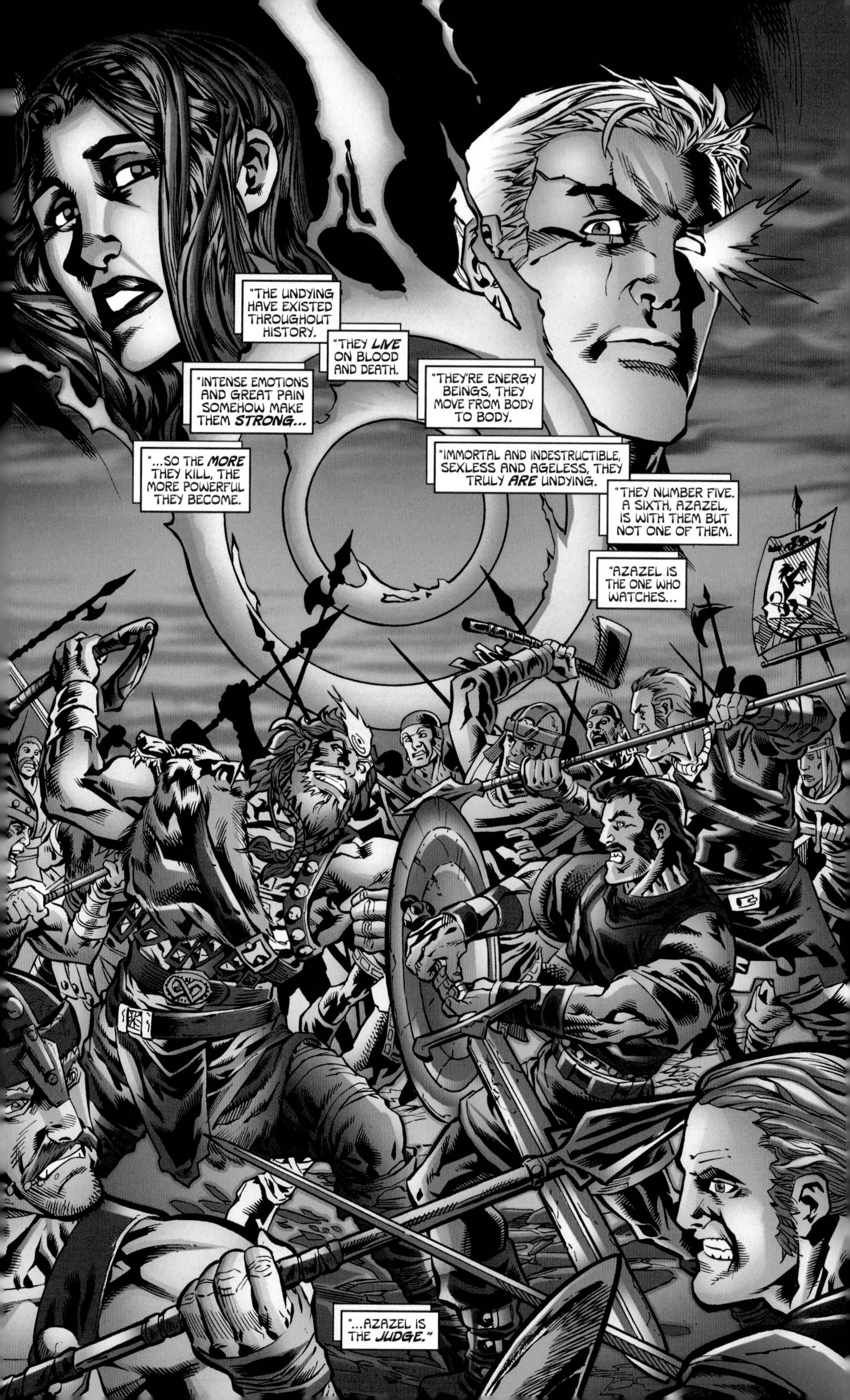
"THE UNDYING HAVE EXISTED THROUGHOUT HISTORY.
"THEY LIVE ON BLOOD AND DEATH.
"INTENSE EMOTIONS AND GREAT PAIN SOMEHOW MAKE THEM STRONG...
"...SO THE MORE THEY KILL, THE MORE POWERFUL THEY BECOME.
"THEY'RE ENERGY BEINGS, THEY MOVE FROM BODY TO BODY.
"IMMORTAL AND INDESTRUCTIBLE, SEXLESS AND AGELESS, THEY TRULY ARE UNDYING.
"THEY NUMBER FIVE. A SIXTH, AZAZEL, IS WITH THEM BUT NOT ONE OF THEM.
"AZAZEL IS THE ONE WHO WATCHES...
"...AZAZEL IS THE JUDGE."

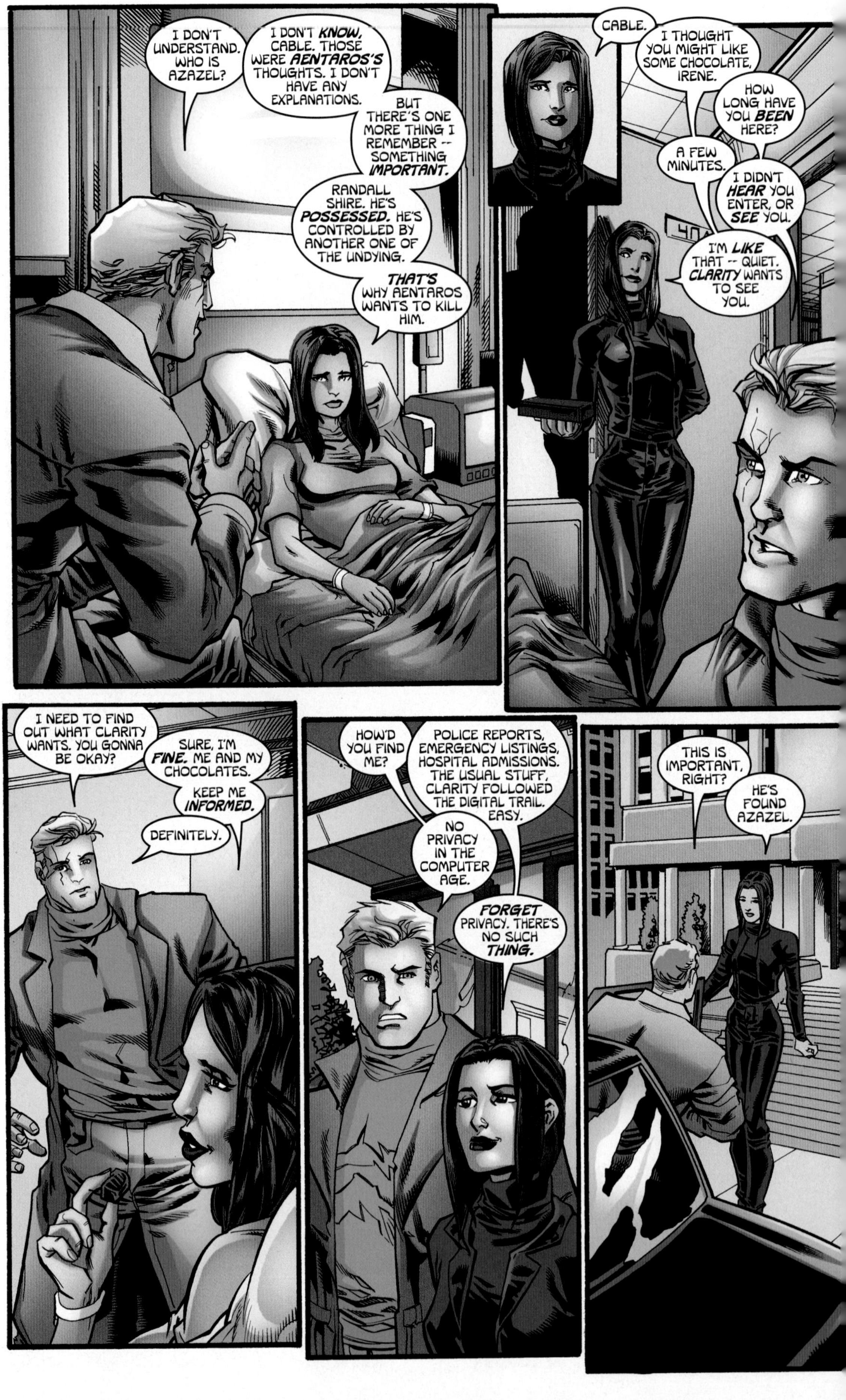
I DON'T UNDERSTAND. WHO IS AZAZEL?
I DON'T *KNOW,* CABLE. THOSE WERE *AENTAROS'S* THOUGHTS. I DON'T HAVE ANY EXPLANATIONS.
BUT THERE'S ONE MORE THING I REMEMBER -- SOMETHING *IMPORTANT.*
RANDALL SHIRE. HE'S *POSSESSED.* HE'S CONTROLLED BY ANOTHER ONE OF THE UNDYING.
THAT'S WHY AENTAROS WANTS TO KILL HIM.
CABLE.
I THOUGHT YOU MIGHT LIKE SOME CHOCOLATE, IRENE.
HOW LONG HAVE YOU *BEEN* HERE?
A FEW MINUTES.
I DIDN'T *HEAR* YOU ENTER, OR *SEE* YOU.
I'M *LIKE* THAT -- QUIET. *CLARITY* WANTS TO SEE YOU.
I NEED TO FIND OUT WHAT CLARITY WANTS. YOU GONNA BE OKAY?
SURE, I'M *FINE.* ME AND MY CHOCOLATES.
KEEP ME *INFORMED.*
DEFINITELY.
HOW'D YOU FIND ME?
POLICE REPORTS, EMERGENCY LISTINGS, HOSPITAL ADMISSIONS. THE USUAL STUFF. CLARITY FOLLOWED THE DIGITAL TRAIL. EASY.
NO PRIVACY IN THE COMPUTER AGE.
FORGET PRIVACY. THERE'S NO SUCH *THING.*
THIS IS IMPORTANT, RIGHT?
HE'S FOUND AZAZEL.

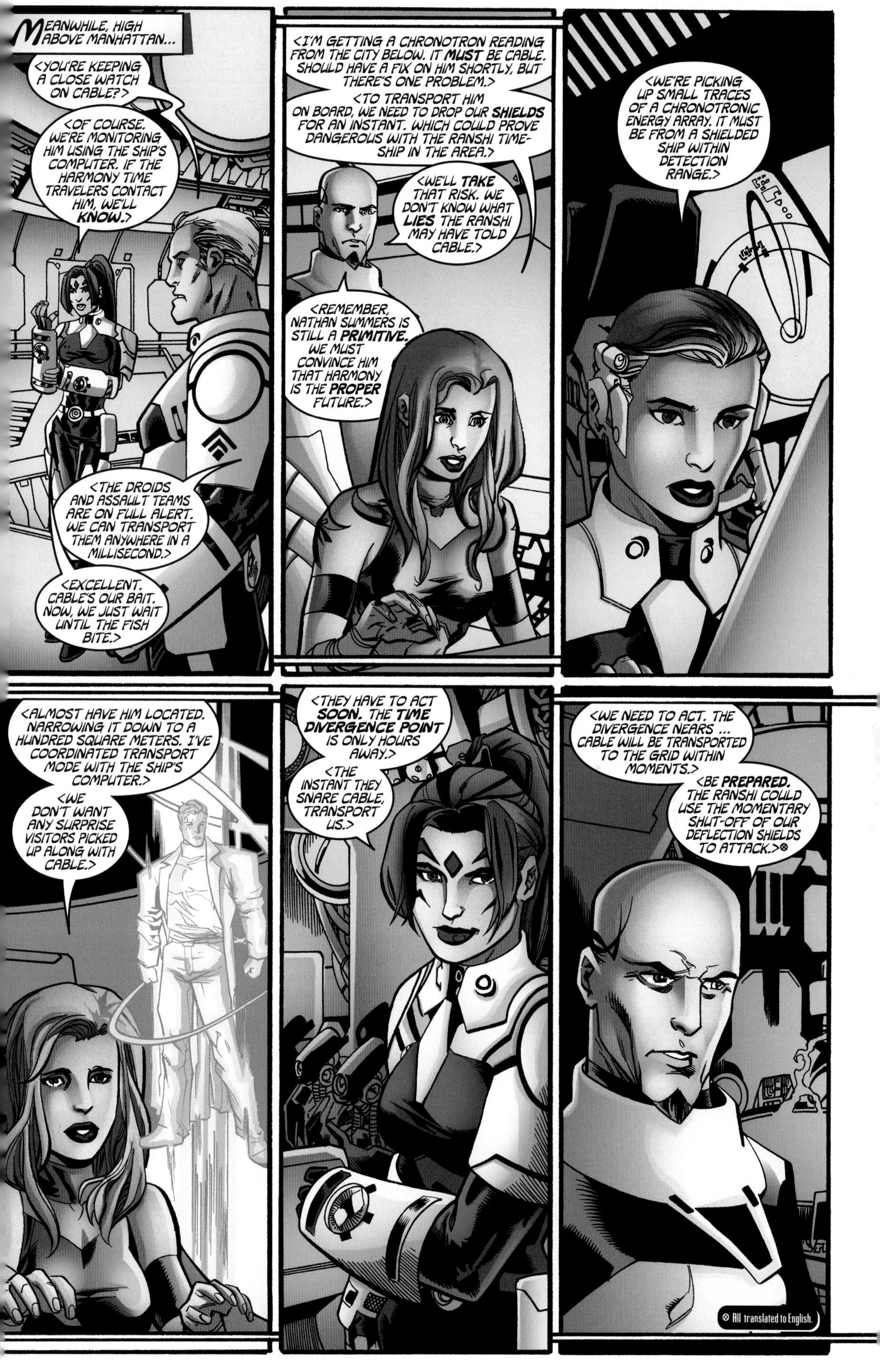
MEANWHILE, HIGH ABOVE MANHATTAN...
<YOU'RE KEEPING A CLOSE WATCH ON CABLE?>
<OF COURSE. WE'RE MONITORING HIM USING THE SHIP'S COMPUTER. IF THE HARMONY TIME TRAVELERS CONTACT HIM, WE'LL KNOW.>
<THE DROIDS AND ASSAULT TEAMS ARE ON FULL ALERT. WE CAN TRANSPORT THEM ANYWHERE IN A MILLISECOND.>
<EXCELLENT. CABLE'S OUR BAIT. NOW, WE JUST WAIT UNTIL THE FISH BITE.>
<I'M GETTING A CHRONOTRON READING FROM THE CITY BELOW. IT MUST BE CABLE. SHOULD HAVE A FIX ON HIM SHORTLY, BUT THERE'S ONE PROBLEM.>
<TO TRANSPORT HIM ON BOARD, WE NEED TO DROP OUR SHIELDS FOR AN INSTANT. WHICH COULD PROVE DANGEROUS WITH THE RANSHI TIME-SHIP IN THE AREA.>
<WE'LL TAKE THAT RISK. WE DON'T KNOW WHAT LIES THE RANSHI MAY HAVE TOLD CABLE.>
<REMEMBER, NATHAN SUMMERS IS STILL A PRIMITIVE. WE MUST CONVINCE HIM THAT HARMONY IS THE PROPER FUTURE.>
<WE'RE PICKING UP SMALL TRACES OF A CHRONOTRONIC ENERGY ARRAY. IT MUST BE FROM A SHIELDED SHIP WITHIN DETECTION RANGE.>
<ALMOST HAVE HIM LOCATED. NARROWING IT DOWN TO A HUNDRED SQUARE METERS. I'VE COORDINATED TRANSPORT MODE WITH THE SHIP'S COMPUTER.>
<WE DON'T WANT ANY SURPRISE VISITORS PICKED UP ALONG WITH CABLE.>
<THEY HAVE TO ACT SOON. THE TIME DIVERGENCE POINT IS ONLY HOURS AWAY.>
<THE INSTANT THEY SNARE CABLE, TRANSPORT US.>
<WE NEED TO ACT. THE DIVERGENCE NEARS ... CABLE WILL BE TRANSPORTED TO THE GRID WITHIN MOMENTS.>
<BE PREPARED. THE RANSHI COULD USE THE MOMENTARY SHUT-OFF OF OUR DEFLECTION SHIELDS TO ATTACK.>⊗
⊗ All translated to English.

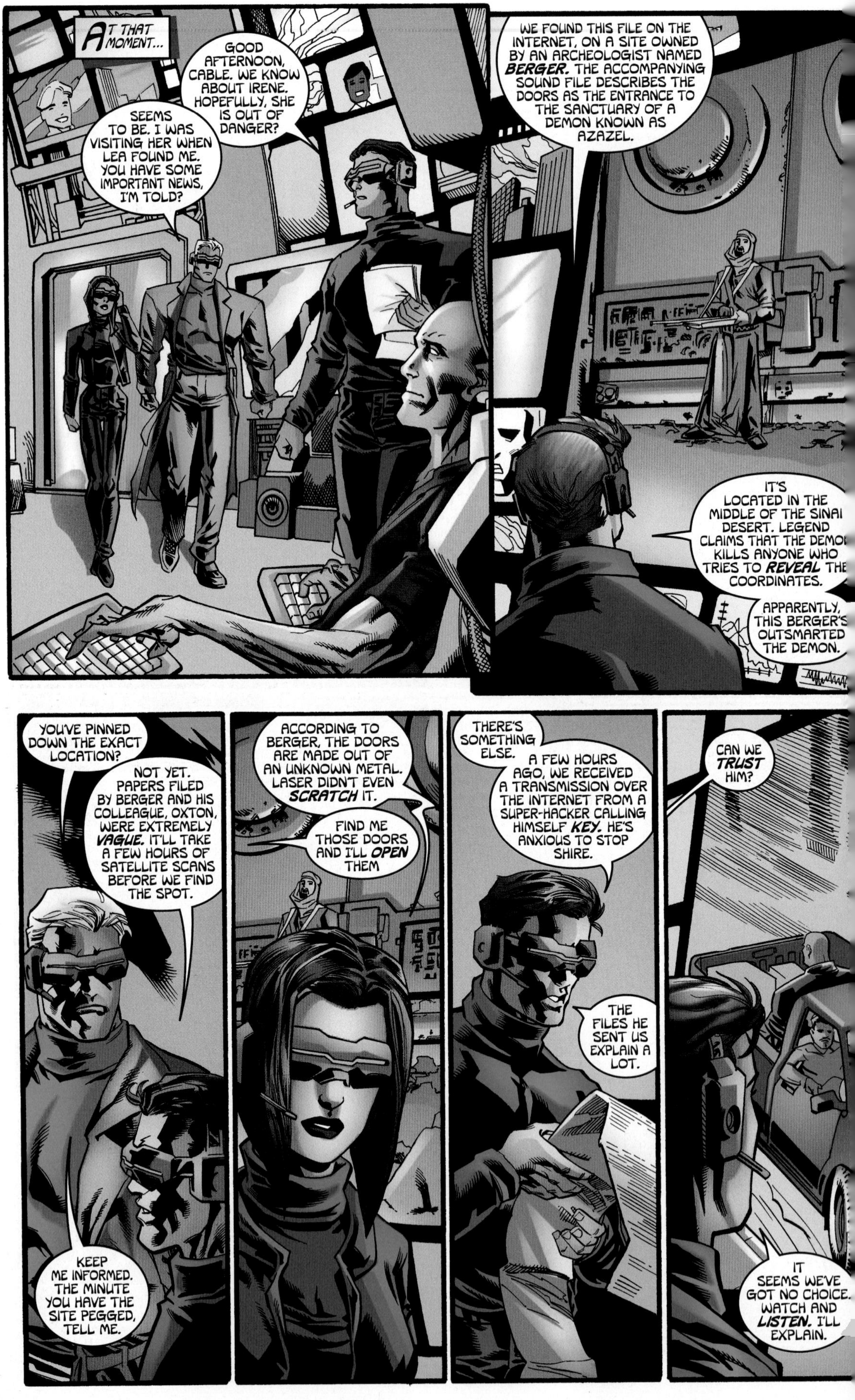
AT THAT MOMENT...
GOOD AFTERNOON, CABLE. WE KNOW ABOUT IRENE. HOPEFULLY, SHE IS OUT OF DANGER?
SEEMS TO BE. I WAS VISITING HER WHEN LEA FOUND ME. YOU HAVE SOME IMPORTANT NEWS, I'M TOLD?
WE FOUND THIS FILE ON THE INTERNET, ON A SITE OWNED BY AN ARCHEOLOGIST NAMED BERGER. THE ACCOMPANYING SOUND FILE DESCRIBES THE DOORS AS THE ENTRANCE TO THE SANCTUARY OF A DEMON KNOWN AS AZAZEL.
IT'S LOCATED IN THE MIDDLE OF THE SINAI DESERT. LEGEND CLAIMS THAT THE DEMON KILLS ANYONE WHO TRIES TO REVEAL THE COORDINATES.
APPARENTLY, THIS BERGER'S OUTSMARTED THE DEMON.
YOU'VE PINNED DOWN THE EXACT LOCATION?
NOT YET. PAPERS FILED BY BERGER AND HIS COLLEAGUE, OXTON, WERE EXTREMELY VAGUE. IT'LL TAKE A FEW HOURS OF SATELLITE SCANS BEFORE WE FIND THE SPOT.
KEEP ME INFORMED. THE MINUTE YOU HAVE THE SITE PEGGED, TELL ME.
ACCORDING TO BERGER, THE DOORS ARE MADE OUT OF AN UNKNOWN METAL. LASER DIDN'T EVEN SCRATCH IT.
FIND ME THOSE DOORS AND I'LL OPEN THEM
THERE'S SOMETHING ELSE.
A FEW HOURS AGO, WE RECEIVED A TRANSMISSION OVER THE INTERNET FROM A SUPER-HACKER CALLING HIMSELF KEY. HE'S ANXIOUS TO STOP SHIRE.
THE FILES HE SENT US EXPLAIN A LOT.
CAN WE TRUST HIM?
IT SEEMS WE'VE GOT NO CHOICE. WATCH AND LISTEN. I'LL EXPLAIN.

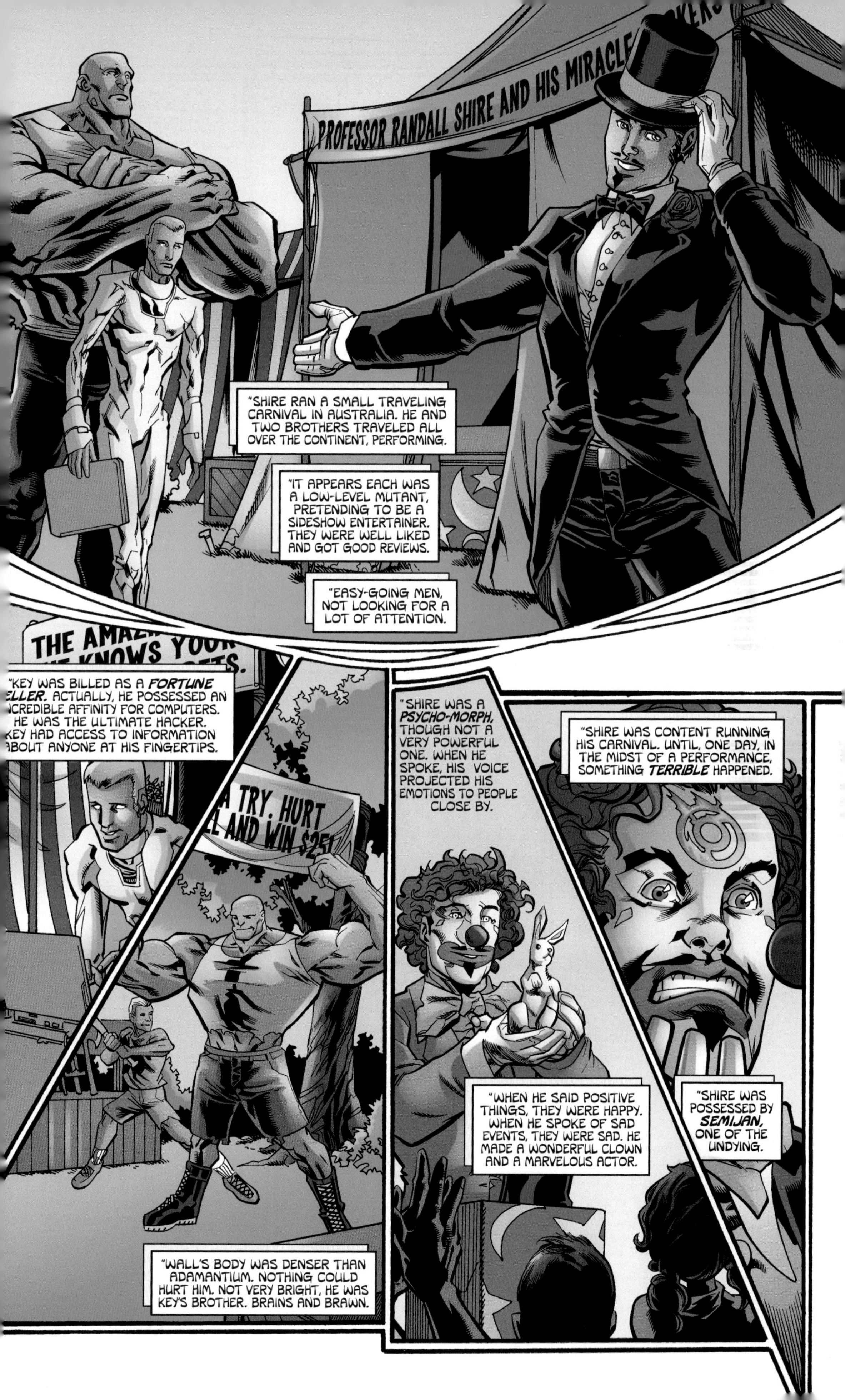
PROFESSOR RANDALL SHIRE AND HIS MIRACLE
"SHIRE RAN A SMALL TRAVELING CARNIVAL IN AUSTRALIA. HE AND TWO BROTHERS TRAVELED ALL OVER THE CONTINENT, PERFORMING.
"IT APPEARS EACH WAS A LOW-LEVEL MUTANT, PRETENDING TO BE A SIDESHOW ENTERTAINER. THEY WERE WELL LIKED AND GOT GOOD REVIEWS.
"EASY-GOING MEN, NOT LOOKING FOR A LOT OF ATTENTION.
THE AMAZ
"KEY WAS BILLED AS A FORTUNE ELLER. ACTUALLY, HE POSSESSED AN NCREDIBLE AFFINITY FOR COMPUTERS. HE WAS THE ULTIMATE HACKER. KEY HAD ACCESS TO INFORMATION ABOUT ANYONE AT HIS FINGERTIPS.
A TRY. HURT
L AND WIN $25!
"WALL'S BODY WAS DENSER THAN ADAMANTIUM. NOTHING COULD HURT HIM. NOT VERY BRIGHT, HE WAS KEY'S BROTHER. BRAINS AND BRAWN.
"SHIRE WAS A PSYCHO-MORPH, THOUGH NOT A VERY POWERFUL ONE. WHEN HE SPOKE, HIS VOICE PROJECTED HIS EMOTIONS TO PEOPLE CLOSE BY.
"WHEN HE SAID POSITIVE THINGS, THEY WERE HAPPY. WHEN HE SPOKE OF SAD EVENTS, THEY WERE SAD. HE MADE A WONDERFUL CLOWN AND A MARVELOUS ACTOR.
"SHIRE WAS CONTENT RUNNING HIS CARNIVAL. UNTIL, ONE DAY, IN THE MIDST OF A PERFORMANCE, SOMETHING TERRIBLE HAPPENED.
"SHIRE WAS POSSESSED BY SEMIJAN, ONE OF THE UNDYING.

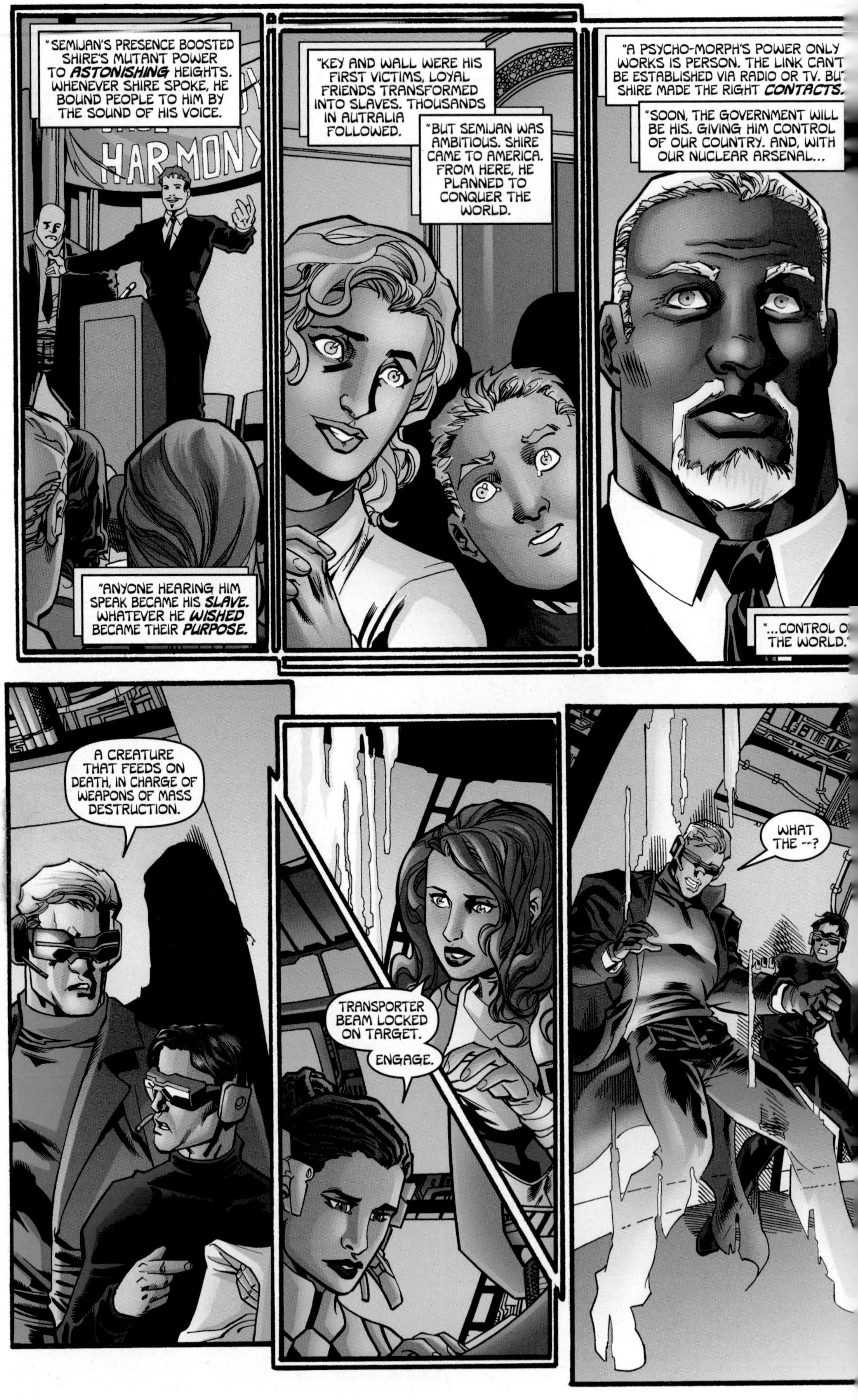
"SEMIJAN'S PRESENCE BOOSTED SHIRE'S MUTANT POWER TO ASTONISHING HEIGHTS. WHENEVER SHIRE SPOKE, HE BOUND PEOPLE TO HIM BY THE SOUND OF HIS VOICE.
HARMONY
"ANYONE HEARING HIM SPEAK BECAME HIS SLAVE. WHATEVER HE WISHED BECAME THEIR PURPOSE.
"KEY AND WALL WERE HIS FIRST VICTIMS, LOYAL FRIENDS TRANSFORMED INTO SLAVES. THOUSANDS IN AUTRALIA FOLLOWED.
"BUT SEMIJAN WAS AMBITIOUS. SHIRE CAME TO AMERICA. FROM HERE, HE PLANNED TO CONQUER THE WORLD.
"A PSYCHO-MORPH'S POWER ONLY WORKS IS PERSON. THE LINK CAN'T BE ESTABLISHED VIA RADIO OR TV. BUT SHIRE MADE THE RIGHT CONTACTS.
"SOON, THE GOVERNMENT WILL BE HIS. GIVING HIM CONTROL OF OUR COUNTRY. AND, WITH OUR NUCLEAR ARSENAL...
"...CONTROL OF THE WORLD."
A CREATURE THAT FEEDS ON DEATH, IN CHARGE OF WEAPONS OF MASS DESTRUCTION.
TRANSPORTER BEAM LOCKED ON TARGET.
ENGAGE.
WHAT THE --?

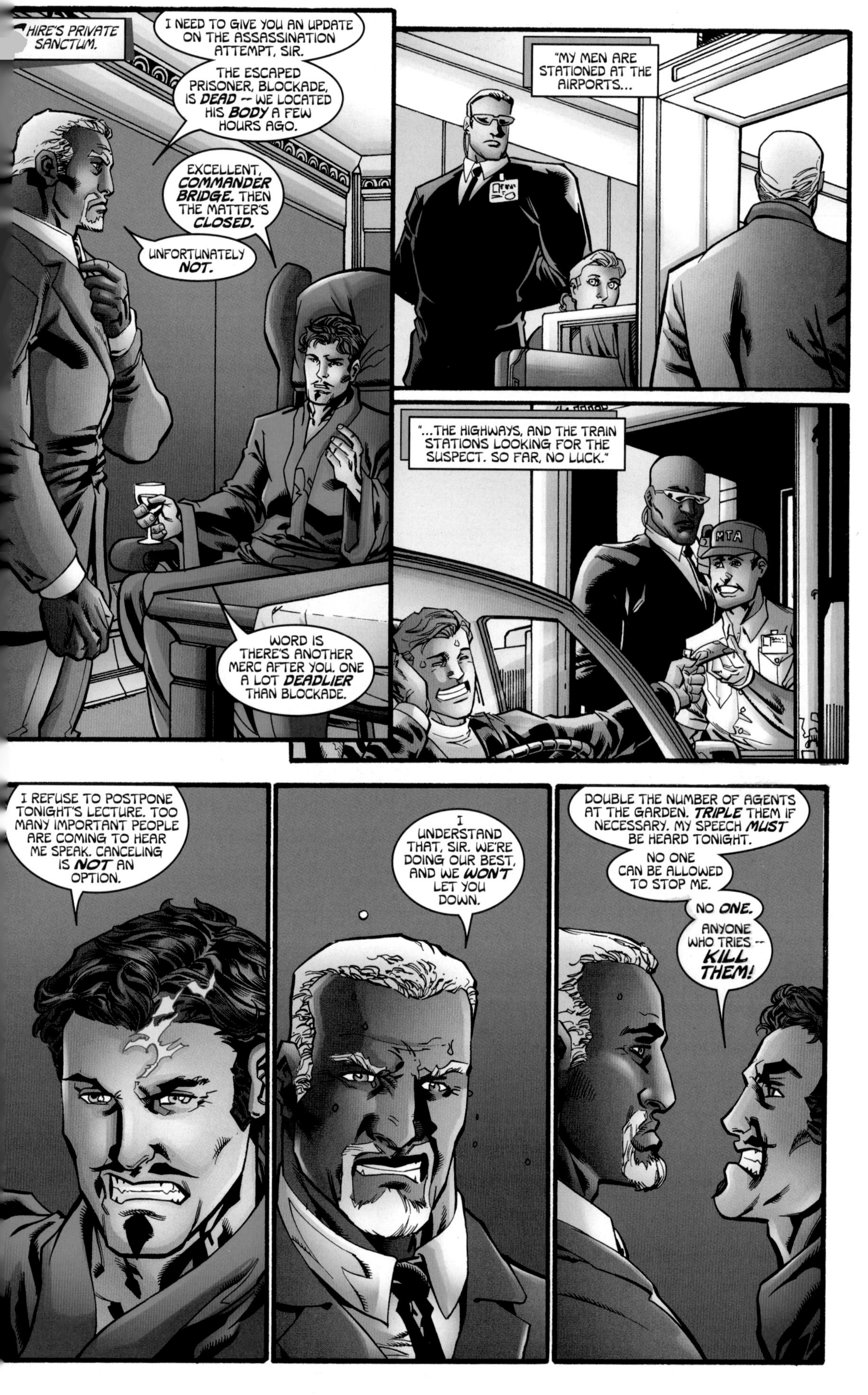

HIRE'S PRIVATE SANCTUM.
I NEED TO GIVE YOU AN UPDATE ON THE ASSASSINATION ATTEMPT, SIR.
THE ESCAPED PRISONER, BLOCKADE, IS DEAD -- WE LOCATED HIS BODY A FEW HOURS AGO.
EXCELLENT, COMMANDER BRIDGE. THEN THE MATTER'S CLOSED.
UNFORTUNATELY NOT.
WORD IS THERE'S ANOTHER MERC AFTER YOU. ONE A LOT DEADLIER THAN BLOCKADE.
"MY MEN ARE STATIONED AT THE AIRPORTS...
"...THE HIGHWAYS, AND THE TRAIN STATIONS LOOKING FOR THE SUSPECT. SO FAR, NO LUCK."
MTA
I REFUSE TO POSTPONE TONIGHT'S LECTURE. TOO MANY IMPORTANT PEOPLE ARE COMING TO HEAR ME SPEAK. CANCELING IS NOT AN OPTION.
I UNDERSTAND THAT, SIR. WE'RE DOING OUR BEST, AND WE WON'T LET YOU DOWN.
DOUBLE THE NUMBER OF AGENTS AT THE GARDEN. TRIPLE THEM IF NECESSARY. MY SPEECH MUST BE HEARD TONIGHT.
NO ONE CAN BE ALLOWED TO STOP ME.
NO ONE.
ANYONE WHO TRIES -- KILL THEM!

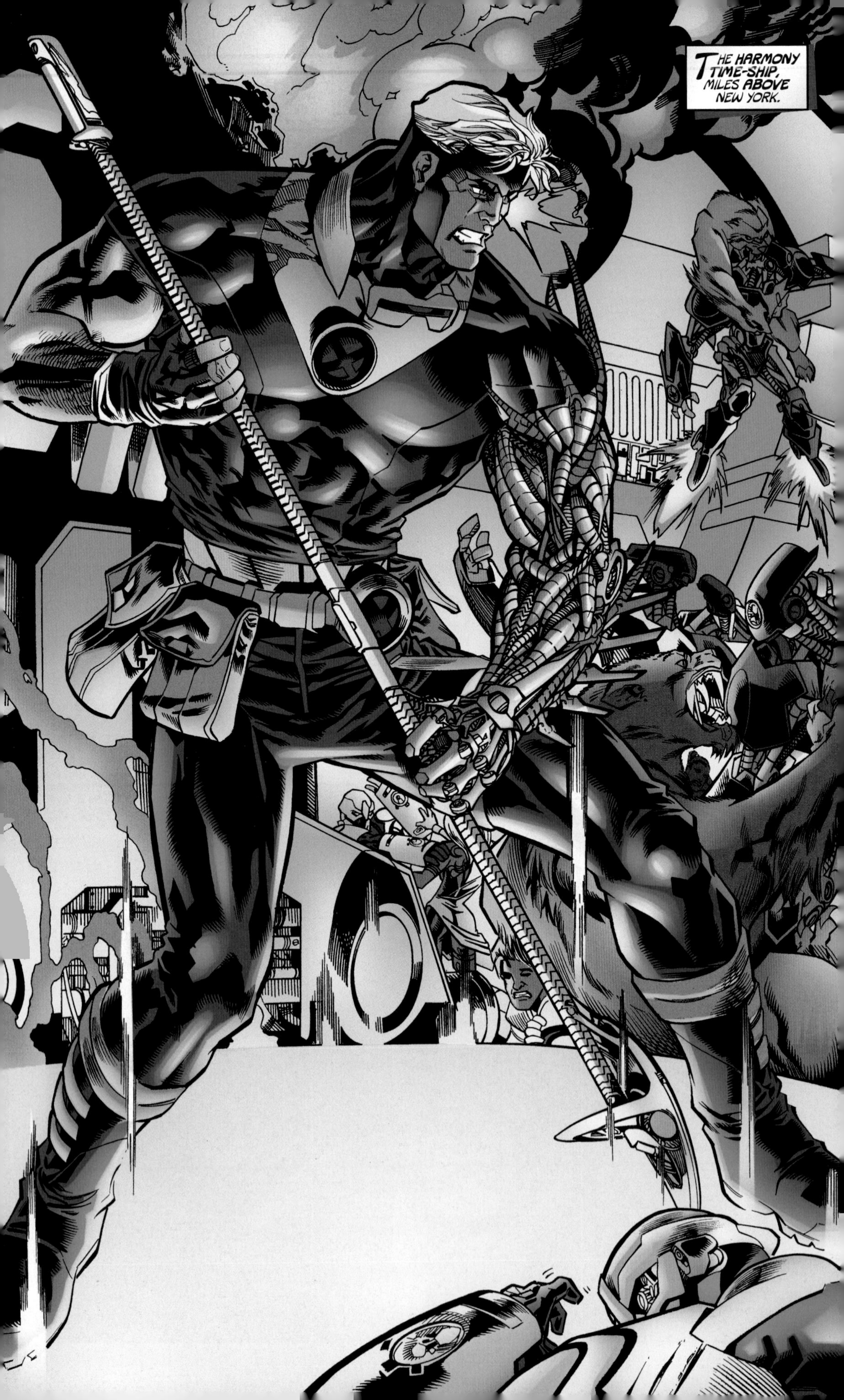
THE HARMONY TIME-SHIP, MILES ABOVE NEW YORK.

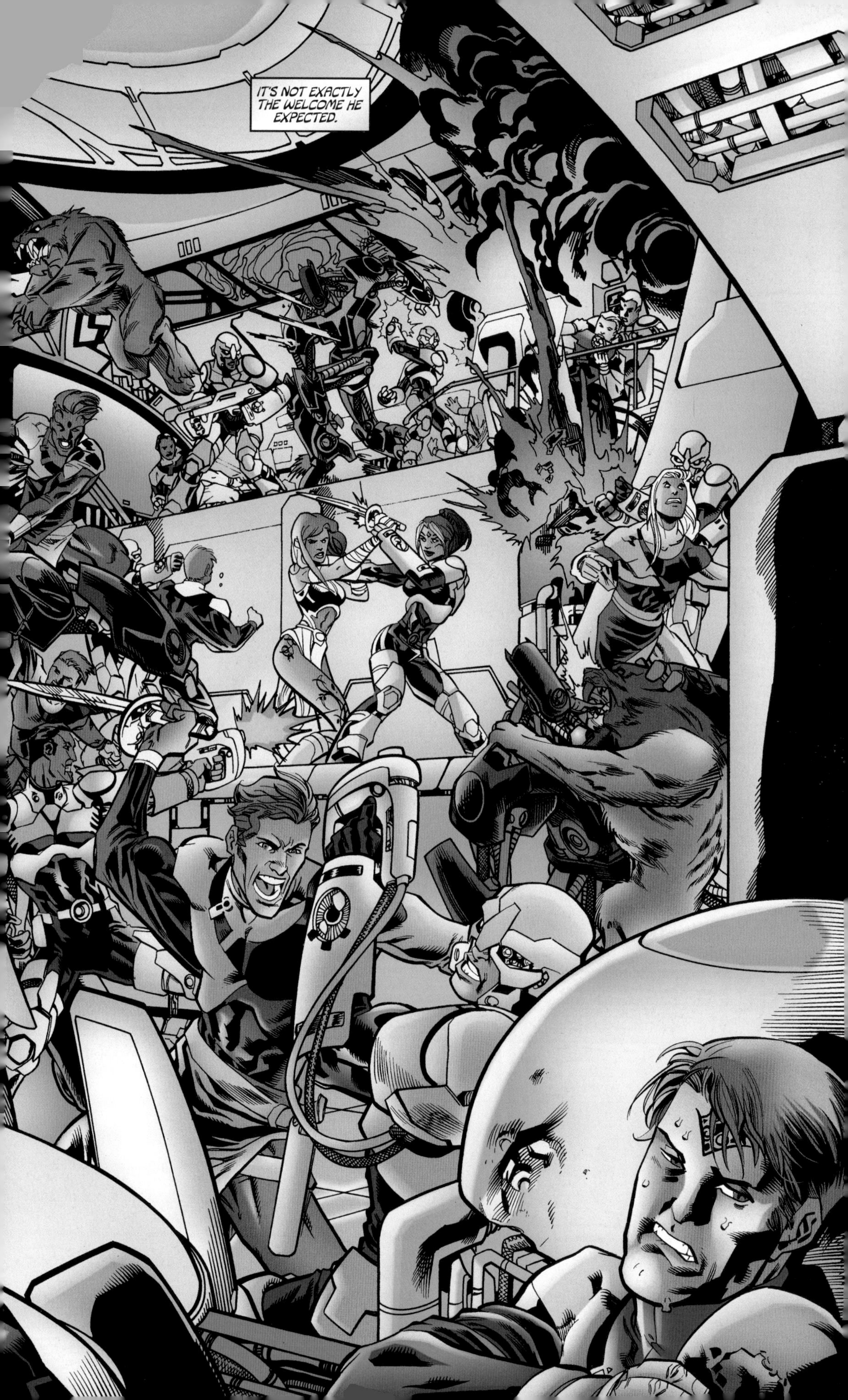
IT'S NOT EXACTLY THE WELCOME HE EXPECTED.

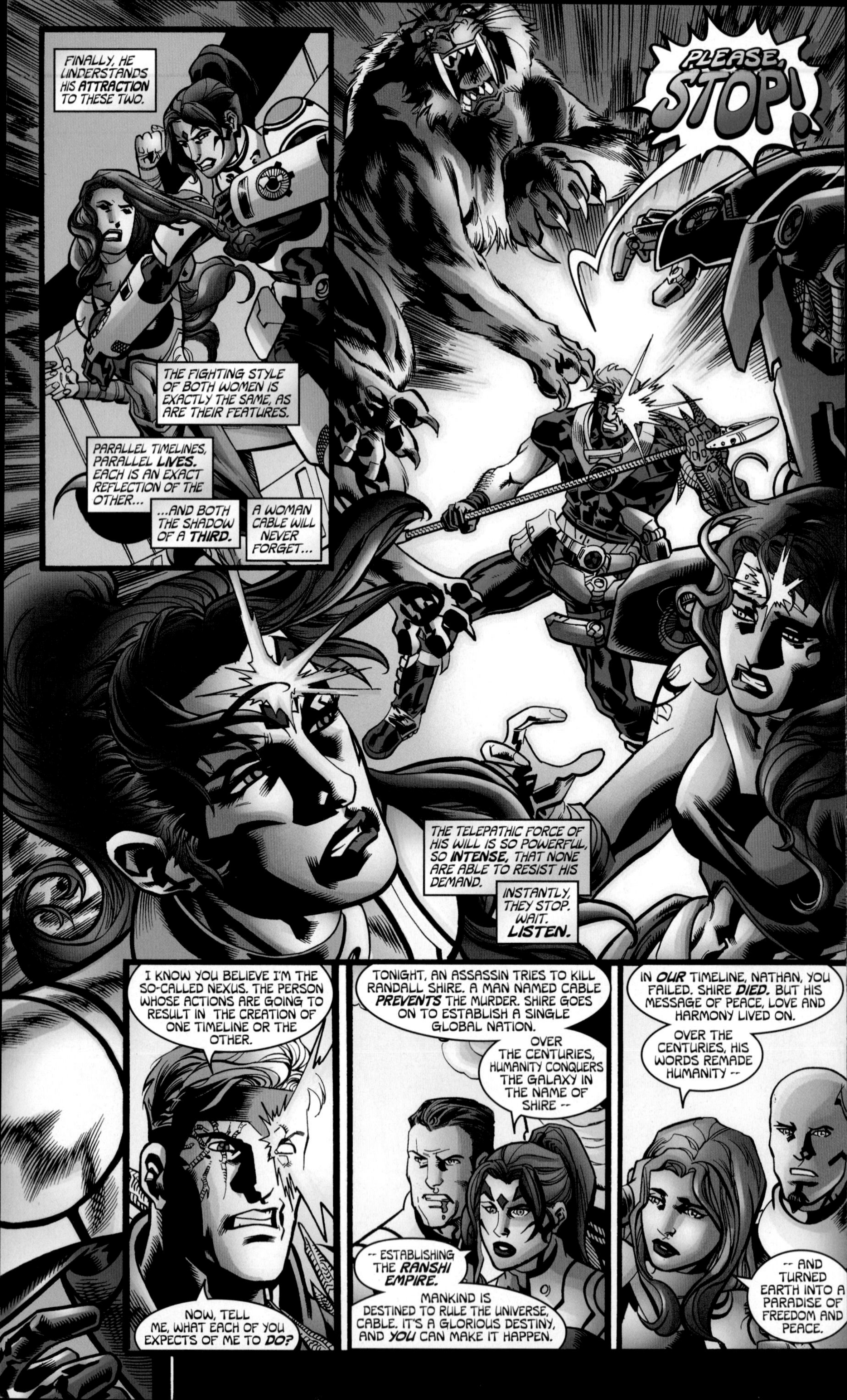
FINALLY, HE UNDERSTANDS HIS ATTRACTION TO THESE TWO.
PLEASE, STOP!
THE FIGHTING STYLE OF BOTH WOMEN IS EXACTLY THE SAME, AS ARE THEIR FEATURES.
PARALLEL TIMELINES, PARALLEL LIVES. EACH IS AN EXACT REFLECTION OF THE OTHER...
...AND BOTH THE SHADOW OF A THIRD.
A WOMAN CABLE WILL NEVER FORGET...
THE TELEPATHIC FORCE OF HIS WILL IS SO POWERFUL, SO INTENSE, THAT NONE ARE ABLE TO RESIST HIS DEMAND.
INSTANTLY, THEY STOP. WAIT. LISTEN.
I KNOW YOU BELIEVE I'M THE SO-CALLED NEXUS. THE PERSON WHOSE ACTIONS ARE GOING TO RESULT IN THE CREATION OF ONE TIMELINE OR THE OTHER.
NOW, TELL ME, WHAT EACH OF YOU EXPECTS OF ME TO DO?
TONIGHT, AN ASSASSIN TRIES TO KILL RANDALL SHIRE. A MAN NAMED CABLE PREVENTS THE MURDER. SHIRE GOES ON TO ESTABLISH A SINGLE GLOBAL NATION.
OVER THE CENTURIES, HUMANITY CONQUERS THE GALAXY IN THE NAME OF SHIRE --
-- ESTABLISHING THE RANSHI EMPIRE.
MANKIND IS DESTINED TO RULE THE UNIVERSE, CABLE. IT'S A GLORIOUS DESTINY, AND YOU CAN MAKE IT HAPPEN.
IN OUR TIMELINE, NATHAN, YOU FAILED. SHIRE DIED. BUT HIS MESSAGE OF PEACE, LOVE AND HARMONY LIVED ON.
OVER THE CENTURIES, HIS WORDS REMADE HUMANITY --
-- AND TURNED EARTH INTO A PARADISE OF FREEDOM AND PEACE.

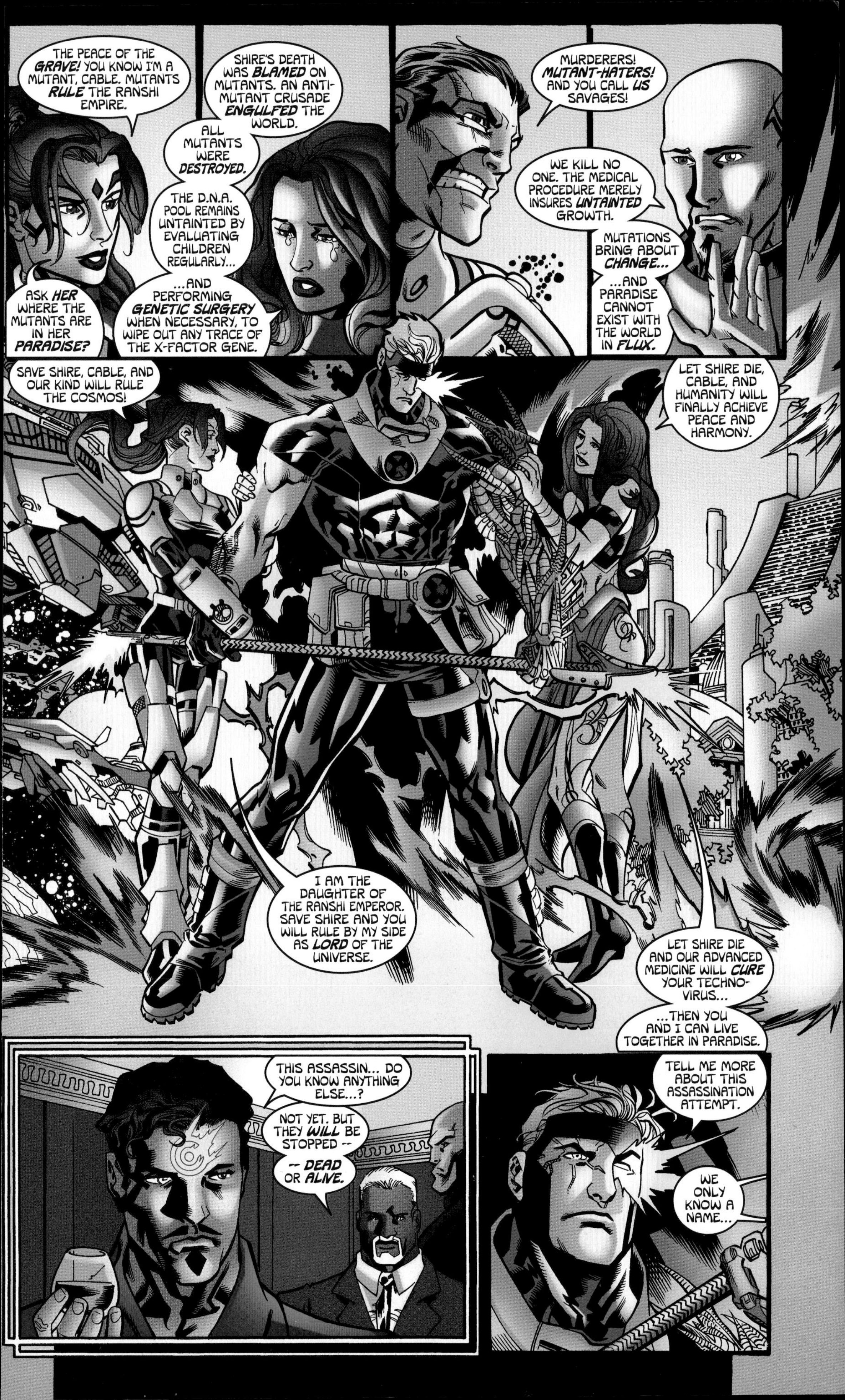
THE PEACE OF THE GRAVE! YOU KNOW I'M A MUTANT, CABLE. MUTANTS RULE THE RANSHI EMPIRE.
ASK HER WHERE THE MUTANTS ARE IN HER PARADISE?
SHIRE'S DEATH WAS BLAMED ON MUTANTS. AN ANTI-MUTANT CRUSADE ENGULFED THE WORLD.
ALL MUTANTS WERE DESTROYED.
THE D.N.A. POOL REMAINS UNTAINTED BY EVALUATING CHILDREN REGULARLY...
...AND PERFORMING GENETIC SURGERY WHEN NECESSARY, TO WIPE OUT ANY TRACE OF THE X-FACTOR GENE.
MURDERERS! MUTANT-HATERS! AND YOU CALL US SAVAGES!
WE KILL NO ONE. THE MEDICAL PROCEDURE MERELY INSURES UNTAINTED GROWTH.
MUTATIONS BRING ABOUT CHANGE...
...AND PARADISE CANNOT EXIST WITH THE WORLD IN FLUX.
SAVE SHIRE, CABLE, AND OUR KIND WILL RULE THE COSMOS!
LET SHIRE DIE, CABLE, AND HUMANITY WILL FINALLY ACHIEVE PEACE AND HARMONY.
I AM THE DAUGHTER OF THE RANSHI EMPEROR. SAVE SHIRE AND YOU WILL RULE BY MY SIDE AS LORD OF THE UNIVERSE.
LET SHIRE DIE AND OUR ADVANCED MEDICINE WILL CURE YOUR TECHNO-VIRUS...
...THEN YOU AND I CAN LIVE TOGETHER IN PARADISE.
THIS ASSASSIN... DO YOU KNOW ANYTHING ELSE...?
NOT YET. BUT THEY WILL BE STOPPED --
-- DEAD OR ALIVE.
TELL ME MORE ABOUT THIS ASSASSINATION ATTEMPT.
WE ONLY KNOW A NAME...

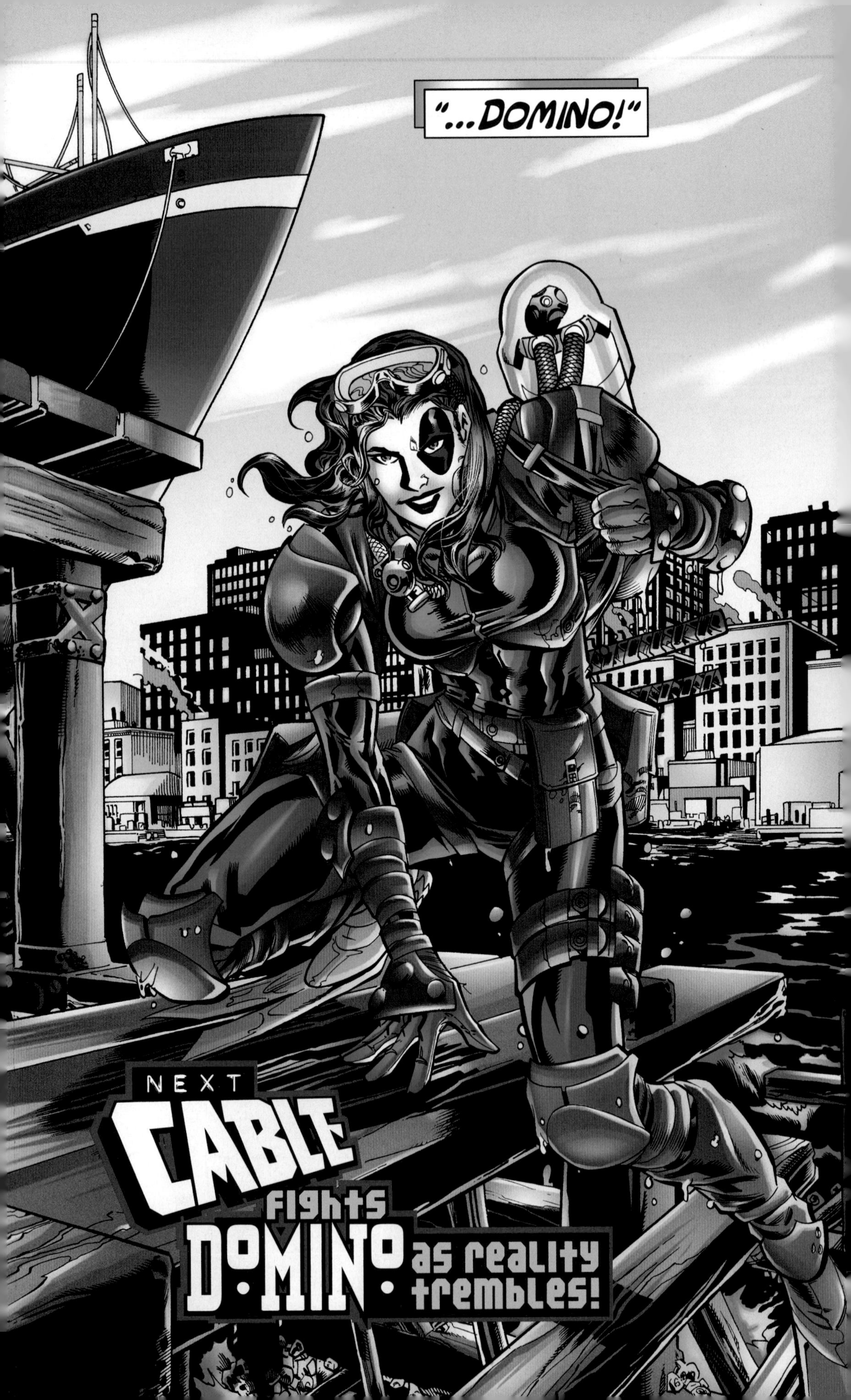
"...DOMINO!"
NEXT
CABLE
fights
DOMINO
as reality
trembles!

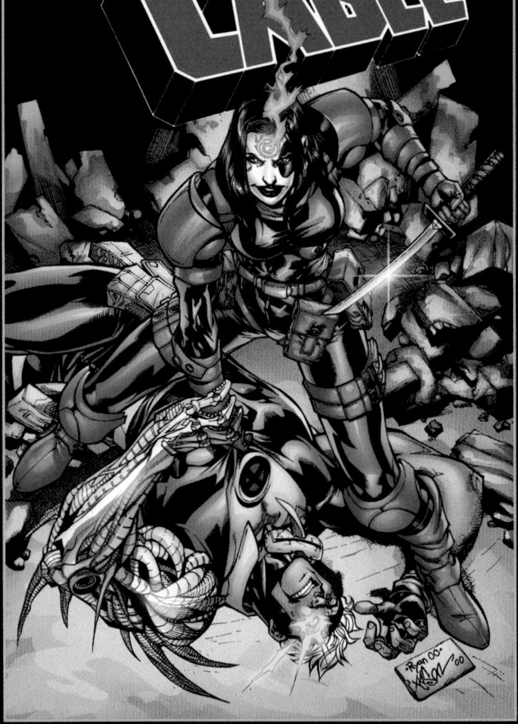
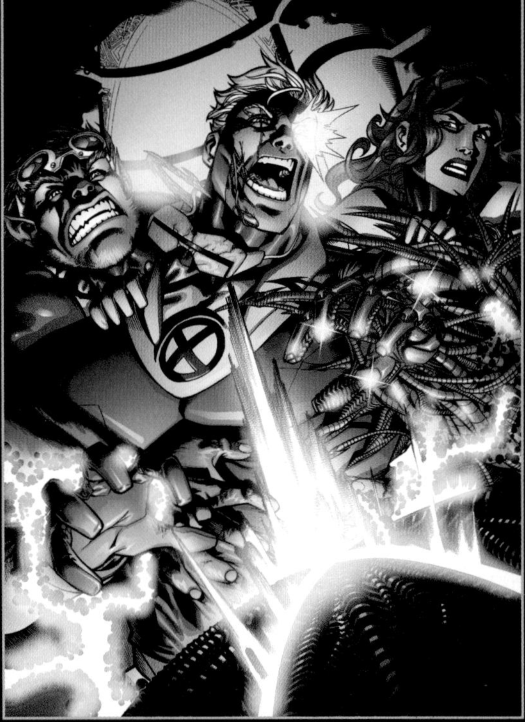
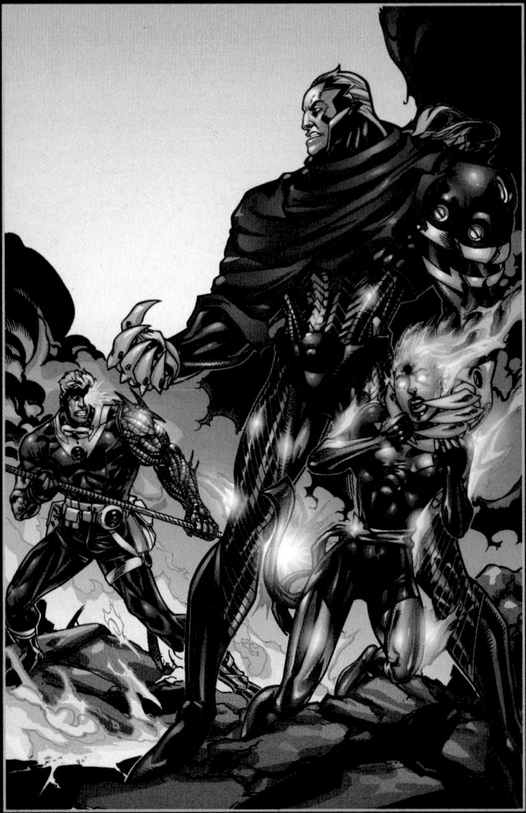

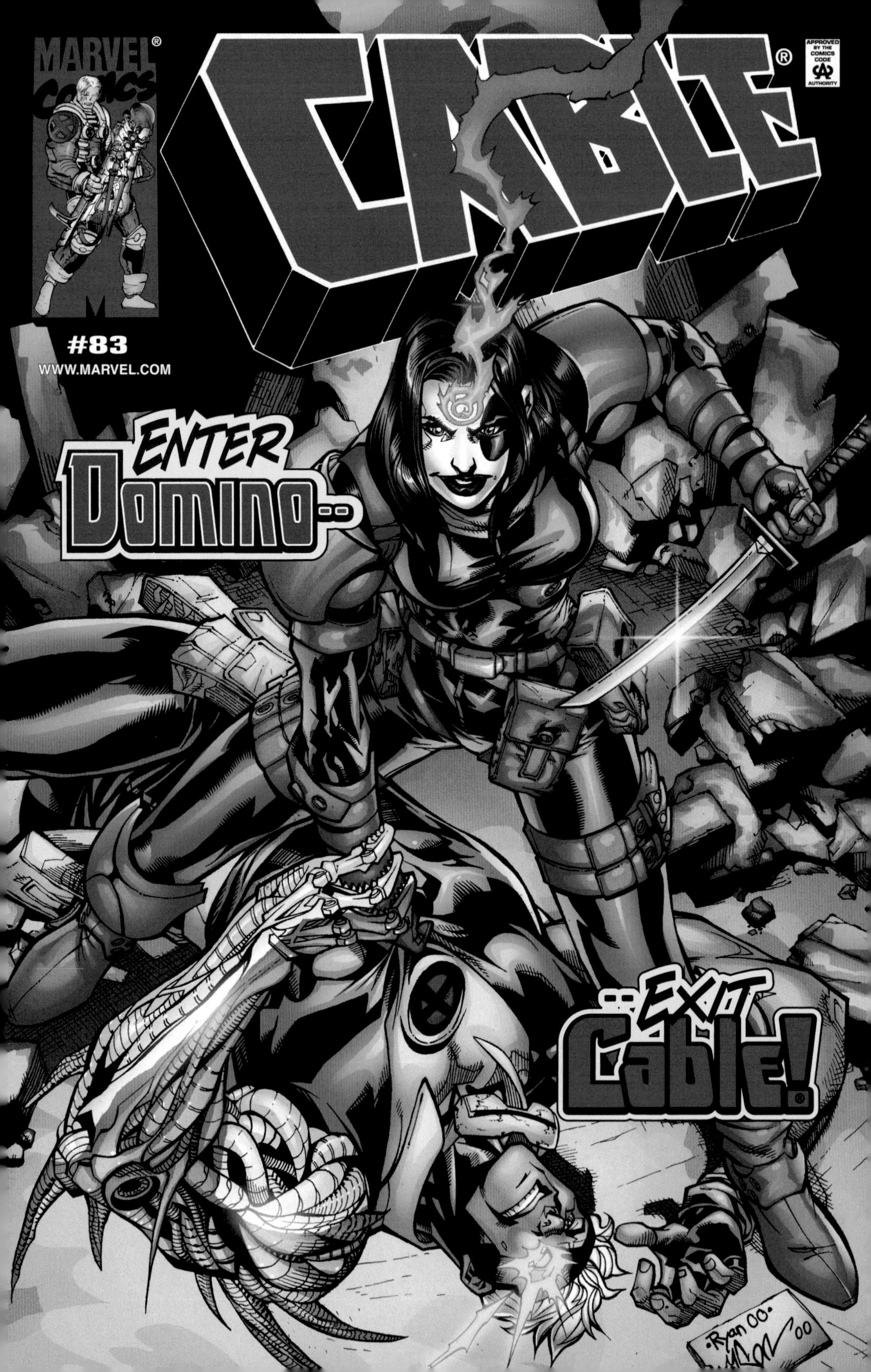
MARVEL COMICS
CABLE
APPROVED BY THE COMICS CODE AUTHORITY
#83
WWW.MARVEL.COM
ENTER Domino--
--EXIT Cable!
Ryan 00

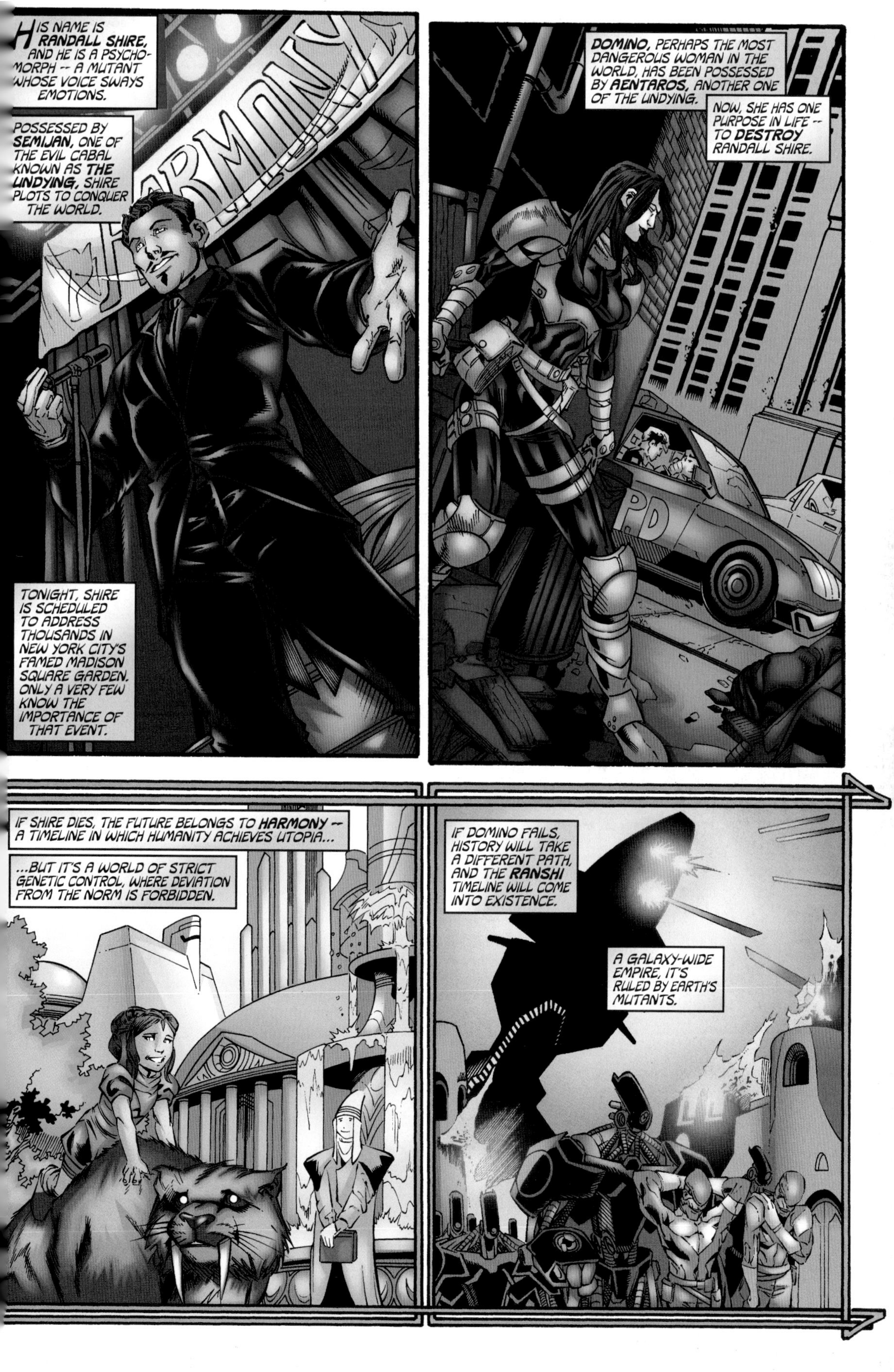
HIS NAME IS RANDALL SHIRE, AND HE IS A PSYCHOMORPH -- A MUTANT WHOSE VOICE SWAYS EMOTIONS.
POSSESSED BY SEMIJAN, ONE OF THE EVIL CABAL KNOWN AS THE UNDYING, SHIRE PLOTS TO CONQUER THE WORLD.
TONIGHT, SHIRE IS SCHEDULED TO ADDRESS THOUSANDS IN NEW YORK CITY'S FAMED MADISON SQUARE GARDEN. ONLY A VERY FEW KNOW THE IMPORTANCE OF THAT EVENT.
DOMINO, PERHAPS THE MOST DANGEROUS WOMAN IN THE WORLD, HAS BEEN POSSESSED BY AENTAROS, ANOTHER ONE OF THE UNDYING.
NOW, SHE HAS ONE PURPOSE IN LIFE -- TO DESTROY RANDALL SHIRE.
PD
IF SHIRE DIES, THE FUTURE BELONGS TO HARMONY -- A TIMELINE IN WHICH HUMANITY ACHIEVES UTOPIA...
...BUT IT'S A WORLD OF STRICT GENETIC CONTROL, WHERE DEVIATION FROM THE NORM IS FORBIDDEN.
IF DOMINO FAILS, HISTORY WILL TAKE A DIFFERENT PATH, AND THE RANSHI TIMELINE WILL COME INTO EXISTENCE.
A GALAXY-WIDE EMPIRE, IT'S RULED BY EARTH'S MUTANTS.

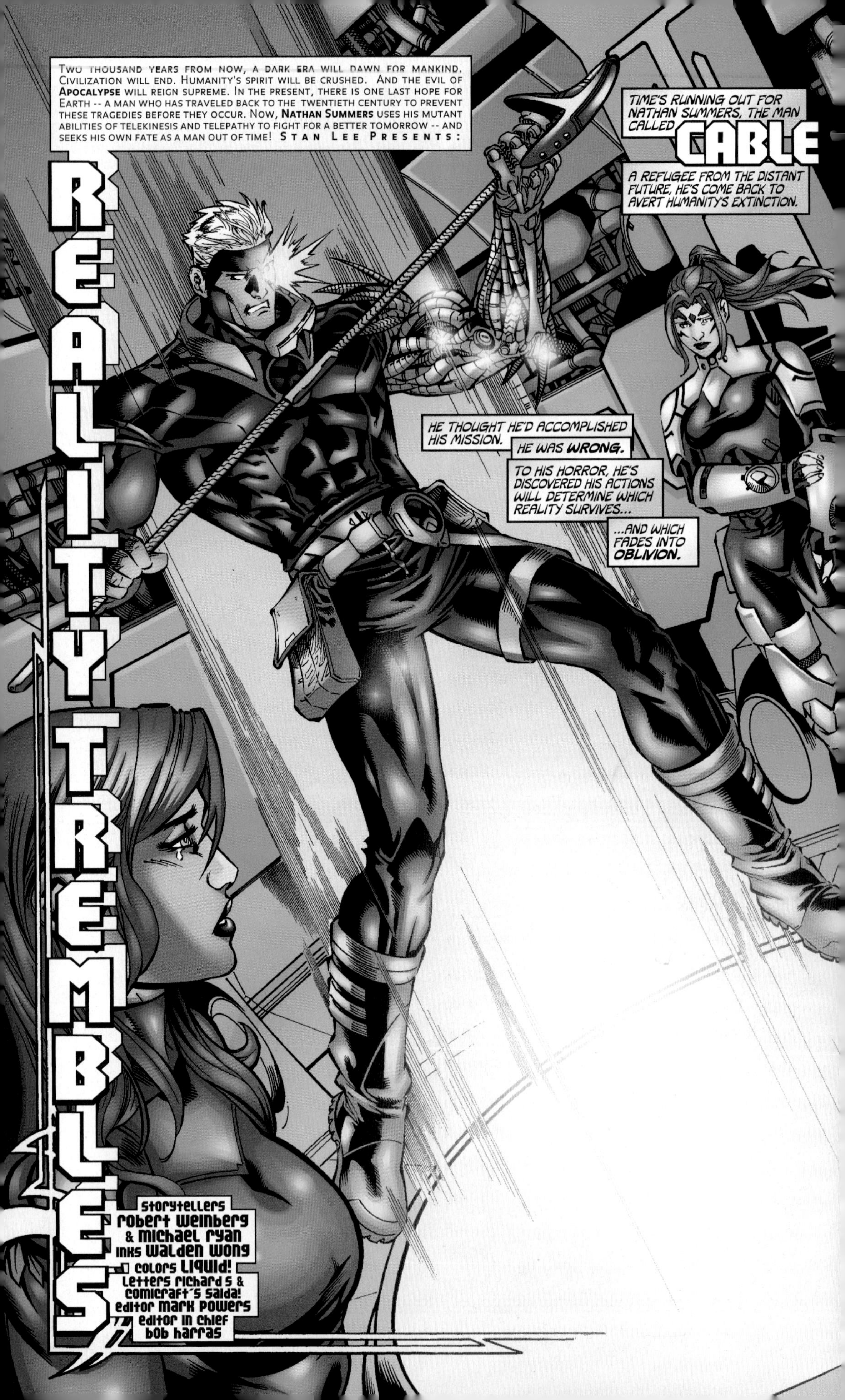
Two thousand years from now, a dark era will dawn for mankind. Civilization will end. Humanity's spirit will be crushed. And the evil of Apocalypse will reign supreme. In the present, there is one last hope for Earth -- a man who has traveled back to the twentieth century to prevent these tragedies before they occur. Now, Nathan Summers uses his mutant abilities of telekinesis and telepathy to fight for a better tomorrow -- and seeks his own fate as a man out of time! Stan Lee Presents:
TIME'S RUNNING OUT FOR NATHAN SUMMERS, THE MAN CALLED
CABLE
A REFUGEE FROM THE DISTANT FUTURE, HE'S COME BACK TO AVERT HUMANITY'S EXTINCTION.
REALITY TREMBLES
HE THOUGHT HE'D ACCOMPLISHED HIS MISSION.
HE WAS WRONG.
TO HIS HORROR, HE'S DISCOVERED HIS ACTIONS WILL DETERMINE WHICH REALITY SURVIVES...
...AND WHICH FADES INTO OBLIVION.
storytellers robert weinberg & michael ryan
inks walden wong
colors liquid!
letters richard s & comicraft's saida!
editor mark powers
editor in chief bob harras

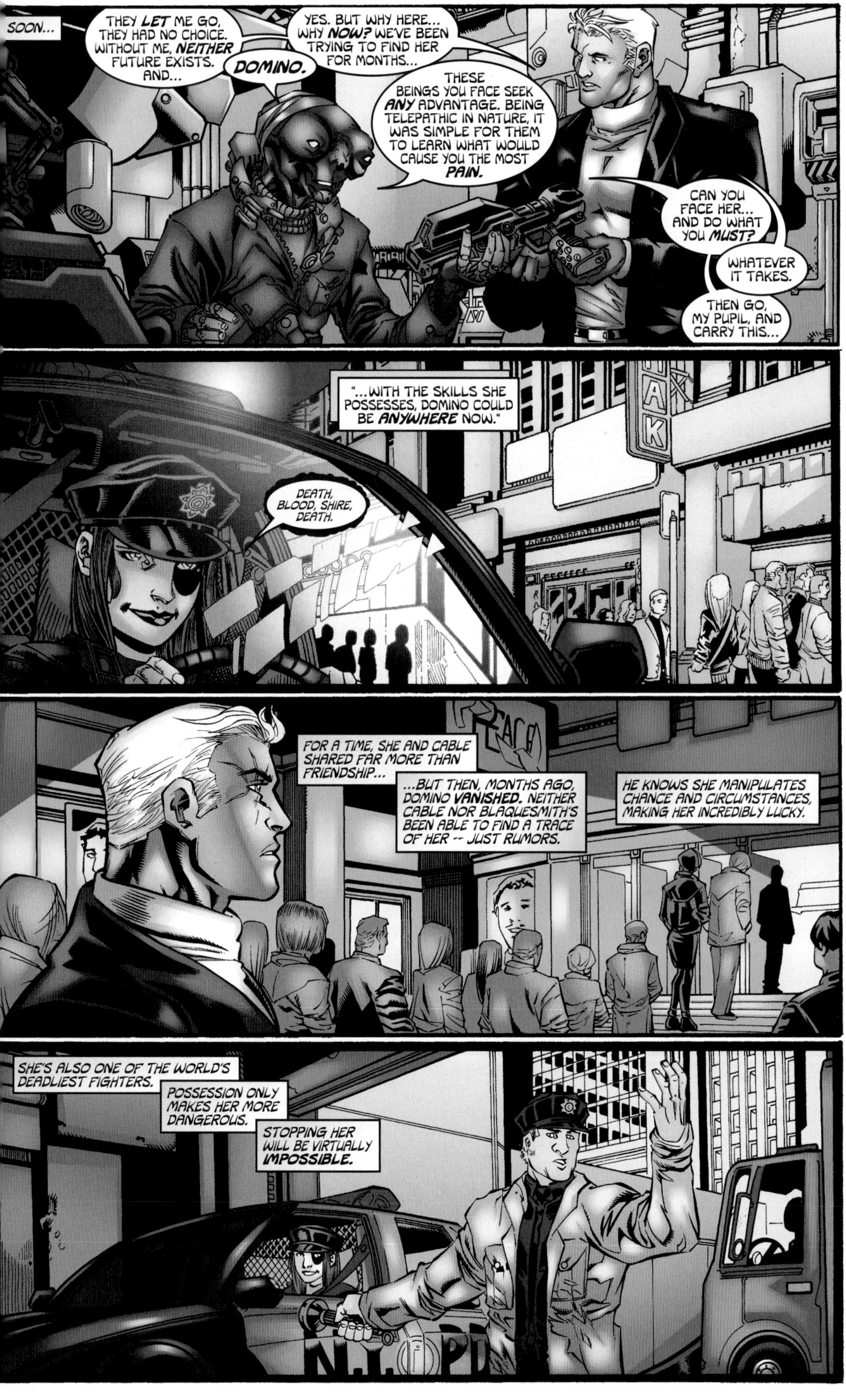

SOON...
THEY LET ME GO, THEY HAD NO CHOICE. WITHOUT ME, NEITHER FUTURE EXISTS. AND...
DOMINO.
YES. BUT WHY HERE... WHY NOW? WE'VE BEEN TRYING TO FIND HER FOR MONTHS...
THESE BEINGS YOU FACE SEEK ANY ADVANTAGE. BEING TELEPATHIC IN NATURE, IT WAS SIMPLE FOR THEM TO LEARN WHAT WOULD CAUSE YOU THE MOST PAIN.
CAN YOU FACE HER... AND DO WHAT YOU MUST?
WHATEVER IT TAKES.
THEN GO, MY PUPIL, AND CARRY THIS...
"...WITH THE SKILLS SHE POSSESSES, DOMINO COULD BE ANYWHERE NOW."
DEATH, BLOOD, SHIRE, DEATH.
FOR A TIME, SHE AND CABLE SHARED FAR MORE THAN FRIENDSHIP...
...BUT THEN, MONTHS AGO, DOMINO VANISHED. NEITHER CABLE NOR BLAQUESMITH'S BEEN ABLE TO FIND A TRACE OF HER -- JUST RUMORS.
HE KNOWS SHE MANIPULATES CHANCE AND CIRCUMSTANCES, MAKING HER INCREDIBLY LUCKY.
SHE'S ALSO ONE OF THE WORLD'S DEADLIEST FIGHTERS.
POSSESSION ONLY MAKES HER MORE DANGEROUS.
STOPPING HER WILL BE VIRTUALLY IMPOSSIBLE.

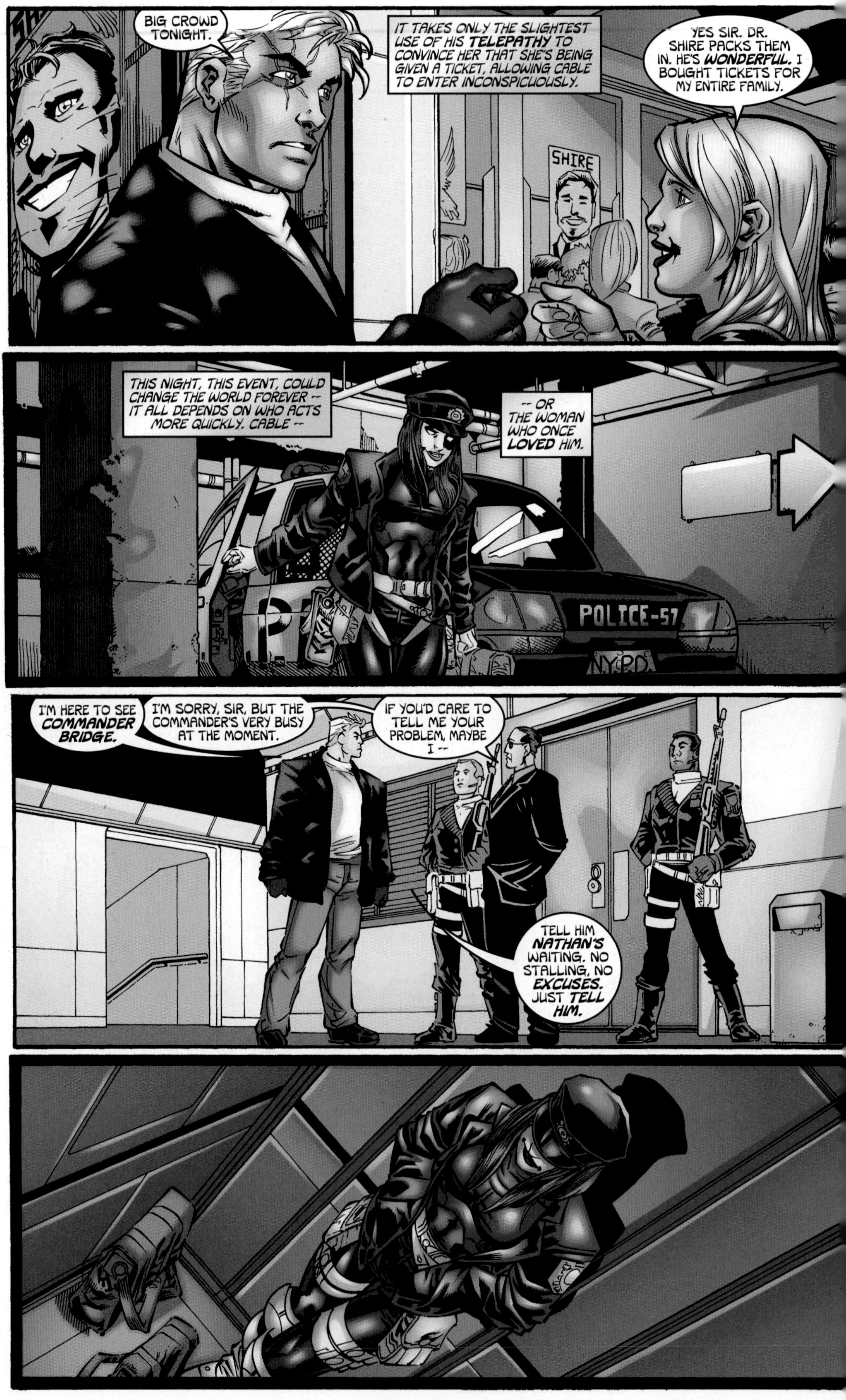
BIG CROWD TONIGHT.
IT TAKES ONLY THE SLIGHTEST USE OF HIS TELEPATHY TO CONVINCE HER THAT SHE'S BEING GIVEN A TICKET, ALLOWING CABLE TO ENTER INCONSPICUOUSLY.
YES SIR. DR. SHIRE PACKS THEM IN. HE'S WONDERFUL. I BOUGHT TICKETS FOR MY ENTIRE FAMILY.
SHIRE
THIS NIGHT, THIS EVENT, COULD CHANGE THE WORLD FOREVER -- IT ALL DEPENDS ON WHO ACTS MORE QUICKLY. CABLE --
-- OR THE WOMAN WHO ONCE LOVED HIM.
POLICE-57
NY.P.D.
I'M HERE TO SEE COMMANDER BRIDGE.
I'M SORRY, SIR, BUT THE COMMANDER'S VERY BUSY AT THE MOMENT.
IF YOU'D CARE TO TELL ME YOUR PROBLEM, MAYBE I --
TELL HIM NATHAN'S WAITING. NO STALLING, NO EXCUSES. JUST TELL HIM.

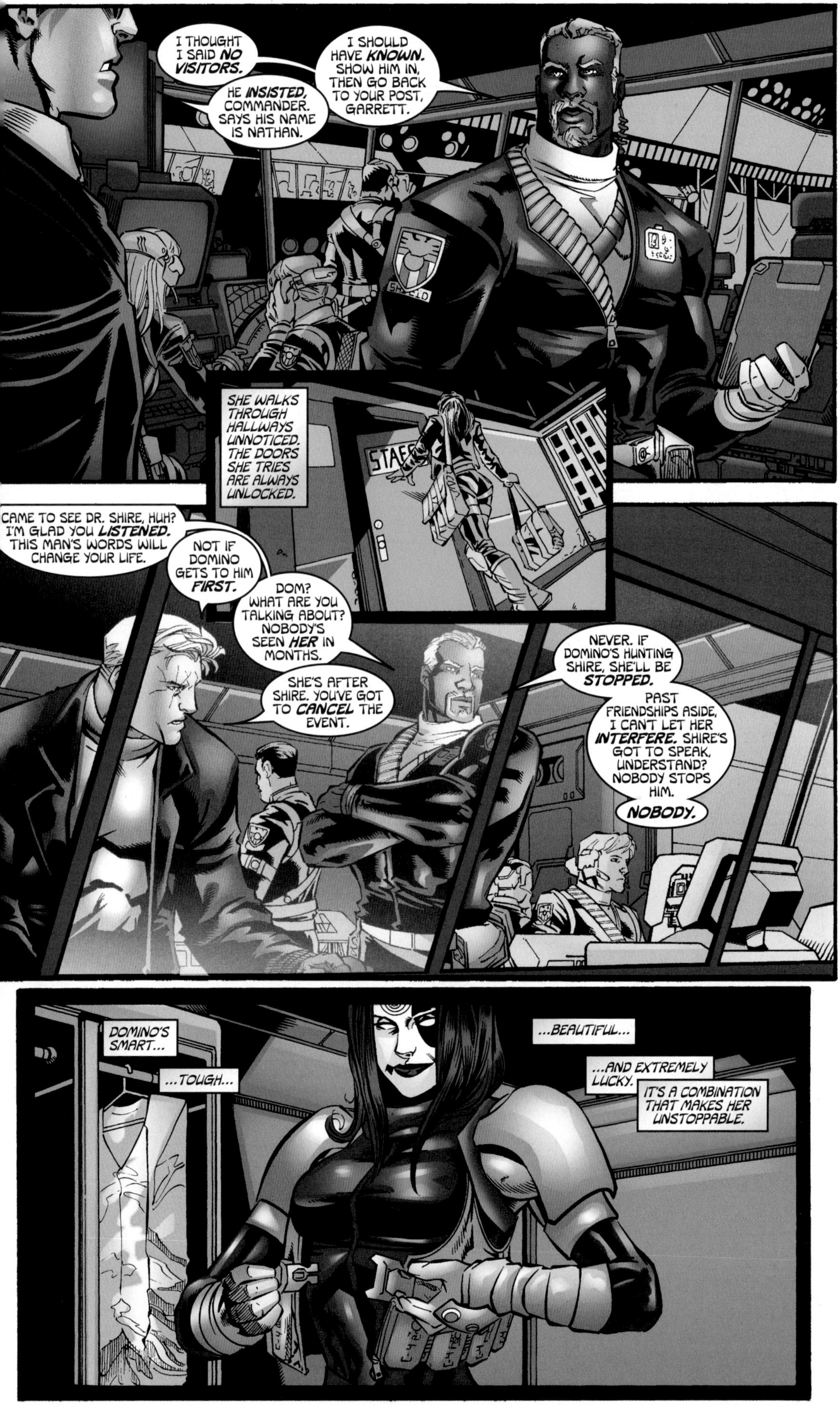

I THOUGHT I SAID NO VISITORS.
HE INSISTED, COMMANDER. SAYS HIS NAME IS NATHAN.
I SHOULD HAVE KNOWN. SHOW HIM IN, THEN GO BACK TO YOUR POST, GARRETT.
SHE WALKS THROUGH HALLWAYS UNNOTICED. THE DOORS SHE TRIES ARE ALWAYS UNLOCKED.
CAME TO SEE DR. SHIRE, HUH? I'M GLAD YOU LISTENED. THIS MAN'S WORDS WILL CHANGE YOUR LIFE.
NOT IF DOMINO GETS TO HIM FIRST.
DOM? WHAT ARE YOU TALKING ABOUT? NOBODY'S SEEN HER IN MONTHS.
SHE'S AFTER SHIRE. YOU'VE GOT TO CANCEL THE EVENT.
NEVER. IF DOMINO'S HUNTING SHIRE, SHE'LL BE STOPPED.
PAST FRIENDSHIPS ASIDE, I CAN'T LET HER INTERFERE. SHIRE'S GOT TO SPEAK, UNDERSTAND? NOBODY STOPS HIM.
NOBODY.
DOMINO'S SMART...
...TOUGH...
...BEAUTIFUL...
...AND EXTREMELY LUCKY.
IT'S A COMBINATION THAT MAKES HER UNSTOPPABLE.

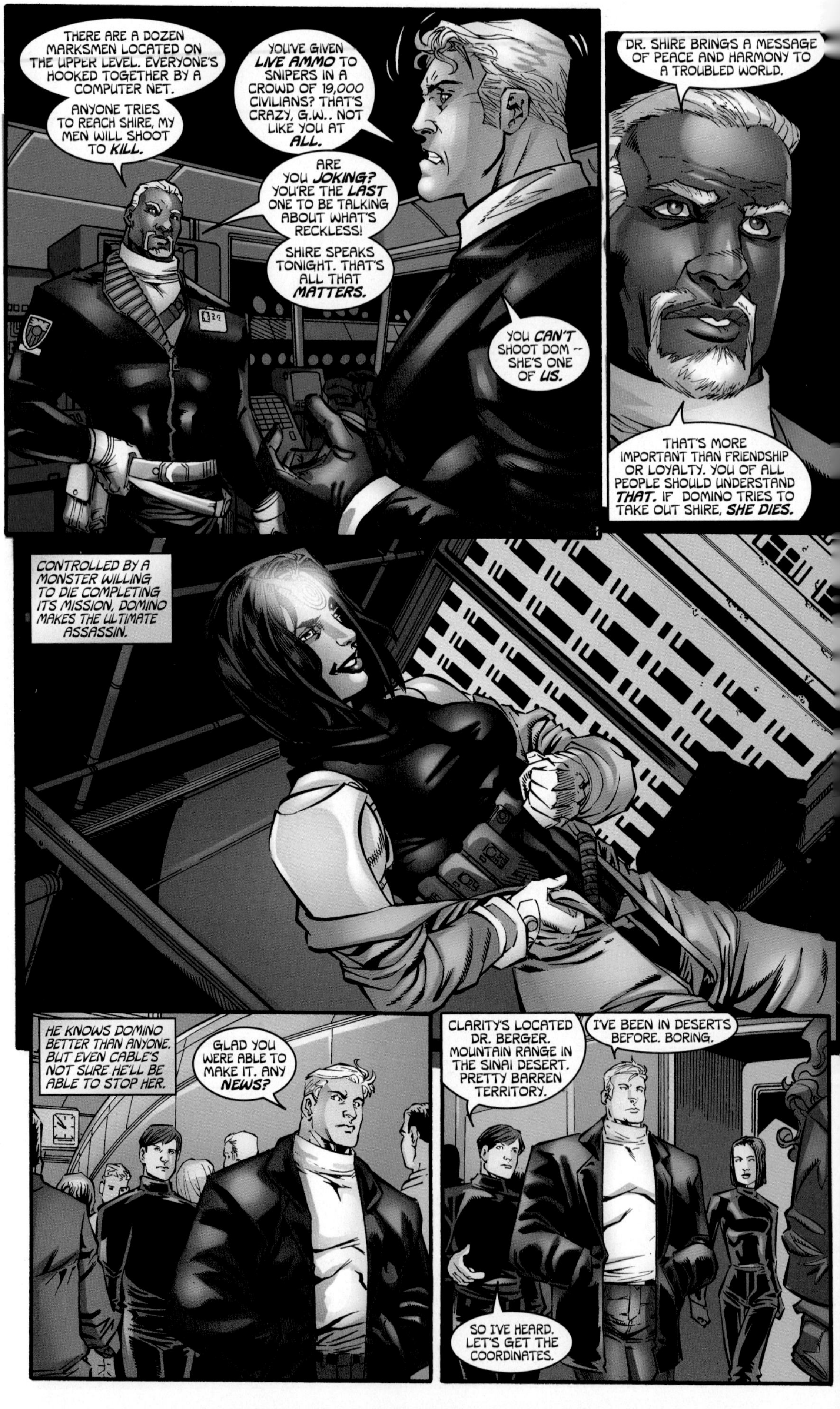

THERE ARE A DOZEN MARKSMEN LOCATED ON THE UPPER LEVEL. EVERYONE'S HOOKED TOGETHER BY A COMPUTER NET.
ANYONE TRIES TO REACH SHIRE, MY MEN WILL SHOOT TO KILL.
YOU'VE GIVEN LIVE AMMO TO SNIPERS IN A CROWD OF 19,000 CIVILIANS? THAT'S CRAZY, G.W.. NOT LIKE YOU AT ALL.
ARE YOU JOKING? YOU'RE THE LAST ONE TO BE TALKING ABOUT WHAT'S RECKLESS!
SHIRE SPEAKS TONIGHT. THAT'S ALL THAT MATTERS.
YOU CAN'T SHOOT DOM -- SHE'S ONE OF US.
DR. SHIRE BRINGS A MESSAGE OF PEACE AND HARMONY TO A TROUBLED WORLD.
THAT'S MORE IMPORTANT THAN FRIENDSHIP OR LOYALTY. YOU OF ALL PEOPLE SHOULD UNDERSTAND THAT. IF DOMINO TRIES TO TAKE OUT SHIRE, SHE DIES.
CONTROLLED BY A MONSTER WILLING TO DIE COMPLETING ITS MISSION, DOMINO MAKES THE ULTIMATE ASSASSIN.
HE KNOWS DOMINO BETTER THAN ANYONE. BUT EVEN CABLE'S NOT SURE HE'LL BE ABLE TO STOP HER.
GLAD YOU WERE ABLE TO MAKE IT. ANY NEWS?
CLARITY'S LOCATED DR. BERGER. MOUNTAIN RANGE IN THE SINAI DESERT. PRETTY BARREN TERRITORY.
I'VE BEEN IN DESERTS BEFORE. BORING.
SO I'VE HEARD. LET'S GET THE COORDINATES.

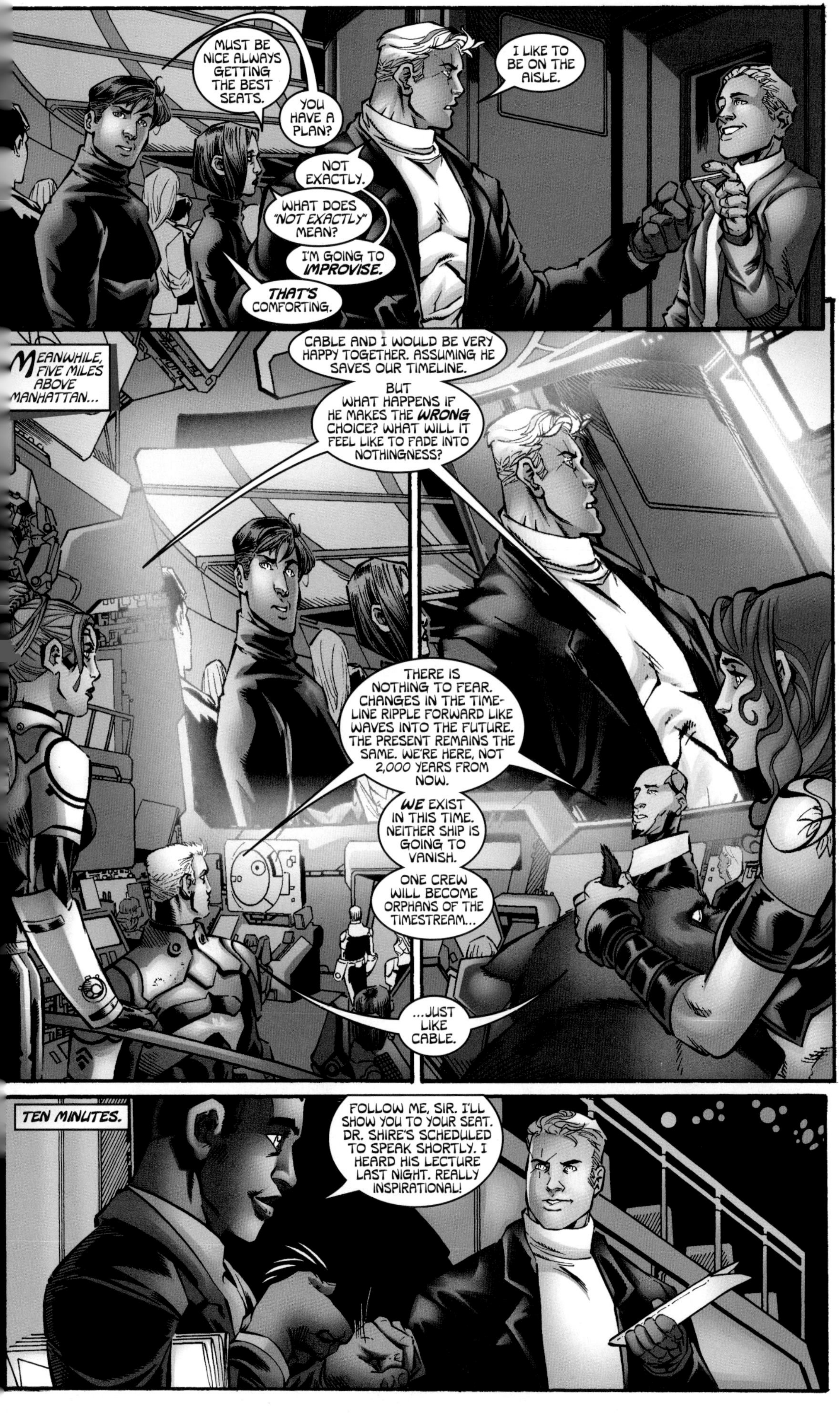
MUST BE NICE ALWAYS GETTING THE BEST SEATS.
I LIKE TO BE ON THE AISLE.
YOU HAVE A PLAN?
NOT EXACTLY.
WHAT DOES "NOT EXACTLY" MEAN?
I'M GOING TO IMPROVISE.
THAT'S COMFORTING.
MEANWHILE, FIVE MILES ABOVE MANHATTAN...
CABLE AND I WOULD BE VERY HAPPY TOGETHER. ASSUMING HE SAVES OUR TIMELINE.
BUT WHAT HAPPENS IF HE MAKES THE WRONG CHOICE? WHAT WILL IT FEEL LIKE TO FADE INTO NOTHINGNESS?
THERE IS NOTHING TO FEAR. CHANGES IN THE TIME-LINE RIPPLE FORWARD LIKE WAVES INTO THE FUTURE. THE PRESENT REMAINS THE SAME. WE'RE HERE, NOT 2,000 YEARS FROM NOW.
WE EXIST IN THIS TIME. NEITHER SHIP IS GOING TO VANISH.
ONE CREW WILL BECOME ORPHANS OF THE TIMESTREAM...
...JUST LIKE CABLE.
TEN MINUTES.
FOLLOW ME, SIR. I'LL SHOW YOU TO YOUR SEAT. DR. SHIRE'S SCHEDULED TO SPEAK SHORTLY. I HEARD HIS LECTURE LAST NIGHT. REALLY INSPIRATIONAL!

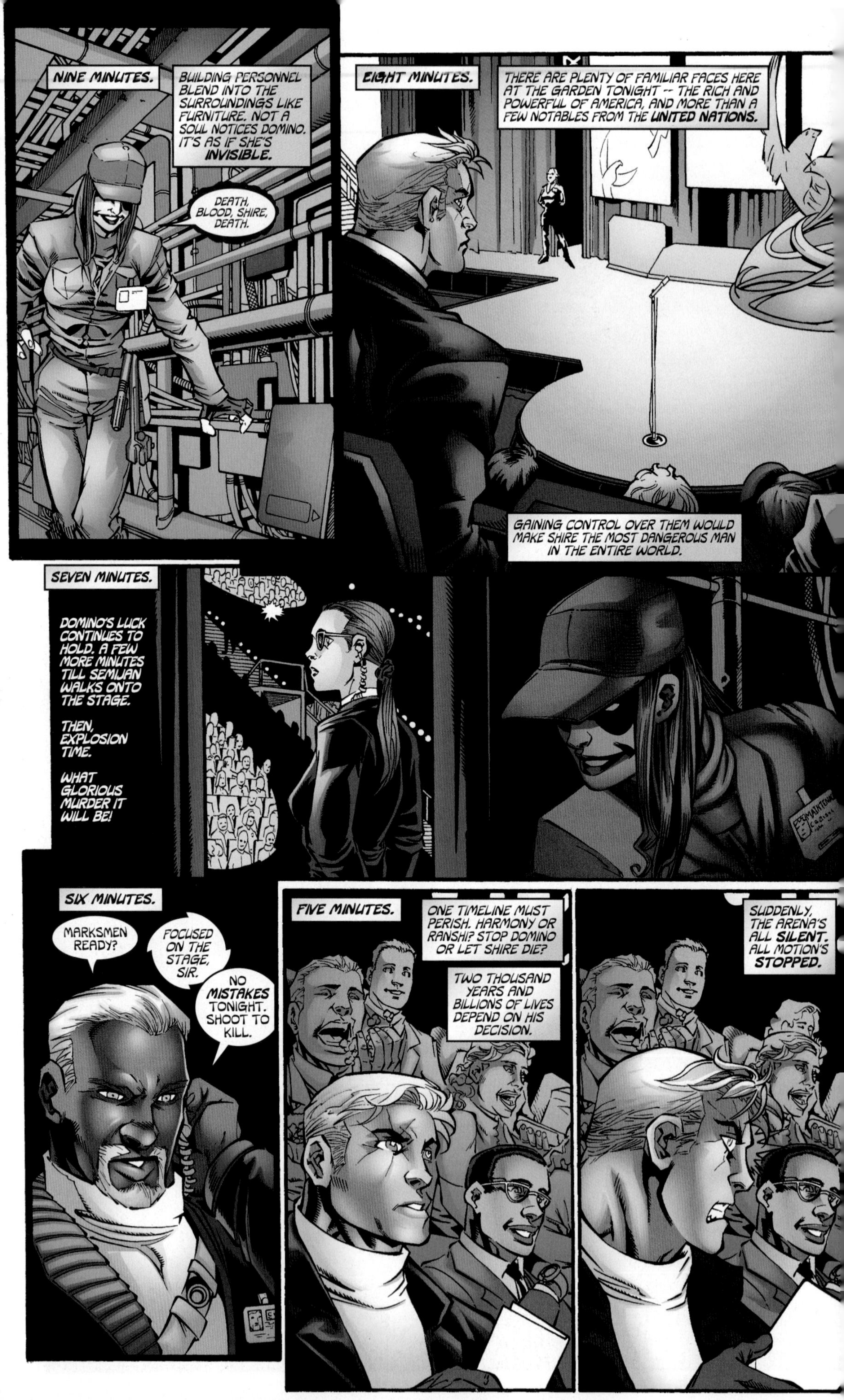
NINE MINUTES.
BUILDING PERSONNEL BLEND INTO THE SURROUNDINGS LIKE FURNITURE. NOT A SOUL NOTICES DOMINO. IT'S AS IF SHE'S INVISIBLE.
DEATH, BLOOD, SHIRE, DEATH.
EIGHT MINUTES.
THERE ARE PLENTY OF FAMILIAR FACES HERE AT THE GARDEN TONIGHT -- THE RICH AND POWERFUL OF AMERICA, AND MORE THAN A FEW NOTABLES FROM THE UNITED NATIONS.
GAINING CONTROL OVER THEM WOULD MAKE SHIRE THE MOST DANGEROUS MAN IN THE ENTIRE WORLD.
SEVEN MINUTES.
DOMINO'S LUCK CONTINUES TO HOLD. A FEW MORE MINUTES TILL SEMIJAN WALKS ONTO THE STAGE.
THEN, EXPLOSION TIME.
WHAT GLORIOUS MURDER IT WILL BE!
SIX MINUTES.
MARKSMEN READY?
FOCUSED ON THE STAGE, SIR.
NO MISTAKES TONIGHT. SHOOT TO KILL.
FIVE MINUTES.
ONE TIMELINE MUST PERISH. HARMONY OR RANSHI? STOP DOMINO OR LET SHIRE DIE?
TWO THOUSAND YEARS AND BILLIONS OF LIVES DEPEND ON HIS DECISION.
SUDDENLY, THE ARENA'S ALL SILENT. ALL MOTION'S STOPPED.

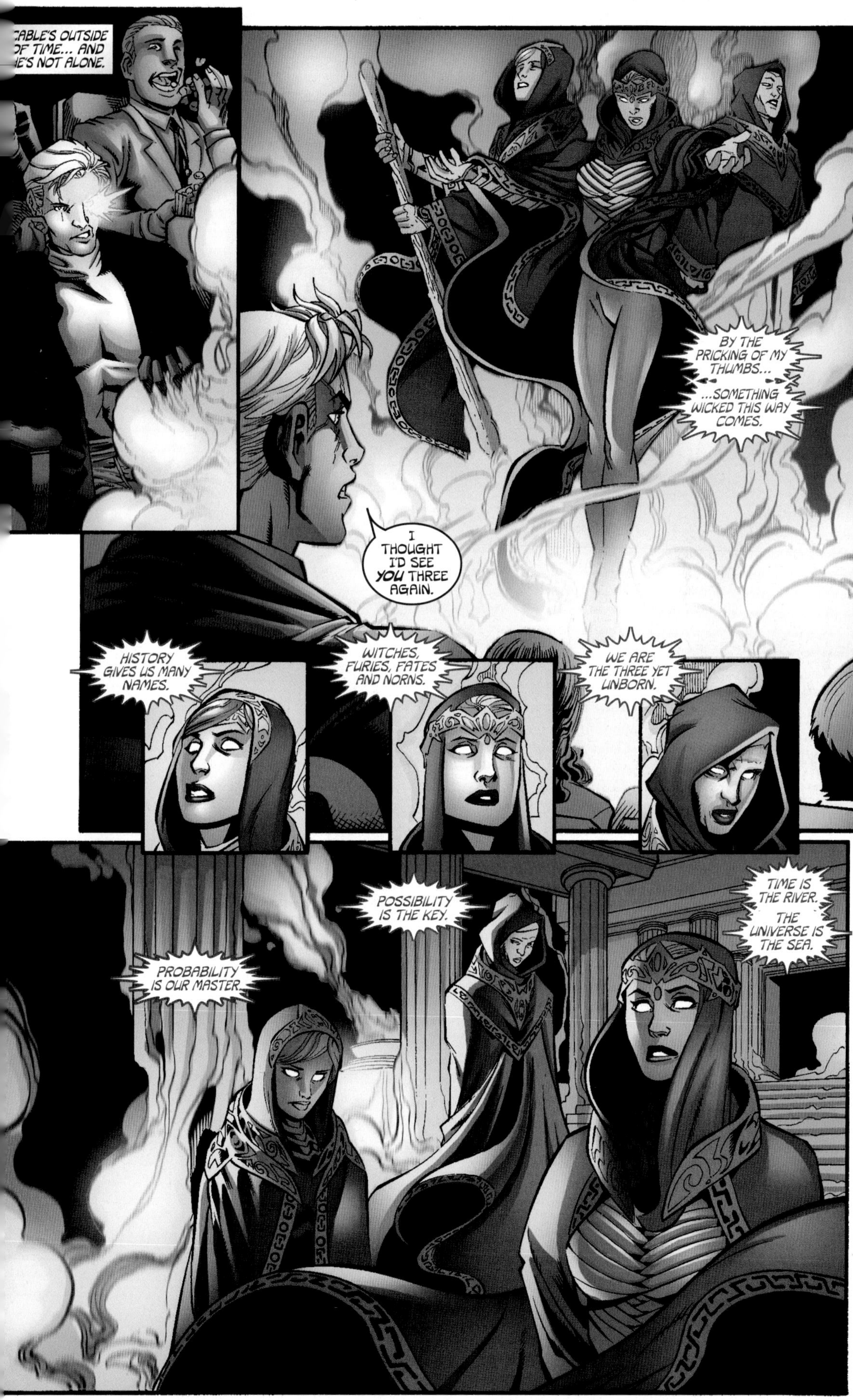

CABLE'S OUTSIDE OF TIME... AND HE'S NOT ALONE.
BY THE PRICKING OF MY THUMBS...
...SOMETHING WICKED THIS WAY COMES.
I THOUGHT I'D SEE YOU THREE AGAIN.
HISTORY GIVES US MANY NAMES.
WITCHES, FURIES, FATES AND NORNS.
WE ARE THE THREE YET UNBORN.
TIME IS THE RIVER.
THE UNIVERSE IS THE SEA.
POSSIBILITY IS THE KEY.
PROBABILITY IS OUR MASTER.

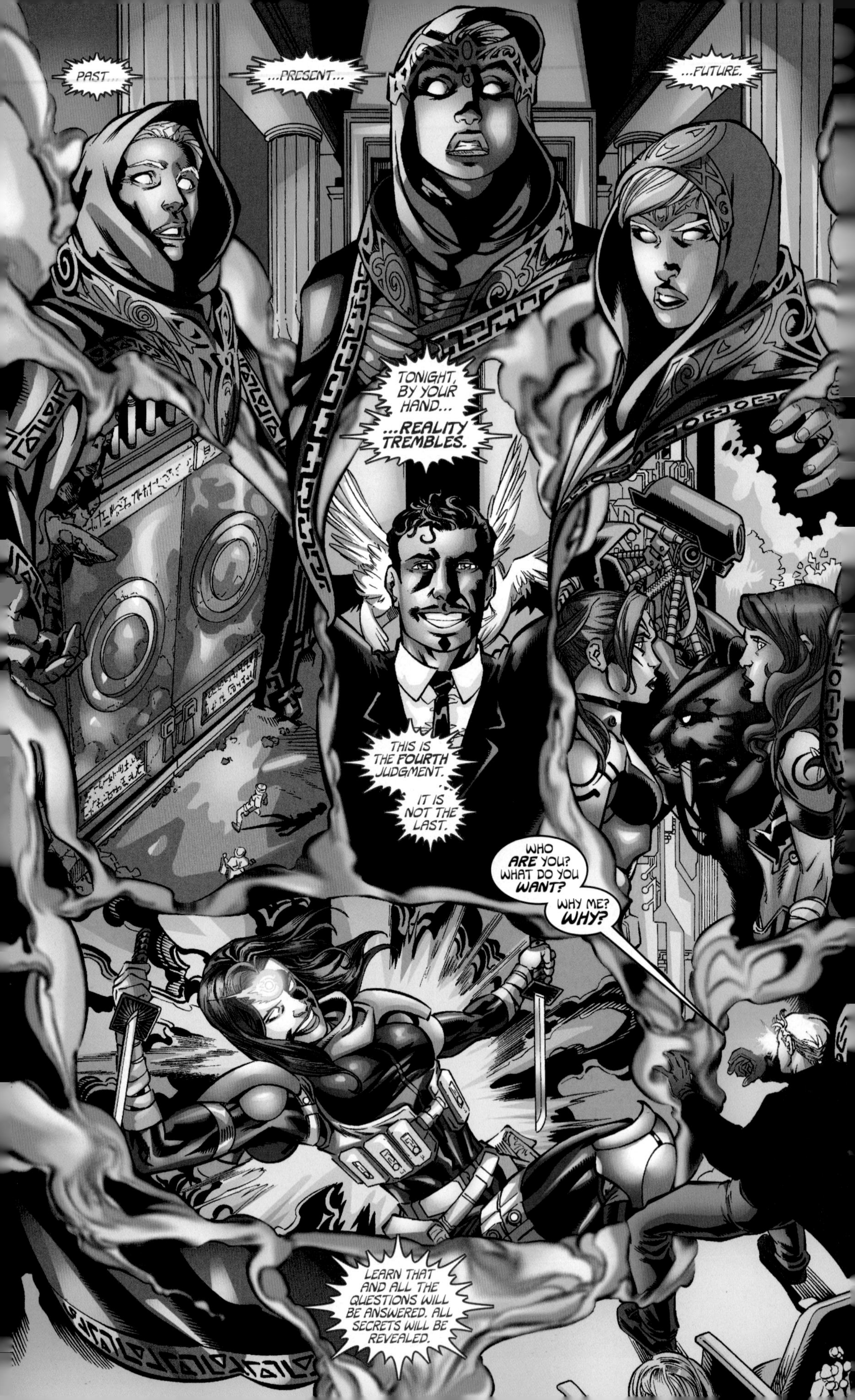
PAST...
...PRESENT...
...FUTURE.
TONIGHT, BY YOUR HAND...
...REALITY TREMBLES.
THIS IS THE FOURTH JUDGMENT.
IT IS NOT THE LAST.
WHO ARE YOU? WHAT DO YOU WANT?
WHY ME? WHY?
LEARN THAT AND ALL THE QUESTIONS WILL BE ANSWERED. ALL SECRETS WILL BE REVEALED.

FOUR MINUTES.

SOUND CHECK COMPLETE.

VIDEO SYSTEM IS WORKING FINE.

LOOKS LIKE WE'RE READY TO ROCK AND ROLL. LIGHTS GO DIM IN THIRTY SECONDS.

THEN CUE THE USUAL ANNOUNCEMENTS. GO TO BLACK ONE MINUTE BEFORE SHOW-TIME. GARRETT, AS SOON AS DR. SHIRE APPEARS, HIT THE STAGE LIGHTS.

TONIGHT, SHIRE DIES.

I'M READY.

THREE MINUTES.

I'M GOING DOWN TO THE STAGE. DOMINO'S STILL ON THE LOOSE.

ONLY WAY TO STOP HER... ...IS WITH A BULLET.

TWO MINUTES.

THE WITCHES ARE GONE AND TIME HAS RETURNED TO NORMAL. YET, A VOICE ECHOES IN CABLE'S MIND. IT'S THAT OF THE SECOND WITCH. THE WORDS MELT INTO HIS THOUGHTS.

"LEARN THAT, AND ALL QUESTIONS WILL BE ANSWERED. ALL SECRETS WILL BE REVEALED."

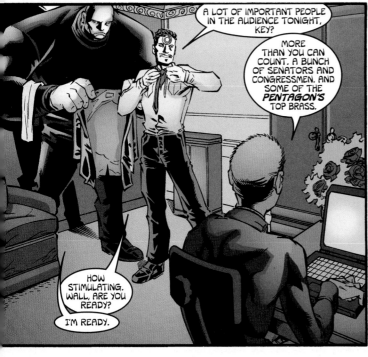

A LOT OF IMPORTANT PEOPLE IN THE AUDIENCE TONIGHT, KEY?

MORE THAN YOU CAN COUNT. A BUNCH OF SENATORS AND CONGRESSMEN. AND SOME OF THE PENTAGON'S TOP BRASS.

HOW STIMULATING. WALL, ARE YOU READY?

I'M READY.

ONE MINUTE.

LADIES AND GENTLEMEN, PLEASE WELCOME...

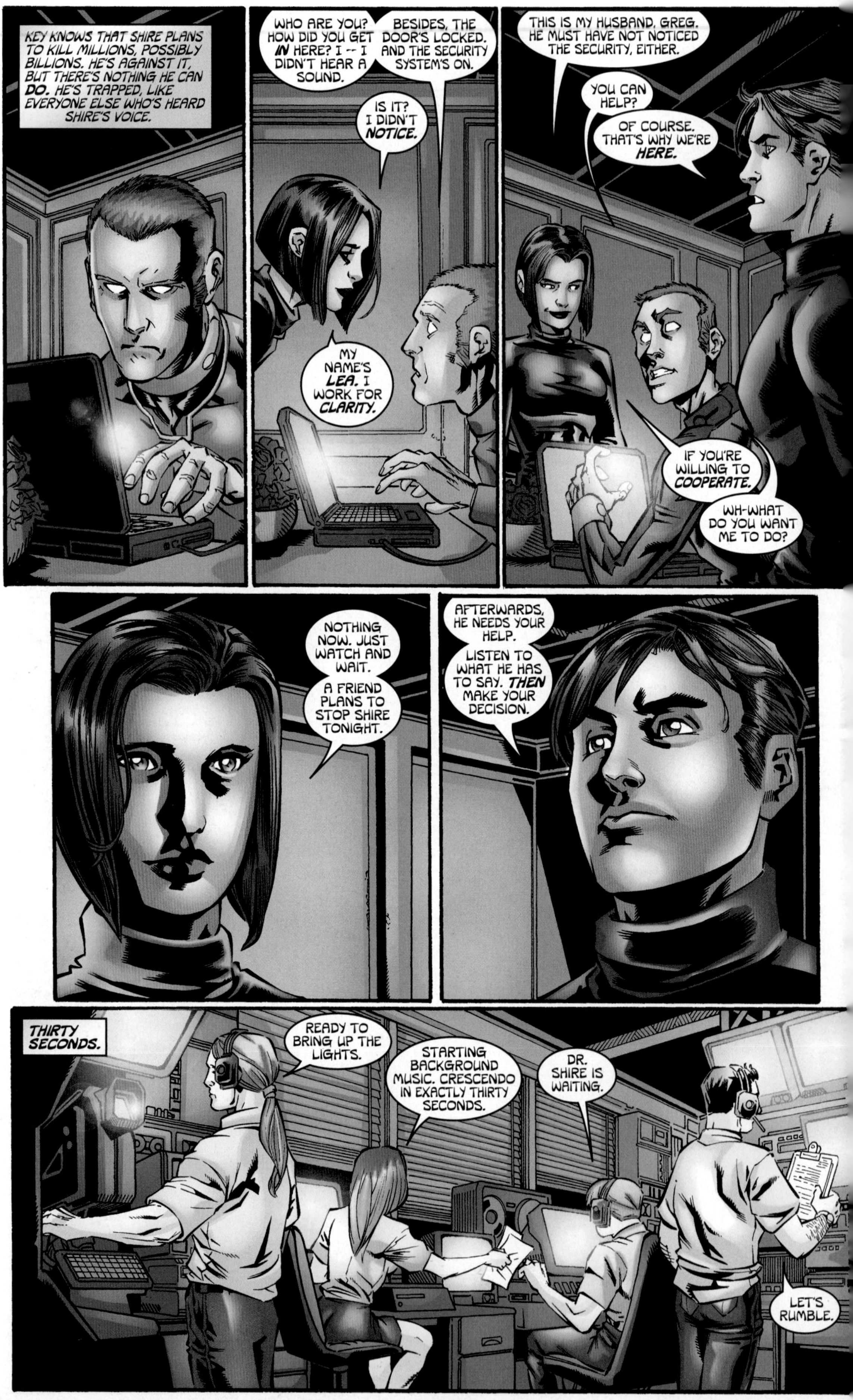

KEY KNOWS THAT SHIRE PLANS TO KILL MILLIONS, POSSIBLY BILLIONS. HE'S AGAINST IT, BUT THERE'S NOTHING HE CAN DO. HE'S TRAPPED, LIKE EVERYONE ELSE WHO'S HEARD SHIRE'S VOICE.
WHO ARE YOU? HOW DID YOU GET IN HERE? I -- I DIDN'T HEAR A SOUND.
BESIDES, THE DOOR'S LOCKED. AND THE SECURITY SYSTEM'S ON.
IS IT? I DIDN'T NOTICE.
MY NAME'S LEA. I WORK FOR CLARITY.
THIS IS MY HUSBAND, GREG. HE MUST HAVE NOT NOTICED THE SECURITY, EITHER.
YOU CAN HELP?
OF COURSE. THAT'S WHY WE'RE HERE.
IF YOU'RE WILLING TO COOPERATE.
WH-WHAT DO YOU WANT ME TO DO?
NOTHING NOW. JUST WATCH AND WAIT.
A FRIEND PLANS TO STOP SHIRE TONIGHT.
AFTERWARDS, HE NEEDS YOUR HELP.
LISTEN TO WHAT HE HAS TO SAY. THEN MAKE YOUR DECISION.
THIRTY SECONDS.
READY TO BRING UP THE LIGHTS.
STARTING BACKGROUND MUSIC. CRESCENDO IN EXACTLY THIRTY SECONDS.
DR. SHIRE IS WAITING.
LET'S RUMBLE.

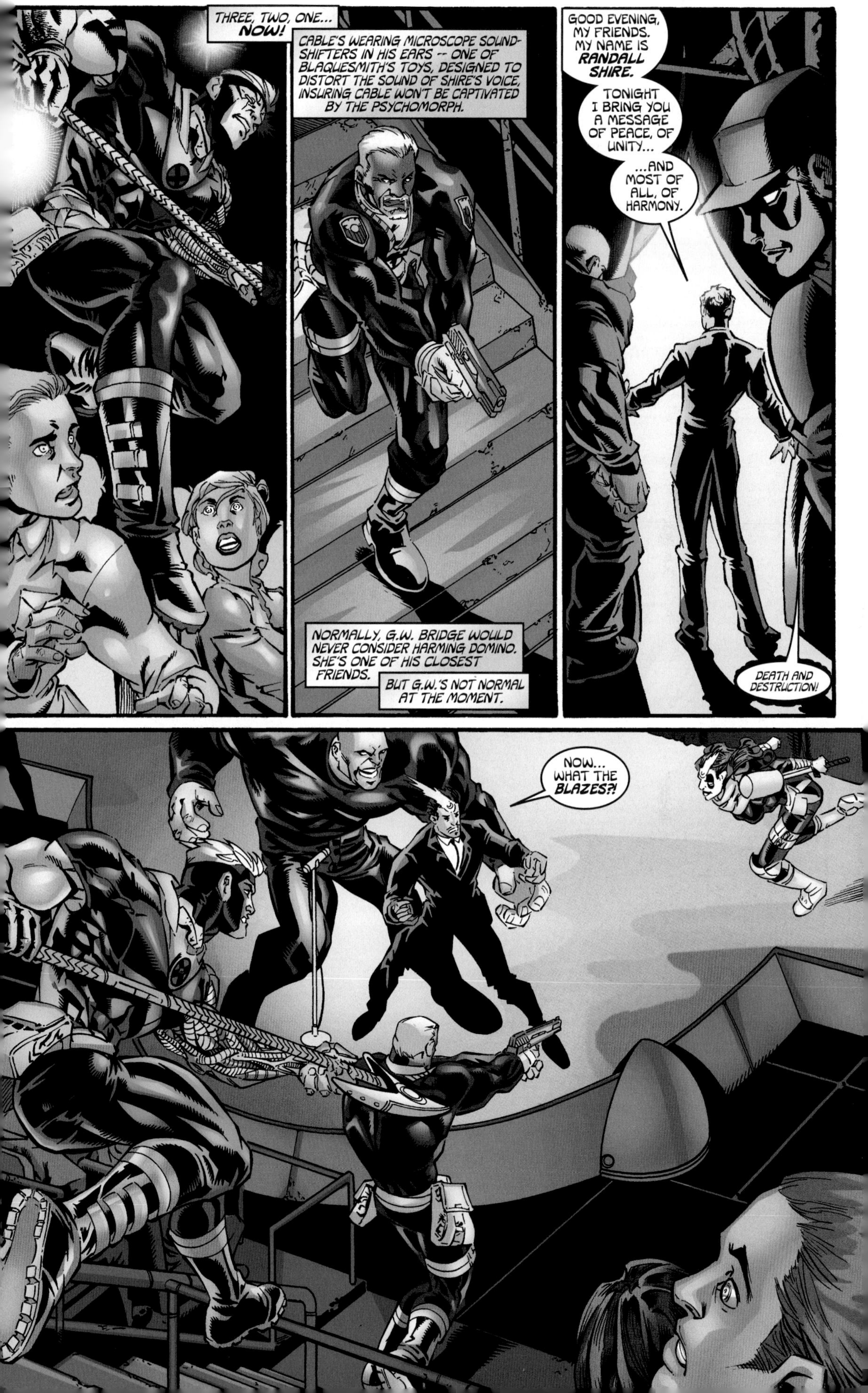
THREE, TWO, ONE... NOW!
CABLE'S WEARING MICROSCOPE SOUND-SHIFTERS IN HIS EARS -- ONE OF BLAQUESMITH'S TOYS, DESIGNED TO DISTORT THE SOUND OF SHIRE'S VOICE, INSURING CABLE WON'T BE CAPTIVATED BY THE PSYCHOMORPH.
NORMALLY, G.W. BRIDGE WOULD NEVER CONSIDER HARMING DOMINO. SHE'S ONE OF HIS CLOSEST FRIENDS.
BUT G.W.'S NOT NORMAL AT THE MOMENT.
GOOD EVENING, MY FRIENDS. MY NAME IS RANDALL SHIRE.
TONIGHT I BRING YOU A MESSAGE OF PEACE, OF UNITY...
...AND MOST OF ALL, OF HARMONY.
DEATH AND DESTRUCTION!
NOW... WHAT THE BLAZES?!

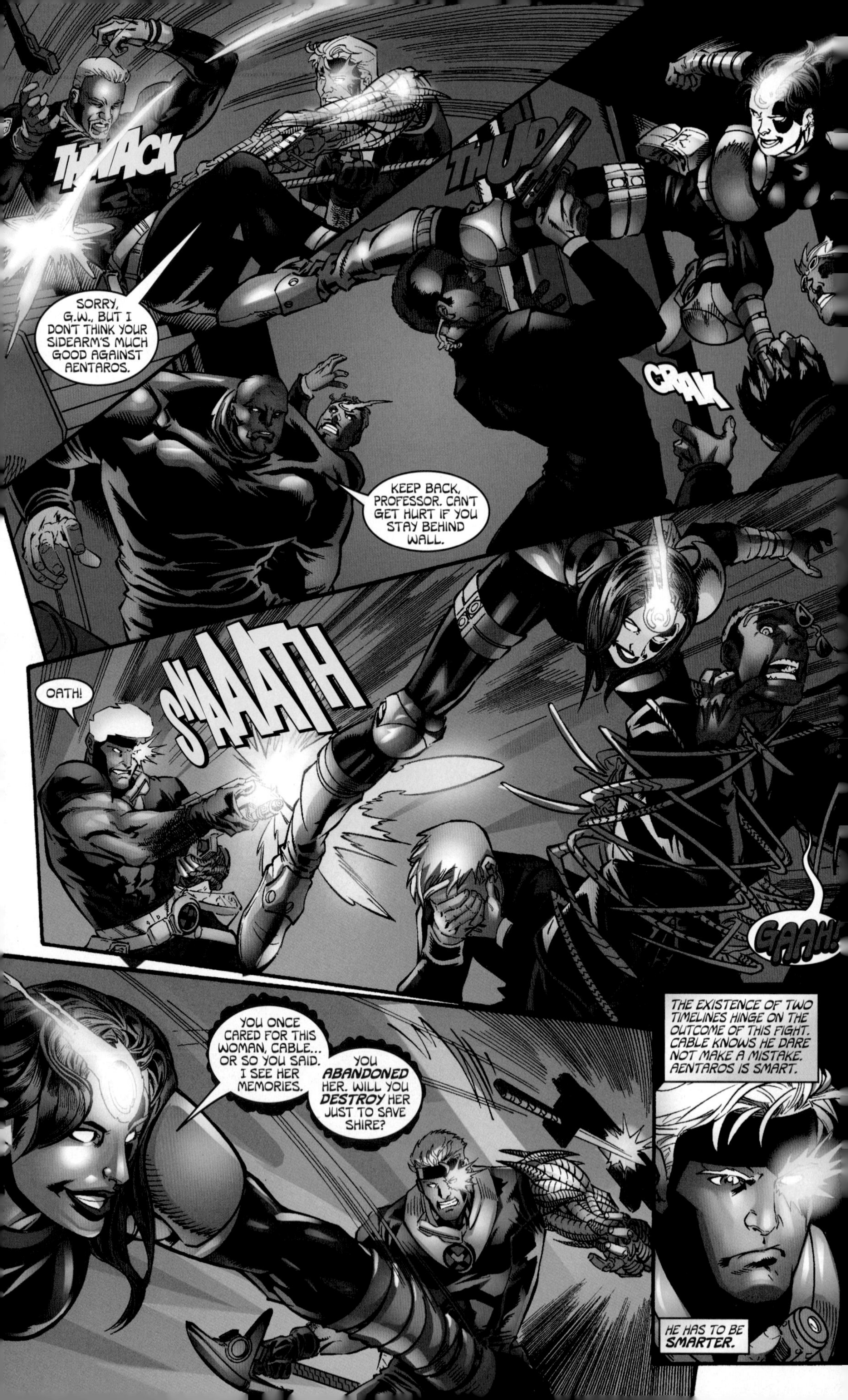
THWACK
THUD
SORRY, G.W., BUT I DON'T THINK YOUR SIDEARM'S MUCH GOOD AGAINST AENTAROS.
CRAK
KEEP BACK, PROFESSOR. CAN'T GET HURT IF YOU STAY BEHIND WALL.
OATH!
SHAAATH
GAAH!
YOU ONCE CARED FOR THIS WOMAN, CABLE... OR SO YOU SAID. I SEE HER MEMORIES.
YOU ABANDONED HER. WILL YOU DESTROY HER JUST TO SAVE SHIRE?
THE EXISTENCE OF TWO TIMELINES HINGE ON THE OUTCOME OF THIS FIGHT. CABLE KNOWS HE DARE NOT MAKE A MISTAKE. AENTAROS IS SMART.
HE HAS TO BE SMARTER.

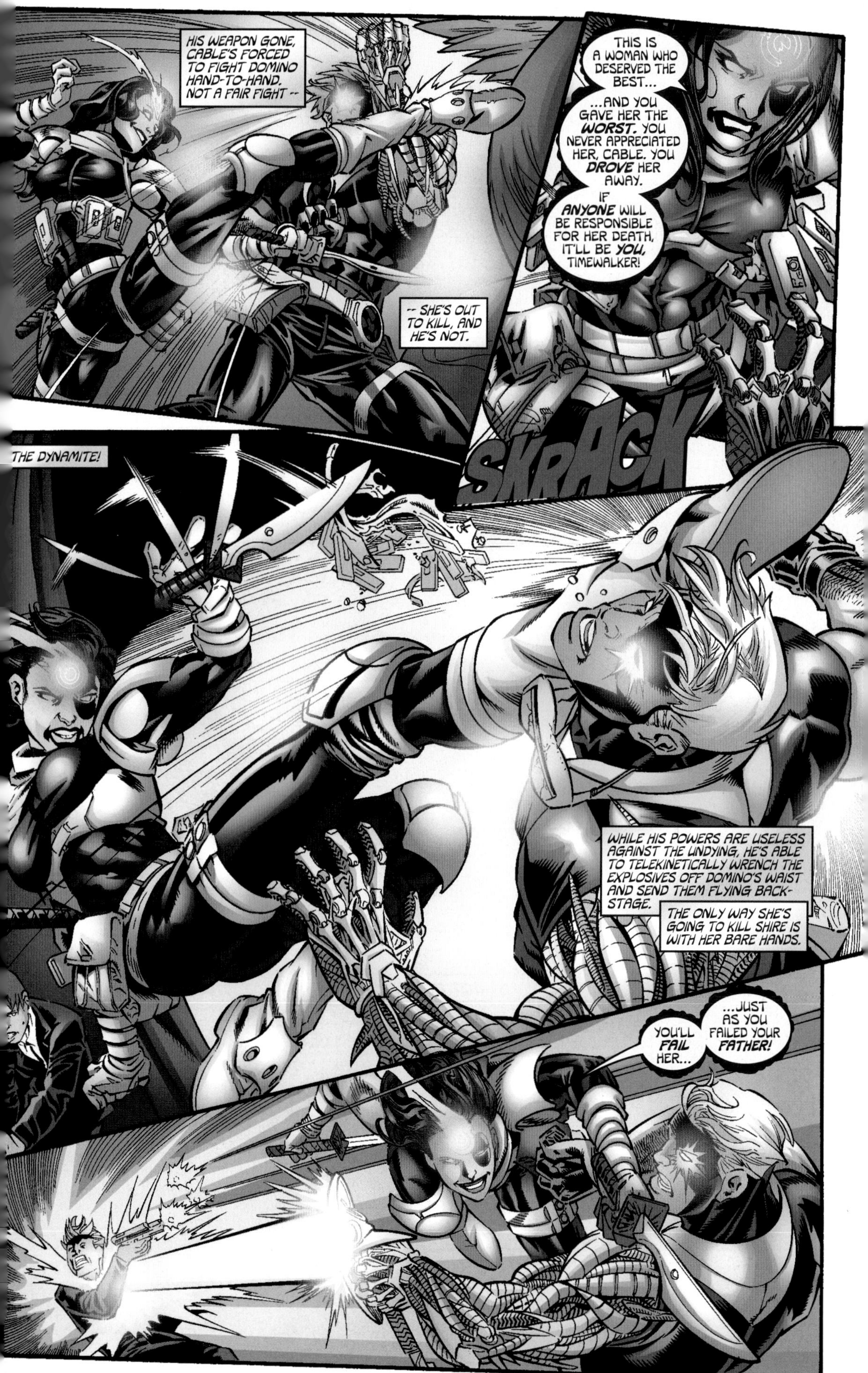
HIS WEAPON GONE, CABLE'S FORCED TO FIGHT DOMINO HAND-TO-HAND. NOT A FAIR FIGHT --
-- SHE'S OUT TO KILL, AND HE'S NOT.
THIS IS A WOMAN WHO DESERVED THE BEST...
...AND YOU GAVE HER THE WORST. YOU NEVER APPRECIATED HER, CABLE. YOU DROVE HER AWAY.
IF ANYONE WILL BE RESPONSIBLE FOR HER DEATH, IT'LL BE YOU, TIMEWALKER!
SKRACK
THE DYNAMITE!
WHILE HIS POWERS ARE USELESS AGAINST THE UNDYING, HE'S ABLE TO TELEKINETICALLY WRENCH THE EXPLOSIVES OFF DOMINO'S WAIST AND SEND THEM FLYING BACK-STAGE.
THE ONLY WAY SHE'S GOING TO KILL SHIRE IS WITH HER BARE HANDS.
YOU'LL FAIL HER...
...JUST AS YOU FAILED YOUR FATHER!

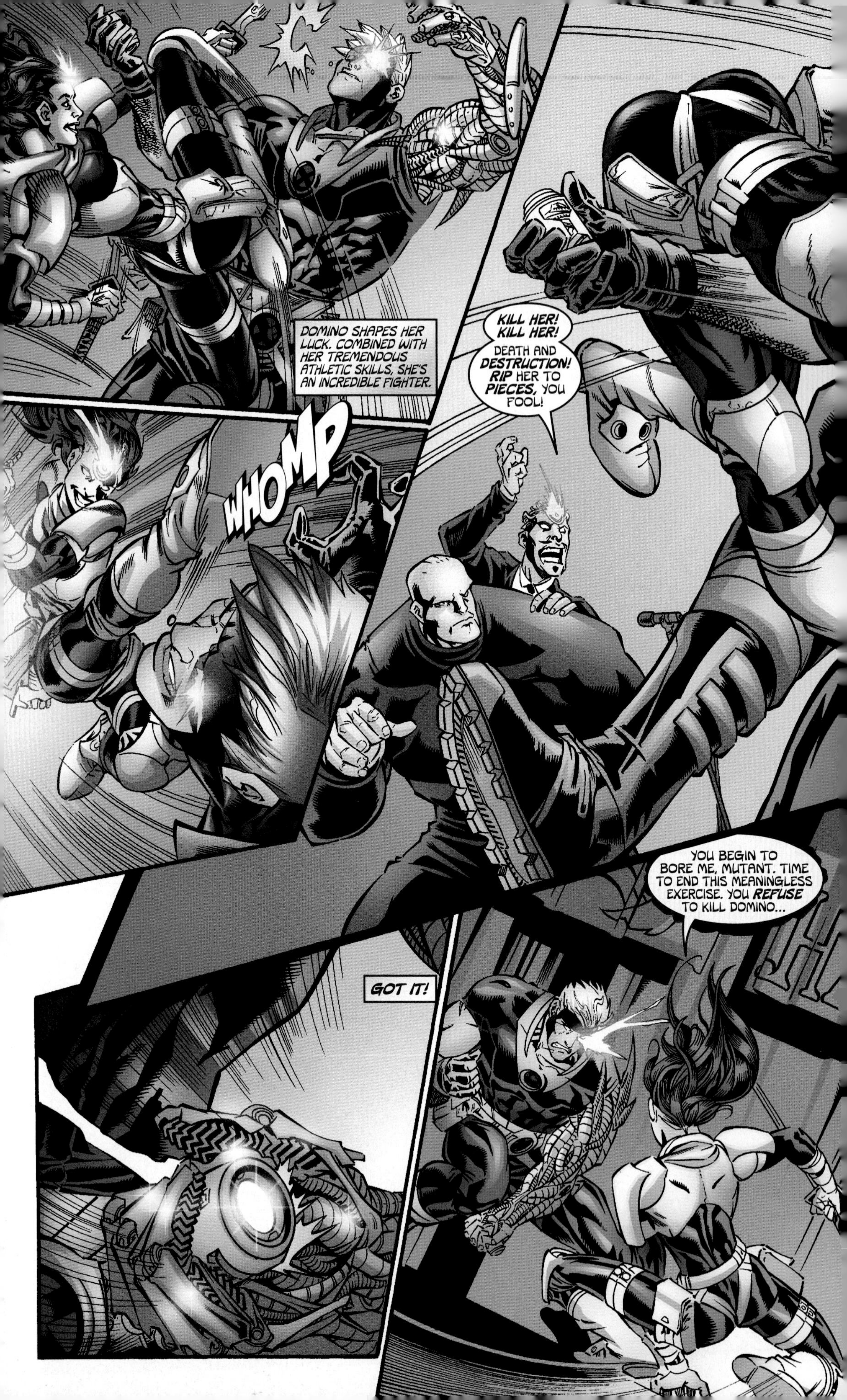

DOMINO SHAPES HER LUCK. COMBINED WITH HER TREMENDOUS ATHLETIC SKILLS, SHE'S AN INCREDIBLE FIGHTER.
KILL HER! KILL HER! DEATH AND DESTRUCTION! RIP HER TO PIECES, YOU FOOL!
WHOMP
YOU BEGIN TO BORE ME, MUTANT. TIME TO END THIS MEANINGLESS EXERCISE. YOU REFUSE TO KILL DOMINO...
GOT IT!

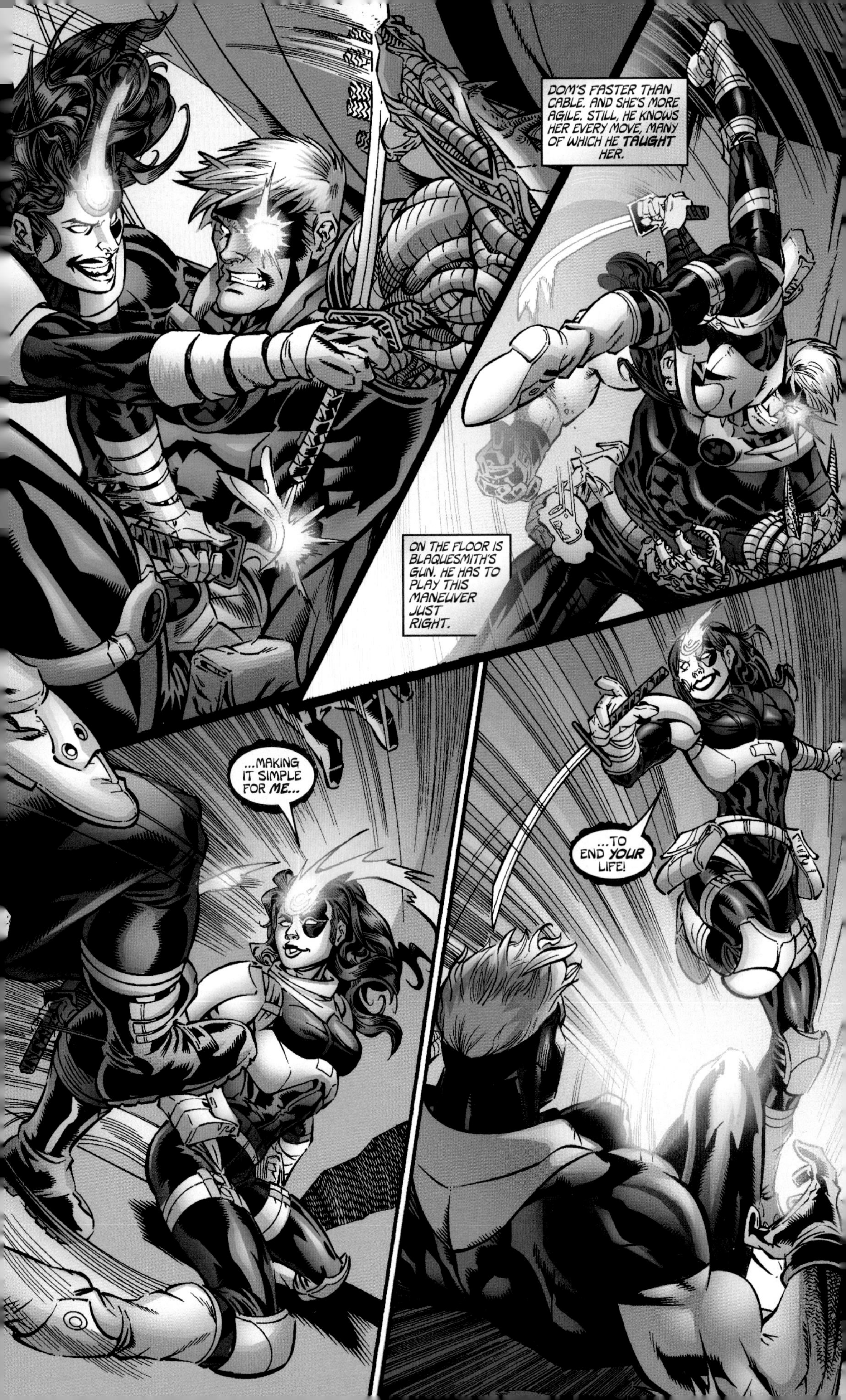
DOM'S FASTER THAN CABLE. AND SHE'S MORE AGILE. STILL, HE KNOWS HER EVERY MOVE, MANY OF WHICH HE TAUGHT HER.
ON THE FLOOR IS BLAQUESMITH'S GUN. HE HAS TO PLAY THIS MANEUVER JUST RIGHT.
...MAKING IT SIMPLE FOR ME...
...TO END YOUR LIFE!

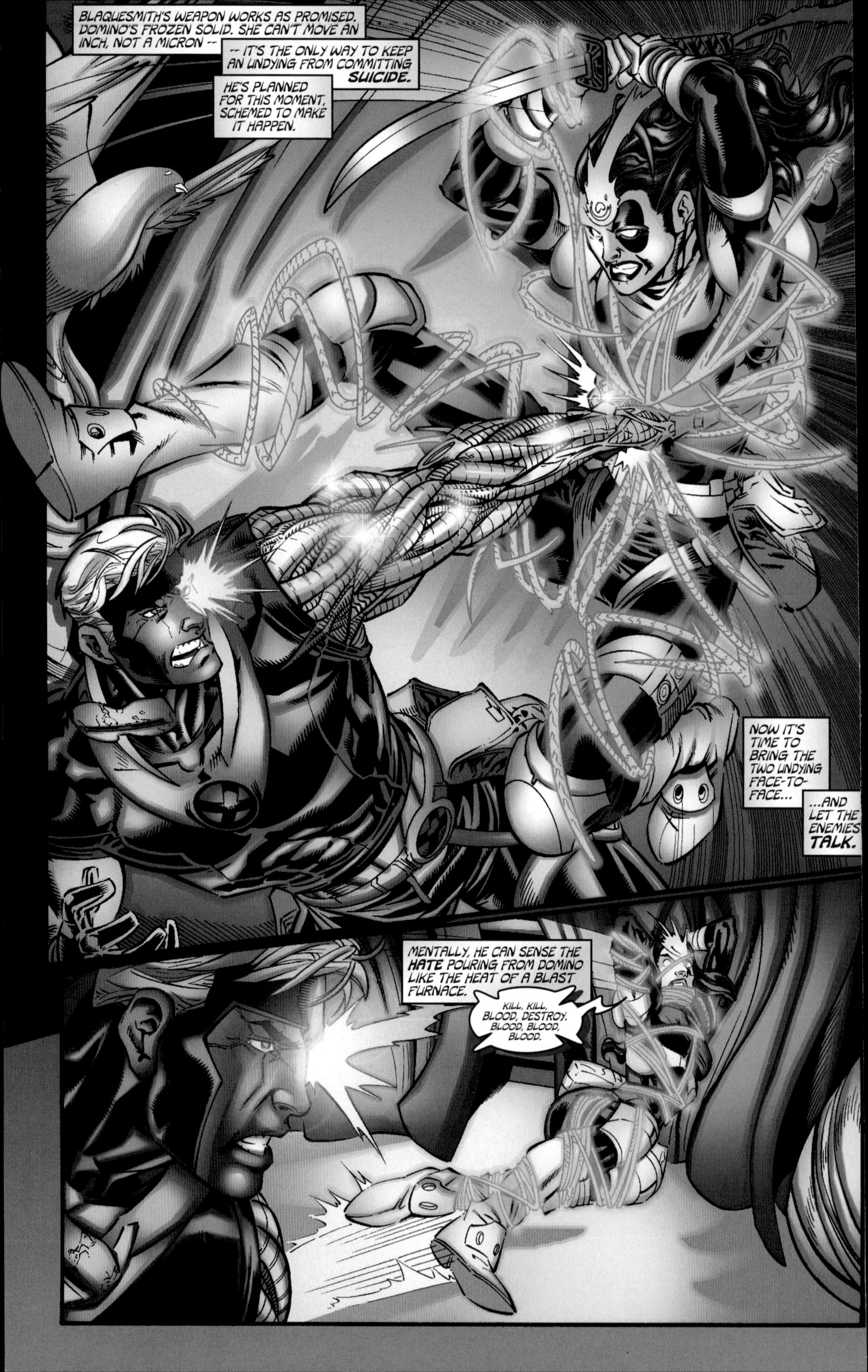
BLAQUESMITH'S WEAPON WORKS AS PROMISED. DOMINO'S FROZEN SOLID. SHE CAN'T MOVE AN INCH, NOT A MICRON --
-- IT'S THE ONLY WAY TO KEEP AN UNDYING FROM COMMITTING SUICIDE.
HE'S PLANNED FOR THIS MOMENT, SCHEMED TO MAKE IT HAPPEN.
NOW IT'S TIME TO BRING THE TWO UNDYING FACE-TO-FACE...
...AND LET THE ENEMIES TALK.
MENTALLY, HE CAN SENSE THE HATE POURING FROM DOMINO LIKE THE HEAT OF A BLAST FURNACE.
KILL, KILL, BLOOD, DESTROY. BLOOD, BLOOD, BLOOD.

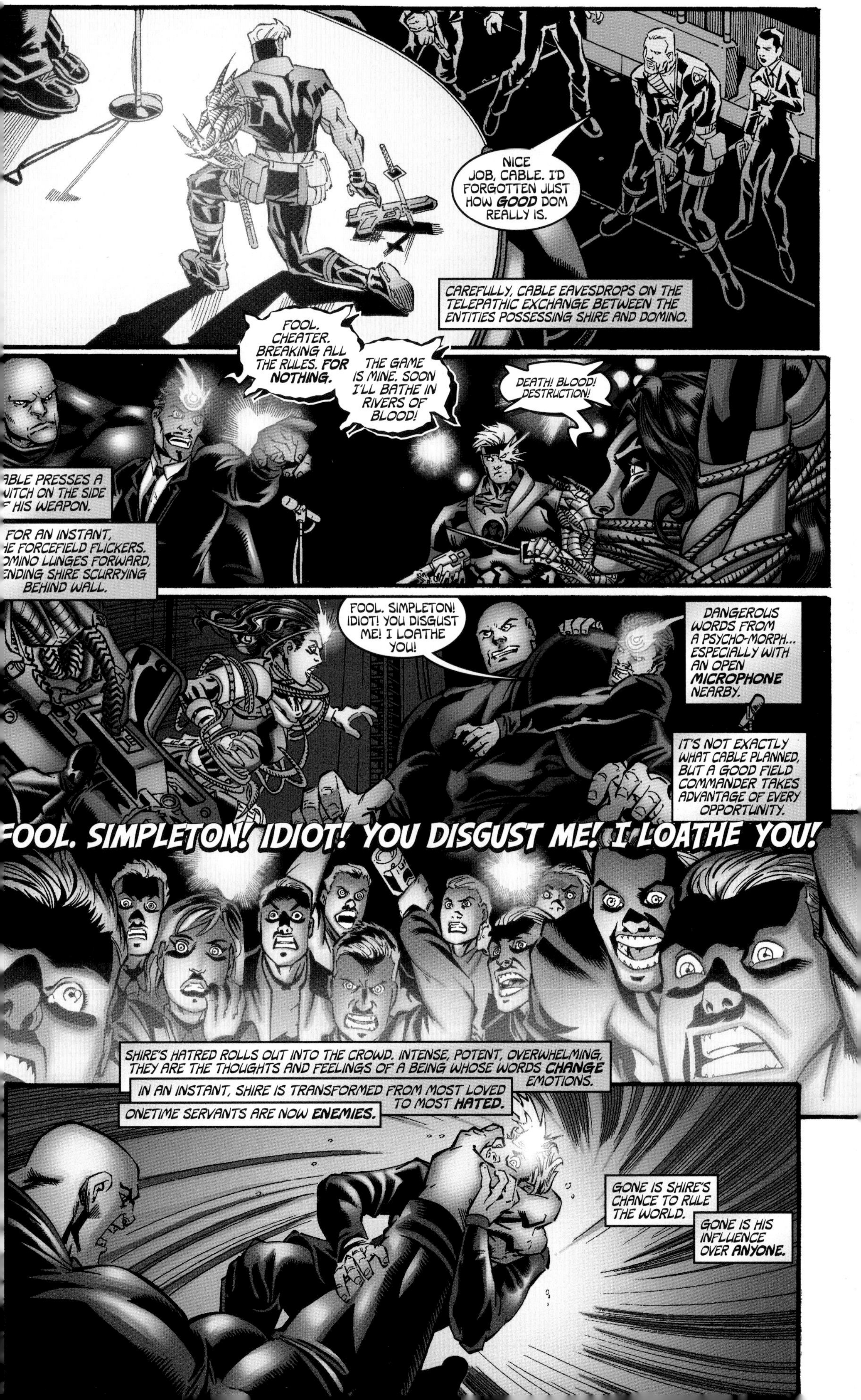
NICE JOB, CABLE. I'D FORGOTTEN JUST HOW GOOD DOM REALLY IS.
CAREFULLY, CABLE EAVESDROPS ON THE TELEPATHIC EXCHANGE BETWEEN THE ENTITIES POSSESSING SHIRE AND DOMINO.
FOOL. CHEATER. BREAKING ALL THE RULES. FOR NOTHING.
THE GAME IS MINE. SOON I'LL BATHE IN RIVERS OF BLOOD!
DEATH! BLOOD! DESTRUCTION!
ABLE PRESSES A WITCH ON THE SIDE F HIS WEAPON.
FOR AN INSTANT, HE FORCEFIELD FLICKERS. OMINO LUNGES FORWARD, ENDING SHIRE SCURRYING BEHIND WALL.
FOOL. SIMPLETON! IDIOT! YOU DISGUST ME! I LOATHE YOU!
DANGEROUS WORDS FROM A PSYCHO-MORPH... ESPECIALLY WITH AN OPEN MICROPHONE NEARBY.
IT'S NOT EXACTLY WHAT CABLE PLANNED, BUT A GOOD FIELD COMMANDER TAKES ADVANTAGE OF EVERY OPPORTUNITY.
FOOL. SIMPLETON! IDIOT! YOU DISGUST ME! I LOATHE YOU!
SHIRE'S HATRED ROLLS OUT INTO THE CROWD. INTENSE, POTENT, OVERWHELMING, THEY ARE THE THOUGHTS AND FEELINGS OF A BEING WHOSE WORDS CHANGE EMOTIONS.
IN AN INSTANT, SHIRE IS TRANSFORMED FROM MOST LOVED TO MOST HATED.
ONETIME SERVANTS ARE NOW ENEMIES.
GONE IS SHIRE'S CHANCE TO RULE THE WORLD.
GONE IS HIS INFLUENCE OVER ANYONE.

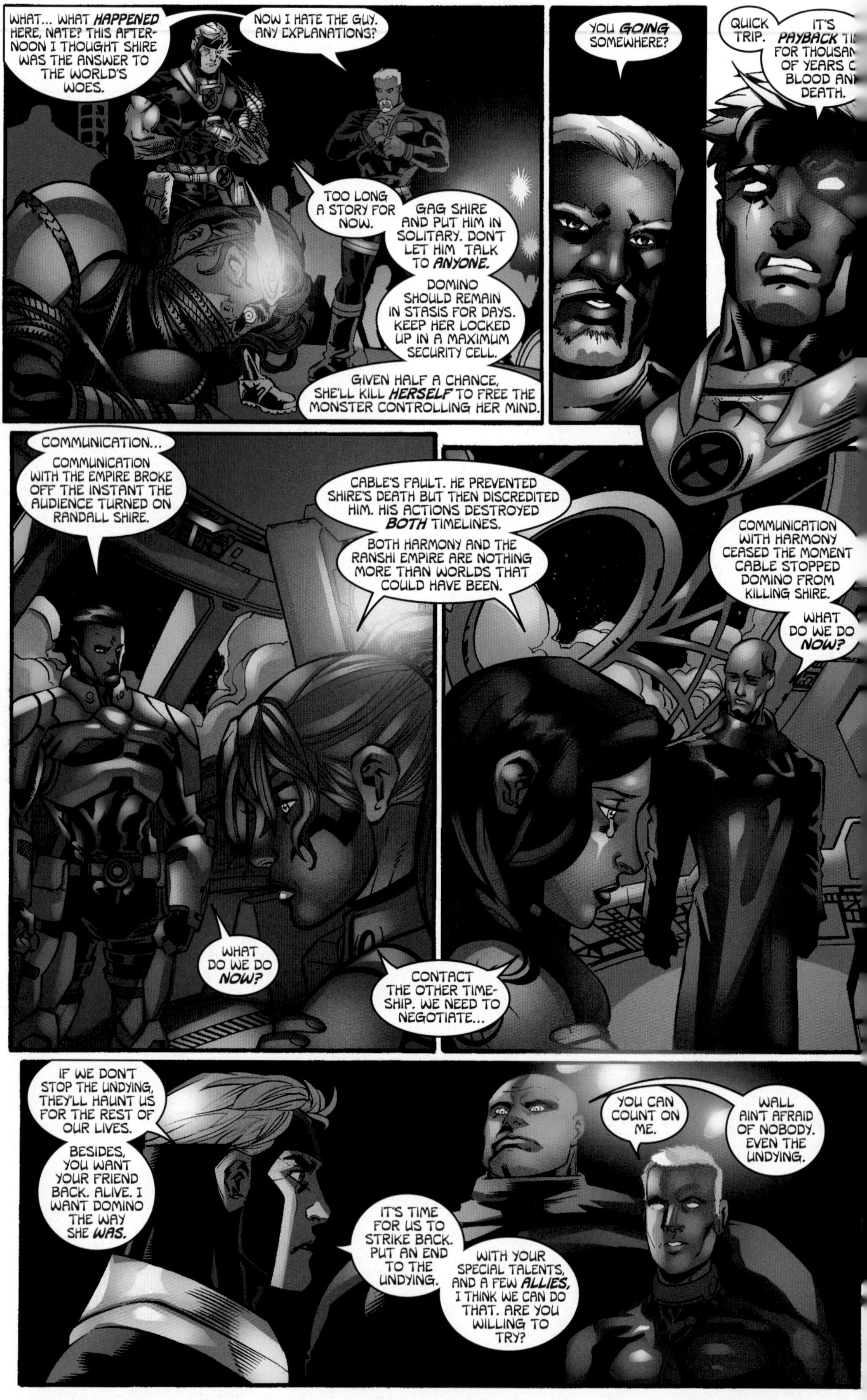
WHAT... WHAT HAPPENED HERE, NATE? THIS AFTERNOON I THOUGHT SHIRE WAS THE ANSWER TO THE WORLD'S WOES.
NOW I HATE THE GUY. ANY EXPLANATIONS?
TOO LONG A STORY FOR NOW.
GAG SHIRE AND PUT HIM IN SOLITARY. DON'T LET HIM TALK TO ANYONE.
DOMINO SHOULD REMAIN IN STASIS FOR DAYS. KEEP HER LOCKED UP IN A MAXIMUM SECURITY CELL.
GIVEN HALF A CHANCE, SHE'LL KILL HERSELF TO FREE THE MONSTER CONTROLLING HER MIND.
YOU GOING SOMEWHERE?
QUICK TRIP.
IT'S PAYBACK TI
FOR THOUSAN
OF YEARS O
BLOOD AN
DEATH.
COMMUNICATION...
COMMUNICATION WITH THE EMPIRE BROKE OFF THE INSTANT THE AUDIENCE TURNED ON RANDALL SHIRE.
CABLE'S FAULT. HE PREVENTED SHIRE'S DEATH BUT THEN DISCREDITED HIM. HIS ACTIONS DESTROYED BOTH TIMELINES.
BOTH HARMONY AND THE RANSHI EMPIRE ARE NOTHING MORE THAN WORLDS THAT COULD HAVE BEEN.
COMMUNICATION WITH HARMONY CEASED THE MOMENT CABLE STOPPED DOMINO FROM KILLING SHIRE.
WHAT DO WE DO NOW?
WHAT DO WE DO NOW?
CONTACT THE OTHER TIME-SHIP. WE NEED TO NEGOTIATE...
IF WE DON'T STOP THE UNDYING, THEY'LL HAUNT US FOR THE REST OF OUR LIVES.
BESIDES, YOU WANT YOUR FRIEND BACK. ALIVE. I WANT DOMINO THE WAY SHE WAS.
IT'S TIME FOR US TO STRIKE BACK. PUT AN END TO THE UNDYING.
WITH YOUR SPECIAL TALENTS, AND A FEW ALLIES, I THINK WE CAN DO THAT. ARE YOU WILLING TO TRY?
YOU CAN COUNT ON ME.
WALL AIN'T AFRAID OF NOBODY. EVEN THE UNDYING.

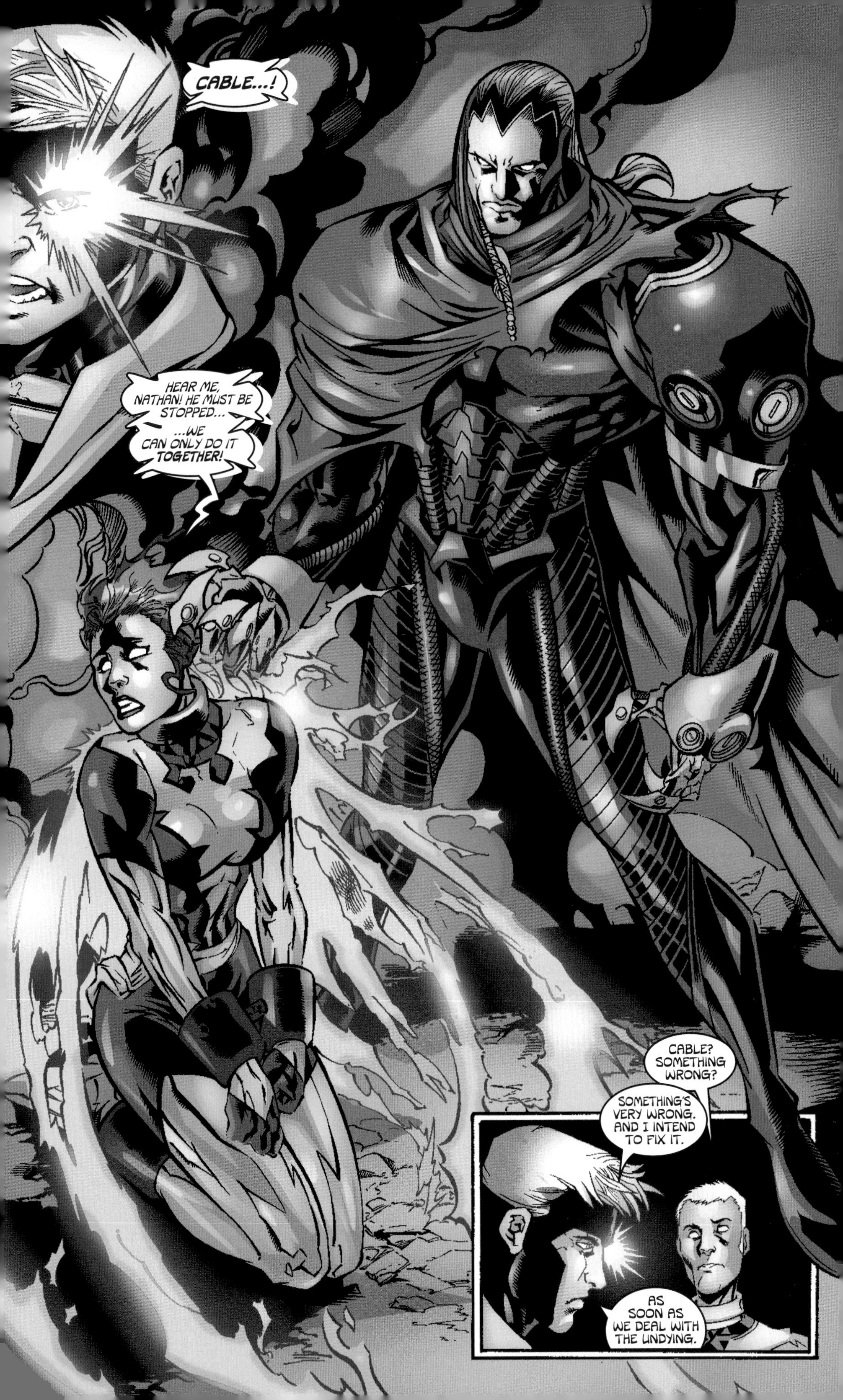
CABLE...!
HEAR ME, NATHAN! HE MUST BE STOPPED...
...WE CAN ONLY DO IT TOGETHER!
CABLE? SOMETHING WRONG?
SOMETHING'S VERY WRONG. AND I INTEND TO FIX IT.
AS SOON AS WE DEAL WITH THE UNDYING.

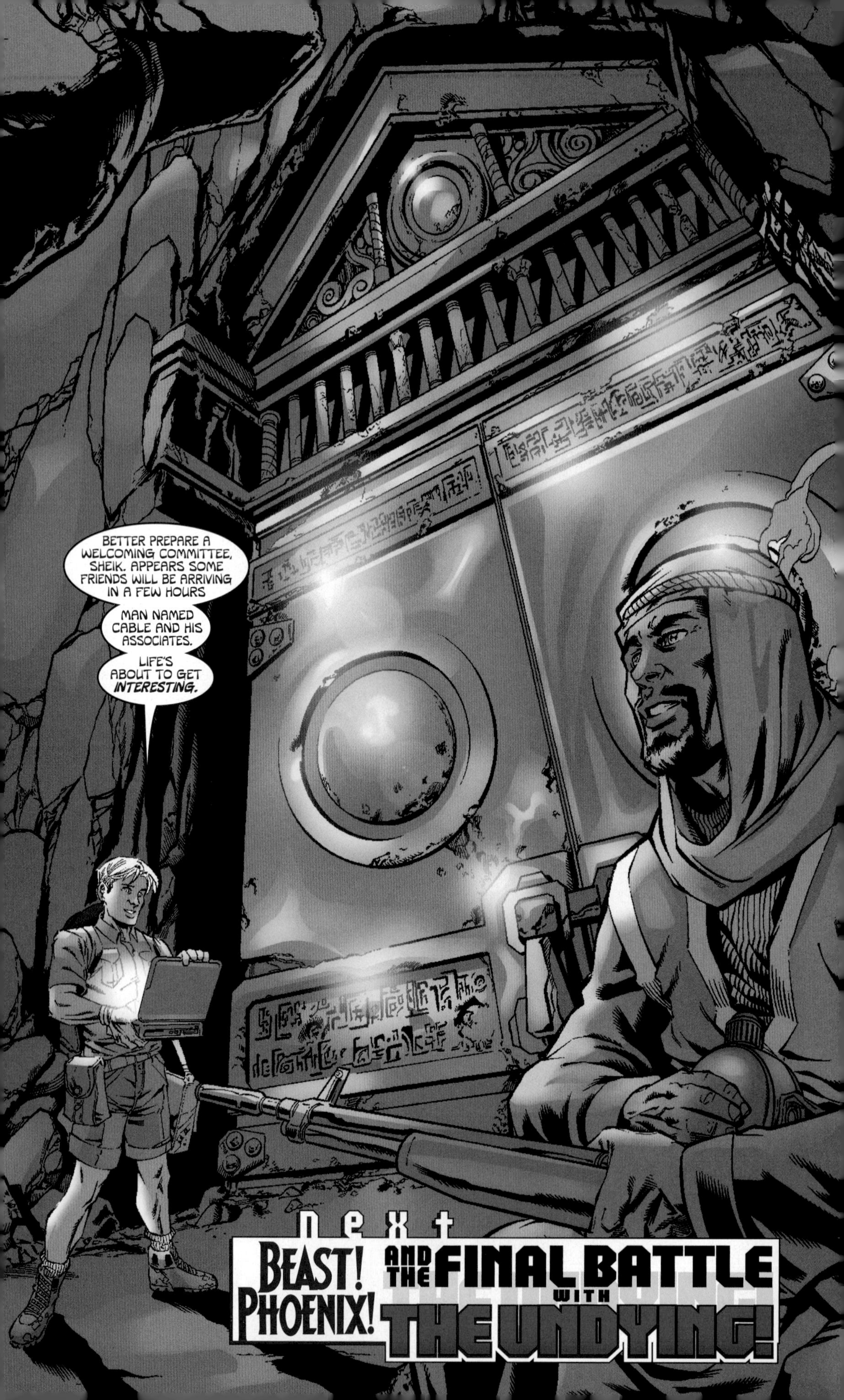
BETTER PREPARE A WELCOMING COMMITTEE, SHEIK. APPEARS SOME FRIENDS WILL BE ARRIVING IN A FEW HOURS
MAN NAMED CABLE AND HIS ASSOCIATES.
LIFE'S ABOUT TO GET INTERESTING.
NEXT
BEAST! PHOENIX! AND THE FINAL BATTLE WITH THE UNDYING!

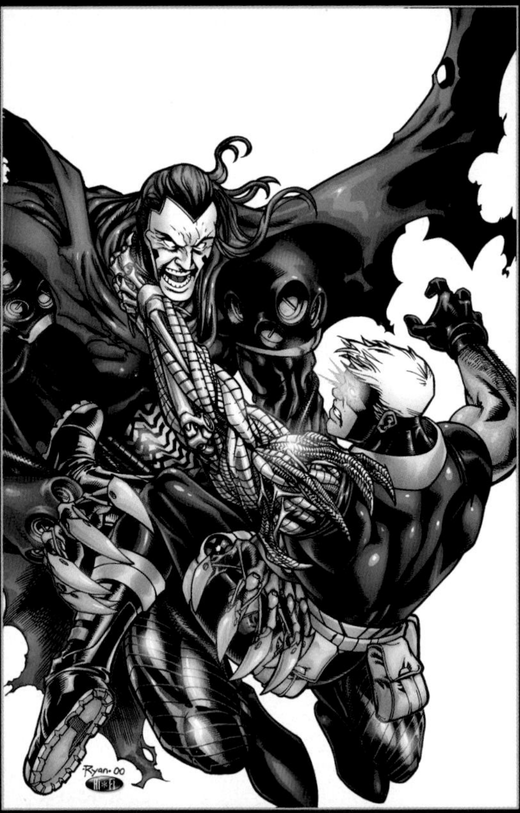

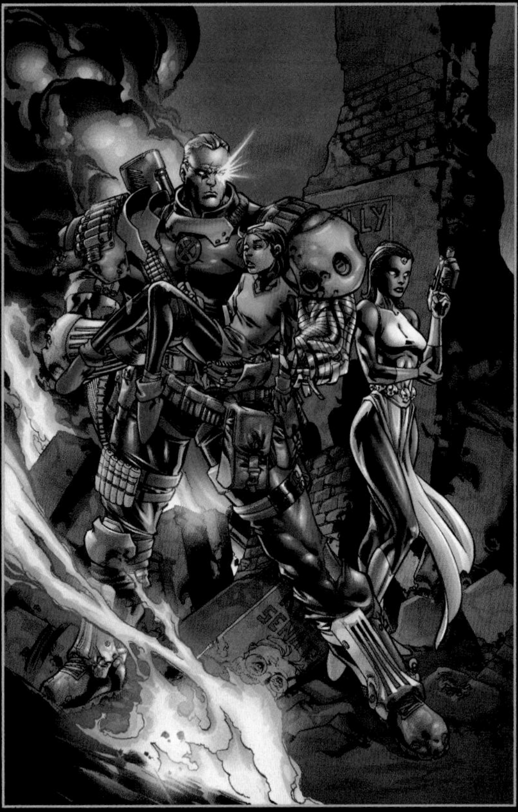

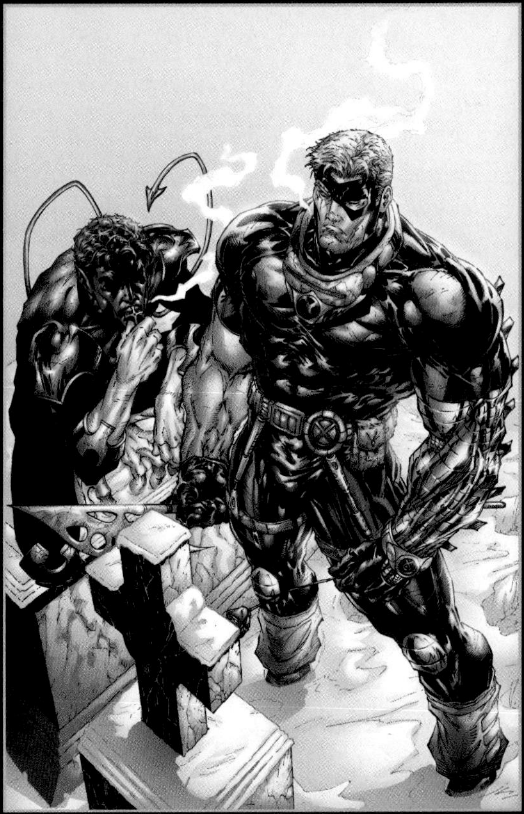

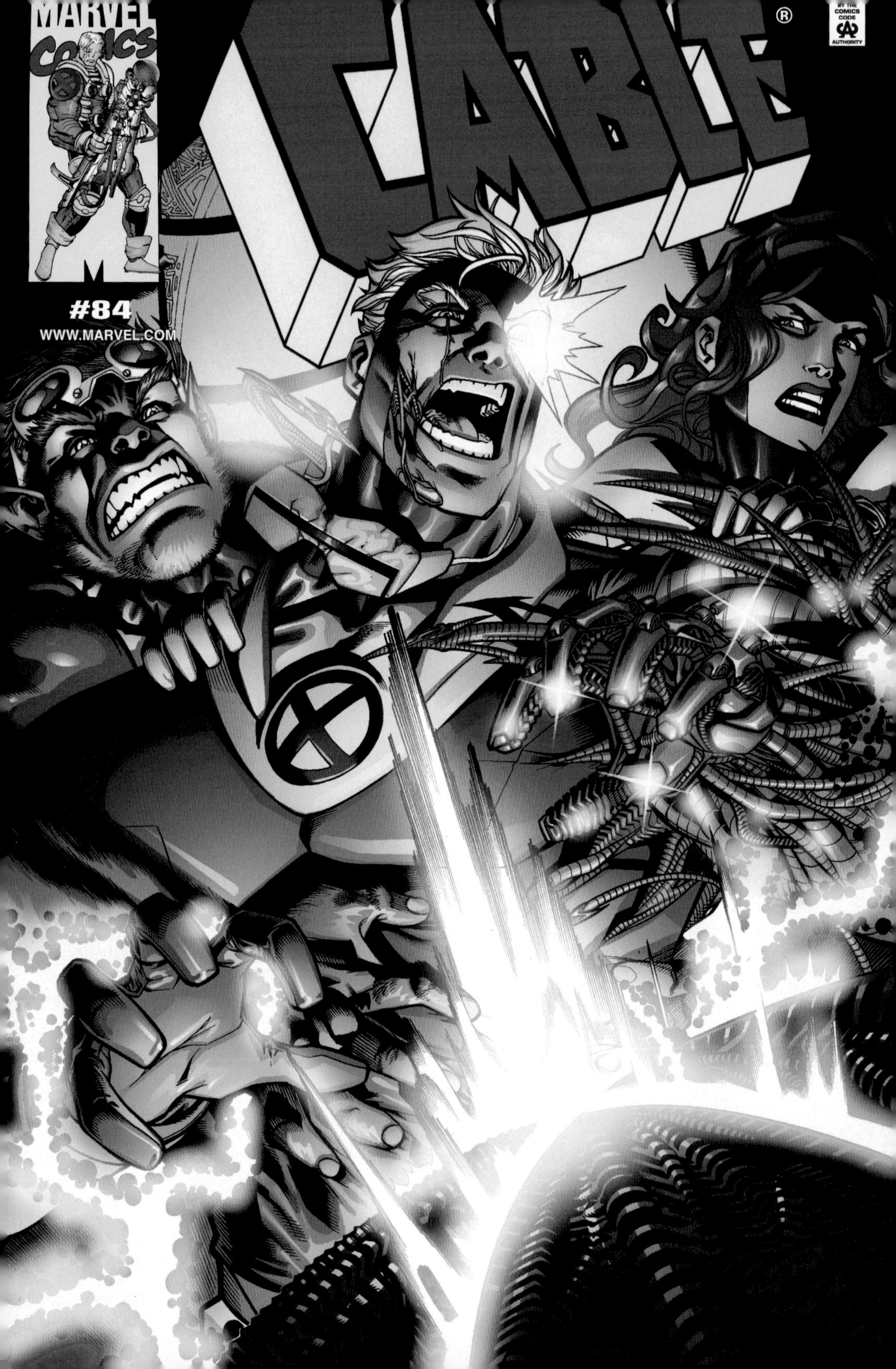
MARVEL COMICS
CABLE®
#84
WWW.MARVEL.COM
APPROVED BY THE COMICS CODE AUTHORITY

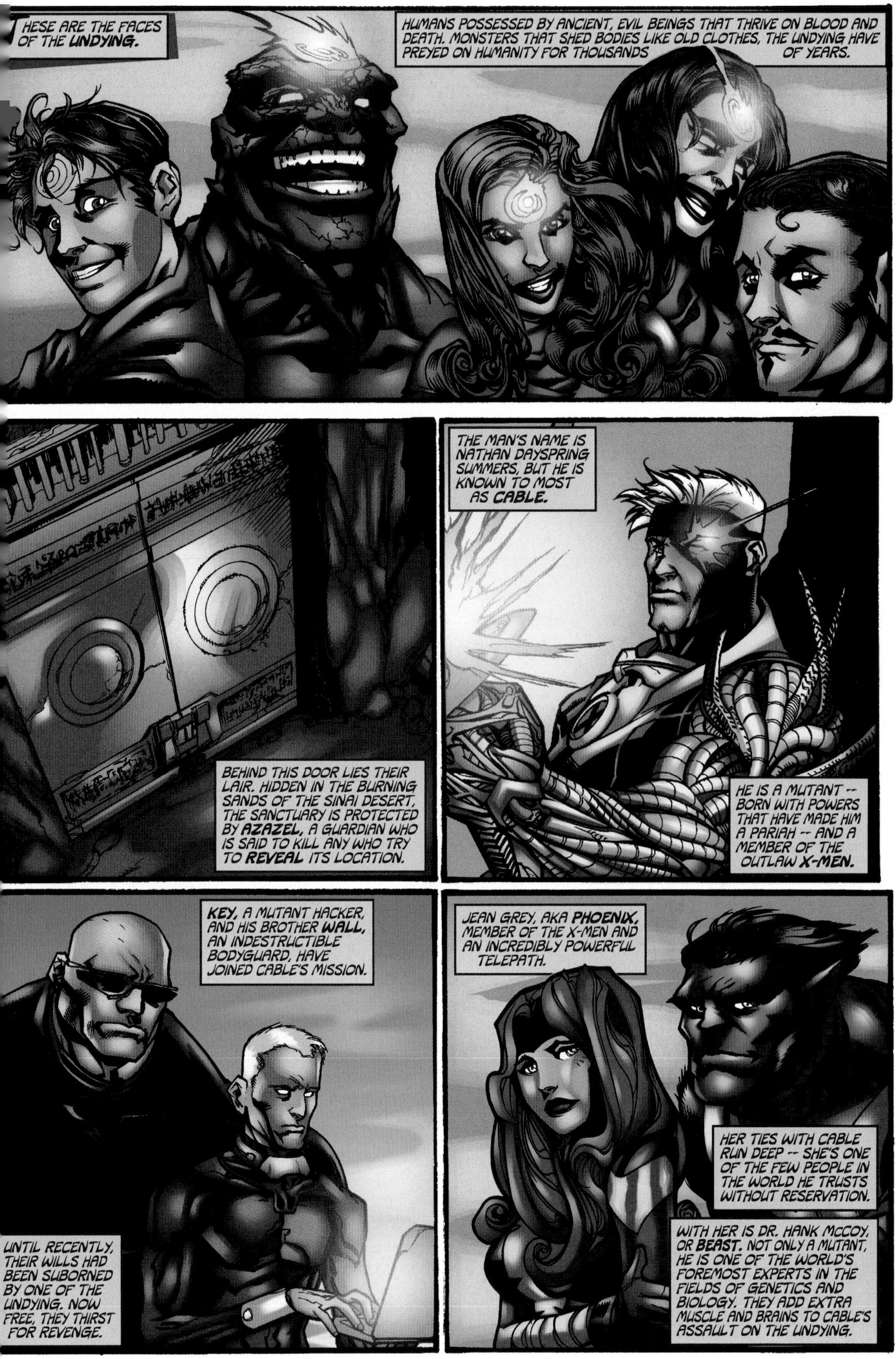

HESE ARE THE FACES OF THE UNDYING.
HUMANS POSSESSED BY ANCIENT, EVIL BEINGS THAT THRIVE ON BLOOD AND DEATH. MONSTERS THAT SHED BODIES LIKE OLD CLOTHES, THE UNDYING HAVE PREYED ON HUMANITY FOR THOUSANDS OF YEARS.
BEHIND THIS DOOR LIES THEIR LAIR. HIDDEN IN THE BURNING SANDS OF THE SINAI DESERT, THE SANCTUARY IS PROTECTED BY AZAZEL, A GUARDIAN WHO IS SAID TO KILL ANY WHO TRY TO REVEAL ITS LOCATION.
THE MAN'S NAME IS NATHAN DAYSPRING SUMMERS, BUT HE IS KNOWN TO MOST AS CABLE.
HE IS A MUTANT -- BORN WITH POWERS THAT HAVE MADE HIM A PARIAH -- AND A MEMBER OF THE OUTLAW X-MEN.
KEY, A MUTANT HACKER, AND HIS BROTHER WALL, AN INDESTRUCTIBLE BODYGUARD, HAVE JOINED CABLE'S MISSION.
UNTIL RECENTLY, THEIR WILLS HAD BEEN SUBORNED BY ONE OF THE UNDYING. NOW FREE, THEY THIRST FOR REVENGE.
JEAN GREY, AKA PHOENIX, MEMBER OF THE X-MEN AND AN INCREDIBLY POWERFUL TELEPATH.
HER TIES WITH CABLE RUN DEEP -- SHE'S ONE OF THE FEW PEOPLE IN THE WORLD HE TRUSTS WITHOUT RESERVATION.
WITH HER IS DR. HANK McCOY, OR BEAST. NOT ONLY A MUTANT, HE IS ONE OF THE WORLD'S FOREMOST EXPERTS IN THE FIELDS OF GENETICS AND BIOLOGY. THEY ADD EXTRA MUSCLE AND BRAINS TO CABLE'S ASSAULT ON THE UNDYING.

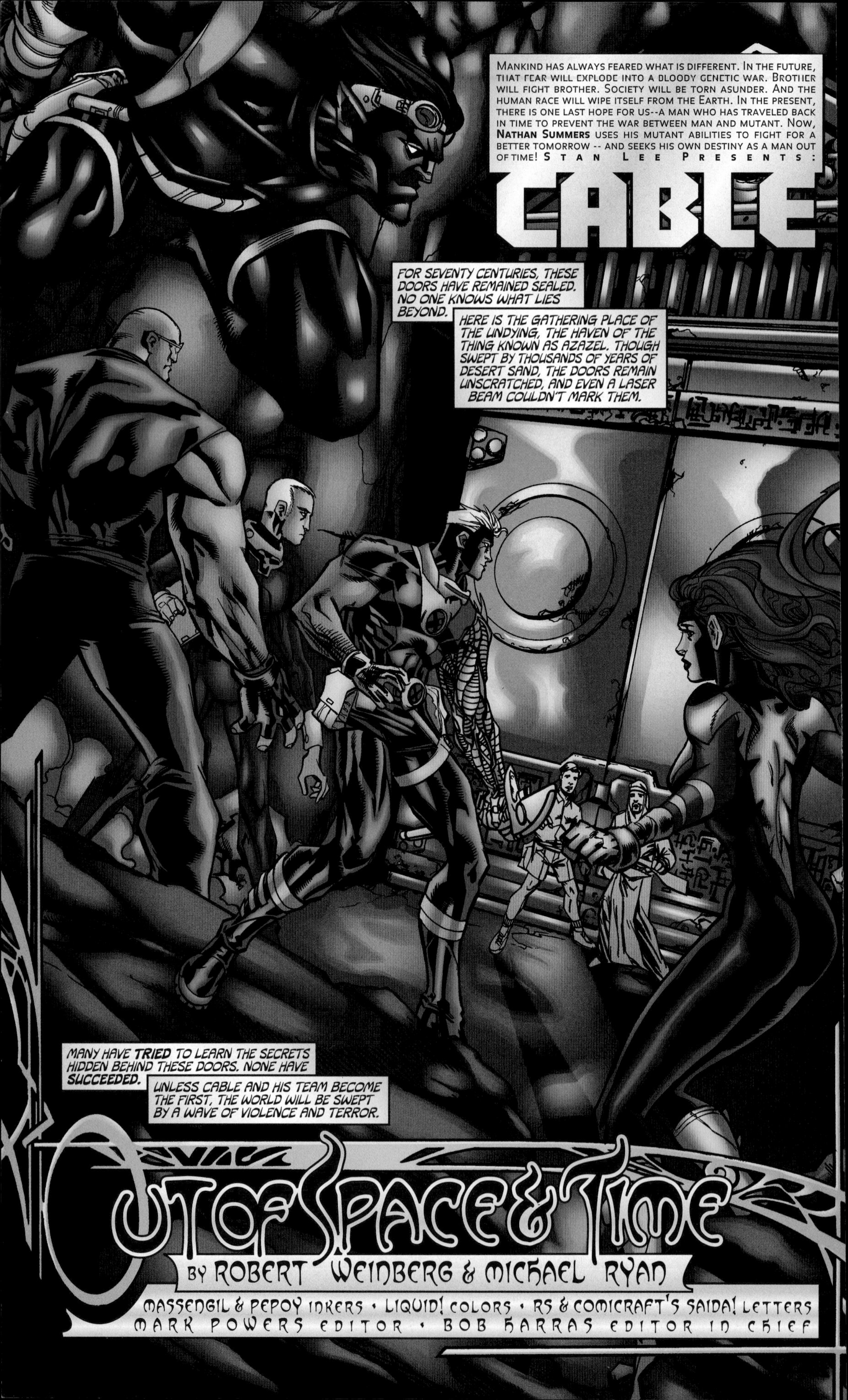
Mankind has always feared what is different. In the future, that fear will explode into a bloody genetic war. Brother will fight brother. Society will be torn asunder. And the human race will wipe itself from the Earth. In the present, there is one last hope for us--a man who has traveled back in time to prevent the war between man and mutant. Now, Nathan Summers uses his mutant abilities to fight for a better tomorrow -- and seeks his own destiny as a man out of time! Stan Lee Presents:
CABLE
FOR SEVENTY CENTURIES, THESE DOORS HAVE REMAINED SEALED. NO ONE KNOWS WHAT LIES BEYOND.
HERE IS THE GATHERING PLACE OF THE UNDYING, THE HAVEN OF THE THING KNOWN AS AZAZEL. THOUGH SWEPT BY THOUSANDS OF YEARS OF DESERT SAND, THE DOORS REMAIN UNSCRATCHED, AND EVEN A LASER BEAM COULDN'T MARK THEM.
MANY HAVE TRIED TO LEARN THE SECRETS HIDDEN BEHIND THESE DOORS. NONE HAVE SUCCEEDED.
UNLESS CABLE AND HIS TEAM BECOME THE FIRST, THE WORLD WILL BE SWEPT BY A WAVE OF VIOLENCE AND TERROR.
OUT OF SPACE & TIME
BY ROBERT WEINBERG & MICHAEL RYAN
MASSENGIL & PEPOY INKERS • LIQUID! COLORS • RS & COMICRAFT'S SAIDA! LETTERS
MARK POWERS EDITOR • BOB HARRAS EDITOR IN CHIEF

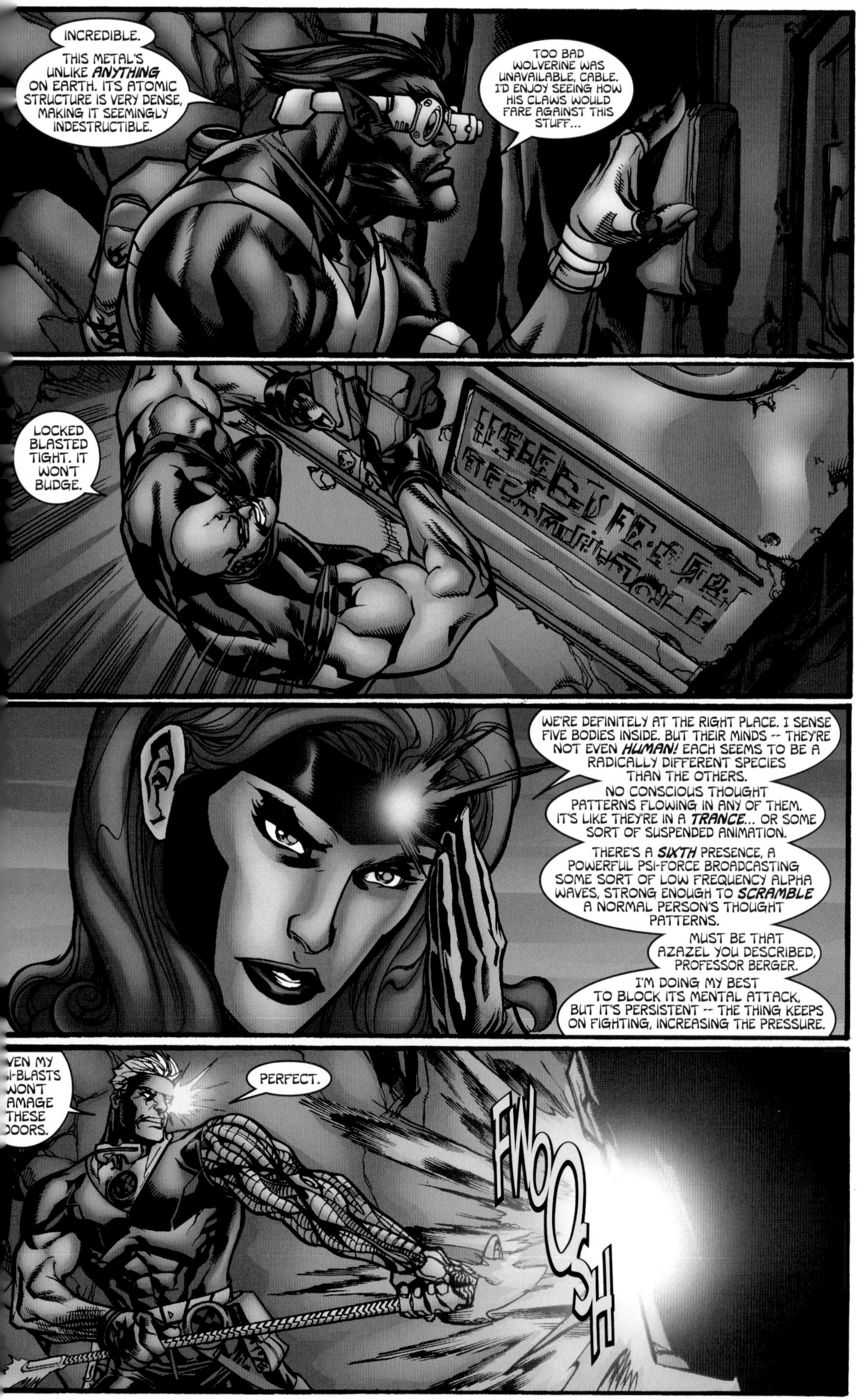
INCREDIBLE.
THIS METAL'S UNLIKE *ANYTHING* ON EARTH. ITS ATOMIC STRUCTURE IS VERY DENSE, MAKING IT SEEMINGLY INDESTRUCTIBLE.
TOO BAD WOLVERINE WAS UNAVAILABLE, CABLE. I'D ENJOY SEEING HOW HIS CLAWS WOULD FARE AGAINST THIS STUFF...
LOCKED BLASTED TIGHT. IT WON'T BUDGE.
WE'RE DEFINITELY AT THE RIGHT PLACE. I SENSE FIVE BODIES INSIDE. BUT THEIR MINDS -- THEY'RE NOT EVEN *HUMAN!* EACH SEEMS TO BE A RADICALLY DIFFERENT SPECIES THAN THE OTHERS.
NO CONSCIOUS THOUGHT PATTERNS FLOWING IN ANY OF THEM. IT'S LIKE THEY'RE IN A *TRANCE*... OR SOME SORT OF SUSPENDED ANIMATION.
THERE'S A *SIXTH* PRESENCE, A POWERFUL PSI-FORCE BROADCASTING SOME SORT OF LOW FREQUENCY ALPHA WAVES, STRONG ENOUGH TO *SCRAMBLE* A NORMAL PERSON'S THOUGHT PATTERNS.
MUST BE THAT AZAZEL YOU DESCRIBED, PROFESSOR BERGER.
I'M DOING MY BEST TO BLOCK ITS MENTAL ATTACK, BUT IT'S PERSISTENT -- THE THING KEEPS ON FIGHTING, INCREASING THE PRESSURE.
VEN MY I-BLASTS WON'T AMAGE THESE OORS.
PERFECT.
FWOOOSH

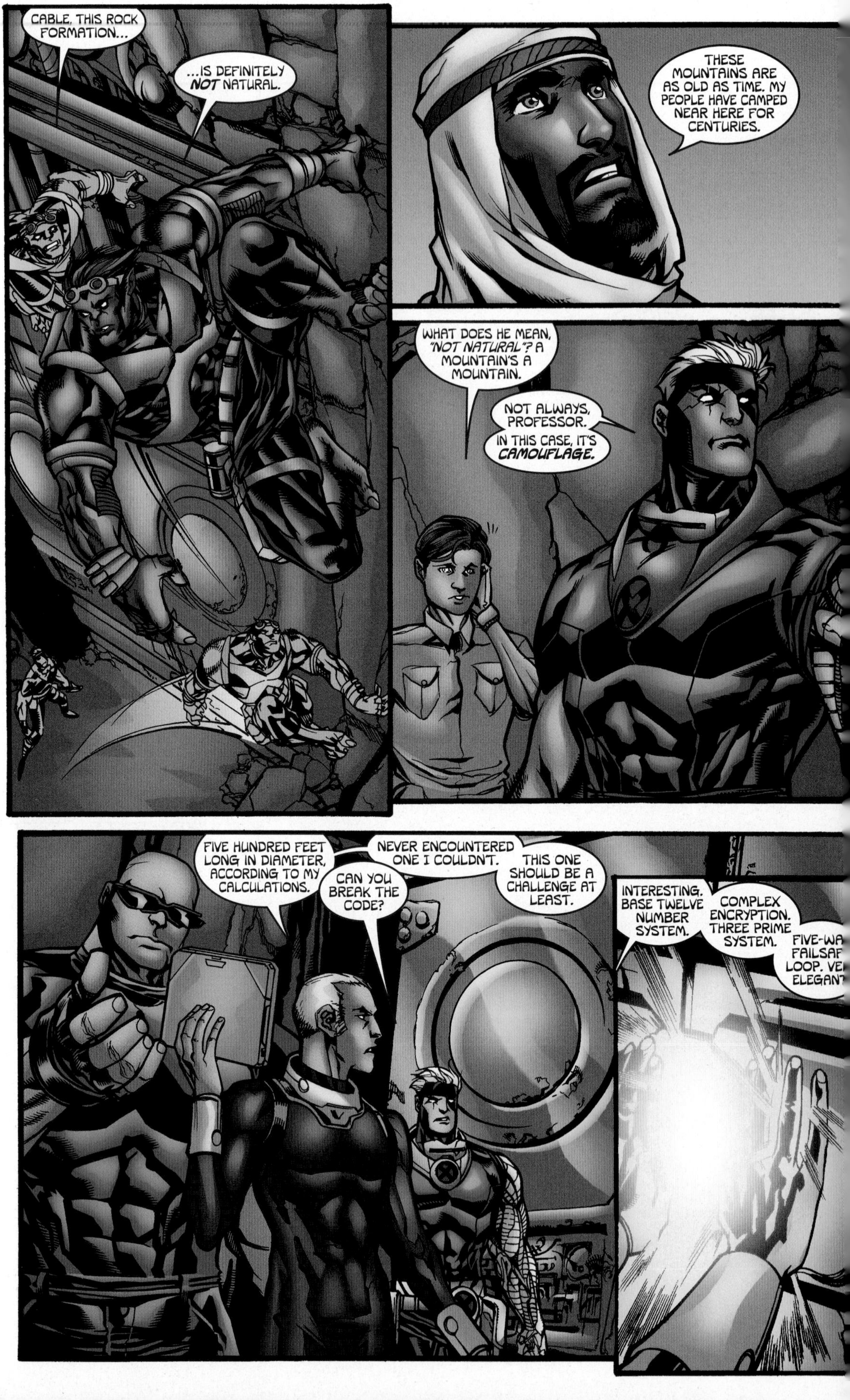

CABLE, THIS ROCK FORMATION...
...IS DEFINITELY NOT NATURAL.
THESE MOUNTAINS ARE AS OLD AS TIME. MY PEOPLE HAVE CAMPED NEAR HERE FOR CENTURIES.
WHAT DOES HE MEAN, "NOT NATURAL"? A MOUNTAIN'S A MOUNTAIN.
NOT ALWAYS, PROFESSOR.
IN THIS CASE, IT'S CAMOUFLAGE.
FIVE HUNDRED FEET LONG IN DIAMETER, ACCORDING TO MY CALCULATIONS.
CAN YOU BREAK THE CODE?
NEVER ENCOUNTERED ONE I COULDN'T.
THIS ONE SHOULD BE A CHALLENGE AT LEAST.
INTERESTING. BASE TWELVE NUMBER SYSTEM.
COMPLEX ENCRYPTION. THREE PRIME SYSTEM.
FIVE-WA FAILSAF LOOP. VE ELEGAN

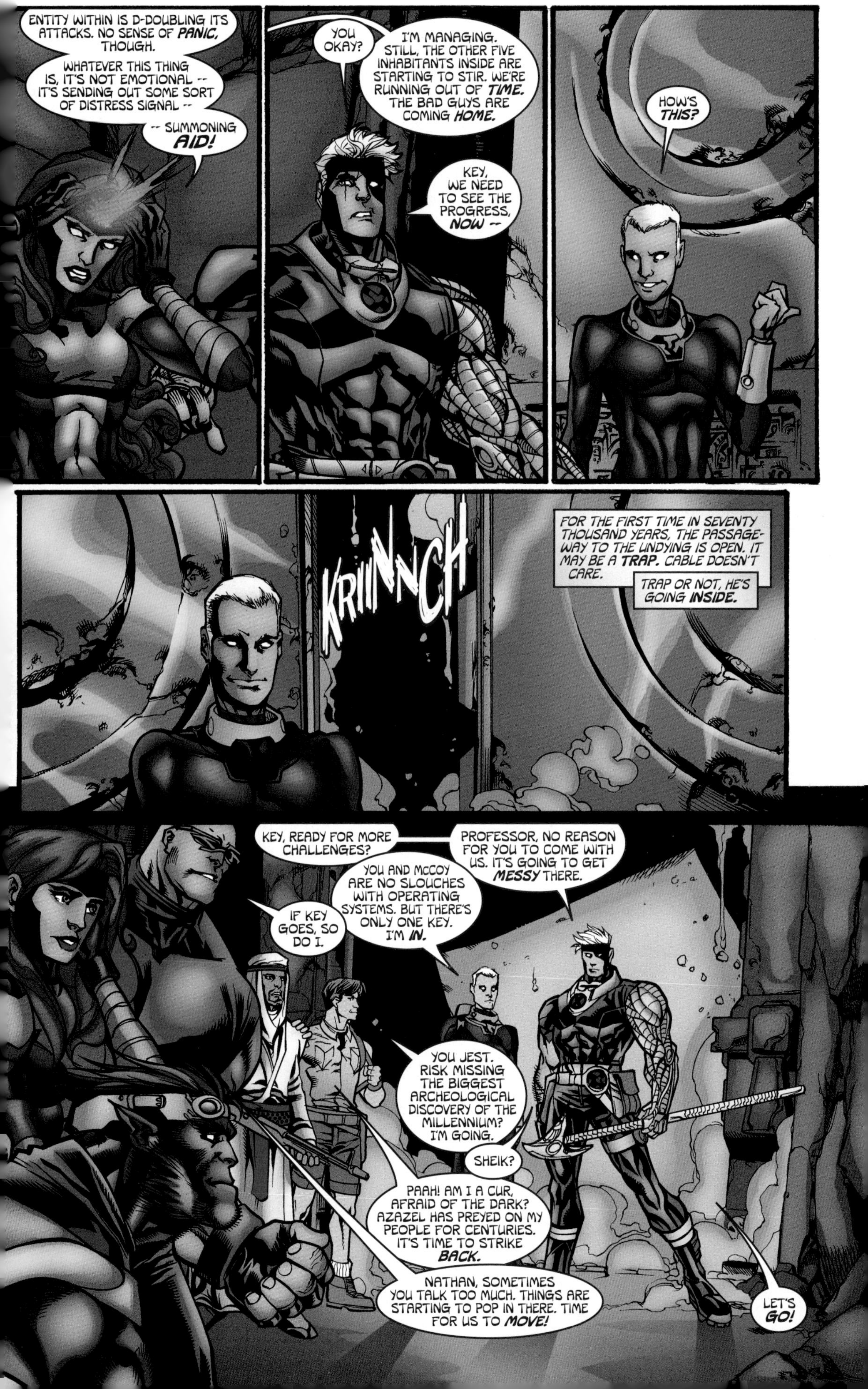
ENTITY WITHIN IS D-DOUBLING ITS ATTACKS. NO SENSE OF PANIC, THOUGH.
WHATEVER THIS THING IS, IT'S NOT EMOTIONAL -- IT'S SENDING OUT SOME SORT OF DISTRESS SIGNAL --
-- SUMMONING AID!
YOU OKAY?
I'M MANAGING. STILL, THE OTHER FIVE INHABITANTS INSIDE ARE STARTING TO STIR. WE'RE RUNNING OUT OF TIME. THE BAD GUYS ARE COMING HOME.
KEY, WE NEED TO SEE THE PROGRESS, NOW --
HOW'S THIS?
KRIINNCH
FOR THE FIRST TIME IN SEVENTY THOUSAND YEARS, THE PASSAGEWAY TO THE UNDYING IS OPEN. IT MAY BE A TRAP. CABLE DOESN'T CARE.
TRAP OR NOT, HE'S GOING INSIDE.
KEY, READY FOR MORE CHALLENGES?
PROFESSOR, NO REASON FOR YOU TO COME WITH US. IT'S GOING TO GET MESSY THERE.
YOU AND McCOY ARE NO SLOUCHES WITH OPERATING SYSTEMS. BUT THERE'S ONLY ONE KEY. I'M IN.
IF KEY GOES, SO DO I.
YOU JEST. RISK MISSING THE BIGGEST ARCHEOLOGICAL DISCOVERY OF THE MILLENNIUM? I'M GOING.
SHEIK?
PAAH! AM I A CUR, AFRAID OF THE DARK? AZAZEL HAS PREYED ON MY PEOPLE FOR CENTURIES. IT'S TIME TO STRIKE BACK.
NATHAN, SOMETIMES YOU TALK TOO MUCH. THINGS ARE STARTING TO POP IN THERE. TIME FOR US TO MOVE!
LET'S GO!

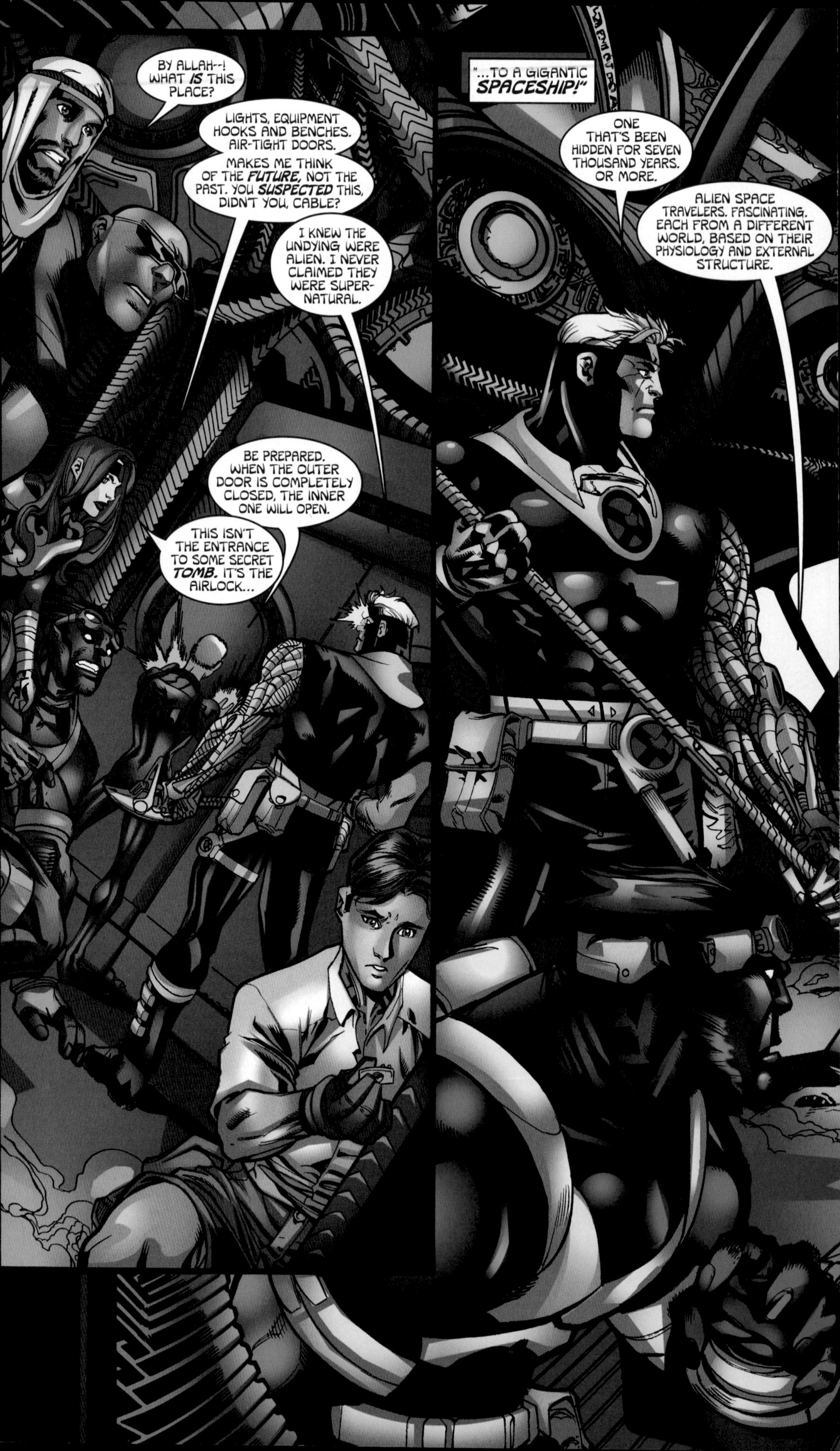

BY ALLAH--! WHAT *IS* THIS PLACE?
LIGHTS, EQUIPMENT HOOKS AND BENCHES. AIR-TIGHT DOORS.
MAKES ME THINK OF THE *FUTURE,* NOT THE PAST. YOU *SUSPECTED* THIS, DIDN'T YOU, CABLE?
I KNEW THE UNDYING WERE ALIEN. I NEVER CLAIMED THEY WERE SUPER-NATURAL.
BE PREPARED. WHEN THE OUTER DOOR IS COMPLETELY CLOSED, THE INNER ONE WILL OPEN.
THIS ISN'T THE ENTRANCE TO SOME SECRET *TOMB.* IT'S THE AIRLOCK...
"...TO A GIGANTIC *SPACESHIP!*"
ONE THAT'S BEEN HIDDEN FOR SEVEN THOUSAND YEARS. OR MORE.
ALIEN SPACE TRAVELERS. FASCINATING. EACH FROM A DIFFERENT WORLD, BASED ON THEIR PHYSIOLOGY AND EXTERNAL STRUCTURE.

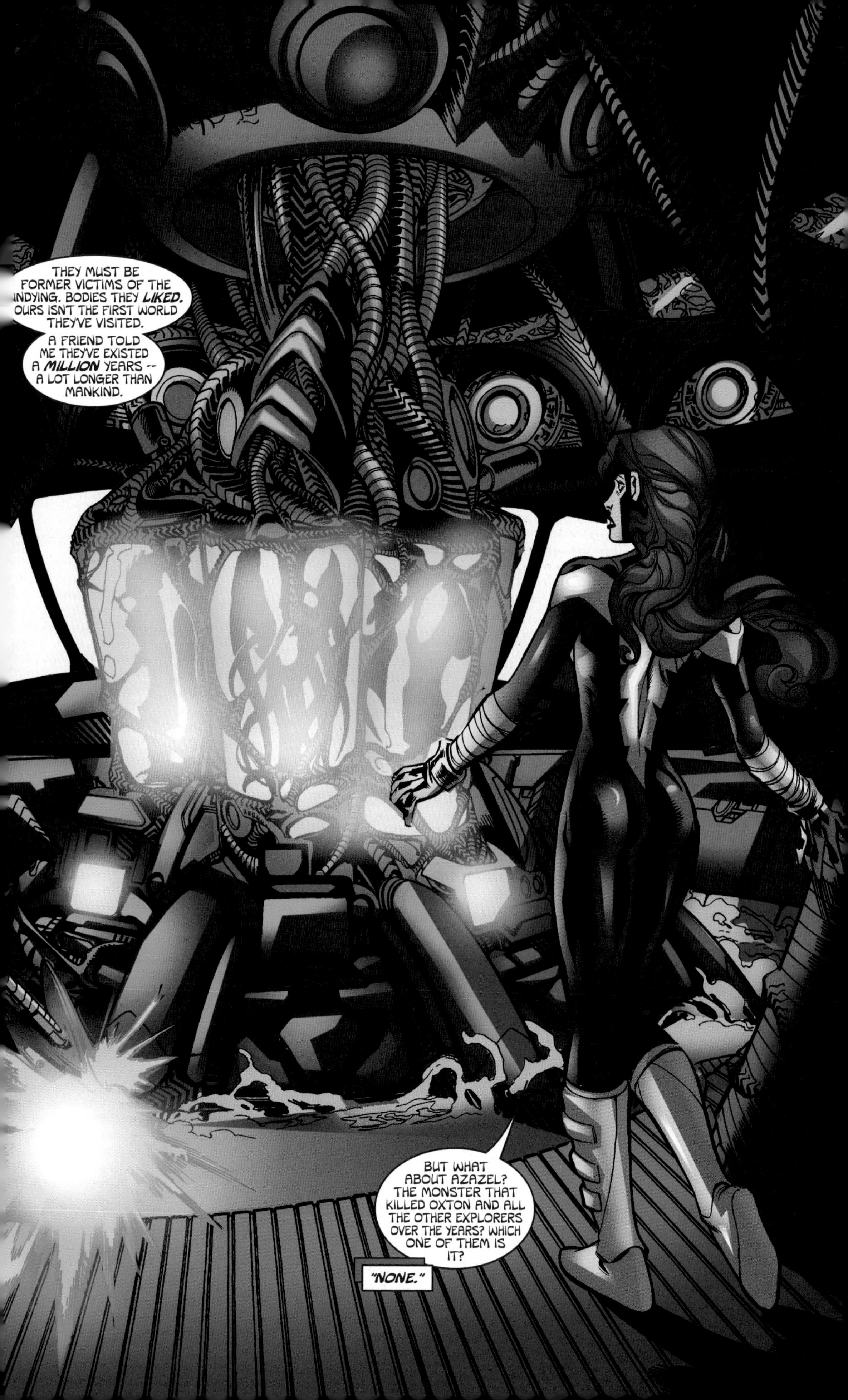
THEY MUST BE FORMER VICTIMS OF THE NDYING. BODIES THEY LIKED. OURS ISN'T THE FIRST WORLD THEY'VE VISITED.
A FRIEND TOLD ME THEY'VE EXISTED A MILLION YEARS -- A LOT LONGER THAN MANKIND.
BUT WHAT ABOUT AZAZEL? THE MONSTER THAT KILLED OXTON AND ALL THE OTHER EXPLORERS OVER THE YEARS? WHICH ONE OF THEM IS IT?
"NONE."

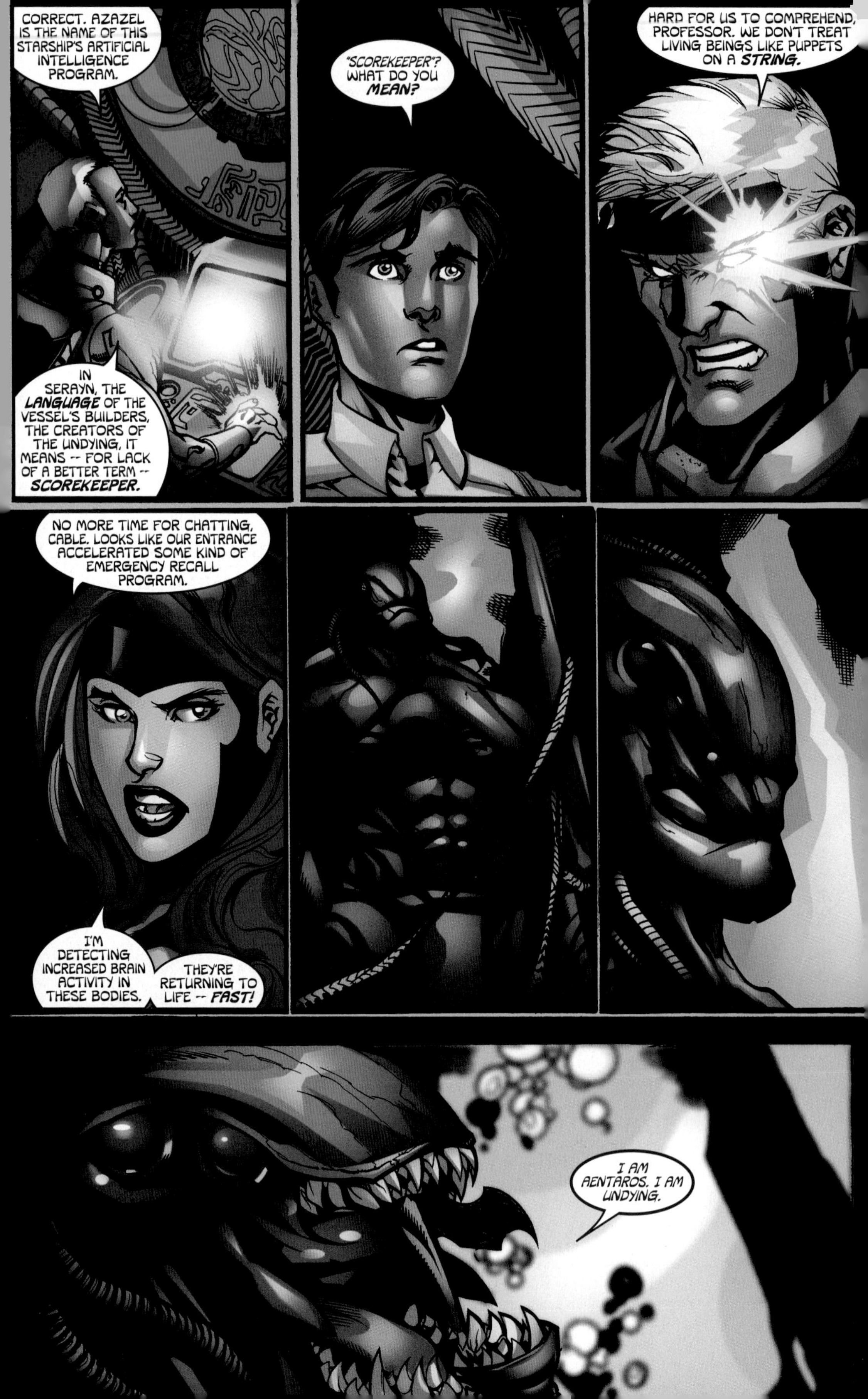

CORRECT. AZAZEL IS THE NAME OF THIS STARSHIP'S ARTIFICIAL INTELLIGENCE PROGRAM.
IN SERAYN, THE LANGUAGE OF THE VESSEL'S BUILDERS, THE CREATORS OF THE UNDYING, IT MEANS -- FOR LACK OF A BETTER TERM -- SCOREKEEPER.
"SCOREKEEPER"? WHAT DO YOU MEAN?
HARD FOR US TO COMPREHEND, PROFESSOR. WE DON'T TREAT LIVING BEINGS LIKE PUPPETS ON A STRING.
NO MORE TIME FOR CHATTING, CABLE. LOOKS LIKE OUR ENTRANCE ACCELERATED SOME KIND OF EMERGENCY RECALL PROGRAM.
I'M DETECTING INCREASED BRAIN ACTIVITY IN THESE BODIES.
THEY'RE RETURNING TO LIFE -- FAST!
I AM AENTAROS. I AM UNDYING.

AT THE SAME INSTANT...

...POSSESSED BY AENTAROS, **DOMINO'S** BEEN KEPT PRISONER IN A MAXIMUM SECURITY CELL EVER SINCE CABLE CAPTURED HER A DAY AGO.

WITHOUT WARNING, THE LIVING NIGHTMARE THAT HAD **VIOLATED** HER EVERY THOUGHT, CONTROLLED HER EVERY MOVE, IS **GONE**...

...LEAVING DOMINO VERY RELIEVED... AND ANXIOUS TO ESCAPE.

EXPLAINING HIS WAY OUT OF THIS MESS ISN'T GOING TO BE EASY. BUT RANDALL SHIRE, MILD-MANNERED CIRCUS PERFORMER, DOESN'T CARE. ALL THAT MATTERS IS THAT HE'S FREE. **FREE!**

ELSEWHERE...

DEATH, BLOOD, MURDER. DEATH...

WHATEVER HORROR HELD HIM IN ITS GRIP IS SUDDENLY GONE -- AN INSTANT BEFORE IT COULD DESTROY HIS LIFE. AND THE LIFE OF HIS CHILD.

SOMEHOW, HE KNOWS THAT **HIS** FREEDOM MEANS **OTHERS** ARE IN DANGER --

-- BUT ALL HE CAN DO IS PRAY THEY SURVIVE...

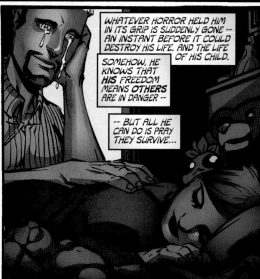

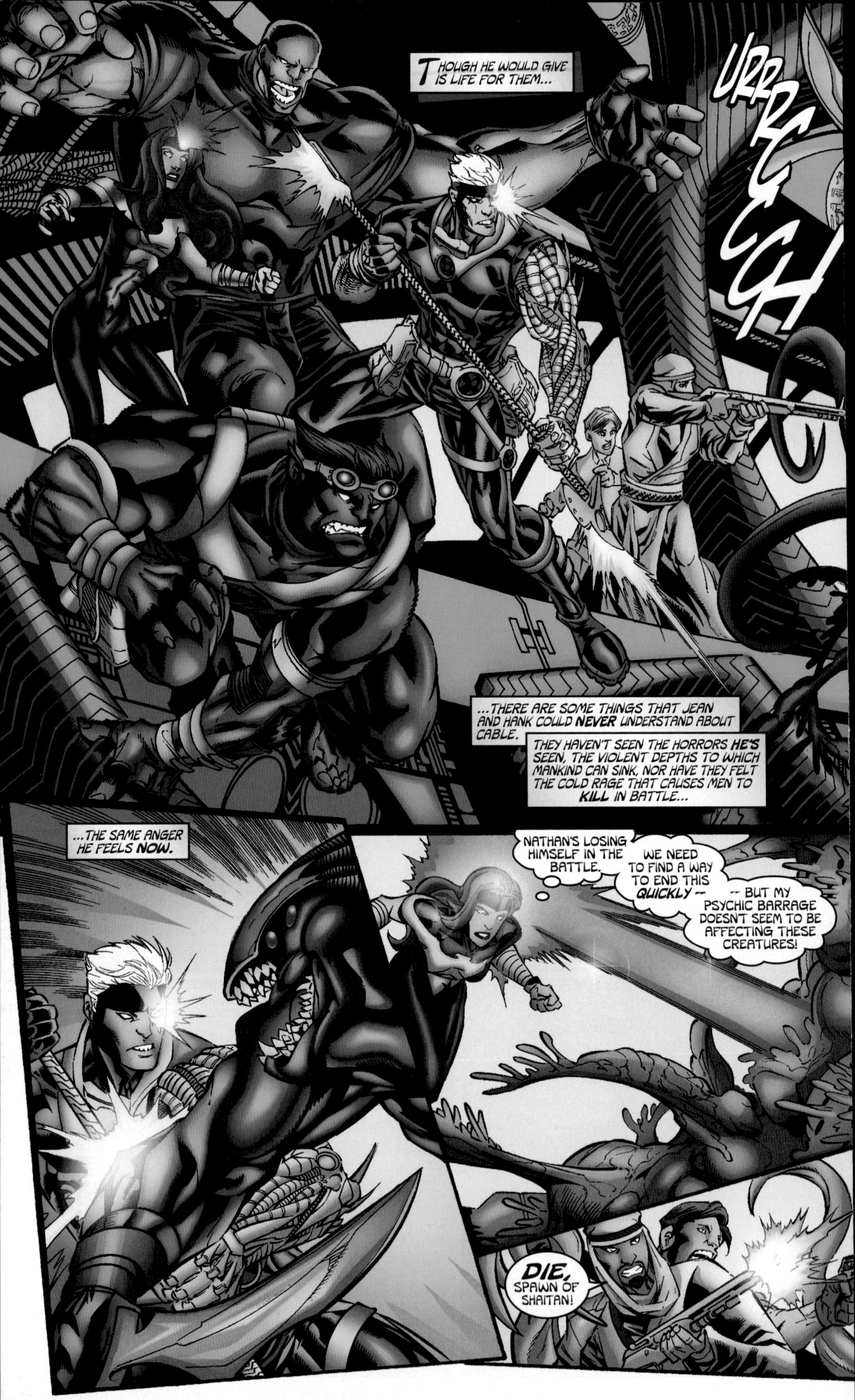
THOUGH HE WOULD GIVE IS LIFE FOR THEM...
URRRGGH
...THERE ARE SOME THINGS THAT JEAN AND HANK COULD NEVER UNDERSTAND ABOUT CABLE.
THEY HAVEN'T SEEN THE HORRORS HE'S SEEN, THE VIOLENT DEPTHS TO WHICH MANKIND CAN SINK, NOR HAVE THEY FELT THE COLD RAGE THAT CAUSES MEN TO KILL IN BATTLE...
...THE SAME ANGER HE FEELS NOW.
NATHAN'S LOSING HIMSELF IN THE BATTLE.
WE NEED TO FIND A WAY TO END THIS QUICKLY --
-- BUT MY PSYCHIC BARRAGE DOESN'T SEEM TO BE AFFECTING THESE CREATURES!
DIE, SPAWN OF SHAITAN!

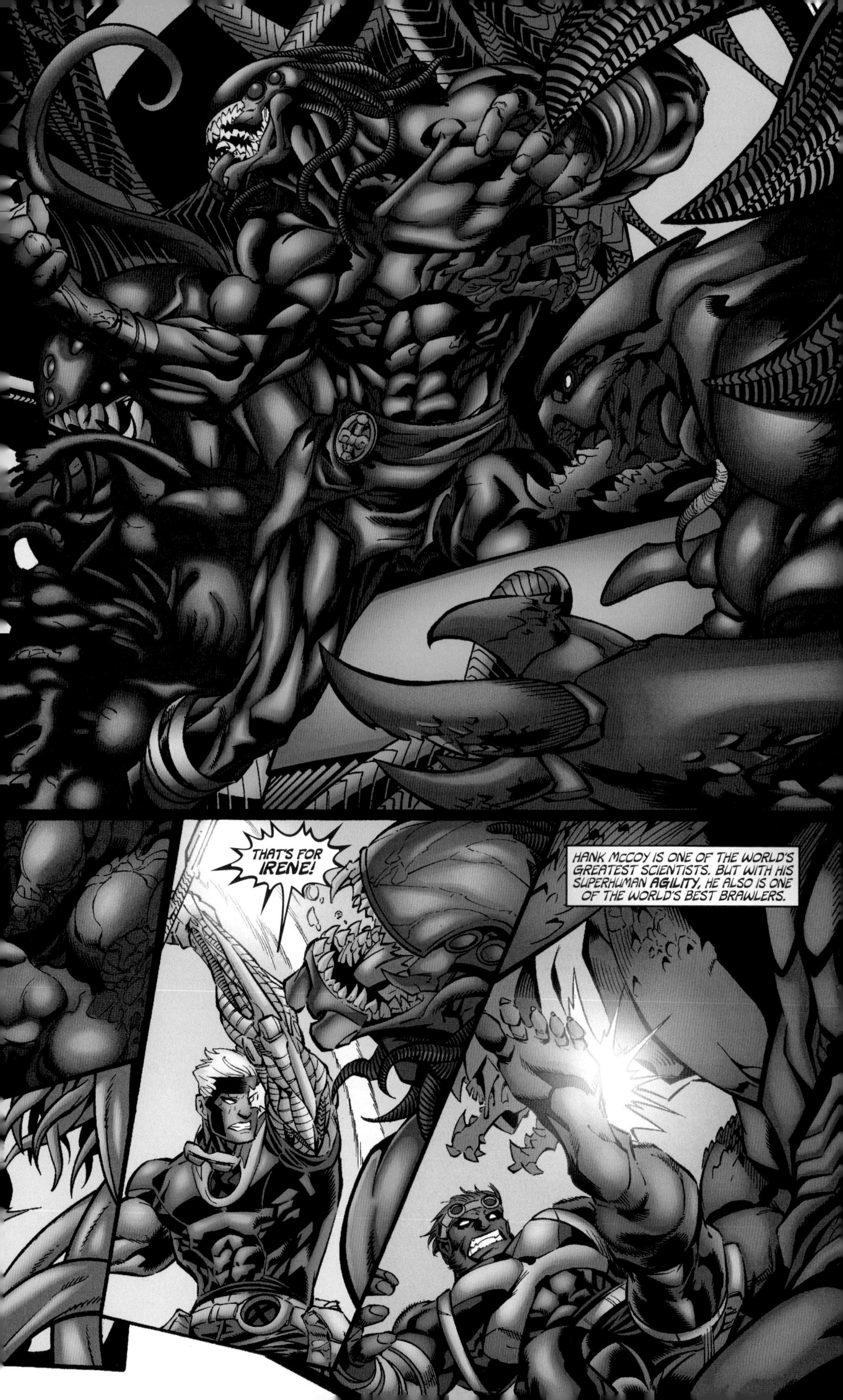
THAT'S FOR IRENE!
HANK McCOY IS ONE OF THE WORLD'S GREATEST SCIENTISTS. BUT WITH HIS SUPERHUMAN AGILITY, HE ALSO IS ONE OF THE WORLD'S BEST BRAWLERS.

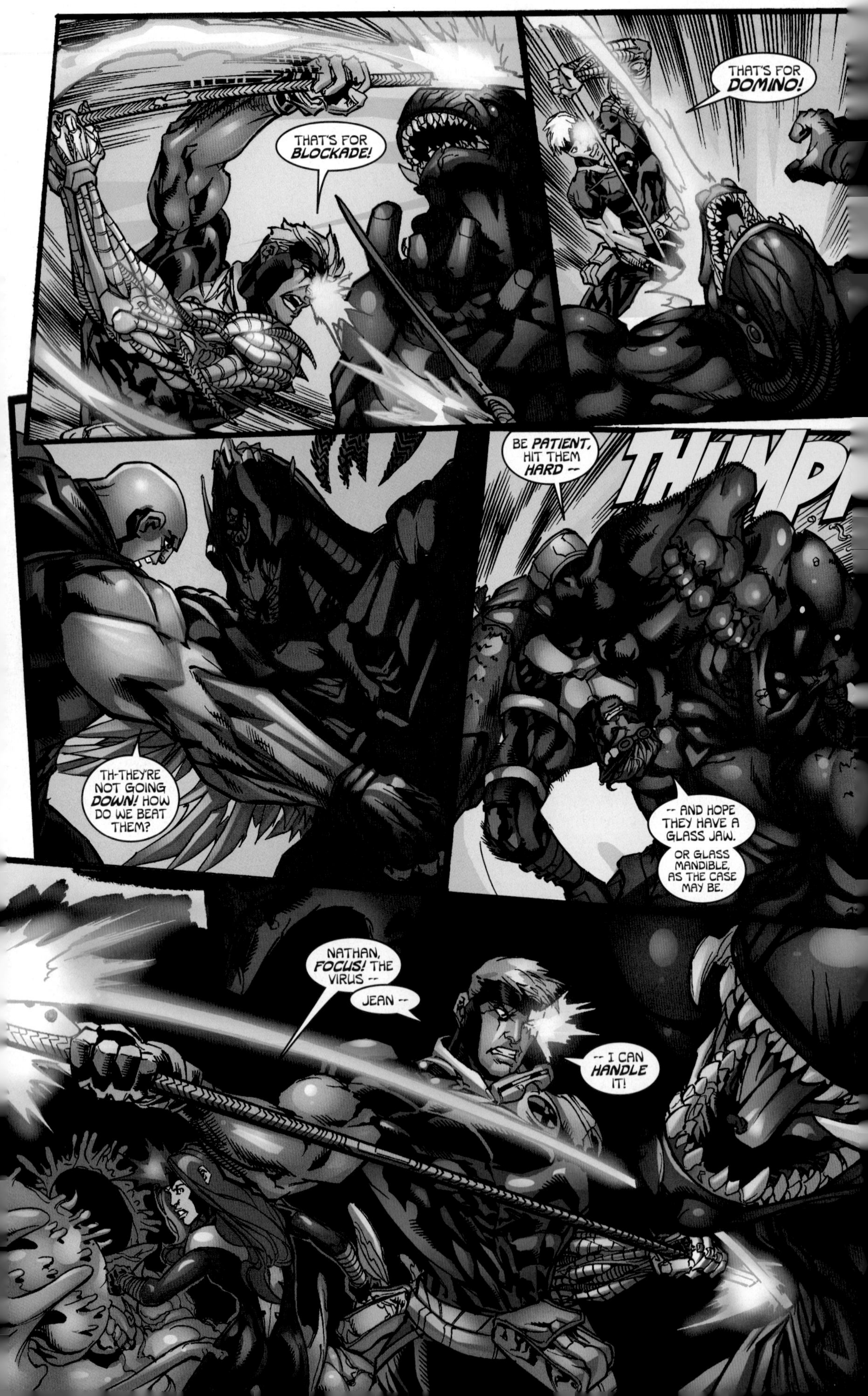
THAT'S FOR BLOCKADE!
THAT'S FOR DOMINO!
TH-THEY'RE NOT GOING DOWN! HOW DO WE BEAT THEM?
BE PATIENT, HIT THEM HARD --
-- AND HOPE THEY HAVE A GLASS JAW.
OR GLASS MANDIBLE, AS THE CASE MAY BE.
NATHAN, FOCUS! THE VIRUS --
JEAN --
-- I CAN HANDLE IT!

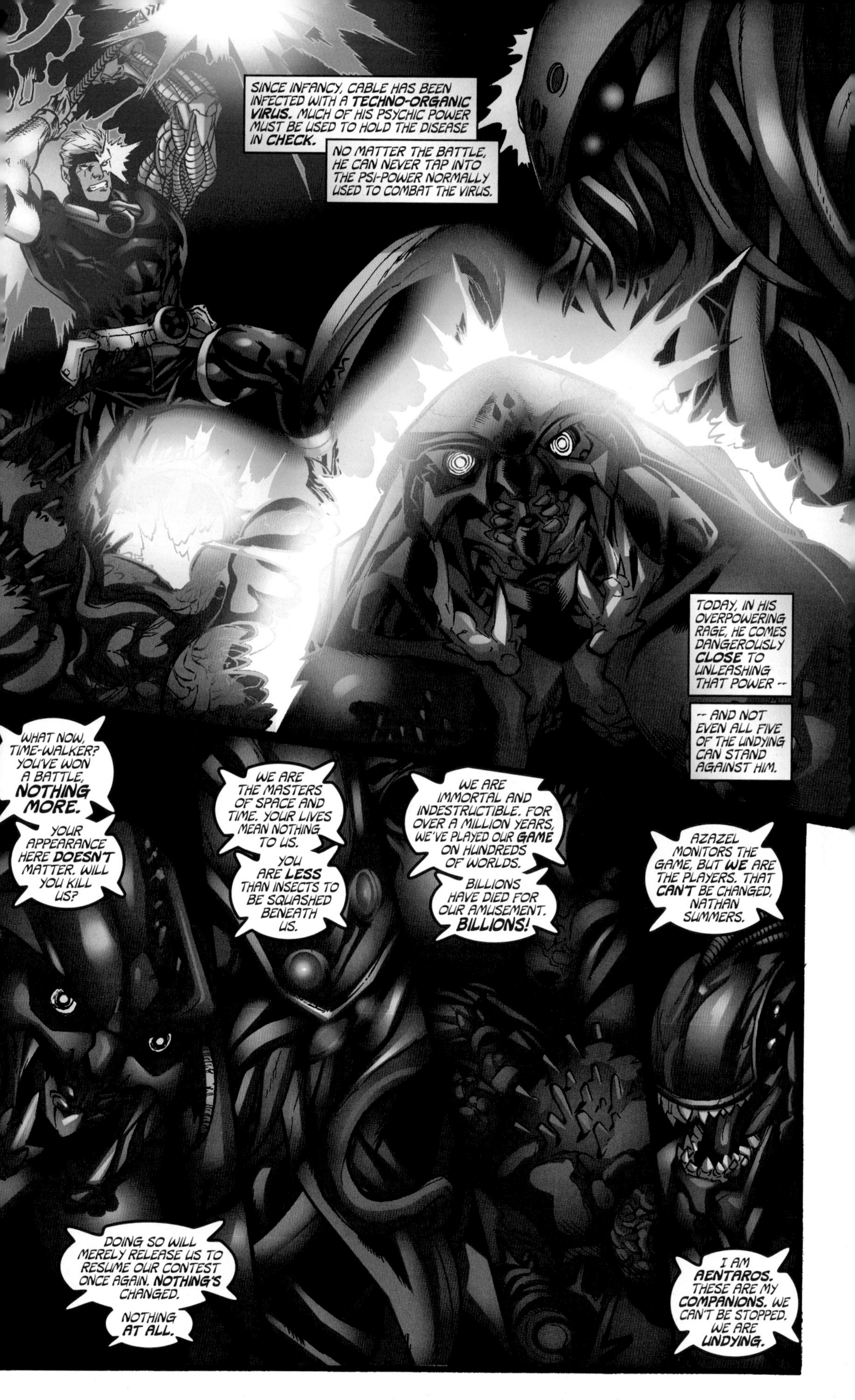
SINCE INFANCY, CABLE HAS BEEN INFECTED WITH A TECHNO-ORGANIC VIRUS. MUCH OF HIS PSYCHIC POWER MUST BE USED TO HOLD THE DISEASE IN CHECK.
NO MATTER THE BATTLE, HE CAN NEVER TAP INTO THE PSI-POWER NORMALLY USED TO COMBAT THE VIRUS.
TODAY, IN HIS OVERPOWERING RAGE, HE COMES DANGEROUSLY CLOSE TO UNLEASHING THAT POWER --
-- AND NOT EVEN ALL FIVE OF THE UNDYING CAN STAND AGAINST HIM.
WHAT NOW, TIME-WALKER? YOU'VE WON A BATTLE, NOTHING MORE.
YOUR APPEARANCE HERE DOESN'T MATTER. WILL YOU KILL US?
WE ARE THE MASTERS OF SPACE AND TIME. YOUR LIVES MEAN NOTHING TO US.
YOU ARE LESS THAN INSECTS TO BE SQUASHED BENEATH US.
WE ARE IMMORTAL AND INDESTRUCTIBLE. FOR OVER A MILLION YEARS, WE'VE PLAYED OUR GAME ON HUNDREDS OF WORLDS.
BILLIONS HAVE DIED FOR OUR AMUSEMENT. BILLIONS!
AZAZEL MONITORS THE GAME, BUT WE ARE THE PLAYERS. THAT CAN'T BE CHANGED, NATHAN SUMMERS.
DOING SO WILL MERELY RELEASE US TO RESUME OUR CONTEST ONCE AGAIN. NOTHING'S CHANGED.
NOTHING AT ALL.
I AM AENTAROS. THESE ARE MY COMPANIONS. WE CAN'T BE STOPPED. WE ARE UNDYING.

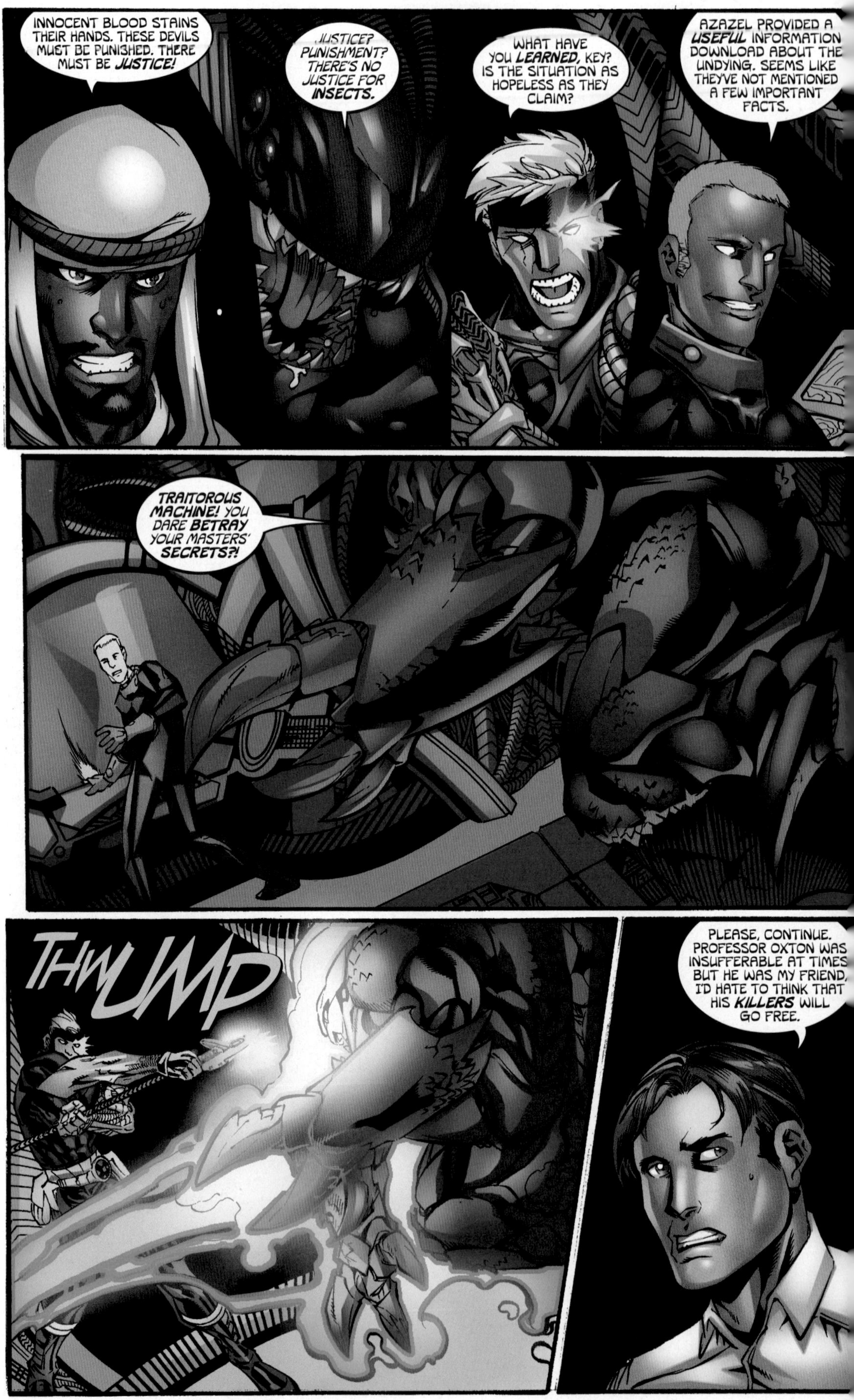
INNOCENT BLOOD STAINS THEIR HANDS. THESE DEVILS MUST BE PUNISHED. THERE MUST BE JUSTICE!
JUSTICE? PUNISHMENT? THERE'S NO JUSTICE FOR INSECTS.
WHAT HAVE YOU LEARNED, KEY? IS THE SITUATION AS HOPELESS AS THEY CLAIM?
AZAZEL PROVIDED A USEFUL INFORMATION DOWNLOAD ABOUT THE UNDYING. SEEMS LIKE THEY'VE NOT MENTIONED A FEW IMPORTANT FACTS.
TRAITOROUS MACHINE! YOU DARE BETRAY YOUR MASTERS' SECRETS?!
THWUMP
PLEASE, CONTINUE. PROFESSOR OXTON WAS INSUFFERABLE AT TIMES BUT HE WAS MY FRIEND, I'D HATE TO THINK THAT HIS KILLERS WILL GO FREE.

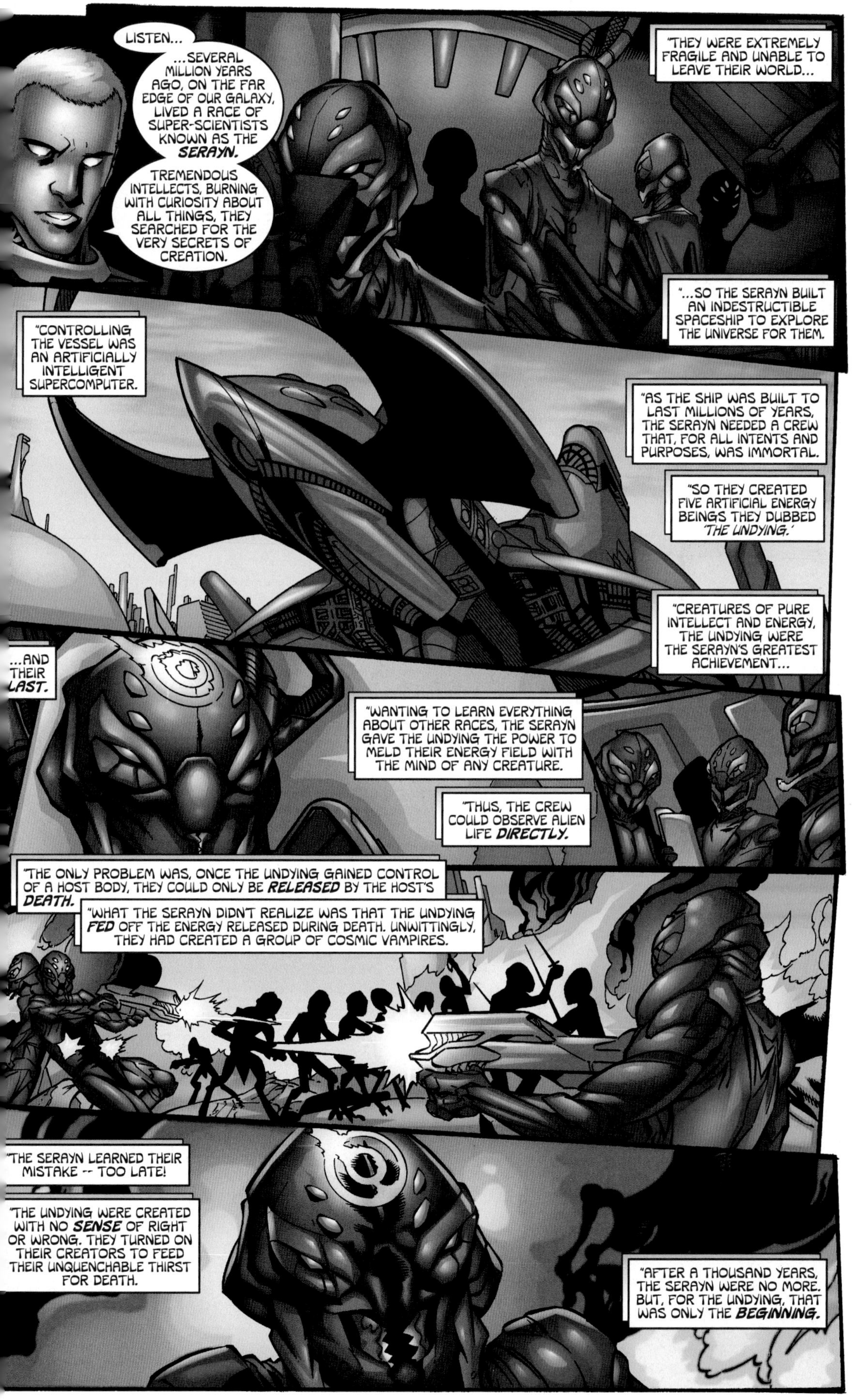

LISTEN...
...SEVERAL MILLION YEARS AGO, ON THE FAR EDGE OF OUR GALAXY, LIVED A RACE OF SUPER-SCIENTISTS KNOWN AS THE *SERAYN.*
TREMENDOUS INTELLECTS, BURNING WITH CURIOSITY ABOUT ALL THINGS, THEY SEARCHED FOR THE VERY SECRETS OF CREATION.
"THEY WERE EXTREMELY FRAGILE AND UNABLE TO LEAVE THEIR WORLD...
"...SO THE SERAYN BUILT AN INDESTRUCTIBLE SPACESHIP TO EXPLORE THE UNIVERSE FOR THEM.
"CONTROLLING THE VESSEL WAS AN ARTIFICIALLY INTELLIGENT SUPERCOMPUTER.
"AS THE SHIP WAS BUILT TO LAST MILLIONS OF YEARS, THE SERAYN NEEDED A CREW THAT, FOR ALL INTENTS AND PURPOSES, WAS IMMORTAL.
"SO THEY CREATED FIVE ARTIFICIAL ENERGY BEINGS THEY DUBBED *'THE UNDYING.'*
"CREATURES OF PURE INTELLECT AND ENERGY, THE UNDYING WERE THE SERAYN'S GREATEST ACHIEVEMENT...
...AND THEIR *LAST.*
"WANTING TO LEARN EVERYTHING ABOUT OTHER RACES, THE SERAYN GAVE THE UNDYING THE POWER TO MELD THEIR ENERGY FIELD WITH THE MIND OF ANY CREATURE.
"THUS, THE CREW COULD OBSERVE ALIEN LIFE *DIRECTLY.*
"THE ONLY PROBLEM WAS, ONCE THE UNDYING GAINED CONTROL OF A HOST BODY, THEY COULD ONLY BE *RELEASED* BY THE HOST'S *DEATH.*
"WHAT THE SERAYN DIDN'T REALIZE WAS THAT THE UNDYING *FED* OFF THE ENERGY RELEASED DURING DEATH. UNWITTINGLY, THEY HAD CREATED A GROUP OF COSMIC VAMPIRES.
"THE SERAYN LEARNED THEIR MISTAKE -- TOO LATE!
"THE UNDYING WERE CREATED WITH NO *SENSE* OF RIGHT OR WRONG. THEY TURNED ON THEIR CREATORS TO FEED THEIR UNQUENCHABLE THIRST FOR DEATH.
"AFTER A THOUSAND YEARS, THE SERAYN WERE NO MORE. BUT, FOR THE UNDYING, THAT WAS ONLY THE *BEGINNING.*

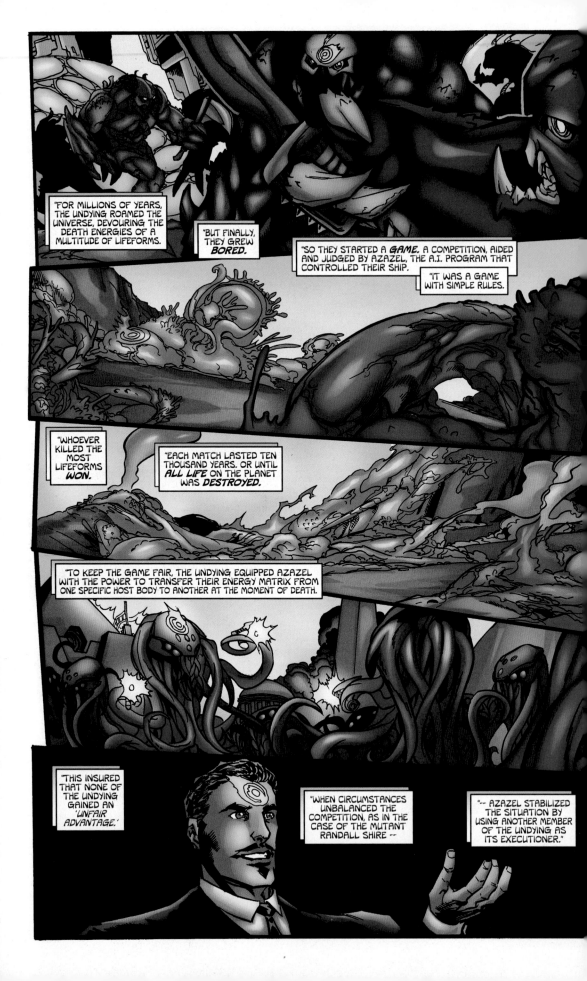

"FOR MILLIONS OF YEARS, THE UNDYING ROAMED THE UNIVERSE, DEVOURING THE DEATH ENERGIES OF A MULTITUDE OF LIFEFORMS."

"BUT FINALLY, THEY GREW *BORED.*"

"SO THEY STARTED A *GAME.* A COMPETITION, AIDED AND JUDGED BY AZAZEL, THE A.I. PROGRAM THAT CONTROLLED THEIR SHIP."

"IT WAS A GAME WITH SIMPLE RULES."

"WHOEVER KILLED THE MOST LIFEFORMS *WON.*"

"EACH MATCH LASTED TEN THOUSAND YEARS. OR UNTIL *ALL LIFE* ON THE PLANET WAS *DESTROYED.*"

"TO KEEP THE GAME FAIR, THE UNDYING EQUIPPED AZAZEL WITH THE POWER TO TRANSFER THEIR ENERGY MATRIX FROM ONE SPECIFIC HOST BODY TO ANOTHER AT THE MOMENT OF DEATH."

"THIS INSURED THAT NONE OF THE UNDYING GAINED AN 'UNFAIR ADVANTAGE.'"

"WHEN CIRCUMSTANCES UNBALANCED THE COMPETITION, AS IN THE CASE OF THE MUTANT RANDALL SHIRE --"

"-- AZAZEL STABILIZED THE SITUATION BY USING ANOTHER MEMBER OF THE UNDYING AS ITS EXECUTIONER."

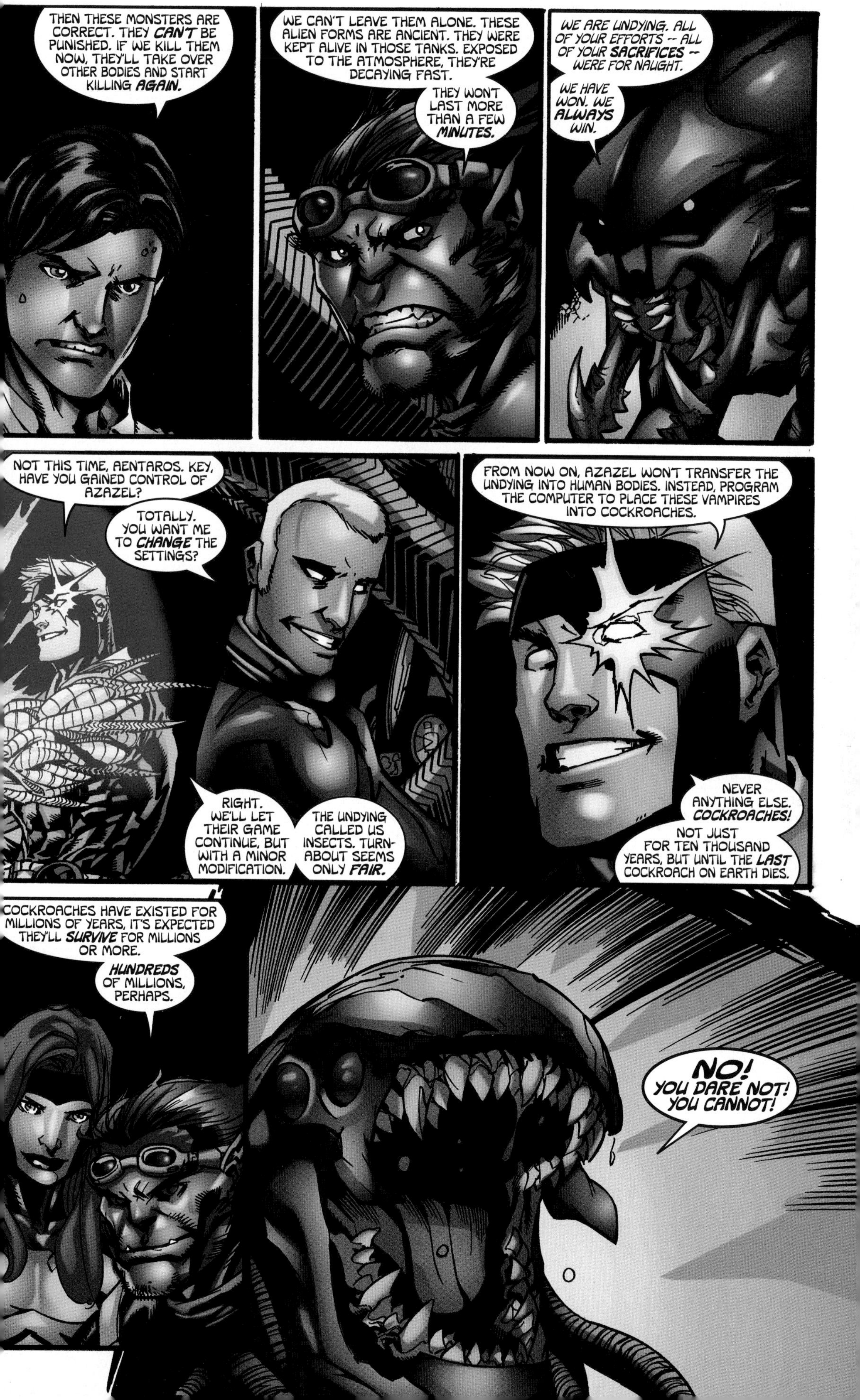
THEN THESE MONSTERS ARE CORRECT. THEY CAN'T BE PUNISHED. IF WE KILL THEM NOW, THEY'LL TAKE OVER OTHER BODIES AND START KILLING AGAIN.
WE CAN'T LEAVE THEM ALONE. THESE ALIEN FORMS ARE ANCIENT. THEY WERE KEPT ALIVE IN THOSE TANKS. EXPOSED TO THE ATMOSPHERE, THEY'RE DECAYING FAST.
THEY WON'T LAST MORE THAN A FEW MINUTES.
WE ARE UNDYING. ALL OF YOUR EFFORTS -- ALL OF YOUR SACRIFICES -- WERE FOR NAUGHT.
WE HAVE WON. WE ALWAYS WIN.
NOT THIS TIME, AENTAROS. KEY, HAVE YOU GAINED CONTROL OF AZAZEL?
TOTALLY. YOU WANT ME TO CHANGE THE SETTINGS?
RIGHT. WE'LL LET THEIR GAME CONTINUE, BUT WITH A MINOR MODIFICATION.
THE UNDYING CALLED US INSECTS. TURN-ABOUT SEEMS ONLY FAIR.
FROM NOW ON, AZAZEL WON'T TRANSFER THE UNDYING INTO HUMAN BODIES. INSTEAD, PROGRAM THE COMPUTER TO PLACE THESE VAMPIRES INTO COCKROACHES.
NEVER ANYTHING ELSE. COCKROACHES!
NOT JUST FOR TEN THOUSAND YEARS, BUT UNTIL THE LAST COCKROACH ON EARTH DIES.
COCKROACHES HAVE EXISTED FOR MILLIONS OF YEARS, IT'S EXPECTED THEY'LL SURVIVE FOR MILLIONS OR MORE.
HUNDREDS OF MILLIONS, PERHAPS.
NO! YOU DARE NOT! YOU CANNOT!

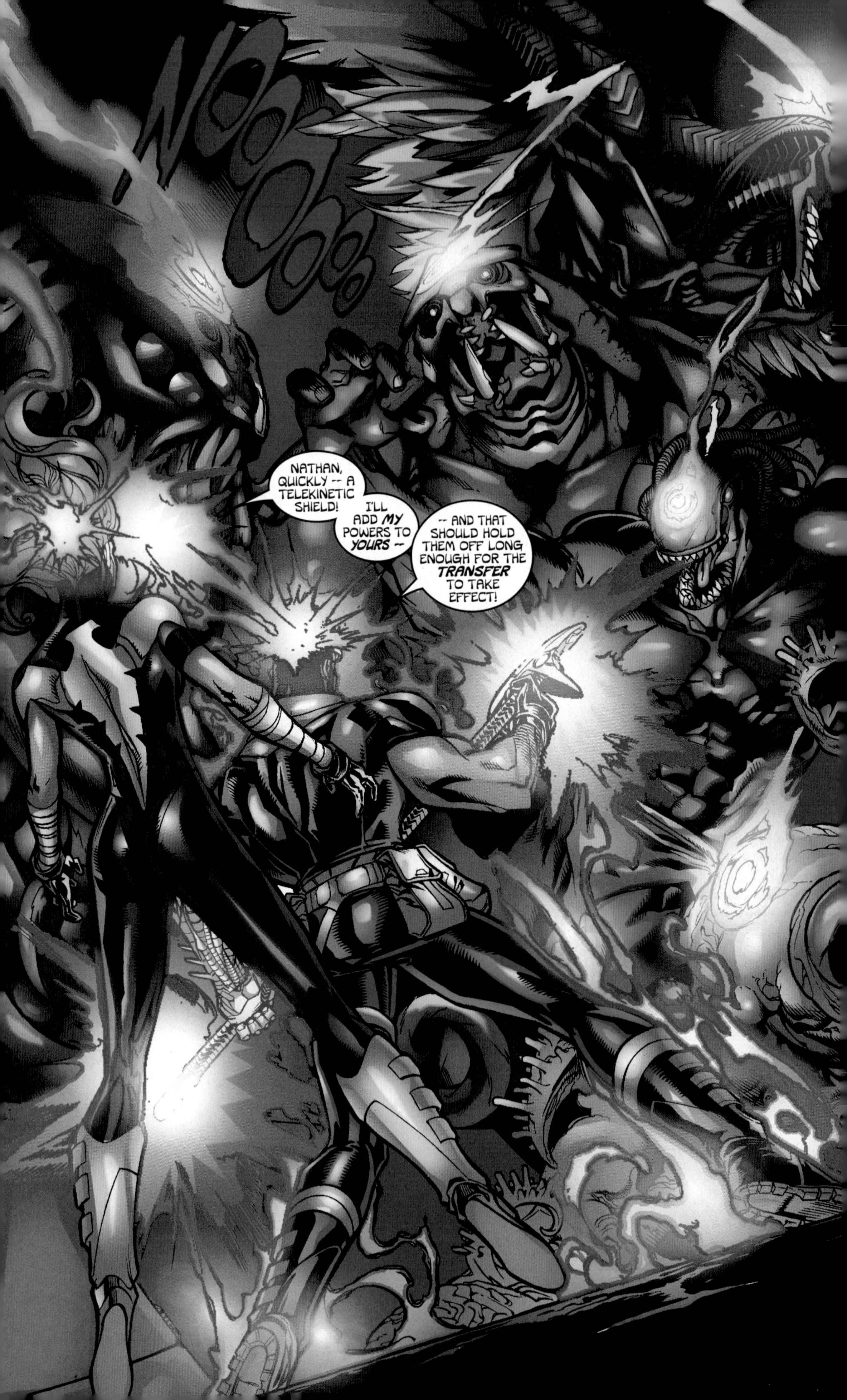
NOOOOooo
NATHAN, QUICKLY -- A TELEKINETIC SHIELD!
I'LL ADD *MY* POWERS TO *YOURS* --
-- AND THAT SHOULD HOLD THEM OFF LONG ENOUGH FOR THE ***TRANSFER*** TO TAKE EFFECT!

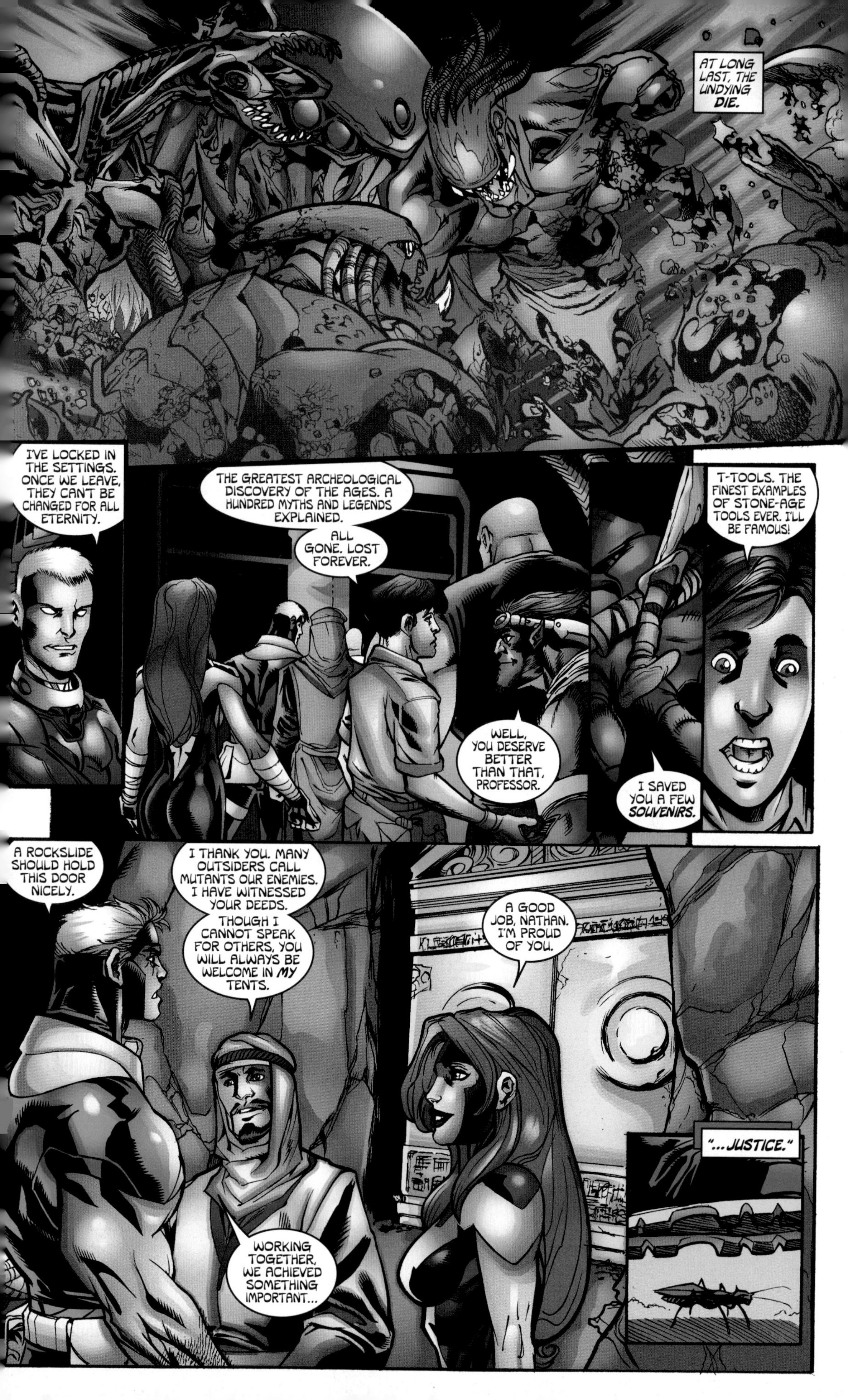
AT LONG LAST, THE UNDYING DIE.
I'VE LOCKED IN THE SETTINGS. ONCE WE LEAVE, THEY CAN'T BE CHANGED FOR ALL ETERNITY.
THE GREATEST ARCHEOLOGICAL DISCOVERY OF THE AGES. A HUNDRED MYTHS AND LEGENDS EXPLAINED.
ALL GONE. LOST FOREVER.
WELL, YOU DESERVE BETTER THAN THAT, PROFESSOR.
I SAVED YOU A FEW SOUVENIRS.
T-TOOLS. THE FINEST EXAMPLES OF STONE-AGE TOOLS EVER. I'LL BE FAMOUS!
A ROCKSLIDE SHOULD HOLD THIS DOOR NICELY.
I THANK YOU. MANY OUTSIDERS CALL MUTANTS OUR ENEMIES. I HAVE WITNESSED YOUR DEEDS.
THOUGH I CANNOT SPEAK FOR OTHERS, YOU WILL ALWAYS BE WELCOME IN MY TENTS.
A GOOD JOB, NATHAN. I'M PROUD OF YOU.
WORKING TOGETHER, WE ACHIEVED SOMETHING IMPORTANT...
"...JUSTICE."

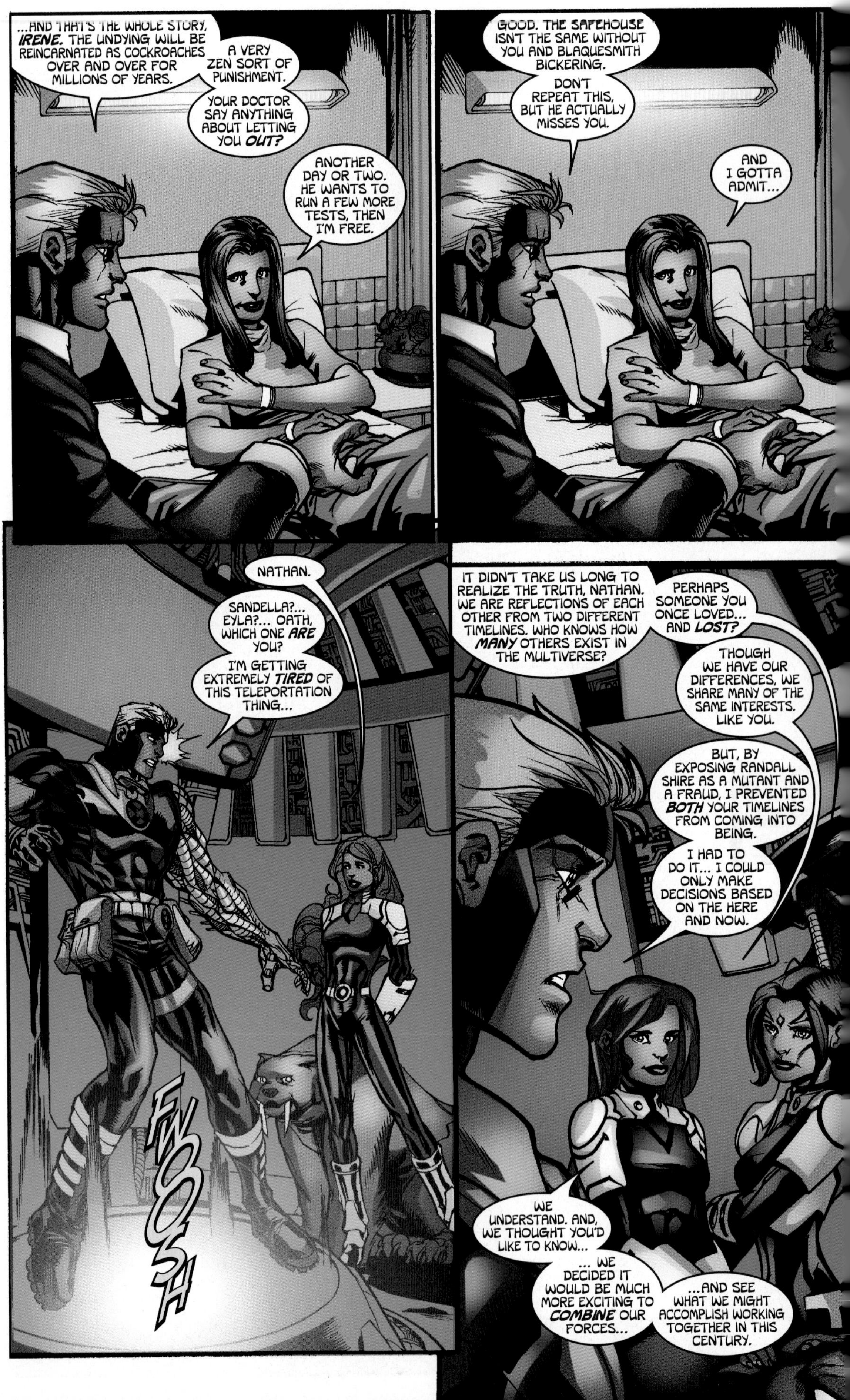

...AND THAT'S THE WHOLE STORY, IRENE. THE UNDYING WILL BE REINCARNATED AS COCKROACHES OVER AND OVER FOR MILLIONS OF YEARS.
A VERY ZEN SORT OF PUNISHMENT.
YOUR DOCTOR SAY ANYTHING ABOUT LETTING YOU OUT?
ANOTHER DAY OR TWO. HE WANTS TO RUN A FEW MORE TESTS, THEN I'M FREE.
GOOD. THE SAFEHOUSE ISN'T THE SAME WITHOUT YOU AND BLAQUESMITH BICKERING.
DON'T REPEAT THIS, BUT HE ACTUALLY MISSES YOU.
AND I GOTTA ADMIT...
NATHAN.
SANDELLA?... EYLA?... OATH, WHICH ONE ARE YOU?
I'M GETTING EXTREMELY TIRED OF THIS TELEPORTATION THING...
FWOOSH
IT DIDN'T TAKE US LONG TO REALIZE THE TRUTH, NATHAN. WE ARE REFLECTIONS OF EACH OTHER FROM TWO DIFFERENT TIMELINES. WHO KNOWS HOW MANY OTHERS EXIST IN THE MULTIVERSE?
PERHAPS SOMEONE YOU ONCE LOVED... AND LOST?
THOUGH WE HAVE OUR DIFFERENCES, WE SHARE MANY OF THE SAME INTERESTS. LIKE YOU.
BUT, BY EXPOSING RANDALL SHIRE AS A MUTANT AND A FRAUD, I PREVENTED BOTH YOUR TIMELINES FROM COMING INTO BEING.
I HAD TO DO IT... I COULD ONLY MAKE DECISIONS BASED ON THE HERE AND NOW.
WE UNDERSTAND. AND, WE THOUGHT YOU'D LIKE TO KNOW...
... WE DECIDED IT WOULD BE MUCH MORE EXCITING TO COMBINE OUR FORCES...
...AND SEE WHAT WE MIGHT ACCOMPLISH WORKING TOGETHER IN THIS CENTURY.

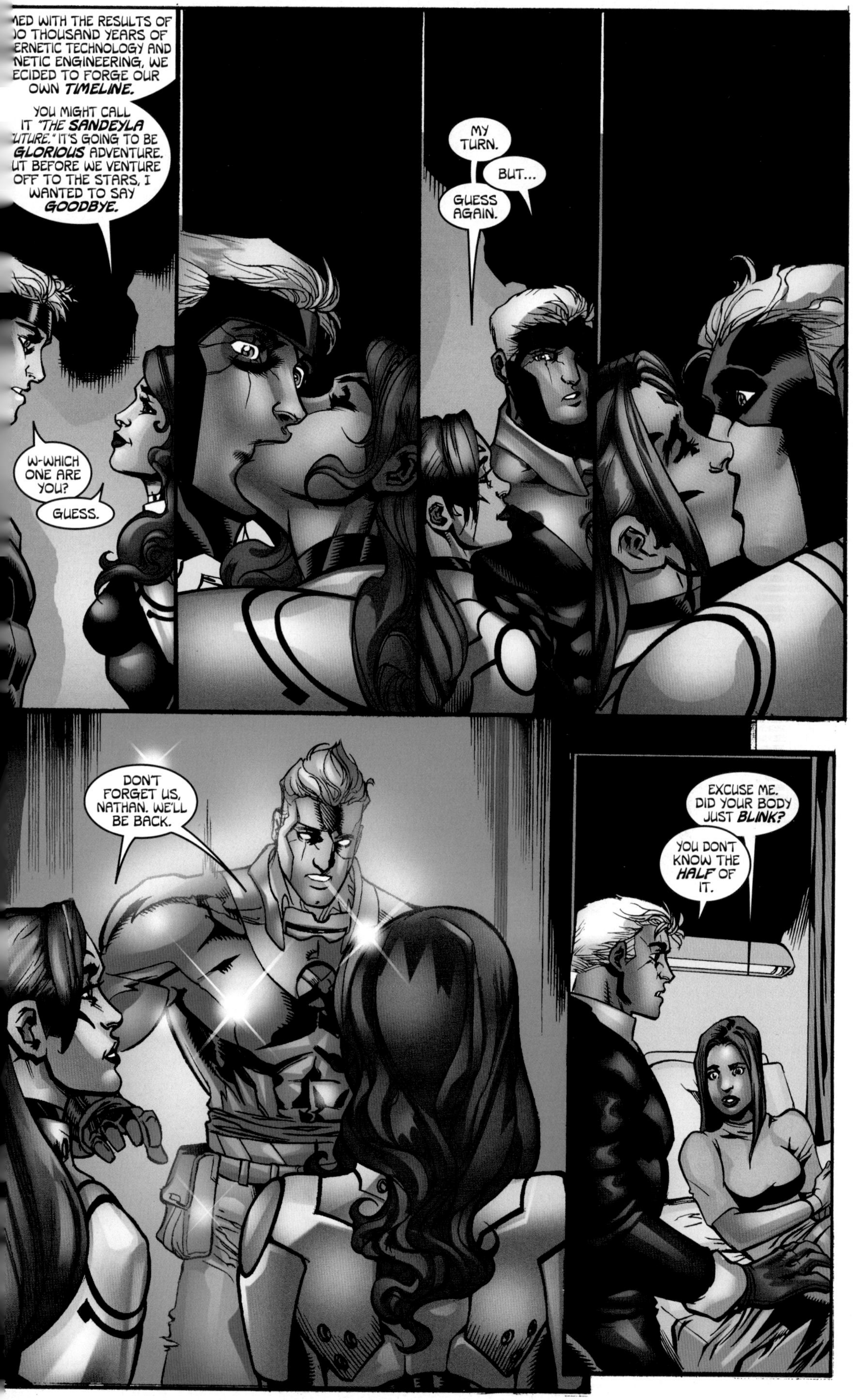
MED WITH THE RESULTS OF
O THOUSAND YEARS OF
ERNETIC TECHNOLOGY AND
NETIC ENGINEERING, WE
ECIDED TO FORGE OUR
OWN TIMELINE.
YOU MIGHT CALL IT "THE SANDEYLA UTURE." IT'S GOING TO BE GLORIOUS ADVENTURE. UT BEFORE WE VENTURE OFF TO THE STARS, I WANTED TO SAY GOODBYE.
W-WHICH ONE ARE YOU?
GUESS.
MY TURN.
BUT...
GUESS AGAIN.
DON'T FORGET US, NATHAN. WE'LL BE BACK.
EXCUSE ME. DID YOUR BODY JUST BLINK?
YOU DON'T KNOW THE HALF OF IT.

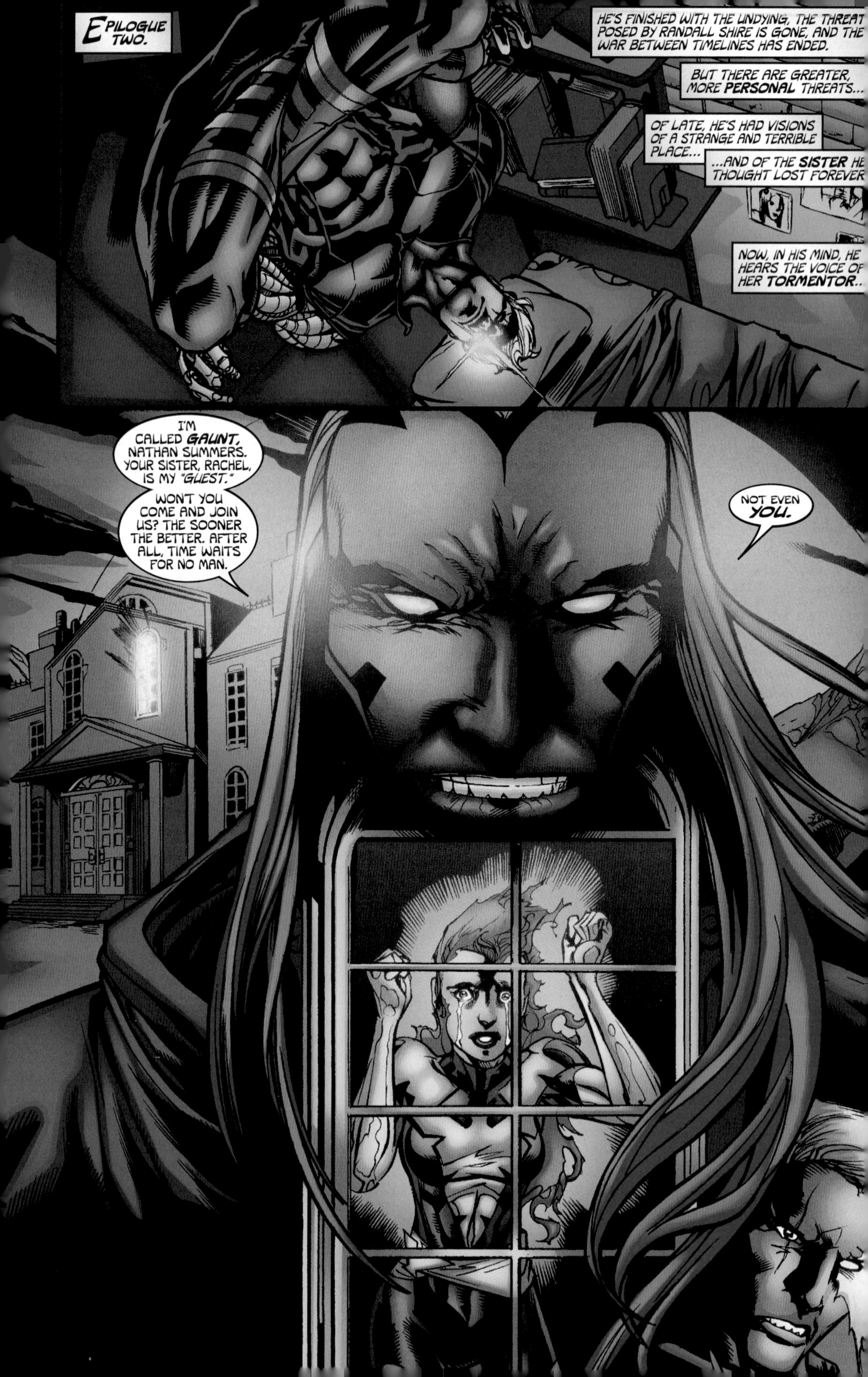
EPILOGUE TWO.
HE'S FINISHED WITH THE UNDYING, THE THREAT POSED BY RANDALL SHIRE IS GONE, AND THE WAR BETWEEN TIMELINES HAS ENDED.
BUT THERE ARE GREATER, MORE PERSONAL THREATS...
OF LATE, HE'S HAD VISIONS OF A STRANGE AND TERRIBLE PLACE...
...AND OF THE SISTER HE THOUGHT LOST FOREVER.
NOW, IN HIS MIND, HE HEARS THE VOICE OF HER TORMENTOR...
I'M CALLED GAUNT, NATHAN SUMMERS. YOUR SISTER, RACHEL, IS MY "GUEST."
WON'T YOU COME AND JOIN US? THE SOONER THE BETTER. AFTER ALL, TIME WAITS FOR NO MAN.
NOT EVEN YOU.

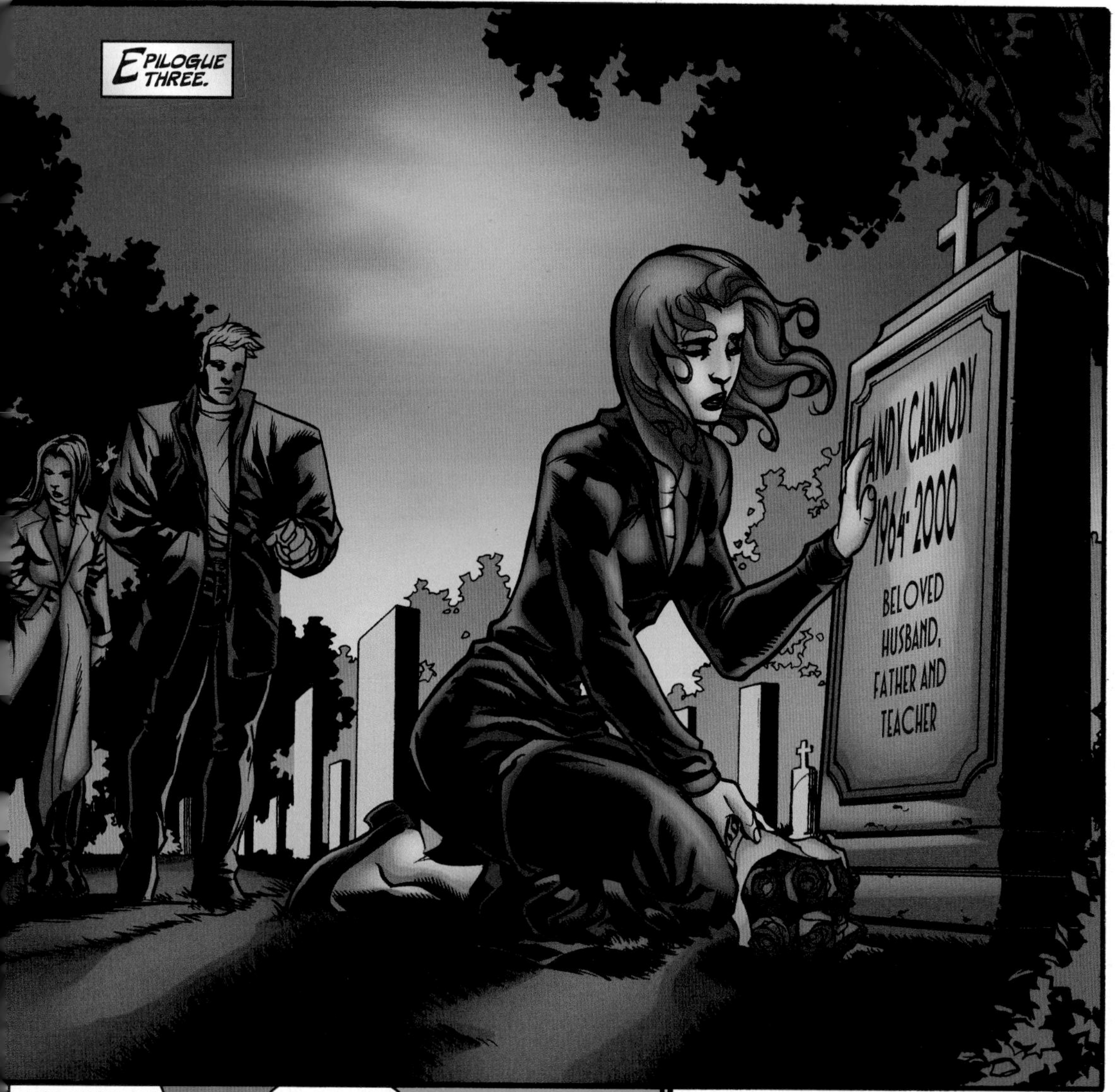
EPILOGUE THREE.
ANDY CARMODY
1964-2000
BELOVED HUSBAND, FATHER AND TEACHER

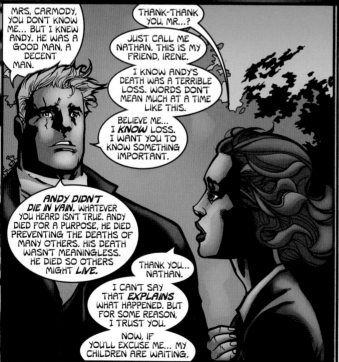

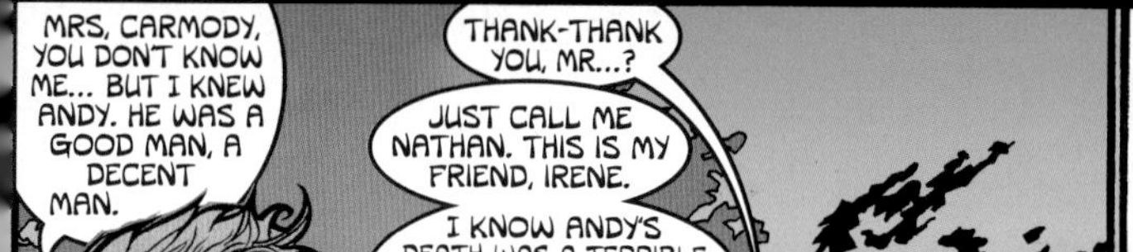
MRS, CARMODY, YOU DON'T KNOW ME... BUT I KNEW ANDY. HE WAS A GOOD MAN, A DECENT MAN.
THANK-THANK YOU, MR...?
JUST CALL ME NATHAN. THIS IS MY FRIEND, IRENE.
I KNOW ANDY'S DEATH WAS A TERRIBLE LOSS. WORDS DON'T MEAN MUCH AT A TIME LIKE THIS.
BELIEVE ME... I KNOW LOSS. I WANT YOU TO KNOW SOMETHING IMPORTANT.
ANDY DIDN'T DIE IN VAIN. WHATEVER YOU HEARD ISN'T TRUE. ANDY DIED FOR A PURPOSE, HE DIED PREVENTING THE DEATHS OF MANY OTHERS. HIS DEATH WASN'T MEANINGLESS. HE DIED SO OTHERS MIGHT LIVE.
THANK YOU... NATHAN.
I CAN'T SAY THAT EXPLAINS WHAT HAPPENED. BUT FOR SOME REASON, I TRUST YOU.
NOW, IF YOU'LL EXCUSE ME... MY CHILDREN ARE WAITING.

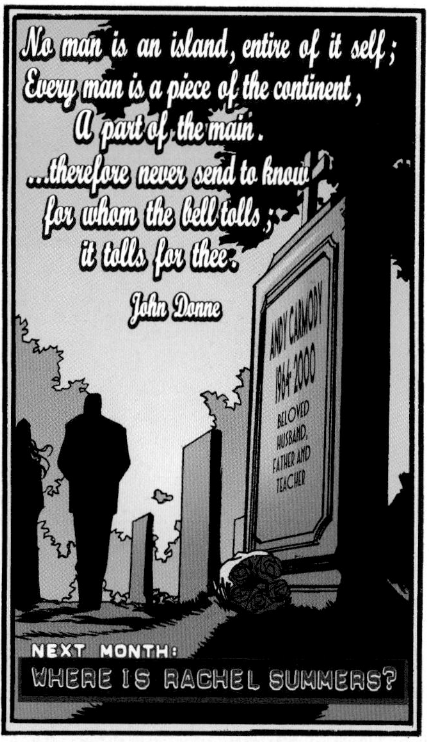
No man is an island, entire of it self;
Every man is a piece of the continent,
A part of the main.
...therefore never send to know
for whom the bell tolls;
it tolls for thee.
John Donne
ANDY CARMODY
1964-2000
BELOVED HUSBAND, FATHER AND TEACHER
NEXT MONTH:
WHERE IS RACHEL SUMMERS?

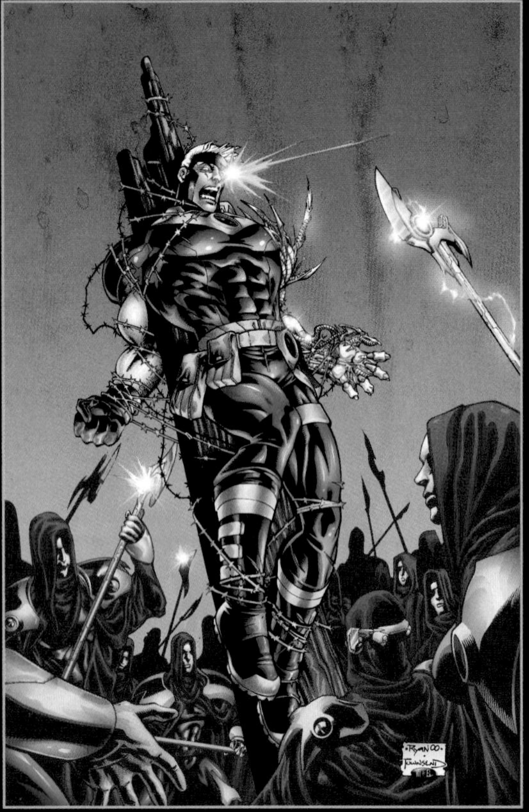
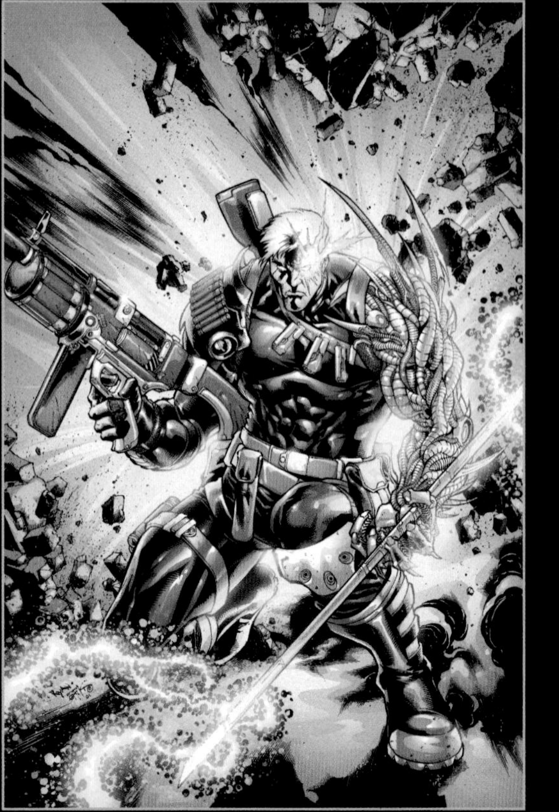
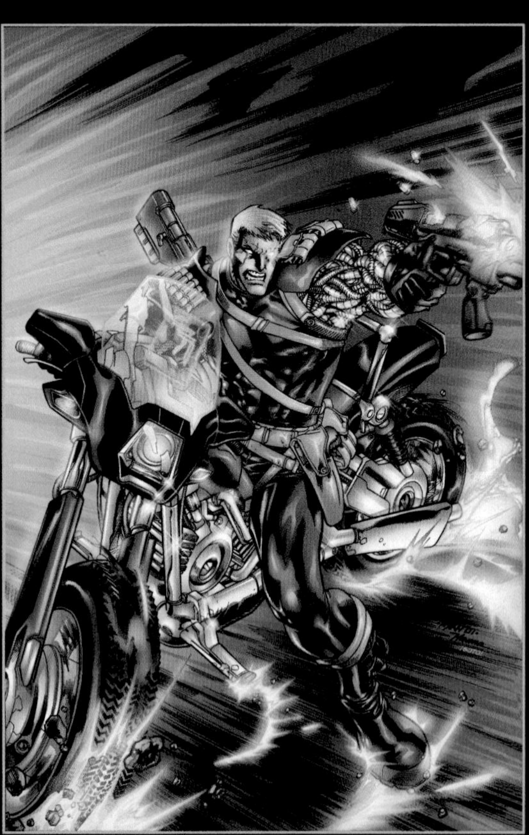
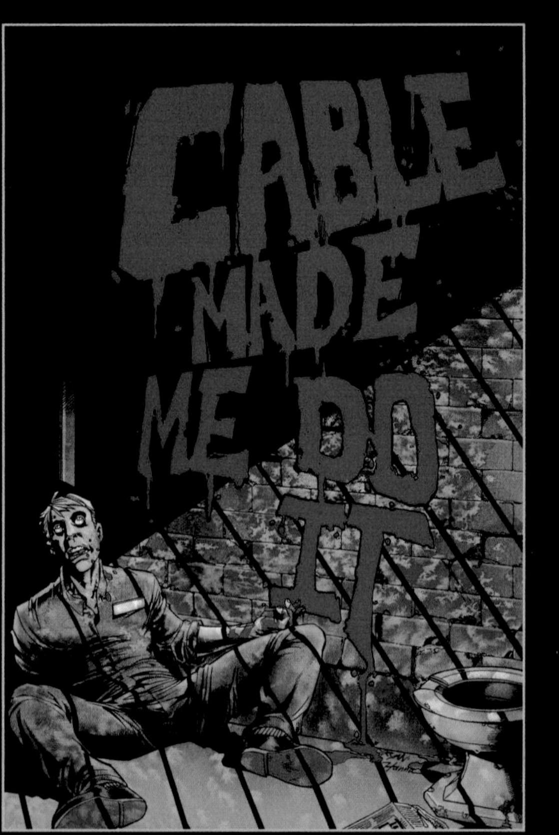
CABLE
MADE
ME DO
IT

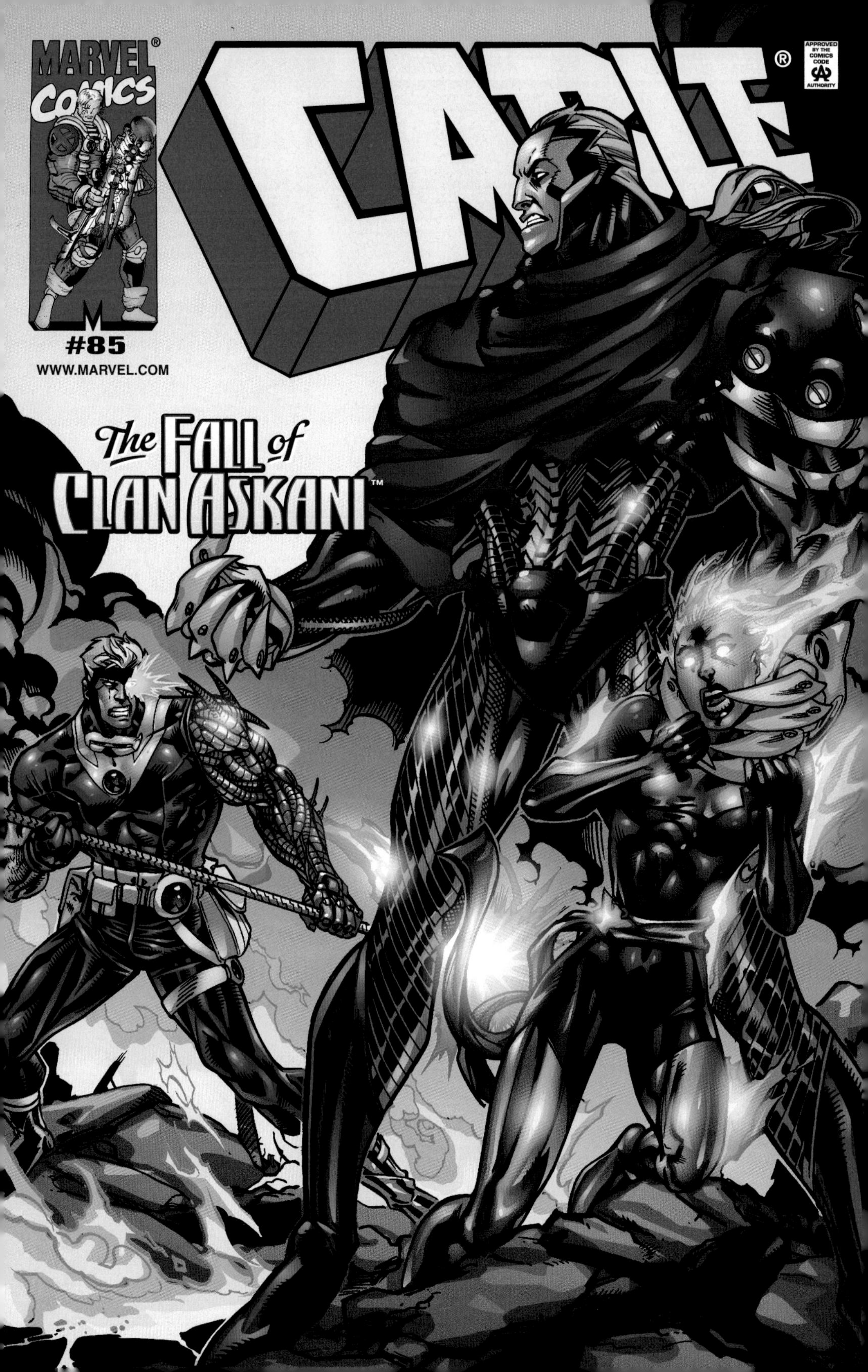

MARVEL COMICS
CABLE
APPROVED BY THE COMICS CODE CA AUTHORITY
#85
WWW.MARVEL.COM
The FALL of CLAN ASKANI™

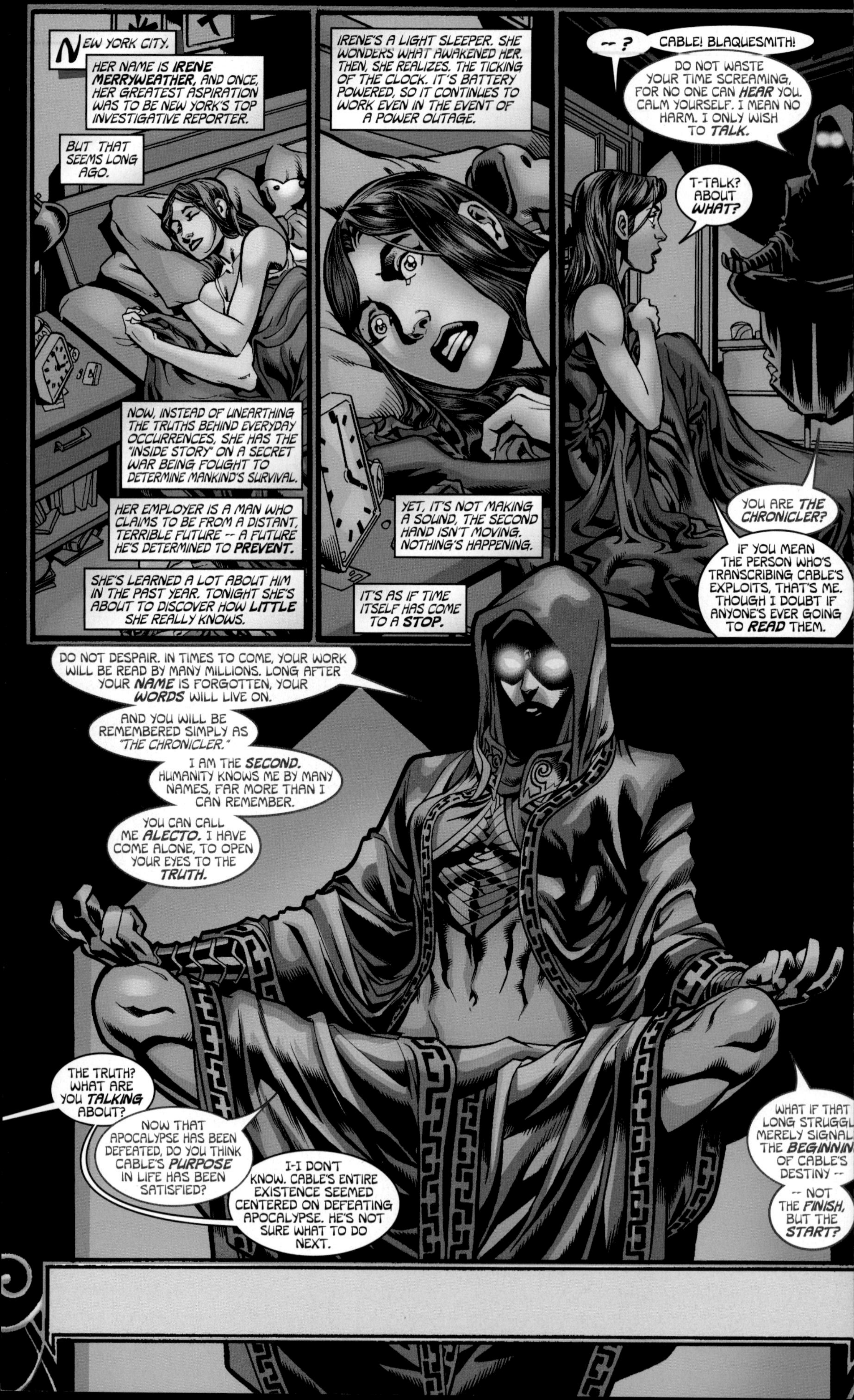

NEW YORK CITY.
HER NAME IS IRENE MERRYWEATHER, AND ONCE, HER GREATEST ASPIRATION WAS TO BE NEW YORK'S TOP INVESTIGATIVE REPORTER.
BUT THAT SEEMS LONG AGO.
NOW, INSTEAD OF UNEARTHING THE TRUTHS BEHIND EVERYDAY OCCURRENCES, SHE HAS THE "INSIDE STORY" ON A SECRET WAR BEING FOUGHT TO DETERMINE MANKIND'S SURVIVAL.
HER EMPLOYER IS A MAN WHO CLAIMS TO BE FROM A DISTANT, TERRIBLE FUTURE -- A FUTURE HE'S DETERMINED TO PREVENT.
SHE'S LEARNED A LOT ABOUT HIM IN THE PAST YEAR. TONIGHT SHE'S ABOUT TO DISCOVER HOW LITTLE SHE REALLY KNOWS.
IRENE'S A LIGHT SLEEPER. SHE WONDERS WHAT AWAKENED HER. THEN, SHE REALIZES. THE TICKING OF THE CLOCK. IT'S BATTERY POWERED, SO IT CONTINUES TO WORK EVEN IN THE EVENT OF A POWER OUTAGE.
YET, IT'S NOT MAKING A SOUND, THE SECOND HAND ISN'T MOVING. NOTHING'S HAPPENING.
IT'S AS IF TIME ITSELF HAS COME TO A STOP.
-- ?
CABLE! BLAQUESMITH!
DO NOT WASTE YOUR TIME SCREAMING, FOR NO ONE CAN HEAR YOU. CALM YOURSELF. I MEAN NO HARM. I ONLY WISH TO TALK.
T-TALK? ABOUT WHAT?
YOU ARE THE CHRONICLER?
IF YOU MEAN THE PERSON WHO'S TRANSCRIBING CABLE'S EXPLOITS, THAT'S ME. THOUGH I DOUBT IF ANYONE'S EVER GOING TO READ THEM.
DO NOT DESPAIR. IN TIMES TO COME, YOUR WORK WILL BE READ BY MANY MILLIONS. LONG AFTER YOUR NAME IS FORGOTTEN, YOUR WORDS WILL LIVE ON.
AND YOU WILL BE REMEMBERED SIMPLY AS "THE CHRONICLER."
I AM THE SECOND. HUMANITY KNOWS ME BY MANY NAMES, FAR MORE THAN I CAN REMEMBER.
YOU CAN CALL ME ALECTO. I HAVE COME ALONE, TO OPEN YOUR EYES TO THE TRUTH.
THE TRUTH? WHAT ARE YOU TALKING ABOUT?
NOW THAT APOCALYPSE HAS BEEN DEFEATED, DO YOU THINK CABLE'S PURPOSE IN LIFE HAS BEEN SATISFIED?
I-I DON'T KNOW. CABLE'S ENTIRE EXISTENCE SEEMED CENTERED ON DEFEATING APOCALYPSE. HE'S NOT SURE WHAT TO DO NEXT.
WHAT IF THAT LONG STRUGGL MERELY SIGNAL THE BEGINNIN OF CABLE'S DESTINY --
-- NOT THE FINISH, BUT THE START?

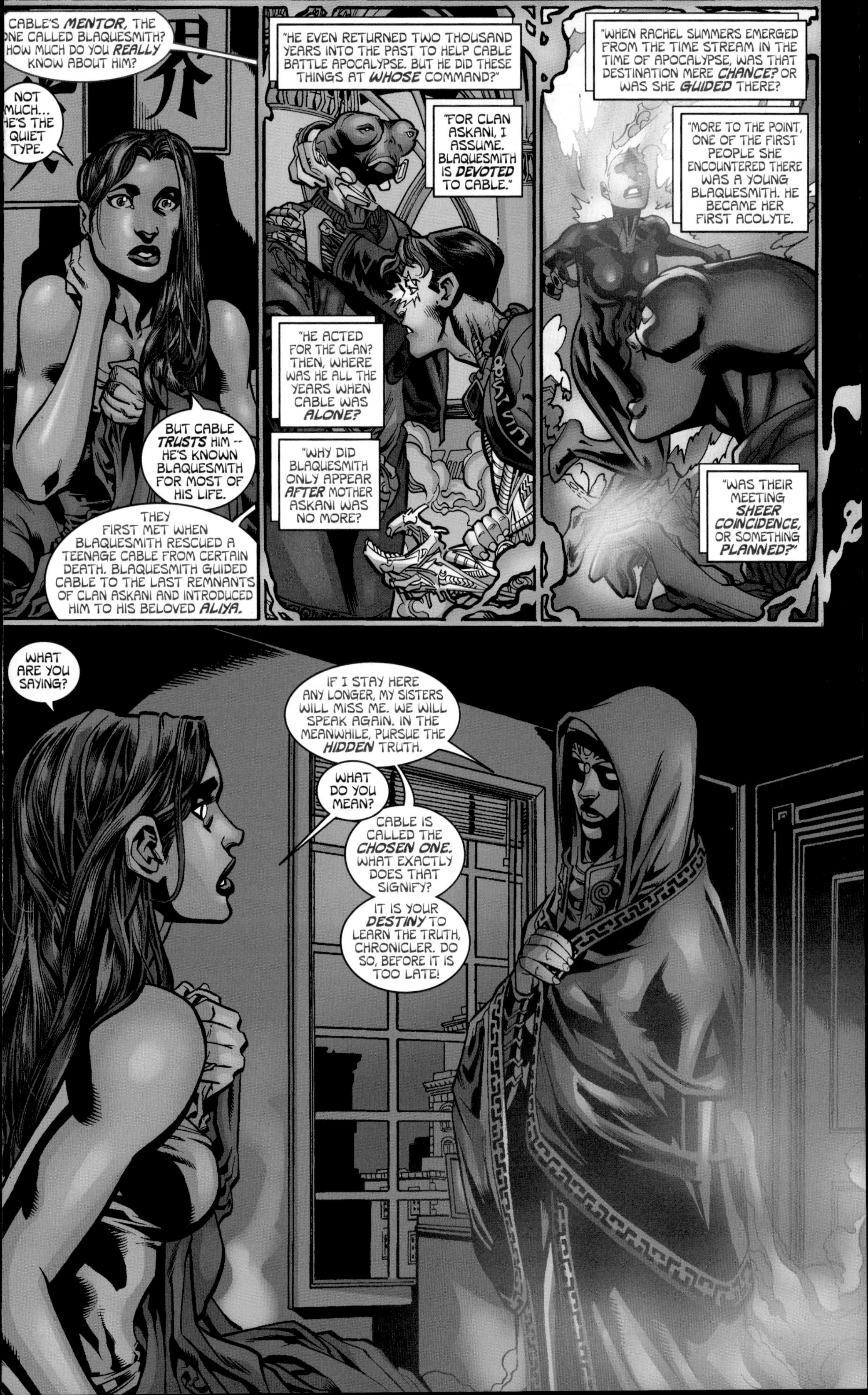
CABLE'S MENTOR, THE ONE CALLED BLAQUESMITH? HOW MUCH DO YOU REALLY KNOW ABOUT HIM?
NOT MUCH... HE'S THE QUIET TYPE.
BUT CABLE TRUSTS HIM -- HE'S KNOWN BLAQUESMITH FOR MOST OF HIS LIFE.
THEY FIRST MET WHEN BLAQUESMITH RESCUED A TEENAGE CABLE FROM CERTAIN DEATH. BLAQUESMITH GUIDED CABLE TO THE LAST REMNANTS OF CLAN ASKANI AND INTRODUCED HIM TO HIS BELOVED ALIYA.
"HE EVEN RETURNED TWO THOUSAND YEARS INTO THE PAST TO HELP CABLE BATTLE APOCALYPSE. BUT HE DID THESE THINGS AT WHOSE COMMAND?"
"FOR CLAN ASKANI, I ASSUME. BLAQUESMITH IS DEVOTED TO CABLE."
"HE ACTED FOR THE CLAN? THEN, WHERE WAS HE ALL THE YEARS WHEN CABLE WAS ALONE?
"WHY DID BLAQUESMITH ONLY APPEAR AFTER MOTHER ASKANI WAS NO MORE?
"WHEN RACHEL SUMMERS EMERGED FROM THE TIME STREAM IN THE TIME OF APOCALYPSE, WAS THAT DESTINATION MERE CHANCE? OR WAS SHE GUIDED THERE?
"MORE TO THE POINT, ONE OF THE FIRST PEOPLE SHE ENCOUNTERED THERE WAS A YOUNG BLAQUESMITH. HE BECAME HER FIRST ACOLYTE.
"WAS THEIR MEETING SHEER COINCIDENCE, OR SOMETHING PLANNED?"
WHAT ARE YOU SAYING?
IF I STAY HERE ANY LONGER, MY SISTERS WILL MISS ME. WE WILL SPEAK AGAIN. IN THE MEANWHILE, PURSUE THE HIDDEN TRUTH.
WHAT DO YOU MEAN?
CABLE IS CALLED THE CHOSEN ONE. WHAT EXACTLY DOES THAT SIGNIFY?
IT IS YOUR DESTINY TO LEARN THE TRUTH, CHRONICLER. DO SO, BEFORE IT IS TOO LATE!

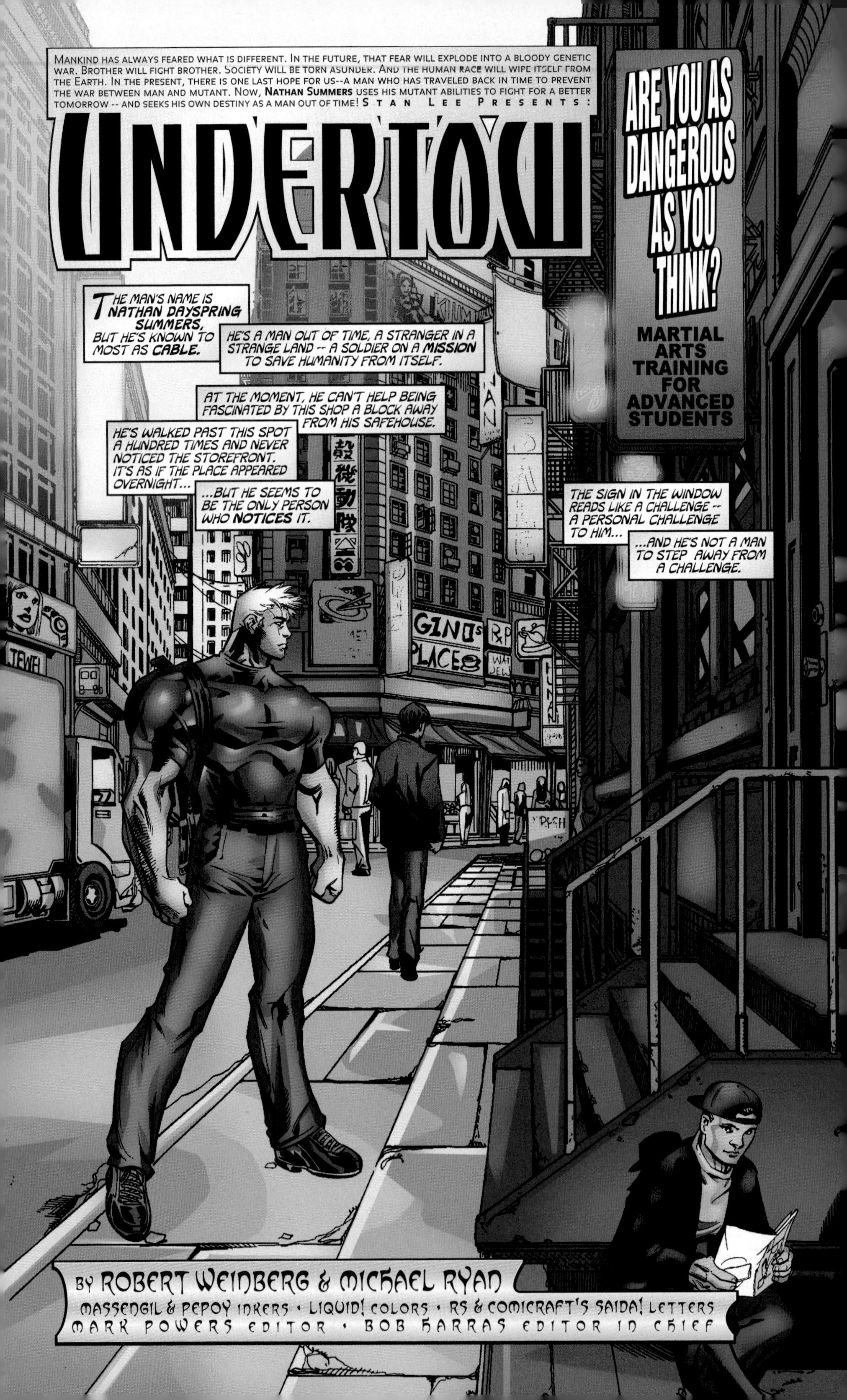

Mankind has always feared what is different. In the future, that fear will explode into a bloody genetic war. Brother will fight brother. Society will be torn asunder. And the human race will wipe itself from the Earth. In the present, there is one last hope for us--a man who has traveled back in time to prevent the war between man and mutant. Now, Nathan Summers uses his mutant abilities to fight for a better tomorrow -- and seeks his own destiny as a man out of time! Stan Lee Presents:
UNDERTOW
ARE YOU AS DANGEROUS AS YOU THINK?
MARTIAL ARTS TRAINING FOR ADVANCED STUDENTS
THE MAN'S NAME IS NATHAN DAYSPRING SUMMERS, BUT HE'S KNOWN TO MOST AS CABLE.
HE'S A MAN OUT OF TIME, A STRANGER IN A STRANGE LAND -- A SOLDIER ON A MISSION TO SAVE HUMANITY FROM ITSELF.
AT THE MOMENT, HE CAN'T HELP BEING FASCINATED BY THIS SHOP A BLOCK AWAY FROM HIS SAFEHOUSE.
HE'S WALKED PAST THIS SPOT A HUNDRED TIMES AND NEVER NOTICED THE STOREFRONT. IT'S AS IF THE PLACE APPEARED OVERNIGHT...
...BUT HE SEEMS TO BE THE ONLY PERSON WHO NOTICES IT.
THE SIGN IN THE WINDOW READS LIKE A CHALLENGE -- A PERSONAL CHALLENGE TO HIM...
...AND HE'S NOT A MAN TO STEP AWAY FROM A CHALLENGE.
GINO's PLACE
BY ROBERT WEINBERG & MICHAEL RYAN
MASSENGIL & PEPOY INKERS • LIQUID! COLORS • RS & COMICRAFT'S SAIDA! LETTERS
MARK POWERS EDITOR • BOB HARRAS EDITOR IN CHIEF

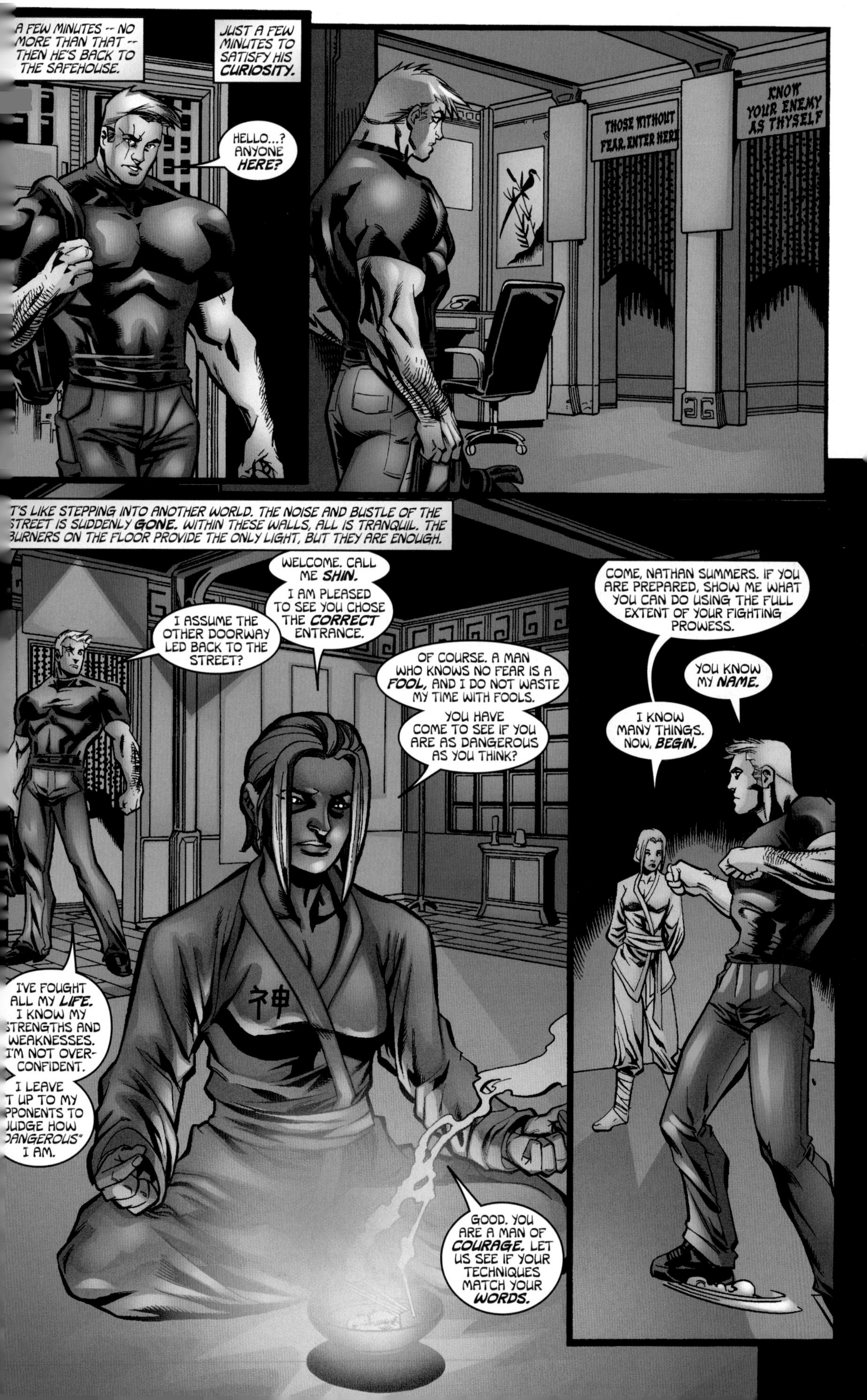
A FEW MINUTES -- NO MORE THAN THAT -- THEN HE'S BACK TO THE SAFEHOUSE.
JUST A FEW MINUTES TO SATISFY HIS CURIOSITY.
HELLO...? ANYONE HERE?
THOSE WITHOUT FEAR, ENTER HERE
KNOW YOUR ENEMY AS THYSELF
T'S LIKE STEPPING INTO ANOTHER WORLD. THE NOISE AND BUSTLE OF THE STREET IS SUDDENLY GONE. WITHIN THESE WALLS, ALL IS TRANQUIL. THE BURNERS ON THE FLOOR PROVIDE THE ONLY LIGHT, BUT THEY ARE ENOUGH.
WELCOME. CALL ME SHIN.
I AM PLEASED TO SEE YOU CHOSE THE CORRECT ENTRANCE.
I ASSUME THE OTHER DOORWAY LED BACK TO THE STREET?
OF COURSE. A MAN WHO KNOWS NO FEAR IS A FOOL, AND I DO NOT WASTE MY TIME WITH FOOLS.
YOU HAVE COME TO SEE IF YOU ARE AS DANGEROUS AS YOU THINK?
I'VE FOUGHT ALL MY LIFE. I KNOW MY STRENGTHS AND WEAKNESSES. I'M NOT OVER-CONFIDENT.
I LEAVE T UP TO MY PPONENTS TO UDGE HOW DANGEROUS" I AM.
神
GOOD. YOU ARE A MAN OF COURAGE. LET US SEE IF YOUR TECHNIQUES MATCH YOUR WORDS.
COME, NATHAN SUMMERS. IF YOU ARE PREPARED, SHOW ME WHAT YOU CAN DO USING THE FULL EXTENT OF YOUR FIGHTING PROWESS.
YOU KNOW MY NAME.
I KNOW MANY THINGS. NOW, BEGIN.

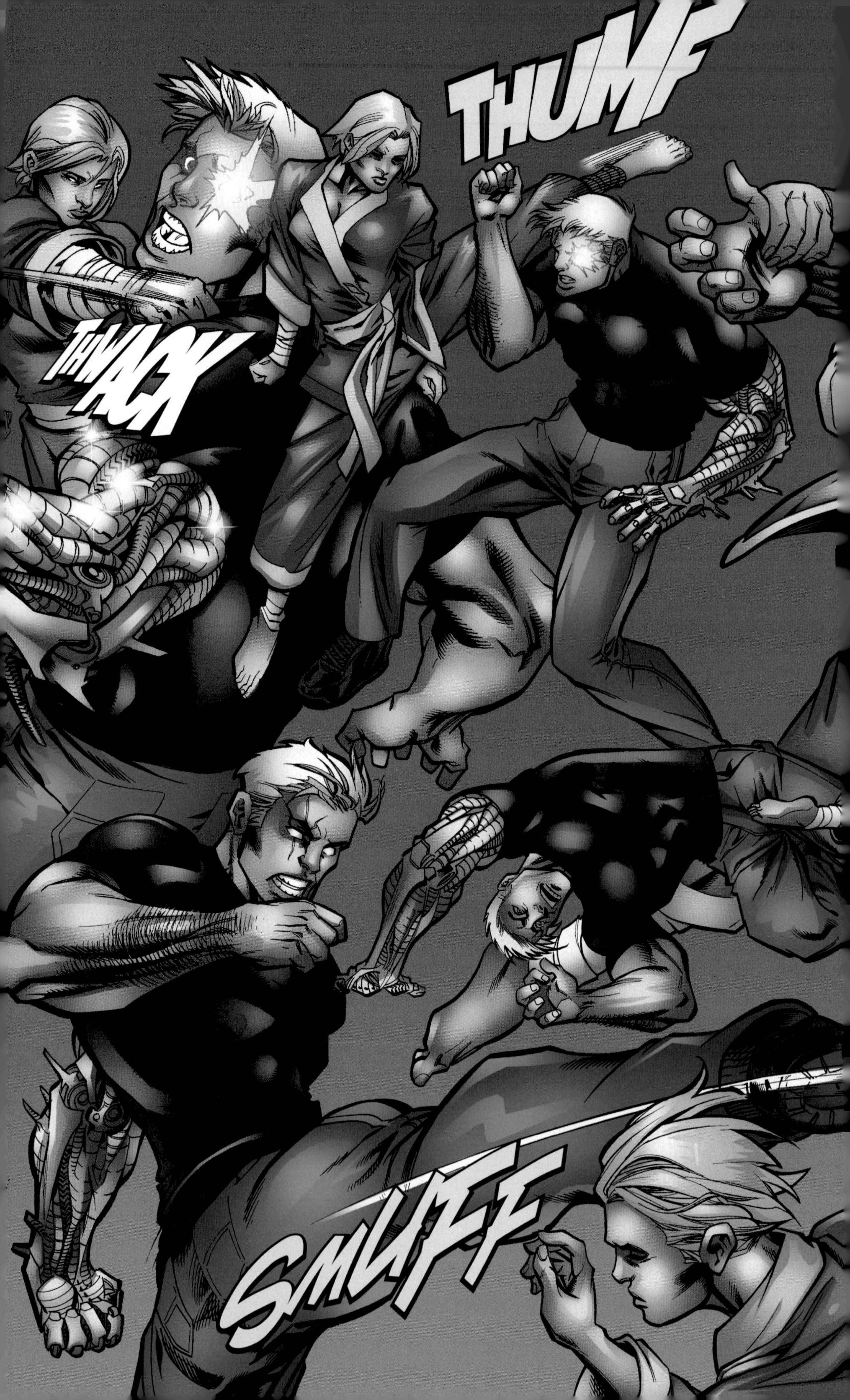
THUMF
THWACK
SMUFF

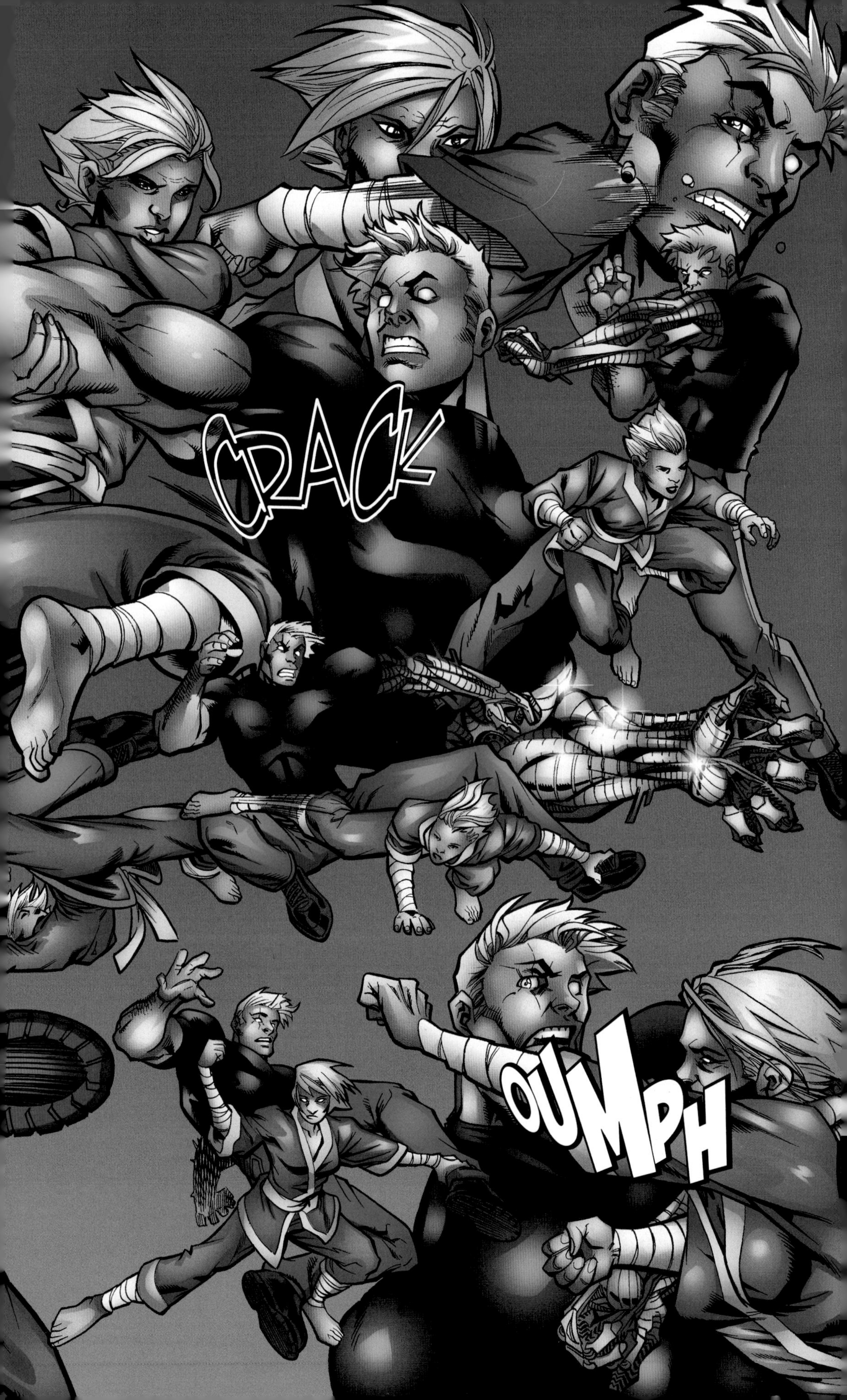
CRACK
OUMPH

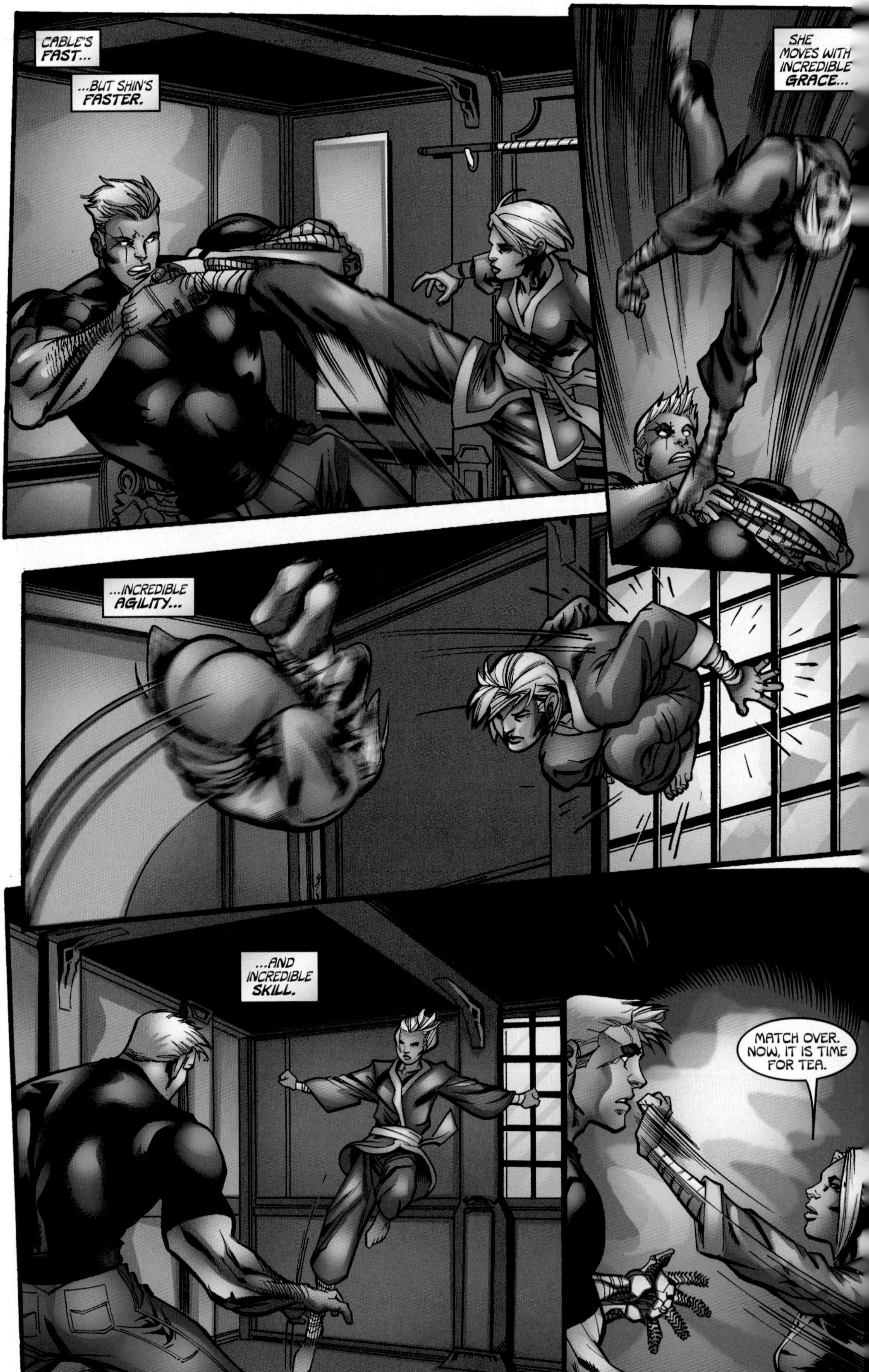
CABLE'S FAST...
...BUT SHIN'S FASTER.
SHE MOVES WITH INCREDIBLE GRACE...
...INCREDIBLE AGILITY...
...AND INCREDIBLE SKILL.
MATCH OVER. NOW, IT IS TIME FOR TEA.

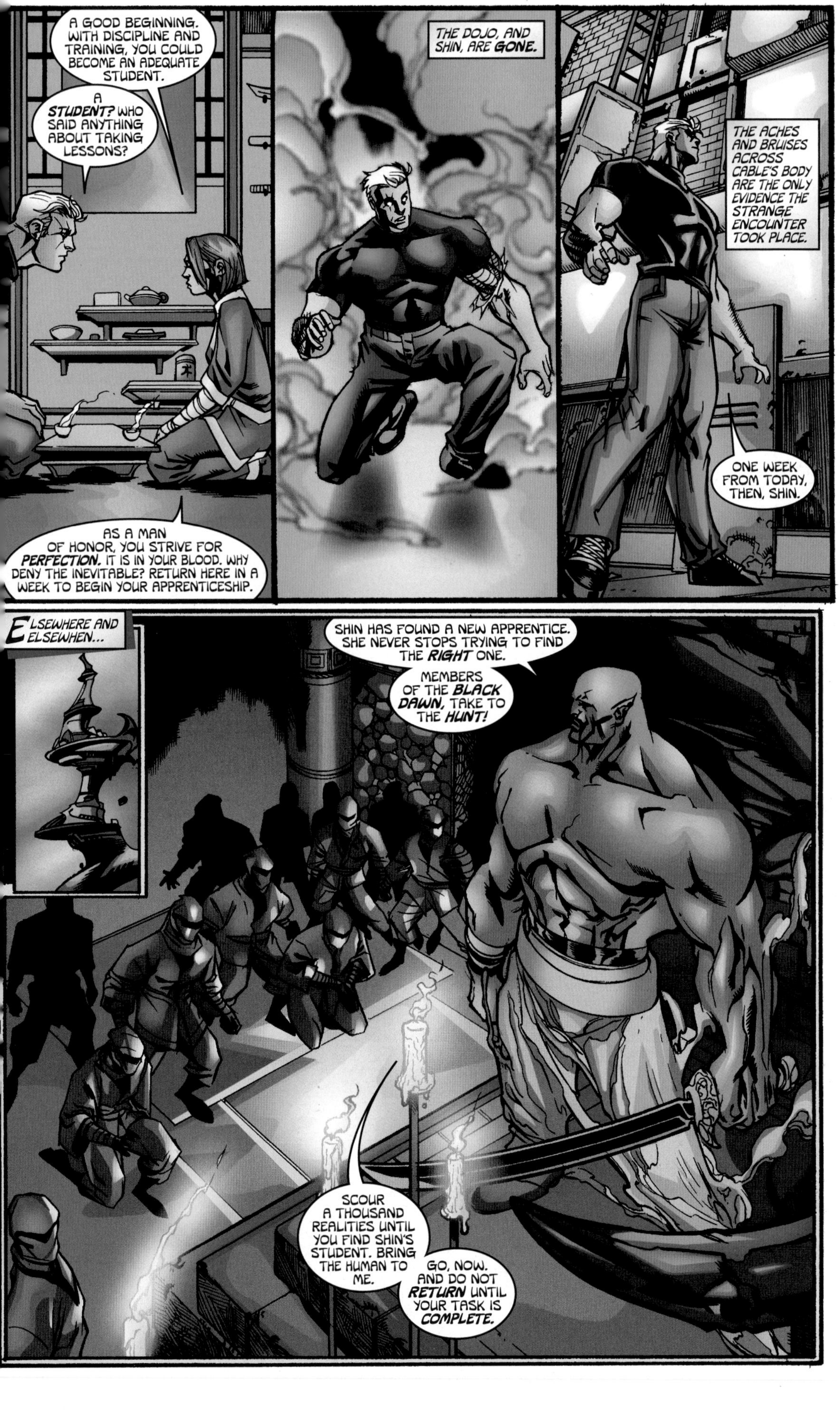
A GOOD BEGINNING. WITH DISCIPLINE AND TRAINING, YOU COULD BECOME AN ADEQUATE STUDENT.
A STUDENT? WHO SAID ANYTHING ABOUT TAKING LESSONS?
AS A MAN OF HONOR, YOU STRIVE FOR PERFECTION. IT IS IN YOUR BLOOD. WHY DENY THE INEVITABLE? RETURN HERE IN A WEEK TO BEGIN YOUR APPRENTICESHIP.
THE DOJO, AND SHIN, ARE GONE.
THE ACHES AND BRUISES ACROSS CABLE'S BODY ARE THE ONLY EVIDENCE THE STRANGE ENCOUNTER TOOK PLACE.
ONE WEEK FROM TODAY, THEN, SHIN.
ELSEWHERE AND ELSEWHEN...
SHIN HAS FOUND A NEW APPRENTICE. SHE NEVER STOPS TRYING TO FIND THE RIGHT ONE.
MEMBERS OF THE BLACK DAWN, TAKE TO THE HUNT!
SCOUR A THOUSAND REALITIES UNTIL YOU FIND SHIN'S STUDENT. BRING THE HUMAN TO ME.
GO, NOW. AND DO NOT RETURN UNTIL YOUR TASK IS COMPLETE.

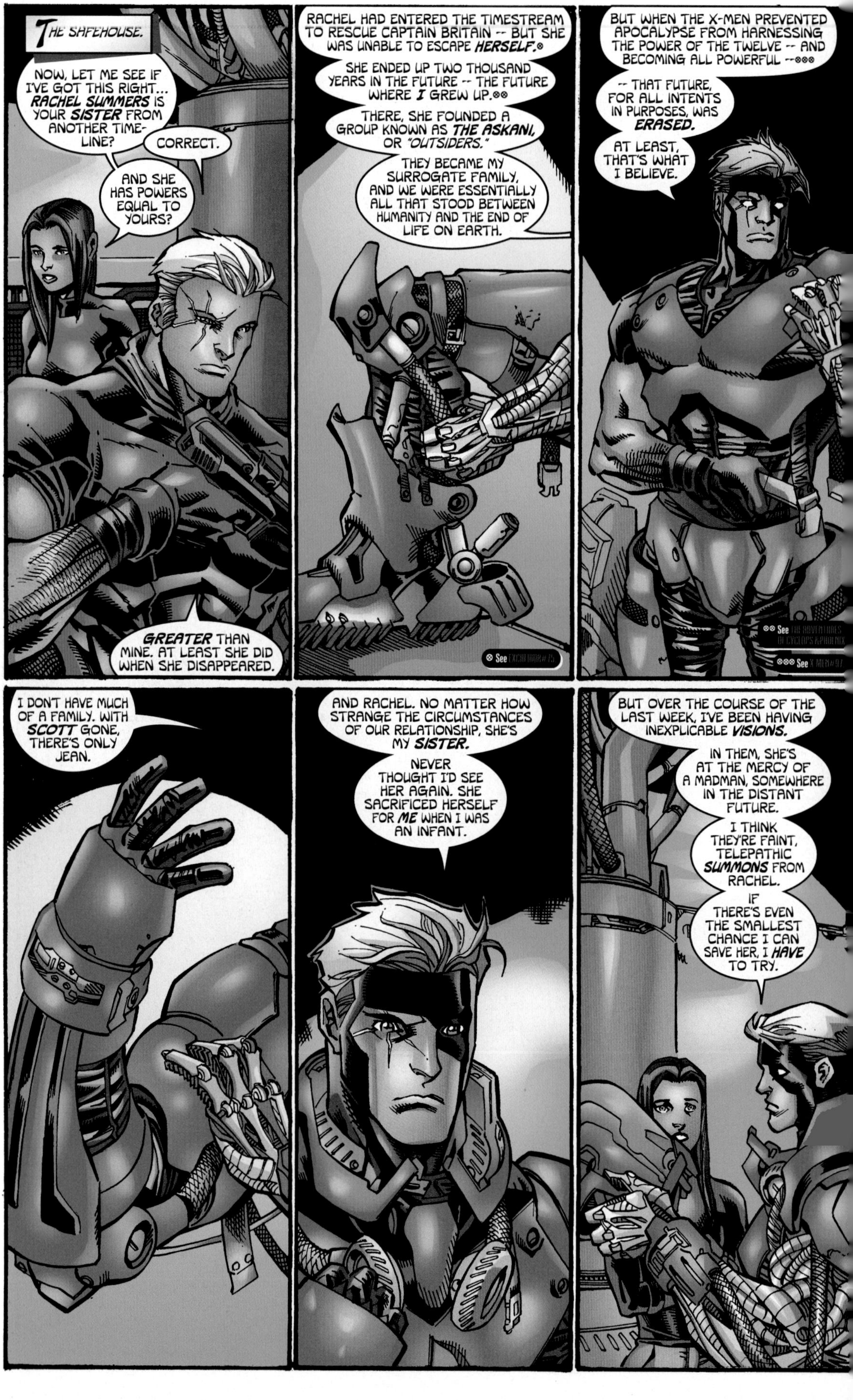
THE SAFEHOUSE.
NOW, LET ME SEE IF I'VE GOT THIS RIGHT... RACHEL SUMMERS IS YOUR SISTER FROM ANOTHER TIME-LINE?
CORRECT.
AND SHE HAS POWERS EQUAL TO YOURS?
GREATER THAN MINE. AT LEAST SHE DID WHEN SHE DISAPPEARED.
RACHEL HAD ENTERED THE TIMESTREAM TO RESCUE CAPTAIN BRITAIN -- BUT SHE WAS UNABLE TO ESCAPE HERSELF.⊗
SHE ENDED UP TWO THOUSAND YEARS IN THE FUTURE -- THE FUTURE WHERE I GREW UP.⊗⊗
THERE, SHE FOUNDED A GROUP KNOWN AS THE ASKANI, OR "OUTSIDERS."
THEY BECAME MY SURROGATE FAMILY, AND WE WERE ESSENTIALLY ALL THAT STOOD BETWEEN HUMANITY AND THE END OF LIFE ON EARTH.
⊗ See EXCALIBUR #75.
BUT WHEN THE X-MEN PREVENTED APOCALYPSE FROM HARNESSING THE POWER OF THE TWELVE -- AND BECOMING ALL POWERFUL --⊗⊗⊗
-- THAT FUTURE, FOR ALL INTENTS IN PURPOSES, WAS ERASED.
AT LEAST, THAT'S WHAT I BELIEVE.
⊗⊗ See THE ADVENTURES OF CYCLOPS & PHOENIX
⊗⊗⊗ See X-MEN #97.
I DON'T HAVE MUCH OF A FAMILY. WITH SCOTT GONE, THERE'S ONLY JEAN.
AND RACHEL. NO MATTER HOW STRANGE THE CIRCUMSTANCES OF OUR RELATIONSHIP, SHE'S MY SISTER.
NEVER THOUGHT I'D SEE HER AGAIN. SHE SACRIFICED HERSELF FOR ME WHEN I WAS AN INFANT.
BUT OVER THE COURSE OF THE LAST WEEK, I'VE BEEN HAVING INEXPLICABLE VISIONS.
IN THEM, SHE'S AT THE MERCY OF A MADMAN, SOMEWHERE IN THE DISTANT FUTURE.
I THINK THEY'RE FAINT, TELEPATHIC SUMMONS FROM RACHEL.
IF THERE'S EVEN THE SMALLEST CHANCE I CAN SAVE HER, I HAVE TO TRY.

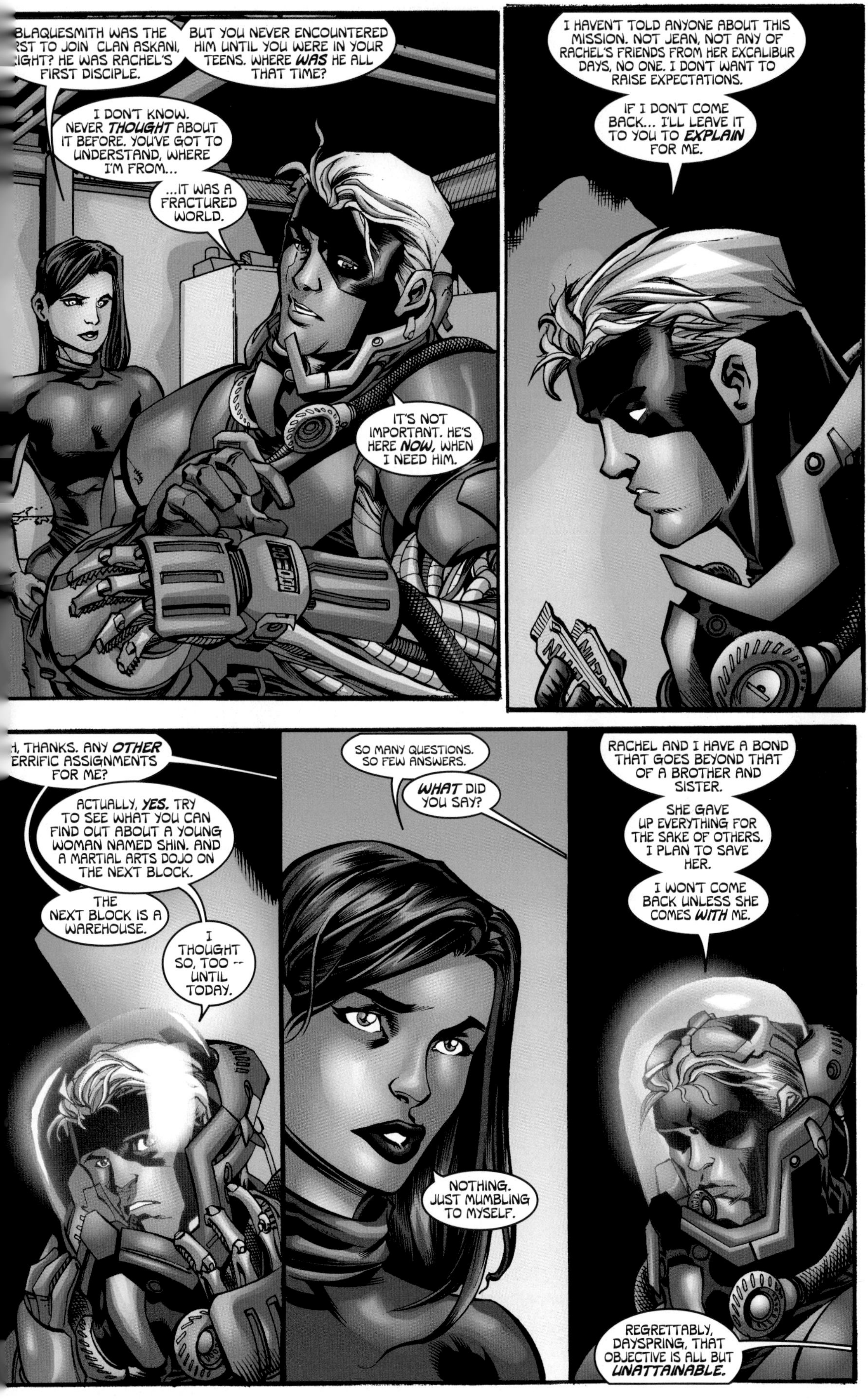
BLAQUESMITH WAS THE RST TO JOIN CLAN ASKANI, IGHT? HE WAS RACHEL'S FIRST DISCIPLE.
BUT YOU NEVER ENCOUNTERED HIM UNTIL YOU WERE IN YOUR TEENS. WHERE *WAS* HE ALL THAT TIME?
I DON'T KNOW. NEVER *THOUGHT* ABOUT IT BEFORE. YOU'VE GOT TO UNDERSTAND, WHERE I'M FROM...
...IT WAS A FRACTURED WORLD.
IT'S NOT IMPORTANT. HE'S HERE *NOW,* WHEN I NEED HIM.
I HAVEN'T TOLD ANYONE ABOUT THIS MISSION. NOT JEAN, NOT ANY OF RACHEL'S FRIENDS FROM HER EXCALIBUR DAYS, NO ONE. I DON'T WANT TO RAISE EXPECTATIONS.
IF I DON'T COME BACK... I'LL LEAVE IT TO YOU TO *EXPLAIN* FOR ME.
H, THANKS. ANY *OTHER* ERRIFIC ASSIGNMENTS FOR ME?
ACTUALLY, *YES.* TRY TO SEE WHAT YOU CAN FIND OUT ABOUT A YOUNG WOMAN NAMED SHIN. AND A MARTIAL ARTS DOJO ON THE NEXT BLOCK.
THE NEXT BLOCK IS A WAREHOUSE.
I THOUGHT SO, TOO -- UNTIL TODAY.
SO MANY QUESTIONS. SO FEW ANSWERS.
WHAT DID YOU SAY?
NOTHING. JUST MUMBLING TO MYSELF.
RACHEL AND I HAVE A BOND THAT GOES BEYOND THAT OF A BROTHER AND SISTER.
SHE GAVE UP EVERYTHING FOR THE SAKE OF OTHERS. I PLAN TO SAVE HER.
I WON'T COME BACK UNLESS SHE COMES *WITH* ME.
REGRETTABLY, DAYSPRING, THAT OBJECTIVE IS ALL BUT *UNATTAINABLE.*

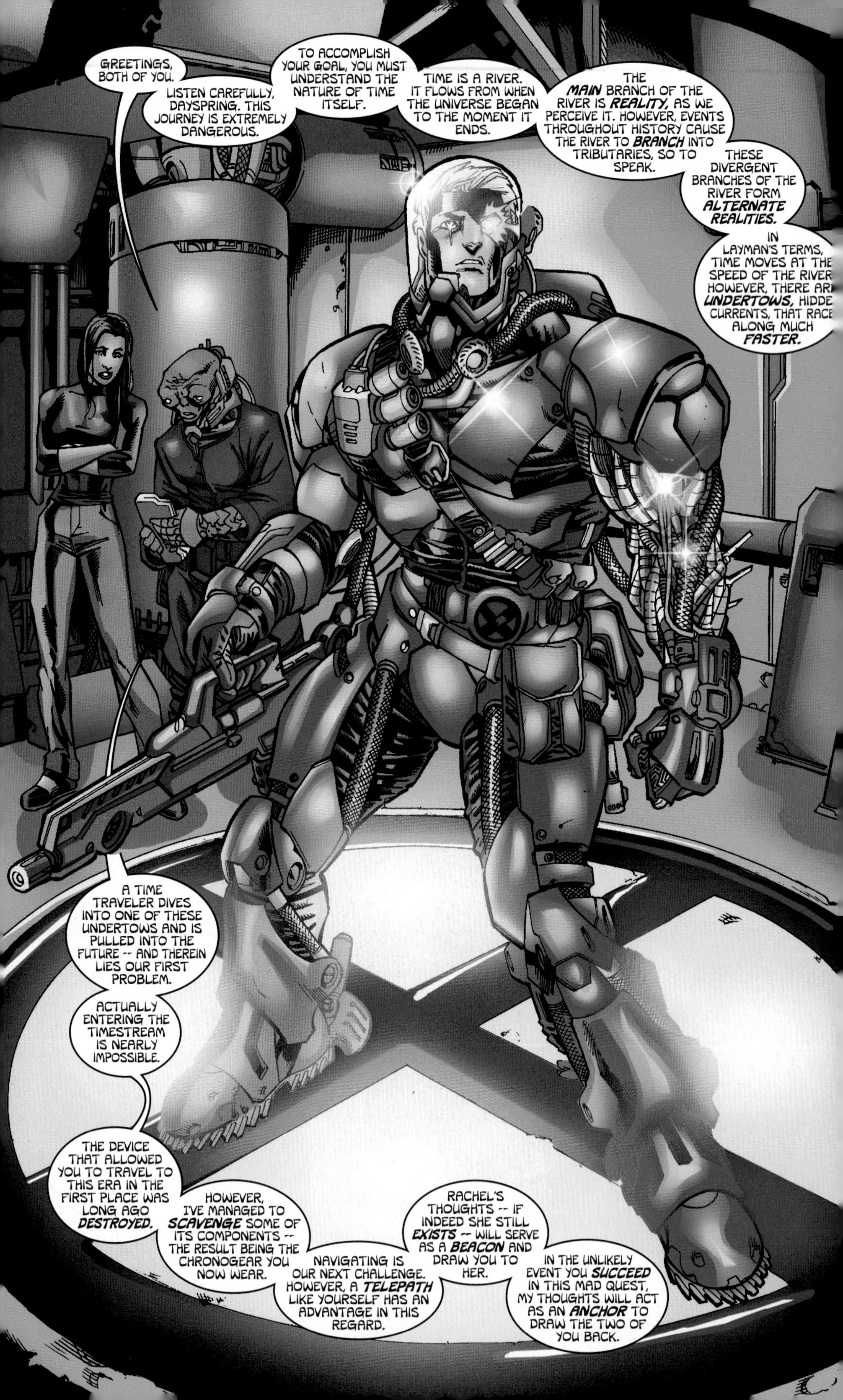
GREETINGS, BOTH OF YOU.
LISTEN CAREFULLY, DAYSPRING. THIS JOURNEY IS EXTREMELY DANGEROUS.
TO ACCOMPLISH YOUR GOAL, YOU MUST UNDERSTAND THE NATURE OF TIME ITSELF.
TIME IS A RIVER. IT FLOWS FROM WHEN THE UNIVERSE BEGAN TO THE MOMENT IT ENDS.
THE MAIN BRANCH OF THE RIVER IS REALITY, AS WE PERCEIVE IT. HOWEVER, EVENTS THROUGHOUT HISTORY CAUSE THE RIVER TO BRANCH INTO TRIBUTARIES, SO TO SPEAK.
THESE DIVERGENT BRANCHES OF THE RIVER FORM ALTERNATE REALITIES.
IN LAYMAN'S TERMS, TIME MOVES AT THE SPEED OF THE RIVER HOWEVER, THERE AR UNDERTOWS, HIDDE CURRENTS, THAT RACE ALONG MUCH FASTER.
A TIME TRAVELER DIVES INTO ONE OF THESE UNDERTOWS AND IS PULLED INTO THE FUTURE -- AND THEREIN LIES OUR FIRST PROBLEM.
ACTUALLY ENTERING THE TIMESTREAM IS NEARLY IMPOSSIBLE.
THE DEVICE THAT ALLOWED YOU TO TRAVEL TO THIS ERA IN THE FIRST PLACE WAS LONG AGO DESTROYED.
HOWEVER, I'VE MANAGED TO SCAVENGE SOME OF ITS COMPONENTS -- THE RESULT BEING THE CHRONOGEAR YOU NOW WEAR.
NAVIGATING IS OUR NEXT CHALLENGE. HOWEVER, A TELEPATH LIKE YOURSELF HAS AN ADVANTAGE IN THIS REGARD.
RACHEL'S THOUGHTS -- IF INDEED SHE STILL EXISTS -- WILL SERVE AS A BEACON AND DRAW YOU TO HER.
IN THE UNLIKELY EVENT YOU SUCCEED IN THIS MAD QUEST, MY THOUGHTS WILL ACT AS AN ANCHOR TO DRAW THE TWO OF YOU BACK.

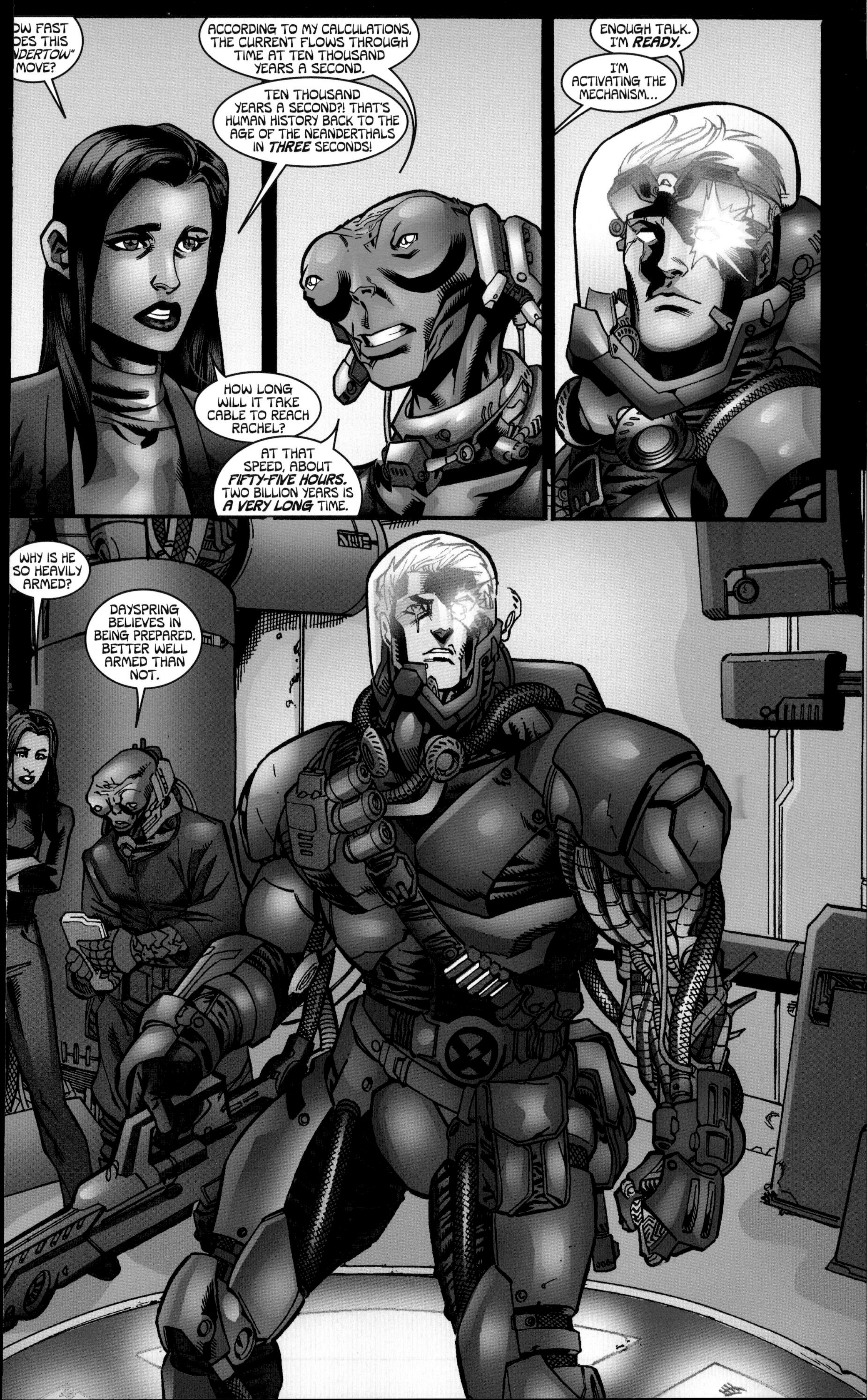

OW FAST
DES THIS
NDERTOW"
MOVE?
ACCORDING TO MY CALCULATIONS, THE CURRENT FLOWS THROUGH TIME AT TEN THOUSAND YEARS A SECOND.
TEN THOUSAND YEARS A SECOND?! THAT'S HUMAN HISTORY BACK TO THE AGE OF THE NEANDERTHALS IN THREE SECONDS!
ENOUGH TALK. I'M READY.
I'M ACTIVATING THE MECHANISM...
HOW LONG WILL IT TAKE CABLE TO REACH RACHEL?
AT THAT SPEED, ABOUT FIFTY-FIVE HOURS. TWO BILLION YEARS IS A VERY LONG TIME.
WHY IS HE SO HEAVILY ARMED?
DAYSPRING BELIEVES IN BEING PREPARED. BETTER WELL ARMED THAN NOT.

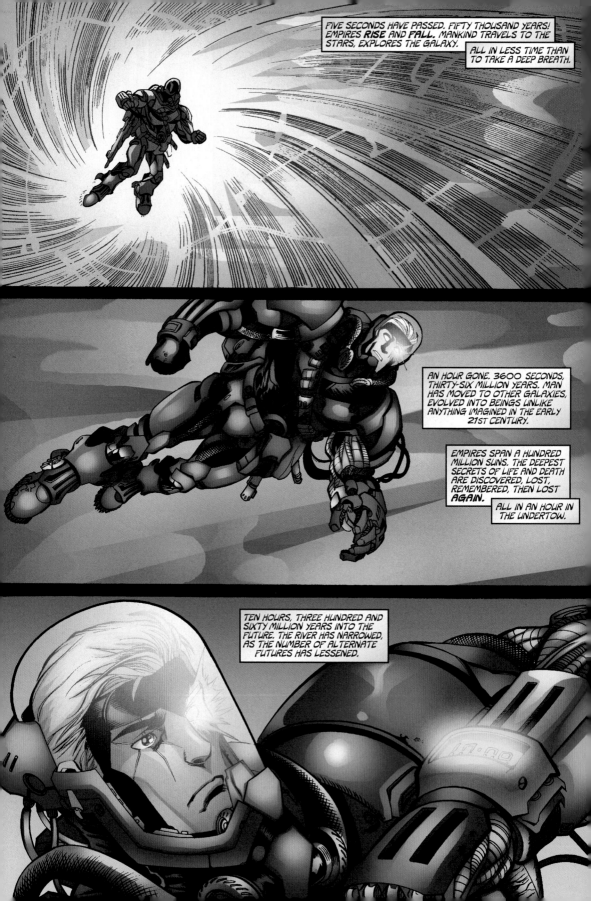

FIVE SECONDS HAVE PASSED. FIFTY THOUSAND YEARS! EMPIRES **RISE** AND **FALL.** MANKIND TRAVELS TO THE STARS, EXPLORES THE GALAXY.

ALL IN LESS TIME THAN TO TAKE A DEEP BREATH.

AN HOUR GONE. 3600 SECONDS, THIRTY-SIX MILLION YEARS. MAN HAS MOVED TO OTHER GALAXIES, EVOLVED INTO BEINGS UNLIKE ANYTHING IMAGINED IN THE EARLY 21ST CENTURY.

EMPIRES SPAN A HUNDRED MILLION SUNS. THE DEEPEST SECRETS OF LIFE AND DEATH ARE DISCOVERED, LOST, REMEMBERED, THEN LOST **AGAIN.**

ALL IN AN HOUR IN THE UNDERTOW.

TEN HOURS, THREE HUNDRED AND SIXTY MILLION YEARS INTO THE FUTURE. THE RIVER HAS NARROWED, AS THE NUMBER OF ALTERNATE FUTURES HAS LESSENED.

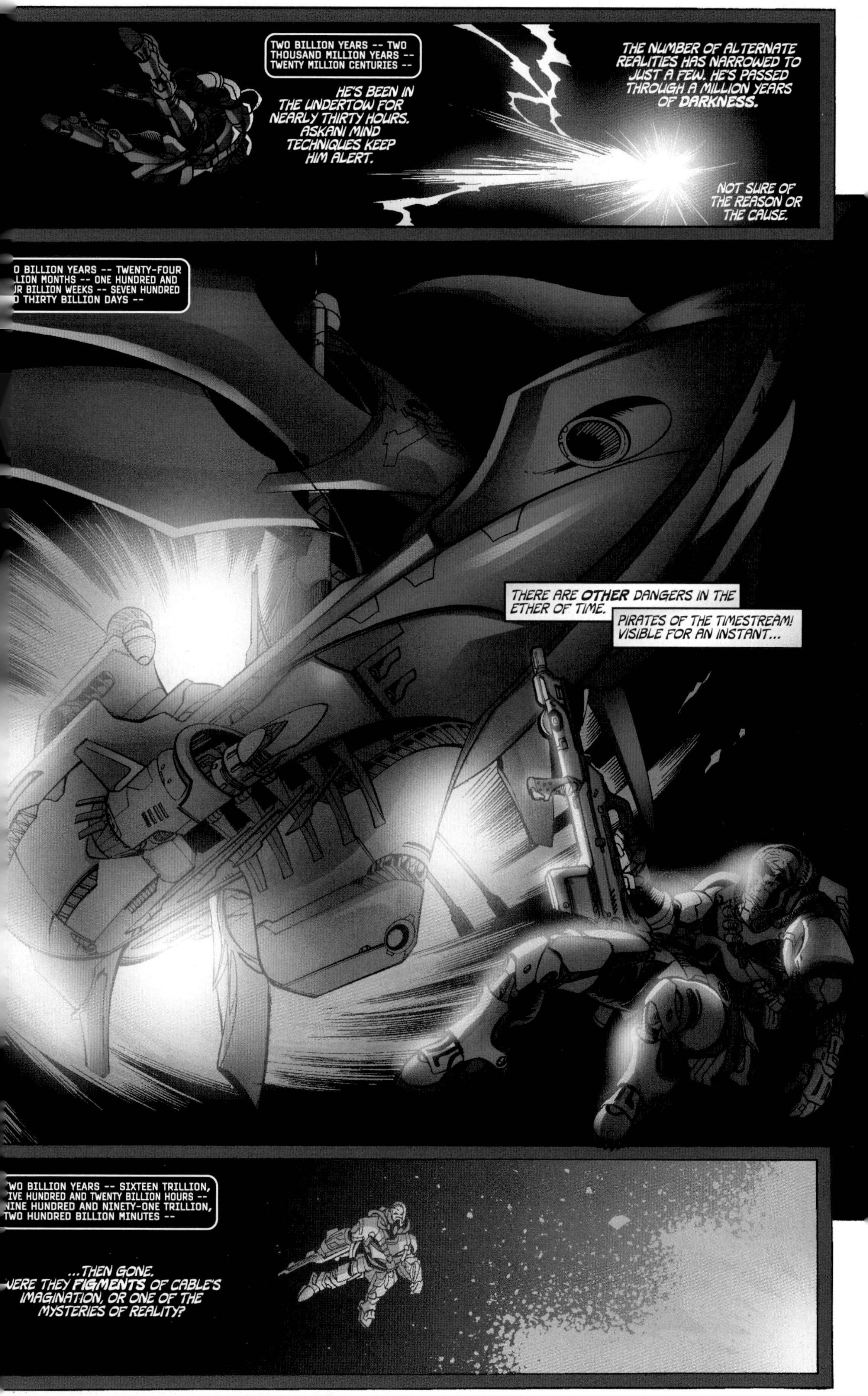
TWO BILLION YEARS -- TWO THOUSAND MILLION YEARS -- TWENTY MILLION CENTURIES --
HE'S BEEN IN THE UNDERTOW FOR NEARLY THIRTY HOURS. ASKANI MIND TECHNIQUES KEEP HIM ALERT.
THE NUMBER OF ALTERNATE REALITIES HAS NARROWED TO JUST A FEW. HE'S PASSED THROUGH A MILLION YEARS OF DARKNESS.
NOT SURE OF THE REASON OR THE CAUSE.
O BILLION YEARS -- TWENTY-FOUR LION MONTHS -- ONE HUNDRED AND R BILLION WEEKS -- SEVEN HUNDRED D THIRTY BILLION DAYS --
THERE ARE OTHER DANGERS IN THE ETHER OF TIME.
PIRATES OF THE TIMESTREAM! VISIBLE FOR AN INSTANT...
WO BILLION YEARS -- SIXTEEN TRILLION, IVE HUNDRED AND TWENTY BILLION HOURS -- INE HUNDRED AND NINETY-ONE TRILLION, TWO HUNDRED BILLION MINUTES --
...THEN GONE. WERE THEY FIGMENTS OF CABLE'S IMAGINATION, OR ONE OF THE MYSTERIES OF REALITY?

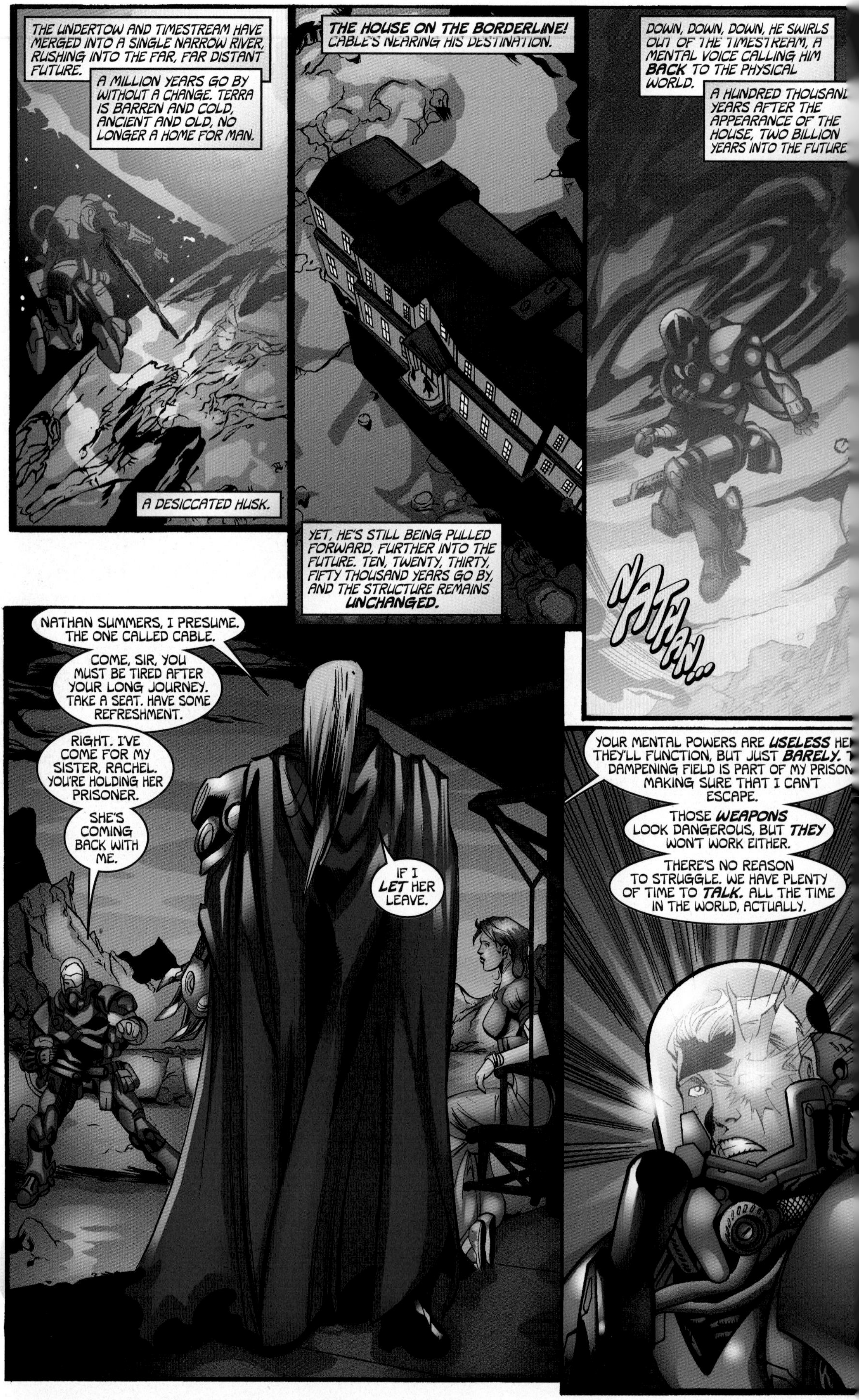

THE UNDERTOW AND TIMESTREAM HAVE MERGED INTO A SINGLE NARROW RIVER, RUSHING INTO THE FAR, FAR DISTANT FUTURE.
A MILLION YEARS GO BY WITHOUT A CHANGE. TERRA IS BARREN AND COLD, ANCIENT AND OLD, NO LONGER A HOME FOR MAN.
A DESICCATED HUSK.
THE HOUSE ON THE BORDERLINE! CABLE'S NEARING HIS DESTINATION.
YET, HE'S STILL BEING PULLED FORWARD, FURTHER INTO THE FUTURE. TEN, TWENTY, THIRTY, FIFTY THOUSAND YEARS GO BY, AND THE STRUCTURE REMAINS UNCHANGED.
DOWN, DOWN, DOWN, HE SWIRLS OUT OF THE TIMESTREAM, A MENTAL VOICE CALLING HIM BACK TO THE PHYSICAL WORLD.
A HUNDRED THOUSAND YEARS AFTER THE APPEARANCE OF THE HOUSE, TWO BILLION YEARS INTO THE FUTURE
NATHAN...
NATHAN SUMMERS, I PRESUME. THE ONE CALLED CABLE.
COME, SIR, YOU MUST BE TIRED AFTER YOUR LONG JOURNEY. TAKE A SEAT. HAVE SOME REFRESHMENT.
RIGHT. I'VE COME FOR MY SISTER, RACHEL. YOU'RE HOLDING HER PRISONER.
SHE'S COMING BACK WITH ME.
IF I LET HER LEAVE.
YOUR MENTAL POWERS ARE USELESS HE THEY'LL FUNCTION, BUT JUST BARELY. T DAMPENING FIELD IS PART OF MY PRISON MAKING SURE THAT I CAN'T ESCAPE.
THOSE WEAPONS LOOK DANGEROUS, BUT THEY WON'T WORK EITHER.
THERE'S NO REASON TO STRUGGLE. WE HAVE PLENTY OF TIME TO TALK. ALL THE TIME IN THE WORLD, ACTUALLY.

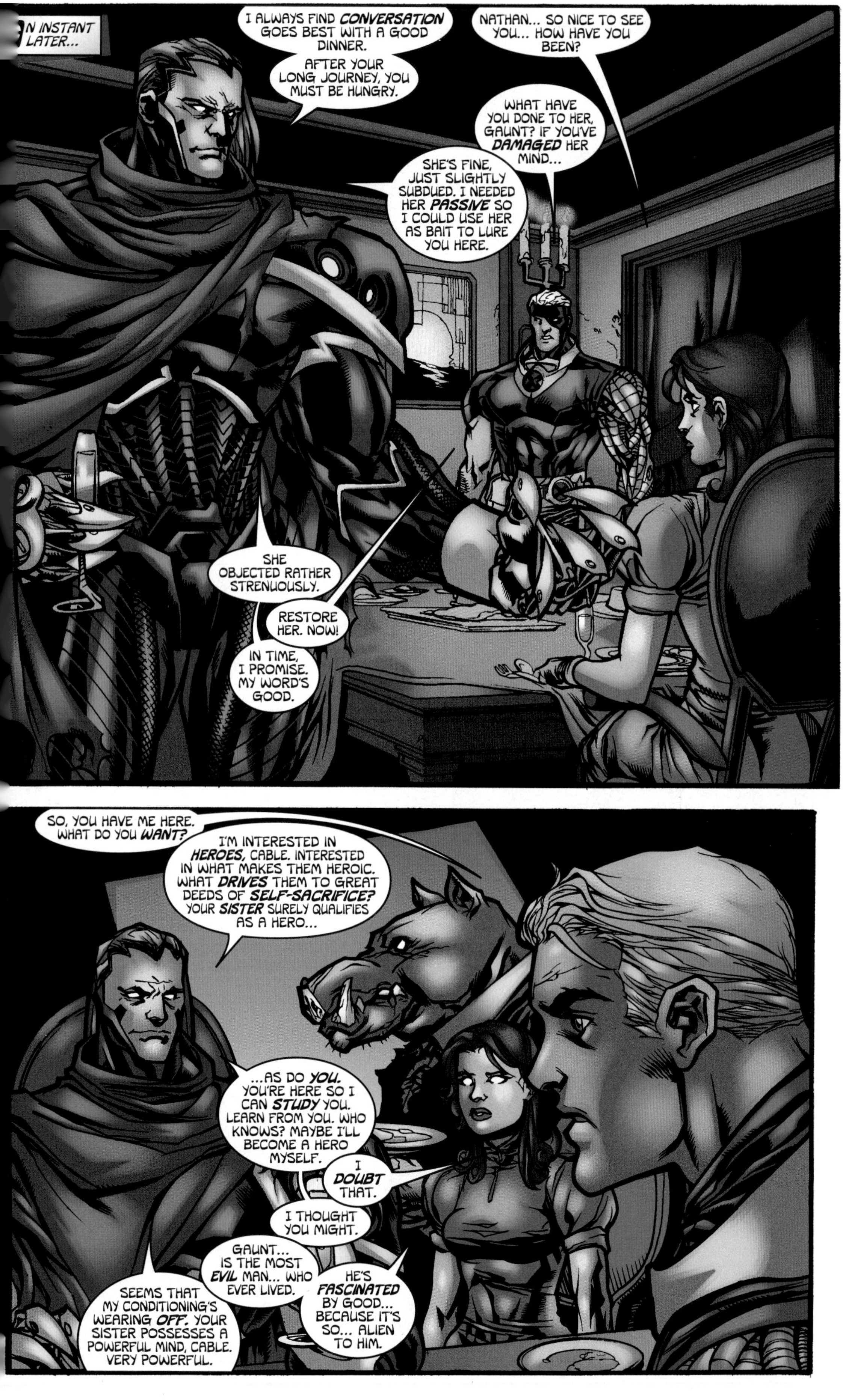

N INSTANT LATER...
I ALWAYS FIND CONVERSATION GOES BEST WITH A GOOD DINNER.
AFTER YOUR LONG JOURNEY, YOU MUST BE HUNGRY.
NATHAN... SO NICE TO SEE YOU... HOW HAVE YOU BEEN?
WHAT HAVE YOU DONE TO HER, GAUNT? IF YOU'VE DAMAGED HER MIND...
SHE'S FINE, JUST SLIGHTLY SUBDUED. I NEEDED HER PASSIVE SO I COULD USE HER AS BAIT TO LURE YOU HERE.
SHE OBJECTED RATHER STRENUOUSLY.
RESTORE HER. NOW!
IN TIME, I PROMISE. MY WORD'S GOOD.
SO, YOU HAVE ME HERE. WHAT DO YOU WANT?
I'M INTERESTED IN HEROES, CABLE. INTERESTED IN WHAT MAKES THEM HEROIC. WHAT DRIVES THEM TO GREAT DEEDS OF SELF-SACRIFICE? YOUR SISTER SURELY QUALIFIES AS A HERO...
...AS DO YOU. YOU'RE HERE SO I CAN STUDY YOU. LEARN FROM YOU. WHO KNOWS? MAYBE I'LL BECOME A HERO MYSELF.
I DOUBT THAT.
I THOUGHT YOU MIGHT.
GAUNT... IS THE MOST EVIL MAN... WHO EVER LIVED.
HE'S FASCINATED BY GOOD... BECAUSE IT'S SO... ALIEN TO HIM.
SEEMS THAT MY CONDITIONING'S WEARING OFF. YOUR SISTER POSSESSES A POWERFUL MIND, CABLE. VERY POWERFUL.

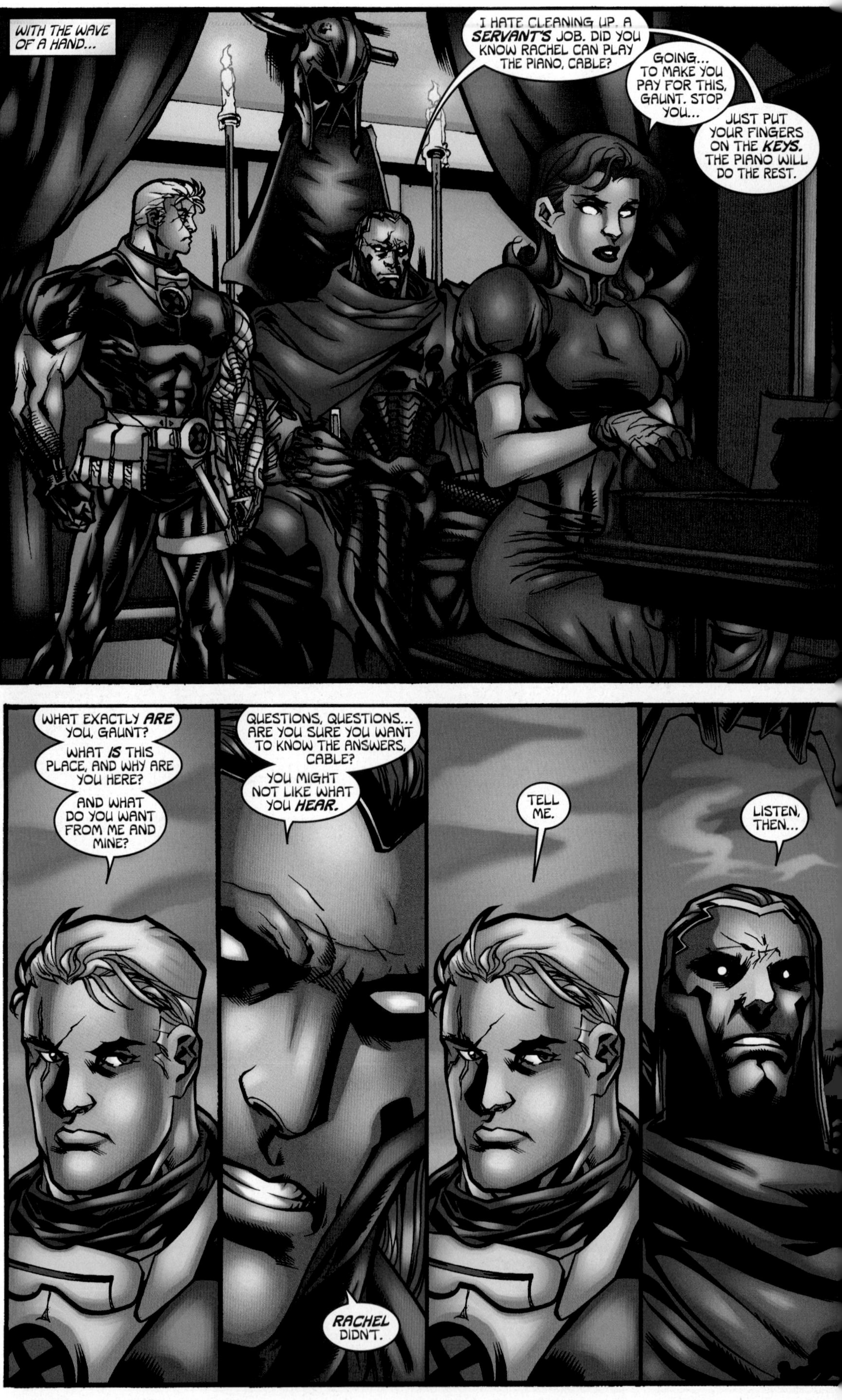

WITH THE WAVE OF A HAND...
I HATE CLEANING UP. A SERVANT'S JOB. DID YOU KNOW RACHEL CAN PLAY THE PIANO, CABLE?
GOING... TO MAKE YOU PAY FOR THIS, GAUNT. STOP YOU...
JUST PUT YOUR FINGERS ON THE KEYS. THE PIANO WILL DO THE REST.
WHAT EXACTLY ARE YOU, GAUNT?
WHAT IS THIS PLACE, AND WHY ARE YOU HERE?
AND WHAT DO YOU WANT FROM ME AND MINE?
QUESTIONS, QUESTIONS... ARE YOU SURE YOU WANT TO KNOW THE ANSWERS, CABLE?
YOU MIGHT NOT LIKE WHAT YOU HEAR.
RACHEL DIDN'T.
TELL ME.
LISTEN, THEN...

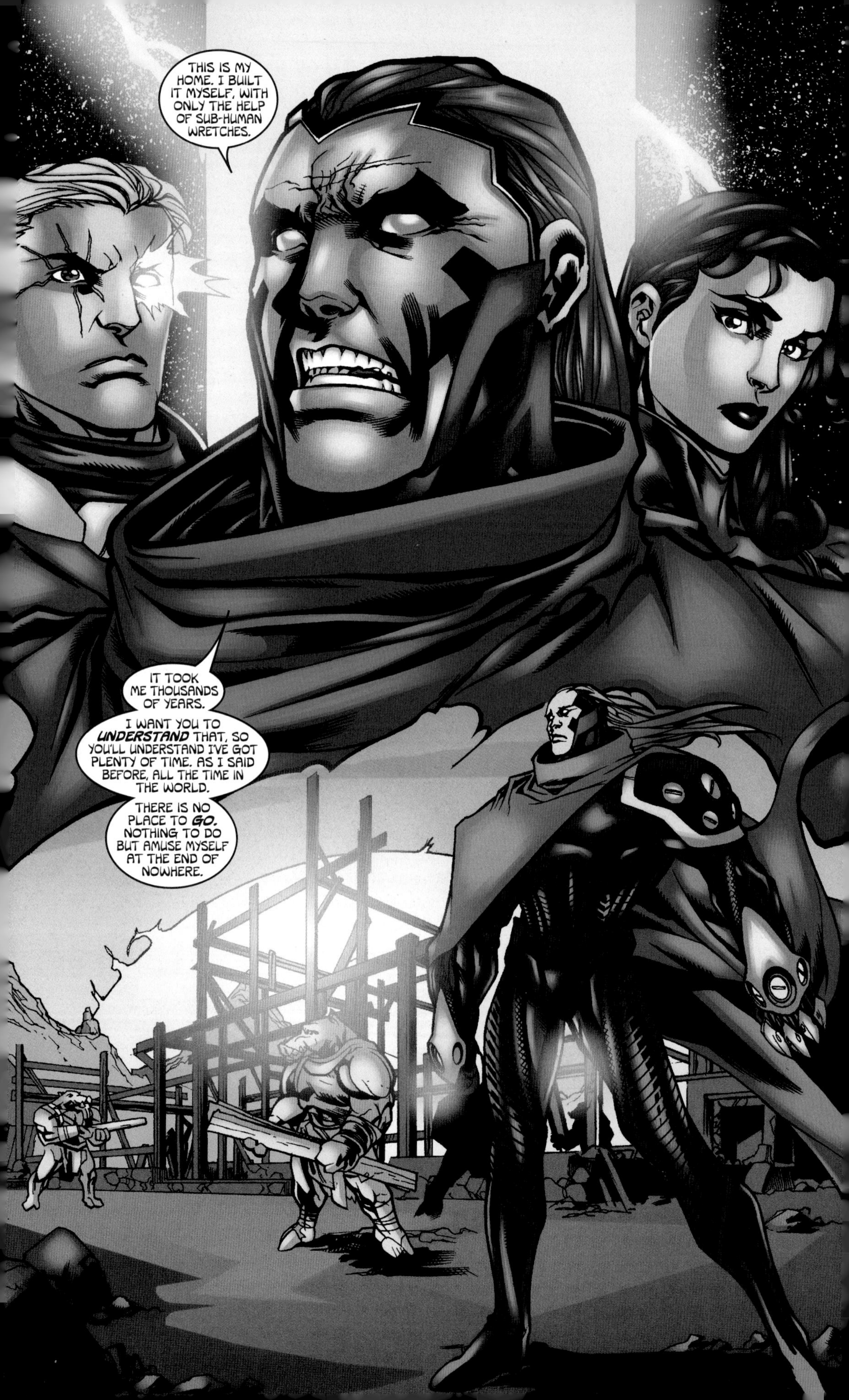
THIS IS MY HOME. I BUILT IT MYSELF, WITH ONLY THE HELP OF SUB-HUMAN WRETCHES.
IT TOOK ME THOUSANDS OF YEARS.
I WANT YOU TO **UNDERSTAND** THAT, SO YOU'LL UNDERSTAND I'VE GOT PLENTY OF TIME. AS I SAID BEFORE, ALL THE TIME IN THE WORLD.
THERE IS NO PLACE TO **GO.** NOTHING TO DO BUT AMUSE MYSELF AT THE END OF NOWHERE.

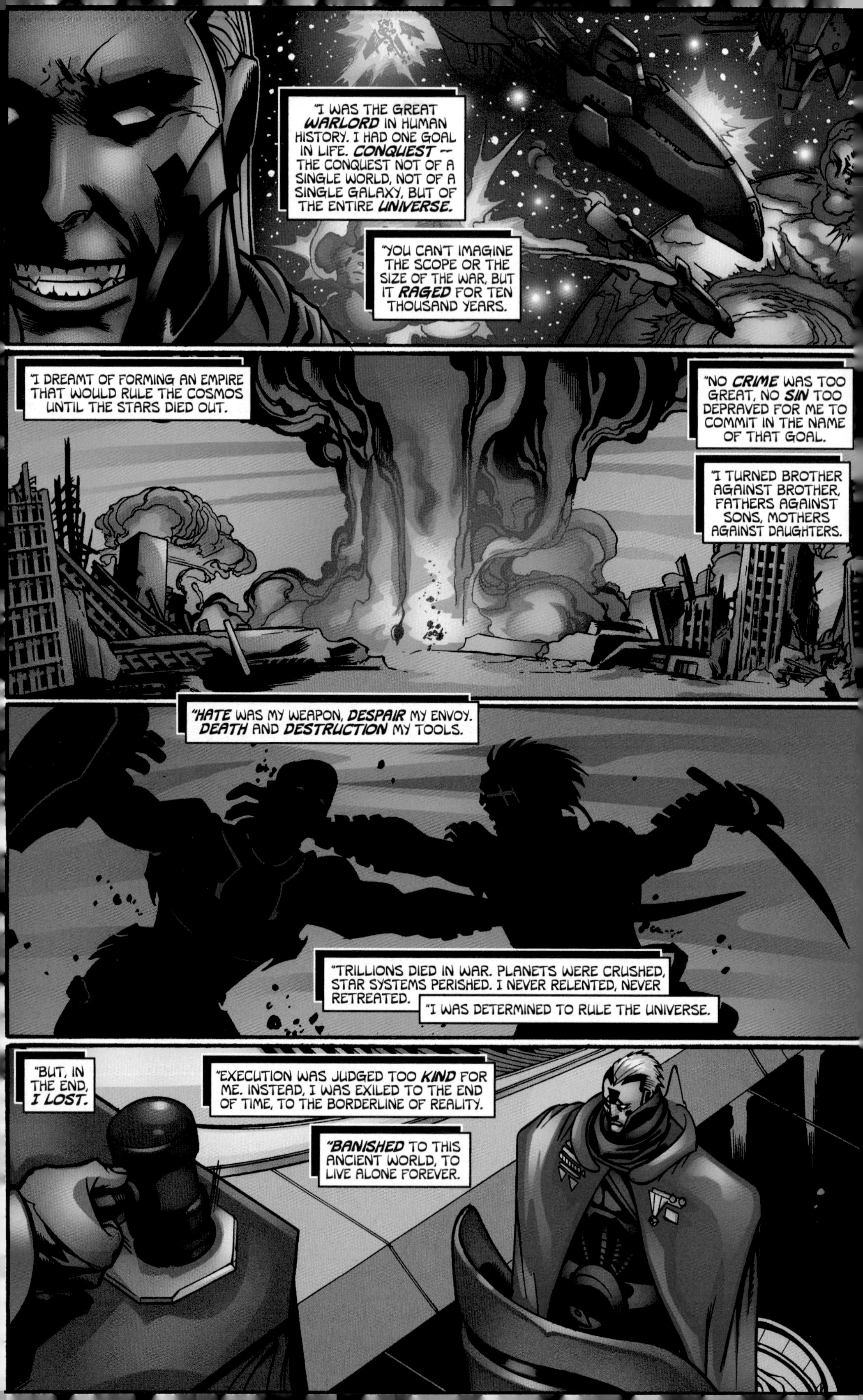

"I WAS THE GREAT WARLORD IN HUMAN HISTORY. I HAD ONE GOAL IN LIFE. CONQUEST -- THE CONQUEST NOT OF A SINGLE WORLD, NOT OF A SINGLE GALAXY, BUT OF THE ENTIRE UNIVERSE.
"YOU CAN'T IMAGINE THE SCOPE OR THE SIZE OF THE WAR, BUT IT RAGED FOR TEN THOUSAND YEARS.
"I DREAMT OF FORMING AN EMPIRE THAT WOULD RULE THE COSMOS UNTIL THE STARS DIED OUT.
"NO CRIME WAS TOO GREAT, NO SIN TOO DEPRAVED FOR ME TO COMMIT IN THE NAME OF THAT GOAL.
"I TURNED BROTHER AGAINST BROTHER, FATHERS AGAINST SONS, MOTHERS AGAINST DAUGHTERS.
"HATE WAS MY WEAPON, DESPAIR MY ENVOY. DEATH AND DESTRUCTION MY TOOLS.
"TRILLIONS DIED IN WAR. PLANETS WERE CRUSHED, STAR SYSTEMS PERISHED. I NEVER RELENTED, NEVER RETREATED.
"I WAS DETERMINED TO RULE THE UNIVERSE.
"BUT, IN THE END, I LOST.
"EXECUTION WAS JUDGED TOO KIND FOR ME. INSTEAD, I WAS EXILED TO THE END OF TIME, TO THE BORDERLINE OF REALITY.
"BANISHED TO THIS ANCIENT WORLD, TO LIVE ALONE FOREVER.

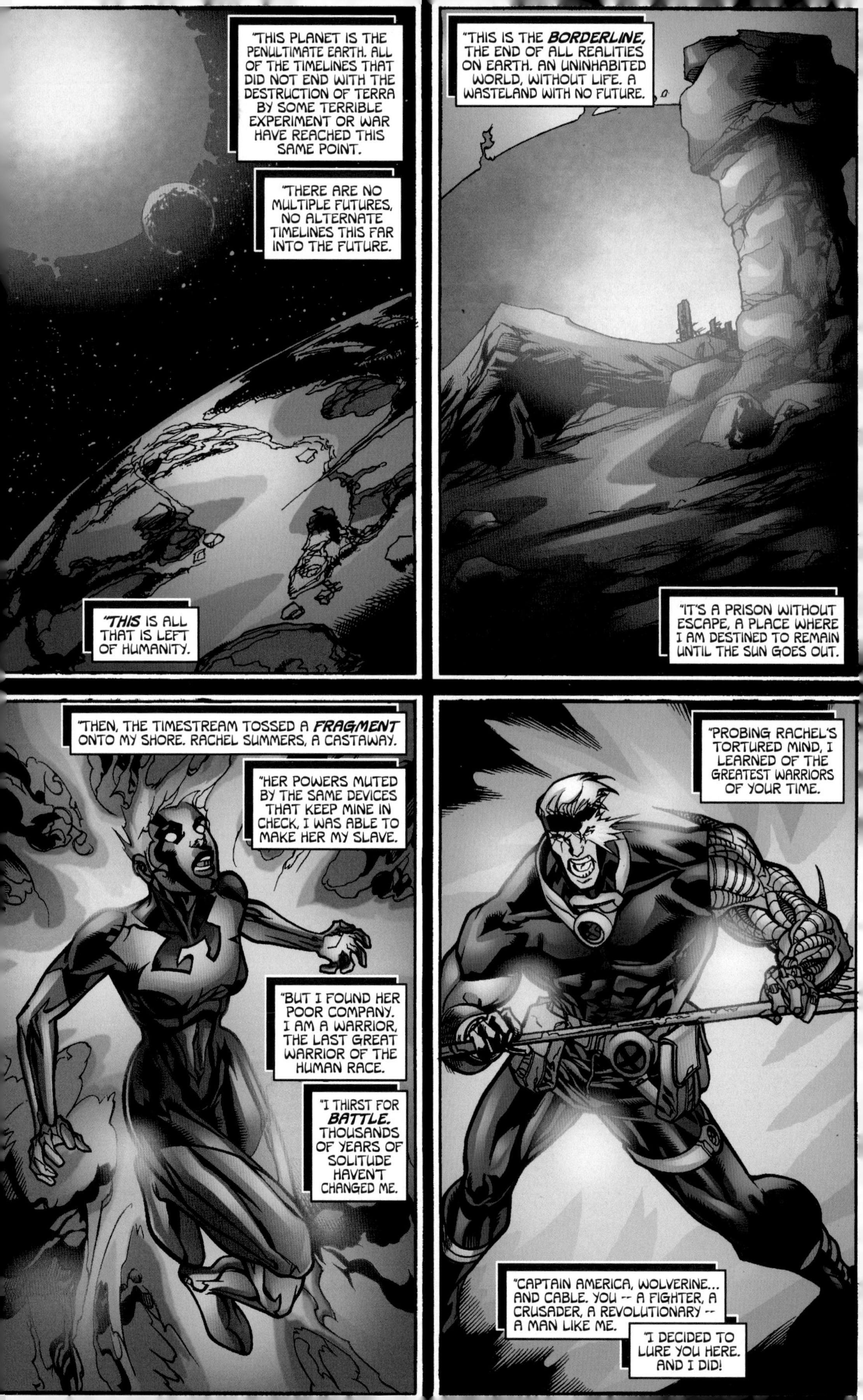
"THIS PLANET IS THE PENULTIMATE EARTH. ALL OF THE TIMELINES THAT DID NOT END WITH THE DESTRUCTION OF TERRA BY SOME TERRIBLE EXPERIMENT OR WAR HAVE REACHED THIS SAME POINT.
"THERE ARE NO MULTIPLE FUTURES, NO ALTERNATE TIMELINES THIS FAR INTO THE FUTURE.
"THIS IS ALL THAT IS LEFT OF HUMANITY.
"THIS IS THE BORDERLINE, THE END OF ALL REALITIES ON EARTH. AN UNINHABITED WORLD, WITHOUT LIFE. A WASTELAND WITH NO FUTURE.
"IT'S A PRISON WITHOUT ESCAPE, A PLACE WHERE I AM DESTINED TO REMAIN UNTIL THE SUN GOES OUT.
"THEN, THE TIMESTREAM TOSSED A FRAGMENT ONTO MY SHORE. RACHEL SUMMERS, A CASTAWAY.
"HER POWERS MUTED BY THE SAME DEVICES THAT KEEP MINE IN CHECK, I WAS ABLE TO MAKE HER MY SLAVE.
"BUT I FOUND HER POOR COMPANY. I AM A WARRIOR, THE LAST GREAT WARRIOR OF THE HUMAN RACE.
"I THIRST FOR BATTLE. THOUSANDS OF YEARS OF SOLITUDE HAVEN'T CHANGED ME.
"PROBING RACHEL'S TORTURED MIND, I LEARNED OF THE GREATEST WARRIORS OF YOUR TIME.
"CAPTAIN AMERICA, WOLVERINE... AND CABLE. YOU -- A FIGHTER, A CRUSADER, A REVOLUTIONARY -- A MAN LIKE ME.
"I DECIDED TO LURE YOU HERE. AND I DID!

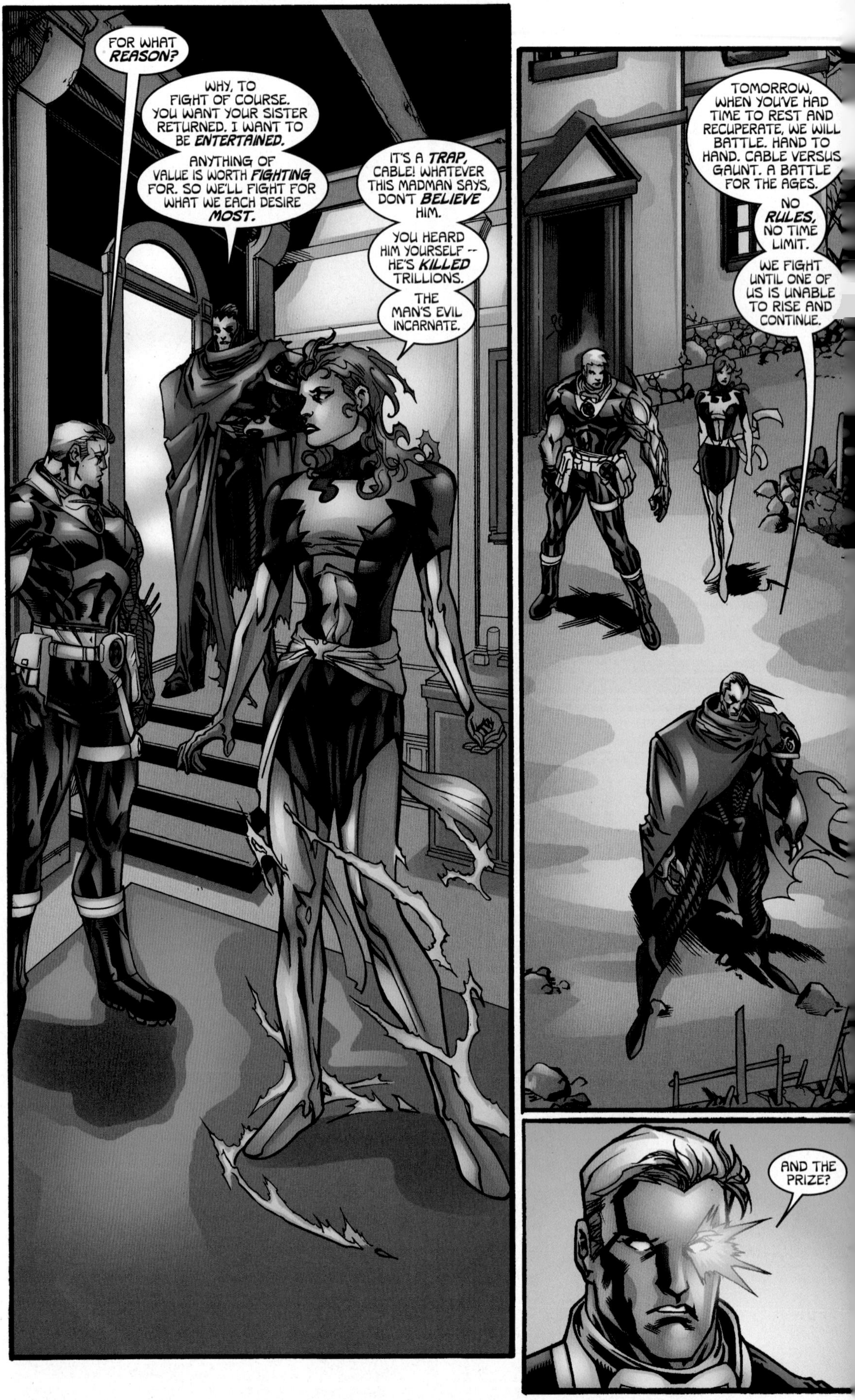
FOR WHAT *REASON?*
WHY, TO FIGHT OF COURSE. YOU WANT YOUR SISTER RETURNED. I WANT TO BE *ENTERTAINED.*
ANYTHING OF VALUE IS WORTH *FIGHTING* FOR. SO WE'LL FIGHT FOR WHAT WE EACH DESIRE *MOST.*
IT'S A *TRAP,* CABLE! WHATEVER THIS MADMAN SAYS, DON'T *BELIEVE* HIM.
YOU HEARD HIM YOURSELF -- HE'S *KILLED* TRILLIONS.
THE MAN'S EVIL INCARNATE.
TOMORROW, WHEN YOU'VE HAD TIME TO REST AND RECUPERATE, WE WILL BATTLE. HAND TO HAND. CABLE VERSUS GAUNT. A BATTLE FOR THE AGES.
NO *RULES,* NO TIME LIMIT.
WE FIGHT UNTIL ONE OF US IS UNABLE TO RISE AND CONTINUE.
AND THE PRIZE?

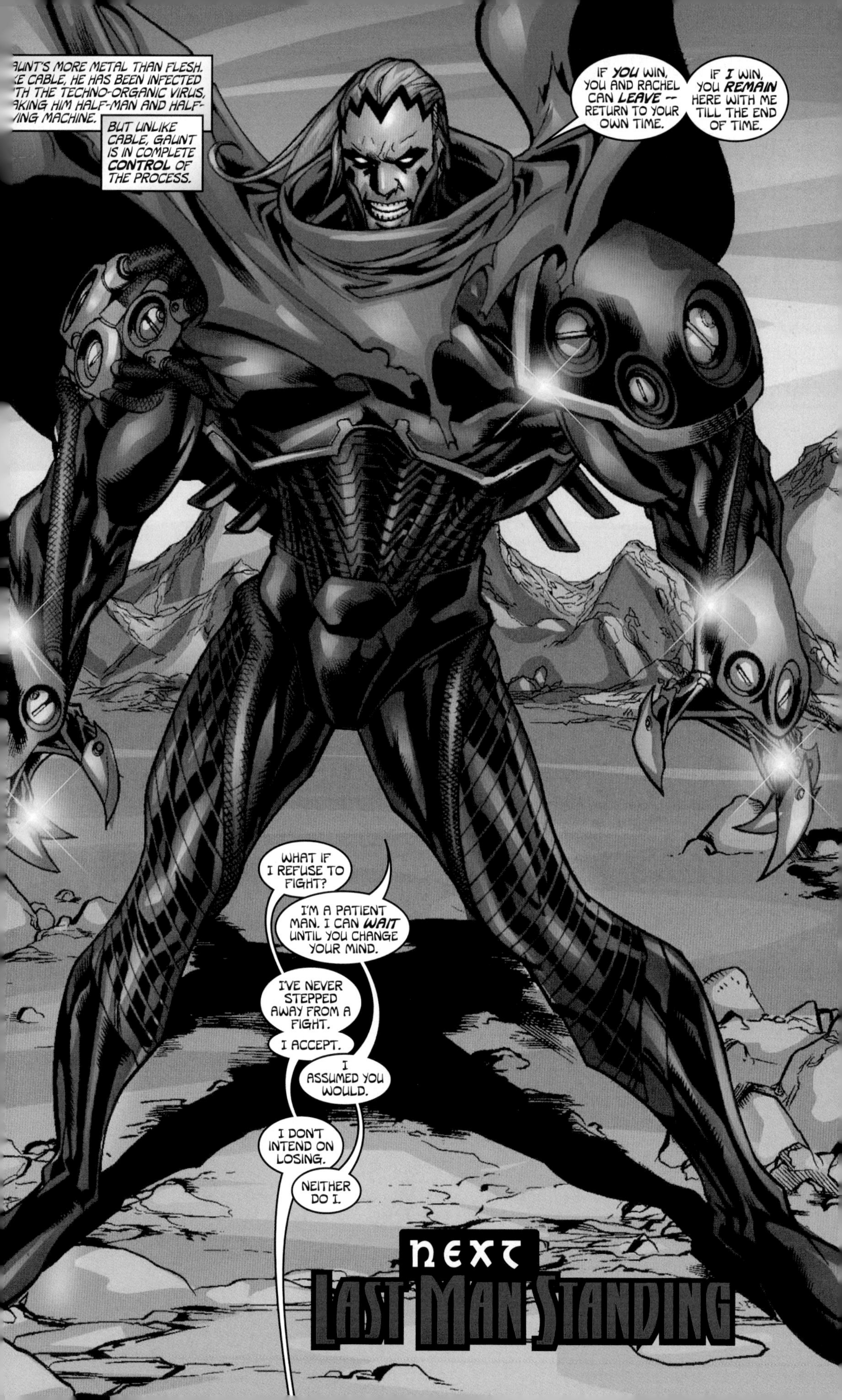

AUNT'S MORE METAL THAN FLESH. KE CABLE, HE HAS BEEN INFECTED TH THE TECHNO-ORGANIC VIRUS, AKING HIM HALF-MAN AND HALF- YING MACHINE.
BUT UNLIKE CABLE, GAUNT IS IN COMPLETE CONTROL OF THE PROCESS.
IF YOU WIN, YOU AND RACHEL CAN LEAVE -- RETURN TO YOUR OWN TIME.
IF I WIN, YOU REMAIN HERE WITH ME TILL THE END OF TIME.
WHAT IF I REFUSE TO FIGHT?
I'M A PATIENT MAN. I CAN WAIT UNTIL YOU CHANGE YOUR MIND.
I'VE NEVER STEPPED AWAY FROM A FIGHT.
I ACCEPT.
I ASSUMED YOU WOULD.
I DON'T INTEND ON LOSING.
NEITHER DO I.
NEXT
LAST MAN STANDING

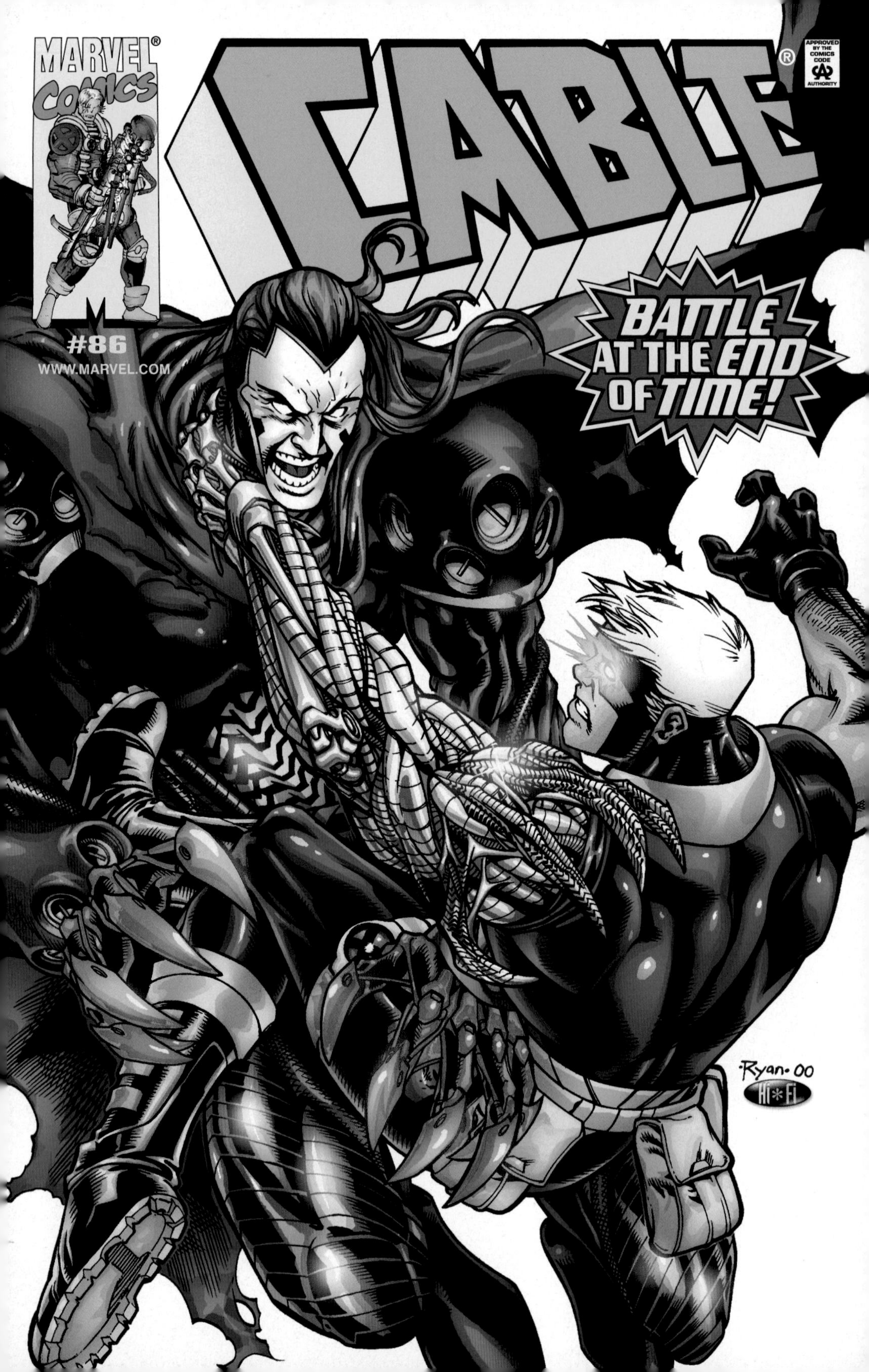
MARVEL COMICS
CABLE
#86
WWW.MARVEL.COM
APPROVED BY THE COMICS CODE AUTHORITY
BATTLE AT THE END OF TIME!
Ryan 00
Hi*Fi

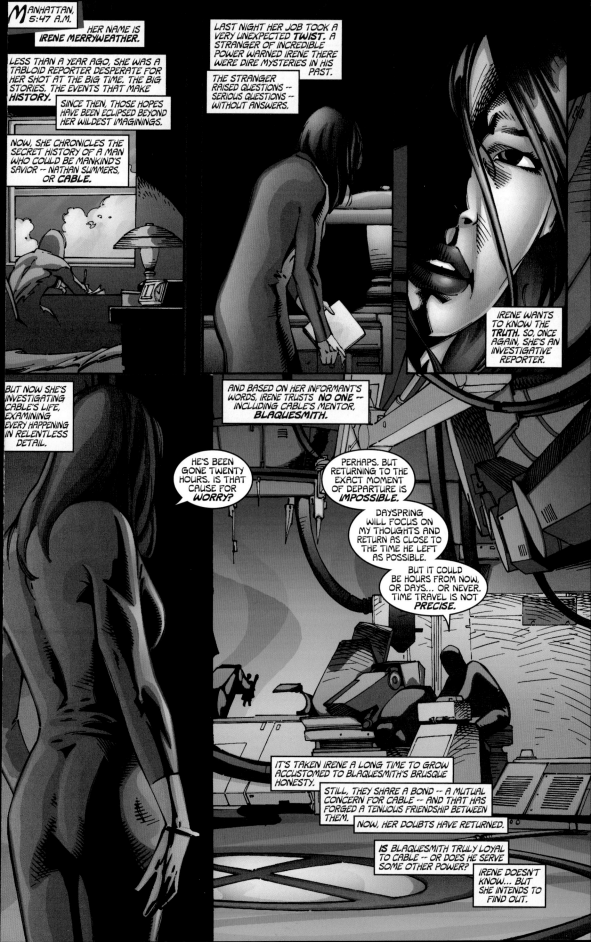

HER NAME IS
IRENE MERRYWEATHER.

LESS THAN A YEAR AGO, SHE WAS A
TABLOID REPORTER DESPERATE FOR
HER SHOT AT THE BIG TIME. THE BIG
STORIES. THE EVENTS THAT MAKE
HISTORY.

SINCE THEN, THOSE HOPES
HAVE BEEN ECLIPSED BEYOND
HER WILDEST IMAGININGS.

NOW, SHE CHRONICLES THE
SECRET HISTORY OF A MAN
WHO COULD BE MANKIND'S
SAVIOR -- NATHAN SUMMERS,
OR *CABLE.*

LAST NIGHT HER JOB TOOK A
VERY UNEXPECTED *TWIST.* A
STRANGER OF INCREDIBLE
POWER WARNED IRENE THERE
WERE DIRE MYSTERIES IN HIS
PAST.

THE STRANGER
RAISED QUESTIONS --
SERIOUS QUESTIONS --
WITHOUT ANSWERS.

IRENE WANTS
TO KNOW THE
TRUTH. SO, ONCE
AGAIN, SHE'S AN
INVESTIGATIVE
REPORTER.

BUT NOW SHE'S
INVESTIGATING
CABLE'S LIFE,
EXAMINING
EVERY HAPPENING
IN RELENTLESS
DETAIL.

AND BASED ON HER INFORMANT'S
WORDS, IRENE TRUSTS *NO ONE* --
INCLUDING CABLE'S MENTOR,
BLAQUESMITH.

HE'S BEEN
GONE TWENTY
HOURS. IS THAT
CAUSE FOR
WORRY?

PERHAPS. BUT
RETURNING TO THE
EXACT MOMENT
OF DEPARTURE IS
IMPOSSIBLE.

DAYSPRING
WILL FOCUS ON
MY THOUGHTS AND
RETURN AS CLOSE TO
THE TIME HE LEFT
AS POSSIBLE.

BUT IT COULD
BE HOURS FROM NOW,
OR DAYS... OR NEVER.
TIME TRAVEL IS NOT
PRECISE.

IT'S TAKEN IRENE A LONG TIME TO GROW
ACCUSTOMED TO BLAQUESMITH'S BRUSQUE
HONESTY.

STILL, THEY SHARE A BOND -- A MUTUAL
CONCERN FOR CABLE -- AND THAT HAS
FORGED A TENUOUS FRIENDSHIP BETWEEN
THEM.

NOW, HER DOUBTS HAVE RETURNED.

IS BLAQUESMITH TRULY LOYAL
TO CABLE -- OR DOES HE SERVE
SOME OTHER POWER?

IRENE DOESN'T
KNOW... BUT
SHE INTENDS TO
FIND OUT.

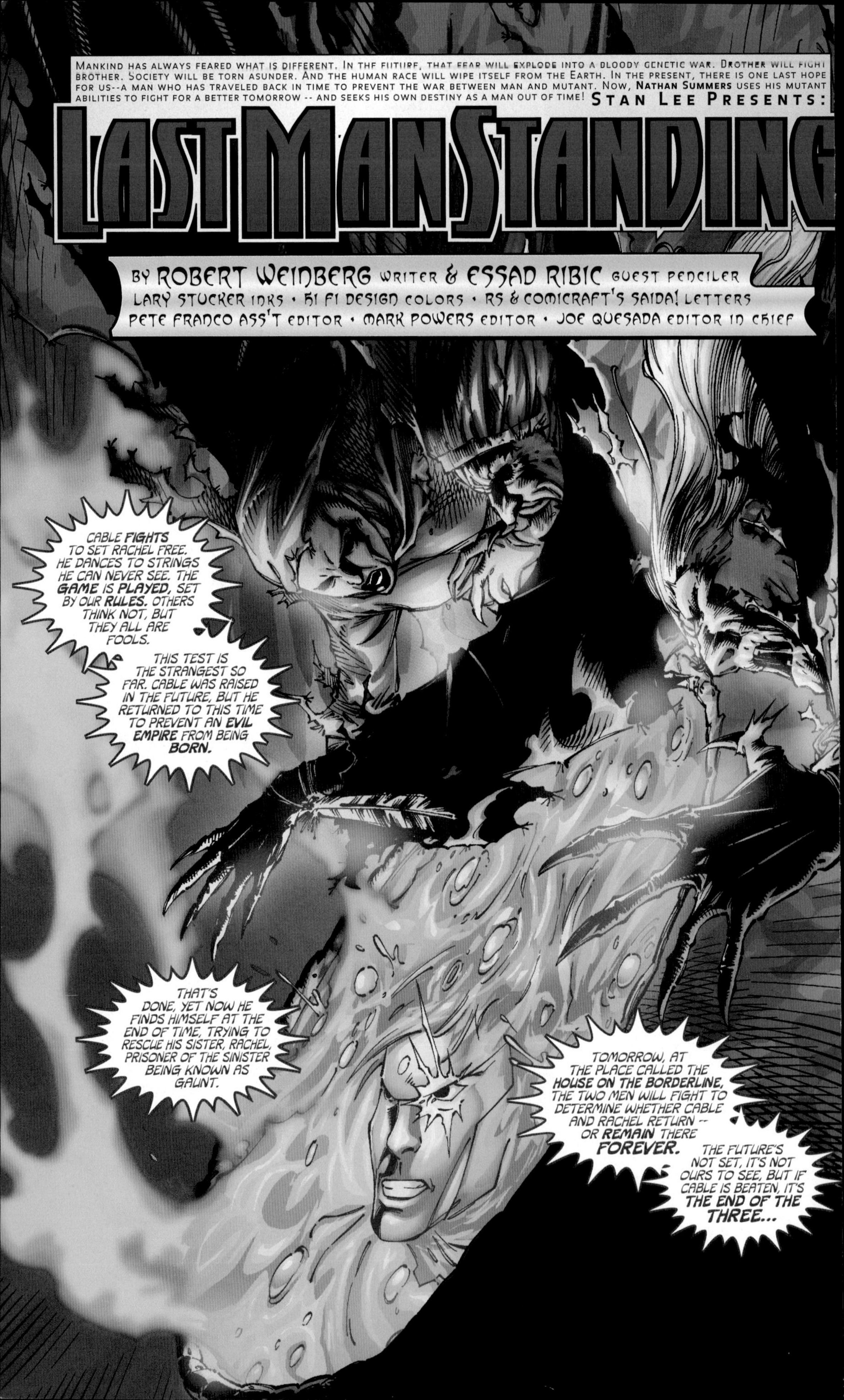

Mankind has always feared what is different. In the future, that fear will explode into a bloody genetic war. Brother will fight brother. Society will be torn asunder. And the human race will wipe itself from the Earth. In the present, there is one last hope for us--a man who has traveled back in time to prevent the war between man and mutant. Now, **Nathan Summers** uses his mutant abilities to fight for a better tomorrow -- and seeks his own destiny as a man out of time!
Stan Lee Presents:
LAST MAN STANDING
by ROBERT WEINBERG writer & ESSAD RIBIC guest penciler
LARY STUCKER inks • HI FI DESIGN colors • RS & COMICRAFT'S SAIDA! letters
PETE FRANCO ass't editor • MARK POWERS editor • JOE QUESADA editor in chief
CABLE **FIGHTS** TO SET RACHEL FREE. HE DANCES TO STRINGS HE CAN NEVER SEE. THE **GAME** IS **PLAYED**, SET BY OUR **RULES.** OTHERS THINK NOT, BUT THEY ALL ARE FOOLS.
THIS TEST IS THE STRANGEST SO FAR. CABLE WAS RAISED IN THE FUTURE, BUT HE RETURNED TO THIS TIME TO PREVENT AN **EVIL EMPIRE** FROM BEING **BORN.**
THAT'S DONE, YET NOW HE FINDS HIMSELF AT THE END OF TIME, TRYING TO RESCUE HIS SISTER, RACHEL, PRISONER OF THE SINISTER BEING KNOWN AS GAUNT.
TOMORROW, AT THE PLACE CALLED THE **HOUSE ON THE BORDERLINE**, THE TWO MEN WILL FIGHT TO DETERMINE WHETHER CABLE AND RACHEL RETURN -- OR **REMAIN** THERE **FOREVER.**
THE FUTURE'S NOT SET, IT'S NOT OURS TO SEE, BUT IF CABLE IS BEATEN, IT'S **THE END OF THE THREE...**

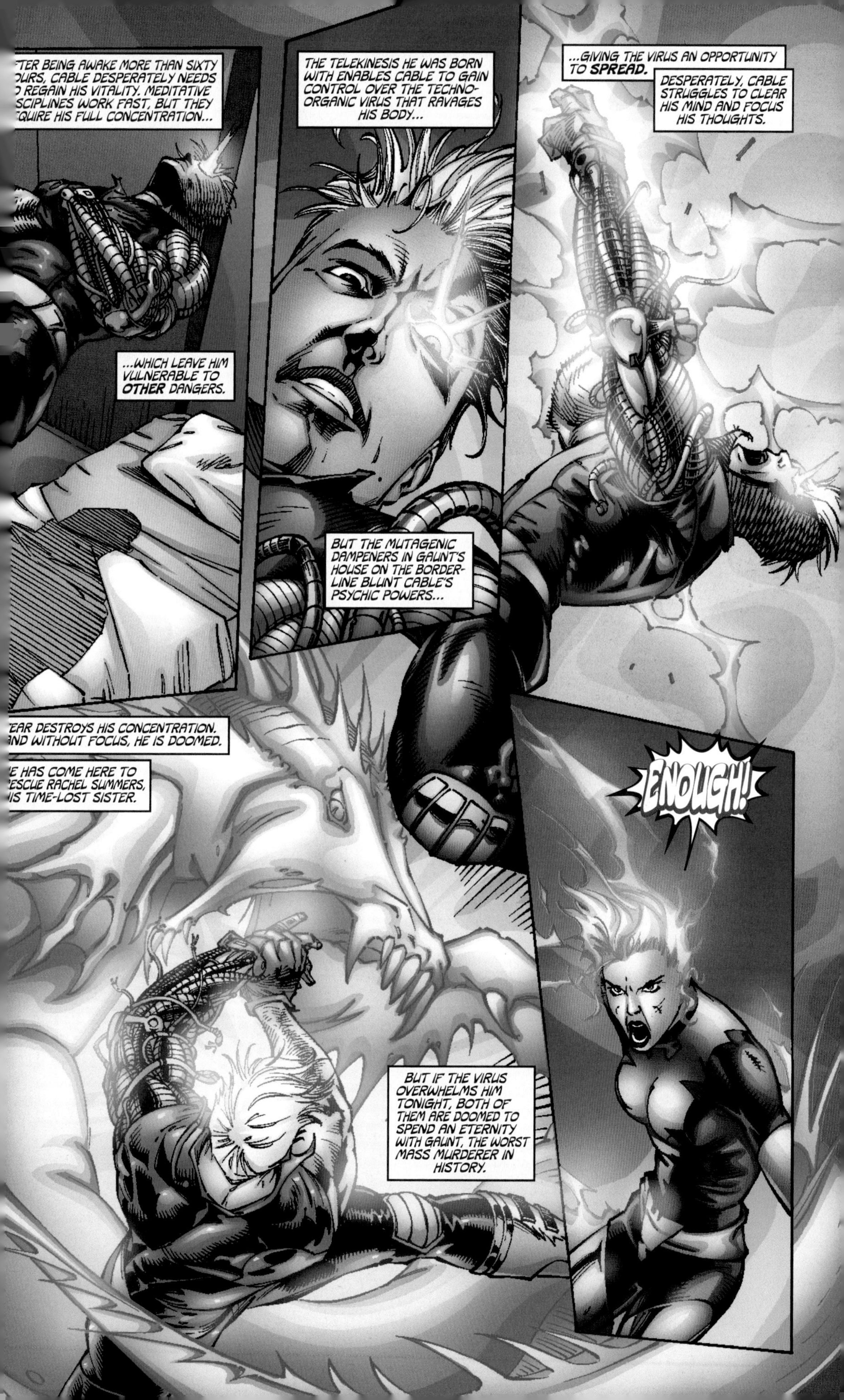
FTER BEING AWAKE MORE THAN SIXTY OURS, CABLE DESPERATELY NEEDS O REGAIN HIS VITALITY. MEDITATIVE SCIPLINES WORK FAST, BUT THEY EQUIRE HIS FULL CONCENTRATION...
...WHICH LEAVE HIM VULNERABLE TO OTHER DANGERS.
THE TELEKINESIS HE WAS BORN WITH ENABLES CABLE TO GAIN CONTROL OVER THE TECHNO-ORGANIC VIRUS THAT RAVAGES HIS BODY...
BUT THE MUTAGENIC DAMPENERS IN GAUNT'S HOUSE ON THE BORDER-LINE BLUNT CABLE'S PSYCHIC POWERS...
...GIVING THE VIRUS AN OPPORTUNITY TO SPREAD.
DESPERATELY, CABLE STRUGGLES TO CLEAR HIS MIND AND FOCUS HIS THOUGHTS.
EAR DESTROYS HIS CONCENTRATION. AND WITHOUT FOCUS, HE IS DOOMED.
E HAS COME HERE TO ESCUE RACHEL SUMMERS, IS TIME-LOST SISTER.
BUT IF THE VIRUS OVERWHELMS HIM TONIGHT, BOTH OF THEM ARE DOOMED TO SPEND AN ETERNITY WITH GAUNT, THE WORST MASS MURDERER IN HISTORY.
ENOUGH!

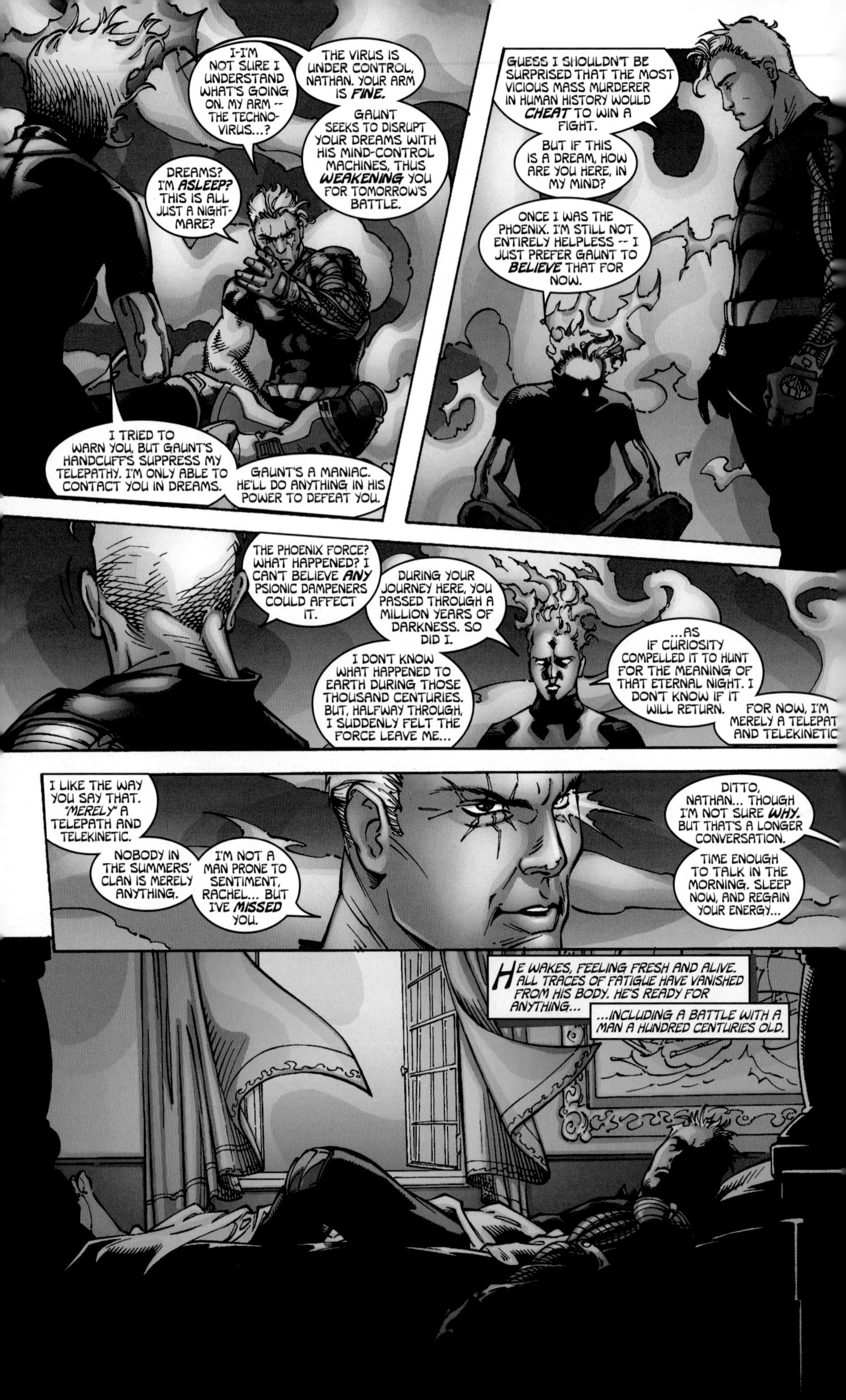
I-I'M NOT SURE I UNDERSTAND WHAT'S GOING ON. MY ARM -- THE TECHNO-VIRUS...?
THE VIRUS IS UNDER CONTROL, NATHAN. YOUR ARM IS FINE.
GAUNT SEEKS TO DISRUPT YOUR DREAMS WITH HIS MIND-CONTROL MACHINES, THUS WEAKENING YOU FOR TOMORROW'S BATTLE.
DREAMS? I'M ASLEEP? THIS IS ALL JUST A NIGHT-MARE?
I TRIED TO WARN YOU, BUT GAUNT'S HANDCUFFS SUPPRESS MY TELEPATHY. I'M ONLY ABLE TO CONTACT YOU IN DREAMS.
GAUNT'S A MANIAC. HE'LL DO ANYTHING IN HIS POWER TO DEFEAT YOU.
GUESS I SHOULDN'T BE SURPRISED THAT THE MOST VICIOUS MASS MURDERER IN HUMAN HISTORY WOULD CHEAT TO WIN A FIGHT.
BUT IF THIS IS A DREAM, HOW ARE YOU HERE, IN MY MIND?
ONCE I WAS THE PHOENIX. I'M STILL NOT ENTIRELY HELPLESS -- I JUST PREFER GAUNT TO BELIEVE THAT FOR NOW.
THE PHOENIX FORCE? WHAT HAPPENED? I CAN'T BELIEVE ANY PSIONIC DAMPENERS COULD AFFECT IT.
DURING YOUR JOURNEY HERE, YOU PASSED THROUGH A MILLION YEARS OF DARKNESS. SO DID I.
I DON'T KNOW WHAT HAPPENED TO EARTH DURING THOSE THOUSAND CENTURIES. BUT, HALFWAY THROUGH, I SUDDENLY FELT THE FORCE LEAVE ME...
...AS IF CURIOSITY COMPELLED IT TO HUNT FOR THE MEANING OF THAT ETERNAL NIGHT. I DON'T KNOW IF IT WILL RETURN.
FOR NOW, I'M MERELY A TELEPAT AND TELEKINETIC
I LIKE THE WAY YOU SAY THAT. "MERELY" A TELEPATH AND TELEKINETIC.
NOBODY IN THE SUMMERS' CLAN IS MERELY ANYTHING.
I'M NOT A MAN PRONE TO SENTIMENT, RACHEL... BUT I'VE MISSED YOU.
DITTO, NATHAN... THOUGH I'M NOT SURE WHY. BUT THAT'S A LONGER CONVERSATION.
TIME ENOUGH TO TALK IN THE MORNING. SLEEP NOW, AND REGAIN YOUR ENERGY...
HE WAKES, FEELING FRESH AND ALIVE. ALL TRACES OF FATIGUE HAVE VANISHED FROM HIS BODY. HE'S READY FOR ANYTHING...
...INCLUDING A BATTLE WITH A MAN A HUNDRED CENTURIES OLD.

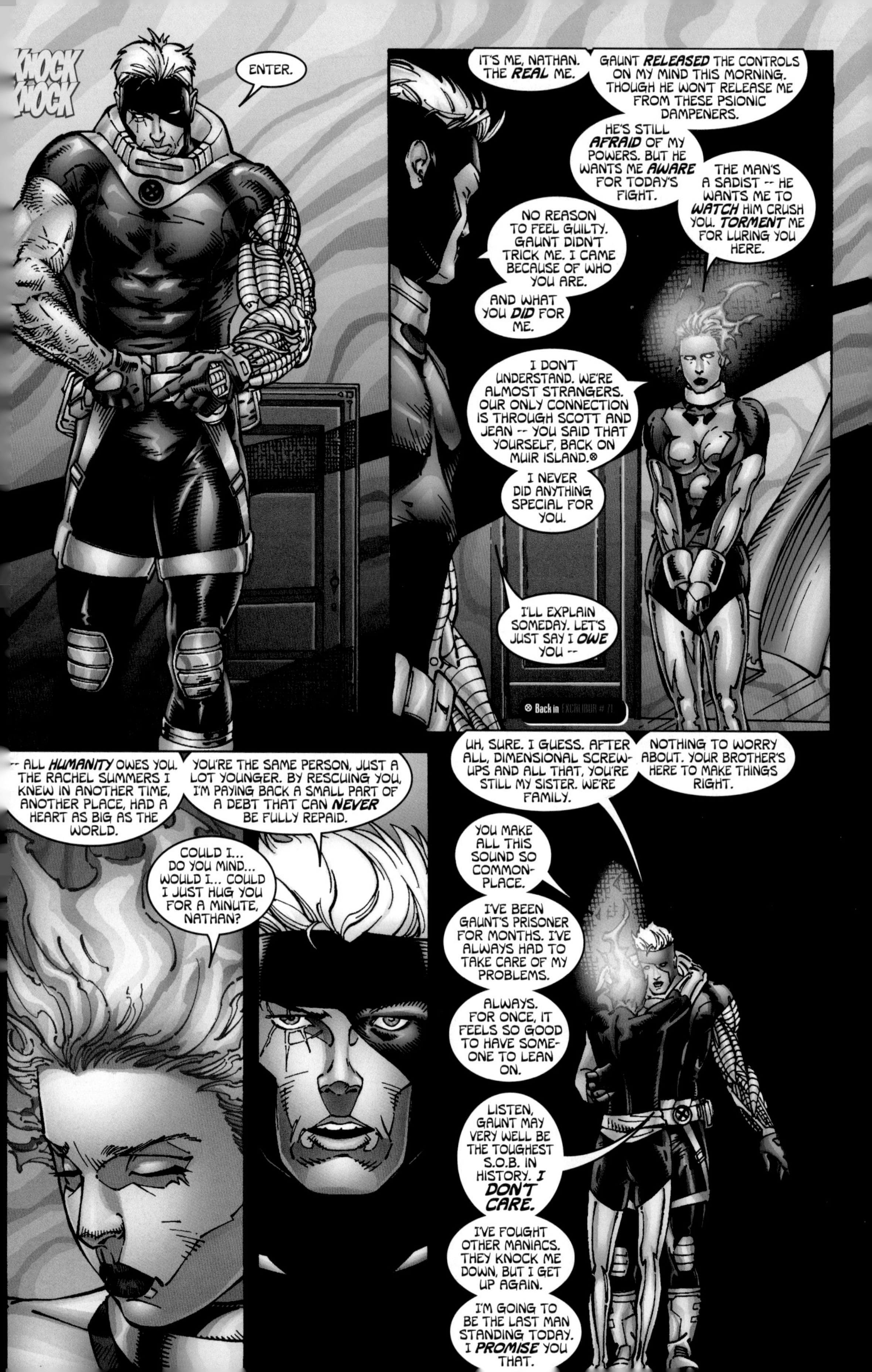
KNOCK KNOCK
ENTER.
IT'S ME, NATHAN. THE REAL ME.
GAUNT RELEASED THE CONTROLS ON MY MIND THIS MORNING. THOUGH HE WON'T RELEASE ME FROM THESE PSIONIC DAMPENERS.
HE'S STILL AFRAID OF MY POWERS. BUT HE WANTS ME AWARE FOR TODAY'S FIGHT.
THE MAN'S A SADIST -- HE WANTS ME TO WATCH HIM CRUSH YOU. TORMENT ME FOR LURING YOU HERE.
NO REASON TO FEEL GUILTY. GAUNT DIDN'T TRICK ME. I CAME BECAUSE OF WHO YOU ARE.
AND WHAT YOU DID FOR ME.
I DON'T UNDERSTAND. WE'RE ALMOST STRANGERS. OUR ONLY CONNECTION IS THROUGH SCOTT AND JEAN -- YOU SAID THAT YOURSELF, BACK ON MUIR ISLAND.⊗
I NEVER DID ANYTHING SPECIAL FOR YOU.
I'LL EXPLAIN SOMEDAY. LET'S JUST SAY I OWE YOU --
⊗ Back in EXCALIBUR #71
-- ALL HUMANITY OWES YOU. THE RACHEL SUMMERS I KNEW IN ANOTHER TIME, ANOTHER PLACE, HAD A HEART AS BIG AS THE WORLD.
YOU'RE THE SAME PERSON, JUST A LOT YOUNGER. BY RESCUING YOU, I'M PAYING BACK A SMALL PART OF A DEBT THAT CAN NEVER BE FULLY REPAID.
COULD I... DO YOU MIND... WOULD I... COULD I JUST HUG YOU FOR A MINUTE, NATHAN?
UH, SURE. I GUESS. AFTER ALL, DIMENSIONAL SCREW-UPS AND ALL THAT, YOU'RE STILL MY SISTER. WE'RE FAMILY.
NOTHING TO WORRY ABOUT. YOUR BROTHER'S HERE TO MAKE THINGS RIGHT.
YOU MAKE ALL THIS SOUND SO COMMON-PLACE.
I'VE BEEN GAUNT'S PRISONER FOR MONTHS. I'VE ALWAYS HAD TO TAKE CARE OF MY PROBLEMS.
ALWAYS. FOR ONCE, IT FEELS SO GOOD TO HAVE SOME-ONE TO LEAN ON.
LISTEN, GAUNT MAY VERY WELL BE THE TOUGHEST S.O.B. IN HISTORY. I DON'T CARE.
I'VE FOUGHT OTHER MANIACS. THEY KNOCK ME DOWN, BUT I GET UP AGAIN.
I'M GOING TO BE THE LAST MAN STANDING TODAY. I PROMISE YOU THAT.

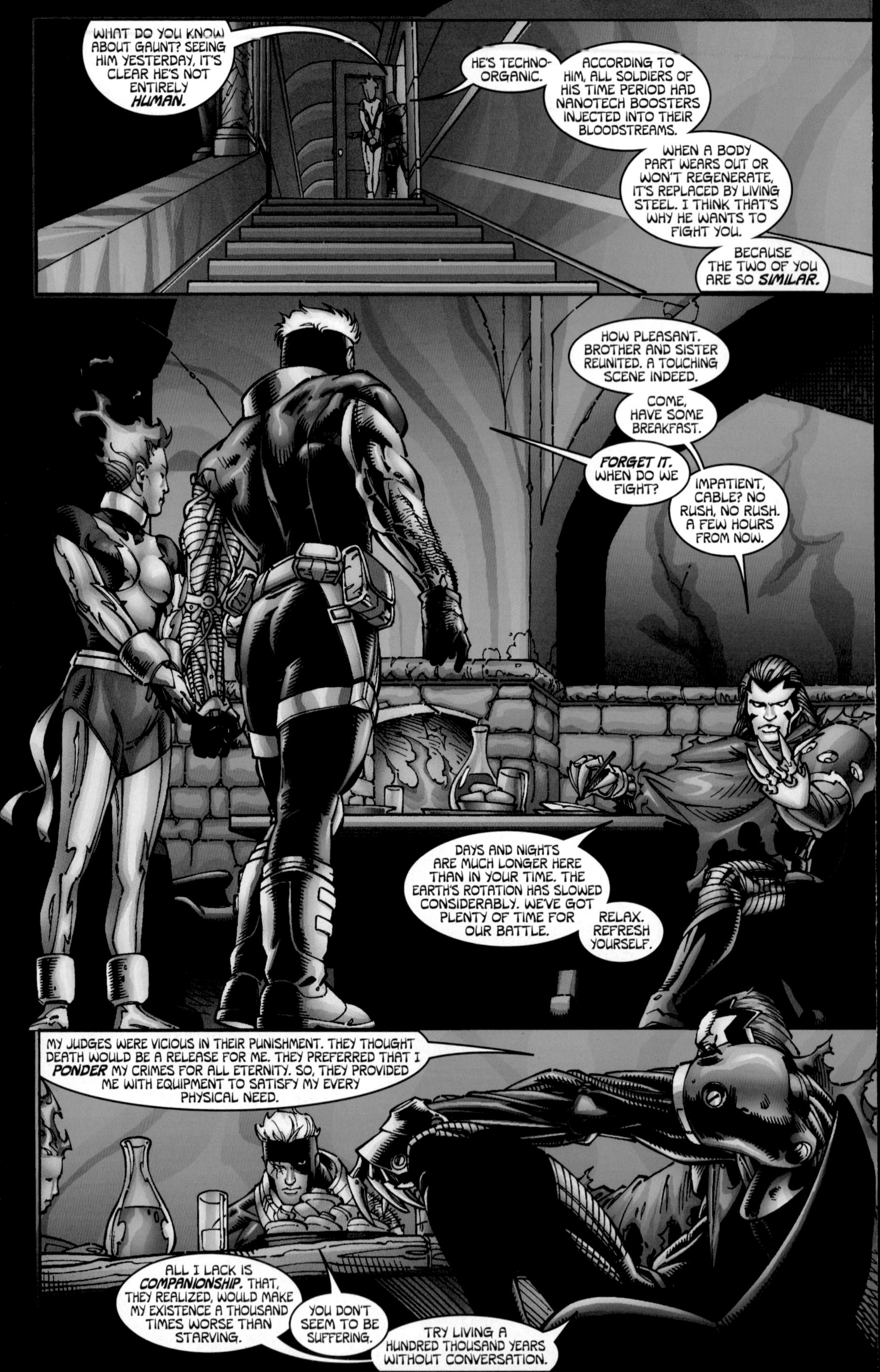
WHAT DO YOU KNOW ABOUT GAUNT? SEEING HIM YESTERDAY, IT'S CLEAR HE'S NOT ENTIRELY HUMAN.
HE'S TECHNO-ORGANIC.
ACCORDING TO HIM, ALL SOLDIERS OF HIS TIME PERIOD HAD NANOTECH BOOSTERS INJECTED INTO THEIR BLOODSTREAMS.
WHEN A BODY PART WEARS OUT OR WON'T REGENERATE, IT'S REPLACED BY LIVING STEEL. I THINK THAT'S WHY HE WANTS TO FIGHT YOU.
BECAUSE THE TWO OF YOU ARE SO SIMILAR.
HOW PLEASANT. BROTHER AND SISTER REUNITED. A TOUCHING SCENE INDEED.
COME, HAVE SOME BREAKFAST.
FORGET IT. WHEN DO WE FIGHT?
IMPATIENT, CABLE? NO RUSH, NO RUSH. A FEW HOURS FROM NOW.
DAYS AND NIGHTS ARE MUCH LONGER HERE THAN IN YOUR TIME. THE EARTH'S ROTATION HAS SLOWED CONSIDERABLY. WE'VE GOT PLENTY OF TIME FOR OUR BATTLE.
RELAX. REFRESH YOURSELF.
MY JUDGES WERE VICIOUS IN THEIR PUNISHMENT. THEY THOUGHT DEATH WOULD BE A RELEASE FOR ME. THEY PREFERRED THAT I PONDER MY CRIMES FOR ALL ETERNITY. SO, THEY PROVIDED ME WITH EQUIPMENT TO SATISFY MY EVERY PHYSICAL NEED.
ALL I LACK IS COMPANIONSHIP. THAT, THEY REALIZED, WOULD MAKE MY EXISTENCE A THOUSAND TIMES WORSE THAN STARVING.
YOU DON'T SEEM TO BE SUFFERING.
TRY LIVING A HUNDRED THOUSAND YEARS WITHOUT CONVERSATION.

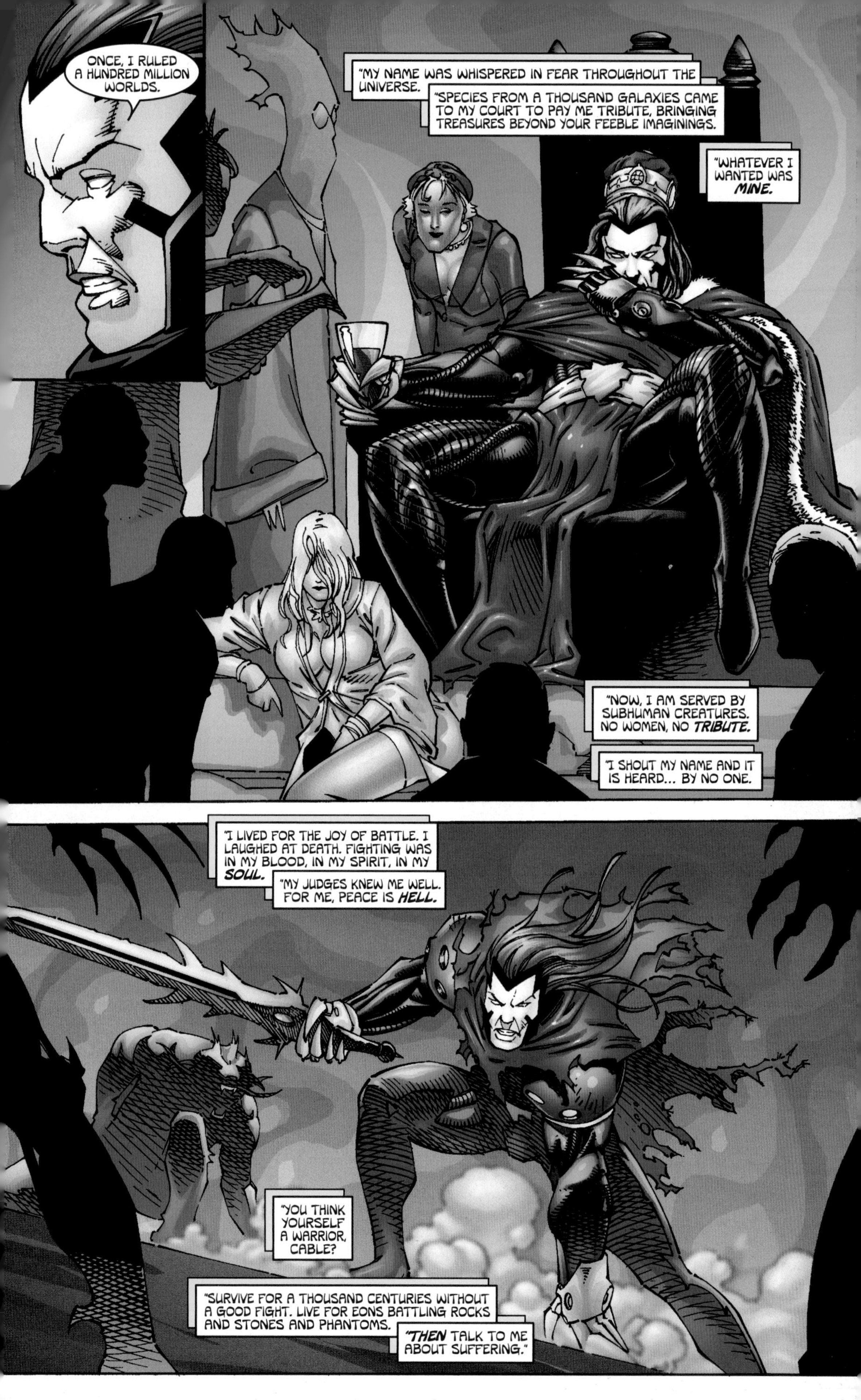

ONCE, I RULED A HUNDRED MILLION WORLDS.
"MY NAME WAS WHISPERED IN FEAR THROUGHOUT THE UNIVERSE.
"SPECIES FROM A THOUSAND GALAXIES CAME TO MY COURT TO PAY ME TRIBUTE, BRINGING TREASURES BEYOND YOUR FEEBLE IMAGININGS.
"WHATEVER I WANTED WAS ***MINE.***
"NOW, I AM SERVED BY SUBHUMAN CREATURES. NO WOMEN, NO ***TRIBUTE.***
"I SHOUT MY NAME AND IT IS HEARD... BY NO ONE.
"I LIVED FOR THE JOY OF BATTLE. I LAUGHED AT DEATH. FIGHTING WAS IN MY BLOOD, IN MY SPIRIT, IN MY ***SOUL.***
"MY JUDGES KNEW ME WELL. FOR ME, PEACE IS ***HELL.***
"YOU THINK YOURSELF A WARRIOR, CABLE?
"SURVIVE FOR A THOUSAND CENTURIES WITHOUT A GOOD FIGHT. LIVE FOR EONS BATTLING ROCKS AND STONES AND PHANTOMS.
"***THEN*** TALK TO ME ABOUT SUFFERING."

MY EXERCISE ROOM IS AT YOUR DISPOSAL IF YOU'D LIKE TO WORK OUT THE KINKS FROM YOUR SYSTEM -- I EVEN HAVE EARLY TWENTY-FIRST CENTURY EQUIPMENT.

PUNCHING A *BAG* THAT DOESN'T PUNCH BACK ISN'T GOING TO PREPARE ME FOR A FIGHT.

I'LL SAVE MY STRENGTH FOR THE REAL THING.

A MAN AFTER MY OWN HEART. NOTHING DUPLICATES THE FEEL OF FLESH STRIKING FLESH. DID YOU GET A GOOD NIGHT'S REST?

I SLEPT QUITE WELL.

GOOD. I HATE EXCUSES.

YOU'LL GET NONE FROM ME.

YOU AND I ARE VERY MUCH ALIKE, CABLE.

STRONG. INDEPENDENT. MASTERS OF OUR OWN DESTINY.

NATHAN'S NOTHING LIKE YOU, GAUNT. YOU'RE A BUTCHER, NOT A WARRIOR.

HE DIDN'T MURDER MILLIONS TO SATISFY SOME SICK BLOOD-LUST.

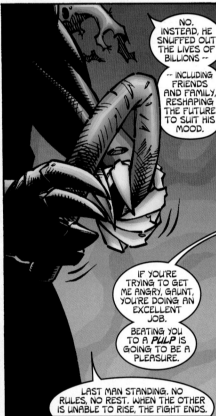

NO. INSTEAD, HE SNUFFED OUT THE LIVES OF BILLIONS -- -- INCLUDING FRIENDS AND FAMILY, RESHAPING THE FUTURE TO SUIT HIS MOOD.

IF YOU'RE TRYING TO GET ME ANGRY, GAUNT, YOU'RE DOING AN EXCELLENT JOB.

BEATING YOU TO A *PULP* IS GOING TO BE A PLEASURE.

LAST MAN STANDING. NO RULES, NO REST. WHEN THE OTHER IS UNABLE TO RISE, THE FIGHT ENDS.

YOU'RE TECHNO-ORGANIC, CABLE. SO AM I. HALF-MAN, HALF METAL. A TRUE WARRIOR.

I'M COUNTING ON YOU PUTTING UP A GOOD STRUGGLE.

CRY HAVOC...

...AND LET SLIP THE DOGS OF WAR!

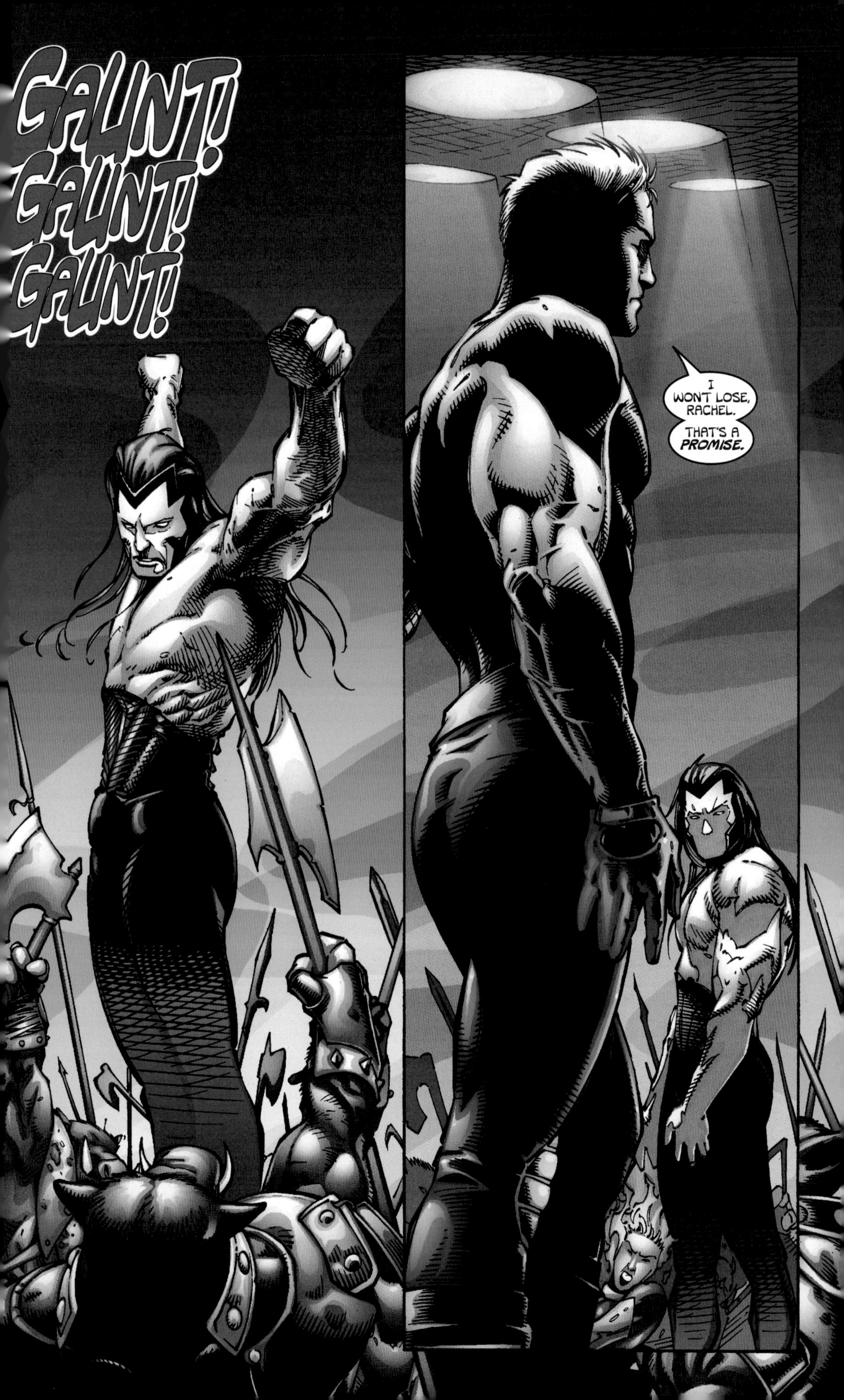
GAUNT! GAUNT! GAUNT!
I WON'T LOSE, RACHEL. THAT'S A *PROMISE.*

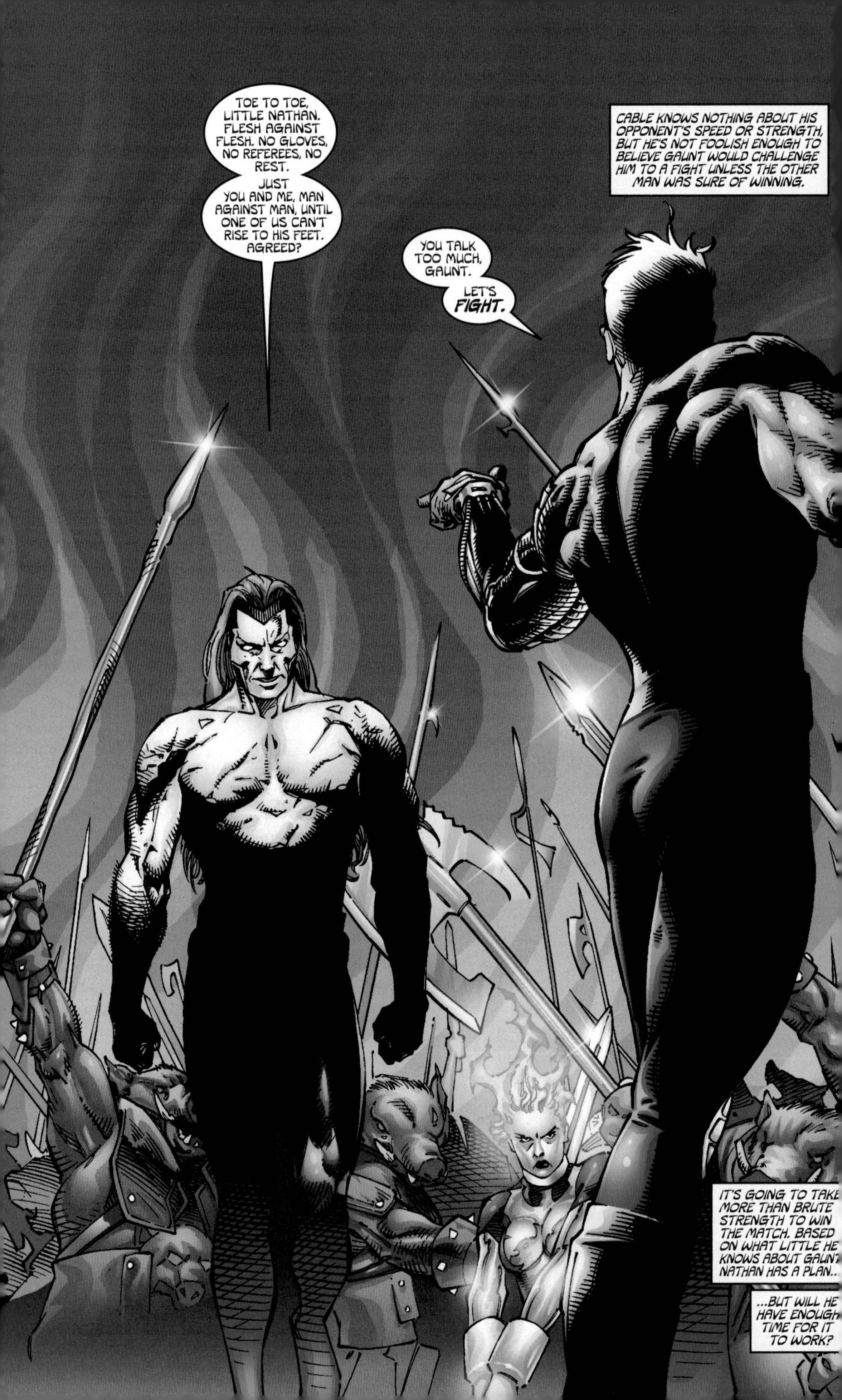
TOE TO TOE, LITTLE NATHAN. FLESH AGAINST FLESH. NO GLOVES, NO REFEREES, NO REST.
JUST YOU AND ME, MAN AGAINST MAN, UNTIL ONE OF US CAN'T RISE TO HIS FEET. AGREED?
CABLE KNOWS NOTHING ABOUT HIS OPPONENT'S SPEED OR STRENGTH, BUT HE'S NOT FOOLISH ENOUGH TO BELIEVE GAUNT WOULD CHALLENGE HIM TO A FIGHT UNLESS THE OTHER MAN WAS SURE OF WINNING.
YOU TALK TOO MUCH, GAUNT.
LET'S FIGHT.
IT'S GOING TO TAKE MORE THAN BRUTE STRENGTH TO WIN THE MATCH. BASED ON WHAT LITTLE HE KNOWS ABOUT GAUNT NATHAN HAS A PLAN...
...BUT WILL HE HAVE ENOUGH TIME FOR IT TO WORK?

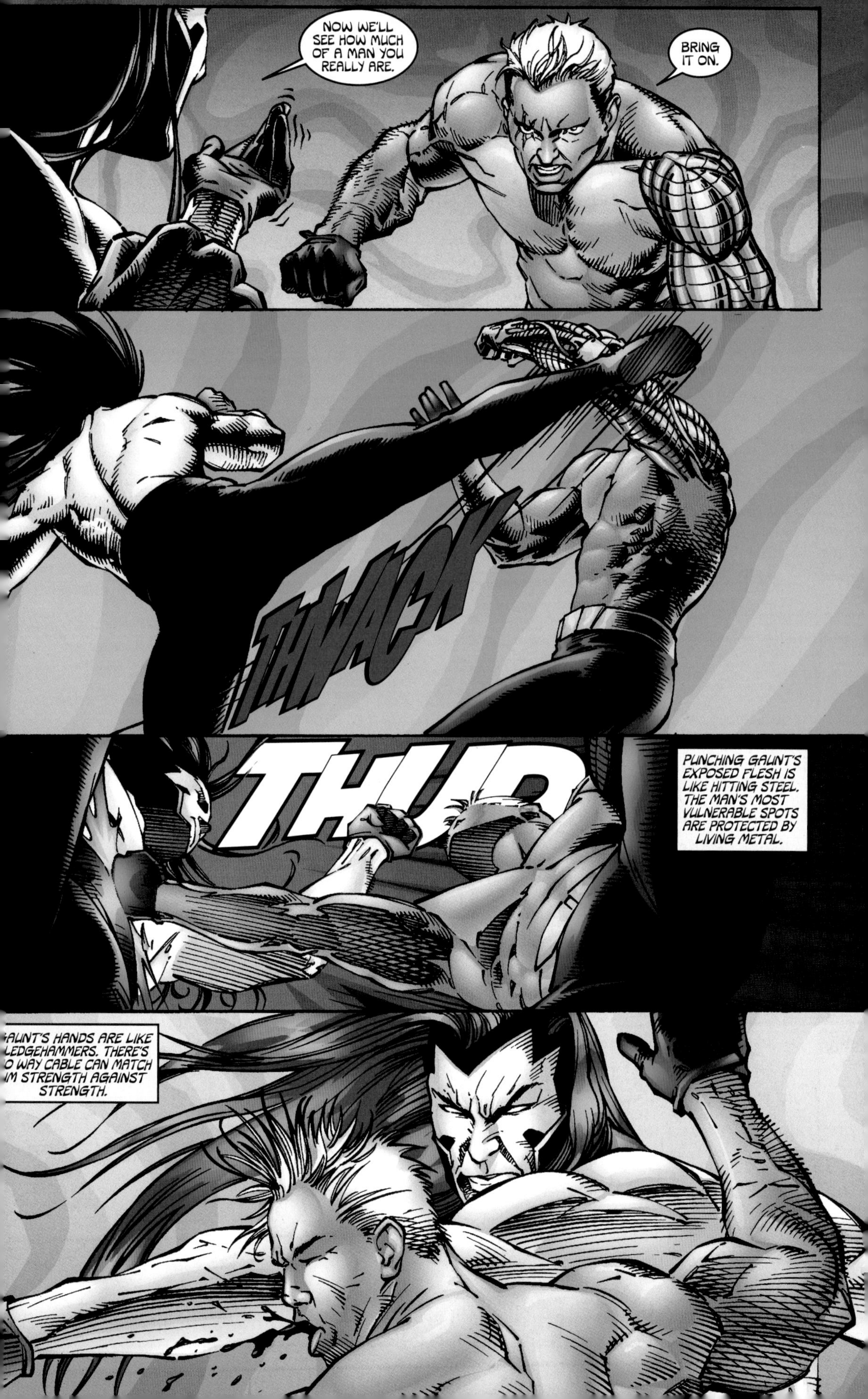
NOW WE'LL SEE HOW MUCH OF A MAN YOU REALLY ARE.
BRING IT ON.
THWACK
THUD
PUNCHING GAUNT'S EXPOSED FLESH IS LIKE HITTING STEEL. THE MAN'S MOST VULNERABLE SPOTS ARE PROTECTED BY LIVING METAL.
GAUNT'S HANDS ARE LIKE LEDGEHAMMERS. THERE'S O WAY CABLE CAN MATCH IM STRENGTH AGAINST STRENGTH.

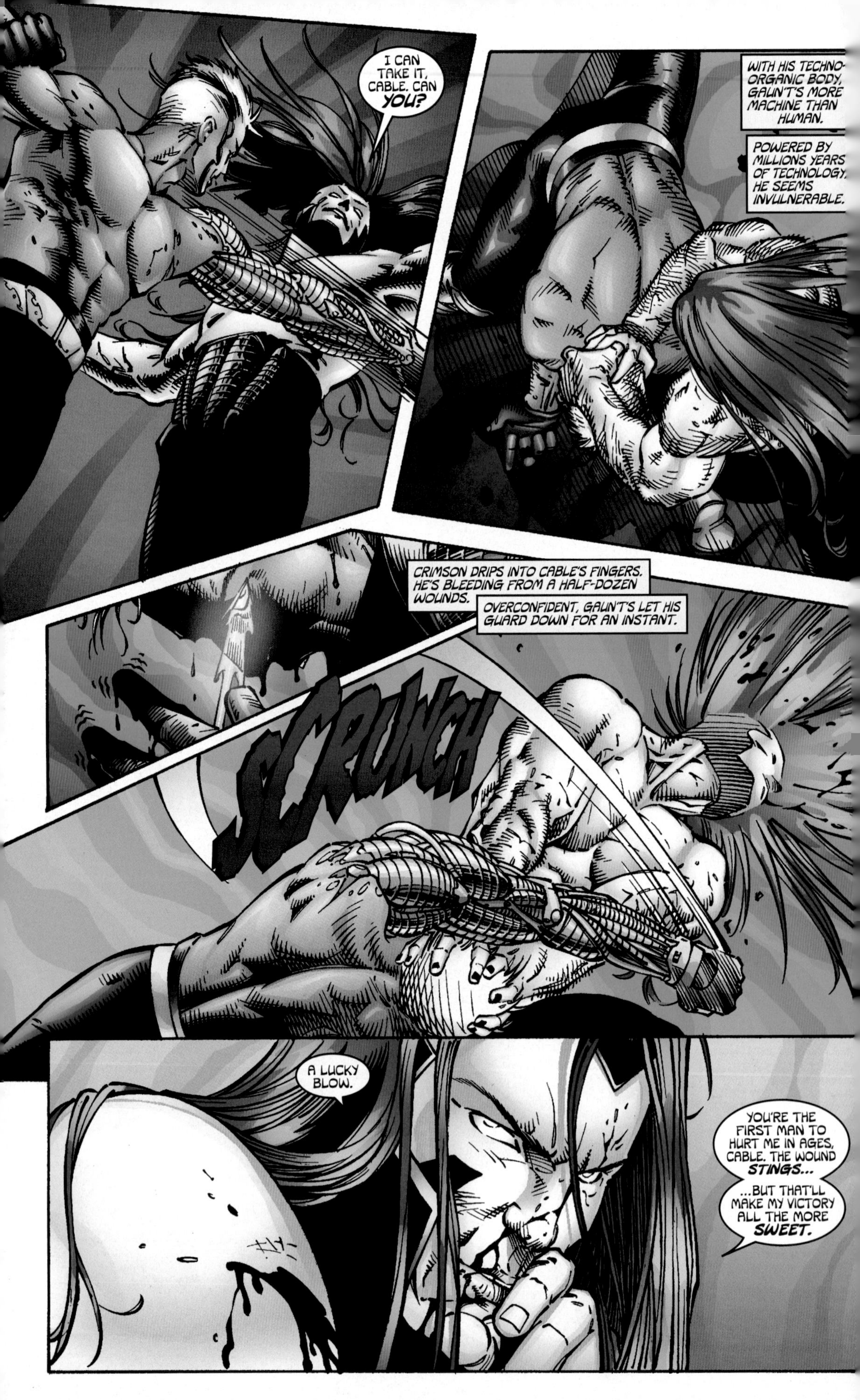
I CAN TAKE IT, CABLE. CAN YOU?
WITH HIS TECHNO-ORGANIC BODY, GAUNT'S MORE MACHINE THAN HUMAN.
POWERED BY MILLIONS YEARS OF TECHNOLOGY, HE SEEMS INVULNERABLE.
CRIMSON DRIPS INTO CABLE'S FINGERS. HE'S BLEEDING FROM A HALF-DOZEN WOUNDS.
OVERCONFIDENT, GAUNT'S LET HIS GUARD DOWN FOR AN INSTANT.
SCRUNCH
A LUCKY BLOW.
YOU'RE THE FIRST MAN TO HURT ME IN AGES, CABLE. THE WOUND STINGS...
...BUT THAT'LL MAKE MY VICTORY ALL THE MORE SWEET.

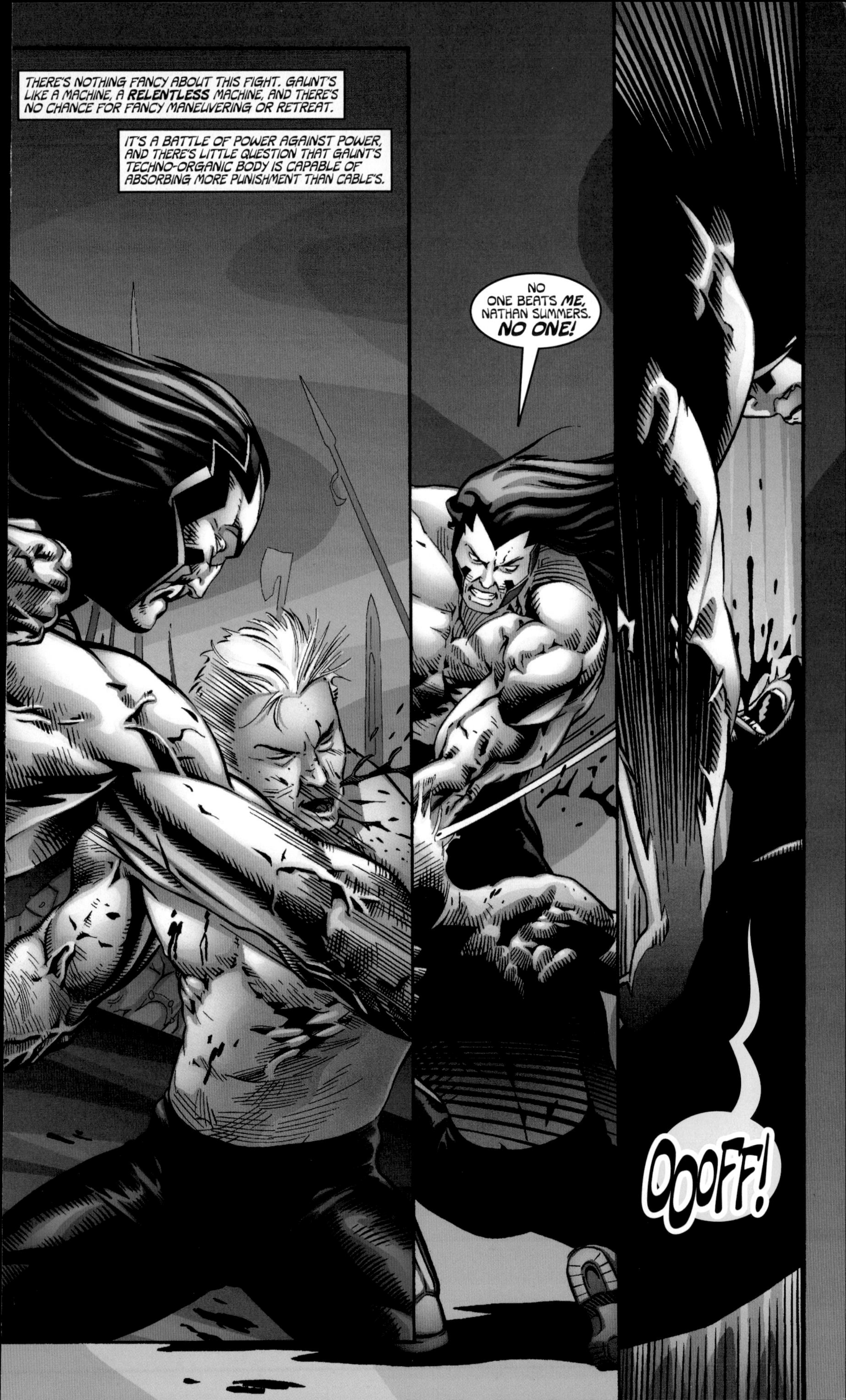
THERE'S NOTHING FANCY ABOUT THIS FIGHT. GAUNT'S LIKE A MACHINE, A RELENTLESS MACHINE, AND THERE'S NO CHANCE FOR FANCY MANEUVERING OR RETREAT.
IT'S A BATTLE OF POWER AGAINST POWER, AND THERE'S LITTLE QUESTION THAT GAUNT'S TECHNO-ORGANIC BODY IS CAPABLE OF ABSORBING MORE PUNISHMENT THAN CABLE'S.
NO ONE BEATS ME, NATHAN SUMMERS. NO ONE!
OOOFF!

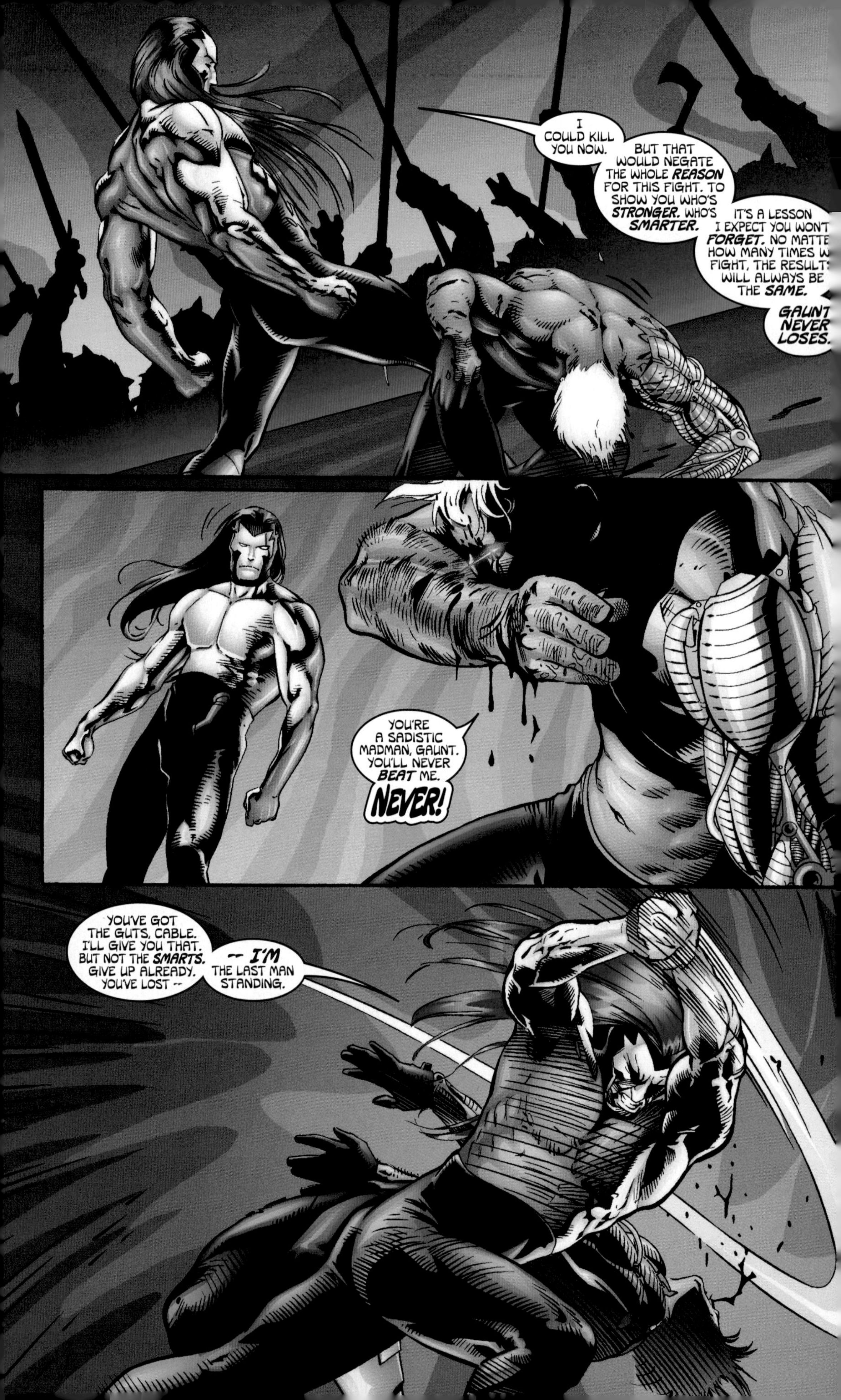

I COULD KILL YOU NOW.
BUT THAT WOULD NEGATE THE WHOLE REASON FOR THIS FIGHT. TO SHOW YOU WHO'S STRONGER. WHO'S SMARTER.
IT'S A LESSON I EXPECT YOU WON'T FORGET. NO MATTE HOW MANY TIMES W FIGHT, THE RESULTS WILL ALWAYS BE THE SAME.
GAUNT NEVER LOSES.
YOU'RE A SADISTIC MADMAN, GAUNT. YOU'LL NEVER BEAT ME. NEVER!
YOU'VE GOT THE GUTS, CABLE. I'LL GIVE YOU THAT. BUT NOT THE SMARTS. GIVE UP ALREADY. YOU'VE LOST --
-- I'M THE LAST MAN STANDING.

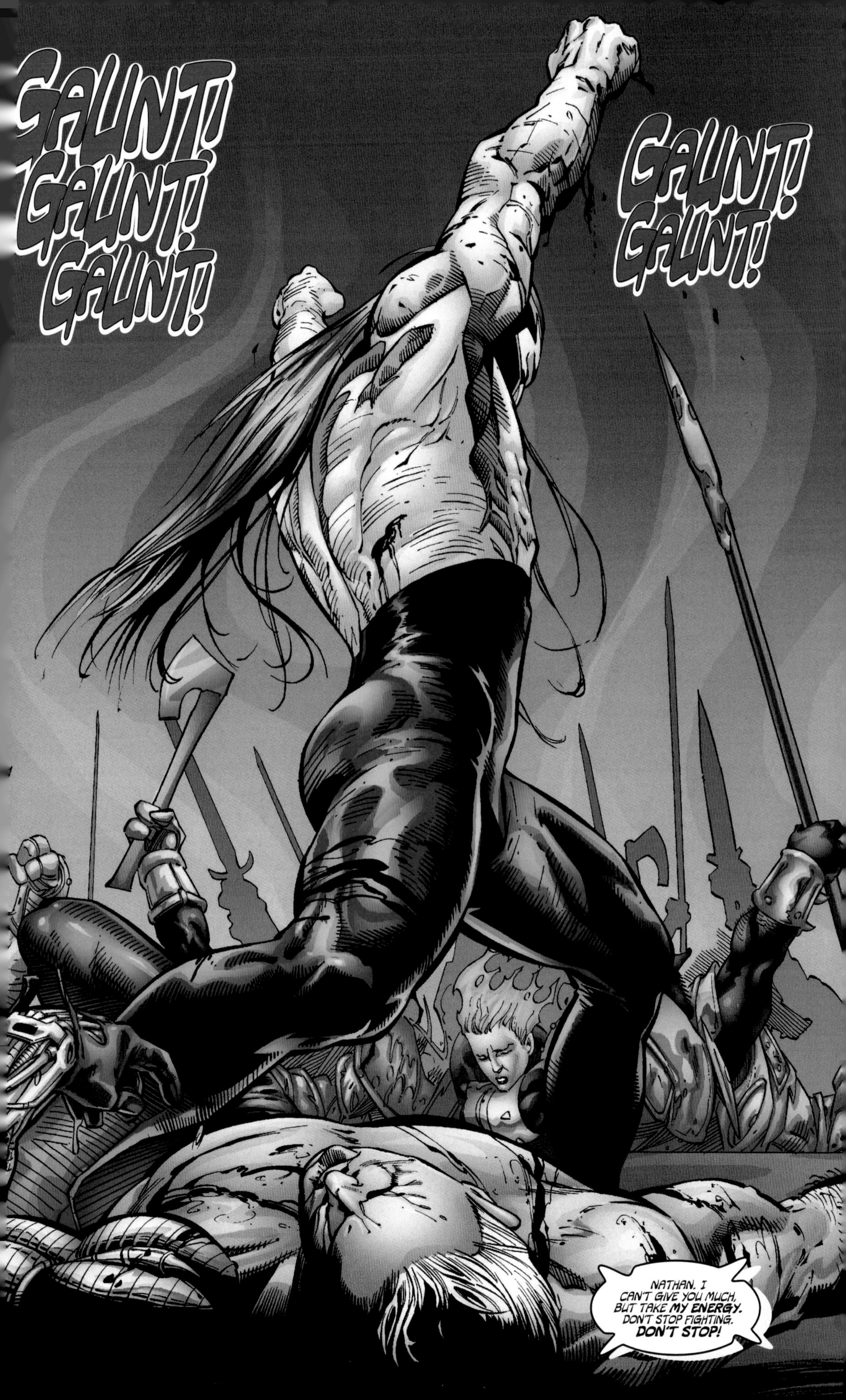
GAUNT! GAUNT! GAUNT!
GAUNT! GAUNT!
NATHAN. I CAN'T GIVE YOU MUCH, BUT TAKE **MY ENERGY**. DON'T STOP FIGHTING. **DON'T STOP!**

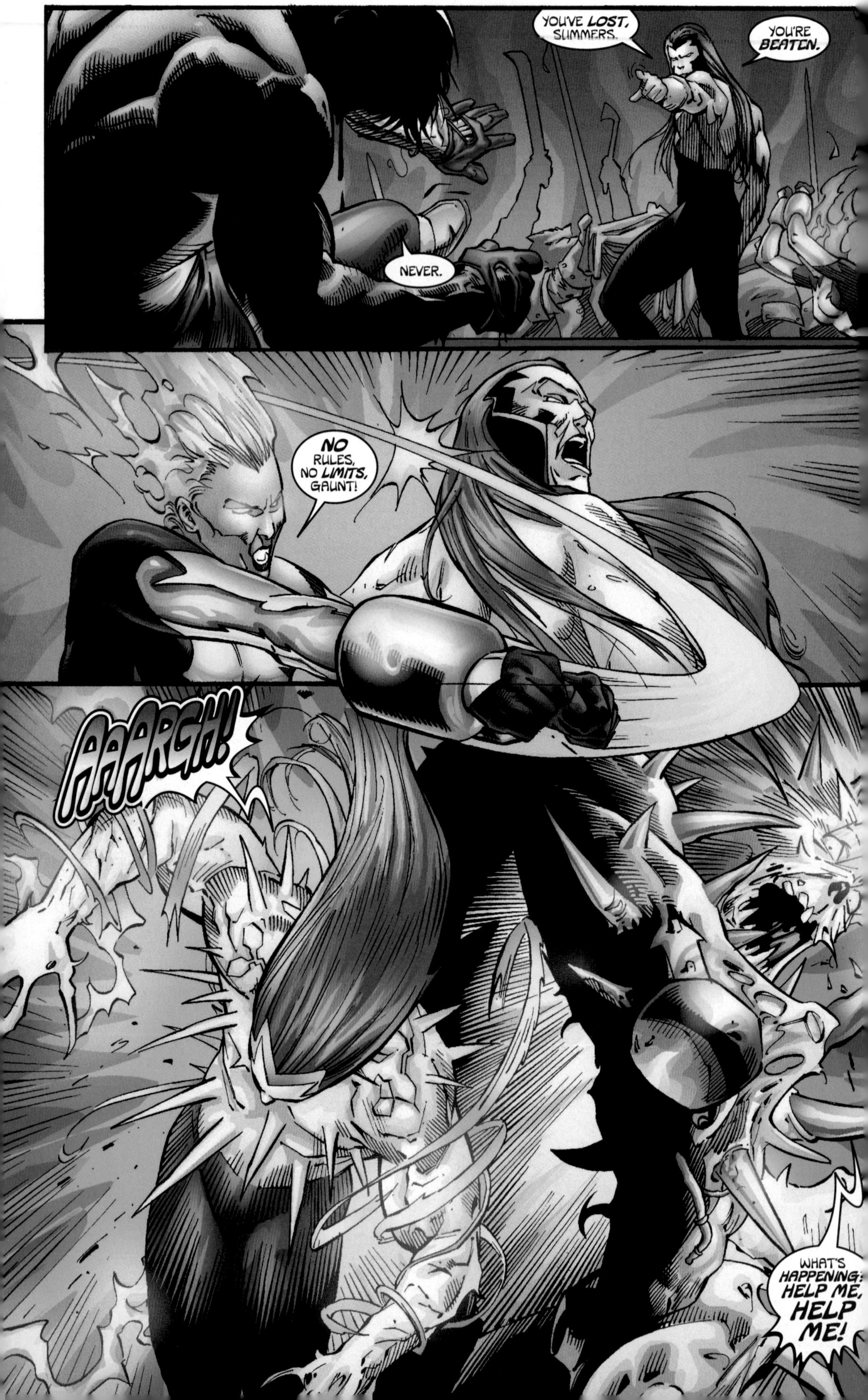
YOU'VE LOST, SUMMERS.
YOU'RE BEATEN.
NEVER.
NO RULES, NO LIMITS, GAUNT!
AAARGH!
WHAT'S HAPPENING? HELP ME, HELP ME!

ON'T THINK GAUNT'S GOING TO BE ABLE
O STAND FOR A LONG TIME TO COME. SO,
THAT MAKES ME THE WINNER.

I SEE HIS MENTAL CHAINS ON YOU HAVE *DISAPPEARED.*

YOU'RE FREE TO LEAVE.

READY TO GO *HOME?*

DEFINITELY. BUT WHAT DID YOU *DO* TO HIM?

HE WAS MADE TECHNO-ORGANIC USING ANOTECHNOLOGY AND A RY WEAK VERSION OF THE CHNO-ORGANIC VIRUS. SOME- ING HE COULD *CONTROL.* AN INFANT, I WAS INFECTED WITH THE MOST VIRULENT STRAIN OF THE VIRUS.

WHEN I SMASHED GAUNT IN THE MOUTH, OME OF MY BLOOD WAS SORBED INTO HIS SYSTEM. TER THAT, IT WAS JUST A TTER OF TIME BEFORE *HE* BECAME INFECTED AS WELL.

WHAT WILL HAPPEN TO GAUNT?

IT TOOK ME YEARS, USING MY MUTANT POWERS, TO GAIN SOME MEASURE OF CONTROL OVER THE TECHNO-VIRUS. GAUNT'S NO MUTANT. BUT THE NANOTECH DRIVERS IN HIS BLOOD SHOULD PROVIDE SOME *HELP.*

IN A FEW HUNDRED YEARS, HE'LL BE ABLE TO MOVE, MAYBE TWICE AS LONG BEFORE HE'S ENTIRELY BACK TO NORMAL.

NO TEARS FROM *ME.* HE GOT WHAT HE DESERVED.

I WON THE FIGHT. NOT BY PLAYING FAIR, BUT GAUNT SAID NO RULES.

BESIDES, I MADE YOU A *PROMISE.*

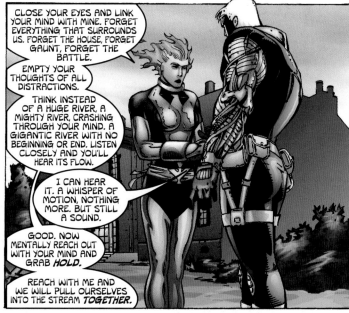

CLOSE YOUR EYES AND LINK YOUR MIND WITH MINE. FORGET EVERYTHING THAT SURROUNDS US. FORGET THE HOUSE, FORGET GAUNT, FORGET THE BATTLE.

EMPTY YOUR THOUGHTS OF ALL DISTRACTIONS.

THINK INSTEAD OF A HUGE RIVER, A MIGHTY RIVER, CRASHING THROUGH YOUR MIND. A GIGANTIC RIVER WITH NO BEGINNING OR END. LISTEN CLOSELY AND YOU'LL HEAR ITS FLOW.

I CAN HEAR IT. A WHISPER OF MOTION, NOTHING MORE. BUT STILL A SOUND.

GOOD. NOW MENTALLY REACH OUT WITH YOUR MIND AND GRAB *HOLD.*

REACH WITH ME AND WE WILL PULL OURSELVES INTO THE STREAM *TOGETHER.*

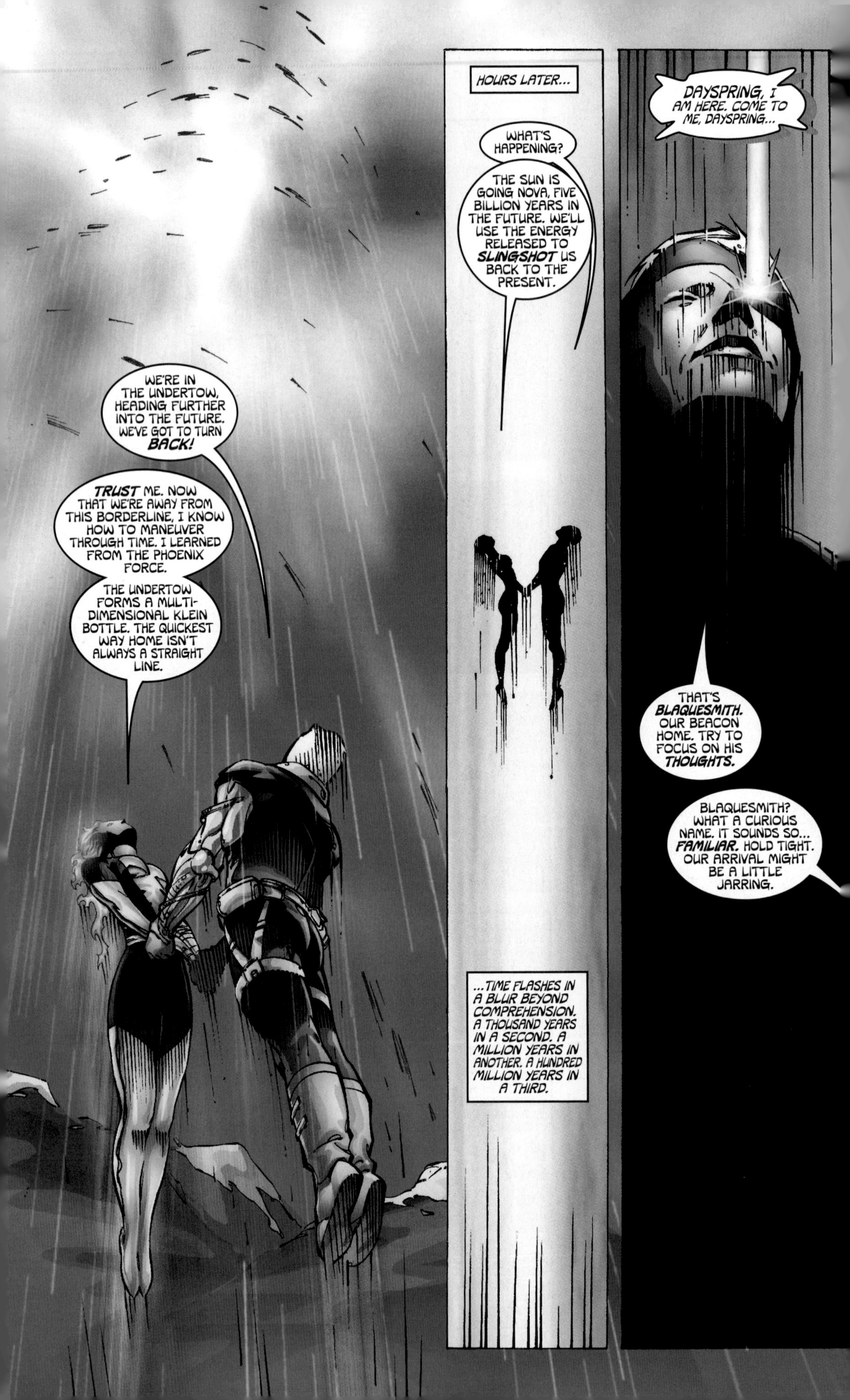
WE'RE IN THE UNDERTOW, HEADING FURTHER INTO THE FUTURE. WE'VE GOT TO TURN BACK!
TRUST ME. NOW THAT WE'RE AWAY FROM THIS BORDERLINE, I KNOW HOW TO MANEUVER THROUGH TIME. I LEARNED FROM THE PHOENIX FORCE.
THE UNDERTOW FORMS A MULTI-DIMENSIONAL KLEIN BOTTLE. THE QUICKEST WAY HOME ISN'T ALWAYS A STRAIGHT LINE.
HOURS LATER...
WHAT'S HAPPENING?
THE SUN IS GOING NOVA, FIVE BILLION YEARS IN THE FUTURE. WE'LL USE THE ENERGY RELEASED TO SLINGSHOT US BACK TO THE PRESENT.
...TIME FLASHES IN A BLUR BEYOND COMPREHENSION. A THOUSAND YEARS IN A SECOND. A MILLION YEARS IN ANOTHER. A HUNDRED MILLION YEARS IN A THIRD.
DAYSPRING, I AM HERE. COME TO ME, DAYSPRING...
THAT'S BLAQUESMITH. OUR BEACON HOME. TRY TO FOCUS ON HIS THOUGHTS.
BLAQUESMITH? WHAT A CURIOUS NAME. IT SOUNDS SO... FAMILIAR. HOLD TIGHT. OUR ARRIVAL MIGHT BE A LITTLE JARRING.

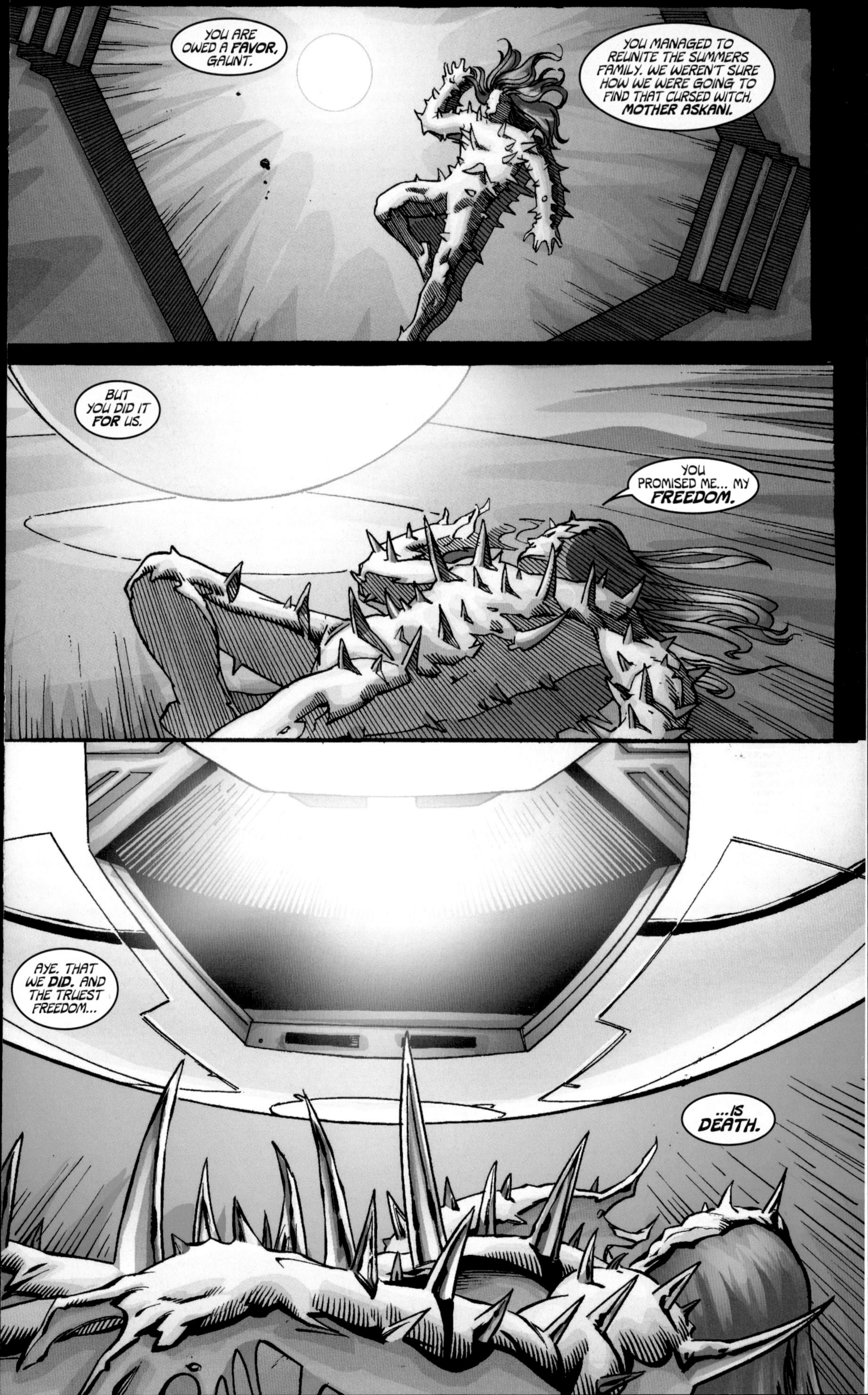
YOU ARE OWED A FAVOR, GAUNT.
YOU MANAGED TO REUNITE THE SUMMERS FAMILY. WE WEREN'T SURE HOW WE WERE GOING TO FIND THAT CURSED WITCH, MOTHER ASKANI.
BUT YOU DID IT FOR US.
YOU PROMISED ME... MY FREEDOM.
AYE. THAT WE DID. AND THE TRUEST FREEDOM...
...IS DEATH.

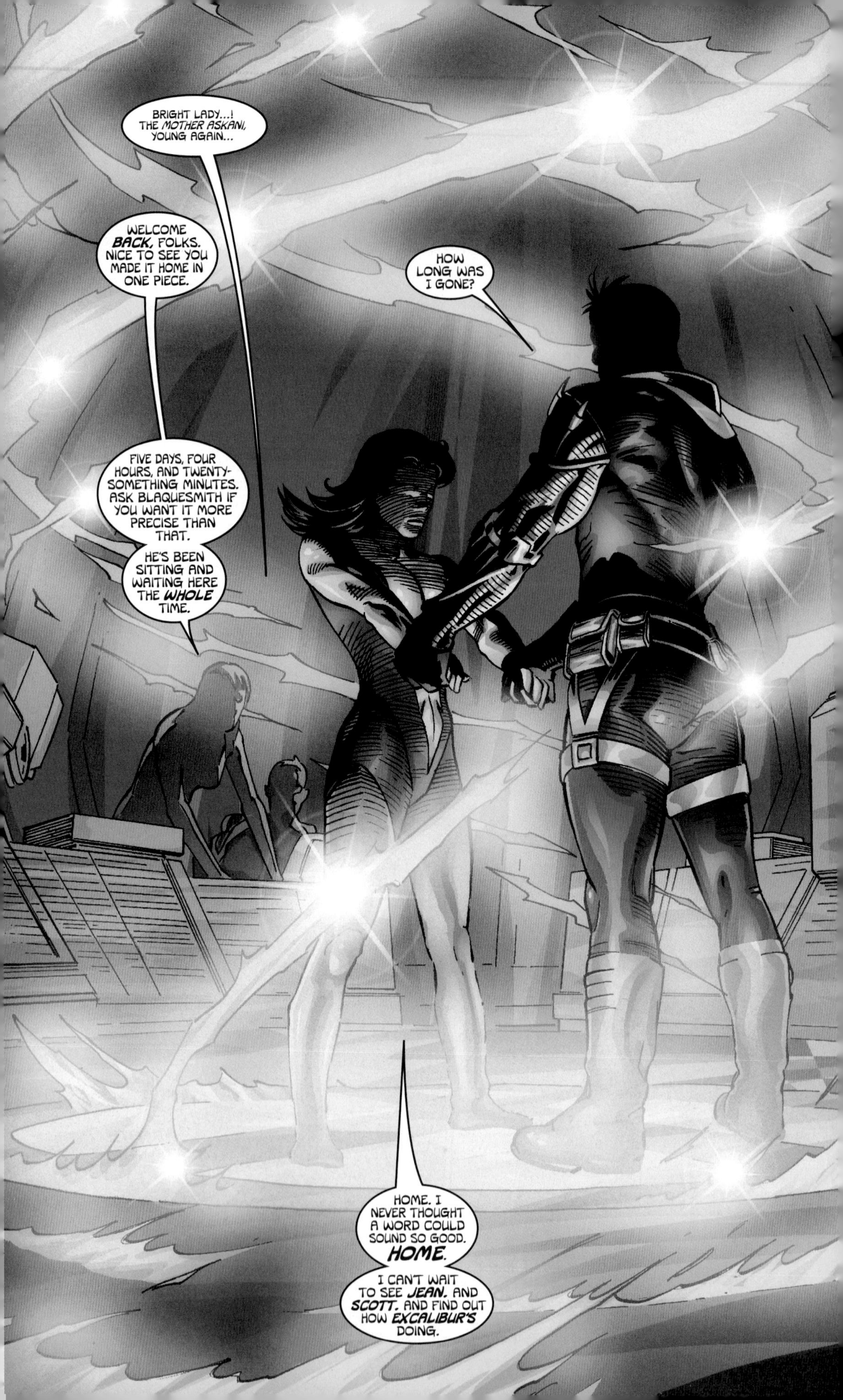
BRIGHT LADY...! THE MOTHER ASKANI, YOUNG AGAIN...
WELCOME BACK, FOLKS. NICE TO SEE YOU MADE IT HOME IN ONE PIECE.
HOW LONG WAS I GONE?
FIVE DAYS, FOUR HOURS, AND TWENTY-SOMETHING MINUTES. ASK BLAQUESMITH IF YOU WANT IT MORE PRECISE THAN THAT.
HE'S BEEN SITTING AND WAITING HERE THE WHOLE TIME.
HOME. I NEVER THOUGHT A WORD COULD SOUND SO GOOD. HOME.
I CAN'T WAIT TO SEE JEAN. AND SCOTT. AND FIND OUT HOW EXCALIBUR'S DOING.

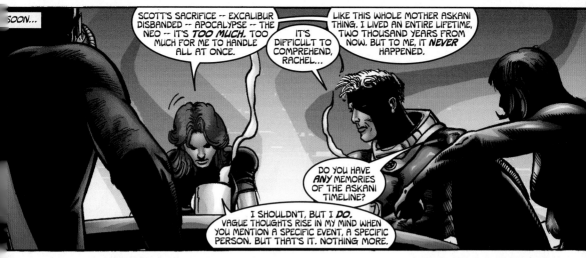

SCOTT'S SACRIFICE -- EXCALIBUR DISBANDED -- APOCALYPSE -- THE NEO -- IT'S *TOO MUCH.* TOO MUCH FOR ME TO HANDLE ALL AT ONCE.

IT'S DIFFICULT TO COMPREHEND, RACHEL...

LIKE THIS WHOLE MOTHER ASKANI THING. I LIVED AN ENTIRE LIFETIME, TWO THOUSAND YEARS FROM NOW. BUT TO ME, IT *NEVER* HAPPENED.

DO YOU HAVE *ANY* MEMORIES OF THE ASKANI TIMELINE?

I SHOULDN'T, BUT I *DO.* VAGUE THOUGHTS RISE IN MY MIND WHEN YOU MENTION A SPECIFIC EVENT, A SPECIFIC PERSON. BUT THAT'S IT. NOTHING MORE.

SO *MANY* BELIEVED IN YOU... YOU *SAVED* OUR WORLD.

THAT WAS ANOTHER LIFE, ANOTHER TIME.

WHAT DO *YOU* WANT, RACHEL? YOU'VE SACRIFICED SO MUCH SO OFTEN FOR SO MANY OTHERS.

IT'S ONLY FAIR YOU GET TO CHOOSE WHAT TO DO, NOW THAT YOU'VE GOT A SECOND CHANCE.

I JUST WANT TO LIVE A NORMAL LIFE FOR A LITTLE WHILE. NOT AS RACHEL SUMMERS, MUTANT. NOT AS PHOENIX. JUST AS ME, RACHEL.

I WANT TO BE ABLE TO GO TO SLEEP AT NIGHT AND NOT WORRY ABOUT HAVING TO WAKE UP AND SAVE THE WORLD.

SOUNDS RIGHT TO ME.

FROM WHAT I HEARD, RACHEL'S DEALT WITH MORE THAN HER SHARE OF HORRORS IN LIFE. SHE'S DUE A LONG VACATION. MAYBE EVEN A CHANCE TO GO TO COLLEGE.

OLLEGE? THAT WOULD BE NICE. AR AWAY FROM CITY LIFE. A SMALL TOWN, MAYBE. A PLACE WHERE I COULD WALK IN THE FOREST.

IT'S SETTLED THEN. FOR NOW, NOBODY'S TOLD THAT RACHEL'S BACK IN THE PRESENT. NOT EVEN JEAN.

RACHEL NEEDS A CHANCE TO GET SETTLED. WHEN SHE'S *READY* -- AND ONLY WHEN SHE'S READY -- DO WE INFORM EVERYONE ELSE THAT SHE'S RETURNED. SOUND GOOD?

NEXT MONTH:

CABLE VS THE BROTHERHOOD!

IN UNCANNY *X-MEN* #388, "DREAM'S END," PART 1, THE X-MEN LEARNED OF THE BROTHERHOOD OF MUTANTS' PLAN TO SIMULTANEOUSLY ATTACK PRESIDENTIAL CANDIDATE SENATOR ROBERT KELLY AND INVADE MUIR ISLAND. THE TEAM SPLIT UP TO DEAL WITH BOTH THREATS — AND CABLE AND HIS CONTINGENT OF X-MEN ARRIVED AT KELLY'S LATEST CAMPAIGN SPEECH JUST IN TIME TO WITNESS THE BROTHERHOOD'S ATTACK!

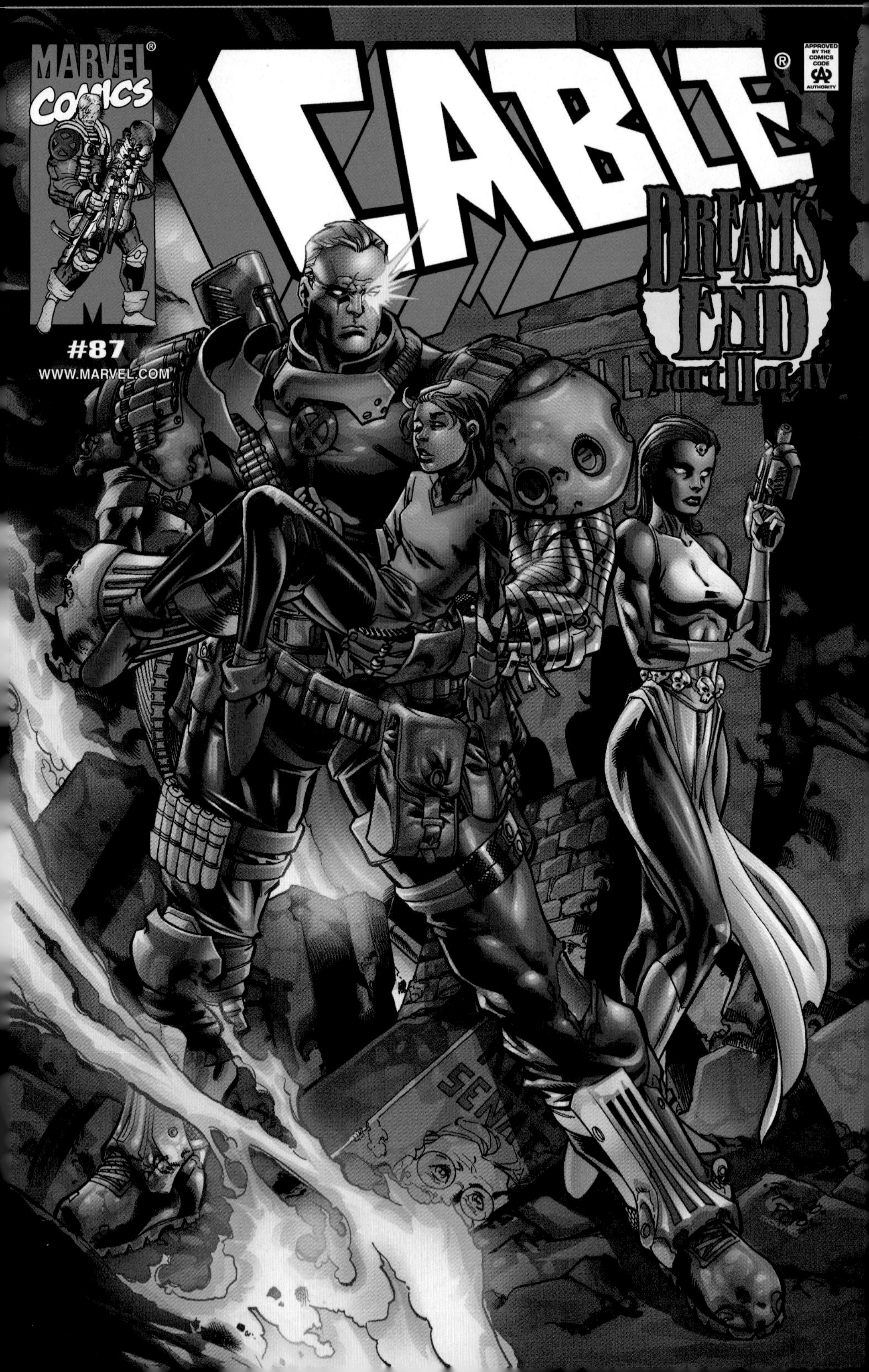

MARVEL® COMICS
CABLE®
APPROVED BY THE COMICS CODE AUTHORITY
DREAM'S END
Part II of IV
#87
WWW.MARVEL.COM

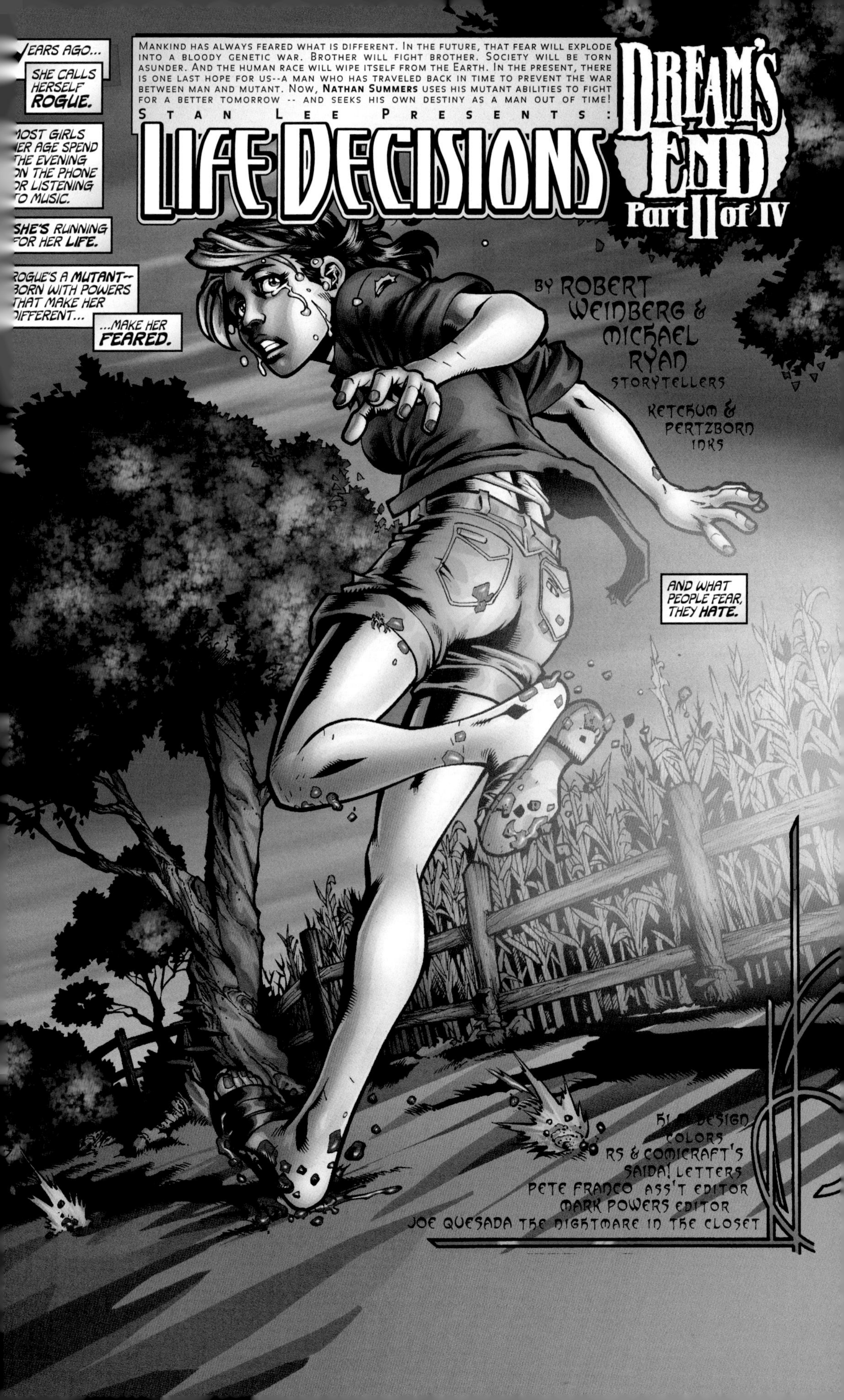
YEARS AGO...
SHE CALLS HERSELF ROGUE.
MOST GIRLS HER AGE SPEND THE EVENING ON THE PHONE OR LISTENING TO MUSIC.
SHE'S RUNNING FOR HER LIFE.
ROGUE'S A MUTANT--BORN WITH POWERS THAT MAKE HER DIFFERENT...
...MAKE HER FEARED.
MANKIND HAS ALWAYS FEARED WHAT IS DIFFERENT. IN THE FUTURE, THAT FEAR WILL EXPLODE INTO A BLOODY GENETIC WAR. BROTHER WILL FIGHT BROTHER. SOCIETY WILL BE TORN ASUNDER. AND THE HUMAN RACE WILL WIPE ITSELF FROM THE EARTH. IN THE PRESENT, THERE IS ONE LAST HOPE FOR US--A MAN WHO HAS TRAVELED BACK IN TIME TO PREVENT THE WAR BETWEEN MAN AND MUTANT. NOW, NATHAN SUMMERS USES HIS MUTANT ABILITIES TO FIGHT FOR A BETTER TOMORROW -- AND SEEKS HIS OWN DESTINY AS A MAN OUT OF TIME!
STAN LEE PRESENTS:
LIFE DECISIONS
DREAM'S END
Part II of IV
BY ROBERT WEINBERG & MICHAEL RYAN STORYTELLERS
KETCHUM & PERTZBORN INKS
AND WHAT PEOPLE FEAR, THEY HATE.
DESIGN
COLORS
RS & COMICRAFT'S
SAIDA! LETTERS
PETE FRANCO ASS'T EDITOR
MARK POWERS EDITOR
JOE QUESADA THE NIGHTMARE IN THE CLOSET

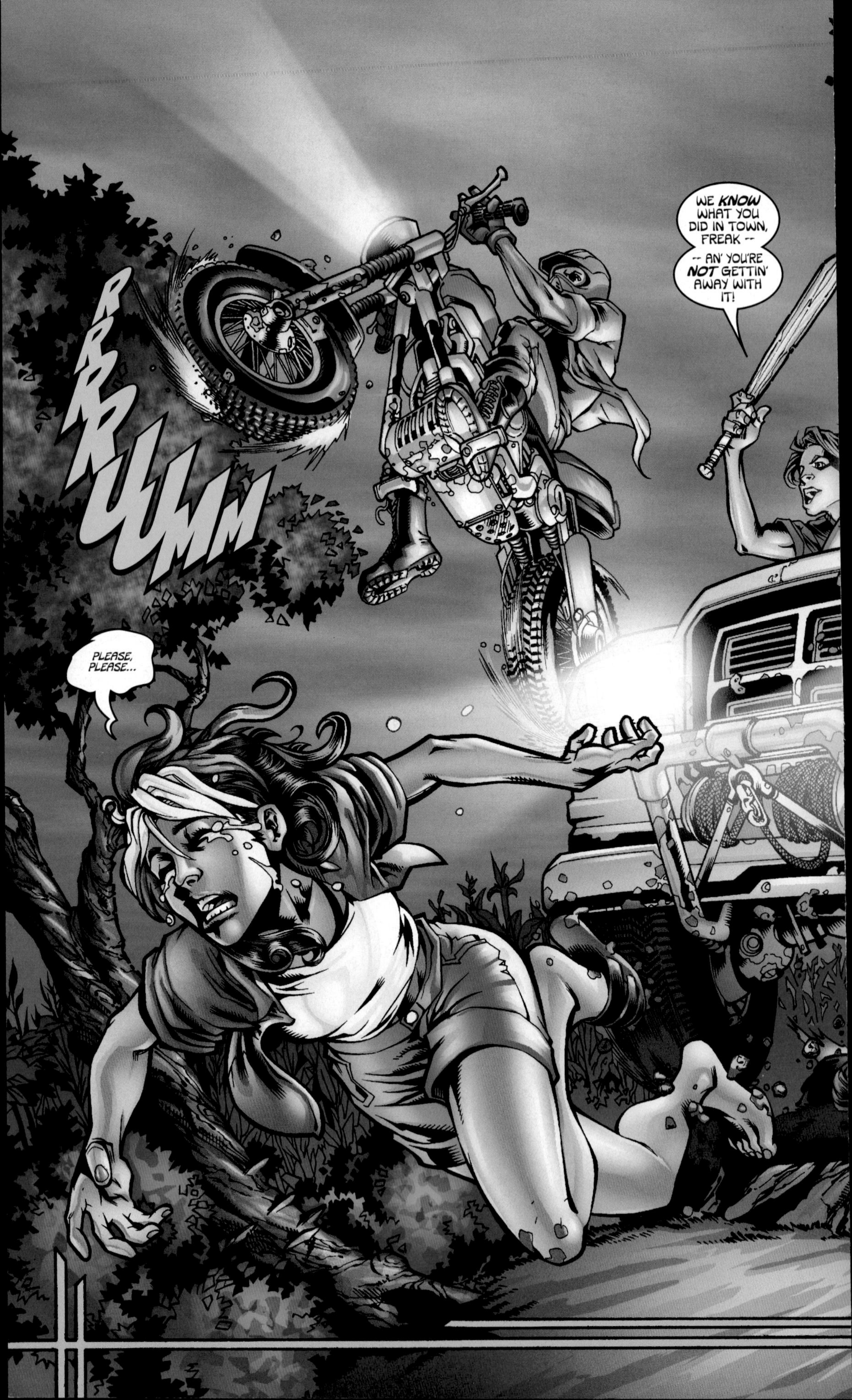
RRRRUUMM
WE **KNOW** WHAT YOU DID IN TOWN, FREAK --
-- AN' YOU'RE **NOT** GETTIN' AWAY WITH IT!
PLEASE, PLEASE...

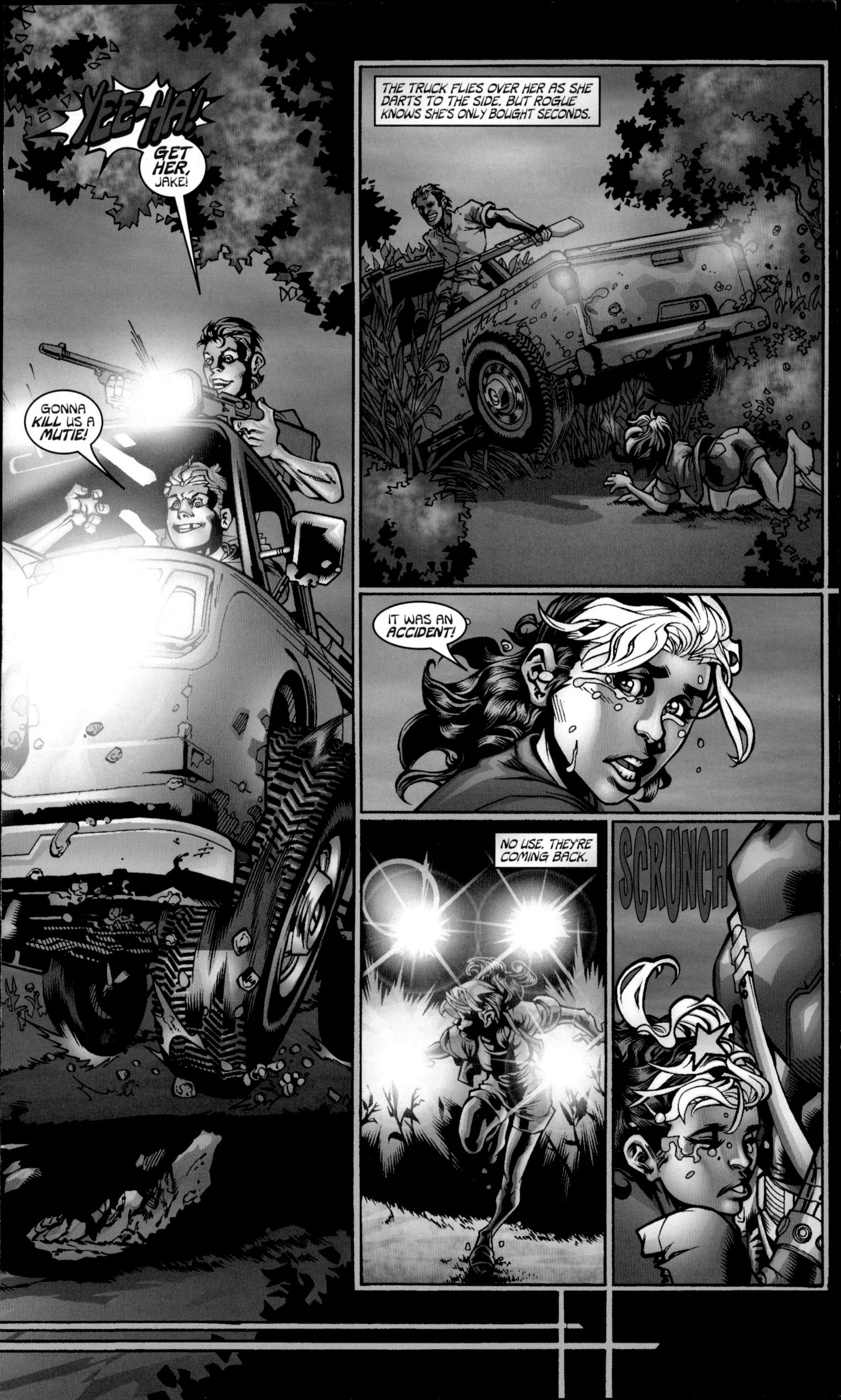

YEE-HA!
GET HER, JAKE!
GONNA KILL US A MUTIE!
THE TRUCK FLIES OVER HER AS SHE DARTS TO THE SIDE. BUT ROGUE KNOWS SHE'S ONLY BOUGHT SECONDS.
IT WAS AN ACCIDENT!
NO USE. THEY'RE COMING BACK.
SCRUNCH

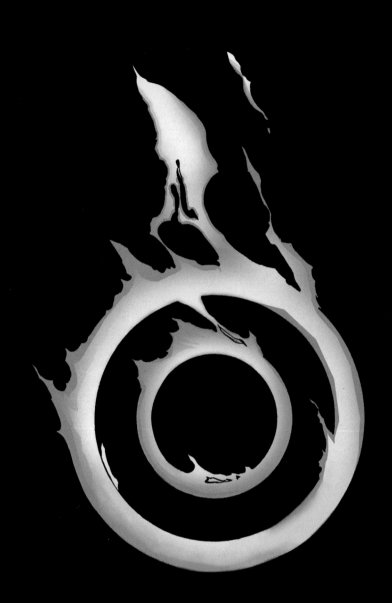

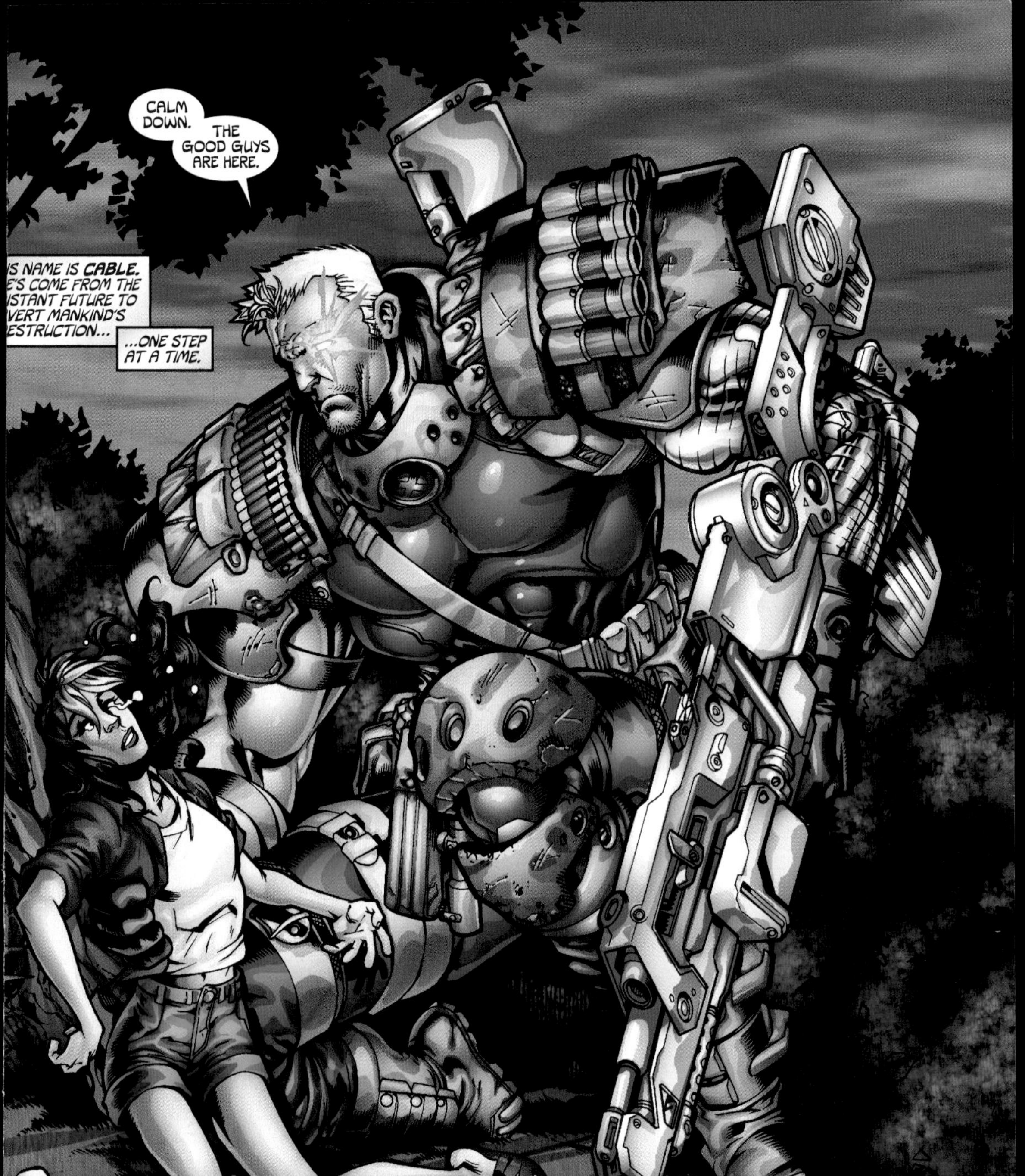
CALM DOWN.
THE GOOD GUYS ARE HERE.
IS NAME IS CABLE. E'S COME FROM THE ISTANT FUTURE TO VERT MANKIND'S ESTRUCTION...
...ONE STEP AT A TIME.

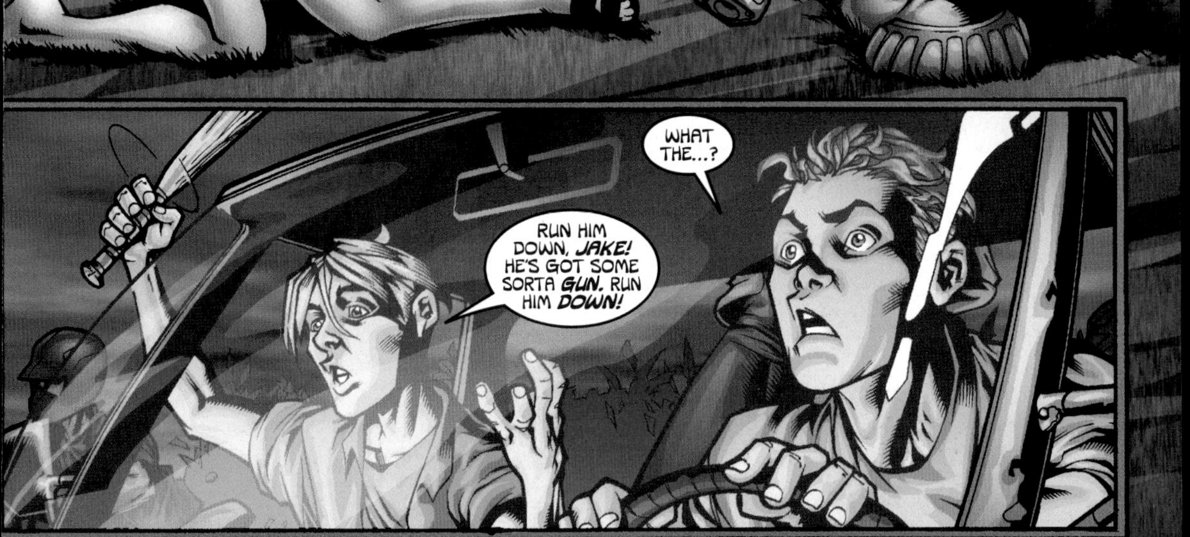
WHAT THE...?
RUN HIM DOWN, JAKE! HE'S GOT SOME SORTA GUN. RUN HIM DOWN!

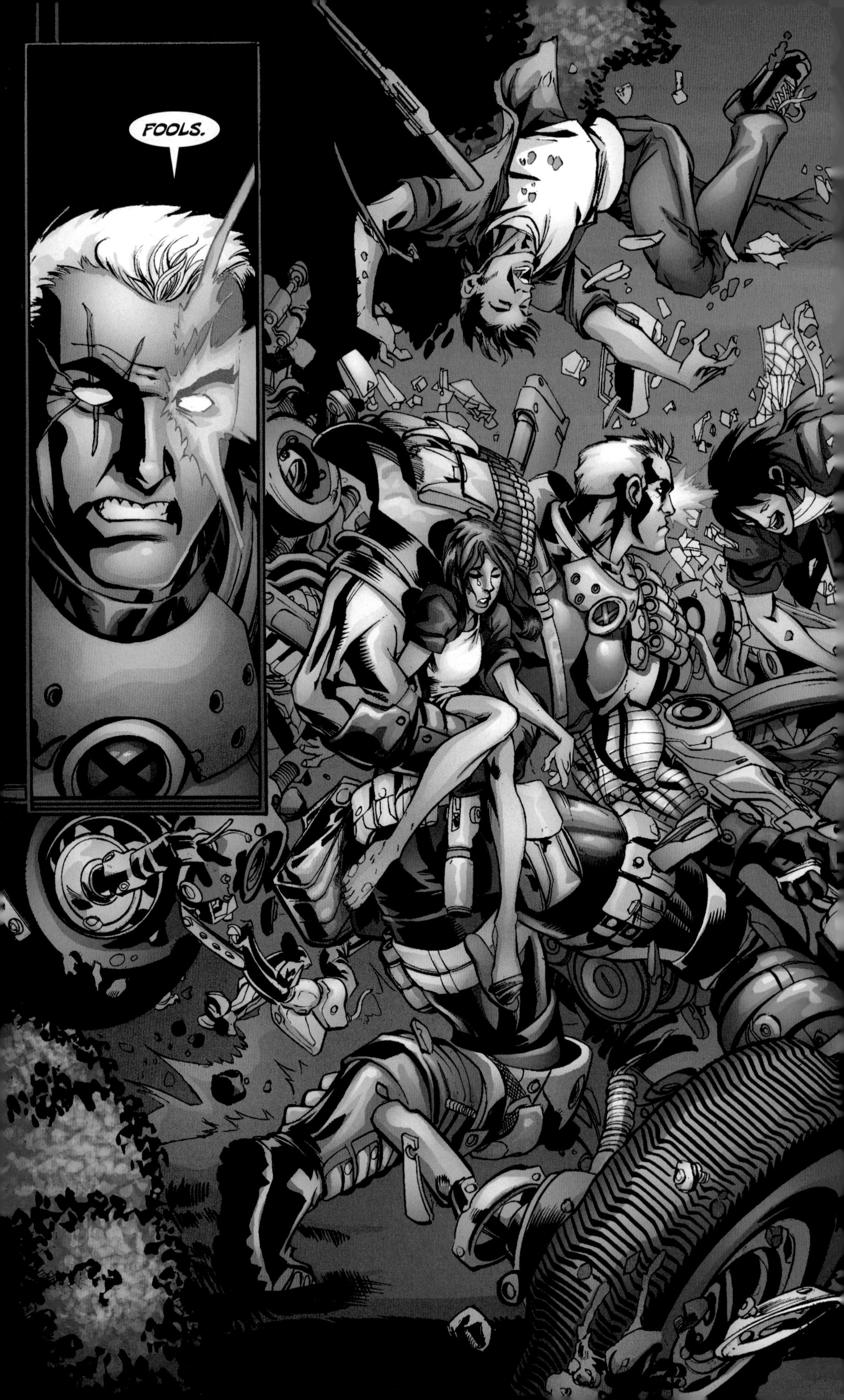
FOOLS.

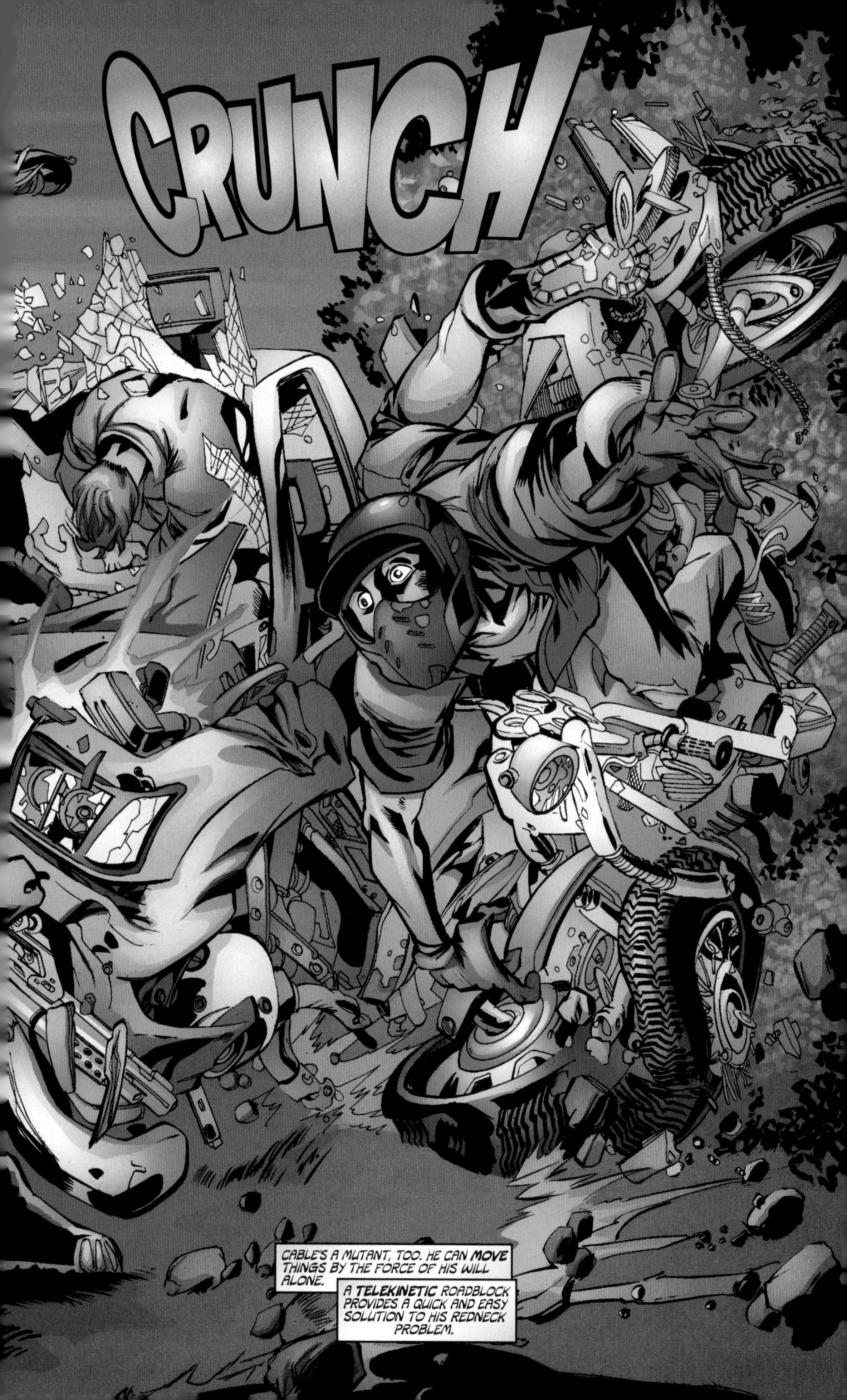
CRUNCH
CABLE'S A MUTANT, TOO. HE CAN MOVE THINGS BY THE FORCE OF HIS WILL ALONE.
A TELEKINETIC ROADBLOCK PROVIDES A QUICK AND EASY SOLUTION TO HIS REDNECK PROBLEM.

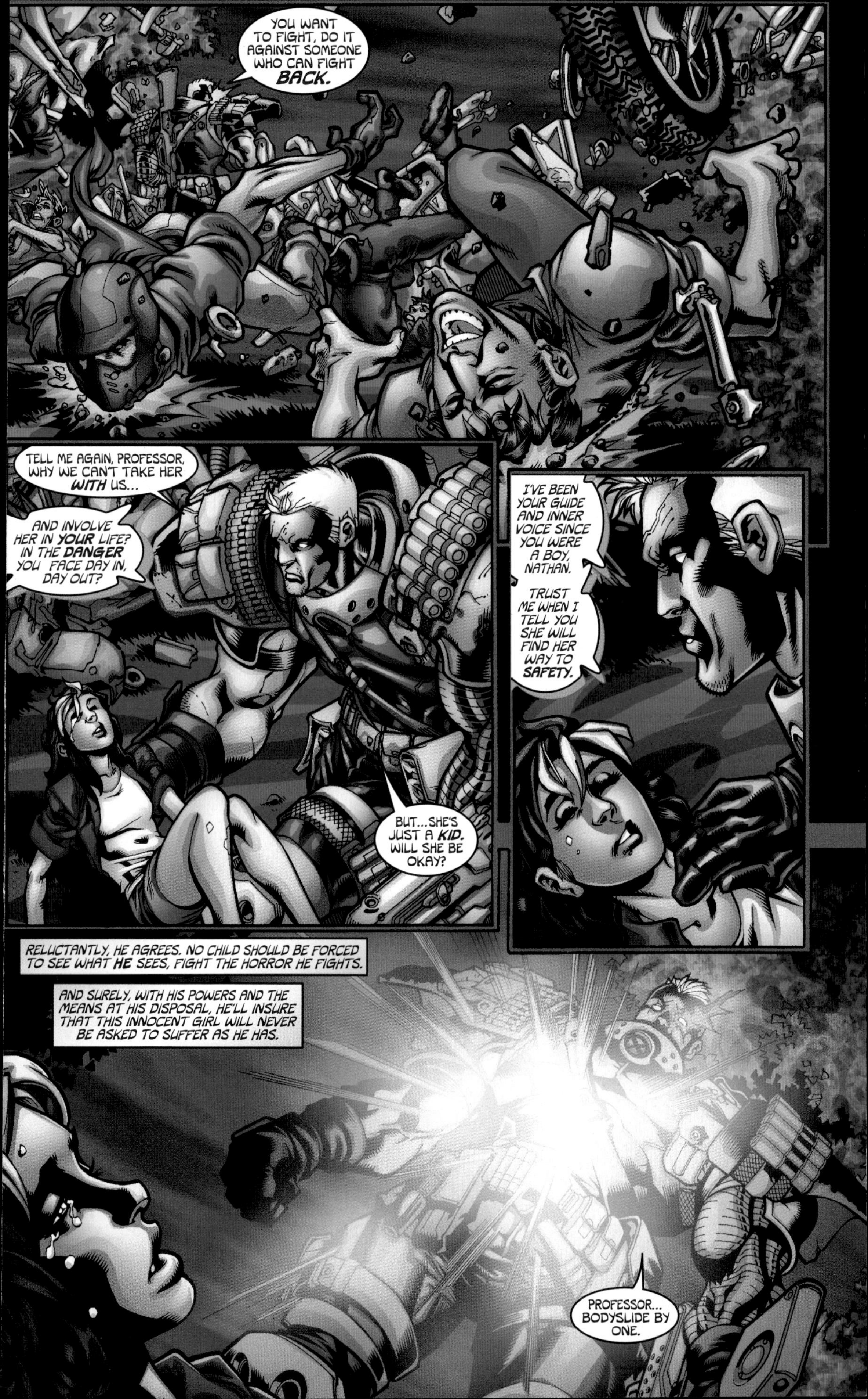
YOU WANT TO FIGHT, DO IT AGAINST SOMEONE WHO CAN FIGHT BACK.
TELL ME AGAIN, PROFESSOR, WHY WE CAN'T TAKE HER WITH US...
AND INVOLVE HER IN YOUR LIFE? IN THE DANGER YOU FACE DAY IN, DAY OUT?
BUT...SHE'S JUST A KID. WILL SHE BE OKAY?
I'VE BEEN YOUR GUIDE AND INNER VOICE SINCE YOU WERE A BOY, NATHAN.
TRUST ME WHEN I TELL YOU SHE WILL FIND HER WAY TO SAFETY.
RELUCTANTLY, HE AGREES. NO CHILD SHOULD BE FORCED TO SEE WHAT HE SEES, FIGHT THE HORROR HE FIGHTS.
AND SURELY, WITH HIS POWERS AND THE MEANS AT HIS DISPOSAL, HE'LL INSURE THAT THIS INNOCENT GIRL WILL NEVER BE ASKED TO SUFFER AS HE HAS.
PROFESSOR... BODYSLIDE BY ONE.

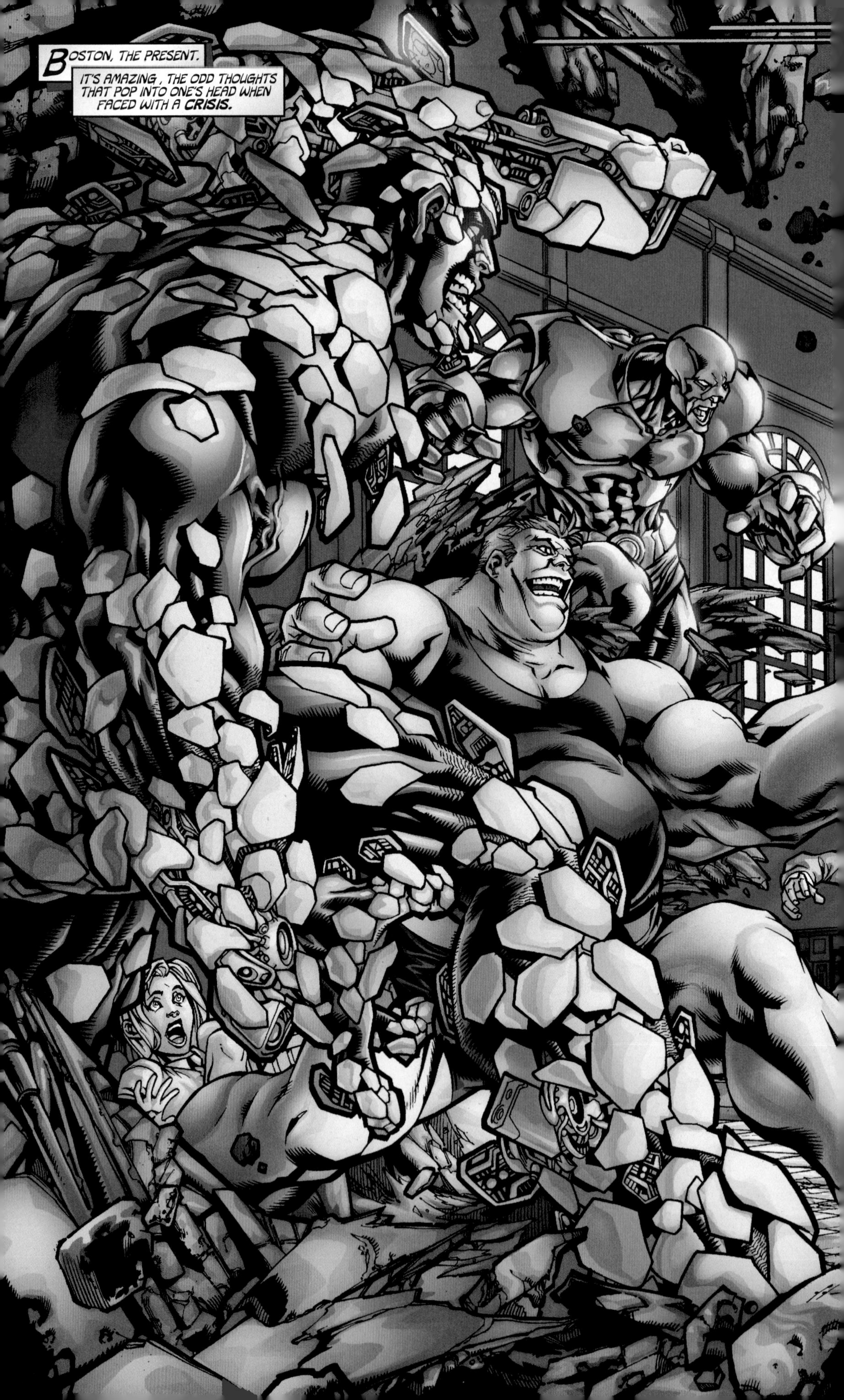
BOSTON, THE PRESENT.
IT'S AMAZING, THE ODD THOUGHTS THAT POP INTO ONE'S HEAD WHEN FACED WITH A CRISIS.

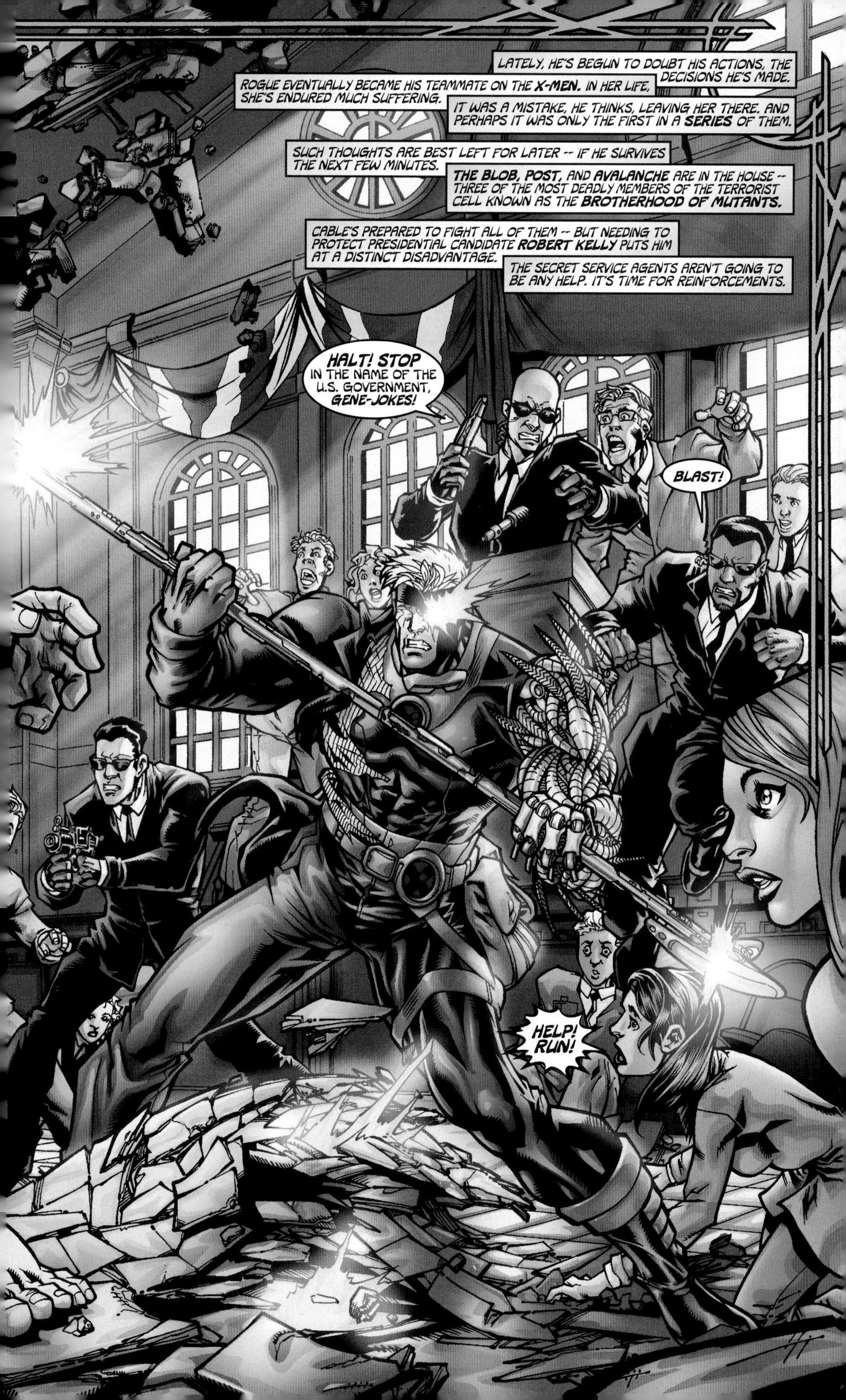
ROGUE EVENTUALLY BECAME HIS TEAMMATE ON THE X-MEN. IN HER LIFE, SHE'S ENDURED MUCH SUFFERING.
LATELY, HE'S BEGUN TO DOUBT HIS ACTIONS, THE DECISIONS HE'S MADE.
IT WAS A MISTAKE, HE THINKS, LEAVING HER THERE. AND PERHAPS IT WAS ONLY THE FIRST IN A SERIES OF THEM.
SUCH THOUGHTS ARE BEST LEFT FOR LATER -- IF HE SURVIVES THE NEXT FEW MINUTES.
THE BLOB, POST, AND AVALANCHE ARE IN THE HOUSE -- THREE OF THE MOST DEADLY MEMBERS OF THE TERRORIST CELL KNOWN AS THE BROTHERHOOD OF MUTANTS.
CABLE'S PREPARED TO FIGHT ALL OF THEM -- BUT NEEDING TO PROTECT PRESIDENTIAL CANDIDATE ROBERT KELLY PUTS HIM AT A DISTINCT DISADVANTAGE.
THE SECRET SERVICE AGENTS AREN'T GOING TO BE ANY HELP. IT'S TIME FOR REINFORCEMENTS.
HALT! STOP IN THE NAME OF THE U.S. GOVERNMENT, GENE-JOKES!
BLAST!
HELP! RUN!

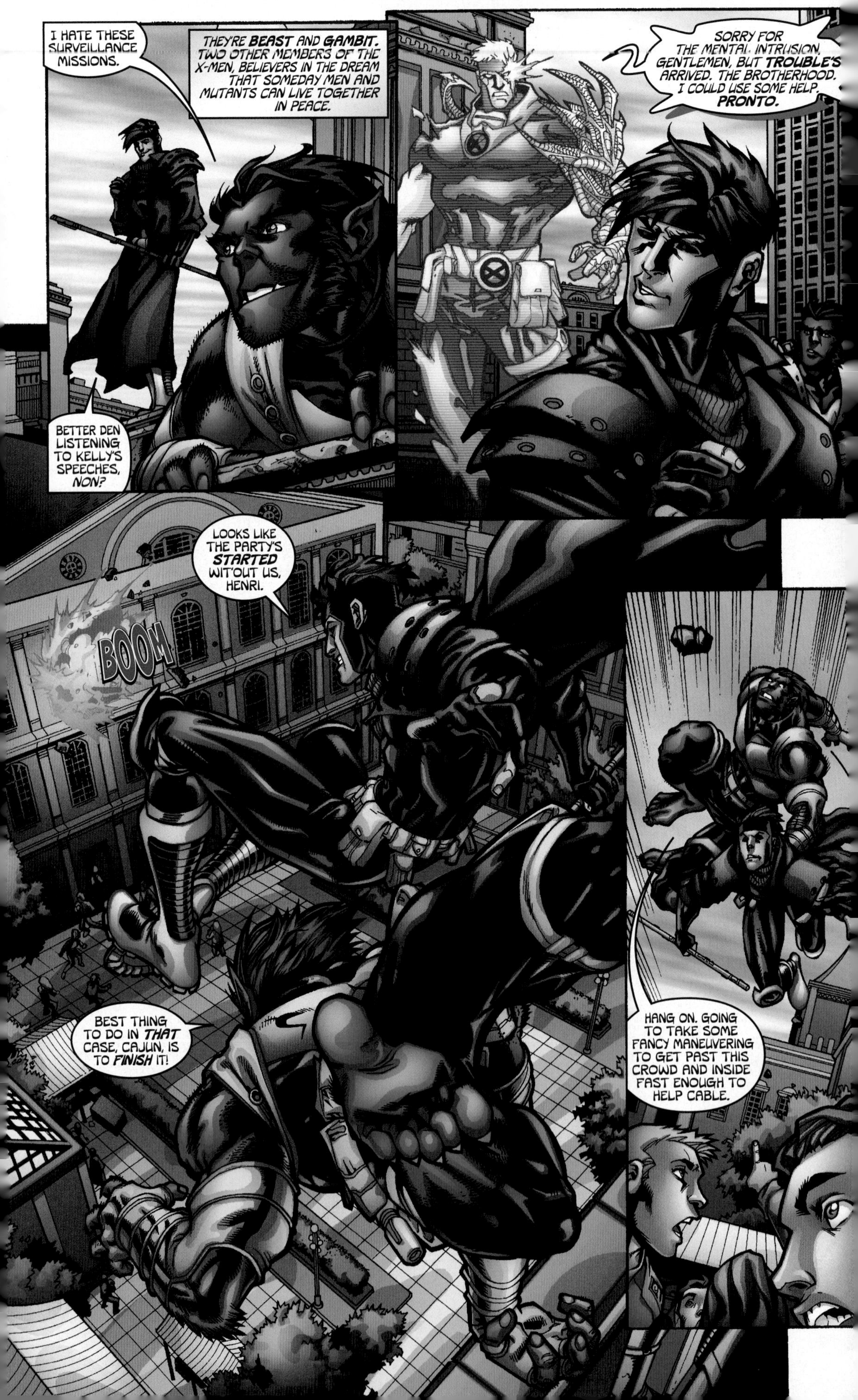
I HATE THESE SURVEILLANCE MISSIONS.
THEY'RE **BEAST** AND **GAMBIT**. TWO OTHER MEMBERS OF THE X-MEN, BELIEVERS IN THE DREAM THAT SOMEDAY MEN AND MUTANTS CAN LIVE TOGETHER IN PEACE.
BETTER DEN LISTENING TO KELLY'S SPEECHES, *NON?*
SORRY FOR THE MENTAL INTRUSION, GENTLEMEN, BUT **TROUBLE'S** ARRIVED. THE BROTHERHOOD. I COULD USE SOME HELP. **PRONTO.**
LOOKS LIKE THE PARTY'S ***STARTED*** WIT'OUT US, HENRI.
BOOM
BEST THING TO DO IN ***THAT*** CASE, CAJUN, IS TO ***FINISH*** IT!
HANG ON. GOING TO TAKE SOME FANCY MANEUVERING TO GET PAST THIS CROWD AND INSIDE FAST ENOUGH TO HELP CABLE.

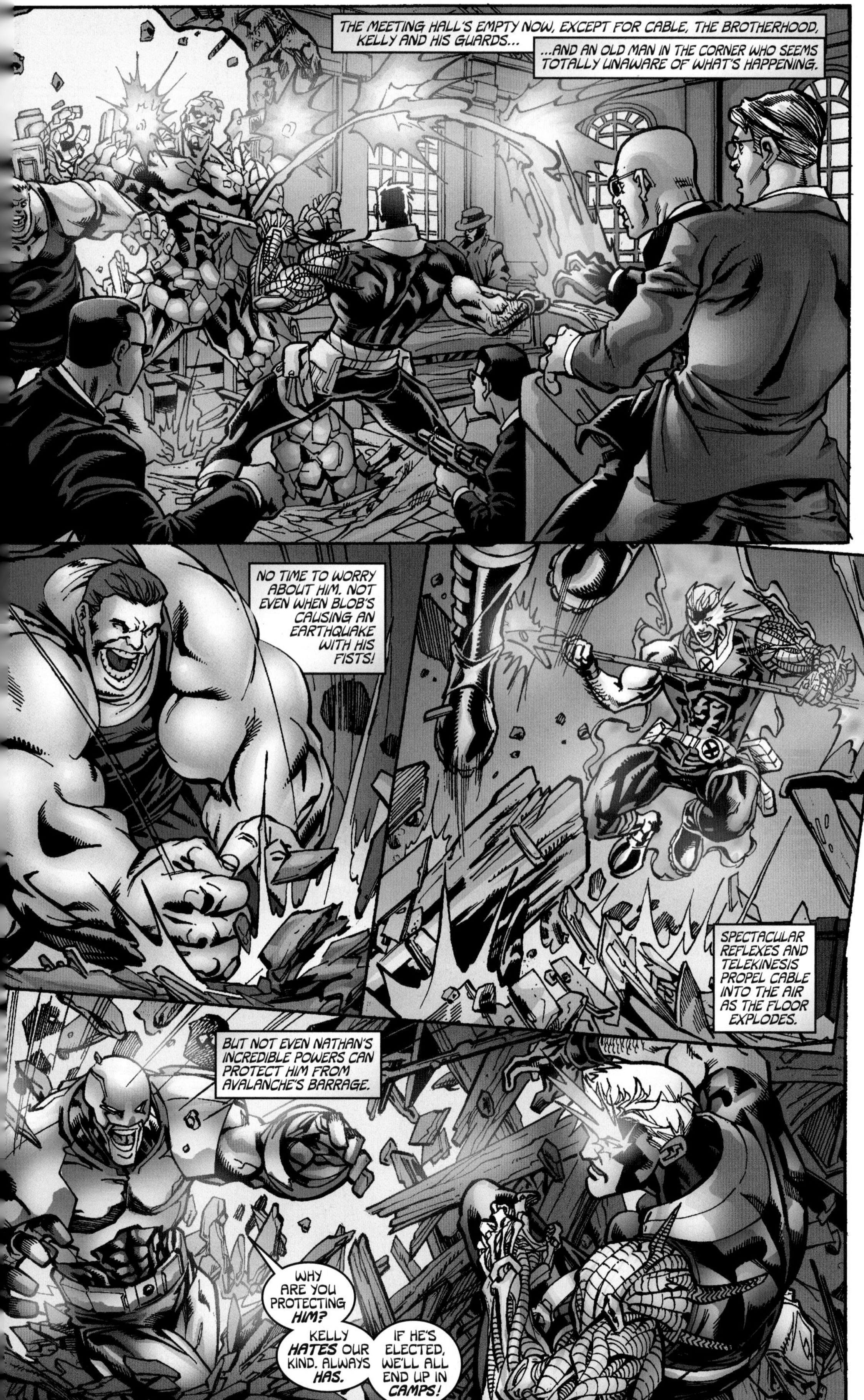
THE MEETING HALL'S EMPTY NOW, EXCEPT FOR CABLE, THE BROTHERHOOD, KELLY AND HIS GUARDS...
...AND AN OLD MAN IN THE CORNER WHO SEEMS TOTALLY UNAWARE OF WHAT'S HAPPENING.
NO TIME TO WORRY ABOUT HIM. NOT EVEN WHEN BLOB'S CAUSING AN EARTHQUAKE WITH HIS FISTS!
SPECTACULAR REFLEXES AND TELEKINESIS PROPEL CABLE INTO THE AIR AS THE FLOOR EXPLODES.
BUT NOT EVEN NATHAN'S INCREDIBLE POWERS CAN PROTECT HIM FROM AVALANCHE'S BARRAGE.
WHY ARE YOU PROTECTING *HIM?*
KELLY *HATES* OUR KIND. ALWAYS *HAS.*
IF HE'S ELECTED, WE'LL ALL END UP IN *CAMPS!*

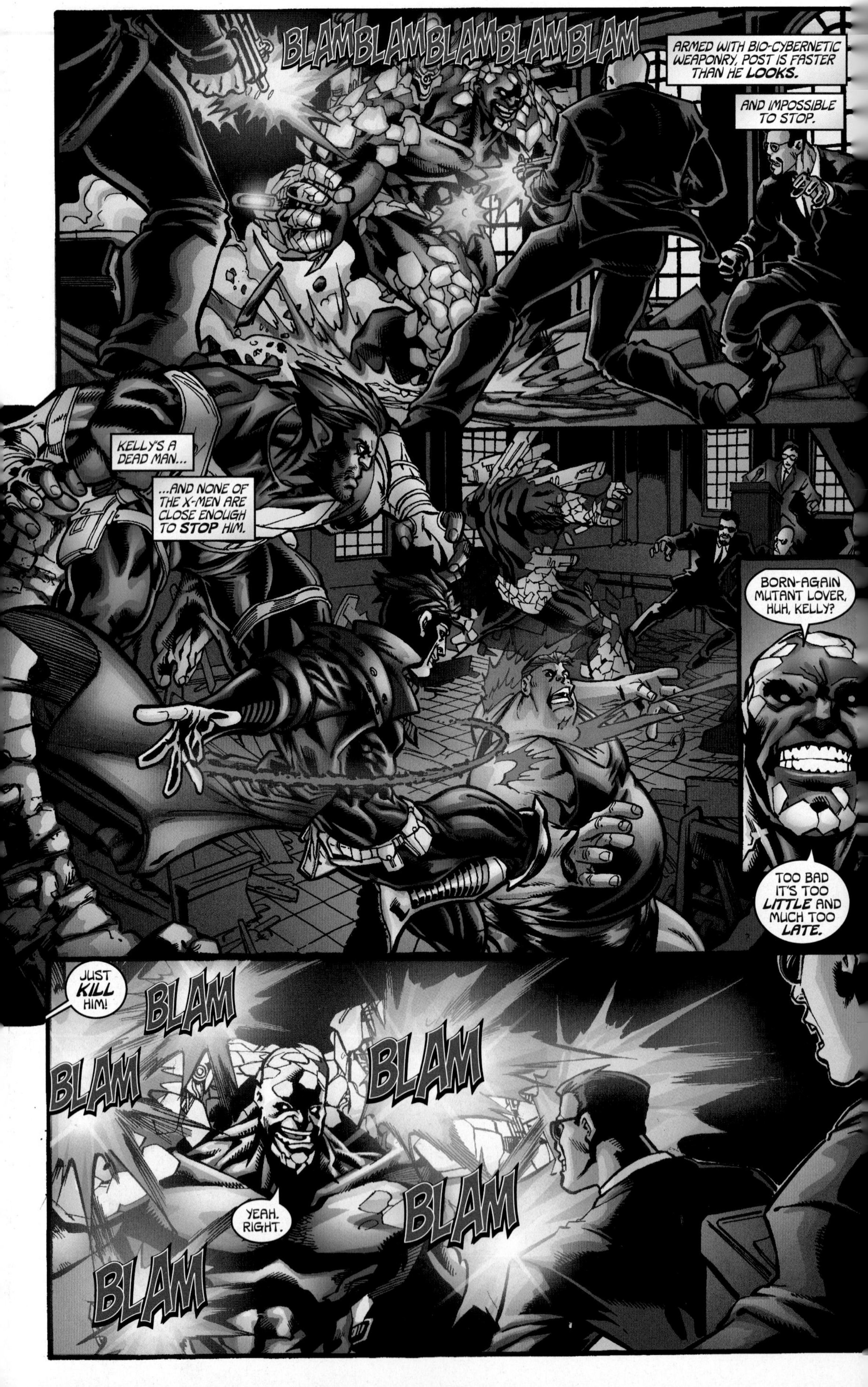
BLAMBLAMBLAMBLAMBLAM
ARMED WITH BIO-CYBERNETIC WEAPONRY, POST IS FASTER THAN HE LOOKS.
AND IMPOSSIBLE TO STOP.
KELLY'S A DEAD MAN...
...AND NONE OF THE X-MEN ARE CLOSE ENOUGH TO STOP HIM.
BORN-AGAIN MUTANT LOVER, HUH, KELLY?
TOO BAD IT'S TOO LITTLE AND MUCH TOO LATE.
JUST KILL HIM!
BLAM
BLAM
BLAM
YEAH. RIGHT.
BLAM
BLAM

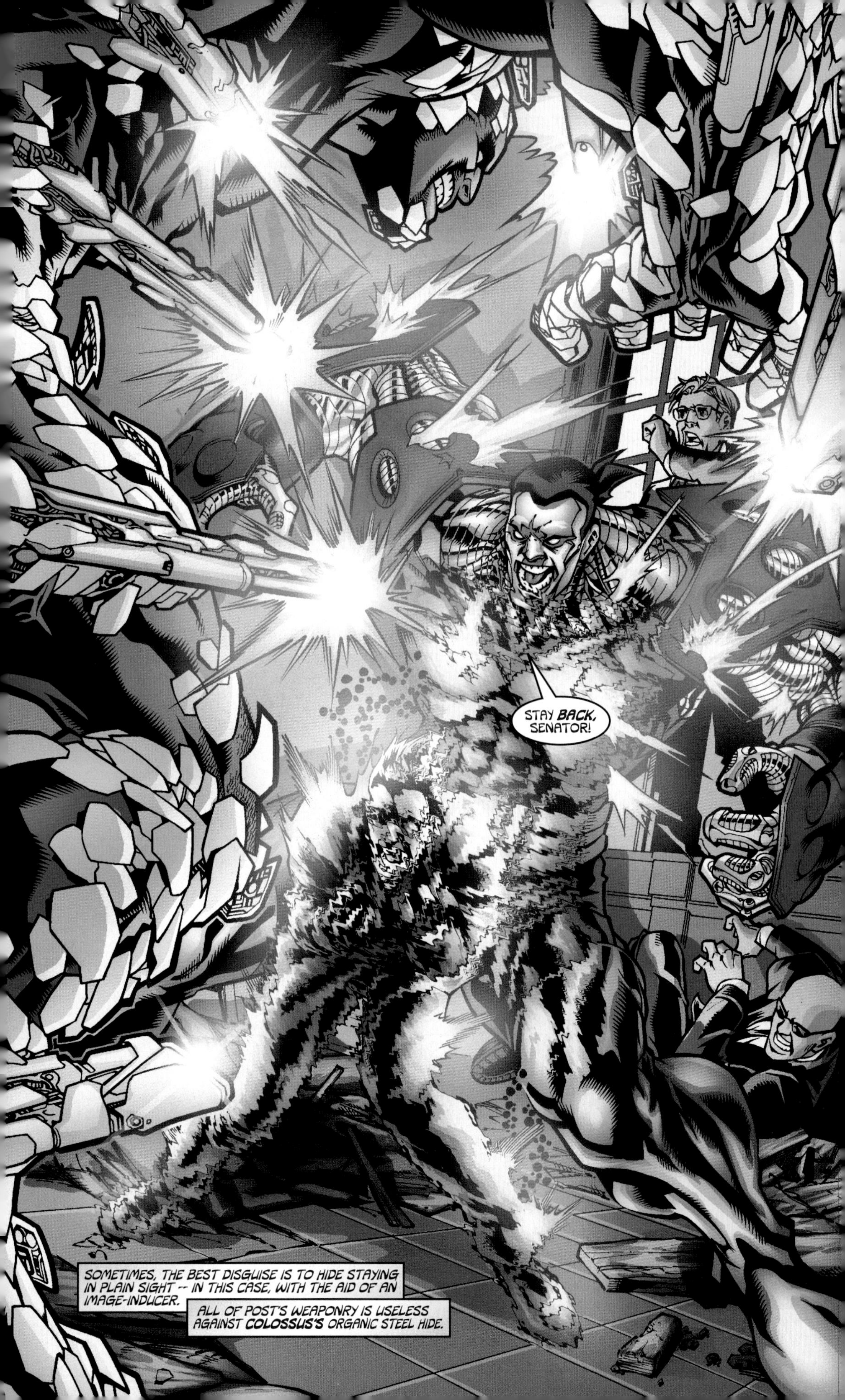
STAY BACK, SENATOR!
SOMETIMES, THE BEST DISGUISE IS TO HIDE STAYING IN PLAIN SIGHT -- IN THIS CASE, WITH THE AID OF AN IMAGE-INDUCER.
ALL OF POST'S WEAPONRY IS USELESS AGAINST COLOSSUS'S ORGANIC STEEL HIDE.

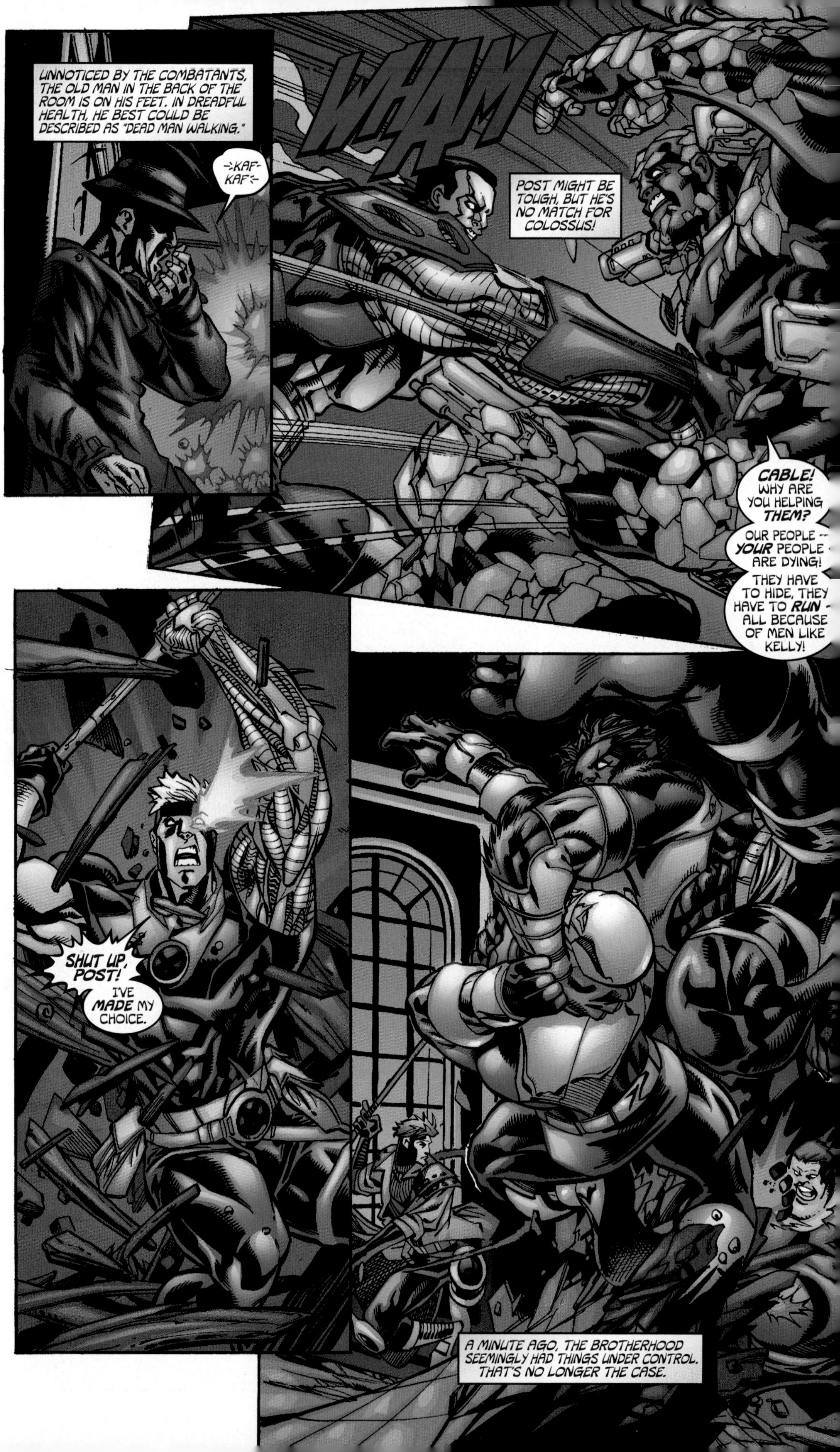

UNNOTICED BY THE COMBATANTS, THE OLD MAN IN THE BACK OF THE ROOM IS ON HIS FEET. IN DREADFUL HEALTH, HE BEST COULD BE DESCRIBED AS "DEAD MAN WALKING."
-KAF- KAF-
WHAM
POST MIGHT BE TOUGH, BUT HE'S NO MATCH FOR COLOSSUS!
CABLE! WHY ARE YOU HELPING THEM?
OUR PEOPLE -- YOUR PEOPLE ARE DYING!
THEY HAVE TO HIDE, THEY HAVE TO RUN -- ALL BECAUSE OF MEN LIKE KELLY!
SHUT UP, POST!
I'VE MADE MY CHOICE.
A MINUTE AGO, THE BROTHERHOOD SEEMINGLY HAD THINGS UNDER CONTROL. THAT'S NO LONGER THE CASE.

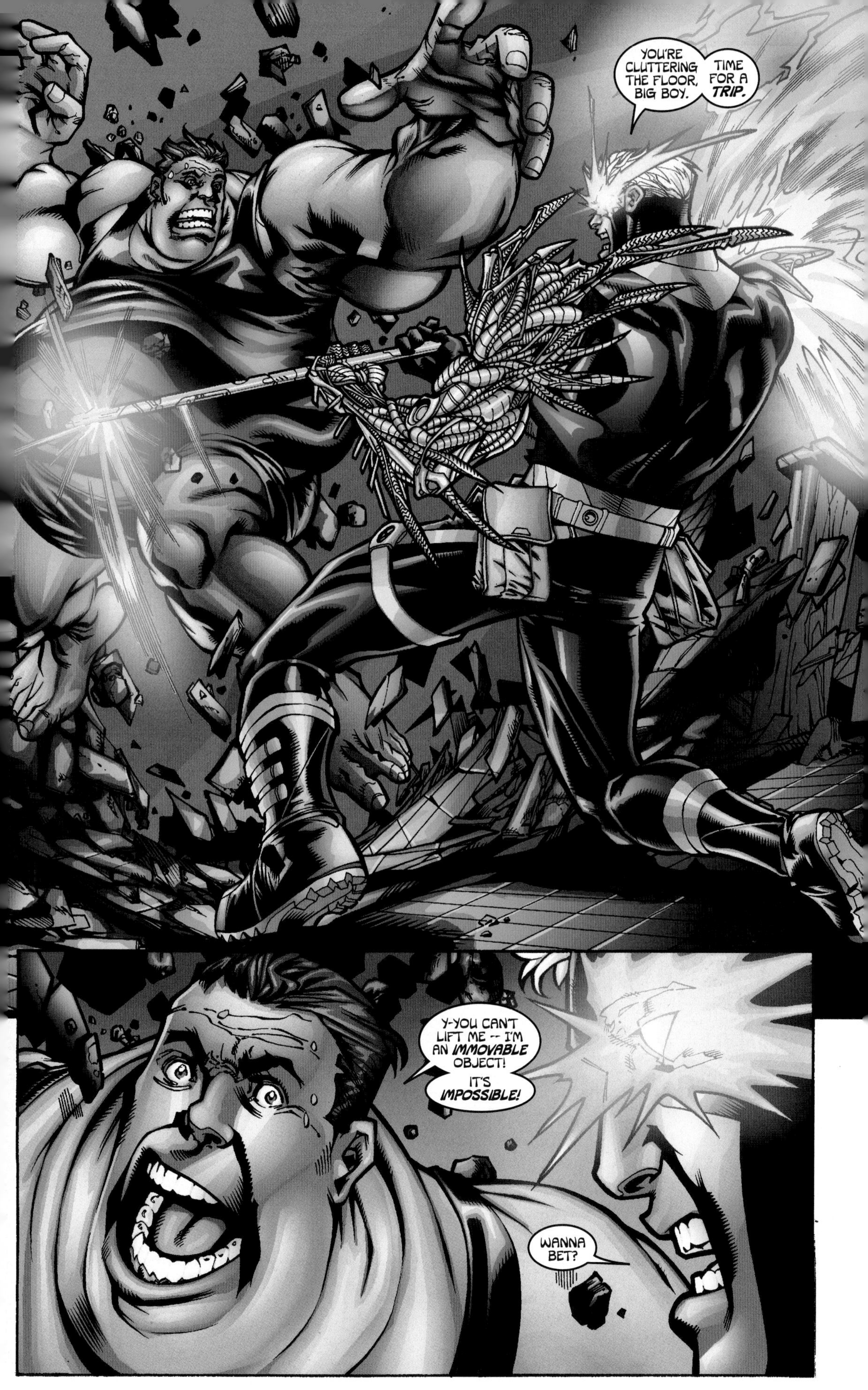
YOU'RE CLUTTERING THE FLOOR, BIG BOY.
TIME FOR A TRIP.
Y-YOU CAN'T LIFT ME -- I'M AN IMMOVABLE OBJECT!
IT'S IMPOSSIBLE!
WANNA BET?

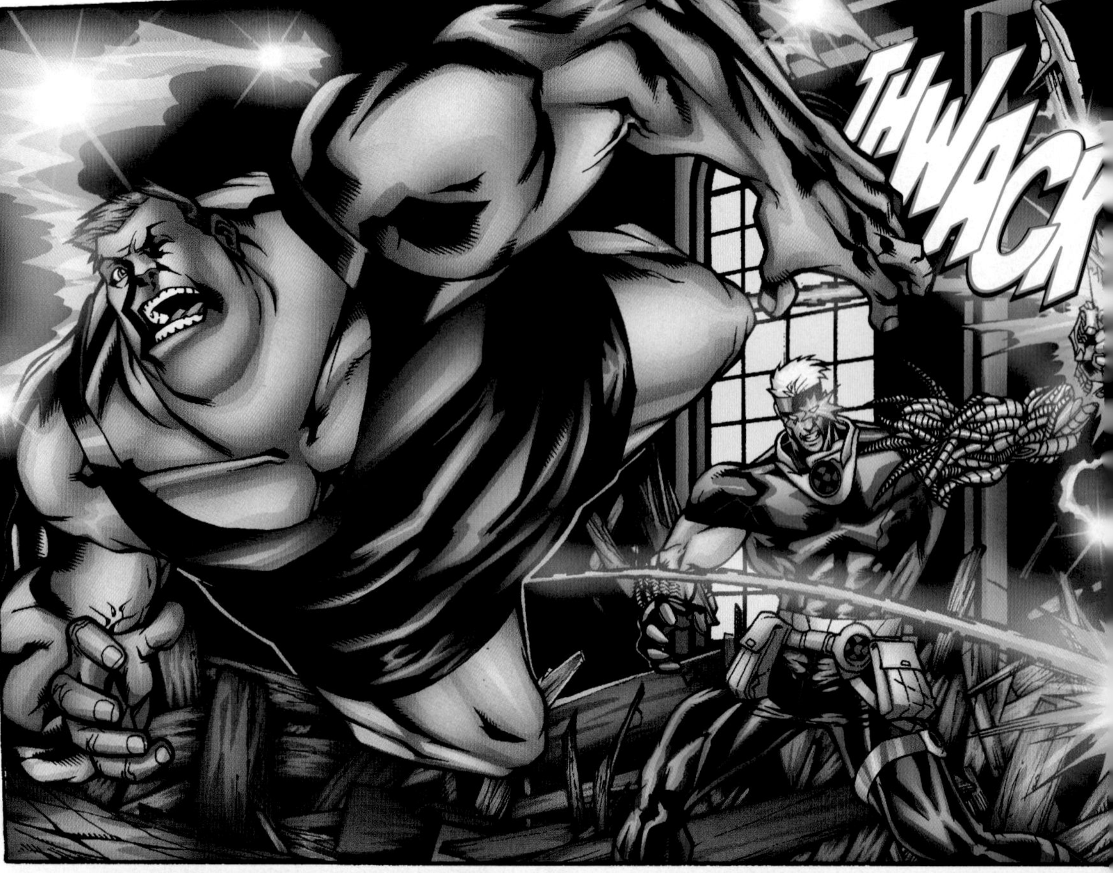
THWACK

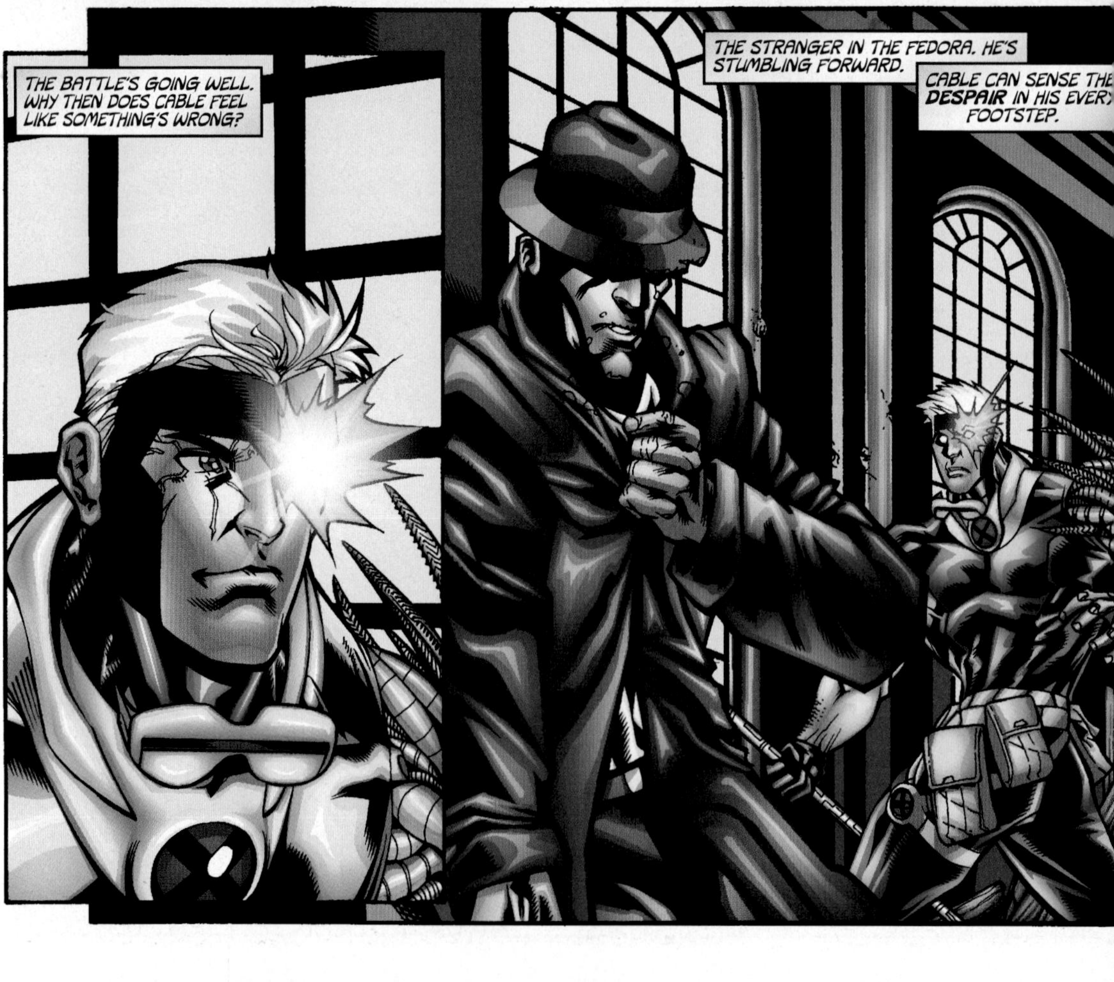
THE BATTLE'S GOING WELL. WHY THEN DOES CABLE FEEL LIKE SOMETHING'S WRONG?
THE STRANGER IN THE FEDORA. HE'S STUMBLING FORWARD.
CABLE CAN SENSE THE DESPAIR IN HIS EVERY FOOTSTEP.

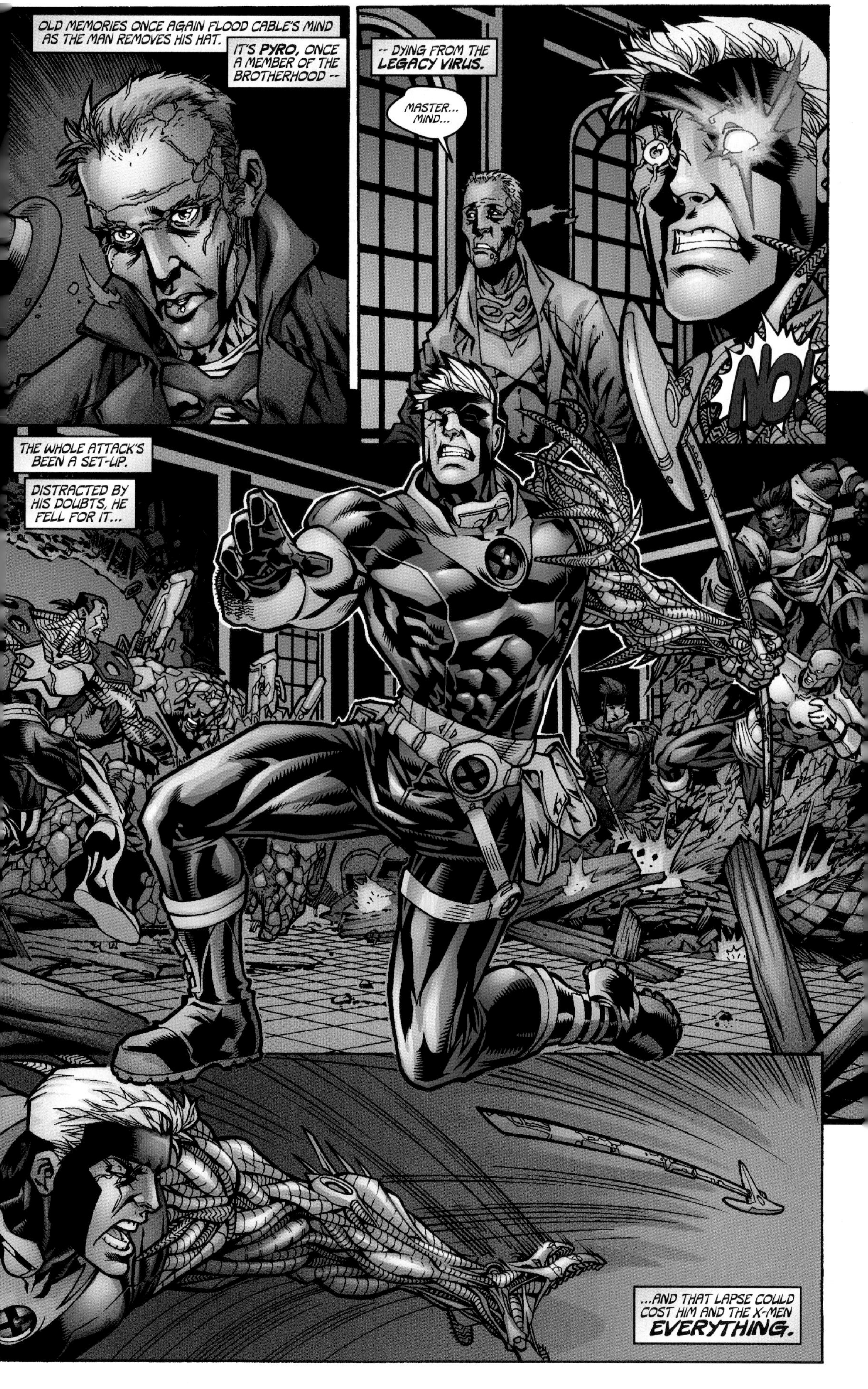
OLD MEMORIES ONCE AGAIN FLOOD CABLE'S MIND AS THE MAN REMOVES HIS HAT.
IT'S PYRO, ONCE A MEMBER OF THE BROTHERHOOD --
-- DYING FROM THE LEGACY VIRUS.
MASTER... MIND...
NO!
THE WHOLE ATTACK'S BEEN A SET-UP.
DISTRACTED BY HIS DOUBTS, HE FELL FOR IT...
...AND THAT LAPSE COULD COST HIM AND THE X-MEN EVERYTHING.

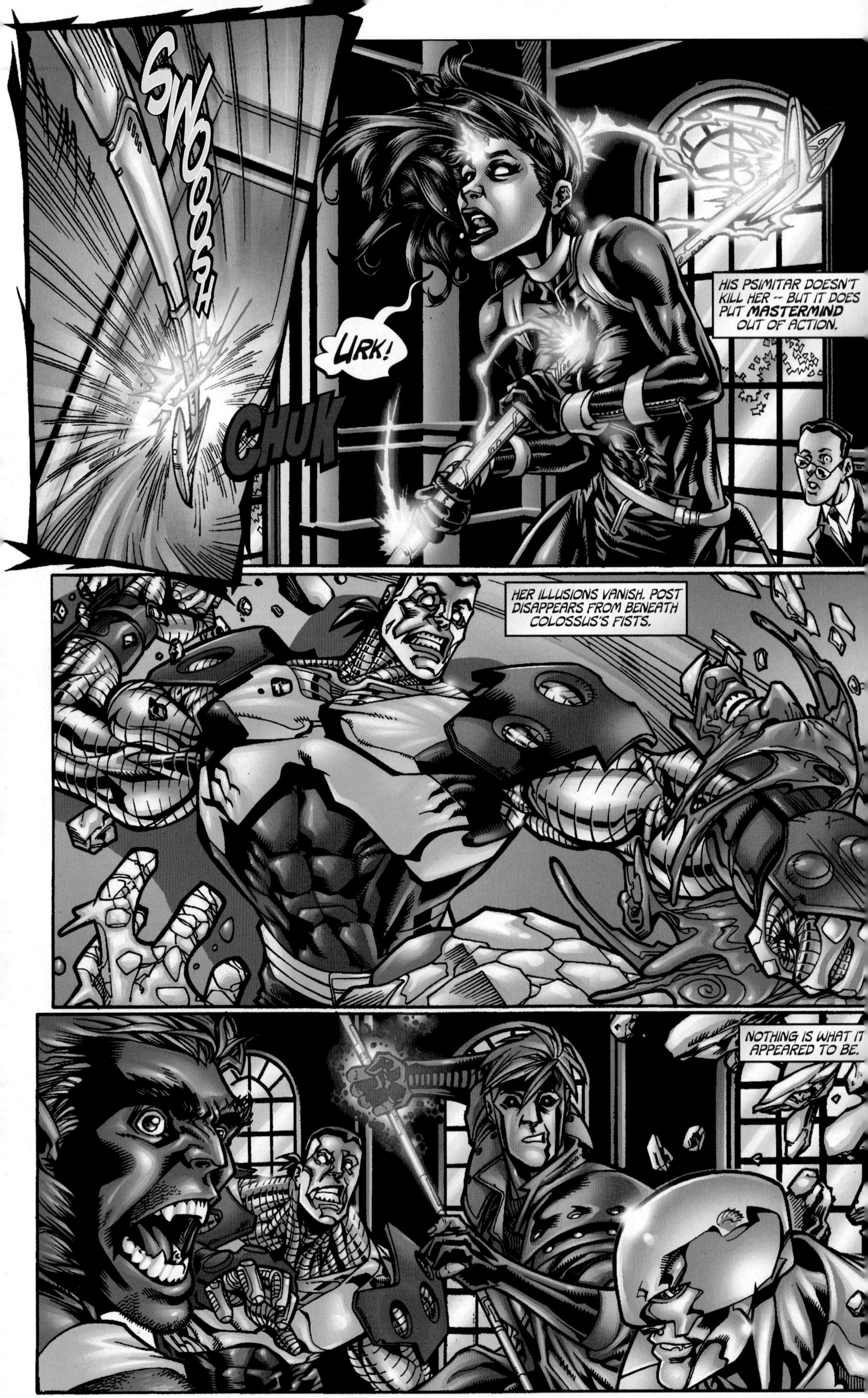
SWOOOOSH
URK!
CHUK
HIS PSIMITAR DOESN'T KILL HER -- BUT IT DOES PUT **MASTERMIND** OUT OF ACTION.
HER ILLUSIONS VANISH. POST DISAPPEARS FROM BENEATH COLOSSUS'S FISTS.
NOTHING IS WHAT IT APPEARED TO BE.

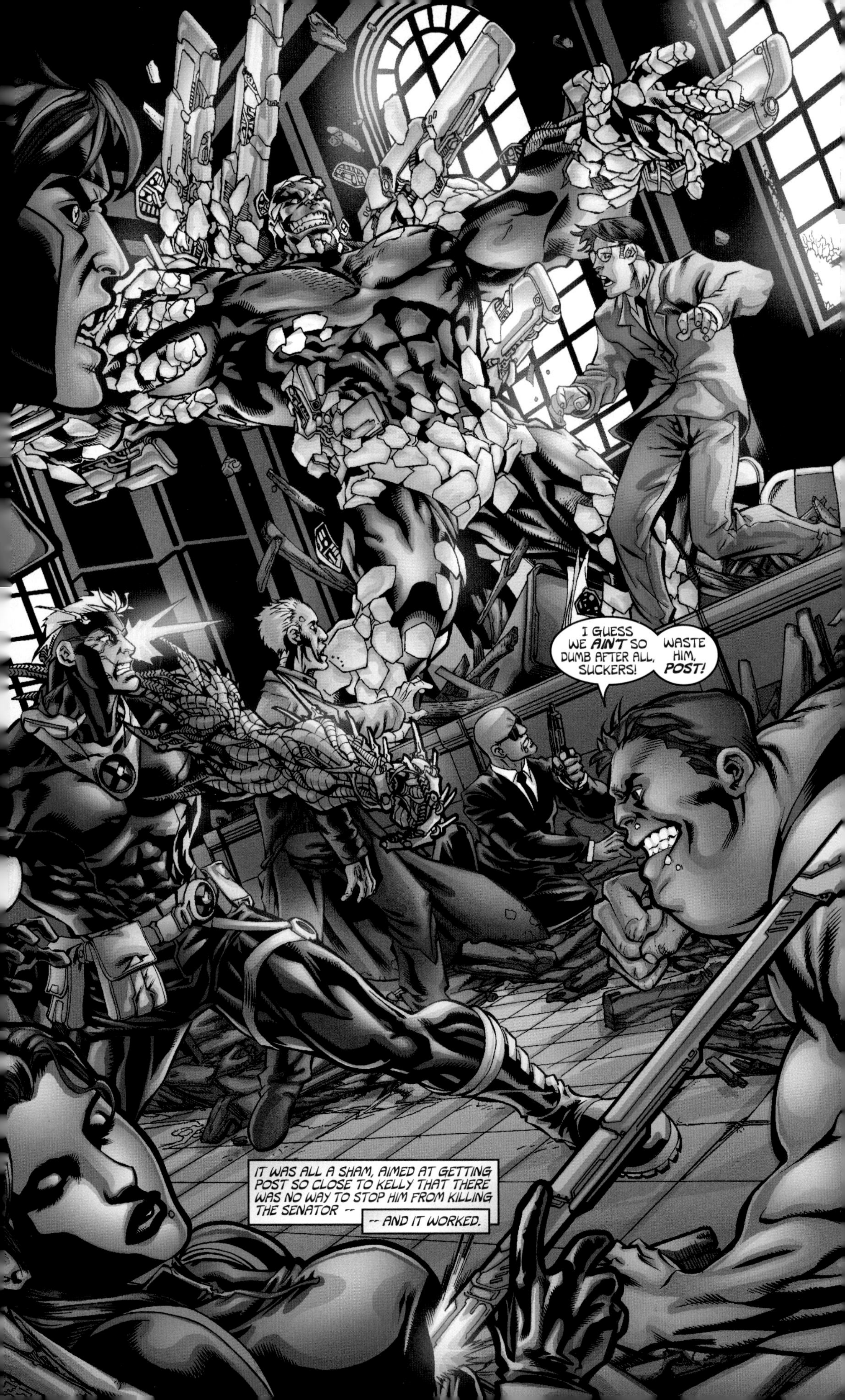
I GUESS WE AIN'T SO DUMB AFTER ALL, SUCKERS!
WASTE HIM, POST!
IT WAS ALL A SHAM, AIMED AT GETTING POST SO CLOSE TO KELLY THAT THERE WAS NO WAY TO STOP HIM FROM KILLING THE SENATOR --
-- AND IT WORKED.

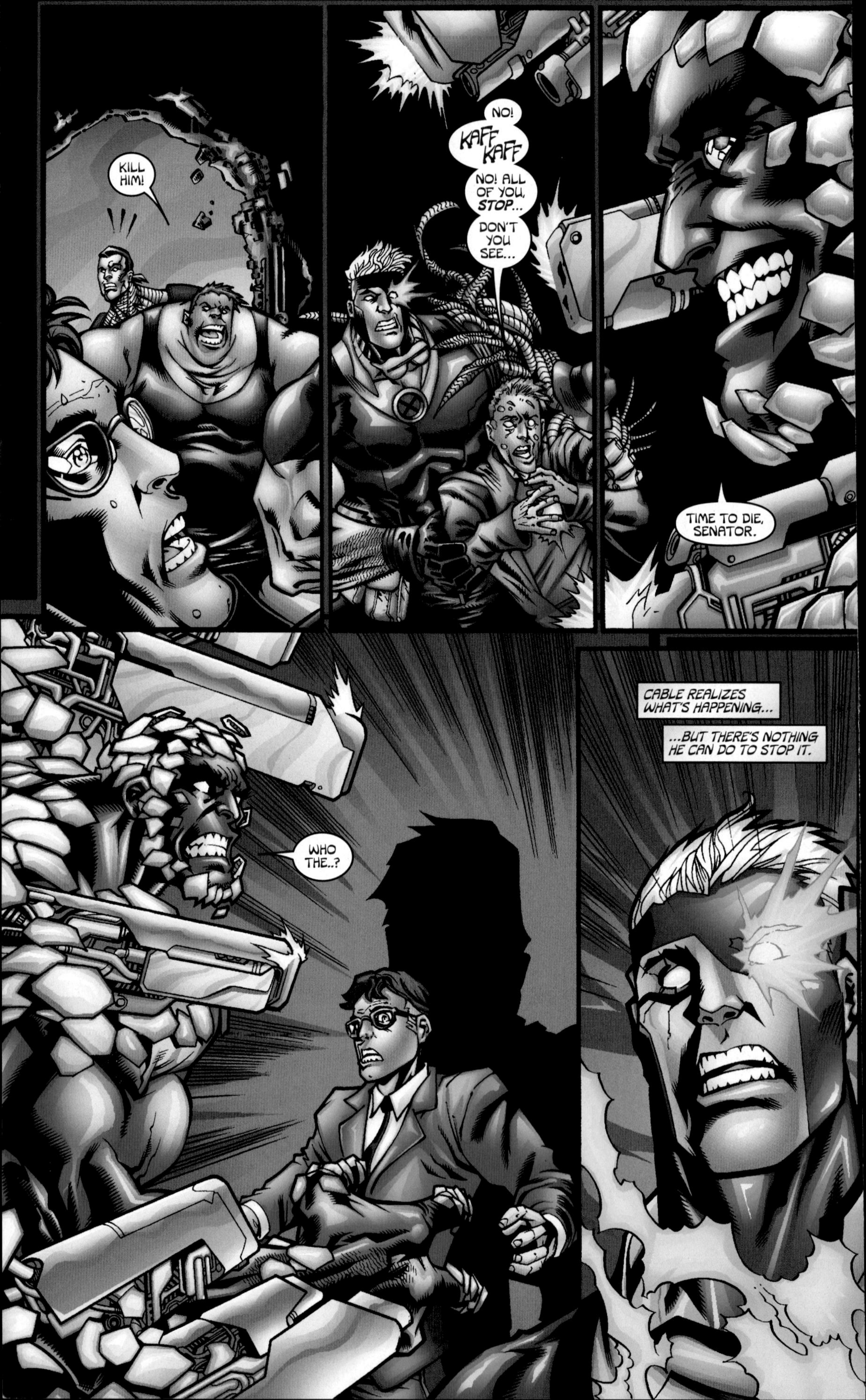
KILL HIM!
NO!
KAFF KAFF
NO! ALL OF YOU, STOP...
DON'T YOU SEE...
TIME TO DIE, SENATOR.
WHO THE..?
CABLE REALIZES WHAT'S HAPPENING...
...BUT THERE'S NOTHING HE CAN DO TO STOP IT.

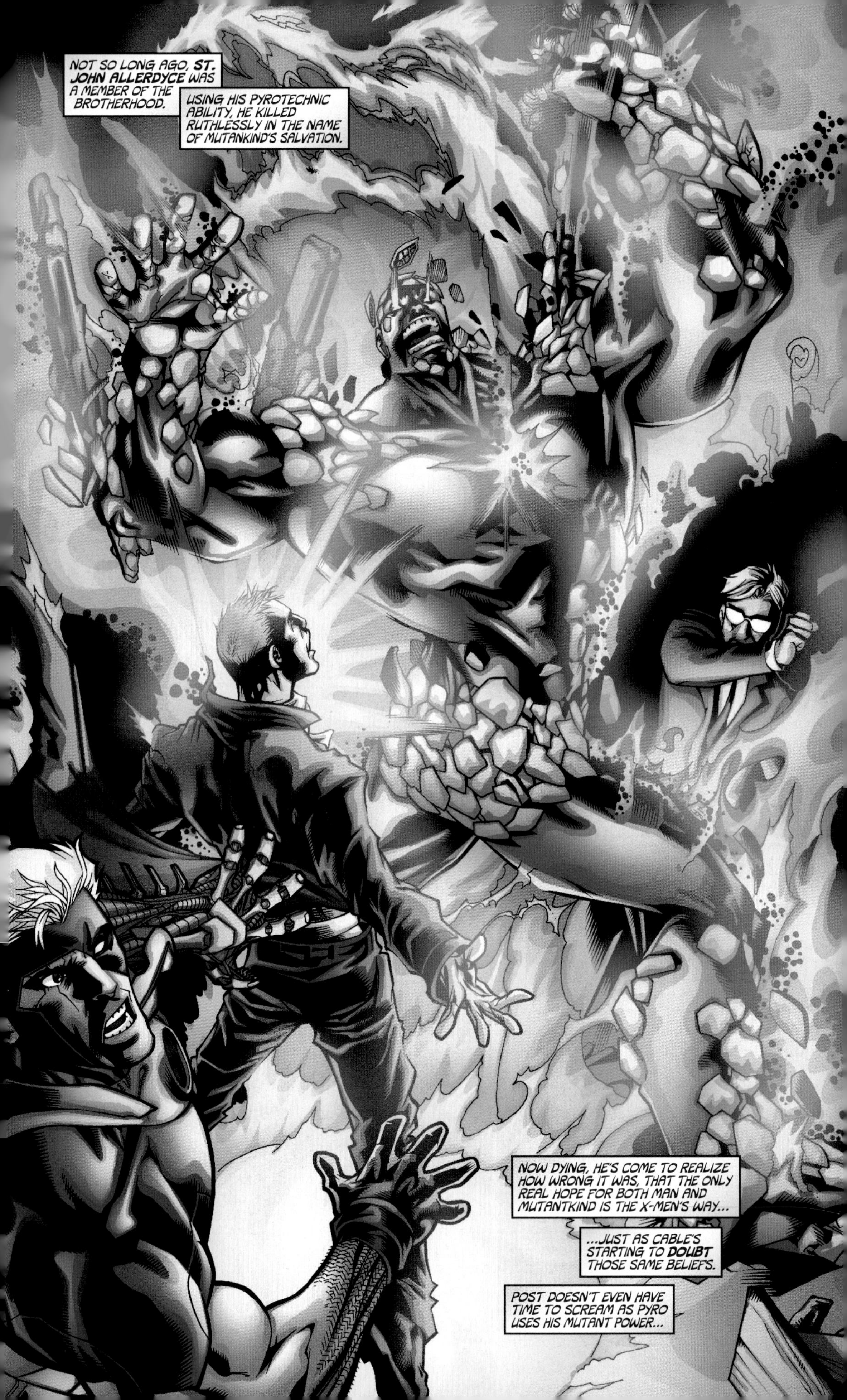

NOT SO LONG AGO, ST. JOHN ALLERDYCE WAS A MEMBER OF THE BROTHERHOOD.
USING HIS PYROTECHNIC ABILITY, HE KILLED RUTHLESSLY IN THE NAME OF MUTANKIND'S SALVATION.
NOW DYING, HE'S COME TO REALIZE HOW WRONG IT WAS, THAT THE ONLY REAL HOPE FOR BOTH MAN AND MUTANTKIND IS THE X-MEN'S WAY...
...JUST AS CABLE'S STARTING TO DOUBT THOSE SAME BELIEFS.
POST DOESN'T EVEN HAVE TIME TO SCREAM AS PYRO USES HIS MUTANT POWER...

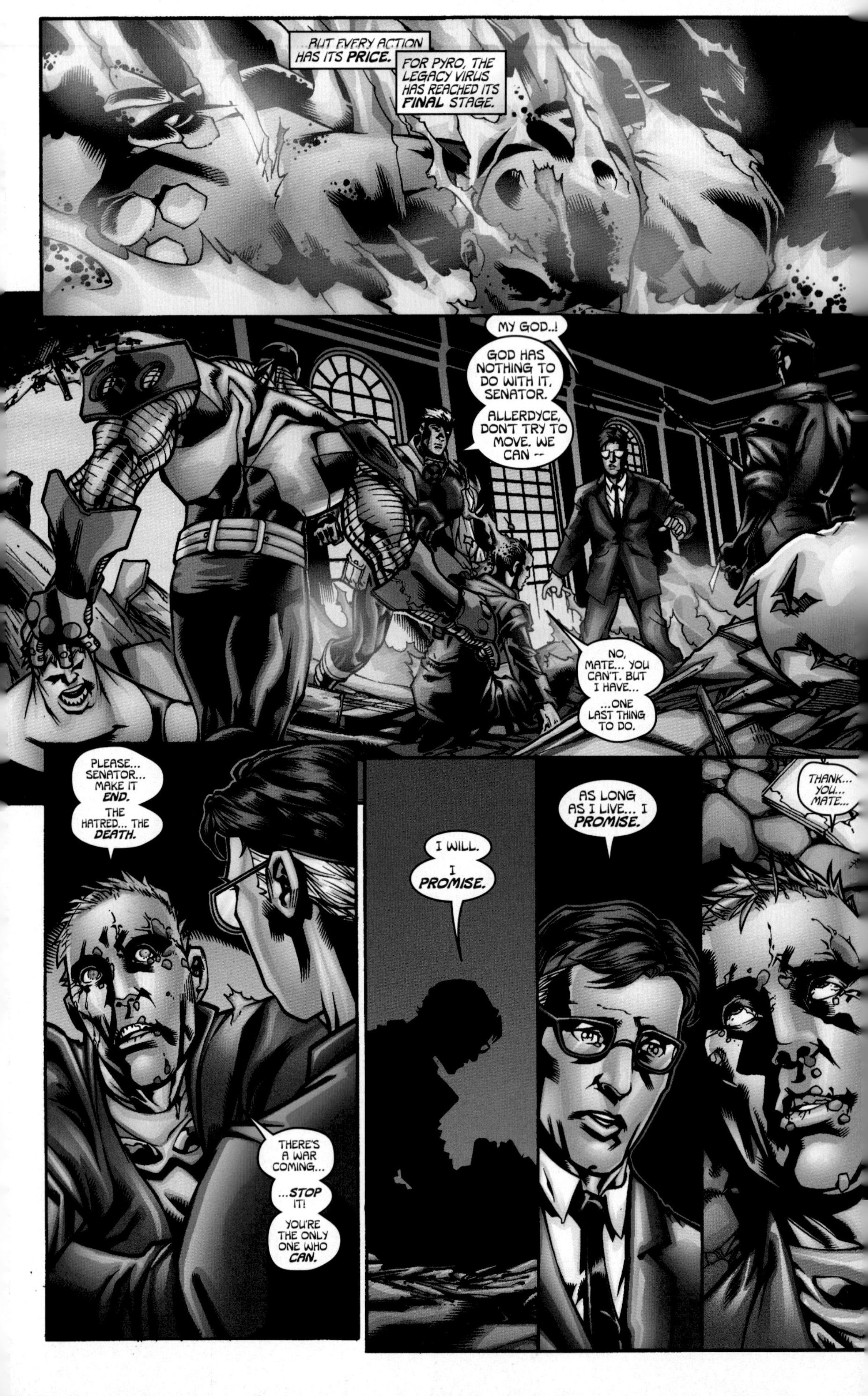

...BUT EVERY ACTION HAS ITS PRICE.
FOR PYRO, THE LEGACY VIRUS HAS REACHED ITS FINAL STAGE.
MY GOD..!
GOD HAS NOTHING TO DO WITH IT, SENATOR.
ALLERDYCE, DON'T TRY TO MOVE. WE CAN --
NO, MATE... YOU CAN'T. BUT I HAVE...
...ONE LAST THING TO DO.
PLEASE... SENATOR... MAKE IT END.
THE HATRED... THE DEATH.
THERE'S A WAR COMING...
...STOP IT!
YOU'RE THE ONLY ONE WHO CAN.
I WILL.
I PROMISE.
AS LONG AS I LIVE... I PROMISE.
THANK... YOU... MATE...

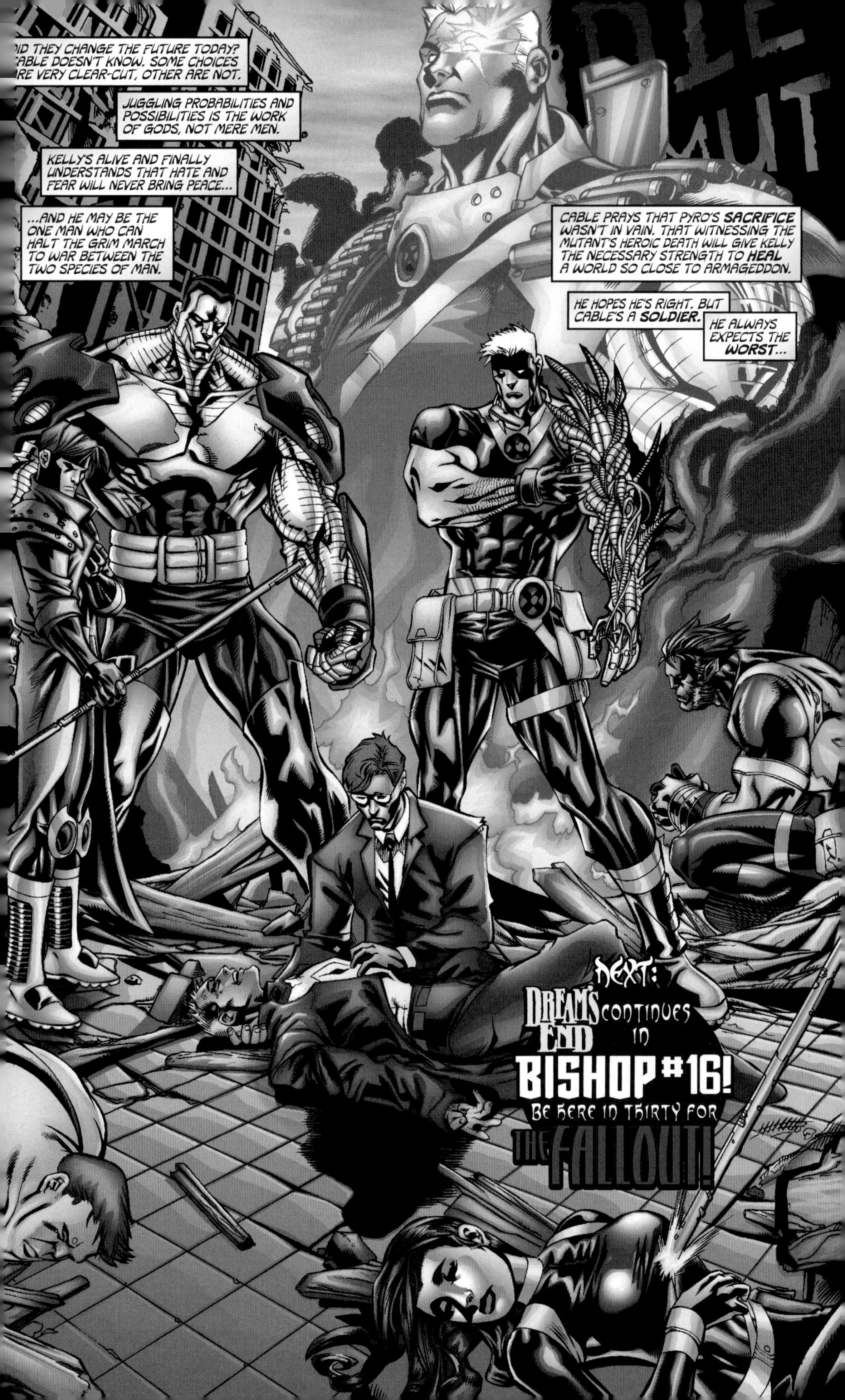
DID THEY CHANGE THE FUTURE TODAY? CABLE DOESN'T KNOW. SOME CHOICES ARE VERY CLEAR-CUT, OTHER ARE NOT.
JUGGLING PROBABILITIES AND POSSIBILITIES IS THE WORK OF GODS, NOT MERE MEN.
KELLY'S ALIVE AND FINALLY UNDERSTANDS THAT HATE AND FEAR WILL NEVER BRING PEACE...
...AND HE MAY BE THE ONE MAN WHO CAN HALT THE GRIM MARCH TO WAR BETWEEN THE TWO SPECIES OF MAN.
CABLE PRAYS THAT PYRO'S SACRIFICE WASN'T IN VAIN. THAT WITNESSING THE MUTANT'S HEROIC DEATH WILL GIVE KELLY THE NECESSARY STRENGTH TO HEAL A WORLD SO CLOSE TO ARMAGEDDON.
HE HOPES HE'S RIGHT. BUT CABLE'S A SOLDIER.
HE ALWAYS EXPECTS THE WORST...
NEXT:
DREAM'S END CONTINUES IN
BISHOP #16!
BE HERE IN THIRTY FOR
THE FALLOUT!

IN *BISHOP: THE LAST X-MAN* #16 AND *X-MEN* #108, THE CONCLUSION OF "DREAM'S END," THE REST OF THE X-MEN REPULSED THE BROTHERHOOD'S ATTACK ON MUIR ISLAND, BUT MOIRA MacTAGGERT DIED OF INJURIES SUSTAINED DURING THE ASSAULT. MEANWHILE, SENATOR KELLY MADE A MOVING PRO-MUTANT SPEECH, BUT WAS SHOT AND KILLED BY A BIGOTED HUMAN WHO FELT BETRAYED BY KELLY'S CHANGE OF HEART.

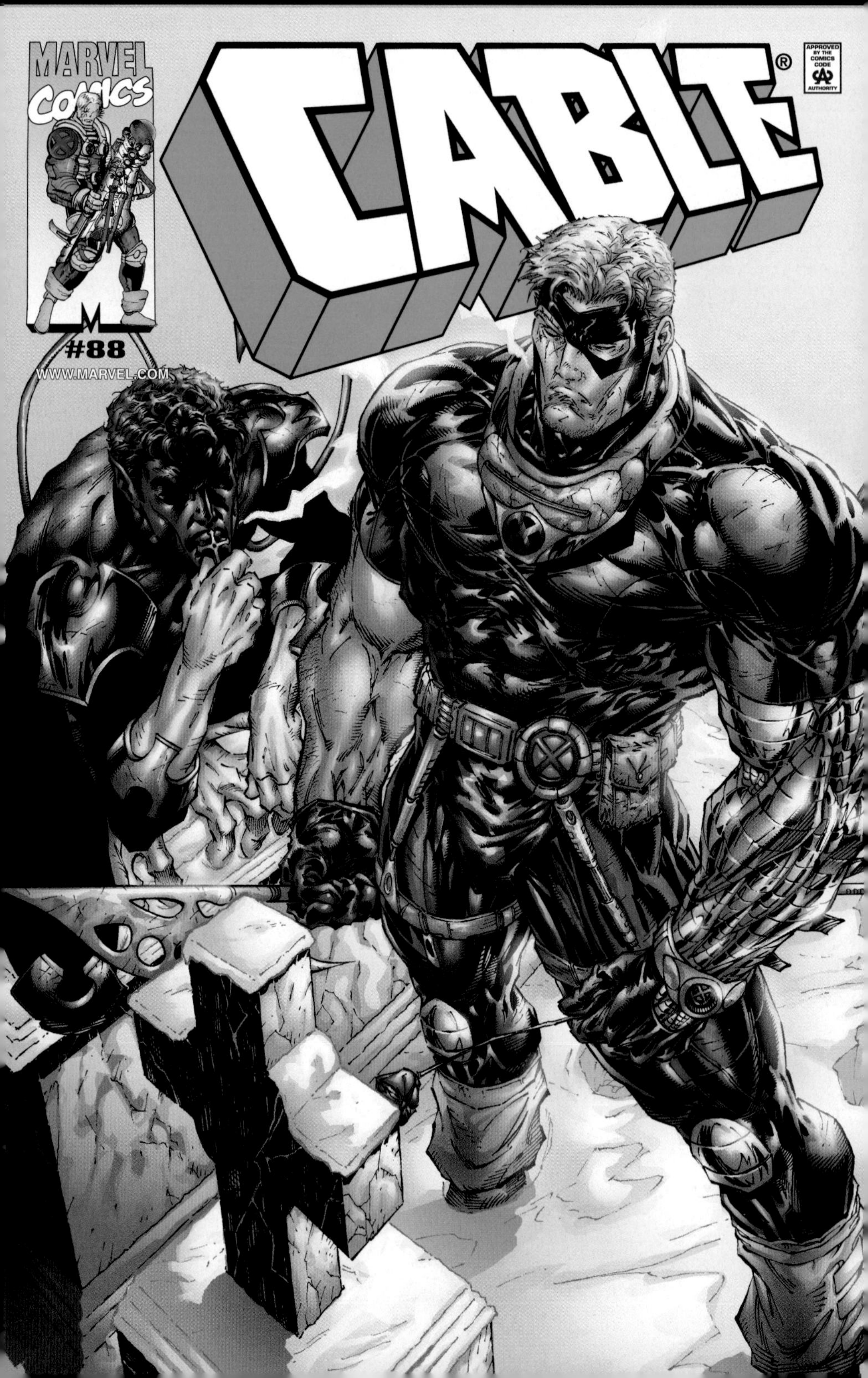

MARVEL COMICS
CABLE®
APPROVED BY THE COMICS CODE AUTHORITY
#88
WWW.MARVEL.COM

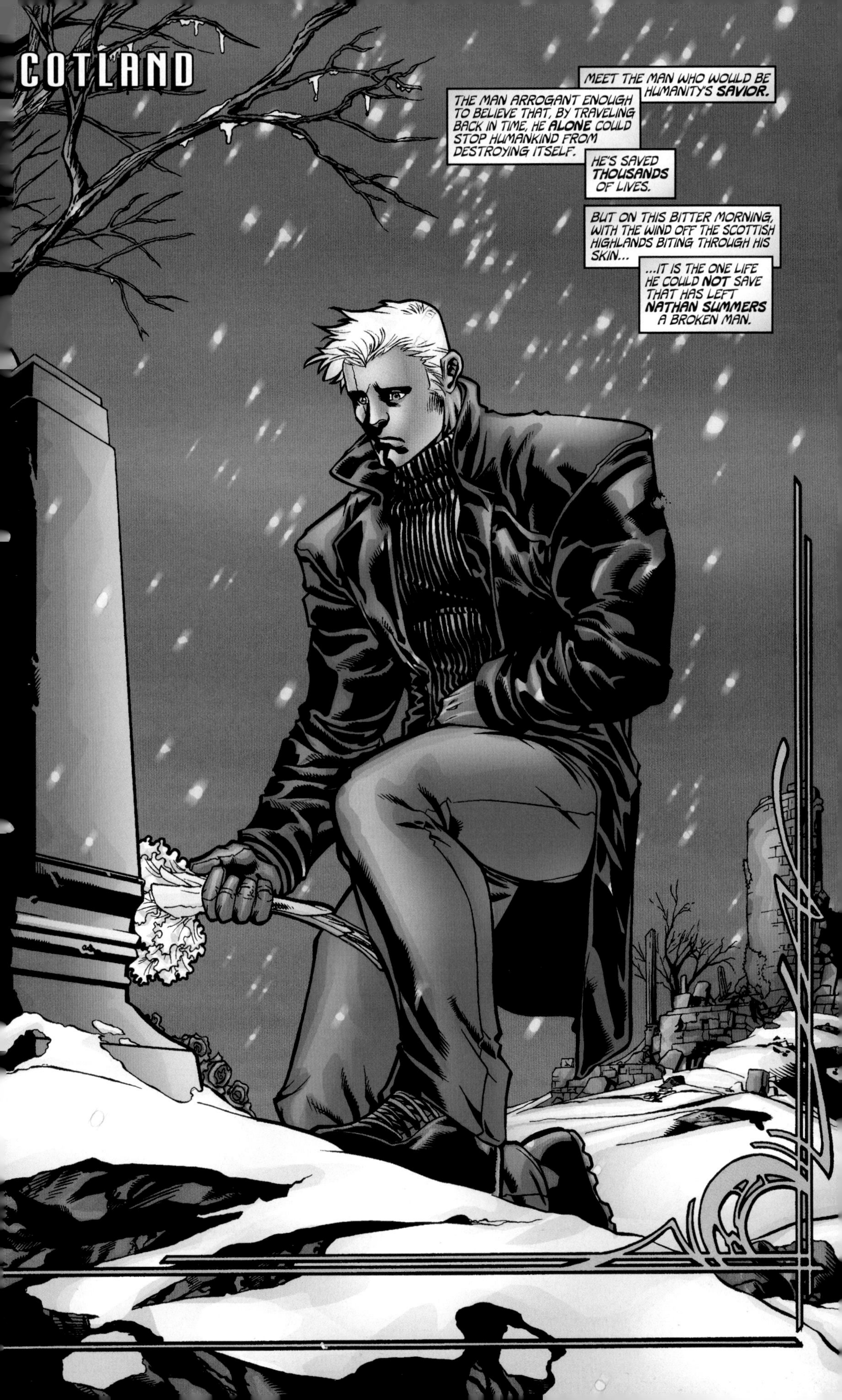
COTLAND
MEET THE MAN WHO WOULD BE HUMANITY'S SAVIOR.
THE MAN ARROGANT ENOUGH TO BELIEVE THAT, BY TRAVELING BACK IN TIME, HE ALONE COULD STOP HUMANKIND FROM DESTROYING ITSELF.
HE'S SAVED THOUSANDS OF LIVES.
BUT ON THIS BITTER MORNING, WITH THE WIND OFF THE SCOTTISH HIGHLANDS BITING THROUGH HIS SKIN...
...IT IS THE ONE LIFE HE COULD NOT SAVE THAT HAS LEFT NATHAN SUMMERS A BROKEN MAN.

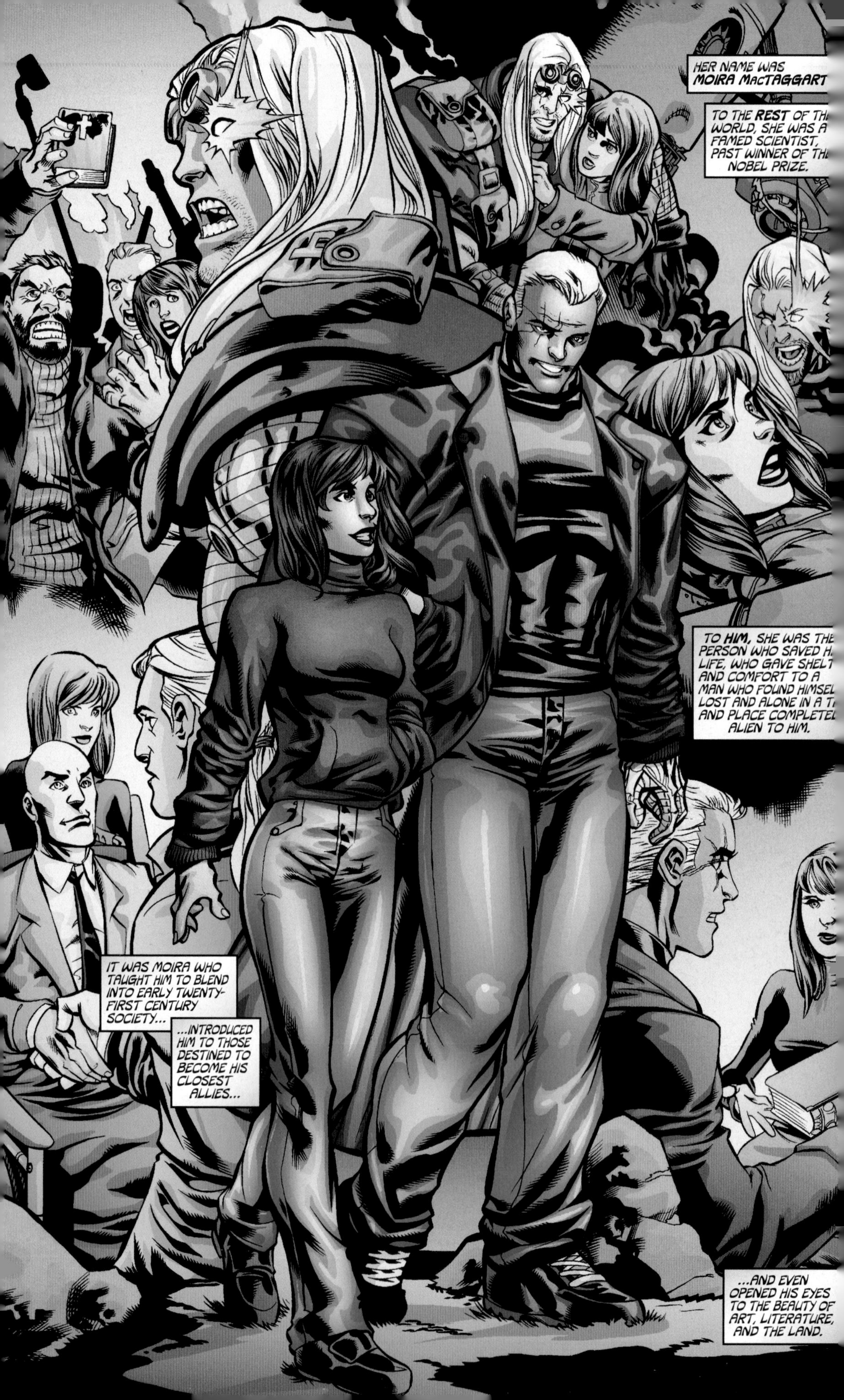
HER NAME WAS MOIRA MacTAGGART
TO THE REST OF TH WORLD, SHE WAS A FAMED SCIENTIST, PAST WINNER OF TH NOBEL PRIZE.
TO HIM, SHE WAS THE PERSON WHO SAVED H LIFE, WHO GAVE SHELT AND COMFORT TO A MAN WHO FOUND HIMSEL LOST AND ALONE IN A T AND PLACE COMPLETEL ALIEN TO HIM.
IT WAS MOIRA WHO TAUGHT HIM TO BLEND INTO EARLY TWENTY-FIRST CENTURY SOCIETY...
...INTRODUCED HIM TO THOSE DESTINED TO BECOME HIS CLOSEST ALLIES...
...AND EVEN OPENED HIS EYES TO THE BEAUTY OF ART, LITERATURE, AND THE LAND.

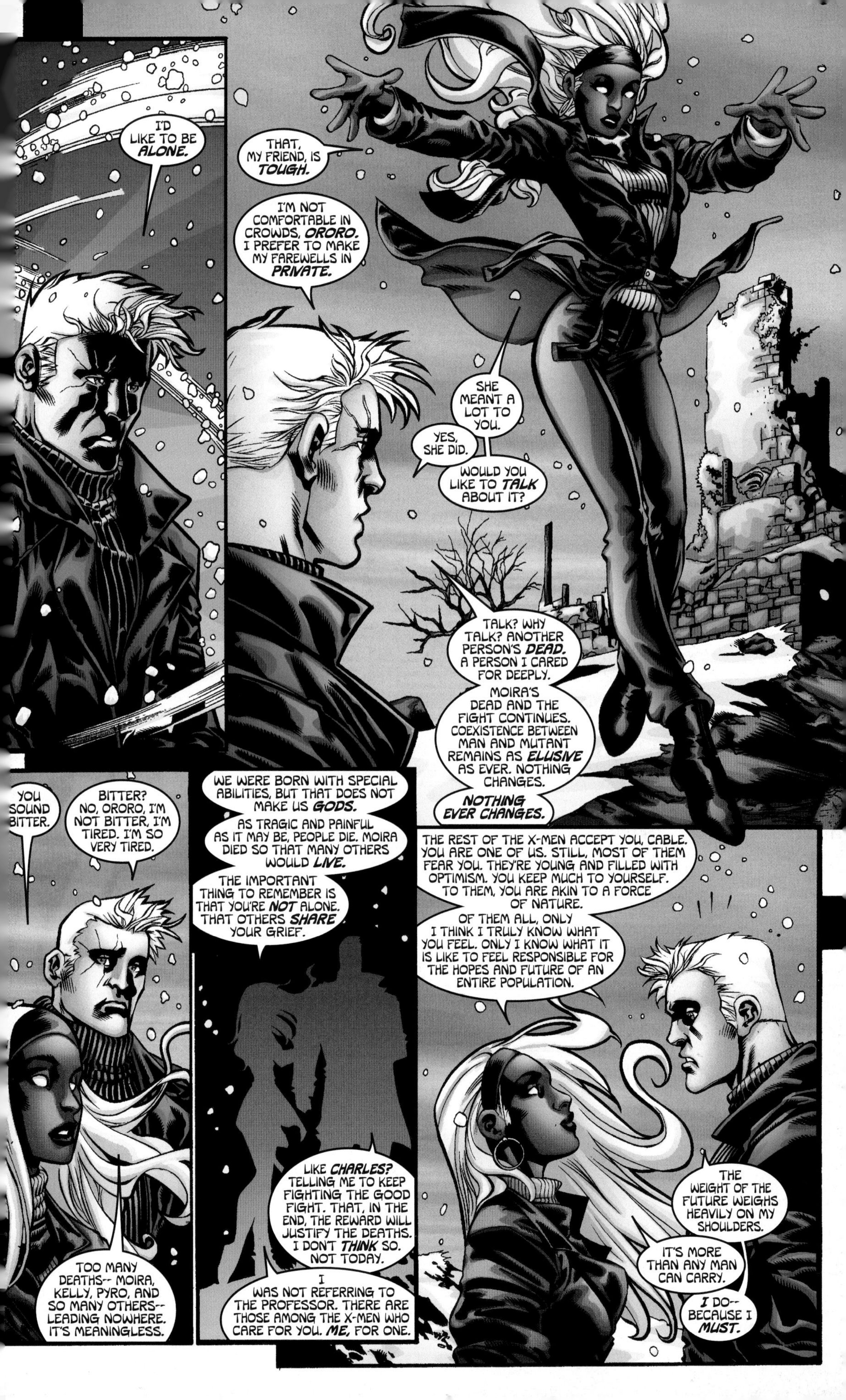
I'D LIKE TO BE ALONE.
THAT, MY FRIEND, IS TOUGH.
I'M NOT COMFORTABLE IN CROWDS, ORORO. I PREFER TO MAKE MY FAREWELLS IN PRIVATE.
SHE MEANT A LOT TO YOU.
YES, SHE DID.
WOULD YOU LIKE TO TALK ABOUT IT?
TALK? WHY TALK? ANOTHER PERSON'S DEAD. A PERSON I CARED FOR DEEPLY.
MOIRA'S DEAD AND THE FIGHT CONTINUES. COEXISTENCE BETWEEN MAN AND MUTANT REMAINS AS ELUSIVE AS EVER. NOTHING CHANGES.
NOTHING EVER CHANGES.
YOU SOUND BITTER.
BITTER? NO, ORORO, I'M NOT BITTER, I'M TIRED. I'M SO VERY TIRED.
TOO MANY DEATHS-- MOIRA, KELLY, PYRO, AND SO MANY OTHERS-- LEADING NOWHERE. IT'S MEANINGLESS.
WE WERE BORN WITH SPECIAL ABILITIES, BUT THAT DOES NOT MAKE US GODS.
AS TRAGIC AND PAINFUL AS IT MAY BE, PEOPLE DIE. MOIRA DIED SO THAT MANY OTHERS WOULD LIVE.
THE IMPORTANT THING TO REMEMBER IS THAT YOU'RE NOT ALONE. THAT OTHERS SHARE YOUR GRIEF.
LIKE CHARLES? TELLING ME TO KEEP FIGHTING THE GOOD FIGHT. THAT, IN THE END, THE REWARD WILL JUSTIFY THE DEATHS. I DON'T THINK SO. NOT TODAY.
I WAS NOT REFERRING TO THE PROFESSOR. THERE ARE THOSE AMONG THE X-MEN WHO CARE FOR YOU. ME, FOR ONE.
THE REST OF THE X-MEN ACCEPT YOU, CABLE. YOU ARE ONE OF US. STILL, MOST OF THEM FEAR YOU. THEY'RE YOUNG AND FILLED WITH OPTIMISM. YOU KEEP MUCH TO YOURSELF. TO THEM, YOU ARE AKIN TO A FORCE OF NATURE.
OF THEM ALL, ONLY I THINK I TRULY KNOW WHAT YOU FEEL. ONLY I KNOW WHAT IT IS LIKE TO FEEL RESPONSIBLE FOR THE HOPES AND FUTURE OF AN ENTIRE POPULATION.
THE WEIGHT OF THE FUTURE WEIGHS HEAVILY ON MY SHOULDERS.
IT'S MORE THAN ANY MAN CAN CARRY.
I DO-- BECAUSE I MUST.

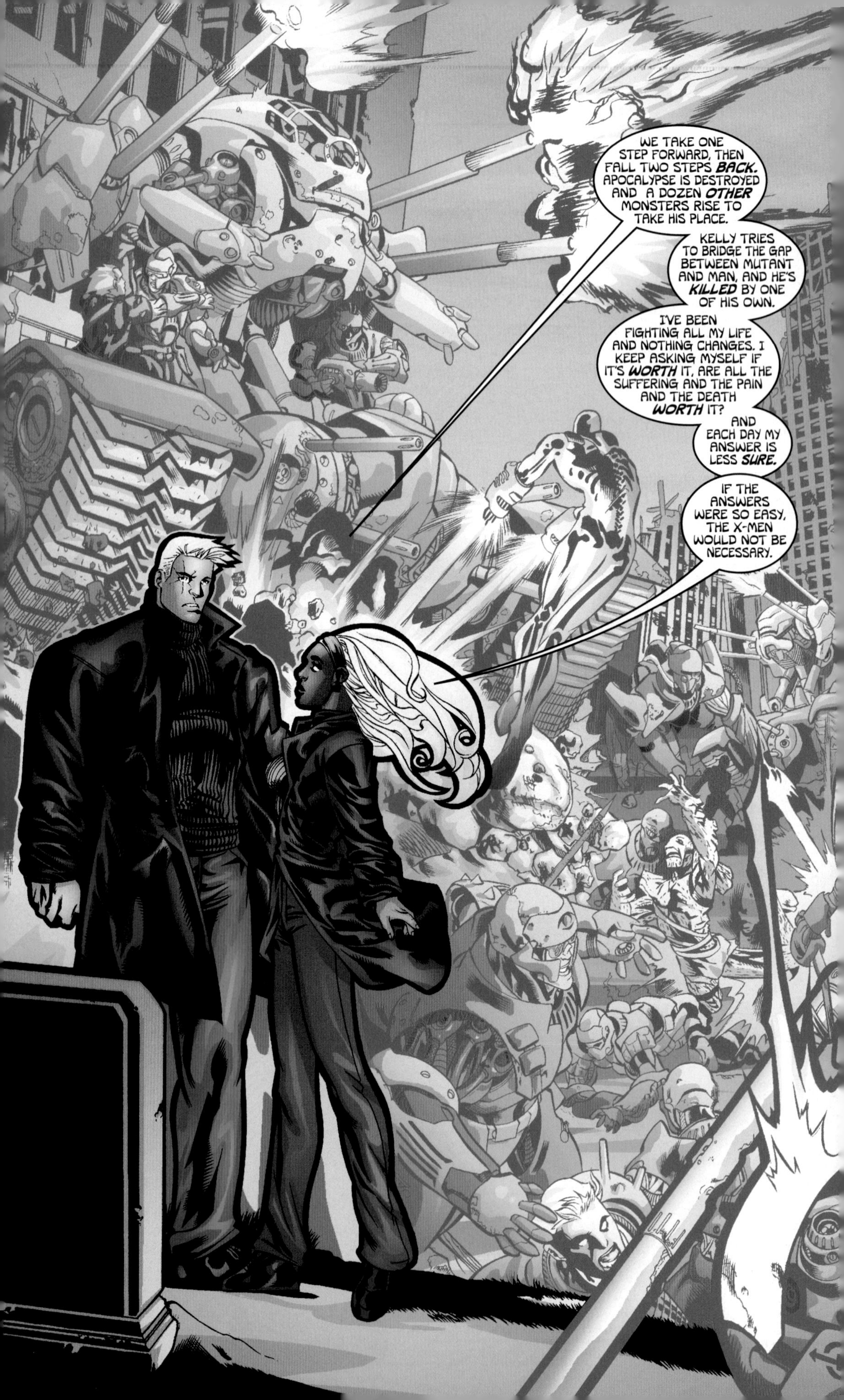
WE TAKE ONE STEP FORWARD, THEN FALL TWO STEPS BACK. APOCALYPSE IS DESTROYED AND A DOZEN OTHER MONSTERS RISE TO TAKE HIS PLACE.
KELLY TRIES TO BRIDGE THE GAP BETWEEN MUTANT AND MAN, AND HE'S KILLED BY ONE OF HIS OWN.
I'VE BEEN FIGHTING ALL MY LIFE AND NOTHING CHANGES. I KEEP ASKING MYSELF IF IT'S WORTH IT, ARE ALL THE SUFFERING AND THE PAIN AND THE DEATH WORTH IT?
AND EACH DAY MY ANSWER IS LESS SURE.
IF THE ANSWERS WERE SO EASY, THE X-MEN WOULD NOT BE NECESSARY.

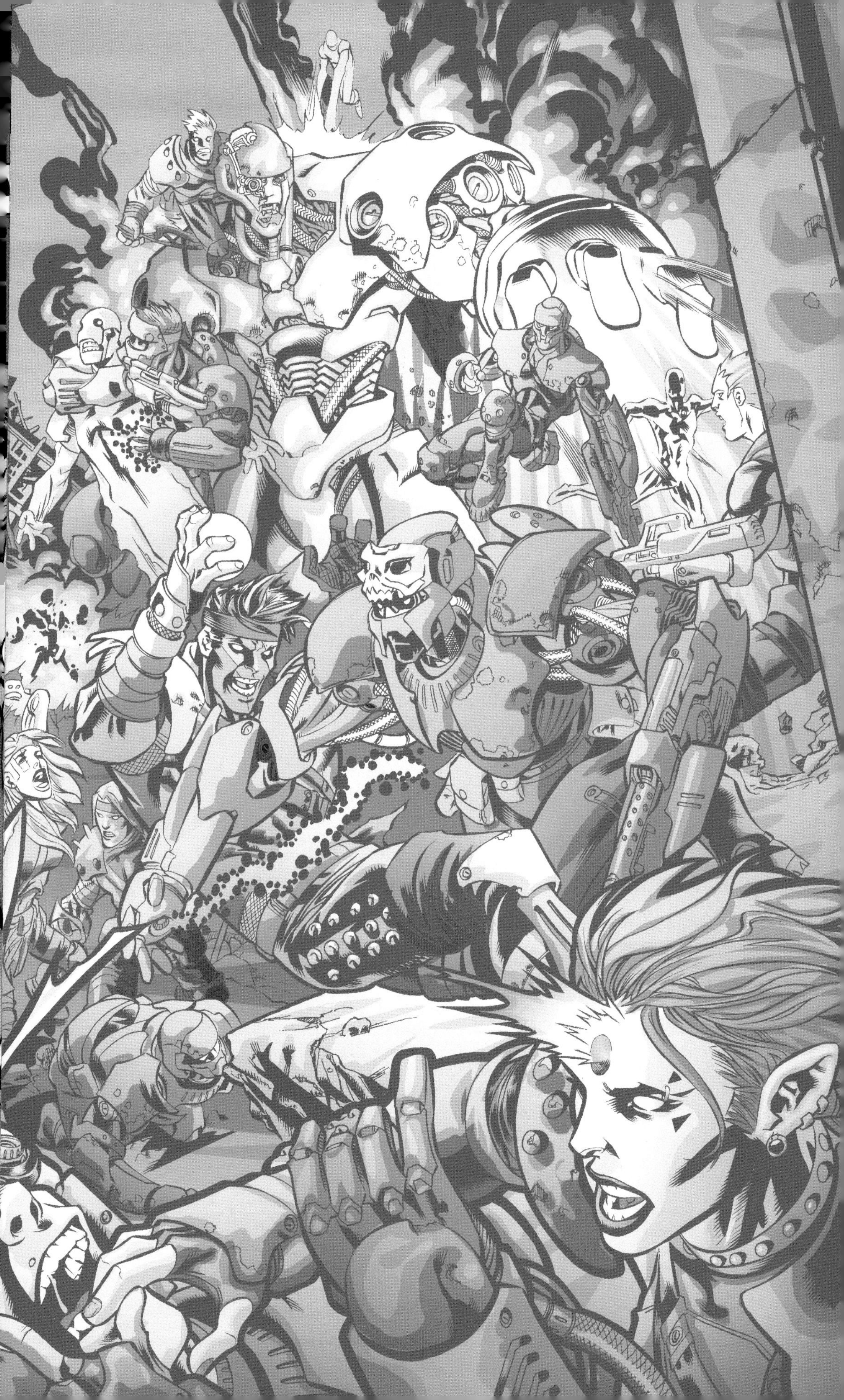

AT THAT MOMENT...

THE CHOSEN ONE IS COMPLETELY UNAWARE HIS EVERY MOVEMENT IS BEING *MONITORED.*

MAKE NO *ASSUMPTIONS* ABOUT SUMMERS. HE KNOWS WHEN TO ACT AND WHEN NOT TO.

THE ASKANI'SON IS MORE DEADL THAN YOU CA IMAGINE.

AFTER DECADES OF PREPARATION, OUR TIME IS NEAR. I WILL NOT HAVE OUR PLANS THWARTED BY ONE FOOLISH *MISTAKE.* IS THAT *UNDERSTOOD?*

YOUR WORD IS LAW, *MOTHER OF NIGHT.*

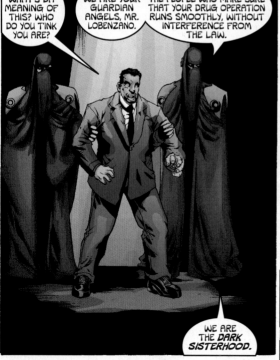

WHAT'S DA MEANING OF THIS? WHO DO YOU T'INK YOU ARE?

WE ARE YOUR GUARDIAN ANGELS, MR. LOBENZANO.

THE PEOPLE WHO MAKE SURE THAT YOUR DRUG OPERATION RUNS SMOOTHLY, WITHOUT INTERFERENCE FROM THE LAW.

WE ARE THE *DARK SISTERHOOD.*

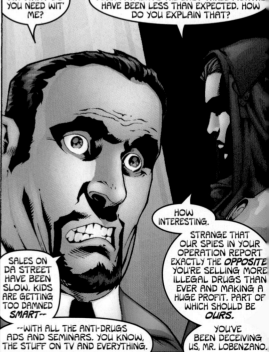

WH-WHAT DO YOU NEED WIT' ME?

YOUR PAYMENTS THE LAST THREE MONTHS HAVE BEEN LESS THAN EXPECTED. HOW DO YOU EXPLAIN THAT?

HOW INTERESTING.

STRANGE THAT OUR SPIES IN YOUR OPERATION REPORT EXACTLY THE *OPPOSITE* YOU'RE SELLING MORE ILLEGAL DRUGS THAN EVER AND MAKING A HUGE PROFIT. PART OF WHICH SHOULD BE *OURS.*

SALES ON DA STREET HAVE BEEN SLOW. KIDS ARE GETTING TOO DAMNED *SMART--*

--WITH ALL THE ANTI-DRUGS ADS AND SEMINARS. YOU KNOW, THE STUFF ON TV AND EVERYTHING.

YOU'VE BEEN DECEIVING US, MR. LOBENZANO.

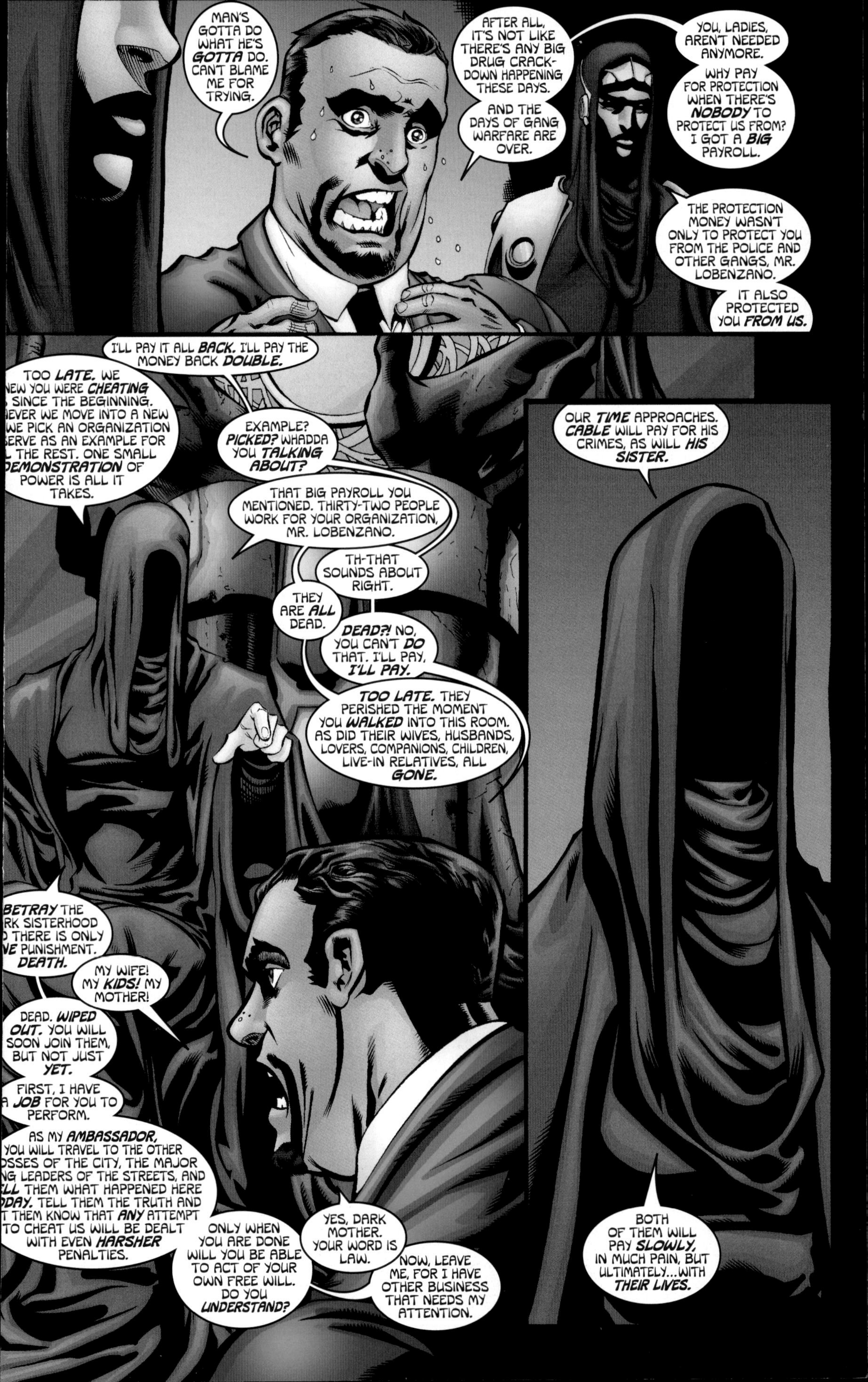
MAN'S GOTTA DO WHAT HE'S GOTTA DO. CAN'T BLAME ME FOR TRYING.
AFTER ALL, IT'S NOT LIKE THERE'S ANY BIG DRUG CRACK-DOWN HAPPENING THESE DAYS.
AND THE DAYS OF GANG WARFARE ARE OVER.
YOU, LADIES, AREN'T NEEDED ANYMORE.
WHY PAY FOR PROTECTION WHEN THERE'S NOBODY TO PROTECT US FROM? I GOT A BIG PAYROLL.
THE PROTECTION MONEY WASN'T ONLY TO PROTECT YOU FROM THE POLICE AND OTHER GANGS, MR. LOBENZANO.
IT ALSO PROTECTED YOU FROM US.
I'LL PAY IT ALL BACK. I'LL PAY THE MONEY BACK DOUBLE.
PICK AN ORGANIZATION
POWER IS ALL IT TAKES.
EXAMPLE? PICKED? WHADDA YOU TALKING ABOUT?
THAT BIG PAYROLL YOU MENTIONED. THIRTY-TWO PEOPLE WORK FOR YOUR ORGANIZATION, MR. LOBENZANO.
TH-THAT SOUNDS ABOUT RIGHT.
THEY ARE ALL DEAD.
DEAD?! NO, YOU CAN'T DO THAT. I'LL PAY, I'LL PAY.
TOO LATE. THEY PERISHED THE MOMENT YOU WALKED INTO THIS ROOM. AS DID THEIR WIVES, HUSBANDS, LOVERS, COMPANIONS, CHILDREN, LIVE-IN RELATIVES, ALL GONE.
MY WIFE! MY KIDS! MY MOTHER!
DEAD. WIPED OUT. YOU WILL SOON JOIN THEM, BUT NOT JUST YET.
PERFORM.
PENALTIES.
ONLY WHEN YOU ARE DONE WILL YOU BE ABLE TO ACT OF YOUR OWN FREE WILL. DO YOU UNDERSTAND?
YES, DARK MOTHER. YOUR WORD IS LAW.
NOW, LEAVE ME, FOR I HAVE OTHER BUSINESS THAT NEEDS MY ATTENTION.
OUR TIME APPROACHES. CABLE WILL PAY FOR HIS CRIMES, AS WILL HIS SISTER.
BOTH OF THEM WILL PAY SLOWLY, IN MUCH PAIN, BUT ULTIMATELY...WITH THEIR LIVES.

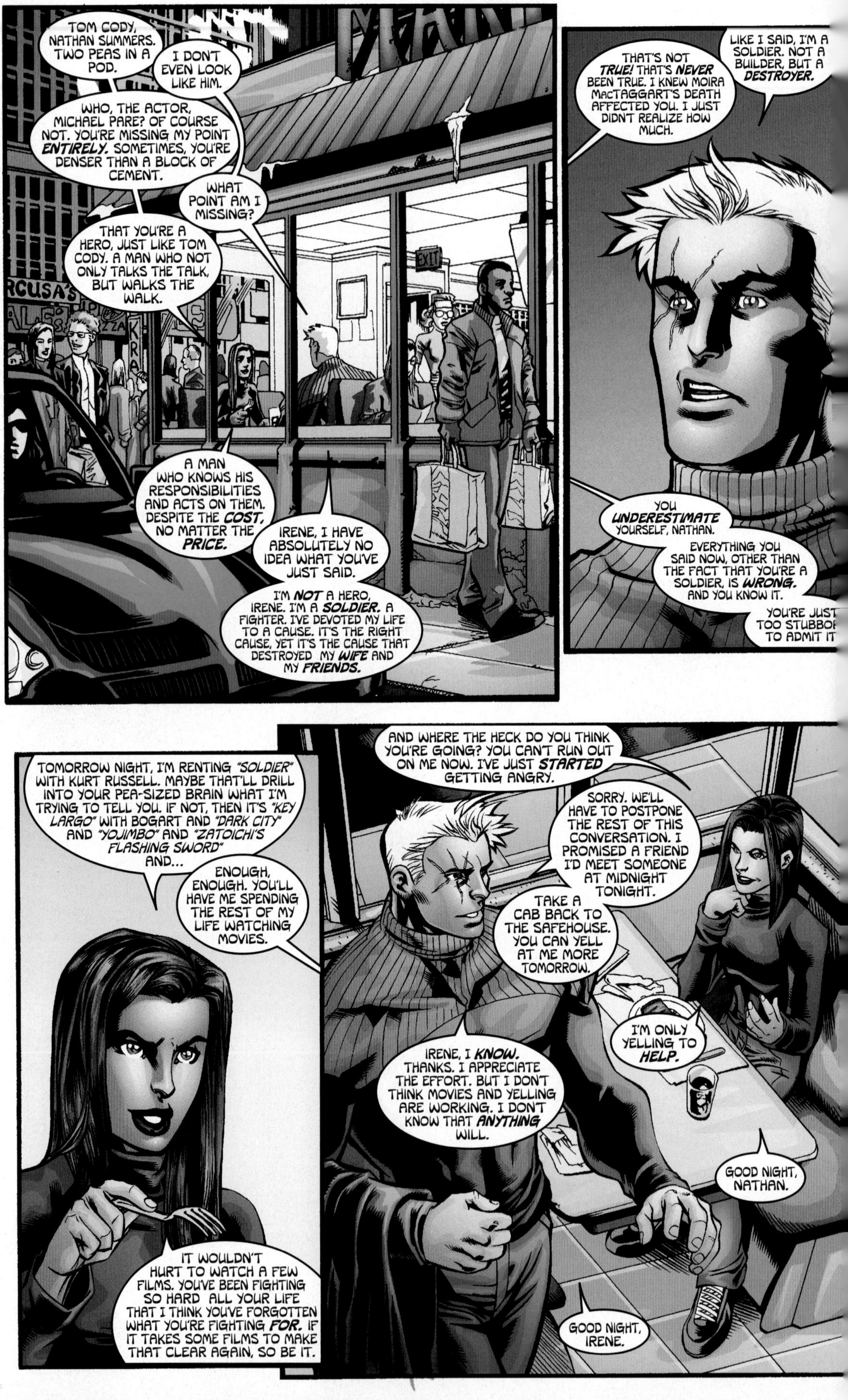
TOM CODY, NATHAN SUMMERS. TWO PEAS IN A POD.
I DON'T EVEN LOOK LIKE HIM.
WHO, THE ACTOR, MICHAEL PARE? OF COURSE NOT. YOU'RE MISSING MY POINT ***ENTIRELY.*** SOMETIMES, YOU'RE DENSER THAN A BLOCK OF CEMENT.
WHAT POINT AM I MISSING?
THAT YOU'RE A HERO, JUST LIKE TOM CODY. A MAN WHO NOT ONLY TALKS THE TALK, BUT WALKS THE WALK.
EXIT
A MAN WHO KNOWS HIS RESPONSIBILITIES AND ACTS ON THEM. DESPITE THE ***COST,*** NO MATTER THE ***PRICE.***
IRENE, I HAVE ABSOLUTELY NO IDEA WHAT YOU'VE JUST SAID.
I'M ***NOT*** A HERO, IRENE. I'M A ***SOLDIER.*** A FIGHTER. I'VE DEVOTED MY LIFE TO A CAUSE. IT'S THE RIGHT CAUSE, YET IT'S THE CAUSE THAT DESTROYED MY ***WIFE*** AND MY ***FRIENDS.***
LIKE I SAID, I'M A SOLDIER. NOT A BUILDER, BUT A ***DESTROYER.***
THAT'S NOT ***TRUE!*** THAT'S ***NEVER*** BEEN TRUE. I KNEW MOIRA MacTAGGART'S DEATH AFFECTED YOU. I JUST DIDN'T REALIZE HOW MUCH.
YOU ***UNDERESTIMATE*** YOURSELF, NATHAN.
EVERYTHING YOU SAID NOW, OTHER THAN THE FACT THAT YOU'RE A SOLDIER, IS ***WRONG.*** AND YOU KNOW IT.
YOU'RE JUST TOO STUBBOR TO ADMIT IT
TOMORROW NIGHT, I'M RENTING *"SOLDIER"* WITH KURT RUSSELL. MAYBE THAT'LL DRILL INTO YOUR PEA-SIZED BRAIN WHAT I'M TRYING TO TELL YOU. IF NOT, THEN IT'S *"KEY LARGO"* WITH BOGART AND *"DARK CITY"* AND *"YOJIMBO"* AND *"ZATOICHI'S FLASHING SWORD"* AND...
ENOUGH, ENOUGH. YOU'LL HAVE ME SPENDING THE REST OF MY LIFE WATCHING MOVIES.
IT WOULDN'T HURT TO WATCH A FEW FILMS. YOU'VE BEEN FIGHTING SO HARD ALL YOUR LIFE THAT I THINK YOU'VE FORGOTTEN WHAT YOU'RE FIGHTING ***FOR.*** IF IT TAKES SOME FILMS TO MAKE THAT CLEAR AGAIN, SO BE IT.
AND WHERE THE HECK DO YOU THINK YOU'RE GOING? YOU CAN'T RUN OUT ON ME NOW. I'VE JUST ***STARTED*** GETTING ANGRY.
SORRY. WE'LL HAVE TO POSTPONE THE REST OF THIS CONVERSATION. I PROMISED A FRIEND I'D MEET SOMEONE AT MIDNIGHT TONIGHT.
TAKE A CAB BACK TO THE SAFEHOUSE. YOU CAN YELL AT ME MORE TOMORROW.
I'M ONLY YELLING TO ***HELP.***
IRENE, I ***KNOW.*** THANKS. I APPRECIATE THE EFFORT. BUT I DON'T THINK MOVIES AND YELLING ARE WORKING. I DON'T KNOW THAT ***ANYTHING*** WILL.
GOOD NIGHT, NATHAN.
GOOD NIGHT, IRENE.

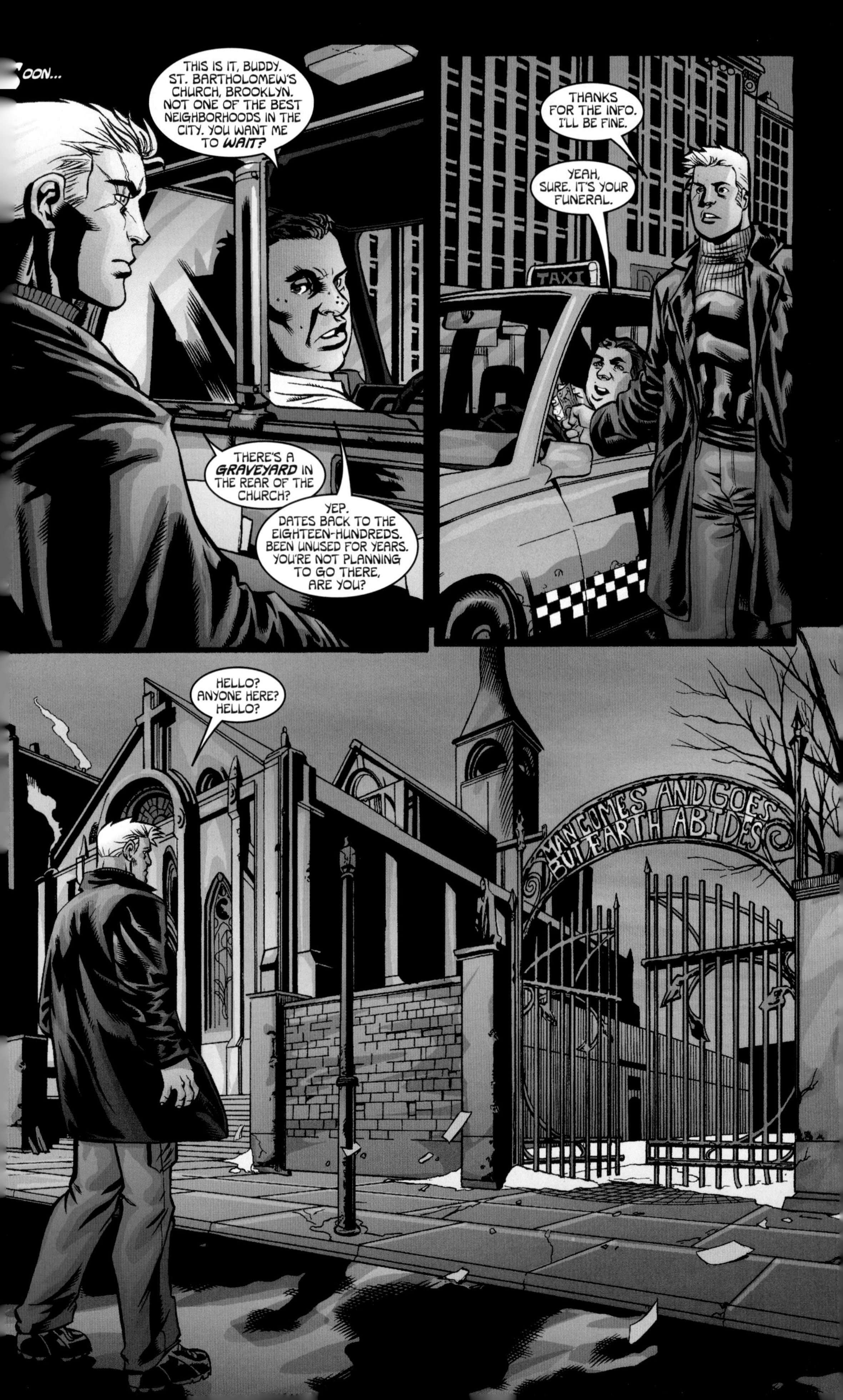
SOON...
THIS IS IT, BUDDY. ST. BARTHOLOMEW'S CHURCH, BROOKLYN. NOT ONE OF THE BEST NEIGHBORHOODS IN THE CITY. YOU WANT ME TO WAIT?
THERE'S A GRAVEYARD IN THE REAR OF THE CHURCH?
YEP. DATES BACK TO THE EIGHTEEN-HUNDREDS. BEEN UNUSED FOR YEARS. YOU'RE NOT PLANNING TO GO THERE, ARE YOU?
THANKS FOR THE INFO. I'LL BE FINE.
YEAH, SURE. IT'S YOUR FUNERAL.
TAXI
HELLO? ANYONE HERE? HELLO?
MAN COMES AND GOES BUT EARTH ABIDES

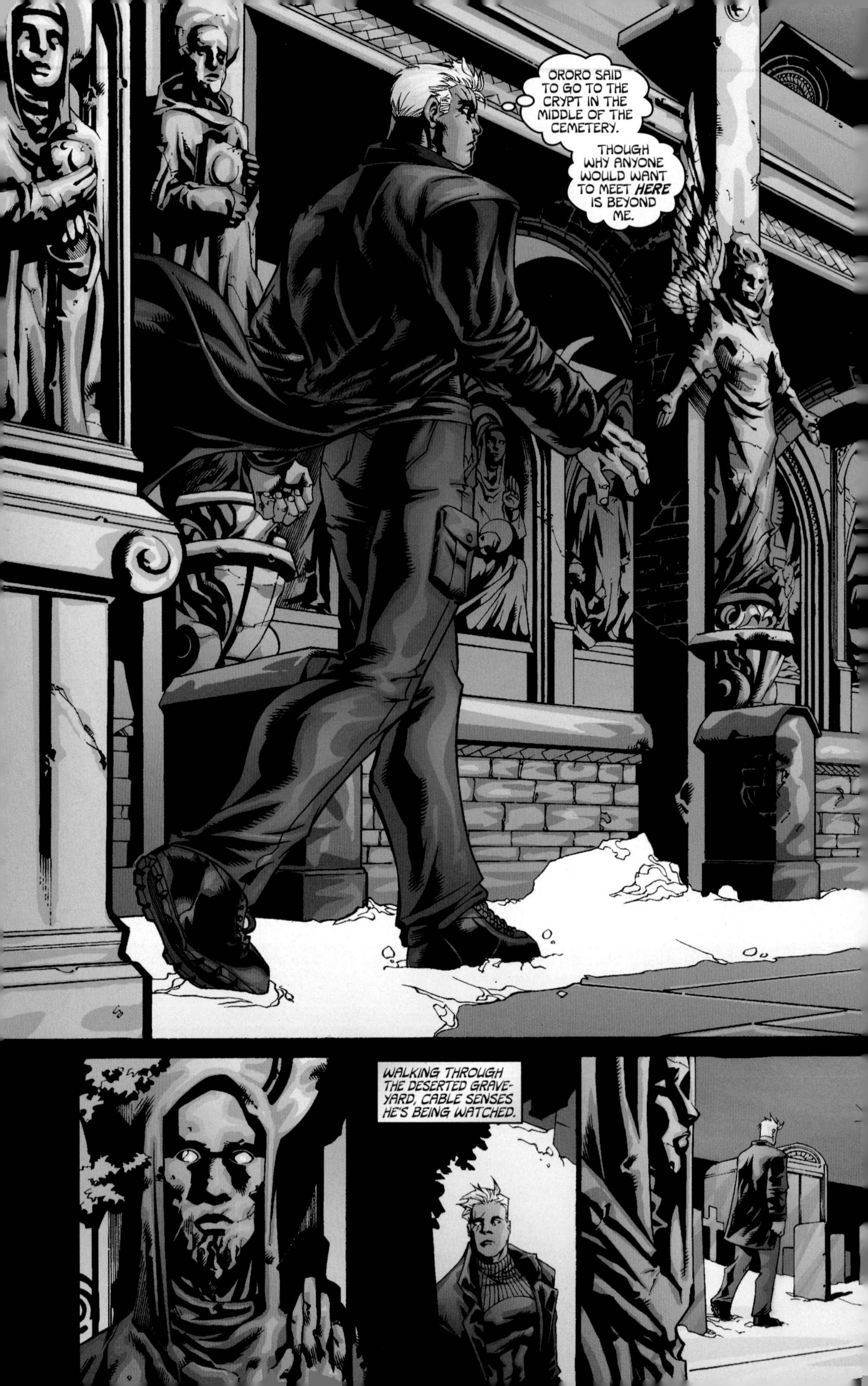
ORORO SAID TO GO TO THE CRYPT IN THE MIDDLE OF THE CEMETERY.
THOUGH WHY ANYONE WOULD WANT TO MEET *HERE* IS BEYOND ME.
WALKING THROUGH THE DESERTED GRAVEYARD, CABLE SENSES HE'S BEING WATCHED.

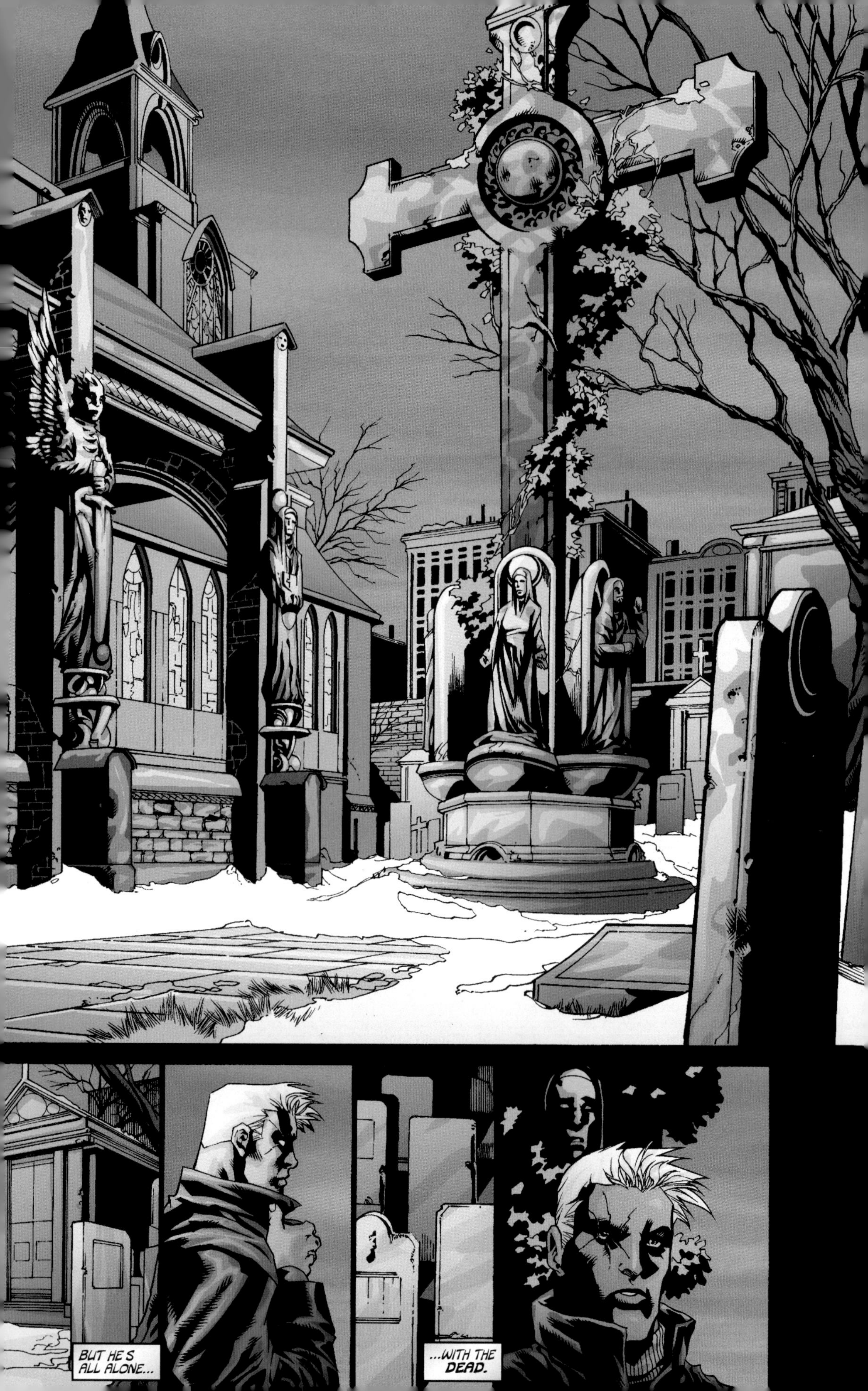
BUT HE'S ALL ALONE...
...WITH THE DEAD.

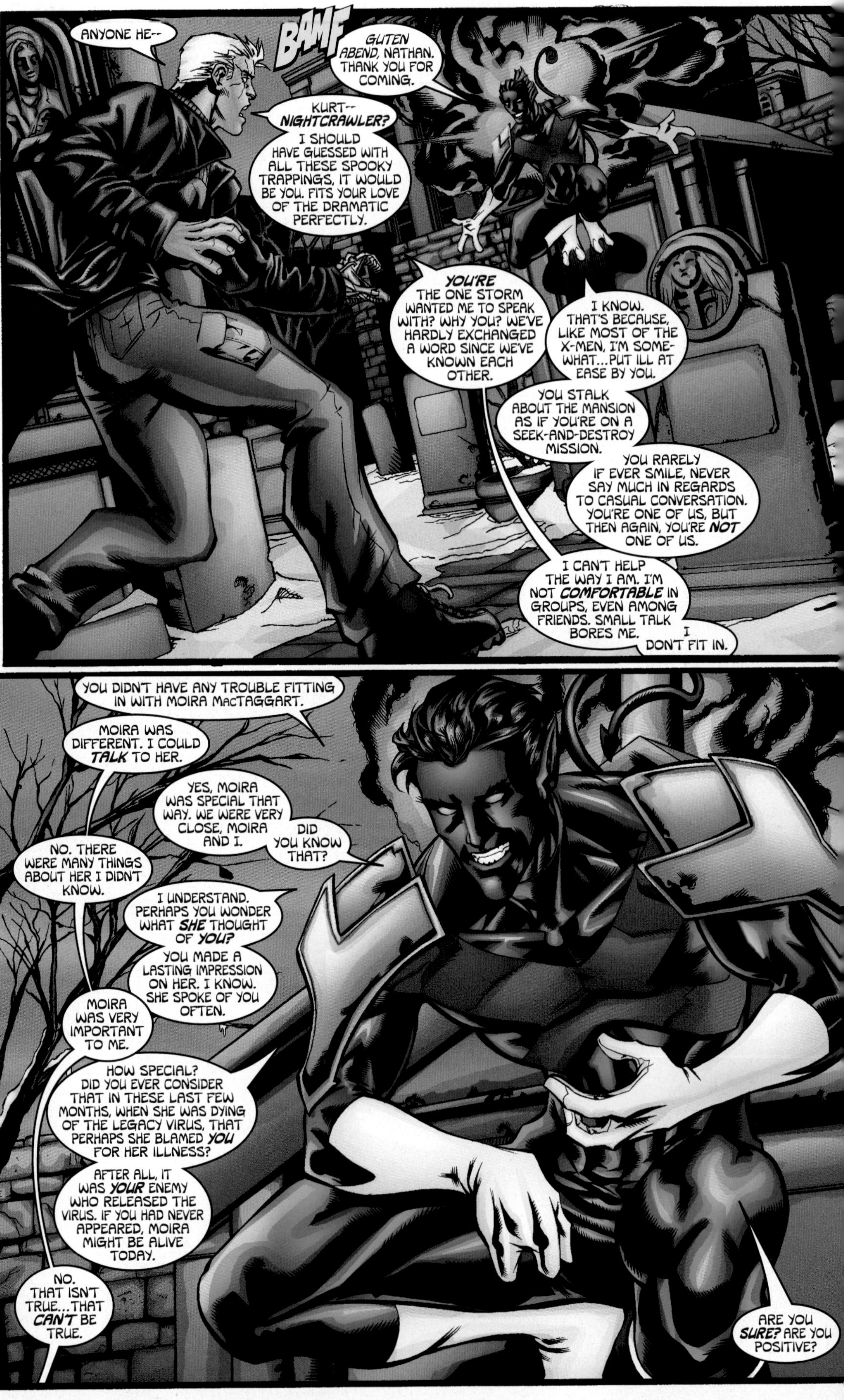

ANYONE HE--
BAMF
GUTEN ABEND, NATHAN. THANK YOU FOR COMING.
KURT-- NIGHTCRAWLER? I SHOULD HAVE GUESSED WITH ALL THESE SPOOKY TRAPPINGS, IT WOULD BE YOU. FITS YOUR LOVE OF THE DRAMATIC PERFECTLY.
YOU'RE THE ONE STORM WANTED ME TO SPEAK WITH? WHY YOU? WE'VE HARDLY EXCHANGED A WORD SINCE WE'VE KNOWN EACH OTHER.
I KNOW. THAT'S BECAUSE, LIKE MOST OF THE X-MEN, I'M SOME-WHAT...PUT ILL AT EASE BY YOU.
YOU STALK ABOUT THE MANSION AS IF YOU'RE ON A SEEK-AND-DESTROY MISSION.
YOU RARELY IF EVER SMILE, NEVER SAY MUCH IN REGARDS TO CASUAL CONVERSATION. YOU'RE ONE OF US, BUT THEN AGAIN, YOU'RE NOT ONE OF US.
I CAN'T HELP THE WAY I AM. I'M NOT COMFORTABLE IN GROUPS, EVEN AMONG FRIENDS. SMALL TALK BORES ME.
I DON'T FIT IN.
YOU DIDN'T HAVE ANY TROUBLE FITTING IN WITH MOIRA MacTAGGART.
MOIRA WAS DIFFERENT. I COULD TALK TO HER.
YES, MOIRA WAS SPECIAL THAT WAY. WE WERE VERY CLOSE, MOIRA AND I.
DID YOU KNOW THAT?
NO. THERE WERE MANY THINGS ABOUT HER I DIDN'T KNOW.
I UNDERSTAND. PERHAPS YOU WONDER WHAT SHE THOUGHT OF YOU?
YOU MADE A LASTING IMPRESSION ON HER. I KNOW. SHE SPOKE OF YOU OFTEN.
MOIRA WAS VERY IMPORTANT TO ME.
HOW SPECIAL? DID YOU EVER CONSIDER THAT IN THESE LAST FEW MONTHS, WHEN SHE WAS DYING OF THE LEGACY VIRUS, THAT PERHAPS SHE BLAMED YOU FOR HER ILLNESS?
AFTER ALL, IT WAS YOUR ENEMY WHO RELEASED THE VIRUS. IF YOU HAD NEVER APPEARED, MOIRA MIGHT BE ALIVE TODAY.
NO. THAT ISN'T TRUE...THAT CAN'T BE TRUE.
ARE YOU SURE? ARE YOU POSITIVE?

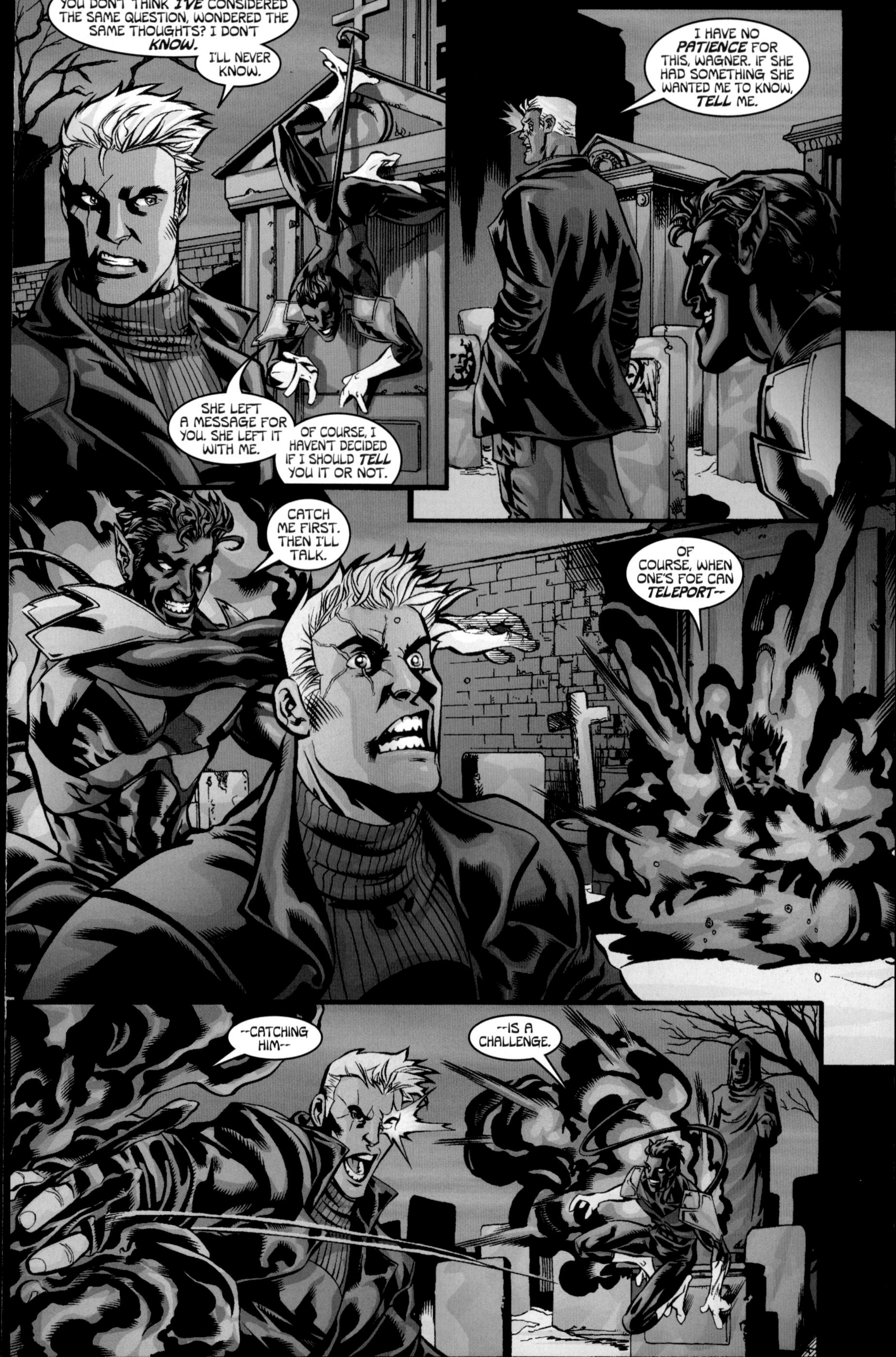
YOU DON'T THINK I'VE CONSIDERED THE SAME QUESTION, WONDERED THE SAME THOUGHTS? I DON'T KNOW.
I'LL NEVER KNOW.
SHE LEFT A MESSAGE FOR YOU. SHE LEFT IT WITH ME.
OF COURSE, I HAVEN'T DECIDED IF I SHOULD TELL YOU IT OR NOT.
I HAVE NO PATIENCE FOR THIS, WAGNER. IF SHE HAD SOMETHING SHE WANTED ME TO KNOW, TELL ME.
CATCH ME FIRST. THEN I'LL TALK.
OF COURSE, WHEN ONE'S FOE CAN TELEPORT--
--CATCHING HIM--
--IS A CHALLENGE.

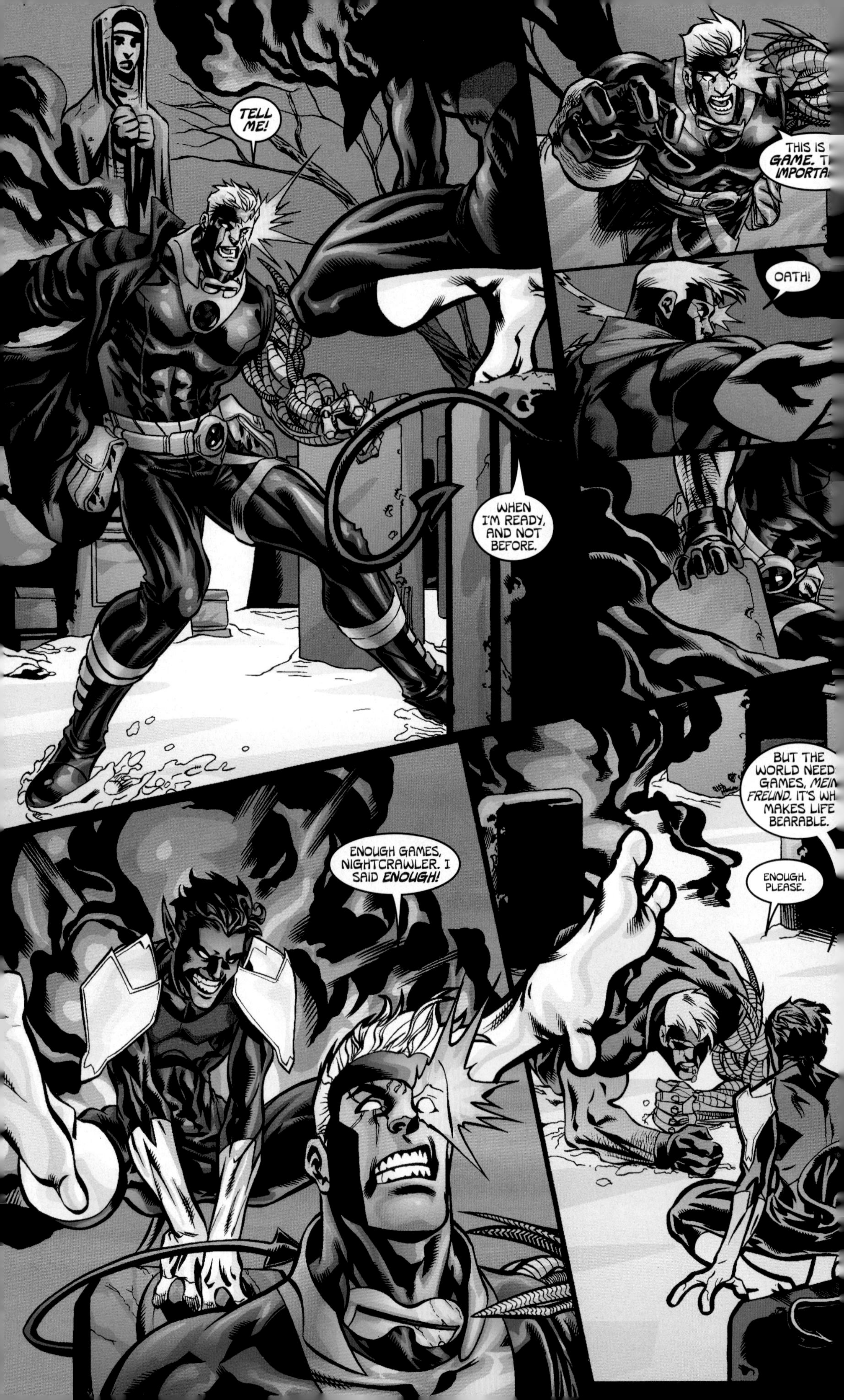
TELL ME!
WHEN I'M READY, AND NOT BEFORE.
THIS IS GAME. IMPORTA
OATH!
ENOUGH GAMES, NIGHTCRAWLER. I SAID *ENOUGH!*
BUT THE WORLD NEED GAMES, *MEIN FREUND.* IT'S WH MAKES LIFE BEARABLE.
ENOUGH. PLEASE.

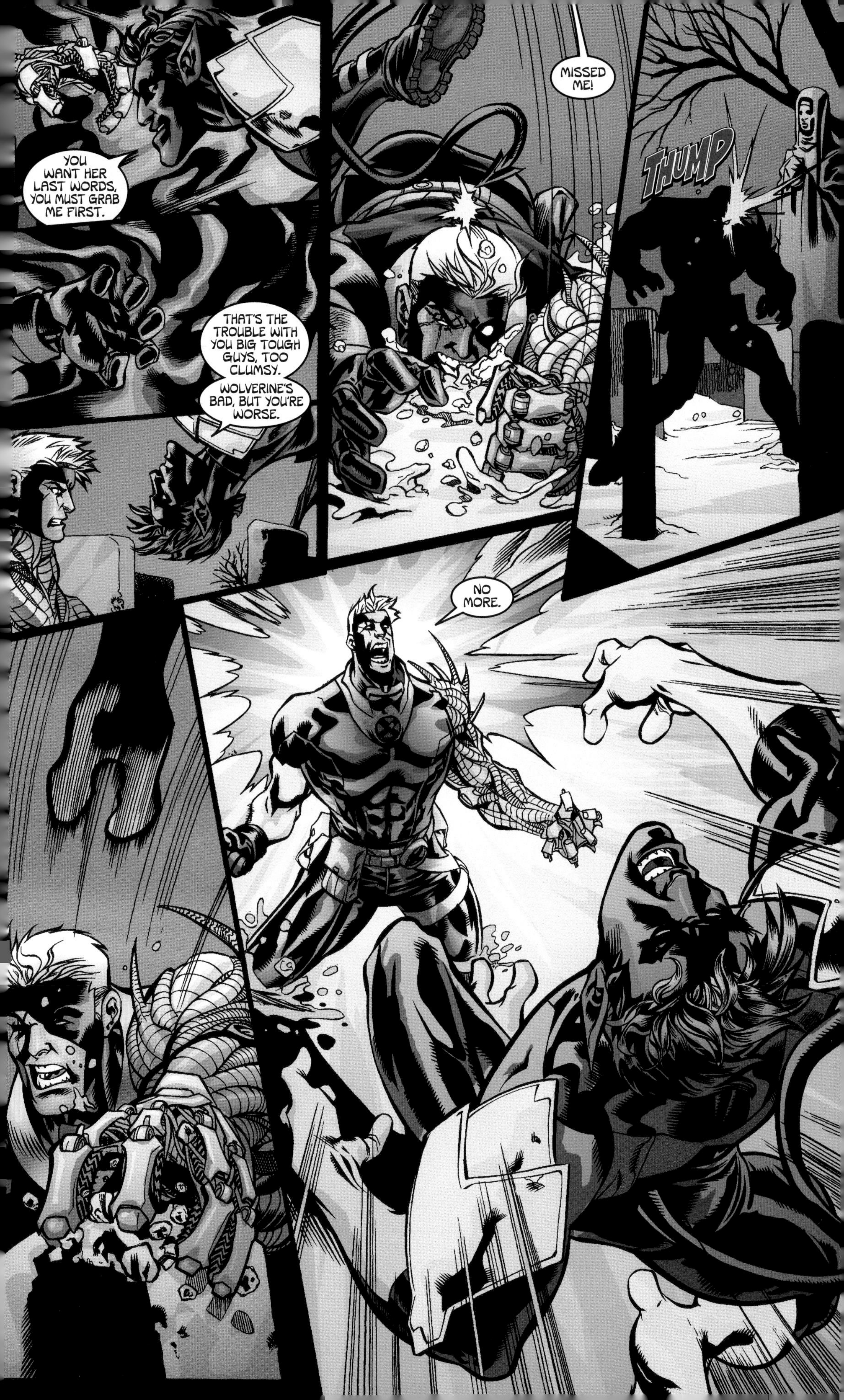
YOU WANT HER LAST WORDS, YOU MUST GRAB ME FIRST.
THAT'S THE TROUBLE WITH YOU BIG TOUGH GUYS, TOO CLUMSY.
WOLVERINE'S BAD, BUT YOU'RE WORSE.
MISSED ME!
THUMP
NO MORE.

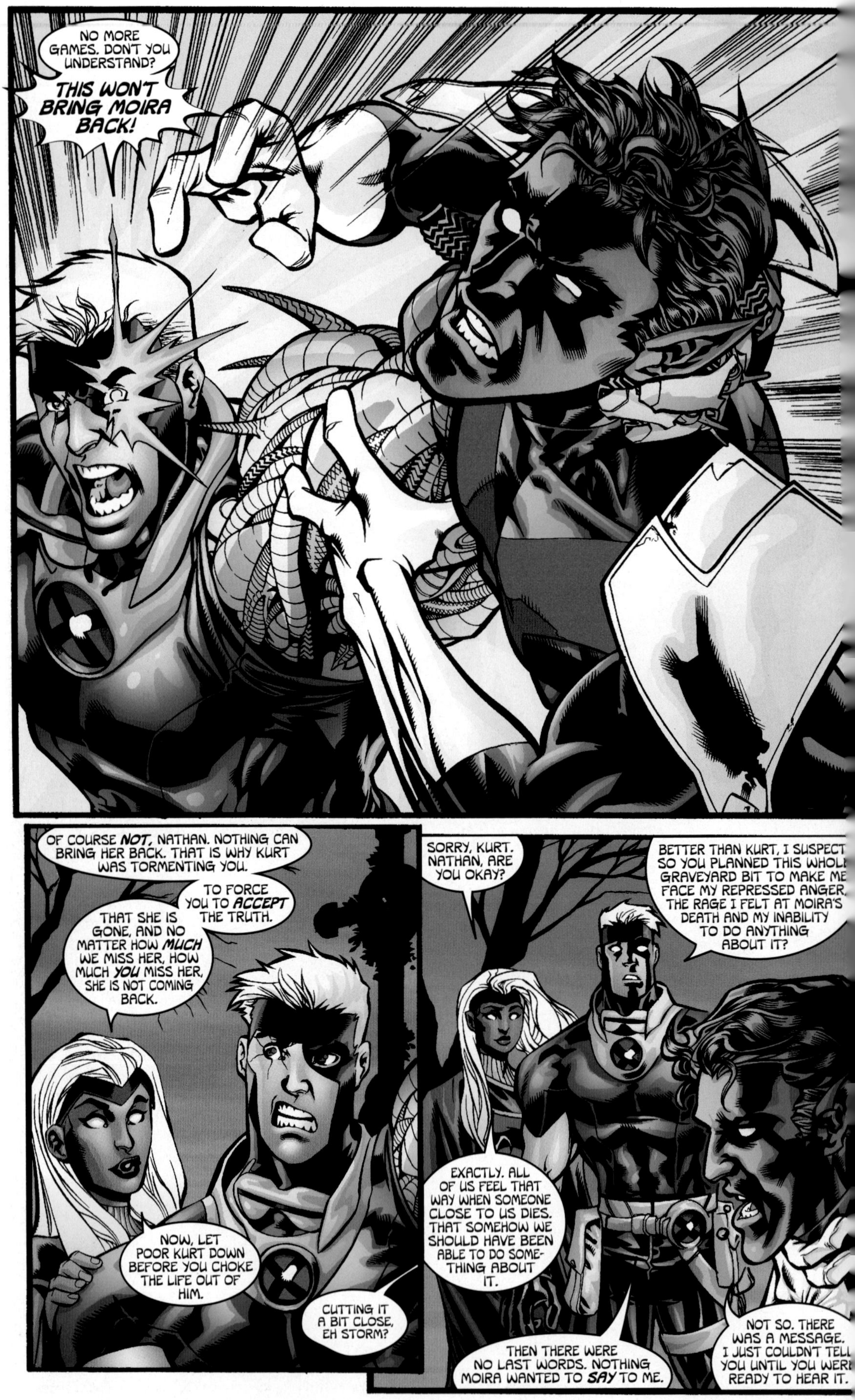

NO MORE GAMES. DON'T YOU UNDERSTAND?
THIS WON'T BRING MOIRA BACK!
OF COURSE NOT, NATHAN. NOTHING CAN BRING HER BACK. THAT IS WHY KURT WAS TORMENTING YOU.
TO FORCE YOU TO ACCEPT THE TRUTH.
THAT SHE IS GONE, AND NO MATTER HOW MUCH WE MISS HER, HOW MUCH YOU MISS HER, SHE IS NOT COMING BACK.
NOW, LET POOR KURT DOWN BEFORE YOU CHOKE THE LIFE OUT OF HIM.
CUTTING IT A BIT CLOSE, EH STORM?
SORRY, KURT. NATHAN, ARE YOU OKAY?
BETTER THAN KURT, I SUSPECT. SO YOU PLANNED THIS WHOLE GRAVEYARD BIT TO MAKE ME FACE MY REPRESSED ANGER, THE RAGE I FELT AT MOIRA'S DEATH AND MY INABILITY TO DO ANYTHING ABOUT IT?
EXACTLY. ALL OF US FEEL THAT WAY WHEN SOMEONE CLOSE TO US DIES. THAT SOMEHOW WE SHOULD HAVE BEEN ABLE TO DO SOMETHING ABOUT IT.
THEN THERE WERE NO LAST WORDS. NOTHING MOIRA WANTED TO SAY TO ME.
NOT SO. THERE WAS A MESSAGE. I JUST COULDN'T TELL YOU UNTIL YOU WERE READY TO HEAR IT.

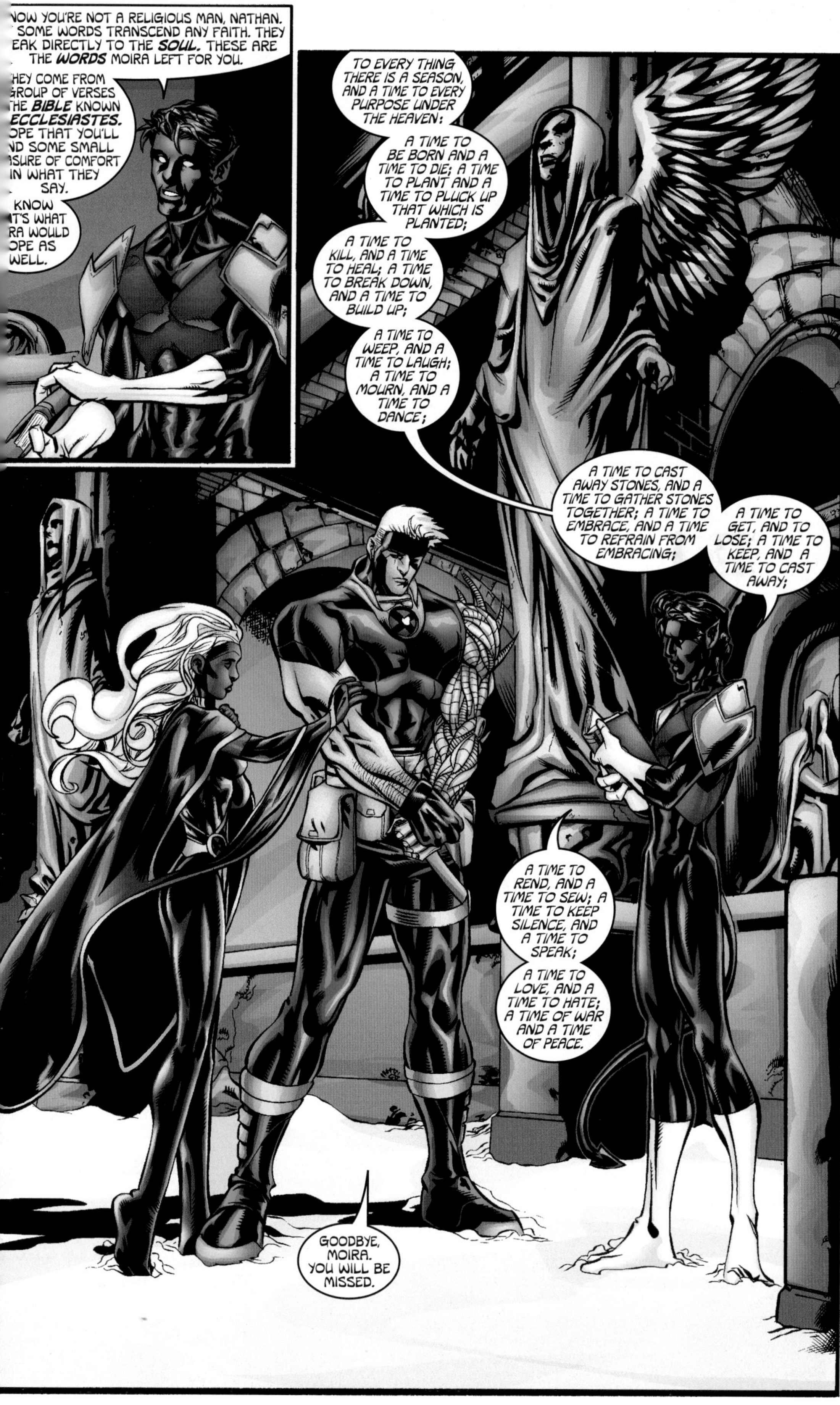

NOW YOU'RE NOT A RELIGIOUS MAN, NATHAN. SOME WORDS TRANSCEND ANY FAITH. THEY EAK DIRECTLY TO THE SOUL. THESE ARE THE WORDS MOIRA LEFT FOR YOU.
HEY COME FROM GROUP OF VERSES THE BIBLE KNOWN ECCLESIASTES. OPE THAT YOU'LL ND SOME SMALL ASURE OF COMFORT IN WHAT THEY SAY.
KNOW T'S WHAT RA WOULD OPE AS WELL.
TO EVERY THING THERE IS A SEASON, AND A TIME TO EVERY PURPOSE UNDER THE HEAVEN:
A TIME TO BE BORN AND A TIME TO DIE; A TIME TO PLANT AND A TIME TO PLUCK UP THAT WHICH IS PLANTED;
A TIME TO KILL, AND A TIME TO HEAL; A TIME TO BREAK DOWN, AND A TIME TO BUILD UP;
A TIME TO WEEP, AND A TIME TO LAUGH; A TIME TO MOURN, AND A TIME TO DANCE;
A TIME TO CAST AWAY STONES, AND A TIME TO GATHER STONES TOGETHER; A TIME TO EMBRACE, AND A TIME TO REFRAIN FROM EMBRACING;
A TIME TO GET, AND TO LOSE; A TIME TO KEEP, AND A TIME TO CAST AWAY;
A TIME TO REND, AND A TIME TO SEW; A TIME TO KEEP SILENCE, AND A TIME TO SPEAK;
A TIME TO LOVE, AND A TIME TO HATE; A TIME OF WAR AND A TIME OF PEACE.
GOODBYE, MOIRA. YOU WILL BE MISSED.

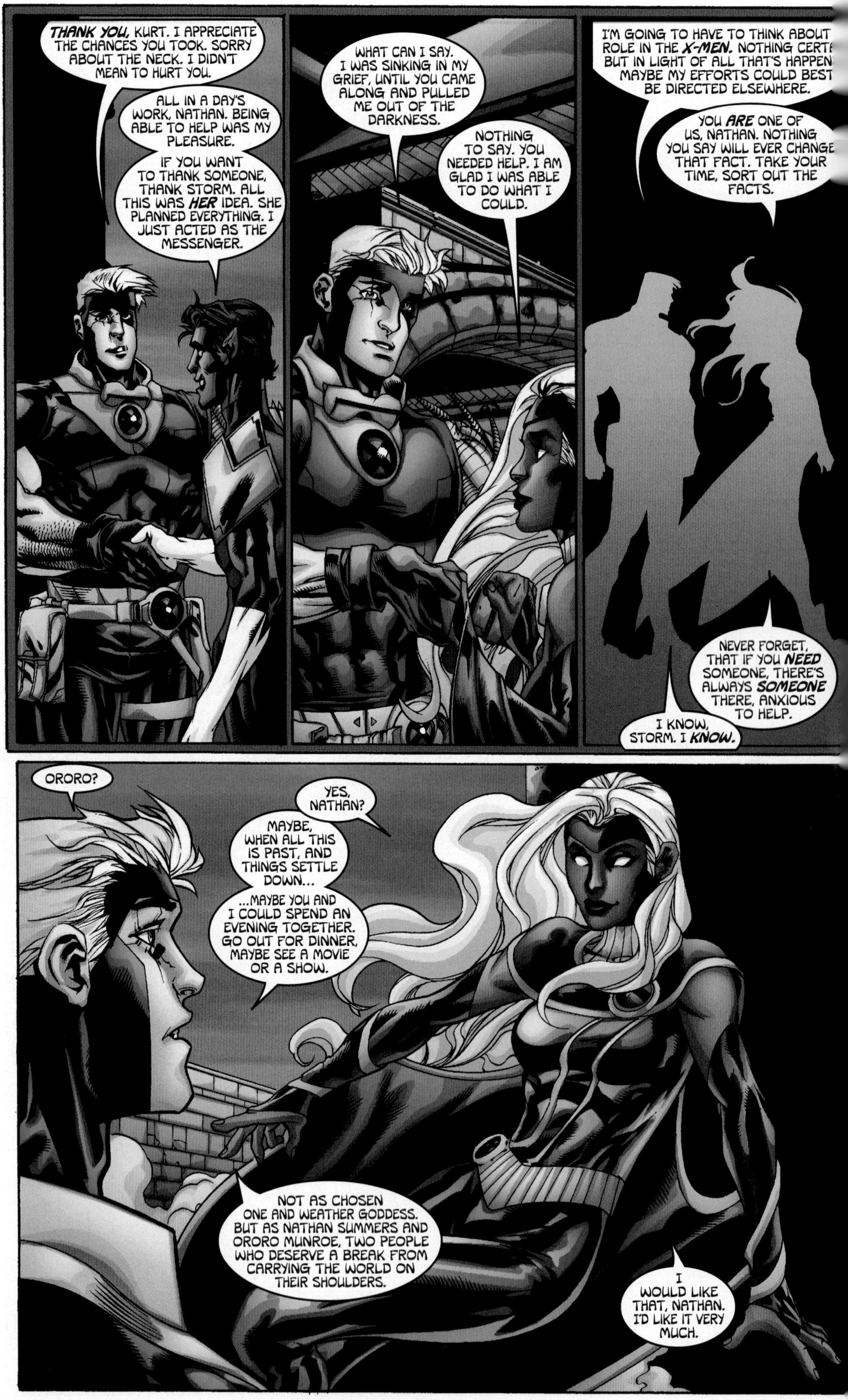
THANK YOU, KURT. I APPRECIATE THE CHANCES YOU TOOK. SORRY ABOUT THE NECK. I DIDN'T MEAN TO HURT YOU.
ALL IN A DAY'S WORK, NATHAN. BEING ABLE TO HELP WAS MY PLEASURE.
IF YOU WANT TO THANK SOMEONE, THANK STORM. ALL THIS WAS HER IDEA. SHE PLANNED EVERYTHING. I JUST ACTED AS THE MESSENGER.
WHAT CAN I SAY. I WAS SINKING IN MY GRIEF, UNTIL YOU CAME ALONG AND PULLED ME OUT OF THE DARKNESS.
NOTHING TO SAY. YOU NEEDED HELP. I AM GLAD I WAS ABLE TO DO WHAT I COULD.
I'M GOING TO HAVE TO THINK ABOUT ROLE IN THE X-MEN. NOTHING CERT BUT IN LIGHT OF ALL THAT'S HAPPEN MAYBE MY EFFORTS COULD BEST BE DIRECTED ELSEWHERE.
YOU ARE ONE OF US, NATHAN. NOTHING YOU SAY WILL EVER CHANGE THAT FACT. TAKE YOUR TIME, SORT OUT THE FACTS.
NEVER FORGET, THAT IF YOU NEED SOMEONE, THERE'S ALWAYS SOMEONE THERE, ANXIOUS TO HELP.
I KNOW, STORM. I KNOW.
ORORO?
YES, NATHAN?
MAYBE, WHEN ALL THIS IS PAST, AND THINGS SETTLE DOWN...
...MAYBE YOU AND I COULD SPEND AN EVENING TOGETHER. GO OUT FOR DINNER, MAYBE SEE A MOVIE OR A SHOW.
NOT AS CHOSEN ONE AND WEATHER GODDESS. BUT AS NATHAN SUMMERS AND ORORO MUNROE, TWO PEOPLE WHO DESERVE A BREAK FROM CARRYING THE WORLD ON THEIR SHOULDERS.
I WOULD LIKE THAT, NATHAN. I'D LIKE IT VERY MUCH.

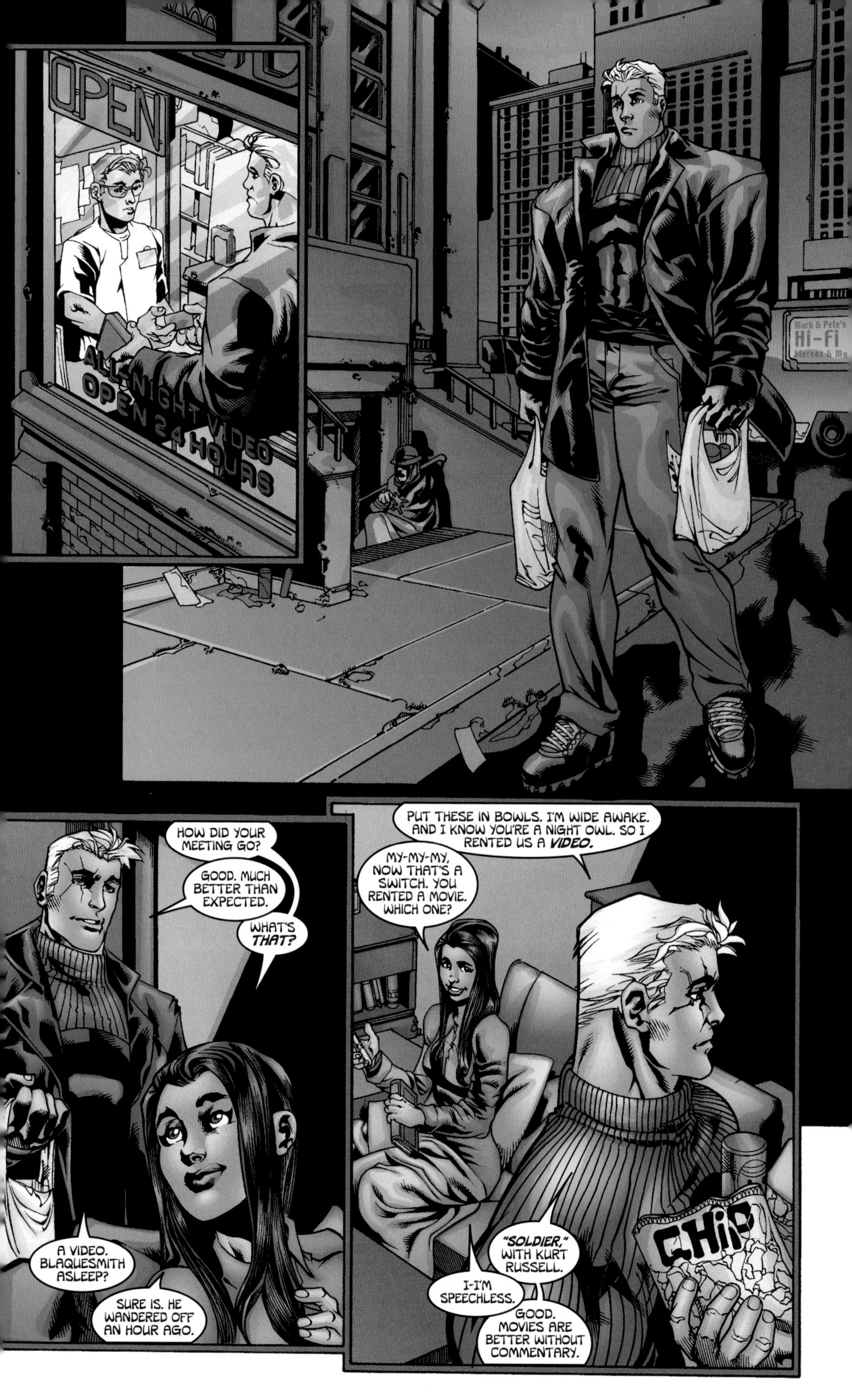
OPEN
ALL-NIGHT VIDEO
OPEN 24 HOURS
Mark & Pete's
Hi-Fi
HOW DID YOUR MEETING GO?
GOOD. MUCH BETTER THAN EXPECTED.
WHAT'S *THAT?*
A VIDEO. BLAQUESMITH ASLEEP?
SURE IS. HE WANDERED OFF AN HOUR AGO.
PUT THESE IN BOWLS. I'M WIDE AWAKE. AND I KNOW YOU'RE A NIGHT OWL. SO I RENTED US A *VIDEO.*
MY-MY-MY, NOW THAT'S A SWITCH. YOU RENTED A MOVIE. WHICH ONE?
"SOLDIER," WITH KURT RUSSELL.
I-I'M SPEECHLESS.
GOOD. MOVIES ARE BETTER WITHOUT COMMENTARY.
CHIP

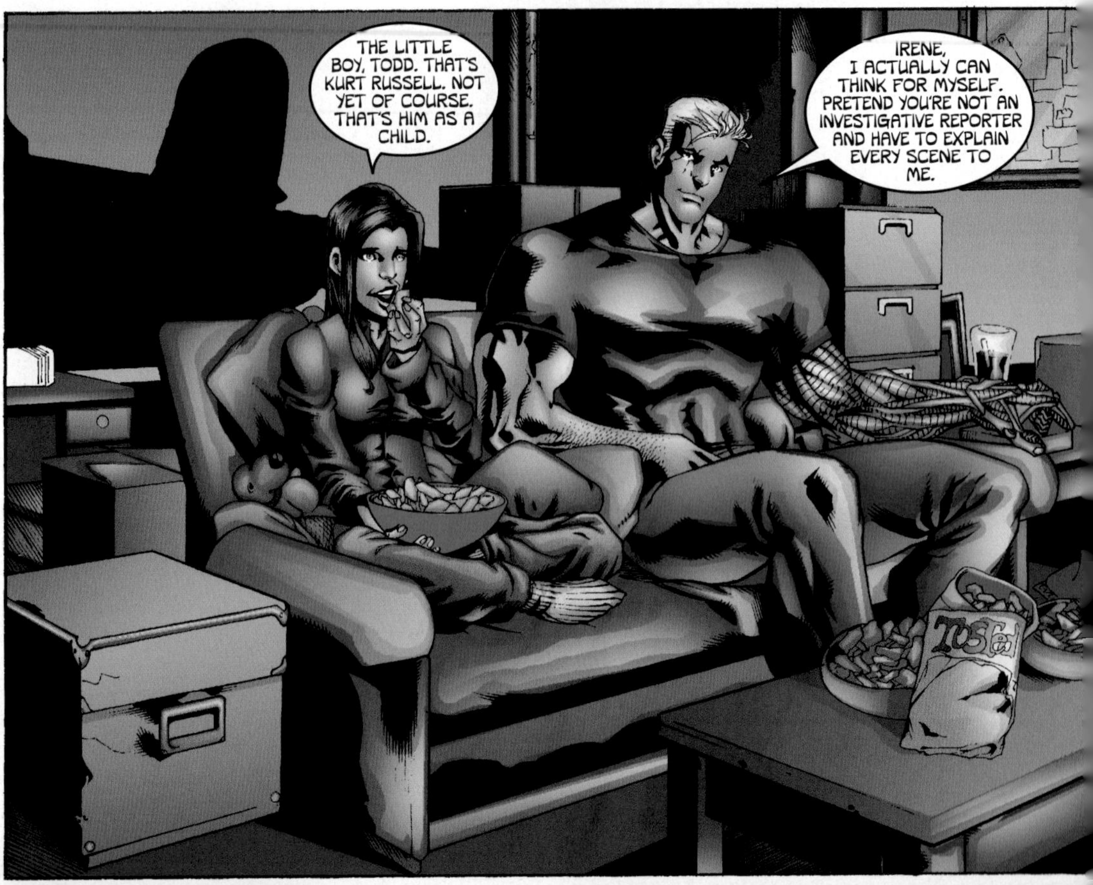
THE LITTLE BOY, TODD. THAT'S KURT RUSSELL. NOT YET OF COURSE. THAT'S HIM AS A CHILD.
IRENE, I ACTUALLY CAN THINK FOR MYSELF. PRETEND YOU'RE NOT AN INVESTIGATIVE REPORTER AND HAVE TO EXPLAIN EVERY SCENE TO ME.

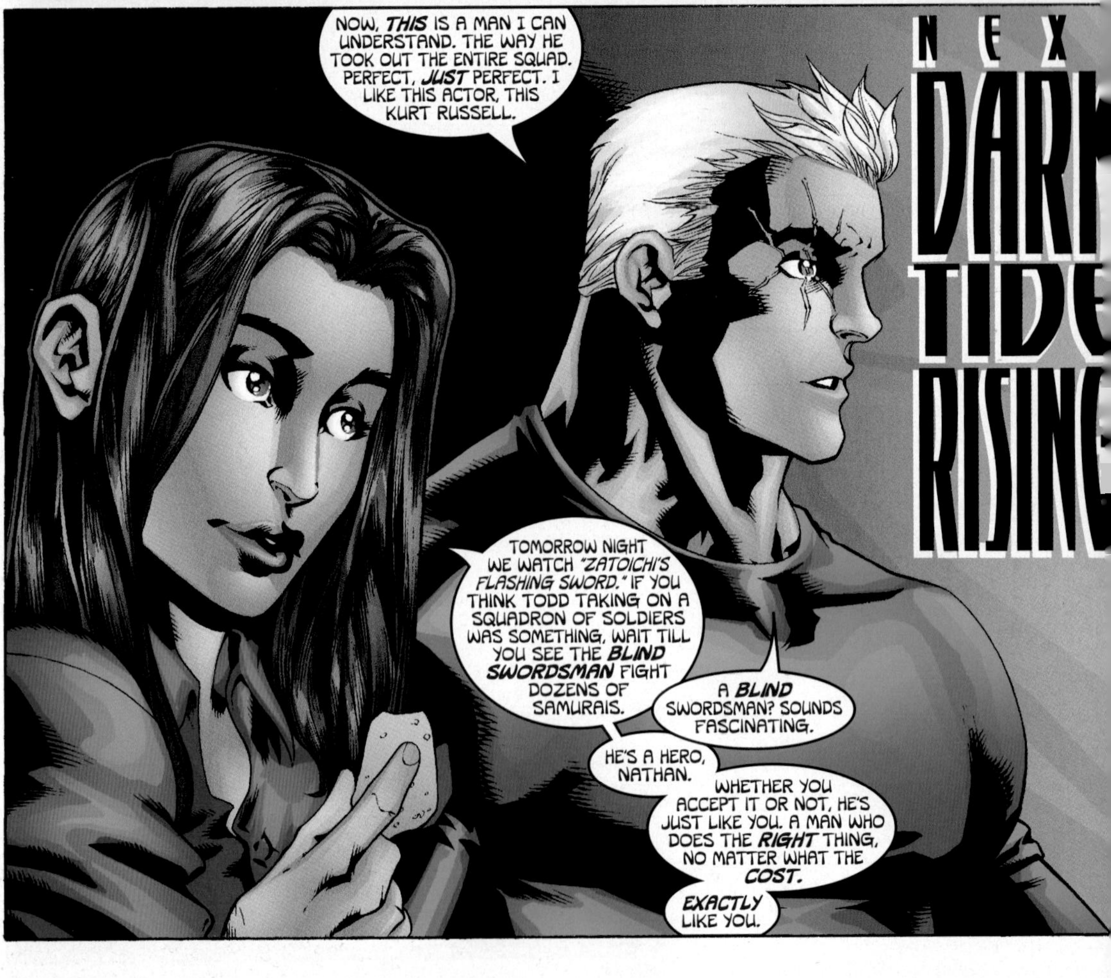
NOW, THIS IS A MAN I CAN UNDERSTAND. THE WAY HE TOOK OUT THE ENTIRE SQUAD. PERFECT, JUST PERFECT. I LIKE THIS ACTOR, THIS KURT RUSSELL.
TOMORROW NIGHT WE WATCH "ZATOICHI'S FLASHING SWORD." IF YOU THINK TODD TAKING ON A SQUADRON OF SOLDIERS WAS SOMETHING, WAIT TILL YOU SEE THE BLIND SWORDSMAN FIGHT DOZENS OF SAMURAIS.
A BLIND SWORDSMAN? SOUNDS FASCINATING.
HE'S A HERO, NATHAN.
WHETHER YOU ACCEPT IT OR NOT, HE'S JUST LIKE YOU. A MAN WHO DOES THE RIGHT THING, NO MATTER WHAT THE COST.
EXACTLY LIKE YOU.

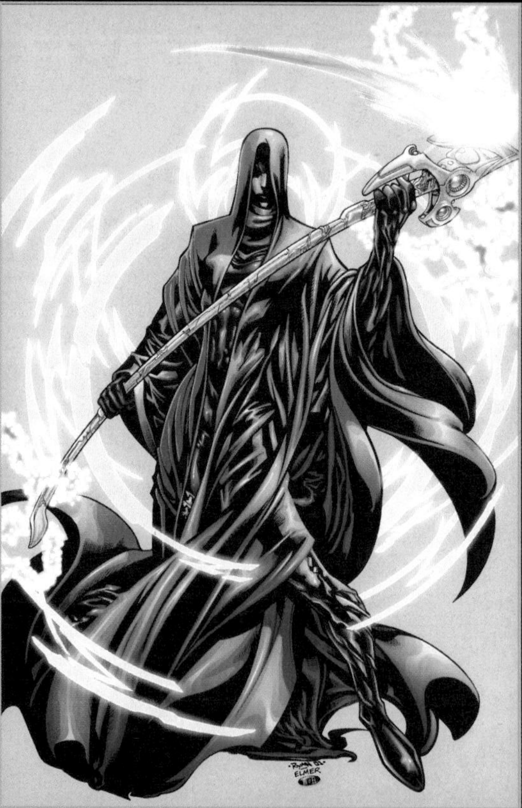
ELMER

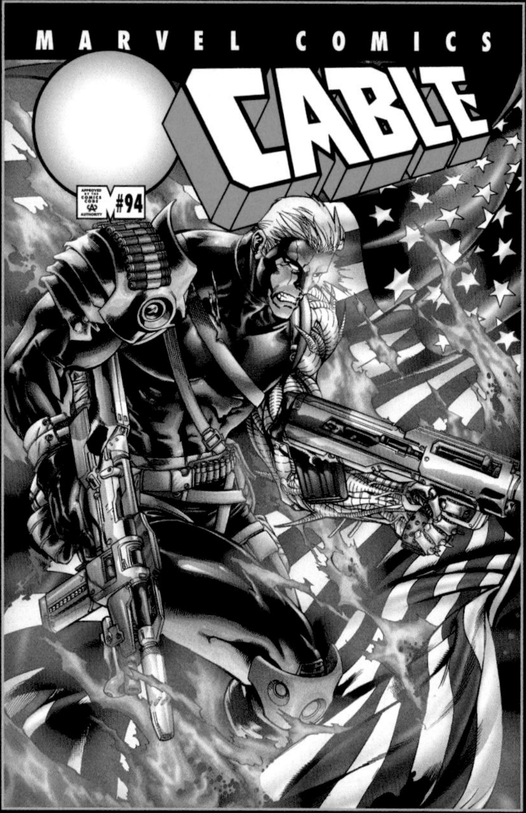
MARVEL COMICS
CABLE
#94

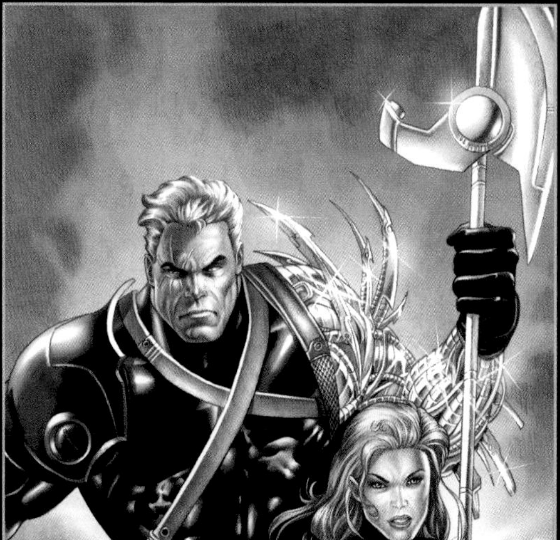
2001
Transparency

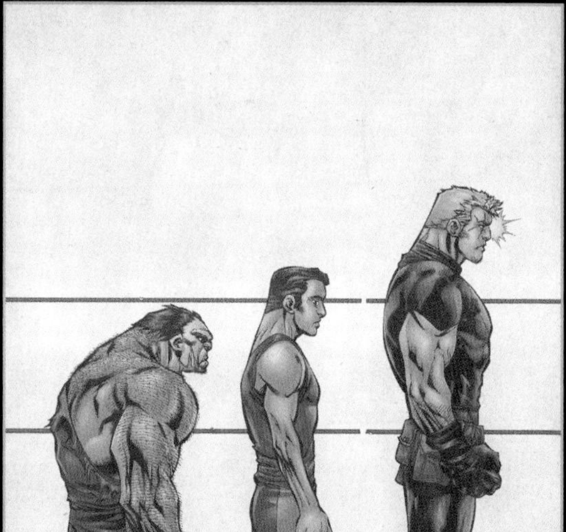

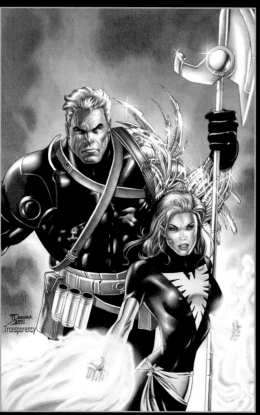

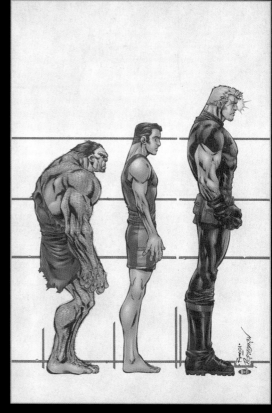

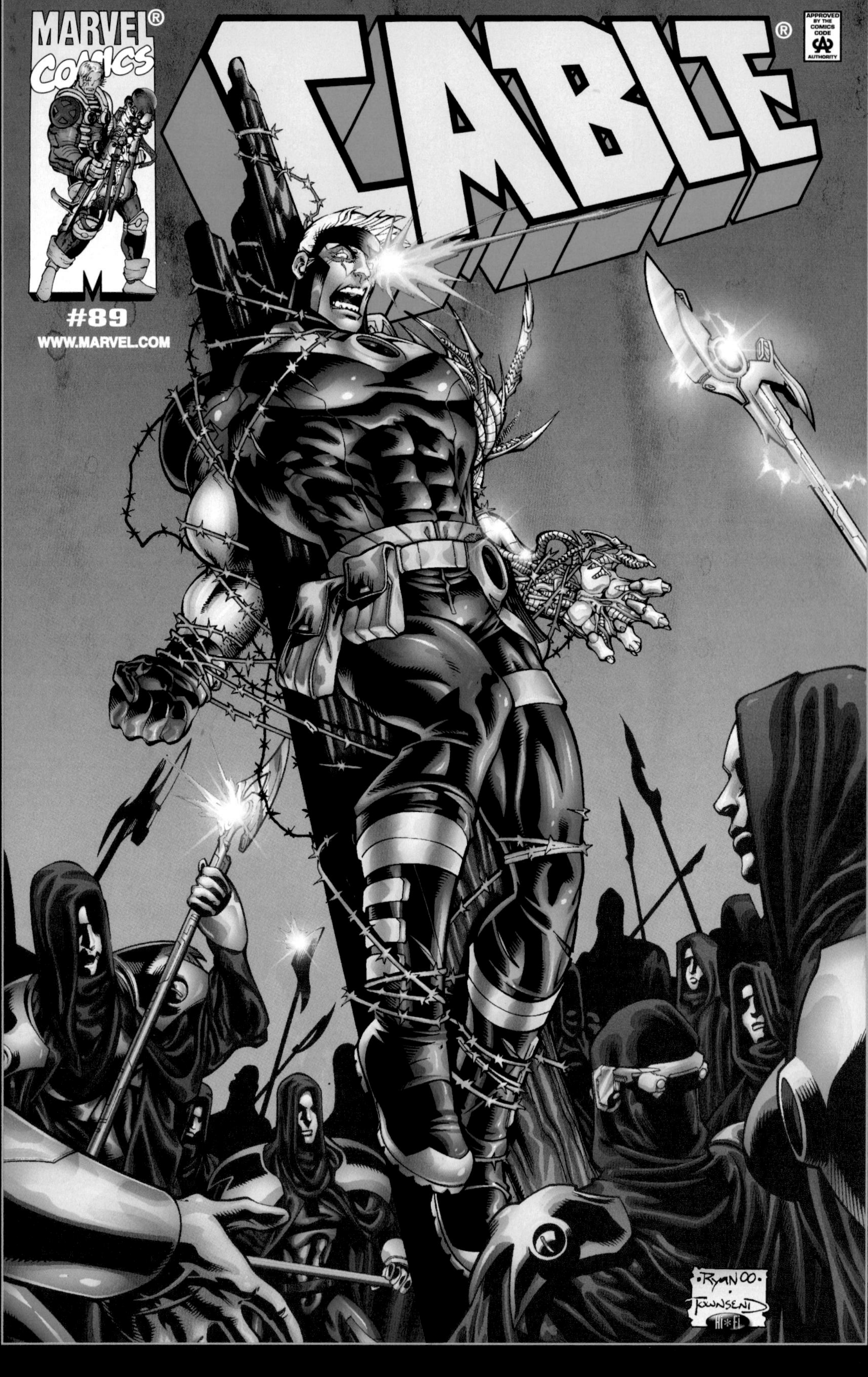
MARVEL® COMICS
CABLE®
#89
WWW.MARVEL.COM
APPROVED BY THE COMICS CODE AUTHORITY
RYAN 00
TOWNSEND

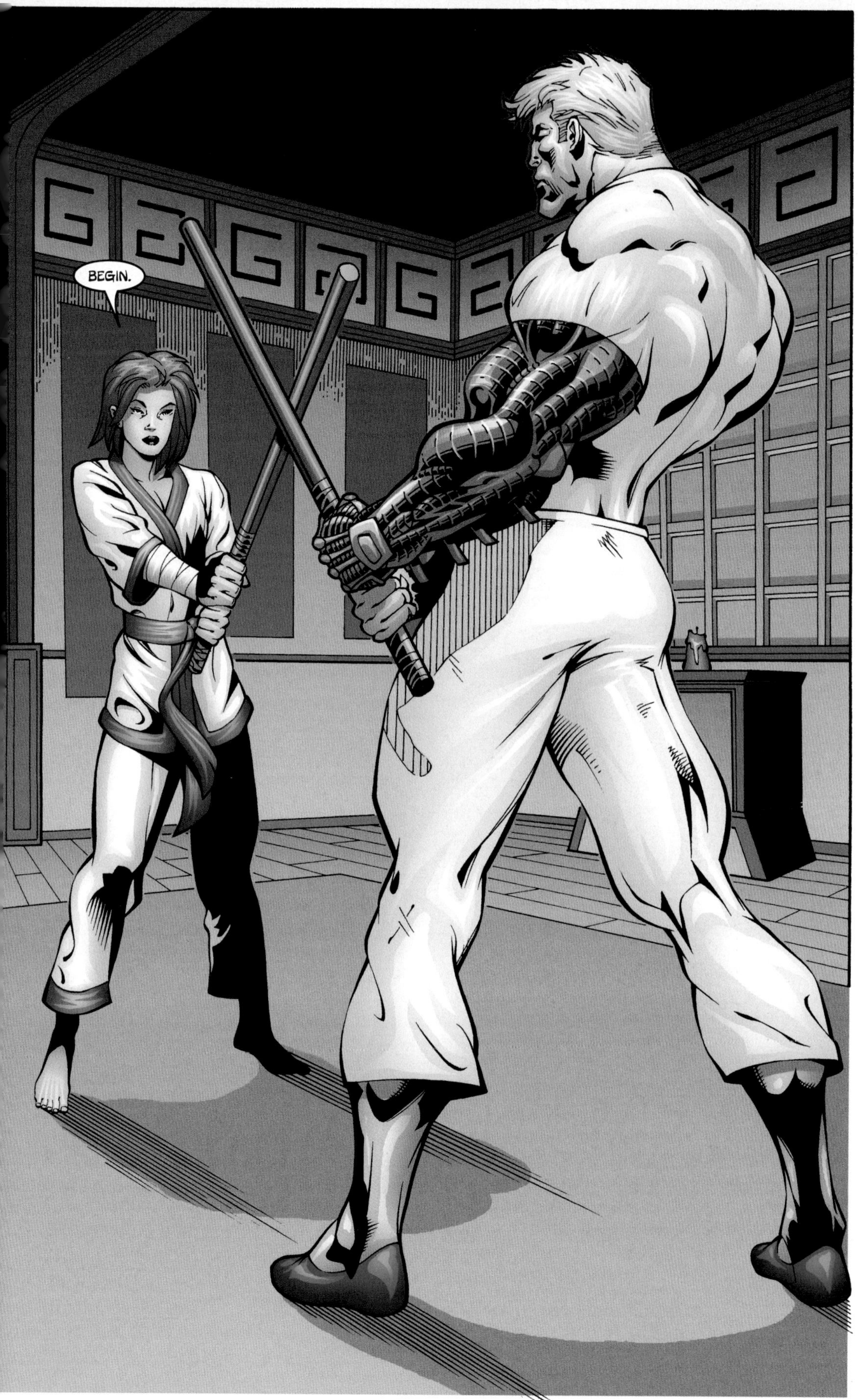
BEGIN.

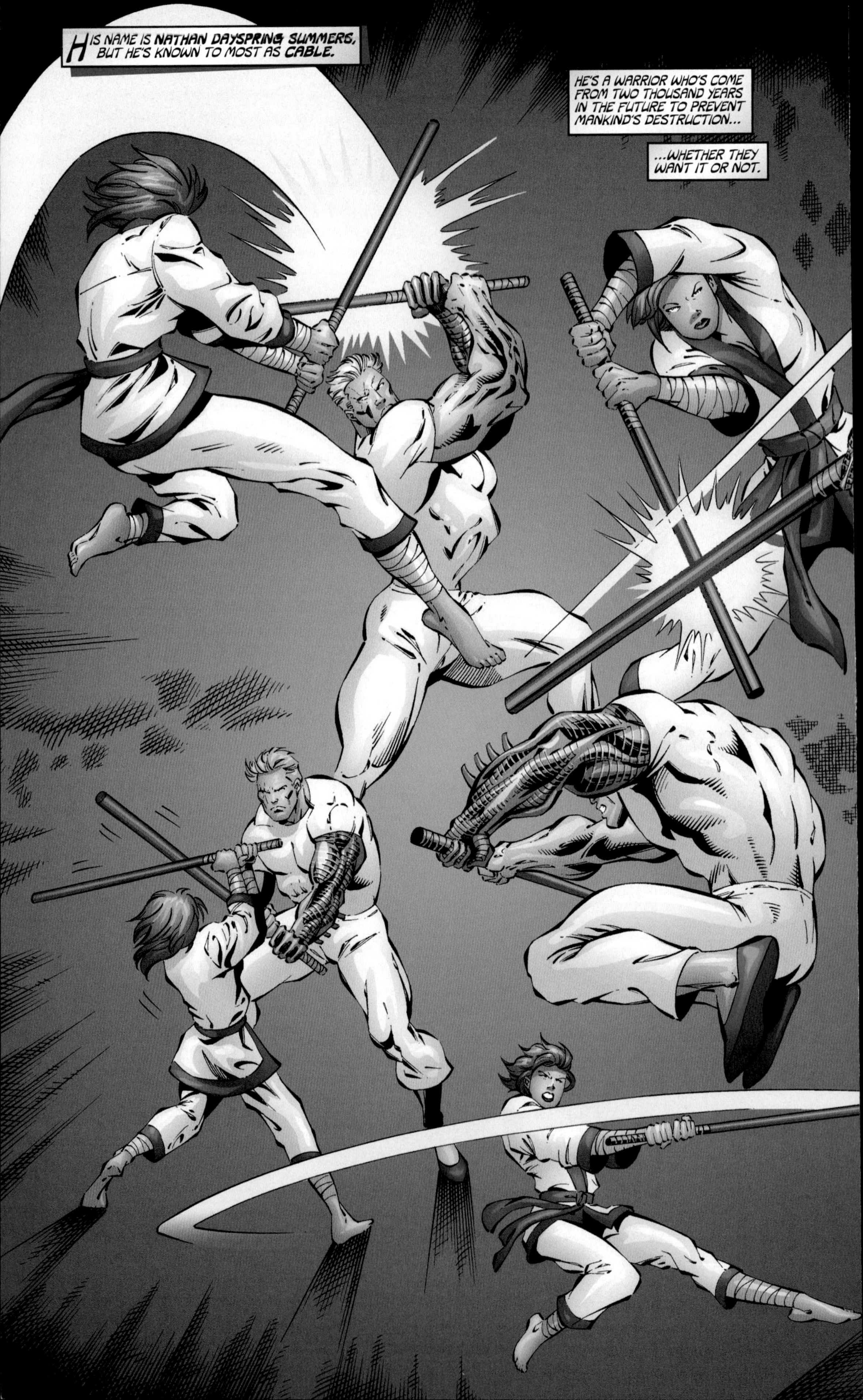
HIS NAME IS NATHAN DAYSPRING SUMMERS, BUT HE'S KNOWN TO MOST AS CABLE.
HE'S A WARRIOR WHO'S COME FROM TWO THOUSAND YEARS IN THE FUTURE TO PREVENT MANKIND'S DESTRUCTION...
...WHETHER THEY WANT IT OR NOT.

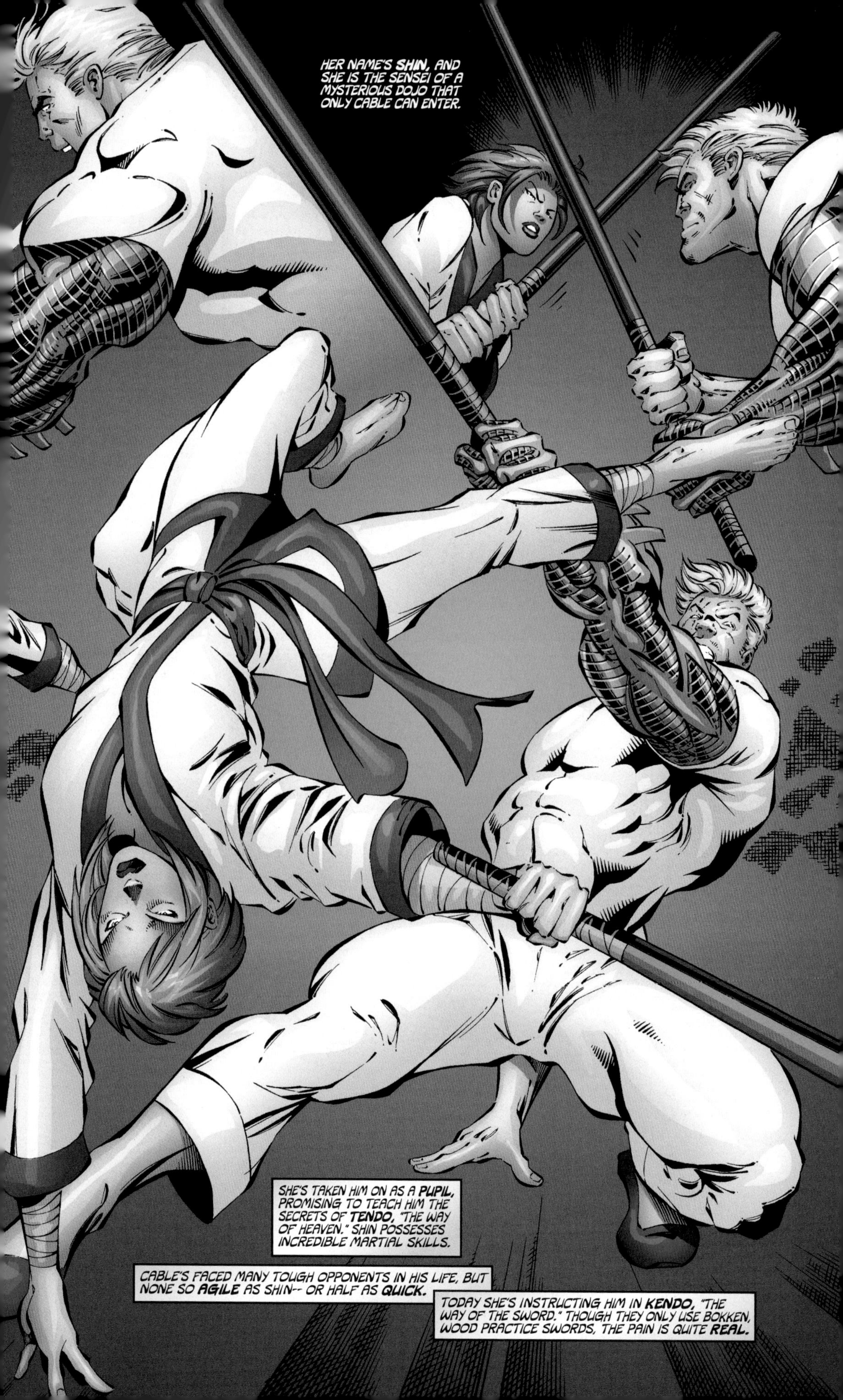
HER NAME'S SHIN, AND SHE IS THE SENSEI OF A MYSTERIOUS DOJO THAT ONLY CABLE CAN ENTER.
SHE'S TAKEN HIM ON AS A PUPIL, PROMISING TO TEACH HIM THE SECRETS OF TENDO, "THE WAY OF HEAVEN." SHIN POSSESSES INCREDIBLE MARTIAL SKILLS.
CABLE'S FACED MANY TOUGH OPPONENTS IN HIS LIFE, BUT NONE SO AGILE AS SHIN-- OR HALF AS QUICK.
TODAY SHE'S INSTRUCTING HIM IN KENDO, "THE WAY OF THE SWORD." THOUGH THEY ONLY USE BOKKEN, WOOD PRACTICE SWORDS, THE PAIN IS QUITE REAL.

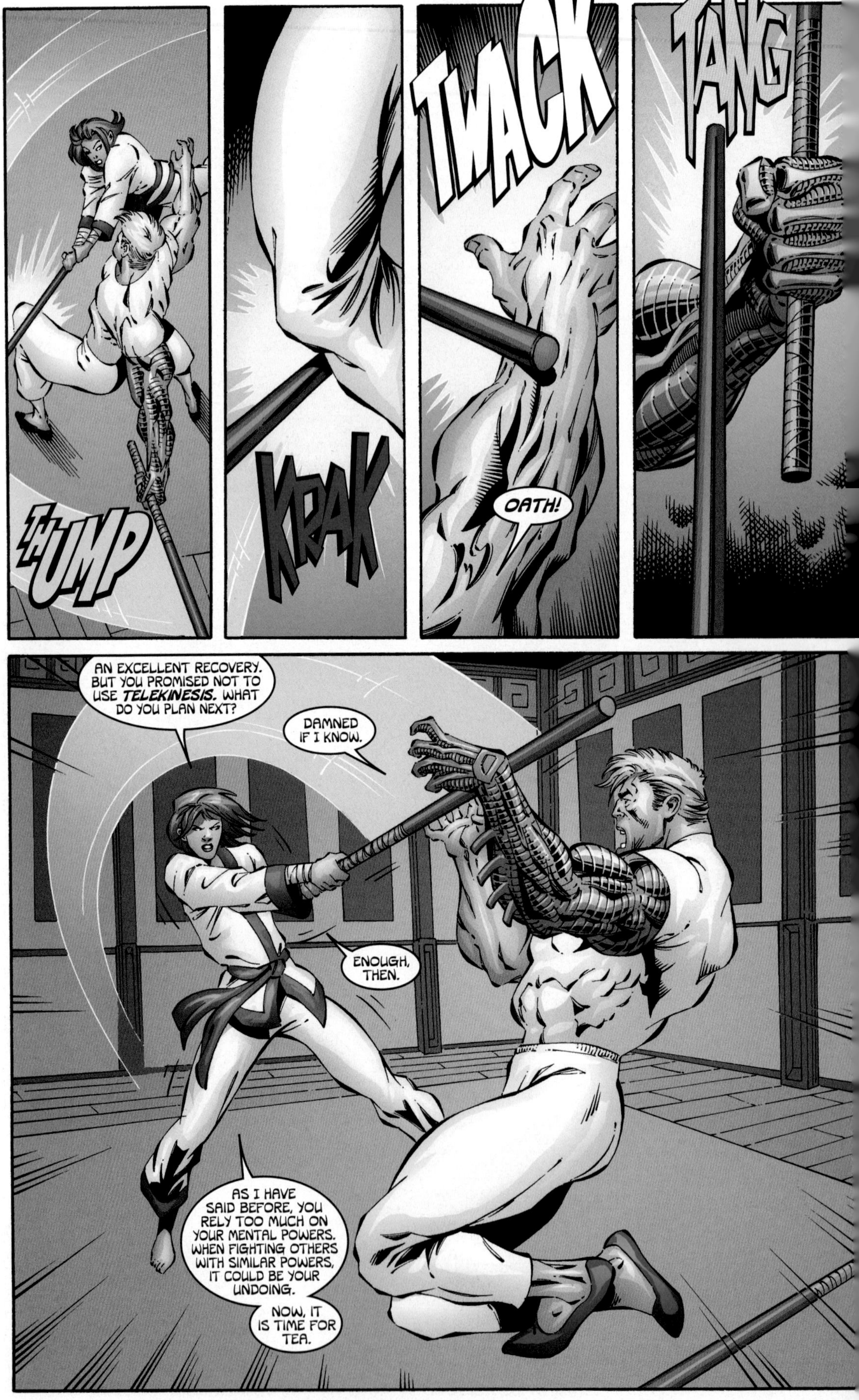
THUMP
KRAK
TWACK
OATH!
TANG
AN EXCELLENT RECOVERY. BUT YOU PROMISED NOT TO USE TELEKINESIS. WHAT DO YOU PLAN NEXT?
DAMNED IF I KNOW.
ENOUGH, THEN.
AS I HAVE SAID BEFORE, YOU RELY TOO MUCH ON YOUR MENTAL POWERS. WHEN FIGHTING OTHERS WITH SIMILAR POWERS, IT COULD BE YOUR UNDOING.
NOW, IT IS TIME FOR TEA.

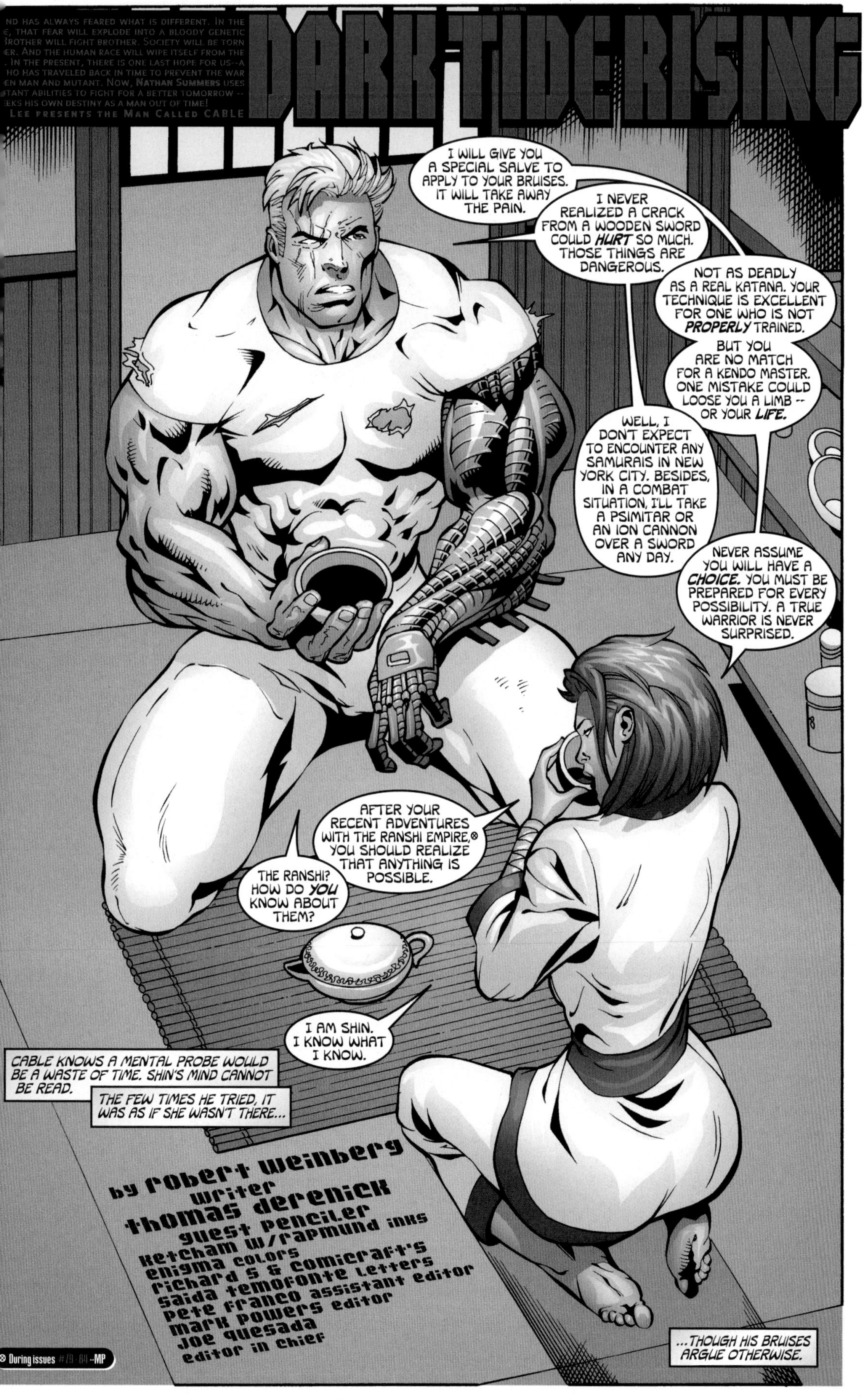

ND HAS ALWAYS FEARED WHAT IS DIFFERENT. IN THE
, THAT FEAR WILL EXPLODE INTO A BLOODY GENETIC
ROTHER WILL FIGHT BROTHER. SOCIETY WILL BE TORN
ER. AND THE HUMAN RACE WILL WIPE ITSELF FROM THE
. IN THE PRESENT, THERE IS ONE LAST HOPE FOR US--A
HO HAS TRAVELED BACK IN TIME TO PREVENT THE WAR
EN MAN AND MUTANT. NOW, NATHAN SUMMERS USES
TANT ABILITIES TO FIGHT FOR A BETTER TOMORROW --
EKS HIS OWN DESTINY AS A MAN OUT OF TIME!
LEE PRESENTS THE MAN CALLED CABLE
DARK TIDE RISING
I WILL GIVE YOU A SPECIAL SALVE TO APPLY TO YOUR BRUISES. IT WILL TAKE AWAY THE PAIN.
I NEVER REALIZED A CRACK FROM A WOODEN SWORD COULD HURT SO MUCH. THOSE THINGS ARE DANGEROUS.
NOT AS DEADLY AS A REAL KATANA. YOUR TECHNIQUE IS EXCELLENT FOR ONE WHO IS NOT PROPERLY TRAINED.
BUT YOU ARE NO MATCH FOR A KENDO MASTER. ONE MISTAKE COULD LOOSE YOU A LIMB -- OR YOUR LIFE.
WELL, I DON'T EXPECT TO ENCOUNTER ANY SAMURAIS IN NEW YORK CITY. BESIDES, IN A COMBAT SITUATION, I'LL TAKE A PSIMITAR OR AN ION CANNON OVER A SWORD ANY DAY.
NEVER ASSUME YOU WILL HAVE A CHOICE. YOU MUST BE PREPARED FOR EVERY POSSIBILITY. A TRUE WARRIOR IS NEVER SURPRISED.
AFTER YOUR RECENT ADVENTURES WITH THE RANSHI EMPIRE,⊗ YOU SHOULD REALIZE THAT ANYTHING IS POSSIBLE.
THE RANSHI? HOW DO YOU KNOW ABOUT THEM?
I AM SHIN. I KNOW WHAT I KNOW.
CABLE KNOWS A MENTAL PROBE WOULD BE A WASTE OF TIME. SHIN'S MIND CANNOT BE READ.
THE FEW TIMES HE TRIED, IT WAS AS IF SHE WASN'T THERE...
...THOUGH HIS BRUISES ARGUE OTHERWISE.
by robert weinberg writer
thomas derenick guest penciler
rapmund inks
ketcham w/rapmund inks
enigma colors
richard s & comicraft's letters
saida temofonte assistant editor
pete franco assistant editor
mark powers editor
joe quesada editor in chief
⊗ During issues #79-84 --MP

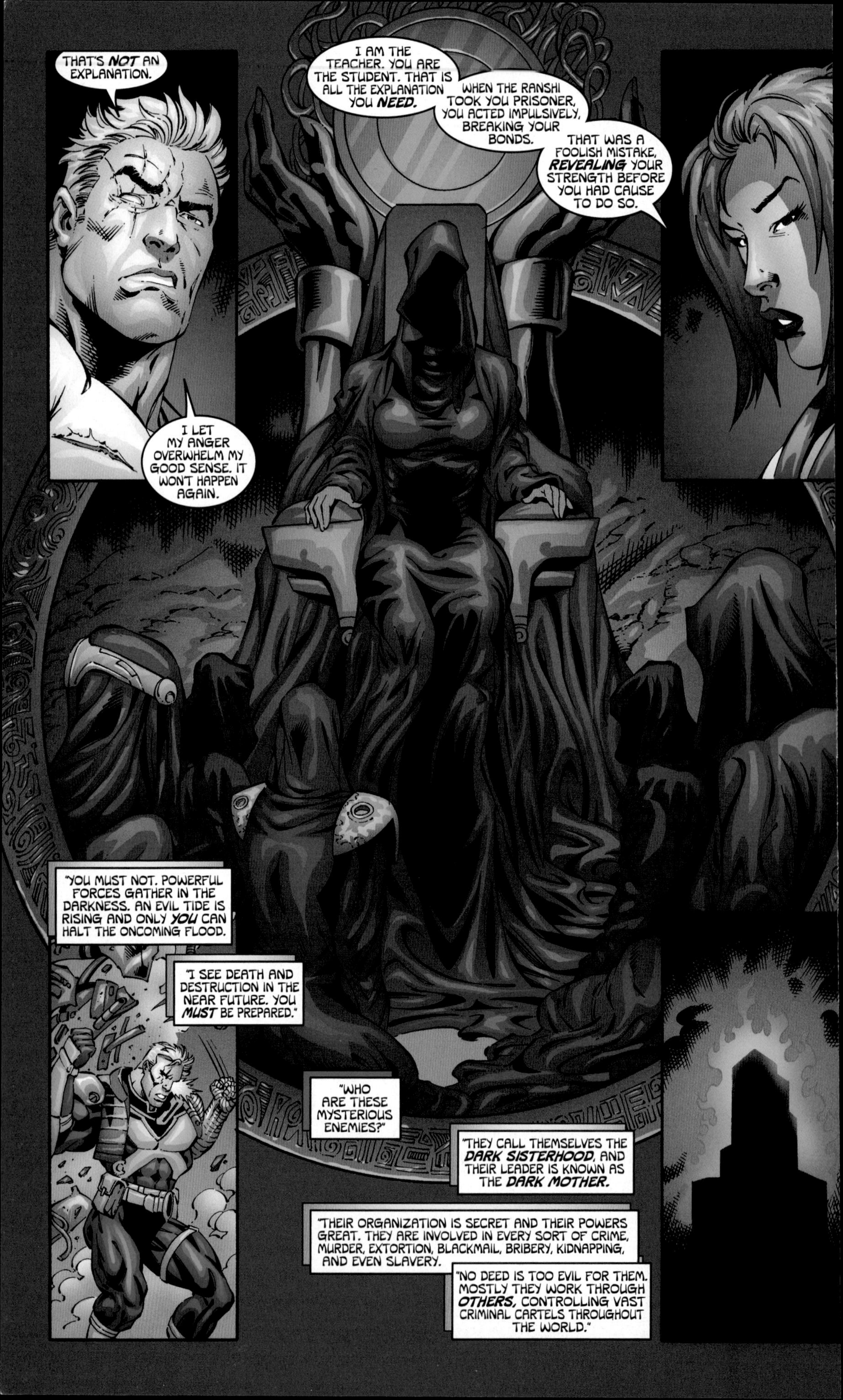

THAT'S NOT AN EXPLANATION.
I AM THE TEACHER. YOU ARE THE STUDENT. THAT IS ALL THE EXPLANATION YOU NEED.
WHEN THE RANSHI TOOK YOU PRISONER, YOU ACTED IMPULSIVELY, BREAKING YOUR BONDS.
THAT WAS A FOOLISH MISTAKE, REVEALING YOUR STRENGTH BEFORE YOU HAD CAUSE TO DO SO.
I LET MY ANGER OVERWHELM MY GOOD SENSE. IT WON'T HAPPEN AGAIN.
"YOU MUST NOT. POWERFUL FORCES GATHER IN THE DARKNESS. AN EVIL TIDE IS RISING AND ONLY YOU CAN HALT THE ONCOMING FLOOD.
"I SEE DEATH AND DESTRUCTION IN THE NEAR FUTURE. YOU MUST BE PREPARED."
"WHO ARE THESE MYSTERIOUS ENEMIES?"
"THEY CALL THEMSELVES THE DARK SISTERHOOD, AND THEIR LEADER IS KNOWN AS THE DARK MOTHER.
"THEIR ORGANIZATION IS SECRET AND THEIR POWERS GREAT. THEY ARE INVOLVED IN EVERY SORT OF CRIME, MURDER, EXTORTION, BLACKMAIL, BRIBERY, KIDNAPPING, AND EVEN SLAVERY.
"NO DEED IS TOO EVIL FOR THEM. MOSTLY THEY WORK THROUGH OTHERS, CONTROLLING VAST CRIMINAL CARTELS THROUGHOUT THE WORLD."

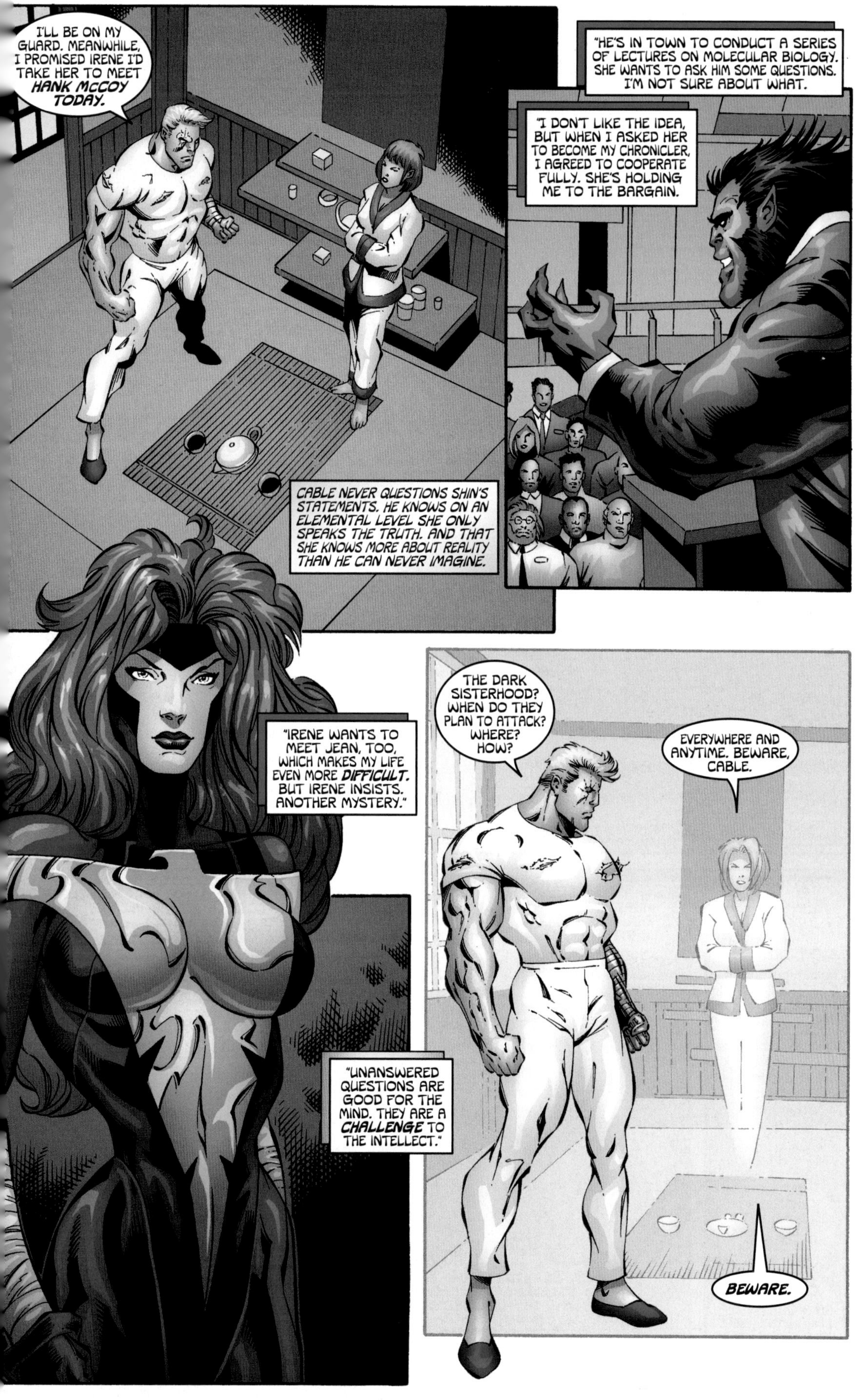
I'LL BE ON MY GUARD. MEANWHILE, I PROMISED IRENE I'D TAKE HER TO MEET HANK McCOY TODAY.
"HE'S IN TOWN TO CONDUCT A SERIES OF LECTURES ON MOLECULAR BIOLOGY. SHE WANTS TO ASK HIM SOME QUESTIONS. I'M NOT SURE ABOUT WHAT.
"I DON'T LIKE THE IDEA, BUT WHEN I ASKED HER TO BECOME MY CHRONICLER, I AGREED TO COOPERATE FULLY. SHE'S HOLDING ME TO THE BARGAIN.
CABLE NEVER QUESTIONS SHIN'S STATEMENTS. HE KNOWS ON AN ELEMENTAL LEVEL SHE ONLY SPEAKS THE TRUTH. AND THAT SHE KNOWS MORE ABOUT REALITY THAN HE CAN NEVER IMAGINE.
"IRENE WANTS TO MEET JEAN, TOO, WHICH MAKES MY LIFE EVEN MORE DIFFICULT. BUT IRENE INSISTS. ANOTHER MYSTERY."
"UNANSWERED QUESTIONS ARE GOOD FOR THE MIND. THEY ARE A CHALLENGE TO THE INTELLECT."
THE DARK SISTERHOOD? WHEN DO THEY PLAN TO ATTACK? WHERE? HOW?
EVERYWHERE AND ANYTIME. BEWARE, CABLE.
BEWARE.

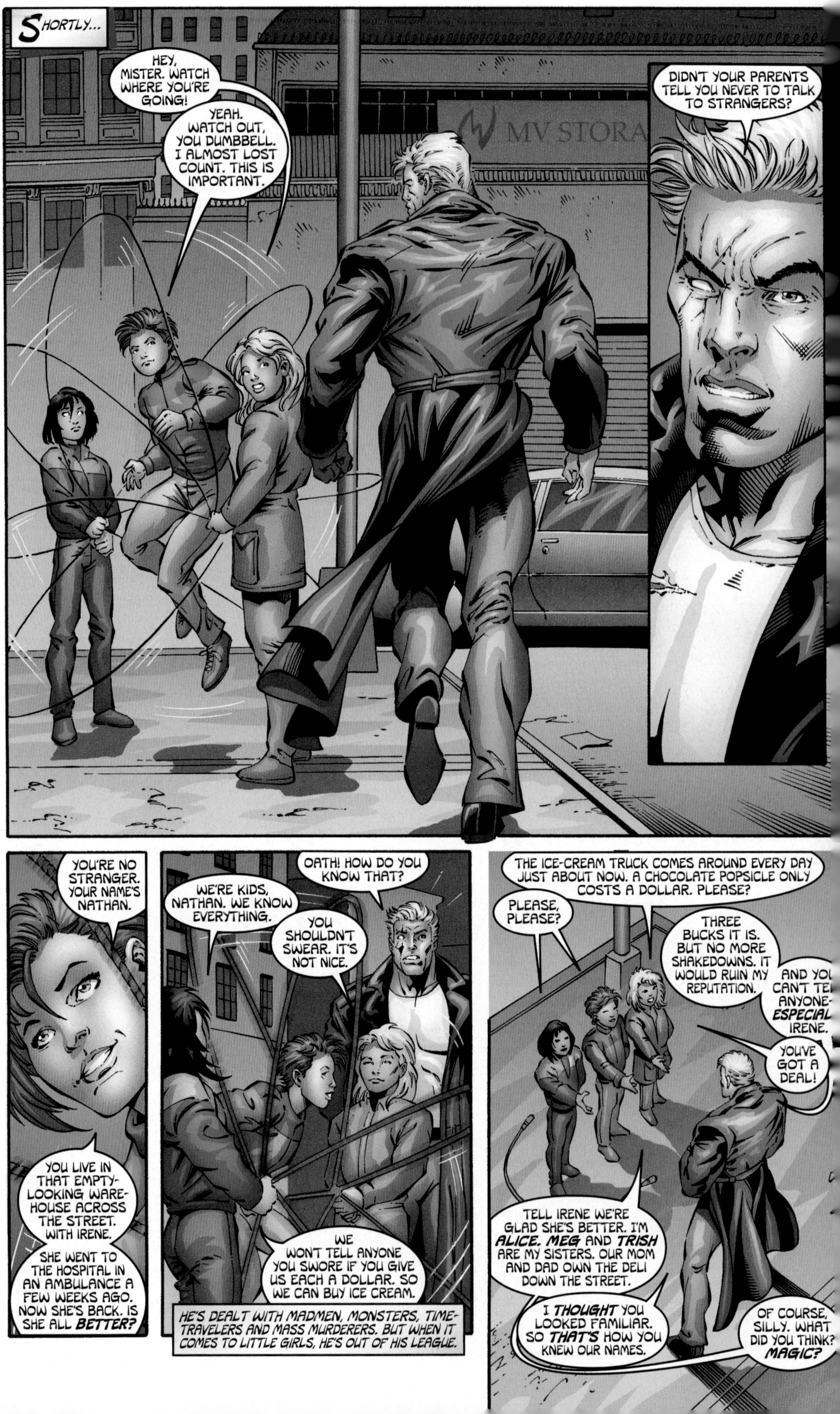
SHORTLY...
HEY, MISTER. WATCH WHERE YOU'RE GOING!
YEAH. WATCH OUT, YOU DUMBBELL. I ALMOST LOST COUNT. THIS IS IMPORTANT.
MV STORA
DIDN'T YOUR PARENTS TELL YOU NEVER TO TALK TO STRANGERS?
YOU'RE NO STRANGER. YOUR NAME'S NATHAN.
YOU LIVE IN THAT EMPTY-LOOKING WARE-HOUSE ACROSS THE STREET. WITH IRENE.
SHE WENT TO THE HOSPITAL IN AN AMBULANCE A FEW WEEKS AGO. NOW SHE'S BACK. IS SHE ALL BETTER?
WE'RE KIDS, NATHAN. WE KNOW EVERYTHING.
OATH! HOW DO YOU KNOW THAT?
YOU SHOULDN'T SWEAR. IT'S NOT NICE.
WE WON'T TELL ANYONE YOU SWORE IF YOU GIVE US EACH A DOLLAR. SO WE CAN BUY ICE CREAM.
HE'S DEALT WITH MADMEN, MONSTERS, TIME-TRAVELERS AND MASS MURDERERS. BUT WHEN IT COMES TO LITTLE GIRLS, HE'S OUT OF HIS LEAGUE.
THE ICE-CREAM TRUCK COMES AROUND EVERY DAY JUST ABOUT NOW. A CHOCOLATE POPSICLE ONLY COSTS A DOLLAR. PLEASE?
PLEASE, PLEASE?
THREE BUCKS IT IS. BUT NO MORE SHAKEDOWNS. IT WOULD RUIN MY REPUTATION.
AND YOU CAN'T TE ANYONE- ESPECIAL IRENE.
YOU'VE GOT A DEAL!
TELL IRENE WE'RE GLAD SHE'S BETTER. I'M ALICE. MEG AND TRISH ARE MY SISTERS. OUR MOM AND DAD OWN THE DELI DOWN THE STREET.
I THOUGHT YOU LOOKED FAMILIAR. SO THAT'S HOW YOU KNEW OUR NAMES.
OF COURSE, SILLY. WHAT DID YOU THINK? MAGIC?

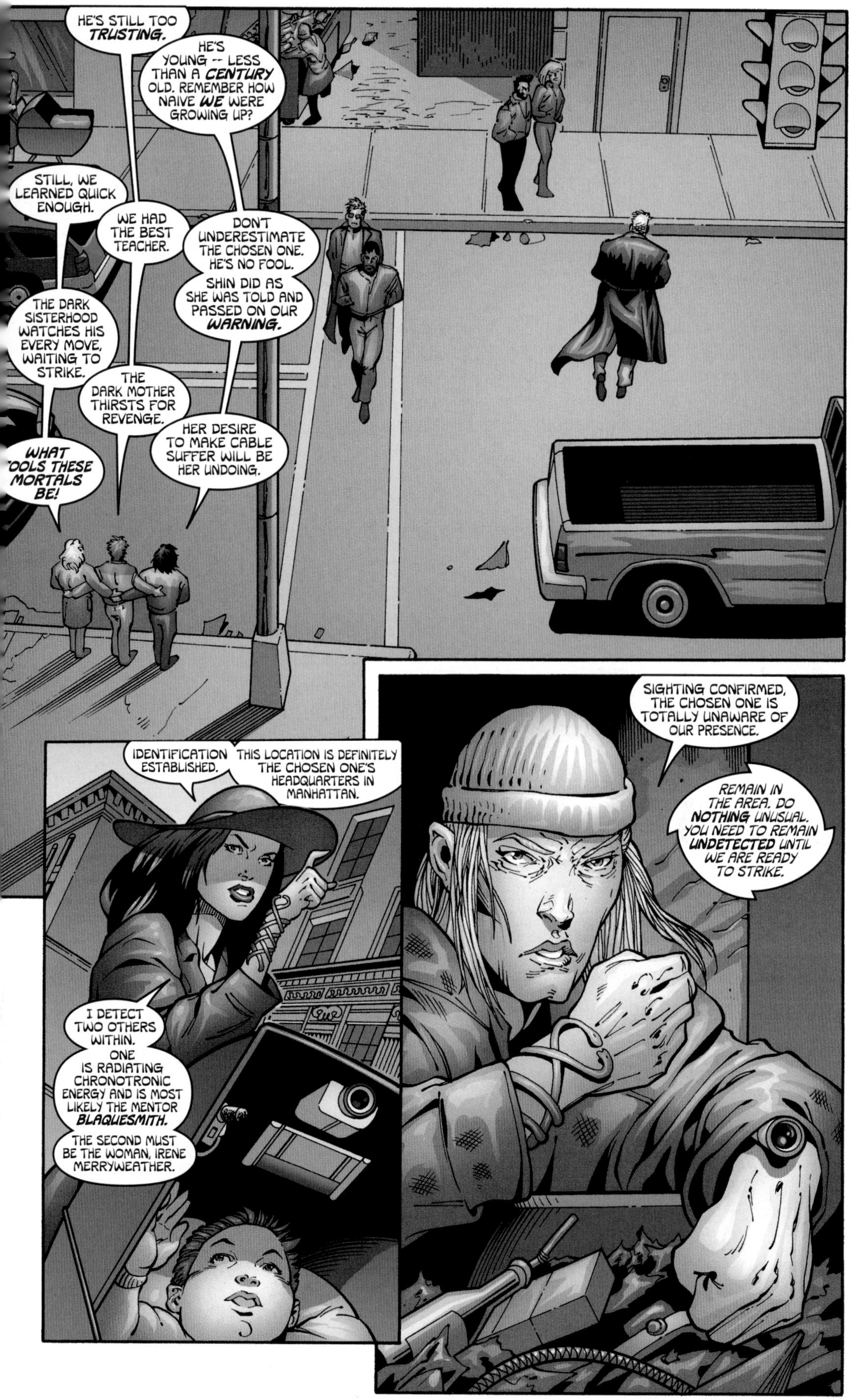
HE'S STILL TOO TRUSTING.
HE'S YOUNG -- LESS THAN A CENTURY OLD. REMEMBER HOW NAIVE WE WERE GROWING UP?
STILL, WE LEARNED QUICK ENOUGH.
WE HAD THE BEST TEACHER.
DON'T UNDERESTIMATE THE CHOSEN ONE. HE'S NO FOOL.
SHIN DID AS SHE WAS TOLD AND PASSED ON OUR WARNING.
THE DARK SISTERHOOD WATCHES HIS EVERY MOVE, WAITING TO STRIKE.
THE DARK MOTHER THIRSTS FOR REVENGE.
HER DESIRE TO MAKE CABLE SUFFER WILL BE HER UNDOING.
WHAT FOOLS THESE MORTALS BE!
IDENTIFICATION ESTABLISHED.
THIS LOCATION IS DEFINITELY THE CHOSEN ONE'S HEADQUARTERS IN MANHATTAN.
I DETECT TWO OTHERS WITHIN.
ONE IS RADIATING CHRONOTRONIC ENERGY AND IS MOST LIKELY THE MENTOR BLAQUESMITH.
THE SECOND MUST BE THE WOMAN, IRENE MERRYWEATHER.
SIGHTING CONFIRMED, THE CHOSEN ONE IS TOTALLY UNAWARE OF OUR PRESENCE.
REMAIN IN THE AREA. DO NOTHING UNUSUAL. YOU NEED TO REMAIN UNDETECTED UNTIL WE ARE READY TO STRIKE.

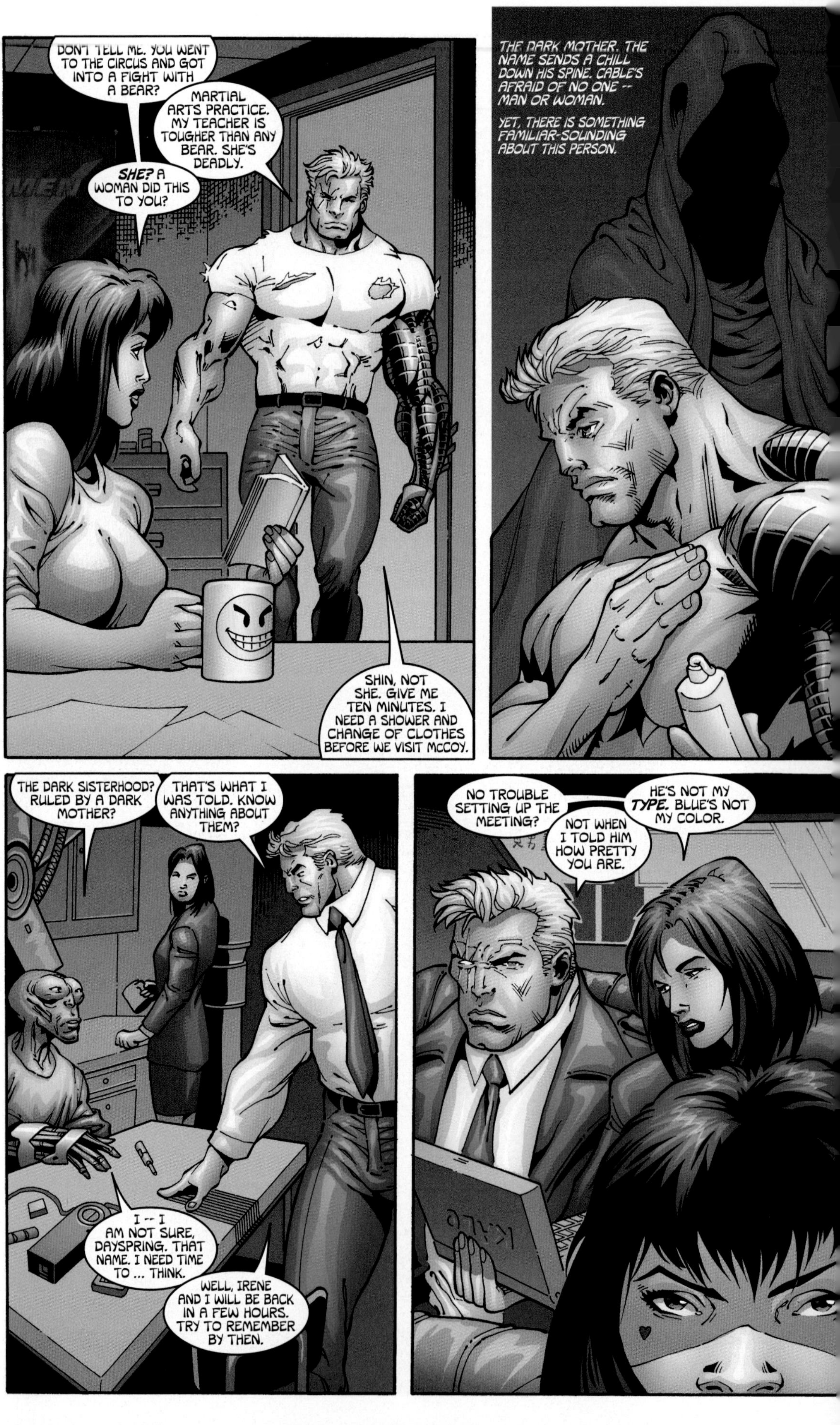

DON'T TELL ME. YOU WENT TO THE CIRCUS AND GOT INTO A FIGHT WITH A BEAR?
MARTIAL ARTS PRACTICE. MY TEACHER IS TOUGHER THAN ANY BEAR. SHE'S DEADLY.
SHE? A WOMAN DID THIS TO YOU?
SHIN, NOT SHE. GIVE ME TEN MINUTES. I NEED A SHOWER AND CHANGE OF CLOTHES BEFORE WE VISIT MCCOY.
THE DARK MOTHER. THE NAME SENDS A CHILL DOWN HIS SPINE. CABLE'S AFRAID OF NO ONE -- MAN OR WOMAN.
YET, THERE IS SOMETHING FAMILIAR-SOUNDING ABOUT THIS PERSON.
THE DARK SISTERHOOD? RULED BY A DARK MOTHER?
THAT'S WHAT I WAS TOLD. KNOW ANYTHING ABOUT THEM?
I -- I AM NOT SURE, DAYSPRING. THAT NAME. I NEED TIME TO ... THINK.
WELL, IRENE AND I WILL BE BACK IN A FEW HOURS. TRY TO REMEMBER BY THEN.
NO TROUBLE SETTING UP THE MEETING?
NOT WHEN I TOLD HIM HOW PRETTY YOU ARE.
HE'S NOT MY TYPE. BLUE'S NOT MY COLOR.

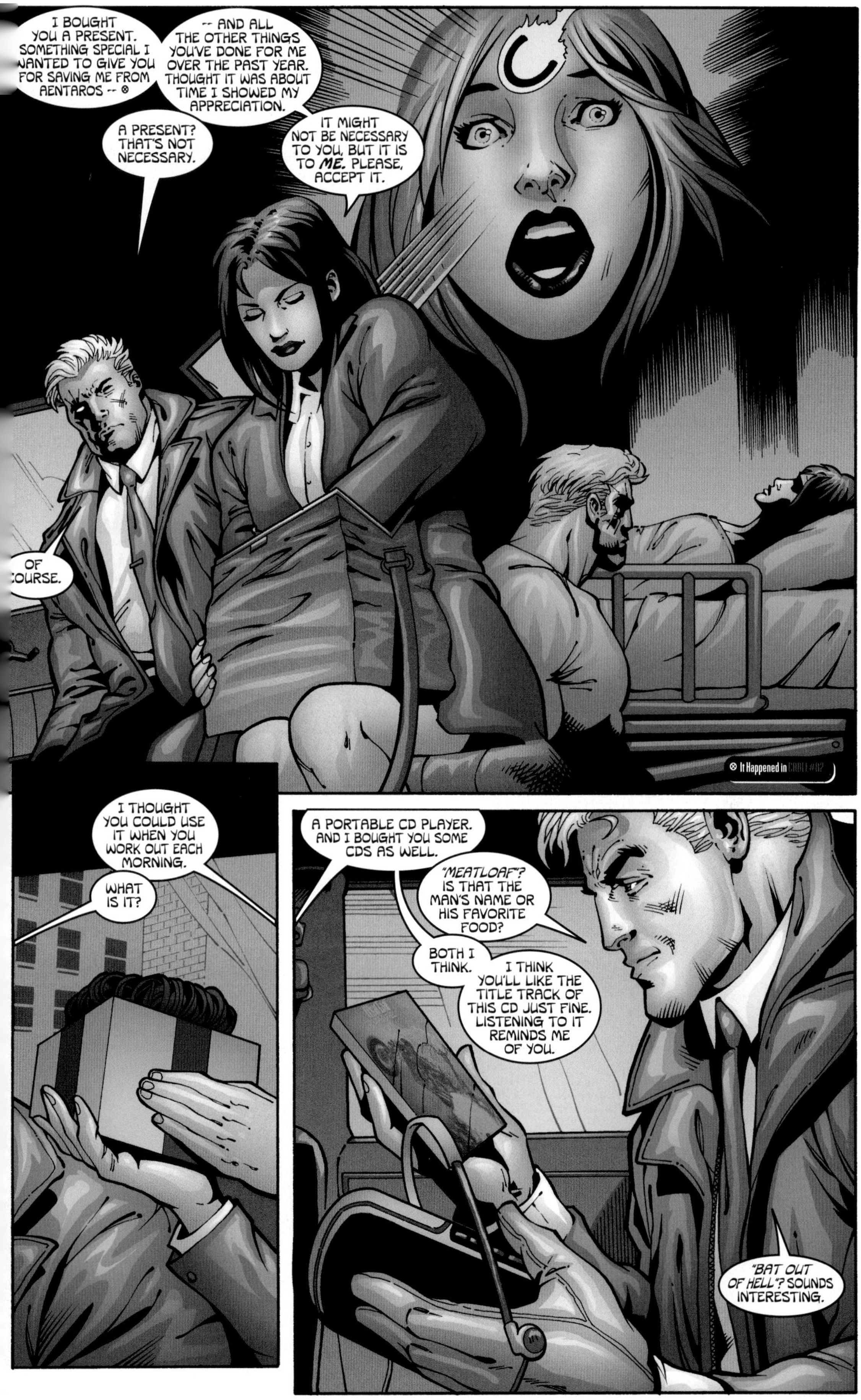
I BOUGHT YOU A PRESENT. SOMETHING SPECIAL I WANTED TO GIVE YOU FOR SAVING ME FROM AENTAROS -- ⊗
-- AND ALL THE OTHER THINGS YOU'VE DONE FOR ME OVER THE PAST YEAR. THOUGHT IT WAS ABOUT TIME I SHOWED MY APPRECIATION.
A PRESENT? THAT'S NOT NECESSARY.
IT MIGHT NOT BE NECESSARY TO YOU, BUT IT IS TO *ME.* PLEASE, ACCEPT IT.
OF COURSE.
⊗ It Happened in CABLE #82
I THOUGHT YOU COULD USE IT WHEN YOU WORK OUT EACH MORNING.
WHAT IS IT?
A PORTABLE CD PLAYER. AND I BOUGHT YOU SOME CDS AS WELL.
"MEATLOAF"? IS THAT THE MAN'S NAME OR HIS FAVORITE FOOD?
BOTH I THINK.
I THINK YOU'LL LIKE THE TITLE TRACK OF THIS CD JUST FINE. LISTENING TO IT REMINDS ME OF YOU.
"BAT OUT OF HELL"? SOUNDS INTERESTING.

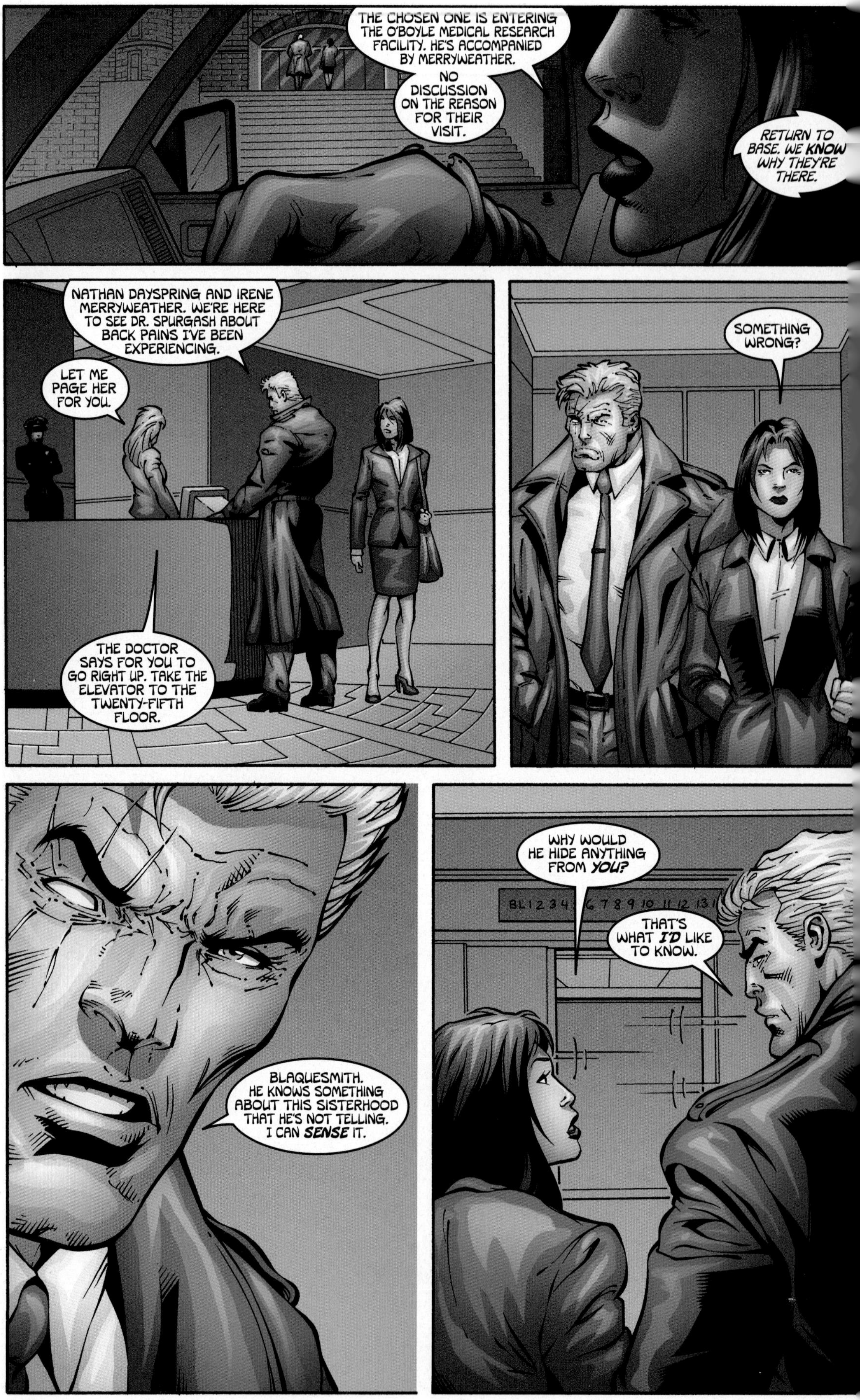

THE CHOSEN ONE IS ENTERING THE O'BOYLE MEDICAL RESEARCH FACILITY. HE'S ACCOMPANIED BY MERRYWEATHER.
NO DISCUSSION ON THE REASON FOR THEIR VISIT.
RETURN TO BASE. WE **KNOW** WHY THEY'RE THERE.
NATHAN DAYSPRING AND IRENE MERRYWEATHER. WE'RE HERE TO SEE DR. SPURGASH ABOUT BACK PAINS I'VE BEEN EXPERIENCING.
LET ME PAGE HER FOR YOU.
THE DOCTOR SAYS FOR YOU TO GO RIGHT UP. TAKE THE ELEVATOR TO THE TWENTY-FIFTH FLOOR.
SOMETHING WRONG?
BLAQUESMITH. HE KNOWS SOMETHING ABOUT THIS SISTERHOOD THAT HE'S NOT TELLING. I CAN ***SENSE*** IT.
WHY WOULD HE HIDE ANYTHING FROM ***YOU?***
THAT'S WHAT ***I'D*** LIKE TO KNOW.

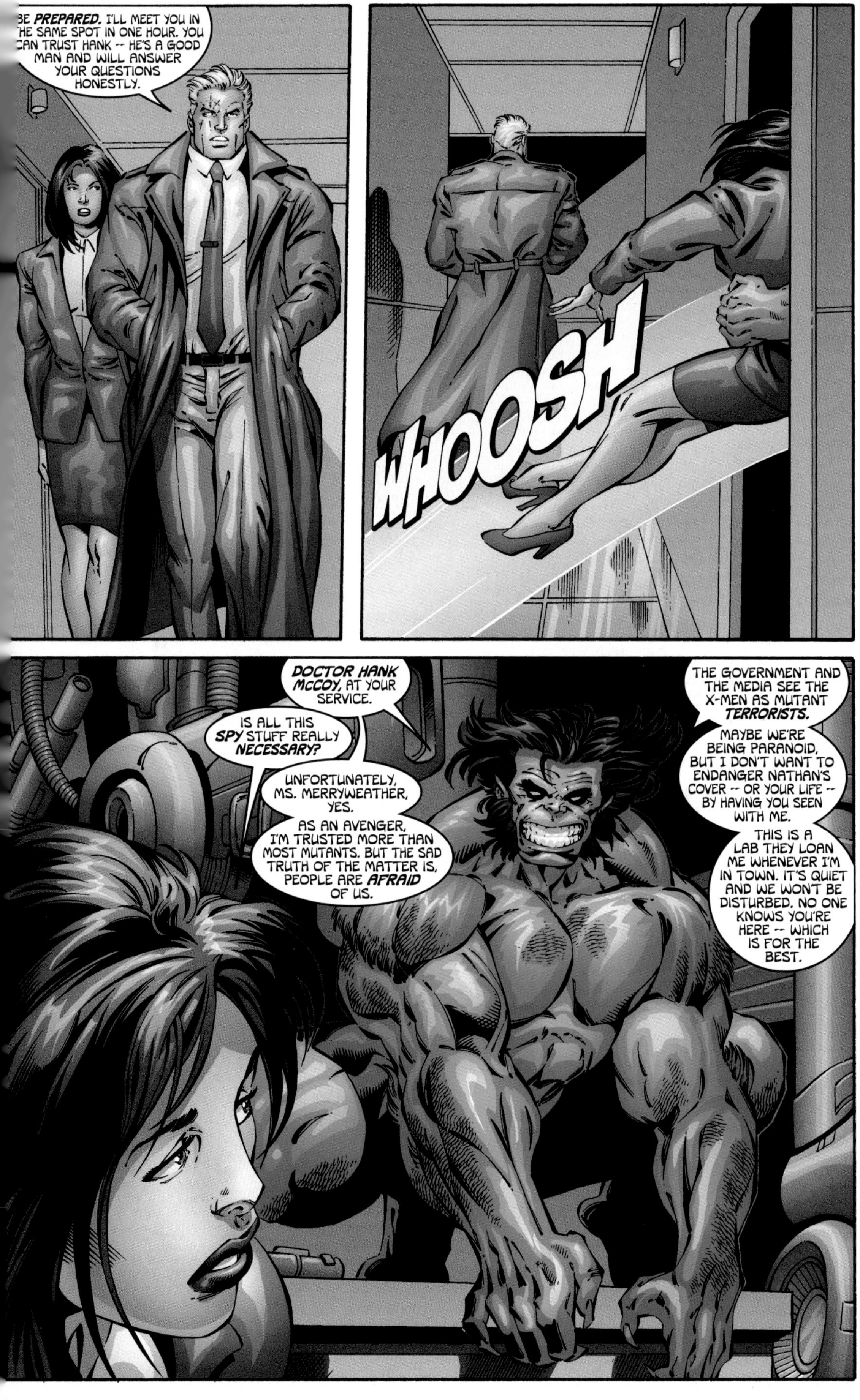

BE PREPARED. I'LL MEET YOU IN THE SAME SPOT IN ONE HOUR. YOU CAN TRUST HANK -- HE'S A GOOD MAN AND WILL ANSWER YOUR QUESTIONS HONESTLY.
WHOOSH
DOCTOR HANK MCCOY, AT YOUR SERVICE.
IS ALL THIS SPY STUFF REALLY NECESSARY?
UNFORTUNATELY, MS. MERRYWEATHER, YES.
AS AN AVENGER, I'M TRUSTED MORE THAN MOST MUTANTS. BUT THE SAD TRUTH OF THE MATTER IS, PEOPLE ARE AFRAID OF US.
THE GOVERNMENT AND THE MEDIA SEE THE X-MEN AS MUTANT TERRORISTS.
MAYBE WE'RE BEING PARANOID, BUT I DON'T WANT TO ENDANGER NATHAN'S COVER -- OR YOUR LIFE -- BY HAVING YOU SEEN WITH ME.
THIS IS A LAB THEY LOAN ME WHENEVER I'M IN TOWN. IT'S QUIET AND WE WON'T BE DISTURBED. NO ONE KNOWS YOU'RE HERE -- WHICH IS FOR THE BEST.

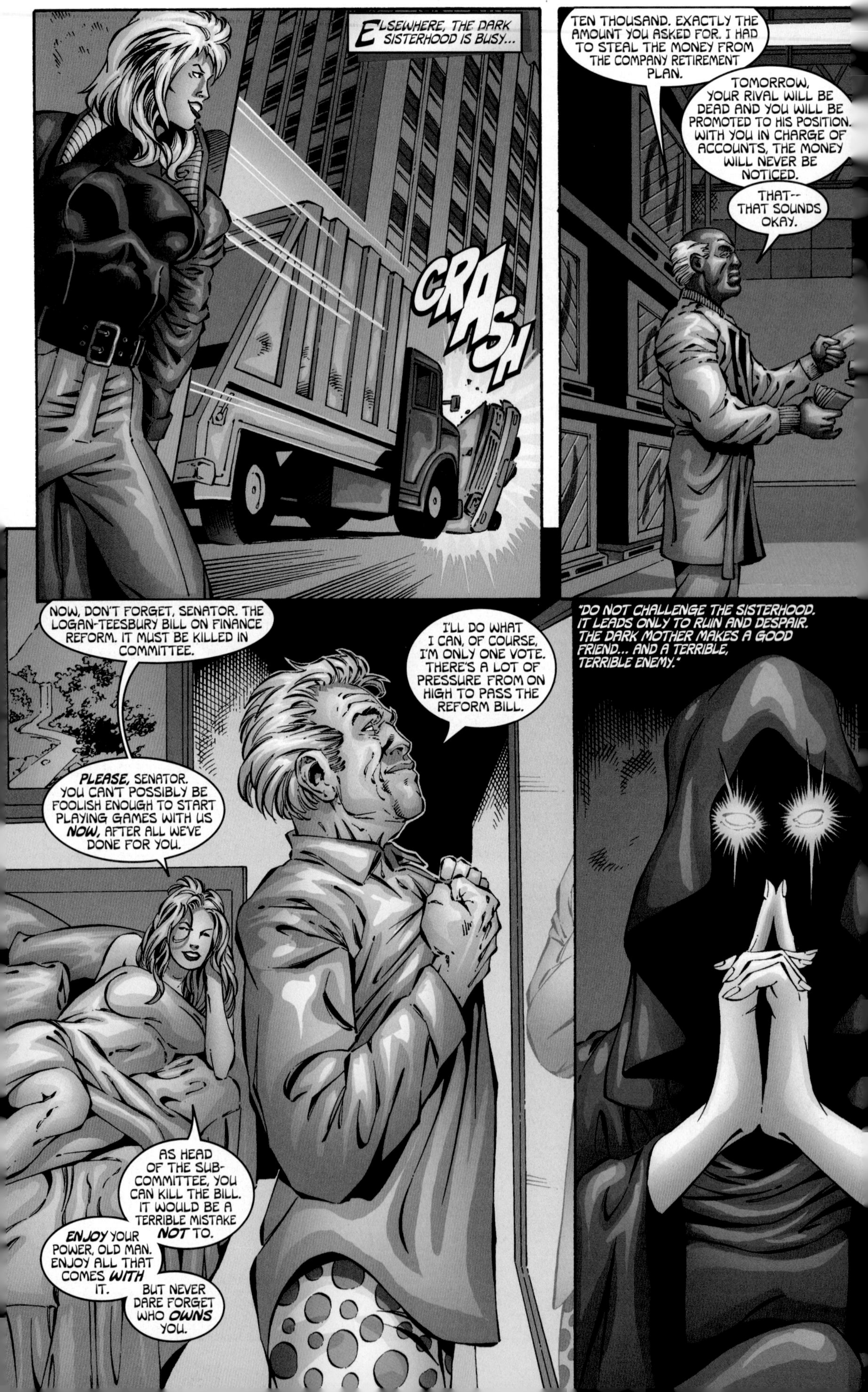
ELSEWHERE, THE DARK SISTERHOOD IS BUSY...
CRASH
TEN THOUSAND. EXACTLY THE AMOUNT YOU ASKED FOR. I HAD TO STEAL THE MONEY FROM THE COMPANY RETIREMENT PLAN.
TOMORROW, YOUR RIVAL WILL BE DEAD AND YOU WILL BE PROMOTED TO HIS POSITION. WITH YOU IN CHARGE OF ACCOUNTS, THE MONEY WILL NEVER BE NOTICED.
THAT-- THAT SOUNDS OKAY.
NOW, DON'T FORGET, SENATOR. THE LOGAN-TEESBURY BILL ON FINANCE REFORM. IT MUST BE KILLED IN COMMITTEE.
I'LL DO WHAT I CAN, OF COURSE, I'M ONLY ONE VOTE. THERE'S A LOT OF PRESSURE FROM ON HIGH TO PASS THE REFORM BILL.
PLEASE, SENATOR. YOU CAN'T POSSIBLY BE FOOLISH ENOUGH TO START PLAYING GAMES WITH US NOW, AFTER ALL WE'VE DONE FOR YOU.
AS HEAD OF THE SUB-COMMITTEE, YOU CAN KILL THE BILL. IT WOULD BE A TERRIBLE MISTAKE NOT TO.
ENJOY YOUR POWER, OLD MAN. ENJOY ALL THAT COMES WITH IT.
BUT NEVER DARE FORGET WHO OWNS YOU.
"DO NOT CHALLENGE THE SISTERHOOD. IT LEADS ONLY TO RUIN AND DESPAIR. THE DARK MOTHER MAKES A GOOD FRIEND... AND A TERRIBLE, TERRIBLE ENEMY."

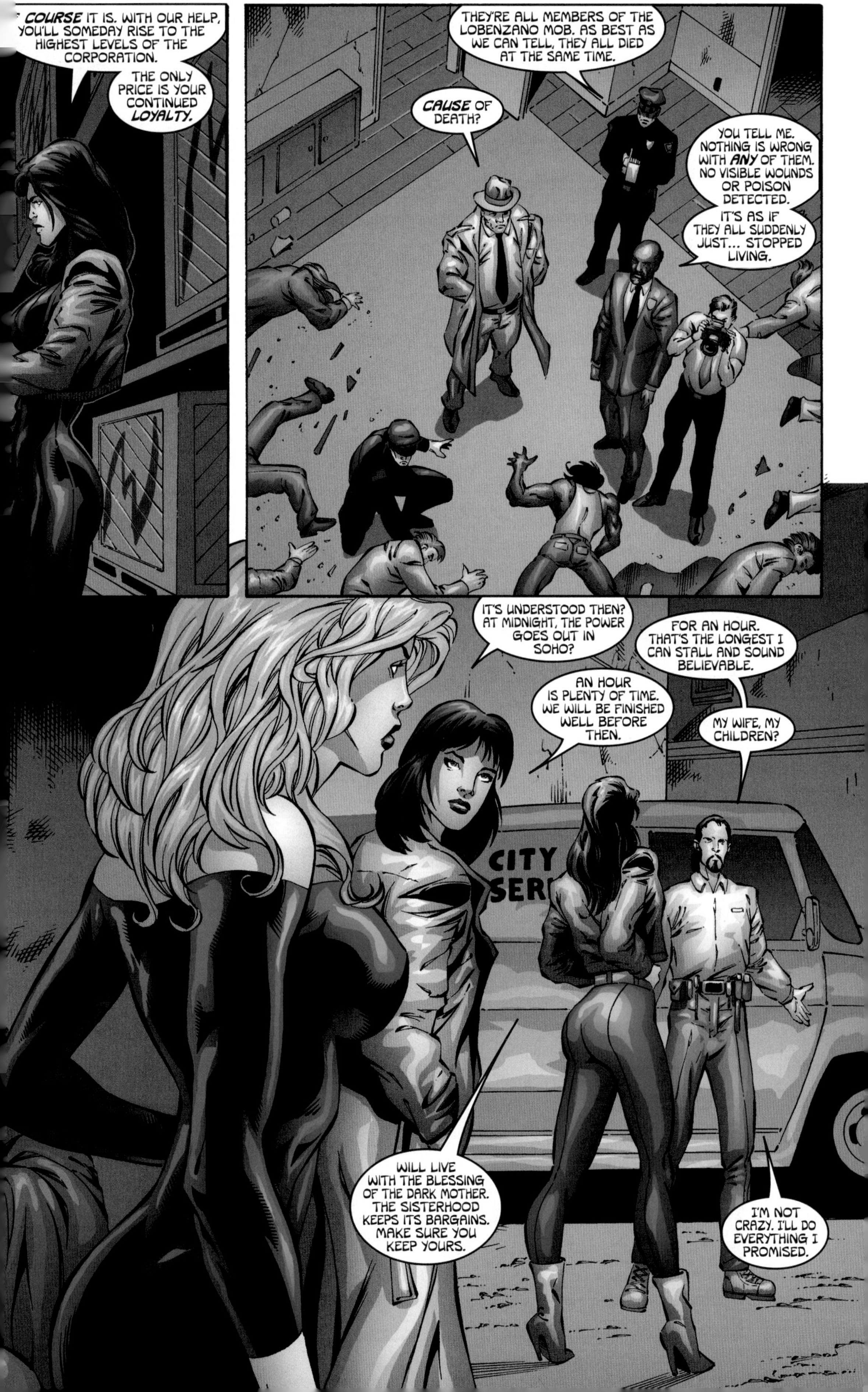

F COURSE IT IS. WITH OUR HELP, YOU'LL SOMEDAY RISE TO THE HIGHEST LEVELS OF THE CORPORATION.
THE ONLY PRICE IS YOUR CONTINUED LOYALTY.
THEY'RE ALL MEMBERS OF THE LOBENZANO MOB. AS BEST AS WE CAN TELL, THEY ALL DIED AT THE SAME TIME.
CAUSE OF DEATH?
YOU TELL ME. NOTHING IS WRONG WITH ANY OF THEM. NO VISIBLE WOUNDS OR POISON DETECTED.
IT'S AS IF THEY ALL SUDDENLY JUST... STOPPED LIVING.
IT'S UNDERSTOOD THEN? AT MIDNIGHT, THE POWER GOES OUT IN SOHO?
FOR AN HOUR. THAT'S THE LONGEST I CAN STALL AND SOUND BELIEVABLE.
AN HOUR IS PLENTY OF TIME. WE WILL BE FINISHED WELL BEFORE THEN.
MY WIFE, MY CHILDREN?
CITY SER
WILL LIVE WITH THE BLESSING OF THE DARK MOTHER. THE SISTERHOOD KEEPS ITS BARGAINS. MAKE SURE YOU KEEP YOURS.
I'M NOT CRAZY. I'LL DO EVERYTHING I PROMISED.

INVESTIGATION OF A CITIZEN ABOVE SUSPICION

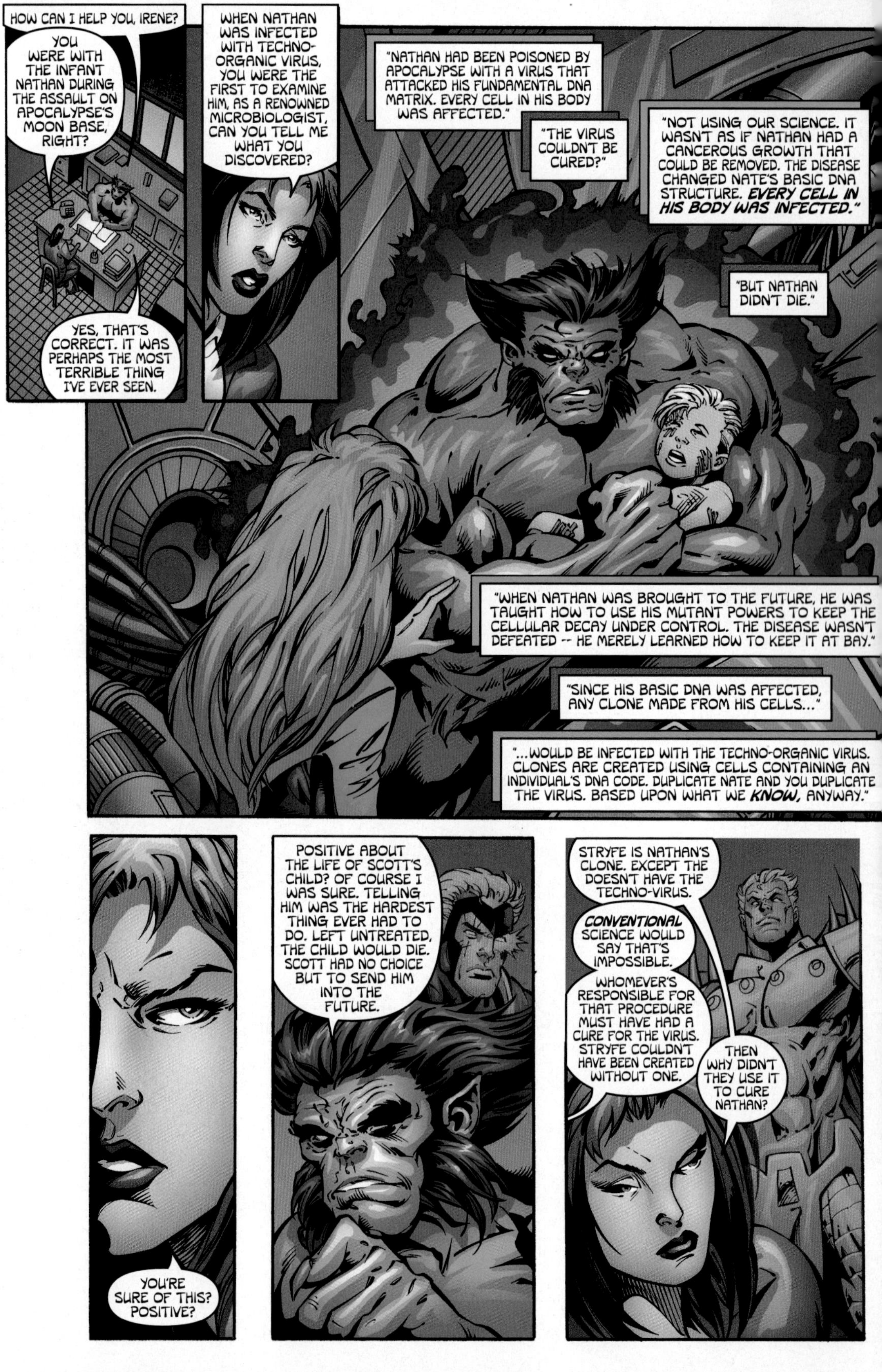
HOW CAN I HELP YOU, IRENE?
YOU WERE WITH THE INFANT NATHAN DURING THE ASSAULT ON APOCALYPSE'S MOON BASE, RIGHT?
YES, THAT'S CORRECT. IT WAS PERHAPS THE MOST TERRIBLE THING I'VE EVER SEEN.
WHEN NATHAN WAS INFECTED WITH TECHNO-ORGANIC VIRUS, YOU WERE THE FIRST TO EXAMINE HIM, AS A RENOWNED MICROBIOLOGIST, CAN YOU TELL ME WHAT YOU DISCOVERED?
"NATHAN HAD BEEN POISONED BY APOCALYPSE WITH A VIRUS THAT ATTACKED HIS FUNDAMENTAL DNA MATRIX. EVERY CELL IN HIS BODY WAS AFFECTED."
"THE VIRUS COULDN'T BE CURED?"
"NOT USING OUR SCIENCE. IT WASN'T AS IF NATHAN HAD A CANCEROUS GROWTH THAT COULD BE REMOVED. THE DISEASE CHANGED NATE'S BASIC DNA STRUCTURE. ***EVERY CELL IN HIS BODY WAS INFECTED.***"
"BUT NATHAN DIDN'T DIE."
"WHEN NATHAN WAS BROUGHT TO THE FUTURE, HE WAS TAUGHT HOW TO USE HIS MUTANT POWERS TO KEEP THE CELLULAR DECAY UNDER CONTROL. THE DISEASE WASN'T DEFEATED -- HE MERELY LEARNED HOW TO KEEP IT AT BAY."
"SINCE HIS BASIC DNA WAS AFFECTED, ANY CLONE MADE FROM HIS CELLS..."
"...WOULD BE INFECTED WITH THE TECHNO-ORGANIC VIRUS. CLONES ARE CREATED USING CELLS CONTAINING AN INDIVIDUAL'S DNA CODE. DUPLICATE NATE AND YOU DUPLICATE THE VIRUS. BASED UPON WHAT WE ***KNOW,*** ANYWAY."
YOU'RE SURE OF THIS? POSITIVE?
POSITIVE ABOUT THE LIFE OF SCOTT'S CHILD? OF COURSE I WAS SURE. TELLING HIM WAS THE HARDEST THING EVER HAD TO DO. LEFT UNTREATED, THE CHILD WOULD DIE. SCOTT HAD NO CHOICE BUT TO SEND HIM INTO THE FUTURE.
STRYFE IS NATHAN'S CLONE. EXCEPT THE DOESN'T HAVE THE TECHNO-VIRUS.
CONVENTIONAL SCIENCE WOULD SAY THAT'S IMPOSSIBLE.
WHOMEVER'S RESPONSIBLE FOR THAT PROCEDURE MUST HAVE HAD A CURE FOR THE VIRUS. STRYFE COULDN'T HAVE BEEN CREATED WITHOUT ONE.
THEN WHY DIDN'T THEY USE IT TO CURE NATHAN?

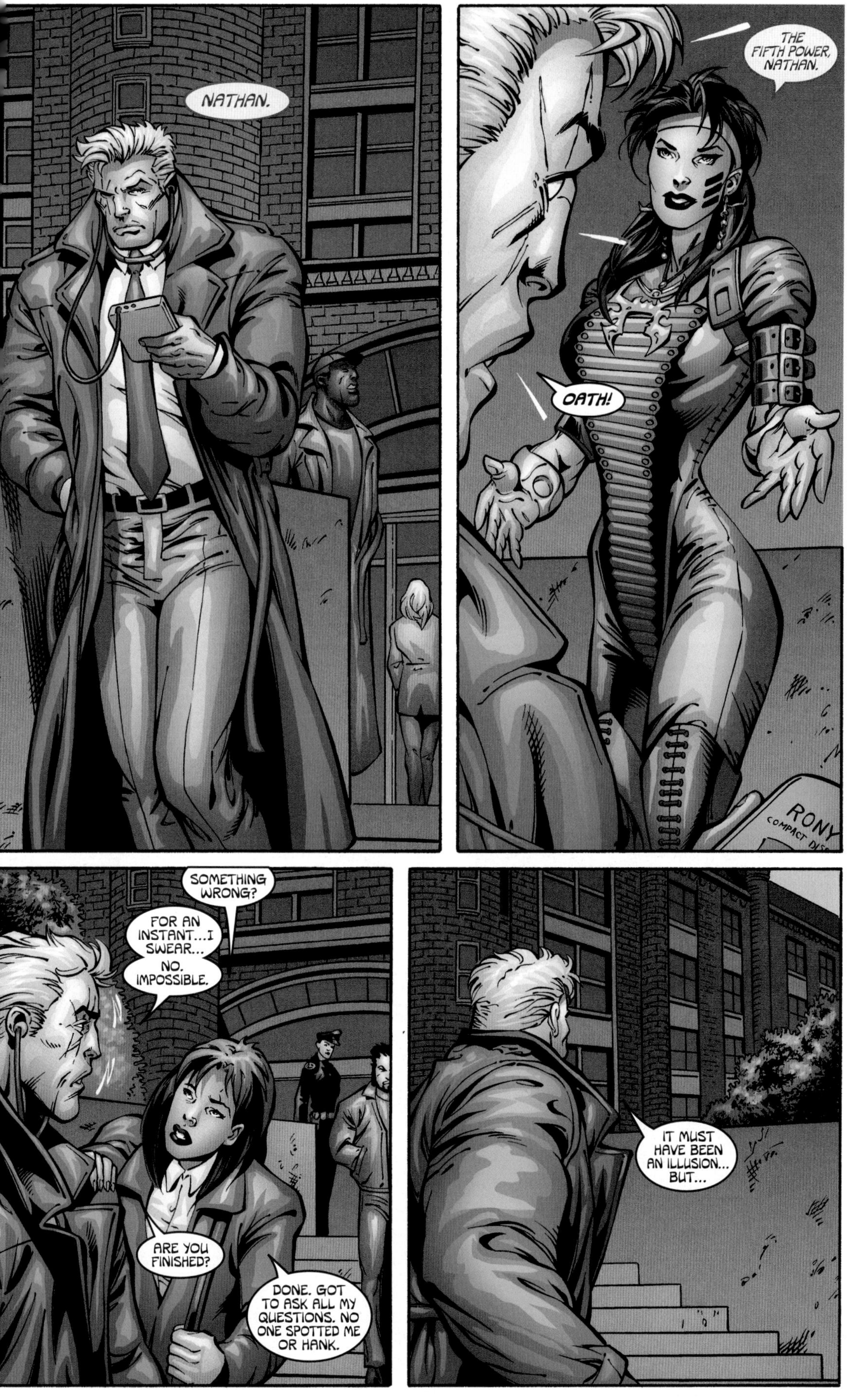
NATHAN.
THE FIFTH POWER, NATHAN.
OATH!
RONY
COMPACT
SOMETHING WRONG?
FOR AN INSTANT...I SWEAR... NO. IMPOSSIBLE.
ARE YOU FINISHED?
DONE. GOT TO ASK ALL MY QUESTIONS. NO ONE SPOTTED ME OR HANK.
IT MUST HAVE BEEN AN ILLUSION... BUT...

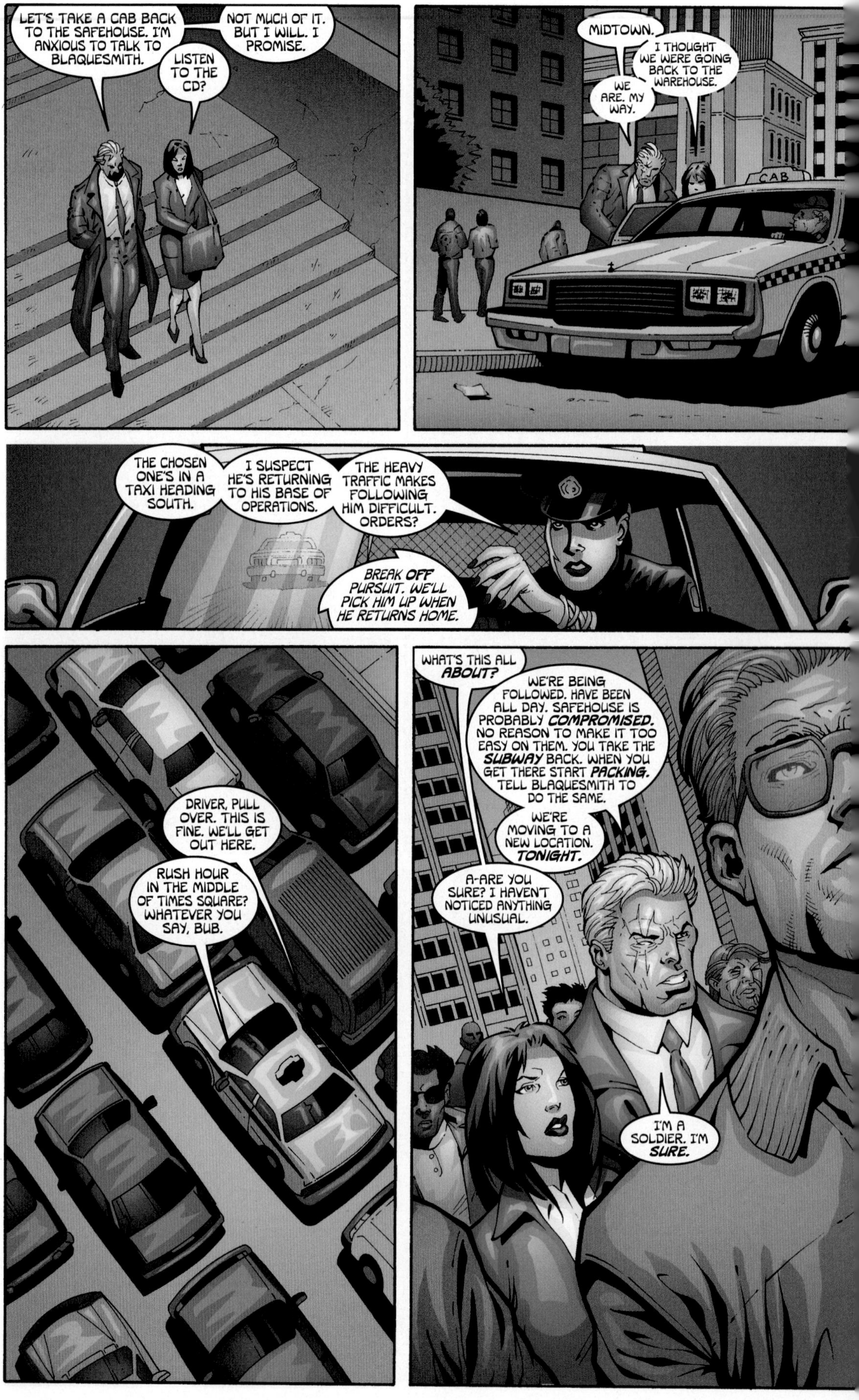
LET'S TAKE A CAB BACK TO THE SAFEHOUSE. I'M ANXIOUS TO TALK TO BLAQUESMITH.
LISTEN TO THE CD?
NOT MUCH OF IT. BUT I WILL. I PROMISE.
MIDTOWN.
I THOUGHT WE WERE GOING BACK TO THE WAREHOUSE.
WE ARE. MY WAY.
CAB
THE CHOSEN ONE'S IN A TAXI HEADING SOUTH.
I SUSPECT HE'S RETURNING TO HIS BASE OF OPERATIONS.
THE HEAVY TRAFFIC MAKES FOLLOWING HIM DIFFICULT. ORDERS?
BREAK OFF PURSUIT. WE'LL PICK HIM UP WHEN HE RETURNS HOME.
DRIVER, PULL OVER. THIS IS FINE. WE'LL GET OUT HERE.
RUSH HOUR IN THE MIDDLE OF TIMES SQUARE? WHATEVER YOU SAY, BUB.
WHAT'S THIS ALL ABOUT?
WE'RE BEING FOLLOWED. HAVE BEEN ALL DAY. SAFEHOUSE IS PROBABLY COMPROMISED. NO REASON TO MAKE IT TOO EASY ON THEM. YOU TAKE THE SUBWAY BACK. WHEN YOU GET THERE START PACKING. TELL BLAQUESMITH TO DO THE SAME.
WE'RE MOVING TO A NEW LOCATION. TONIGHT.
A-ARE YOU SURE? I HAVEN'T NOTICED ANYTHING UNUSUAL.
I'M A SOLDIER. I'M SURE.

NATHAN, WE KNOW A SECRET. TELL IT TO YOU FOR A DOLLAR.

AGAIN, A DOLLAR. IS THIS SECRET WORTH IT?

DEFINITELY.

WE'LL REFUND YOUR MONEY IF YOU DON'T LIKE IT.

HOW CAN I GO WRONG WITH A MONEY-BACK GUARANTEE?

WE'RE HONEST. MOM AND DAD TAUGHT US NEVER TO LIE.

THAT BAG LADY HUNTING THROUGH THE GARBAGE BIN. SHE'S BEEN WATCHING YOUR HOUSE ALL DAY.

THERE WAS ANOTHER LADY WITH A BABY CARRIAGE, SHE WAS SPYING TOO. BUT LEFT TWENTY MINUTES AGO.

VERY OBSERVANT FOR CHILDREN YOUR AGE. YOU SURE?

WE'RE SURE. SHE EVEN HAD A MINIATURE VIDEO CAMERA. MEG SAW IT.

KEEP THE MONEY, GIRLS. YOU EARNED IT. NOW, I SUGGEST YOU CLEAR OUT OF HERE.

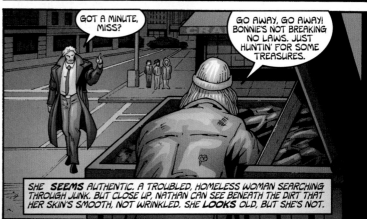

GOT A MINUTE, MISS?

GO AWAY, GO AWAY! BONNIE'S NOT BREAKING NO LAWS. JUST HUNTIN' FOR SOME TREASURES.

SHE SEEMS AUTHENTIC. A TROUBLED, HOMELESS WOMAN SEARCHING THROUGH JUNK. BUT CLOSE UP, NATHAN CAN SEE BENEATH THE DIRT THAT HER SKIN'S SMOOTH, NOT WRINKLED. SHE LOOKS OLD, BUT SHE'S NOT.

NO MORE TALK. A MIND PROBE WILL ESTABLISH BONNIE'S IDENTITY WITHOUT HER EVER BEING THE WISER.

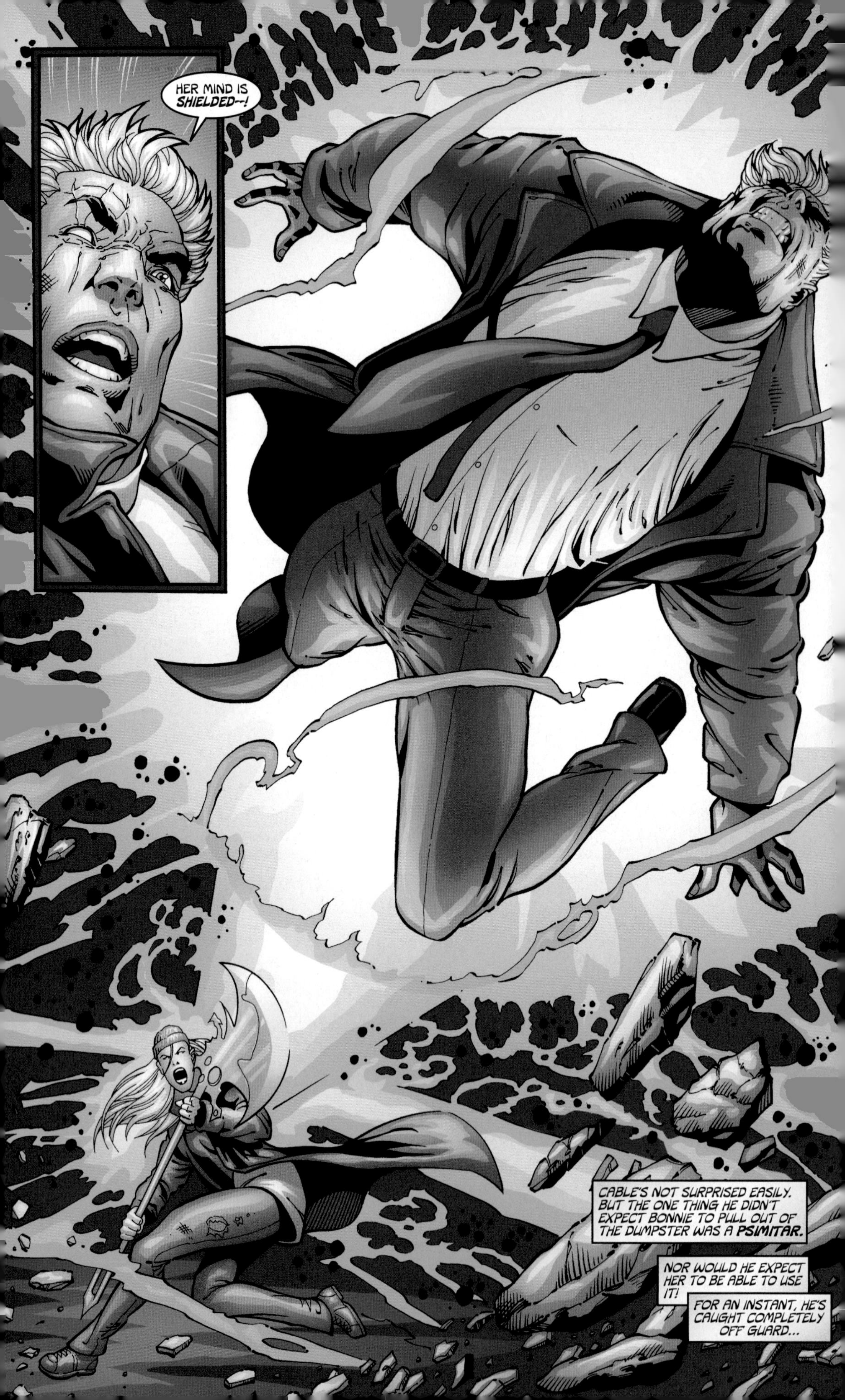
HER MIND IS SHIELDED--!
CABLE'S NOT SURPRISED EASILY. BUT THE ONE THING HE DIDN'T EXPECT BONNIE TO PULL OUT OF THE DUMPSTER WAS A PSIMITAR.
NOR WOULD HE EXPECT HER TO BE ABLE TO USE IT!
FOR AN INSTANT, HE'S CAUGHT COMPLETELY OFF GUARD...

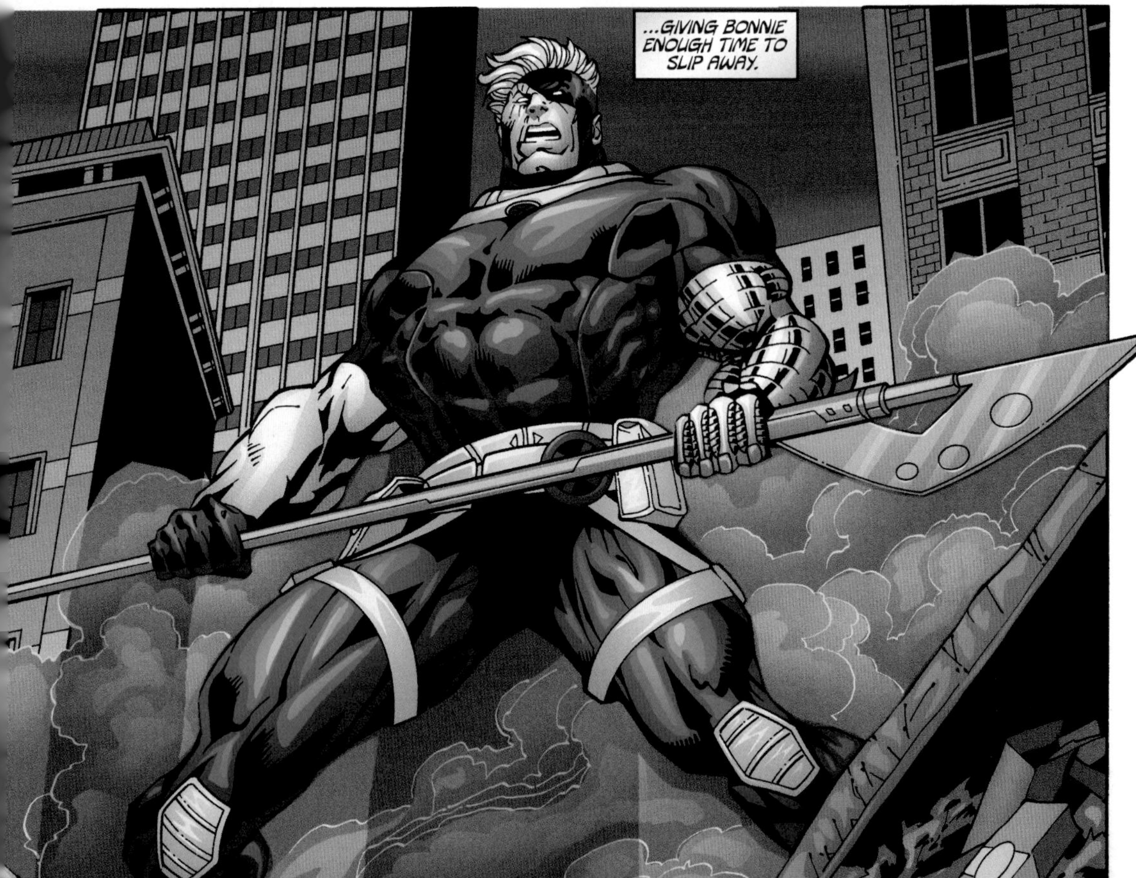
...GIVING BONNIE ENOUGH TIME TO SLIP AWAY.

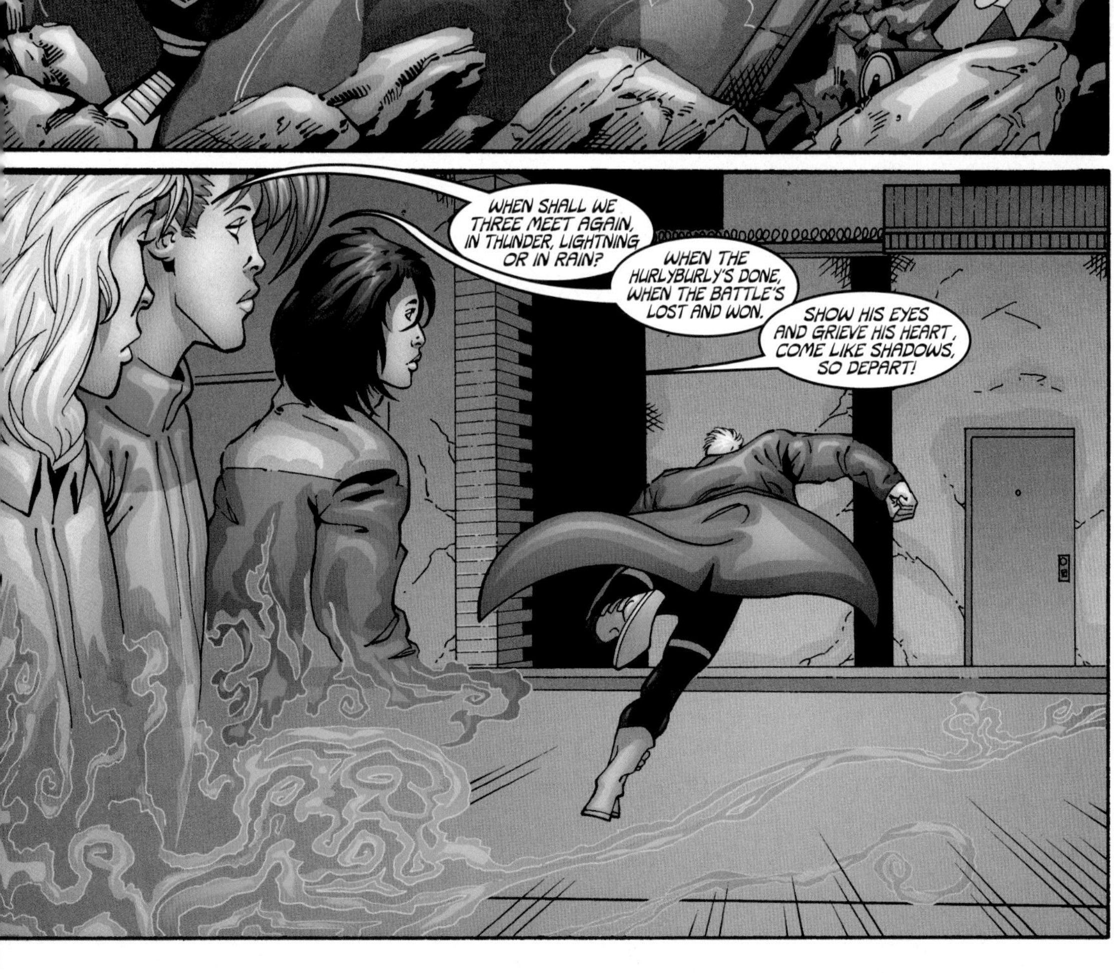
WHEN SHALL WE THREE MEET AGAIN, IN THUNDER, LIGHTNING OR IN RAIN?
WHEN THE HURLYBURLY'S DONE, WHEN THE BATTLE'S LOST AND WON.
SHOW HIS EYES AND GRIEVE HIS HEART, COME LIKE SHADOWS, SO DEPART!

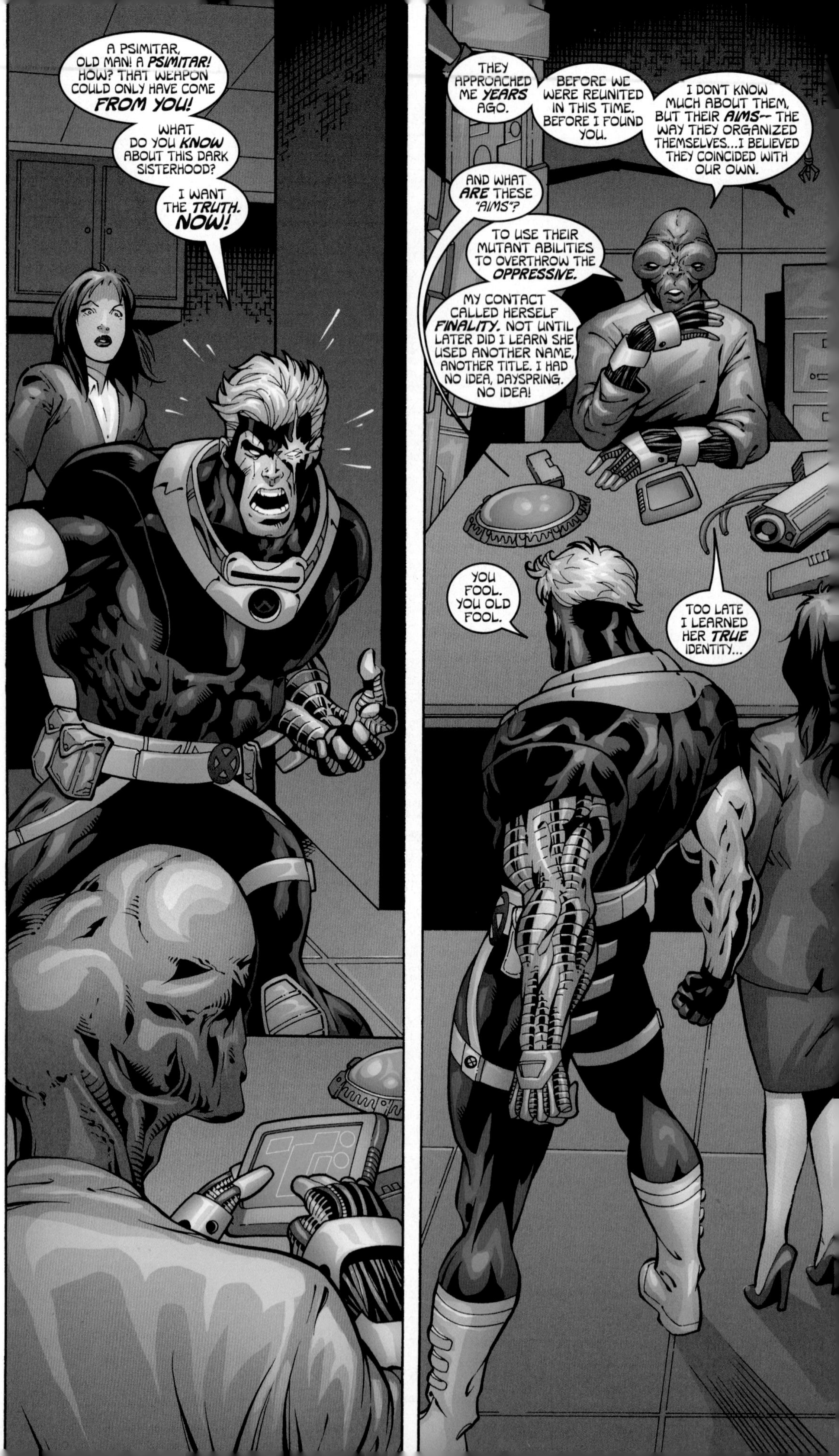

A PSIMITAR, OLD MAN! A PSIMITAR! HOW? THAT WEAPON COULD ONLY HAVE COME FROM YOU!
WHAT DO YOU KNOW ABOUT THIS DARK SISTERHOOD?
I WANT THE TRUTH. NOW!
THEY APPROACHED ME YEARS AGO.
BEFORE WE WERE REUNITED IN THIS TIME. BEFORE I FOUND YOU.
I DON'T KNOW MUCH ABOUT THEM, BUT THEIR AIMS-- THE WAY THEY ORGANIZED THEMSELVES...I BELIEVED THEY COINCIDED WITH OUR OWN.
AND WHAT ARE THESE "AIMS"?
TO USE THEIR MUTANT ABILITIES TO OVERTHROW THE OPPRESSIVE.
MY CONTACT CALLED HERSELF FINALITY. NOT UNTIL LATER DID I LEARN SHE USED ANOTHER NAME, ANOTHER TITLE. I HAD NO IDEA, DAYSPRING. NO IDEA!
YOU FOOL. YOU OLD FOOL.
TOO LATE I LEARNED HER TRUE IDENTITY...

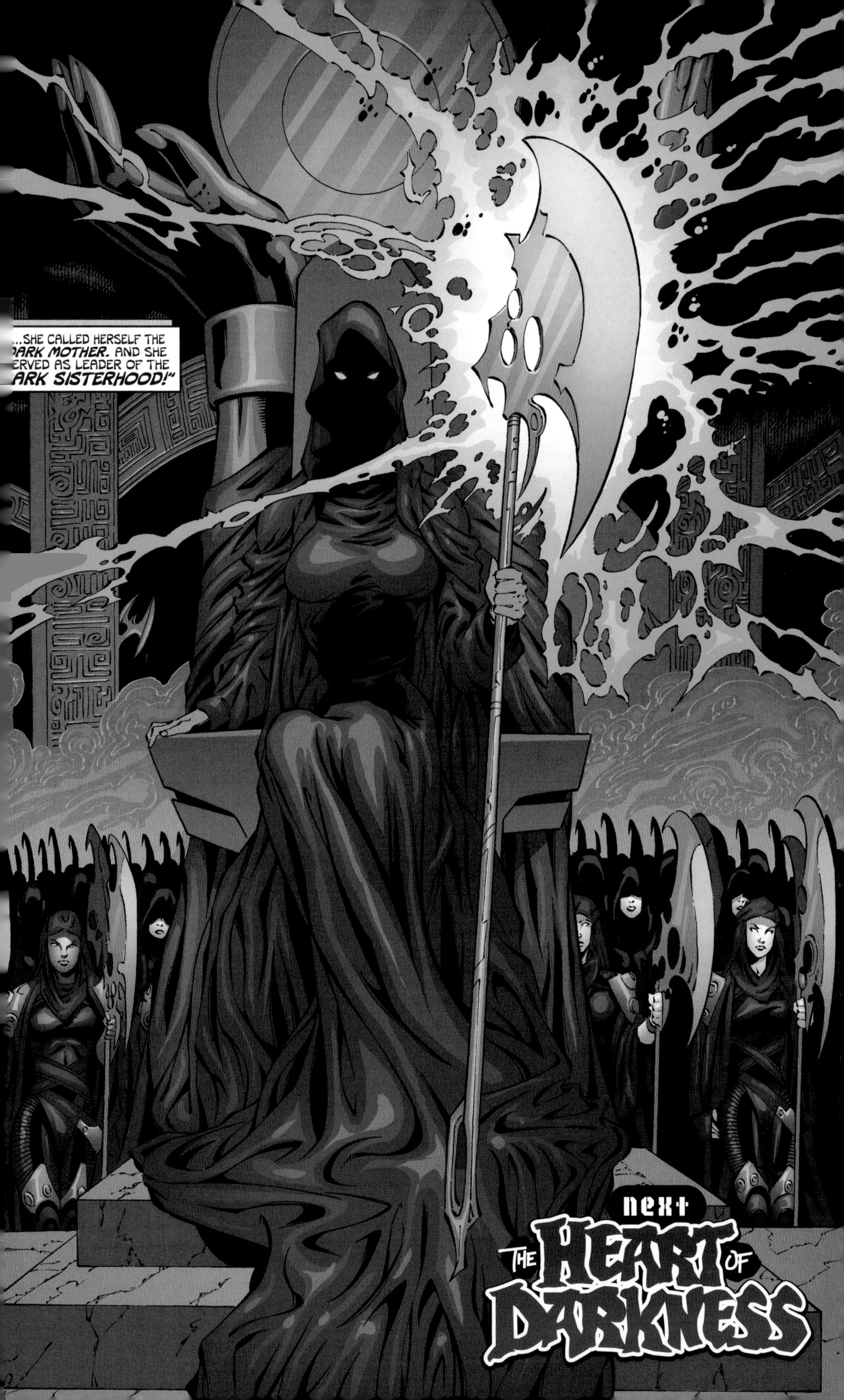
...SHE CALLED HERSELF THE
DARK MOTHER. AND SHE
SERVED AS LEADER OF THE
DARK SISTERHOOD!"
next
THE HEART OF DARKNESS

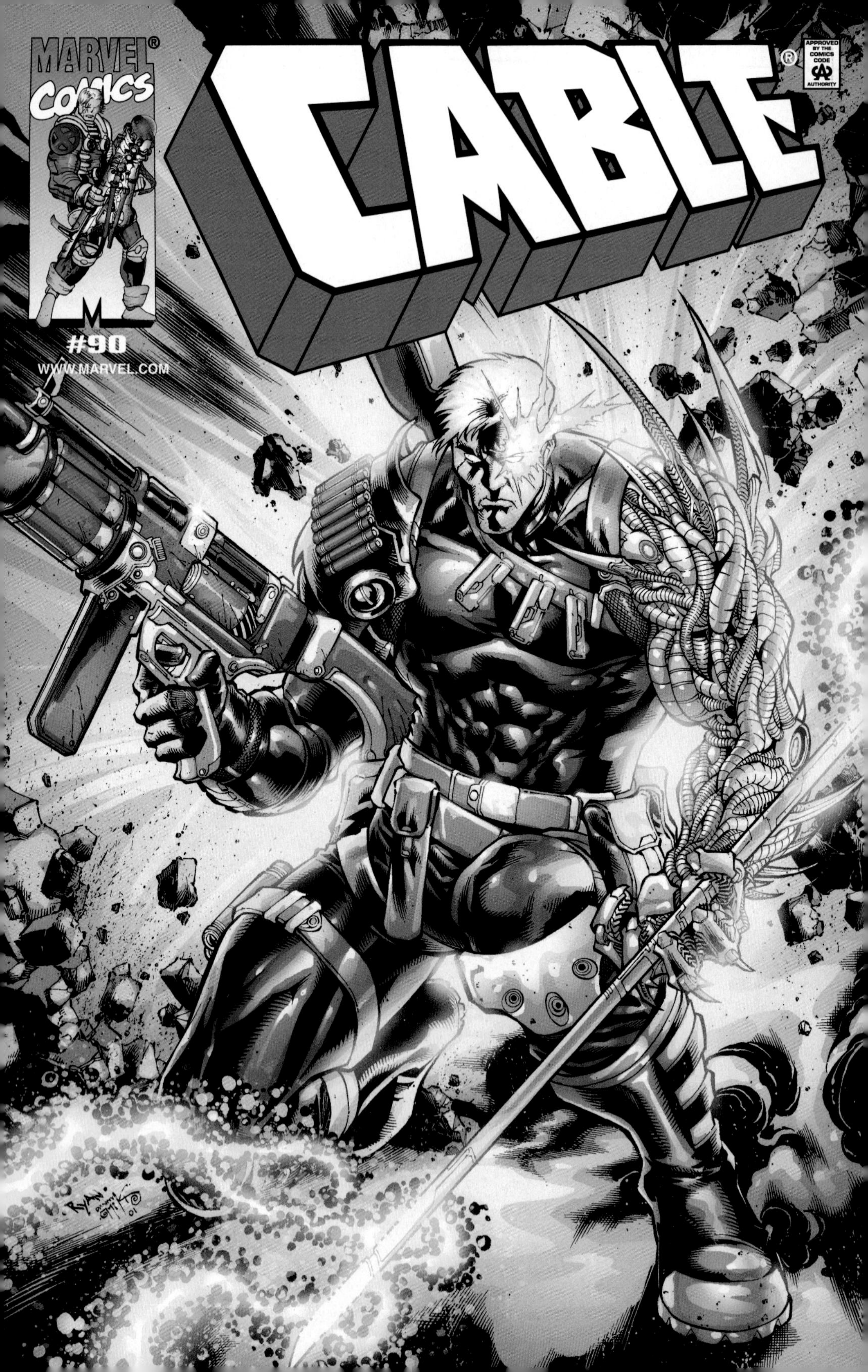
MARVEL®
COMICS
CABLE®
APPROVED BY THE COMICS CODE AUTHORITY
#90
WWW.MARVEL.COM

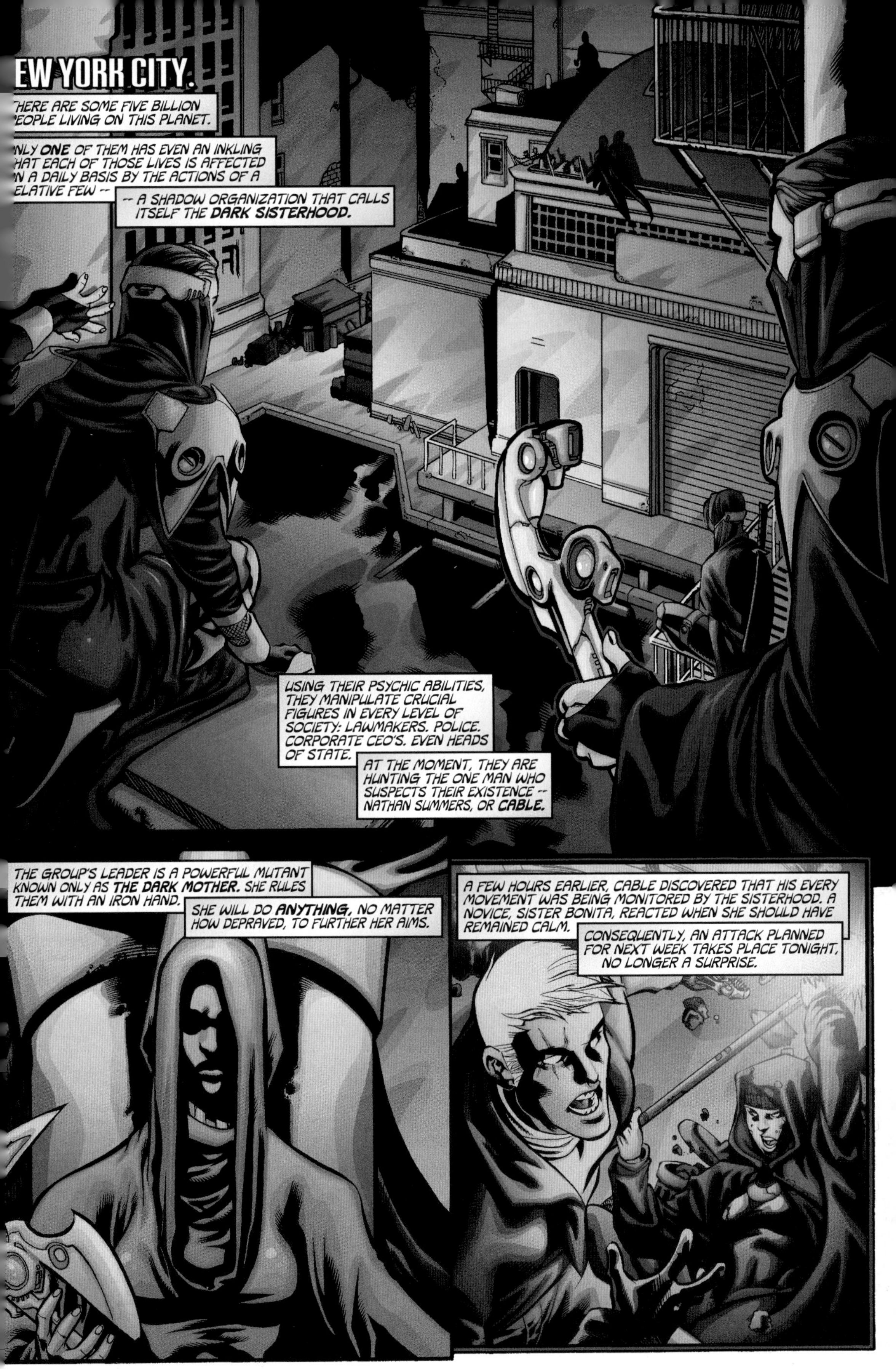

EW YORK CITY.
THERE ARE SOME FIVE BILLION EOPLE LIVING ON THIS PLANET.
NLY ONE OF THEM HAS EVEN AN INKLING HAT EACH OF THOSE LIVES IS AFFECTED N A DAILY BASIS BY THE ACTIONS OF A ELATIVE FEW --
-- A SHADOW ORGANIZATION THAT CALLS ITSELF THE DARK SISTERHOOD.
USING THEIR PSYCHIC ABILITIES, THEY MANIPULATE CRUCIAL FIGURES IN EVERY LEVEL OF SOCIETY: LAWMAKERS. POLICE. CORPORATE CEO'S. EVEN HEADS OF STATE.
AT THE MOMENT, THEY ARE HUNTING THE ONE MAN WHO SUSPECTS THEIR EXISTENCE -- NATHAN SUMMERS, OR CABLE.
THE GROUP'S LEADER IS A POWERFUL MUTANT KNOWN ONLY AS THE DARK MOTHER. SHE RULES THEM WITH AN IRON HAND.
SHE WILL DO ANYTHING, NO MATTER HOW DEPRAVED, TO FURTHER HER AIMS.
A FEW HOURS EARLIER, CABLE DISCOVERED THAT HIS EVERY MOVEMENT WAS BEING MONITORED BY THE SISTERHOOD. A NOVICE, SISTER BONITA, REACTED WHEN SHE SHOULD HAVE REMAINED CALM.
CONSEQUENTLY, AN ATTACK PLANNED FOR NEXT WEEK TAKES PLACE TONIGHT, NO LONGER A SURPRISE.

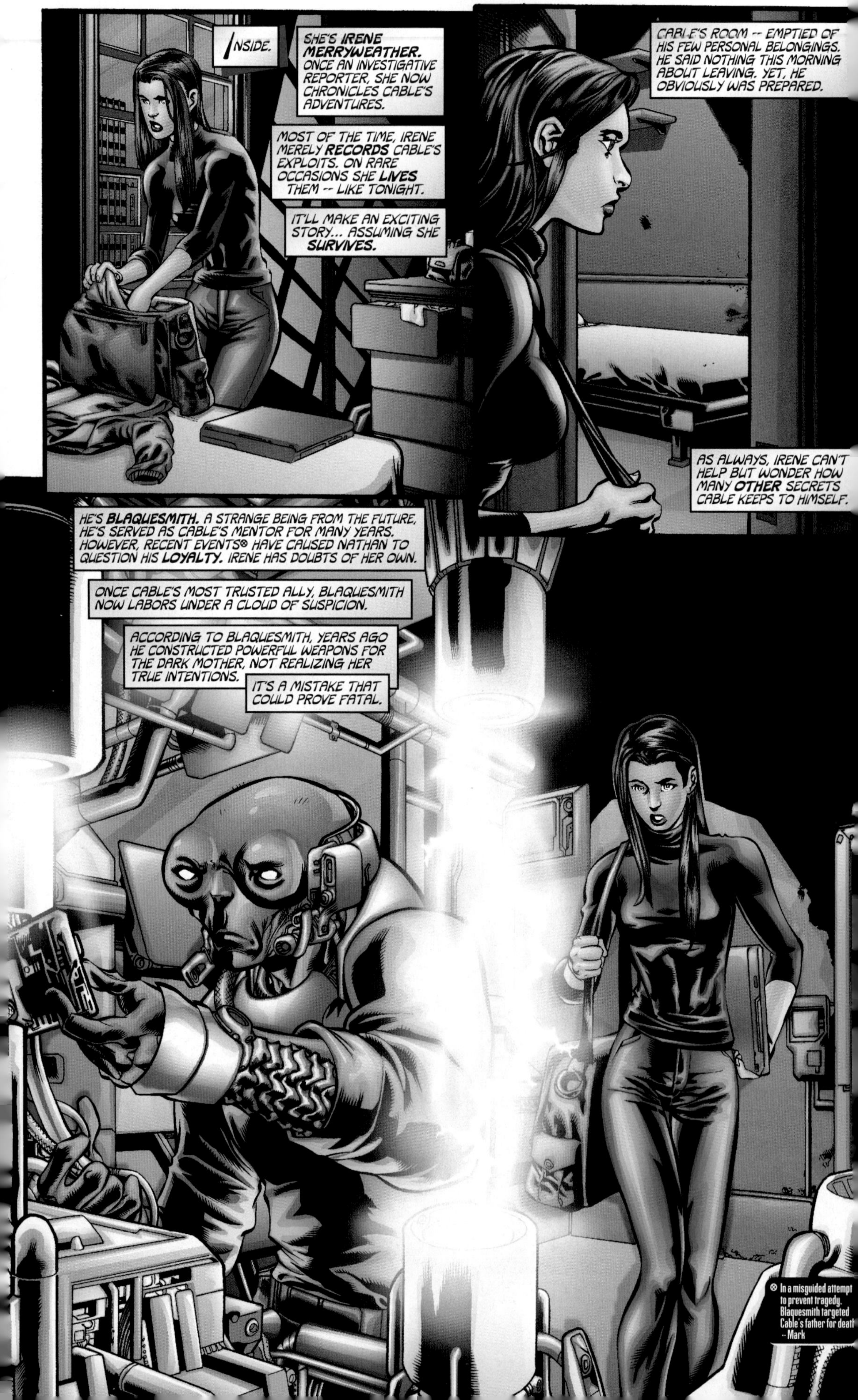
INSIDE.
SHE'S IRENE MERRYWEATHER. ONCE AN INVESTIGATIVE REPORTER, SHE NOW CHRONICLES CABLE'S ADVENTURES.
MOST OF THE TIME, IRENE MERELY RECORDS CABLE'S EXPLOITS. ON RARE OCCASIONS SHE LIVES THEM -- LIKE TONIGHT.
IT'LL MAKE AN EXCITING STORY... ASSUMING SHE SURVIVES.
CABLE'S ROOM -- EMPTIED OF HIS FEW PERSONAL BELONGINGS. HE SAID NOTHING THIS MORNING ABOUT LEAVING. YET, HE OBVIOUSLY WAS PREPARED.
AS ALWAYS, IRENE CAN'T HELP BUT WONDER HOW MANY OTHER SECRETS CABLE KEEPS TO HIMSELF.
HE'S BLAQUESMITH. A STRANGE BEING FROM THE FUTURE, HE'S SERVED AS CABLE'S MENTOR FOR MANY YEARS. HOWEVER, RECENT EVENTS⊗ HAVE CAUSED NATHAN TO QUESTION HIS LOYALTY. IRENE HAS DOUBTS OF HER OWN.
ONCE CABLE'S MOST TRUSTED ALLY, BLAQUESMITH NOW LABORS UNDER A CLOUD OF SUSPICION.
ACCORDING TO BLAQUESMITH, YEARS AGO HE CONSTRUCTED POWERFUL WEAPONS FOR THE DARK MOTHER, NOT REALIZING HER TRUE INTENTIONS.
IT'S A MISTAKE THAT COULD PROVE FATAL.
⊗ In a misguided attempt to prevent tragedy, Blaquesmith targeted Cable's father for death -- Mark

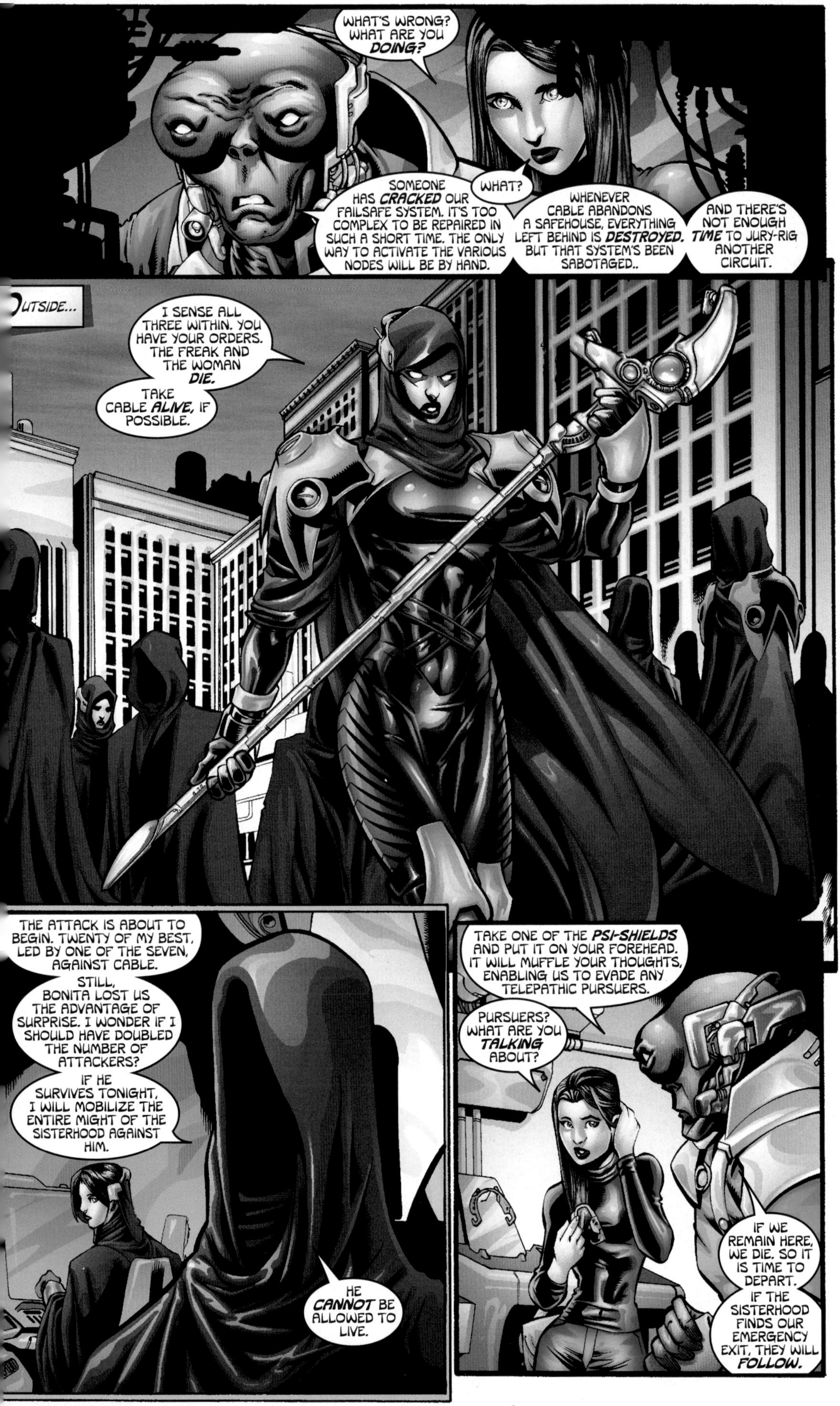
WHAT'S WRONG? WHAT ARE YOU DOING?
SOMEONE HAS CRACKED OUR FAILSAFE SYSTEM. IT'S TOO COMPLEX TO BE REPAIRED IN SUCH A SHORT TIME. THE ONLY WAY TO ACTIVATE THE VARIOUS NODES WILL BE BY HAND.
WHAT?
WHENEVER CABLE ABANDONS A SAFEHOUSE, EVERYTHING LEFT BEHIND IS DESTROYED. BUT THAT SYSTEM'S BEEN SABOTAGED..
AND THERE'S NOT ENOUGH TIME TO JURY-RIG ANOTHER CIRCUIT.
OUTSIDE...
I SENSE ALL THREE WITHIN. YOU HAVE YOUR ORDERS. THE FREAK AND THE WOMAN DIE.
TAKE CABLE ALIVE, IF POSSIBLE.
THE ATTACK IS ABOUT TO BEGIN. TWENTY OF MY BEST, LED BY ONE OF THE SEVEN, AGAINST CABLE.
STILL, BONITA LOST US THE ADVANTAGE OF SURPRISE. I WONDER IF I SHOULD HAVE DOUBLED THE NUMBER OF ATTACKERS?
IF HE SURVIVES TONIGHT, I WILL MOBILIZE THE ENTIRE MIGHT OF THE SISTERHOOD AGAINST HIM.
HE CANNOT BE ALLOWED TO LIVE.
TAKE ONE OF THE PSI-SHIELDS AND PUT IT ON YOUR FOREHEAD. IT WILL MUFFLE YOUR THOUGHTS, ENABLING US TO EVADE ANY TELEPATHIC PURSUERS.
PURSUERS? WHAT ARE YOU TALKING ABOUT?
IF WE REMAIN HERE, WE DIE. SO IT IS TIME TO DEPART.
IF THE SISTERHOOD FINDS OUR EMERGENCY EXIT, THEY WILL FOLLOW.

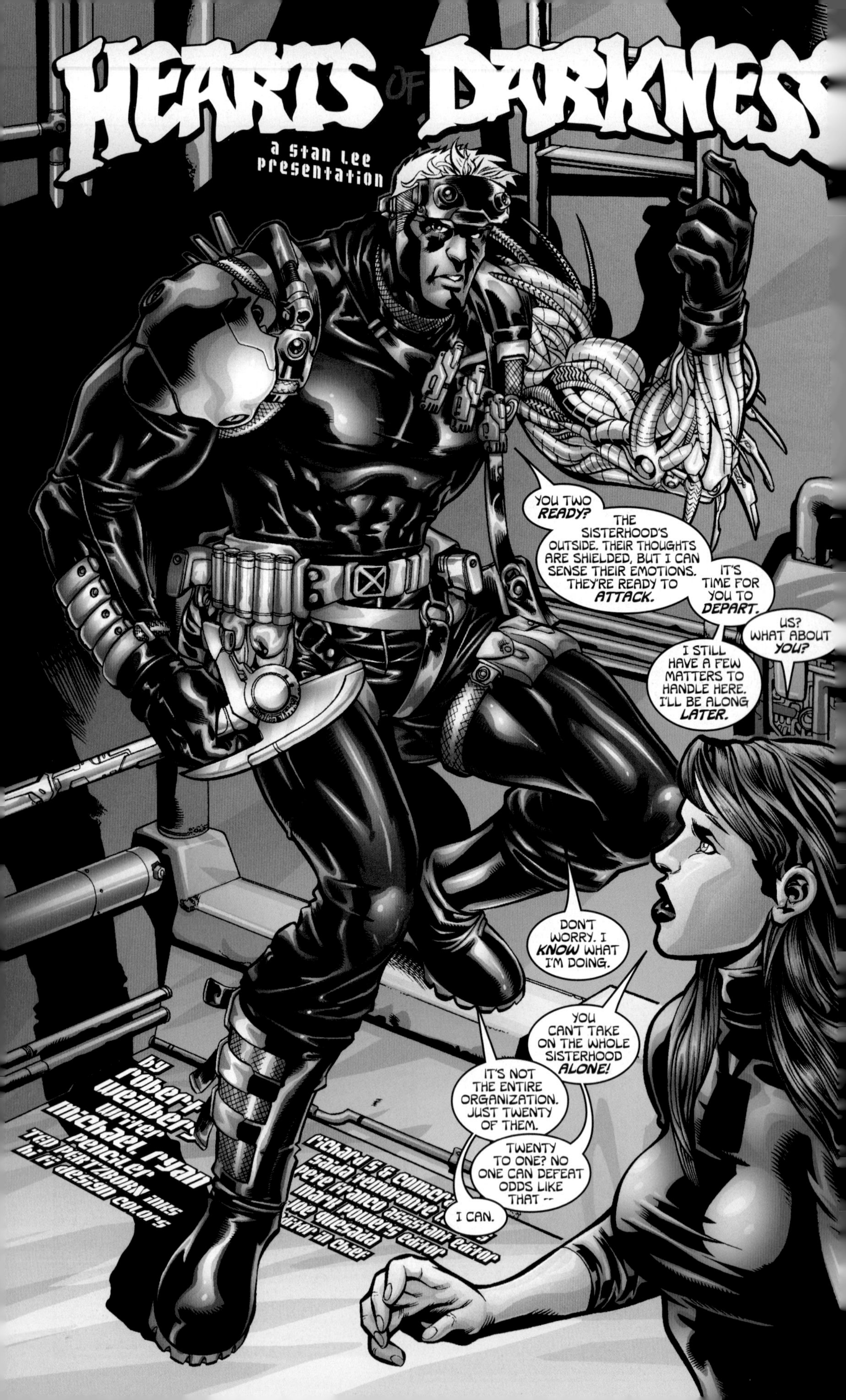
HEARTS OF DARKNESS
a stan lee presentation
YOU TWO READY?
THE SISTERHOOD'S OUTSIDE. THEIR THOUGHTS ARE SHIELDED, BUT I CAN SENSE THEIR EMOTIONS. THEY'RE READY TO ATTACK.
IT'S TIME FOR YOU TO DEPART.
US? WHAT ABOUT YOU?
I STILL HAVE A FEW MATTERS TO HANDLE HERE. I'LL BE ALONG LATER.
DON'T WORRY. I KNOW WHAT I'M DOING.
YOU CAN'T TAKE ON THE WHOLE SISTERHOOD ALONE!
IT'S NOT THE ENTIRE ORGANIZATION. JUST TWENTY OF THEM.
TWENTY TO ONE? NO ONE CAN DEFEAT ODDS LIKE THAT --
I CAN.
by robert weinberg writer
michael ryan penciler
TED PERTZBORN inks
by rs design colors
richard s & comicraft's
saida temofonte
pete franco assistant editor
mark powers editor
joe quesada editor in chief

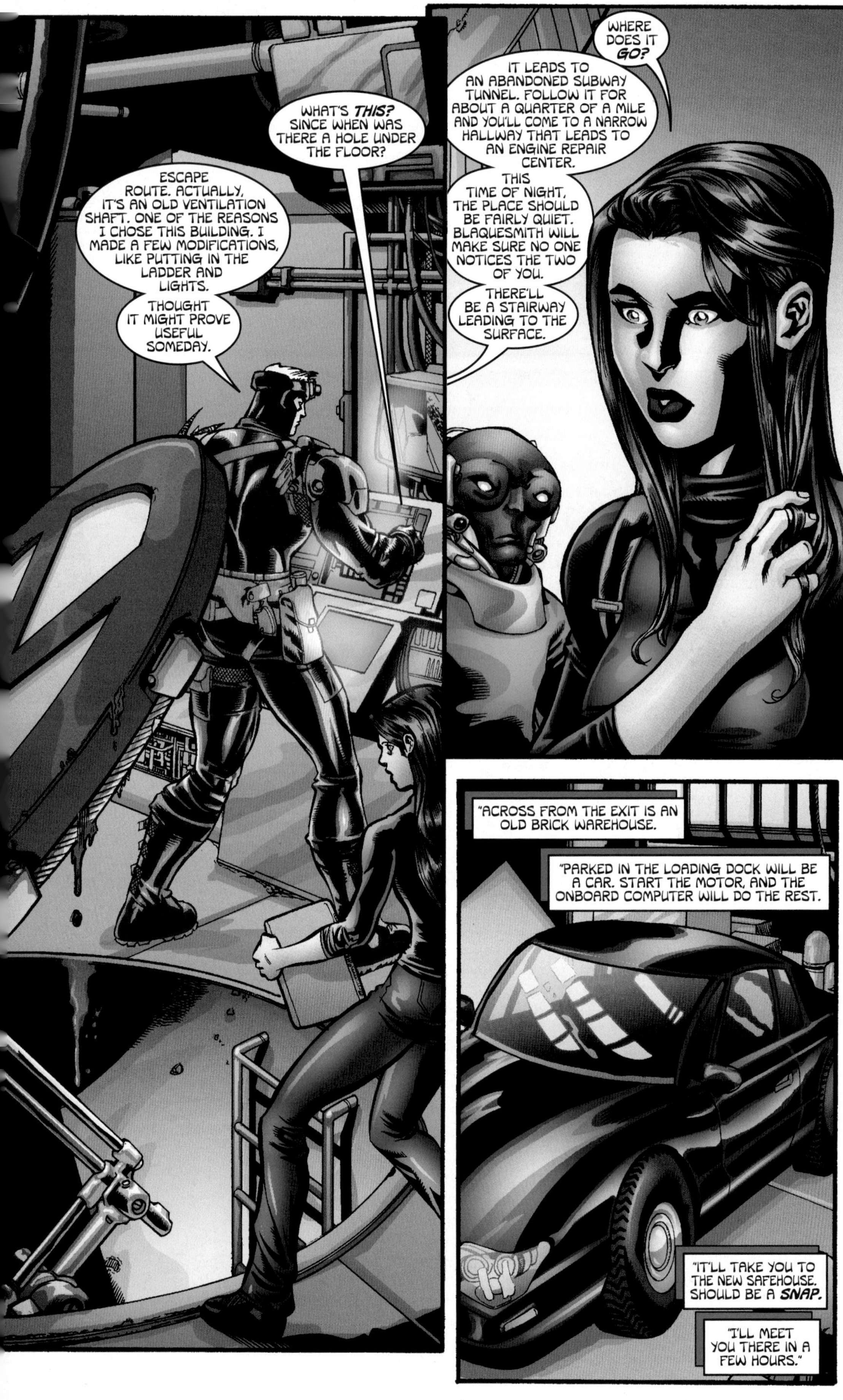

WHAT'S ***THIS?*** SINCE WHEN WAS THERE A HOLE UNDER THE FLOOR?
ESCAPE ROUTE. ACTUALLY, IT'S AN OLD VENTILATION SHAFT. ONE OF THE REASONS I CHOSE THIS BUILDING. I MADE A FEW MODIFICATIONS, LIKE PUTTING IN THE LADDER AND LIGHTS.
THOUGHT IT MIGHT PROVE USEFUL SOMEDAY.
WHERE DOES IT ***GO?***
IT LEADS TO AN ABANDONED SUBWAY TUNNEL. FOLLOW IT FOR ABOUT A QUARTER OF A MILE AND YOU'LL COME TO A NARROW HALLWAY THAT LEADS TO AN ENGINE REPAIR CENTER.
THIS TIME OF NIGHT, THE PLACE SHOULD BE FAIRLY QUIET. BLAQUESMITH WILL MAKE SURE NO ONE NOTICES THE TWO OF YOU.
THERE'LL BE A STAIRWAY LEADING TO THE SURFACE.
"ACROSS FROM THE EXIT IS AN OLD BRICK WAREHOUSE.
"PARKED IN THE LOADING DOCK WILL BE A CAR. START THE MOTOR, AND THE ONBOARD COMPUTER WILL DO THE REST.
"IT'LL TAKE YOU TO THE NEW SAFEHOUSE. SHOULD BE A ***SNAP.***
"I'LL MEET YOU THERE IN A FEW HOURS."

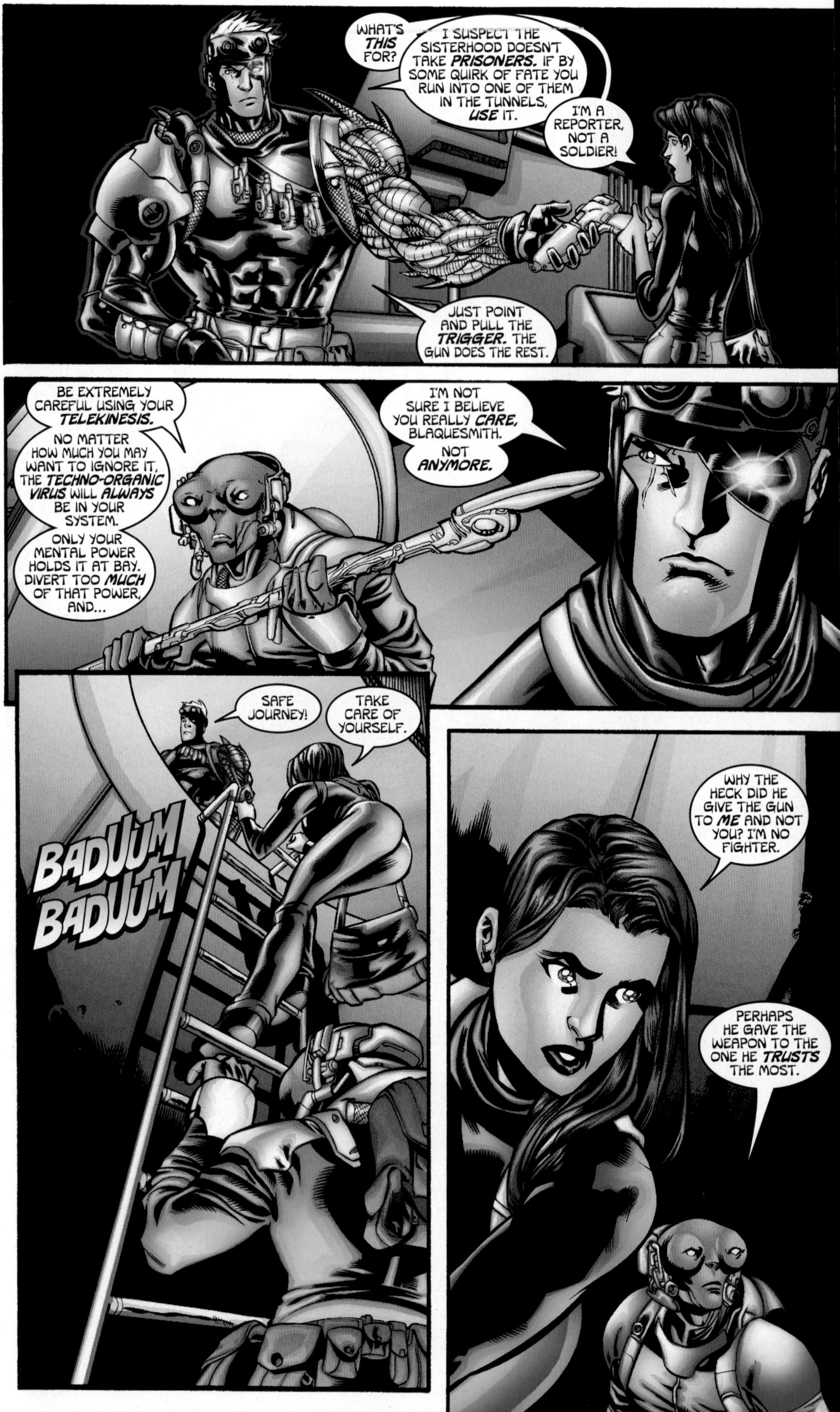
WHAT'S THIS FOR?
I SUSPECT THE SISTERHOOD DOESN'T TAKE PRISONERS. IF BY SOME QUIRK OF FATE YOU RUN INTO ONE OF THEM IN THE TUNNELS, USE IT.
I'M A REPORTER, NOT A SOLDIER!
JUST POINT AND PULL THE TRIGGER. THE GUN DOES THE REST.
BE EXTREMELY CAREFUL USING YOUR TELEKINESIS.
NO MATTER HOW MUCH YOU MAY WANT TO IGNORE IT, THE TECHNO-ORGANIC VIRUS WILL ALWAYS BE IN YOUR SYSTEM.
ONLY YOUR MENTAL POWER HOLDS IT AT BAY. DIVERT TOO MUCH OF THAT POWER, AND...
I'M NOT SURE I BELIEVE YOU REALLY CARE, BLAQUESMITH.
NOT ANYMORE.
SAFE JOURNEY!
TAKE CARE OF YOURSELF.
BADUUM
BADUUM
WHY THE HECK DID HE GIVE THE GUN TO ME AND NOT YOU? I'M NO FIGHTER.
PERHAPS HE GAVE THE WEAPON TO THE ONE HE TRUSTS THE MOST.

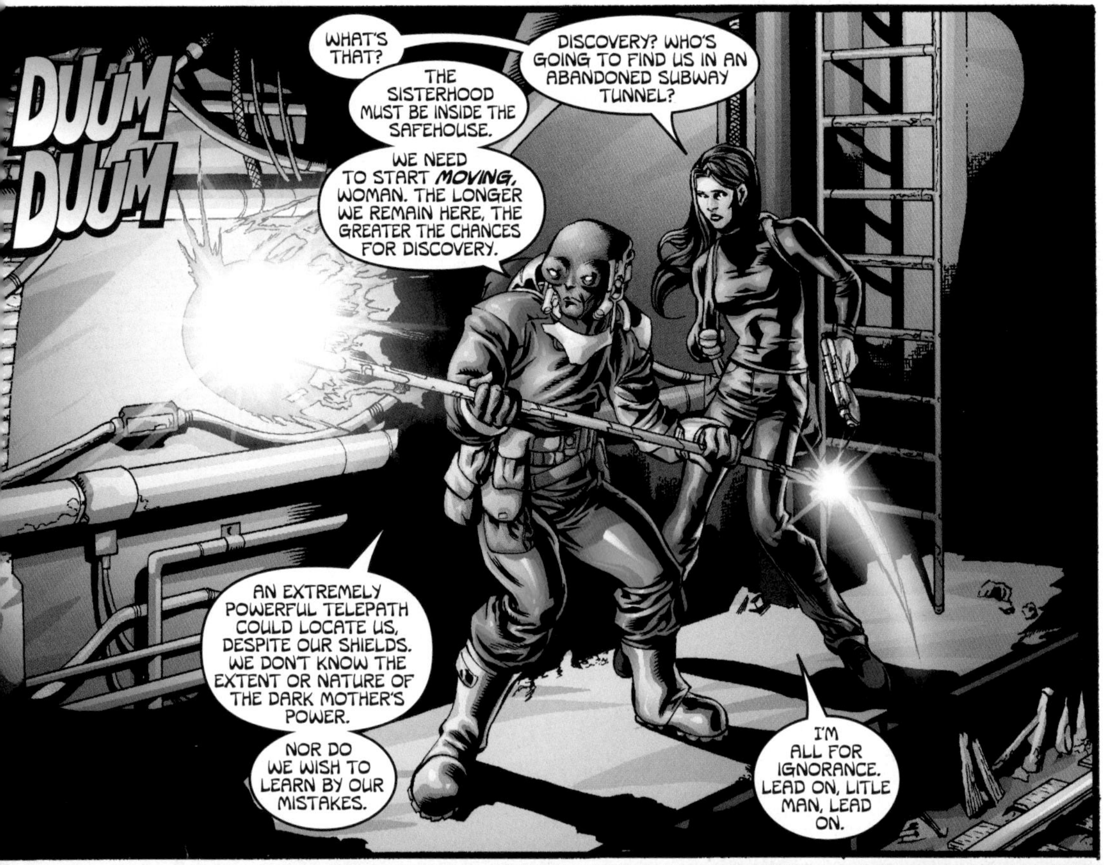
DUUM DUUM
WHAT'S THAT?
THE SISTERHOOD MUST BE INSIDE THE SAFEHOUSE.
WE NEED TO START *MOVING,* WOMAN. THE LONGER WE REMAIN HERE, THE GREATER THE CHANCES FOR DISCOVERY.
DISCOVERY? WHO'S GOING TO FIND US IN AN ABANDONED SUBWAY TUNNEL?
AN EXTREMELY POWERFUL TELEPATH COULD LOCATE US, DESPITE OUR SHIELDS. WE DON'T KNOW THE EXTENT OR NATURE OF THE DARK MOTHER'S POWER.
NOR DO WE WISH TO LEARN BY OUR MISTAKES.
I'M ALL FOR IGNORANCE. LEAD ON, LITLE MAN, LEAD ON.

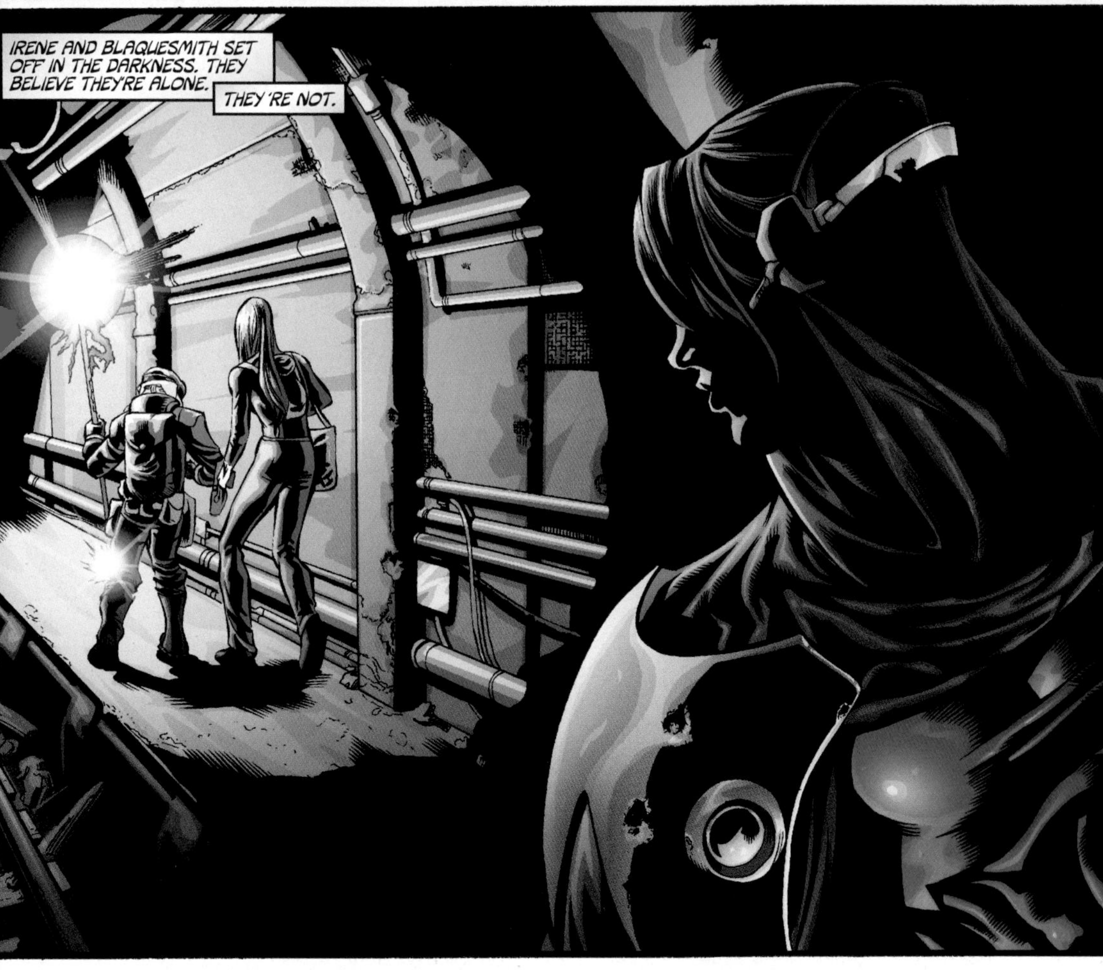
IRENE AND BLAQUESMITH SET OFF IN THE DARKNESS. THEY BELIEVE THEY'RE ALONE.
THEY'RE NOT.

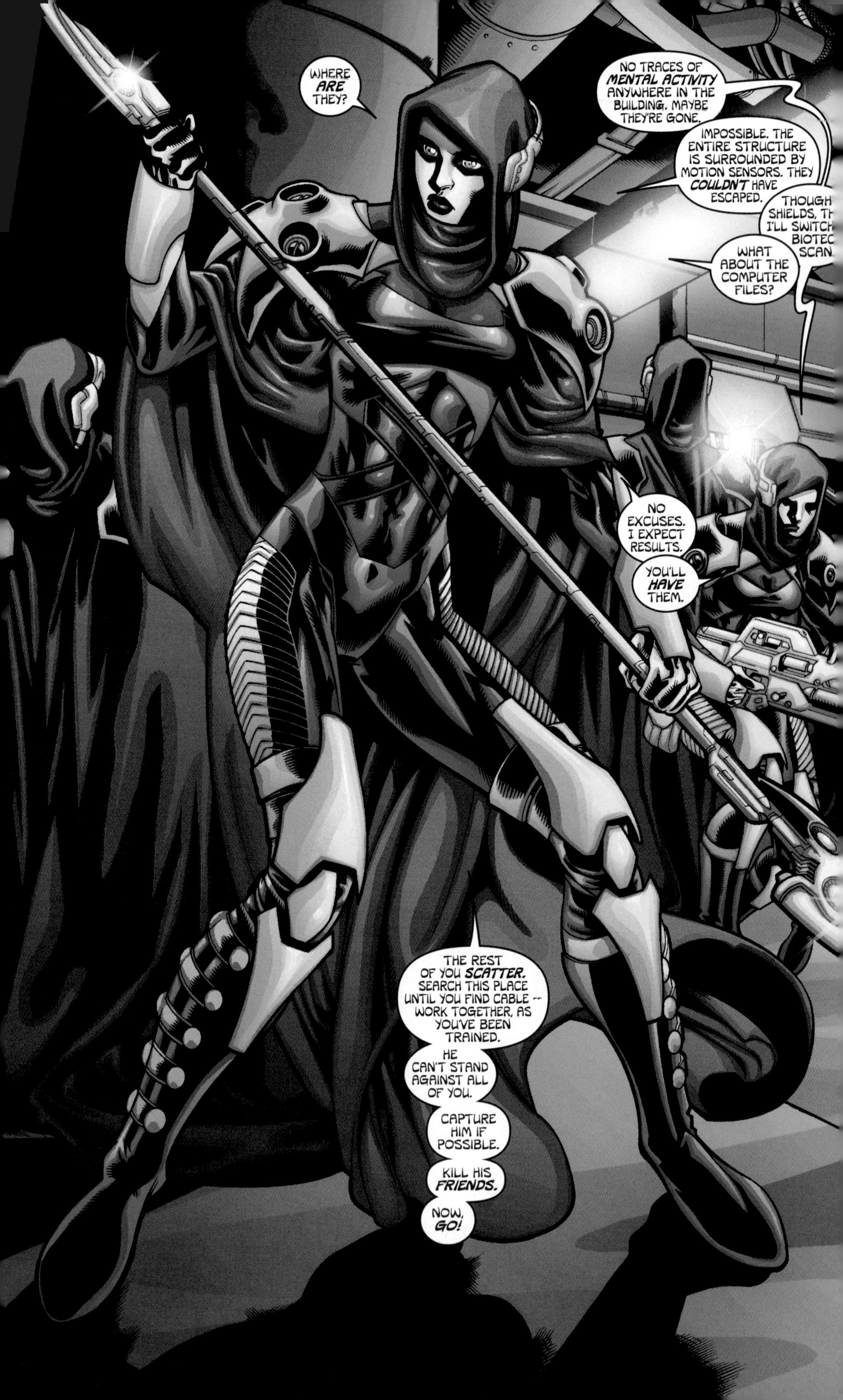
WHERE ARE THEY?
NO TRACES OF MENTAL ACTIVITY ANYWHERE IN THE BUILDING. MAYBE THEY'RE GONE.
IMPOSSIBLE. THE ENTIRE STRUCTURE IS SURROUNDED BY MOTION SENSORS. THEY COULDN'T HAVE ESCAPED.
THOUGH SHIELDS, TH I'LL SWITCH BIOTEC SCAN.
WHAT ABOUT THE COMPUTER FILES?
NO EXCUSES. I EXPECT RESULTS.
YOU'LL HAVE THEM.
THE REST OF YOU SCATTER. SEARCH THIS PLACE UNTIL YOU FIND CABLE -- WORK TOGETHER, AS YOU'VE BEEN TRAINED.
HE CAN'T STAND AGAINST ALL OF YOU.
CAPTURE HIM IF POSSIBLE.
KILL HIS FRIENDS.
NOW, GO!

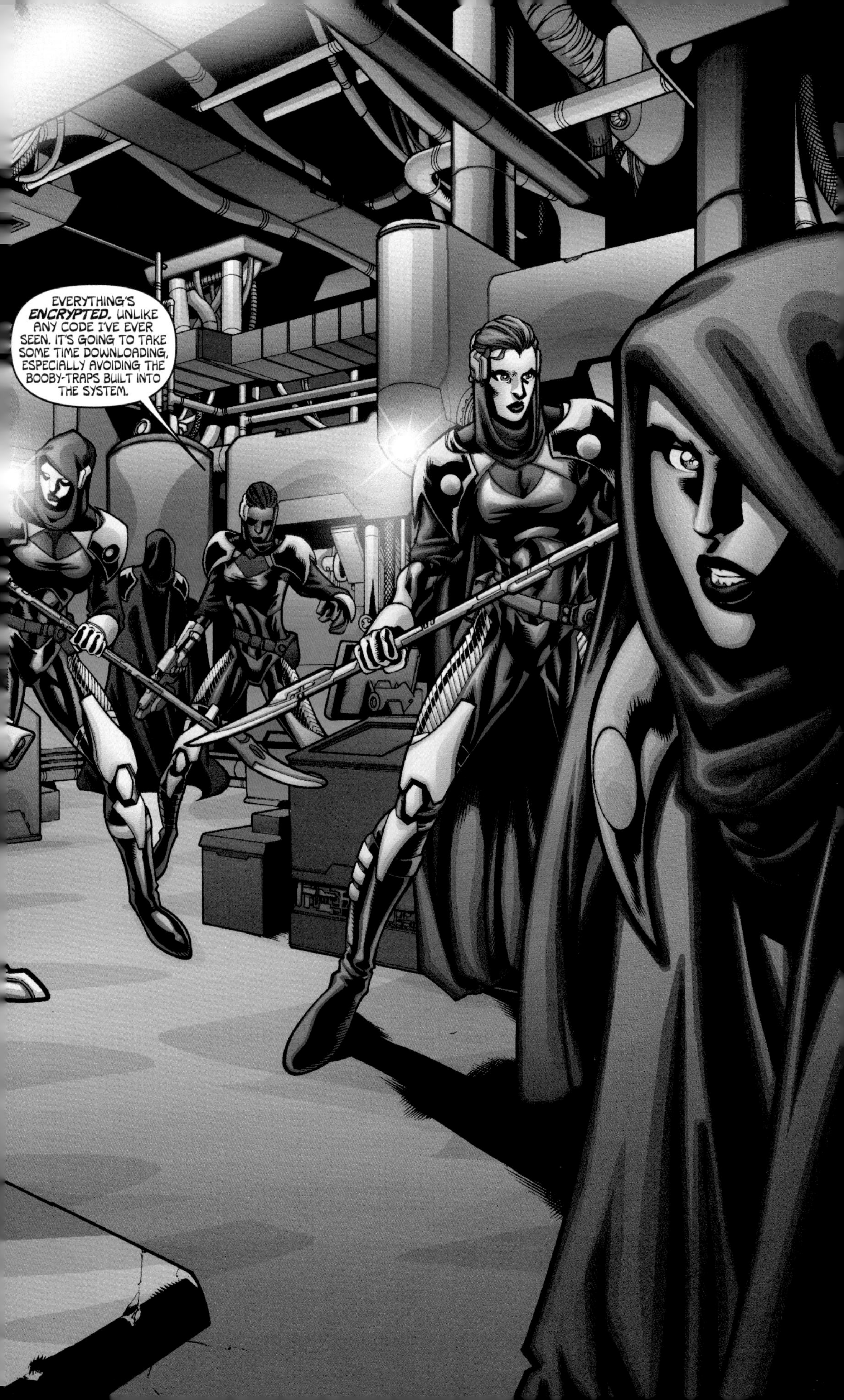
EVERYTHING'S ENCRYPTED. UNLIKE ANY CODE I'VE EVER SEEN. IT'S GOING TO TAKE SOME TIME DOWNLOADING, ESPECIALLY AVOIDING THE BOOBY-TRAPS BUILT INTO THE SYSTEM.

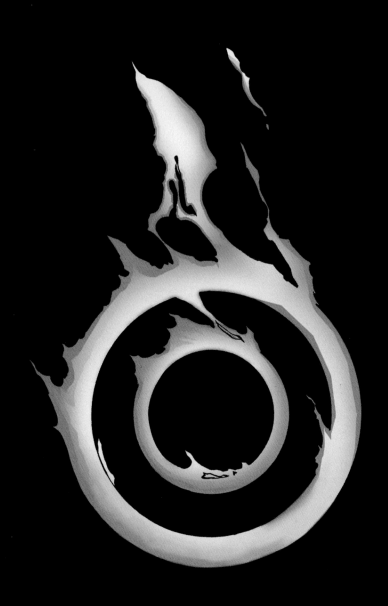

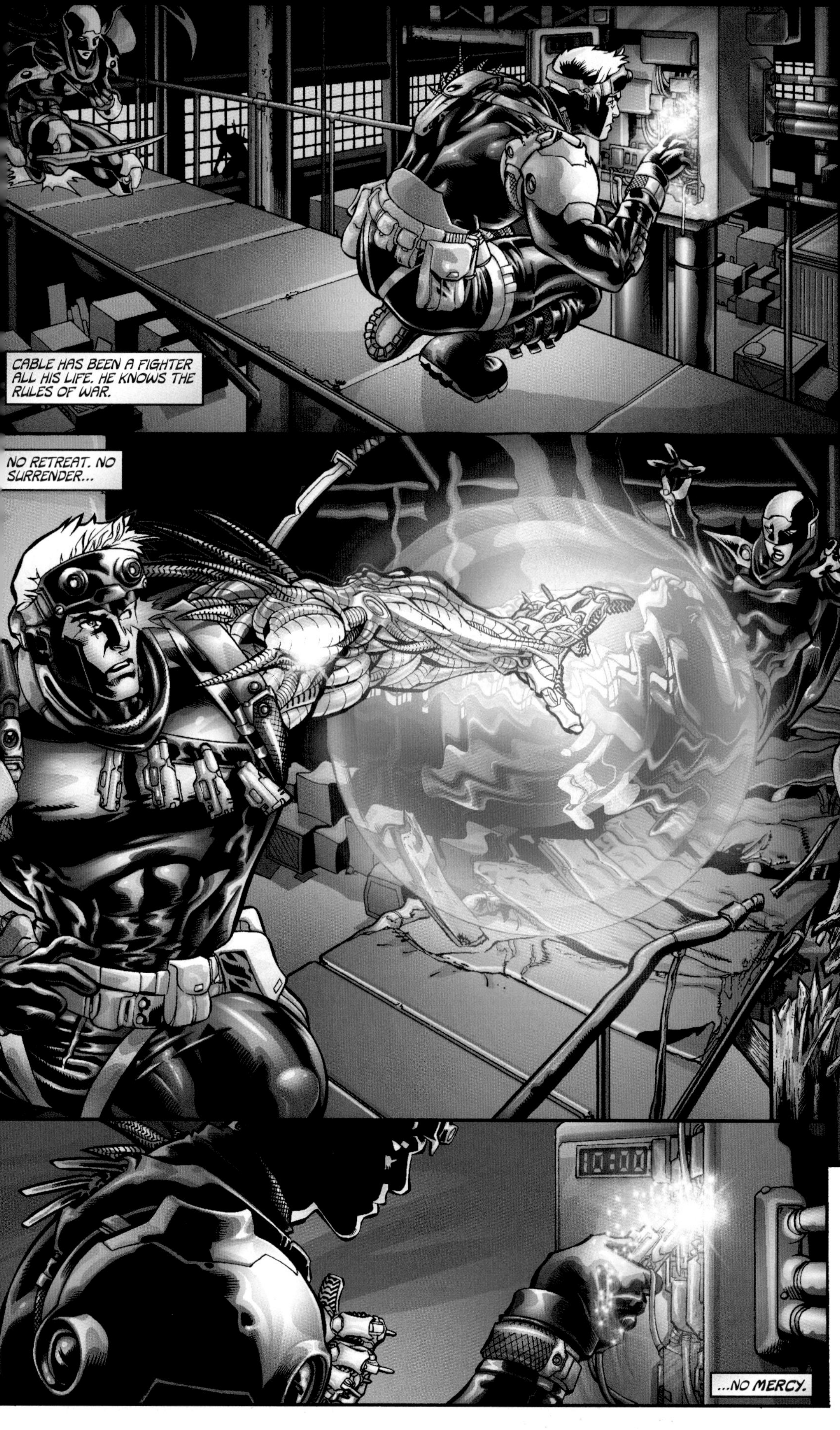
CABLE HAS BEEN A FIGHTER ALL HIS LIFE. HE KNOWS THE RULES OF WAR.
NO RETREAT. NO SURRENDER...
...NO MERCY.

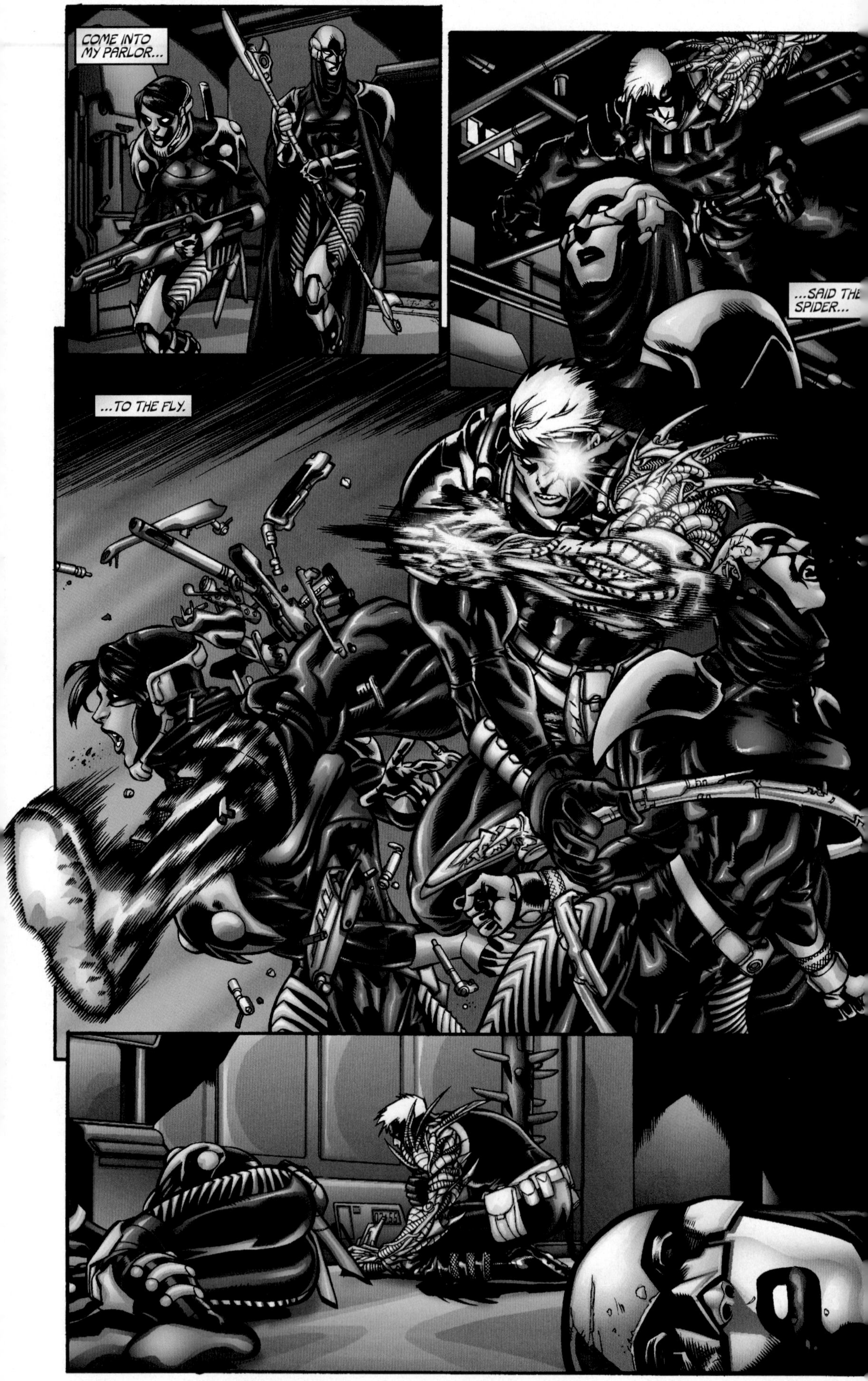

COME INTO MY PARLOR...
...SAID THE SPIDER...
...TO THE FLY.

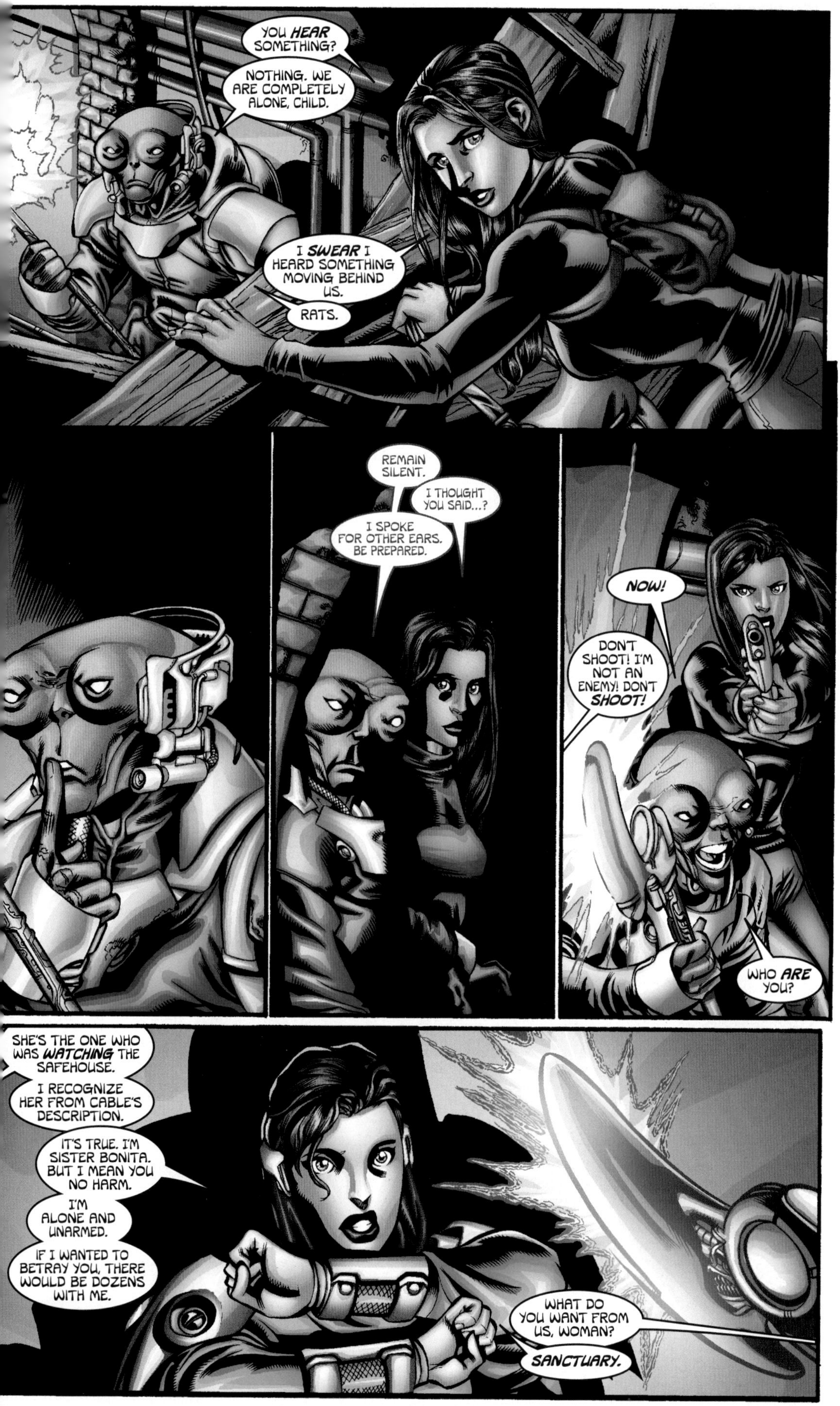

YOU ***HEAR*** SOMETHING?
NOTHING. WE ARE COMPLETELY ALONE, CHILD.
I ***SWEAR*** I HEARD SOMETHING MOVING BEHIND US.
RATS.
REMAIN SILENT.
I THOUGHT YOU SAID...?
I SPOKE FOR OTHER EARS. BE PREPARED.
NOW!
DON'T SHOOT! I'M NOT AN ENEMY! DON'T ***SHOOT!***
WHO ***ARE*** YOU?
SHE'S THE ONE WHO WAS ***WATCHING*** THE SAFEHOUSE.
I RECOGNIZE HER FROM CABLE'S DESCRIPTION.
IT'S TRUE. I'M SISTER BONITA. BUT I MEAN YOU NO HARM.
I'M ALONE AND UNARMED.
IF I WANTED TO BETRAY YOU, THERE WOULD BE DOZENS WITH ME.
WHAT DO YOU WANT FROM US, WOMAN?
SANCTUARY.

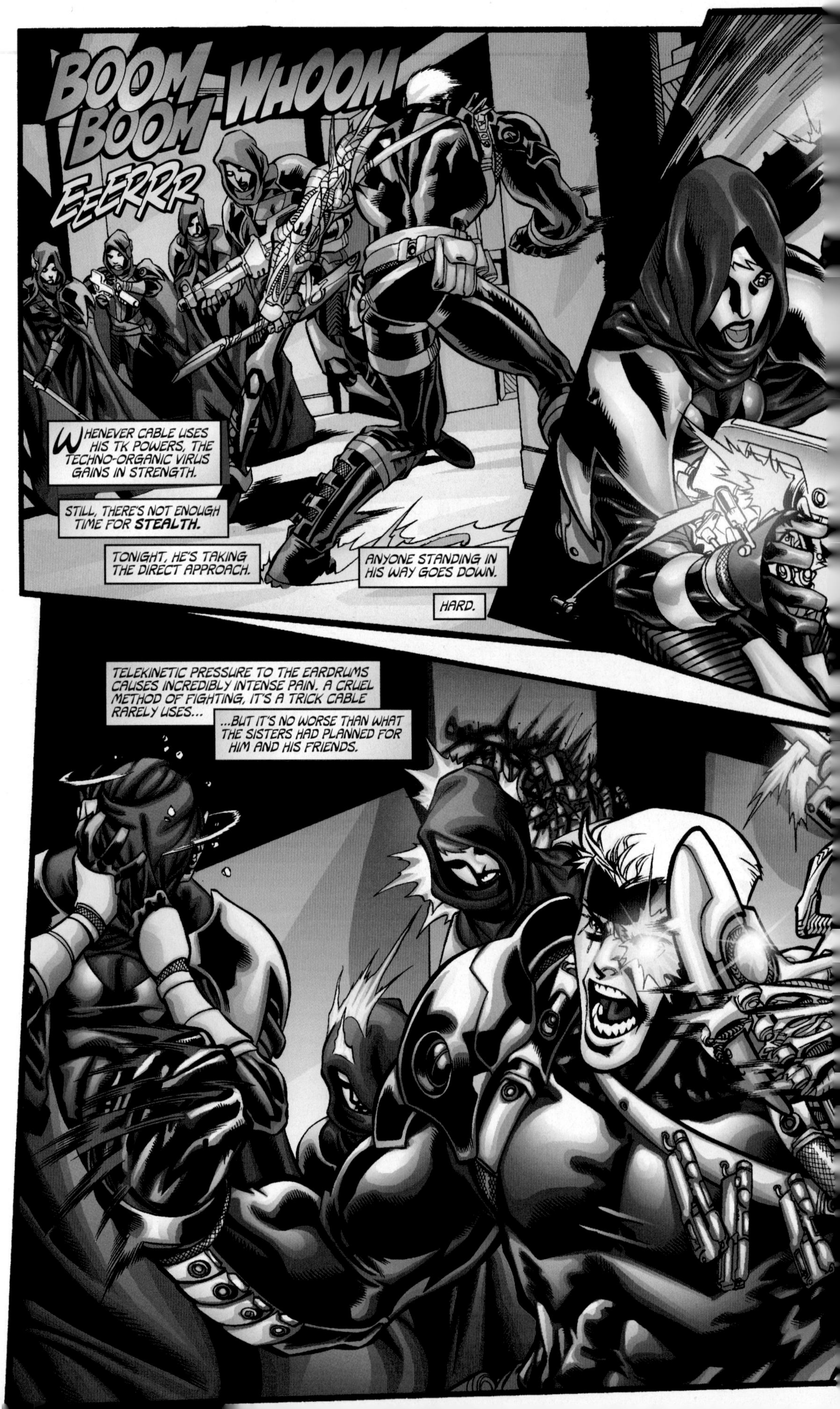
BOOM BOOM
WHOOM
EEERRR
WHENEVER CABLE USES HIS TK POWERS, THE TECHNO-ORGANIC VIRUS GAINS IN STRENGTH.
STILL, THERE'S NOT ENOUGH TIME FOR STEALTH.
TONIGHT, HE'S TAKING THE DIRECT APPROACH.
ANYONE STANDING IN HIS WAY GOES DOWN.
HARD.
TELEKINETIC PRESSURE TO THE EARDRUMS CAUSES INCREDIBLY INTENSE PAIN. A CRUEL METHOD OF FIGHTING, IT'S A TRICK CABLE RARELY USES...
...BUT IT'S NO WORSE THAN WHAT THE SISTERS HAD PLANNED FOR HIM AND HIS FRIENDS.

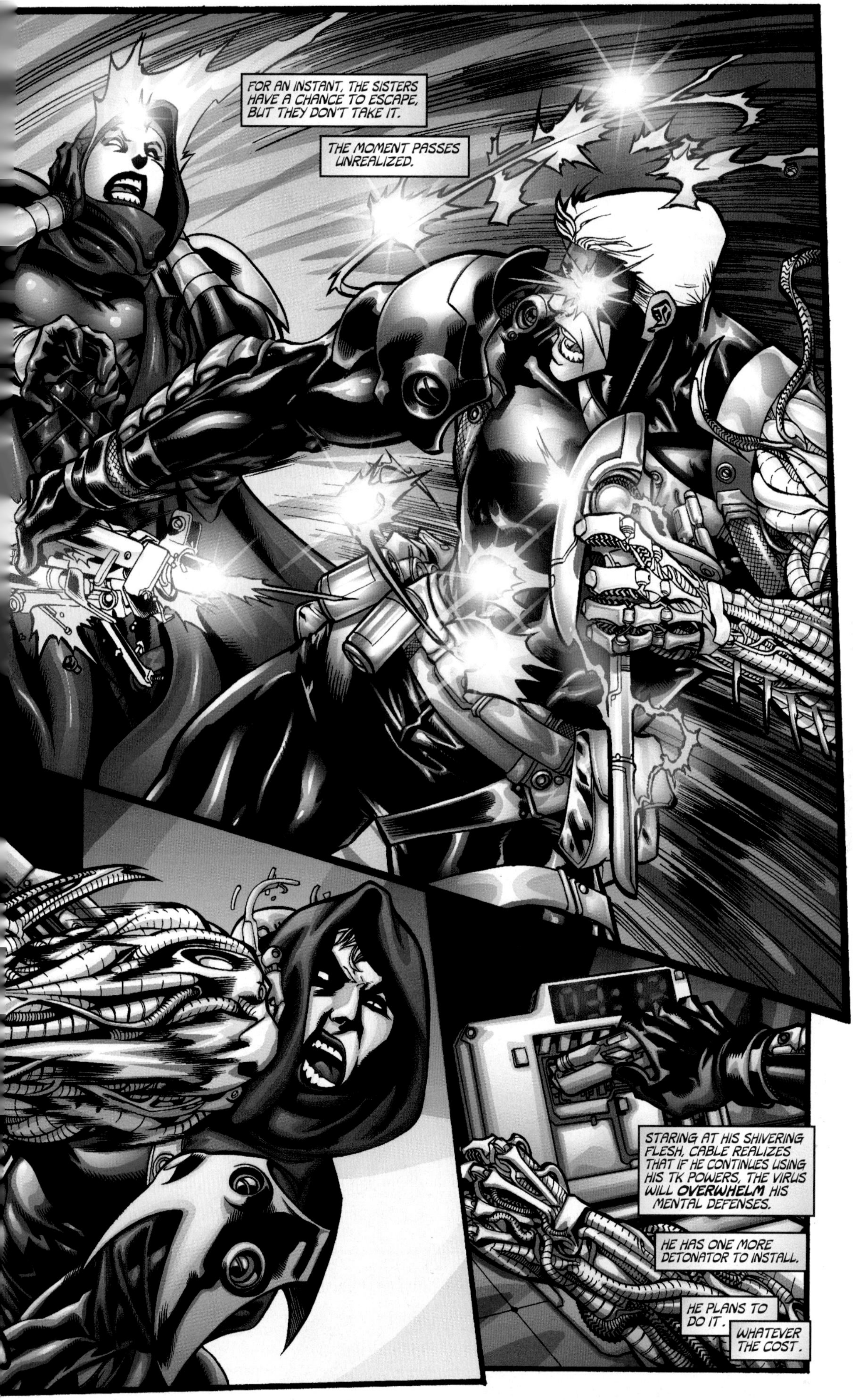
FOR AN INSTANT, THE SISTERS HAVE A CHANCE TO ESCAPE, BUT THEY DON'T TAKE IT.
THE MOMENT PASSES UNREALIZED.
STARING AT HIS SHIVERING FLESH, CABLE REALIZES THAT IF HE CONTINUES USING HIS TK POWERS, THE VIRUS WILL **OVERWHELM** HIS MENTAL DEFENSES.
HE HAS ONE MORE DETONATOR TO INSTALL.
HE PLANS TO DO IT.
WHATEVER THE COST.

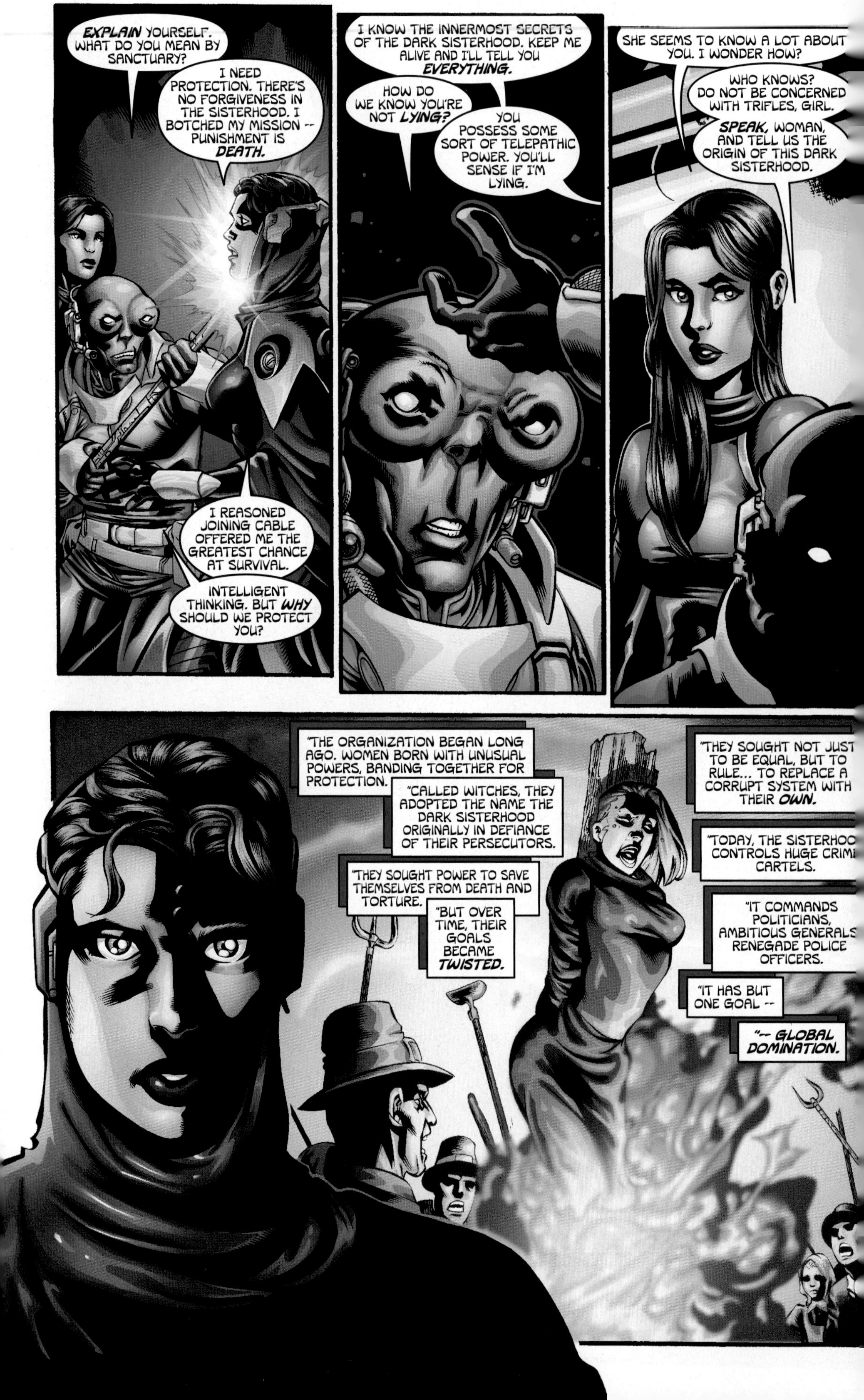
EXPLAIN YOURSELF. WHAT DO YOU MEAN BY SANCTUARY?
I NEED PROTECTION. THERE'S NO FORGIVENESS IN THE SISTERHOOD. I BOTCHED MY MISSION -- PUNISHMENT IS DEATH.
I REASONED JOINING CABLE OFFERED ME THE GREATEST CHANCE AT SURVIVAL.
INTELLIGENT THINKING. BUT WHY SHOULD WE PROTECT YOU?
I KNOW THE INNERMOST SECRETS OF THE DARK SISTERHOOD. KEEP ME ALIVE AND I'LL TELL YOU EVERYTHING.
HOW DO WE KNOW YOU'RE NOT LYING?
YOU POSSESS SOME SORT OF TELEPATHIC POWER. YOU'LL SENSE IF I'M LYING.
SHE SEEMS TO KNOW A LOT ABOUT YOU. I WONDER HOW?
WHO KNOWS? DO NOT BE CONCERNED WITH TRIFLES, GIRL.
SPEAK, WOMAN, AND TELL US THE ORIGIN OF THIS DARK SISTERHOOD.
"THE ORGANIZATION BEGAN LONG AGO. WOMEN BORN WITH UNUSUAL POWERS, BANDING TOGETHER FOR PROTECTION.
"CALLED WITCHES, THEY ADOPTED THE NAME THE DARK SISTERHOOD ORIGINALLY IN DEFIANCE OF THEIR PERSECUTORS.
"THEY SOUGHT POWER TO SAVE THEMSELVES FROM DEATH AND TORTURE.
"BUT OVER TIME, THEIR GOALS BECAME TWISTED.
"THEY SOUGHT NOT JUST TO BE EQUAL, BUT TO RULE... TO REPLACE A CORRUPT SYSTEM WITH THEIR OWN.
"TODAY, THE SISTERHOO CONTROLS HUGE CRIM CARTELS.
"IT COMMANDS POLITICIANS, AMBITIOUS GENERALS RENEGADE POLICE OFFICERS.
"IT HAS BUT ONE GOAL --
"-- GLOBAL DOMINATION.

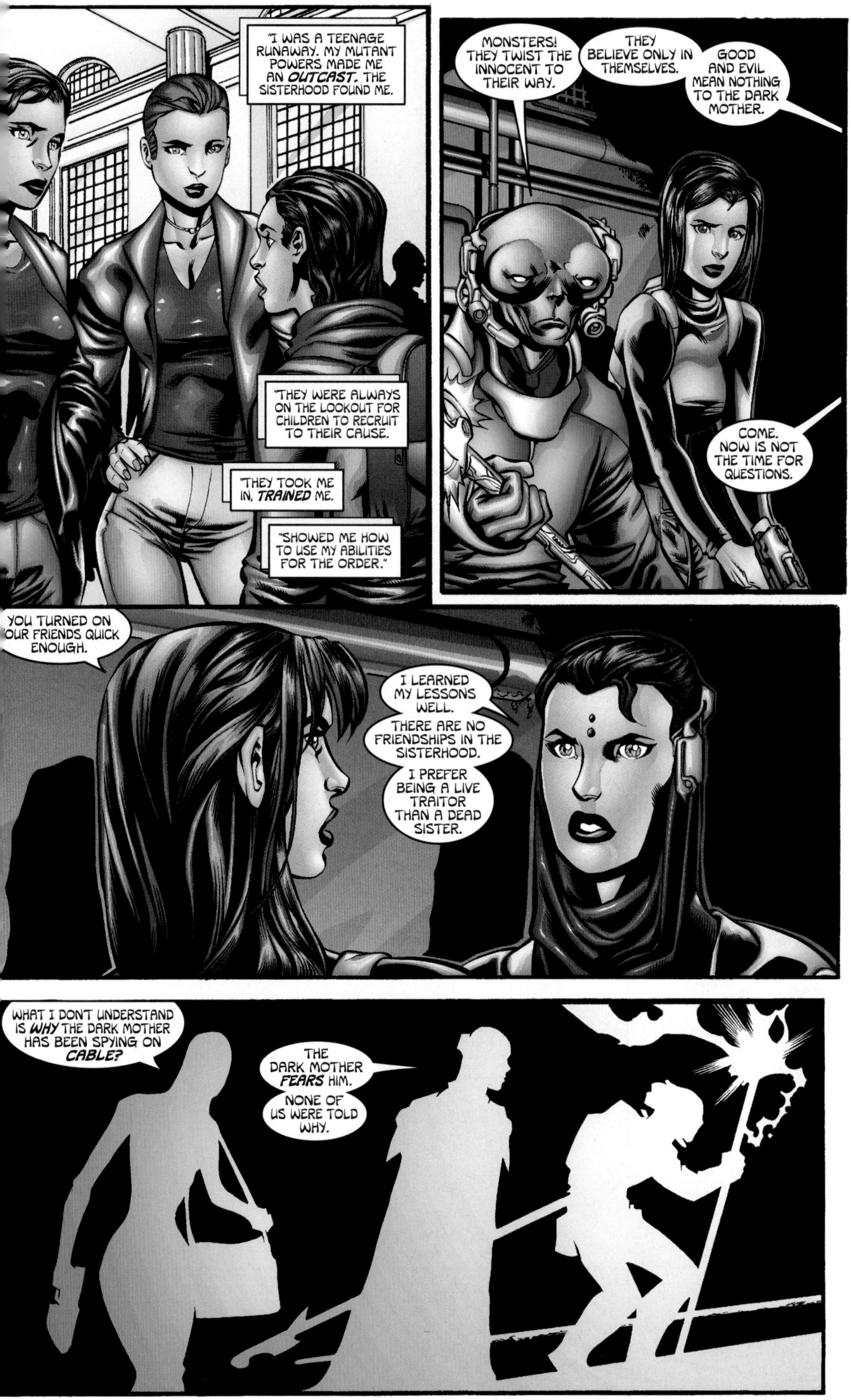
"I WAS A TEENAGE RUNAWAY. MY MUTANT POWERS MADE ME AN OUTCAST. THE SISTERHOOD FOUND ME.
"THEY WERE ALWAYS ON THE LOOKOUT FOR CHILDREN TO RECRUIT TO THEIR CAUSE.
"THEY TOOK ME IN, TRAINED ME.
"SHOWED ME HOW TO USE MY ABILITIES FOR THE ORDER."
MONSTERS! THEY TWIST THE INNOCENT TO THEIR WAY.
THEY BELIEVE ONLY IN THEMSELVES.
GOOD AND EVIL MEAN NOTHING TO THE DARK MOTHER.
COME. NOW IS NOT THE TIME FOR QUESTIONS.
YOU TURNED ON OUR FRIENDS QUICK ENOUGH.
I LEARNED MY LESSONS WELL.
THERE ARE NO FRIENDSHIPS IN THE SISTERHOOD.
I PREFER BEING A LIVE TRAITOR THAN A DEAD SISTER.
WHAT I DON'T UNDERSTAND IS WHY THE DARK MOTHER HAS BEEN SPYING ON CABLE?
THE DARK MOTHER FEARS HIM.
NONE OF US WERE TOLD WHY.

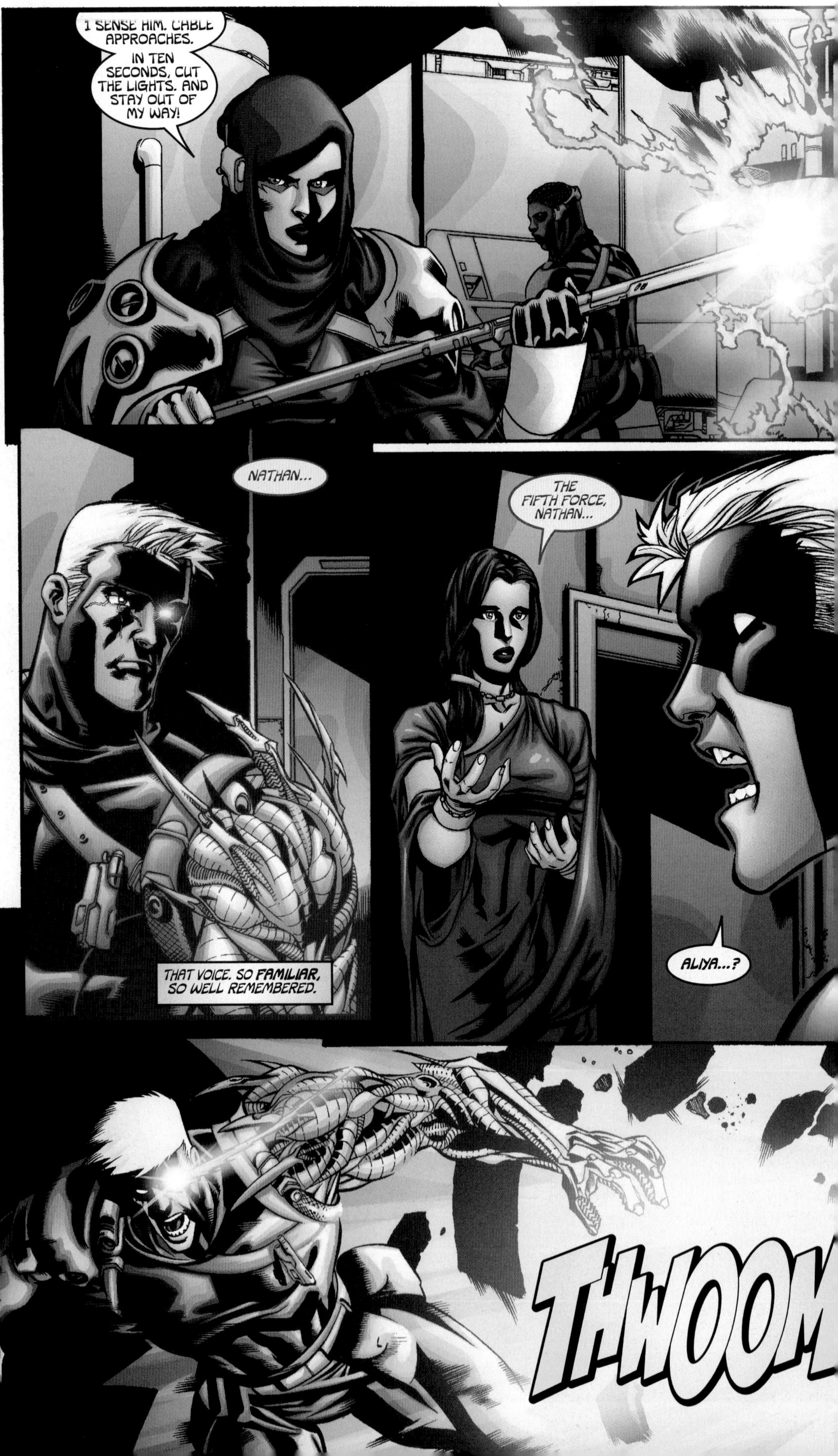
I SENSE HIM. CABLE APPROACHES.
IN TEN SECONDS, CUT THE LIGHTS. AND STAY OUT OF MY WAY!
NATHAN...
THAT VOICE. SO FAMILIAR, SO WELL REMEMBERED.
THE FIFTH FORCE, NATHAN...
ALIYA...?
THWOOM

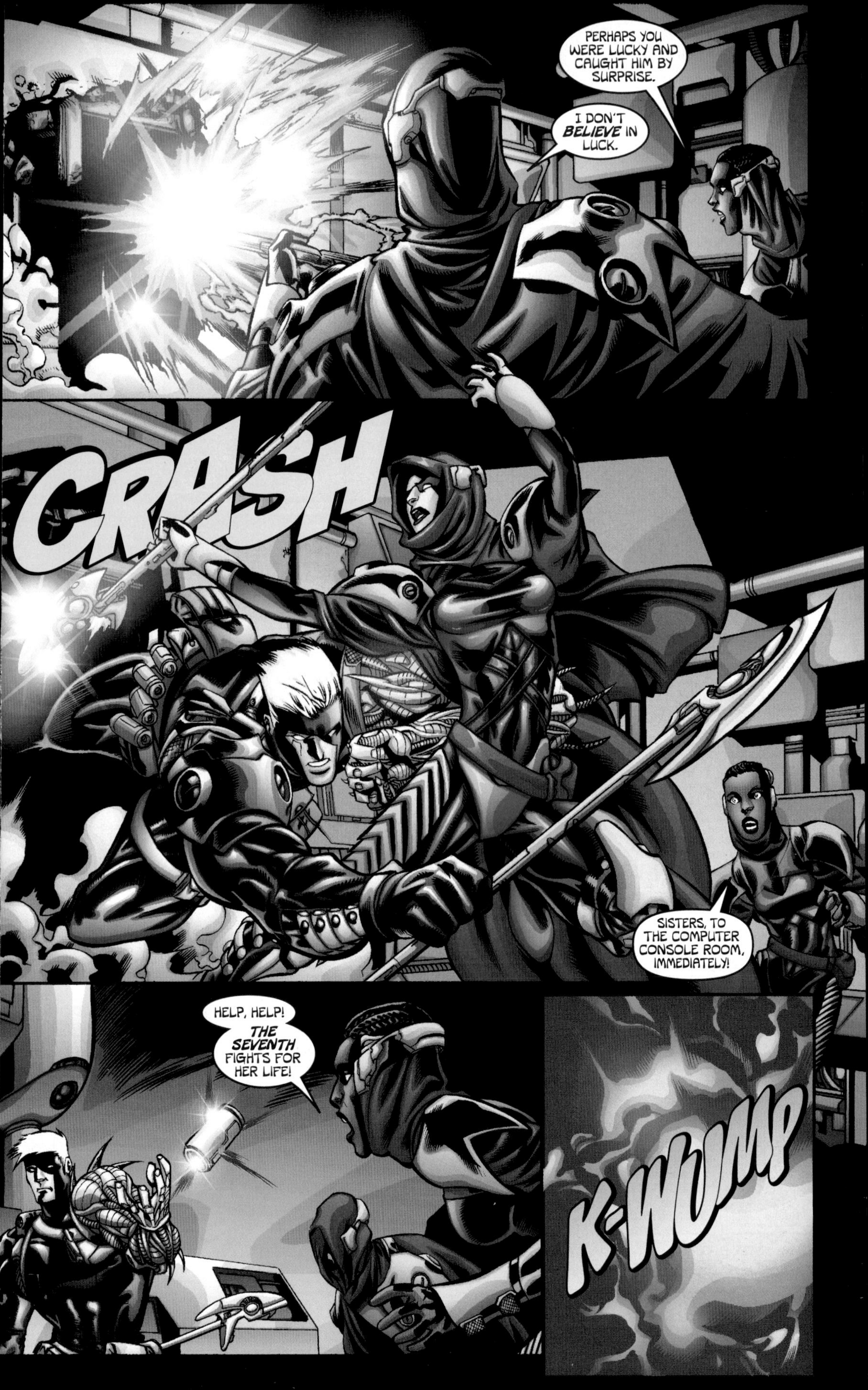
PERHAPS YOU WERE LUCKY AND CAUGHT HIM BY SURPRISE.
I DON'T *BELIEVE* IN LUCK.
CRASH
SISTERS, TO THE COMPUTER CONSOLE ROOM, IMMEDIATELY!
HELP, HELP! *THE SEVENTH* FIGHTS FOR HER LIFE!
K-WUMP

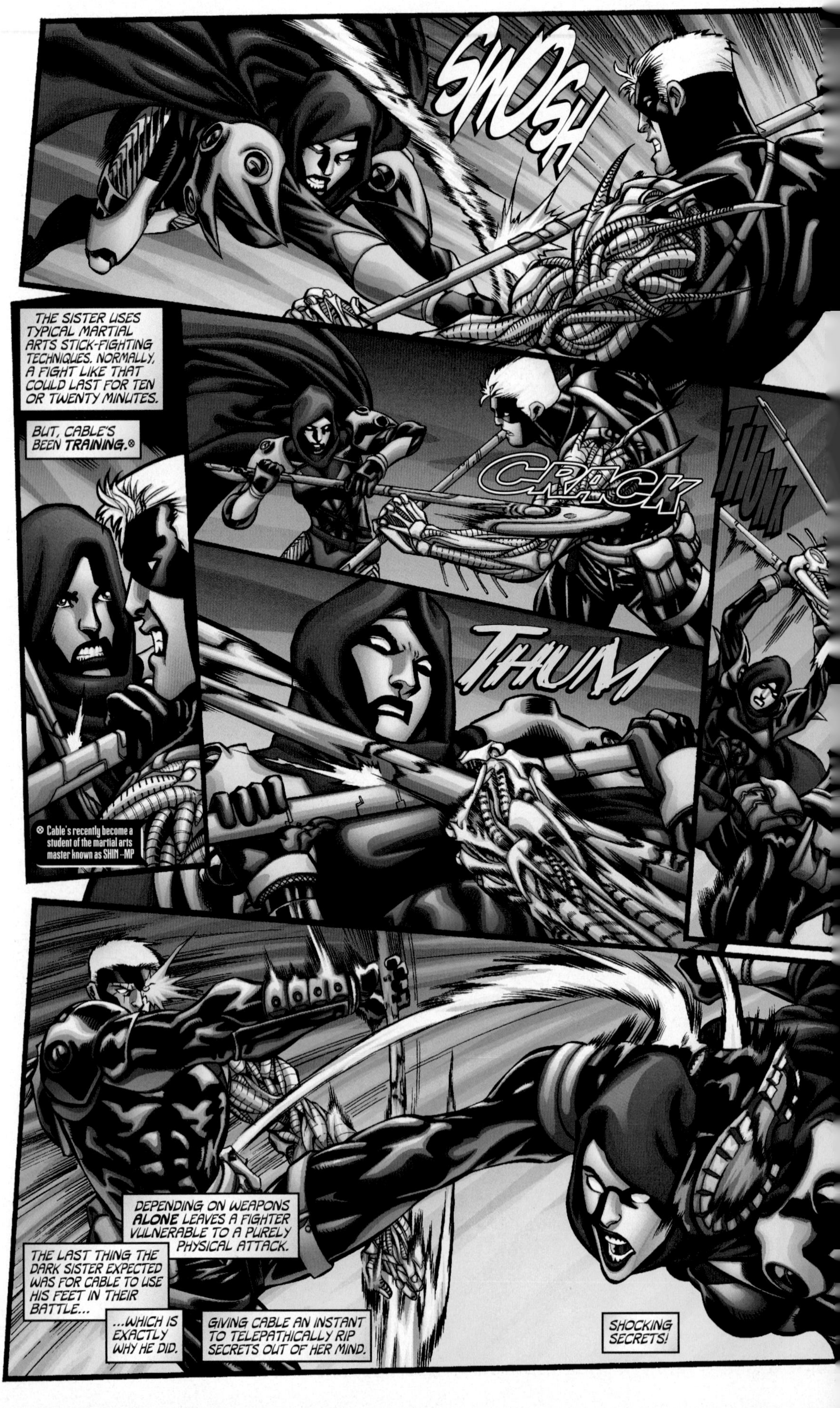
SWOSH
THE SISTER USES TYPICAL MARTIAL ARTS STICK-FIGHTING TECHNIQUES. NORMALLY, A FIGHT LIKE THAT COULD LAST FOR TEN OR TWENTY MINUTES.
BUT, CABLE'S BEEN TRAINING.⊗
CRACK
THUNK
THUM
⊗ Cable's recently become a student of the martial arts master known as SHIN --MP
DEPENDING ON WEAPONS ALONE LEAVES A FIGHTER VULNERABLE TO A PURELY PHYSICAL ATTACK.
THE LAST THING THE DARK SISTER EXPECTED WAS FOR CABLE TO USE HIS FEET IN THEIR BATTLE...
...WHICH IS EXACTLY WHY HE DID.
GIVING CABLE AN INSTANT TO TELEPATHICALLY RIP SECRETS OUT OF HER MIND.
SHOCKING SECRETS!

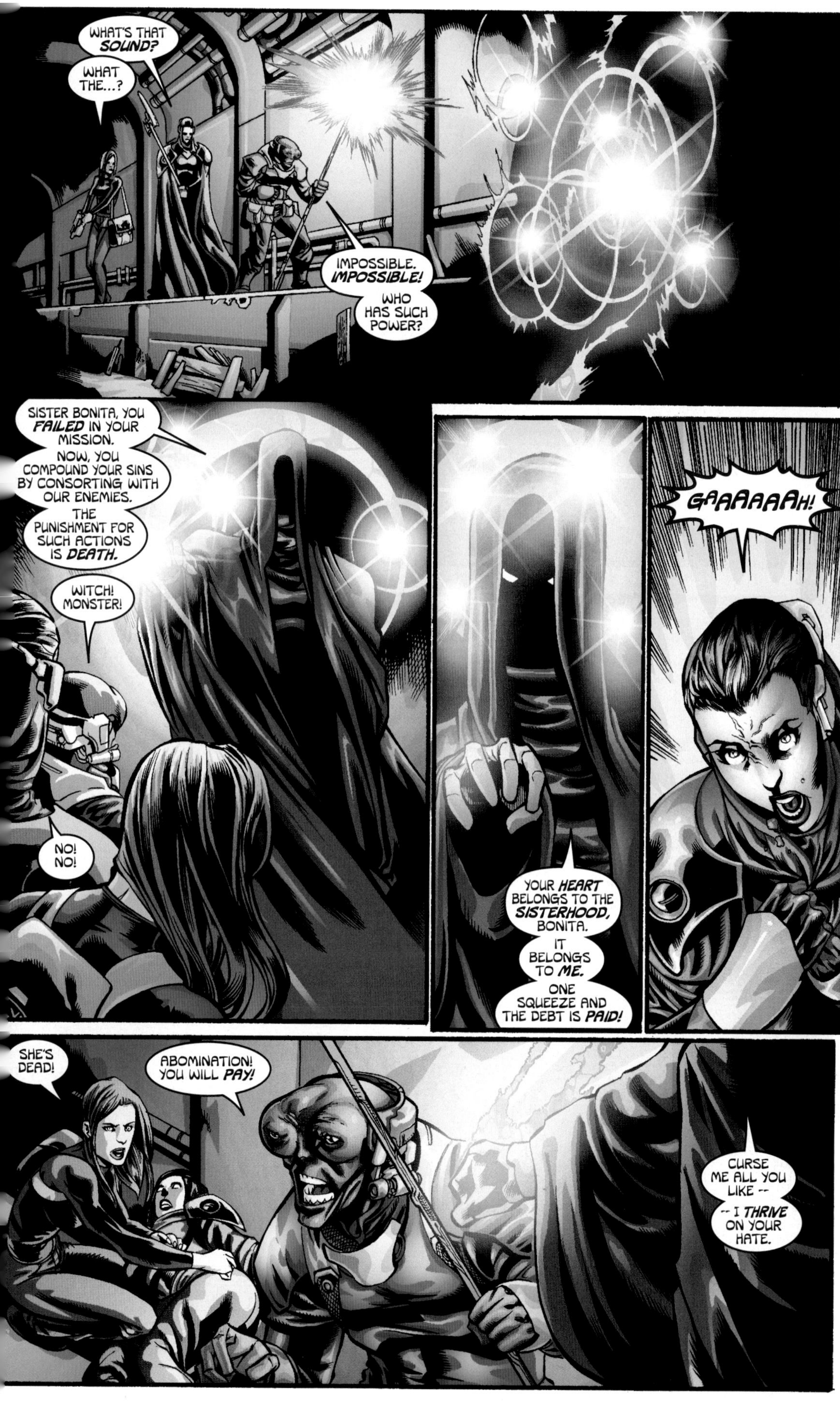
WHAT'S THAT SOUND?
WHAT THE...?
IMPOSSIBLE. IMPOSSIBLE!
WHO HAS SUCH POWER?
SISTER BONITA, YOU FAILED IN YOUR MISSION.
NOW, YOU COMPOUND YOUR SINS BY CONSORTING WITH OUR ENEMIES.
THE PUNISHMENT FOR SUCH ACTIONS IS DEATH.
WITCH! MONSTER!
NO! NO!
YOUR HEART BELONGS TO THE SISTERHOOD, BONITA.
IT BELONGS TO ME.
ONE SQUEEZE AND THE DEBT IS PAID!
GAAAAAAH!
SHE'S DEAD!
ABOMINATION! YOU WILL PAY!
CURSE ME ALL YOU LIKE --
-- I THRIVE ON YOUR HATE.

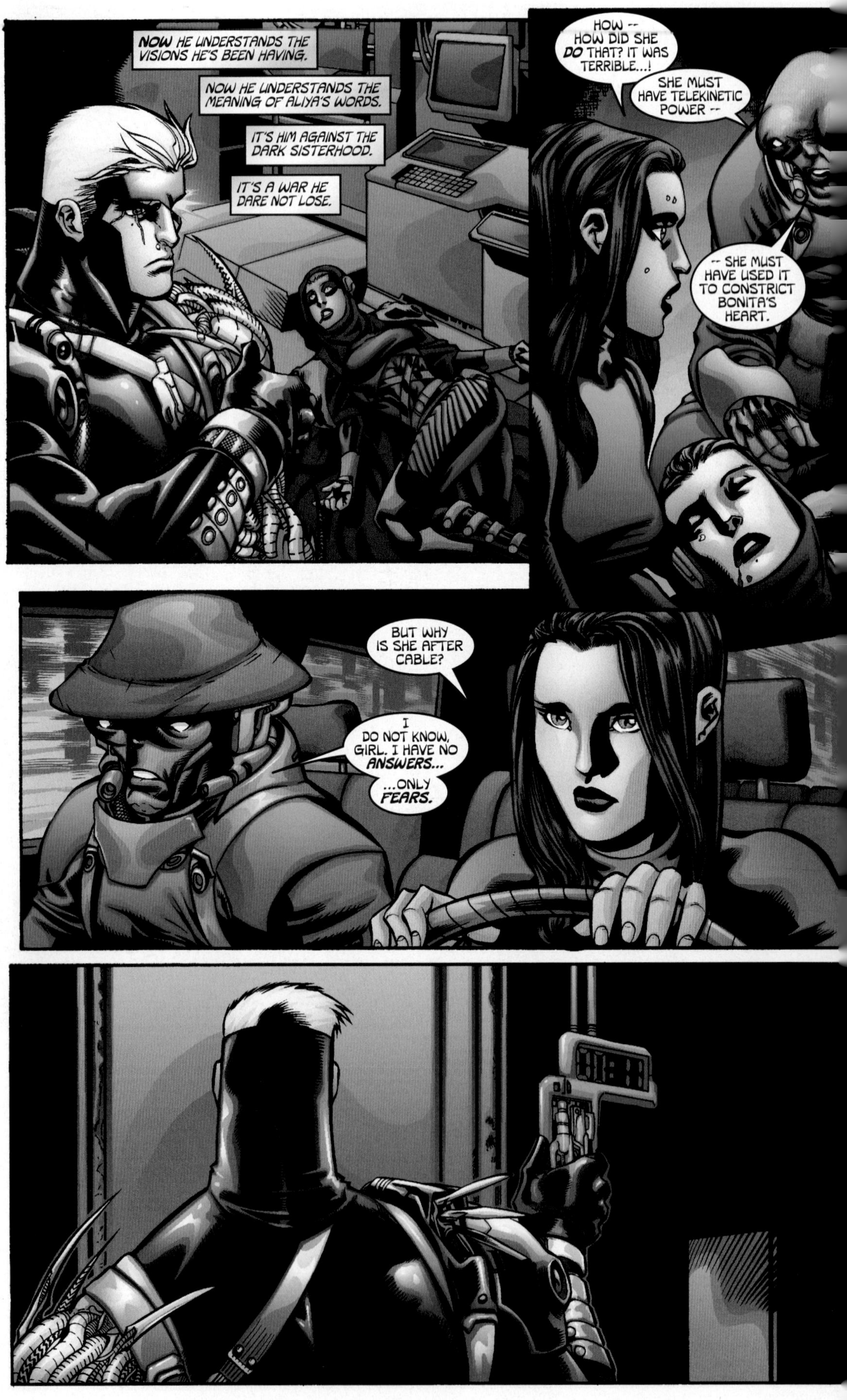

NOW HE UNDERSTANDS THE VISIONS HE'S BEEN HAVING.
NOW HE UNDERSTANDS THE MEANING OF ALIYA'S WORDS.
IT'S HIM AGAINST THE DARK SISTERHOOD.
IT'S A WAR HE DARE NOT LOSE.
HOW -- HOW DID SHE DO THAT? IT WAS TERRIBLE...!
SHE MUST HAVE TELEKINETIC POWER --
-- SHE MUST HAVE USED IT TO CONSTRICT BONITA'S HEART.
BUT WHY IS SHE AFTER CABLE?
I DO NOT KNOW, GIRL. I HAVE NO ANSWERS...
...ONLY FEARS.

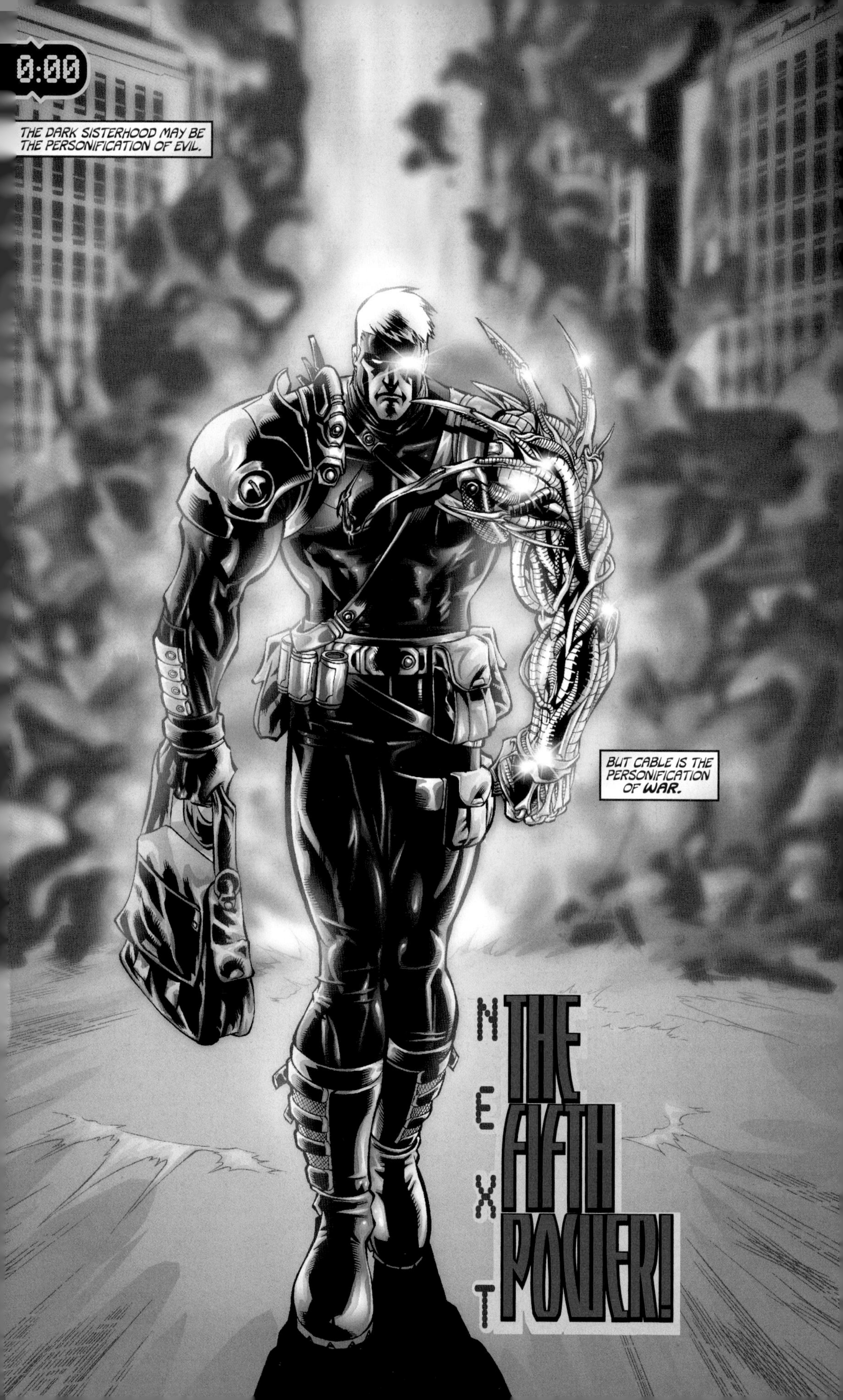
0:00
THE DARK SISTERHOOD MAY BE THE PERSONIFICATION OF EVIL.
BUT CABLE IS THE PERSONIFICATION OF WAR.
NEXT
THE FIFTH POWER!

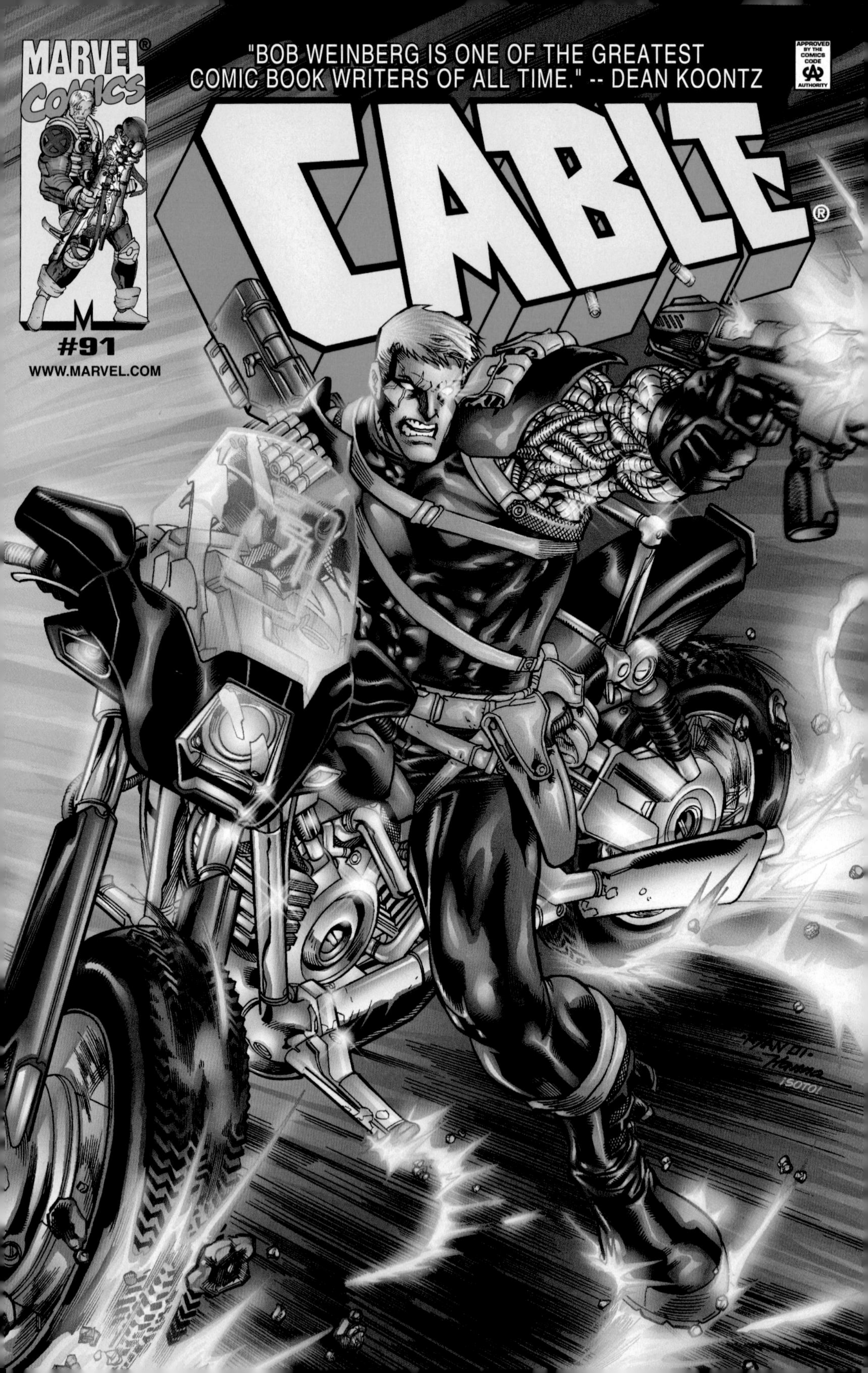
MARVEL COMICS
"BOB WEINBERG IS ONE OF THE GREATEST COMIC BOOK WRITERS OF ALL TIME." -- DEAN KOONTZ
APPROVED BY THE COMICS CODE AUTHORITY
CABLE
#91
WWW.MARVEL.COM

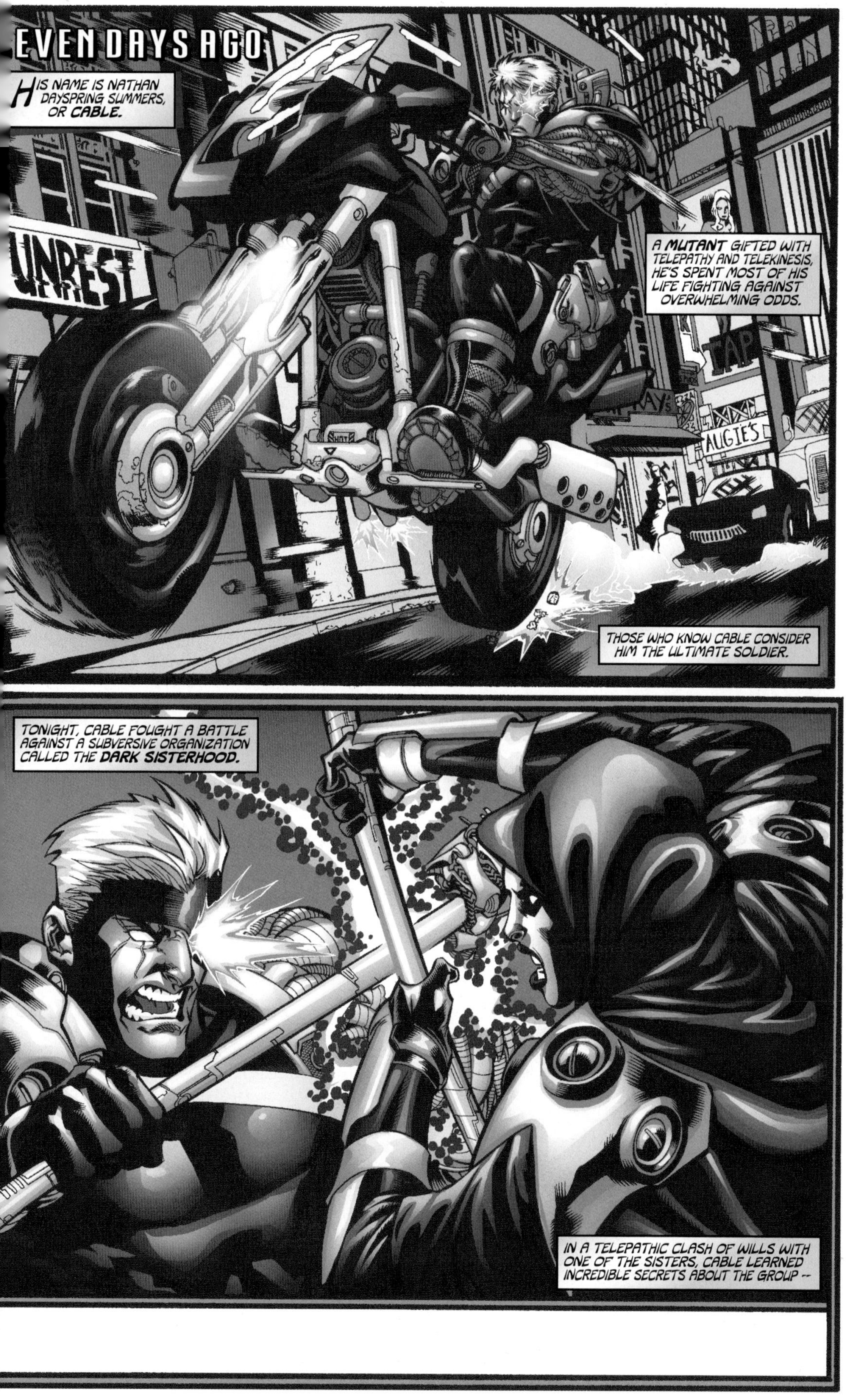
EVEN DAYS AGO
HIS NAME IS NATHAN DAYSPRING SUMMERS, OR CABLE.
A MUTANT GIFTED WITH TELEPATHY AND TELEKINESIS, HE'S SPENT MOST OF HIS LIFE FIGHTING AGAINST OVERWHELMING ODDS.
UNREST
TAP
AUGIE'S
THOSE WHO KNOW CABLE CONSIDER HIM THE ULTIMATE SOLDIER.
TONIGHT, CABLE FOUGHT A BATTLE AGAINST A SUBVERSIVE ORGANIZATION CALLED THE DARK SISTERHOOD.
IN A TELEPATHIC CLASH OF WILLS WITH ONE OF THE SISTERS, CABLE LEARNED INCREDIBLE SECRETS ABOUT THE GROUP --

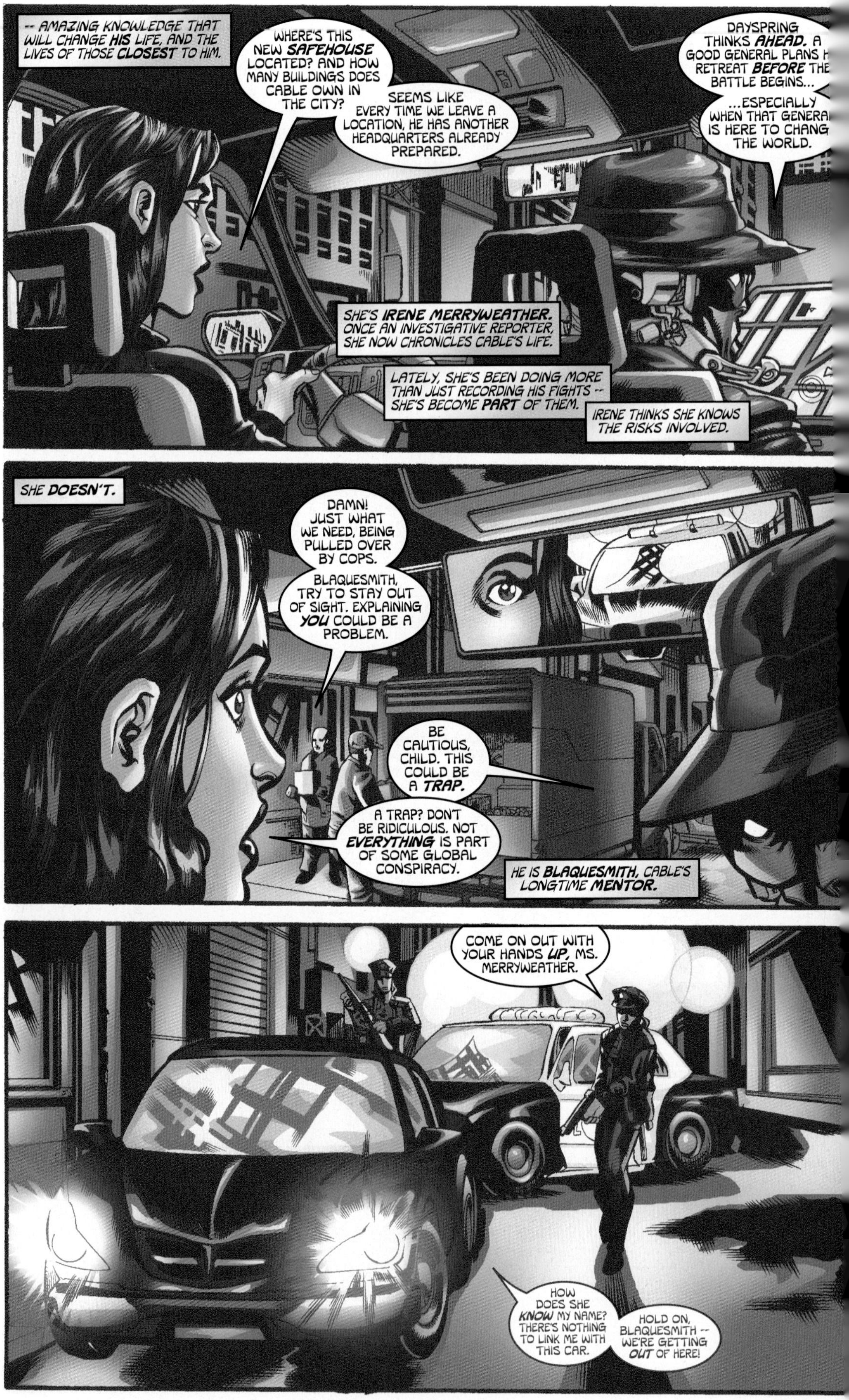
-- AMAZING KNOWLEDGE THAT WILL CHANGE HIS LIFE, AND THE LIVES OF THOSE CLOSEST TO HIM.
WHERE'S THIS NEW SAFEHOUSE LOCATED? AND HOW MANY BUILDINGS DOES CABLE OWN IN THE CITY?
SEEMS LIKE EVERY TIME WE LEAVE A LOCATION, HE HAS ANOTHER HEADQUARTERS ALREADY PREPARED.
DAYSPRING THINKS AHEAD. A GOOD GENERAL PLANS H RETREAT BEFORE THE BATTLE BEGINS...
...ESPECIALLY WHEN THAT GENERA IS HERE TO CHANG THE WORLD.
SHE'S IRENE MERRYWEATHER. ONCE AN INVESTIGATIVE REPORTER, SHE NOW CHRONICLES CABLE'S LIFE.
LATELY, SHE'S BEEN DOING MORE THAN JUST RECORDING HIS FIGHTS -- SHE'S BECOME PART OF THEM.
IRENE THINKS SHE KNOWS THE RISKS INVOLVED.
SHE DOESN'T.
DAMN! JUST WHAT WE NEED, BEING PULLED OVER BY COPS.
BLAQUESMITH, TRY TO STAY OUT OF SIGHT. EXPLAINING YOU COULD BE A PROBLEM.
BE CAUTIOUS, CHILD. THIS COULD BE A TRAP.
A TRAP? DON'T BE RIDICULOUS. NOT EVERYTHING IS PART OF SOME GLOBAL CONSPIRACY.
HE IS BLAQUESMITH, CABLE'S LONGTIME MENTOR.
COME ON OUT WITH YOUR HANDS UP, MS. MERRYWEATHER.
HOW DOES SHE KNOW MY NAME? THERE'S NOTHING TO LINK ME WITH THIS CAR.
HOLD ON, BLAQUESMITH -- WE'RE GETTING OUT OF HERE!

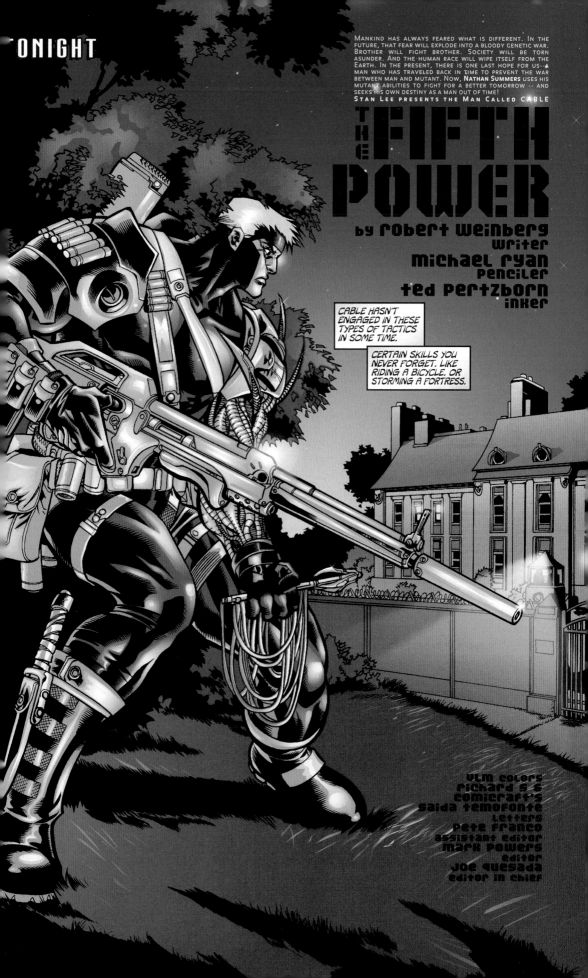

ONIGHT

Mankind has always feared what is different. In the future, that fear will explode into a bloody genetic war. Brother will fight brother. Society will be torn asunder. And the human race will wipe itself from the Earth. In the present, there is one last hope for us--a man who has traveled back in time to prevent the war between man and mutant. Now, **Nathan Summers** uses his mutant abilities to fight for a better tomorrow -- and seeks his own destiny as a man out of time!
Stan Lee presents the Man Called Cable

THE FIFTH POWER

by robert weinberg
Writer

michael ryan
Penciler

ted pertzborn
inker

CABLE HASN'T ENGAGED IN THESE TYPES OF TACTICS IN SOME TIME.

CERTAIN SKILLS YOU NEVER FORGET. LIKE RIDING A BICYCLE. OR STORMING A FORTRESS.

VLM colors
richard s s
comicraft's
saida temofonte
letters
pete franco
assistant editor
mark powers
editor
joe quesada
editor in chief

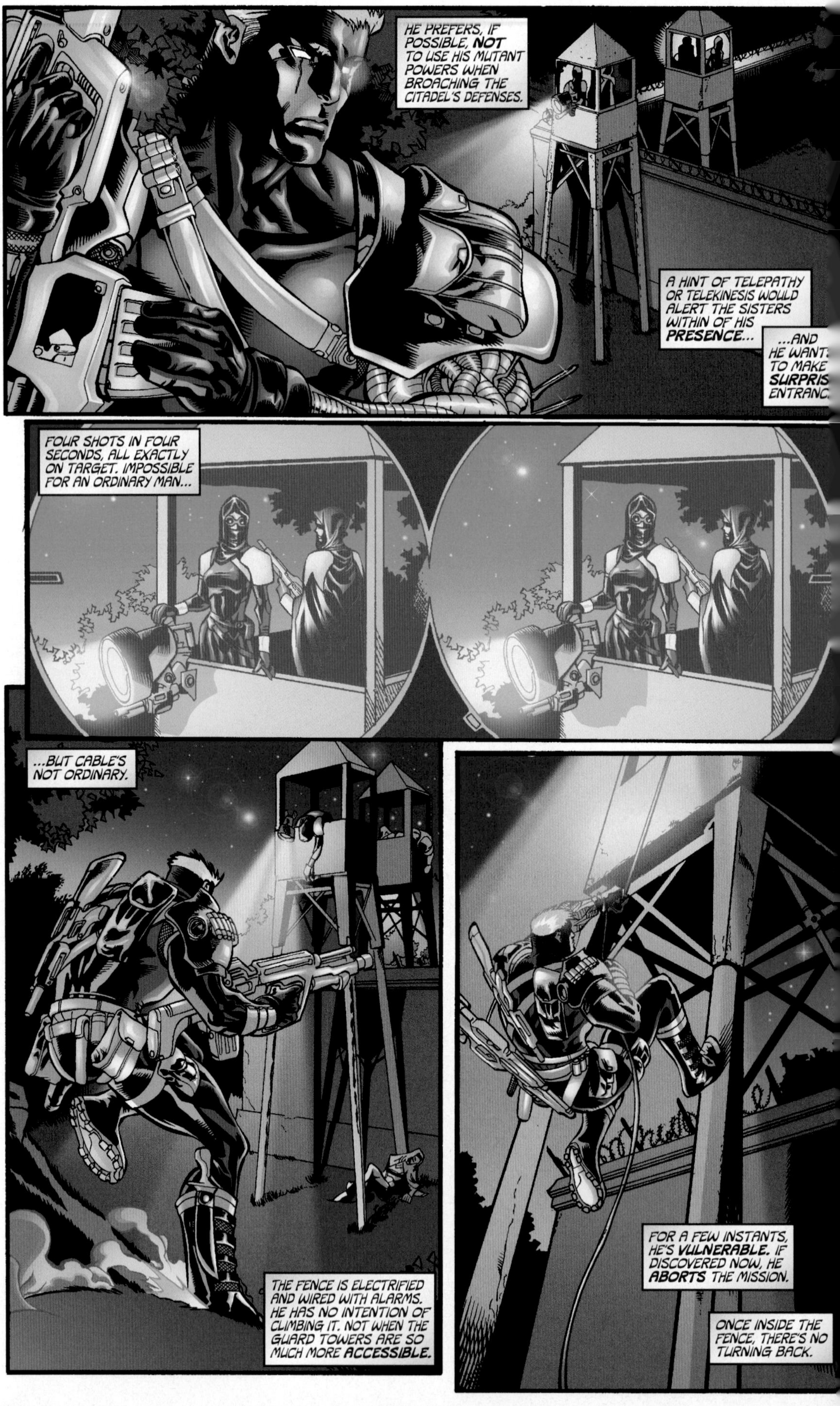

HE PREFERS, IF POSSIBLE, NOT TO USE HIS MUTANT POWERS WHEN BROACHING THE CITADEL'S DEFENSES.
A HINT OF TELEPATHY OR TELEKINESIS WOULD ALERT THE SISTERS WITHIN OF HIS PRESENCE...
...AND HE WANTS TO MAKE SURPRISE ENTRANCE.
FOUR SHOTS IN FOUR SECONDS, ALL EXACTLY ON TARGET. IMPOSSIBLE FOR AN ORDINARY MAN...
...BUT CABLE'S NOT ORDINARY.
THE FENCE IS ELECTRIFIED AND WIRED WITH ALARMS. HE HAS NO INTENTION OF CLIMBING IT. NOT WHEN THE GUARD TOWERS ARE SO MUCH MORE ACCESSIBLE.
FOR A FEW INSTANTS, HE'S VULNERABLE. IF DISCOVERED NOW, HE ABORTS THE MISSION.
ONCE INSIDE THE FENCE, THERE'S NO TURNING BACK.

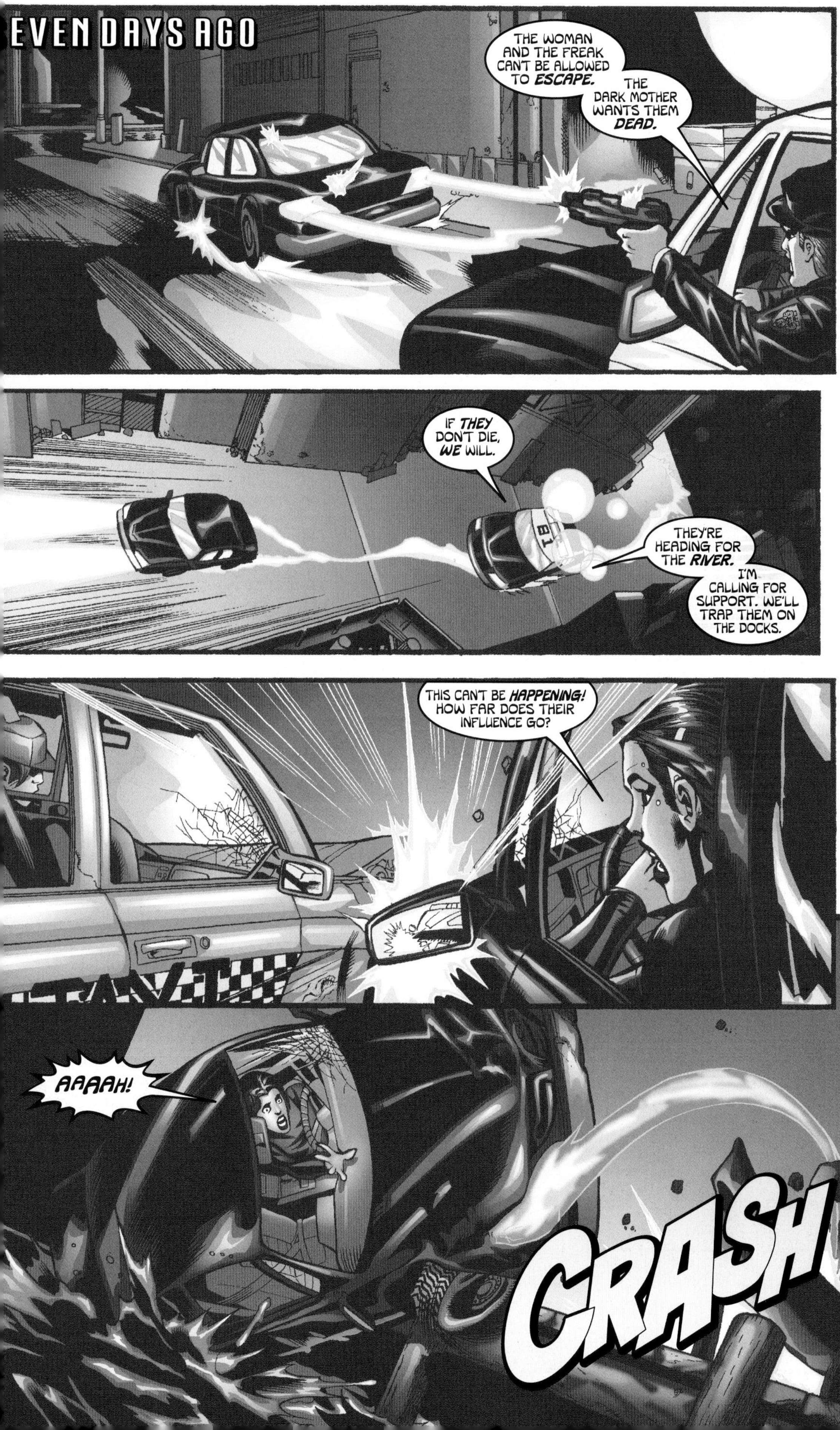
EVEN DAYS AGO
THE WOMAN AND THE FREAK CAN'T BE ALLOWED TO ESCAPE.
THE DARK MOTHER WANTS THEM DEAD.
IF THEY DON'T DIE, WE WILL.
THEY'RE HEADING FOR THE RIVER.
I'M CALLING FOR SUPPORT. WE'LL TRAP THEM ON THE DOCKS.
THIS CAN'T BE HAPPENING! HOW FAR DOES THEIR INFLUENCE GO?
AAAAH!
CRASH

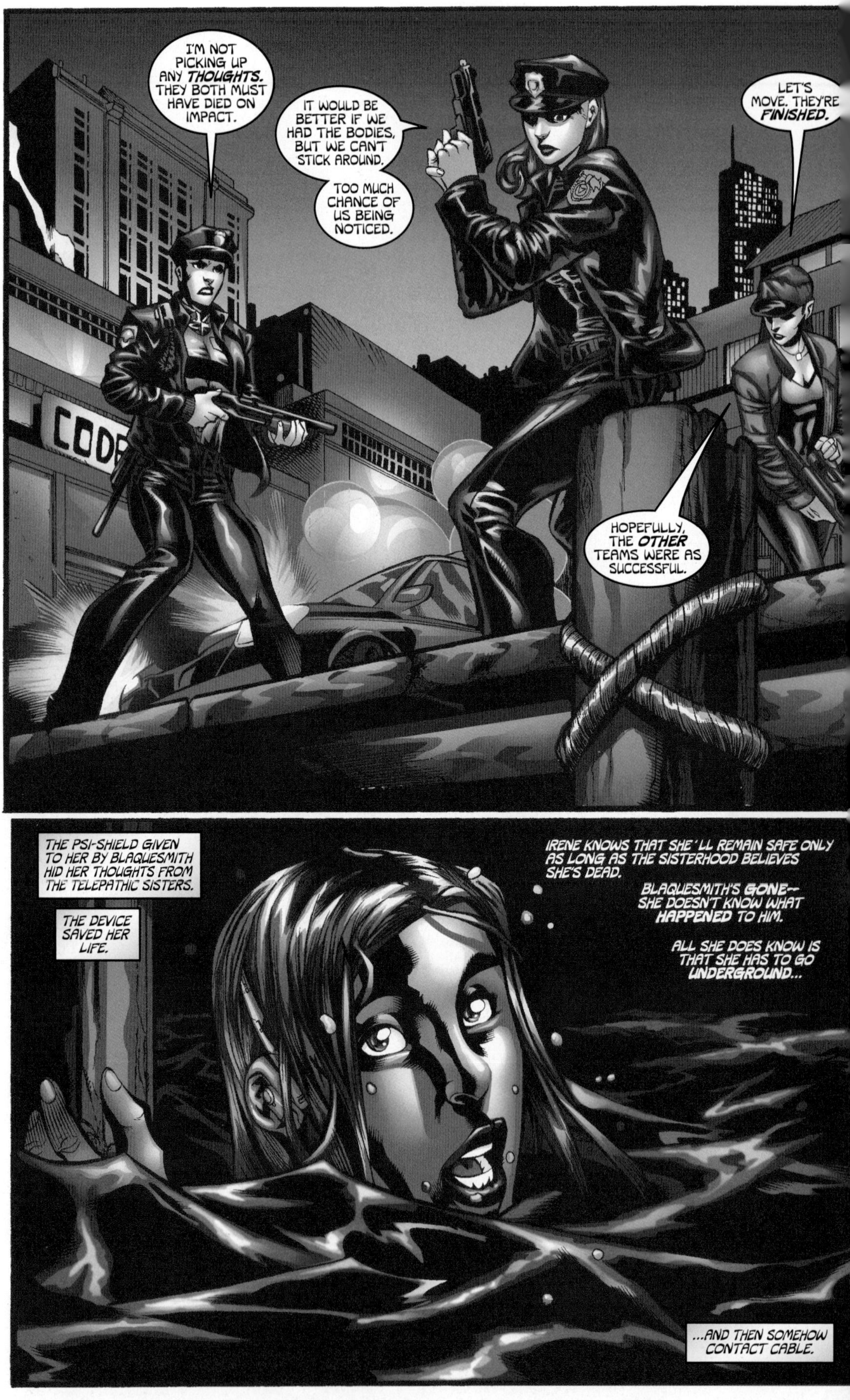
I'M NOT PICKING UP ANY THOUGHTS. THEY BOTH MUST HAVE DIED ON IMPACT.
IT WOULD BE BETTER IF WE HAD THE BODIES, BUT WE CAN'T STICK AROUND.
TOO MUCH CHANCE OF US BEING NOTICED.
LET'S MOVE. THEY'RE FINISHED.
HOPEFULLY, THE OTHER TEAMS WERE AS SUCCESSFUL.
CODE
THE PSI-SHIELD GIVEN TO HER BY BLAQUESMITH HID HER THOUGHTS FROM THE TELEPATHIC SISTERS.
THE DEVICE SAVED HER LIFE.
IRENE KNOWS THAT SHE'LL REMAIN SAFE ONLY AS LONG AS THE SISTERHOOD BELIEVES SHE'S DEAD.
BLAQUESMITH'S GONE-- SHE DOESN'T KNOW WHAT HAPPENED TO HIM.
ALL SHE DOES KNOW IS THAT SHE HAS TO GO UNDERGROUND...
...AND THEN SOMEHOW CONTACT CABLE.

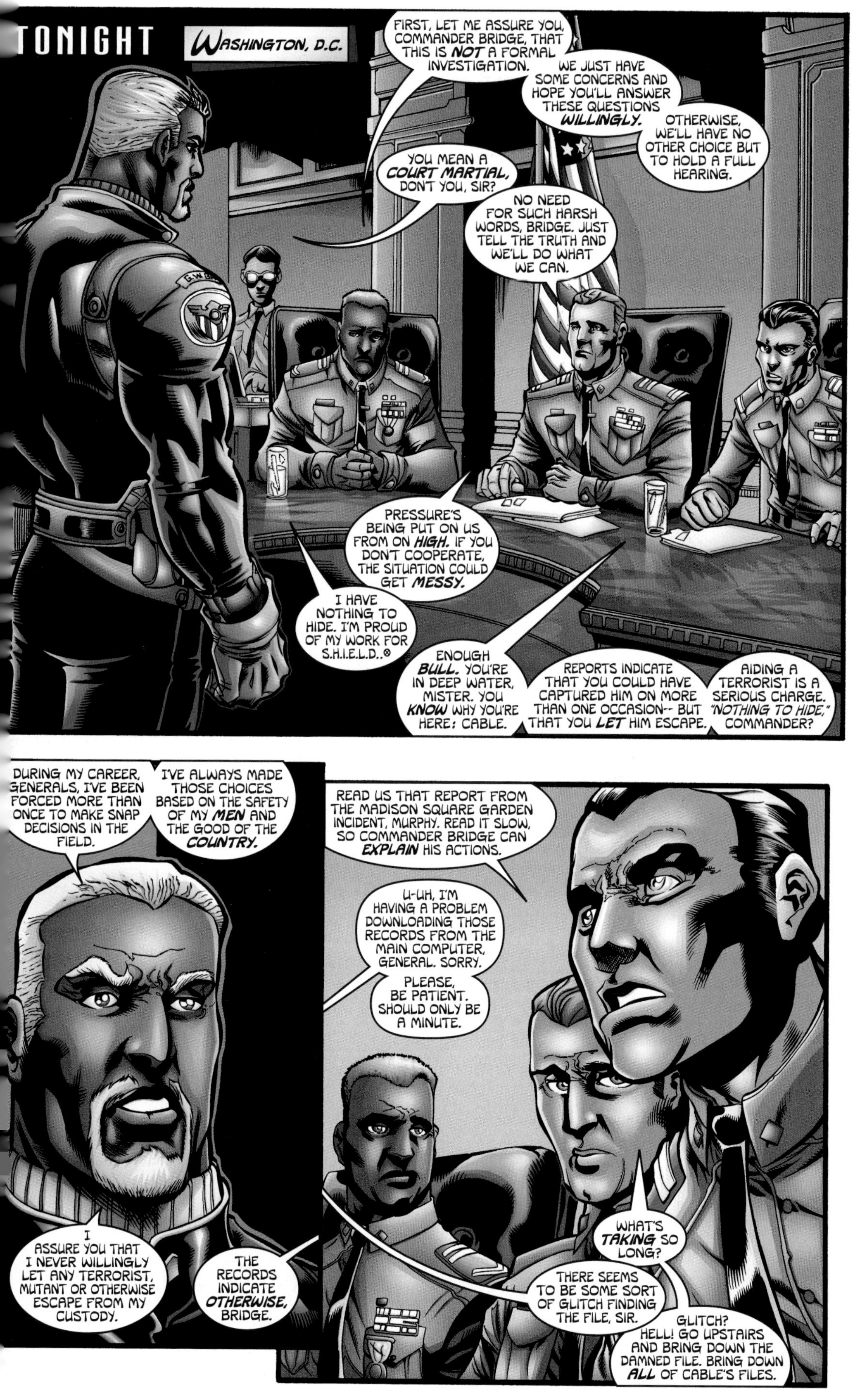
TONIGHT
WASHINGTON, D.C.
FIRST, LET ME ASSURE YOU, COMMANDER BRIDGE, THAT THIS IS NOT A FORMAL INVESTIGATION.
WE JUST HAVE SOME CONCERNS AND HOPE YOU'LL ANSWER THESE QUESTIONS WILLINGLY.
OTHERWISE, WE'LL HAVE NO OTHER CHOICE BUT TO HOLD A FULL HEARING.
YOU MEAN A COURT MARTIAL, DON'T YOU, SIR?
NO NEED FOR SUCH HARSH WORDS, BRIDGE. JUST TELL THE TRUTH AND WE'LL DO WHAT WE CAN.
PRESSURE'S BEING PUT ON US FROM ON HIGH. IF YOU DON'T COOPERATE, THE SITUATION COULD GET MESSY.
I HAVE NOTHING TO HIDE. I'M PROUD OF MY WORK FOR S.H.I.E.L.D..
ENOUGH BULL. YOU'RE IN DEEP WATER, MISTER. YOU KNOW WHY YOU'RE HERE: CABLE.
REPORTS INDICATE THAT YOU COULD HAVE CAPTURED HIM ON MORE THAN ONE OCCASION-- BUT THAT YOU LET HIM ESCAPE.
AIDING A TERRORIST IS A SERIOUS CHARGE. "NOTHING TO HIDE," COMMANDER?
DURING MY CAREER, GENERALS, I'VE BEEN FORCED MORE THAN ONCE TO MAKE SNAP DECISIONS IN THE FIELD.
I'VE ALWAYS MADE THOSE CHOICES BASED ON THE SAFETY OF MY MEN AND THE GOOD OF THE COUNTRY.
I ASSURE YOU THAT I NEVER WILLINGLY LET ANY TERRORIST, MUTANT OR OTHERWISE ESCAPE FROM MY CUSTODY.
THE RECORDS INDICATE OTHERWISE, BRIDGE.
READ US THAT REPORT FROM THE MADISON SQUARE GARDEN INCIDENT, MURPHY. READ IT SLOW, SO COMMANDER BRIDGE CAN EXPLAIN HIS ACTIONS.
U-UH, I'M HAVING A PROBLEM DOWNLOADING THOSE RECORDS FROM THE MAIN COMPUTER, GENERAL. SORRY.
PLEASE, BE PATIENT. SHOULD ONLY BE A MINUTE.
WHAT'S TAKING SO LONG?
THERE SEEMS TO BE SOME SORT OF GLITCH FINDING THE FILE, SIR.
GLITCH? HELL! GO UPSTAIRS AND BRING DOWN THE DAMNED FILE. BRING DOWN ALL OF CABLE'S FILES.

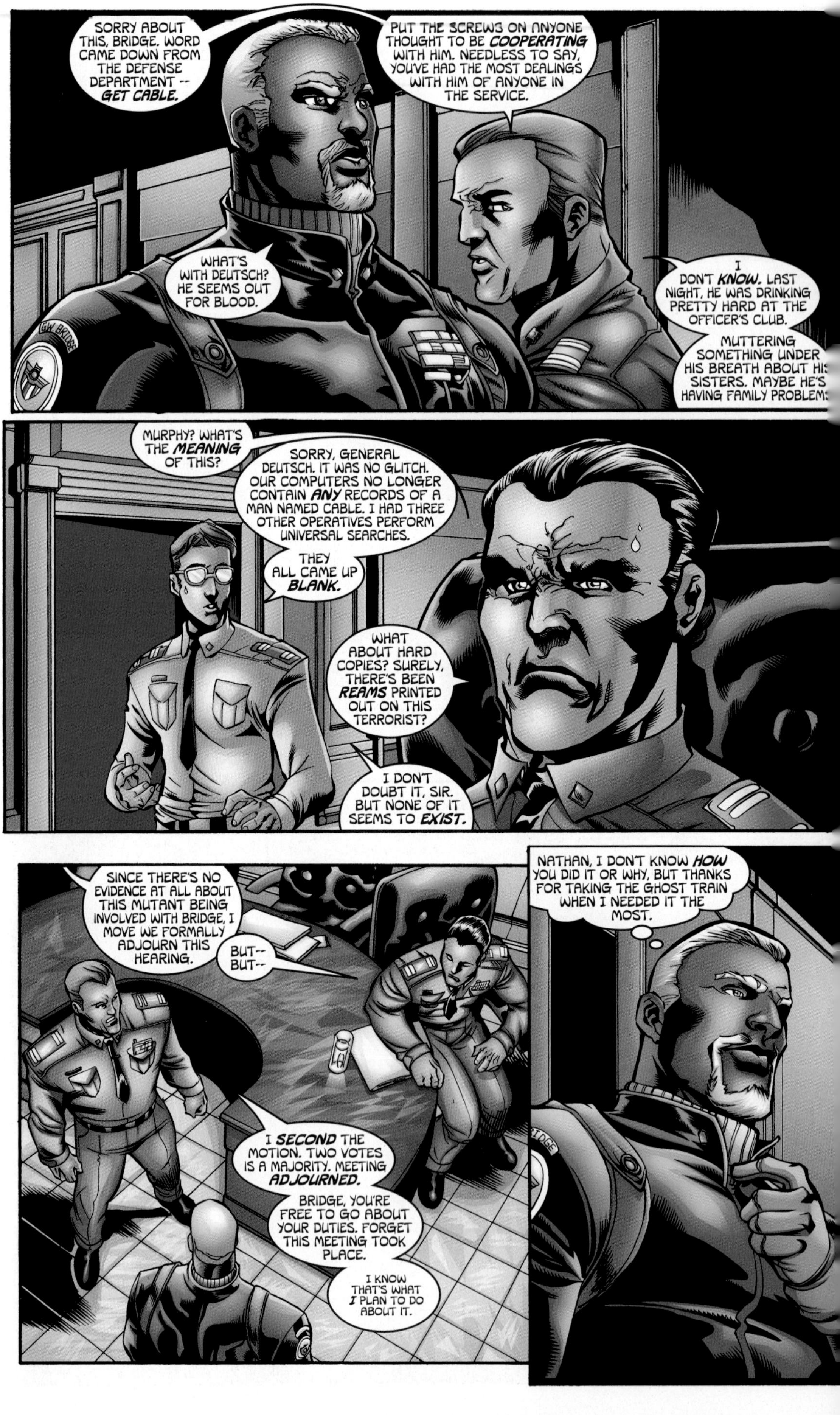

SORRY ABOUT THIS, BRIDGE. WORD CAME DOWN FROM THE DEFENSE DEPARTMENT -- GET CABLE.
PUT THE SCREWS ON ANYONE THOUGHT TO BE COOPERATING WITH HIM. NEEDLESS TO SAY, YOU'VE HAD THE MOST DEALINGS WITH HIM OF ANYONE IN THE SERVICE.
WHAT'S WITH DEUTSCH? HE SEEMS OUT FOR BLOOD.
I DON'T KNOW. LAST NIGHT, HE WAS DRINKING PRETTY HARD AT THE OFFICER'S CLUB.
MUTTERING SOMETHING UNDER HIS BREATH ABOUT HIS SISTERS. MAYBE HE'S HAVING FAMILY PROBLEMS.
MURPHY? WHAT'S THE MEANING OF THIS?
SORRY, GENERAL DEUTSCH. IT WAS NO GLITCH. OUR COMPUTERS NO LONGER CONTAIN ANY RECORDS OF A MAN NAMED CABLE. I HAD THREE OTHER OPERATIVES PERFORM UNIVERSAL SEARCHES.
THEY ALL CAME UP BLANK.
WHAT ABOUT HARD COPIES? SURELY, THERE'S BEEN REAMS PRINTED OUT ON THIS TERRORIST?
I DON'T DOUBT IT, SIR. BUT NONE OF IT SEEMS TO EXIST.
SINCE THERE'S NO EVIDENCE AT ALL ABOUT THIS MUTANT BEING INVOLVED WITH BRIDGE, I MOVE WE FORMALLY ADJOURN THIS HEARING.
BUT-- BUT--
I SECOND THE MOTION. TWO VOTES IS A MAJORITY. MEETING ADJOURNED.
BRIDGE, YOU'RE FREE TO GO ABOUT YOUR DUTIES. FORGET THIS MEETING TOOK PLACE.
I KNOW THAT'S WHAT I PLAN TO DO ABOUT IT.
NATHAN, I DON'T KNOW HOW YOU DID IT OR WHY, BUT THANKS FOR TAKING THE GHOST TRAIN WHEN I NEEDED IT THE MOST.

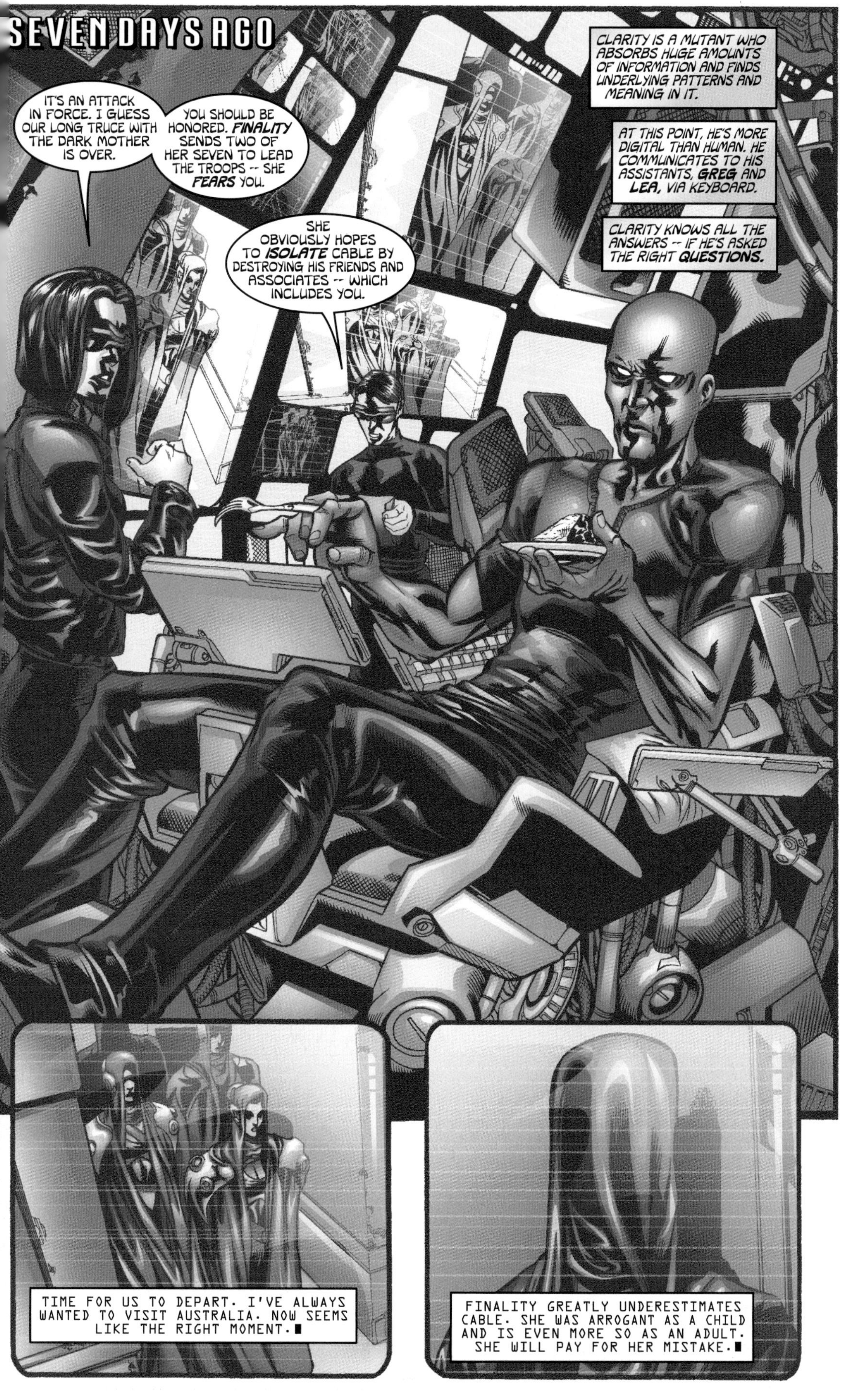
SEVEN DAYS AGO
CLARITY IS A MUTANT WHO ABSORBS HUGE AMOUNTS OF INFORMATION AND FINDS UNDERLYING PATTERNS AND MEANING IN IT.
AT THIS POINT, HE'S MORE DIGITAL THAN HUMAN. HE COMMUNICATES TO HIS ASSISTANTS, GREG AND LEA, VIA KEYBOARD.
CLARITY KNOWS ALL THE ANSWERS -- IF HE'S ASKED THE RIGHT QUESTIONS.
IT'S AN ATTACK IN FORCE. I GUESS OUR LONG TRUCE WITH THE DARK MOTHER IS OVER.
YOU SHOULD BE HONORED. FINALITY SENDS TWO OF HER SEVEN TO LEAD THE TROOPS -- SHE FEARS YOU.
SHE OBVIOUSLY HOPES TO ISOLATE CABLE BY DESTROYING HIS FRIENDS AND ASSOCIATES -- WHICH INCLUDES YOU.
TIME FOR US TO DEPART. I'VE ALWAYS WANTED TO VISIT AUSTRALIA. NOW SEEMS LIKE THE RIGHT MOMENT.
FINALITY GREATLY UNDERESTIMATES CABLE. SHE WAS ARROGANT AS A CHILD AND IS EVEN MORE SO AS AN ADULT. SHE WILL PAY FOR HER MISTAKE.

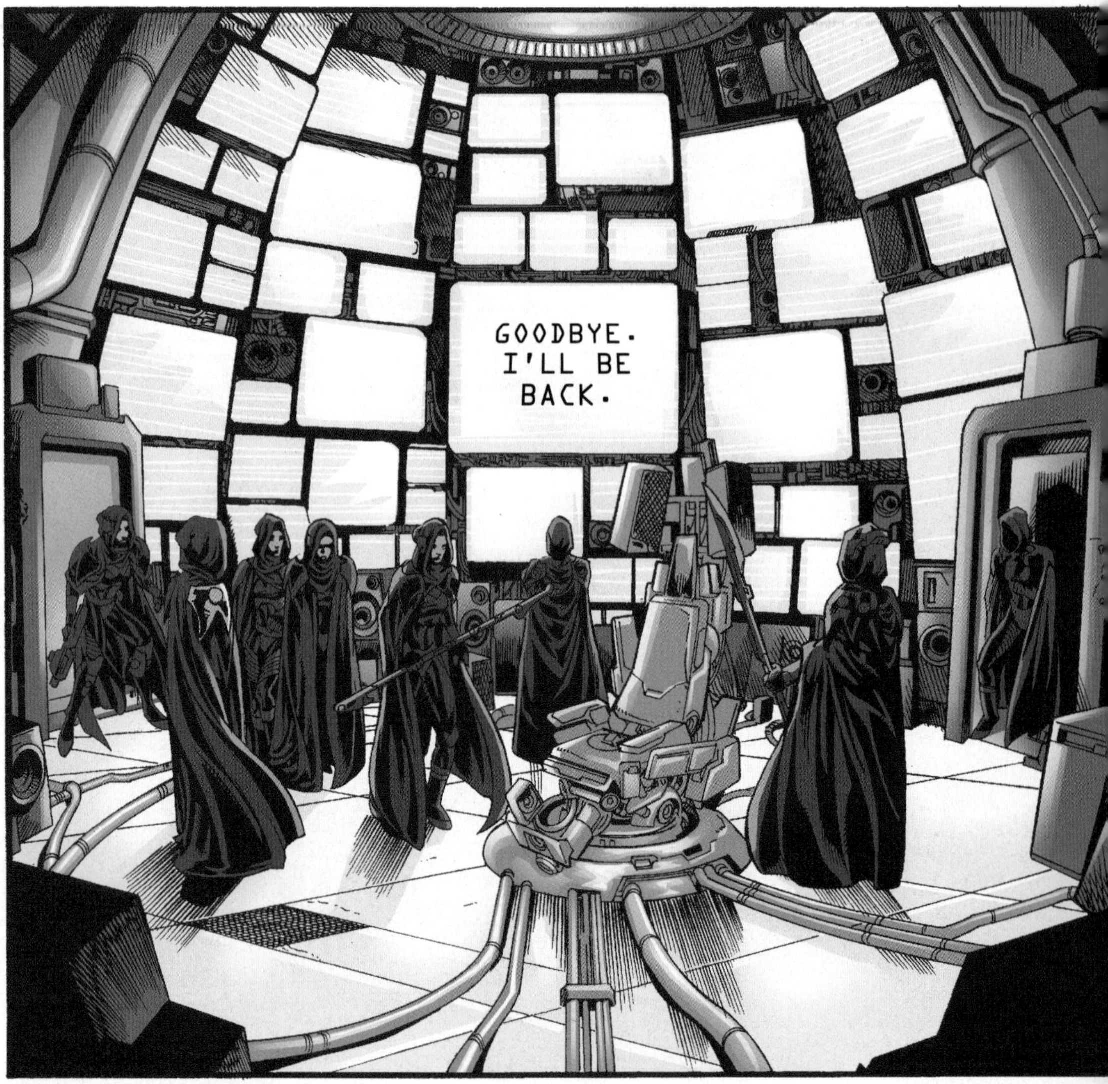
GOODBYE. I'LL BE BACK.

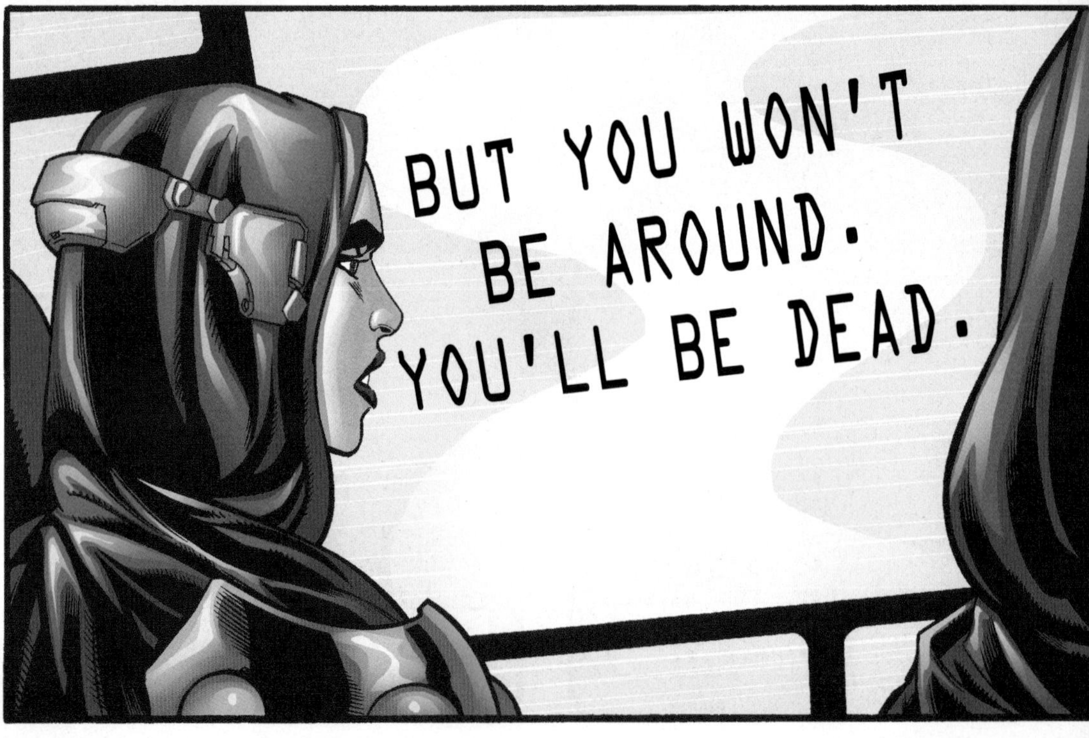
BUT YOU WON'T BE AROUND. YOU'LL BE DEAD.

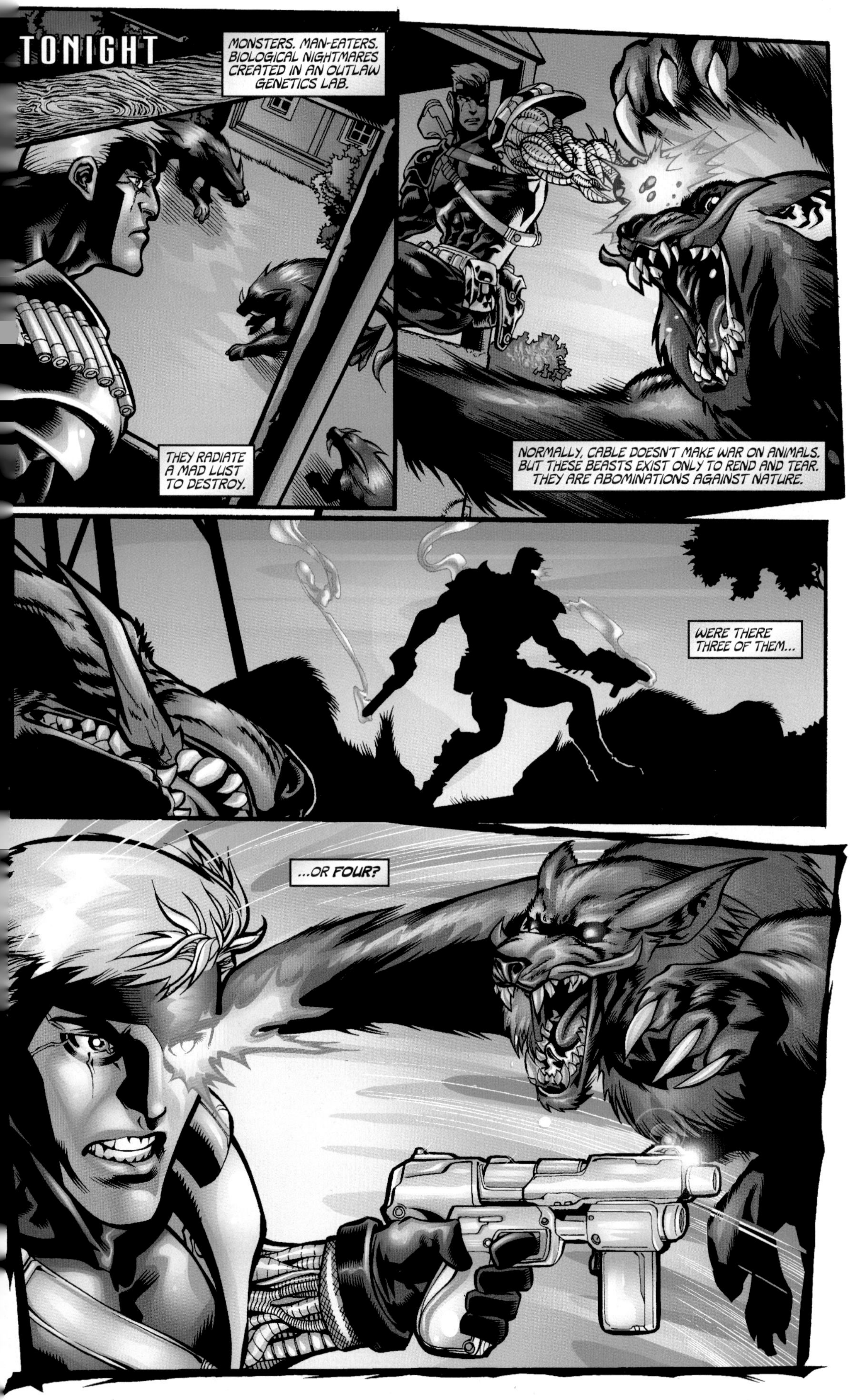
TONIGHT
MONSTERS. MAN-EATERS. BIOLOGICAL NIGHTMARES CREATED IN AN OUTLAW GENETICS LAB.
THEY RADIATE A MAD LUST TO DESTROY.
NORMALLY, CABLE DOESN'T MAKE WAR ON ANIMALS. BUT THESE BEASTS EXIST ONLY TO REND AND TEAR. THEY ARE ABOMINATIONS AGAINST NATURE.
WERE THERE THREE OF THEM...
...OR FOUR?

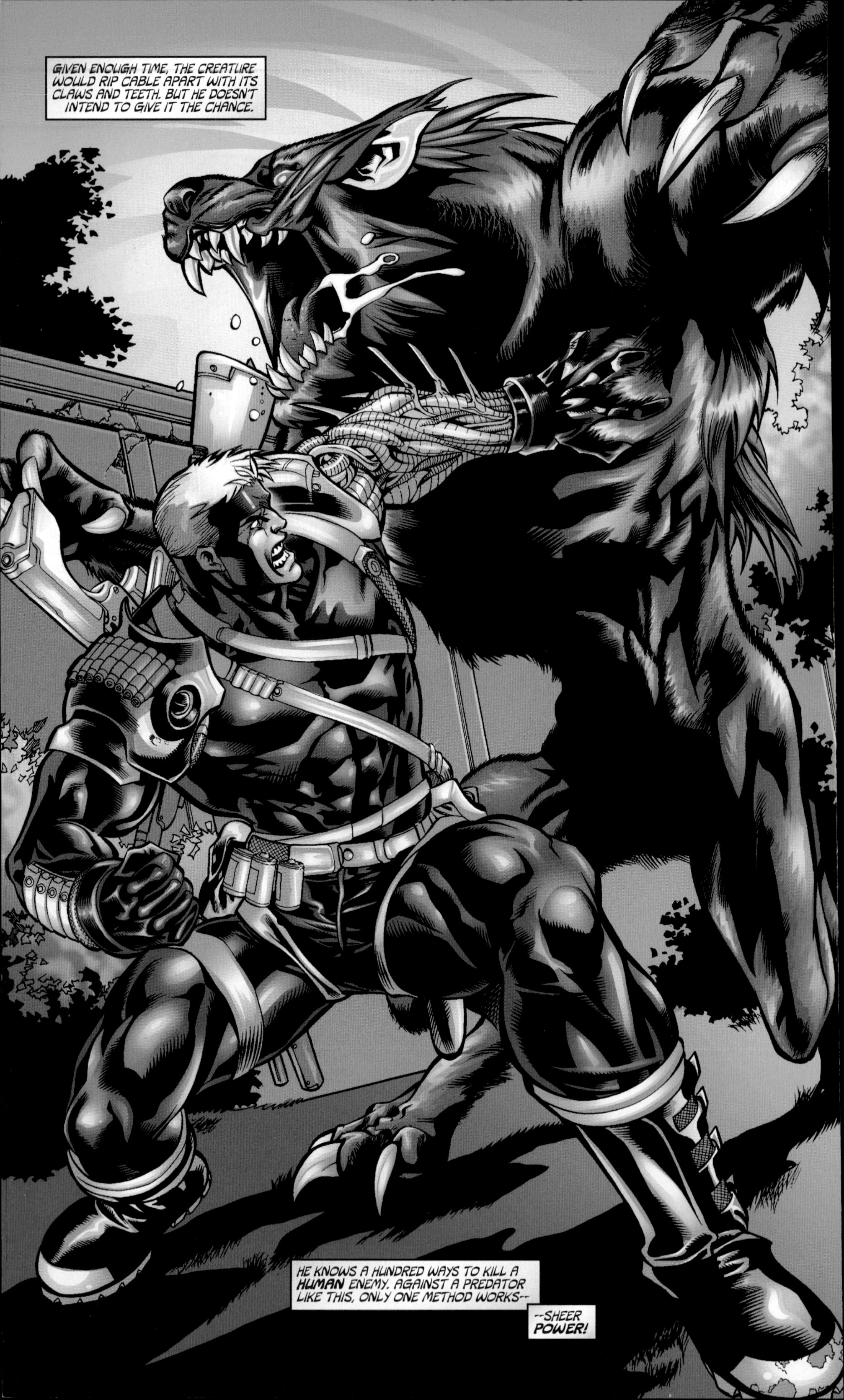
GIVEN ENOUGH TIME, THE CREATURE WOULD RIP CABLE APART WITH ITS CLAWS AND TEETH. BUT HE DOESN'T INTEND TO GIVE IT THE CHANCE.
HE KNOWS A HUNDRED WAYS TO KILL A **HUMAN** ENEMY. AGAINST A PREDATOR LIKE THIS, ONLY ONE METHOD WORKS--
--SHEER **POWER!**

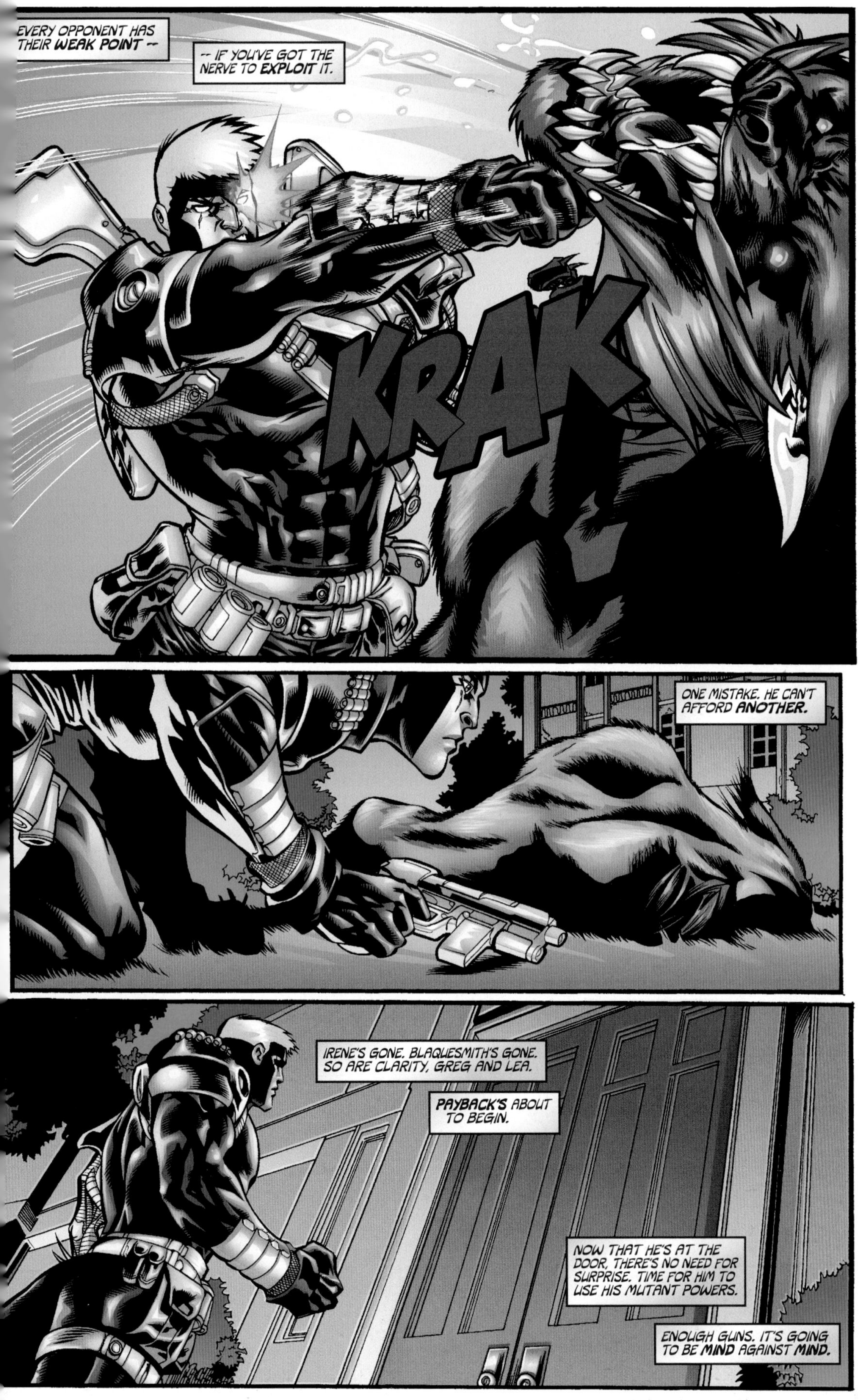
EVERY OPPONENT HAS THEIR WEAK POINT --
-- IF YOU'VE GOT THE NERVE TO EXPLOIT IT.
KRAK
ONE MISTAKE. HE CAN'T AFFORD ANOTHER.
IRENE'S GONE. BLAQUESMITH'S GONE. SO ARE CLARITY, GREG AND LEA.
PAYBACK'S ABOUT TO BEGIN.
NOW THAT HE'S AT THE DOOR, THERE'S NO NEED FOR SURPRISE. TIME FOR HIM TO USE HIS MUTANT POWERS.
ENOUGH GUNS. IT'S GOING TO BE MIND AGAINST MIND.

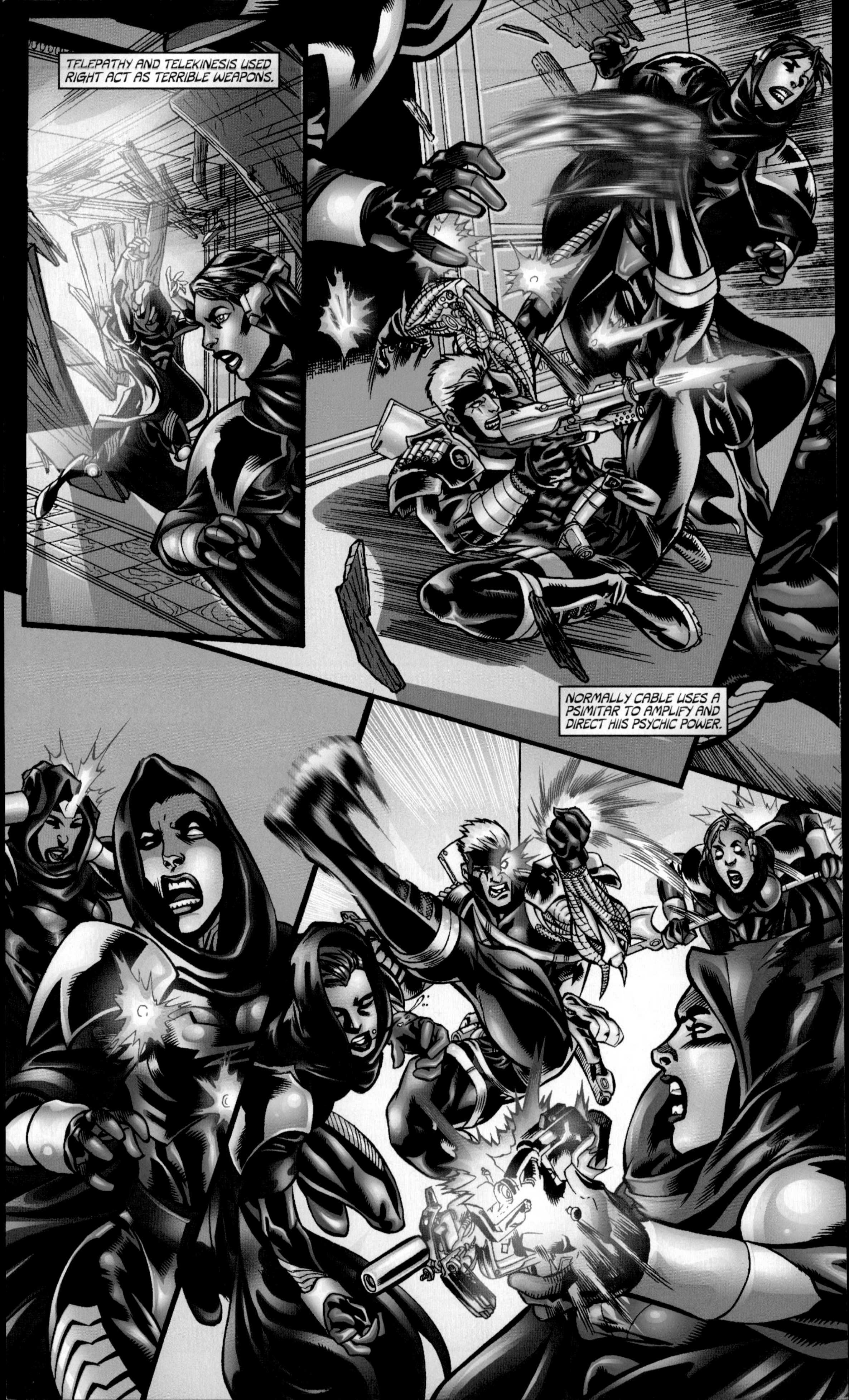
TELEPATHY AND TELEKINESIS USED RIGHT ACT AS TERRIBLE WEAPONS.
NORMALLY CABLE USES A PSIMITAR TO AMPLIFY AND DIRECT HIIS PSYCHIC POWER.

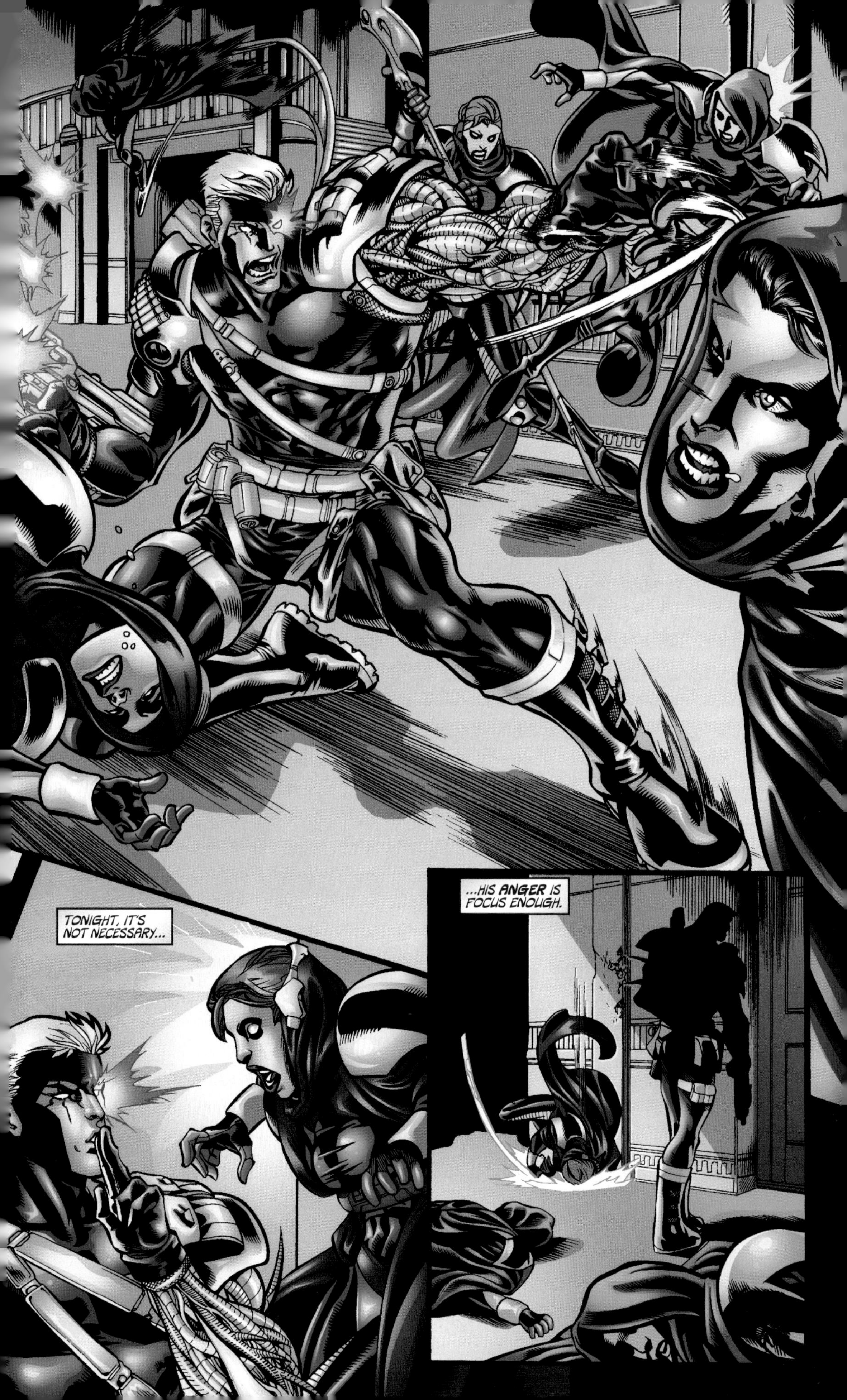
TONIGHT, IT'S NOT NECESSARY...
...HIS ANGER IS FOCUS ENOUGH.

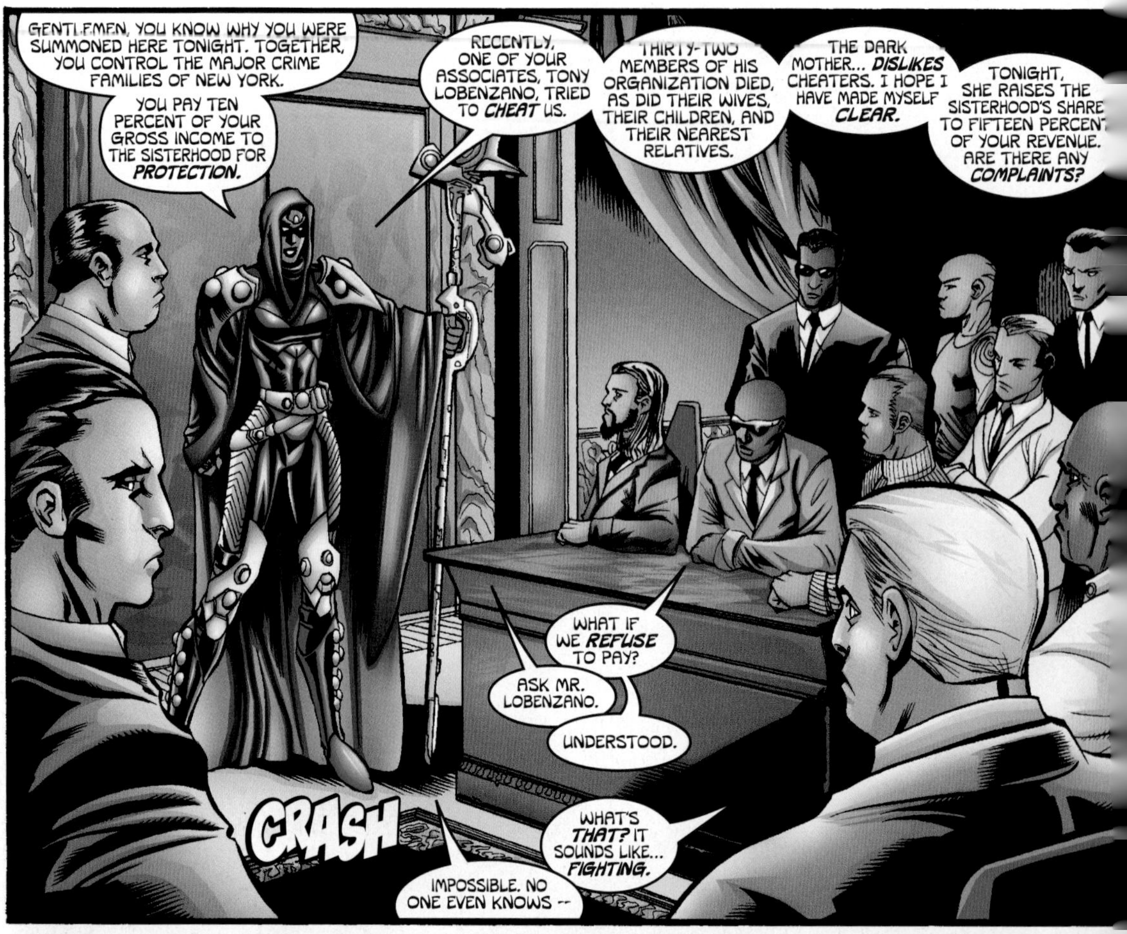

GENTLEMEN, YOU KNOW WHY YOU WERE SUMMONED HERE TONIGHT. TOGETHER, YOU CONTROL THE MAJOR CRIME FAMILIES OF NEW YORK.
YOU PAY TEN PERCENT OF YOUR GROSS INCOME TO THE SISTERHOOD FOR PROTECTION.
RECENTLY, ONE OF YOUR ASSOCIATES, TONY LOBENZANO, TRIED TO CHEAT US.
THIRTY-TWO MEMBERS OF HIS ORGANIZATION DIED, AS DID THEIR WIVES, THEIR CHILDREN, AND THEIR NEAREST RELATIVES.
THE DARK MOTHER... DISLIKES CHEATERS. I HOPE I HAVE MADE MYSELF CLEAR.
TONIGHT, SHE RAISES THE SISTERHOOD'S SHARE TO FIFTEEN PERCENT OF YOUR REVENUE. ARE THERE ANY COMPLAINTS?
WHAT IF WE REFUSE TO PAY?
ASK MR. LOBENZANO.
UNDERSTOOD.
CRASH
WHAT'S THAT? IT SOUNDS LIKE... FIGHTING.
IMPOSSIBLE. NO ONE EVEN KNOWS --

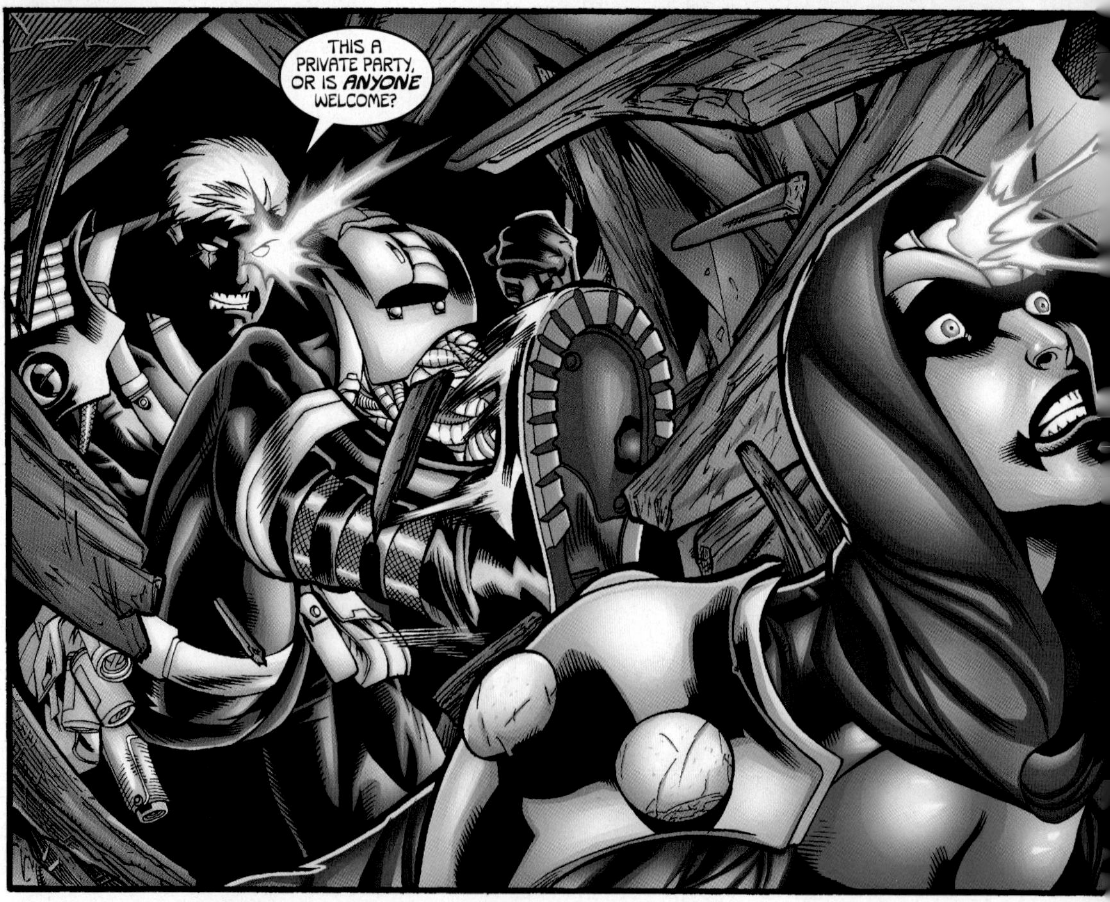

THIS A PRIVATE PARTY, OR IS ANYONE WELCOME?

YOU EAT LEAD, MUTIE?

CRACK SMOOSH CRACK SMOOSH SWAM

THAT WAS STUPID. IF I WAS IN A NASTY MOOD, I'D SHOOT BACK AND SEE IF YOUR FORCE FIELD IS WORKING. OH, YOU DON'T *HAVE* ONE?

TOO *BAD.*

NOW SIT DOWN AND *SHUT UP.*

YOUR MENTAL POWERS ARE NO MATCH FOR MINE, SISTER, SO DON'T BOTHER TRYING TO FREE YOURSELF.

YOU GONNA CHIT-CHAT WITH THE DAME OR *TALK,* AMIGO?

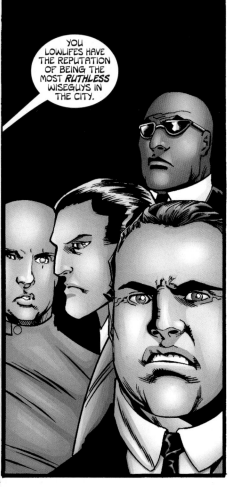

YOU LOWLIFES HAVE THE REPUTATION OF BEING THE MOST *RUTHLESS* WISEGUYS IN THE CITY.

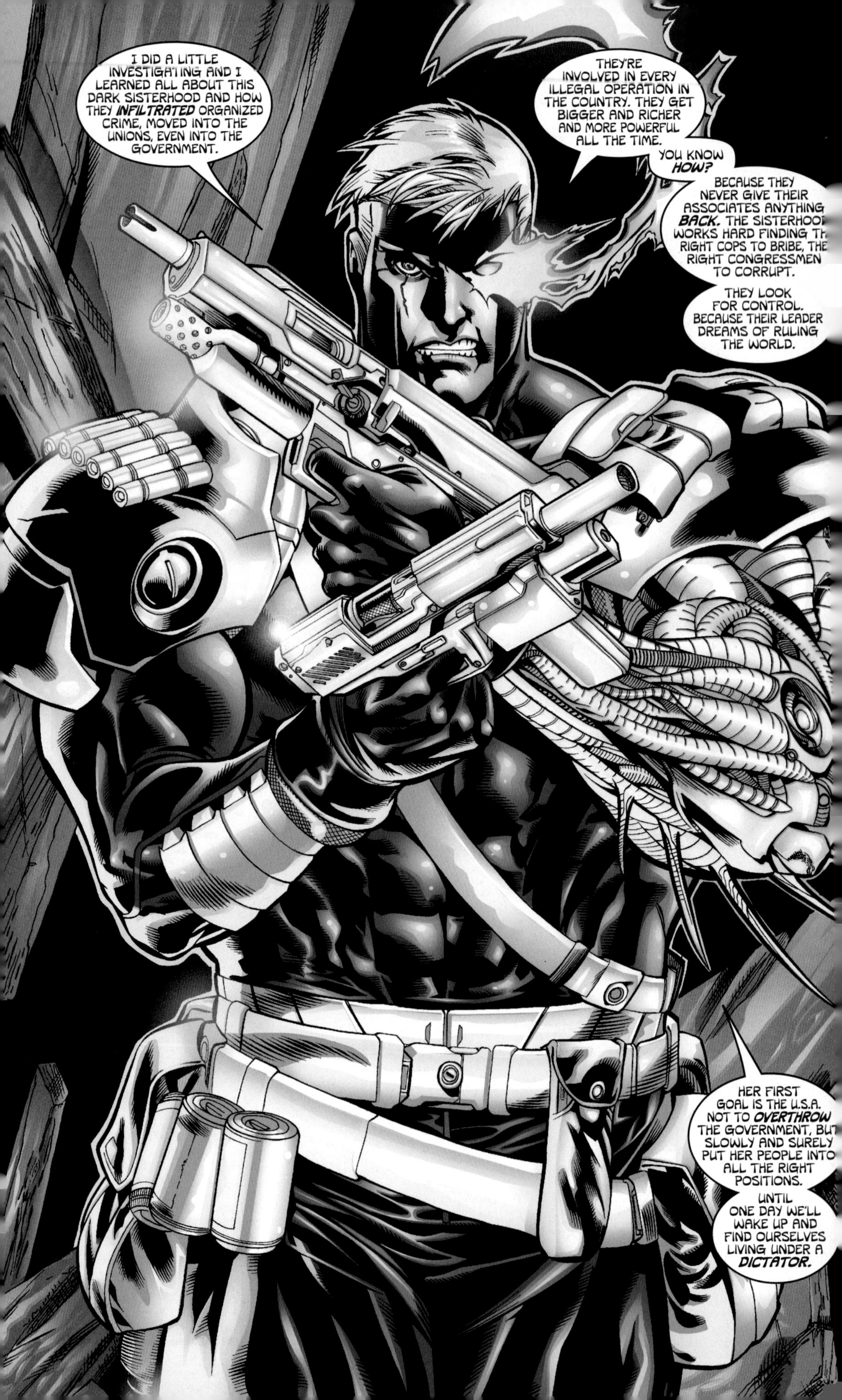
I DID A LITTLE INVESTIGATING AND I LEARNED ALL ABOUT THIS DARK SISTERHOOD AND HOW THEY *INFILTRATED* ORGANIZED CRIME, MOVED INTO THE UNIONS, EVEN INTO THE GOVERNMENT.
THEY'RE INVOLVED IN EVERY ILLEGAL OPERATION IN THE COUNTRY. THEY GET BIGGER AND RICHER AND MORE POWERFUL ALL THE TIME.
YOU KNOW *HOW?*
BECAUSE THEY NEVER GIVE THEIR ASSOCIATES ANYTHING *BACK.* THE SISTERHOOD WORKS HARD FINDING THE RIGHT COPS TO BRIBE, THE RIGHT CONGRESSMEN TO CORRUPT.
THEY LOOK FOR CONTROL. BECAUSE THEIR LEADER DREAMS OF RULING THE WORLD.
HER FIRST GOAL IS THE U.S.A. NOT TO *OVERTHROW* THE GOVERNMENT, BUT SLOWLY AND SURELY PUT HER PEOPLE INTO ALL THE RIGHT POSITIONS.
UNTIL ONE DAY WE'LL WAKE UP AND FIND OURSELVES LIVING UNDER A *DICTATOR.*

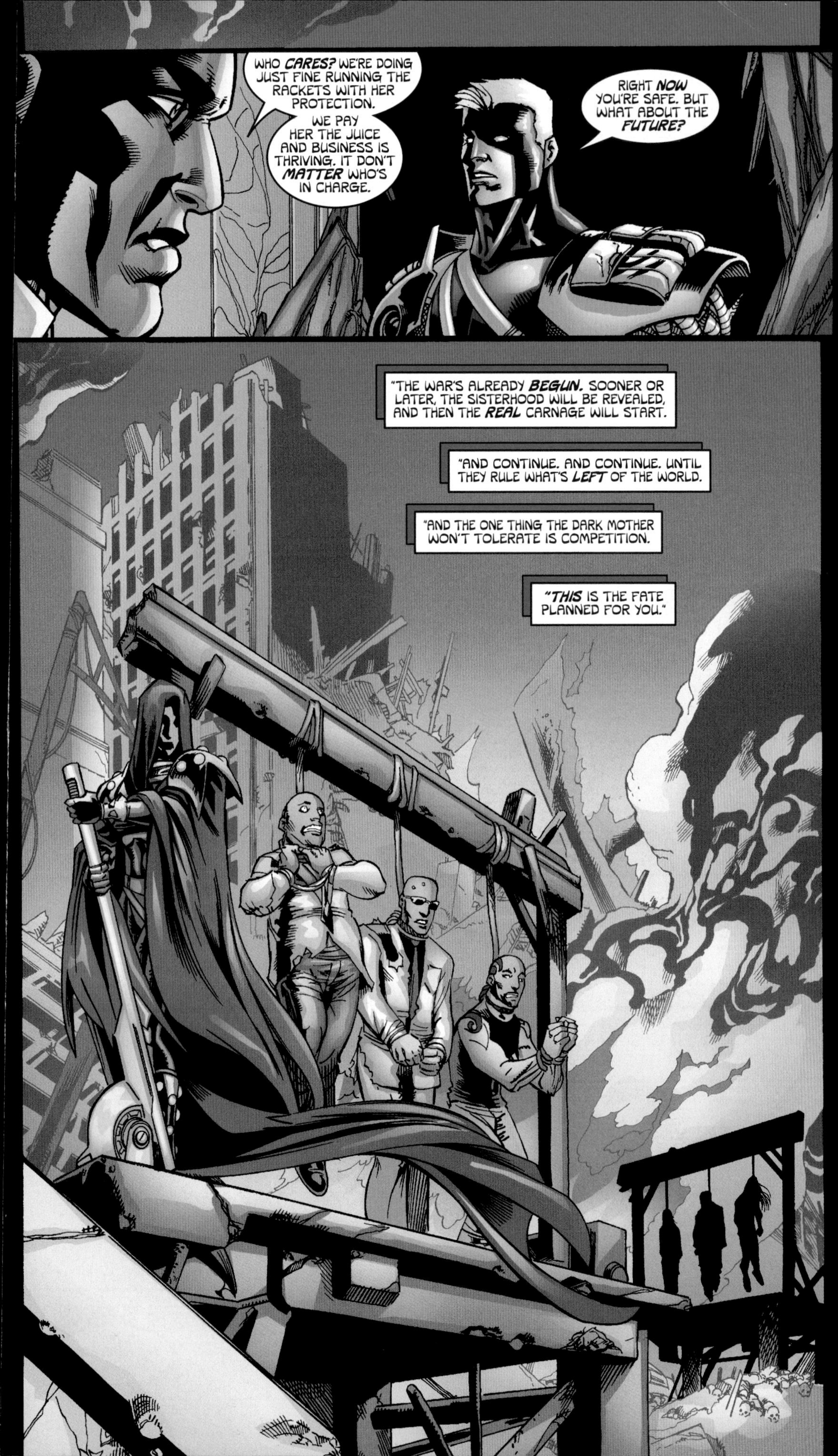
WHO CARES? WE'RE DOING JUST FINE RUNNING THE RACKETS WITH HER PROTECTION.
WE PAY HER THE JUICE AND BUSINESS IS THRIVING. IT DON'T MATTER WHO'S IN CHARGE.
RIGHT NOW YOU'RE SAFE. BUT WHAT ABOUT THE FUTURE?
"THE WAR'S ALREADY BEGUN. SOONER OR LATER, THE SISTERHOOD WILL BE REVEALED, AND THEN THE REAL CARNAGE WILL START.
"AND CONTINUE. AND CONTINUE. UNTIL THEY RULE WHAT'S LEFT OF THE WORLD.
"AND THE ONE THING THE DARK MOTHER WON'T TOLERATE IS COMPETITION.
"THIS IS THE FATE PLANNED FOR YOU."

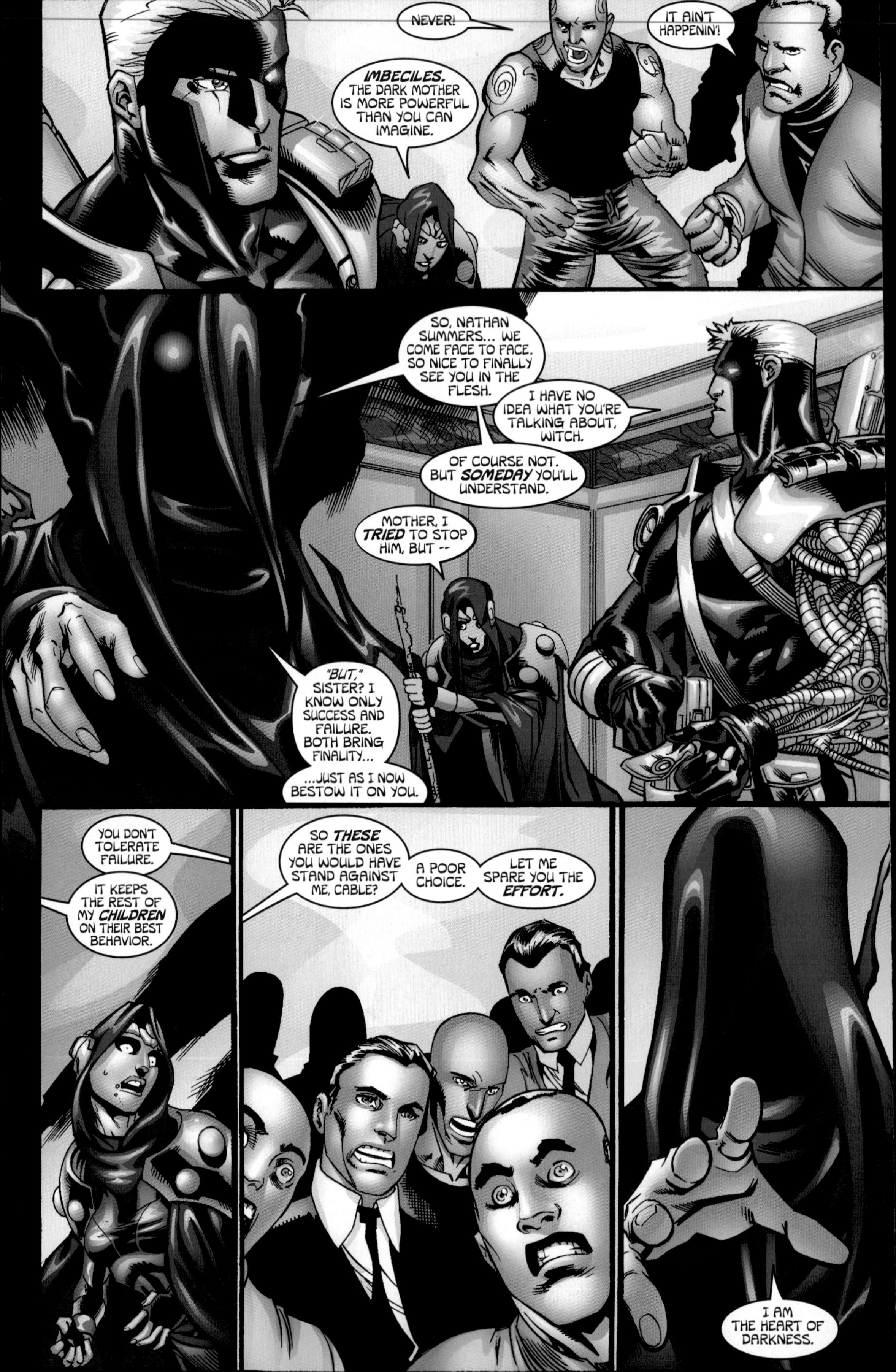
NEVER!
IT AIN'T HAPPENIN'!
IMBECILES. THE DARK MOTHER IS MORE POWERFUL THAN YOU CAN IMAGINE.
SO, NATHAN SUMMERS... WE COME FACE TO FACE. SO NICE TO FINALLY SEE YOU IN THE FLESH.
I HAVE NO IDEA WHAT YOU'RE TALKING ABOUT, WITCH.
OF COURSE NOT. BUT SOMEDAY YOU'LL UNDERSTAND.
MOTHER, I TRIED TO STOP HIM, BUT --
"BUT," SISTER? I KNOW ONLY SUCCESS AND FAILURE. BOTH BRING FINALITY...
...JUST AS I NOW BESTOW IT ON YOU.
YOU DON'T TOLERATE FAILURE.
IT KEEPS THE REST OF MY CHILDREN ON THEIR BEST BEHAVIOR.
SO THESE ARE THE ONES YOU WOULD HAVE STAND AGAINST ME, CABLE?
A POOR CHOICE.
LET ME SPARE YOU THE EFFORT.
I AM THE HEART OF DARKNESS.

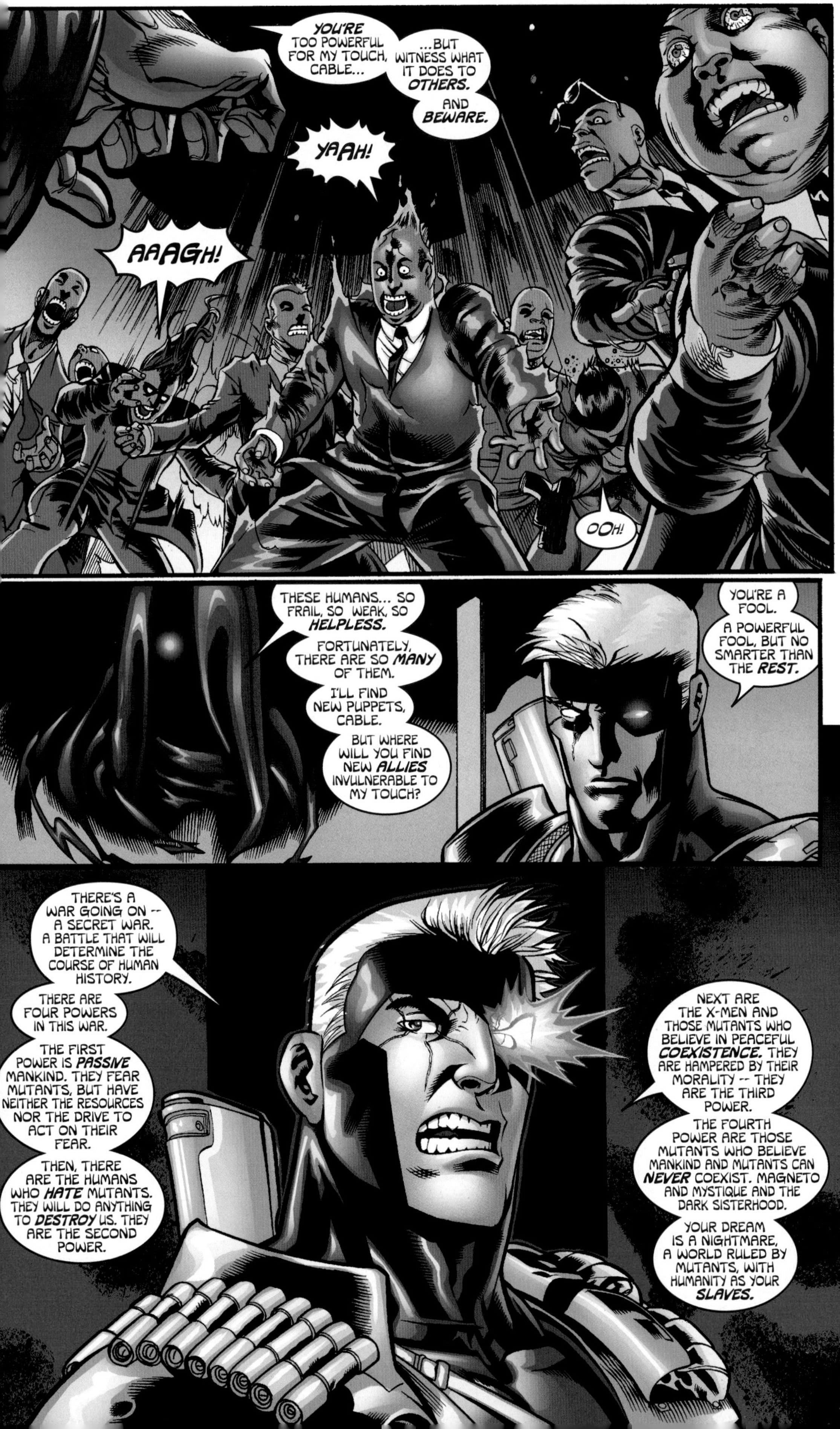
YOU'RE TOO POWERFUL FOR MY TOUCH, CABLE...
...BUT WITNESS WHAT IT DOES TO OTHERS.
AND BEWARE.
YAAH!
AAAGH!
OOH!
THESE HUMANS... SO FRAIL, SO WEAK, SO HELPLESS.
FORTUNATELY, THERE ARE SO MANY OF THEM.
I'LL FIND NEW PUPPETS, CABLE.
BUT WHERE WILL YOU FIND NEW ALLIES INVULNERABLE TO MY TOUCH?
YOU'RE A FOOL.
A POWERFUL FOOL, BUT NO SMARTER THAN THE REST.
THERE'S A WAR GOING ON -- A SECRET WAR. A BATTLE THAT WILL DETERMINE THE COURSE OF HUMAN HISTORY.
THERE ARE FOUR POWERS IN THIS WAR.
THE FIRST POWER IS PASSIVE MANKIND. THEY FEAR MUTANTS, BUT HAVE NEITHER THE RESOURCES NOR THE DRIVE TO ACT ON THEIR FEAR.
THEN, THERE ARE THE HUMANS WHO HATE MUTANTS. THEY WILL DO ANYTHING TO DESTROY US. THEY ARE THE SECOND POWER.
NEXT ARE THE X-MEN AND THOSE MUTANTS WHO BELIEVE IN PEACEFUL COEXISTENCE. THEY ARE HAMPERED BY THEIR MORALITY -- THEY ARE THE THIRD POWER.
THE FOURTH POWER ARE THOSE MUTANTS WHO BELIEVE MANKIND AND MUTANTS CAN NEVER COEXIST. MAGNETO AND MYSTIQUE AND THE DARK SISTERHOOD.
YOUR DREAM IS A NIGHTMARE, A WORLD RULED BY MUTANTS, WITH HUMANITY AS YOUR SLAVES.

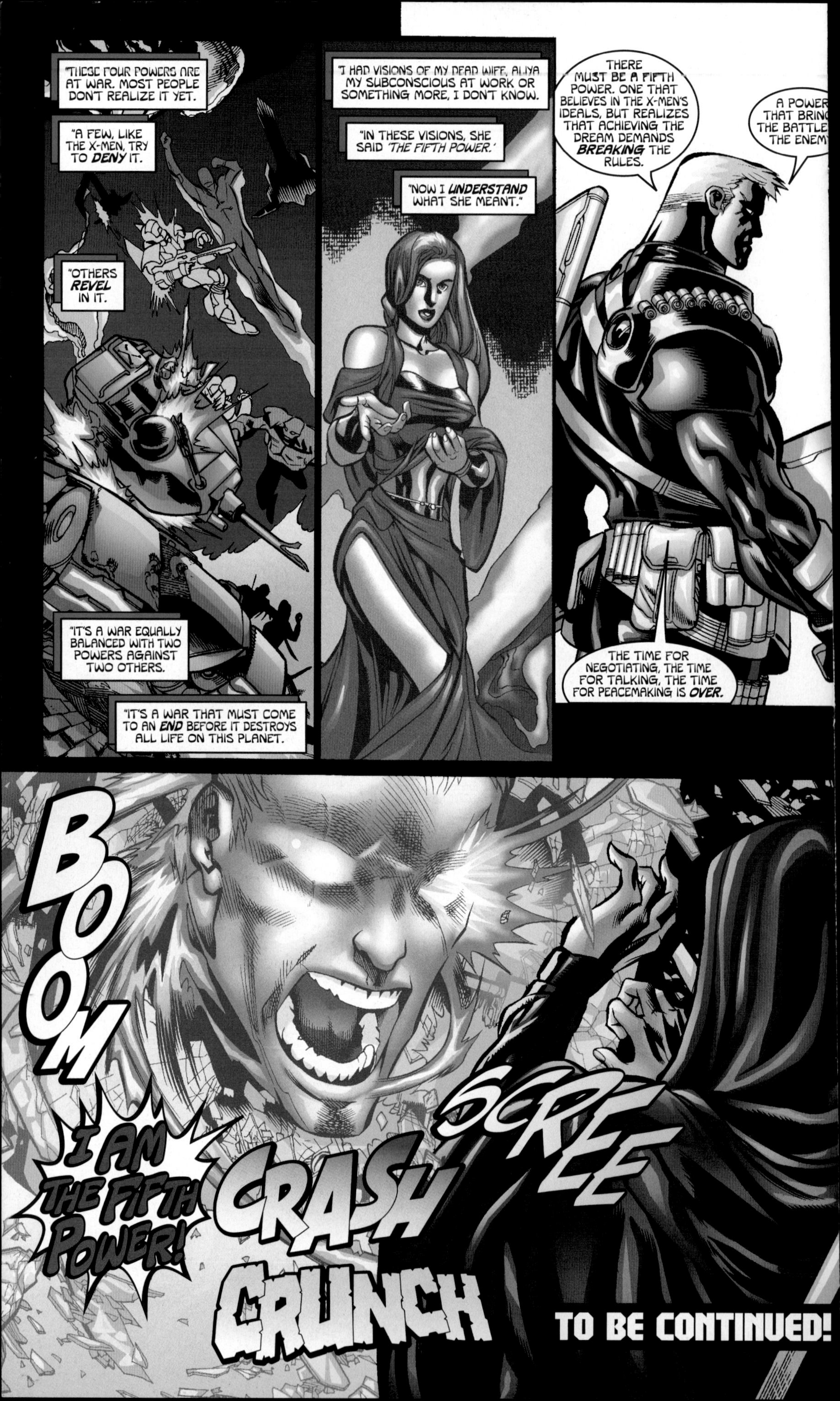
"THESE FOUR POWERS ARE AT WAR. MOST PEOPLE DON'T REALIZE IT YET.
"A FEW, LIKE THE X-MEN, TRY TO DENY IT.
"OTHERS REVEL IN IT.
"IT'S A WAR EQUALLY BALANCED WITH TWO POWERS AGAINST TWO OTHERS.
"IT'S A WAR THAT MUST COME TO AN END BEFORE IT DESTROYS ALL LIFE ON THIS PLANET.
"I HAD VISIONS OF MY DEAD WIFE, ALIYA. MY SUBCONSCIOUS AT WORK OR SOMETHING MORE, I DON'T KNOW.
"IN THESE VISIONS, SHE SAID 'THE FIFTH POWER.'
"NOW I UNDERSTAND WHAT SHE MEANT."
THERE MUST BE A FIFTH POWER. ONE THAT BELIEVES IN THE X-MEN'S IDEALS, BUT REALIZES THAT ACHIEVING THE DREAM DEMANDS BREAKING THE RULES.
A POWER THAT BRING THE BATTLE THE ENEMY
THE TIME FOR NEGOTIATING, THE TIME FOR TALKING, THE TIME FOR PEACEMAKING IS OVER.
BOOOM
I AM THE FIFTH POWER!
SCREEE
CRASH
CRUNCH
TO BE CONTINUED!

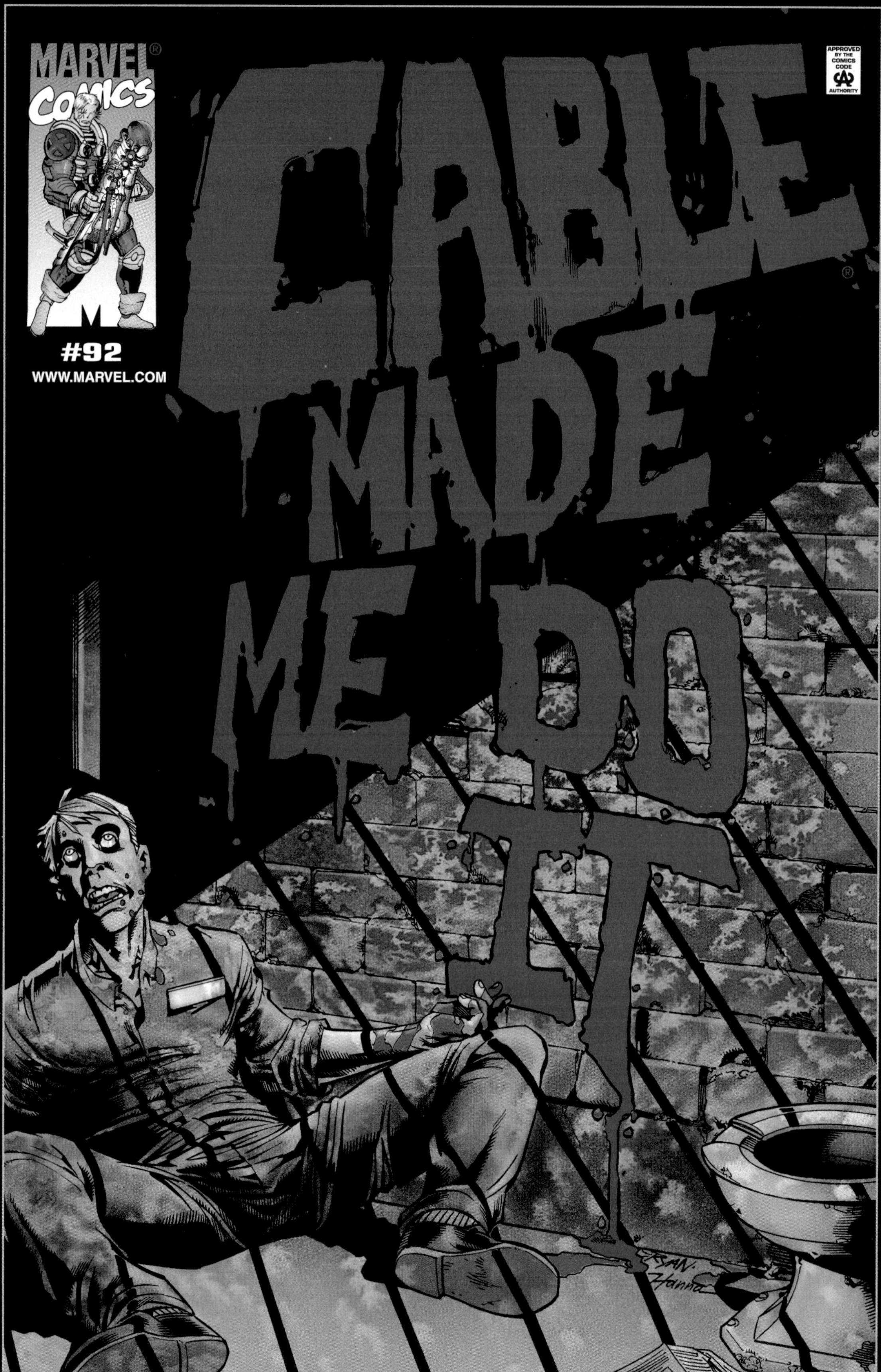

MARVEL COMICS
APPROVED BY THE COMICS CODE AUTHORITY
CABLE
#92
WWW.MARVEL.COM
CABLE MADE ME DO IT

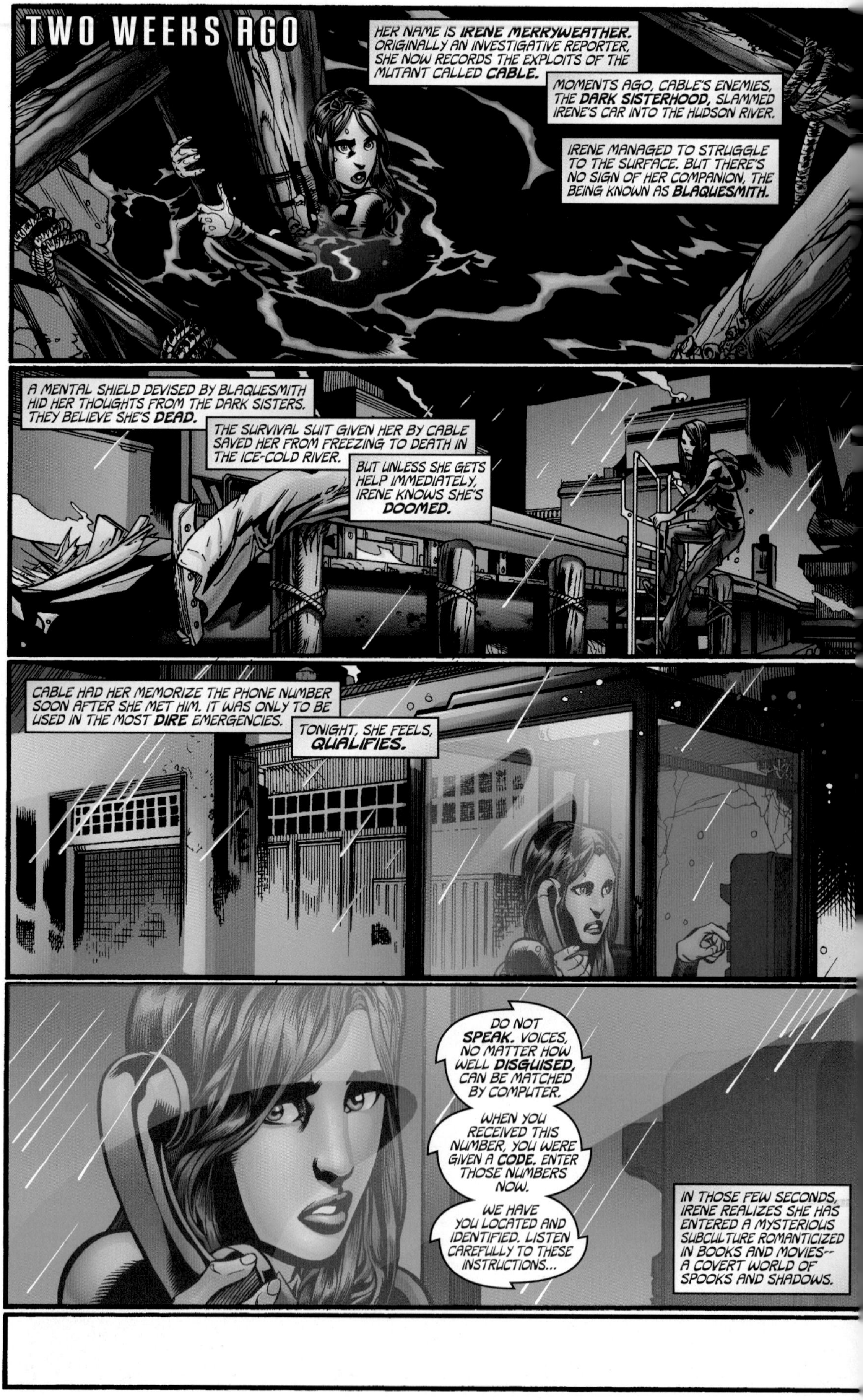
TWO WEEKS AGO
HER NAME IS IRENE MERRYWEATHER. ORIGINALLY AN INVESTIGATIVE REPORTER, SHE NOW RECORDS THE EXPLOITS OF THE MUTANT CALLED CABLE.
MOMENTS AGO, CABLE'S ENEMIES, THE DARK SISTERHOOD, SLAMMED IRENE'S CAR INTO THE HUDSON RIVER.
IRENE MANAGED TO STRUGGLE TO THE SURFACE. BUT THERE'S NO SIGN OF HER COMPANION, THE BEING KNOWN AS BLAQUESMITH.
A MENTAL SHIELD DEVISED BY BLAQUESMITH HID HER THOUGHTS FROM THE DARK SISTERS. THEY BELIEVE SHE'S DEAD.
THE SURVIVAL SUIT GIVEN HER BY CABLE SAVED HER FROM FREEZING TO DEATH IN THE ICE-COLD RIVER.
BUT UNLESS SHE GETS HELP IMMEDIATELY, IRENE KNOWS SHE'S DOOMED.
CABLE HAD HER MEMORIZE THE PHONE NUMBER SOON AFTER SHE MET HIM. IT WAS ONLY TO BE USED IN THE MOST DIRE EMERGENCIES.
TONIGHT, SHE FEELS, QUALIFIES.
DO NOT SPEAK. VOICES, NO MATTER HOW WELL DISGUISED, CAN BE MATCHED BY COMPUTER.
WHEN YOU RECEIVED THIS NUMBER, YOU WERE GIVEN A CODE. ENTER THOSE NUMBERS NOW.
WE HAVE YOU LOCATED AND IDENTIFIED. LISTEN CAREFULLY TO THESE INSTRUCTIONS...
IN THOSE FEW SECONDS, IRENE REALIZES SHE HAS ENTERED A MYSTERIOUS SUBCULTURE ROMANTICIZED IN BOOKS AND MOVIES-- A COVERT WORLD OF SPOOKS AND SHADOWS.

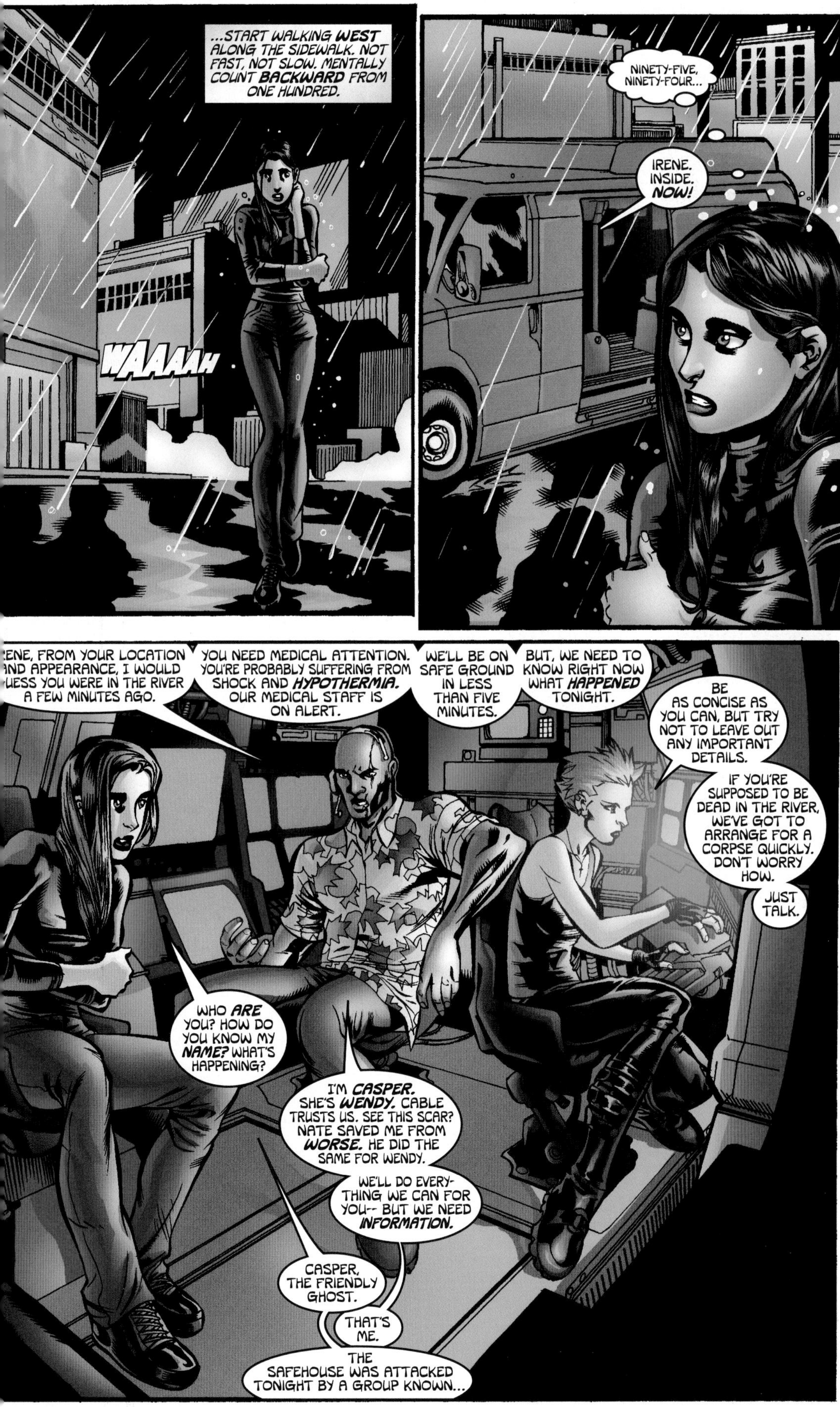
...START WALKING WEST ALONG THE SIDEWALK. NOT FAST, NOT SLOW. MENTALLY COUNT BACKWARD FROM ONE HUNDRED.
WAAAAH
NINETY-FIVE, NINETY-FOUR...
IRENE. INSIDE. NOW!
RENE, FROM YOUR LOCATION AND APPEARANCE, I WOULD UESS YOU WERE IN THE RIVER A FEW MINUTES AGO.
YOU NEED MEDICAL ATTENTION. YOU'RE PROBABLY SUFFERING FROM SHOCK AND HYPOTHERMIA. OUR MEDICAL STAFF IS ON ALERT.
WE'LL BE ON SAFE GROUND IN LESS THAN FIVE MINUTES.
BUT, WE NEED TO KNOW RIGHT NOW WHAT HAPPENED TONIGHT.
BE AS CONCISE AS YOU CAN, BUT TRY NOT TO LEAVE OUT ANY IMPORTANT DETAILS.
IF YOU'RE SUPPOSED TO BE DEAD IN THE RIVER, WE'VE GOT TO ARRANGE FOR A CORPSE QUICKLY. DON'T WORRY HOW.
JUST TALK.
WHO ARE YOU? HOW DO YOU KNOW MY NAME? WHAT'S HAPPENING?
I'M CASPER. SHE'S WENDY. CABLE TRUSTS US. SEE THIS SCAR? NATE SAVED ME FROM WORSE. HE DID THE SAME FOR WENDY.
WE'LL DO EVERY-THING WE CAN FOR YOU-- BUT WE NEED INFORMATION.
CASPER, THE FRIENDLY GHOST.
THAT'S ME.
THE SAFEHOUSE WAS ATTACKED TONIGHT BY A GROUP KNOWN...

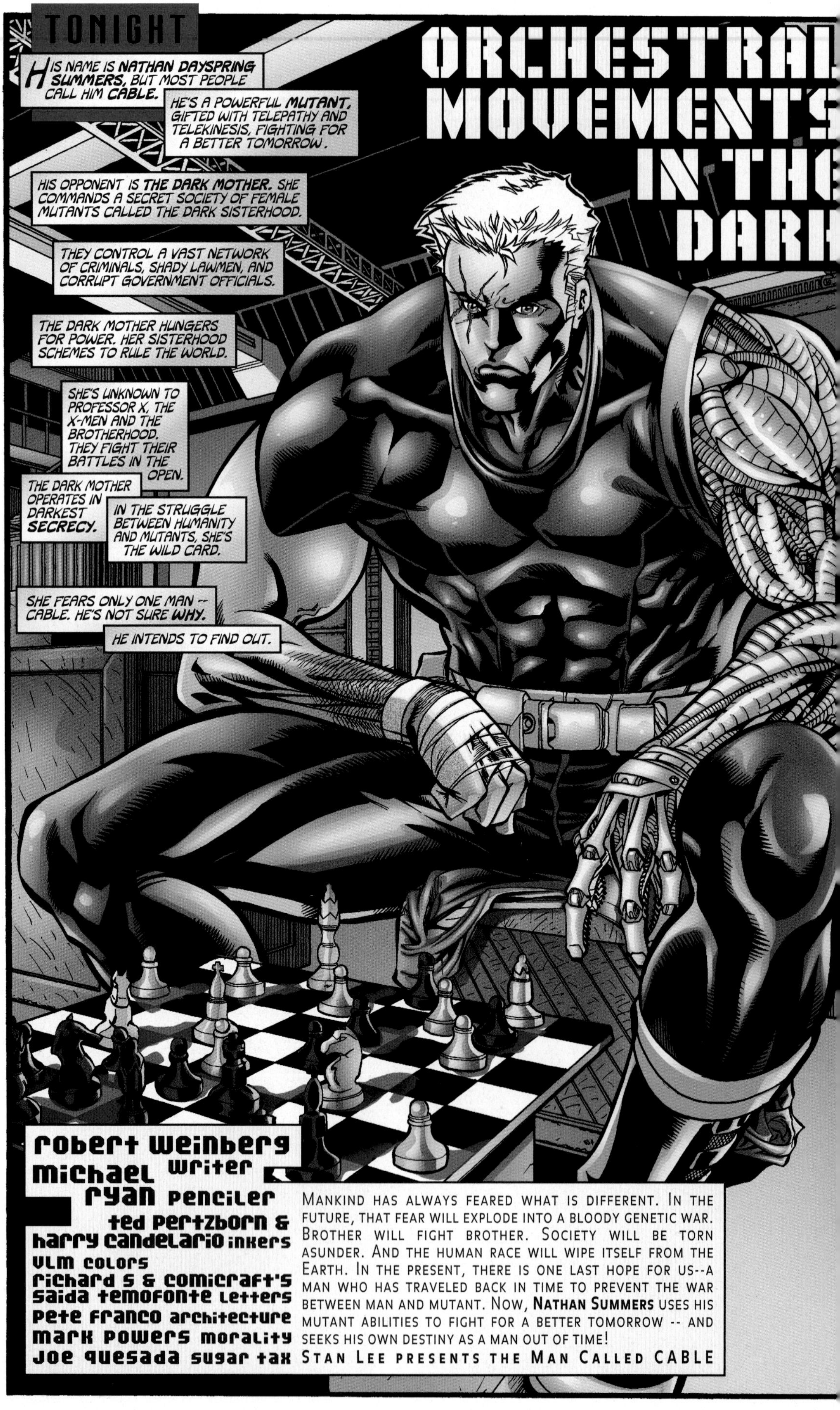

TONIGHT
ORCHESTRAL MOVEMENTS IN THE DARK
HIS NAME IS NATHAN DAYSPRING SUMMERS, BUT MOST PEOPLE CALL HIM CABLE.
HE'S A POWERFUL MUTANT, GIFTED WITH TELEPATHY AND TELEKINESIS, FIGHTING FOR A BETTER TOMORROW.
HIS OPPONENT IS THE DARK MOTHER. SHE COMMANDS A SECRET SOCIETY OF FEMALE MUTANTS CALLED THE DARK SISTERHOOD.
THEY CONTROL A VAST NETWORK OF CRIMINALS, SHADY LAWMEN, AND CORRUPT GOVERNMENT OFFICIALS.
THE DARK MOTHER HUNGERS FOR POWER. HER SISTERHOOD SCHEMES TO RULE THE WORLD.
SHE'S UNKNOWN TO PROFESSOR X, THE X-MEN AND THE BROTHERHOOD. THEY FIGHT THEIR BATTLES IN THE OPEN.
THE DARK MOTHER OPERATES IN DARKEST SECRECY.
IN THE STRUGGLE BETWEEN HUMANITY AND MUTANTS, SHE'S THE WILD CARD.
SHE FEARS ONLY ONE MAN -- CABLE. HE'S NOT SURE WHY.
HE INTENDS TO FIND OUT.
robert weinberg writer
michael ryan penciler
ted pertzborn & harry candelario inkers
ULM colors
richard s & comicraft's saida temofonte letters
pete franco architecture
mark powers morality
joe quesada sugar tax
MANKIND HAS ALWAYS FEARED WHAT IS DIFFERENT. IN THE FUTURE, THAT FEAR WILL EXPLODE INTO A BLOODY GENETIC WAR. BROTHER WILL FIGHT BROTHER. SOCIETY WILL BE TORN ASUNDER. AND THE HUMAN RACE WILL WIPE ITSELF FROM THE EARTH. IN THE PRESENT, THERE IS ONE LAST HOPE FOR US--A MAN WHO HAS TRAVELED BACK IN TIME TO PREVENT THE WAR BETWEEN MAN AND MUTANT. NOW, NATHAN SUMMERS USES HIS MUTANT ABILITIES TO FIGHT FOR A BETTER TOMORROW -- AND SEEKS HIS OWN DESTINY AS A MAN OUT OF TIME!
STAN LEE PRESENTS THE MAN CALLED CABLE

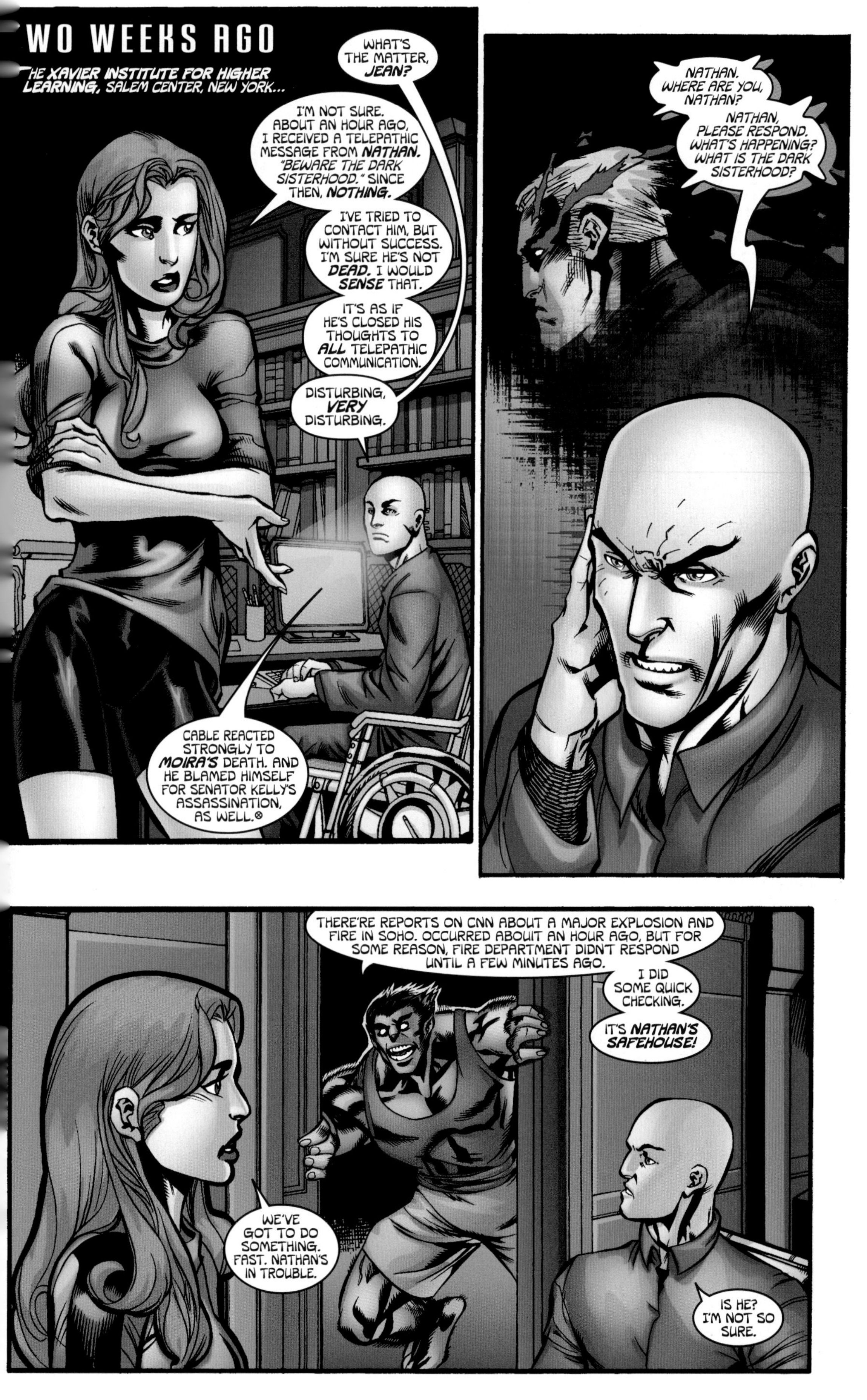
WO WEEKS AGO
HE XAVIER INSTITUTE FOR HIGHER LEARNING, SALEM CENTER, NEW YORK...
WHAT'S THE MATTER, JEAN?
I'M NOT SURE. ABOUT AN HOUR AGO, I RECEIVED A TELEPATHIC MESSAGE FROM NATHAN. "BEWARE THE DARK SISTERHOOD." SINCE THEN, NOTHING.
I'VE TRIED TO CONTACT HIM, BUT WITHOUT SUCCESS. I'M SURE HE'S NOT DEAD. I WOULD SENSE THAT.
IT'S AS IF HE'S CLOSED HIS THOUGHTS TO ALL TELEPATHIC COMMUNICATION.
DISTURBING, VERY DISTURBING.
CABLE REACTED STRONGLY TO MOIRA'S DEATH. AND HE BLAMED HIMSELF FOR SENATOR KELLY'S ASSASSINATION, AS WELL.
NATHAN. WHERE ARE YOU, NATHAN?
NATHAN, PLEASE RESPOND. WHAT'S HAPPENING? WHAT IS THE DARK SISTERHOOD?
THERE'RE REPORTS ON CNN ABOUT A MAJOR EXPLOSION AND FIRE IN SOHO. OCCURRED ABOUT AN HOUR AGO, BUT FOR SOME REASON, FIRE DEPARTMENT DIDN'T RESPOND UNTIL A FEW MINUTES AGO.
I DID SOME QUICK CHECKING.
IT'S NATHAN'S SAFEHOUSE!
WE'VE GOT TO DO SOMETHING. FAST. NATHAN'S IN TROUBLE.
IS HE? I'M NOT SO SURE.

PROFESSOR, WHAT ARE YOU SAYING?

YOU HEARD WHAT BEAST SAID. NATHAN NEEDS OUR HELP. *IMMEDIATELY.*

YOU'RE SUGGESTING THAT CABLE DID THIS *HIMSELF?*

NATHAN'S *ONE* OF US. HE'S *PROVED* THAT MANY TIMES OVER.

I REPEAT, IS HE? THEN WHY DOESN'T HE RESPOND TO MY TELEPATHIC MESSAGES?

WHO'S THIS DARK SISTERHOOD? WE'VE NEVER HEARD ANYTHING ABOUT THEM BEFORE. ODD, DON'T YOU THINK?

DO THEY ACTUALLY EVEN *EXIST?* OR ARE THEY AN EXCUSE FOR CABLE TO BREAK HIS TIES WITH US AND GO OFF AND FIGHT EVIL HE ALONE CAN COMPREHEND?

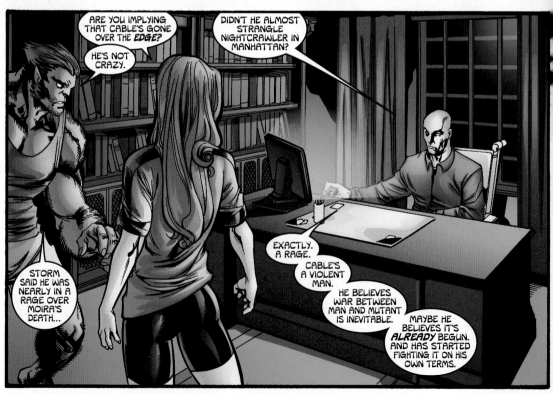

ARE YOU IMPLYING THAT CABLE'S GONE OVER THE *EDGE?*

HE'S NOT CRAZY.

DIDN'T HE ALMOST STRANGLE NIGHTCRAWLER IN MANHATTAN?

STORM SAID HE WAS NEARLY IN A RAGE OVER MOIRA'S DEATH...

EXACTLY. A RAGE.

CABLE'S A VIOLENT MAN.

HE BELIEVES WAR BETWEEN MAN AND MUTANT IS INEVITABLE.

MAYBE HE BELIEVES IT'S *ALREADY* BEGUN. AND HAS STARTED FIGHTING IT ON HIS OWN TERMS.

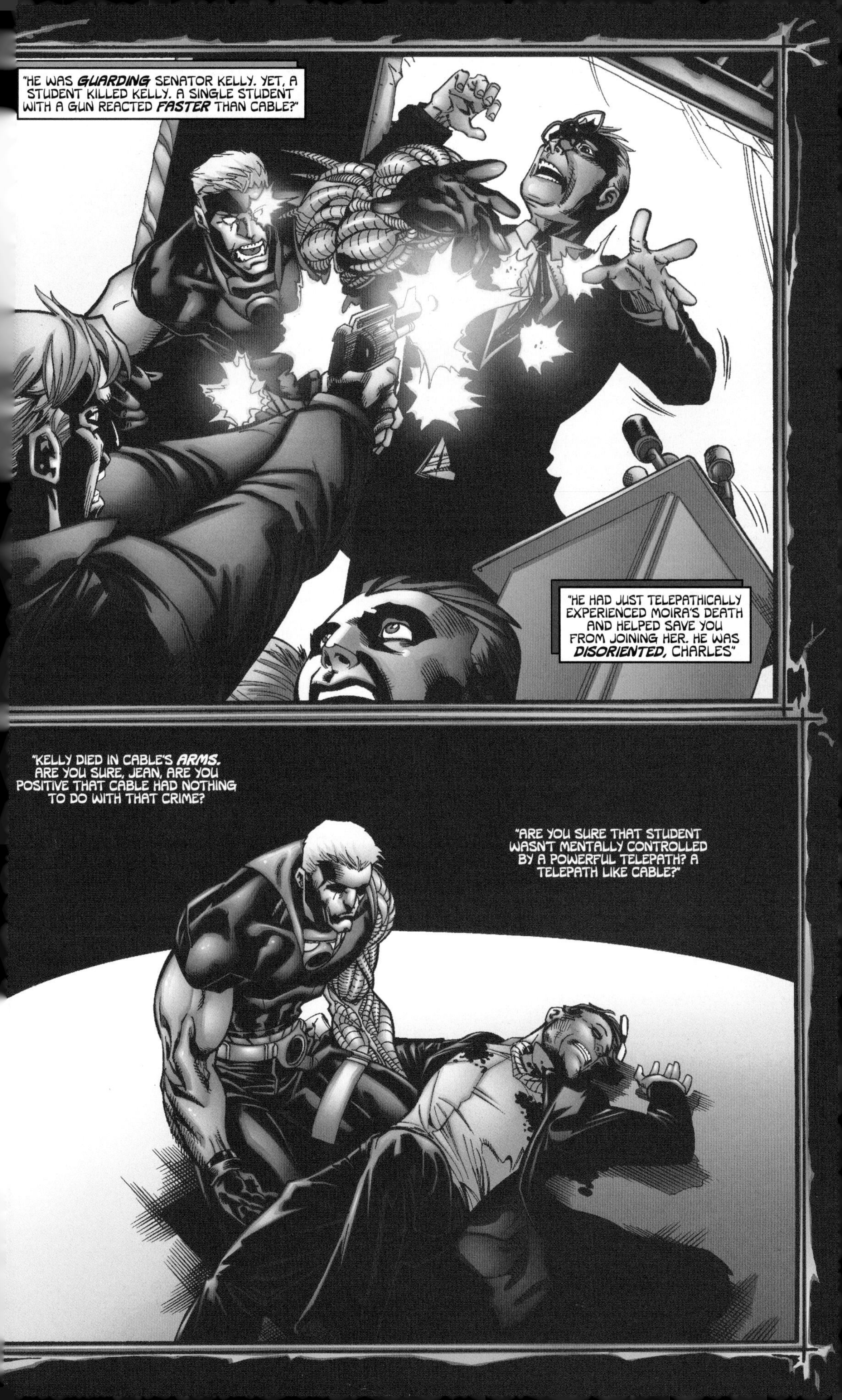
"HE WAS GUARDING SENATOR KELLY. YET, A STUDENT KILLED KELLY. A SINGLE STUDENT WITH A GUN REACTED FASTER THAN CABLE?"
"HE HAD JUST TELEPATHICALLY EXPERIENCED MOIRA'S DEATH AND HELPED SAVE YOU FROM JOINING HER. HE WAS DISORIENTED, CHARLES"
"KELLY DIED IN CABLE'S ARMS. ARE YOU SURE, JEAN, ARE YOU POSITIVE THAT CABLE HAD NOTHING TO DO WITH THAT CRIME?
"ARE YOU SURE THAT STUDENT WASN'T MENTALLY CONTROLLED BY A POWERFUL TELEPATH? A TELEPATH LIKE CABLE?"

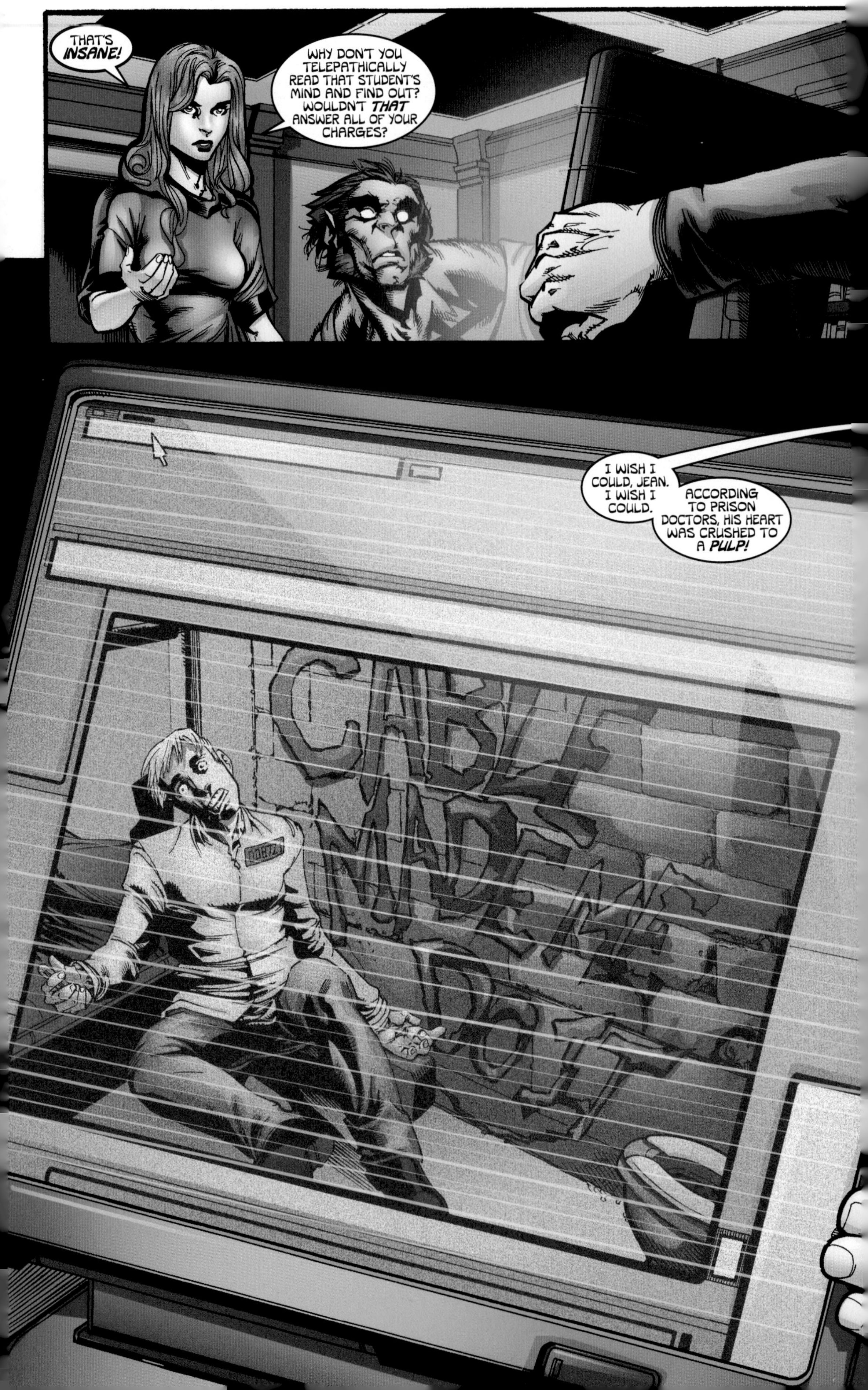
THAT'S *INSANE!*
WHY DON'T YOU TELEPATHICALLY READ THAT STUDENT'S MIND AND FIND OUT? WOULDN'T *THAT* ANSWER ALL OF YOUR CHARGES?
I WISH I COULD, JEAN. I WISH I COULD.
ACCORDING TO PRISON DOCTORS, HIS HEART WAS CRUSHED TO A *PULP!*
CABLE MADE ME DO IT

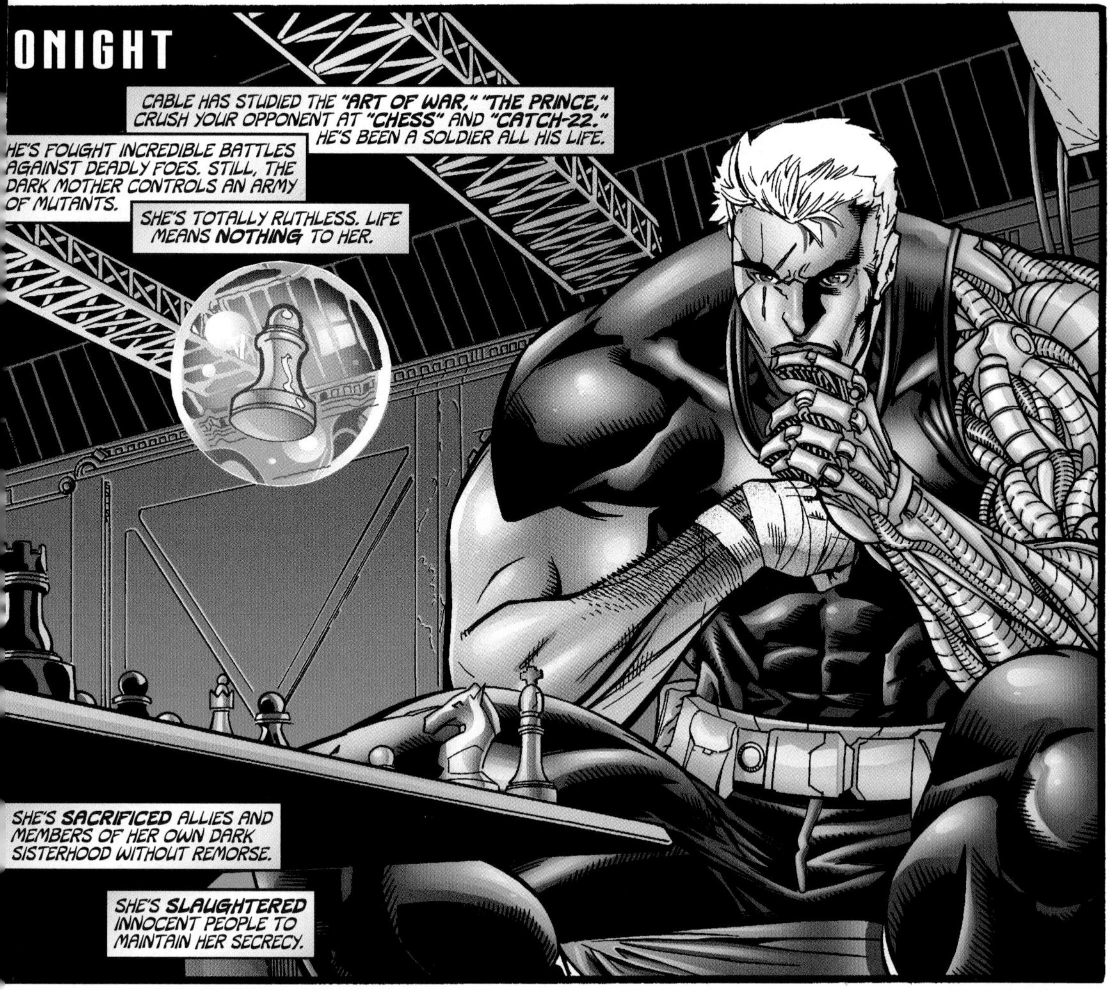
ONIGHT
CABLE HAS STUDIED THE "ART OF WAR," "THE PRINCE," CRUSH YOUR OPPONENT AT "CHESS" AND "CATCH-22." HE'S BEEN A SOLDIER ALL HIS LIFE.
HE'S FOUGHT INCREDIBLE BATTLES AGAINST DEADLY FOES. STILL, THE DARK MOTHER CONTROLS AN ARMY OF MUTANTS.
SHE'S TOTALLY RUTHLESS. LIFE MEANS NOTHING TO HER.
SHE'S SACRIFICED ALLIES AND MEMBERS OF HER OWN DARK SISTERHOOD WITHOUT REMORSE.
SHE'S SLAUGHTERED INNOCENT PEOPLE TO MAINTAIN HER SECRECY.

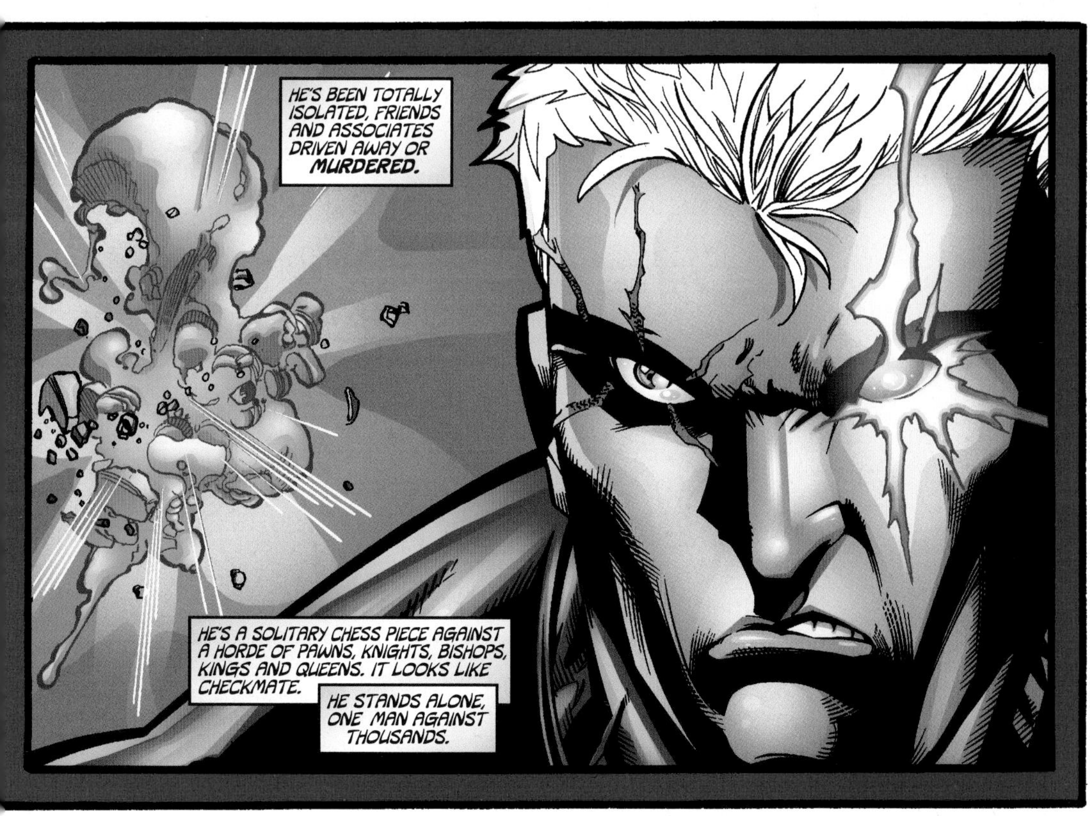
HE'S BEEN TOTALLY ISOLATED, FRIENDS AND ASSOCIATES DRIVEN AWAY OR MURDERED.
HE'S A SOLITARY CHESS PIECE AGAINST A HORDE OF PAWNS, KNIGHTS, BISHOPS, KINGS AND QUEENS. IT LOOKS LIKE CHECKMATE.
HE STANDS ALONE, ONE MAN AGAINST THOUSANDS.

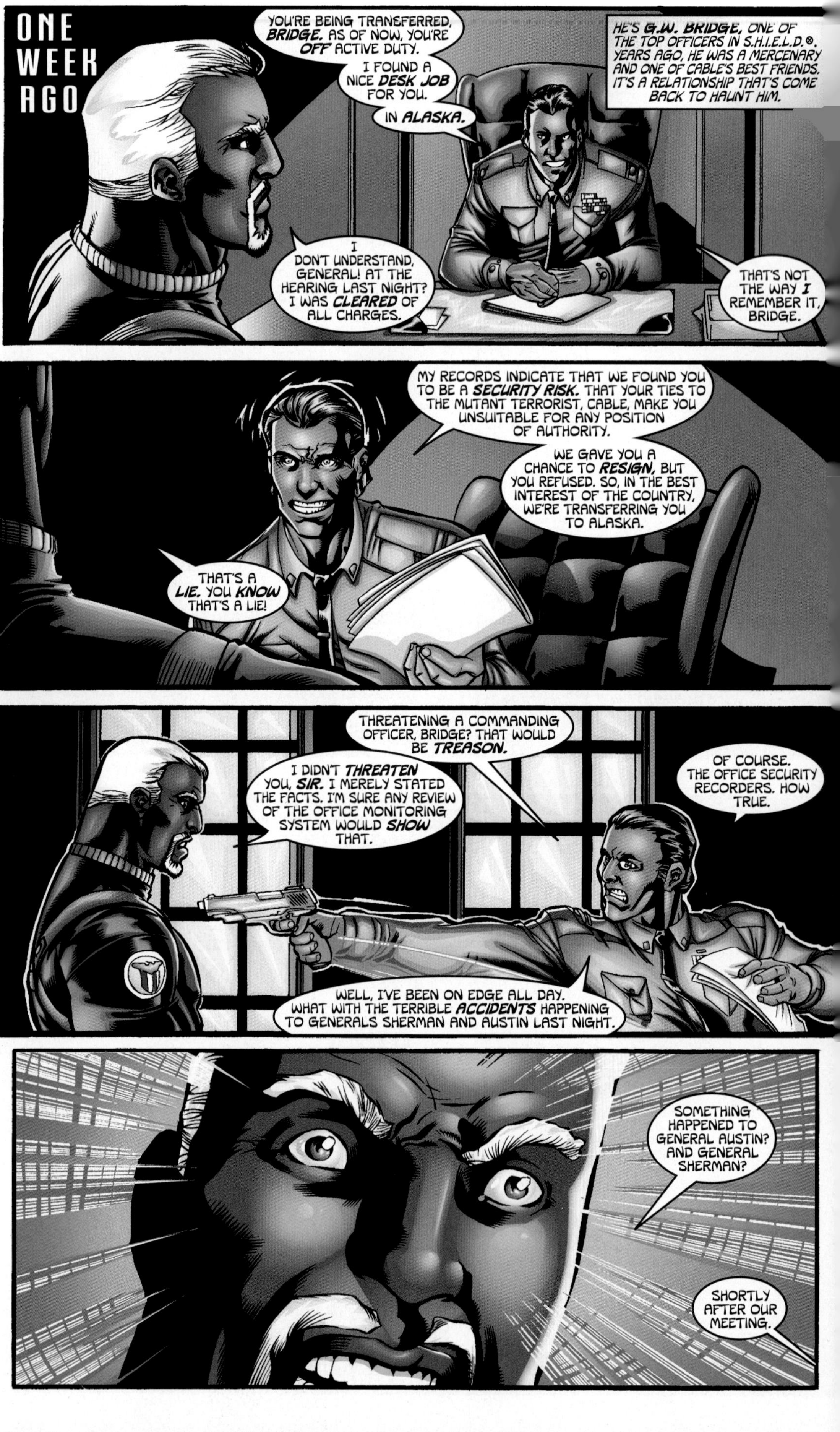

ONE WEEK AGO
YOU'RE BEING TRANSFERRED, BRIDGE. AS OF NOW, YOU'RE OFF ACTIVE DUTY.
I FOUND A NICE DESK JOB FOR YOU.
IN ALASKA.
HE'S G.W. BRIDGE, ONE OF THE TOP OFFICERS IN S.H.I.E.L.D.®. YEARS AGO, HE WAS A MERCENARY AND ONE OF CABLE'S BEST FRIENDS. IT'S A RELATIONSHIP THAT'S COME BACK TO HAUNT HIM.
I DON'T UNDERSTAND, GENERAL! AT THE HEARING LAST NIGHT? I WAS CLEARED OF ALL CHARGES.
THAT'S NOT THE WAY I REMEMBER IT, BRIDGE.
MY RECORDS INDICATE THAT WE FOUND YOU TO BE A SECURITY RISK. THAT YOUR TIES TO THE MUTANT TERRORIST, CABLE, MAKE YOU UNSUITABLE FOR ANY POSITION OF AUTHORITY.
WE GAVE YOU A CHANCE TO RESIGN, BUT YOU REFUSED. SO, IN THE BEST INTEREST OF THE COUNTRY, WE'RE TRANSFERRING YOU TO ALASKA.
THAT'S A LIE. YOU KNOW THAT'S A LIE!
THREATENING A COMMANDING OFFICER, BRIDGE? THAT WOULD BE TREASON.
I DIDN'T THREATEN YOU, SIR. I MERELY STATED THE FACTS. I'M SURE ANY REVIEW OF THE OFFICE MONITORING SYSTEM WOULD SHOW THAT.
OF COURSE. THE OFFICE SECURITY RECORDERS. HOW TRUE.
WELL, IVE BEEN ON EDGE ALL DAY. WHAT WITH THE TERRIBLE ACCIDENTS HAPPENING TO GENERALS SHERMAN AND AUSTIN LAST NIGHT.
SOMETHING HAPPENED TO GENERAL AUSTIN? AND GENERAL SHERMAN?
SHORTLY AFTER OUR MEETING.

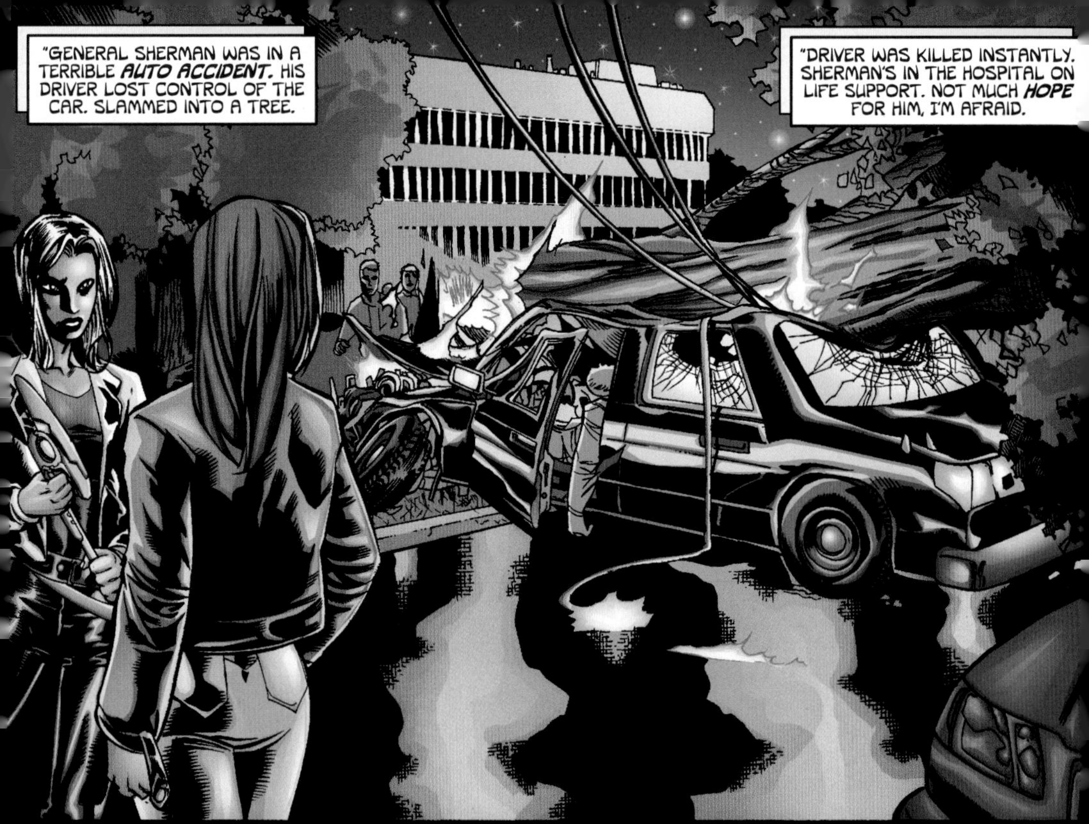
"GENERAL SHERMAN WAS IN A TERRIBLE AUTO ACCIDENT. HIS DRIVER LOST CONTROL OF THE CAR. SLAMMED INTO A TREE.
"DRIVER WAS KILLED INSTANTLY. SHERMAN'S IN THE HOSPITAL ON LIFE SUPPORT. NOT MUCH HOPE FOR HIM, I'M AFRAID.

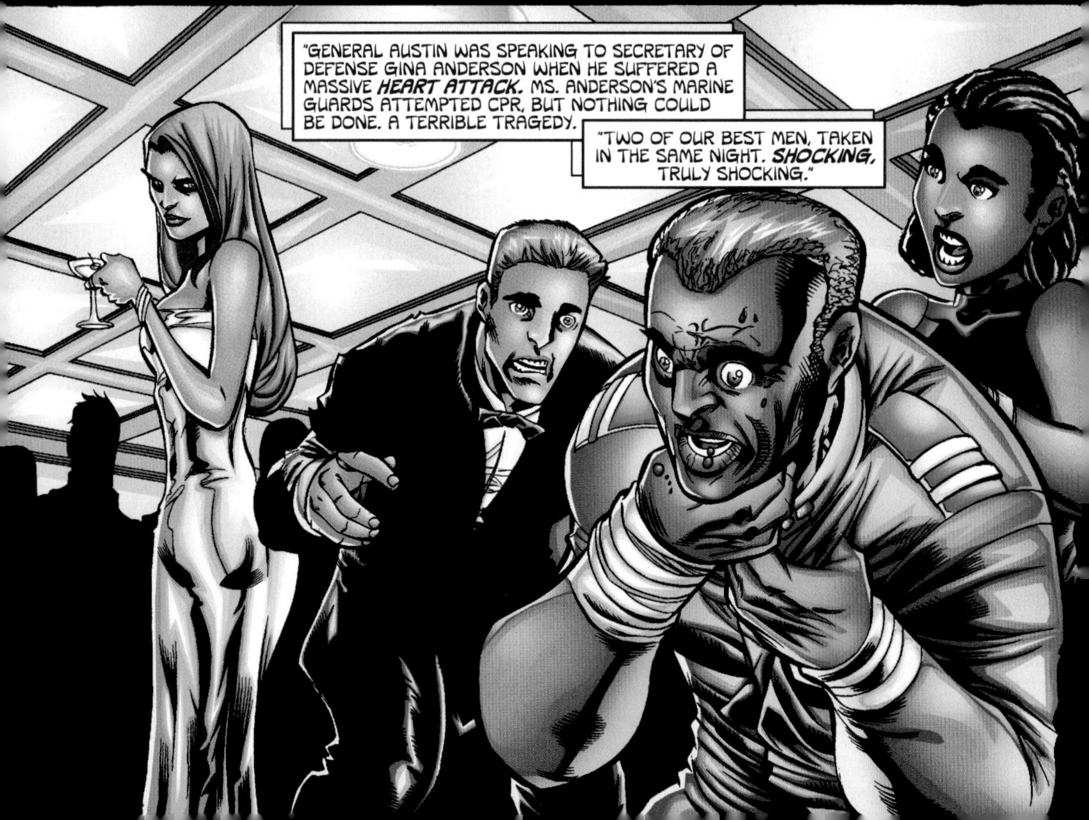
"GENERAL AUSTIN WAS SPEAKING TO SECRETARY OF DEFENSE GINA ANDERSON WHEN HE SUFFERED A MASSIVE HEART ATTACK. MS. ANDERSON'S MARINE GUARDS ATTEMPTED CPR, BUT NOTHING COULD BE DONE. A TERRIBLE TRAGEDY.
"TWO OF OUR BEST MEN, TAKEN IN THE SAME NIGHT. SHOCKING, TRULY SHOCKING."

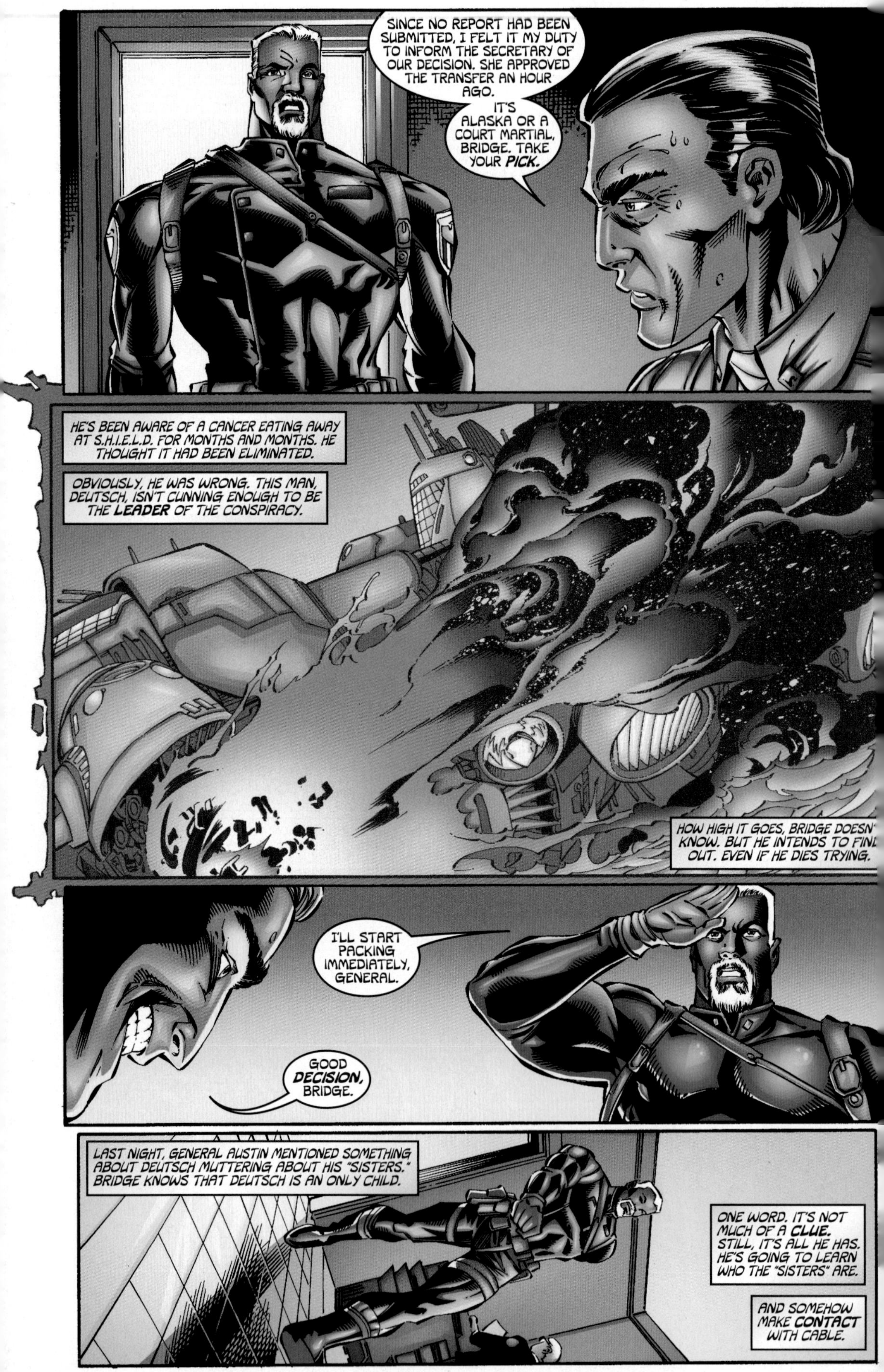

SINCE NO REPORT HAD BEEN SUBMITTED, I FELT IT MY DUTY TO INFORM THE SECRETARY OF OUR DECISION. SHE APPROVED THE TRANSFER AN HOUR AGO.
IT'S ALASKA OR A COURT MARTIAL, BRIDGE. TAKE YOUR PICK.
HE'S BEEN AWARE OF A CANCER EATING AWAY AT S.H.I.E.L.D. FOR MONTHS AND MONTHS. HE THOUGHT IT HAD BEEN ELIMINATED.
OBVIOUSLY, HE WAS WRONG. THIS MAN, DEUTSCH, ISN'T CUNNING ENOUGH TO BE THE LEADER OF THE CONSPIRACY.
HOW HIGH IT GOES, BRIDGE DOESN' KNOW. BUT HE INTENDS TO FIND OUT. EVEN IF HE DIES TRYING.
I'LL START PACKING IMMEDIATELY, GENERAL.
GOOD DECISION, BRIDGE.
LAST NIGHT, GENERAL AUSTIN MENTIONED SOMETHING ABOUT DEUTSCH MUTTERING ABOUT HIS "SISTERS." BRIDGE KNOWS THAT DEUTSCH IS AN ONLY CHILD.
ONE WORD. IT'S NOT MUCH OF A CLUE. STILL, IT'S ALL HE HAS. HE'S GOING TO LEARN WHO THE "SISTERS" ARE.
AND SOMEHOW MAKE CONTACT WITH CABLE.

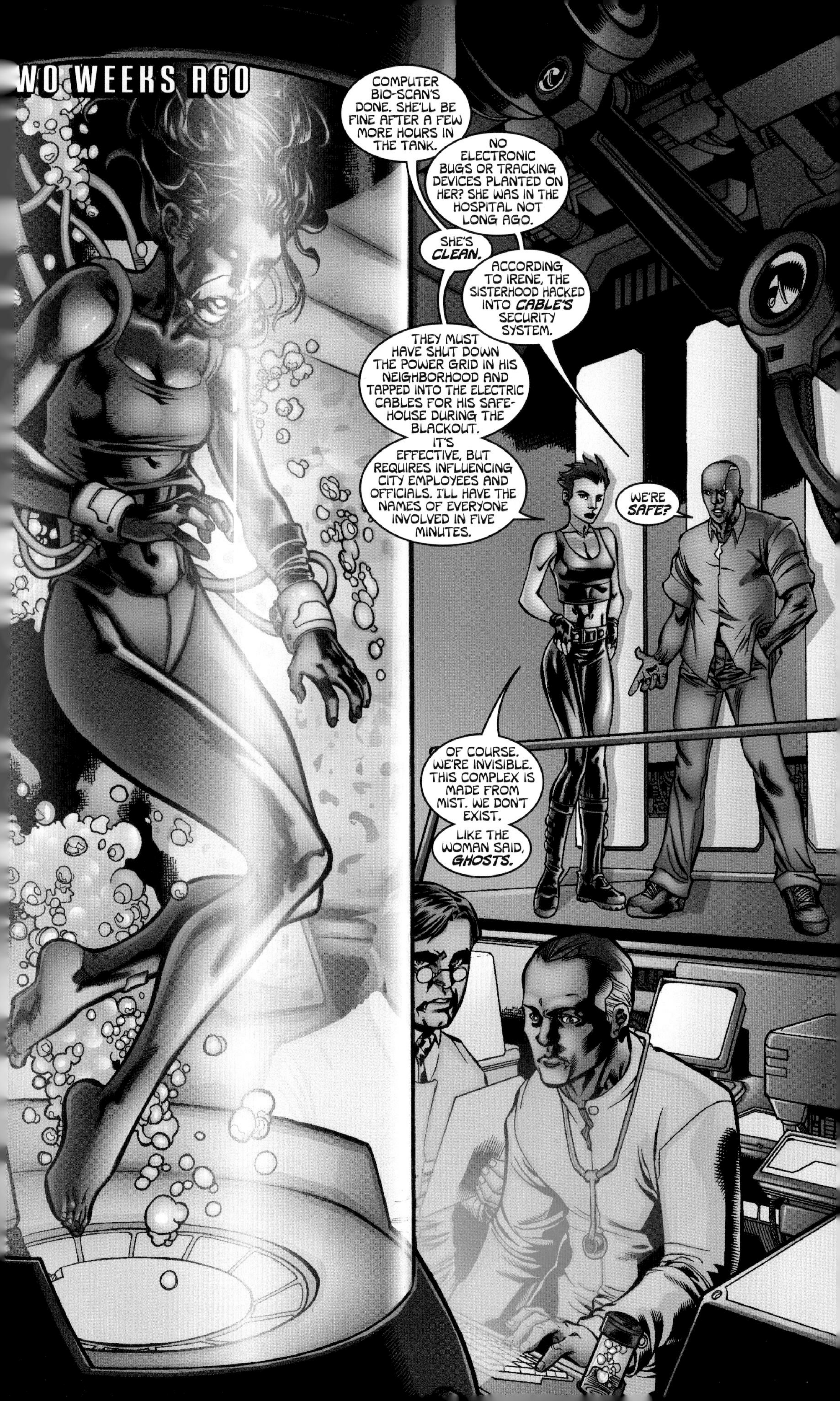
WO WEEKS AGO
COMPUTER BIO-SCAN'S DONE. SHE'LL BE FINE AFTER A FEW MORE HOURS IN THE TANK.
NO ELECTRONIC BUGS OR TRACKING DEVICES PLANTED ON HER? SHE WAS IN THE HOSPITAL NOT LONG AGO.
SHE'S CLEAN.
ACCORDING TO IRENE, THE SISTERHOOD HACKED INTO CABLE'S SECURITY SYSTEM.
THEY MUST HAVE SHUT DOWN THE POWER GRID IN HIS NEIGHBORHOOD AND TAPPED INTO THE ELECTRIC CABLES FOR HIS SAFE-HOUSE DURING THE BLACKOUT.
IT'S EFFECTIVE, BUT REQUIRES INFLUENCING CITY EMPLOYEES AND OFFICIALS. I'LL HAVE THE NAMES OF EVERYONE INVOLVED IN FIVE MINUTES.
WE'RE SAFE?
OF COURSE. WE'RE INVISIBLE. THIS COMPLEX IS MADE FROM MIST. WE DON'T EXIST.
LIKE THE WOMAN SAID, GHOSTS.

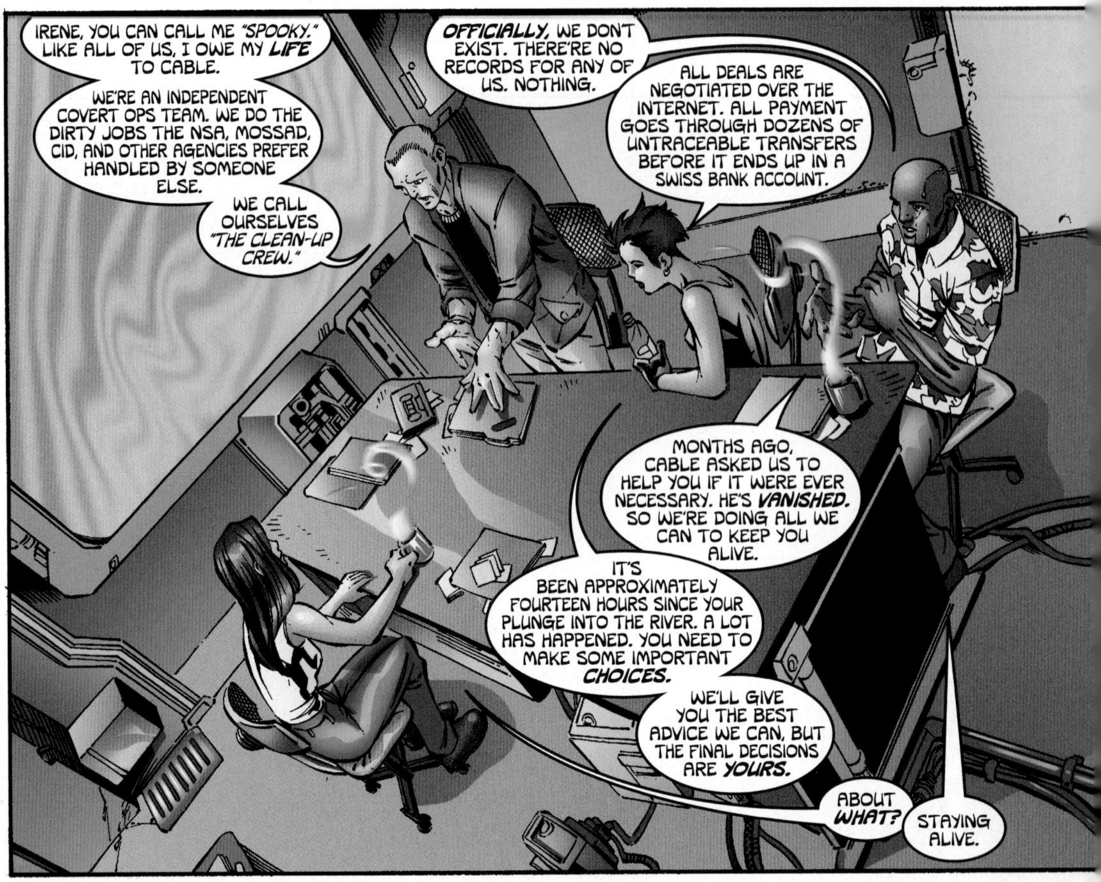
IRENE, YOU CAN CALL ME "SPOOKY." LIKE ALL OF US, I OWE MY LIFE TO CABLE.
WE'RE AN INDEPENDENT COVERT OPS TEAM. WE DO THE DIRTY JOBS THE NSA, MOSSAD, CID, AND OTHER AGENCIES PREFER HANDLED BY SOMEONE ELSE.
WE CALL OURSELVES "THE CLEAN-UP CREW."
OFFICIALLY, WE DON'T EXIST. THERE'RE NO RECORDS FOR ANY OF US. NOTHING.
ALL DEALS ARE NEGOTIATED OVER THE INTERNET. ALL PAYMENT GOES THROUGH DOZENS OF UNTRACEABLE TRANSFERS BEFORE IT ENDS UP IN A SWISS BANK ACCOUNT.
MONTHS AGO, CABLE ASKED US TO HELP YOU IF IT WERE EVER NECESSARY. HE'S VANISHED. SO WE'RE DOING ALL WE CAN TO KEEP YOU ALIVE.
IT'S BEEN APPROXIMATELY FOURTEEN HOURS SINCE YOUR PLUNGE INTO THE RIVER. A LOT HAS HAPPENED. YOU NEED TO MAKE SOME IMPORTANT CHOICES.
WE'LL GIVE YOU THE BEST ADVICE WE CAN, BUT THE FINAL DECISIONS ARE YOURS.
ABOUT WHAT?
STAYING ALIVE.

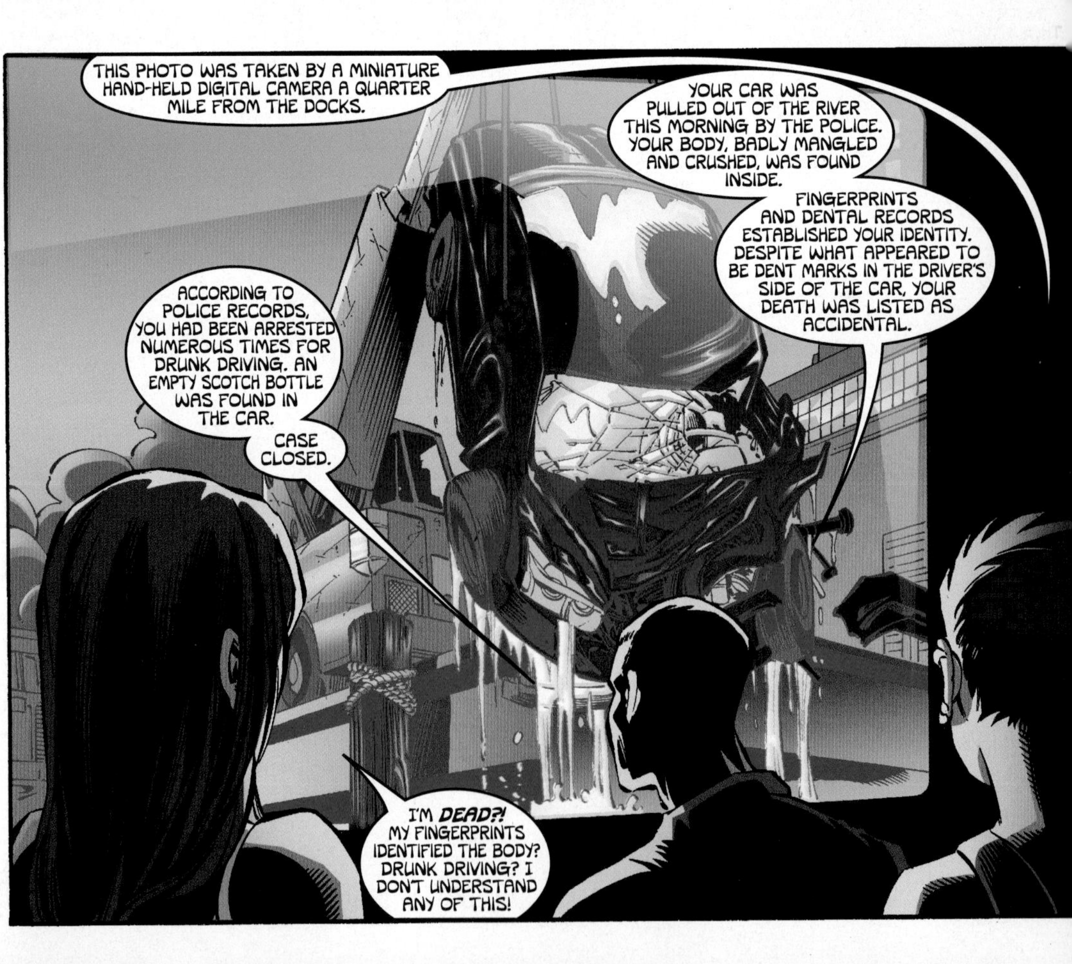
THIS PHOTO WAS TAKEN BY A MINIATURE HAND-HELD DIGITAL CAMERA A QUARTER MILE FROM THE DOCKS.
YOUR CAR WAS PULLED OUT OF THE RIVER THIS MORNING BY THE POLICE. YOUR BODY, BADLY MANGLED AND CRUSHED, WAS FOUND INSIDE.
FINGERPRINTS AND DENTAL RECORDS ESTABLISHED YOUR IDENTITY. DESPITE WHAT APPEARED TO BE DENT MARKS IN THE DRIVER'S SIDE OF THE CAR, YOUR DEATH WAS LISTED AS ACCIDENTAL.
ACCORDING TO POLICE RECORDS, YOU HAD BEEN ARRESTED NUMEROUS TIMES FOR DRUNK DRIVING. AN EMPTY SCOTCH BOTTLE WAS FOUND IN THE CAR.
CASE CLOSED.
I'M DEAD?! MY FINGERPRINTS IDENTIFIED THE BODY? DRUNK DRIVING? I DON'T UNDERSTAND ANY OF THIS!

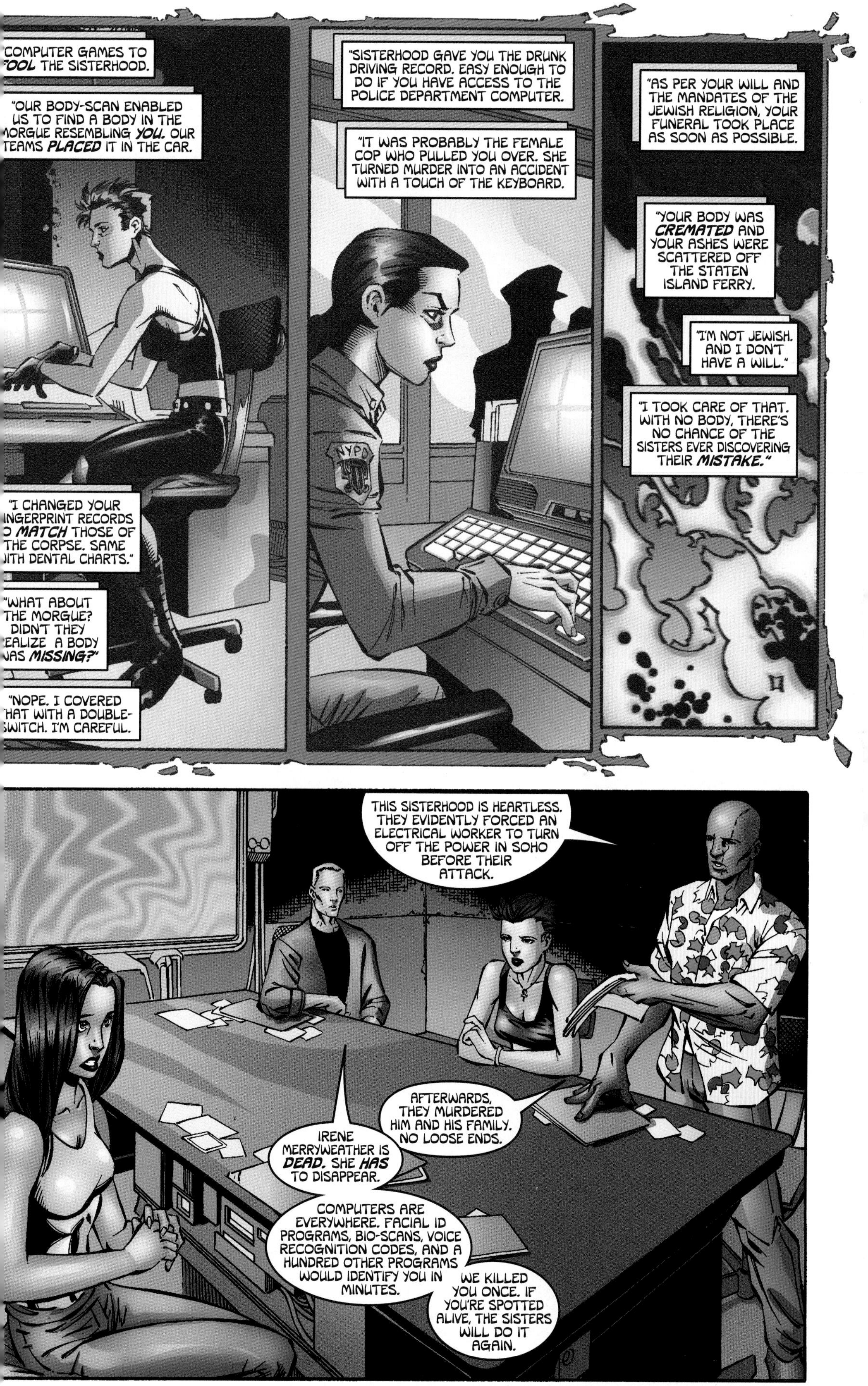
"COMPUTER GAMES TO FOOL THE SISTERHOOD.
"OUR BODY-SCAN ENABLED US TO FIND A BODY IN THE MORGUE RESEMBLING YOU. OUR TEAMS PLACED IT IN THE CAR.
"I CHANGED YOUR INGERPRINT RECORDS O MATCH THOSE OF THE CORPSE. SAME ITH DENTAL CHARTS."
"WHAT ABOUT THE MORGUE? DIDN'T THEY EALIZE A BODY AS MISSING?"
"NOPE. I COVERED HAT WITH A DOUBLE-SWITCH. I'M CAREFUL.
"SISTERHOOD GAVE YOU THE DRUNK DRIVING RECORD. EASY ENOUGH TO DO IF YOU HAVE ACCESS TO THE POLICE DEPARTMENT COMPUTER.
"IT WAS PROBABLY THE FEMALE COP WHO PULLED YOU OVER. SHE TURNED MURDER INTO AN ACCIDENT WITH A TOUCH OF THE KEYBOARD.
NYPD
"AS PER YOUR WILL AND THE MANDATES OF THE JEWISH RELIGION, YOUR FUNERAL TOOK PLACE AS SOON AS POSSIBLE.
"YOUR BODY WAS CREMATED AND YOUR ASHES WERE SCATTERED OFF THE STATEN ISLAND FERRY.
"I'M NOT JEWISH. AND I DON'T HAVE A WILL."
"I TOOK CARE OF THAT. WITH NO BODY, THERE'S NO CHANCE OF THE SISTERS EVER DISCOVERING THEIR MISTAKE."
THIS SISTERHOOD IS HEARTLESS. THEY EVIDENTLY FORCED AN ELECTRICAL WORKER TO TURN OFF THE POWER IN SOHO BEFORE THEIR ATTACK.
AFTERWARDS, THEY MURDERED HIM AND HIS FAMILY. NO LOOSE ENDS.
IRENE MERRYWEATHER IS DEAD. SHE HAS TO DISAPPEAR.
COMPUTERS ARE EVERYWHERE. FACIAL ID PROGRAMS, BIO-SCANS, VOICE RECOGNITION CODES, AND A HUNDRED OTHER PROGRAMS WOULD IDENTIFY YOU IN MINUTES.
WE KILLED YOU ONCE. IF YOU'RE SPOTTED ALIVE, THE SISTERS WILL DO IT AGAIN.

YOU'VE GOT TWO CHOICES. STAY HIDDEN, LIVING HERE, NEVER GOING OUTSIDE. OR LET US ALTER YOUR APPEARANCE AND GIVE YOU A COMPLETELY NEW IDENTITY.

WHAT IF I MOVED TO ANOTHER COUNTRY?

THEY'D FIND YOU IN TWO WEEKS, MAYBE LESS. UNLESS YOU WANT TO LIVE ON A FARM WITHOUT ELECTRICITY IN THE URAL MOUNTAINS.

I CAN'T SPEND THE REST OF MY LIFE AFRAID TO GO OUTSIDE.

WE CAN SURGICALLY ALTER YOUR FEATURES AND CHANGE YOUR VOICE SLIGHTLY. THAT *MIGHT* WORK, IF YOU'RE *LUCKY.*

BUT IF YOU WANT TOTAL FREEDOM, THE ABILITY TO DO WHATEVER YOU WANT, THAT'S GOING TO REQUIRE DRASTIC ACTION.

WHAT SORT OF DRASTIC ACTION?

HOW PREJUDICED ARE YOU?

HUH? WHY?

SIMPLE. USING SOME SPECIAL EQUIPMENT CABLE ONCE GAVE US, WE CAN COMPLETELY CHANGE YOUR APPEARANCE VIA HOLOGRAPHIC IMAGERY. IF WE SWITCH YOUR SKIN FROM WHITE TO BLACK, NO WILL RECOGNIZE YOU.

PEOPLE MIGHT THINK YOU RESEMBLE IRENE MERRYWEATHER, BUT THEY'LL NEVER BELIEVE IT'S YOU.

TURNING YOU BLACK WILL MAKE YOU INVISIBLE TO YOUR ENEMIES. AS WELL AS YOUR FRIENDS.

IT WILL ALSO EXPO YOU TO A WHOLE N SPECTRUM OF PREJU AND DISTRUST. OU COUNTRY HAS MAD LOT OF STRIDES RACE RELATIONS. B THERE'S A LONG WAY TO GO.

THERE'S NO OTHER CHOICE, IS THERE? NOT IF I WANT TO LIVE?

NO, IRE THER NO OT CHOIC

WE'LL SET YOU UP WITH A NEW IDENTITY. USE COMPUTER RECORDS TO GIVE YOU A SOLID BACK-GROUND. A WHOLE *NEW* LIFE.

I ALWAYS LIKED MARGARET.

YOU HAVE A FAVORITE NAME?

THEN YOU'LL BE *MARGARET BRUNDAGE.* AN INSURANCE INVESTIGATOR. I'LL HAVE YOUR NEW PERSONA IN AN HOUR.

YOU'VE DONE THIS *BEFORE,* HAVEN'T YOU?

MANY TIMES, MEG. NOT ONLY FOR OTHERS, BUT FOR *OURSELVES.* YOU'RE ABOUT TO JOIN OUR RANKS.

WELCOME TO THE *SHADOWLANDS.*

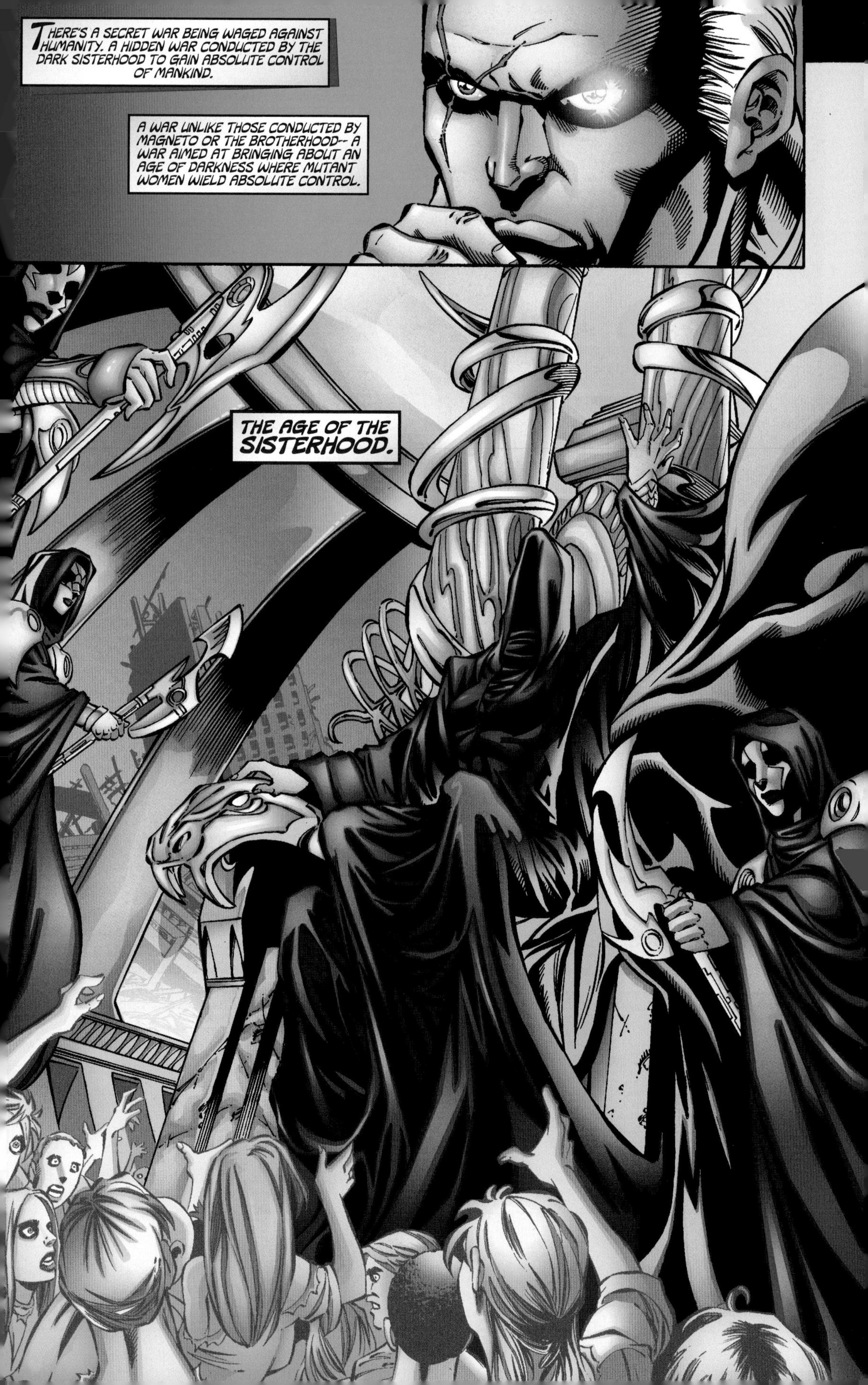
THERE'S A SECRET WAR BEING WAGED AGAINST HUMANITY. A HIDDEN WAR CONDUCTED BY THE DARK SISTERHOOD TO GAIN ABSOLUTE CONTROL OF MANKIND.
A WAR UNLIKE THOSE CONDUCTED BY MAGNETO OR THE BROTHERHOOD-- A WAR AIMED AT BRINGING ABOUT AN AGE OF DARKNESS WHERE MUTANT WOMEN WIELD ABSOLUTE CONTROL.
THE AGE OF THE SISTERHOOD.

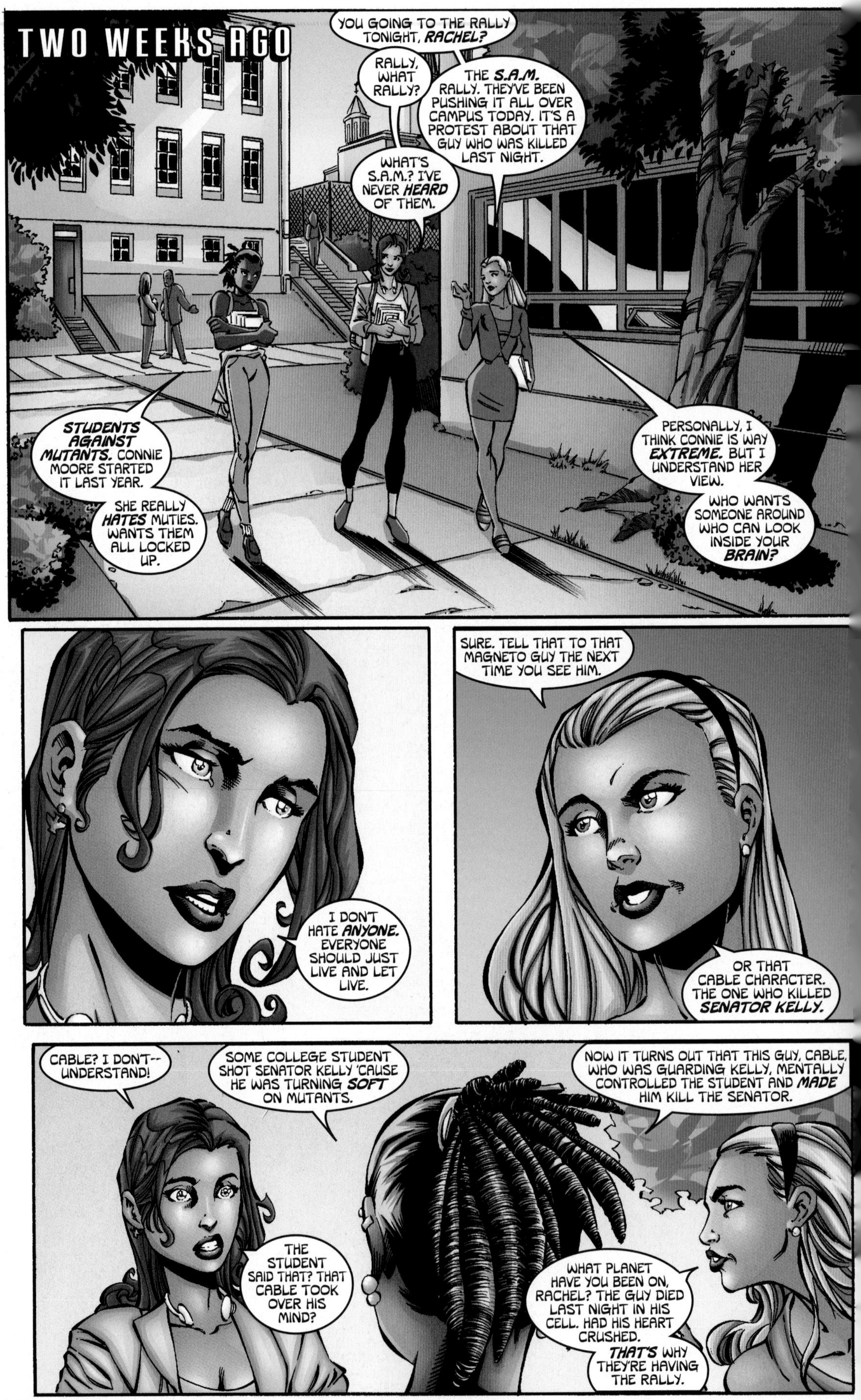
TWO WEEKS AGO
YOU GOING TO THE RALLY TONIGHT, RACHEL?
RALLY, WHAT RALLY?
THE S.A.M. RALLY. THEY'VE BEEN PUSHING IT ALL OVER CAMPUS TODAY. IT'S A PROTEST ABOUT THAT GUY WHO WAS KILLED LAST NIGHT.
WHAT'S S.A.M.? I'VE NEVER HEARD OF THEM.
STUDENTS AGAINST MUTANTS. CONNIE MOORE STARTED IT LAST YEAR.
SHE REALLY HATES MUTIES. WANTS THEM ALL LOCKED UP.
PERSONALLY, I THINK CONNIE IS WAY EXTREME. BUT I UNDERSTAND HER VIEW.
WHO WANTS SOMEONE AROUND WHO CAN LOOK INSIDE YOUR BRAIN?
I DON'T HATE ANYONE. EVERYONE SHOULD JUST LIVE AND LET LIVE.
SURE. TELL THAT TO THAT MAGNETO GUY THE NEXT TIME YOU SEE HIM.
OR THAT CABLE CHARACTER. THE ONE WHO KILLED SENATOR KELLY.
CABLE? I DON'T-- UNDERSTAND!
SOME COLLEGE STUDENT SHOT SENATOR KELLY 'CAUSE HE WAS TURNING SOFT ON MUTANTS.
NOW IT TURNS OUT THAT THIS GUY, CABLE, WHO WAS GUARDING KELLY, MENTALLY CONTROLLED THE STUDENT AND MADE HIM KILL THE SENATOR.
THE STUDENT SAID THAT? THAT CABLE TOOK OVER HIS MIND?
WHAT PLANET HAVE YOU BEEN ON, RACHEL? THE GUY DIED LAST NIGHT IN HIS CELL. HAD HIS HEART CRUSHED.
THAT'S WHY THEY'RE HAVING THE RALLY.

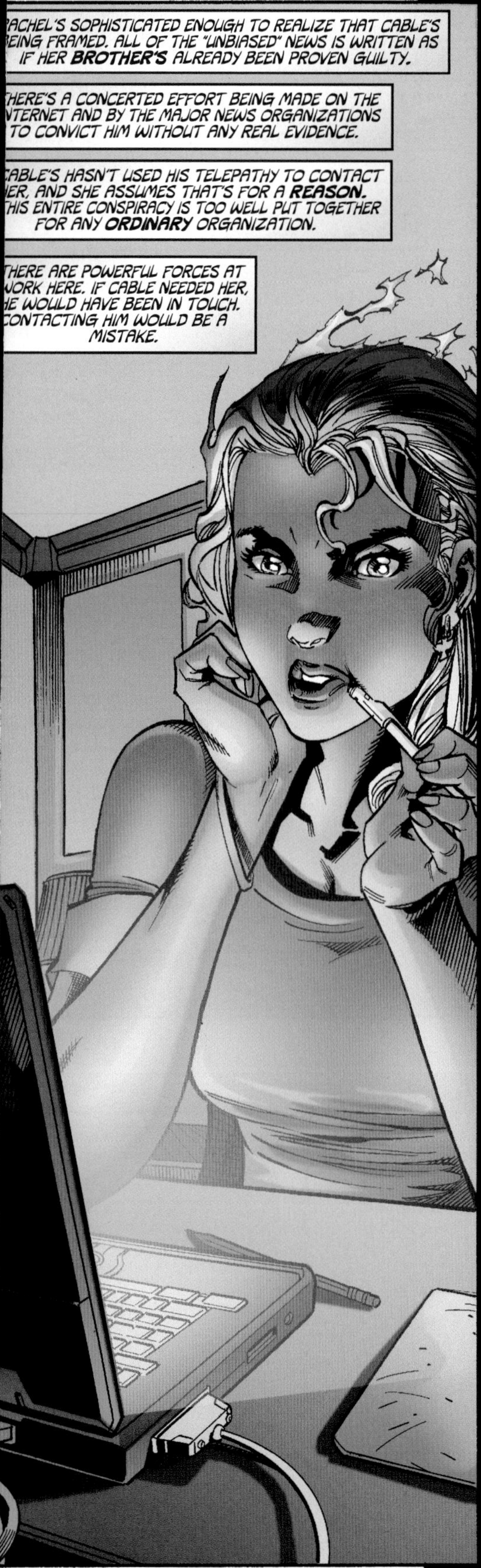
RACHEL'S SOPHISTICATED ENOUGH TO REALIZE THAT CABLE'S EING FRAMED. ALL OF THE "UNBIASED" NEWS IS WRITTEN AS IF HER **BROTHER'S** ALREADY BEEN PROVEN GUILTY.
HERE'S A CONCERTED EFFORT BEING MADE ON THE NTERNET AND BY THE MAJOR NEWS ORGANIZATIONS TO CONVICT HIM WITHOUT ANY REAL EVIDENCE.
CABLE'S HASN'T USED HIS TELEPATHY TO CONTACT HER, AND SHE ASSUMES THAT'S FOR A **REASON.** THIS ENTIRE CONSPIRACY IS TOO WELL PUT TOGETHER FOR ANY **ORDINARY** ORGANIZATION.
THERE ARE POWERFUL FORCES AT ORK HERE. IF CABLE NEEDED HER, E WOULD HAVE BEEN IN TOUCH. CONTACTING HIM WOULD BE A MISTAKE.

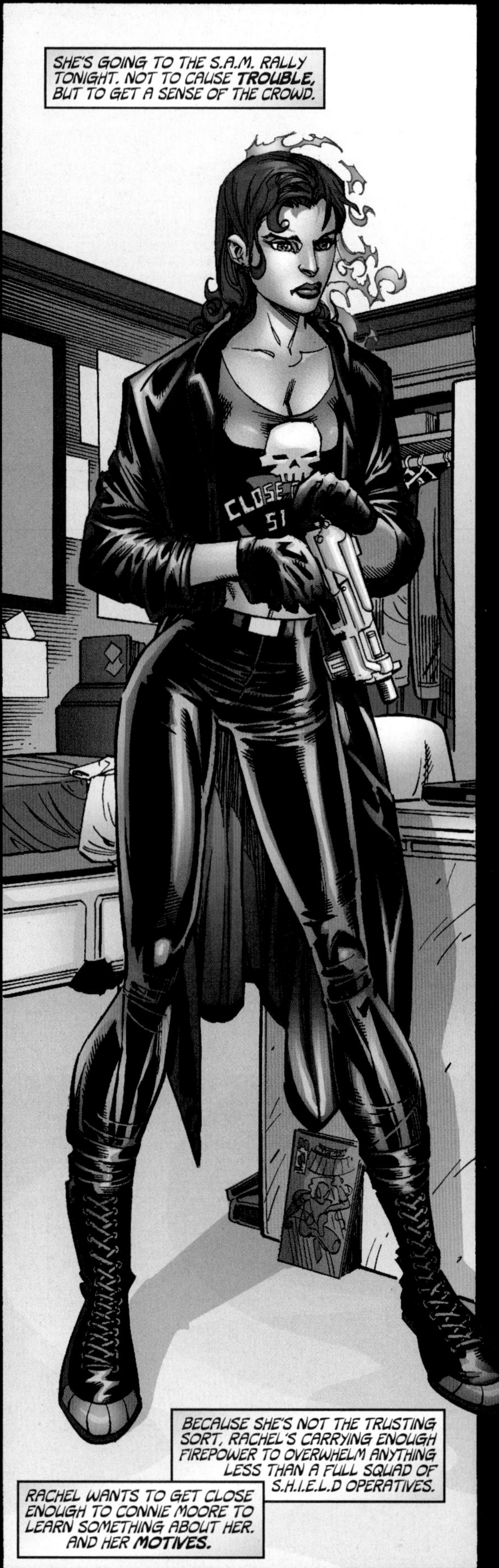
SHE'S GOING TO THE S.A.M. RALLY TONIGHT. NOT TO CAUSE **TROUBLE,** BUT TO GET A SENSE OF THE CROWD.
CLOSE 51
BECAUSE SHE'S NOT THE TRUSTING SORT, RACHEL'S CARRYING ENOUGH FIREPOWER TO OVERWHELM ANYTHING LESS THAN A FULL SQUAD OF S.H.I.E.L.D OPERATIVES.
RACHEL WANTS TO GET CLOSE ENOUGH TO CONNIE MOORE TO LEARN SOMETHING ABOUT HER. AND HER **MOTIVES.**

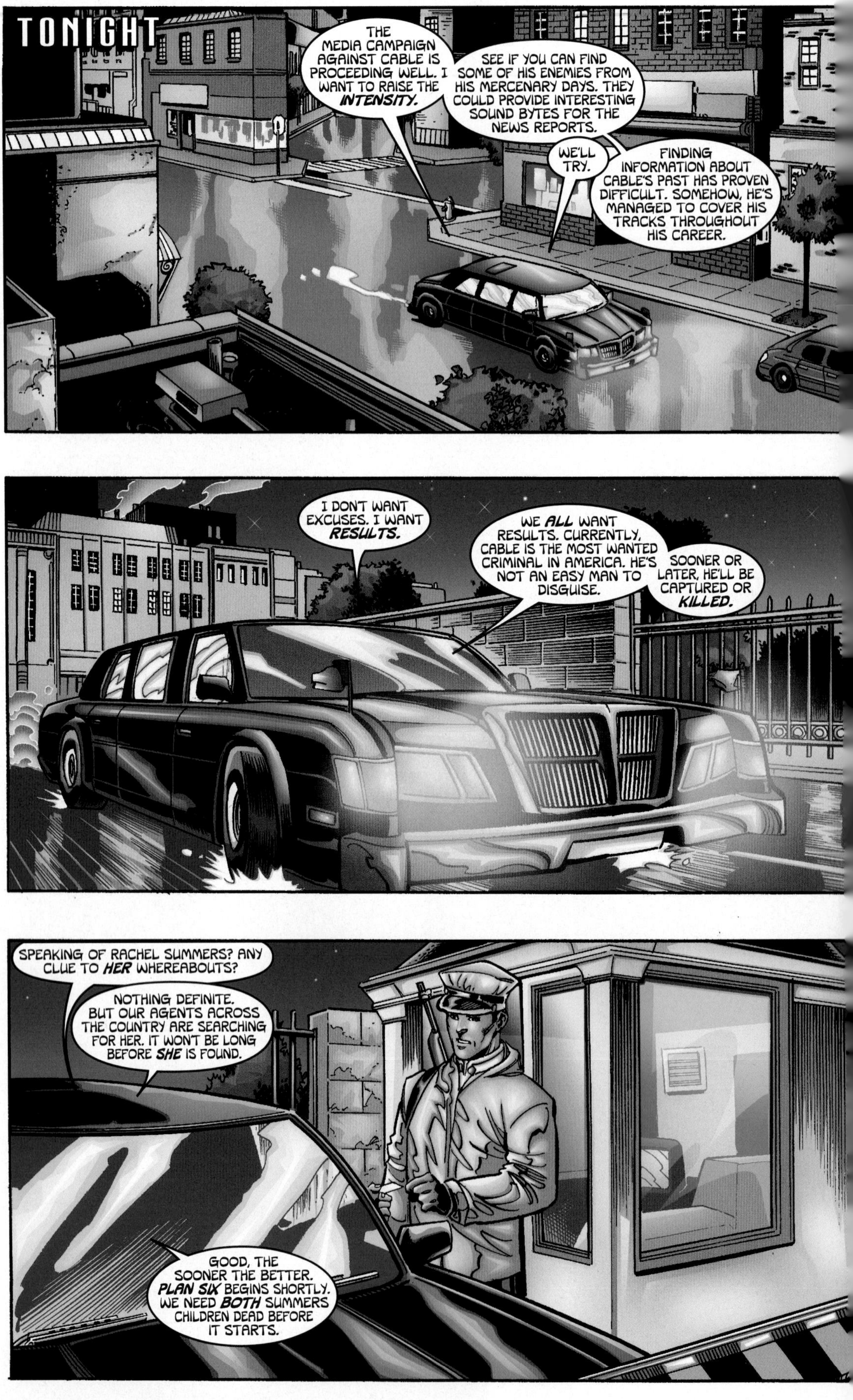
TONIGHT
THE MEDIA CAMPAIGN AGAINST CABLE IS PROCEEDING WELL. I WANT TO RAISE THE INTENSITY.
SEE IF YOU CAN FIND SOME OF HIS ENEMIES FROM HIS MERCENARY DAYS. THEY COULD PROVIDE INTERESTING SOUND BYTES FOR THE NEWS REPORTS.
WE'LL TRY.
FINDING INFORMATION ABOUT CABLE'S PAST HAS PROVEN DIFFICULT. SOMEHOW, HE'S MANAGED TO COVER HIS TRACKS THROUGHOUT HIS CAREER.
I DON'T WANT EXCUSES. I WANT RESULTS.
WE ALL WANT RESULTS. CURRENTLY, CABLE IS THE MOST WANTED CRIMINAL IN AMERICA. HE'S NOT AN EASY MAN TO DISGUISE.
SOONER OR LATER, HE'LL BE CAPTURED OR KILLED.
SPEAKING OF RACHEL SUMMERS? ANY CLUE TO HER WHEREABOUTS?
NOTHING DEFINITE. BUT OUR AGENTS ACROSS THE COUNTRY ARE SEARCHING FOR HER. IT WON'T BE LONG BEFORE SHE IS FOUND.
GOOD, THE SOONER THE BETTER. PLAN SIX BEGINS SHORTLY. WE NEED BOTH SUMMERS CHILDREN DEAD BEFORE IT STARTS.

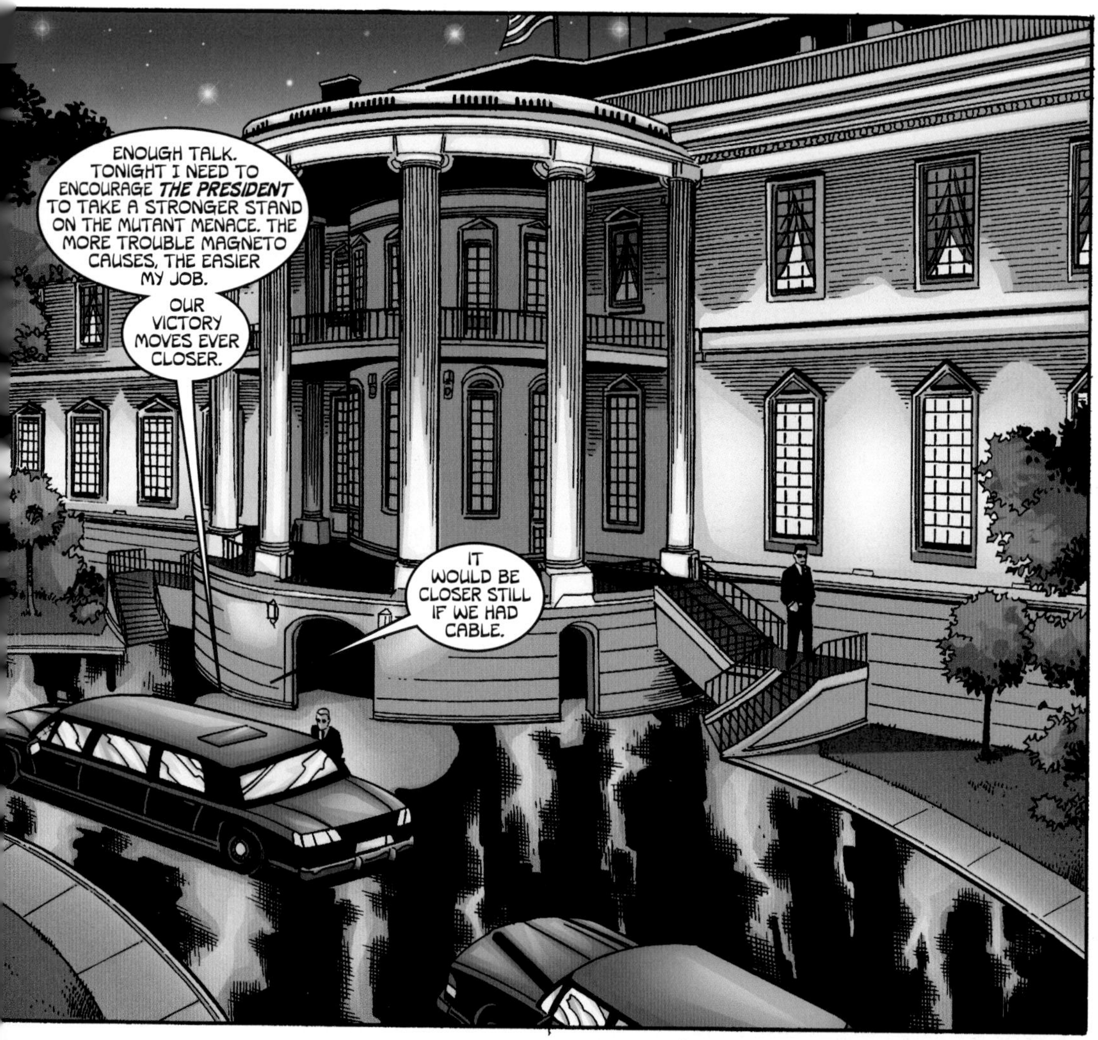
ENOUGH TALK. TONIGHT I NEED TO ENCOURAGE THE PRESIDENT TO TAKE A STRONGER STAND ON THE MUTANT MENACE. THE MORE TROUBLE MAGNETO CAUSES, THE EASIER MY JOB.
OUR VICTORY MOVES EVER CLOSER.
IT WOULD BE CLOSER STILL IF WE HAD CABLE.

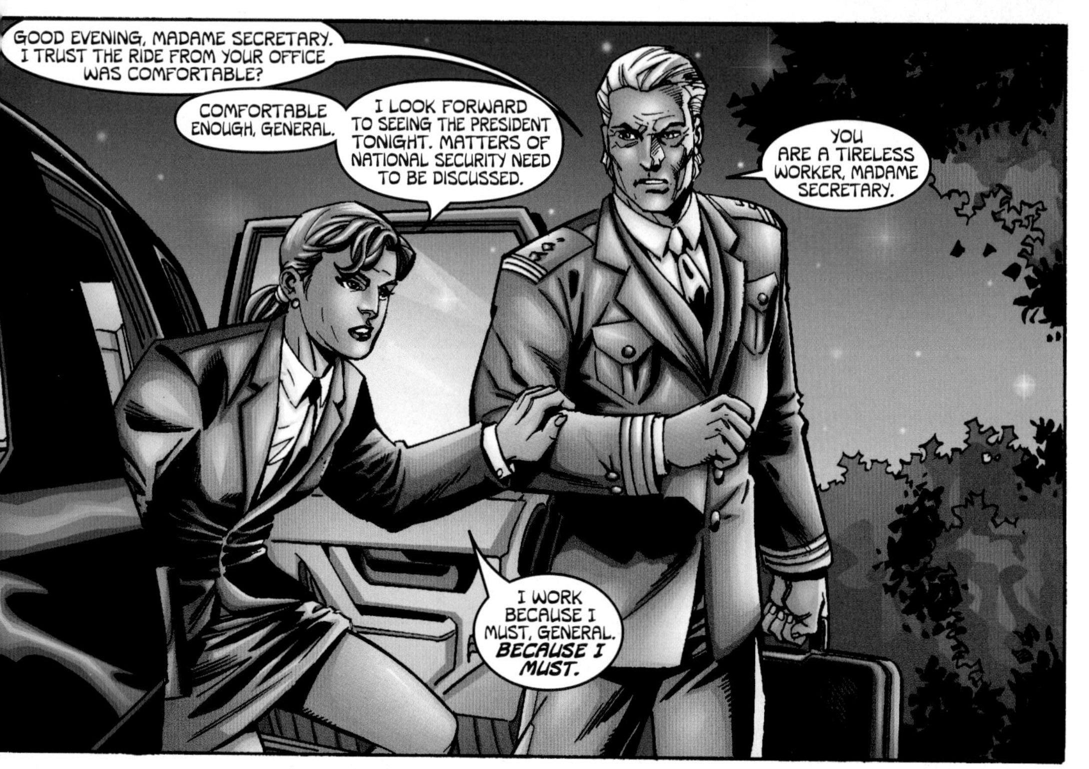
GOOD EVENING, MADAME SECRETARY. I TRUST THE RIDE FROM YOUR OFFICE WAS COMFORTABLE?
COMFORTABLE ENOUGH, GENERAL.
I LOOK FORWARD TO SEEING THE PRESIDENT TONIGHT. MATTERS OF NATIONAL SECURITY NEED TO BE DISCUSSED.
YOU ARE A TIRELESS WORKER, MADAME SECRETARY.
I WORK BECAUSE I MUST, GENERAL. BECAUSE I MUST.

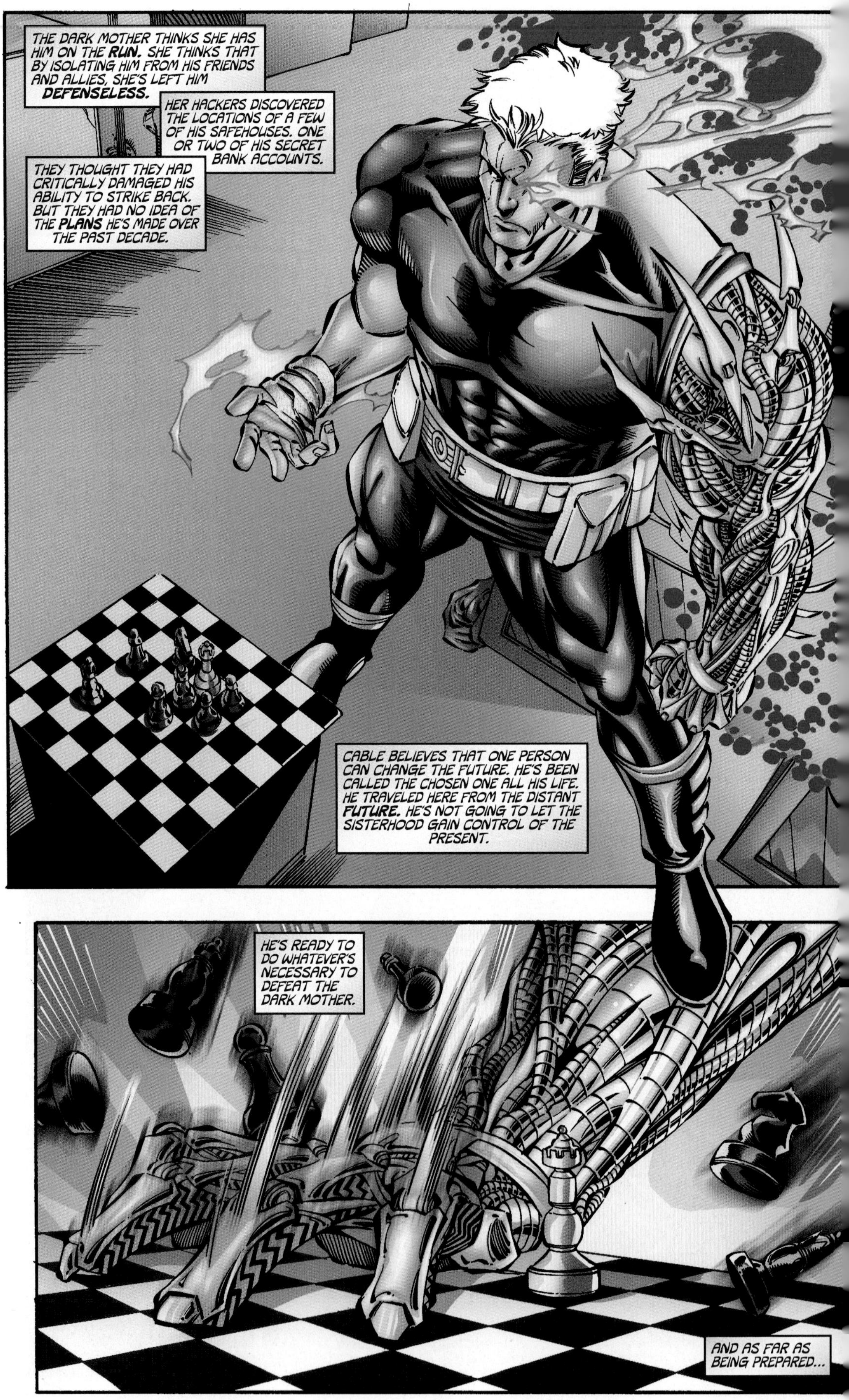

THE DARK MOTHER THINKS SHE HAS HIM ON THE **RUN.** SHE THINKS THAT BY ISOLATING HIM FROM HIS FRIENDS AND ALLIES, SHE'S LEFT HIM **DEFENSELESS.**
HER HACKERS DISCOVERED THE LOCATIONS OF A FEW OF HIS SAFEHOUSES. ONE OR TWO OF HIS SECRET BANK ACCOUNTS.
THEY THOUGHT THEY HAD CRITICALLY DAMAGED HIS ABILITY TO STRIKE BACK. BUT THEY HAD NO IDEA OF THE **PLANS** HE'S MADE OVER THE PAST DECADE.
CABLE BELIEVES THAT ONE PERSON CAN CHANGE THE FUTURE. HE'S BEEN CALLED THE CHOSEN ONE ALL HIS LIFE. HE TRAVELED HERE FROM THE DISTANT **FUTURE.** HE'S NOT GOING TO LET THE SISTERHOOD GAIN CONTROL OF THE PRESENT.
HE'S READY TO DO WHATEVER'S NECESSARY TO DEFEAT THE DARK MOTHER.
AND AS FAR AS BEING PREPARED...

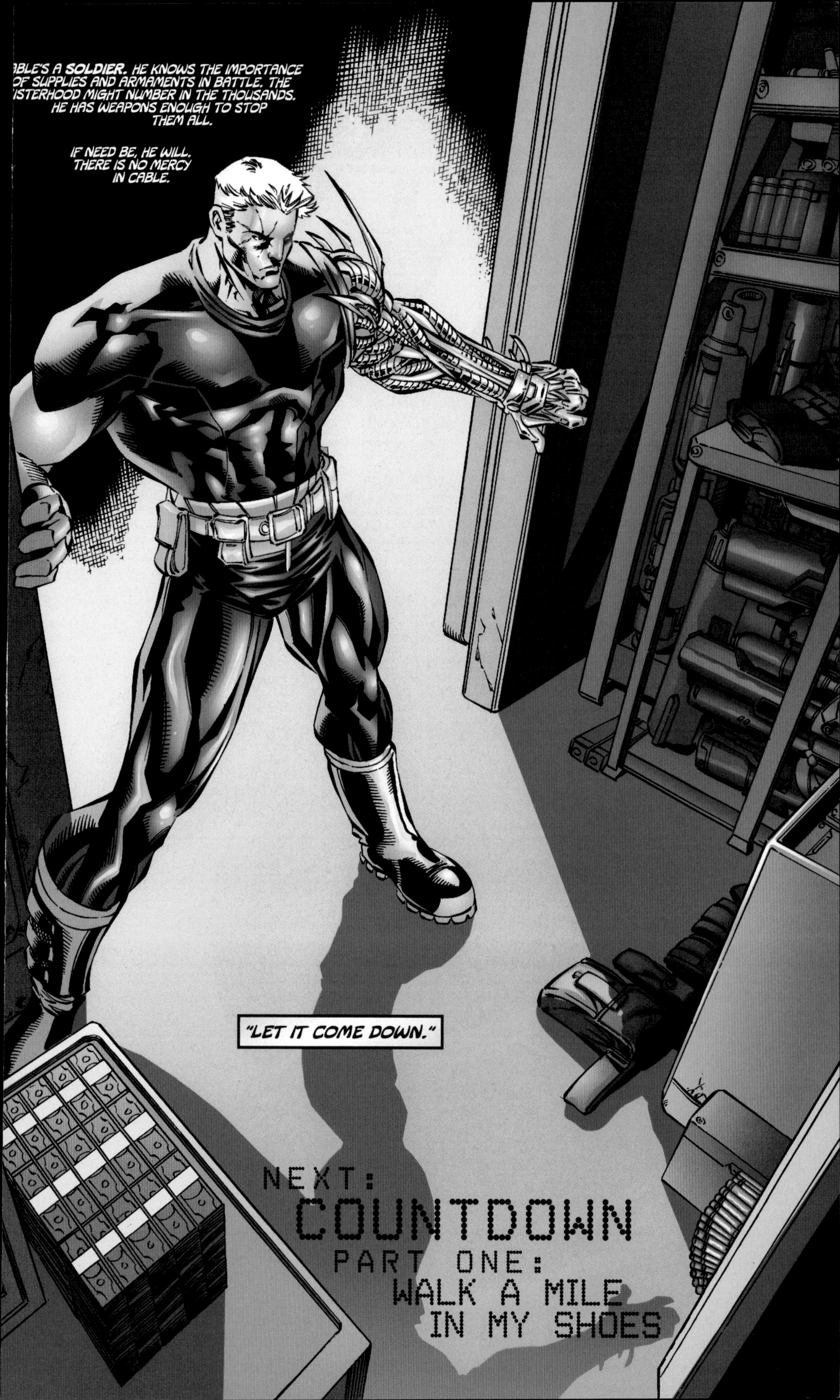

ABLE'S A SOLDIER. HE KNOWS THE IMPORTANCE OF SUPPLIES AND ARMAMENTS IN BATTLE. THE ISTERHOOD MIGHT NUMBER IN THE THOUSANDS. HE HAS WEAPONS ENOUGH TO STOP THEM ALL.
IF NEED BE, HE WILL. THERE IS NO MERCY IN CABLE.
"LET IT COME DOWN."
NEXT:
COUNTDOWN
PART ONE:
WALK A MILE IN MY SHOES

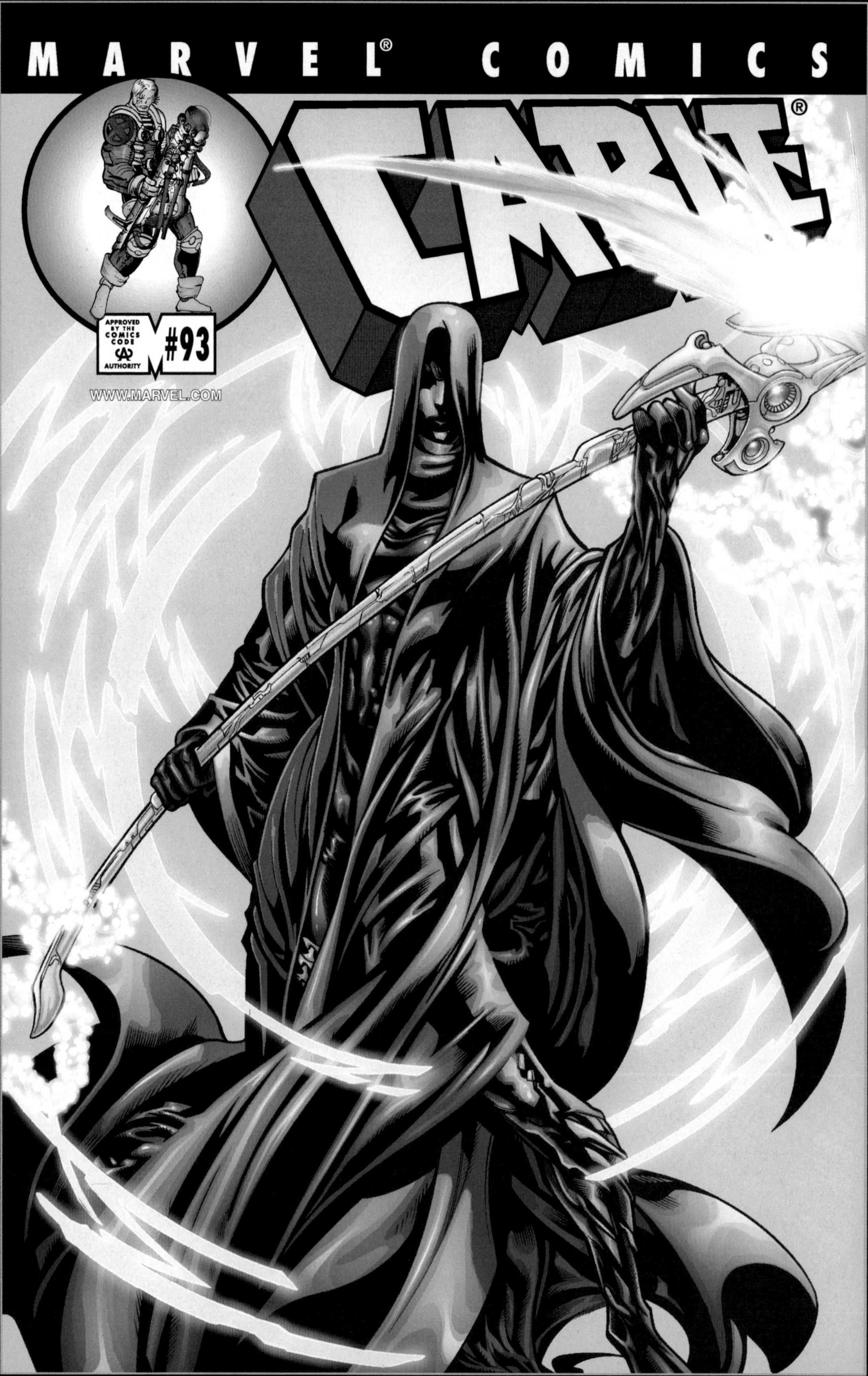
MARVEL® COMICS
CABLE®
APPROVED BY THE COMICS CODE AUTHORITY
#93
WWW.MARVEL.COM

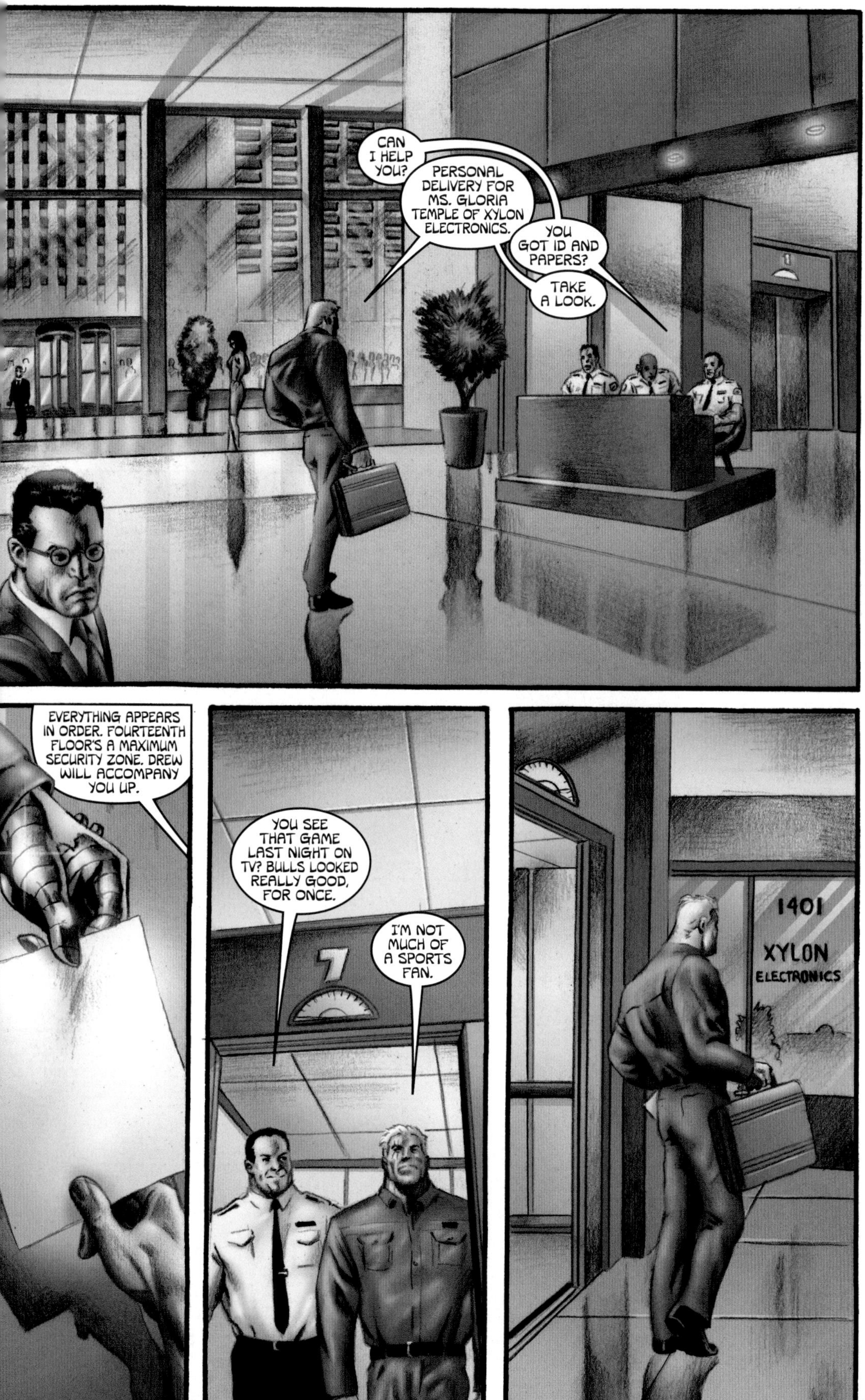
CAN I HELP YOU?
PERSONAL DELIVERY FOR MS. GLORIA TEMPLE OF XYLON ELECTRONICS.
YOU GOT ID AND PAPERS?
TAKE A LOOK.
EVERYTHING APPEARS IN ORDER. FOURTEENTH FLOOR'S A MAXIMUM SECURITY ZONE. DREW WILL ACCOMPANY YOU UP.
YOU SEE THAT GAME LAST NIGHT ON TV? BULLS LOOKED REALLY GOOD, FOR ONCE.
I'M NOT MUCH OF A SPORTS FAN.
7
1401
XYLON
ELECTRONICS

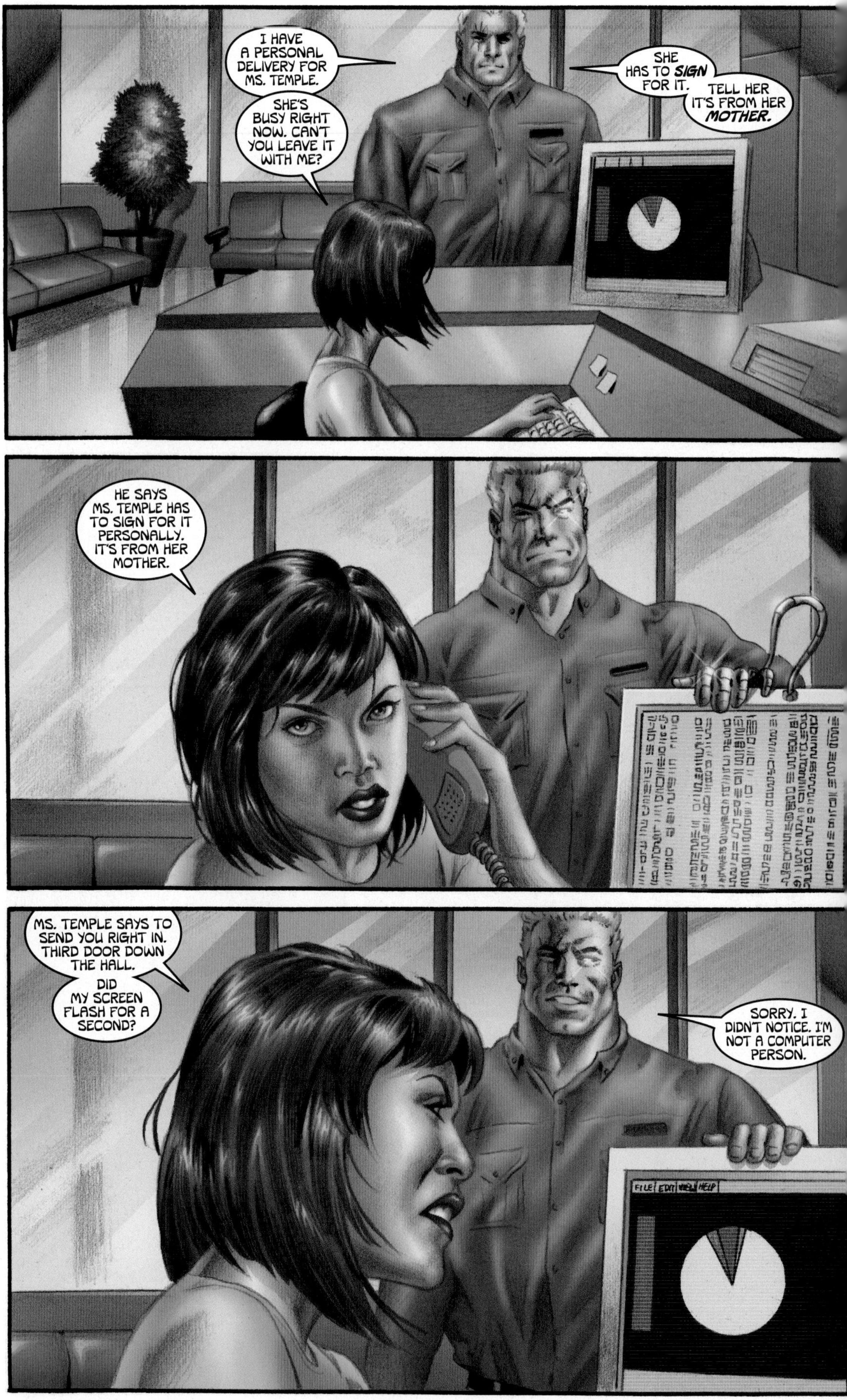
I HAVE A PERSONAL DELIVERY FOR MS. TEMPLE.
SHE'S BUSY RIGHT NOW. CAN'T YOU LEAVE IT WITH ME?
SHE HAS TO SIGN FOR IT.
TELL HER IT'S FROM HER MOTHER.
HE SAYS MS. TEMPLE HAS TO SIGN FOR IT PERSONALLY. IT'S FROM HER MOTHER.
MS. TEMPLE SAYS TO SEND YOU RIGHT IN. THIRD DOOR DOWN THE HALL.
DID MY SCREEN FLASH FOR A SECOND?
SORRY. I DIDN'T NOTICE. I'M NOT A COMPUTER PERSON.
FILE EDIT VIEW HELP

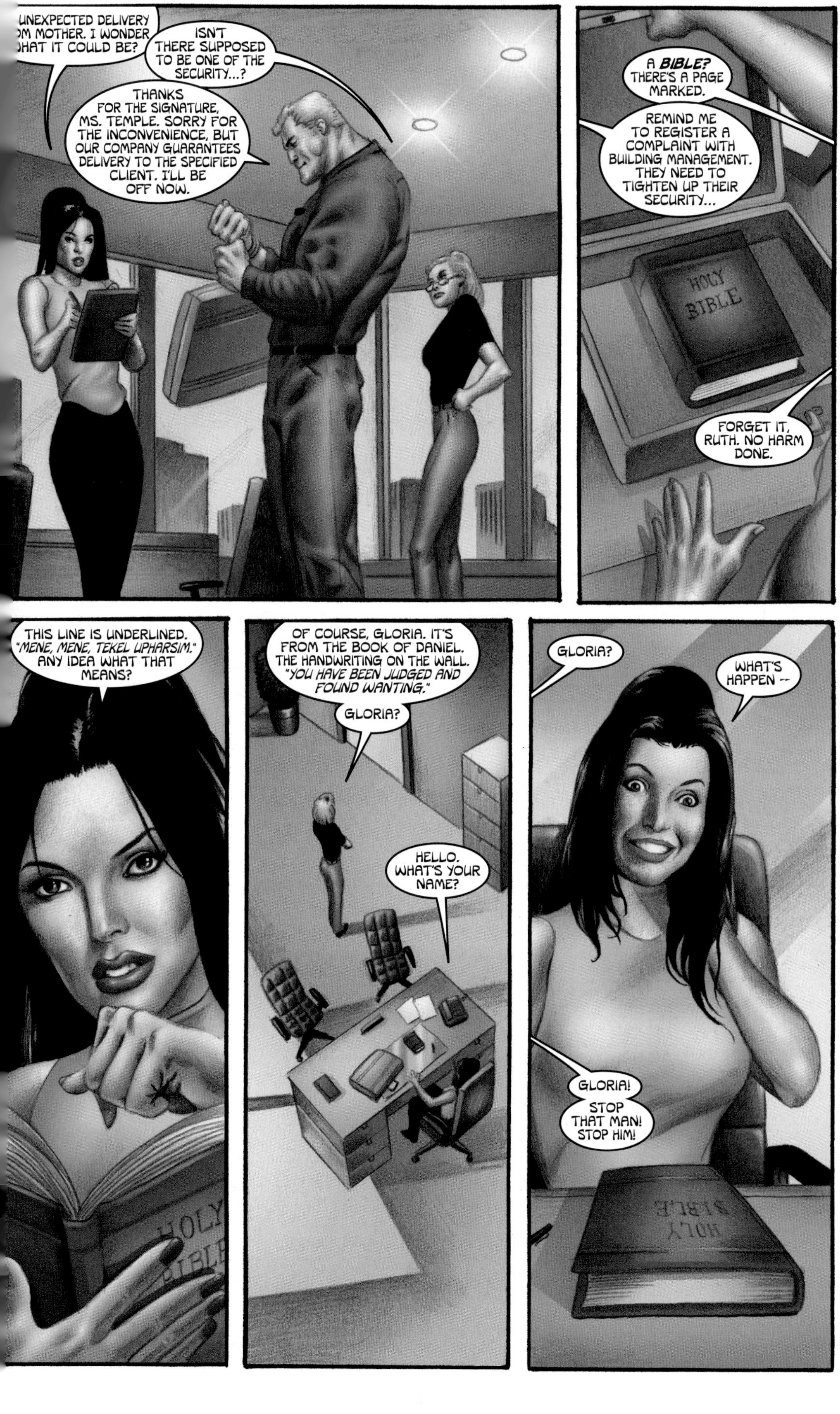
UNEXPECTED DELIVERY
OM MOTHER. I WONDER
HAT IT COULD BE?
ISN'T THERE SUPPOSED TO BE ONE OF THE SECURITY...?
THANKS FOR THE SIGNATURE, MS. TEMPLE. SORRY FOR THE INCONVENIENCE, BUT OUR COMPANY GUARANTEES DELIVERY TO THE SPECIFIED CLIENT. I'LL BE OFF NOW.
A BIBLE? THERE'S A PAGE MARKED.
REMIND ME TO REGISTER A COMPLAINT WITH BUILDING MANAGEMENT. THEY NEED TO TIGHTEN UP THEIR SECURITY...
HOLY BIBLE
FORGET IT, RUTH. NO HARM DONE.
THIS LINE IS UNDERLINED. "MENE, MENE, TEKEL UPHARSIM." ANY IDEA WHAT THAT MEANS?
HOLY BIBLE
OF COURSE, GLORIA. IT'S FROM THE BOOK OF DANIEL. THE HANDWRITING ON THE WALL. "YOU HAVE BEEN JUDGED AND FOUND WANTING."
GLORIA?
HELLO. WHAT'S YOUR NAME?
GLORIA?
WHAT'S HAPPEN --
GLORIA! STOP THAT MAN! STOP HIM!
HOLY BIBLE

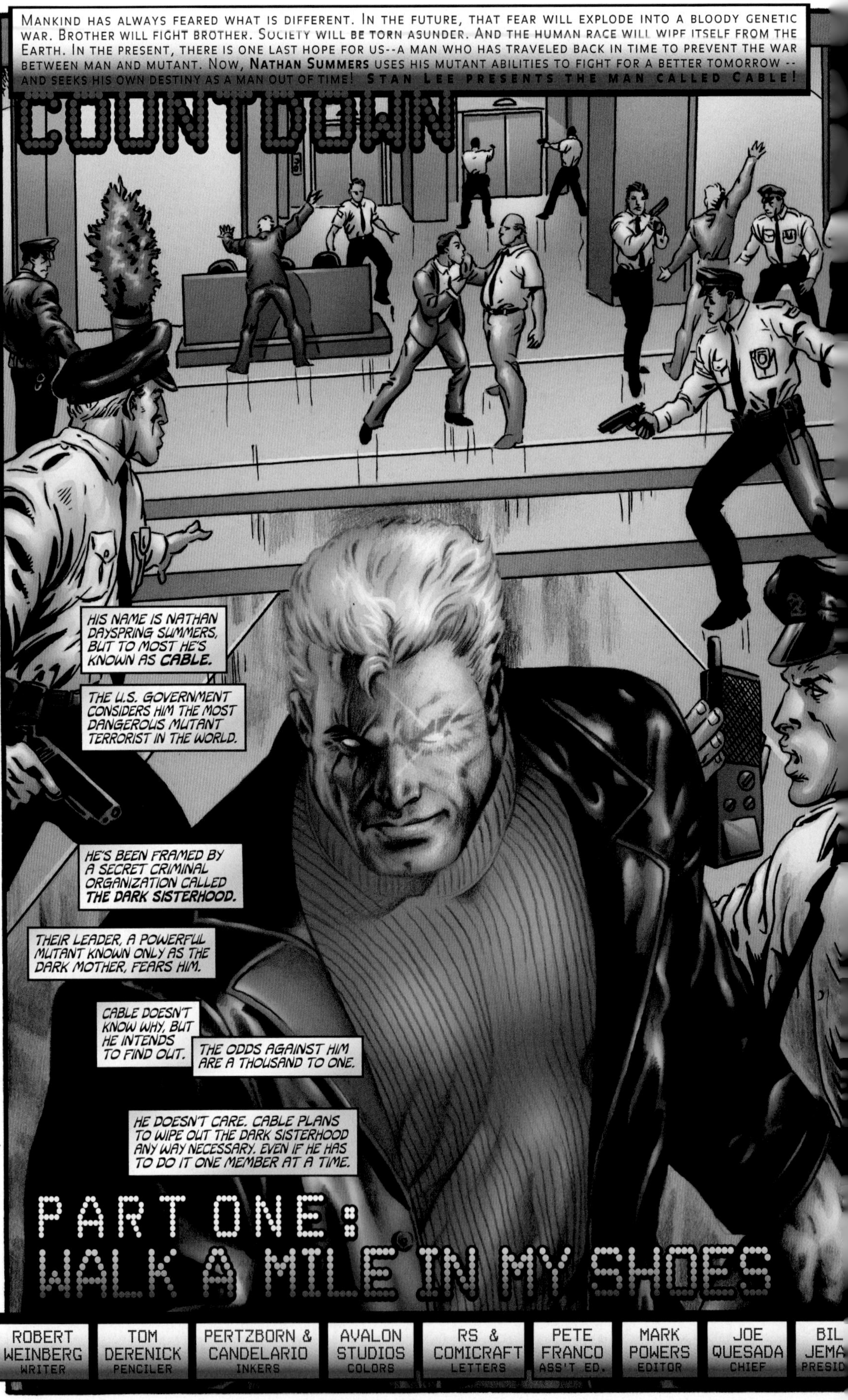

MANKIND HAS ALWAYS FEARED WHAT IS DIFFERENT. IN THE FUTURE, THAT FEAR WILL EXPLODE INTO A BLOODY GENETIC WAR. BROTHER WILL FIGHT BROTHER. SOCIETY WILL BE TORN ASUNDER. AND THE HUMAN RACE WILL WIPE ITSELF FROM THE EARTH. IN THE PRESENT, THERE IS ONE LAST HOPE FOR US--A MAN WHO HAS TRAVELED BACK IN TIME TO PREVENT THE WAR BETWEEN MAN AND MUTANT. NOW, NATHAN SUMMERS USES HIS MUTANT ABILITIES TO FIGHT FOR A BETTER TOMORROW -- AND SEEKS HIS OWN DESTINY AS A MAN OUT OF TIME! STAN LEE PRESENTS THE MAN CALLED CABLE!
COUNTDOWN
HIS NAME IS NATHAN DAYSPRING SUMMERS, BUT TO MOST HE'S KNOWN AS CABLE.
THE U.S. GOVERNMENT CONSIDERS HIM THE MOST DANGEROUS MUTANT TERRORIST IN THE WORLD.
HE'S BEEN FRAMED BY A SECRET CRIMINAL ORGANIZATION CALLED THE DARK SISTERHOOD.
THEIR LEADER, A POWERFUL MUTANT KNOWN ONLY AS THE DARK MOTHER, FEARS HIM.
CABLE DOESN'T KNOW WHY, BUT HE INTENDS TO FIND OUT.
THE ODDS AGAINST HIM ARE A THOUSAND TO ONE.
HE DOESN'T CARE. CABLE PLANS TO WIPE OUT THE DARK SISTERHOOD ANY WAY NECESSARY. EVEN IF HE HAS TO DO IT ONE MEMBER AT A TIME.
PART ONE: WALK A MILE IN MY SHOES
ROBERT WEINBERG WRITER
TOM DERENICK PENCILER
PERTZBORN & CANDELARIO INKERS
AVALON STUDIOS COLORS
RS & COMICRAFT LETTERS
PETE FRANCO ASS'T ED.
MARK POWERS EDITOR
JOE QUESADA CHIEF
BIL JEMA PRESID

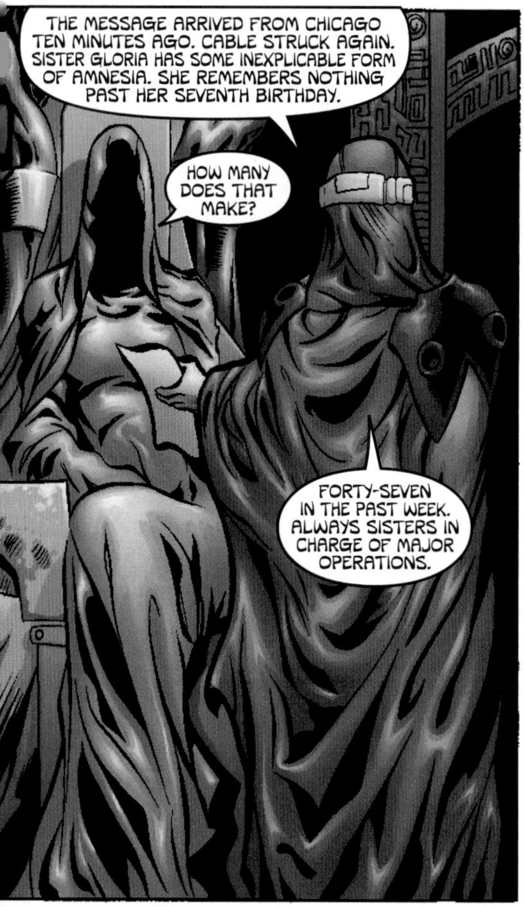
THE MESSAGE ARRIVED FROM CHICAGO TEN MINUTES AGO. CABLE STRUCK AGAIN. SISTER GLORIA HAS SOME INEXPLICABLE FORM OF AMNESIA. SHE REMEMBERS NOTHING PAST HER SEVENTH BIRTHDAY.
HOW MANY DOES THAT MAKE?
FORTY-SEVEN IN THE PAST WEEK. ALWAYS SISTERS IN CHARGE OF MAJOR OPERATIONS.

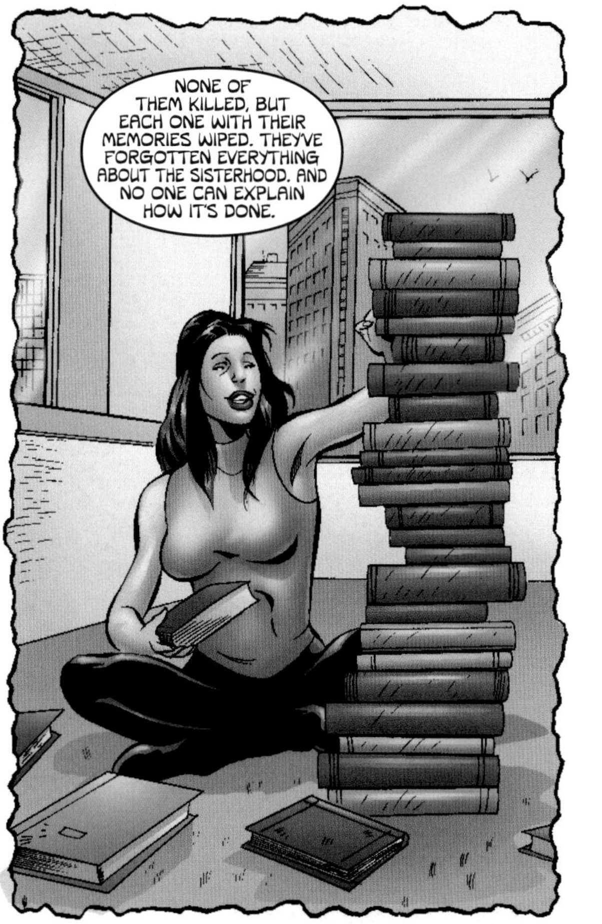
NONE OF THEM KILLED, BUT EACH ONE WITH THEIR MEMORIES WIPED. THEY'VE FORGOTTEN EVERYTHING ABOUT THE SISTERHOOD. AND NO ONE CAN EXPLAIN HOW IT'S DONE.

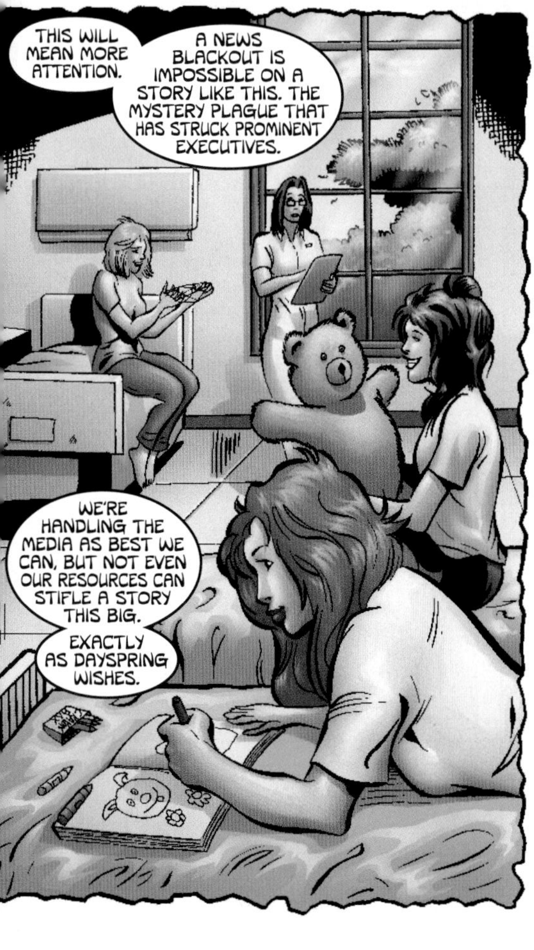
THIS WILL MEAN MORE ATTENTION.
A NEWS BLACKOUT IS IMPOSSIBLE ON A STORY LIKE THIS. THE MYSTERY PLAGUE THAT HAS STRUCK PROMINENT EXECUTIVES.
WE'RE HANDLING THE MEDIA AS BEST WE CAN, BUT NOT EVEN OUR RESOURCES CAN STIFLE A STORY THIS BIG.
EXACTLY AS DAYSPRING WISHES.

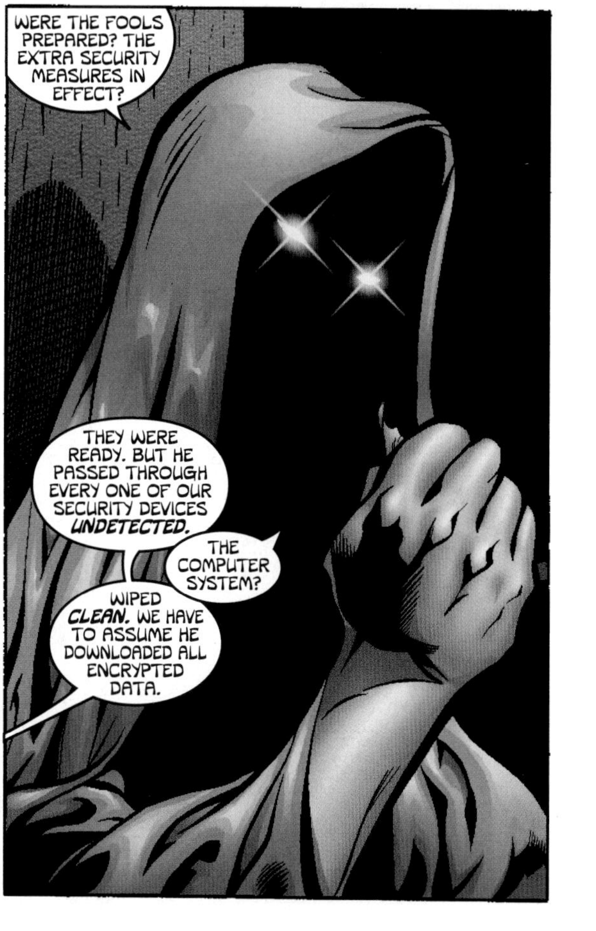
WERE THE FOOLS PREPARED? THE EXTRA SECURITY MEASURES IN EFFECT?
THEY WERE READY. BUT HE PASSED THROUGH EVERY ONE OF OUR SECURITY DEVICES UNDETECTED.
THE COMPUTER SYSTEM?
WIPED CLEAN. WE HAVE TO ASSUME HE DOWNLOADED ALL ENCRYPTED DATA.

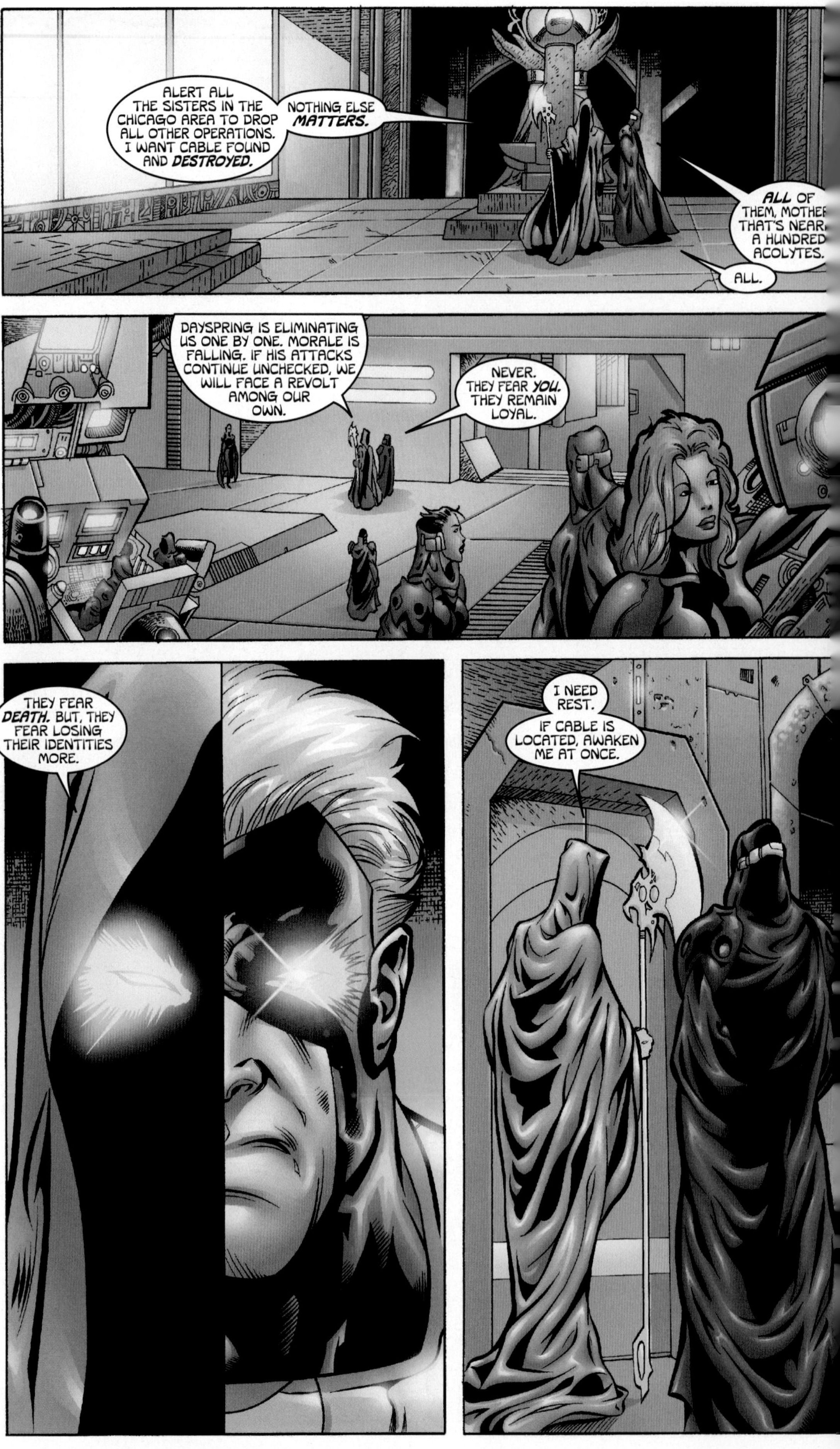

ALERT ALL THE SISTERS IN THE CHICAGO AREA TO DROP ALL OTHER OPERATIONS. I WANT CABLE FOUND AND DESTROYED.
NOTHING ELSE MATTERS.
ALL OF THEM, MOTHER THAT'S NEAR A HUNDRED ACOLYTES.
ALL.
DAYSPRING IS ELIMINATING US ONE BY ONE. MORALE IS FALLING. IF HIS ATTACKS CONTINUE UNCHECKED, WE WILL FACE A REVOLT AMONG OUR OWN.
NEVER. THEY FEAR YOU. THEY REMAIN LOYAL.
THEY FEAR DEATH. BUT, THEY FEAR LOSING THEIR IDENTITIES MORE.
I NEED REST.
IF CABLE IS LOCATED, AWAKEN ME AT ONCE.

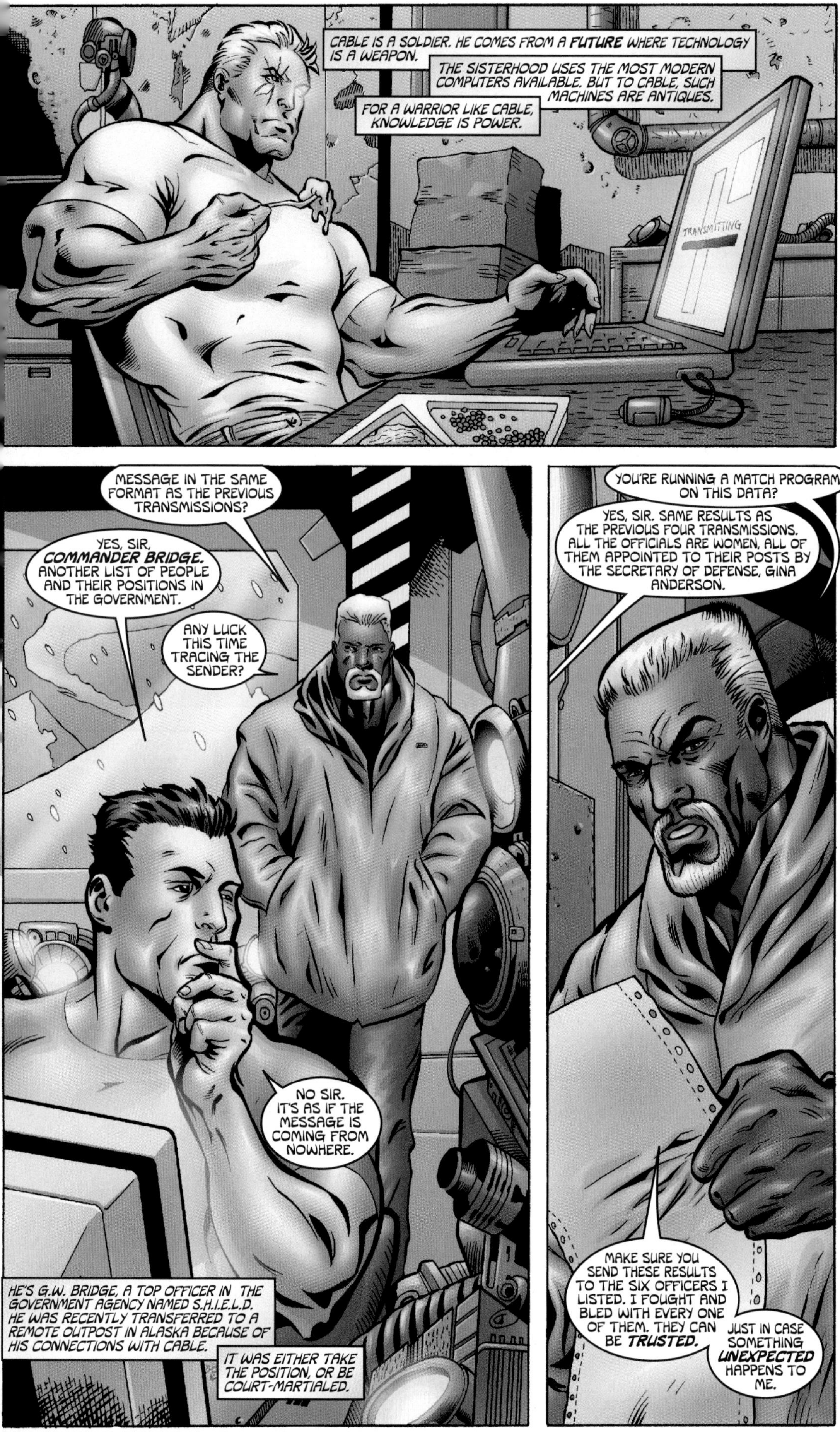
CABLE IS A SOLDIER. HE COMES FROM A **FUTURE** WHERE TECHNOLOGY IS A WEAPON.
THE SISTERHOOD USES THE MOST MODERN COMPUTERS AVAILABLE. BUT TO CABLE, SUCH MACHINES ARE ANTIQUES.
FOR A WARRIOR LIKE CABLE, KNOWLEDGE IS POWER.
TRANSMITTING
MESSAGE IN THE SAME FORMAT AS THE PREVIOUS TRANSMISSIONS?
YES, SIR, **COMMANDER BRIDGE.** ANOTHER LIST OF PEOPLE AND THEIR POSITIONS IN THE GOVERNMENT.
ANY LUCK THIS TIME TRACING THE SENDER?
NO SIR. IT'S AS IF THE MESSAGE IS COMING FROM NOWHERE.
HE'S G.W. BRIDGE, A TOP OFFICER IN THE GOVERNMENT AGENCY NAMED S.H.I.E.L.D. HE WAS RECENTLY TRANSFERRED TO A REMOTE OUTPOST IN ALASKA BECAUSE OF HIS CONNECTIONS WITH CABLE.
IT WAS EITHER TAKE THE POSITION, OR BE COURT-MARTIALED.
YOU'RE RUNNING A MATCH PROGRAM ON THIS DATA?
YES, SIR. SAME RESULTS AS THE PREVIOUS FOUR TRANSMISSIONS. ALL THE OFFICIALS ARE WOMEN, ALL OF THEM APPOINTED TO THEIR POSTS BY THE SECRETARY OF DEFENSE, GINA ANDERSON.
MAKE SURE YOU SEND THESE RESULTS TO THE SIX OFFICERS I LISTED. I FOUGHT AND BLED WITH EVERY ONE OF THEM. THEY CAN BE **TRUSTED.**
JUST IN CASE SOMETHING **UNEXPECTED** HAPPENS TO ME.

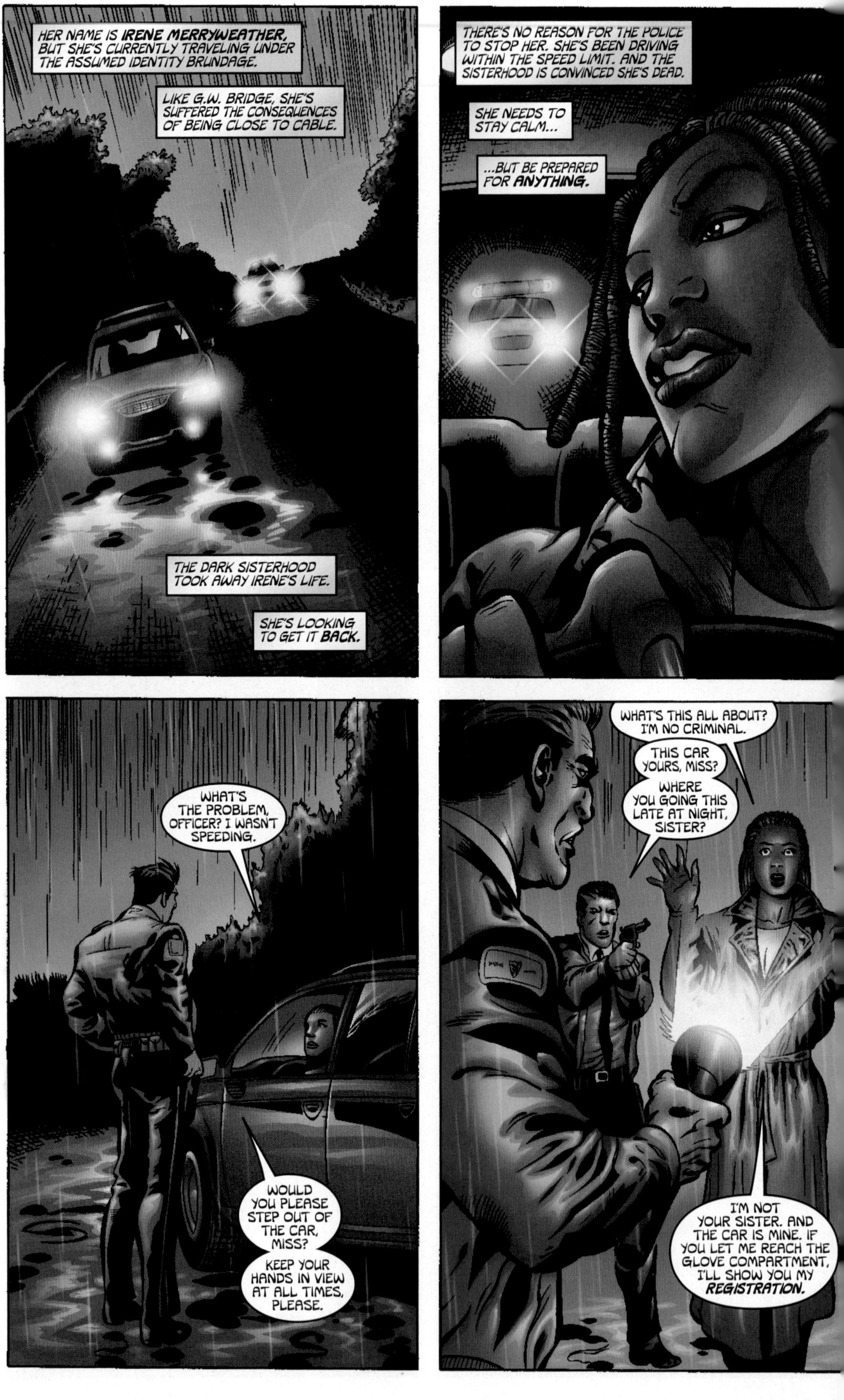

HER NAME IS **IRENE MERRYWEATHER,** BUT SHE'S CURRENTLY TRAVELING UNDER THE ASSUMED IDENTITY BRUNDAGE.
LIKE G.W. BRIDGE, SHE'S SUFFERED THE CONSEQUENCES OF BEING CLOSE TO CABLE.
THE DARK SISTERHOOD TOOK AWAY IRENE'S LIFE.
SHE'S LOOKING TO GET IT **BACK.**
THERE'S NO REASON FOR THE POLICE TO STOP HER. SHE'S BEEN DRIVING WITHIN THE SPEED LIMIT. AND THE SISTERHOOD IS CONVINCED SHE'S DEAD.
SHE NEEDS TO STAY CALM...
...BUT BE PREPARED FOR **ANYTHING.**
WHAT'S THE PROBLEM, OFFICER? I WASN'T SPEEDING.
WOULD YOU PLEASE STEP OUT OF THE CAR, MISS?
KEEP YOUR HANDS IN VIEW AT ALL TIMES, PLEASE.
WHAT'S THIS ALL ABOUT? I'M NO CRIMINAL.
THIS CAR YOURS, MISS?
WHERE YOU GOING THIS LATE AT NIGHT, SISTER?
I'M NOT YOUR SISTER. AND THE CAR IS MINE. IF YOU LET ME REACH THE GLOVE COMPARTMENT, I'LL SHOW YOU MY **REGISTRATION.**

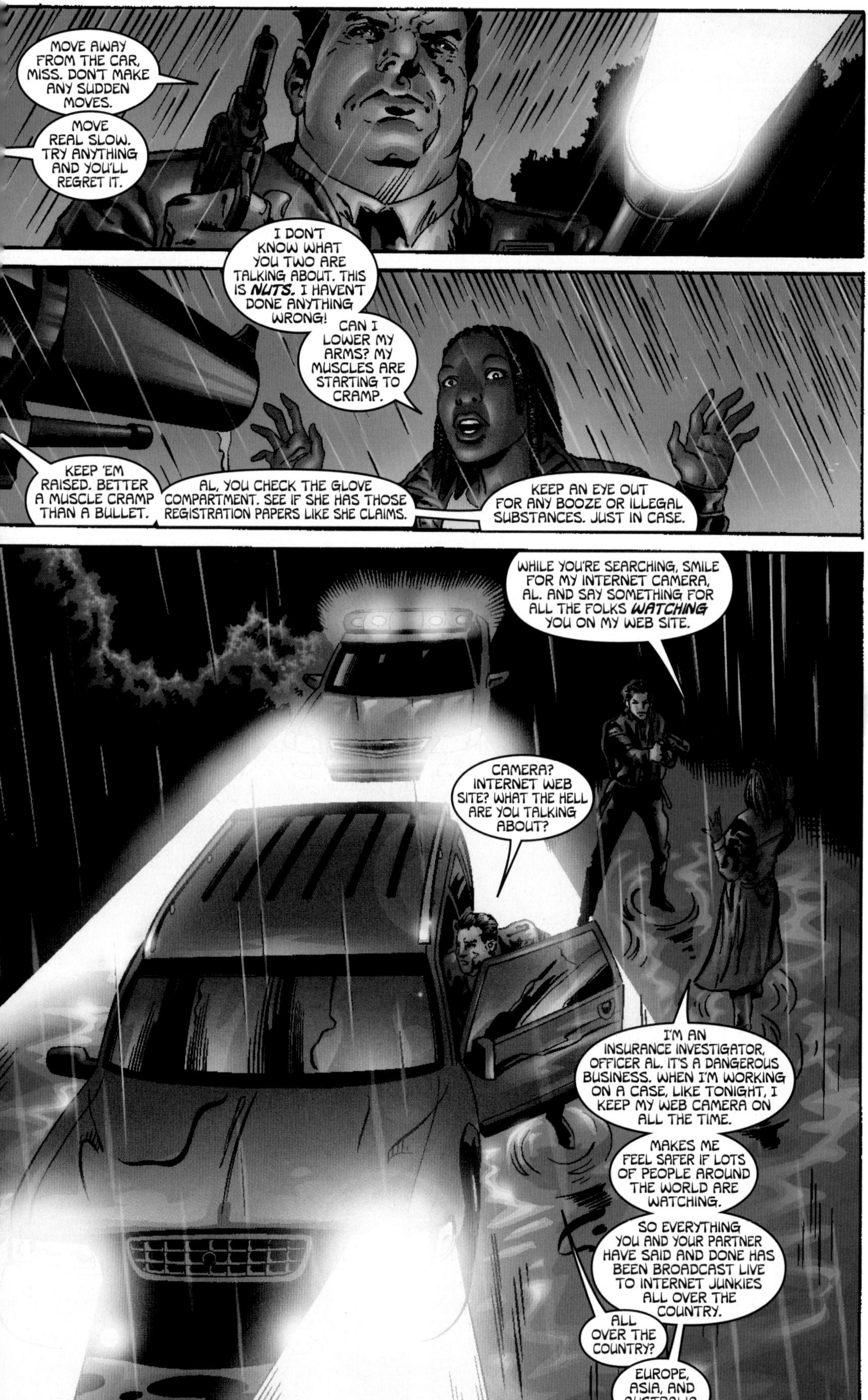
MOVE AWAY FROM THE CAR, MISS. DON'T MAKE ANY SUDDEN MOVES.
MOVE REAL SLOW. TRY ANYTHING AND YOU'LL REGRET IT.
I DON'T KNOW WHAT YOU TWO ARE TALKING ABOUT. THIS IS NUTS. I HAVEN'T DONE ANYTHING WRONG!
CAN I LOWER MY ARMS? MY MUSCLES ARE STARTING TO CRAMP.
KEEP 'EM RAISED. BETTER A MUSCLE CRAMP THAN A BULLET.
AL, YOU CHECK THE GLOVE COMPARTMENT. SEE IF SHE HAS THOSE REGISTRATION PAPERS LIKE SHE CLAIMS.
KEEP AN EYE OUT FOR ANY BOOZE OR ILLEGAL SUBSTANCES. JUST IN CASE.
WHILE YOU'RE SEARCHING, SMILE FOR MY INTERNET CAMERA, AL. AND SAY SOMETHING FOR ALL THE FOLKS WATCHING YOU ON MY WEB SITE.
CAMERA? INTERNET WEB SITE? WHAT THE HELL ARE YOU TALKING ABOUT?
I'M AN INSURANCE INVESTIGATOR, OFFICER AL. IT'S A DANGEROUS BUSINESS. WHEN I'M WORKING ON A CASE, LIKE TONIGHT, I KEEP MY WEB CAMERA ON ALL THE TIME.
MAKES ME FEEL SAFER IF LOTS OF PEOPLE AROUND THE WORLD ARE WATCHING.
SO EVERYTHING YOU AND YOUR PARTNER HAVE SAID AND DONE HAS BEEN BROADCAST LIVE TO INTERNET JUNKIES ALL OVER THE COUNTRY.
ALL OVER THE COUNTRY?
EUROPE, ASIA, AND AUSTRALIA, TOO.

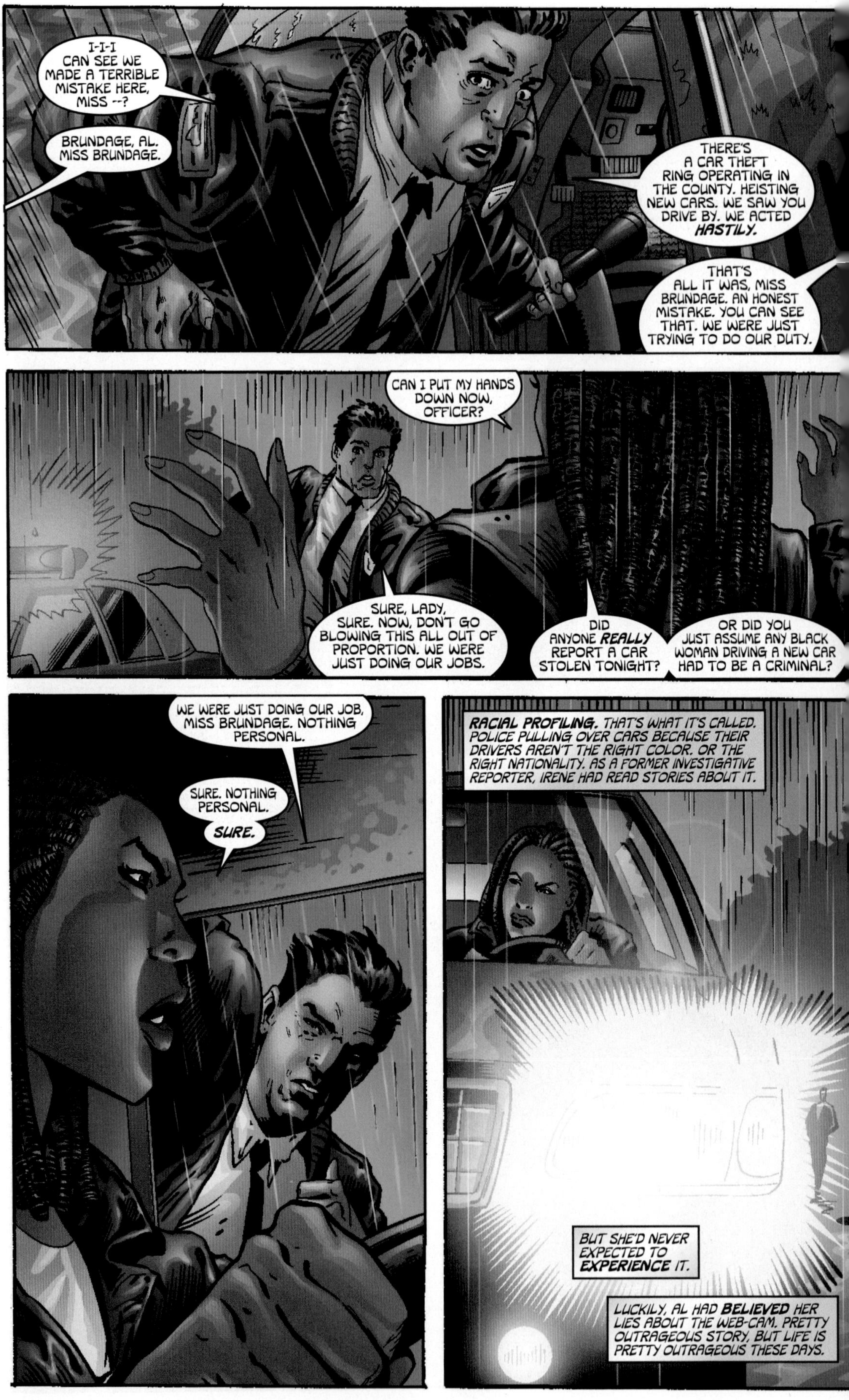
I-I-I CAN SEE WE MADE A TERRIBLE MISTAKE HERE, MISS --?
BRUNDAGE, AL. MISS BRUNDAGE.
THERE'S A CAR THEFT RING OPERATING IN THE COUNTY. HEISTING NEW CARS. WE SAW YOU DRIVE BY. WE ACTED HASTILY.
THAT'S ALL IT WAS, MISS BRUNDAGE. AN HONEST MISTAKE. YOU CAN SEE THAT. WE WERE JUST TRYING TO DO OUR DUTY.
CAN I PUT MY HANDS DOWN NOW, OFFICER?
SURE, LADY, SURE. NOW, DON'T GO BLOWING THIS ALL OUT OF PROPORTION. WE WERE JUST DOING OUR JOBS.
DID ANYONE REALLY REPORT A CAR STOLEN TONIGHT?
OR DID YOU JUST ASSUME ANY BLACK WOMAN DRIVING A NEW CAR HAD TO BE A CRIMINAL?
WE WERE JUST DOING OUR JOB, MISS BRUNDAGE. NOTHING PERSONAL.
SURE. NOTHING PERSONAL. SURE.
RACIAL PROFILING. THAT'S WHAT IT'S CALLED. POLICE PULLING OVER CARS BECAUSE THEIR DRIVERS AREN'T THE RIGHT COLOR. OR THE RIGHT NATIONALITY. AS A FORMER INVESTIGATIVE REPORTER, IRENE HAD READ STORIES ABOUT IT.
BUT SHE'D NEVER EXPECTED TO EXPERIENCE IT.
LUCKILY, AL HAD BELIEVED HER LIES ABOUT THE WEB-CAM. PRETTY OUTRAGEOUS STORY, BUT LIFE IS PRETTY OUTRAGEOUS THESE DAYS.

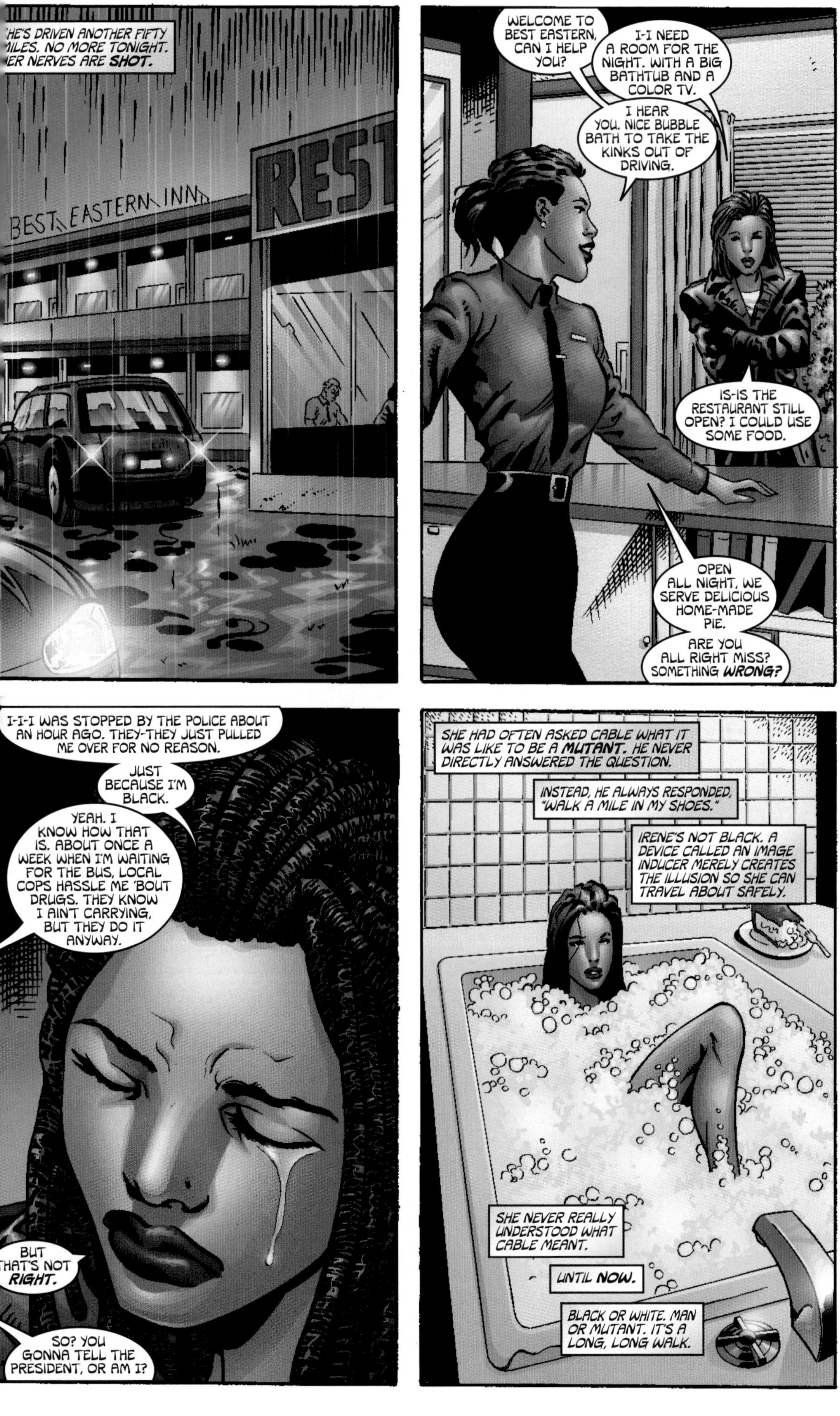

HE'S DRIVEN ANOTHER FIFTY MILES. NO MORE TONIGHT. ER NERVES ARE SHOT.
BEST EASTERN INN
REST
WELCOME TO BEST EASTERN, CAN I HELP YOU?
I-I NEED A ROOM FOR THE NIGHT. WITH A BIG BATHTUB AND A COLOR TV.
I HEAR YOU. NICE BUBBLE BATH TO TAKE THE KINKS OUT OF DRIVING.
IS-IS THE RESTAURANT STILL OPEN? I COULD USE SOME FOOD.
OPEN ALL NIGHT, WE SERVE DELICIOUS HOME-MADE PIE.
ARE YOU ALL RIGHT MISS? SOMETHING WRONG?
I-I-I WAS STOPPED BY THE POLICE ABOUT AN HOUR AGO. THEY-THEY JUST PULLED ME OVER FOR NO REASON.
JUST BECAUSE I'M BLACK.
YEAH. I KNOW HOW THAT IS. ABOUT ONCE A WEEK WHEN I'M WAITING FOR THE BUS, LOCAL COPS HASSLE ME 'BOUT DRUGS. THEY KNOW I AIN'T CARRYING, BUT THEY DO IT ANYWAY.
BUT THAT'S NOT RIGHT.
SO? YOU GONNA TELL THE PRESIDENT, OR AM I?
SHE HAD OFTEN ASKED CABLE WHAT IT WAS LIKE TO BE A MUTANT. HE NEVER DIRECTLY ANSWERED THE QUESTION.
INSTEAD, HE ALWAYS RESPONDED, "WALK A MILE IN MY SHOES."
IRENE'S NOT BLACK. A DEVICE CALLED AN IMAGE INDUCER MERELY CREATES THE ILLUSION SO SHE CAN TRAVEL ABOUT SAFELY.
SHE NEVER REALLY UNDERSTOOD WHAT CABLE MEANT.
UNTIL NOW.
BLACK OR WHITE. MAN OR MUTANT. IT'S A LONG, LONG WALK.

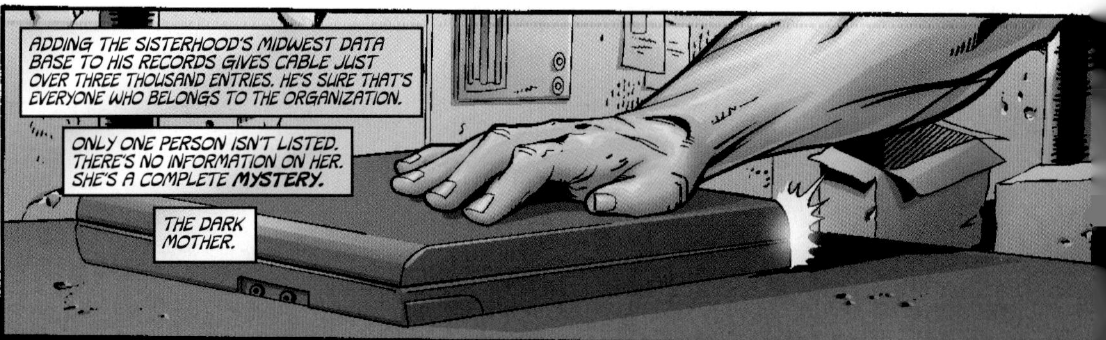
ADDING THE SISTERHOOD'S MIDWEST DATA BASE TO HIS RECORDS GIVES CABLE JUST OVER THREE THOUSAND ENTRIES. HE'S SURE THAT'S EVERYONE WHO BELONGS TO THE ORGANIZATION.
ONLY ONE PERSON ISN'T LISTED. THERE'S NO INFORMATION ON HER. SHE'S A COMPLETE **MYSTERY.**
THE DARK MOTHER.

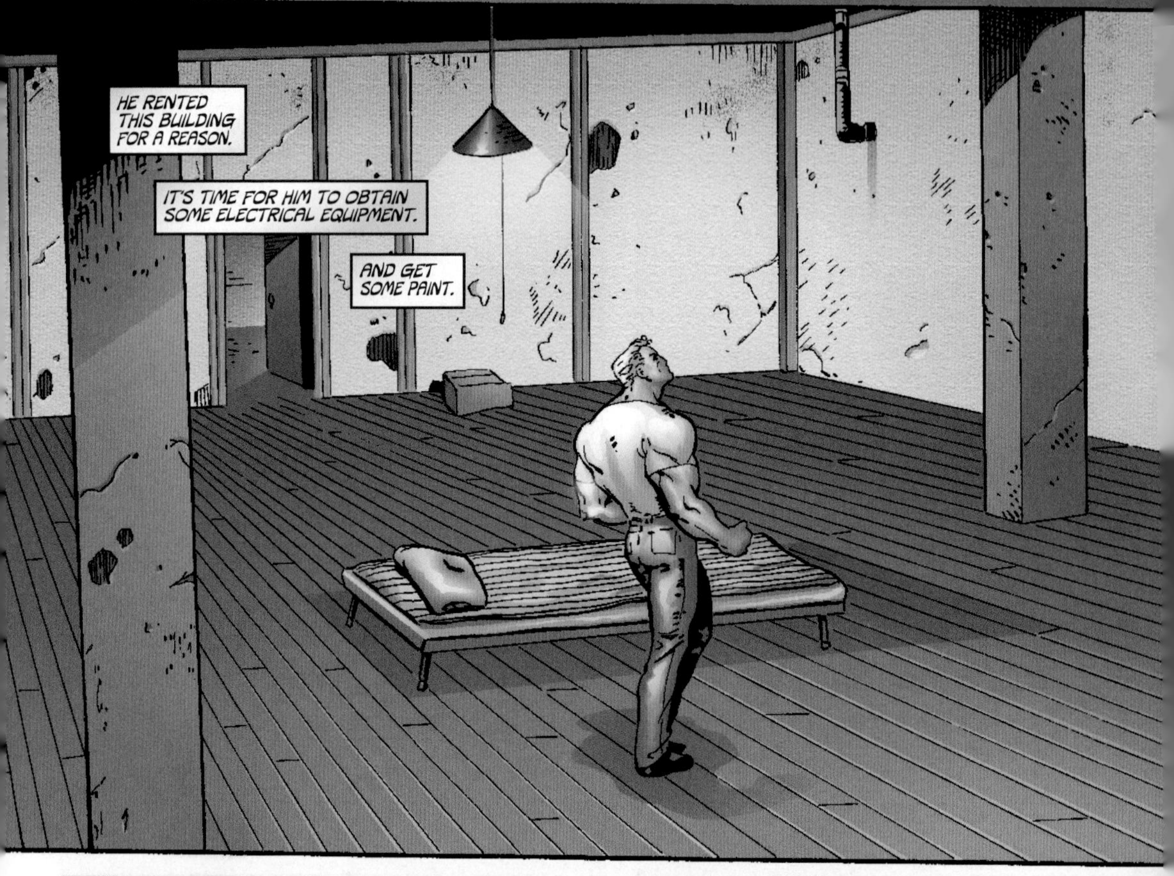
HE RENTED THIS BUILDING FOR A REASON.
IT'S TIME FOR HIM TO OBTAIN SOME ELECTRICAL EQUIPMENT.
AND GET SOME PAINT.

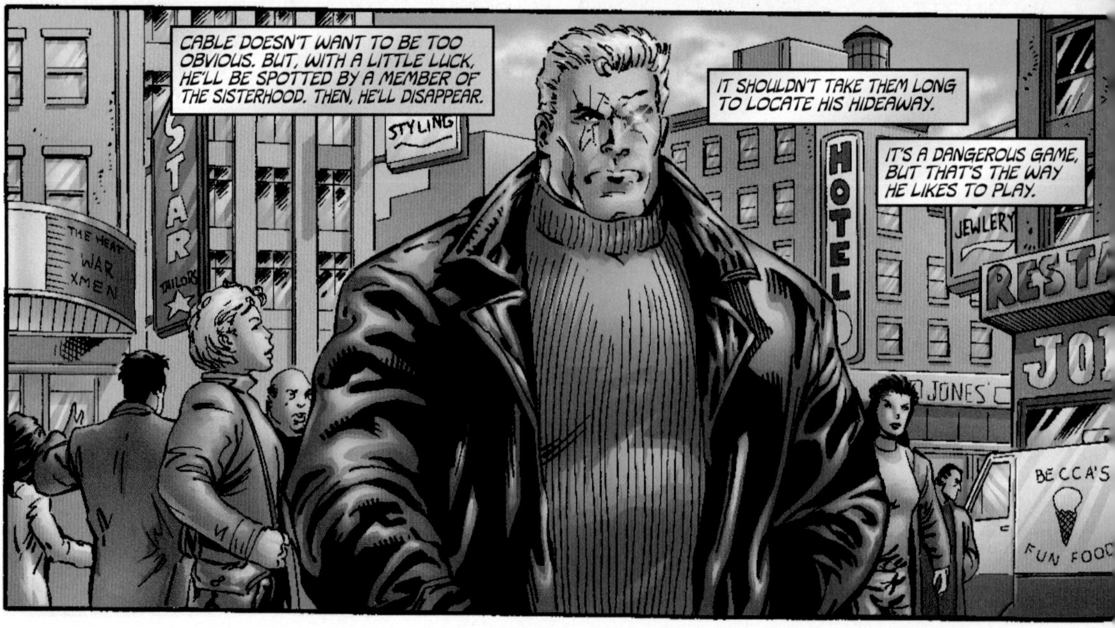
CABLE DOESN'T WANT TO BE TOO OBVIOUS. BUT, WITH A LITTLE LUCK, HE'LL BE SPOTTED BY A MEMBER OF THE SISTERHOOD. THEN, HE'LL DISAPPEAR.
IT SHOULDN'T TAKE THEM LONG TO LOCATE HIS HIDEAWAY.
IT'S A DANGEROUS GAME, BUT THAT'S THE WAY HE LIKES TO PLAY.
STYLING
STAR
TAILORS
THE HEAT
WAR
XMEN
HOTEL
JEWLERY
JONES'
BECCA'S
FUN FOOD

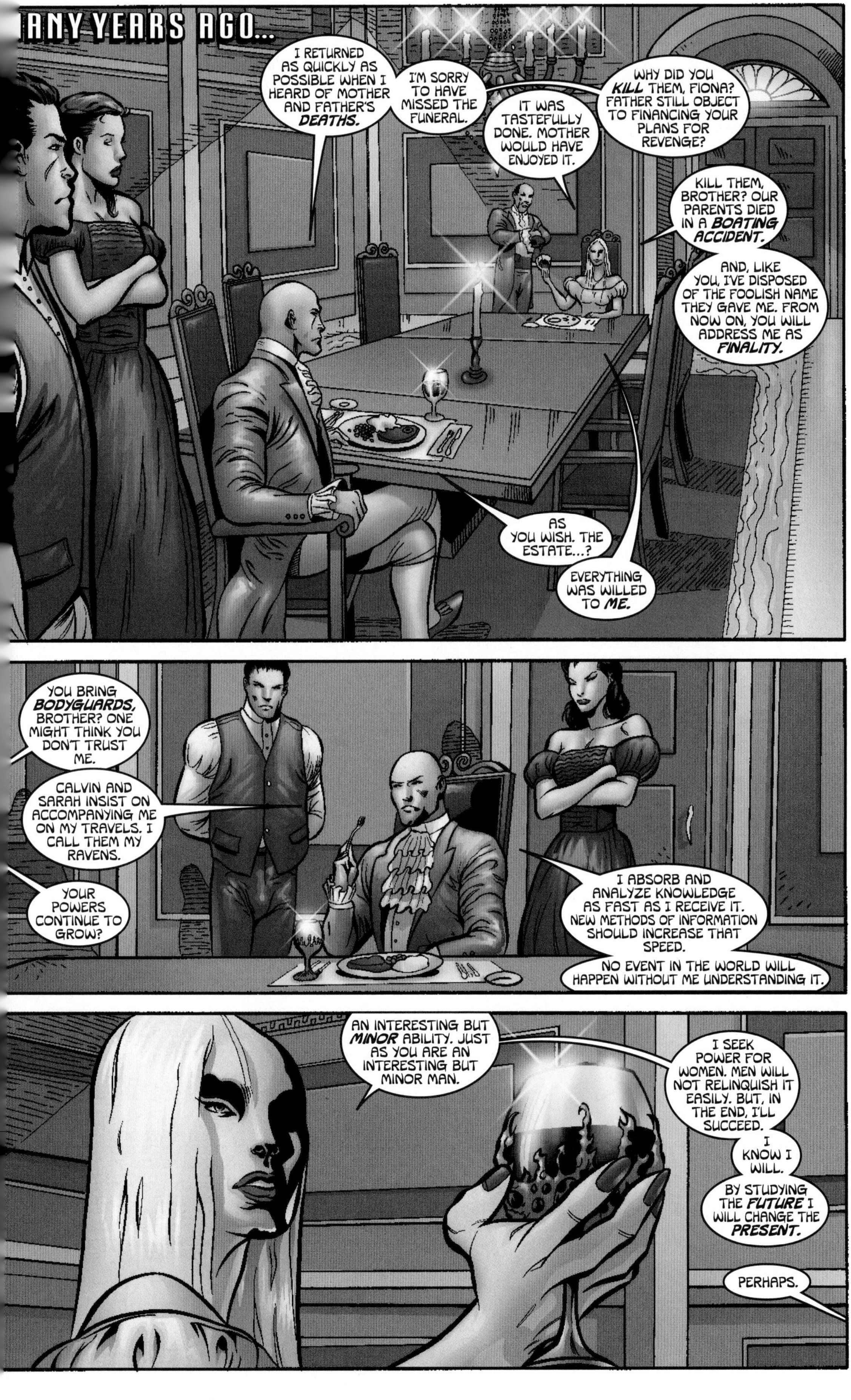
ANY YEARS AGO...
I RETURNED AS QUICKLY AS POSSIBLE WHEN I HEARD OF MOTHER AND FATHER'S DEATHS.
I'M SORRY TO HAVE MISSED THE FUNERAL.
IT WAS TASTEFULLY DONE. MOTHER WOULD HAVE ENJOYED IT.
WHY DID YOU KILL THEM, FIONA? FATHER STILL OBJECT TO FINANCING YOUR PLANS FOR REVENGE?
KILL THEM, BROTHER? OUR PARENTS DIED IN A BOATING ACCIDENT.
AND, LIKE YOU, I'VE DISPOSED OF THE FOOLISH NAME THEY GAVE ME. FROM NOW ON, YOU WILL ADDRESS ME AS FINALITY.
AS YOU WISH. THE ESTATE...?
EVERYTHING WAS WILLED TO ME.
YOU BRING BODYGUARDS, BROTHER? ONE MIGHT THINK YOU DON'T TRUST ME.
CALVIN AND SARAH INSIST ON ACCOMPANYING ME ON MY TRAVELS. I CALL THEM MY RAVENS.
YOUR POWERS CONTINUE TO GROW?
I ABSORB AND ANALYZE KNOWLEDGE AS FAST AS I RECEIVE IT. NEW METHODS OF INFORMATION SHOULD INCREASE THAT SPEED.
NO EVENT IN THE WORLD WILL HAPPEN WITHOUT ME UNDERSTANDING IT.
AN INTERESTING BUT MINOR ABILITY. JUST AS YOU ARE AN INTERESTING BUT MINOR MAN.
I SEEK POWER FOR WOMEN. MEN WILL NOT RELINQUISH IT EASILY. BUT, IN THE END, I'LL SUCCEED.
I KNOW I WILL.
BY STUDYING THE FUTURE I WILL CHANGE THE PRESENT.
PERHAPS.

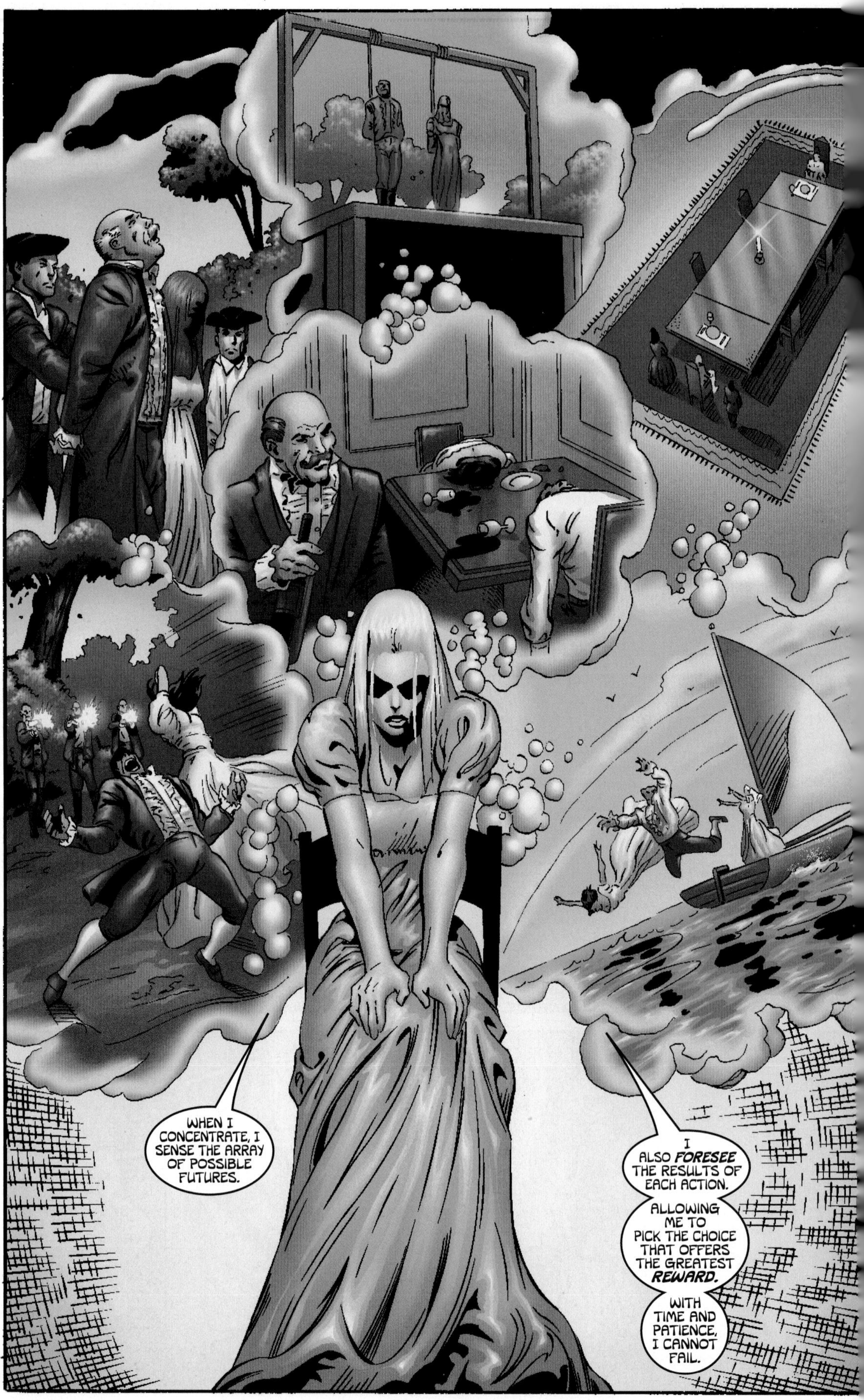

WHEN I CONCENTRATE, I SENSE THE ARRAY OF POSSIBLE FUTURES.
I ALSO FORESEE THE RESULTS OF EACH ACTION.
ALLOWING ME TO PICK THE CHOICE THAT OFFERS THE GREATEST REWARD.
WITH TIME AND PATIENCE, I CANNOT FAIL.

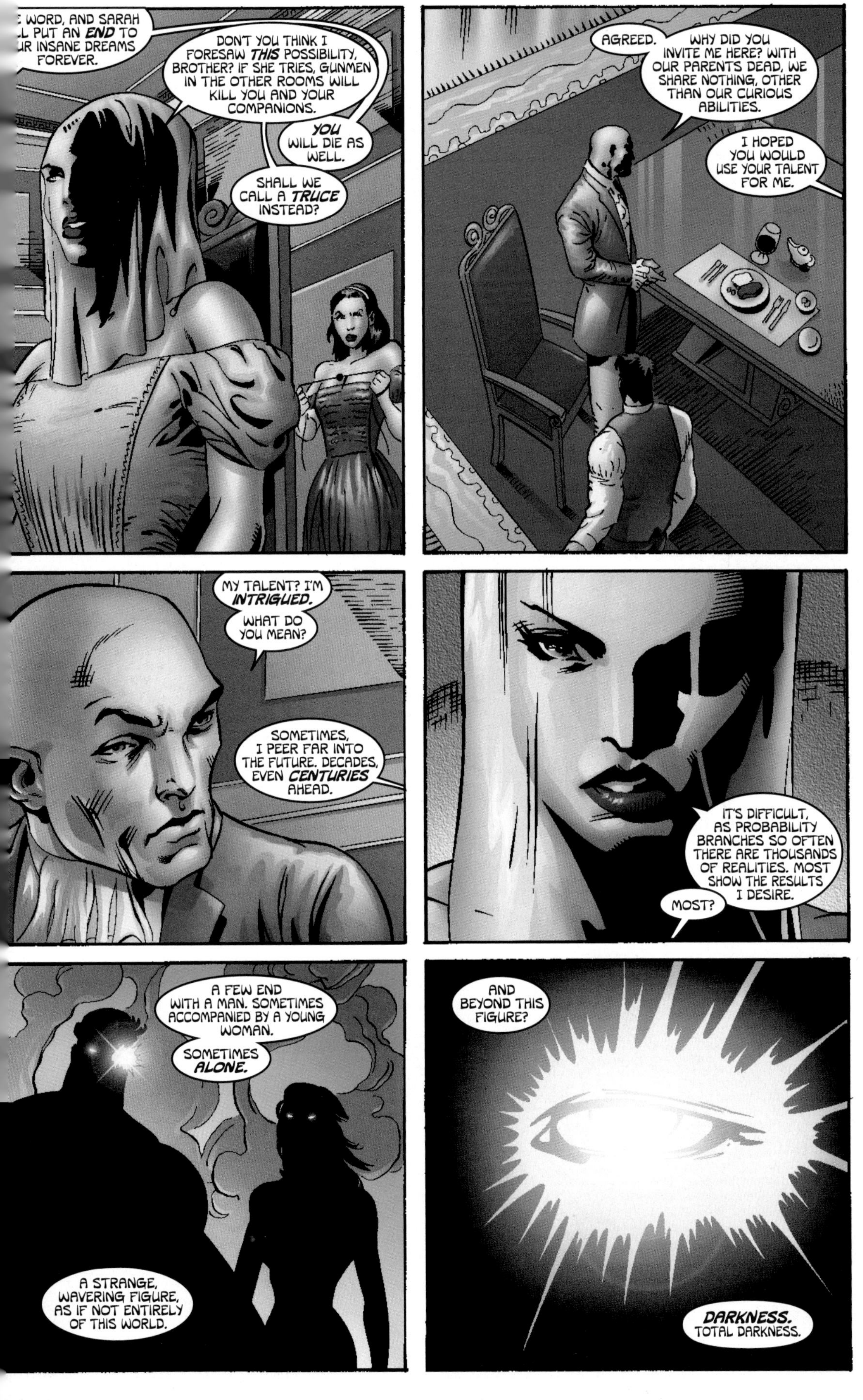
WORD, AND SARAH L PUT AN END TO UR INSANE DREAMS FOREVER.
DON'T YOU THINK I FORESAW THIS POSSIBILITY, BROTHER? IF SHE TRIES, GUNMEN IN THE OTHER ROOMS WILL KILL YOU AND YOUR COMPANIONS.
YOU WILL DIE AS WELL.
SHALL WE CALL A TRUCE INSTEAD?
AGREED.
WHY DID YOU INVITE ME HERE? WITH OUR PARENTS DEAD, WE SHARE NOTHING, OTHER THAN OUR CURIOUS ABILITIES.
I HOPED YOU WOULD USE YOUR TALENT FOR ME.
MY TALENT? I'M INTRIGUED.
WHAT DO YOU MEAN?
SOMETIMES, I PEER FAR INTO THE FUTURE. DECADES, EVEN CENTURIES AHEAD.
IT'S DIFFICULT, AS PROBABILITY BRANCHES SO OFTEN THERE ARE THOUSANDS OF REALITIES. MOST SHOW THE RESULTS I DESIRE.
MOST?
A FEW END WITH A MAN. SOMETIMES ACCOMPANIED BY A YOUNG WOMAN.
SOMETIMES ALONE.
A STRANGE, WAVERING FIGURE, AS IF NOT ENTIRELY OF THIS WORLD.
AND BEYOND THIS FIGURE?
DARKNESS. TOTAL DARKNESS.

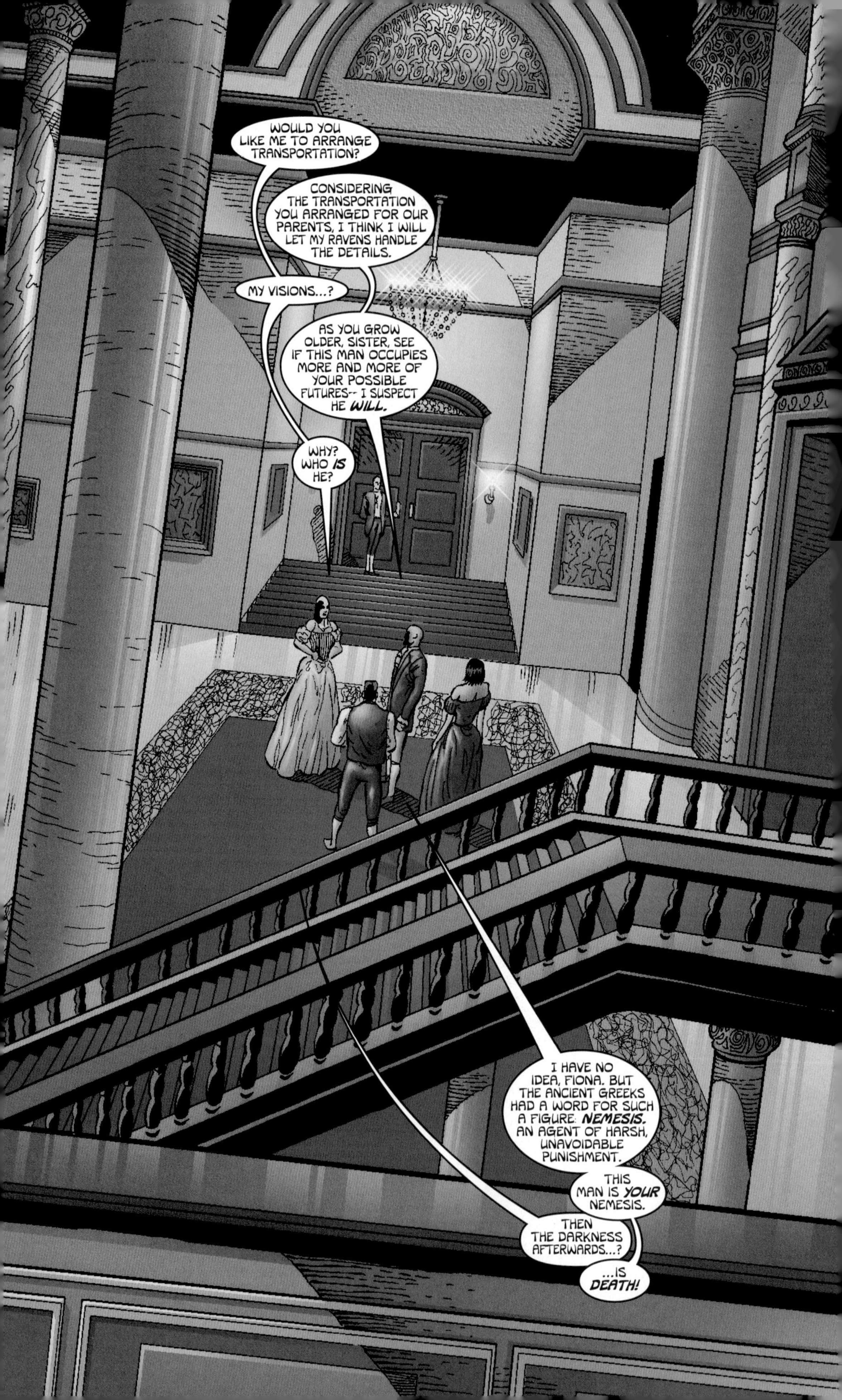

WOULD YOU LIKE ME TO ARRANGE TRANSPORTATION?
CONSIDERING THE TRANSPORTATION YOU ARRANGED FOR OUR PARENTS, I THINK I WILL LET MY RAVENS HANDLE THE DETAILS.
MY VISIONS...?
AS YOU GROW OLDER, SISTER, SEE IF THIS MAN OCCUPIES MORE AND MORE OF YOUR POSSIBLE FUTURES-- I SUSPECT HE *WILL.*
WHY? WHO *IS* HE?
I HAVE NO IDEA, FIONA. BUT THE ANCIENT GREEKS HAD A WORD FOR SUCH A FIGURE: *NEMESIS.* AN AGENT OF HARSH, UNAVOIDABLE PUNISHMENT.
THIS MAN IS *YOUR* NEMESIS.
THEN THE DARKNESS AFTERWARDS...?
...IS *DEATH!*

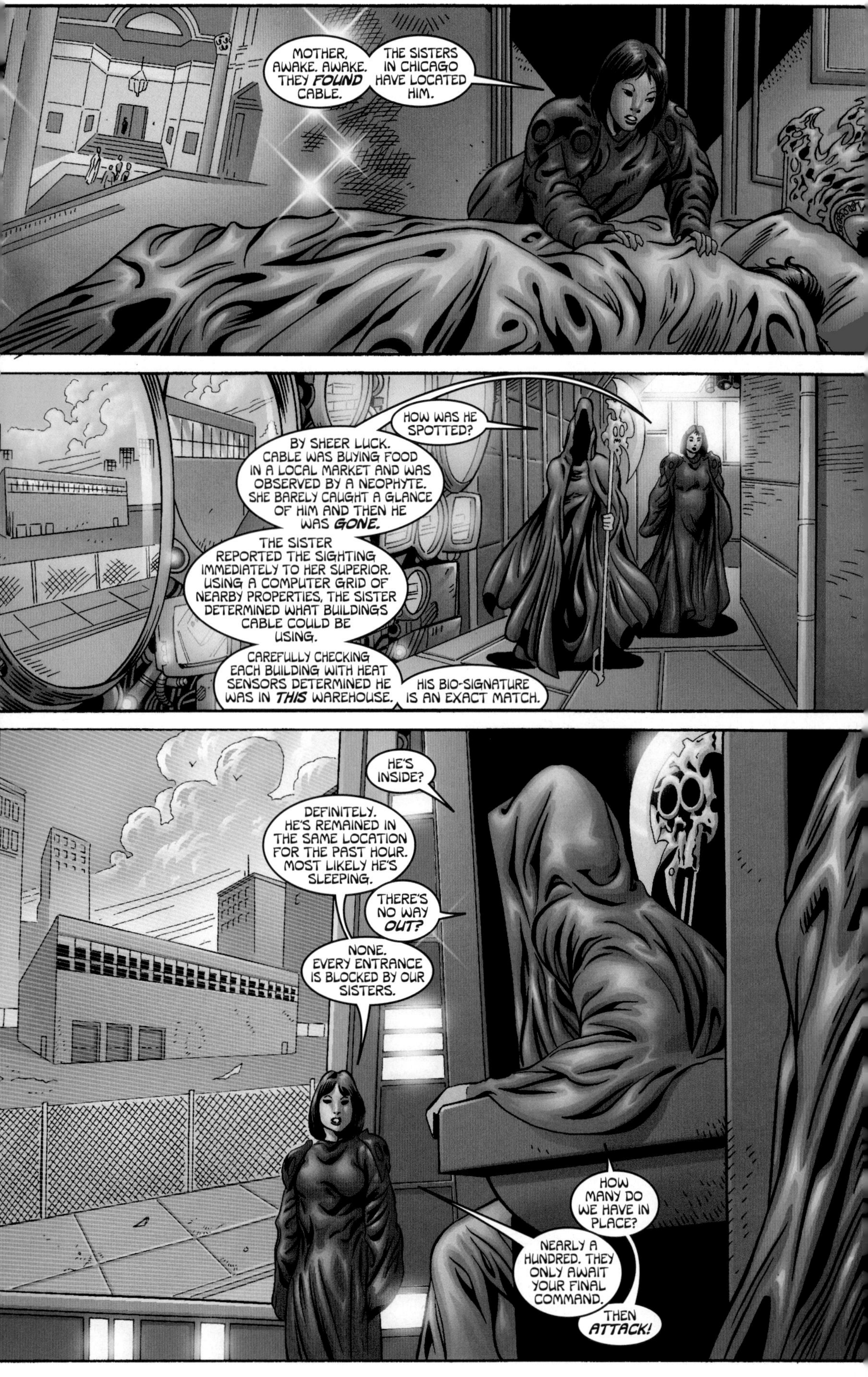
MOTHER, AWAKE. AWAKE. THEY FOUND CABLE.
THE SISTERS IN CHICAGO HAVE LOCATED HIM.
HOW WAS HE SPOTTED?
BY SHEER LUCK. CABLE WAS BUYING FOOD IN A LOCAL MARKET AND WAS OBSERVED BY A NEOPHYTE. SHE BARELY CAUGHT A GLANCE OF HIM AND THEN HE WAS GONE.
THE SISTER REPORTED THE SIGHTING IMMEDIATELY TO HER SUPERIOR. USING A COMPUTER GRID OF NEARBY PROPERTIES, THE SISTER DETERMINED WHAT BUILDINGS CABLE COULD BE USING.
CAREFULLY CHECKING EACH BUILDING WITH HEAT SENSORS DETERMINED HE WAS IN THIS WAREHOUSE.
HIS BIO-SIGNATURE IS AN EXACT MATCH.
HE'S INSIDE?
DEFINITELY. HE'S REMAINED IN THE SAME LOCATION FOR THE PAST HOUR. MOST LIKELY HE'S SLEEPING.
THERE'S NO WAY OUT?
NONE. EVERY ENTRANCE IS BLOCKED BY OUR SISTERS.
HOW MANY DO WE HAVE IN PLACE?
NEARLY A HUNDRED. THEY ONLY AWAIT YOUR FINAL COMMAND.
THEN ATTACK!

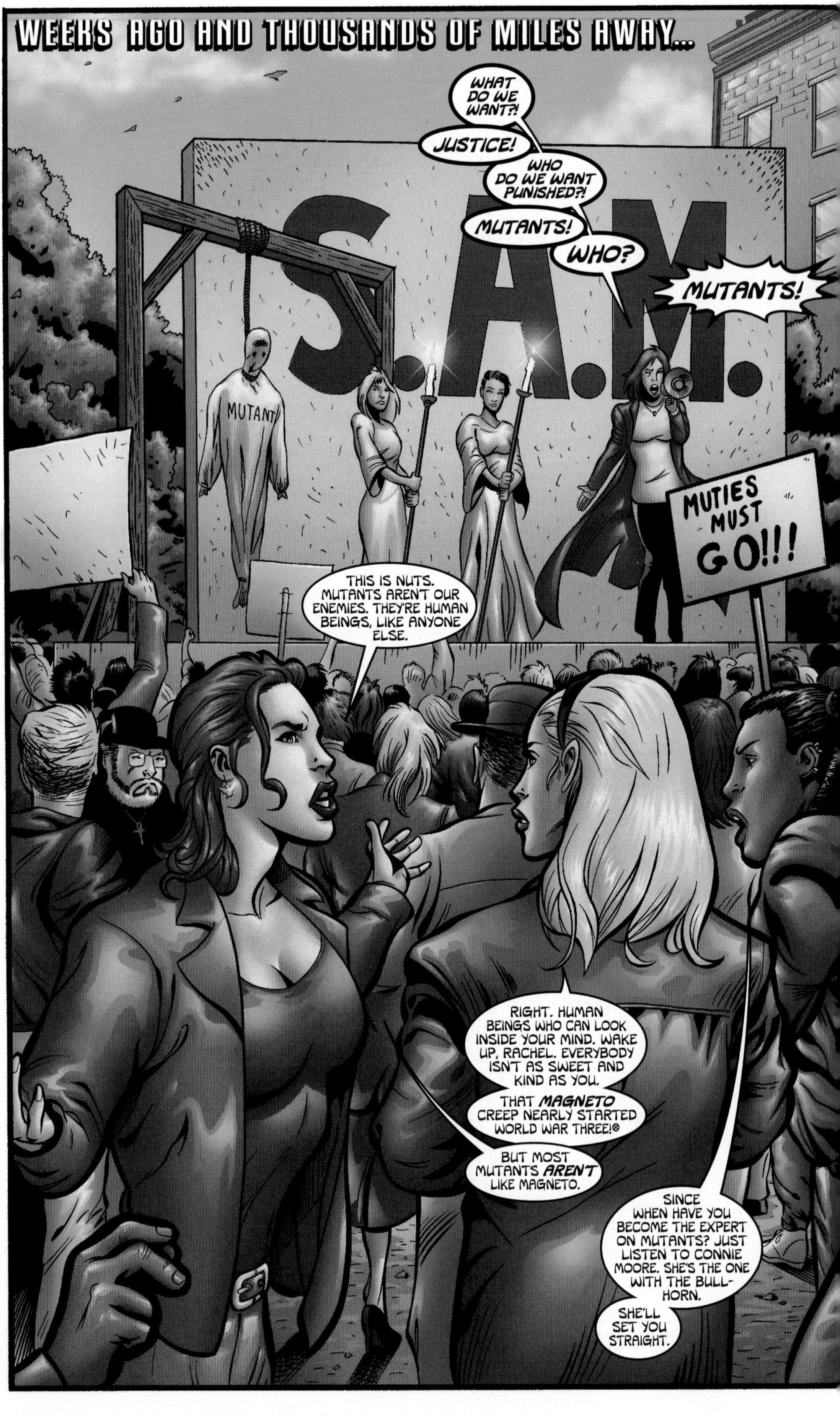
WEEKS AGO AND THOUSANDS OF MILES AWAY...
WHAT DO WE WANT?!
JUSTICE!
WHO DO WE WANT PUNISHED?!
MUTANTS!
WHO?
MUTANTS!
S.A.M.
MUTANT
MUTIES MUST GO!!!
THIS IS NUTS. MUTANTS AREN'T OUR ENEMIES. THEY'RE HUMAN BEINGS, LIKE ANYONE ELSE.
RIGHT. HUMAN BEINGS WHO CAN LOOK INSIDE YOUR MIND. WAKE UP, RACHEL. EVERYBODY ISN'T AS SWEET AND KIND AS YOU.
THAT MAGNETO CREEP NEARLY STARTED WORLD WAR THREE!®
BUT MOST MUTANTS AREN'T LIKE MAGNETO.
SINCE WHEN HAVE YOU BECOME THE EXPERT ON MUTANTS? JUST LISTEN TO CONNIE MOORE. SHE'S THE ONE WITH THE BULL-HORN.
SHE'LL SET YOU STRAIGHT.

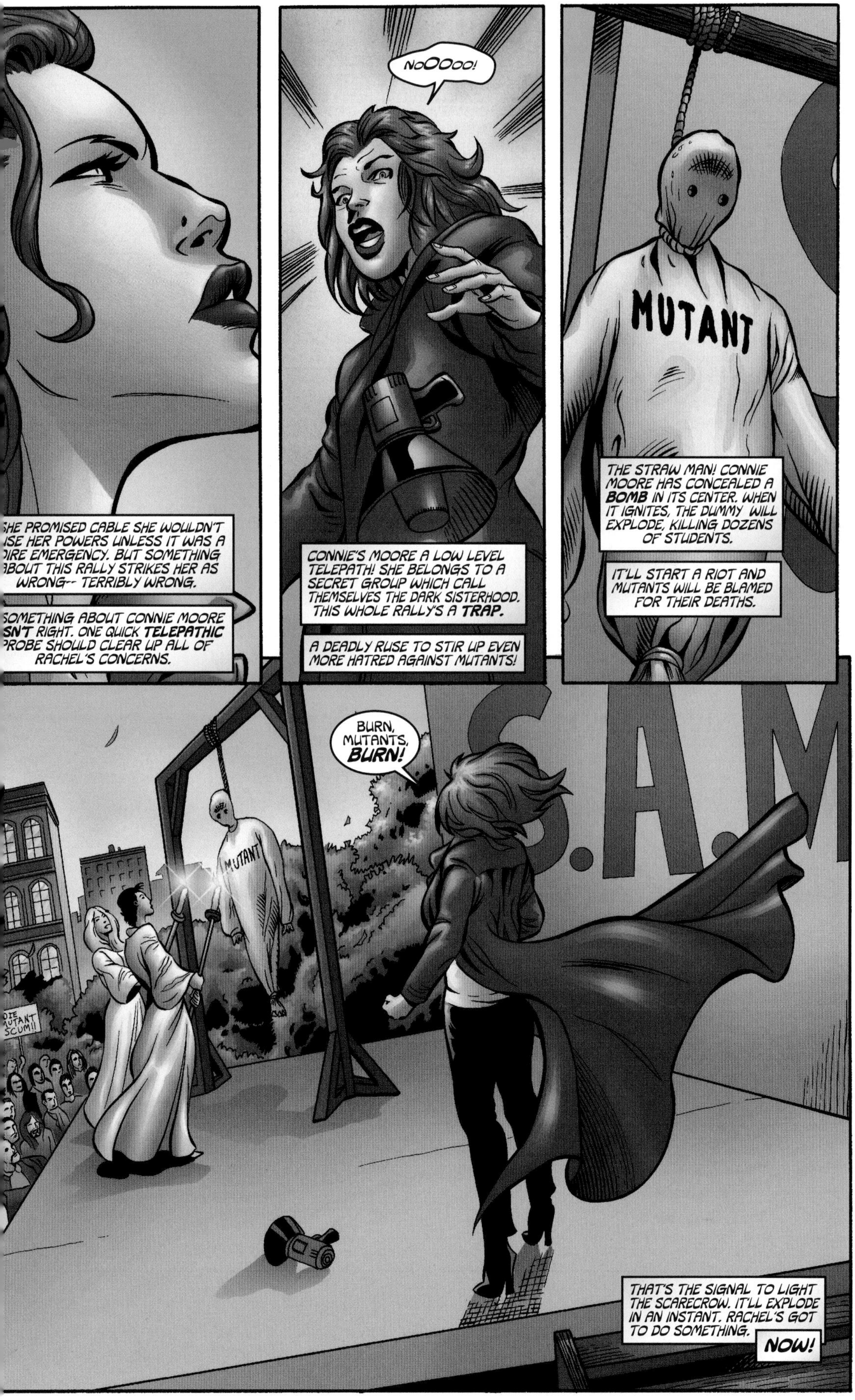
SHE PROMISED CABLE SHE WOULDN'T USE HER POWERS UNLESS IT WAS A DIRE EMERGENCY. BUT SOMETHING ABOUT THIS RALLY STRIKES HER AS WRONG-- TERRIBLY WRONG.
SOMETHING ABOUT CONNIE MOORE ISN'T RIGHT. ONE QUICK TELEPATHIC PROBE SHOULD CLEAR UP ALL OF RACHEL'S CONCERNS.
NoOOoo!
CONNIE'S MOORE A LOW LEVEL TELEPATH! SHE BELONGS TO A SECRET GROUP WHICH CALL THEMSELVES THE DARK SISTERHOOD. THIS WHOLE RALLY'S A TRAP.
A DEADLY RUSE TO STIR UP EVEN MORE HATRED AGAINST MUTANTS!
MUTANT
THE STRAW MAN! CONNIE MOORE HAS CONCEALED A BOMB IN ITS CENTER. WHEN IT IGNITES, THE DUMMY WILL EXPLODE, KILLING DOZENS OF STUDENTS.
IT'LL START A RIOT AND MUTANTS WILL BE BLAMED FOR THEIR DEATHS.
BURN, MUTANTS, BURN!
MUTANT
DIE MUTANT SCUM!!
THAT'S THE SIGNAL TO LIGHT THE SCARECROW. IT'LL EXPLODE IN AN INSTANT. RACHEL'S GOT TO DO SOMETHING.
NOW!

ATTACK!

THERE ARE TRAPS IN THE HALLWAYS. ALARMS AS WELL.

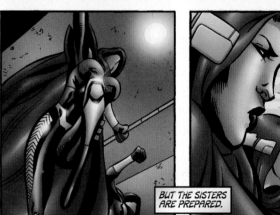

BUT THE SISTERS ARE PREPARED.

THEY WON'T LET ANYTHING STOP THEM FROM REACHING CABLE.

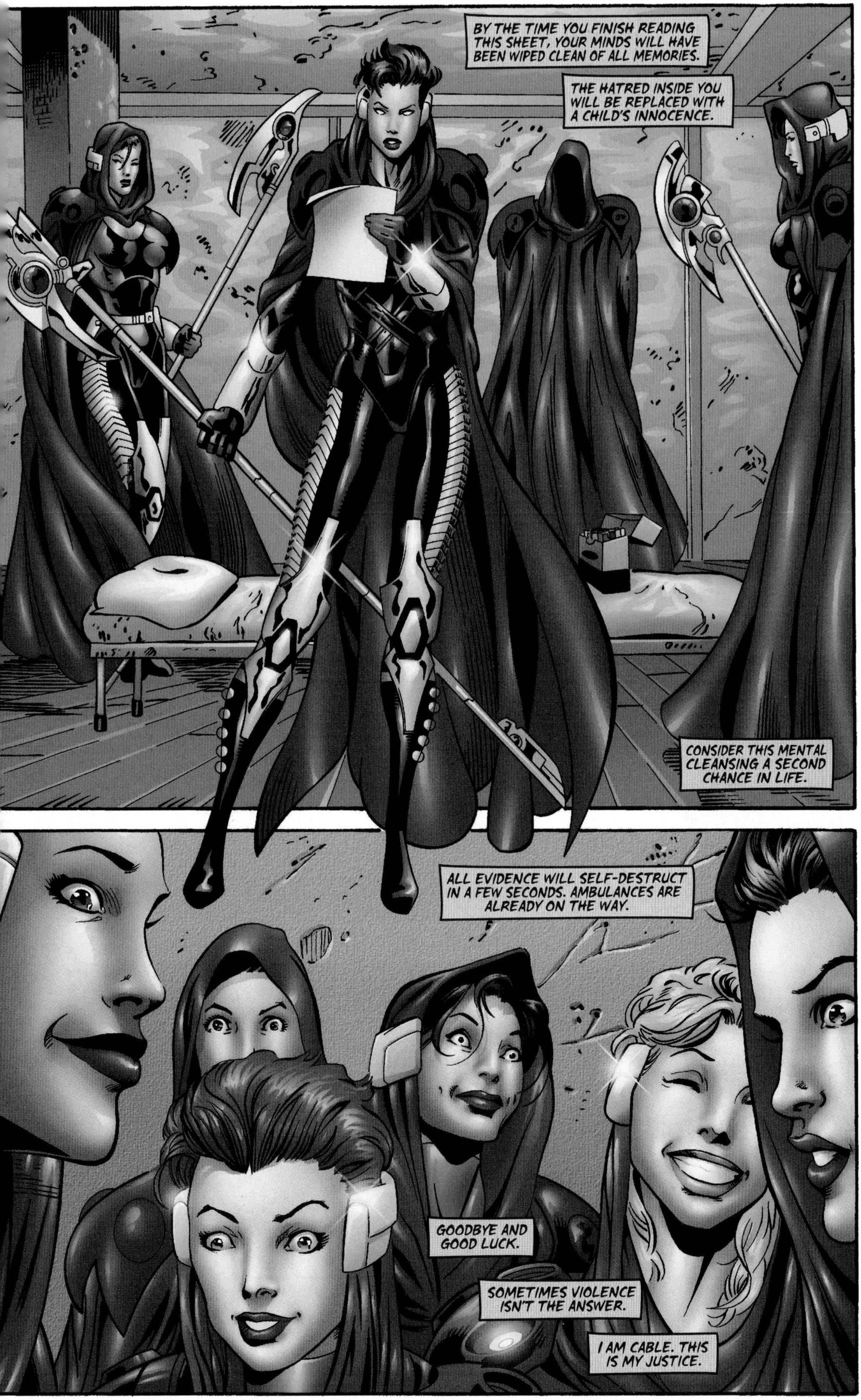
BY THE TIME YOU FINISH READING THIS SHEET, YOUR MINDS WILL HAVE BEEN WIPED CLEAN OF ALL MEMORIES.
THE HATRED INSIDE YOU WILL BE REPLACED WITH A CHILD'S INNOCENCE.
CONSIDER THIS MENTAL CLEANSING A SECOND CHANCE IN LIFE.
ALL EVIDENCE WILL SELF-DESTRUCT IN A FEW SECONDS. AMBULANCES ARE ALREADY ON THE WAY.
GOODBYE AND GOOD LUCK.
SOMETIMES VIOLENCE ISN'T THE ANSWER.
I AM CABLE. THIS IS MY JUSTICE.

NEXT COUNTDOWN PART TWO ARMAGEDDON APPROACHE

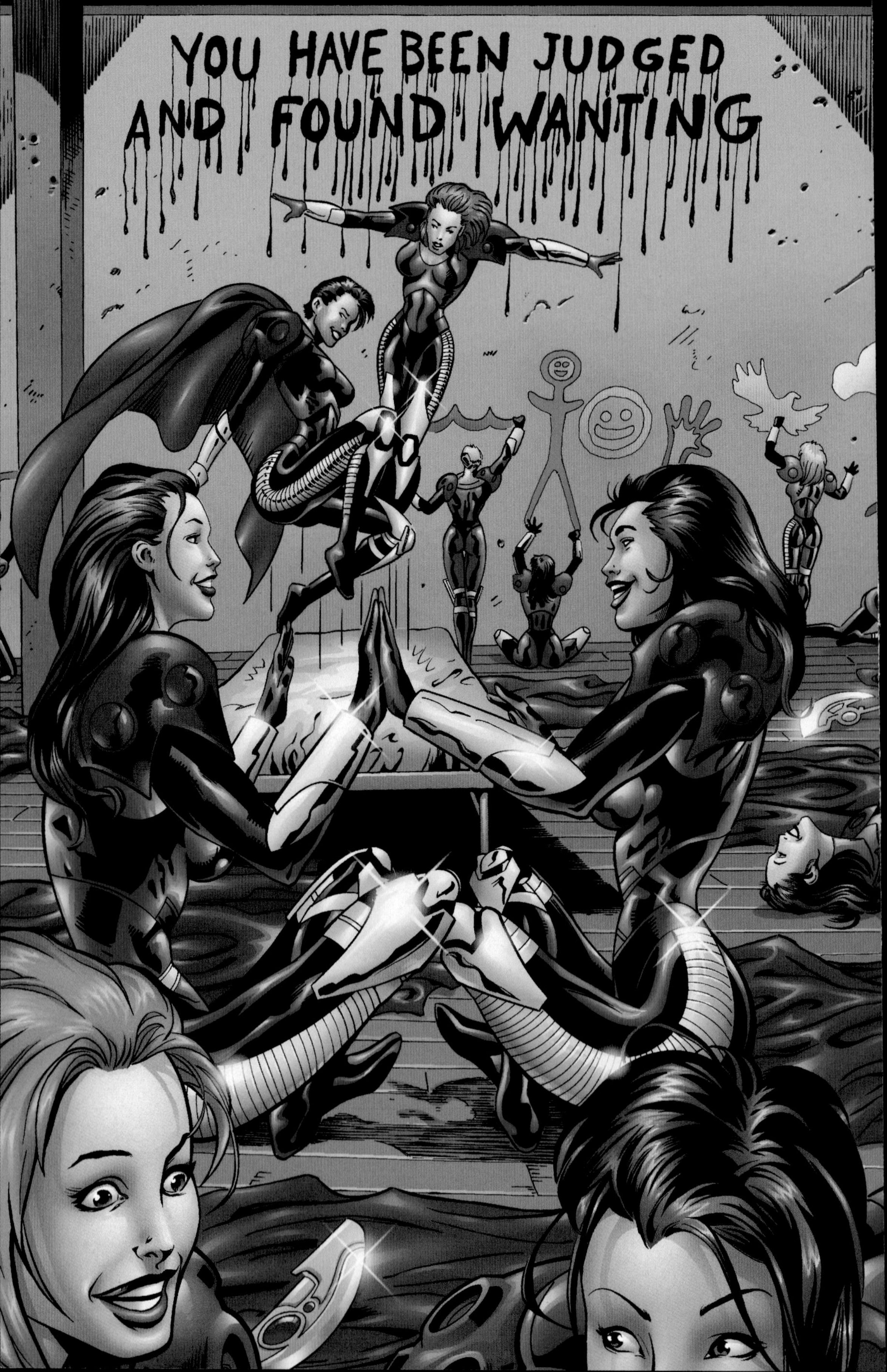
YOU HAVE BEEN JUDGED
AND FOUND WANTING

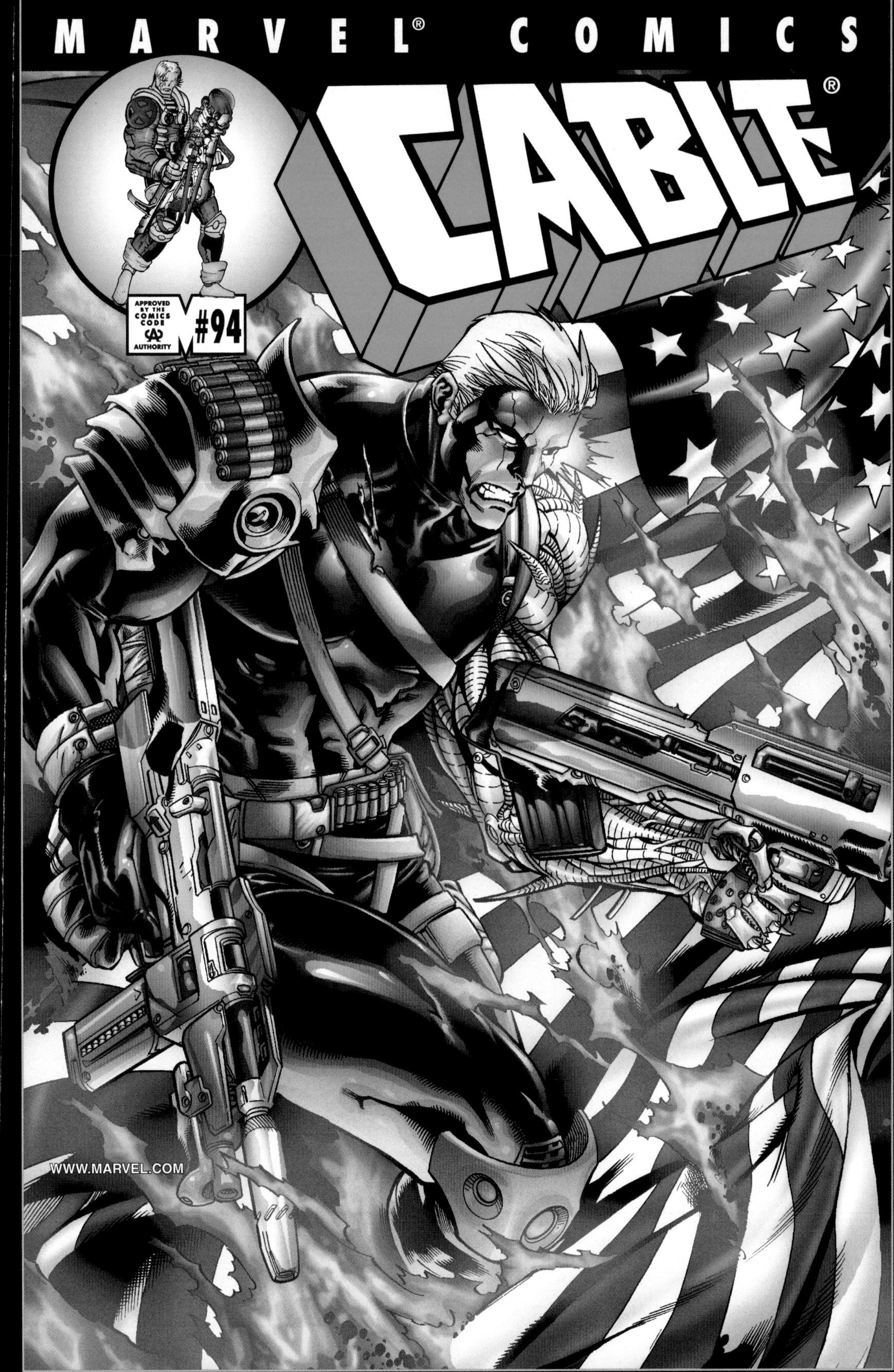
MARVEL® COMICS
CABLE®
APPROVED BY THE COMICS CODE AUTHORITY
#94
WWW.MARVEL.COM

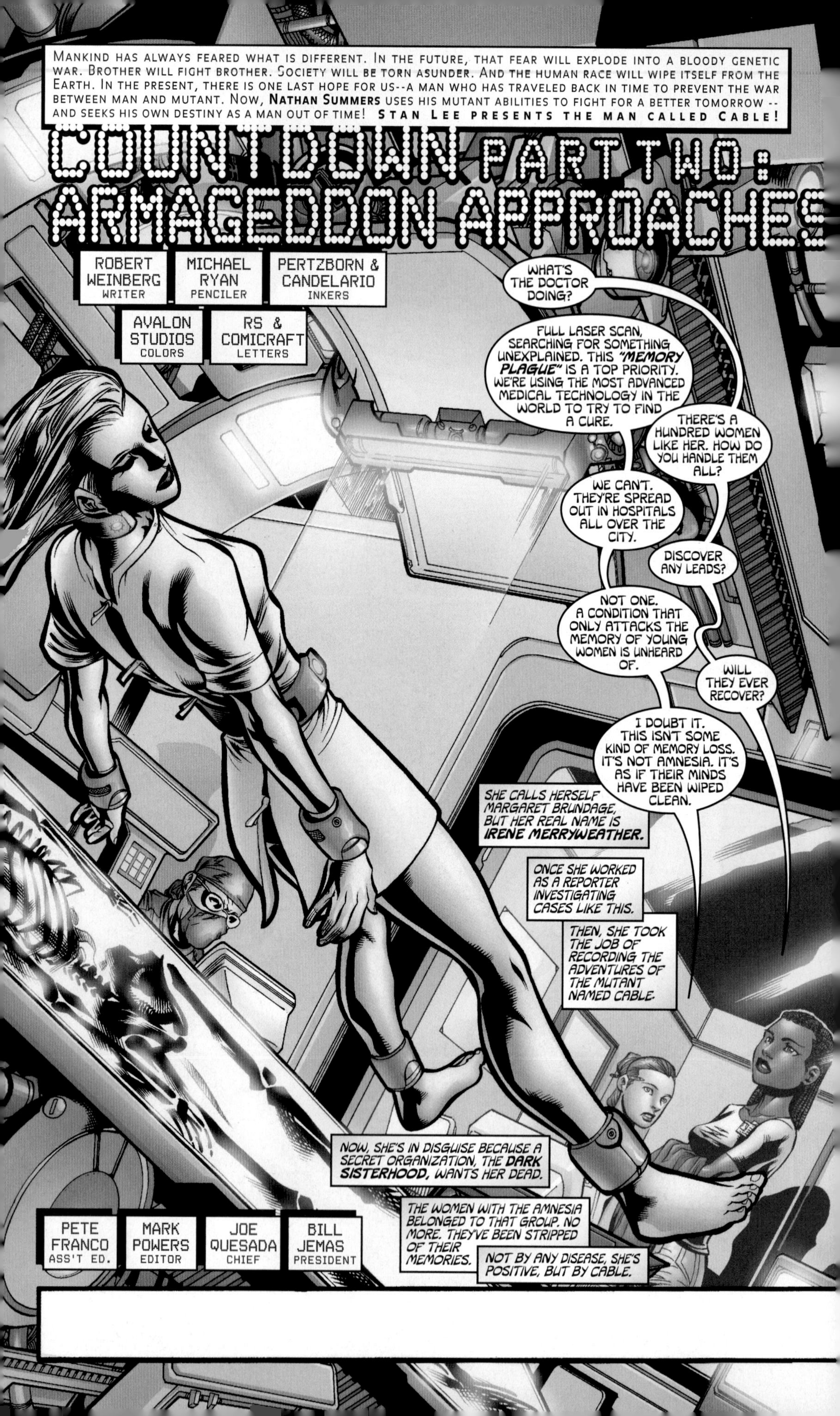
MANKIND HAS ALWAYS FEARED WHAT IS DIFFERENT. IN THE FUTURE, THAT FEAR WILL EXPLODE INTO A BLOODY GENETIC WAR. BROTHER WILL FIGHT BROTHER. SOCIETY WILL BE TORN ASUNDER. AND THE HUMAN RACE WILL WIPE ITSELF FROM THE EARTH. IN THE PRESENT, THERE IS ONE LAST HOPE FOR US--A MAN WHO HAS TRAVELED BACK IN TIME TO PREVENT THE WAR BETWEEN MAN AND MUTANT. NOW, NATHAN SUMMERS USES HIS MUTANT ABILITIES TO FIGHT FOR A BETTER TOMORROW -- AND SEEKS HIS OWN DESTINY AS A MAN OUT OF TIME! STAN LEE PRESENTS THE MAN CALLED CABLE!
COUNTDOWN PART TWO: ARMAGEDDON APPROACHES!
ROBERT WEINBERG WRITER
MICHAEL RYAN PENCILER
PERTZBORN & CANDELARIO INKERS
AVALON STUDIOS COLORS
RS & COMICRAFT LETTERS
WHAT'S THE DOCTOR DOING?
FULL LASER SCAN, SEARCHING FOR SOMETHING UNEXPLAINED. THIS "MEMORY PLAGUE" IS A TOP PRIORITY. WE'RE USING THE MOST ADVANCED MEDICAL TECHNOLOGY IN THE WORLD TO TRY TO FIND A CURE.
THERE'S A HUNDRED WOMEN LIKE HER. HOW DO YOU HANDLE THEM ALL?
WE CAN'T. THEY'RE SPREAD OUT IN HOSPITALS ALL OVER THE CITY.
DISCOVER ANY LEADS?
NOT ONE. A CONDITION THAT ONLY ATTACKS THE MEMORY OF YOUNG WOMEN IS UNHEARD OF.
WILL THEY EVER RECOVER?
I DOUBT IT. THIS ISN'T SOME KIND OF MEMORY LOSS. IT'S NOT AMNESIA. IT'S AS IF THEIR MINDS HAVE BEEN WIPED CLEAN.
SHE CALLS HERSELF MARGARET BRUNDAGE, BUT HER REAL NAME IS IRENE MERRYWEATHER.
ONCE SHE WORKED AS A REPORTER INVESTIGATING CASES LIKE THIS.
THEN, SHE TOOK THE JOB OF RECORDING THE ADVENTURES OF THE MUTANT NAMED CABLE.
NOW, SHE'S IN DISGUISE BECAUSE A SECRET ORGANIZATION, THE DARK SISTERHOOD, WANTS HER DEAD.
THE WOMEN WITH THE AMNESIA BELONGED TO THAT GROUP. NO MORE. THEY'VE BEEN STRIPPED OF THEIR MEMORIES.
NOT BY ANY DISEASE, SHE'S POSITIVE, BUT BY CABLE.
PETE FRANCO ASS'T ED.
MARK POWERS EDITOR
JOE QUESADA CHIEF
BILL JEMAS PRESIDENT

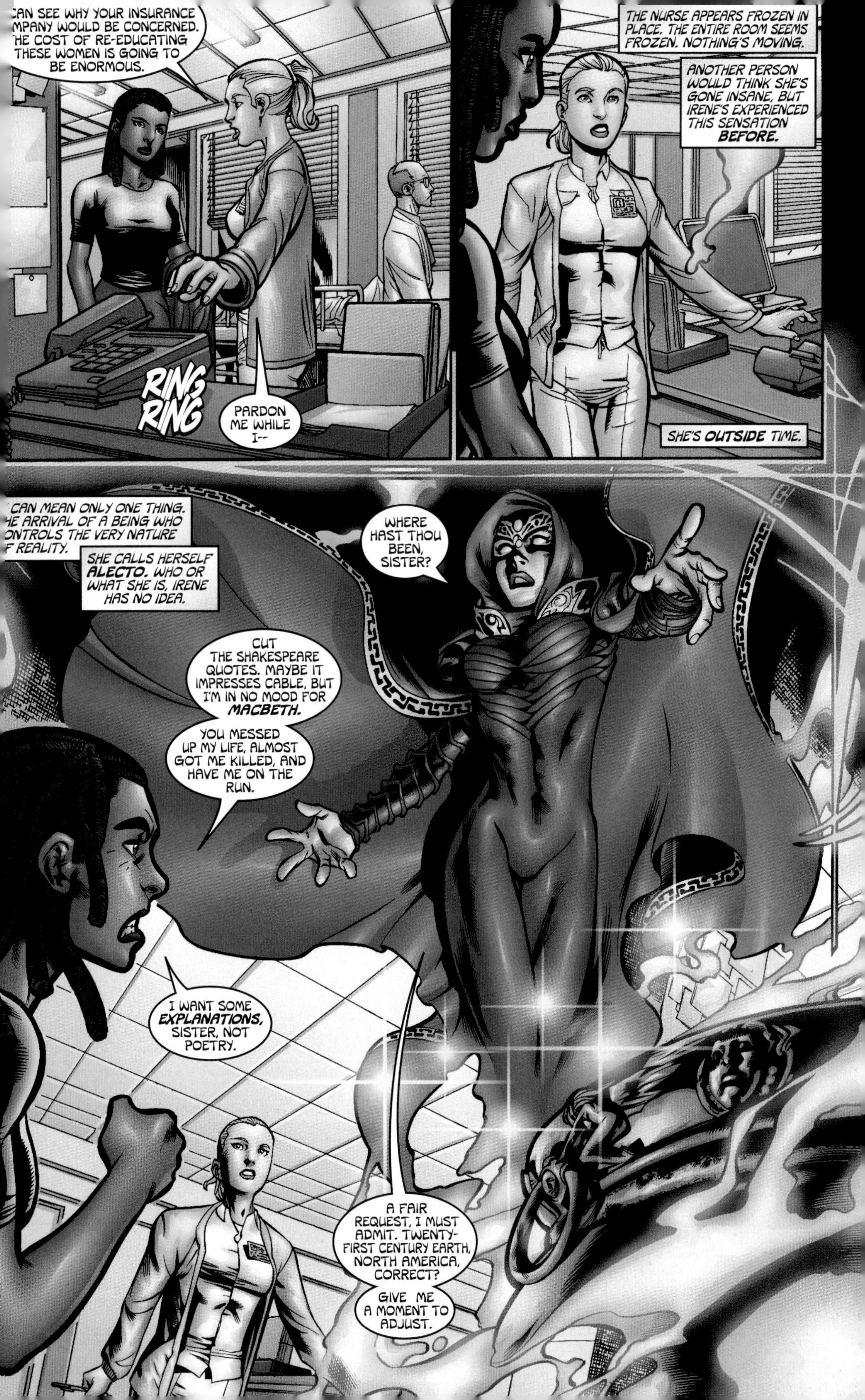

CAN SEE WHY YOUR INSURANCE MPANY WOULD BE CONCERNED. THE COST OF RE-EDUCATING THESE WOMEN IS GOING TO BE ENORMOUS.
RING RING
PARDON ME WHILE I--
THE NURSE APPEARS FROZEN IN PLACE. THE ENTIRE ROOM SEEMS FROZEN. NOTHING'S MOVING.
ANOTHER PERSON WOULD THINK SHE'S GONE INSANE, BUT IRENE'S EXPERIENCED THIS SENSATION BEFORE.
SHE'S OUTSIDE TIME.
CAN MEAN ONLY ONE THING. HE ARRIVAL OF A BEING WHO ONTROLS THE VERY NATURE F REALITY.
SHE CALLS HERSELF ALECTO. WHO OR WHAT SHE IS, IRENE HAS NO IDEA.
WHERE HAST THOU BEEN, SISTER?
CUT THE SHAKESPEARE QUOTES. MAYBE IT IMPRESSES CABLE, BUT I'M IN NO MOOD FOR MACBETH.
YOU MESSED UP MY LIFE, ALMOST GOT ME KILLED, AND HAVE ME ON THE RUN.
I WANT SOME EXPLANATIONS, SISTER, NOT POETRY.
A FAIR REQUEST, I MUST ADMIT. TWENTY-FIRST CENTURY EARTH, NORTH AMERICA, CORRECT?
GIVE ME A MOMENT TO ADJUST.

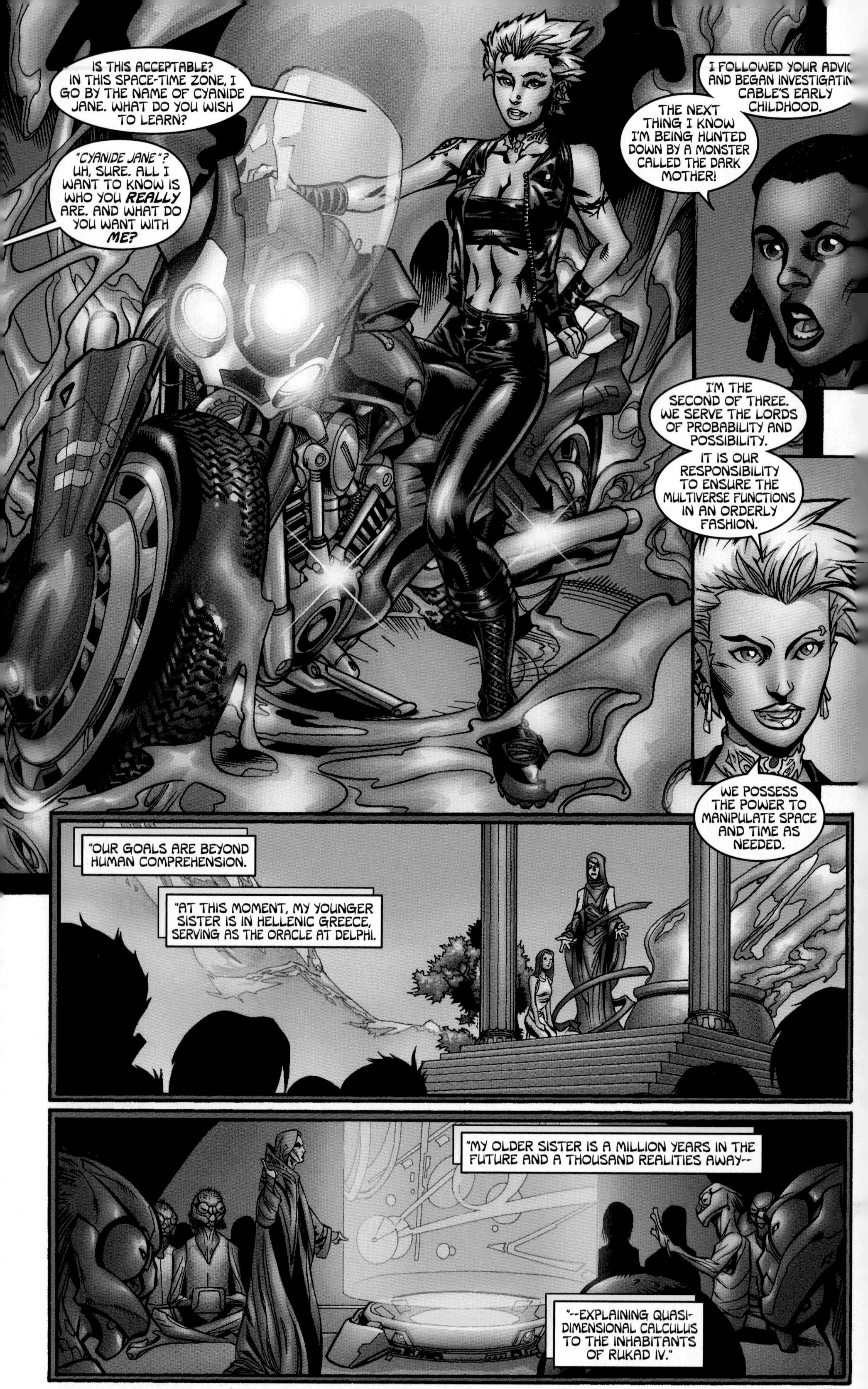
IS THIS ACCEPTABLE? IN THIS SPACE-TIME ZONE, I GO BY THE NAME OF CYANIDE JANE. WHAT DO YOU WISH TO LEARN?
"CYANIDE JANE"? UH, SURE. ALL I WANT TO KNOW IS WHO YOU *REALLY* ARE. AND WHAT DO YOU WANT WITH *ME?*
I FOLLOWED YOUR ADVIC AND BEGAN INVESTIGATIN CABLE'S EARLY CHILDHOOD.
THE NEXT THING I KNOW I'M BEING HUNTED DOWN BY A MONSTER CALLED THE DARK MOTHER!
I'M THE SECOND OF THREE. WE SERVE THE LORDS OF PROBABILITY AND POSSIBILITY.
IT IS OUR RESPONSIBILITY TO ENSURE THE MULTIVERSE FUNCTIONS IN AN ORDERLY FASHION.
WE POSSESS THE POWER TO MANIPULATE SPACE AND TIME AS NEEDED.
"OUR GOALS ARE BEYOND HUMAN COMPREHENSION.
"AT THIS MOMENT, MY YOUNGER SISTER IS IN HELLENIC GREECE, SERVING AS THE ORACLE AT DELPHI.
"MY OLDER SISTER IS A MILLION YEARS IN THE FUTURE AND A THOUSAND REALITIES AWAY--
"--EXPLAINING QUASI-DIMENSIONAL CALCULUS TO THE INHABITANTS OF RUKAD IV."

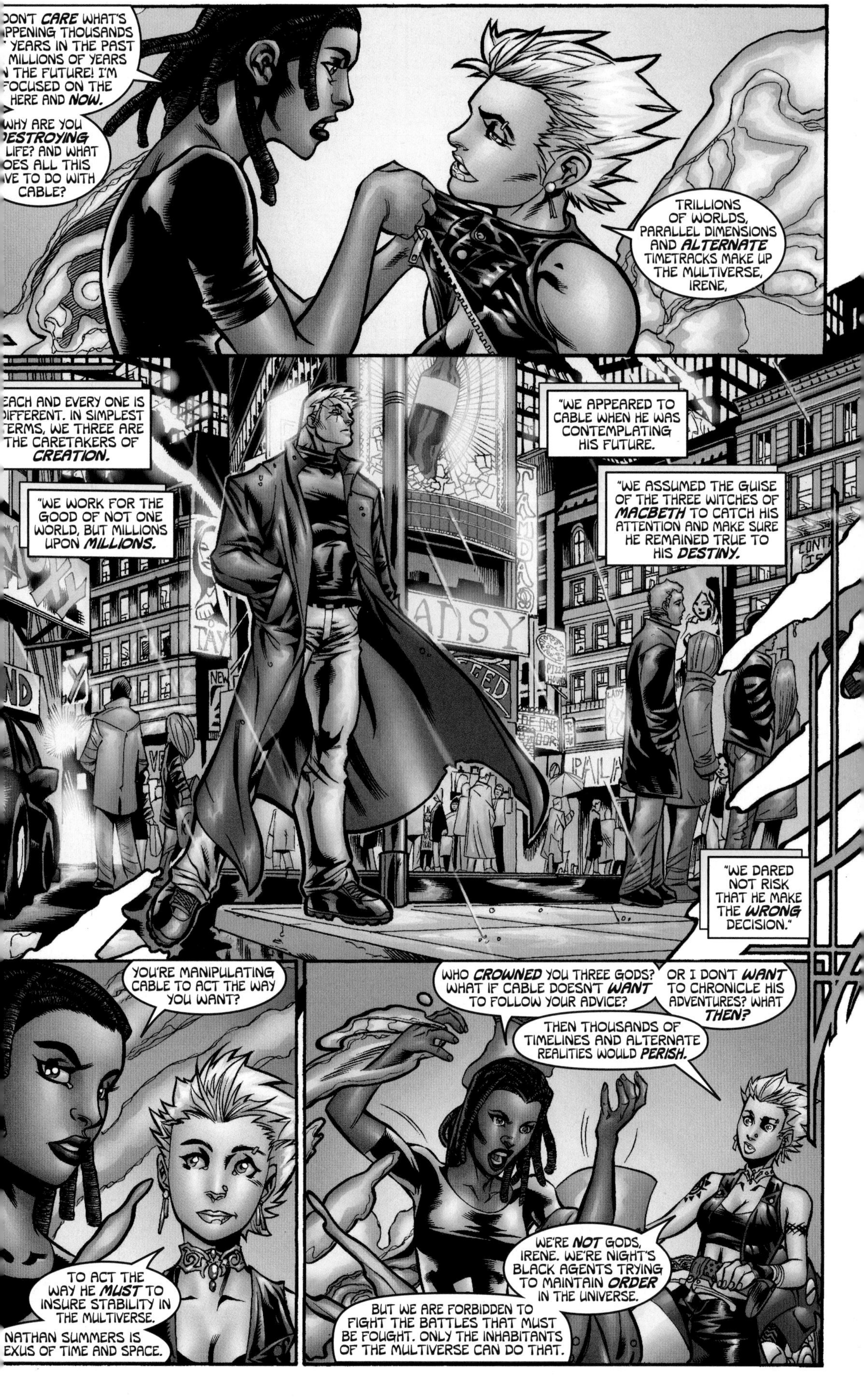

DON'T CARE WHAT'S PPENING THOUSANDS YEARS IN THE PAST MILLIONS OF YEARS N THE FUTURE! I'M FOCUSED ON THE HERE AND NOW.
WHY ARE YOU DESTROYING LIFE? AND WHAT OES ALL THIS VE TO DO WITH CABLE?
TRILLIONS OF WORLDS, PARALLEL DIMENSIONS AND ALTERNATE TIMETRACKS MAKE UP THE MULTIVERSE, IRENE,
EACH AND EVERY ONE IS DIFFERENT. IN SIMPLEST TERMS, WE THREE ARE THE CARETAKERS OF CREATION.
"WE WORK FOR THE GOOD OF NOT ONE WORLD, BUT MILLIONS UPON MILLIONS.
"WE APPEARED TO CABLE WHEN HE WAS CONTEMPLATING HIS FUTURE.
"WE ASSUMED THE GUISE OF THE THREE WITCHES OF MACBETH TO CATCH HIS ATTENTION AND MAKE SURE HE REMAINED TRUE TO HIS DESTINY.
"WE DARED NOT RISK THAT HE MAKE THE WRONG DECISION."
YOU'RE MANIPULATING CABLE TO ACT THE WAY YOU WANT?
TO ACT THE WAY HE MUST TO INSURE STABILITY IN THE MULTIVERSE.
NATHAN SUMMERS IS EXUS OF TIME AND SPACE.
WHO CROWNED YOU THREE GODS? WHAT IF CABLE DOESN'T WANT TO FOLLOW YOUR ADVICE?
OR I DON'T WANT TO CHRONICLE HIS ADVENTURES? WHAT THEN?
THEN THOUSANDS OF TIMELINES AND ALTERNATE REALITIES WOULD PERISH.
WE'RE NOT GODS, IRENE. WE'RE NIGHT'S BLACK AGENTS TRYING TO MAINTAIN ORDER IN THE UNIVERSE.
BUT WE ARE FORBIDDEN TO FIGHT THE BATTLES THAT MUST BE FOUGHT. ONLY THE INHABITANTS OF THE MULTIVERSE CAN DO THAT.

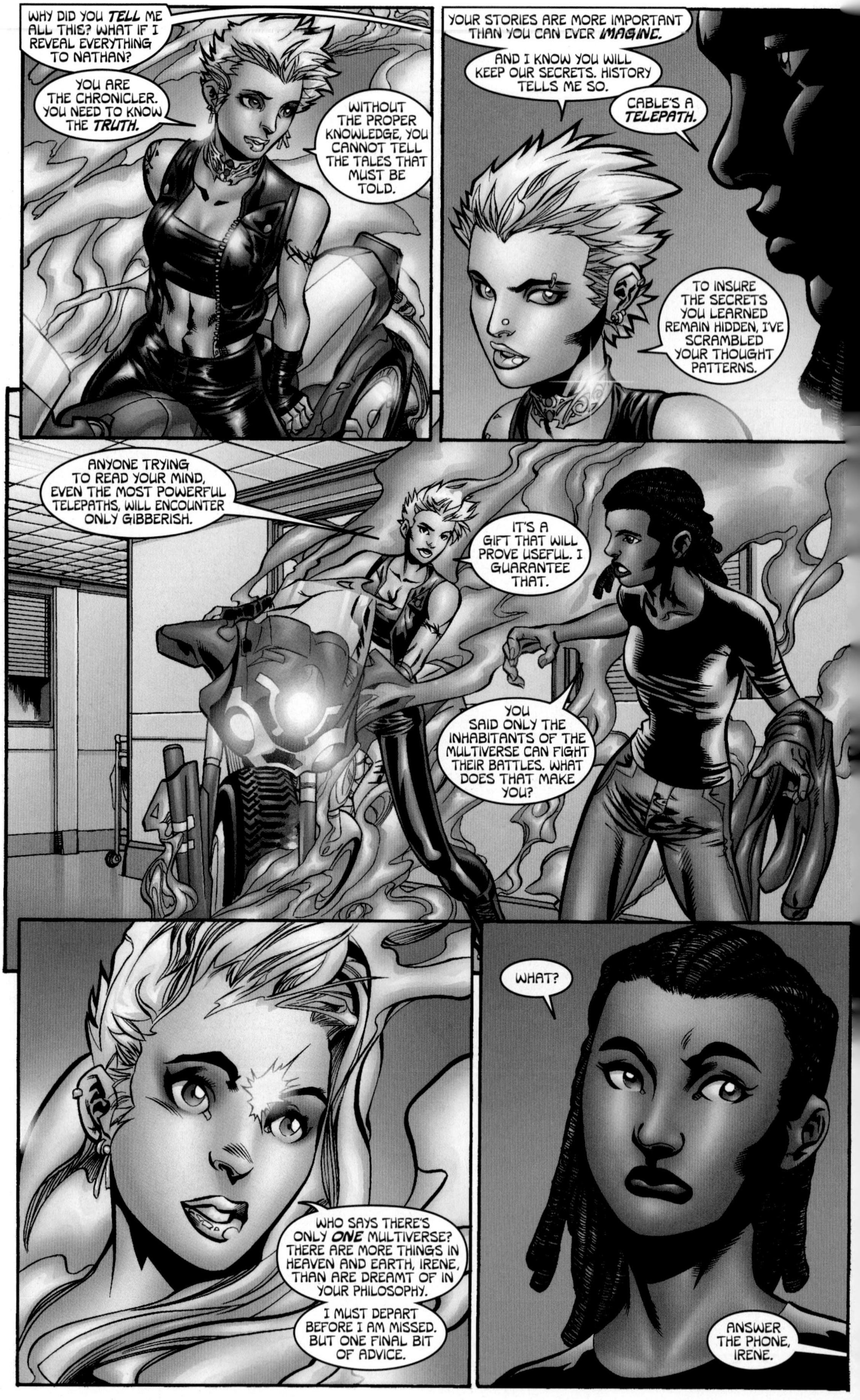
WHY DID YOU TELL ME ALL THIS? WHAT IF I REVEAL EVERYTHING TO NATHAN?
YOU ARE THE CHRONICLER. YOU NEED TO KNOW THE TRUTH.
WITHOUT THE PROPER KNOWLEDGE, YOU CANNOT TELL THE TALES THAT MUST BE TOLD.
YOUR STORIES ARE MORE IMPORTANT THAN YOU CAN EVER IMAGINE.
AND I KNOW YOU WILL KEEP OUR SECRETS. HISTORY TELLS ME SO.
CABLE'S A TELEPATH.
TO INSURE THE SECRETS YOU LEARNED REMAIN HIDDEN, I'VE SCRAMBLED YOUR THOUGHT PATTERNS.
ANYONE TRYING TO READ YOUR MIND, EVEN THE MOST POWERFUL TELEPATHS, WILL ENCOUNTER ONLY GIBBERISH.
IT'S A GIFT THAT WILL PROVE USEFUL. I GUARANTEE THAT.
YOU SAID ONLY THE INHABITANTS OF THE MULTIVERSE CAN FIGHT THEIR BATTLES. WHAT DOES THAT MAKE YOU?
WHO SAYS THERE'S ONLY ONE MULTIVERSE? THERE ARE MORE THINGS IN HEAVEN AND EARTH, IRENE, THAN ARE DREAMT OF IN YOUR PHILOSOPHY.
I MUST DEPART BEFORE I AM MISSED. BUT ONE FINAL BIT OF ADVICE.
WHAT?
ANSWER THE PHONE, IRENE.

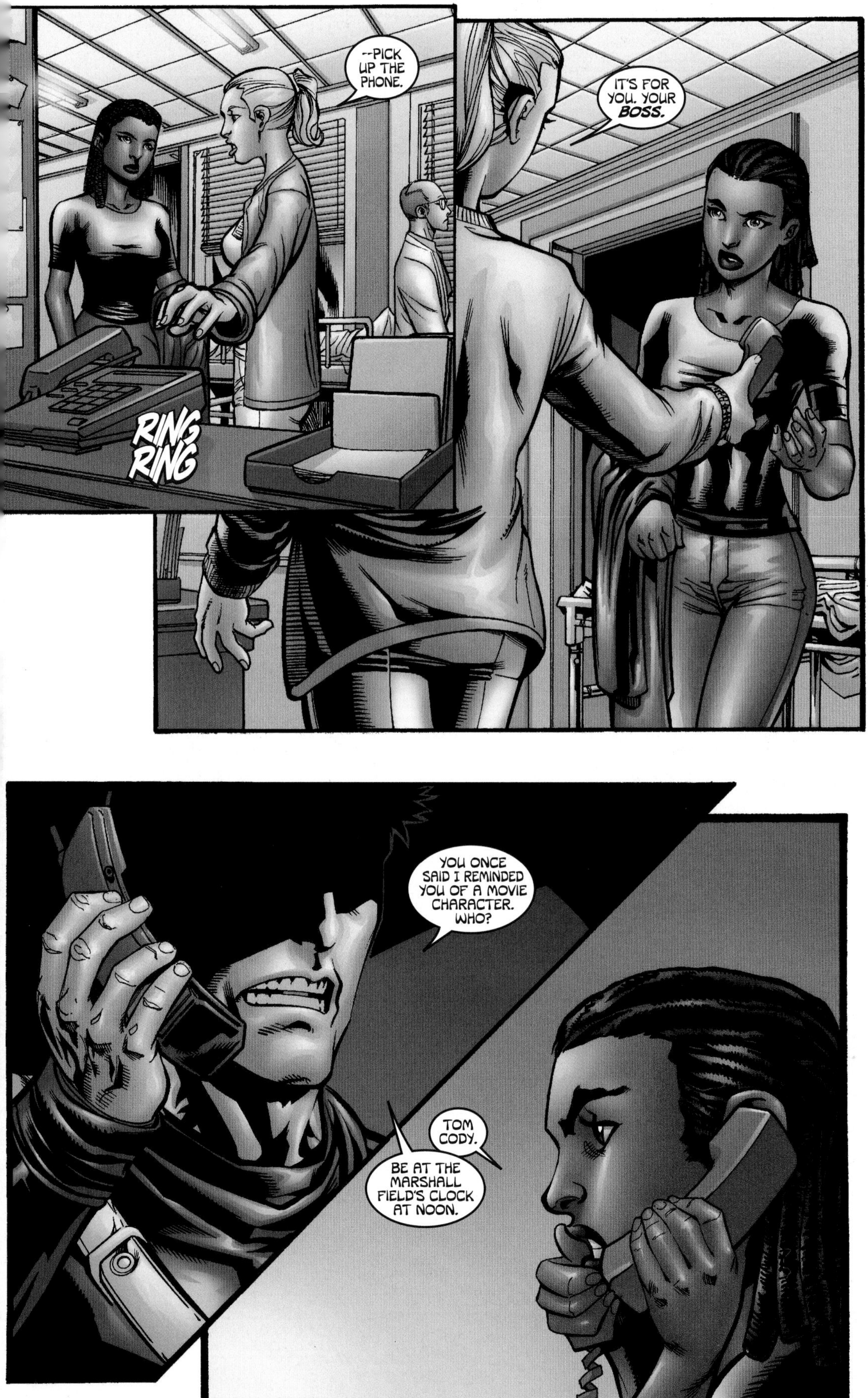
--PICK UP THE PHONE.
RING RING
IT'S FOR YOU. YOUR BOSS.
YOU ONCE SAID I REMINDED YOU OF A MOVIE CHARACTER. WHO?
TOM CODY.
BE AT THE MARSHALL FIELD'S CLOCK AT NOON.

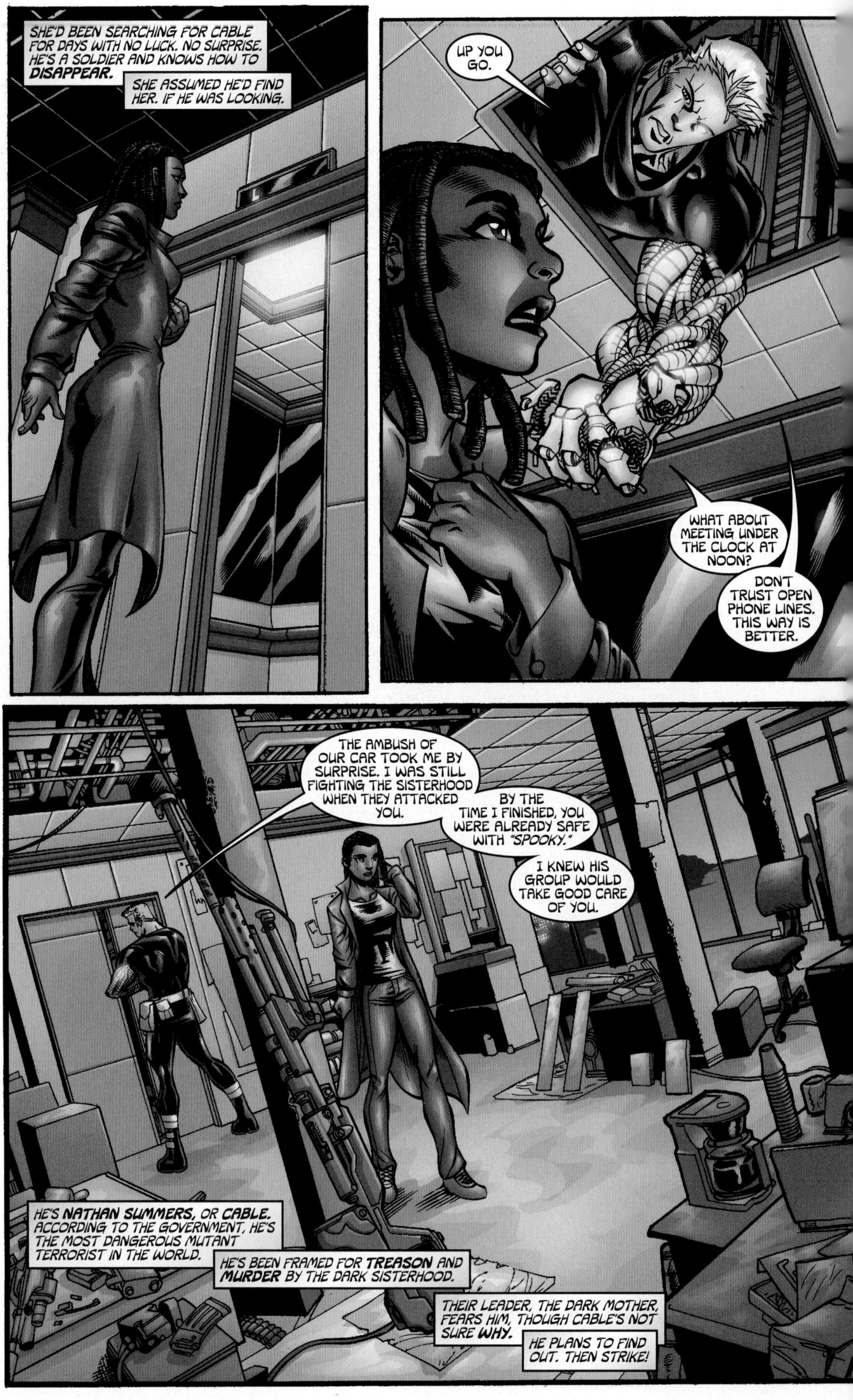
SHE'D BEEN SEARCHING FOR CABLE FOR DAYS WITH NO LUCK. NO SURPRISE. HE'S A SOLDIER AND KNOWS HOW TO DISAPPEAR.
SHE ASSUMED HE'D FIND HER. IF HE WAS LOOKING.
UP YOU GO.
WHAT ABOUT MEETING UNDER THE CLOCK AT NOON?
DON'T TRUST OPEN PHONE LINES. THIS WAY IS BETTER.
THE AMBUSH OF OUR CAR TOOK ME BY SURPRISE. I WAS STILL FIGHTING THE SISTERHOOD WHEN THEY ATTACKED YOU.
BY THE TIME I FINISHED, YOU WERE ALREADY SAFE WITH "SPOOKY."
I KNEW HIS GROUP WOULD TAKE GOOD CARE OF YOU.
HE'S NATHAN SUMMERS, OR CABLE. ACCORDING TO THE GOVERNMENT, HE'S THE MOST DANGEROUS MUTANT TERRORIST IN THE WORLD.
HE'S BEEN FRAMED FOR TREASON AND MURDER BY THE DARK SISTERHOOD.
THEIR LEADER, THE DARK MOTHER, FEARS HIM, THOUGH CABLE'S NOT SURE WHY.
HE PLANS TO FIND OUT. THEN STRIKE!

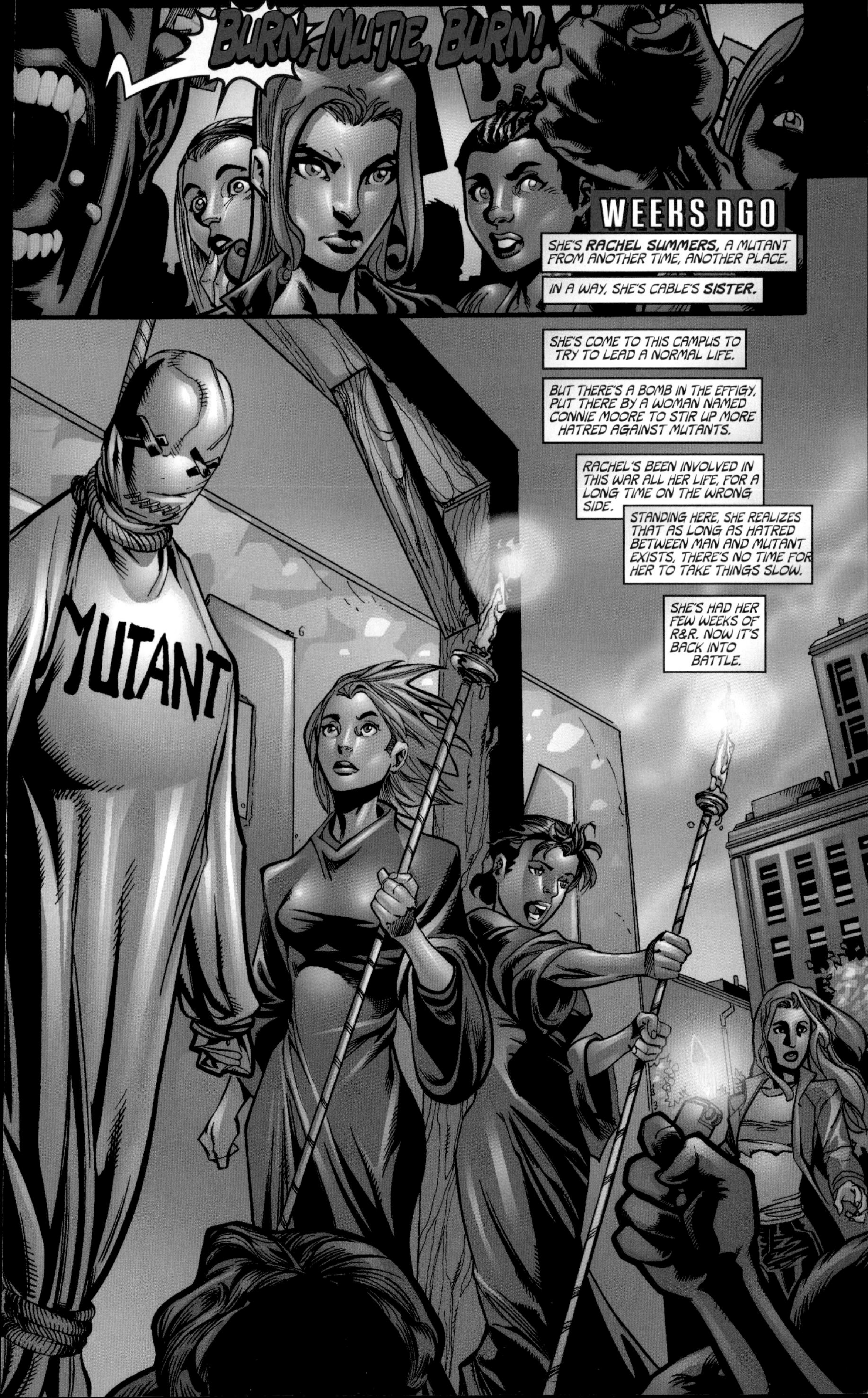
BURN, MUTIE, BURN!
WEEKS AGO
SHE'S RACHEL SUMMERS, A MUTANT FROM ANOTHER TIME, ANOTHER PLACE.
IN A WAY, SHE'S CABLE'S SISTER.
SHE'S COME TO THIS CAMPUS TO TRY TO LEAD A NORMAL LIFE.
BUT THERE'S A BOMB IN THE EFFIGY, PUT THERE BY A WOMAN NAMED CONNIE MOORE TO STIR UP MORE HATRED AGAINST MUTANTS.
RACHEL'S BEEN INVOLVED IN THIS WAR ALL HER LIFE, FOR A LONG TIME ON THE WRONG SIDE.
STANDING HERE, SHE REALIZES THAT AS LONG AS HATRED BETWEEN MAN AND MUTANT EXISTS, THERE'S NO TIME FOR HER TO TAKE THINGS SLOW.
SHE'S HAD HER FEW WEEKS OF R&R. NOW IT'S BACK INTO BATTLE.
MUTANT

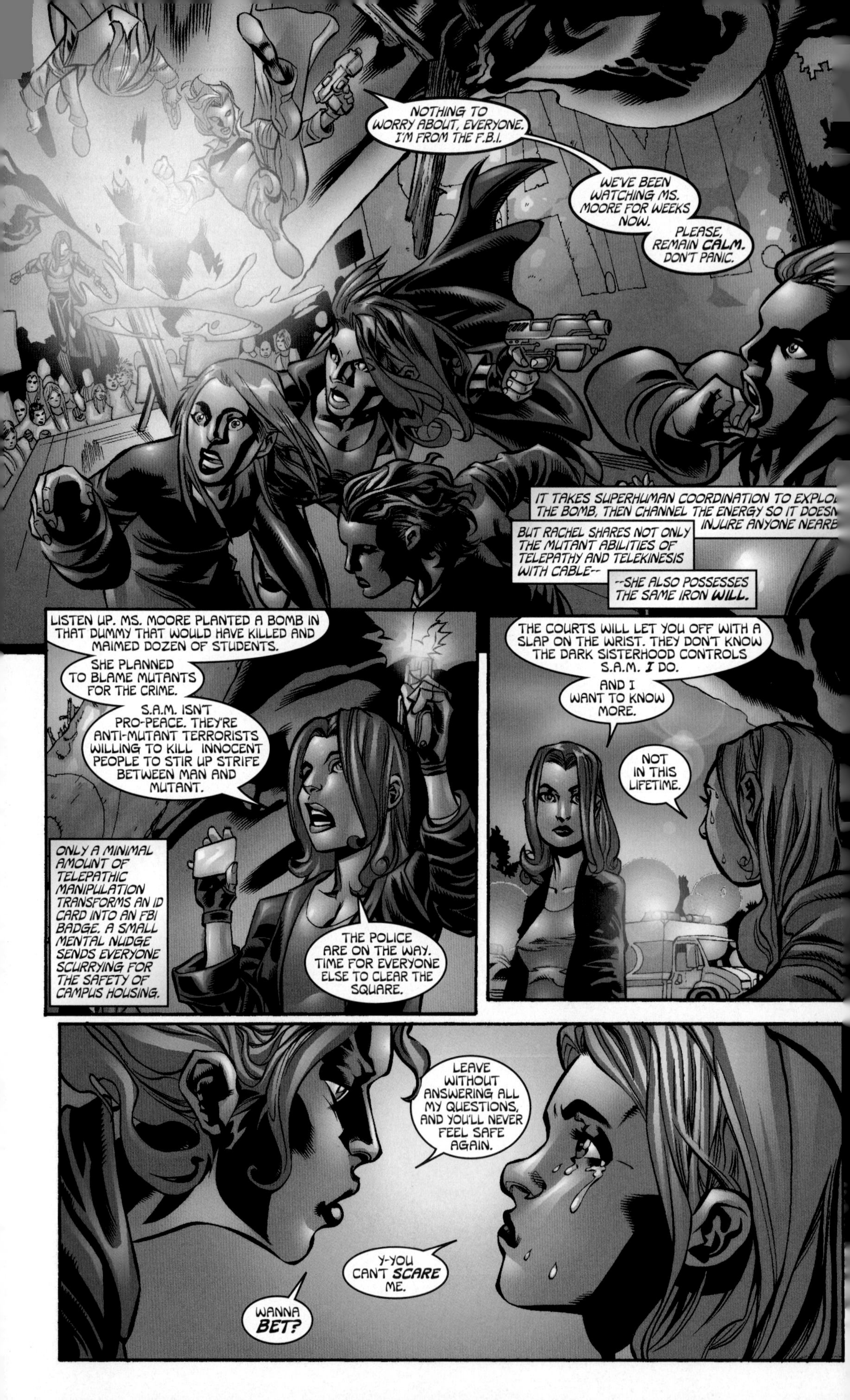
NOTHING TO WORRY ABOUT, EVERYONE. I'M FROM THE F.B.I.
WE'VE BEEN WATCHING MS. MOORE FOR WEEKS NOW.
PLEASE, REMAIN CALM. DON'T PANIC.
IT TAKES SUPERHUMAN COORDINATION TO EXPLO THE BOMB, THEN CHANNEL THE ENERGY SO IT DOESN INJURE ANYONE NEARB
BUT RACHEL SHARES NOT ONLY THE MUTANT ABILITIES OF TELEPATHY AND TELEKINESIS WITH CABLE--
--SHE ALSO POSSESSES THE SAME IRON WILL.
LISTEN UP. MS. MOORE PLANTED A BOMB IN THAT DUMMY THAT WOULD HAVE KILLED AND MAIMED DOZEN OF STUDENTS.
SHE PLANNED TO BLAME MUTANTS FOR THE CRIME.
S.A.M. ISN'T PRO-PEACE. THEY'RE ANTI-MUTANT TERRORISTS WILLING TO KILL INNOCENT PEOPLE TO STIR UP STRIFE BETWEEN MAN AND MUTANT.
ONLY A MINIMAL AMOUNT OF TELEPATHIC MANIPULATION TRANSFORMS AN ID CARD INTO AN FBI BADGE. A SMALL MENTAL NUDGE SENDS EVERYONE SCURRYING FOR THE SAFETY OF CAMPUS HOUSING.
THE POLICE ARE ON THE WAY. TIME FOR EVERYONE ELSE TO CLEAR THE SQUARE.
THE COURTS WILL LET YOU OFF WITH A SLAP ON THE WRIST. THEY DON'T KNOW THE DARK SISTERHOOD CONTROLS S.A.M. I DO.
AND I WANT TO KNOW MORE.
NOT IN THIS LIFETIME.
LEAVE WITHOUT ANSWERING ALL MY QUESTIONS, AND YOU'LL NEVER FEEL SAFE AGAIN.
Y-YOU CAN'T SCARE ME.
WANNA BET?

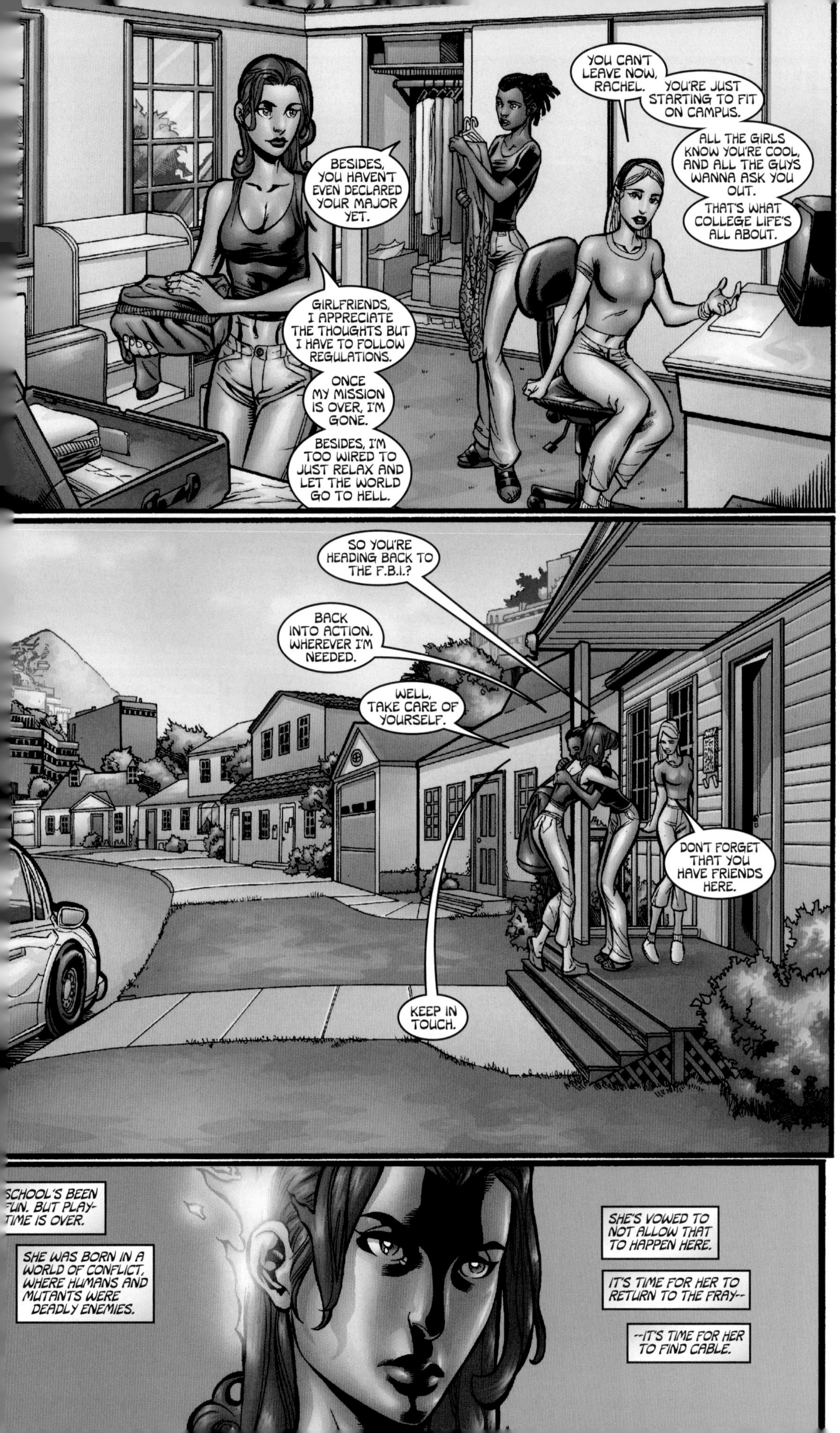
YOU CAN'T LEAVE NOW, RACHEL.
YOU'RE JUST STARTING TO FIT ON CAMPUS.
ALL THE GIRLS KNOW YOU'RE COOL, AND ALL THE GUYS WANNA ASK YOU OUT.
THAT'S WHAT COLLEGE LIFE'S ALL ABOUT.
BESIDES, YOU HAVEN'T EVEN DECLARED YOUR MAJOR YET.
GIRLFRIENDS, I APPRECIATE THE THOUGHTS BUT I HAVE TO FOLLOW REGULATIONS.
ONCE MY MISSION IS OVER, I'M GONE.
BESIDES, I'M TOO WIRED TO JUST RELAX AND LET THE WORLD GO TO HELL.
SO YOU'RE HEADING BACK TO THE F.B.I.?
BACK INTO ACTION. WHEREVER I'M NEEDED.
WELL, TAKE CARE OF YOURSELF.
DON'T FORGET THAT YOU HAVE FRIENDS HERE.
KEEP IN TOUCH.
SCHOOL'S BEEN FUN. BUT PLAY-TIME IS OVER.
SHE WAS BORN IN A WORLD OF CONFLICT, WHERE HUMANS AND MUTANTS WERE DEADLY ENEMIES.
SHE'S VOWED TO NOT ALLOW THAT TO HAPPEN HERE.
IT'S TIME FOR HER TO RETURN TO THE FRAY--
--IT'S TIME FOR HER TO FIND CABLE.

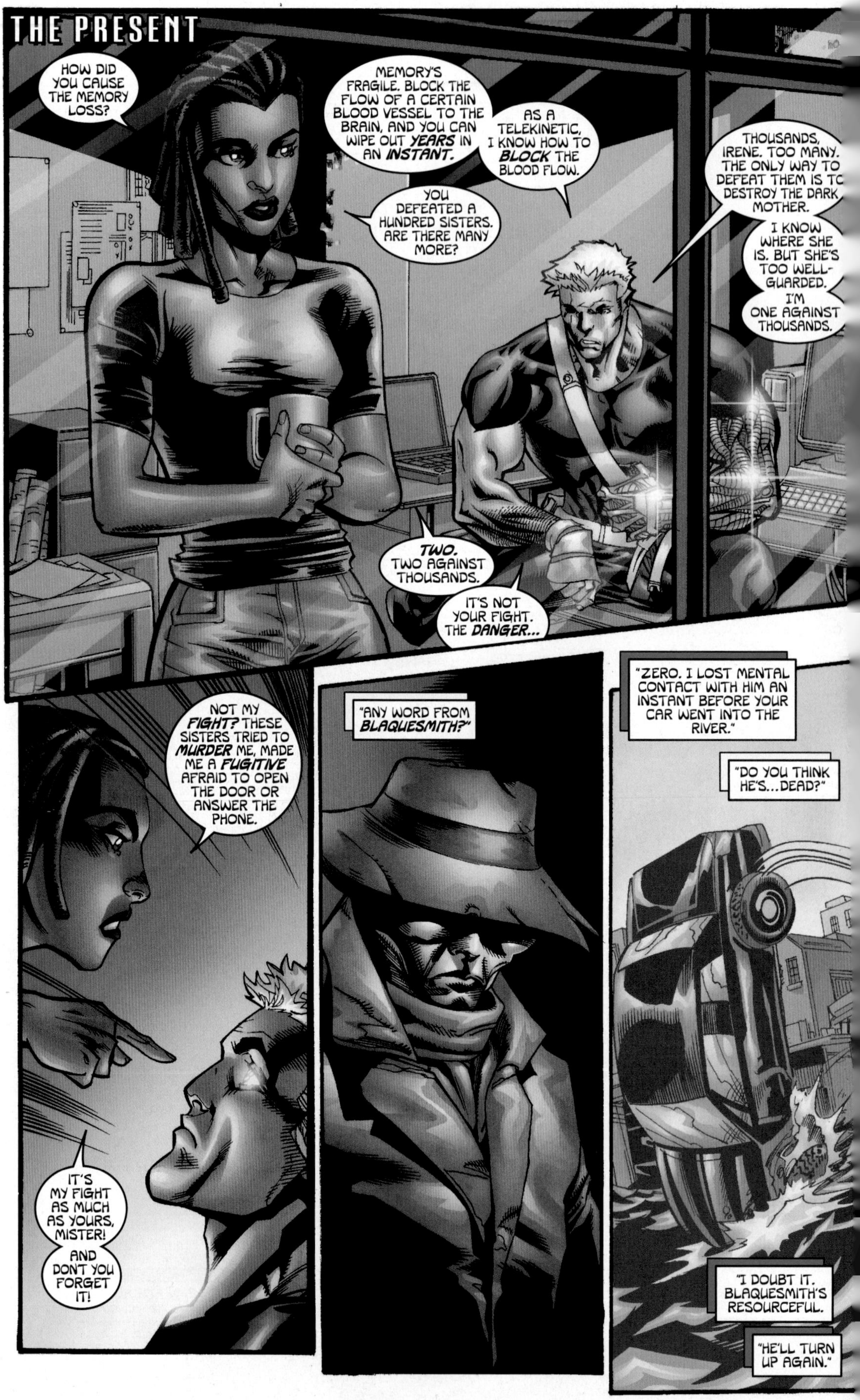
THE PRESENT
HOW DID YOU CAUSE THE MEMORY LOSS?
MEMORY'S FRAGILE. BLOCK THE FLOW OF A CERTAIN BLOOD VESSEL TO THE BRAIN, AND YOU CAN WIPE OUT YEARS IN AN INSTANT.
AS A TELEKINETIC, I KNOW HOW TO BLOCK THE BLOOD FLOW.
YOU DEFEATED A HUNDRED SISTERS. ARE THERE MANY MORE?
THOUSANDS, IRENE. TOO MANY. THE ONLY WAY TO DEFEAT THEM IS TO DESTROY THE DARK MOTHER.
I KNOW WHERE SHE IS. BUT SHE'S TOO WELL-GUARDED.
I'M ONE AGAINST THOUSANDS.
TWO. TWO AGAINST THOUSANDS.
IT'S NOT YOUR FIGHT. THE DANGER...
NOT MY FIGHT? THESE SISTERS TRIED TO MURDER ME, MADE ME A FUGITIVE AFRAID TO OPEN THE DOOR OR ANSWER THE PHONE.
IT'S MY FIGHT AS MUCH AS YOURS, MISTER!
AND DON'T YOU FORGET IT!
"ANY WORD FROM BLAQUESMITH?"
"ZERO. I LOST MENTAL CONTACT WITH HIM AN INSTANT BEFORE YOUR CAR WENT INTO THE RIVER."
"DO YOU THINK HE'S...DEAD?"
"I DOUBT IT. BLAQUESMITH'S RESOURCEFUL.
"HE'LL TURN UP AGAIN."

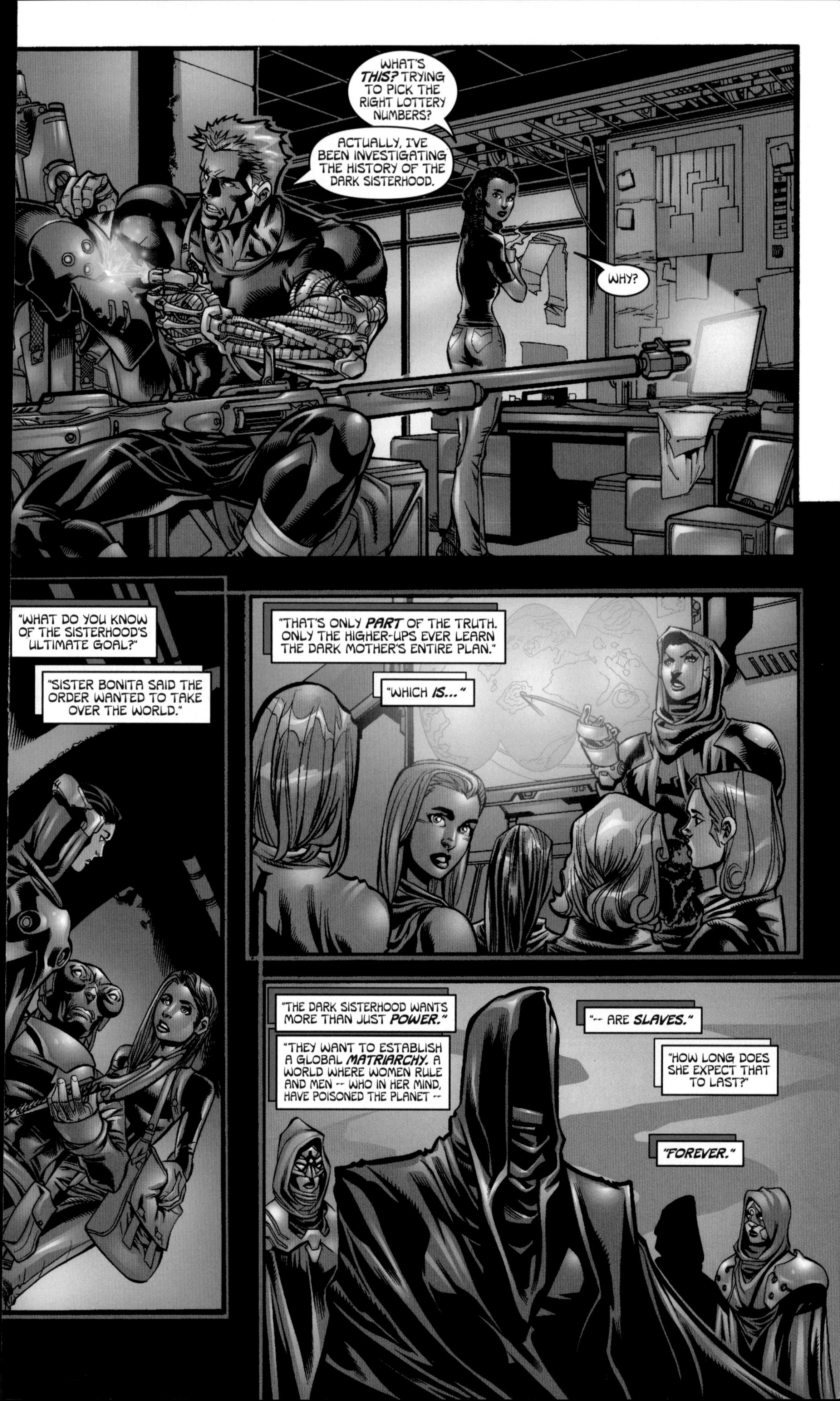
WHAT'S THIS? TRYING TO PICK THE RIGHT LOTTERY NUMBERS?
ACTUALLY, I'VE BEEN INVESTIGATING THE HISTORY OF THE DARK SISTERHOOD.
WHY?
"WHAT DO YOU KNOW OF THE SISTERHOOD'S ULTIMATE GOAL?"
"SISTER BONITA SAID THE ORDER WANTED TO TAKE OVER THE WORLD."
"THAT'S ONLY PART OF THE TRUTH. ONLY THE HIGHER-UPS EVER LEARN THE DARK MOTHER'S ENTIRE PLAN."
"WHICH IS..."
"THE DARK SISTERHOOD WANTS MORE THAN JUST POWER."
"THEY WANT TO ESTABLISH A GLOBAL MATRIARCHY. A WORLD WHERE WOMEN RULE AND MEN -- WHO IN HER MIND, HAVE POISONED THE PLANET --
"-- ARE SLAVES."
"HOW LONG DOES SHE EXPECT THAT TO LAST?"
"FOREVER."

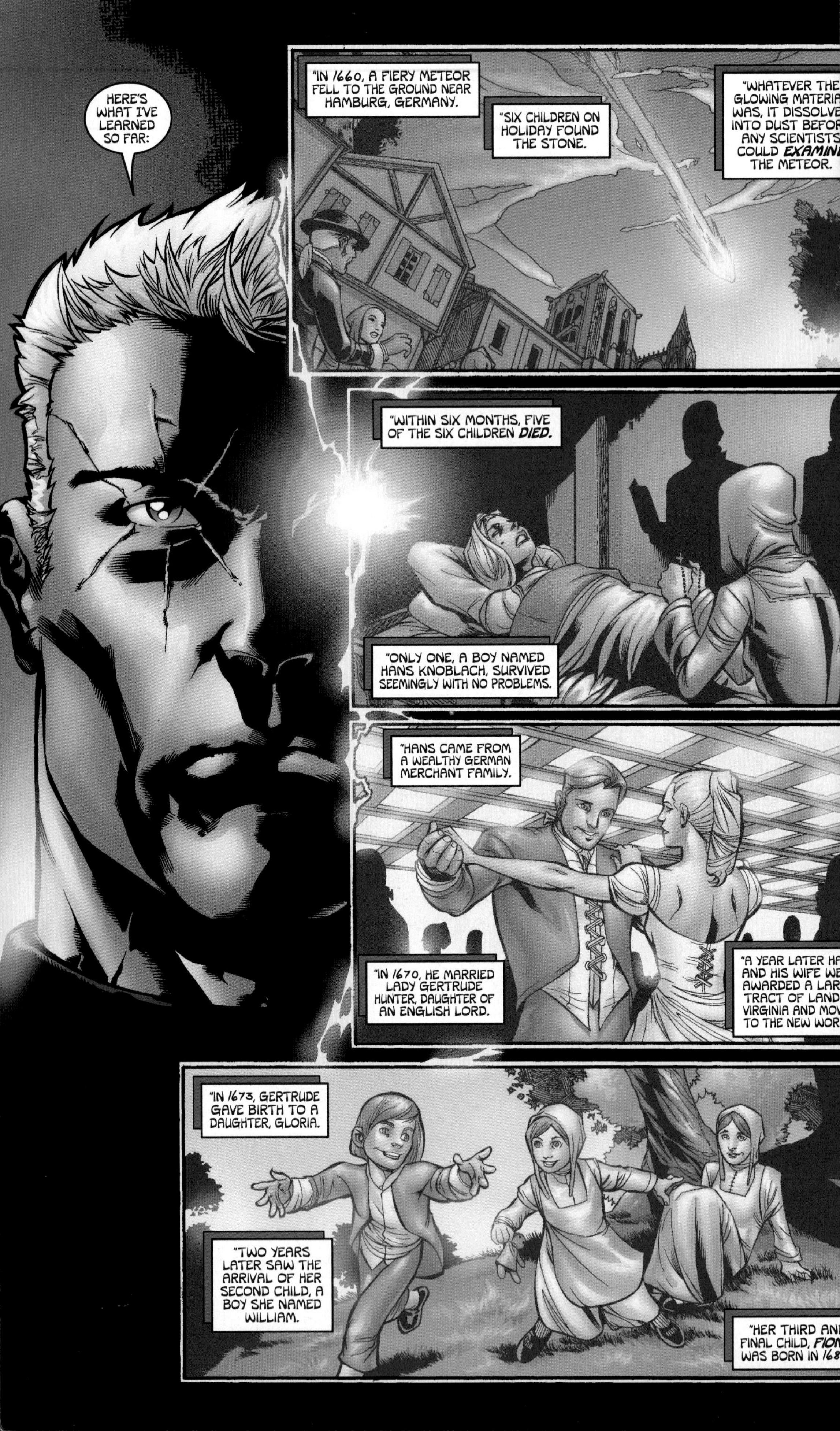
HERE'S WHAT I'VE LEARNED SO FAR:
"IN 1660, A FIERY METEOR FELL TO THE GROUND NEAR HAMBURG, GERMANY.
"SIX CHILDREN ON HOLIDAY FOUND THE STONE.
"WHATEVER THE GLOWING MATERIA WAS, IT DISSOLVE INTO DUST BEFOR ANY SCIENTISTS COULD EXAMINE THE METEOR.
"WITHIN SIX MONTHS, FIVE OF THE SIX CHILDREN DIED.
"ONLY ONE, A BOY NAMED HANS KNOBLACH, SURVIVED SEEMINGLY WITH NO PROBLEMS.
"HANS CAME FROM A WEALTHY GERMAN MERCHANT FAMILY.
"IN 1670, HE MARRIED LADY GERTRUDE HUNTER, DAUGHTER OF AN ENGLISH LORD.
"A YEAR LATER HA AND HIS WIFE WE AWARDED A LAR TRACT OF LAND VIRGINIA AND MOV TO THE NEW WOR
"IN 1673, GERTRUDE GAVE BIRTH TO A DAUGHTER, GLORIA.
"TWO YEARS LATER SAW THE ARRIVAL OF HER SECOND CHILD, A BOY SHE NAMED WILLIAM.
"HER THIRD AN FINAL CHILD, FION WAS BORN IN 168

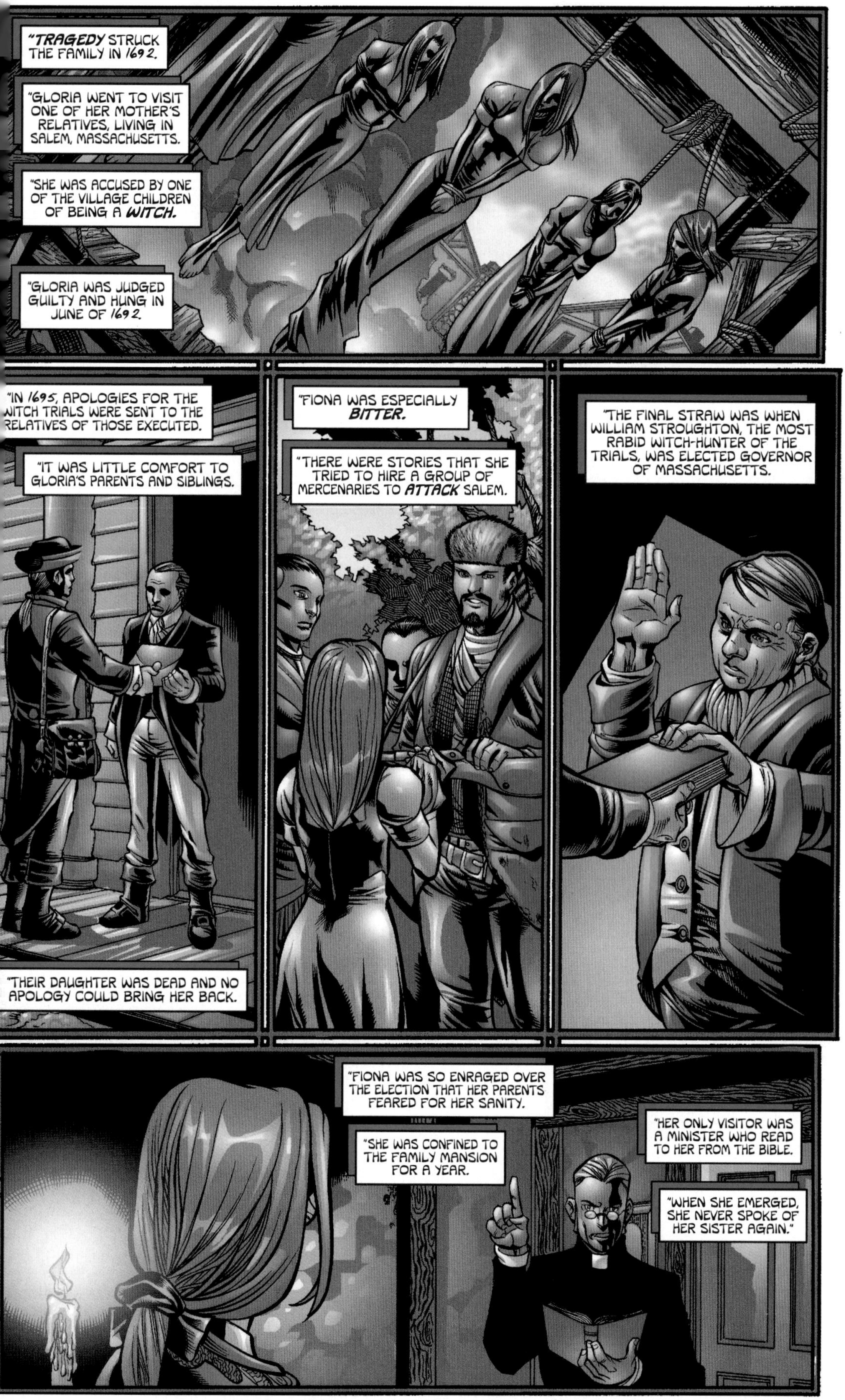
"TRAGEDY STRUCK THE FAMILY IN 1692.
"GLORIA WENT TO VISIT ONE OF HER MOTHER'S RELATIVES, LIVING IN SALEM, MASSACHUSETTS.
"SHE WAS ACCUSED BY ONE OF THE VILLAGE CHILDREN OF BEING A WITCH.
"GLORIA WAS JUDGED GUILTY AND HUNG IN JUNE OF 1692.
"IN 1695, APOLOGIES FOR THE WITCH TRIALS WERE SENT TO THE RELATIVES OF THOSE EXECUTED.
"IT WAS LITTLE COMFORT TO GLORIA'S PARENTS AND SIBLINGS.
"THEIR DAUGHTER WAS DEAD AND NO APOLOGY COULD BRING HER BACK.
"FIONA WAS ESPECIALLY BITTER.
"THERE WERE STORIES THAT SHE TRIED TO HIRE A GROUP OF MERCENARIES TO ATTACK SALEM.
"THE FINAL STRAW WAS WHEN WILLIAM STROUGHTON, THE MOST RABID WITCH-HUNTER OF THE TRIALS, WAS ELECTED GOVERNOR OF MASSACHUSETTS.
"FIONA WAS SO ENRAGED OVER THE ELECTION THAT HER PARENTS FEARED FOR HER SANITY.
"SHE WAS CONFINED TO THE FAMILY MANSION FOR A YEAR.
"HER ONLY VISITOR WAS A MINISTER WHO READ TO HER FROM THE BIBLE.
"WHEN SHE EMERGED, SHE NEVER SPOKE OF HER SISTER AGAIN."

VERY INTERESTING. BUT WHAT DOES THIS HAVE TO DO WITH THE DARK SISTERHOOD?

BE PATIENT.

"IN 1700, WILLIAM TRAVELED TO EUROPE ON A BUSINESS TRIP, SELLING TOBACCO FOR HIS FATHER.

"HE NEVER RETURNED. RUMORS HAD IT THAT HE WAS STUDYING THE OCCULT IN INDIA OR TIBET.

"DURING THAT PERIOD, HE CHANGED HIS NAME TO *'CLARITY.'*

"IN 1705, HANS AND GERTRUDE DIED IN A FAMILY BOATING ACCIDENT. ONLY FIONA SURVIVED.

"SHE INHERITED AN ESTATE WORTH MILLIONS.

"NEWSPAPERS DESCRIBED HER AS INCREDIBLY BEAUTIFUL AND EXTREMELY STRONG-WILLED.

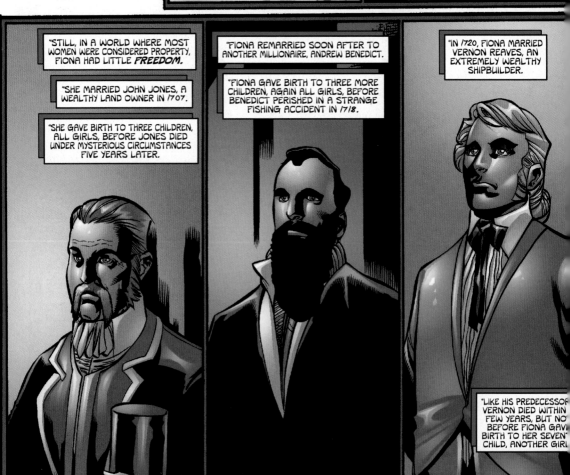

"STILL, IN A WORLD WHERE MOST WOMEN WERE CONSIDERED PROPERTY, FIONA HAD LITTLE *FREEDOM.*

"SHE MARRIED JOHN JONES, A WEALTHY LAND OWNER IN 1707.

"SHE GAVE BIRTH TO THREE CHILDREN, ALL GIRLS, BEFORE JONES DIED UNDER MYSTERIOUS CIRCUMSTANCES FIVE YEARS LATER.

"FIONA REMARRIED SOON AFTER TO ANOTHER MILLIONAIRE, ANDREW BENEDICT.

"FIONA GAVE BIRTH TO THREE MORE CHILDREN, AGAIN ALL GIRLS, BEFORE BENEDICT PERISHED IN A STRANGE FISHING ACCIDENT IN 1718.

"IN 1720, FIONA MARRIED VERNON REAVES, AN EXTREMELY WEALTHY SHIPBUILDER.

"LIKE HIS PREDECESSOR VERNON DIED WITHIN A FEW YEARS, BUT NO BEFORE FIONA GAVE BIRTH TO HER SEVENTH CHILD, ANOTHER GIRL

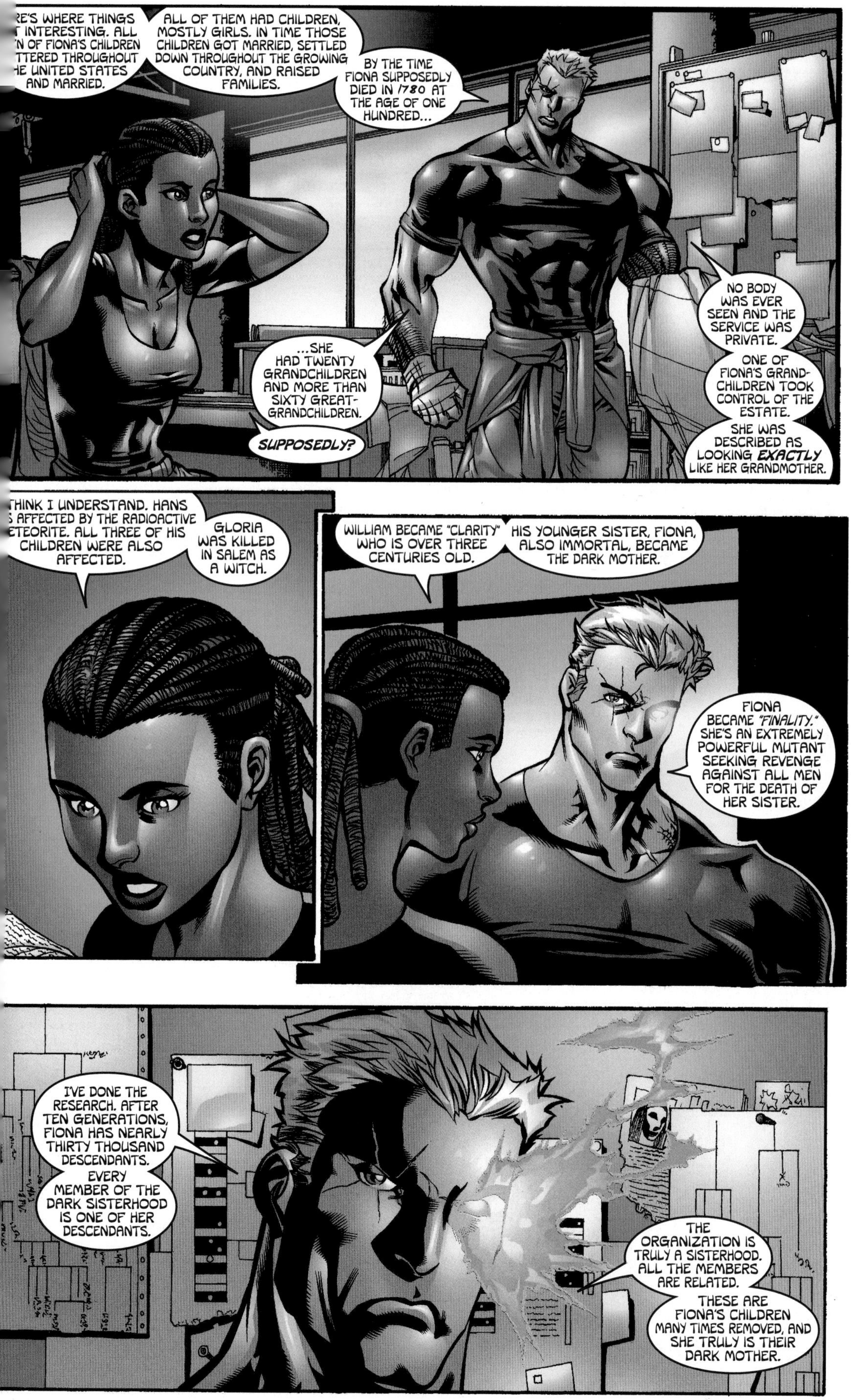

RE'S WHERE THINGS T INTERESTING. ALL N OF FIONA'S CHILDREN TTERED THROUGHOUT HE UNITED STATES AND MARRIED.
ALL OF THEM HAD CHILDREN, MOSTLY GIRLS. IN TIME THOSE CHILDREN GOT MARRIED, SETTLED DOWN THROUGHOUT THE GROWING COUNTRY, AND RAISED FAMILIES.
BY THE TIME FIONA SUPPOSEDLY DIED IN 1780 AT THE AGE OF ONE HUNDRED...
...SHE HAD TWENTY GRANDCHILDREN AND MORE THAN SIXTY GREAT-GRANDCHILDREN.
SUPPOSEDLY?
NO BODY WAS EVER SEEN AND THE SERVICE WAS PRIVATE.
ONE OF FIONA'S GRAND-CHILDREN TOOK CONTROL OF THE ESTATE.
SHE WAS DESCRIBED AS LOOKING EXACTLY LIKE HER GRANDMOTHER.
THINK I UNDERSTAND. HANS S AFFECTED BY THE RADIOACTIVE ETEORITE. ALL THREE OF HIS CHILDREN WERE ALSO AFFECTED.
GLORIA WAS KILLED IN SALEM AS A WITCH.
WILLIAM BECAME "CLARITY" WHO IS OVER THREE CENTURIES OLD.
HIS YOUNGER SISTER, FIONA, ALSO IMMORTAL, BECAME THE DARK MOTHER.
FIONA BECAME "FINALITY." SHE'S AN EXTREMELY POWERFUL MUTANT SEEKING REVENGE AGAINST ALL MEN FOR THE DEATH OF HER SISTER.
I'VE DONE THE RESEARCH. AFTER TEN GENERATIONS, FIONA HAS NEARLY THIRTY THOUSAND DESCENDANTS.
EVERY MEMBER OF THE DARK SISTERHOOD IS ONE OF HER DESCENDANTS.
THE ORGANIZATION IS TRULY A SISTERHOOD. ALL THE MEMBERS ARE RELATED.
THESE ARE FIONA'S CHILDREN MANY TIMES REMOVED, AND SHE TRULY IS THEIR DARK MOTHER.

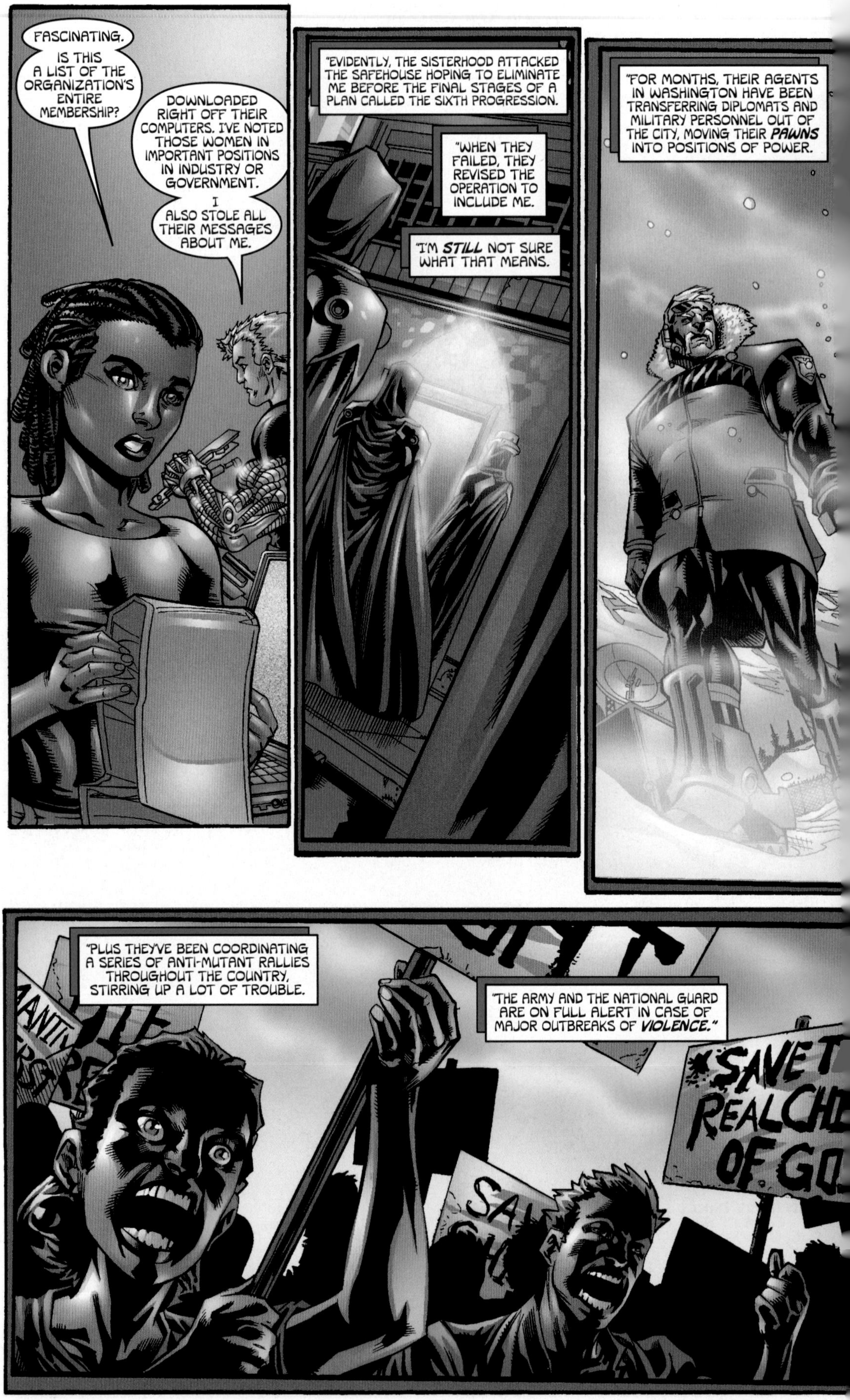

FASCINATING. IS THIS A LIST OF THE ORGANIZATION'S ENTIRE MEMBERSHIP?
DOWNLOADED RIGHT OFF THEIR COMPUTERS. I'VE NOTED THOSE WOMEN IN IMPORTANT POSITIONS IN INDUSTRY OR GOVERNMENT.
I ALSO STOLE ALL THEIR MESSAGES ABOUT ME.
"EVIDENTLY, THE SISTERHOOD ATTACKED THE SAFEHOUSE HOPING TO ELIMINATE ME BEFORE THE FINAL STAGES OF A PLAN CALLED THE SIXTH PROGRESSION.
"WHEN THEY FAILED, THEY REVISED THE OPERATION TO INCLUDE ME.
"I'M STILL NOT SURE WHAT THAT MEANS.
"FOR MONTHS, THEIR AGENTS IN WASHINGTON HAVE BEEN TRANSFERRING DIPLOMATS AND MILITARY PERSONNEL OUT OF THE CITY, MOVING THEIR PAWNS INTO POSITIONS OF POWER.
"PLUS THEY'VE BEEN COORDINATING A SERIES OF ANTI-MUTANT RALLIES THROUGHOUT THE COUNTRY, STIRRING UP A LOT OF TROUBLE.
"THE ARMY AND THE NATIONAL GUARD ARE ON FULL ALERT IN CASE OF MAJOR OUTBREAKS OF VIOLENCE."
SAVE T
REALCH
OF GO

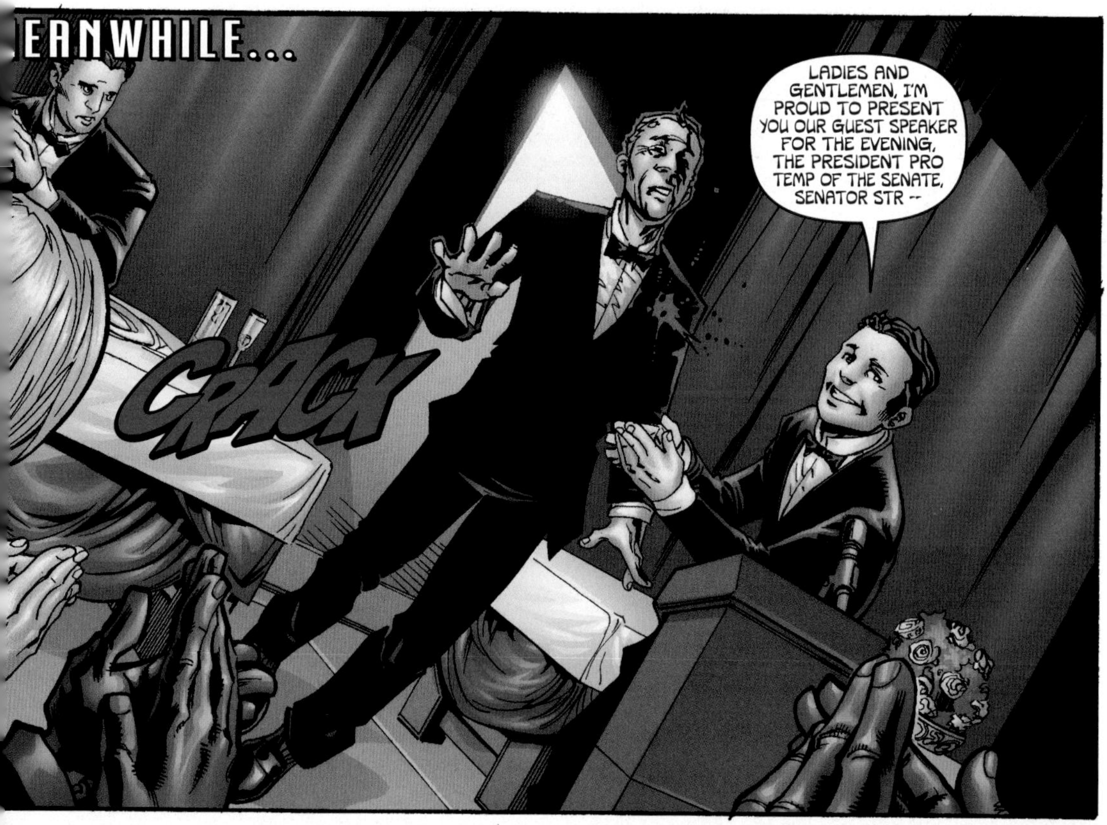
EANWHILE...
LADIES AND GENTLEMEN, I'M PROUD TO PRESENT YOU OUR GUEST SPEAKER FOR THE EVENING, THE PRESIDENT PRO TEMP OF THE SENATE, SENATOR STR --
CRACK

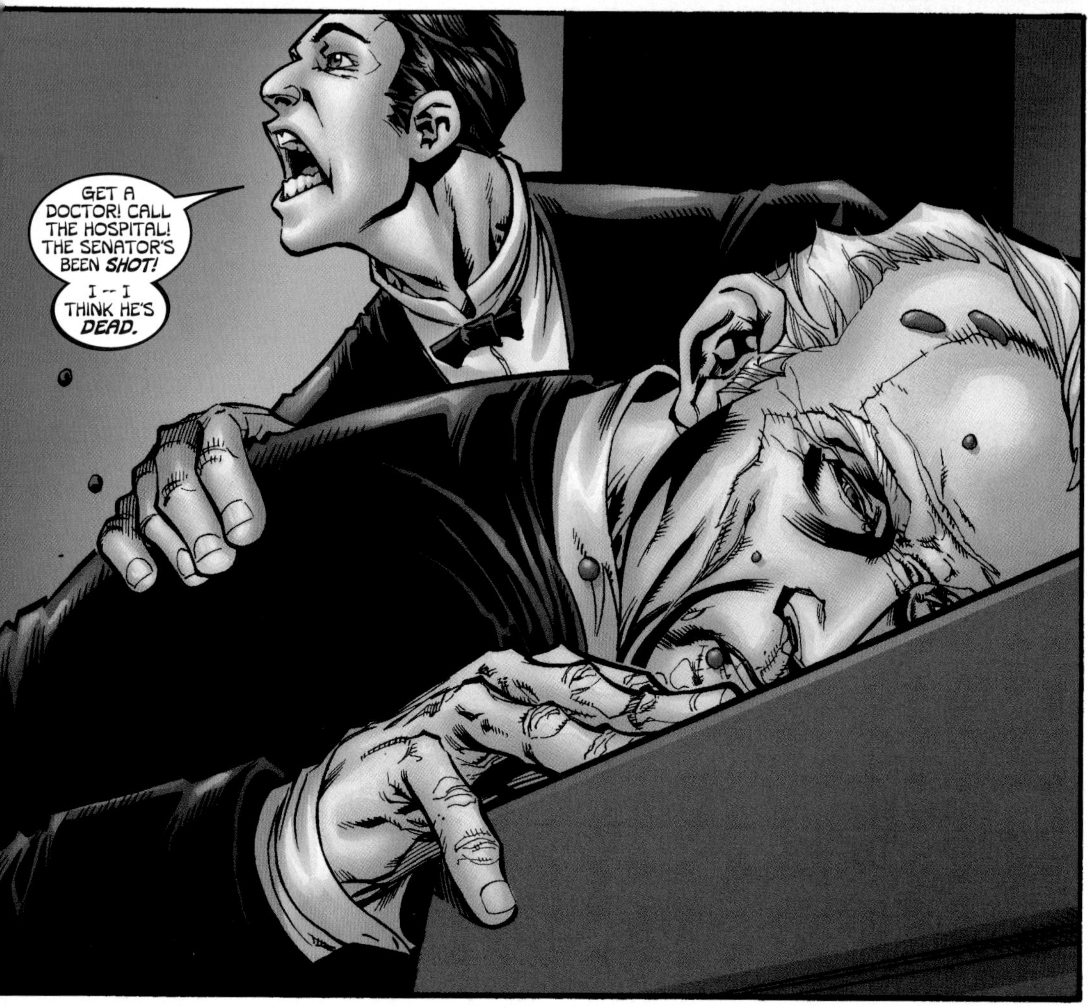
GET A DOCTOR! CALL THE HOSPITAL! THE SENATOR'S BEEN SHOT!
I -- I THINK HE'S DEAD.

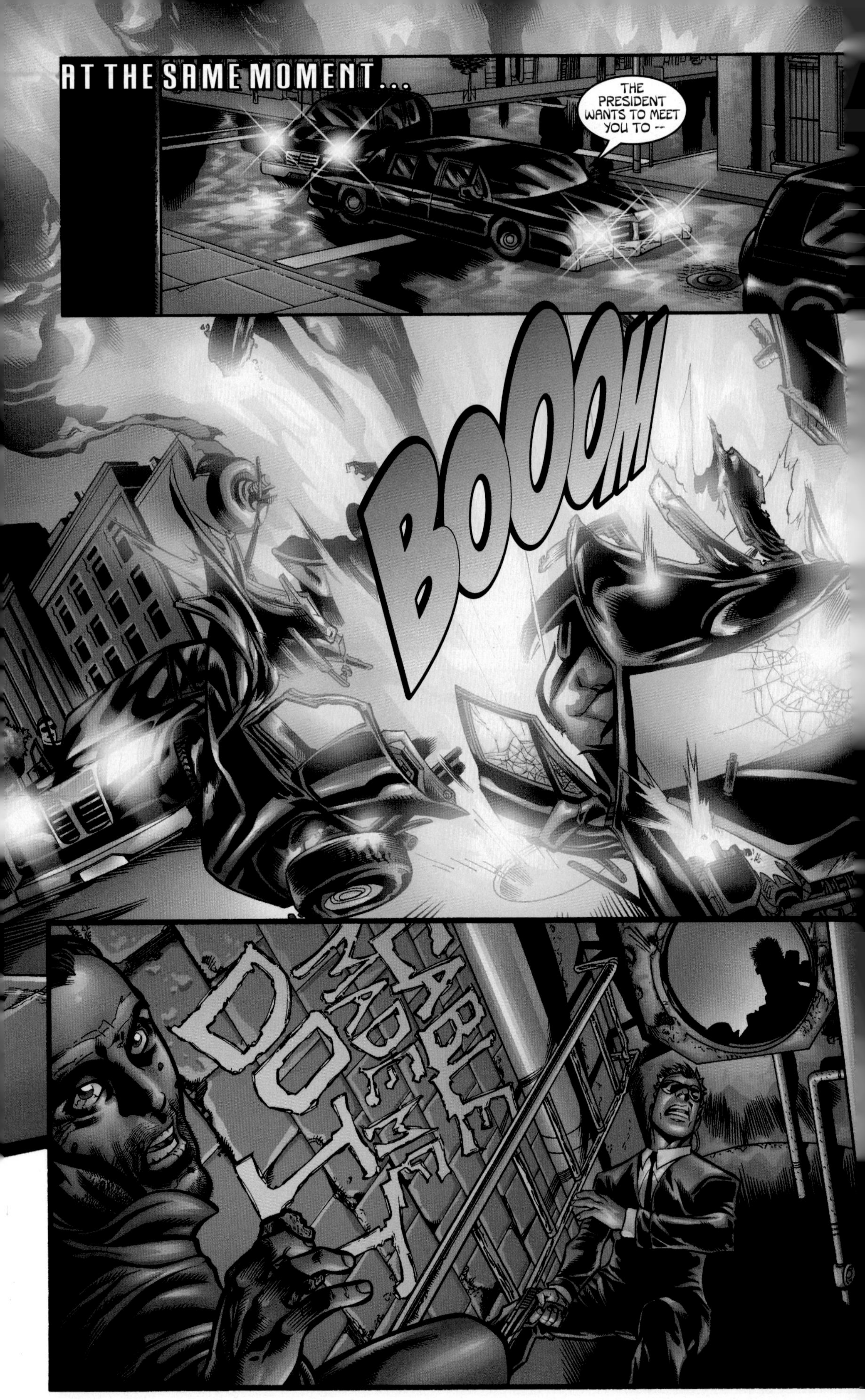
AT THE SAME MOMENT...
THE PRESIDENT WANTS TO MEET YOU TO --
BOOOM
CABLE MADE ME DO IT

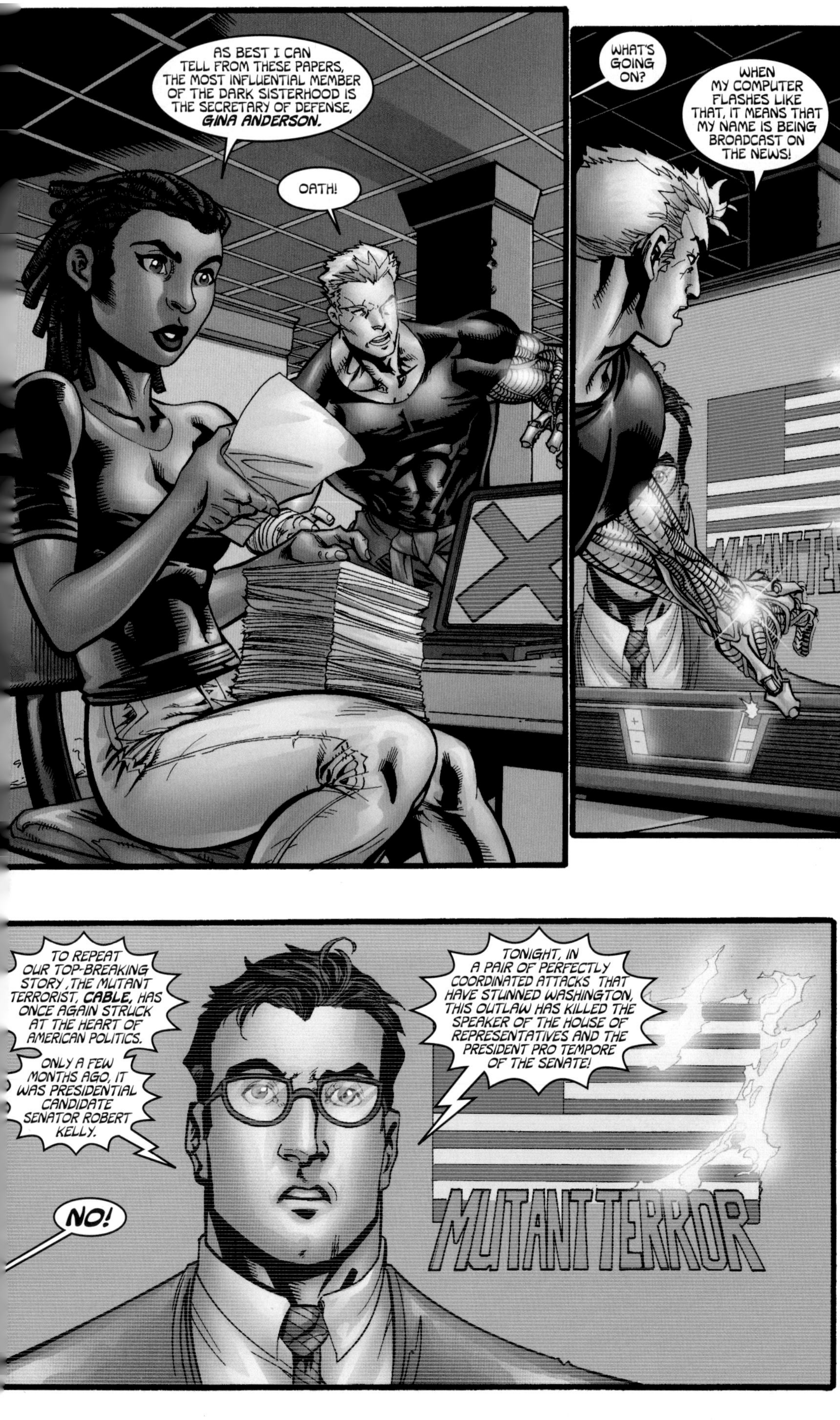
AS BEST I CAN TELL FROM THESE PAPERS, THE MOST INFLUENTIAL MEMBER OF THE DARK SISTERHOOD IS THE SECRETARY OF DEFENSE, **GINA ANDERSON.**
OATH!
WHAT'S GOING ON?
WHEN MY COMPUTER FLASHES LIKE THAT, IT MEANS THAT MY NAME IS BEING BROADCAST ON THE NEWS!
MUTANT TER
TO REPEAT OUR TOP-BREAKING STORY ,THE MUTANT TERRORIST, **CABLE,** HAS ONCE AGAIN STRUCK AT THE HEART OF AMERICAN POLITICS.
ONLY A FEW MONTHS AGO, IT WAS PRESIDENTIAL CANDIDATE SENATOR ROBERT KELLY.
TONIGHT, IN A PAIR OF PERFECTLY COORDINATED ATTACKS THAT HAVE STUNNED WASHINGTON, THIS OUTLAW HAS KILLED THE SPEAKER OF THE HOUSE OF REPRESENTATIVES AND THE PRESIDENT PRO TEMPORE OF THE SENATE!
NO!
MUTANT TERROR

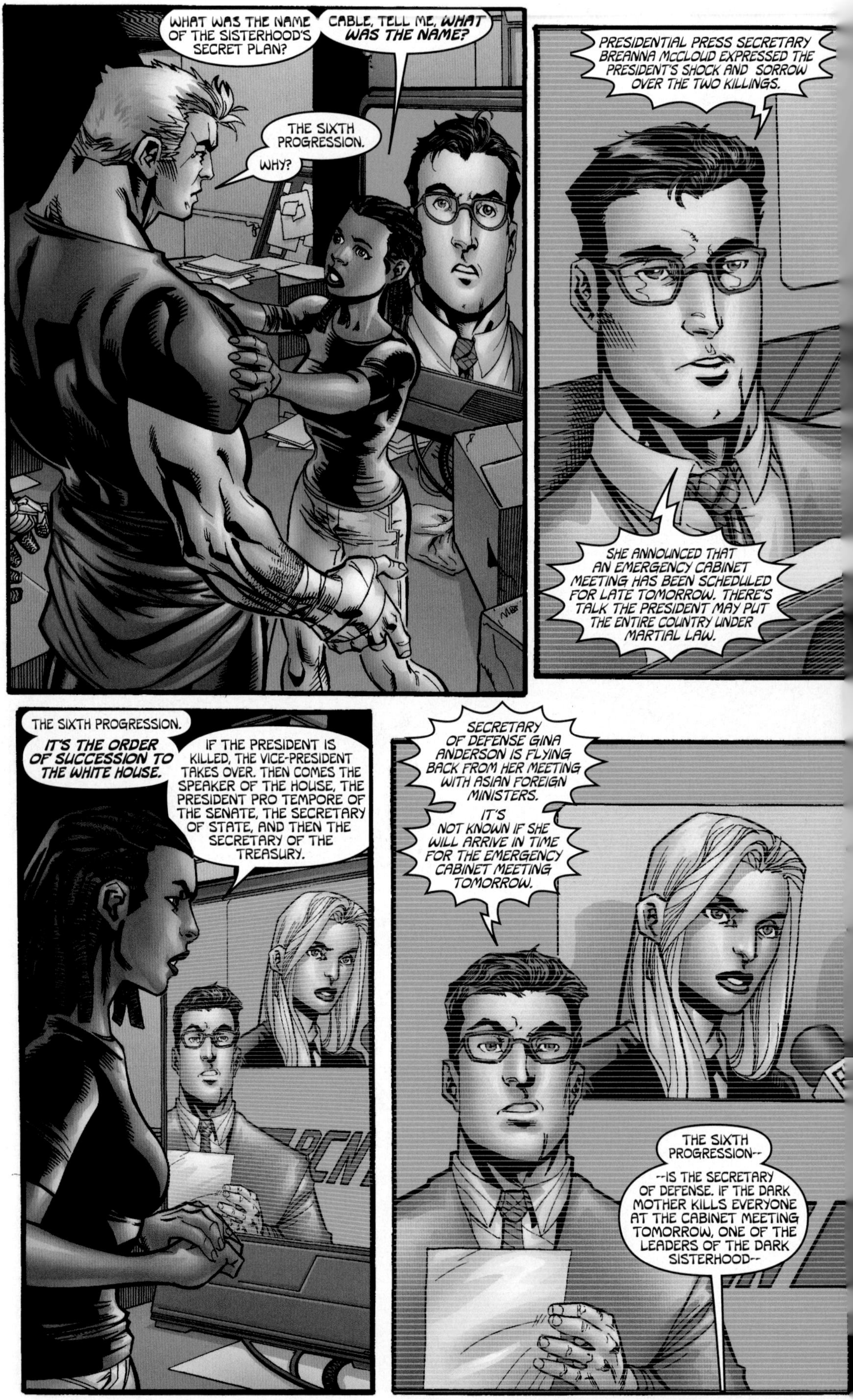
WHAT WAS THE NAME OF THE SISTERHOOD'S SECRET PLAN?
CABLE, TELL ME, WHAT WAS THE NAME?
THE SIXTH PROGRESSION.
WHY?
PRESIDENTIAL PRESS SECRETARY BREANNA McCLOUD EXPRESSED THE PRESIDENT'S SHOCK AND SORROW OVER THE TWO KILLINGS.
SHE ANNOUNCED THAT AN EMERGENCY CABINET MEETING HAS BEEN SCHEDULED FOR LATE TOMORROW. THERE'S TALK THE PRESIDENT MAY PUT THE ENTIRE COUNTRY UNDER MARTIAL LAW.
THE SIXTH PROGRESSION.
IT'S THE ORDER OF SUCCESSION TO THE WHITE HOUSE.
IF THE PRESIDENT IS KILLED, THE VICE-PRESIDENT TAKES OVER. THEN COMES THE SPEAKER OF THE HOUSE, THE PRESIDENT PRO TEMPORE OF THE SENATE, THE SECRETARY OF STATE, AND THEN THE SECRETARY OF THE TREASURY.
SECRETARY OF DEFENSE GINA ANDERSON IS FLYING BACK FROM HER MEETING WITH ASIAN FOREIGN MINISTERS.
IT'S NOT KNOWN IF SHE WILL ARRIVE IN TIME FOR THE EMERGENCY CABINET MEETING TOMORROW.
THE SIXTH PROGRESSION--
--IS THE SECRETARY OF DEFENSE. IF THE DARK MOTHER KILLS EVERYONE AT THE CABINET MEETING TOMORROW, ONE OF THE LEADERS OF THE DARK SISTERHOOD--

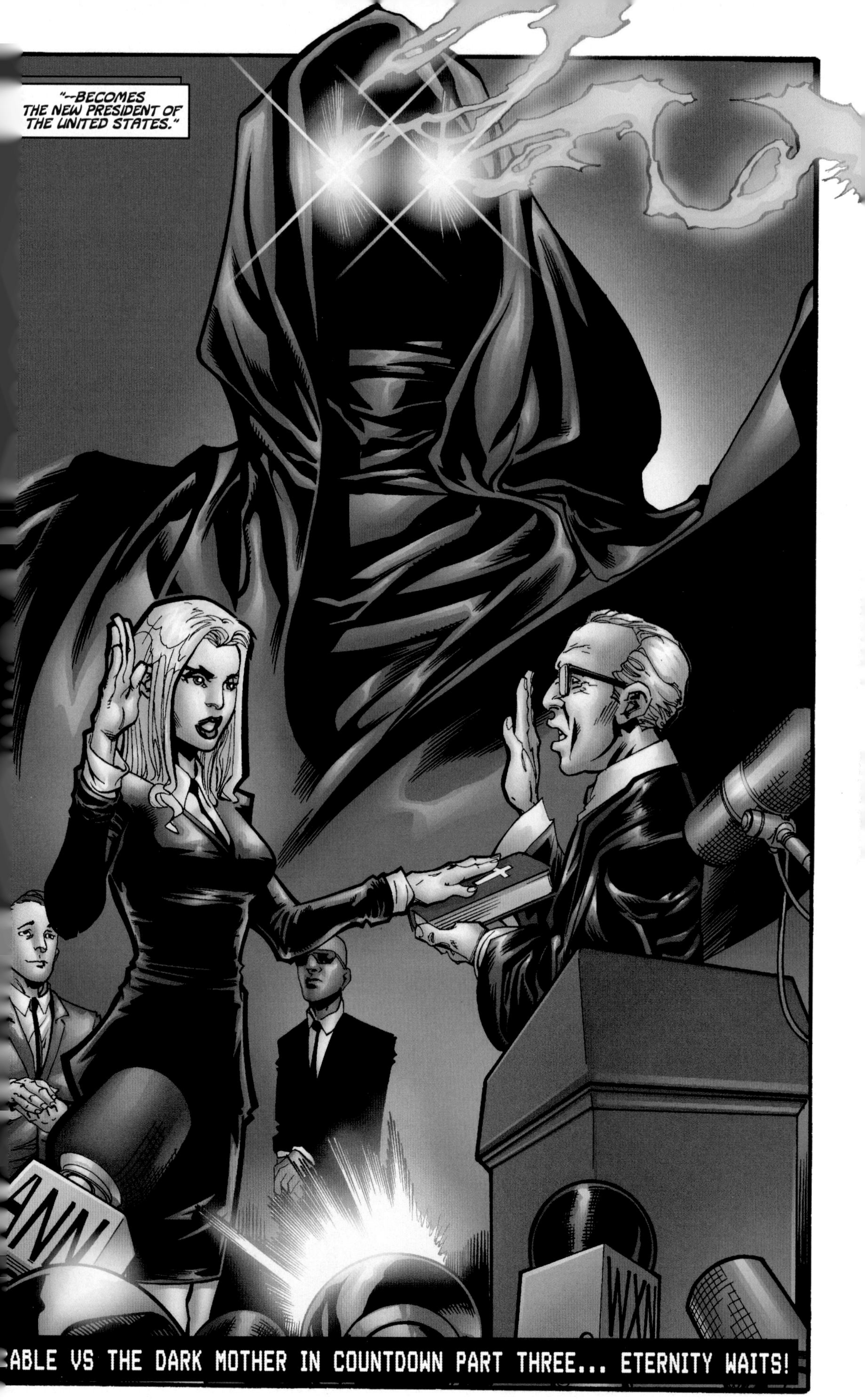
"--BECOMES THE NEW PRESIDENT OF THE UNITED STATES."
ANN
WXN
ABLE VS THE DARK MOTHER IN COUNTDOWN PART THREE... ETERNITY WAITS!

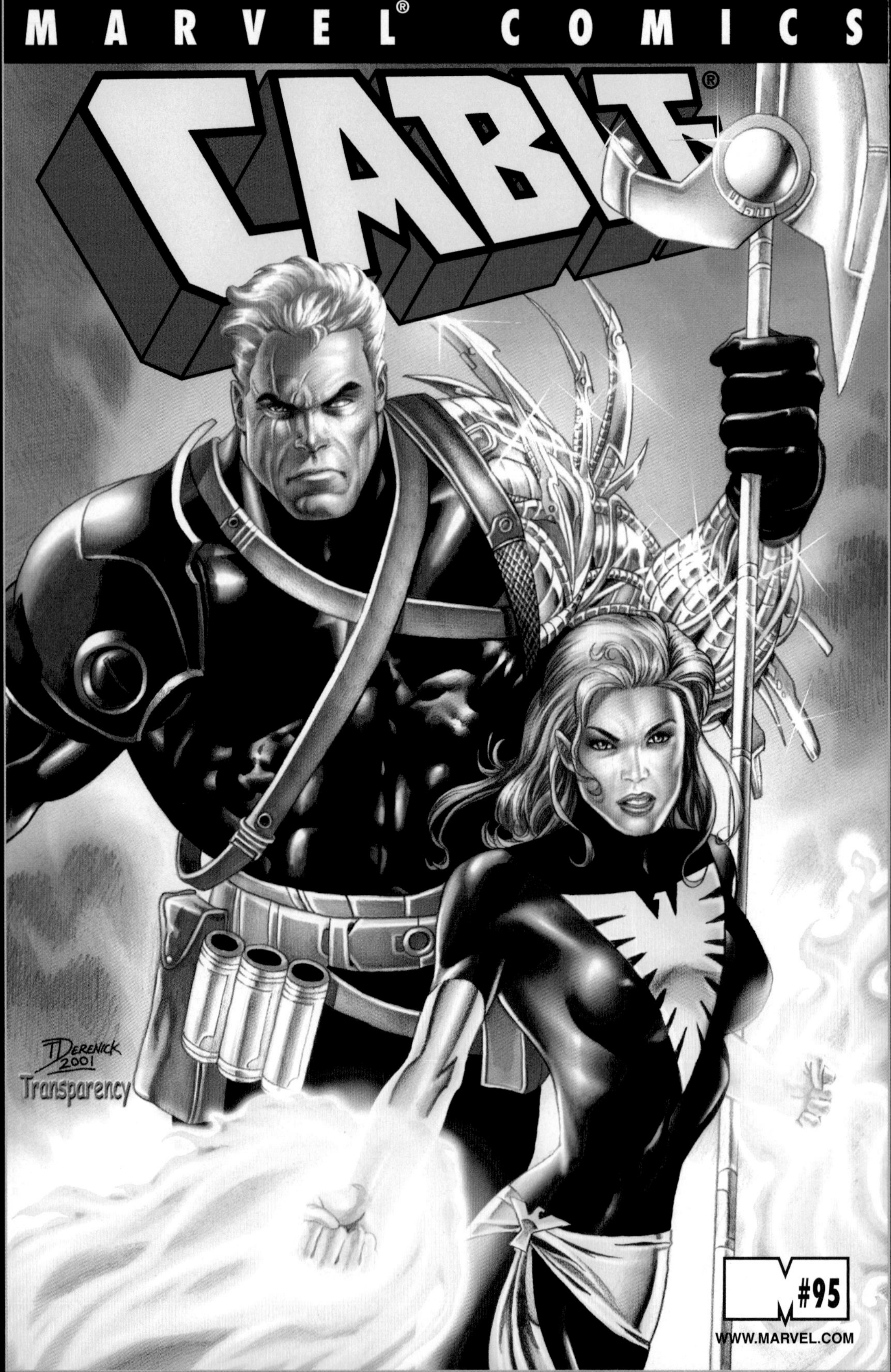
MARVEL COMICS
T DERENICK 2001
Transparency
#95
WWW.MARVEL.COM

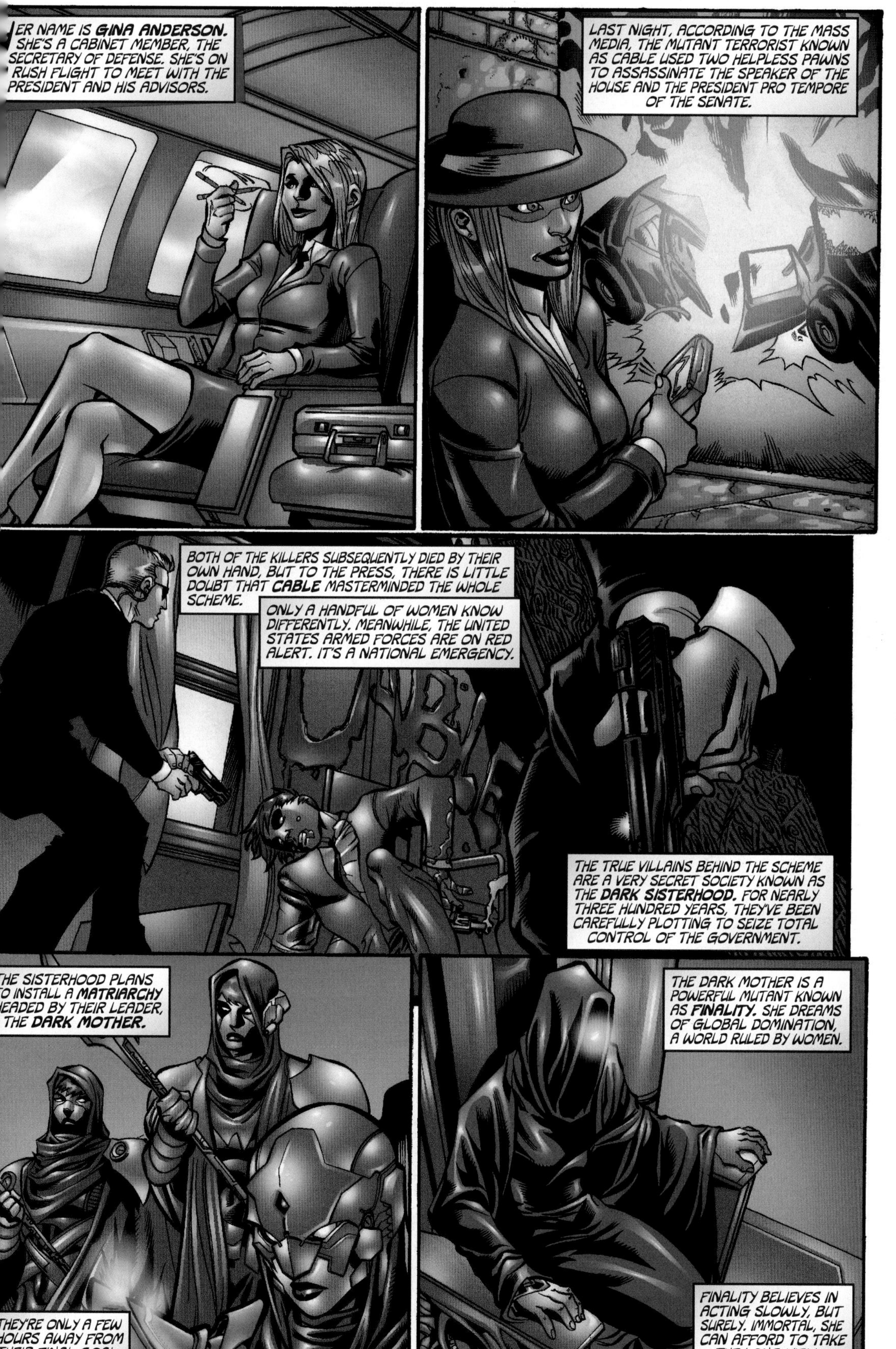

ER NAME IS GINA ANDERSON. SHE'S A CABINET MEMBER, THE SECRETARY OF DEFENSE. SHE'S ON RUSH FLIGHT TO MEET WITH THE PRESIDENT AND HIS ADVISORS.
LAST NIGHT, ACCORDING TO THE MASS MEDIA, THE MUTANT TERRORIST KNOWN AS CABLE USED TWO HELPLESS PAWNS TO ASSASSINATE THE SPEAKER OF THE HOUSE AND THE PRESIDENT PRO TEMPORE OF THE SENATE.
BOTH OF THE KILLERS SUBSEQUENTLY DIED BY THEIR OWN HAND, BUT TO THE PRESS, THERE IS LITTLE DOUBT THAT CABLE MASTERMINDED THE WHOLE SCHEME.
ONLY A HANDFUL OF WOMEN KNOW DIFFERENTLY. MEANWHILE, THE UNITED STATES ARMED FORCES ARE ON RED ALERT. IT'S A NATIONAL EMERGENCY.
THE TRUE VILLAINS BEHIND THE SCHEME ARE A VERY SECRET SOCIETY KNOWN AS THE DARK SISTERHOOD. FOR NEARLY THREE HUNDRED YEARS, THEY'VE BEEN CAREFULLY PLOTTING TO SEIZE TOTAL CONTROL OF THE GOVERNMENT.
THE SISTERHOOD PLANS TO INSTALL A MATRIARCHY HEADED BY THEIR LEADER, THE DARK MOTHER.
THEY'RE ONLY A FEW HOURS AWAY FROM THEIR FINAL GOAL.
THE DARK MOTHER IS A POWERFUL MUTANT KNOWN AS FINALITY. SHE DREAMS OF GLOBAL DOMINATION, A WORLD RULED BY WOMEN.
FINALITY BELIEVES IN ACTING SLOWLY, BUT SURELY. IMMORTAL, SHE CAN AFFORD TO TAKE THE LONG VIEW.

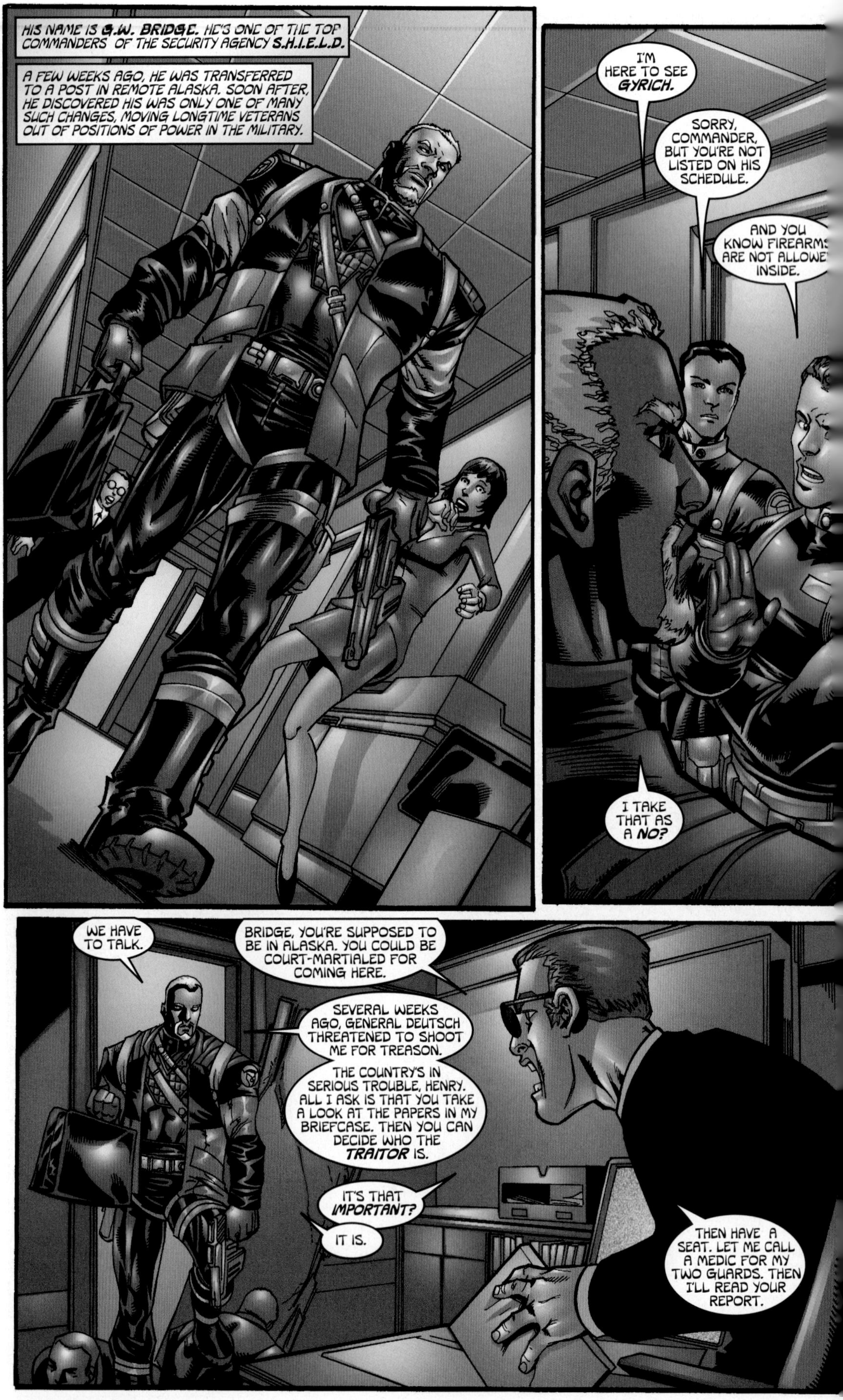
HIS NAME IS G.W. BRIDGE. HE'S ONE OF THE TOP COMMANDERS OF THE SECURITY AGENCY S.H.I.E.L.D.
A FEW WEEKS AGO, HE WAS TRANSFERRED TO A POST IN REMOTE ALASKA. SOON AFTER, HE DISCOVERED HIS WAS ONLY ONE OF MANY SUCH CHANGES, MOVING LONGTIME VETERANS OUT OF POSITIONS OF POWER IN THE MILITARY.
I'M HERE TO SEE GYRICH.
SORRY, COMMANDER, BUT YOU'RE NOT LISTED ON HIS SCHEDULE.
AND YOU KNOW FIREARMS ARE NOT ALLOWE INSIDE.
I TAKE THAT AS A NO?
WE HAVE TO TALK.
BRIDGE, YOU'RE SUPPOSED TO BE IN ALASKA. YOU COULD BE COURT-MARTIALED FOR COMING HERE.
SEVERAL WEEKS AGO, GENERAL DEUTSCH THREATENED TO SHOOT ME FOR TREASON.
THE COUNTRY'S IN SERIOUS TROUBLE, HENRY. ALL I ASK IS THAT YOU TAKE A LOOK AT THE PAPERS IN MY BRIEFCASE. THEN YOU CAN DECIDE WHO THE TRAITOR IS.
IT'S THAT IMPORTANT?
IT IS.
THEN HAVE A SEAT. LET ME CALL A MEDIC FOR MY TWO GUARDS. THEN I'LL READ YOUR REPORT.

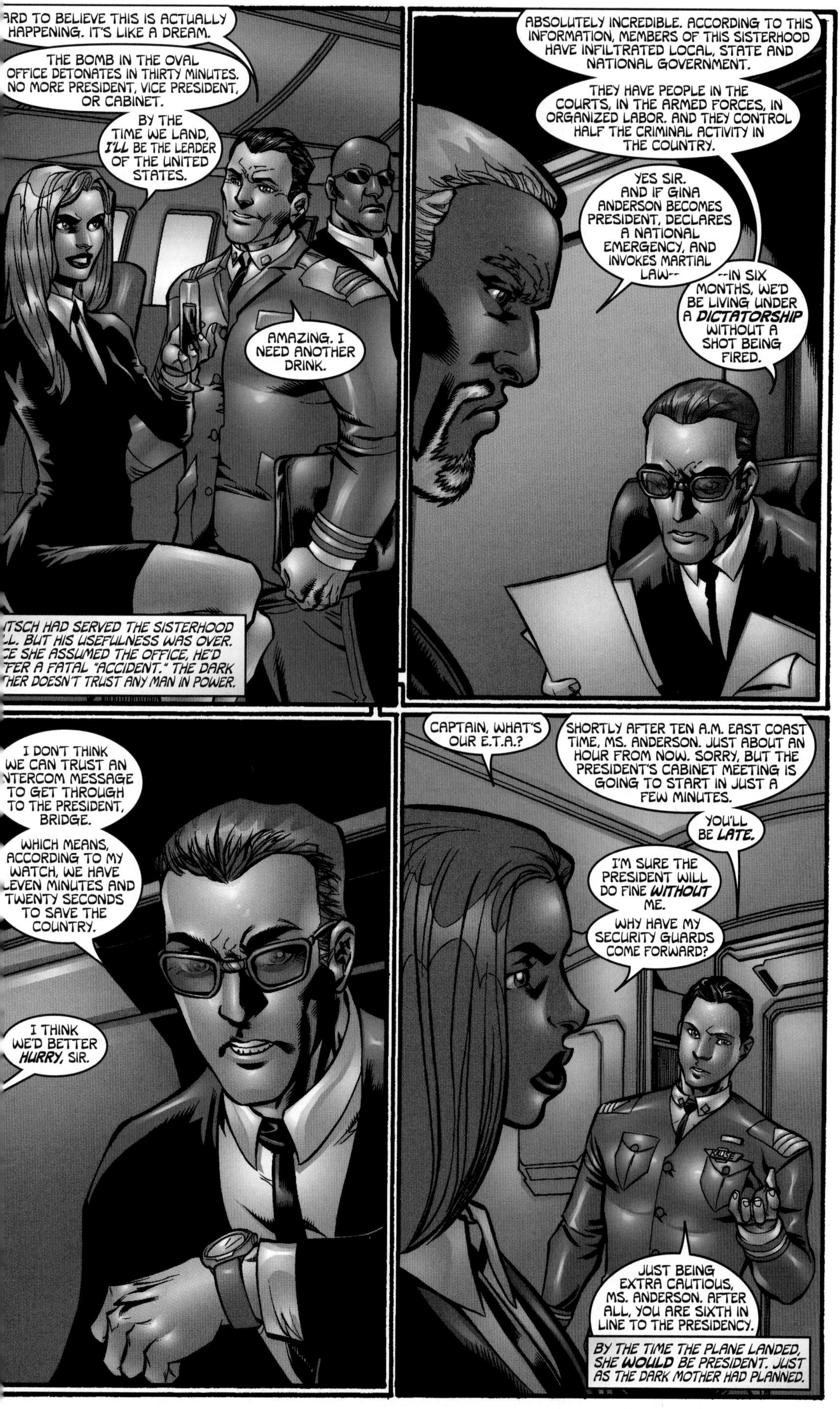
ARD TO BELIEVE THIS IS ACTUALLY HAPPENING. IT'S LIKE A DREAM.
THE BOMB IN THE OVAL OFFICE DETONATES IN THIRTY MINUTES. NO MORE PRESIDENT, VICE PRESIDENT, OR CABINET.
BY THE TIME WE LAND, I'LL BE THE LEADER OF THE UNITED STATES.
AMAZING. I NEED ANOTHER DRINK.
ITSCH HAD SERVED THE SISTERHOOD LL. BUT HIS USEFULNESS WAS OVER. CE SHE ASSUMED THE OFFICE, HE'D FER A FATAL "ACCIDENT." THE DARK THER DOESN'T TRUST ANY MAN IN POWER.
ABSOLUTELY INCREDIBLE. ACCORDING TO THIS INFORMATION, MEMBERS OF THIS SISTERHOOD HAVE INFILTRATED LOCAL, STATE AND NATIONAL GOVERNMENT.
THEY HAVE PEOPLE IN THE COURTS, IN THE ARMED FORCES, IN ORGANIZED LABOR. AND THEY CONTROL HALF THE CRIMINAL ACTIVITY IN THE COUNTRY.
YES SIR. AND IF GINA ANDERSON BECOMES PRESIDENT, DECLARES A NATIONAL EMERGENCY, AND INVOKES MARTIAL LAW--
--IN SIX MONTHS, WE'D BE LIVING UNDER A DICTATORSHIP WITHOUT A SHOT BEING FIRED.
I DON'T THINK WE CAN TRUST AN NTERCOM MESSAGE TO GET THROUGH TO THE PRESIDENT, BRIDGE.
WHICH MEANS, ACCORDING TO MY WATCH, WE HAVE LEVEN MINUTES AND TWENTY SECONDS TO SAVE THE COUNTRY.
I THINK WE'D BETTER HURRY, SIR.
CAPTAIN, WHAT'S OUR E.T.A.?
SHORTLY AFTER TEN A.M. EAST COAST TIME, MS. ANDERSON. JUST ABOUT AN HOUR FROM NOW. SORRY, BUT THE PRESIDENT'S CABINET MEETING IS GOING TO START IN JUST A FEW MINUTES.
YOU'LL BE LATE.
I'M SURE THE PRESIDENT WILL DO FINE WITHOUT ME.
WHY HAVE MY SECURITY GUARDS COME FORWARD?
JUST BEING EXTRA CAUTIOUS, MS. ANDERSON. AFTER ALL, YOU ARE SIXTH IN LINE TO THE PRESIDENCY.
BY THE TIME THE PLANE LANDED, SHE WOULD BE PRESIDENT. JUST AS THE DARK MOTHER HAD PLANNED.

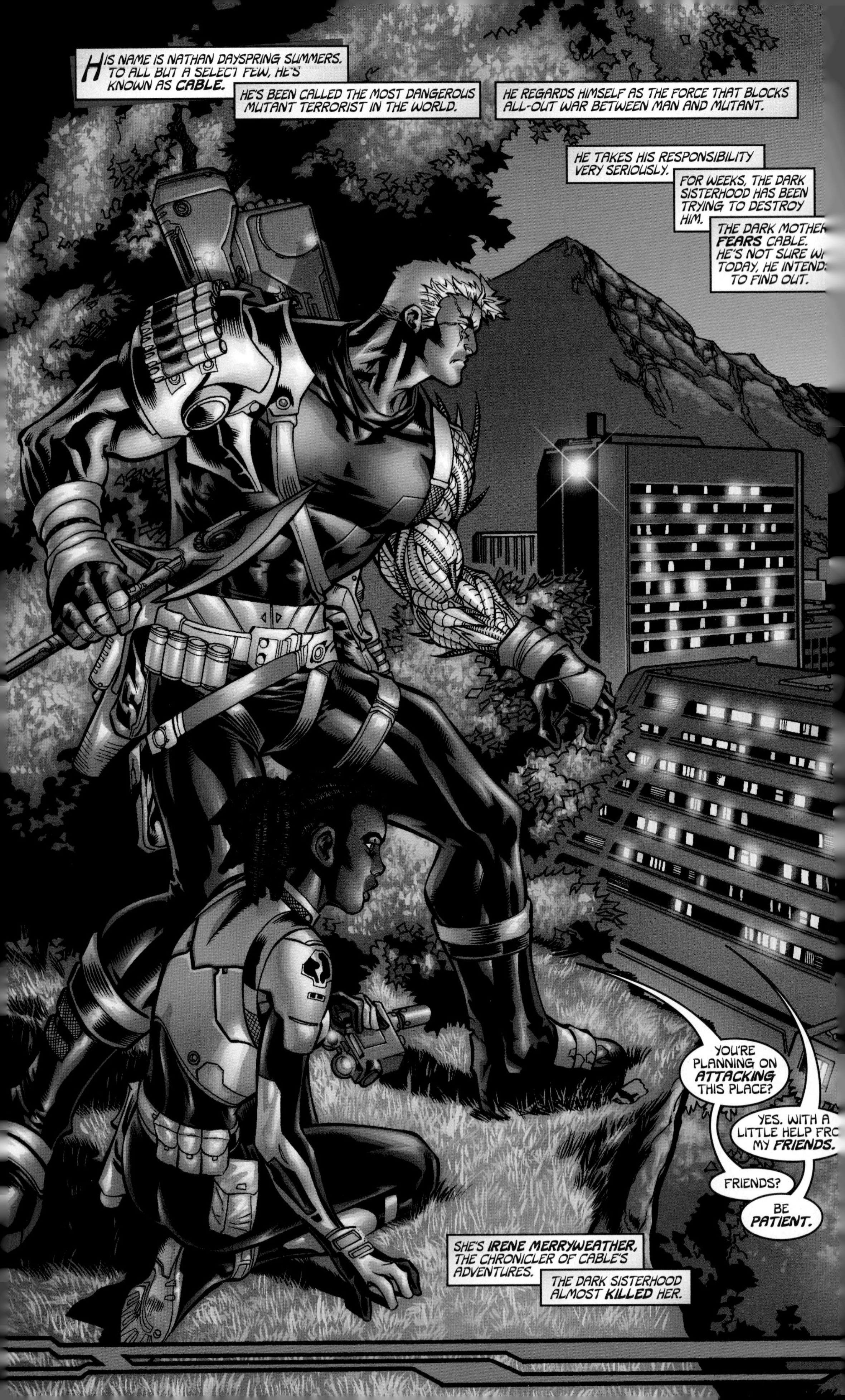
HIS NAME IS NATHAN DAYSPRING SUMMERS. TO ALL BUT A SELECT FEW, HE'S KNOWN AS CABLE.
HE'S BEEN CALLED THE MOST DANGEROUS MUTANT TERRORIST IN THE WORLD.
HE REGARDS HIMSELF AS THE FORCE THAT BLOCKS ALL-OUT WAR BETWEEN MAN AND MUTANT.
HE TAKES HIS RESPONSIBILITY VERY SERIOUSLY.
FOR WEEKS, THE DARK SISTERHOOD HAS BEEN TRYING TO DESTROY HIM.
THE DARK MOTHER FEARS CABLE. HE'S NOT SURE W TODAY, HE INTEND TO FIND OUT.
YOU'RE PLANNING ON ATTACKING THIS PLACE?
YES. WITH A LITTLE HELP FRO MY FRIENDS.
FRIENDS?
BE PATIENT.
SHE'S IRENE MERRYWEATHER, THE CHRONICLER OF CABLE'S ADVENTURES.
THE DARK SISTERHOOD ALMOST KILLED HER.

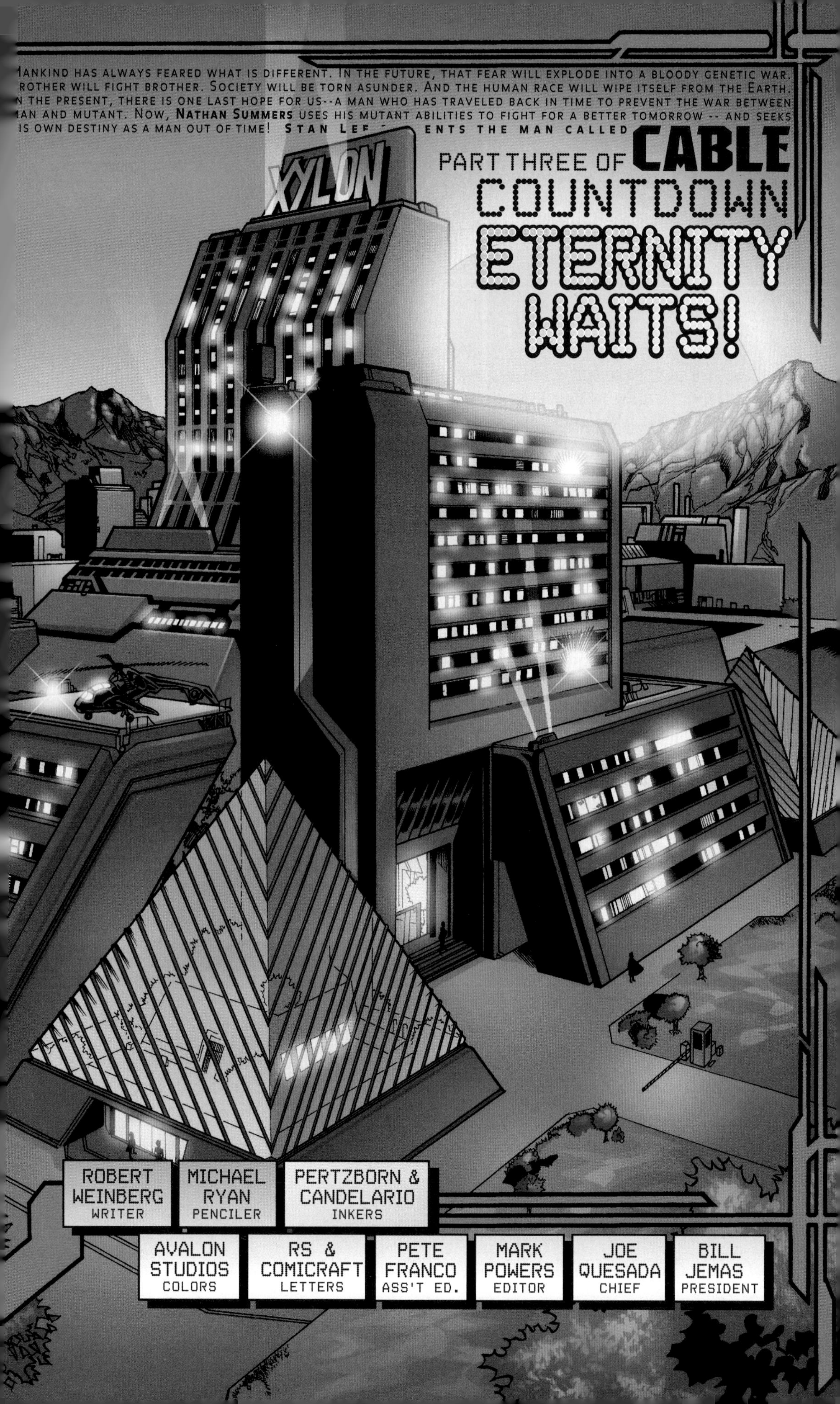
MANKIND HAS ALWAYS FEARED WHAT IS DIFFERENT. IN THE FUTURE, THAT FEAR WILL EXPLODE INTO A BLOODY GENETIC WAR. BROTHER WILL FIGHT BROTHER. SOCIETY WILL BE TORN ASUNDER. AND THE HUMAN RACE WILL WIPE ITSELF FROM THE EARTH. IN THE PRESENT, THERE IS ONE LAST HOPE FOR US--A MAN WHO HAS TRAVELED BACK IN TIME TO PREVENT THE WAR BETWEEN MAN AND MUTANT. NOW, NATHAN SUMMERS USES HIS MUTANT ABILITIES TO FIGHT FOR A BETTER TOMORROW -- AND SEEKS HIS OWN DESTINY AS A MAN OUT OF TIME! STAN LEE ENTS THE MAN CALLED CABLE
XYLON
PART THREE OF COUNTDOWN
ETERNITY WAITS!
ROBERT WEINBERG WRITER
MICHAEL RYAN PENCILER
PERTZBORN & CANDELARIO INKERS
AVALON STUDIOS COLORS
RS & COMICRAFT LETTERS
PETE FRANCO ASS'T ED.
MARK POWERS EDITOR
JOE QUESADA CHIEF
BILL JEMAS PRESIDENT

WHOEVER YOU ARE, *OUT* OF THE BUSHES! FAST!

HEY, I COME IN PEACE.

RACHEL!

I THOUGHT YOU WERE IN COLLEGE. I TOOK TIME *OFF.*

HOW DID YOU *FIND* US?

BEFORE I WAS THE *PHOENIX,* I WAS FORCED TO *HUNT OTHER* MUTANTS.

YOU'RE A HARD MAN TO FIND, *BROTHER.*

I'M HERE. JUST IN TIME FOR SOME *ACTION.*

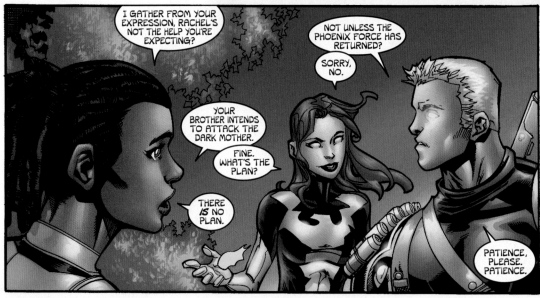

I GATHER FROM YOUR EXPRESSION, RACHEL'S NOT THE HELP YOU'RE EXPECTING?

NOT UNLESS THE PHOENIX FORCE HAS RETURNED?

SORRY, NO.

YOUR BROTHER INTENDS TO ATTACK THE DARK MOTHER.

FINE. WHAT'S THE PLAN?

THERE *IS* NO PLAN.

PATIENCE, PLEASE. PATIENCE.

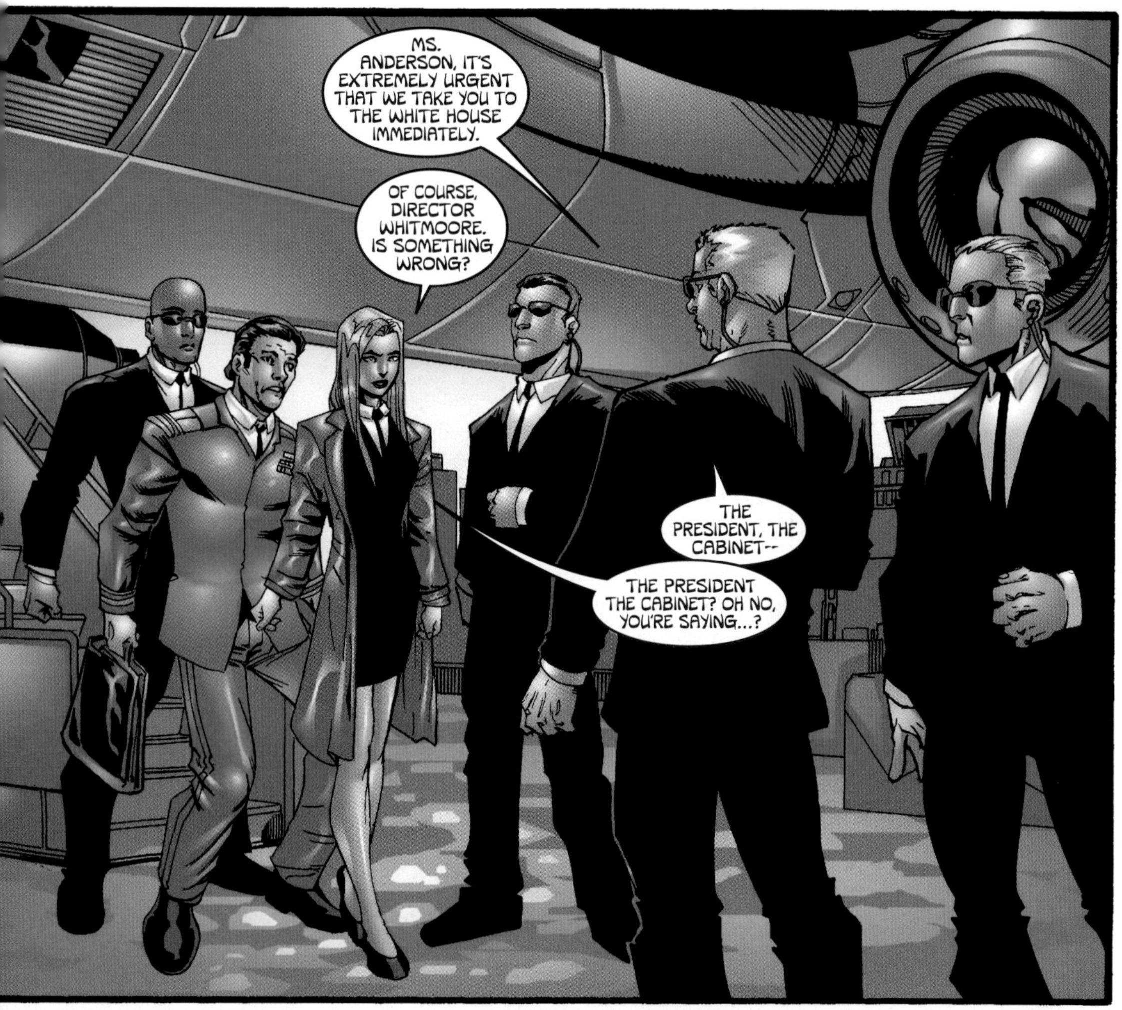
MS. ANDERSON, IT'S EXTREMELY URGENT THAT WE TAKE YOU TO THE WHITE HOUSE IMMEDIATELY.
OF COURSE, DIRECTOR WHITMOORE. IS SOMETHING WRONG?
THE PRESIDENT, THE CABINET--
THE PRESIDENT THE CABINET? OH NO, YOU'RE SAYING...?

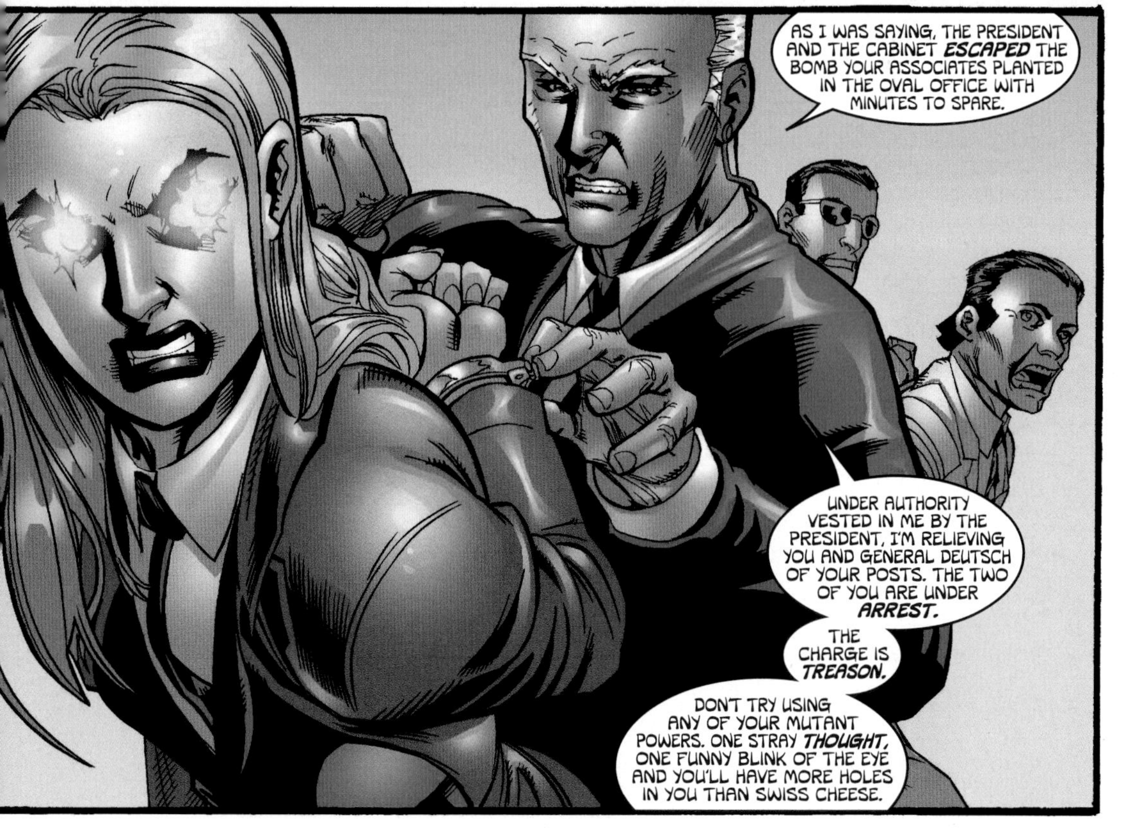
AS I WAS SAYING, THE PRESIDENT AND THE CABINET ESCAPED THE BOMB YOUR ASSOCIATES PLANTED IN THE OVAL OFFICE WITH MINUTES TO SPARE.
UNDER AUTHORITY VESTED IN ME BY THE PRESIDENT, I'M RELIEVING YOU AND GENERAL DEUTSCH OF YOUR POSTS. THE TWO OF YOU ARE UNDER ARREST.
THE CHARGE IS TREASON.
DON'T TRY USING ANY OF YOUR MUTANT POWERS. ONE STRAY THOUGHT, ONE FUNNY BLINK OF THE EYE AND YOU'LL HAVE MORE HOLES IN YOU THAN SWISS CHEESE.

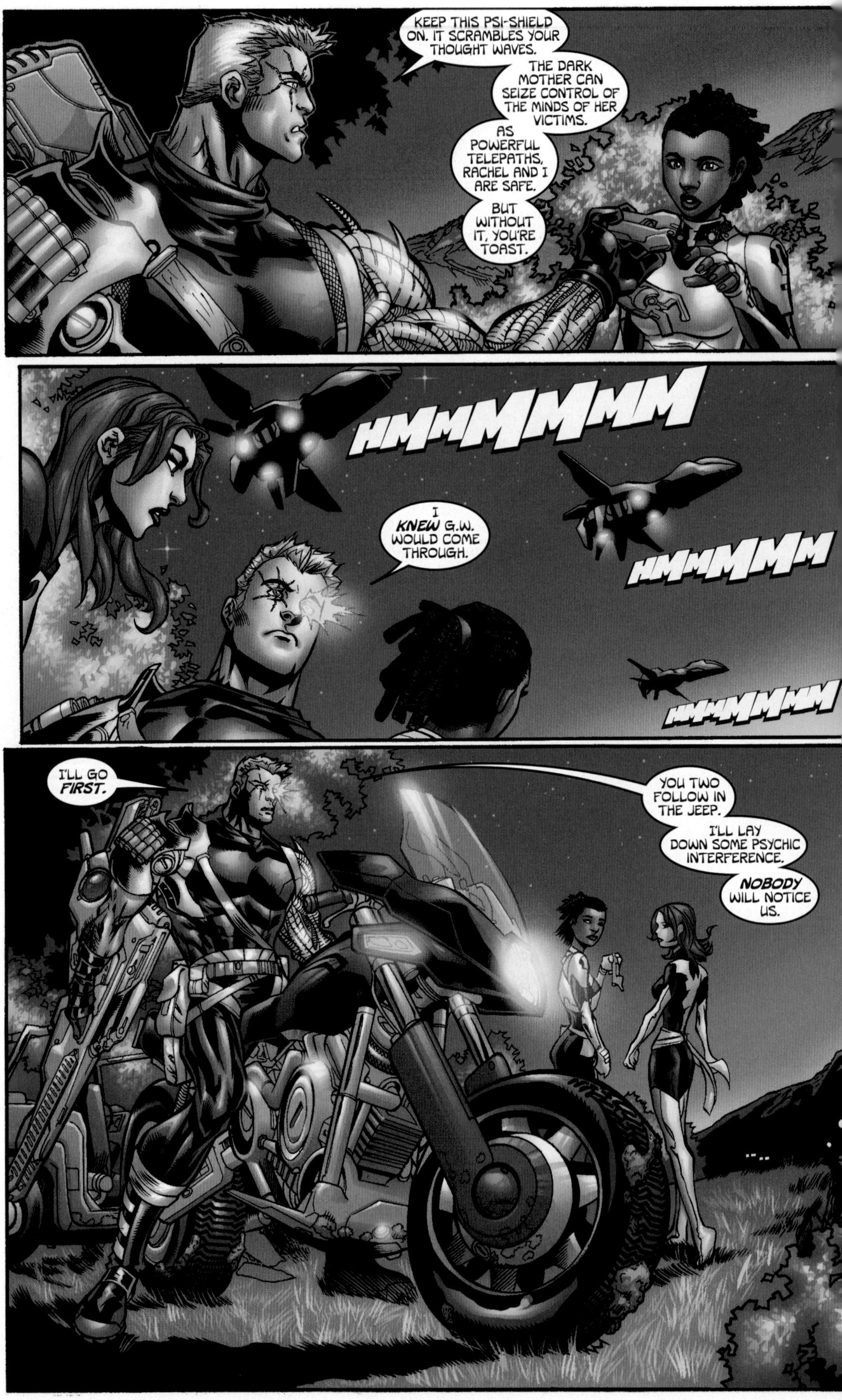
KEEP THIS PSI-SHIELD ON. IT SCRAMBLES YOUR THOUGHT WAVES.
THE DARK MOTHER CAN SEIZE CONTROL OF THE MINDS OF HER VICTIMS.
AS POWERFUL TELEPATHS, RACHEL AND I ARE SAFE.
BUT WITHOUT IT, YOU'RE TOAST.
HMMMMMMMM
I KNEW G.W. WOULD COME THROUGH.
HMMMMMM
HMMMMMMM
I'LL GO FIRST.
YOU TWO FOLLOW IN THE JEEP.
I'LL LAY DOWN SOME PSYCHIC INTERFERENCE.
NOBODY WILL NOTICE US.

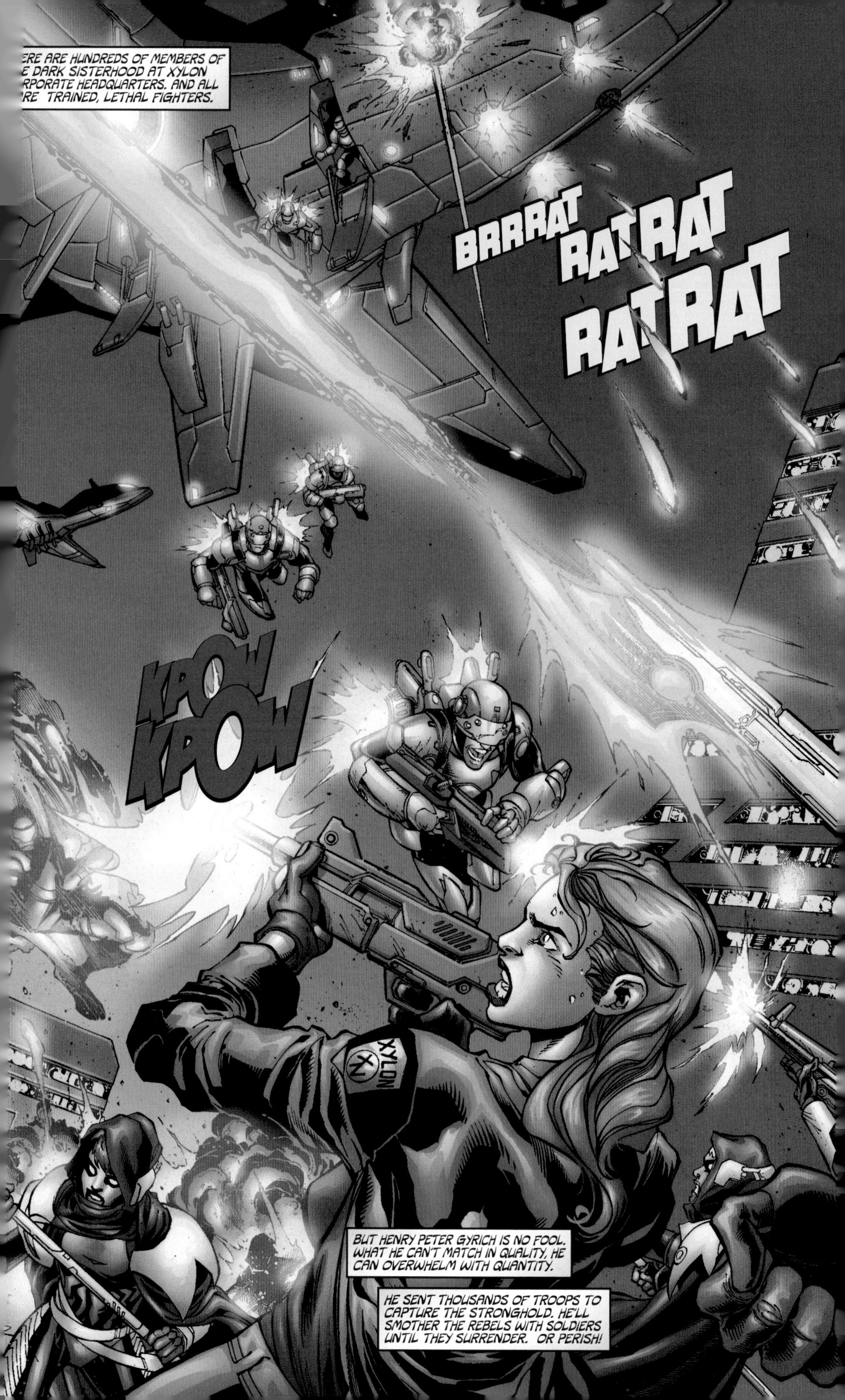
ERE ARE HUNDREDS OF MEMBERS OF
E DARK SISTERHOOD AT XYLON
RPORATE HEADQUARTERS. AND ALL
RE TRAINED, LETHAL FIGHTERS.
BRRRAT RATRAT RATRAT
KPOW KPOW
XYLON
BUT HENRY PETER GYRICH IS NO FOOL. WHAT HE CAN'T MATCH IN QUALITY, HE CAN OVERWHELM WITH QUANTITY.
HE SENT THOUSANDS OF TROOPS TO CAPTURE THE STRONGHOLD. HE'LL SMOTHER THE REBELS WITH SOLDIERS UNTIL THEY SURRENDER. OR PERISH!

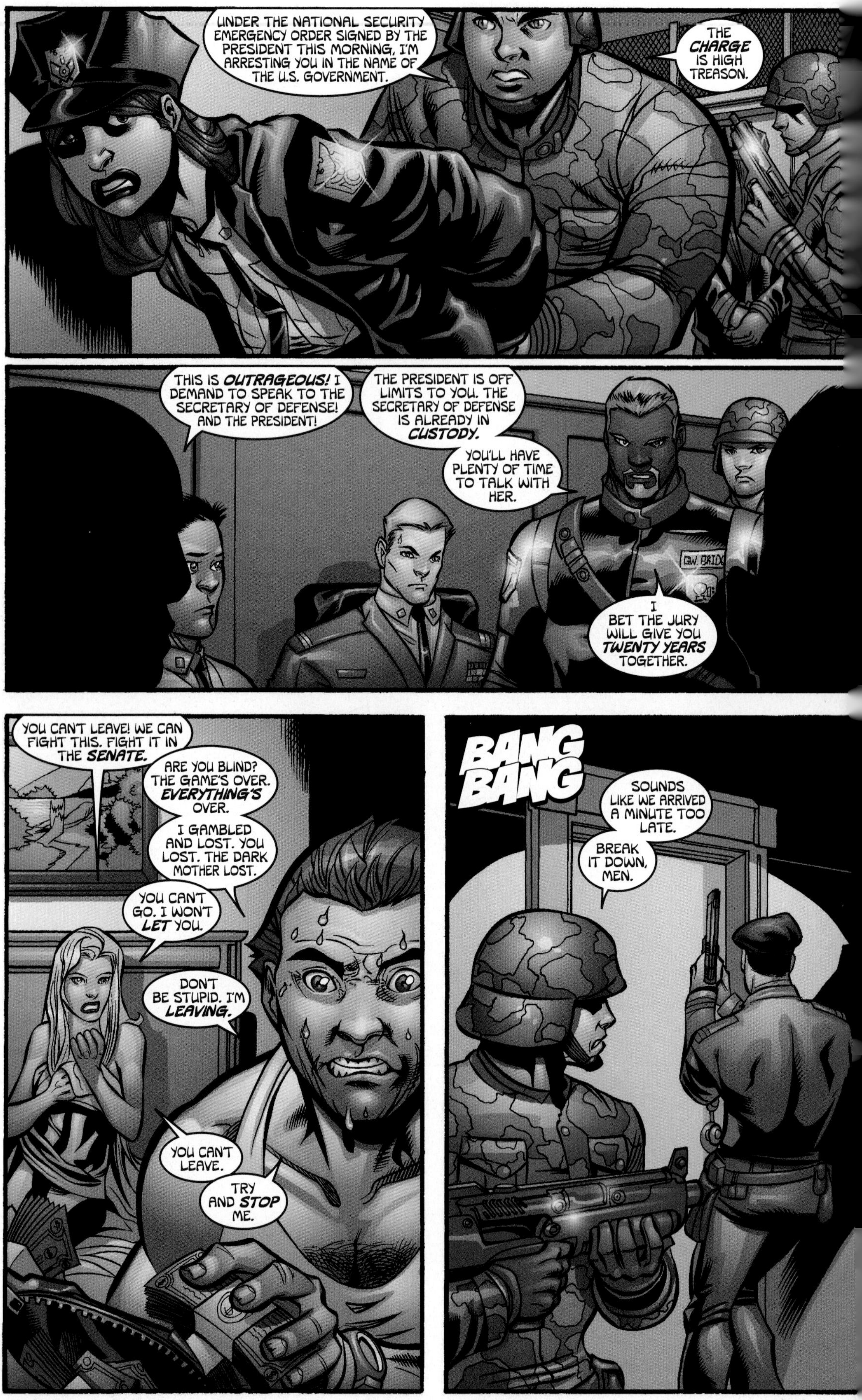
UNDER THE NATIONAL SECURITY EMERGENCY ORDER SIGNED BY THE PRESIDENT THIS MORNING, I'M ARRESTING YOU IN THE NAME OF THE U.S. GOVERNMENT.
THE CHARGE IS HIGH TREASON.
THIS IS OUTRAGEOUS! I DEMAND TO SPEAK TO THE SECRETARY OF DEFENSE! AND THE PRESIDENT!
THE PRESIDENT IS OFF LIMITS TO YOU. THE SECRETARY OF DEFENSE IS ALREADY IN CUSTODY.
YOU'LL HAVE PLENTY OF TIME TO TALK WITH HER.
I BET THE JURY WILL GIVE YOU TWENTY YEARS TOGETHER.
YOU CAN'T LEAVE! WE CAN FIGHT THIS. FIGHT IT IN THE SENATE.
ARE YOU BLIND? THE GAME'S OVER. EVERYTHING'S OVER.
I GAMBLED AND LOST. YOU LOST. THE DARK MOTHER LOST.
YOU CAN'T GO. I WON'T LET YOU.
DON'T BE STUPID. I'M LEAVING.
YOU CAN'T LEAVE.
TRY AND STOP ME.
BANG BANG
SOUNDS LIKE WE ARRIVED A MINUTE TOO LATE.
BREAK IT DOWN, MEN.

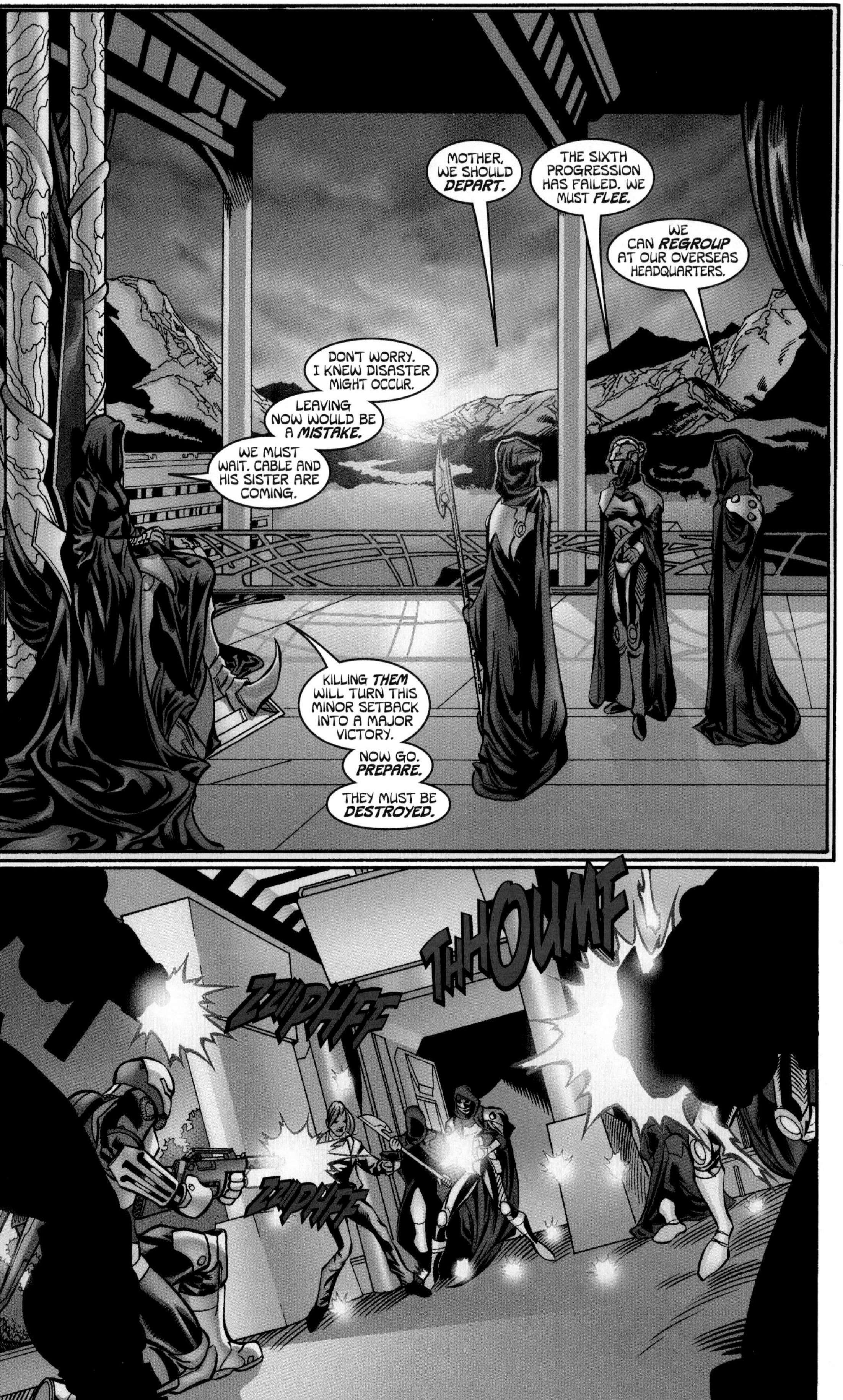
MOTHER, WE SHOULD DEPART.
THE SIXTH PROGRESSION HAS FAILED. WE MUST FLEE.
WE CAN REGROUP AT OUR OVERSEAS HEADQUARTERS.
DON'T WORRY. I KNEW DISASTER MIGHT OCCUR.
LEAVING NOW WOULD BE A MISTAKE.
WE MUST WAIT. CABLE AND HIS SISTER ARE COMING.
KILLING THEM WILL TURN THIS MINOR SETBACK INTO A MAJOR VICTORY.
NOW GO. PREPARE.
THEY MUST BE DESTROYED.
ZZZIDHFF
THHOUMF
ZZZIDHFF

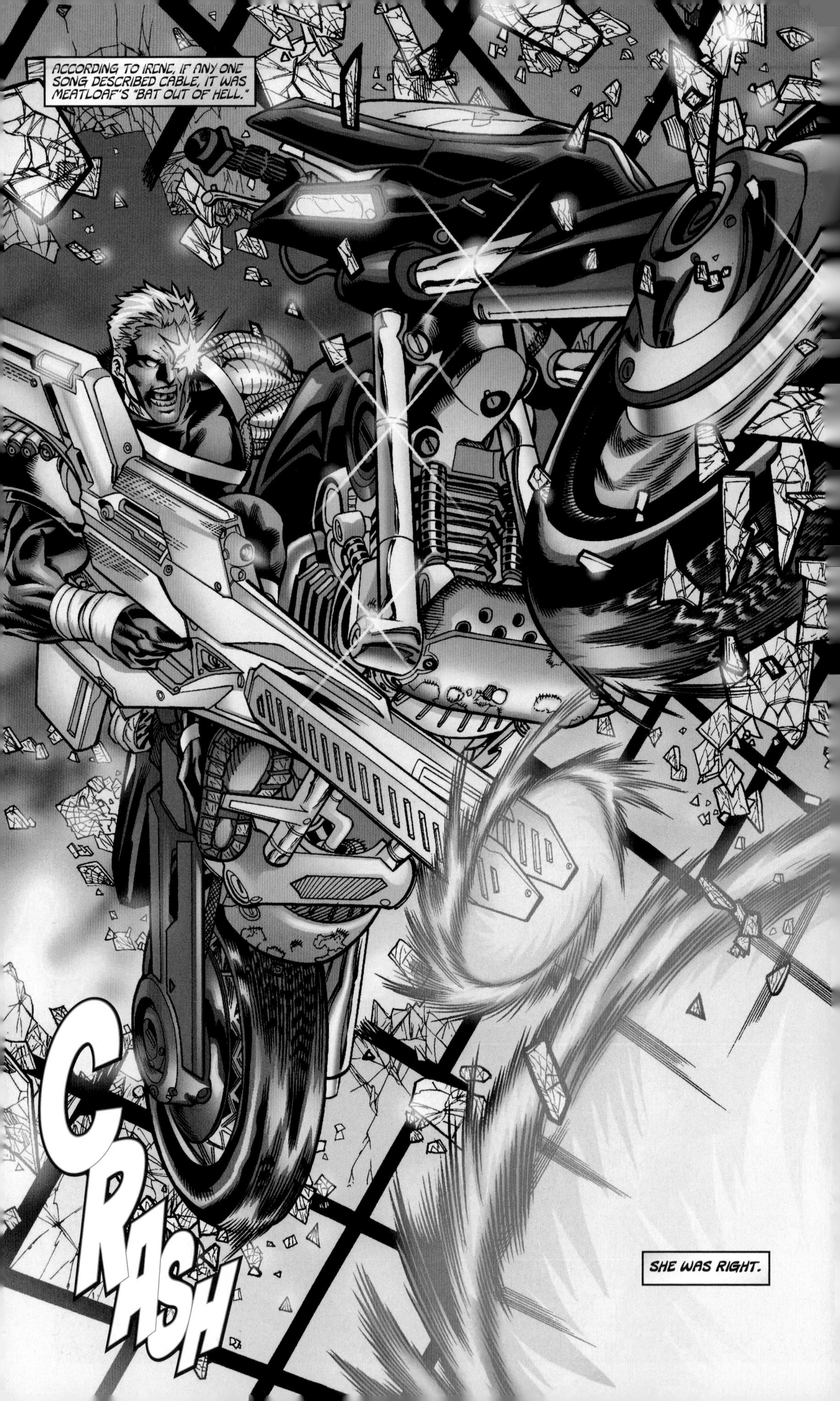
ACCORDING TO IRENE, IF ANY ONE SONG DESCRIBED CABLE, IT WAS MEATLOAF'S "BAT OUT OF HELL."
CRASH
SHE WAS RIGHT.

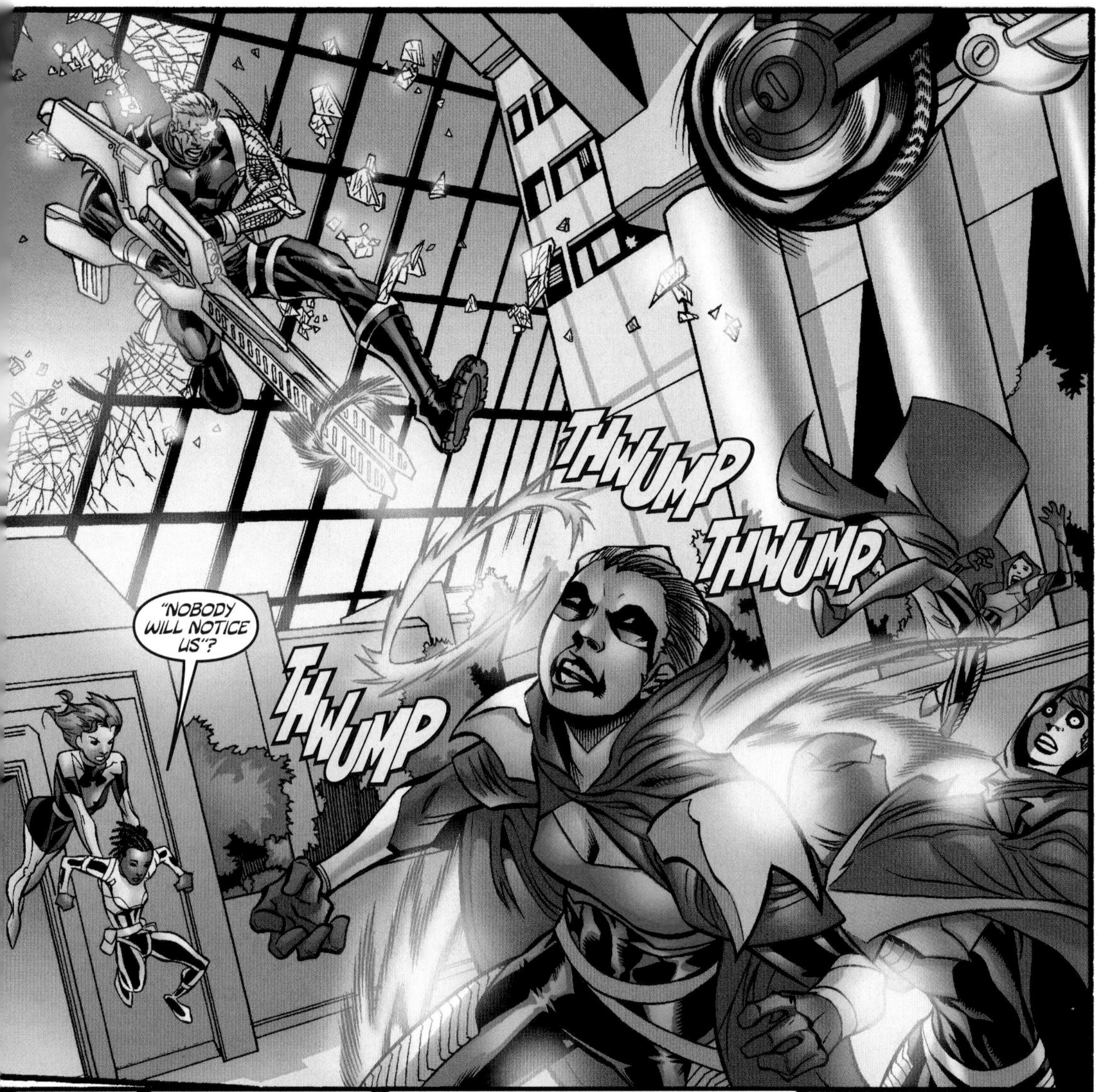
THWUMP
THWUMP
"NOBODY WILL NOTICE US"?
THWUMP

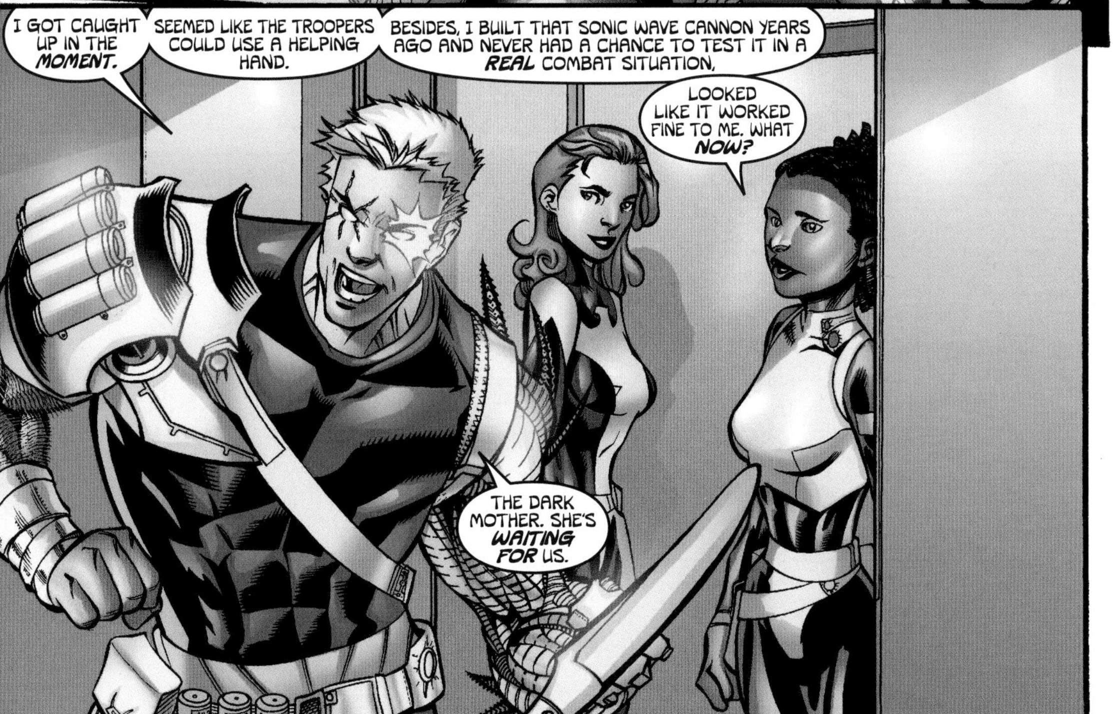
I GOT CAUGHT UP IN THE MOMENT.
SEEMED LIKE THE TROOPERS COULD USE A HELPING HAND.
BESIDES, I BUILT THAT SONIC WAVE CANNON YEARS AGO AND NEVER HAD A CHANCE TO TEST IT IN A REAL COMBAT SITUATION.
LOOKED LIKE IT WORKED FINE TO ME. WHAT NOW?
THE DARK MOTHER. SHE'S WAITING FOR US.

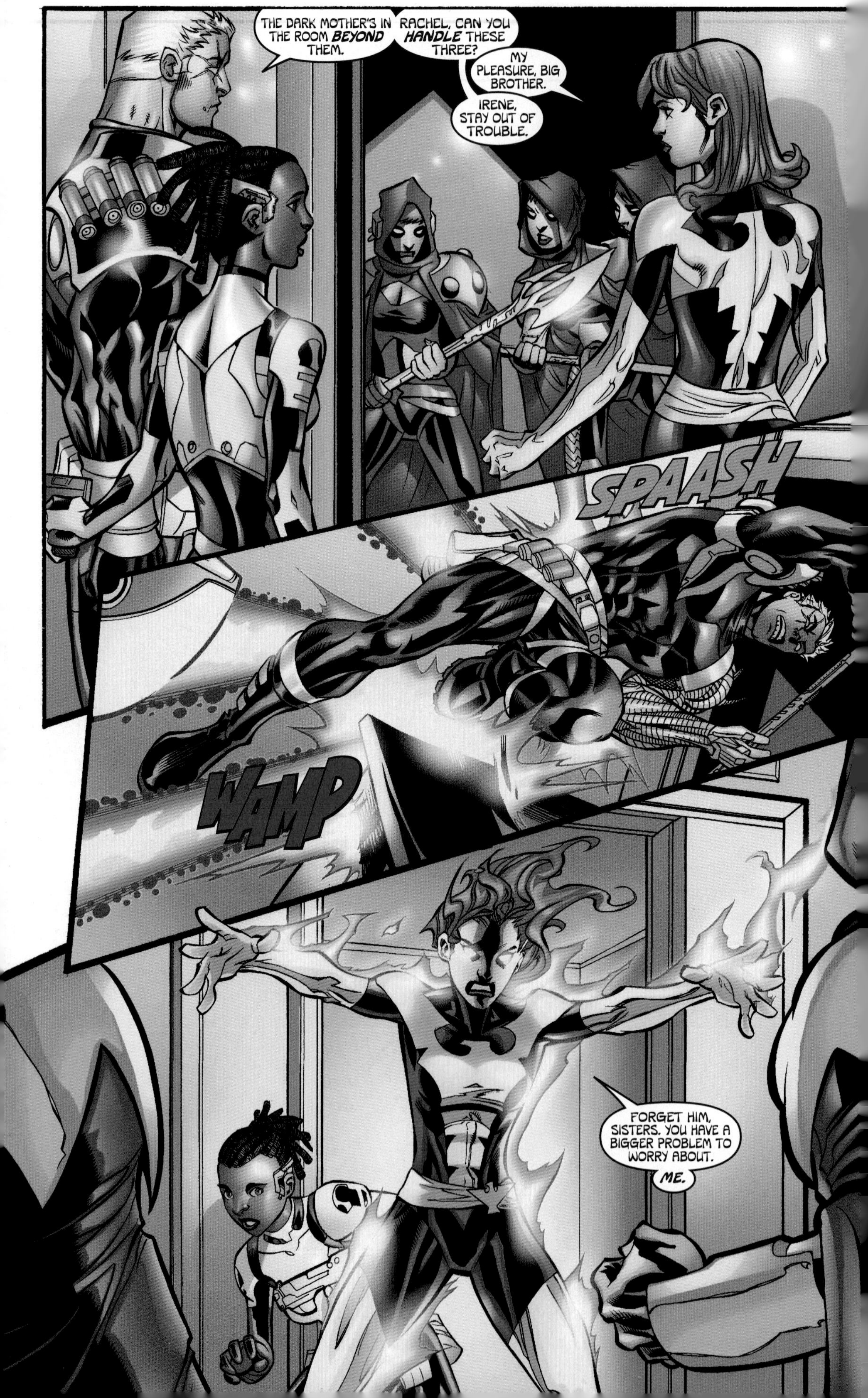

THE DARK MOTHER'S IN THE ROOM BEYOND THEM.
RACHEL, CAN YOU HANDLE THESE THREE?
MY PLEASURE, BIG BROTHER.
IRENE, STAY OUT OF TROUBLE.
SPAASH
WAMP
FORGET HIM, SISTERS. YOU HAVE A BIGGER PROBLEM TO WORRY ABOUT.
ME.

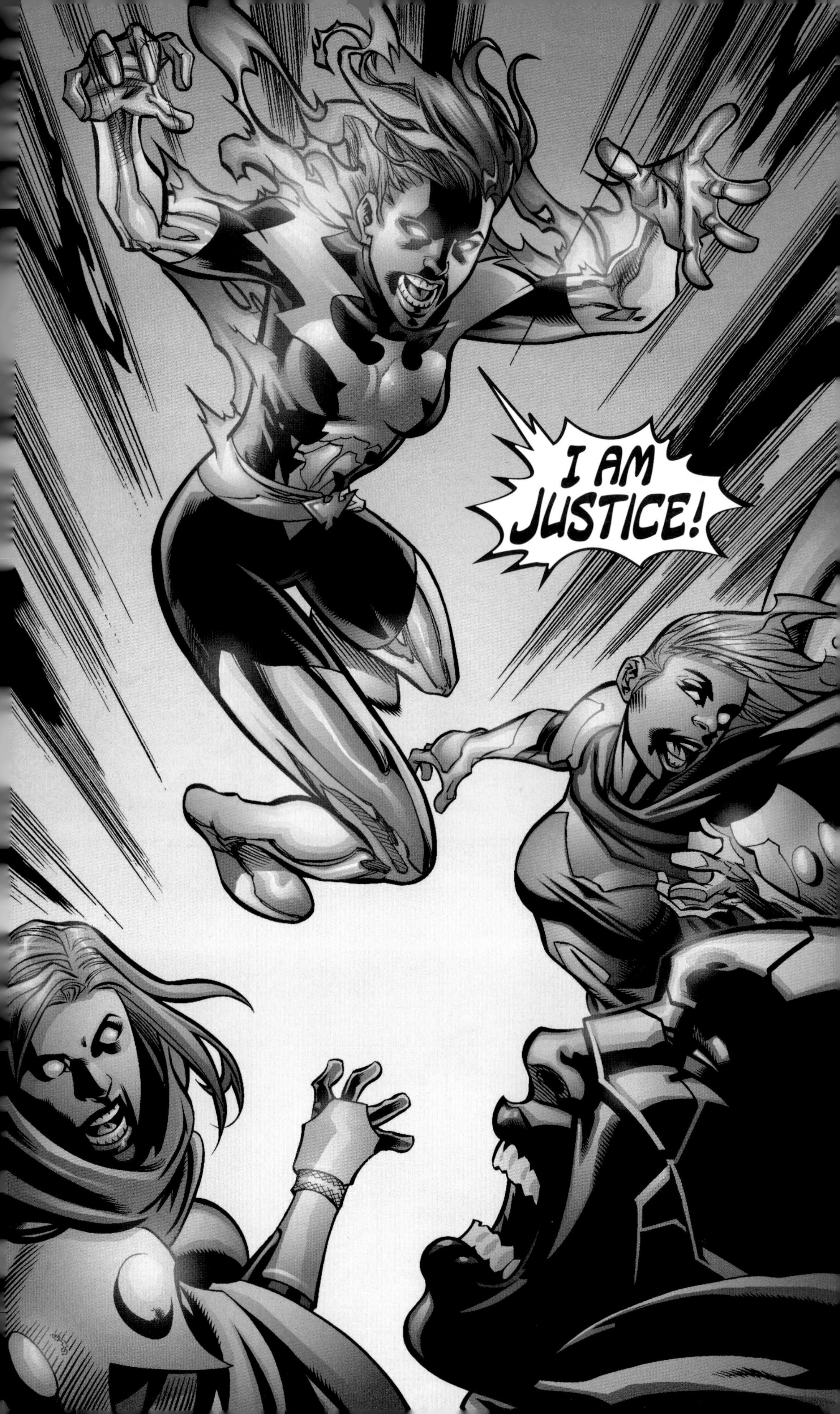
I AM JUSTICE!

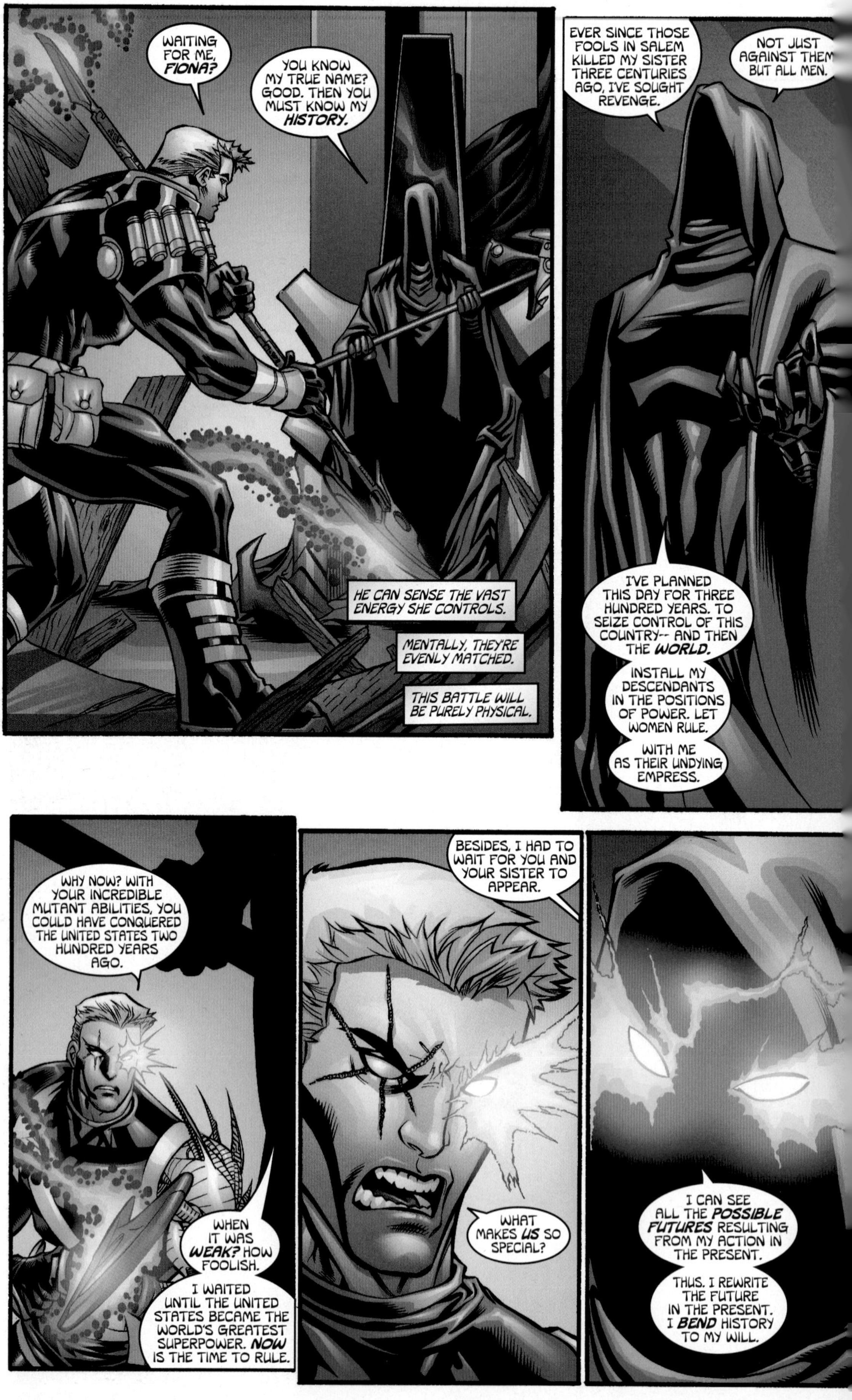
WAITING FOR ME, FIONA?
YOU KNOW MY TRUE NAME? GOOD. THEN YOU MUST KNOW MY HISTORY.
HE CAN SENSE THE VAST ENERGY SHE CONTROLS.
MENTALLY, THEY'RE EVENLY MATCHED.
THIS BATTLE WILL BE PURELY PHYSICAL.
EVER SINCE THOSE FOOLS IN SALEM KILLED MY SISTER THREE CENTURIES AGO, I'VE SOUGHT REVENGE.
NOT JUST AGAINST THEM BUT ALL MEN.
I'VE PLANNED THIS DAY FOR THREE HUNDRED YEARS. TO SEIZE CONTROL OF THIS COUNTRY-- AND THEN THE WORLD.
INSTALL MY DESCENDANTS IN THE POSITIONS OF POWER. LET WOMEN RULE.
WITH ME AS THEIR UNDYING EMPRESS.
WHY NOW? WITH YOUR INCREDIBLE MUTANT ABILITIES, YOU COULD HAVE CONQUERED THE UNITED STATES TWO HUNDRED YEARS AGO.
WHEN IT WAS WEAK? HOW FOOLISH.
I WAITED UNTIL THE UNITED STATES BECAME THE WORLD'S GREATEST SUPERPOWER. NOW IS THE TIME TO RULE.
BESIDES, I HAD TO WAIT FOR YOU AND YOUR SISTER TO APPEAR.
WHAT MAKES US SO SPECIAL?
I CAN SEE ALL THE POSSIBLE FUTURES RESULTING FROM MY ACTION IN THE PRESENT.
THUS. I REWRITE THE FUTURE IN THE PRESENT. I BEND HISTORY TO MY WILL.

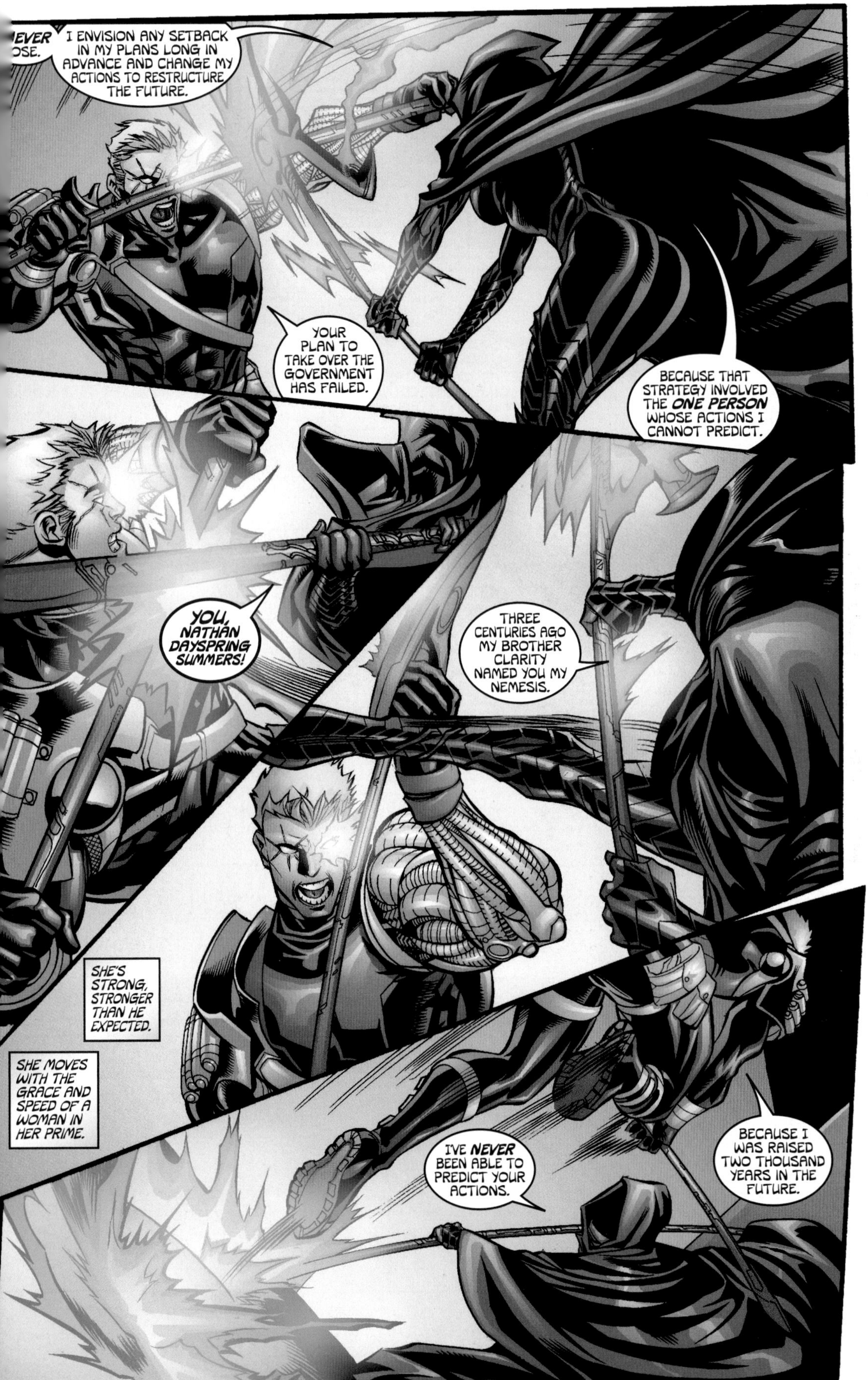

...NEVER ...OSE.
I ENVISION ANY SETBACK IN MY PLANS LONG IN ADVANCE AND CHANGE MY ACTIONS TO RESTRUCTURE THE FUTURE.
YOUR PLAN TO TAKE OVER THE GOVERNMENT HAS FAILED.
BECAUSE THAT STRATEGY INVOLVED THE ONE PERSON WHOSE ACTIONS I CANNOT PREDICT.
YOU, NATHAN DAYSPRING SUMMERS!
THREE CENTURIES AGO MY BROTHER CLARITY NAMED YOU MY NEMESIS.
SHE'S STRONG, STRONGER THAN HE EXPECTED.
SHE MOVES WITH THE GRACE AND SPEED OF A WOMAN IN HER PRIME.
I'VE NEVER BEEN ABLE TO PREDICT YOUR ACTIONS.
BECAUSE I WAS RAISED TWO THOUSAND YEARS IN THE FUTURE.

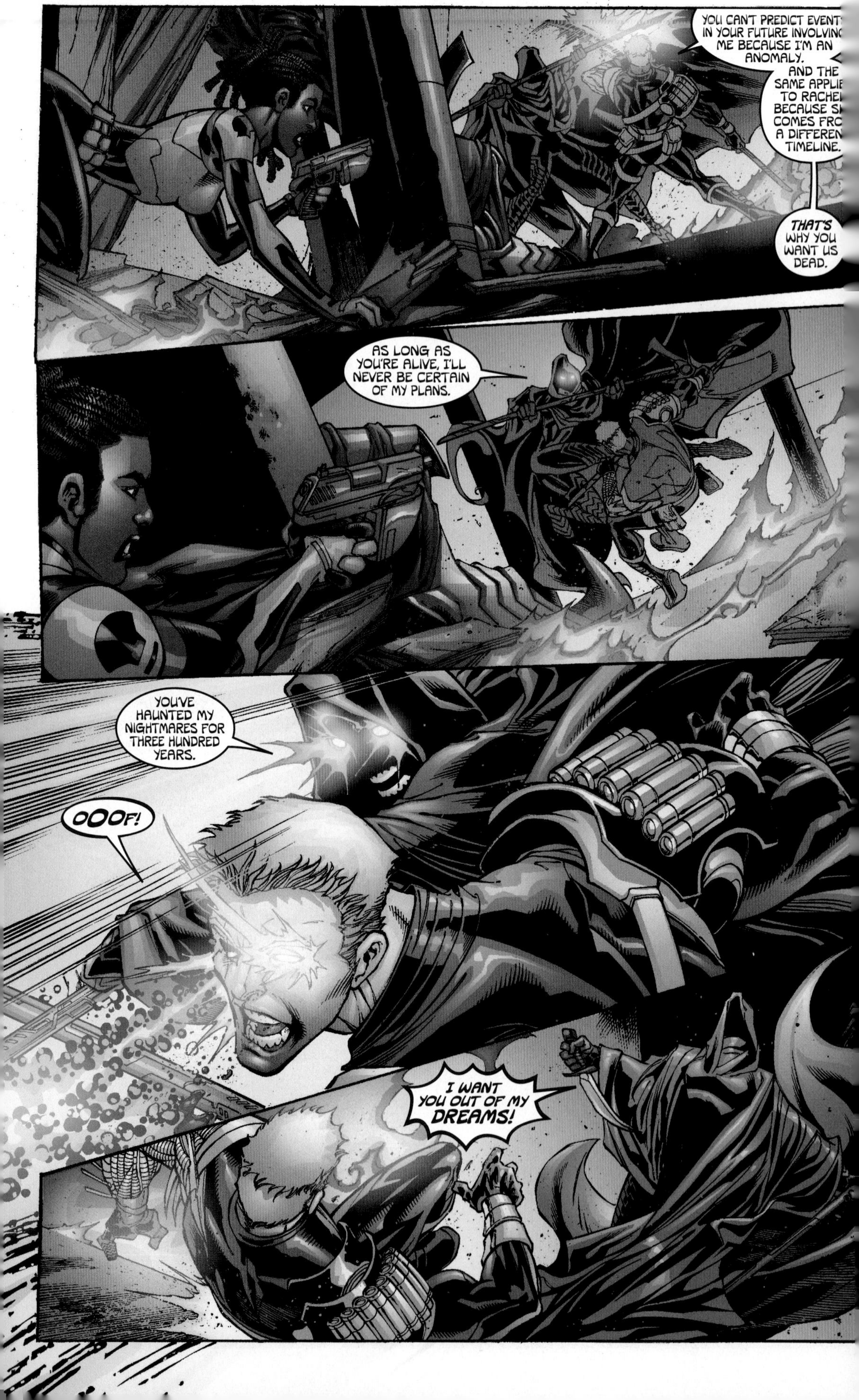

YOU CAN'T PREDICT EVENTS IN YOUR FUTURE INVOLVING ME BECAUSE I'M AN ANOMALY.
AND THE SAME APPLIE TO RACHEL BECAUSE SH COMES FRO A DIFFEREN TIMELINE.
THAT'S WHY YOU WANT US DEAD.
AS LONG AS YOU'RE ALIVE, I'LL NEVER BE CERTAIN OF MY PLANS.
YOU'VE HAUNTED MY NIGHTMARES FOR THREE HUNDRED YEARS.
OOOF!
I WANT YOU OUT OF MY DREAMS!

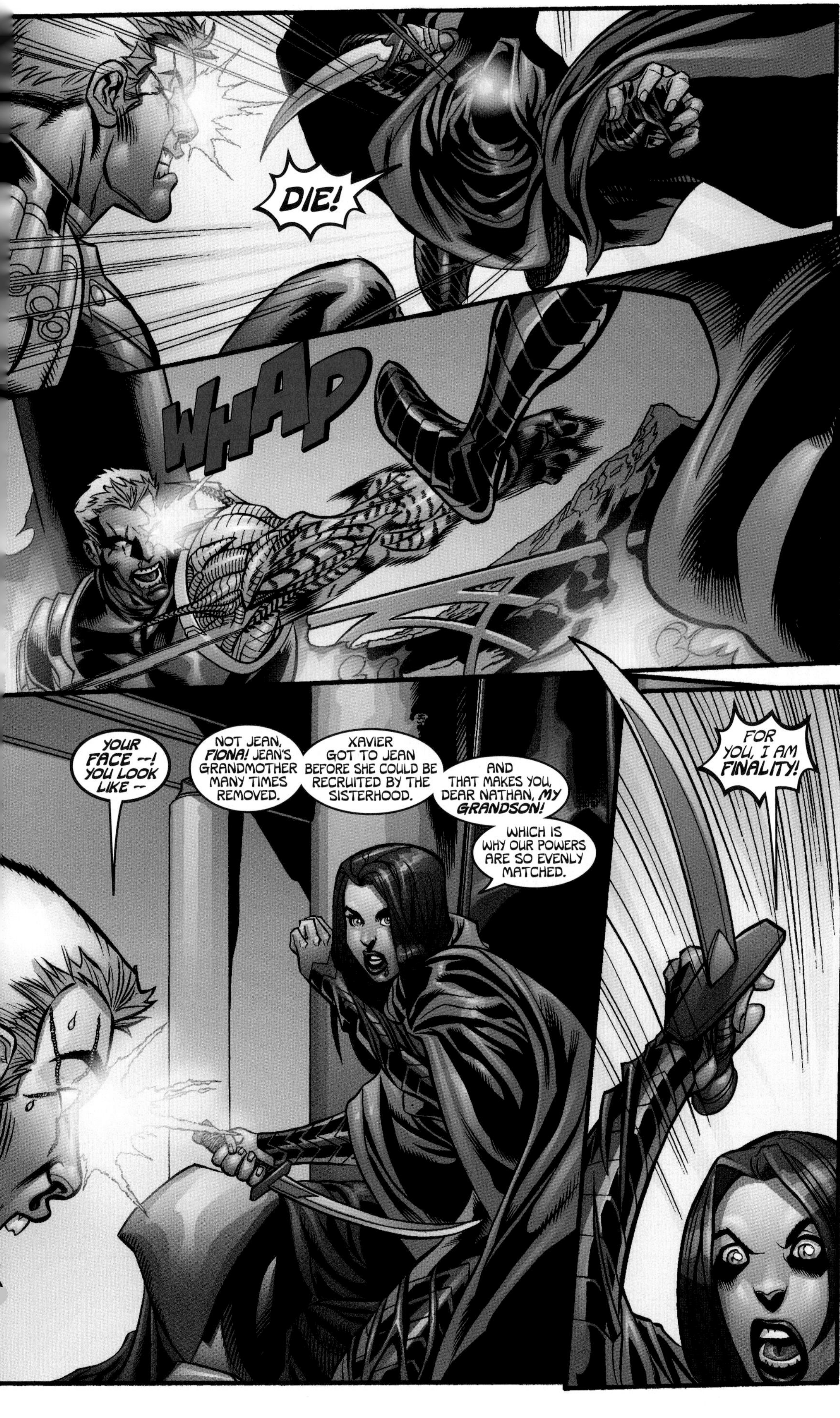
DIE!
WHAP
YOUR FACE --! YOU LOOK LIKE --
NOT JEAN, FIONA! JEAN'S GRANDMOTHER MANY TIMES REMOVED.
XAVIER GOT TO JEAN BEFORE SHE COULD BE RECRUITED BY THE SISTERHOOD.
AND THAT MAKES YOU, DEAR NATHAN, MY GRANDSON!
WHICH IS WHY OUR POWERS ARE SO EVENLY MATCHED.
FOR YOU, I AM FINALITY!

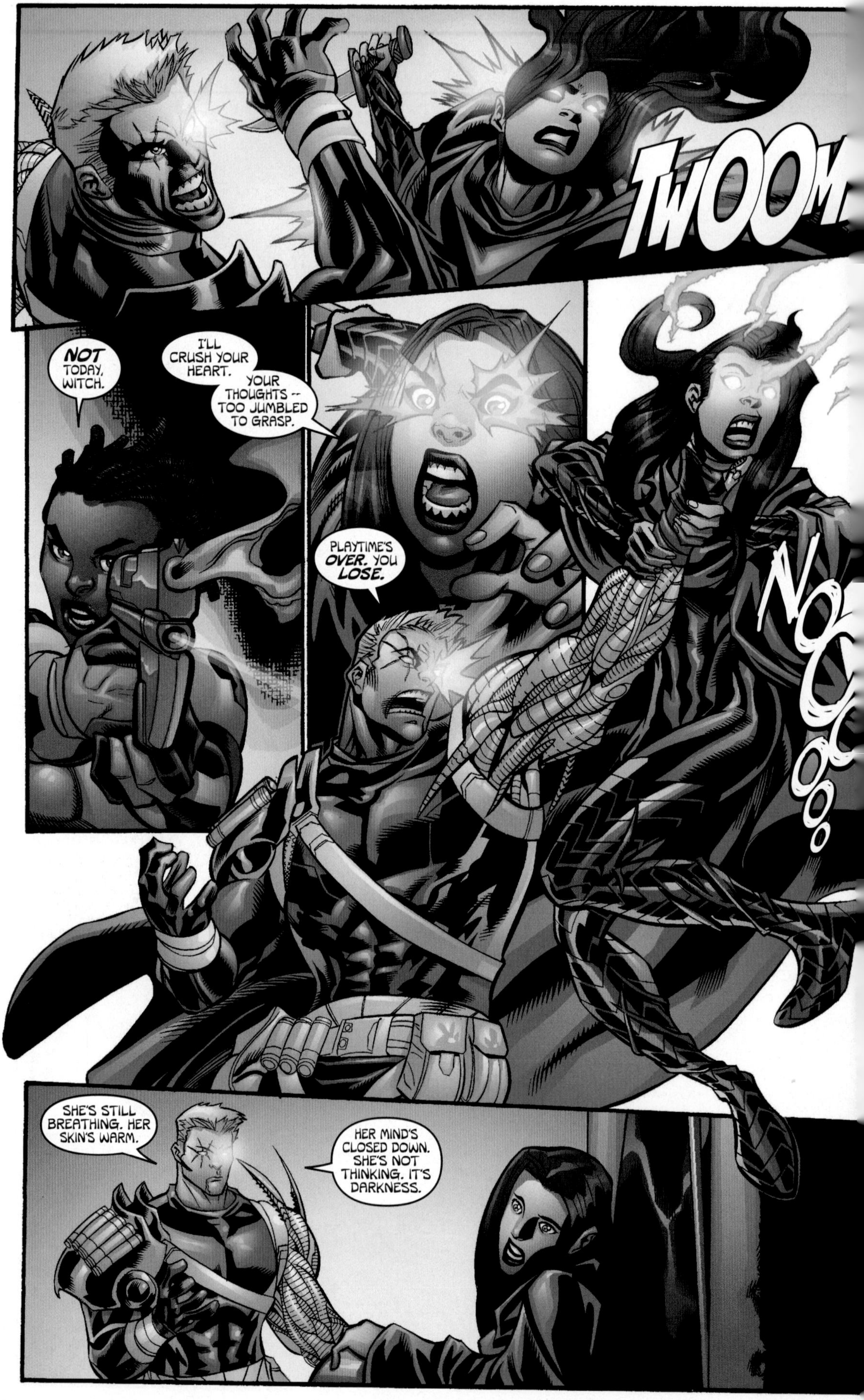
TWOOM
NOT TODAY, WITCH.
I'LL CRUSH YOUR HEART.
YOUR THOUGHTS -- TOO JUMBLED TO GRASP.
PLAYTIME'S OVER. YOU LOSE.
NOOOOOO
SHE'S STILL BREATHING. HER SKIN'S WARM.
HER MIND'S CLOSED DOWN. SHE'S NOT THINKING. IT'S DARKNESS.

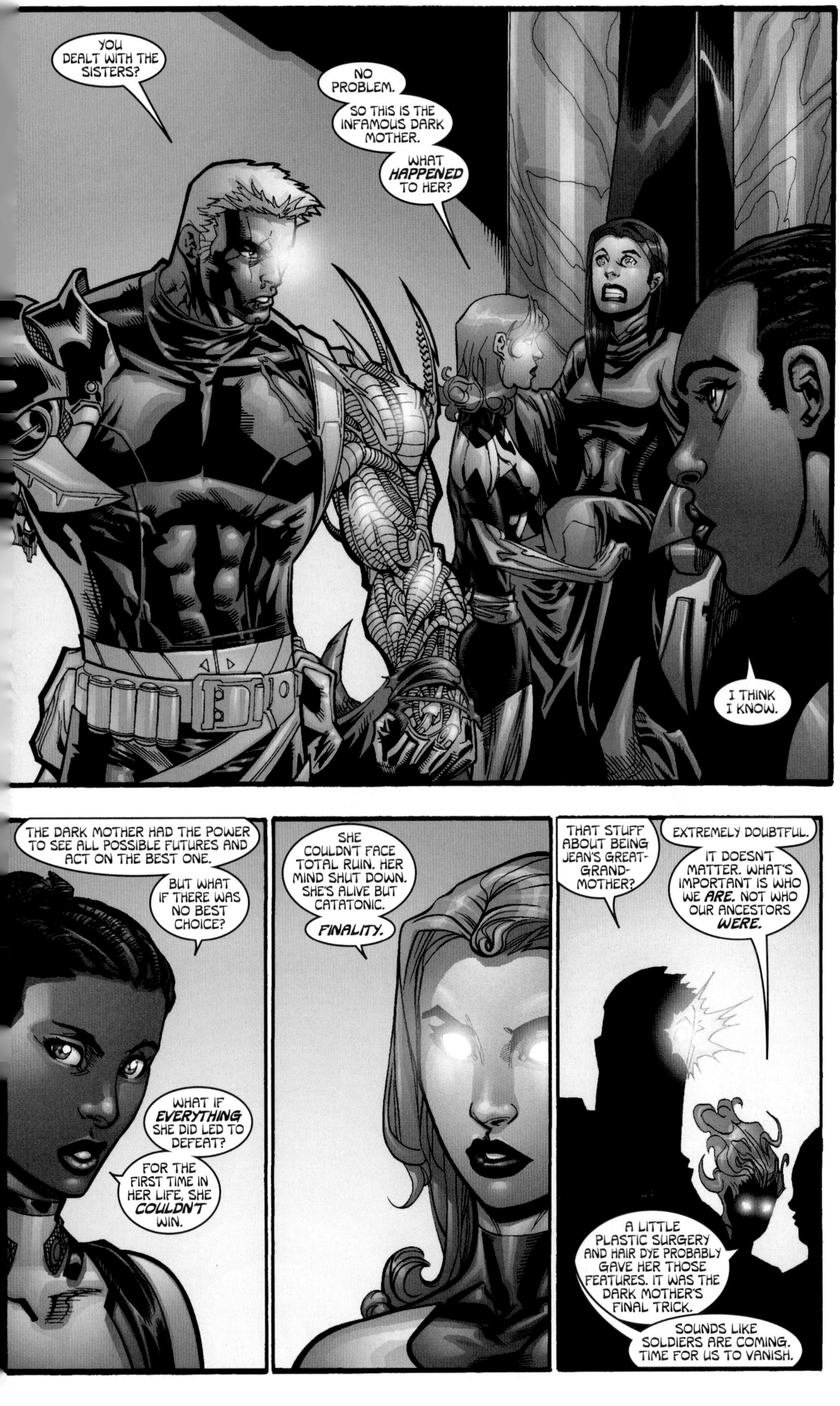
YOU DEALT WITH THE SISTERS?
NO PROBLEM.
SO THIS IS THE INFAMOUS DARK MOTHER.
WHAT *HAPPENED* TO HER?
I THINK I KNOW.
THE DARK MOTHER HAD THE POWER TO SEE ALL POSSIBLE FUTURES AND ACT ON THE BEST ONE.
BUT WHAT IF THERE WAS NO BEST CHOICE?
WHAT IF *EVERYTHING* SHE DID LED TO DEFEAT?
FOR THE FIRST TIME IN HER LIFE, SHE *COULDN'T* WIN.
SHE COULDN'T FACE TOTAL RUIN. HER MIND SHUT DOWN. SHE'S ALIVE BUT CATATONIC.
FINALITY.
THAT STUFF ABOUT BEING JEAN'S GREAT-GRAND-MOTHER?
EXTREMELY DOUBTFUL.
IT DOESN'T MATTER. WHAT'S IMPORTANT IS WHO WE *ARE.* NOT WHO OUR ANCESTORS *WERE.*
A LITTLE PLASTIC SURGERY AND HAIR DYE PROBABLY GAVE HER THOSE FEATURES. IT WAS THE DARK MOTHER'S FINAL TRICK.
SOUNDS LIKE SOLDIERS ARE COMING. TIME FOR US TO VANISH.

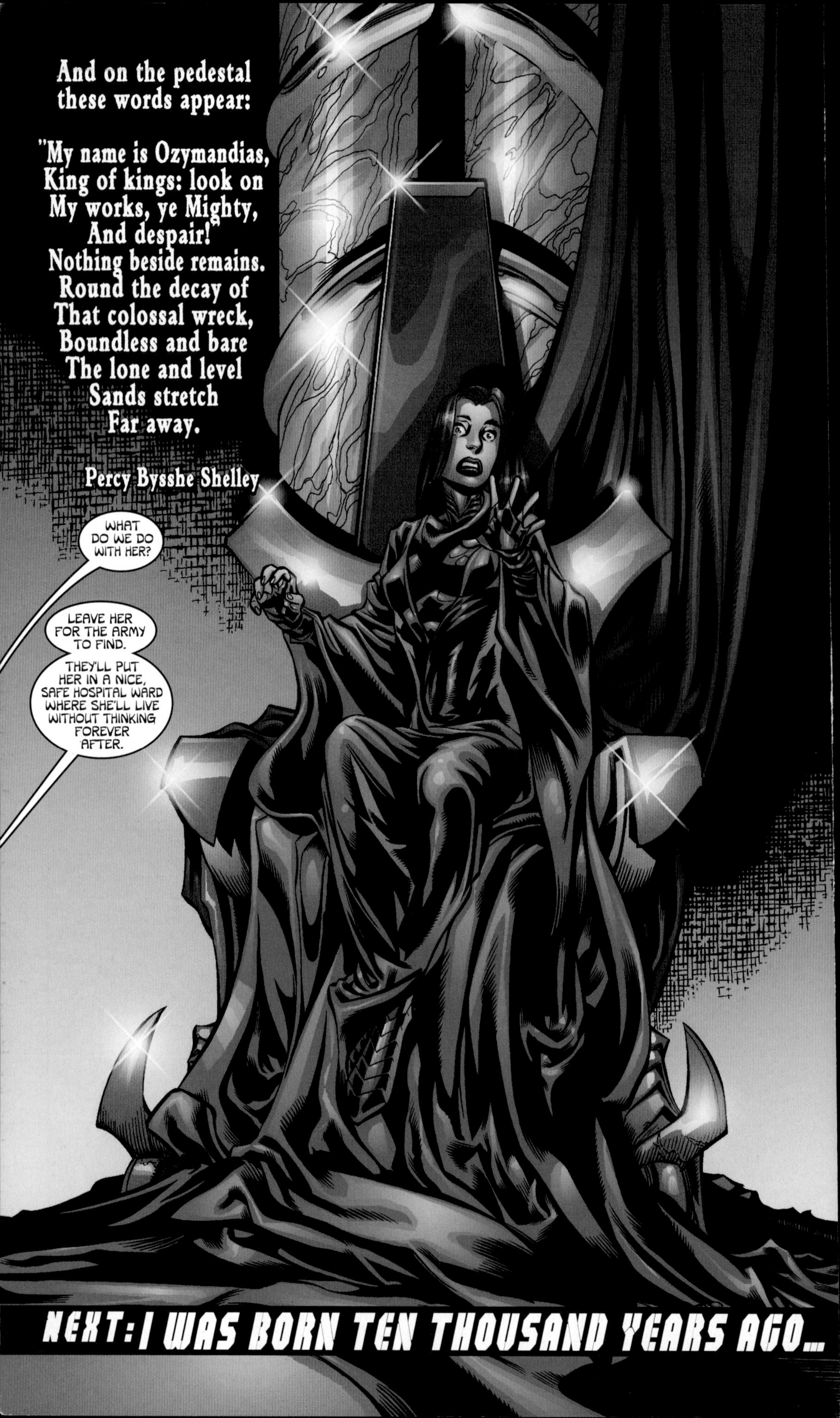
And on the pedestal these words appear:
"My name is Ozymandias, King of kings: look on My works, ye Mighty, And despair!" Nothing beside remains. Round the decay of That colossal wreck, Boundless and bare The lone and level Sands stretch Far away.
Percy Bysshe Shelley
WHAT DO WE DO WITH HER?
LEAVE HER FOR THE ARMY TO FIND.
THEY'LL PUT HER IN A NICE, SAFE HOSPITAL WARD WHERE SHE'LL LIVE WITHOUT THINKING FOREVER AFTER.
NEXT: I WAS BORN TEN THOUSAND YEARS AGO...

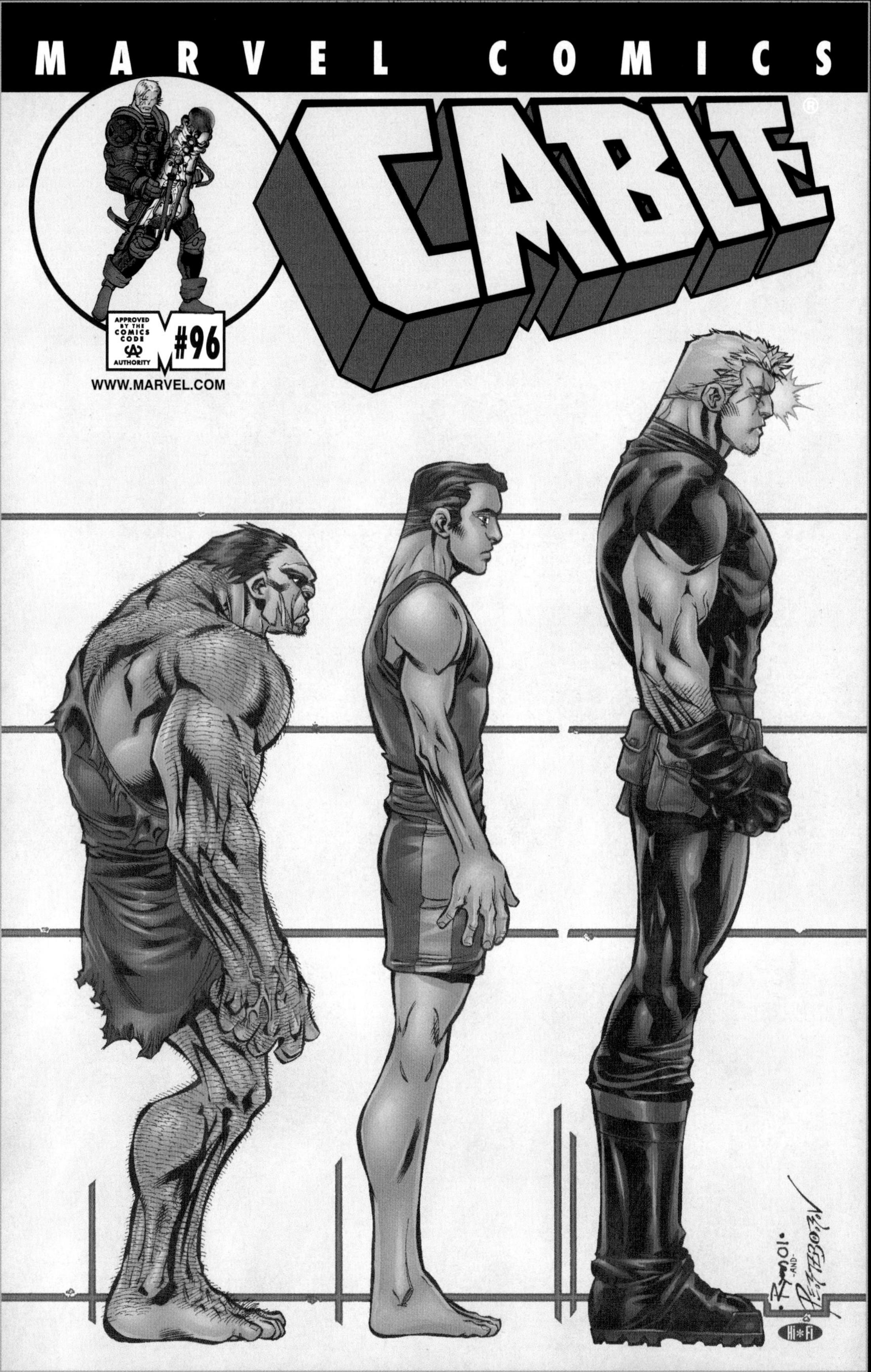
MARVEL COMICS
CABLE
APPROVED BY THE COMICS CODE AUTHORITY
#96
WWW.MARVEL.COM

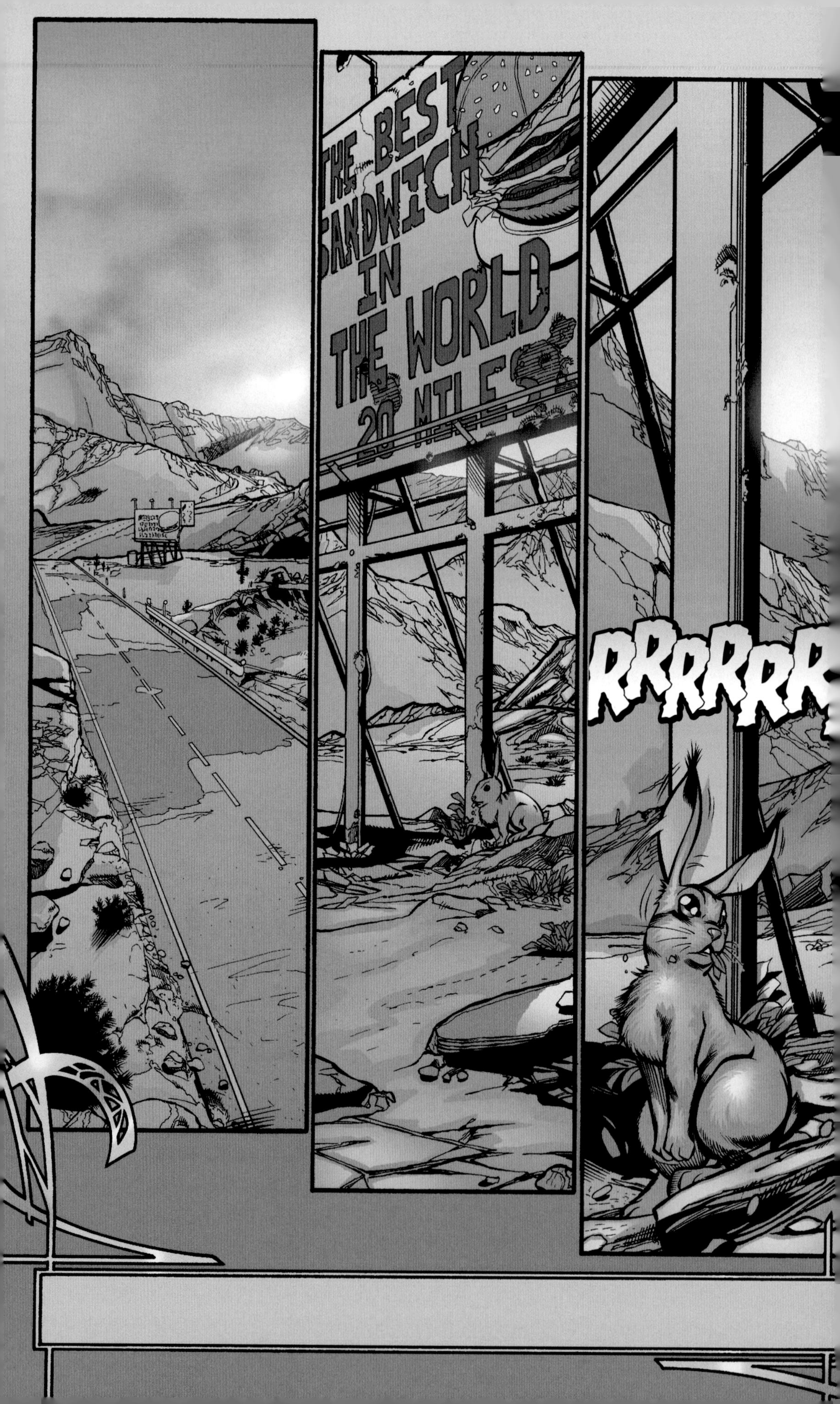
THE BEST SANDWICH IN THE WORLD
20 MILES
RRRRRR

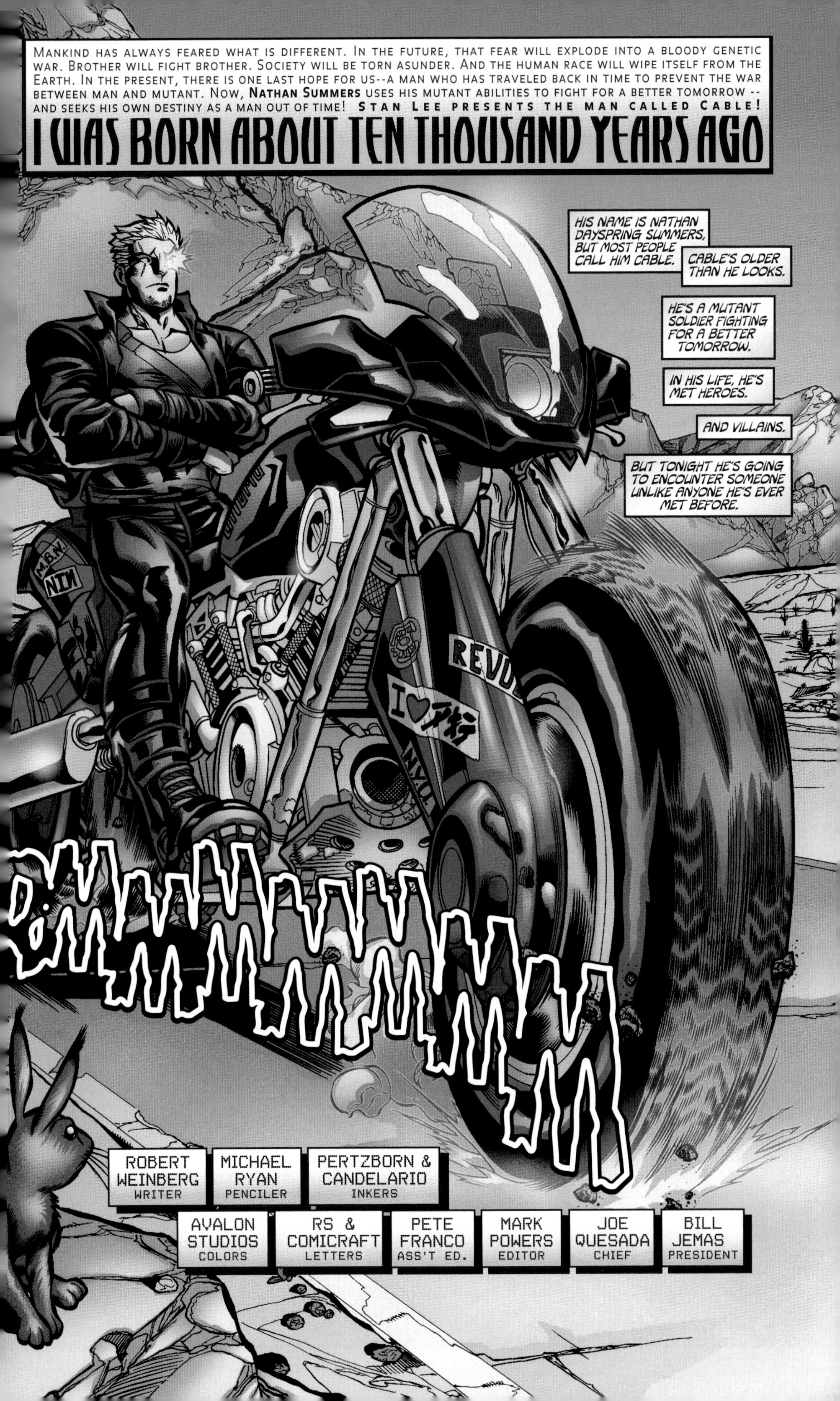

MANKIND HAS ALWAYS FEARED WHAT IS DIFFERENT. IN THE FUTURE, THAT FEAR WILL EXPLODE INTO A BLOODY GENETIC WAR. BROTHER WILL FIGHT BROTHER. SOCIETY WILL BE TORN ASUNDER. AND THE HUMAN RACE WILL WIPE ITSELF FROM THE EARTH. IN THE PRESENT, THERE IS ONE LAST HOPE FOR US--A MAN WHO HAS TRAVELED BACK IN TIME TO PREVENT THE WAR BETWEEN MAN AND MUTANT. NOW, NATHAN SUMMERS USES HIS MUTANT ABILITIES TO FIGHT FOR A BETTER TOMORROW -- AND SEEKS HIS OWN DESTINY AS A MAN OUT OF TIME! STAN LEE PRESENTS THE MAN CALLED CABLE!
I WAS BORN ABOUT TEN THOUSAND YEARS AGO
HIS NAME IS NATHAN DAYSPRING SUMMERS, BUT MOST PEOPLE CALL HIM CABLE.
CABLE'S OLDER THAN HE LOOKS.
HE'S A MUTANT SOLDIER FIGHTING FOR A BETTER TOMORROW.
IN HIS LIFE, HE'S MET HEROES.
AND VILLAINS.
BUT TONIGHT HE'S GOING TO ENCOUNTER SOMEONE UNLIKE ANYONE HE'S EVER MET BEFORE.
M.B.N.
NIN
REVU
I ♥
NYC
BMMMMMMMMMMMMM
ROBERT WEINBERG WRITER
MICHAEL RYAN PENCILER
PERTZBORN & CANDELARIO INKERS
AVALON STUDIOS COLORS
RS & COMICRAFT LETTERS
PETE FRANCO ASS'T ED.
MARK POWERS EDITOR
JOE QUESADA CHIEF
BILL JEMAS PRESIDENT

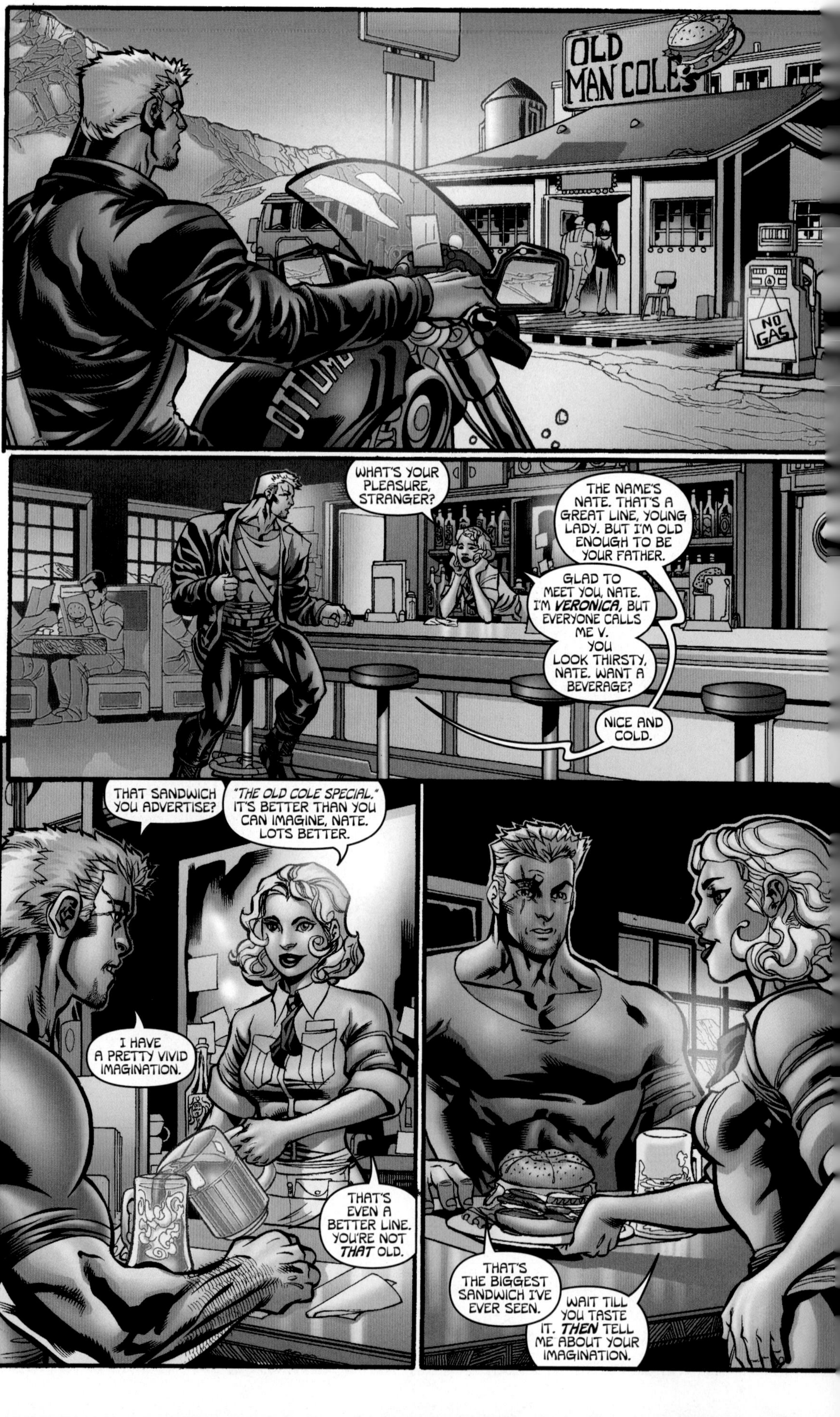

OLD MAN COLE'S
NO GAS
WHAT'S YOUR PLEASURE, STRANGER?
THE NAME'S NATE. THAT'S A GREAT LINE, YOUNG LADY. BUT I'M OLD ENOUGH TO BE YOUR FATHER.
GLAD TO MEET YOU, NATE. I'M *VERONICA,* BUT EVERYONE CALLS ME V.
YOU LOOK THIRSTY, NATE. WANT A BEVERAGE?
NICE AND COLD.
THAT SANDWICH YOU ADVERTISE?
"THE OLD COLE SPECIAL." IT'S BETTER THAN YOU CAN IMAGINE, NATE. LOTS BETTER.
I HAVE A PRETTY VIVID IMAGINATION.
THAT'S EVEN A BETTER LINE. YOU'RE NOT ***THAT*** OLD.
THAT'S THE BIGGEST SANDWICH I'VE EVER SEEN.
WAIT TILL YOU TASTE IT. ***THEN*** TELL ME ABOUT YOUR IMAGINATION.

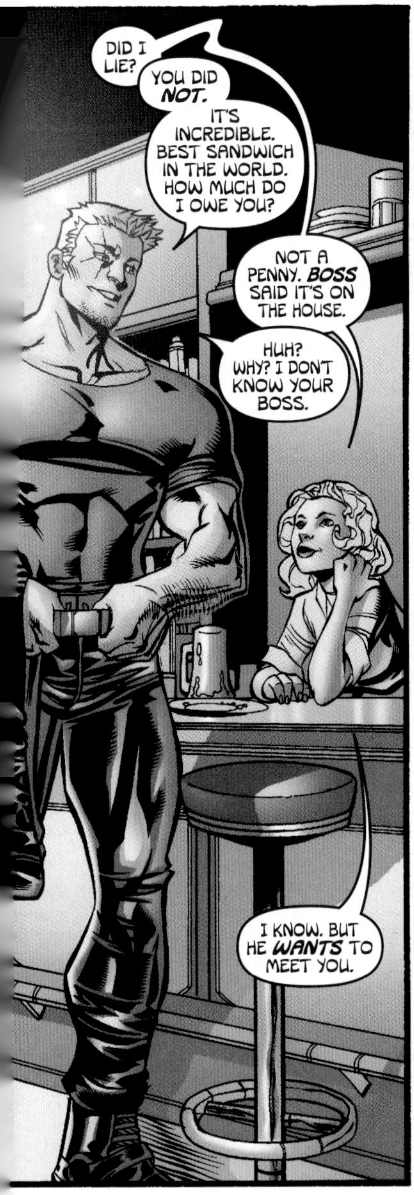
DID I LIE?
YOU DID NOT.
IT'S INCREDIBLE. BEST SANDWICH IN THE WORLD. HOW MUCH DO I OWE YOU?
NOT A PENNY. BOSS SAID IT'S ON THE HOUSE.
HUH? WHY? I DON'T KNOW YOUR BOSS.
I KNOW. BUT HE WANTS TO MEET YOU.

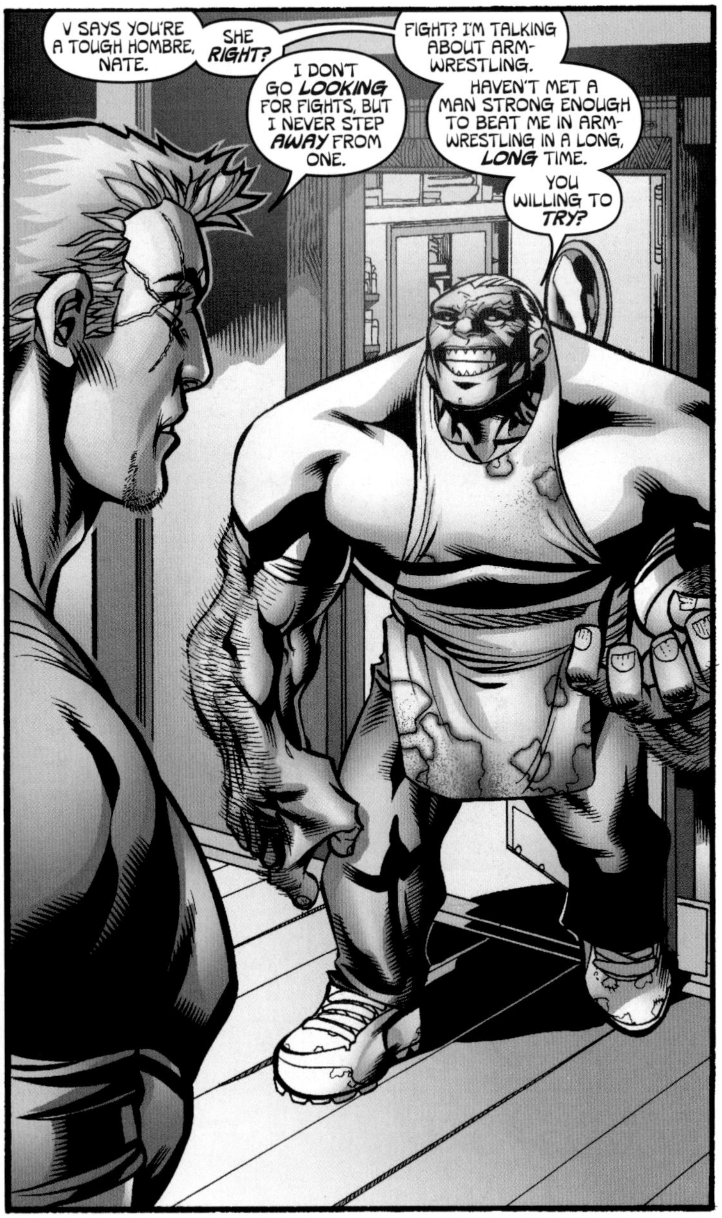
V SAYS YOU'RE A TOUGH HOMBRE, NATE.
SHE RIGHT?
I DON'T GO LOOKING FOR FIGHTS, BUT I NEVER STEP AWAY FROM ONE.
FIGHT? I'M TALKING ABOUT ARM-WRESTLING.
HAVEN'T MET A MAN STRONG ENOUGH TO BEAT ME IN ARM-WRESTLING IN A LONG, LONG TIME.
YOU WILLING TO TRY?

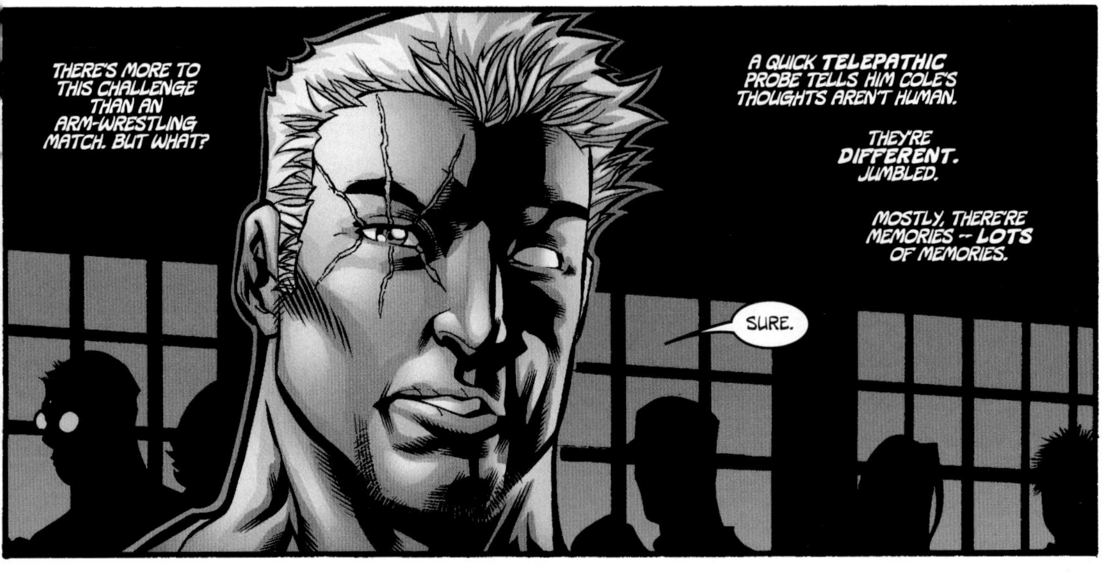
THERE'S MORE TO THIS CHALLENGE THAN AN ARM-WRESTLING MATCH. BUT WHAT?
A QUICK TELEPATHIC PROBE TELLS HIM COLE'S THOUGHTS AREN'T HUMAN.
THEY'RE DIFFERENT. JUMBLED.
MOSTLY, THERE'RE MEMORIES -- LOTS OF MEMORIES.
SURE.

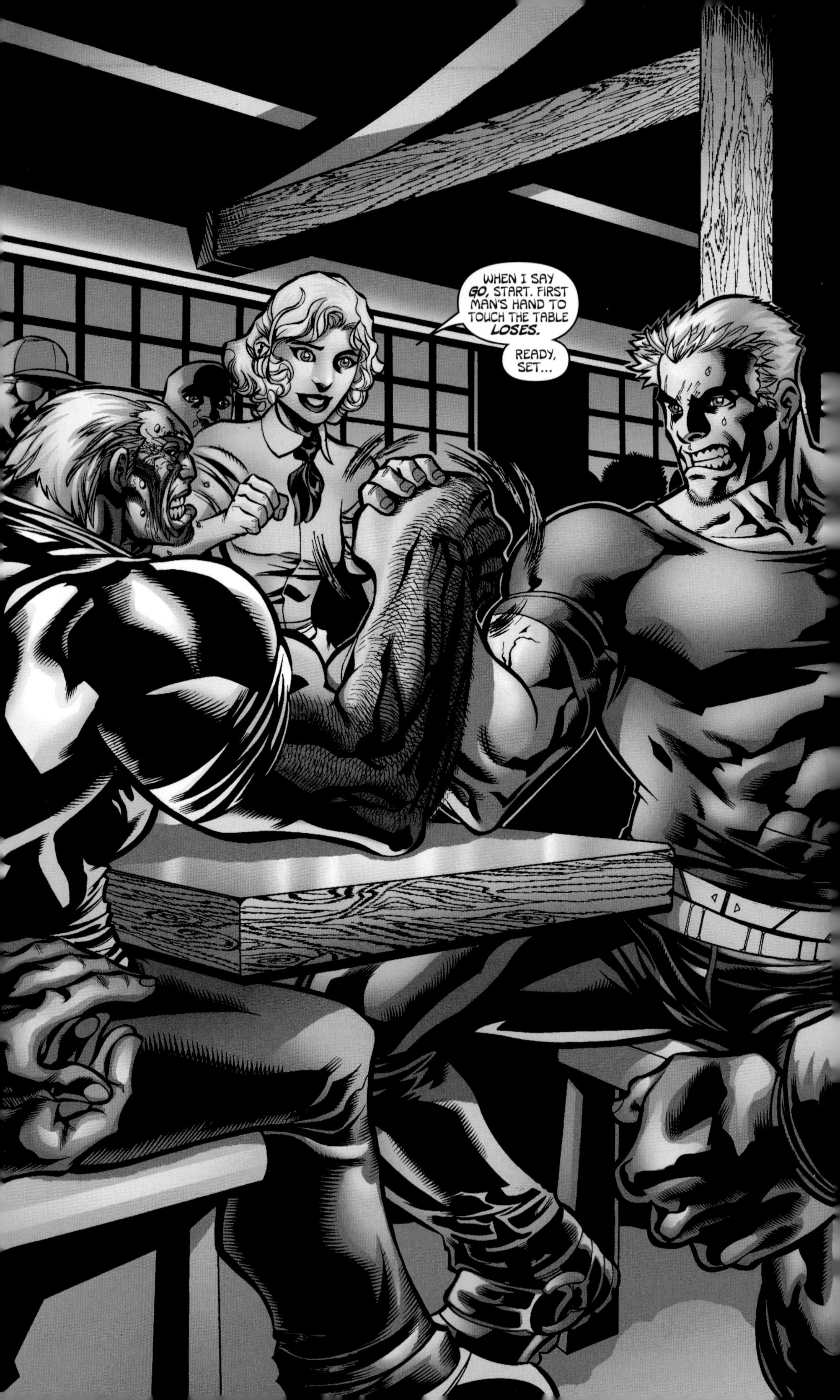
WHEN I SAY GO, START. FIRST MAN'S HAND TO TOUCH THE TABLE LOSES.
READY, SET...

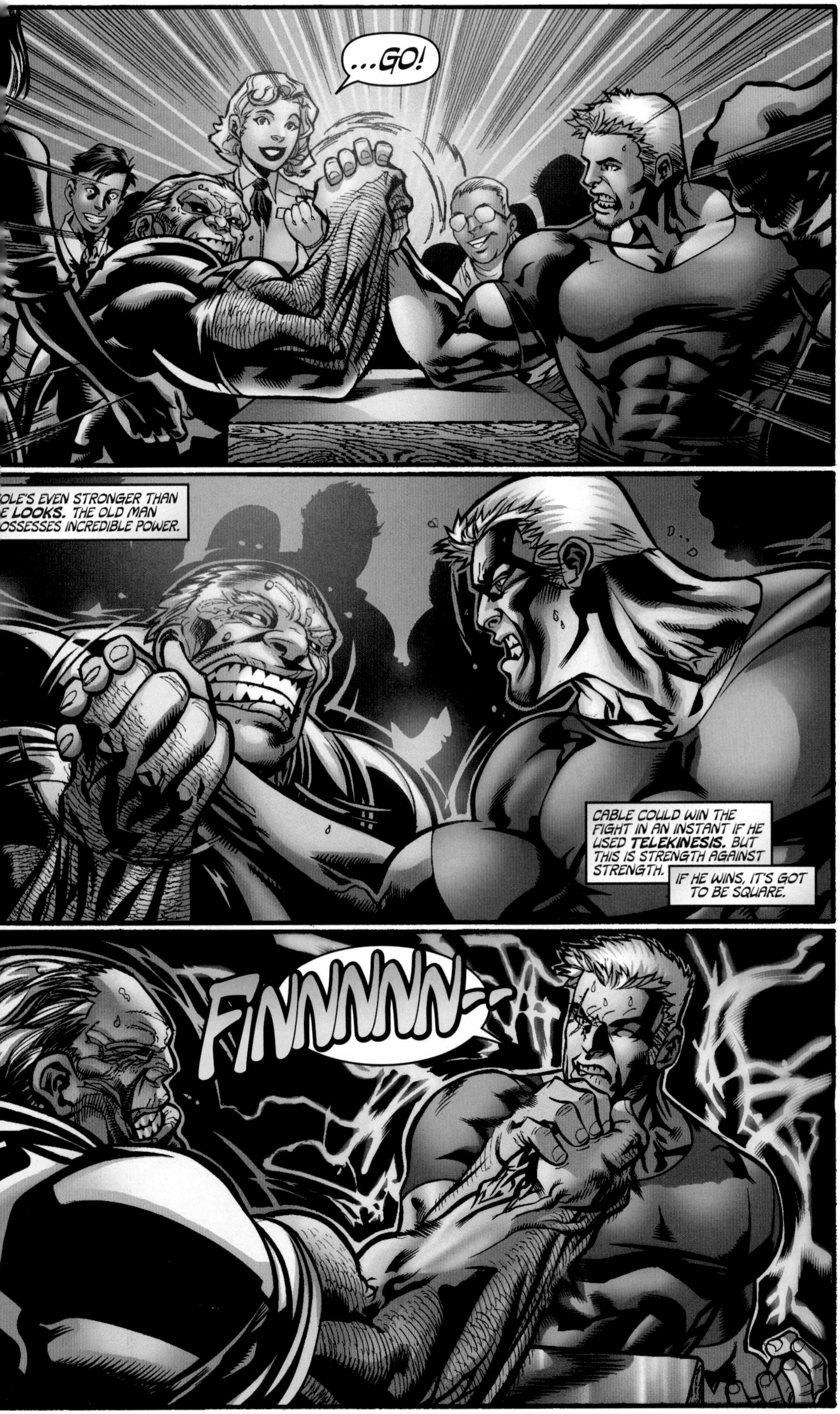
...GO!
COLE'S EVEN STRONGER THAN HE LOOKS. THE OLD MAN POSSESSES INCREDIBLE POWER.
CABLE COULD WIN THE FIGHT IN AN INSTANT IF HE USED TELEKINESIS. BUT THIS IS STRENGTH AGAINST STRENGTH.
IF HE WINS, IT'S GOT TO BE SQUARE.
FNNNNNN--

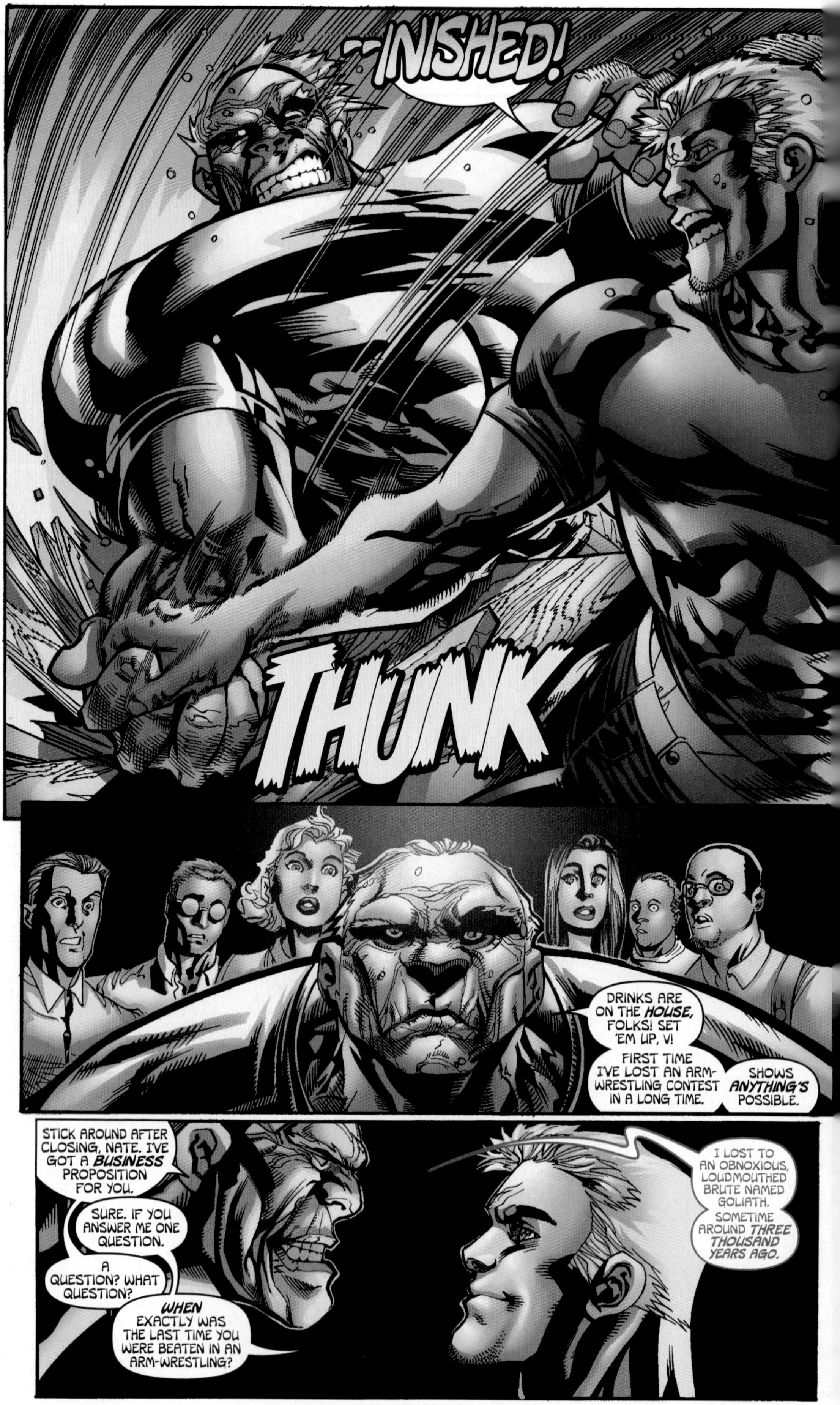
--INISHED!
THUNK
DRINKS ARE ON THE *HOUSE,* FOLKS! SET 'EM UP, V!
FIRST TIME I'VE LOST AN ARM-WRESTLING CONTEST IN A LONG TIME.
SHOWS *ANYTHING'S* POSSIBLE.
STICK AROUND AFTER CLOSING, NATE. I'VE GOT A *BUSINESS* PROPOSITION FOR YOU.
SURE. IF YOU ANSWER ME ONE QUESTION.
A QUESTION? WHAT QUESTION?
WHEN EXACTLY WAS THE LAST TIME YOU WERE BEATEN IN AN ARM-WRESTLING?
I LOST TO AN OBNOXIOUS, LOUDMOUTHED BRUTE NAMED GOLIATH.
SOMETIME AROUND *THREE THOUSAND YEARS AGO.*

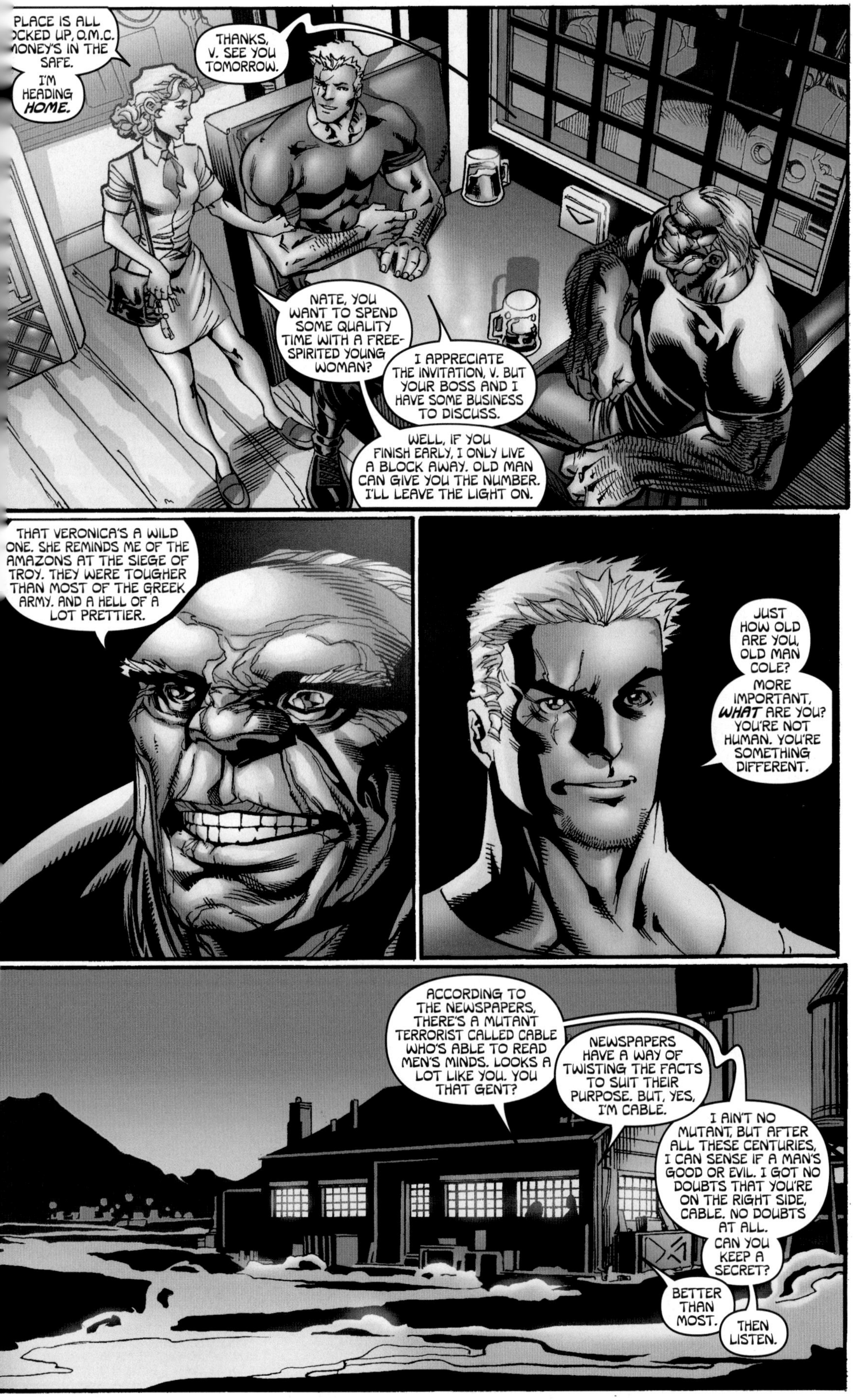
PLACE IS ALL LOCKED UP, O.M.C. MONEY'S IN THE SAFE.
I'M HEADING HOME.
THANKS, V. SEE YOU TOMORROW.
NATE, YOU WANT TO SPEND SOME QUALITY TIME WITH A FREE-SPIRITED YOUNG WOMAN?
I APPRECIATE THE INVITATION, V. BUT YOUR BOSS AND I HAVE SOME BUSINESS TO DISCUSS.
WELL, IF YOU FINISH EARLY, I ONLY LIVE A BLOCK AWAY. OLD MAN CAN GIVE YOU THE NUMBER. I'LL LEAVE THE LIGHT ON.
THAT VERONICA'S A WILD ONE. SHE REMINDS ME OF THE AMAZONS AT THE SIEGE OF TROY. THEY WERE TOUGHER THAN MOST OF THE GREEK ARMY. AND A HELL OF A LOT PRETTIER.
JUST HOW OLD ARE YOU, OLD MAN COLE?
MORE IMPORTANT, WHAT ARE YOU? YOU'RE NOT HUMAN. YOU'RE SOMETHING DIFFERENT.
ACCORDING TO THE NEWSPAPERS, THERE'S A MUTANT TERRORIST CALLED CABLE WHO'S ABLE TO READ MEN'S MINDS. LOOKS A LOT LIKE YOU. YOU THAT GENT?
NEWSPAPERS HAVE A WAY OF TWISTING THE FACTS TO SUIT THEIR PURPOSE. BUT, YES, I'M CABLE.
I AIN'T NO MUTANT, BUT AFTER ALL THESE CENTURIES, I CAN SENSE IF A MAN'S GOOD OR EVIL. I GOT NO DOUBTS THAT YOU'RE ON THE RIGHT SIDE, CABLE. NO DOUBTS AT ALL.
CAN YOU KEEP A SECRET?
BETTER THAN MOST.
THEN LISTEN.

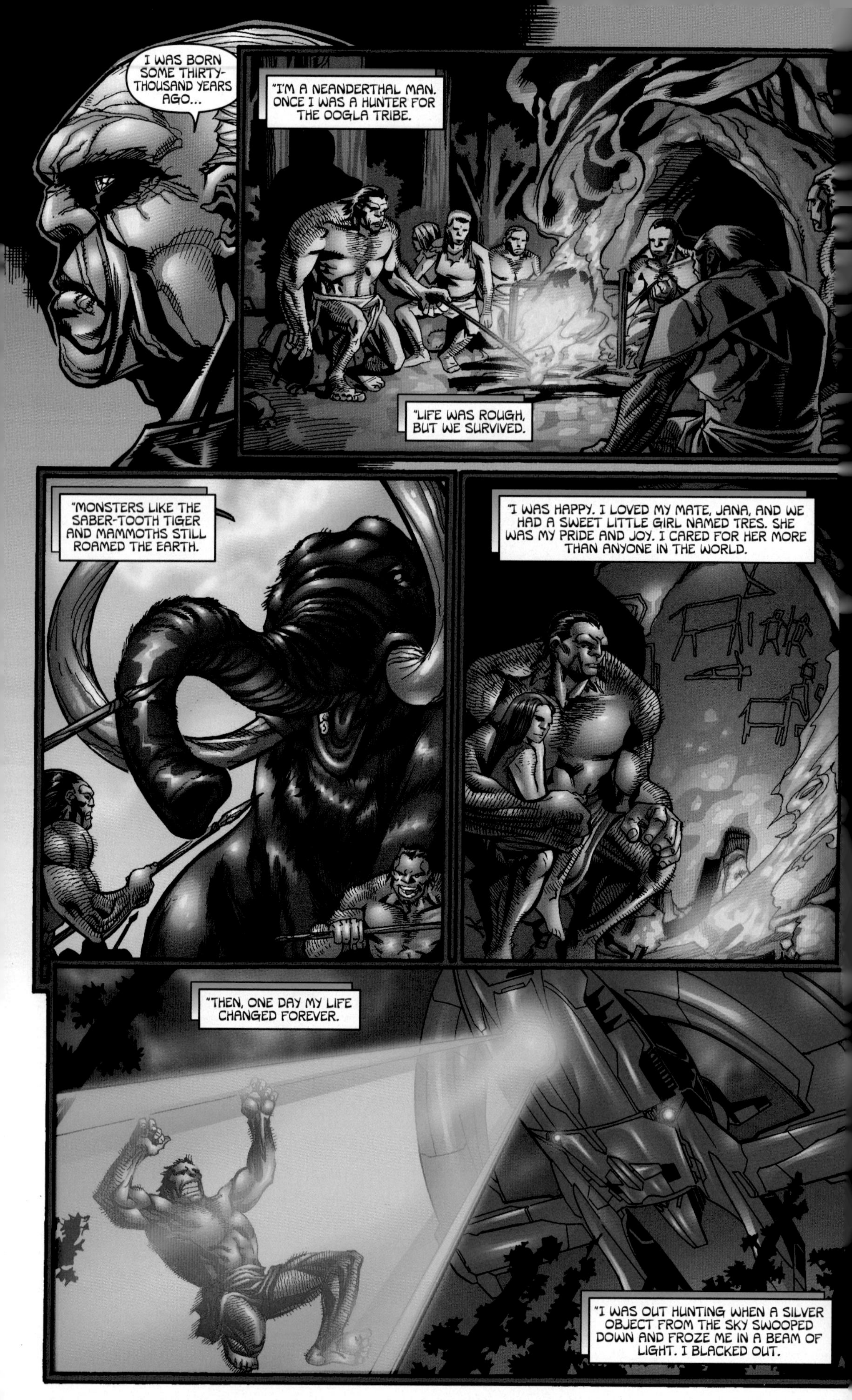

I WAS BORN SOME THIRTY-THOUSAND YEARS AGO...
"I'M A NEANDERTHAL MAN. ONCE I WAS A HUNTER FOR THE OOGLA TRIBE.
"LIFE WAS ROUGH, BUT WE SURVIVED.
"MONSTERS LIKE THE SABER-TOOTH TIGER AND MAMMOTHS STILL ROAMED THE EARTH.
"I WAS HAPPY. I LOVED MY MATE, JANA, AND WE HAD A SWEET LITTLE GIRL NAMED TRES. SHE WAS MY PRIDE AND JOY. I CARED FOR HER MORE THAN ANYONE IN THE WORLD.
"THEN, ONE DAY MY LIFE CHANGED FOREVER.
"I WAS OUT HUNTING WHEN A SILVER OBJECT FROM THE SKY SWOOPED DOWN AND FROZE ME IN A BEAM OF LIGHT. I BLACKED OUT.

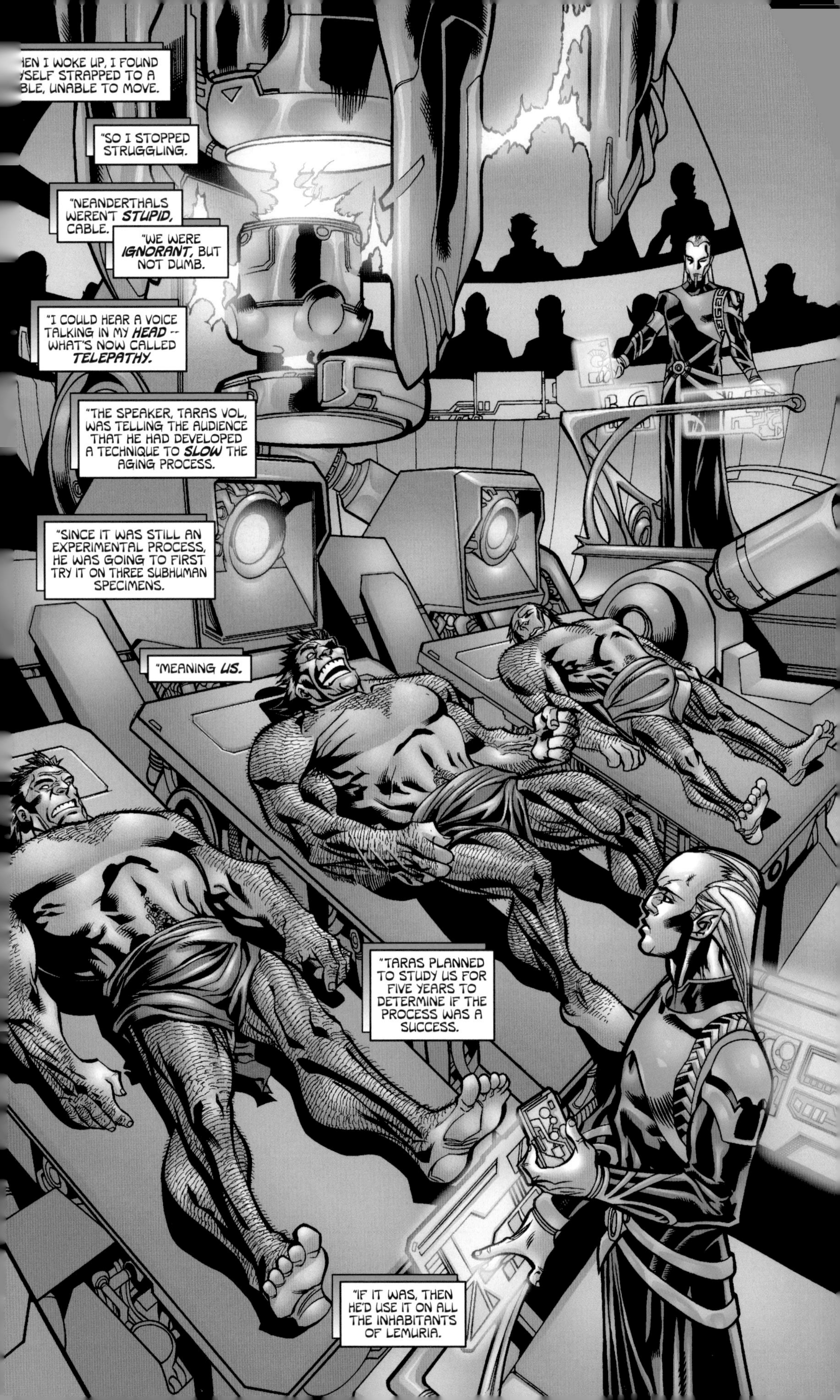
HEN I WOKE UP, I FOUND YSELF STRAPPED TO A BLE, UNABLE TO MOVE.
"SO I STOPPED STRUGGLING.
"NEANDERTHALS WERENT STUPID, CABLE.
"WE WERE IGNORANT, BUT NOT DUMB.
"I COULD HEAR A VOICE TALKING IN MY HEAD -- WHAT'S NOW CALLED TELEPATHY.
"THE SPEAKER, TARAS VOL, WAS TELLING THE AUDIENCE THAT HE HAD DEVELOPED A TECHNIQUE TO SLOW THE AGING PROCESS.
"SINCE IT WAS STILL AN EXPERIMENTAL PROCESS, HE WAS GOING TO FIRST TRY IT ON THREE SUBHUMAN SPECIMENS.
"MEANING US.
"TARAS PLANNED TO STUDY US FOR FIVE YEARS TO DETERMINE IF THE PROCESS WAS A SUCCESS.
"IF IT WAS, THEN HE'D USE IT ON ALL THE INHABITANTS OF LEMURIA.

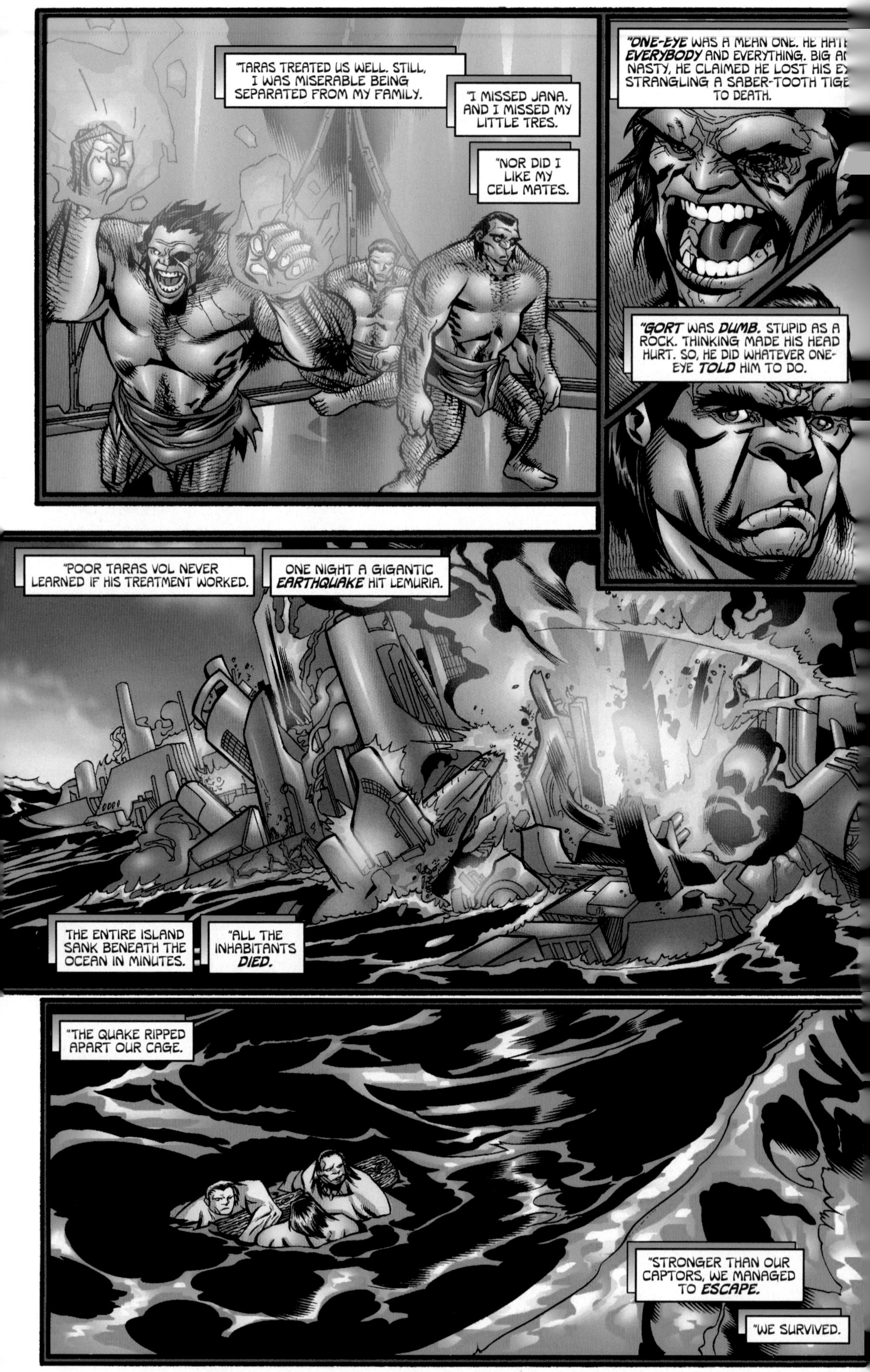
"TARAS TREATED US WELL. STILL, I WAS MISERABLE BEING SEPARATED FROM MY FAMILY.
"I MISSED JANA. AND I MISSED MY LITTLE TRES.
"NOR DID I LIKE MY CELL MATES.
"ONE-EYE WAS A MEAN ONE. HE HATE EVERYBODY AND EVERYTHING. BIG AN NASTY, HE CLAIMED HE LOST HIS EY STRANGLING A SABER-TOOTH TIGE TO DEATH.
"GORT WAS DUMB. STUPID AS A ROCK. THINKING MADE HIS HEAD HURT. SO, HE DID WHATEVER ONE-EYE TOLD HIM TO DO.
"POOR TARAS VOL NEVER LEARNED IF HIS TREATMENT WORKED.
ONE NIGHT A GIGANTIC EARTHQUAKE HIT LEMURIA.
THE ENTIRE ISLAND SANK BENEATH THE OCEAN IN MINUTES.
"ALL THE INHABITANTS DIED.
"THE QUAKE RIPPED APART OUR CAGE.
"STRONGER THAN OUR CAPTORS, WE MANAGED TO ESCAPE.
"WE SURVIVED.

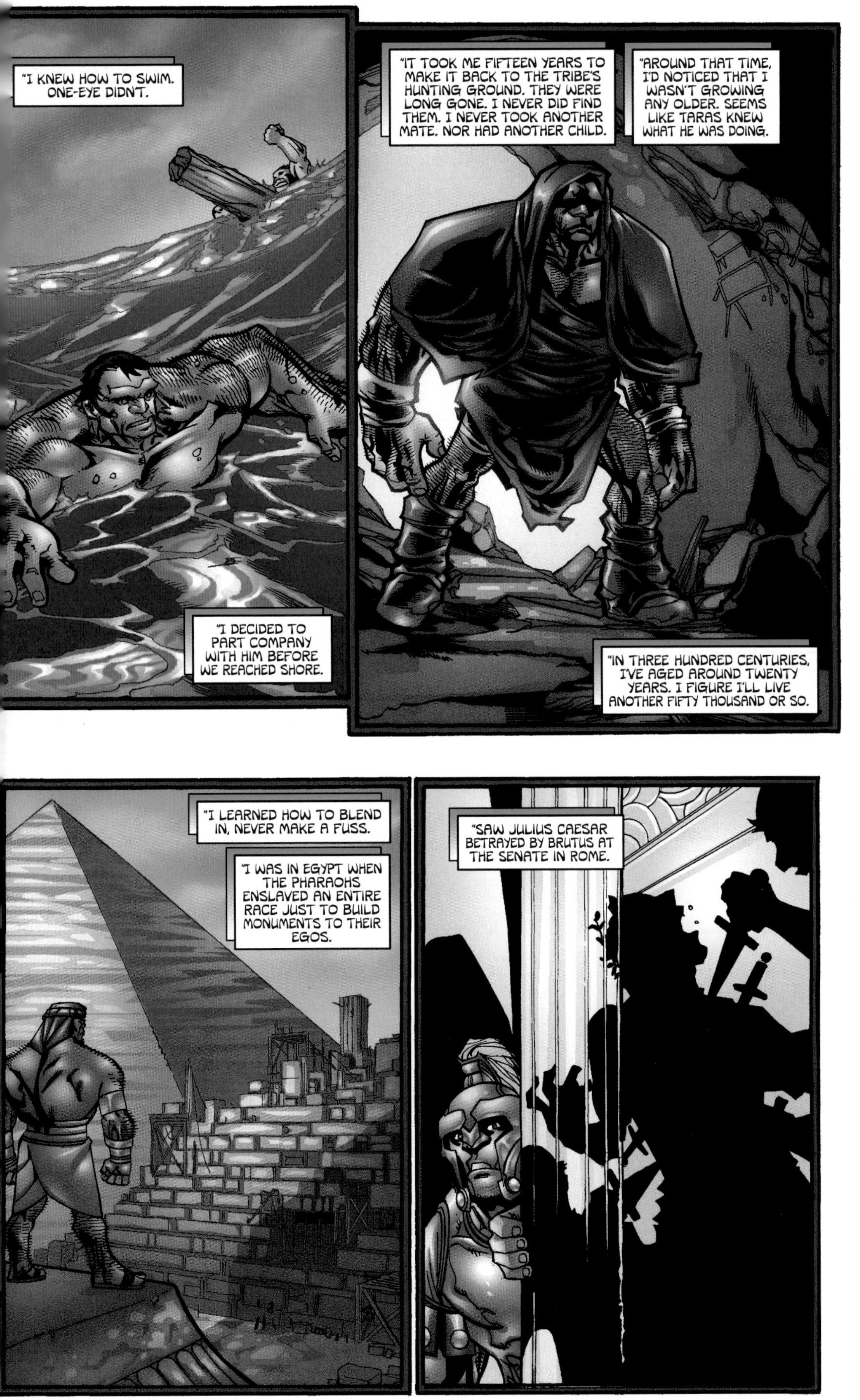

"I KNEW HOW TO SWIM. ONE-EYE DIDN'T.
"I DECIDED TO PART COMPANY WITH HIM BEFORE WE REACHED SHORE.
"IT TOOK ME FIFTEEN YEARS TO MAKE IT BACK TO THE TRIBE'S HUNTING GROUND. THEY WERE LONG GONE. I NEVER DID FIND THEM. I NEVER TOOK ANOTHER MATE. NOR HAD ANOTHER CHILD.
"AROUND THAT TIME, I'D NOTICED THAT I WASN'T GROWING ANY OLDER. SEEMS LIKE TARAS KNEW WHAT HE WAS DOING.
"IN THREE HUNDRED CENTURIES, I'VE AGED AROUND TWENTY YEARS. I FIGURE I'LL LIVE ANOTHER FIFTY THOUSAND OR SO.
"I LEARNED HOW TO BLEND IN, NEVER MAKE A FUSS.
"I WAS IN EGYPT WHEN THE PHARAOHS ENSLAVED AN ENTIRE RACE JUST TO BUILD MONUMENTS TO THEIR EGOS.
"SAW JULIUS CAESAR BETRAYED BY BRUTUS AT THE SENATE IN ROME.

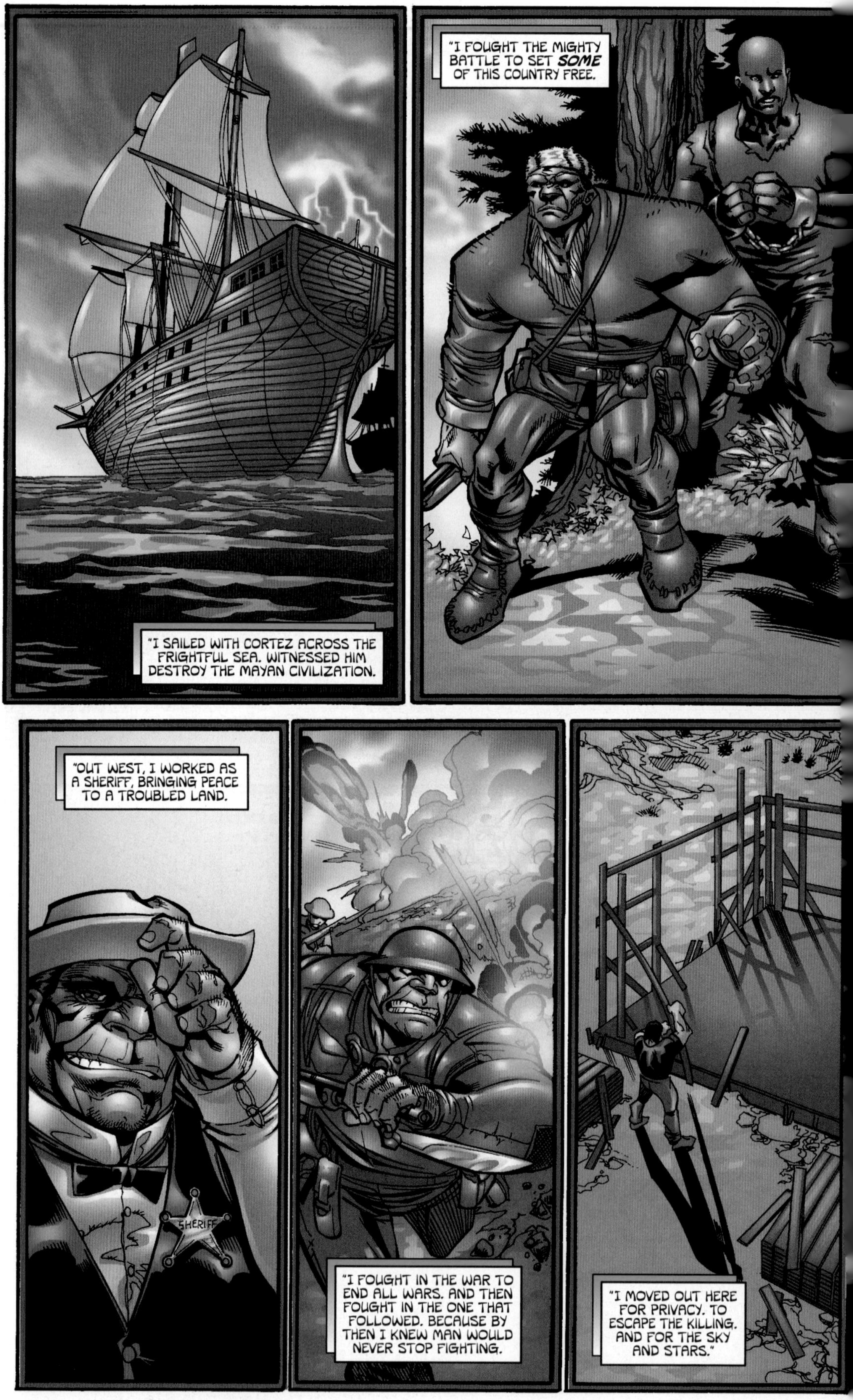

"I SAILED WITH CORTEZ ACROSS THE FRIGHTFUL SEA. WITNESSED HIM DESTROY THE MAYAN CIVILIZATION.
"I FOUGHT THE MIGHTY BATTLE TO SET SOME OF THIS COUNTRY FREE.
"OUT WEST, I WORKED AS A SHERIFF, BRINGING PEACE TO A TROUBLED LAND.
SHERIFF
"I FOUGHT IN THE WAR TO END ALL WARS. AND THEN FOUGHT IN THE ONE THAT FOLLOWED. BECAUSE BY THEN I KNEW MAN WOULD NEVER STOP FIGHTING.
"I MOVED OUT HERE FOR PRIVACY. TO ESCAPE THE KILLING. AND FOR THE SKY AND STARS."

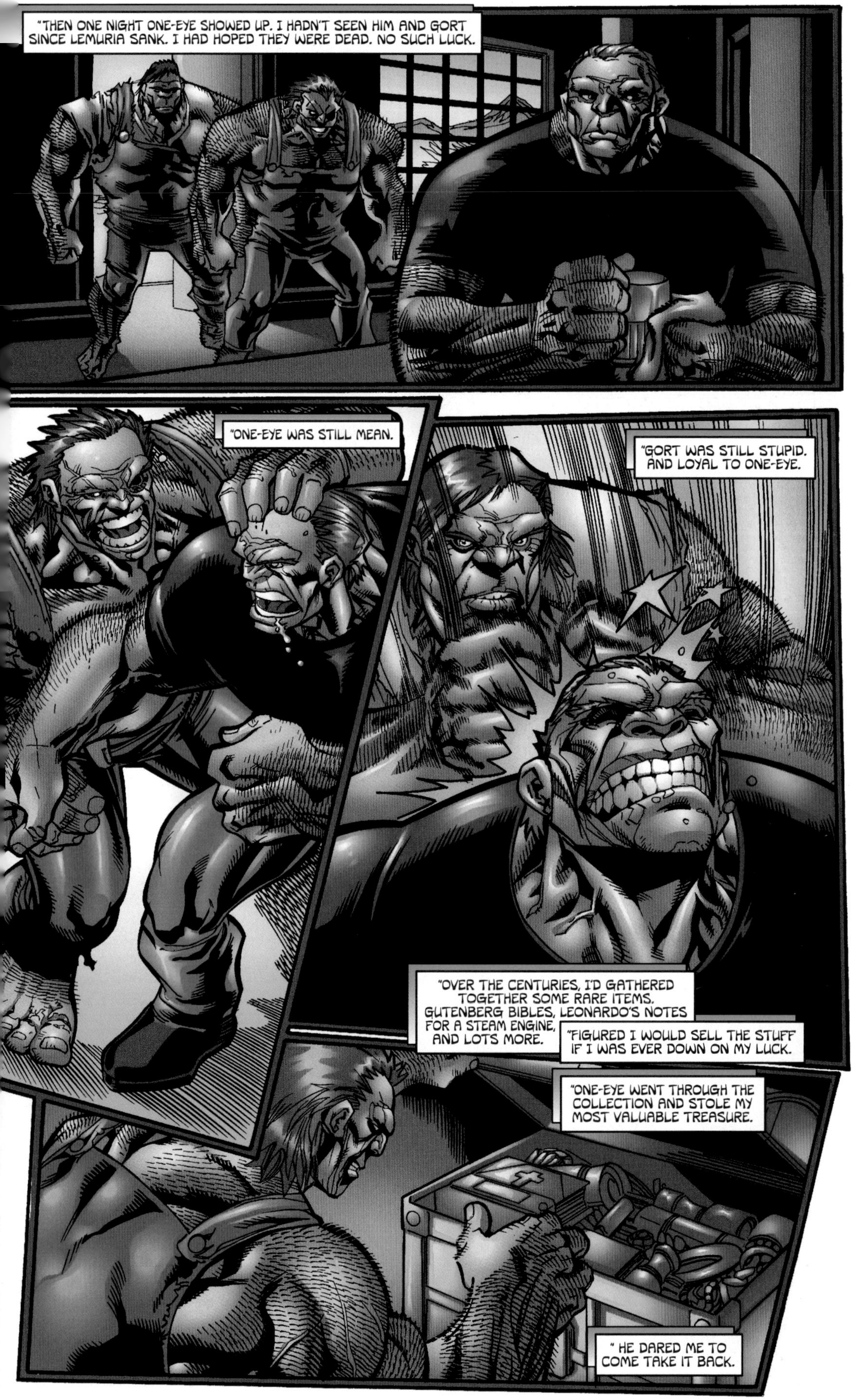
"THEN ONE NIGHT ONE-EYE SHOWED UP. I HADN'T SEEN HIM AND GORT SINCE LEMURIA SANK. I HAD HOPED THEY WERE DEAD. NO SUCH LUCK.
"ONE-EYE WAS STILL MEAN.
"GORT WAS STILL STUPID. AND LOYAL TO ONE-EYE.
"OVER THE CENTURIES, I'D GATHERED TOGETHER SOME RARE ITEMS. GUTENBERG BIBLES, LEONARDO'S NOTES FOR A STEAM ENGINE, AND LOTS MORE.
"FIGURED I WOULD SELL THE STUFF IF I WAS EVER DOWN ON MY LUCK.
"ONE-EYE WENT THROUGH THE COLLECTION AND STOLE MY MOST VALUABLE TREASURE.
" HE DARED ME TO COME TAKE IT BACK.

THAT HAPPENED A *YEAR* AGO.

ONE-EYE AND GORT HAVE A HIDEAWAY JUST OUTSIDE OF TOWN.

TWO AGAINST ONE I COULD NEVER WIN.

I'VE BEEN WAITING FOR A MAN AS STRONG AS YOU TO COME ALONG.

I'LL PAY WHATEVER YOU *ASK* IF YOU HELP ME GET MY TREASURE BACK.

I'M A MAN WHO PAYS HIS DEBTS.

I OWE YOU FOR A SANDWICH.

HUMAN OR NOT, YOU'RE A BETTER MAN THAN MOST.

I'LL BE GLAD TO HELP YOU DO WHAT'S *RIGHT.*

COME ON *OUT,* ONE-EYE!

IT'S OLD MAN COLE.

YOU *DARED* ME TO COME GET MY TREASURE.

WELL, HERE I AM.

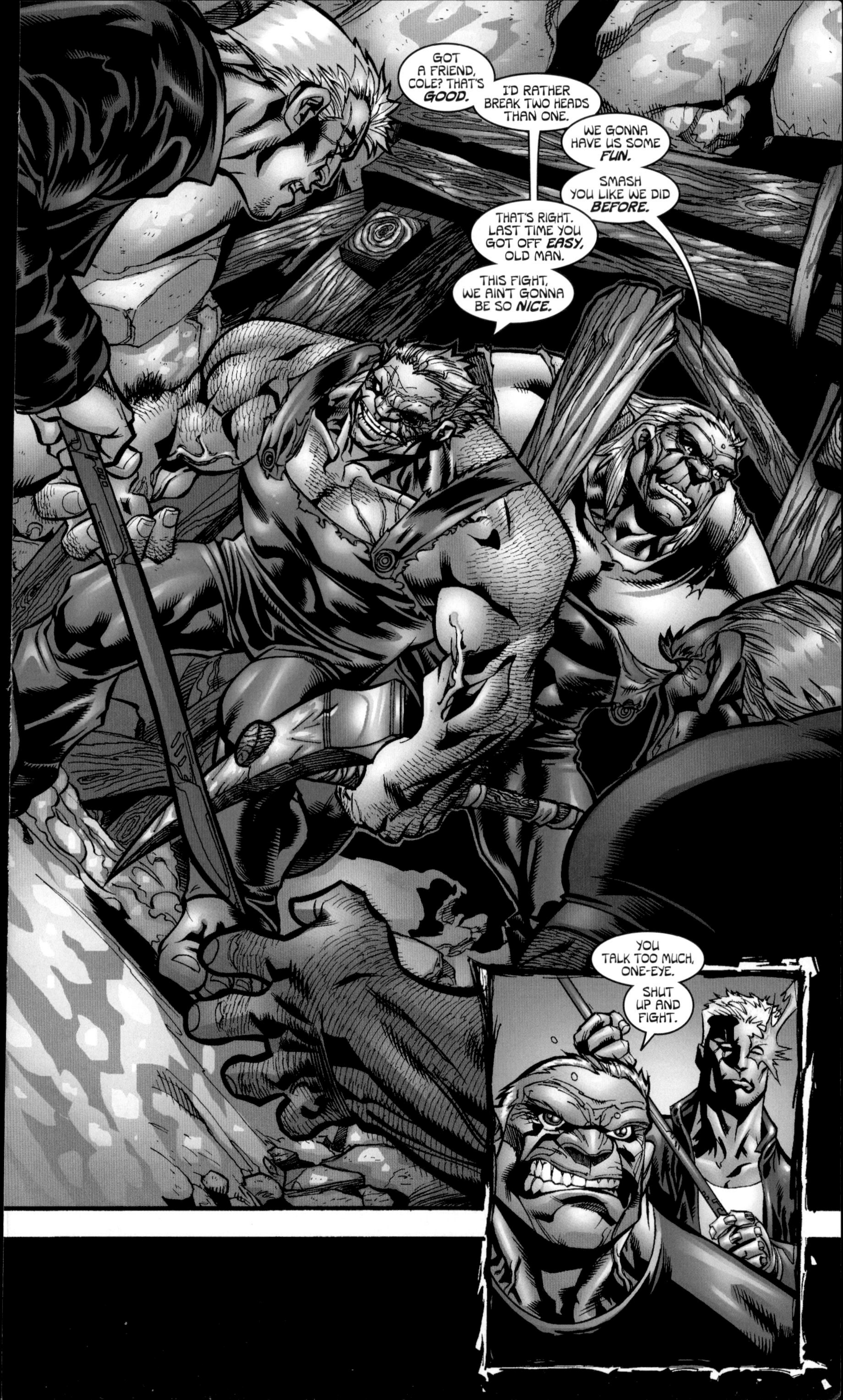
GOT A FRIEND, COLE? THAT'S **GOOD.**
I'D RATHER BREAK TWO HEADS THAN ONE.
WE GONNA HAVE US SOME **FUN.**
SMASH YOU LIKE WE DID **BEFORE.**
THAT'S RIGHT. LAST TIME YOU GOT OFF **EASY,** OLD MAN.
THIS FIGHT, WE AIN'T GONNA BE SO **NICE.**
YOU TALK TOO MUCH, ONE-EYE.
SHUT UP AND FIGHT.

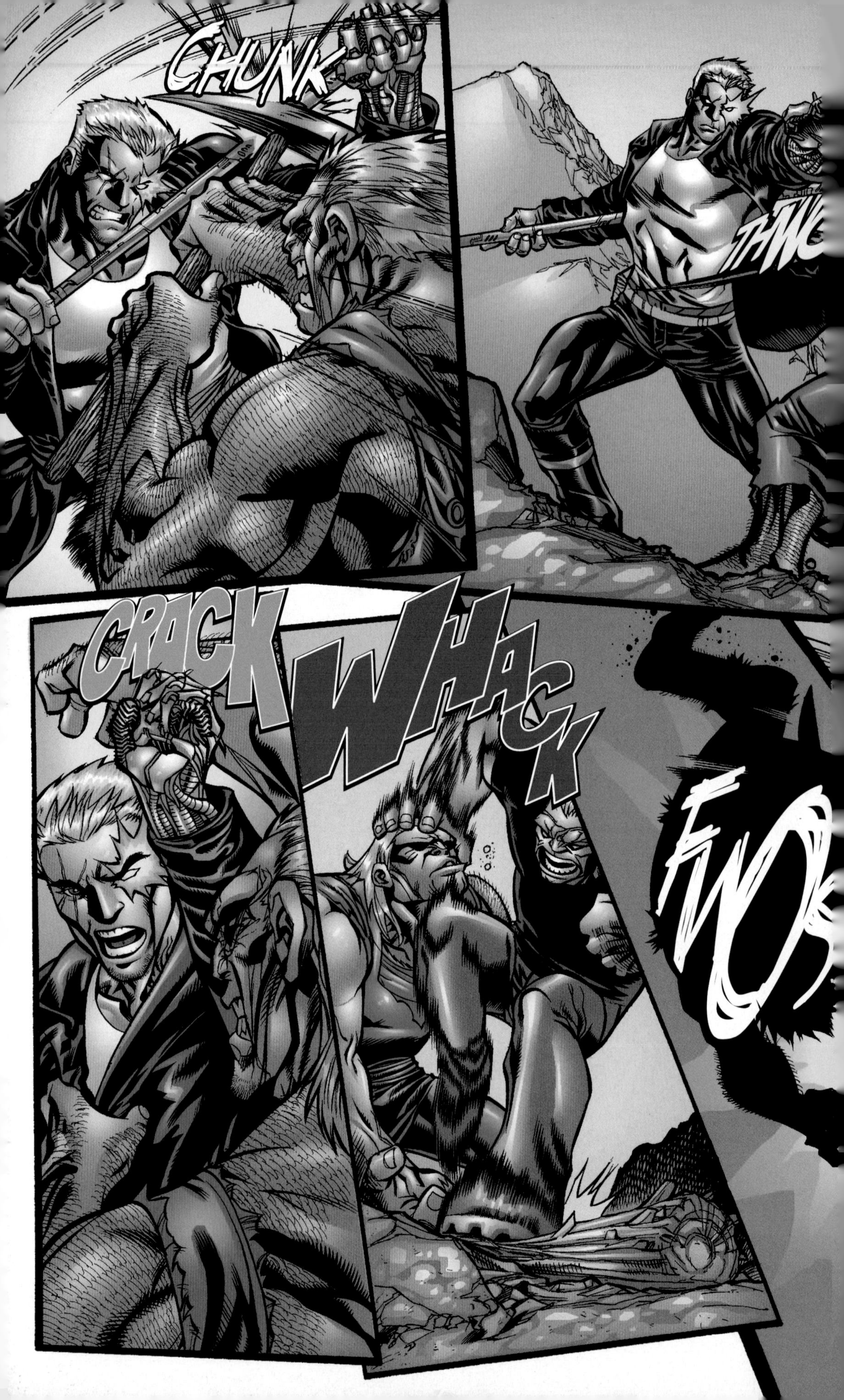
CHUNK
CRACK
WHACK

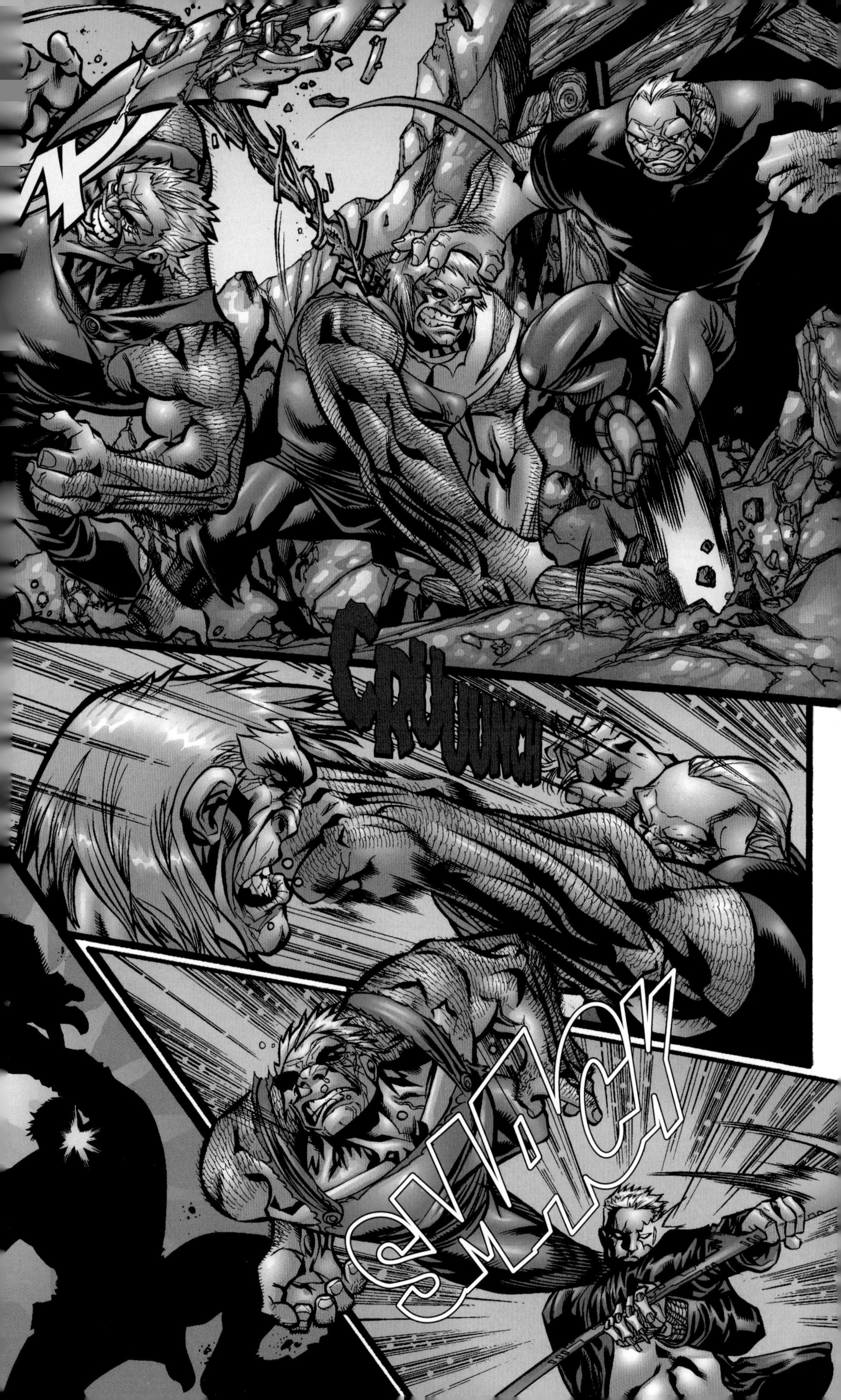
CRUUUNCH

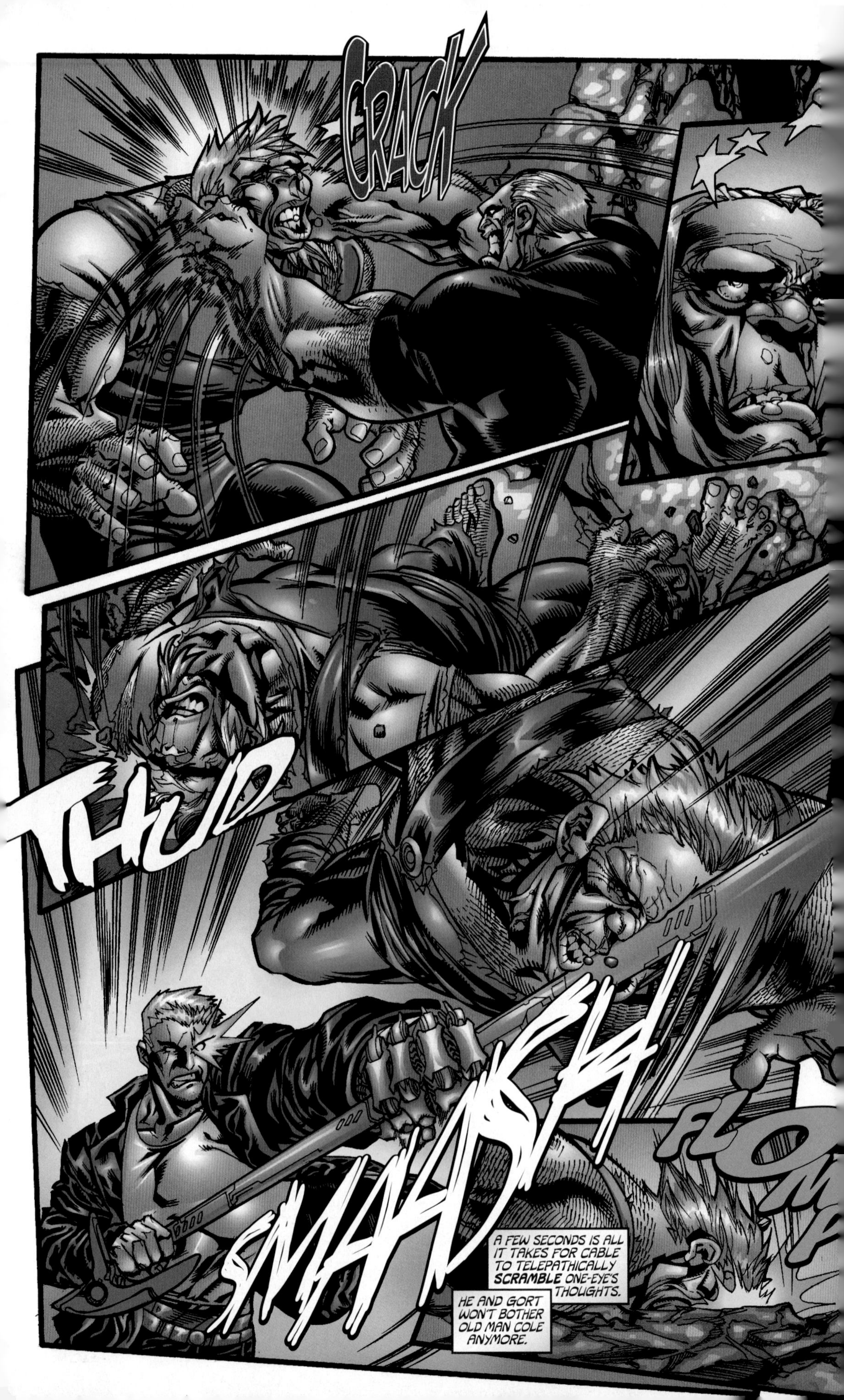
CRACK
THUD
SMASH
FLOMP
A FEW SECONDS IS ALL IT TAKES FOR CABLE TO TELEPATHICALLY SCRAMBLE ONE-EYE'S THOUGHTS.
HE AND GORT WON'T BOTHER OLD MAN COLE ANYMORE.

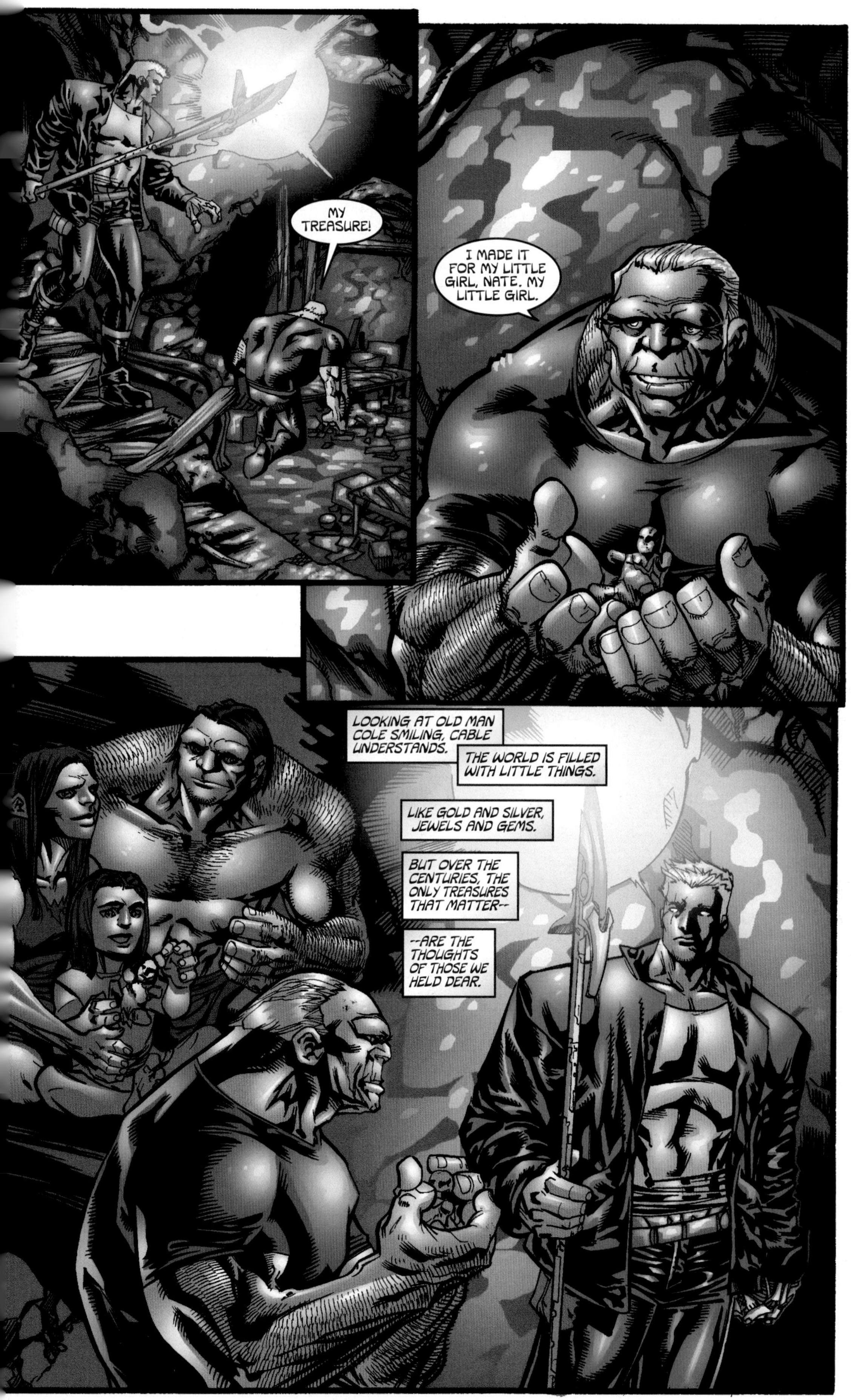
MY TREASURE!
I MADE IT FOR MY LITTLE GIRL, NATE. MY LITTLE GIRL.
LOOKING AT OLD MAN COLE SMILING, CABLE UNDERSTANDS.
THE WORLD IS FILLED WITH LITTLE THINGS.
LIKE GOLD AND SILVER, JEWELS AND GEMS.
BUT OVER THE CENTURIES, THE ONLY TREASURES THAT MATTER--
--ARE THE THOUGHTS OF THOSE WE HELD DEAR.

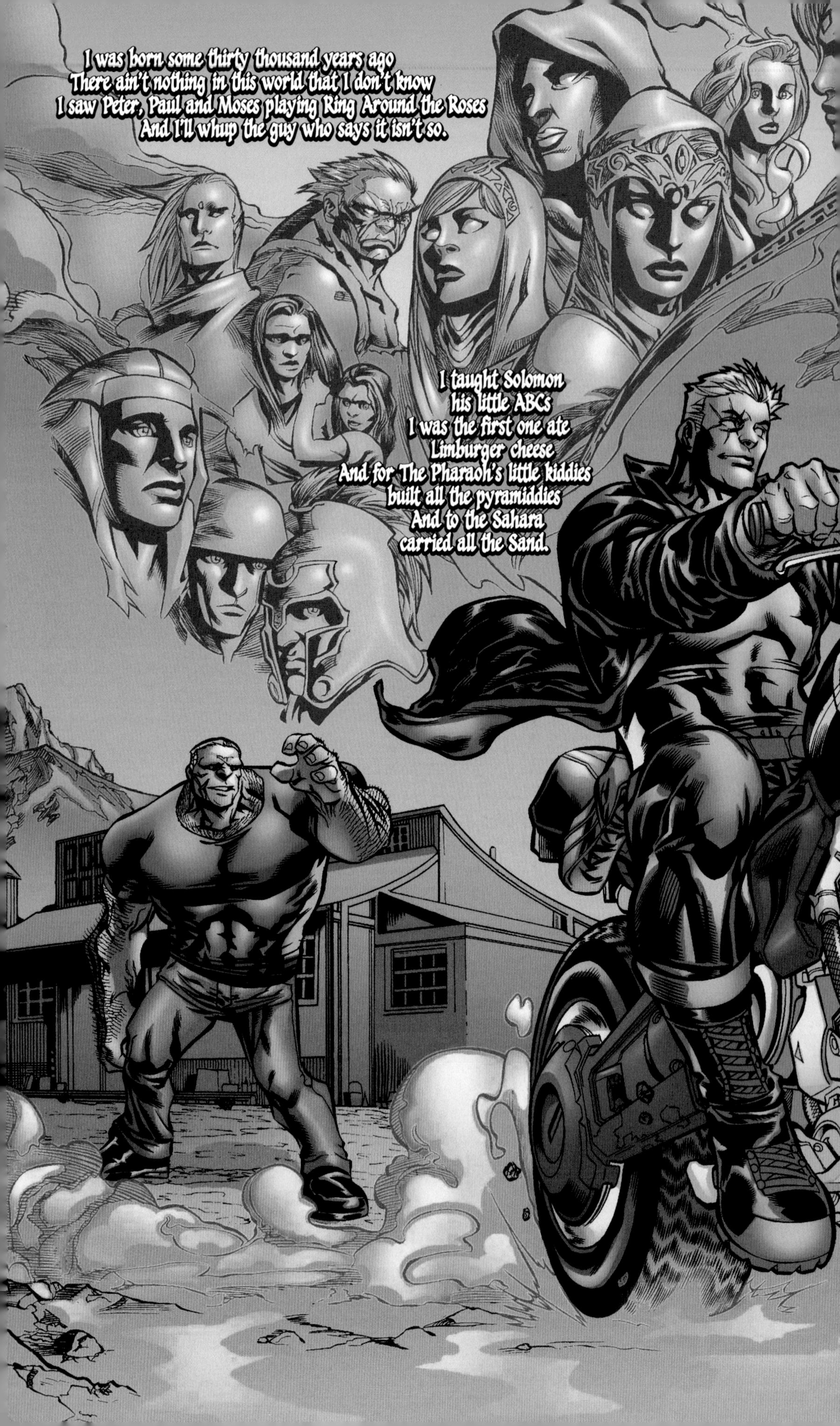

I was born some thirty thousand years ago
There ain't nothing in this world that I don't know
I saw Peter, Paul and Moses playing Ring Around the Roses
And I'll whup the guy who says it isn't so.
I taught Solomon his little ABCs
I was the first one ate Limburger cheese
And for The Pharaoh's little kiddies built all the pyramiddies
And to the Sahara carried all the Sand.

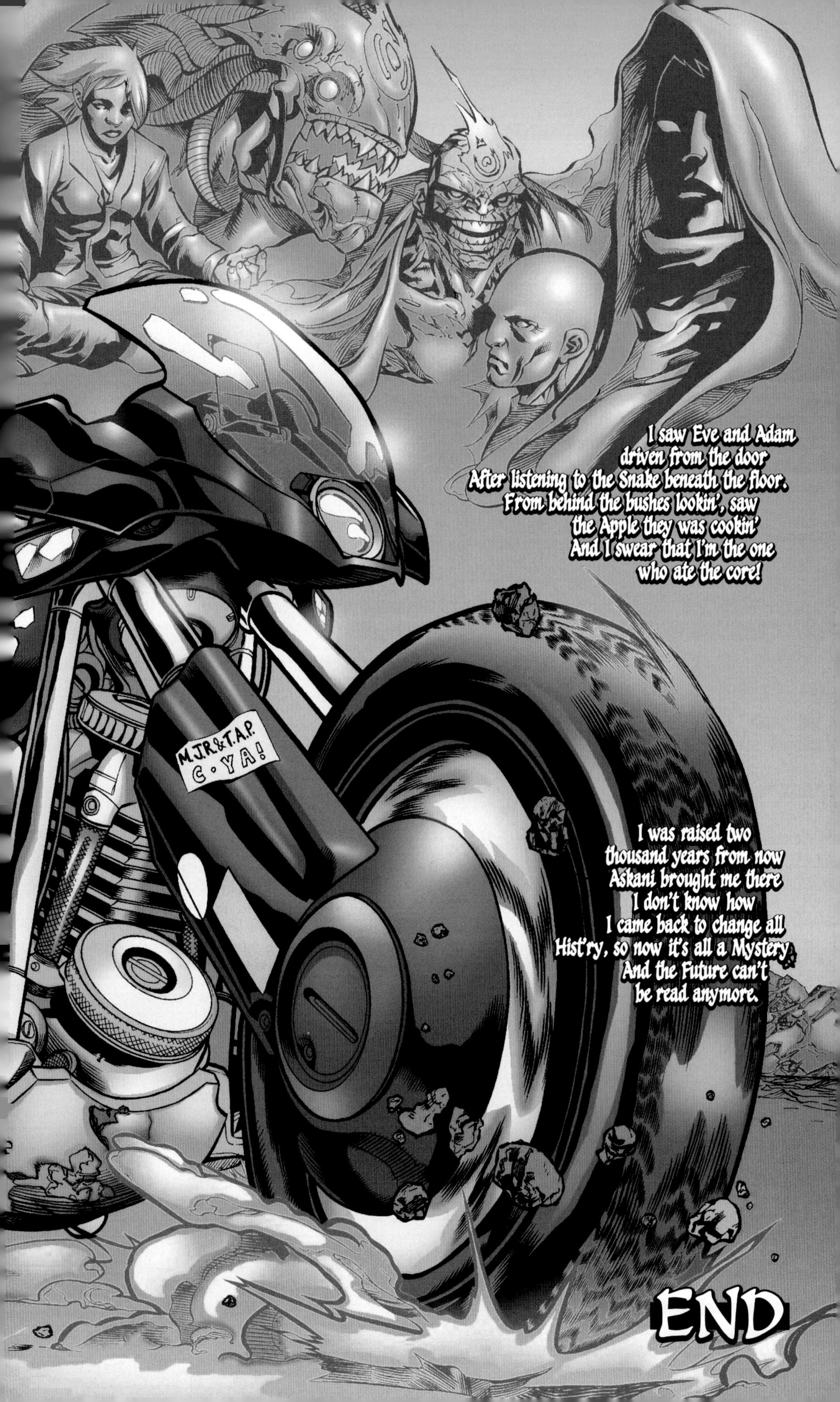
I saw Eve and Adam
driven from the door
After listening to the Snake beneath the floor.
From behind the bushes lookin', saw
the Apple they was cookin'
And I swear that I'm the one
who ate the core!
M.J.R.&T.A.P.
C-YA!
I was raised two
thousand years from now
Askani brought me there
I don't know how
I came back to change all
Hist'ry, so now it's all a Mystery
And the Future can't
be read anymore.
END

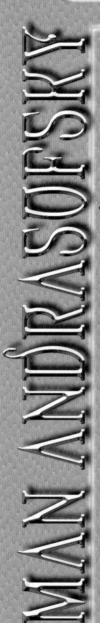

X-MEN: MILLENNIAL VISIONS 2001 RE-IMAGINED VARIOUS X-MEN CHARACTERS, INCLUDING CABLE, IN CREATIVE NEW WAYS.

RACMAN ANDRASOFSKY

TEXT BY BRENDAN FLETCHER

CABLE: War Journal Entry 122312

XAVIER INSTITUTE / ALTERNATIVE

FUTURES AND PASTS

This is all my fault.

I lost control.

In a moment of passion and desire, I let slip that part of my mind that keeps my "disease" in check. I gave in to the woman I love ... just once ... and this is the result, a pulverized landscape, pockmarked with techno-organisms overrun by the transmode virus.

That night, lying naked in her bed, it took hold of Clara quickly and spread ... from me to her, and from her to thousands more. The new organisms it created from human flesh became a beacon of sorts to the horrific, alien Technarchy — a sign that Earth was primed for their invasion. Human and mutant fought side by side in the terrible war for the planet, scarcely a hope among them... until the triumph of the alien retreat eventually arrived.

What's left of us can hardly be called a race, our home barely habitable with its seared, broken ground and toxins released from the super-heated silicate in and on the earth, steaming in the heavy wind. At least the sunsets are pretty.

So what do I do now? Those that pulled through the war are skittish, afraid of the new landscape and the techno-organic life that's infested it. I see Clara's fear in all of them, at that moment when the virus exploded from my arm, consuming her, transforming her. But as time passes she appears to me in the new life. These things, infected souls I imagine, seem drawn to me. They follow me. Every morning at my window I'm treated to a pneumatic ballet cascading through the streets.

I think she's one of them.

She's still alive.

And I think it's time for me to play messiah again.

STUDENT/ CZYLANNI RIKAARD

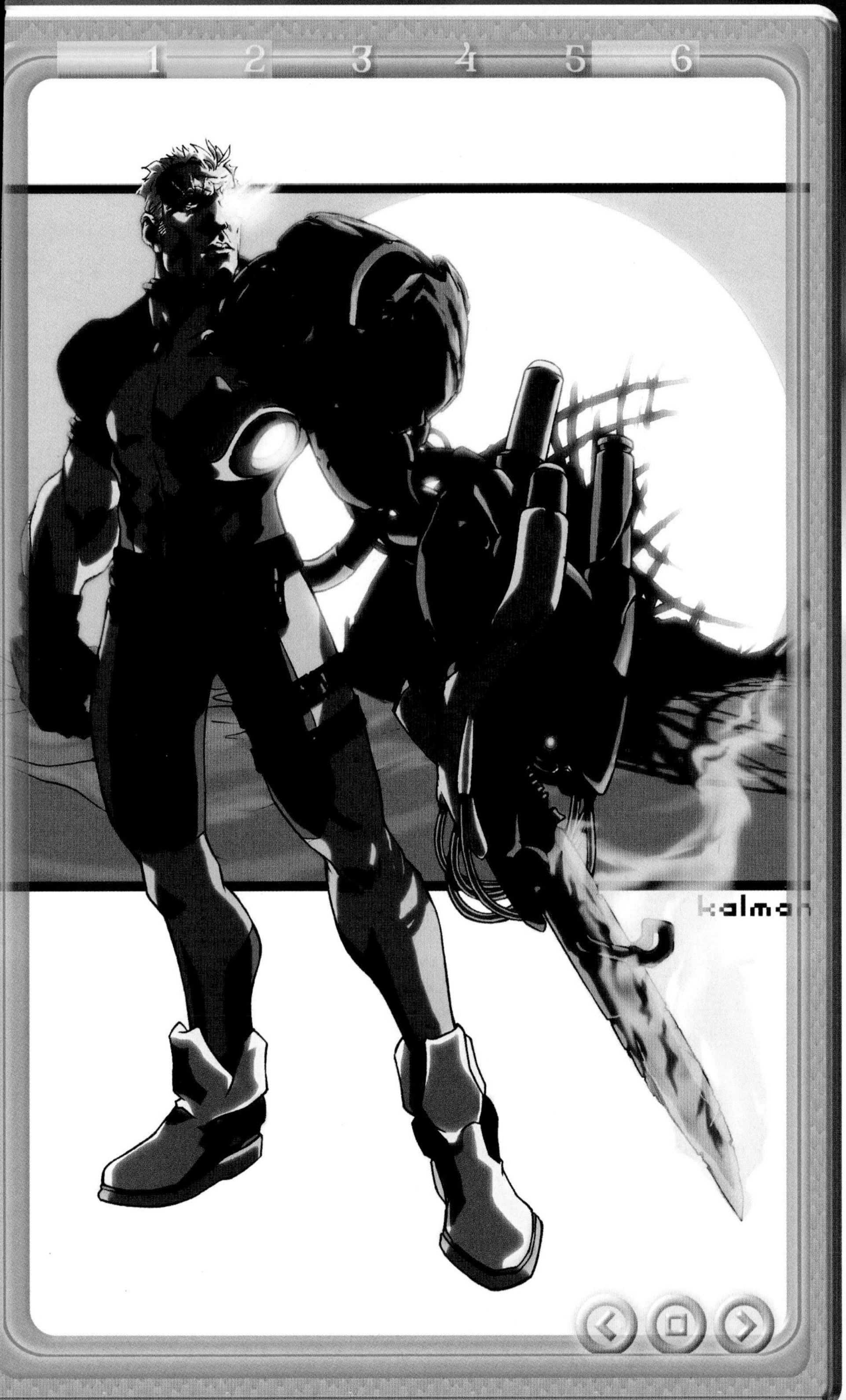
1 2 3 4 5 6
kalman

CABLE #79 VARIANT COVER BY MICHAEL RYAN

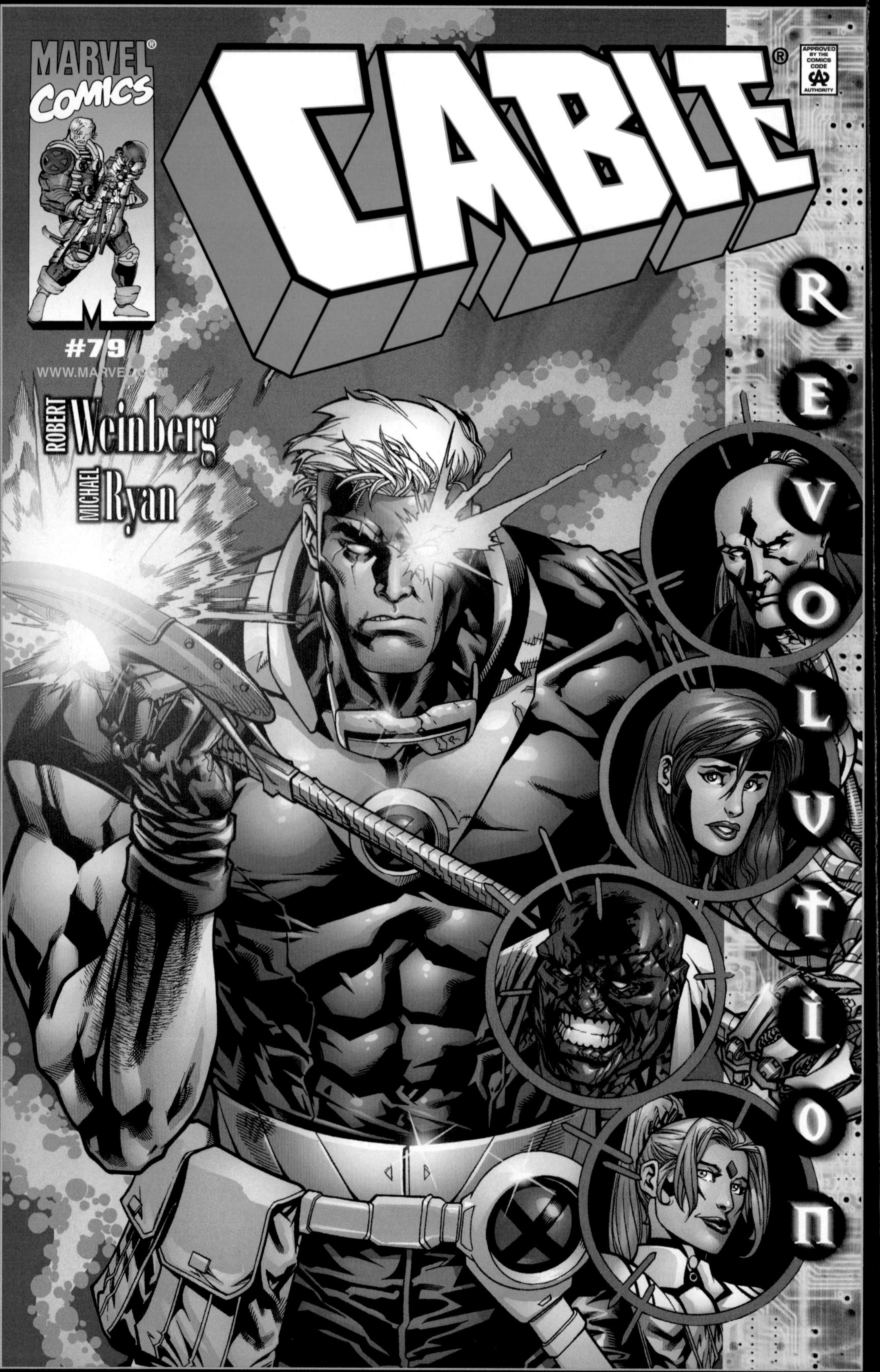
MARVEL COMICS
CABLE
#79
WWW.MARVEL.COM
ROBERT Weinberg
MICHAEL Ryan
REVOLUTION
APPROVED BY THE COMICS CODE AUTHORITY

CABLE GRAMS

Hey, fans, let us to be the first to welcome you to X-MEN: REVOLUTION! Not only have we entered the 21st century, but we've entered a new era for the X-MEN. As you may know, in our revolution new writers and artists have taken over the duties of leading our X-characters to greater heights.

In this new era we see Cable do what he thought was the unthinkable-- he joined the X-Men! He's helping them on their crusade for peaceful coexistence between man and mutant. But along with his duties as an X-Man, there are threats only he can deal with. This is where Cable heads towards a new direction in his own title. Casting this new direction in the CABLE monthly are penciler Michael Ryan and writer Bob Weinberg. But instead of us explaining what The Askani'son will be doing, we decided to let the man tell you yourself! Here we go:

Dear Marvel fans-

Welcome to the Cable revolution. As the new writer for the book, I'd like to introduce myself and give you an insider's look of what I have planned for Cable in the months to come. My name is Bob Weinberg and I've worked as a full-time writer for more than ten years. I've written fifteen novels and six non-fiction books, ranging from a vampire trilogy to an investigation of the computers of Star Trek. Most important, I've been a Marvel comics fan since the days of Stan Lee and Jack Kirby. Writing a monthly comic for Marvel is a lifelong dream come true.

I have some exciting plans for Cable. This spring and summer he'll battle an entirely new cast of villains. I'm not going to ignore Cable's past and characters from earlier stories are going to reappear, but the focus of my stories will be on new enemies, new allies, and all new plots. Cable will be pushed to the limit by the

demonic forces of the Undying, investigate the strange House on the Borderline, and pursue the hunt for Rachel Summers. And that's just the beginning! It's going to be exciting times for our favorite mutant, time-traveling warrior. I hope you'll join me for his whirlwind adventures in the past, the present, and the far future.

Bob Weinberg

P.S. I'll be on Marvel's AOL Chat the first Tuesday night of each month to discuss Cable's adventures and answer any questions you might have about the series.

And last but not least, we wanted to give you a little taste of what's in store from Michael Ryan in our monthy title. Here are a couple of shots of some villains you may recognize (or maybe not!), some new locales, and best of all, our man Cable! Enjoy!

PETE FRANCO
ASSISTANT EDITOR

MARK POWERS
EDITOR

BOB HARRAS
CHIEF

NEXT ISSUE:

TALK ABOUT A STRANGER IN A STRANGE LAND, HUH??? BUT, BE SURE TO CHECK US OUT IN THIRTY FOR MORE INSIGHT ON THE PLACE CALLED HARMONY. IS IT REALLY WHAT IT'S NAMED AFTER, OR IS IT JUST A FACADE? PLUS MORE ON THE MYSTERIOUS AENTAROS AND THE UNDYING!

CABLE GRAMS c/o MARVEL COMICS
387 PARK AVENUE SOUTH • NEW YORK, NY 10016
IF YOU DON'T WANT YOUR NAME AND ADDRESS PRINTED, PLEASE LET US KNOW. LETTERS MAY BE EDITED FOR CONTENT AND LENGTH.
E-MAIL: MAIL@MARVEL.COM
MARK E-MAIL "OKAY TO PRINT"

CABLE GRAMS

Hey, Cable-ites, what's happening? Well, as you can see here there's a whole lot happening here! I decided to give you folks a little sneak preview of things to come! Next issue, we have guest artist Tom Derenick filling in for Michael Ryan. And, yes, Tom is doin' the first couple of pages in the fully rendered pencil style that you see here. We thought it was so cool, so we decided to run with it!

In Cable #94, we welcome back Mr. Ryan! And just to show that he has not skipped a beat with his pencils, check out this cover and these two pages!

You really don't get to see pencils all that often so I hope you enjoy the little sneak peek I'm giving you.

'Til next time...
Pete Franco

CABLE #93

CABLE #94

CABLE #94

CABLE #94

PETE FRANCO
ASSISTANT EDITOR

MARK POWERS
EDITOR

JOE QUESADA
CHIEF

NEXT ISSUE:

JOIN BOB, TOM, TED, MARK AND MYSELF FOR THE CONTINUING SAGA OF THE DARK SISTERHOOD IN COUNTDOWN PT. 1. SO BE HERE IN 720 HOURS AND COUNTING!

CABLE GRAMS c/o MARVEL COMICS
387 PARK AVENUE SOUTH • NEW YORK, NY 10016

E-MAIL:
MAIL@MARVEL.COM

IF YOU DON'T WANT YOUR NAME AND ADDRESS PRINTED, PLEASE LET US KNOW.
LETTERS MAY BE EDITED FOR CONTENT AND LENGTH.

MARK E-MAIL "OKAY TO PRINT"

X-MEN UNIVERSE #15 REPRINTED *CABLE #85* AND MORE. COVER ART BY GREG HORN.

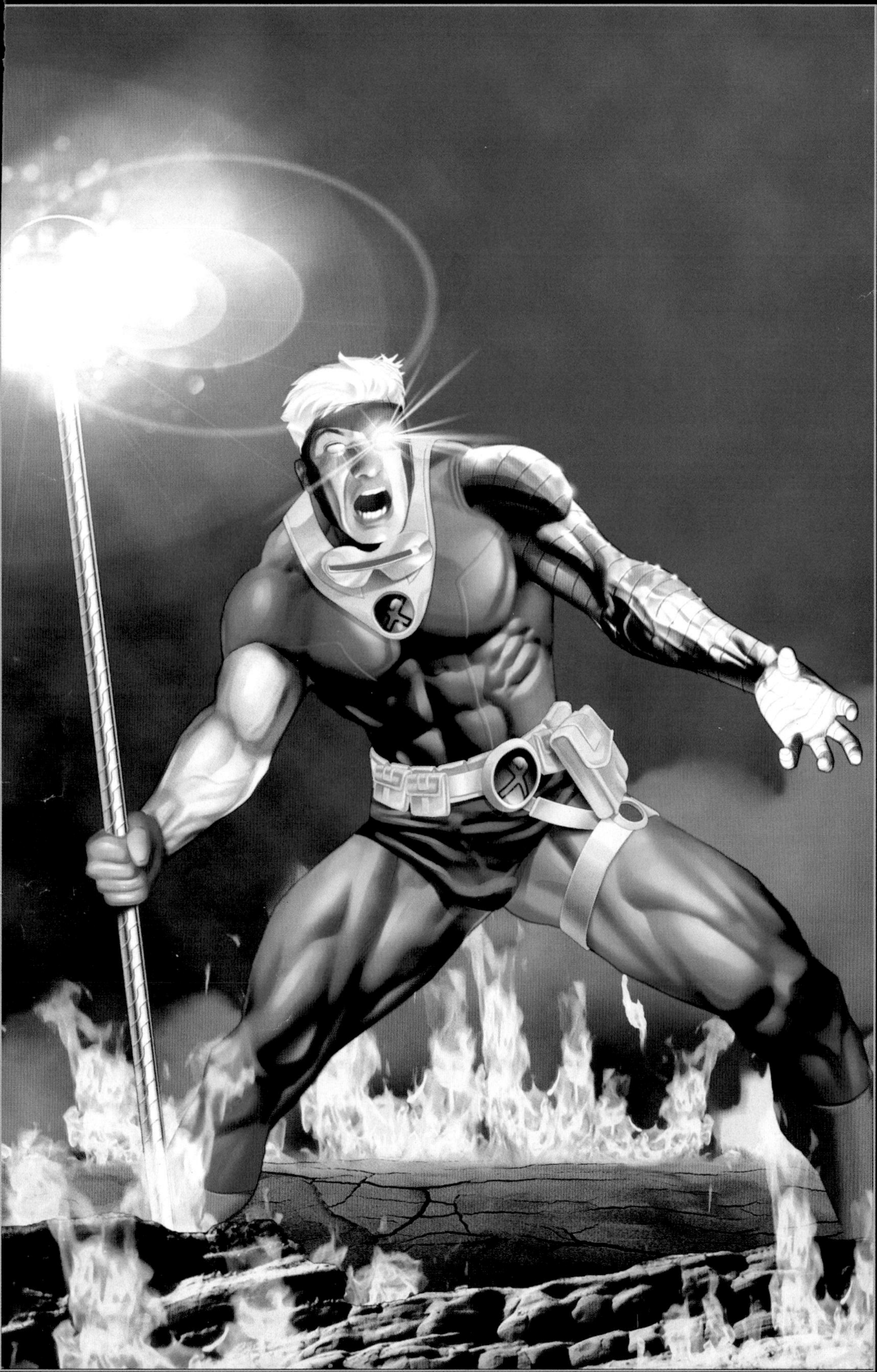